YORBA LINDA PUBLIC LIBRARY

W9-AVS-622

FEB 0 7 2021

336.2
GUID
2021

2021
Guidebook to
CALIFORNIA
TAXES

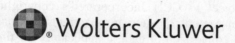

. Wolters Kluwer

YORBA LINDA PUBLIC LIBRARY
CITY OF YORBA LINDA
4852 LAKEVIEW AVE.
YORBA LINDA CA, 92886-3433

Wolters Kluwer Editorial Staff Publication

Editors . . . . Carol Kokinis-Graves, Carolyn Kwock
Production Coordinator . . . . Govardhan. L
Production Editors . . . . Ravikishore. M and Shashikant. G

This publication is designed to provide accurate and authoritative information in regard to the subject matter covered. It is sold with the understanding that the publisher is not engaged in rendering legal, accounting or other professional service. If legal advice or other expert assistance is required, the services of a competent professional person should be sought. All views expressed in this publication are those of the author and not necessarily those of the publisher or any other person.

ISBN: 978-0-8080-5356-9

©2020 CCH Incorporated and its affiliates. All rights reserved.

2700 Lake Cook Road
Riverwoods, IL 60015
800 344 3734
CCHCPELink.com

No claim is made to original government works; however, within this publication, the following are subject to CCH Incorporated's copyright: (1) the gathering, compilation, and arrangement of such government materials; (2) the magnetic translation and digital conversion of data, if applicable; (3) the historical, statutory and other notes and references; and (4) the commentary and other materials.

Do not send returns to the above address. If for any reason you are not satisfied with your book purchase, it can easily be returned within 30 days of shipment. Please go to *support.cch.com/returns* to initiate your return. If you require further assistance with your return, please call: (800) 344-3734 M-F, 8 a.m. – 6 p.m. CT.

Printed in the United States of America

PREFACE

This *Guidebook* gives a general picture of the taxes imposed by the state of California and the general property tax levied by the local governments. All 2020 legislative amendments received as of press time are reflected, and references to California and federal laws are to the laws as of the date of publication of this book.

The emphasis is on the law applicable to the filing of income tax returns in 2021 for the 2020 tax year. However, if legislation has made changes effective after 2020, we have tried to note this also, with an indication of the effective date to avoid confusion.

The taxes of major interest—income and sales and use—are discussed in detail. Other California taxes are summarized, with particular emphasis on application, exemptions, returns, and payment.

Throughout the *Guidebook,* tax tips are highlighted to help practitioners avoid pitfalls and use the tax laws to their best advantage.

The *Guidebook* is designed as a quick reference work, describing the general provisions of the various tax laws, regulations, and administrative practices. It is useful to tax practitioners, business persons, and others who prepare or file California returns or who are required to deal with California taxes.

The *Guidebook* is not designed to eliminate the necessity of referring to the law and regulations for answers to complicated problems, nor is it intended to take the place of detailed reference works such as the CCH CALIFORNIA TAX REPORTS. By assuming some knowledge of federal taxes, the *Guidebook* is able to provide a concise, readable treatment of California taxes that will supply a complete answer to most questions and will serve as a time-saving aid where it does not provide the complete answer.

SCOPE OF THE BOOK

This *Guidebook* is designed to:

—Give a general picture of the impact and pattern of all taxes levied by the state of California and the general property tax levied by local governmental units.

—Provide a readable quick-reference work for the personal income tax and the tax on corporate income. As such, it explains briefly what the California law provides and indicates whether the California provision is the same as federal law.

—Analyze and explain the differences, in most cases, between California and federal law.

HIGHLIGHTS OF 2020 CALIFORNIA TAX CHANGES

The most important 2020 California tax changes received by press time are noted in the "Highlights of 2020 California Tax Changes" section of the *Guidebook,* beginning on page 7. This useful reference gives the practitioner up-to-the-minute information on changes in tax legislation.

FINDERS

The practitioner may find the information wanted by consulting the general Table of Contents at the beginning of the *Guidebook.*

November 2020

CONTENTS

HIGHLIGHTS OF 2020 CALIFORNIA TAX CHANGES

Highlights of the 2020 California tax changes are noted below.

Multiple Taxes

• *Net operating loss deductions suspended*

For tax years beginning on or after January 1, 2020, and before January 1, 2023, California generally suspends NOL deductions for personal income and corporate tax purposes, except for certain small businesses. For any NOL for which a deduction is denied because of the suspension, California will extend the carryover period. See ¶10-805, ¶16-310. (Ch. 8 (A.B. 85), Laws 2020)

• *Business tax credits limited*

For tax years beginning on or after January 1, 2020, and before January 1, 2023, taxpayers can use no more than $5 million of business tax credits, including carry-overs, per year to offset their personal income tax, corporate tax, or insurance premiums tax. The amount of any credit not allowed because of the limit will remain a credit carryover. California will extend the credit carryover period by the number of tax years the credit or any part of it was not allowed. See ¶12-001, ¶16-805, ¶88-300. (Ch. 8 (A.B. 85), Laws 2020)

• *LPs, LLPs, and LLCs exempted from minimum tax in first year*

For tax years beginning on or after January 1, 2021, and before January 1, 2024, limited partnerships, limited liability partnerships, and limited liability companies are exempted from the minimum tax in their first taxable year, with the exemption contingent on a state budget appropriation to the FTB for its associated administrative costs. See ¶10-225, ¶10-240, ¶10-380. (Ch. 8 (A.B. 85), Laws 2020)

• *Forgiven PPP loan amounts excluded from gross income*

For tax years beginning on and after January 1, 2020, California conforms to federal law excluding certain forgiven Paycheck Protection Program loan amounts from gross income. See ¶10-918, ¶15-680. (A.B. 1577, Laws 2020)

• *Small business hiring credit enacted*

California has enacted a small business hiring credit for taxable years beginning on or after January 1, 2020, and before January 1, 2021. The credit provides some financial relief to small businesses for the economic disruptions resulting from COVID-19 that have led to unprecedented job losses. Qualified small business employers may claim the credit against corporate and personal income taxes. Or, they may elect instead to apply the credit against qualified sales and use taxes. See ¶12-001, ¶16-805. (S. B. 1447, Laws 2020)

• *Film and television tax credit carryover period extended*

The carryover period for film and television tax credits under Program 2.0 was extended to nine years. See ¶12-001, ¶16-805. (Ch. 8 (A.B. 85), Laws 2020)

Personal Income Taxes

• *Worker classification legislation enacted*

A.B. 5, Laws 2019, took effect on January 1, 2020, requiring application of a 3-part test to determine if workers in California are employees or independent contractors for purposes of the Labor Code, the Unemployment Insurance Code, and Industrial Welfare Commission (IWC) wage orders. The provisions will also be used to determine whether workers are employees or independent contractors for income tax purposes. Subsequent legislation expanded the exemptions from A.B. 5. See ¶16-615. (Ch. 38 (A.B. 2257), Laws 2020)

- *App-based rideshare and delivery drivers to be classified as independent contractors*

Voters approved Proposition 22, which classifies app-based rideshare and delivery drivers as independent contractors, rather than employees or agents of the companies that hire them. See ¶16-615. (Proposition 22, approved by voters at the November 3, 2020 general election)

- *Earned income tax credit and young child tax credit expanded*

For tax years beginning on or after January 1, 2020, California workers with Individual Taxpayer Identification Numbers (ITINs) may claim the earned income and young child tax credits, regardless of whether they have a qualifying child under 6 years old. See ¶16-805. (A.B. 1876, Laws 2020)

- *Alternate identifying information allowed for dependent credit*

Retroactively for tax years beginning on or after January 1, 2018, for California dependent exemption credit purposes, a taxpayer may provide alternate identifying information for a dependent who is ineligible to receive a federal individual taxpayer identification number (ITIN). See ¶16-805. (A.B. 2247, Laws 2020)

- *Nonresident group return for nonresident aliens authorized*

For tax years beginning on or after January 1, 2021, and until January 1, 2026, California will allow the filing of a nonresident group return on behalf of electing nonresident aliens receiving California source income. See ¶89-102. (A.B. 2660, Laws 2020)

- *Individual shared responsibility penalty limited*

The maximum monthly individual shared responsibility penalty for an individual with a household size of five or more is limited to the same amount as for an individual with a household size of five. See ¶89-206. (Ch. 8 (A.B. 85), Laws 2020)

- *Electronic withholding orders allowed*

Beginning January 1, 2021, the FTB may serve continuous orders to withhold, earnings withholding orders for taxes, earnings withholding orders, and related notices or documents by electronic technology. See ¶89-176. (A.B. 3372, Laws 2020)

Corporation Franchise and Income Taxes

- *Unintended termination of water's-edge elections prevented*

For tax years beginning on or after January 1, 2021, when a unitary foreign affiliate becomes a California taxpayer solely due to the "doing business" statute, California will treat that corporation as having made a water's-edge election with other members of the unitary group. This prevents the unintended termination of an otherwise valid water's-edge election. See ¶11-550. (A.B. 3372, Laws 2020)

- *Exempt organization filing fees eliminated*

Effective January 1, 2021, California has eliminated the $25 fee payable with an application for tax-exempt status and the $10 fee for filing an exempt organization annual information return. See ¶10-245. (S.B. 934, Laws 2020)

Sales and Use Taxes

- *Hiring credit enacted for qualified small business employers*

A hiring credit against California sales and use taxes is enacted for qualified small business employers. A qualified small business employer must submit an application to the California Department of Tax and Fee Administration (CDTFA) for a tentative credit reservation amount for the small business hiring tax credit allowed to such an employer. See ¶ 61-270. (S.B. 1447, Laws 2020, effective September 9, 2020, and applicable as noted; *Senate Floor Analysis*, California State Senate, August 31, 2020; *News Release*, Office of California Gov. Gavin Newsom, September 9, 2020)

• *Cannabis 2020-2021 budget trailer bill enacted*

The California cannabis trailer bill for the 2020-21 budget, which contains changes necessary to implement the budget, including prohibitions on the CDTFA regarding the mark-up amount and the cannabis cultivation tax rate, is enacted for cannabis excise and cultivation tax purposes. See ¶ 60-250. (Ch. 93 (A.B. 1872), Laws 2020, effective September 18, 2020, and applicable as noted)

• *Taxpayer lacked standing to challenge retailer's tax collection practices*

A California sales and use taxpayer lacked standing to challenge a retailer's tax collection practices on bundled transactions. See ¶ 89-236. (*Adame v. Apple Inc.*, Court of Appeal of California, Fourth District, No. D073567, December 31, 2019)

• *Taxpayer may not avoid pay first litigate later rule by filing for declaratory relief*

A California sales and use taxpayer could avoid the "pay first litigate later" rule by filing a claim for declaratory relief. See ¶ 61-220. (*California Department of Tax and Fee Administration v. Superior Court*, Court of Appeal of California, Second District, No. B294400, May 7, 2020)

• *Used motor vehicle dealer requirements enacted; sunset of exemptions extended*

Certain requirements are imposed on used motor vehicle dealers and the sunset date of sales and use tax exemptions for diapers and menstrual hygiene products are extended. See ¶ 60-570 and ¶ 60-520. (Ch. 8 (A.B. 85), Laws 2020, effective June 29, 2020, and applicable as noted)

• *Aircraft jet fuel retailers must file quarterly information returns*

Beginning January 1, 2020, on or before the last day of the month next following each quarterly period, a retailer of aircraft jet fuel must provide a quarterly information return to the California Department of Tax and Fee Administration (CDTFA) for sales and use tax purposes. See ¶ 60-560. (Ch. 17 (A.B. 90), Laws 2020, effective June 29, 2020)

Property Taxes

• *Proposition 19 approved by voters at November 3, 2020, general election*

California voters approved Proposition 19, which was on the ballot in California on November 3, 2020, as a legislatively referred constitutional amendment. The approved ballot measure proposed an amendment to the California Constitution that added the "Home Protection for Seniors, Severely Disabled, Families, and Victims of Wildfire or Natural Disasters Act" to Article XIIIA. See ¶ 20-610, (*State Ballot Measures—Statewide Results*, California Secretary of State, November 4, 2020; as proposed by Ch. 31 (A.C.A. 11), Laws 2020, effective November 3, 2020, upon approval of Proposition 19 at the November 3, 2020, general election, and operative as noted)

• *New construction exclusion enacted*

A new construction California property tax exclusion is enacted for property damaged or destroyed by a Governor-declared disaster. See ¶ 20-150. (Ch. 124 (A.B. 2013), Laws 2020, effective January 1, 2021, and applicable as noted)

• *Tax sale regarding surface rights did not include oil and gas rights*

A California property tax sale of real property, described in the deed as pertaining to surface rights, did not include oil and gas rights which are restrictions of record in a previously recorded oil and gas lease. See ¶ 20-270. (*Leiper v. Gallegos*, Court of Appeal of California, Second District, No. B292905, November 20, 2019)

Motor Fuel Taxes

• *Rate on dimethyl ether set*

Applicable July 1, 2021, the California excise tax under the Use Fuel Tax Law on dimethyl ether (DME) and DME-liquified petroleum gas fuel blend is set. See ¶ 40-007. (Ch. 117 (A.B. 2663), Laws 2020, effective January 1, 2021, and applicable as noted)

CORPORATION FRANCHISE (INCOME)

[¶10-050]

FEDERAL/MULTISTATE ISSUES

[¶10-055] Comparison of Federal/State Key Features

The following is a comparison of key features of federal income tax laws that have been enacted as of March 27, 2020, and California corporation income tax laws. California incorporates by reference numerous Internal Revenue Code (IRC) provisions as of a specified date (see ¶10-515). Some federal provisions are incorporated by reference with specific modifications, others are incorporated without any modifications, and some are not incorporated at all. State modifications to federal taxable income required by law differences are listed at ¶10-600 for additions and ¶10-800 for subtractions.

- *Foreign Tax Credit (IRC Sec. 27)*

California has no equivalent to the federal foreign tax credit (IRC Sec. 27).

- *Alcohol Fuels Credit (IRC Sec. 40)*

California has no equivalent to the federal alcohol fuels credit (IRC Sec. 40).

- *Incremental Research Expenditures Credit (IRC Sec. 41)*

California allows a credit for research expenditures that is generally based on the federal credit (IRC Sec. 41). However, California does not adopt federal changes that (1) increase the credit for amounts paid to eligible small businesses, universities, and federal laboratories; (2) allow a credit for amounts paid to a research consortium for energy research; (3) increase the rates used to compute the alternative incremental credit and allow taxpayers to elect to compute the credit under a third method, the alternative simplified credit; (4) repeal the alternative incremental credit election or the 14% alternative simplified credit calculation; (5) specify how qualified research expenses are allocated in transactions involving acquisitions or between members of a controlled group of businesses; (6) allow qualifying small businesses to apply a specified amount of the credit against payroll taxes; (7) allow the credit to be applied against alternative minimum tax liability; or (8) require research and experimental expenditures paid or incurred in tax years beginning after 2021 be amortized ratably over five years (15 years for foreign research expenditures).

California incorporates the federal provision that disallows a deduction for that portion of qualified research expenses or basic research expenses that equals the credit amount allowed for such expenses under IRC Sec. 41.

- *Low-Income Housing (IRC Sec. 42)*

California allows a low-income housing credit that is generally based on the federal credit (IRC Sec. 42). However, California does not conform to federal law regarding use of the Chained Consumer Price Index for All Urban Consumers (C-CPI-U) in making annual adjustments for inflation for tax years beginning after 2017.

- *Disabled Access Credit (IRC Sec. 44)*

California allows a disabled access expenditures credit that is generally based on the federal credit (IRC Sec. 44).

• *Indian Employment Credit (IRC Sec. 45A)*

California has no equivalent to the Indian employment credit (IRC Sec. 45A). Taxpayers may deduct expenses for which a federal Indian employment credit was claimed (see ¶ 10-855).

• *Employer Social Security Credit (IRC Sec. 45B)*

California has no equivalent to the employer social security credit (IRC Sec. 45B).

• *Orphan Drug Credit (IRC Sec. 45C)*

California has no equivalent to the orphan drug credit (IRC Sec. 45C). California incorporates the federal provision that disallows a deduction for the portion of qualified clinical testing expenses for which a credit is claimed under IRC Sec. 45C (see ¶ 10-855).

• *New Markets Credit (IRC Sec. 45D)*

California has no equivalent to the new market credit (IRC Sec. 45D). However, California does provide a credit for deposits made to certain community development financial institutions.

• *Small Business Pension Start-Up Costs Credit (IRC Sec. 45E)*

California has no equivalent to the small employer pension plan startup costs Credit (IRC Sec. 45E).

• *Employer-Provided Child Care Credit (IRC Sec. 45F)*

California has no equivalent to the federal employer-provide child care credit (IRC Sec. 45F).

• *Fuel from Nonconventional Source Credit (IRC Sec. 45K)*

California has no equivalent to the federal fuel-from-nonconventional-source credit (IRC Sec. 45K).

• *New Energy-Efficient Homes Credit (IRC Sec. 45L)*

California has no equivalent to the federal new energy-efficient homes credit (IRC Sec. 45L).

• *Energy Efficient Appliance Credit (IRC Sec. 45M)*

California has no equivalent to the federal new energy-efficient appliance credit (IRC Sec. 45M).

• *Investment Credit (Former Law) (IRC Sec. 46 — IRC Sec. 49)*

California has no equivalent to the former federal investment credit (repealed effective for property placed in service after 1985) or to the current federal investment credits (IRC Sec. 47, IRC Sec. 48, IRC Sec. 48A, IRC Sec. 48B, IRC Sec. 48C). California does not provide an exclusion for grants received in lieu of the IRC Sec. 48 credit.

• *Wage Credits (IRC Secs. 51 — 52 and IRC Sec. 1396)*

California has no equivalent to the federal work opportunity credit (IRC Sec. 51—IRC Sec. 52) or the empowerment zone employment credit (IRC Sec. 1396). However, California allows a deduction for wages disallowed under federal law when the credits are claimed (see ¶ 10-855). California also allows credits to employers in certain areas for wages paid to qualified employees.

¶10-055

• *Alternative Minimum Tax (IRC Sec. 55 — IRC Sec. 59)*

California imposes an alternative minimum tax (AMT) that is a modified version of the federal AMT (IRC Sec. 55—IRC Sec. 59). However, California has not adopted the federal provision allowing an alternative maximum capital gains tax rate for qualified timber gain of a C corporation for a tax year beginning in 2016.

The federal AMT for corporations is repealed for tax years beginning after 2017. Any unused minimum tax credit of a corporation may be used to offset regular tax liability for any tax year. In addition, a portion of unused minimum tax credit is refundable in the 2018 to 2021 tax years. California has not provided guidance on how the federal AMT repeal will impact its version of the AMT.

• *Base Erosion and Anti-Abuse Tax (BEAT) (IRC Sec. 59A)*

California does not follow federal law imposing a base erosion minimum tax (IRC Sec. 59A).

• *Deemed Dividends (IRC Sec. 78)*

California allows a deduction from gross income for the amount of dividend gross-up included in federal gross income (IRC Sec. 78) when a corporation claims a federal foreign tax credit (see ¶10-810).

• *Interest on Federal Obligations*

Interest on federal obligations is taxable under the California franchise tax, but exempt under the corporate income tax (see ¶10-610).

• *Interest on State Obligations (IRC Sec. 103)*

Under California's franchise tax, all state and municipal bond interest, including California's, is taxable and must be added back to federal taxable income (see ¶10-610). California bond interest is exempt under the corporate income tax and may be subtracted from federal taxable income (see ¶10-815).

• *Discharge of Indebtedness (IRC Sec. 108)*

California generally follows the federal treatment of discharge of indebtedness (IRC Sec. 108), with modifications concerning the reduction of tax attributes (see ¶10-701). California does not adopt the federal provision allowing taxpayers to defer the recognition of discharge of indebtedness income arising from a qualified reacquisition of corporate or business debt instruments issued by the taxpayer or a related person (see ¶10-701 and ¶10-918)

• *Contributions to the Capital of a Corporation (IRC Sec. 118)*

California's treatment of contributions to the capital of a corporation is generally the same as federal because IRC Sec. 118 is incorporated by reference (see ¶10-515). However, due to its conformity date, California does not conform to federal amendments modifying the definition of contribution to capital, which excludes contributions by any governmental entity or civic group that are not made by a shareholder in its capacity as a shareholder, and the elimination of special rules for contributions to water and sewage disposal utilities.

• *Certain Excessive Employee Remuneration (IRC Sec. 162(m))*

California generally follows the federal limitations on excessive employee remuneration because IRC Sec. 162(m) is incorporated by reference (see ¶10-515). However, under federal law, a transition rule applies to changes made by the TCJA. The federal grandfathering period applies to compensation provided pursuant to a written binding contract which was in effect on November 2, 2017, that has not been modified in any material respect. The relevant date for California purposes is March 31, 2019.

• *Interest on Indebtedness (IRC Sec. 163)*

California's treatment of interest on indebtedness is the same as federal because IRC Sec. 163 is incorporated by reference (see ¶ 10-515). However, California has not adopted (1) the repeal of the exception from the registration requirements for foreign targeted obligations under IRC Sec. 163(f); or (2) the federal amendment (IRC Sec. 163(j)) limiting the deduction of business interest for tax years beginning after 2017 to the sum of the taxpayer's business interest income, floor plan financing, and 30% of adjusted taxable income (50% for any tax year beginning in 2019 or 2020) (see ¶ 10-815).

• *Income and Franchise Tax Deductions (IRC Sec. 164)*

California does not allow a subtraction for state, federal, or foreign taxes on or measured by income (see ¶ 10-615).

• *Losses (IRC Sec. 165)*

Generally, California's treatment of losses is the same as federal because IRC Sec. 165 is incorporated by reference (see ¶ 10-515). California, but not federal, law also allows 100% of any excess loss resulting from specified disasters to be carried forward to the next succeeding 15 years (see ¶ 10-820).

• *Bad Debts (IRC Sec. 166)*

California's treatment of bad debts is the same as federal because IRC Sec. 166 is incorporated by reference (see ¶ 10-685 and ¶ 10-875).

• *Depreciation (IRC Secs. 167, 168, and 1400N)*

California does not follow federal ACRS or MACRS depreciation with respect to corporate taxpayers (IRC Sec. 167 and IRC Sec. 168). The pre-ACRS federal Asset Depreciation Range System (ADR) is applicable in California. Consequently, neither federal bonus depreciation nor the limits placed on sales-in, lease out (SILO) transactions or the shortened recovery periods for qualified improvement property apply in California. Although California does allow the income forecast method of depreciation, it has not incorporated the special federal treatment provided to distribution costs and participations and residuals. California also does not adopt various federal provisions, including those relating to (1) amortization of geological and geophysical expenses, electric transmission property, and natural gas lines; (2) the shortening of the recovery period for young racehorses, electric meter systems, and electric grid systems; and (3) the accelerated write-offs for biomass ethanol plant property, reuse and recycling property, and qualified disaster assistance property (see ¶ 10-670 and ¶ 10-900).

• *Safe Harbor Leasing (Pre-1984 Leases) (IRC Sec. 168(f))*

California recognizes safe harbor leases under former IRC Sec. 168(f) (see ¶ 10-900).

¶10-055

- *Pollution Control Facilities Amortization (IRC Sec. 169)*

California's treatment of pollution control facilities is the same as federal (IRC Sec. 169) because the IRC is incorporated by reference, except that the facility must be located in California (see ¶10-665).

- *Charitable Contributions (IRC Sec. 170)*

California and federal laws are generally parallel. However, there are differences in the (1) income from which the contributions are deducted, (2) types of contributions eligible for the deduction, and (3) treatment of appreciated property (see ¶10-650 and ¶10-880). For example, California does not follow the special rules for deductions of charitable contributions of real property for conservation purposes (which were made available to native corporations under the Alaska Native Claims Settlement Act after 2015). However, California does offer a credit for donations of real property for conservation purposes. In addition, California does not follow federal provisions that limit the charitable contribution deduction for patents and most other intellectual property, increase the substantiation requirements for donations of $500 or more, and limit the deductions for donations of vehicles, boats, and aircraft while simultaneously increasing the substantiation requirements. California has also not conformed to federal provisions that allow enhanced deductions for donations of food inventory (see ¶10-650 and ¶10-880).

California allows a credit for the costs of transporting donated agricultural products to nonprofit charitable organizations.

- *Amortizable Bond Premium (IRC Sec. 171)*

The California provisions are generally the same as federal law (IRC Sec. 171). However, a rule in the California provision for computing the amount of amortizable bond premium for the year in which a bond having a call date is actually called differs from the federal rule (see ¶10-610).

- *Net Operating Loss (IRC Secs. 172 and 1400N)*

California permits the deduction of an apportioned and allocated NOL, generally in accord with the federal provisions (IRC Sec. 172), except that (1) NOLs may be carried forward for 20 years (10 years if incurred between 2000 and 2007, or five years if incurred before 2000); (2) a two-year carryback is allowed for tax years 2013-2018; (3) California suspended NOL deductions for the 2008-2011 and 2020-2022 taxable years; (4) California does not follow the federal expanded NOL (IRC Sec. 1400N) for qualified hurricane and tornado disaster victims or federal disaster victims; (5) only a specified percentage of pre-2004 NOLs could be carried over (an exception was provided for losses of businesses located in economic incentive areas and certain new businesses and small businesses); (6) the extended federal carryback for farm losses does not apply (although special NOL treatment is available for farming businesses whose crops were impacted by Pierce's disease); and (7) California does not conform to the limitation of NOL deductions to 80% of taxable income (see ¶10-805).

California also does not conform to the NOL modifications allowing a five-year carryback period and an unlimited carryforward period for NOLs arising in tax years beginning in 2018, 2019, and 2020.

- *Research and Experimental Expenditures (IRC Sec. 174)*

California's treatment of research and experimental expenditures is generally the same as federal because IRC Sec. 174 is incorporated by reference. However, California does not conform to the federal requirement that research and experimental expenditures paid or incurred in taxable years beginning after 2021 be amortized ratably over five years (15 years for foreign research) (see ¶ 10-905).

- *Asset Expense Election (IRC Sec. 179)*

California allows a limited asset expense election (IRC Sec. 179) for corporation franchise and income tax purposes that is limited to $25,000, and reduced if the cost of all IRC Sec. 179 property placed in service during the taxable year is more than $200,000. California does not allow an expanded asset expense election for disaster assistance property, nor does it permit revocation of an election without approval after 2014. California also does not allow the expensing of off-the-shelf computer software, air conditioning units, and heating units. In addition, California does not conform to federal changes that repealed the limitation on the amount of Sec. 179 property that can be attributable to qualified real property and the corresponding provision on carryforwards of disallowed amounts attributable to qualified real property. Furthermore, California has not adopted the redefinition of "qualified real property" eligible for expensing to include improvements to the interior of any nonresidential real property; roofs, heating, ventilation, and air-conditioning property; fire protection and alarm systems; and security systems. Finally, California does not conform to the elimination of the exclusion for tangible personal property used in connection with lodging facilities and the post-2018 inflation adjustment of the $25,000 expensing limit on certain heavy vehicles (see ¶ 10-900).

- *Energy Efficient Commercial Building Deduction (IRC Sec. 179D)*

California does not incorporate the federal provisions allowing qualified taxpayers to claim a deduction for energy efficiency improvements installed on U.S. commercial property (IRC Sec. 179D) (see ¶ 10-665).

- *Deduction for Barriers Removal (IRC Sec. 190)*

The California provision is generally the same as the federal provision (IRC Sec. 190), except that under California law, but not federal law, the deduction is extended to cover the costs of installing a qualified emergency exit/safe area refuge system (see ¶ 10-660).

- *Start-Up Expenses (IRC Sec. 195)*

California's treatment of start-up expenditures is the same as federal because IRC Sec. 195 is incorporated by reference (see ¶ 10-515). However, California does not allow the increased deduction and threshold amounts for the 2010 tax year (see ¶ 10-645).

- *Amortization of Intangibles (IRC Sec. 197)*

California's treatment of amortization of intangibles is the same as federal because IRC Sec. 197 is incorporated by reference (see ¶ 10-515).

- *Domestic Production Activities Deduction (IRC Sec. 199)*

California does not allow the domestic production activities deduction (IRC Sec. 199). Since the federal deduction is repealed for tax years beginning after 2017, the addback to federal taxable income for California purposes is no longer required after 2017 (see ¶ 10-660).

¶10-055

• *Reporting for the Qualified Business Income Deduction (Pass-Through Deduction) (IRC Sec. 199A)*

California has no equivalent to the federal pass-through deduction (IRC Sec. 199A).

• *Dividends Received Deduction (IRC Sec. 243 — IRC Sec. 245)*

California does not incorporate the federal dividends received deduction (IRC Sec. 243—IRC Sec. 245), but does allow a deduction for intercompany dividends and a deduction for dividends received from an insurance company subsidiary (see ¶10-810).

• *Participation Dividends Received Deduction (IRC Sec. 245A)*

California does not incorporate the participation dividends received deduction for the foreign-source portion of dividends received from specified 10% owned foreign corporations by U.S. corporate shareholders (IRC Sec. 245A) (see ¶10-515).

• *Organizational Expenditures (IRC Sec. 248)*

California law is similar, but not identical to the federal provision (IRC Sec. 248) regarding the treatment of organizational expenditures (see ¶10-515).

• *Foreign-Derived Intangible Income and Global Intangible Low-Taxed Income (IRC Sec. 250)*

California does not conform to the federal deduction allowed for foreign-derived intangible income (FDII) and global intangible low-taxed income (GILTI) (IRC Sec. 250) (see ¶10-515).

• *Corporate Distributions and Adjustments (IRC Sec. 301 — IRC Sec. 385)*

Generally, California's treatment of corporate distributions and adjustments is the same as federal (IRC Sec. 301—IRC Sec. 385) with minor modifications. However, California has not incorporated amendments made to IRC Sec. 382 that provide an exception to the rule that limits the offset of taxable income post-change tax years by pre-change net operating losses, certain built-in gains, and deductions for a loss corporation that experiences an ownership change as a result of specified restructuring plans required by the Treasury Department (see ¶10-805). In addition, while California incorporates IRC Sec. 355 as of its conformity date, California has not adopted amendments effective generally for distributions on or after December 7, 2015, providing that IRC Sec. 355 will not apply to any distribution if either the distributing corporation or the controlled corporation is a real estate investment trust (REIT). Furthermore, California has not adopted the repeal of the active trade or business exception to the IRC Sec. 367(a) outbound transfer rules, which is effective for transfers after 2017.

• *Accounting Periods and Methods (IRC Sec. 441 — IRC Sec. 483)*

Generally, California's accounting periods and methods are the same as federal because California automatically incorporates most federal changes made to IRC Sec. 457. The incorporation of IRC Sec. 482 gives the state tax agency the authority to allocate income and deductions among related taxpayers to avoid evasion of tax or to clearly reflect income. California does not incorporate IRC Sec. 457A, which provides rules for compensation from nonqualified deferred compensation plans maintained by foreign corporations. California also has not conformed to the provision of IRC Sec. 451(i) that allows a taxpayer to elect to recognize qualified gain from a qualifying electric transmission transaction over an eight-year period. In addition, California differs from IRC Sec. 469 for personal holding companies and closely held corporations with regard to special rules for rental real estate activities engaged in by real estate businesses, passive activity credits that are eligible to be carried over, the disposition of a passive activity in a taxable transaction, and the offset for rental real estate activities (see ¶ 10-635). Furthermore, California has not adopted the single $25 million gross receipts test for determining whether certain taxpayers qualify as small taxpayers that can use the cash method of accounting, are not required to use inventories, are not required to apply the UNICAP rules, and are not required to use the percentage of completion method for a small construction contract. California also has not adopted federal modifications to income recognition rules for accrual-method taxpayers, the normalization method of accounting, the maximum deferral amount for length-of-service award exclusion, or the IRC Sec. 481(a) adjustment resulting from an accounting method change that is attributable to an eligible S corporation's revocation of its S corporation election.

- *Exempt Organizations (IRC Sec. 501 — IRC Sec. 530)*

The California provisions are similar, but not identical to the federal provisions (IRC Sec. 501—IRC Sec. 530). California incorporates the federal provisions regarding taxation of unrelated business income (IRC Sec. 512—IRC Sec. 514) with modifications. However, California has not adopted federal provisions requiring exempt organizations with more than one unrelated business to calculate unrelated business taxable income (UBTI) separately for each unrelated trade or business (see ¶ 10-245).

- *Corporations Used to Avoid Shareholder Taxation (IRC Sec. 531 — IRC Sec. 547)*

California has no provisions comparable to the federal provisions regarding corporations used to avoid shareholder taxation (IRC Sec. 531—IRC Sec. 547). California does not impose a tax on accumulated earnings or on personal holding companies.

- *Banking Institutions (IRC Sec. 581 — IRC Sec. 597)*

California incorporates IRC Sec. 582, regarding bad debts, gains and losses involving securities or bonds. California has some provisions regarding financial institutions that are similar to the federal provisions but, in some instances, California has no comparable provisions (see ¶ 10-340).

- *Natural Resources (IRC Sec. 611 — IRC Sec. 638)*

California's treatment of natural resources is generally the same as federal because IRC Sec. 611—IRC Sec. 638 are incorporated by reference (see ¶ 10-515). However, California did not incorporate the IRC Sec. 613A suspension of the 100% taxable income limit on percentage depletion deductions for oil and gas production from marginal properties or the modifications to the depletion deduction refinery exemption for independent producers that applied prior to 2012 (see ¶ 10-625).

- *Insurance Companies (IRC Sec. 801 — IRC Sec. 848)*

There is no equivalent to the federal provisions relating to insurance companies (IRC Sec. 801—IRC Sec. 848). A gross premiums tax is imposed on foreign and domestic insurers in lieu of the corporation income tax (see ¶ 10-335).

- *RICs, REITs, REMICs, and FASITs (IRC Sec. 851 — IRC Sec. 860L)*

California incorporates, with certain exceptions, the federal provisions on RICs, REITs, REMICs, and former FASITs. However, due to its conformity date, California has not adopted federal provisions (1) increasing the amount of property that a REIT may sell in a tax year under a safe harbor from the 100% prohibited transactions tax, and (2) defining "undistributed capital gain" for purposes of the taxation of REITs on net capital gains.

- *Foreign Source Income (IRC Sec. 861 — IRC Sec. 865)*

California does not follow the foreign sourcing rules (IRC Sec. 861—IRC Sec. 865). Multistate and international businesses that conduct business both inside and outside California utilize the state's allocation (see ¶ 11-515) and apportionment rules (see ¶ 11-520) for determining whether income is attributable to state sources. California allows a subtraction from taxable income for income derived from the operation of aircraft or ships by a foreign corporation (see ¶ 10-913).

- *Foreign Tax Credit (IRC Sec. 901 — IRC Sec. 908)*

California has no provisions comparable to those relating to the foreign tax credit (IRC Sec. 901—IRC Sec. 908).

- *Global Intangible Low-Taxed Income (GILTI) (IRC Sec. 951A)*

California does not incorporate the current year inclusion of global intangible low-taxed income (GILTI) by a U.S. shareholder of a controlled foreign corporation required by IRC Sec. 951A (see ¶ 10-515).

- *Transition (Repatriation) Tax (IRC Sec. 965)*

California does not incorporate the federal transition (repatriation) tax on accumulated foreign earnings imposed by IRC Sec. 965 (see ¶ 10-515).

- *Gain or Loss on Disposition of Property (IRC Sec. 1001 — IRC Sec. 1092)*

California specifically incorporates several federal provisions; has some provisions that are similar to the federal provisions; and in some cases, has no comparable provisions. For corporate income tax purposes, California has no comparable provision to IRC Sec. 1014, concerning the basis of property acquired from a decedent. California has not incorporated federal amendments that (1) extend the IRC Sec. 1033 replacement period for nonrecognition of gain as a result of an involuntary conversion of business property from two years to five years for property converted by Hurricane Katrina or by the 2007 Kansas tornadoes; (2) provide for the nonrecognition of gain from the exchange of certain long-term care contracts; (3) require capital gain passed through to fund managers via a partnership profits interest (carried interest) in exchange for investment management services to meet an extended three-year holding period to qualify for long-term capital gain treatment; and (4) repeal the election to defer recognition of capital gain realized on the sale of publicly traded securities if the taxpayer used the sale proceeds to purchase common stock or a partnership interest in a specialized small business investment company (SSBIC) after 2017.

For tax years beginning after 2018, and for exchanges completed after January 10, 2019, California will generally conform to the TCJA amendments to IRC Sec. 1031 limiting nonrecognition of gain or loss on like-kind exchanges to real property.

- *Alternative Capital Gains Tax (IRC Sec. 1201)*

California does not provide for an alternative tax rate on capital gains.

¶10-055

• *Capital Losses (IRC Secs. 1211 and 1212)*

California's treatment of capital loss carryovers is the same as federal because IRC Sec. 1211 and IRC Sec. 1212 are incorporated by reference. However, California does not allow capital loss carrybacks.

• *Determining Capital Gains and Losses (IRC Sec. 1221 — IRC Sec. 1260)*

Generally, California's determination of capital gains and losses is the same as federal because IRC Sec. 1221—IRC Sec. 1260 are incorporated by reference. However, California has not adopted federal provisions that (1) exclude certain self-created property (e.g., patents, inventions, models, designs, or secret formulas or process) from the definition of a "capital asset" for dispositions after 2017, or (2) treat certain amounts received by a domestic corporation upon the sale or exchange of stock in a foreign corporation as dividends for purposes of the participation dividends-received deduction for distributions made after 2017 (see ¶ 10-640).

• *S Corporations (IRC Sec. 1361 — IRC Sec. 1379)*

California adopts federal treatment of S corporations and their shareholders (IRC Sec. 1361—IRC Sec. 1379), but imposes a 1.5% tax on S corporation net income prior to its pass-through to shareholders (see ¶ 10-215). California did not adopt the amendment to IRC Sec. 1367, regarding the basis reduction in stock of a shareholder as the result of a charitable contribution or amendments that changed this rule so that the basis reduction does not apply to a charitable contribution of appreciated property to the extent that the shareholder's pro rata share of the contribution exceeds the shareholder's pro rata share of the adjusted basis of the property. California conforms to IRC Sec. 1361 and IRC Sec. 1362 that impact eligibility, elections, and terminations, as those provisions are currently in effect for federal purposes, but does not conform to other amendments made to those IRC sections. Furthermore, California does not conform to the five-year recognition period for built-in gains under IRC Sec. 1374 and, instead, uses a ten-year recognition period. California also has not adopted federal amendments providing that an adjustment resulting from an accounting method change attributable to the revocation of certain S corporation elections will be taken into account ratably over a six-year period (see ¶ 10-215).

• *Empowerment Zones and Renewal Communities (IRC Secs. 1391 — 1397F and IRC Secs. 1400E — 1400J)*

California has no provisions directly comparable to the federal provisions regarding empowerment zones and renewal communities (IRC Sec. 1391—IRC Sec. 1400J). However, prior to the 2014 tax year, California provided its own tax incentives for taxpayers conducting business activities within geographically targeted economic development areas (EDAs), including enterprise zones, manufacturing enhancement areas, targeted tax areas, and local agency military base recovery areas. The California EDA hiring credits are generally not operative for tax years beginning after 2013; however, the credits continue to apply for tax years beginning on or after January 1, 2014, with respect to qualified employees who are employed by qualified taxpayers within the 60-month period immediately preceding that date. Beginning with the 2014 tax year, a hiring credit is available to businesses hiring full-time employees for work in a designated census tract area or an economic development area.

Taxpayers may deduct expenses for which a federal empowerment zone employment credit was claimed (see ¶ 10-885).

¶10-055

• *Consolidated Returns (IRC Sec. 1501 — IRC Sec. 1504)*

Except for certain affiliated groups of railroad corporations, California does not incorporate the federal provisions allowing affiliated corporations to file consolidated returns.

[¶10-075] Nexus--P.L. 86-272--Doing Business in State

What is the California nexus standard?

California's corporation franchise tax nexus standard is not based on the physical presence of an out-of-state corporation in the state. A corporation is subject to California corporation franchise tax if it is doing business in California. "Doing business" means actively engaging in any transaction for financial or pecuniary gain or profit. (Sec. 23101(a), Rev. & Tax. Code) In addition, California applies a factor-based nexus standard, under which a corporation is considered to be doing business in the state for a taxable year if:

— it is organized or commercially domiciled in California;

— its California sales, including sales by an agent or independent contractor, exceed the lesser of $610,395 for 2020 ($601,967 for 2019; $583,867 for 2018; $561,951 for 2017, $547,711 for 2016; $536,446 for 2015; $529,562 for 2014; $518,162 for 2013; $509,500 for 2012; $500,000 for 2011) or 25% percent of its total sales;

— its California real property and tangible personal property exceed the lesser of $61,040 for 2020 ($60,197 for 2019; $58,387 for 2018; $56,195 for 2017, $54,771 for 2016; $53,644 for 2015; $52,956 for 2014; $51,816 for 2013; $50,950 for 2012; $50,000 for 2011) or 25% of its total real property and tangible personal property; or

— the amount the corporation paid in California for compensation exceeds the lesser of $61,040 for 2020 ($60,197 for 2019; $58,387 for 2018; $56,195 for 2017, $54,771 for 2016; $53,644 for 2015; $52,956 for 2014; $51,816 for 2013; $50,950 for 2012; $50,000 for 2011) or 25% of the total compensation paid.

The figures are adjusted annually for inflation. (Sec. 23101(b), Rev. & Tax. Code; Instructions, Form 100, Corporation Franchise or Income Tax Return; *Memorandum*, California Franchise Tax Board, September 1, 2020) A taxpayer's sales, property, and payroll include its pro rata or distributive share of amounts from partnerships or S corporations. (Sec. 23101(d), Rev. & Tax. Code)

PLANNING NOTE: Water's-edge elections.—The FTB has explained how it will treat an otherwise valid water's-edge election (see ¶11-550) when a unitary foreign affiliate of the water's-edge combined reporting group later becomes a taxpayer "doing business" in California under factor-based thresholds. Corporations that are doing business in California are subject to tax (i.e., they are taxpayers). Consequently, a corporation that was not previously subject to California tax before 2011 could become subject to the state's tax (i.e., become a taxpayer) after 2011 under the factor-based thresholds. According to the FTB, if certain conditions are met, it will not seek to terminate the water's-edge election of the water's-edge combined reporting group that is unitary with a foreign affiliate that is now a taxpayer. (*FTB Notice 2016-02*, California Franchise Tax Board, September 9, 2016; *FTB Notice 2017-04*, California Franchise Tax Board, October 16, 2017; *FTB Notice 2019-02*, California Franchise Tax Board, June 26, 2019) Legislation enacted in 2020 codified this practice for water's-edge groups with a unitary foreign affiliate that becomes a California taxpayer due to the "doing business" statute in a taxable year beginning on or after January 1, 2021.

CCH PRACTICE TIP: Multiple interests in pass-through entities.—A taxpayer that owns multiple interests in several California pass-through entities must aggregate the property, payroll, and sales from each pass-through entity to determine if its property, payroll, or sales exceed the threshold amounts. A taxpayer may also be doing business in California even if the thresholds are not met, because partnerships, other than investment partnerships, and limited liability companies (LLCs) are automatically doing business in California if they have general partners or members in California. Also, partners and members are doing business in California if the partnership or LLC is doing business in California, regardless of whether the threshold levels are met. (*General Information on New Rules for Doing Business in California*, California Franchise Tax Board, March 4, 2011)

If an LLC that is classified as a partnership for tax purposes has members that are business entities and is doing business in California, then the members are themselves generally considered to be doing business in California. However, a narrow exception may apply in limited circumstances. If an LLC is only registered to do business in California or organized in California, but has no activities or factor presence in California sufficient to constitute doing business in the state, then the LLC will have a California return filing requirement and be subject to the LLC tax and fee, but the members will not have a California return filing requirement or be subject to California tax as a result of their membership interests in the LLC. If a member's distributive share of the California sales of the LLC exceeds the statutory threshold in Sec. 23101(b), then the member will be doing business in the state on that basis, as well as on the basis of its membership interest in the LLC. (*Legal Ruling 2014-01*, California Franchise Tax Board, July 22, 2014; as modified by *Legal Ruling 2018-01*, California Franchise Tax Board, October 19, 2018)

CCH POINTER: Doing business without meeting factor-based thresholds.—An out-of-state taxpayer that has less than the threshold amounts of property, payroll, or sales in California may still be doing business in California if it actively engages in any transaction for the purpose of financial gain or profit in California. For example, an out-of-state partnership whose only connection with California is its employees, who work out of their homes in California selling and providing warranty work to California customers, may still be doing business in California, even if the property, payroll, and sales in California fall below the threshold amounts, because its employees are actively engaging in transactions for profit on its behalf. (*General Information on New Rules for Doing Business in California*, California Franchise Tax Board, March 4, 2011)

PRACTICAL ANALYSIS: Single member LLC.—When a single member LLC that is disregarded for income tax purposes has as its only asset a personal vacation home located outside California, the California residence of the sole member or the LLC, without more, will not cause the LLC to be "doing business" in California. However, if the member, as a member of the LLC, actively engaged in a transaction in California for financial gain or profit, the LLC would be "doing business" in California. Also, if the property was ever rented or advertised for rent, then there might be a basis for determining that the LLC was "doing business" in California, depending on whether the member actively engaged in a rent-related activity in California. However, if the member used the residence only personally, expenses associated with ownership of the property, like paying taxes, would not usually cause the LLC to be "doing business." in the state. (*Tax News*, California Franchise Tax Board, May 2010)

PRACTICE NOTE: *Employee teleworking in state due to COVID-19.*—California will not tax an out-of-state corporation whose only connection to California is an employee teleworking in California due to Executive Order N-33-20. This tax treatment will continue to apply until the order is no longer in effect. Due to the order, intended to prevent the spread of COVID-19, many individuals living in California who ordinarily did not telework from home began to do so. In some instances, the individuals living in California and now teleworking from home might be employed by corporations that previously had no connections with California. According to the Franchise Tax Board (FTB), California will not treat an out-of-state corporation as doing business in the state if its only connection with California is an employee teleworking in California due to the order. California will not treat the corporation as actively engaging in a transaction for financial or pecuniary gain or profit in the state. California also will not include the compensation attributable to the employee in the computation of the payroll threshold for doing business in the state. In addition, an employee teleworking in California due to the order will not cause an out-of-state corporation to exceed the protections of P.L. 86-272 (see discussion of P.L. 86-272 below). California will treat the presence of an employee teleworking in California due to the order as engaging in de minimis activities for purposes of P.L. 86-272 protection. (COVID-19 Frequently Asked Questions for Tax Relief and Assistance, California Franchise Tax Board, September 11, 2020)

A corporation may petition the FTB to determine that it is not doing business in California. The FTB may determine that a corporation is not doing business in California if:

— the corporation's activity in California is limited to purchasing personal property or services solely for its own use or an affiliate's use outside the state, and it has no more than 100 employees in California (up to 200 employees if the personal property or services are used to build or modify a physical plant or facility located outside California) whose duties are limited to solicitation, negotiation, liaison, monitoring, auditing, and inspecting the personal property or services; or

— the corporation has employees in California solely to attend a public or private school, college, or university.

For corporations engaged in a unitary business, the 100- or 200-employee limitation applies to the total of all corporations in the unitary group. (Sec. 23101.5, Rev. & Tax. Code)

An FTB determination that a corporation is not doing business in California remains in effect for five years, if the corporation continues to meet the prescribed criteria. A corporation must annually confirm with the FTB that the facts relevant to the determination remain unchanged. Also, each taxpayer that sells property or services to a corporation with more than 100 employees in California, and concerning which a determination has been made, must file a report with the FTB. (Sec. 23101.5, Rev. & Tax. Code)

COMPLIANCE NOTE: When a taxpayer is unsure whether its activities constitute "doing business" in California under the general rule of Sec. 23101(a), the FTB will accept requests for written advice on that issue. However, the FTB will not rule on whether the specific factual threshold tests of Sec. 23101(b) have been met. As explained in *FTB Notice 2009-08*, the FTB may issue Chief Counsel Rulings that interpret and apply California law to a specific set of facts. However, there are certain instances when the FTB will not provide written advice, like when the answer to a question depends principally on factual issues. This does not affect the statutory process in place under Sec. 23101.5 for petitioning the FTB for a determination of whether a corporation is "not doing business." That FTB will continue to review petitions brought forward under that section. (FTB Notice 2011-06, California Franchise Tax Board, October 12, 2011)

Corporations organized only to hold stock or bonds in other corporations, and that do not trade in those stocks or bonds, are not doing business in California if they engage in no activity other than the receipt and distribution of interest and dividends from those holdings. (Sec. 23102, Rev. & Tax. Code)

While a corporation that is not doing business in California is not subject to the corporation franchise tax, it may be subject to the corporation income tax on income derived from sources in California. (Sec. 23501, Rev. & Tax. Code)

California's application of P.L. 86-272. P.L. 86-272 prohibits California from imposing income tax on the income that an out-of-state taxpayer derives in California from interstate commerce if the taxpayer's activities in California are limited solely to the solicitation of orders for sales of tangible personal property except for de minimis activities and activities conducted by independent contractors. "Solicitation" means speech or conduct that explicitly or implicitly invites an order, or activities that neither explicitly nor implicitly invite an order but are entirely ancillary to requests for an order.

— **Ancillary activities.** Ancillary activities serve no independent business function apart from their connection to the solicitation of orders. Activities that seek to promote sales are not ancillary activities.

— **De minimis activities.** De minimis activities establish only a trivial connection with the state. Any activity conducted in the state on a regular or systematic basis, or under a company policy, normally will not have a trivial connection with the state. Whether an activity establishes a trivial or non-trivial connection with California must be measured on a qualitative and a quantitative basis. If the activity either qualitatively or quantitatively creates a non-trivial connection with California, then the activity exceeds the protection of P.L. 86-272. Establishing that the disqualifying activity only accounts for a relatively small part of the business conducted in California does not determine whether a de minimis level of activity exists.

— **Activities of independent contractors.** Independent contractors may engage in limited activities in California without causing a taxpayer to lose its P.L. 86-272 protection from taxation. These activities include soliciting sales, making sales, and maintaining an office. Sales representatives who represent a single business are not considered independent contractors. Also, an independent contractor's maintaining a stock of goods in California, except for display and solicitation, is not a protected activity.

— **Activities in foreign commerce.** P.L. 86-272 specifically applies to interstate commerce and does not directly apply to foreign commerce. "Interstate commerce"" includes commerce between the 50 states and Puerto Rico.

— **Unprotected activities during part of tax year.** Protection under P.L. 86-272 is determined on a tax year by tax year basis. If, at any time during a tax year, a taxpayer conducts activities in California that are not protected under P.L. 86–272, then none of the sales the taxpayer makes in California or income the taxpayer earns in California during any part of the tax year will be protected by P.L. 86–272.

(FTB 1050, Application and Interpretation of Public Law 86-272)

CCH PRACTICE TIP: Although P.L. 86-272 exempts qualified taxpayers engaged in selling tangible personal property from tax if their only connection to the state is solicitation of sales, P.L. 86-272 does not provide immunity from the minimum tax, because the minimum tax is not based on net income. Taxpayers are required to file returns and pay the minimum tax if they are doing business in California, even if their activities are otherwise protected by P.L. 86-272. (*General Information on New Rules for Doing Business in California*, California Franchise Tax Board, March 4, 2011) Also, P.L. 86-272 does not provide protection from the LLC fee (see ¶ 10-240). (*Tax News*, California Franchise Tax Board, September 2013)

Activities in California not protected by P.L. 86-272. If they are more than de minimis, then the following activities in California are not protected by P.L. 86-272 and may create corporation franchise tax nexus for an out-of-state taxpayer:

— leasing, renting, or licensing tangible personal property;

— transactions involving intangibles, like franchises, patents, copyrights, trademarks, and service marks;

— sale or delivery, and solicitation for sale or delivery, of any type of service that is not either ancillary to solicitation or listed as a protected activity;

— making repairs or providing maintenance or service to property being sold;

— collecting current or delinquent accounts, directly or by third parties;

— investigating credit worthiness;

— installation or supervising installation during or after shipment or delivery;

— conducting training courses, seminars, or lectures for personnel other than those involved only in solicitation;

— providing technical assistance or service, including engineering assistance or design service, for a purpose other than facilitating the solicitation of orders;

— investigating, handling, or otherwise assisting in resolving customer complaints (other than mediating direct customer complaints if the sole purpose is to ingratiate the sales personnel with the customer);

— approving or accepting orders;

— repossessing property;

— securing deposits on sales;

— picking up or replacing damaged or returned property;

— hiring, training, or supervising personnel, other than personnel involved only in solicitation;

— sales personnel using agency stock checks or any other process to make sales in California;

— maintaining a sample or display room for more than 14 days at any one location in California during the tax year;

— carrying samples for sale, exchange, or distribution subject to a charge;

— owning, leasing, using, or maintaining any of the following facilities or property in California: repair shop; parts department; office other than an "in-home" office; warehouse; meeting place for directors, officers, or employees; stock of goods other than samples for sales personnel or ancillary items; telephone answering service that is publicly attributed to the company or to the company's employees or agents as representatives; mobile stores; or real property or fixtures to real property;

— consigning tangible personal property to anyone, including an independent contractor, for sale;

— an employee or other representative maintaining an office or place of business (other than an "in-home" office located in the employee's or representative's residence that (i) is not publicly attributed to the company or to the employee or representative in a representative capacity and (2) is used only for soliciting and receiving orders from customers, transmitting orders outside California for acceptance or rejection by the company, or other protected activities);

— entering into franchising or licensing agreements, selling or otherwise disposing of franchises and licenses, or selling or otherwise transferring tangible personal property under a franchise or license in California; and

— conducting any activity not listed as a protected activity under P.L. 86-272 that is not entirely ancillary to requests for orders, even if the activity helps to increase purchases.

(FTB 1050, Application and Interpretation of Public Law 86-272)

CCH POINTER: In a nonprecedential summary decision, the California State Board of Equalization (BOE) held that P.L. 86-272 did not provide protection from taxable nexus for an out-of-state media firm with a California employee who sold advertising to California customers, because the solicitation of the advertising sales involved sales of a service and not sales of tangible personal property. According to the BOE, the parties bargained for the right to have an advertiser's images and words appear in the taxpayer's magazine, which was likely to be read by an audience of the advertiser's probable customers. Thus, the sales transactions did not involve the transfer to the advertisers of a tangible medium, like the magazines themselves. As P.L. 86-272 protects only solicitations for sales of tangible personal property, it did not apply in this case. (*Personal Selling Power, Inc.*, California State Board of Equalization, March 16, 2009)

Activities in California protected by P.L. 86-272. The following activities in California are protected under P.L. 86-272 and are not sufficient to create corporation franchise tax nexus for an out-of-state taxpayer:

— advertising to solicit orders;

— soliciting orders through California resident employees or representatives that do not have an office or other place of business in the state other than an "in-home" office;

— carrying samples and promotional materials only for display or free distribution;

— furnishing or setting up display racks and advising customers on the display of products without charge;

— providing automobiles to sales personnel to use in conducting protected activities;

— passing orders, inquiries, and complaints on to the home office;

— missionary sales activities;

— coordinating shipment or delivery without charge and providing related information before or after an order is placed;

— checking customers' inventories without any charge for reorders, but not for other purposes like quality control;

— maintaining a sample or display room for 14 days or less at any one location in California during the tax year;

— recruiting, training, or evaluating sales personnel, including occasionally using homes, hotels, or similar places for meetings with sales personnel;

— mediating direct customer complaints solely to ingratiate the sales representative with the customer and facilitate requests for orders;

— owning, leasing, using, or maintaining personal property for use in an employee's or representative's "in-home" office or automobile solely to conduct protected activities; and

— merely registering or qualifying to do business in California.

(FTB 1050, Application and Interpretation of Public Law 86-272)

[¶10-200]

BUSINESS ENTITIES

[¶10-210] C Corporations

Corporations are subject to Subchapter C of Chapter 1 of Subtitle A of the Internal Revenue Code relating to corporate distributions and adjustments, which is comprised of IRC Sec. 301—IRC Sec. 385. California incorporates this federal law with regard to corporate formation, operations, distributions, reorganizations, liquidations, and dissolutions, generally as of California's federal conformity date (see ¶10-515 Federal Conformity). (Sec. 24451, Rev. & Tax. Code)

• *Interaction of federal and state provisions*

The California Corporation Tax Law applies to all corporations and corporate-like business entities and financial corporations (including banks). The California

¶10-210

Corporation Law imposes a franchise tax on all corporations incorporated in California, qualified through the California Secretary of State, or nonqualified corporations "doing business" in California. (Sec. 23151, Rev. & Tax. Code) Foreign corporations not subject to the franchise tax due to protection under Public Law 86-272 are subject to the income tax if they derive income from sources within California or from activities carried on in the state. Foreign corporations engaged only in soliciting orders for goods to be shipped to California customers from points outside the state are not subject to the income tax. (Sec. 23501, Rev. & Tax. Code)

The term "corporation" applies to all corporations, other than those specifically exempted by the California Revenue and Taxation Code or the California Constitution. Also, certain unincorporated associations, trusts, professional corporations, and limited liability companies (LLCs) are treated as corporations. (Sec. 23038, Rev. & Tax. Code)

California incorporates IRC Sec. 7704, under which a publicly traded partnership is treated as a corporation unless at least 90% of its gross income consists of "qualifying income." (Sec. 23038.5, Rev. & Tax. Code)

Generally, California incorporates federal tax law, as of California's federal conformity date see ¶ 10-515 Federal Conformity relating to corporate organization, distributions, reorganizations, and liquidations. (Sec. 24451, Rev. & Tax. Code)

Unmodified IRC sections.—The California corporation franchise and income tax provisions of the Revenue and Taxation Code incorporate by reference numerous IRS Code provisions without modification, as discussed below.

Formation.—California law conforms to the federal rules (also known as check-the-box regulations) for the classification of business entities. The regulations issued by the Franchise Tax Board (FTB) related to the classification of a business entity must be consistent with the federal regulations as in effect May 1, 2014. (Sec. 23038, Rev. & Tax. Code) In general, the classification of an eligible business entity for purposes of California income and franchise tax is the same as the classification of the entity for federal tax purposes. Any election to change the classification of an eligible business entity for federal purposes is also applicable for California purposes. Except for certain entities (such as business trusts and single member entities that filed as partnerships) in existence prior to 1997, there is no separate California election regarding the classification of an entity for tax purposes. (*California's Corporation Taxes, Frequently Asked Questions*, California Franchise Tax Board Publication 1083, June 2003)

The FTB has issued Pub. 1060, Guide for Corporations Starting Business in California (May 2018), which addresses many of the questions that arise during a corporation's first year, such as minimum franchise tax liability, estimated taxes, election of annual accounting periods and methods, and filing returns.

Distributions.—California incorporates without modification (as of a specified date, see ¶ 10-515 Federal Conformity) the following IRS provisions relating to corporate distributions (Sec. 24451, Rev. & Tax. Code):

— IRC Sec. 303, which requires that stocks redeemed by a corporation from a decedent's estate be treated as a taxable sale and exchange;

— IRC Sec. 304, which treats proceeds from stock sales between a brother-sister corporation as distributions in redemption of the stock of the acquiring corporation;

— IRC Sec. 305, which excludes from gross income, with specified exceptions, distributions by a corporation of its own shares to its shareholders;

— IRC Sec. 307, which requires that in determining the basis of the new stock received in an exempt distribution that the adjusted basis of old stock be allocated between the old stock and the new stock;

— IRC Sec. 311, which allows nonrecognition of gain or loss on stock or property distributions to shareholders, with specified exceptions;

— IRC Sec. 312, which provides rules for the computation of corporate earnings and profits as a result of corporate distributions;

— IRC Sec. 316, as amended by the Regulated Investment Company Modernization Act of 2010 (Public Law 111-325), which defines the term "dividend;"

— IRC Sec. 317, which provides definitions of "property" and "redemptions;" and

— IRC Sec. 318, which provides rules for attributing stock ownership to an individual, partnership, estate, trust, or corporation where such stock is actually owned by other individuals or entities.

Reorganizations.—California conforms to the following IRC provisions relating to reorganizations as of a specified date (Sec. 24451, Rev. & Tax. Code):

— IRC Sec. 354, regarding the tax-free exchange of stock and securities in certain reorganizations;

— IRC Sec. 361, regarding nonrecognition of gain or loss to corporations that exchange property solely for stock or securities in another corporation as part of a reorganization;

— IRC Sec. 368, which provides the definition of "reorganization."

Liquidations.—California directly incorporates without modification the following IRC sections as of a specified date (Sec. 24451, Rev. & Tax. Code):

— IRC Sec. 331, regarding the requirement that shareholders recognize gain or loss on amounts distributed during a complete corporate liquidation;

— IRC Sec. 332, providing that the basis of property received by a parent corporation in the complete liquidation of its subsidiary is the subsidiary's basis in the property, unless the liquidated subsidiary recognizes gain or loss on the transfer;

— IRC Sec. 334, regarding the basis of property received in liquidation;

— IRC Sec. 336, regarding the requirement that a corporation recognize gain or loss on distributions of property in a complete liquidation;

— IRC Sec. 337, providing that no gain or loss is recognized by a liquidating subsidiary on distributions to an 80% distributee;

— IRC Sec. 338, providing that an acquiring corporation may make an irrevocable election to treat qualified stock purchases as asset acquisitions in a complete liquidation; and

— IRC Sec. 346, providing that a distribution is a complete liquidation of a corporation if the distribution is one of a planned series of distributions in redemption of all of the corporation's stock.

Modifications to IRC sections.—Some IRC provisions are incorporated by reference with specific modifications made by California law.

Formation.—IRC Sec. 195, which addresses start-up expenditures, is incorporated as of California's current IRC conformity date, with modifications to internal references. A California taxpayer may elect to treat currently deduct up to $5,000 in start-up expenditures and ratably deduction any remainder over a 15-year period. (Sec. 24414, Rev. & Tax. Code)

The tax for a corporation's first taxable year is computed according to or measured by its net income for the taxable year. (Sec. 23151.1, Rev. & Tax. Code) New corporations are exempt from the minimum franchise tax. (Sec. 23153(f), Rev. & Tax. Code)

A corporation that commenced doing business before 1972 is entitled to a credit for the franchise tax paid during its first full year of doing business. The credit may be taken only in the year of dissolution or withdrawal and is equal to the amount by which the tax paid for the first full taxable year of 12 months exceeds the minimum franchise tax payable for the same time period. (Sec. 23201, Rev. & Tax. Code)

Distributions.—California incorporates IRC Sec. 301, which addresses distributions of property, but requires that a taxpayer qualify for the California dividends received deduction under Sec. 24402, Rev. & Tax. Code, rather than the federal dividends received deductions when determining whether a taxpayer is treated as a 20% corporate shareholder, subject to the special rules outlined in IRC Sec. 301(e). (Sec. 24452, Rev. & Tax. Code) But see ¶10-810 Subtractions—Dividends, for a discussion of a California Court of Appeal's ruling that Sec. 24402, Rev. & Tax. Code is unconstitutional.

California incorporates IRC Sec. 302 regarding distributions in redemption of stock, but replaces references to federal statutes of limitations with references to the corresponding California statutes for determining the period in which an assessment may be issued in situations involving termination of a family-member shareholder's interest. (Sec. 24451, Rev. & Tax. Code; Sec. 24453, Rev. & Tax. Code; Former Sec. 24452.1, Rev. & Tax. Code)

California conforms to IRC Sec. 306, regarding the dispositions of certain stock, which treats proceeds from the sale or redemption of so-called IRC Sec. 306 stock as ordinary income, but does not adopt IRC Sec. 306(f), relating to the source of gain. (Sec. 24456, Rev. & Tax. Code)

Liquidations.—California does not modify any of the IRC provisions relating to corporate liquidations.

Dissolution.—For corporation franchise and income tax purposes, a California corporation is dissolved on the date on which a certificate of winding up and dissolution is filed in the Secretary of State's office or on the date a court decree declaring the corporation duly wound-up and dissolved is filed in the Secretary of State's office. (Sec. 23331, Rev. & Tax. Code) When a corporation files a final franchise tax return, the FTB is required to send the taxpayer information regarding all documents required to be filed with the FTB and the Secretary of State's Office in order to effectuate a dissolution or withdrawal. (Sec. 23335, Rev. & Tax. Code)

The franchise and income tax payable by a corporation dissolving or withdrawing from the state is measured either by the income of the year it ceased business, unless that income has already been included in the measure of tax, or the minimum tax. (Sec. 23151.2, Rev. & Tax. Code)

For corporate income tax purposes, a foreign corporation surrenders its right to transact interstate business on the date a certificate of withdrawal is filed in the office of the Secretary of State. (Sec. 23331, Rev. & Tax. Code) Foreign corporations qualified to do interstate business that wish to withdraw must also obtain a tax clearance certificate from the FTB to establish that all corporation income taxes are paid or secured. (Sec. 23561, Rev. & Tax. Code)

For further details, see FTB Pub. 1038, Guide to Dissolve, Surrender, or Cancel a California Business Entity.

Suspension.—A corporation's powers to act may be suspended or a foreign corporation's forfeited if the corporation fails to pay taxes or file a return. The corporation is still permitted to amend its articles of incorporation to set forth a new name, to file an application for exempt status, or to amend its articles of incorporation to perfect the application for exempt status. (Sec. 23301.5, Rev. & Tax. Code) However, the corporation may not dissolve during a period of suspension or forfeiture. (FTB Pub. 1038, Guide to Dissolve, Surrender, or Cancel a California Business Entity)

PRACTICE NOTE: Suspension procedures.—Before the FTB can suspend or forfeit a corporation, the FTB must notify the corporation that it is in danger of being suspended, being forfeited, or having its contracts become voidable. The FTB first sends FTB 4974BC M (corporation), Final Notice Before Suspension/Forfeiture. If the entity does not comply within 60 days after the FTB sends the first notice, the FTB sends FTB 2520BC M (corporation), Notice of Suspension or Forfeiture. Finally, if the entity still does not comply, suspension or forfeiture will occur, generally on the first working day of the month. (*Tax News*, Franchise Tax Board, August 2010)

The powers of a suspended corporation may be restored by payment of all taxes, penalties, and interest and the filing of all tax returns due at the time of an application for a certificate of revivor is filed. (Sec. 23305, Rev. & Tax. Code)

PLANNING NOTE: Expedited Requests for Corporate Revivor.—The fee for submitting expedited service requests for corporation revivor requests is $56 and must be paid by certified checks, money orders, or cash. Personal checks will not be accepted. Corporation revivor requests are made by submitting Form FTB 3557A (Application for Certificate of Revivor --Walk-Through) along with the necessary returns and payments at one of the FTB district offices that accept walk through applications, including the Los Angeles, Oakland, Sacramento, San Diego, San Francisco, or Santa Ana district offices. (Reg. 19591; FTB Notice 2004-09, FTB, December 17, 2004)

A corporation that has suffered suspension or forfeiture of its corporate powers, rights, and privileges for nonpayment of taxes or the failure to file a return and than is revived in a subsequent taxable year is required to pay a franchise tax for the year of revivor based on the income for the year preceding the suspension or forfeiture if it was doing business in that year. If it was not doing business in that year, it is subject to the minimum franchise tax, which must be prepaid in addition to payment of all delinquent taxes, interest, and penalties, as a condition precedent to the issuance of a certificate of revivor. (Sec. 23282, Rev. & Tax. Code)

Cessation of business activities.—The tax for the taxable year, including the taxable year of cessation, is imposed on the corporation's net income for the taxable year. A corporation that ceases business during a given year but does not legally dissolve or withdraw from the state nor resume doing business during a succeeding year is subject only to the minimum tax for years subsequent to that in which it ceased to do business, unless it qualifies for the exception granted if certain conditions are met. A corporation that opens and discontinues business in the same taxable year, whether or not it dissolves or withdraws in the same year, measures its tax on its earnings for that year. (Sec. 23151.1, Rev. & Tax. Code) A foreign corporation that ceases to do business in California for franchise tax purposes and does not withdraw but continues to have income from California sources is subject to the franchise tax for the year of change. (Sec. 23504, Rev. & Tax. Code)

Voluntary administrative dissolution procedures.—Effective January 1, 2019, procedures are established for voluntary dissolution of domestic corporations and LLCs. Involuntary dissolution procedures are discussed at ¶ 89-206, Civil Penalties.

A voluntary dissolution option is available to businesses that (1) have never done business or have ceased doing business in California; (2) have paid all taxes due for years when it was in operation; and (3) filed all required returns before stopping business operations. Businesses applying for administrative dissolution must:

— request abatement of any unpaid minimum franchise or annual tax, interest, and penalties;

— file dissolution paperwork with the Secretary of State before abatement of the unpaid tax, interest, and penalties; and

— show that it has stopped all business activity and has no remaining assets when it files the request for abatement.

The abatement of unpaid tax, interest, and penalties is conditioned on the prior dissolution of the business. (Sec. 23310, Rev. & Tax. Code) However, the total tax, interest, and penalties that are abated will immediately be due and payable if the business continues to do business or has any remaining assets that were not disclosed with the request for abatement. In addition, a penalty equal to 50% of the total tax abated, plus interest, will be imposed. This penalty is in addition to any other penalty imposed. (Sec. 23311, Rev. & Tax. Code)

• *Federal income tax provisions*

Every corporation that is taxed under subchapter C of the tax code is called a C corporation. A C corporation is a separate taxpaying entity independent from its shareholders. It is organized under state law by filing a corporate charter with the competent state authorities. The corporation must also comply with other state law formalities such as the holding of an organizational meeting and issuance of stock. Individuals, corporations or non-corporate business entities may become shareholders in a corporation by contributing money or other property to the corporation's capital in exchange for its stock. There is no limitation on the number of shareholders, and any changes in the type or the number of shareholders do not affect the existence of the corporation. The liability of the shareholders for the corporation's debts is limited to their investment in the corporation's capital.

Federal tax law rather than state law determines if a corporation exists for tax purposes. State law determines if relationships essential to the federal tax concept of a corporation exist. An entity that qualifies as a corporation under state law is usually taxed as a corporation, unless it is a sham, inactive or organized solely for tax avoidance purposes. On the other hand, a business entity that fails to comply with some of the corporate organization formalities under state law may be treated as a corporation for federal tax purposes.

A C corporation pays a corporate income tax on its annual taxable income at specified corporate tax rates. The shareholders are taxed if and when the corporation's earned income is distributed in the form of dividends. Thus, the distributed corporate income of a C corporation may be subject to double taxation, first at a corporate level and then at a shareholder level. The corporation may also be subject to additional taxes, such as the accumulated earnings tax and the personal holding company tax.

[¶10-215] S Corporations

California generally adopts the federal income tax treatment of an S corporation and its shareholders as of the current California conformity date (see ¶10-515), but with substantial modifications. (Sec. 23800(a), Rev. & Tax. Code) Most significantly, although California usually follows the federal pass-through concept, it does tax an S corporation at the entity level, but at a lower rate than that imposed on other corporations (*i.e.*, with some qualification, 1.5%). However, income and losses, including net operating losses (NOLs) of the S corporation flow to its shareholders.

> **COMPLIANCE NOTE:** *Treatment of S corporation items on shareholder's return.*—A shareholder of an S corporation must treat an S corporation item on the shareholder's return in a manner that is consistent with the treatment of the item on the corporate return unless (1) the S corporation has not filed a return or, if the S corporation has filed a return, the shareholder's treatment of the item on the shareholder's return is, or may be, inconsistent with the treatment of the item on the corporate return; and (2) the shareholder files a statement with the FTB identifying the inconsistency. (Sec. 18601(e)(2), Rev. & Tax. Code)

Furthermore, although California only technically incorporates federal law as of the California's current conformity date (see ¶10-515), because S corporations that have a valid S corporation election for federal purposes are treated as an S corporation for California corporation franchise and income tax purposes (Sec. 23801(a), Rev. & Tax. Code), California essentially incorporates the IRC provisions governing S corporation qualifications, elections, and terminations (IRC Sec. 1361 and IRC Sec. 1362) as currently amended.

> **PLANNING NOTE:** *Timing of election.*—Taxpayers considering making an S corporation election may want to consider the timing of making the election or change. If they make an election mid-year, they will have to file two short-year returns and pay for two entities. (*Tax News*, California Franchise Tax Board, February 2010)

S corporations file a Form 100S, S Corporation Franchise or Income Tax Return.

• *Interaction of federal and state provisions*

The IRC sections incorporated by California without amendment and the various state modifications to the federal income tax provisions are discussed below.

Unmodified IRC sections.—IRC Sec. 1368, which address the tax consequenses of an S corporation's distributions and IRC Sec. 1378, which addresses the tax year of an S corporation, are incorporated by California without amendment.

Modifications to IRC Sec. 1361.—IRC Sec. 1361 defines an S corporation for federal income tax purposes.

IRC Sec. 1361(b)(3), which allows an S corporation to own a qualified Subchapter S subsidiary (QSub), is modified to provide that, although, under California law, a

QSub is not treated as a separate corporation from the parent S corporation, the QSub is still subject to the California corporate minimum tax if the entity is:

— incorporated in California;

— qualified to transact business in the state; or

— doing business in California.

Furthermore, the QSub's activities will be imputed to the parent S corporation for purposes of determining whether the parent S corporation is "doing business" in California. (23800.5(b)(1)) Finally, a parent S corporation's election to treat a subsidiary as a QSub for federal income tax purposes is binding for California franchise and income tax purposes and a separate California election is not allowed. (23800.5(b)(3))

COMPLIANCE POINTER: Reporting QSub election and items of income, deductions, etc.—An S corporation parent must attach a copy of the federal Form 8869, Qualified Subchapter S Subsidiary Election, for each QSub qualified to do business or doing business in California to the return for the taxable year during which the QSub election was made. (Instructions, Form 100S, S Corporation Franchise or Income Tax Return)

An S corporation that owns a QSub does not file a combined return. Instead the QSub is disregarded and the QSubs' activities, assets, liabilities, income, deductions, and credits are considered to be the S corporation's assets, liabilities, income, and credits. If the QSub is not unitary with the S corporation then it is treated as a separate division and separate computations must be made to compute business income and apportionment factors for the two entities. (Instructions, Form 100S, S Corporation Franchise or Income Tax Return) Numerous examples of how to attribute income, deductions, and credits between an S corporation and its QSub are provided in FTB Pub. 1093, Frequently Asked Questions: Qualified Subchapter S Subsidiaries (QSubs), revised May 2000.

Because of California's IRC conformity history, California did not incorporate the following a by the Small Business and Work Opportunity Tax Act of 2007 (SBWOTA) (P.L. 110-28) until the 2010 tax year:

— an amendment that allows a bank changing from the reserve method of accounting for bad debts for its first tax year for which it is an S corporation to elect to take into account all IRC Sec. 481 adjustments in the last tax year it was a C corporation, effective for federal purposes beginning with the 2007 tax year; and

— an amendment that provides that an S corporation's sale of a QSub's stock is treated as a sale of an undivided interest in the QSub's assets followed by a deemed creation of the subsidiary in an IRC Sec. 351 transaction, effective for federal purposes beginning with the 2007 tax year.

— a provision that eliminates a corporation's accumulated earnings and profits that arose during its pre-1983 S corporation years even if the corporation was not an S corporation for its first tax year beginning after 1996, applicable for federal purposes to taxable years beginning after May 25, 2007.

(Analysis of Small Business Work and Opportunity Tax Act of 2007, California Franchise Tax Board, July 25, 2007) Additional amendments made by the SBWOTA were previously incorporated by California because these provisions impacted S corporation eligibility. (Sec. 23800.5(a)(3)(A), Rev. & Tax. Code; Sec. 23801(a), Rev. & Tax. Code)

(Sec. 23800.5, Rev. & Tax. Code)

Modifications to IRC Sec. 1362.—IRC Sec. 1362 makes provision for the election, revocation, and termination of S corporation status. corporation that has in effect a valid federal S corporation election is treated as an S corporation for California tax purposes and no separate election is allowed. (Sec. 23801(a), Rev. & Tax. Code) The federal election applies for purposes of determining the shareholders' California franchise and income tax liability, even if the corporation is not qualified to do business in California or is not incorporated in the state. Likewise, a termination of a federal S corporation election that is not an inadvertent termination, simultaneously terminates the entity's S corporation election for California tax purposes. (Sec. 23801(e)(1), Rev. & Tax. Code)

The federal provision relating to the termination of S corporation status when a corporation has passive investment income exceeding 25% of gross receipts for three consecutive tax years and also has accumulated earnings and profits only applies at the state level if it applies at the federal level and the federal S corporation status is terminated. (Sec. 23801(g), Rev. & Tax. Code)

Like the IRS at the federal level, at the state level, the FTB may validate an invalid election that results from an entity's:

— inadvertent failure to qualify as a small business corporation;

— failure to obtain the required shareholder consents; or

— late filing of an election with reasonable cause.

However, a corporation itself may perfect an S corporation election for California tax purposes, if for any taxable year the corporation merely failed to timely file a federal S corporation election (federal Form 2553 Election by a Small Business Corporation) if the corporation and all of its shareholders filed for IRS relief and received IRS notification of the acceptance of an untimely filed federal S corporation election (Sec. 23801(h)(2), Rev. & Tax. Code)

While ordinarily a California S corporation may not be included in a combined report (Sec. 23801(c), Rev. & Tax. Code), the FTB may apply methods of unitary combination if the FTB determines that the reported income or loss of a group of commonly owned or controlled corporations, which includes one or more S corporations, does not clearly reflect income or loss, or represents an evasion of tax. (Sec. 23801(d)(1), Rev. & Tax. Code)

A C corporation resulting from an S corporation termination must annualize its taxable income for the short taxable year under both California and federal law. However, taxpayers must annualize their income on a monthly basis for California corporation franchise and income tax purposes and on a daily basis for federal income tax purposes. (Sec. 23801(f), Rev. & Tax. Code)

Modifications to IRC Sec. 1363.—IRC Sec. 1363 describes the effect of an S corporation election upon the corporate entity. California has not adopted IRC Sec. 1363(a), which generally exempts an S corporation from an entity-level income tax. Instead, the state subjects all S corporations except financial corporations to the franchise and income tax at a special 1.5% rate. (Secs. 23802(a) and (b)(1), Rev. & Tax. Code) A financial S corporation is taxed at a higher 3.5% rate. (Sec. 23802(b)(2), Rev. & Tax. Code) Regardless of income, an S corporation and a QSub are also subject to California's minimum franchise tax (Sec. 23802(c), Rev. & Tax. Code), but not to the alternative minimum tax.

Note that an S corporation's deduction for amortization and depreciation is computed under the provisions of the Personal Income Tax Law. (Sec. 23802(f)(1), Rev. & Tax. Code)

The treatment of net operating loss carryover following the conversion of a C corporation to an S corporation is covered in the discussion of subtractions from taxable income for NOLs that may be claimed when computing California corporation franchise and income tax liability. (see ¶ 10-805)

Also, an S corporation is subject to the IRC Sec. 465 at-risk rules and the IRC Sec. 469 passive activity rules in the same manner as these rules are applied to an individual. (Secs. 23802(f)(2) and (f)(3)(A), Rev. & Tax. Code) However, for purposes of determining whether the passive activity limitations apply, an S corporation is subject to a slightly modified version of the "material participation" standard applicable to a closely held C corporation or personal service corporation. (Sec. 23802(f)(3)(A), Rev. & Tax. Code)

The gross income exclusion that is allowed to an individual for any gain on the sale of specified small business stock is not allowed to an S corporation. (Sec. 23802(f)(4), Rev. & Tax. Code)

The deduction for bad debts under Sec. 24348(a)(2), Rev. & Tax. Code, is not allowed to an S corporation. (Sec. 23802(f)(5), Rev. & Tax. Code)

Finally, California conforms to the federal exclusion of the last-in, first out (LIFO) recapture tax from estimated tax payment requirements. (Sec. 23802(g), Rev. & Tax. Code) The LIFO tax is imposed against an S corporation that deferred income by using the LIFO inventory method when it was a C corporation. Upon conversion to an S corporation, the S corporation is required to pay tax on the deferred income. Under federal law, these tax payments are not included in the estimated tax payment requirements, whereas, previously, California required such income to be included in estimated tax for California corporation franchise and income tax purposes.

Modifications to IRC Sec. 1366.—IRC Sec. 1366 provides for the passthrough of corporate tax items to an S corporation's shareholders. See Sec. 23802.5, Rev. & Tax. Code and Sec. 23803(b), Rev. & Tax. Code, for specific information regarding California's modifications to this federal statute.

Modifications to IRC Sec. 1367.—IRC Sec. 1367 provides for certain adjustments to the basis of an S corporation shareholder's stock. See Sec. 23804, Rev. & Tax. Code for California's tax treatment of such adjustments. As a result of California's current IRC conformity date (see ¶ 10-515), California has not adopted amendments made by the American Taxpayer Relief Act of 2012 and the Tax Increase Prevention Act of 2014 that extend the requirement that a shareholder's basis in the stock of an S corporation making a charitable contribution of property be reduced by the shareholder's pro rata share of the adjusted basis of the contributed property for contributions made in tax years beginning before January 1, 2015. Consequently, for California purposes the amount of the reduction of a shareholder's basis in the S corporation's stock by reason of the S corporation's charitable contribution of property is equal to the shareholder's pro rata share of the fair market value of the contributed property.

PRACTICE NOTE: *Basis calculations.*—The FTB has issued a technical advise memorandum (TAM) that addresses how a shareholder's basis in an S corporation is calculated when some years are closed by the statute of limitations. The TAM concludes that in situations when an S corporation has both items of income and deduction for the closed years and the shareholder failed to report these items on the shareholder's personal income tax return for the closed years, the shareholder's basis is not increased for items of income but basis is decreased for items of deduction but not below zero. Because the shareholder has not reported the items of loss or deduction, the shareholder may carry over any items of loss or deduction in excess of basis to future years. In instances when an S corporation has both items of income and deduction for the closed years and the shareholder reports all of these items on the shareholder's personal income tax return, basis is increased for items of income and basis decreased for items of loss and deduction but not below zero. Because the shareholder has reported and received the benefit of claiming these items of loss or deduction, the shareholder may carry not over any items of loss or deduction in excess of basis to future years. (Technical Advice Memorandum 2003-305, FTB, June 4, 2005)

The FTB has taken the position that IRC Sec. 1016, the duty of consistency and/or the tax benefit rule does not require a shareholder that reported items of loss and deduction in excess of the shareholder's basis in a closed year to increase the shareholder's income in an open year by the amount of the erroneous items of income and loss reported. In addition, a worthless loss deduction claimed in an open tax year generated from income items in an open tax year is not a double deduction even if a shareholder reported losses in excess of basis in a closed year. The worthless loss deduction is not a double deduction with respect to the previous loss deductions. The basis that permits the taxpayer to take a deduction was generated from the income items in the open year. It is not attributable to any basis that was previously used. (Technical Advice Memorandum 2003-305, FTB, June 4, 2005)

Modifications to IRC Sec. 1371.—IRC Sec. 1371 helps to coordinate Subchapter S of the IRC with Subchapter C of the IRC. California tax law, but not federal tax law (IRC Sec. 1371(b)), allows a C corporation that elects S corporation status to carryover unused C corporation credits and to apply them against the S corporation's tax liability. However, this credit carryover from the C corporation is subject to a one-third limitation for the S corporation. (Sec. 23803, Rev. & Tax. Code) See the *Credits* discussion, below.

Furthermore, IRC Sec. 1371(d), which provides for coordination with investment credit recapture, does not apply. (Sec. 23806(c), Rev. & Tax. Code)

Finally, see Sec. 23802(d)(2), Rev. & Tax. Code, for an instance in which IRC Sec. 1371(b) specifically does not apply.

Modifications to IRC Sec. 1372.—IRC Sec. 1372, concerning the partnership tax rules that apply for fringe benefit purposes, is modified so that the references to partnership treatment are to IRC provisions as modified by California tax law. (Sec. 23807, Rev. & Tax. Code)

Modifications to IRC Sec. 1373.—IRC Sec. 1373, which addresses the tax treatment of foreign income in the S corporation context, is inapplicable for California franchise and income tax purposes. (Sec. 23808, Rev. & Tax. Code)

Modifications to IRC Sec. 1374.—For California tax purposes, IRC Sec. 1374, concerning the tax imposed on certain built-in gains, is modified to apply the applicable California corporate tax rate to any built-in gains instead of the federal tax rate. (Sec. 23809(a), Rev. & Tax. Code) In addition, the federal provisions of IRC Sec. 1374(b)(4) relating to coordination with IRC Sec. 1201(a) do not apply for California tax purposes. (Sec. 23809(c), Rev. & Tax. Code) Furthermore, because of California's current IRC conformity date (see ¶10-515), California does not conform to the five-year recognition period for built-in gains under IRC Sec. 1374(d)(7) and, instead, uses a ten-year recognition period. (Instructions, Form 100S, S Corporation Franchise or Income Tax Return)

> **COMPLIANCE NOTE:** *Apportionment.*—When an apportioning S corporation sells property generating net recognized built-in gain under IRC Sec. 1374, the income should be apportioned for California tax purposes according to the factors in the year of the sale, rather than according to the factors in the year of the S corporation conversion. (*Technical Advice Memorandum 2017-02*, California Franchise Tax Board, April 3, 2017)

Modifications to IRC Sec. 1375.—IRC Sec. 1375 imposes a tax when an S corporation with accumulated earnings and profits has passive investment income in excess of 25% of its gross receipts. California law modifies this provisions to substitute the applicable California corporation franchise or income tax rate. (Sec. 23811(b), Rev. & Tax. Code) Note that these taxes may not be reduced by any credits. (Sec. 23811(c), Rev. & Tax. Code) Only income from California sources is subject to the state's passive investment income tax. Finally, the tax is not imposed on an S corporation that has no excess net passive income, as defined by IRC Sec. 1375. (Sec. 23811(a), Rev. & Tax. Code)

The California tax on excess passive investment income is imposed only on S corporations that have subchapter C earnings and profits attributable to California sources. (Secs. 23811(d), Rev. & Tax. Code) A corporation that elects California S corporation status for its first taxable year for which it has a federal S election in effect may deduct from its California subchapter C earnings and profits at the close of any taxable year the amount of any consent dividend paid after the close of that taxable year. The amount of the consent dividend cannot exceed the difference between subchapter C earnings and profits attributable to California sources at the close of the taxable year and subchapter C earnings and profits for federal income tax purposes at the same date. The corporation must pay the consent dividend within 90 days after the date of determination that it has subchapter C earnings and profits. For this purposes, the determination date is the effective date of a closing agreement with the FTB, the date an assessment of tax becomes final, or the date the corporation executes an agreement with the FTB relating to liability for the tax on excess passive investment income. (Secs. 23811(e), Rev. & Tax. Code)

A corporation that distributes a consent dividend must claim the deduction from earnings and profits by filing a claim with the FTB within 120 days after the date of determination that the corporation has California subchapter C earnings and profits. The collection of the tax on excess passive investment income is stayed for 120 days after the date of determination. If the corporation files a claim with the FTB for the deduction of consent dividends, collection of the tax is further stayed until the FTB acts on the claim. Filing a claim also suspends the statute of limitations for assessments and for actions to collect the tax for a period of two years after the date of determination. (Sec. 23811(e), Rev. & Tax. Code)

Modifications to IRC Sec. 1377.—Among other purposes, IRC Sec. 1377 provides definitions for relevant S corporation concepts. The IRC Sec. 1377(b)(2) definition of "determination" is modified by California for the purpose of defining when the post-termination transition period commences to include a:

— final decision by the California State Board of Equalization (BOE);

— closing agreement; and

— final FTB disposition of a refund claim.

(Sec. 23813, Rev. & Tax. Code)

Modifications to IRC Sec. 1379.—IRC Sec. 1379, which provided transitional rules upon the initial federal enactment of Subchapter S, is inapplicable for California franchise (income) tax purposes. (Sec. 23808, Rev. & Tax. Code)

• *Nonresident S corporation shareholders*

An S corporation may file a group (composite) return and make composite tax payments on behalf of electing nonresident shareholders. (Sec. 18535(c), Rev. & Tax. Code) In addition, S corporations are required to withhold tax on distributions of California source income paid to their nonresident shareholders, see ¶ 89-104 for details. (Sec. 18662, Rev. & Tax. Code)

• *Credits*

Under California law, an S corporation is limited to one-third of the amount of any credit otherwise allowable to reduce the tax imposed upon it as a corporation. If any portion of this allowable one-third goes unused, then the S corporation may carry it forward to subsequent tax years without further restriction; but no carryforward of the remaining two-thirds is permitted. Credits carried forward for tax years beginning prior to the first tax year in which the corporation receives California S corporation treatment are subject to the one-third limitation for the first tax year, but not in subsequent years. Also, no credit is allowed against the minimum franchise tax, the built-in gains tax, excess net passive income tax, credit recaptures, the increase in tax imposed for the deferral of installment sale income, or an installment of a LIFO tax. (Instructions, Form 100S, S Corporation Franchise or Income Tax Return) Furthermore, credits that are allowed only under the Corporation Tax Law may not be passed through to shareholders. However, with respect to any credit that is allowed under both the Corporation Tax Law and the Personal Income Tax Law, shareholders may take the entire credit to which they are entitled under the Personal Income Tax Law, with no one-third limitation. (Sec. 23803, Rev. & Tax. Code)

• *Federal income tax provisions*

An S corporation is a small business corporation that satisfies the requirements of Subchapter S of the tax code and has elected to be taxed under those rules. In order to qualify as a small business corporation, the corporation must be a domestic corporation and is restricted on the number and types of shareholders it can have and on the type of stock that it can issue.

The difference between an S corporation and a regular corporation is that the S corporation has elected to be taxed similarly to a partnership for federal tax purposes. After making the S election, the income, losses, tax credits, and other tax items of the corporation flow through the corporation to the shareholders. Thus, income is only taxed once, at the shareholder level. However, an S corporation that was formerly a C corporation may be subject to taxes at the corporate level for LIFO recapture, excessive net passive income, and built-in gains.

[¶10-220] General Partnerships

California incorporates, with modifications, as of the current federal conformity date (see ¶ 10-515), the federal income tax provisions addressing partners and their partnerships in IRC Sec. 701 through IRC Sec. 761. (Sec. 17851, Rev. & Tax. Code; and Sec. 17851.5, Rev. & Tax. Code—Sec. 17857, Rev. & Tax. Code) Under these provisions, income and losses, including net operating losses (NOLs) of the partnership flow to its partners.

Also, a federal election to pay the imputed underpayment resulting from a federal partnership-level audit adjustment or to pass the underpayment through to partners generally will apply for California purposes, with some exceptions. (Sec. 18622.5, Rev. & Tax. Code)

• *Interaction of federal and state provisions*

The IRC sections incorporated without amendment and the various modifications are discussed below. Special provisions unique to California regarding the computation of income and the filing of returns by nonresident partners are also discussed.

Unmodified IRC sections.—Other than IRC Secs. 702, which addresses a partner's income and credits; 703, concerning partnership computations; 705, involving the basis determination for a partner's interest; 707, describing the tax consequences of transactions between a partner and the partnership; 751, addressing the tax treatment of certain unrealized receivables and inventory items; and 761, which provides definitions for certain applicable terms; the rest of the Subchapter K provisions of the IRC, as amended through the current conformity date (see ¶ 10-515), relating to the taxation of general partnerships and their partners, are incorporated by reference into California tax law without amendment. (Sec. 17851, Rev. & Tax. Code)

PRACTICE NOTE: As part of its tax gap strategy to close "abusive" tax shelter transactions, the California Franchise Tax Board (FTB) is closely scrutinizing the use of bogus optional basis transactions (BOB) transactions, in which a partnership uses an IRC Sec. 754 election to inappropriately increase the basis of its property. In some cases, the basis of assets is increased before their disposition. In other cases, taxpayers are using the additional basis to claim increased depreciation or amortization deductions. Although BOB transactions may be structured in various ways, their ultimate objective is to avoid gain on asset dispositions or to create deductions that offset income. Depending upon the facts and circumstances, a BOB transaction may be disregarded or be recast to properly reflect California income, or the basis step-up might be disallowed. Also, the FTB may add substantial penalties to any additional tax due. However, a taxpayer may be able to avoid certain penalties by filing an amended return to restate the taxpayer's proper tax liability. The amended return should be mailed to ATTN: 343: MS F-150, Franchise Tax Board, PO Box 942867, Sacramento CA 94267-0001. To ensure proper handling, "BOB TS" should be written on the top right margin of the first page. (*Tax News*, California Franchise Tax Board, September 2007)

Modifications to IRC Sec. 702.—IRC Sec. 702 addresses the income and credits of a partner. The list of items that each partner in a general partnership must take into account separately as the partner's distributive share (see IRC Secs. 702(a)(6)) is modified for California tax purposes by the deletion of foreign taxes paid. (Sec. 17024.5(b)(7), Rev. & Tax. Code) Furthermore, while IRC Sec. 702(a)(5) requires the separate statement of dividends qualifying for a special deduction for corporations, California has not incorporated this special corporate deduction. California tax law does not address the federal changes instituted by IRC Sec. 1(h)(11).

Modifications to IRC Sec. 703.—IRC Sec. 703 deals with partnership computations. IRC Sec. 703(a)(2) is modified for California tax purposes to provide that a partnership may not claim a deduction for taxes paid to another state. (Sec. 17853, Rev. & Tax. Code) Instead, the partners are allowed a credit against California personal income tax for taxes paid to another state by the partnership. Furthermore, while IRC Sec. 703(a)(2)(A) addresses a deduction for personal exemptions, California law allows a credit in lieu of personal exemptions and therefore this federal tax provision is inapplicable to California. Finally, IRC Sec. 703(b) requires that an election affecting the computation of taxable income derived from a partnership be made by the partnership. However, for California tax purposes, when the partnership makes an election relating to the computation of depreciation, each partner must take into account that partner's distributive share of the amount computed under such an election. (Sec. 17858, Rev. & Tax. Code)

CAUTION NOTE: Limitation on partner losses.—Because of California's current federal conformity date (see ¶ 10-515), California does not conform to federal law (IRC Sec. 704(d)(3)) providing that charitable contributions and foreign taxes are taken into account in determining the basis limitation on partner losses. (*2017 Summary of Federal Income Tax Changes*, California Franchise Tax Board, May 16, 2018)

Modifications to IRC Sec. 705.—IRC Sec. 705 deals with the basis determination for a partner's interest. While IRC Sec. 705(a)(3) requires a decrease in a partner's basis for any depletion deducted, California's depletion deductions differ from the federal allowances. Accordingly, basis differences for federal and state income tax purposes may arise.

Modifications to IRC Sec. 707.—IRC Sec. 707 establishes the tax consequences of certain transactions between a partner and the partnership. Under IRC Sec. 707(c), a guaranteed payment to a partner for services or the use of capital are considered as made to a non-partner to the extent that such payments are determined without regard to partnership income. Accordingly, such payments constitute ordinary income to the person receiving them, and are a business expense to the partnership paying them. For purposes of computing the taxable income of a nonresident partner, a guaranteed payment to such a partner must be included in that computation as gross income to the payee from sources within the state in the same manner as if those payments were distributive shares of the partnership. (Sec. 17854, Rev. & Tax. Code) This state tax provision has no federal counterpart.

CAUTION NOTE: Definition of substantial built-in loss.—Because of California's current federal conformity date (see ¶ 10-515), California does not conform to the federal modification of the definition of substantial built-in loss in the case of the transfer of partnership interests after December 31, 2017. (*2017 Summary of Federal Income Tax Changes*, California Franchise Tax Board, May 16, 2018)

Modifications to IRC Sec. 708.—IRC Sec. 708 deals with the continuation of a partnership. For tax years beginning after December 31, 2017, the rule for technical terminations for partnerships or entities treated as partnerships (IRC Sec. 708(b)(1)(B)) is repealed. California conforms to the repeal of the technical termination of a partnership for tax years beginning after 2018. Taxpayers may elect to apply the changes for tax years beginning after 2017 and before 2019. The California Franchise Tax Board (FTB) is in the process of developing formal procedures for taxpayers to make the election. (Sec. 17859(a), Rev. & Tax. Code)

Modifications to IRC Sec. 751.—IRC Sec. 751 addresses the tax treatment of certain unrealized receivables and inventory items. IRC Sec. 751(c) and (d) define "unrealized receivables" and "inventory items." These definitions, however, are modified for California tax purposes. For federal income tax purposes, unrealized receivables include the right to payment for stock in a domestic international sales corporation (DISC), but this item is not considered to be an unrealized receivable for California tax purposes. (Sec. 17024.5(b)(2), Rev. & Tax. Code) Stock in certain foreign corporations and oil, gas, or geothermal property are also considered to be unrealized receivables under federal tax law, but not under California tax law. (Sec. 17855, Rev. & Tax. Code) Furthermore, IRC Sec. 751(d)(3) includes any other property of the partnership that, if sold by the partnership, would result in gain on foreign investment company stock taxable under IRC Sec. 1246 in the definition of federal "inventory items." However, California does not incorporate the IRC provisions concerning foreign investment companies. (Sec. 17024.5(b)(5), Rev. & Tax. Code; Sec. 17856, Rev. & Tax. Code)

Furthermore, IRC Sec. 751(e), concerning the limitation on tax attributable to deemed sales of IRC Sec. 1248 stock, is inapplicable for California tax purposes. (Sec. 17857, Rev. & Tax. Code)

Modifications to IRC Sec. 761.—IRC Sec. 761 provides definitions for certain terms in the context of partnership taxation. California's general definition of "partnership" is the same as the definitions contained in IRC Secs. 761 and 7701(a)(2), except that California has an added provision explicitly recognizing a partner who owns a capital interest in a partnership in which capital is a material income-producing factor, whether the interest was derived by purchase or gift. (Sec. 17008, Rev. & Tax. Code)

Modifications to federal partnership return provisions.—Every partnership doing business in California must file an annual return of partnership income (Form 565) by the 15th day of the third month following the close of its tax year (15th day of fourth month following the close of its tax year for tax years prior to 2016). A partnership also must furnish each of its partners with certain information, as specified in regulations, from the partnership return. This applies to electing investment partnerships as well. In addition, the information required to be provided to partners must be provided to persons holding partnership interests as nominees for others. For California tax purposes, a person holding a partnership interest as a nominee for another must disclose the name and address of that other person (along with any other information required by the FTB) to the partnership, and must provide the other person with a copy of the partnership return information. (Sec. 18633, Rev. & Tax. Code)

These reporting requirements are comparable to IRC Sec. 6031, but California imposes the following additional requirements:

— California requires that those listed as entitled to share in net income be designated as resident or nonresident;

— except in the case of electronic filing, California requires a declaration that the return is made under penalty of perjury, signed by one of the partners. (Sec. 18633, Rev. & Tax. Code)

Also, California incorporates IRC Sec. 6031(d), which requires that the unrelated business taxable income of a partnership be separately stated to the partners. (Sec. 18633(d), Rev. & Tax. Code)

However, California does not conform to a provision in IRC Sec. 6011(e)(2), which requires a partnership having more than 100 partners to file its returns on magnetic media. (Sec. 18409(b)(2), Rev. & Tax. Code)

Nonresident partners.—As is the case for other nonresident taxpayers, a nonresident partner's gross income includes only the gross income from sources within California. A nonresident partner's income from stocks, bonds, or other intangible personal property is not income from sources within the state unless:

— the property has acquired a business situs in California;

— the nonresident partnership buys or sells such property in the state; or

— the nonresident partnership places orders with California brokers to buy or sell such property so regularly, systematically, and continuously as to constitute doing business in the state.

(Sec. 17951, Rev. & Tax. Code; Sec. 17952, Rev. & Tax. Code)

The income from estates or trusts distributed to nonresident partnerships is deemed to be income from sources within the state only if the distributed income was derived from sources within the state. (Sec. 17953, Rev. & Tax. Code) Finally, gross income from sources within and without California is allocated and apportioned under rules prescribed by the FTB. (Sec. 17954, Rev. & Tax. Code)

In certain circumstances, nonresident partners of a partnership doing business in California or deriving income from sources in California may elect to file a group income tax return in lieu of filing individual returns. If the election is made, the tax rate applicable to each electing partner's distributive share is the highest marginal income tax rate. Except as noted below, no deductions are allowed except those necessary to determine each partner's distributive share, and no credits are allowed except those directly attributable to the partnership. As agent for the electing partners, the partnership must make payments of tax, additions to tax, interest, and penalties otherwise required to be paid by the electing partners. (Sec. 18535(a), Rev. & Tax. Code)

A partnership that pays personal income tax on behalf of a nonresident partner under a group return election may deduct the amount of any items that would otherwise be deductible by the partner under deferred compensation provisions, but only if the partner certifies to the FTB that the partner has no earned income from any other source. (Sec. 18535(b), Rev. & Tax. Code)

The FTB may adjust the income of a nonresident partner included in a group return if the FTB has reason to believe that the income attributable to that partner does not properly reflect the partner's taxable income. (Sec. 18535(e), Rev. & Tax. Code)

Federal partnership-level audit adjustments.—A federal election to pay the imputed underpayment resulting from a federal partnership-level audit adjustment or to pass the underpayment through to partners generally will apply for California purposes, with no separate state election allowed. This applies for California purposes to final federal determinations assessed under the federal partnership audit rules as in effect January 1, 2018. However, a unitary partner whose share of a partnership's income and apportionment factors is includible as business income on the partner's original California return is not bound by the federal election. The partner will be treated as having filed an amended federal return and must file an amended state return to separately report its California share of the adjustments. Also, any partnership can file a request to make a state election different from its federal election. The FTB must grant such requests as follows:

— where the partnership makes a federal election for alternative payment, if the partnership properly computes the amount of California tax due; or

— where the partnership pays the tax at the federal level, if the partnership can demonstrate that the FTB's tax collection ability would not be impeded and the partnership follows the partnership reporting provisions.

(Sec. 18622.5, Rev. & Tax. Code)

If a federal partnership-level audit adjustment increases the amount of tax due and the partnership does not elect to pass the adjustment through to its partners, the partnership (rather than its partners) must pay California tax calculated as the sum of the following:

— for corporate partners or tax-exempt partners, the total share of all adjustments and positive reallocation adjustments after apportionment and allocation to California, multiplied by the highest marginal corporate tax rate (see ¶ 10-380) for the reviewed year;

— for tiered partners, nonresident individual partners, or nonresident fiduciary partners, the total share of all adjustments and positive reallocation adjustments that is California source income, multiplied by the highest marginal personal income tax rate (see ¶ 15-355) for the reviewed year; and

— for resident partners, resident fiduciary partners, or other partners, the total share of all adjustments and positive reallocations, multiplied by the highest marginal personal income tax rate (see ¶ 15-355) for the reviewed year.

(Sec. 18622.5, Rev. & Tax. Code)

Partnerships may remove the following items from the tax calculation:

— the share of the adjustments made to a tax-exempt partner that is not unrelated business taxable income; and

— the share of the adjustments made to a partner that has filed an amended return reporting a share of the adjustments and paid any additional state tax due.

(Sec. 18622.5, Rev. & Tax. Code)

• *Federal income tax provisions*

A partnership is a pass-through entity that does not pay tax on its income. Instead, the partnership passes along its income or loss, gains, deductions, and credits to the partners. Each partner reports a percentage of the partnership income and other items on the partner's own tax return.

A partnership does not pay tax, but it does compute income, deductions and credits on an annual basis. Information about the business is reported to the IRS on Form 1065 and to the individual partners on separate Schedules K-1. The partners report the partnership income on their own returns and pay any taxes due based on their own tax rates.

[¶10-225] Limited Partnerships; Limited Liability Partnerships

California generally incorporates by reference IRC Sec. 701 through IRC Sec. 761, the federal income tax provisions addressing partners and their limited partnerships, as of a fixed date (see ¶ 15-515 Federal Conformity). (Sec. 17851, Rev. & Tax. Code) A number of these federal tax provisions, however, have been modified for state tax purposes, as discussed more fully at ¶ 10-220 General Partnerships. However, income and losses, including net operating losses (NOLs) of the partnership flow to its partners.

• *Applicable state business laws*

California has enacted a number of business law provisions specifically addressing limited partnerships (Sec. 15507, Corp. Code through Sec. 15692, Corp. Code) and LLPs. (Sec. 16951, Corp. Code through Sec. 16959, Corp. Code) These provisions are briefly addressed below.

The Uniform Limited Partnership Act (ULPA) of 2008 generally governs all limited partnerships. (Sec. 15912.06, Corp. Code) (Sec. 15534, Corp. Code; Sec. 15724, Corp. Code)

Limited partnership.—For business law purposes, a limited partnership combines the characteristics of a corporation with that of a general partnership. Like a corporation, a limited partnership is recognized as a business form, possesses a separate legal status, and will generally form only upon substantial compliance with the respective state requirements. Among other rules, a certificate of limited partnership must be executed and filed (see Sec. 15621, Corp. Code; Sec. 15902.01, Corp. Code), special naming provisions must be followed, and the names of each general and limited partner must be included. Special rules also apply for a foreign limited partnership. (Sec. 15692, Corp. Code; Sec. 15909.02, Corp. Code) These provisions must be satisfied in order to provide the limited partners with limited contractual and tort liability.

A limited partnership consists of one or more general partners, who manage the business and have unlimited personal responsibility for all business debts (see Sec. 15509, Corp. Code; Sec. 15904.04, Corp. Code), and one or more limited partners, who contribute capital and share in business profits, but who do not take an active part in running the business, and possess only "limited liability" (*i.e.*, a limited partner does not incur any liability with respect to the limited partnerships debts beyond the limited partner's actual or promised monetary and/or property contributions). (Sec. 15507, Corp. Code; Sec. 15903.03, Corp. Code) Oftentimes, a limited partner's primary concern is simply the return on investment. But while a limited partner shares many of the same liability advantages as a corporate shareholder, unlike a shareholder, the limited partner may also benefit from the passthrough of the income, gain, loss, credits, and deductions of the partnership entity, subject to the limitations of a few federal income tax provisions, such as the IRC Sec. 465 at-risk rules and the IRC Sec. 469 passive activity limitations. In contrast, the corporate entity generally does not provide for the passthrough of such income items. (See ¶ 10-210 C Corporations and ¶ 10-215 S Corporations for further information on these corporate entities.)

Limited liability partnership (LLP).—In recent years, all 50 states and the District of Columbia have modified their partnership acts to authorize the formation, registration, and operation of certain general partnerships as registered limited liability partnerships (LLPs). For California purposes, see Sec. 16951, Corp. Code, et seq. As stated above, the general partners of a general partnership are usually jointly and severally liable for all of the debts and obligations of the partnership. However, upon the proper registration of an eligible general partnership as an LLP (see Sec. 16953, Corp. Code), each general partner becomes immune to the tortious, negligent, and wrongful conduct of the other general partners and of the employees, agents, and representatives of the partnership not under the partner's direct supervision and control. Although the traditional vicarious liability of general partners is thus limited, a general partner remains liable for the partner's own tortious, negligent, and wrongful conduct and that of those employees, agents, and representatives under the partner's direct supervision and control. For California specifics, see Sec. 16306, Corp. Code. Some states require an LLP to possess sufficient security for potential injured parties. For California purposes, see Sec. 16956, Corp. Code. An increasing number of states even permit the general partners in an LLP to shield themselves from the contractual debts and obligations of the LLP as well. Aside from this statutory protection from vicarious, and sometimes contractual, liability, an LLP and its general partners operate, are liable, and are taxed like any other general partnership and its partners. Note that registration as an LLP does not require the partnership to change its partnership agreement or the way that it conducts its business.

In general, to register as an LLP, a general partnership need only file an application, with the requisite information, with the appropriate state authority (usually the secretary of state), and pay a designated fee. In most states, the name of the partnership must include the words "registered limited liability partnership" or the initials "L.L.P." to alert third parties that the partners of the LLP are not personally liable for many of the debts and obligations normally associated with a general partnership. Specifically, to register as an LLP in California, a partnership must file a registration statement with the Secretary of State and pay a fee of $70. In addition, as part of the registration requirement, a California LLP must provide specified amounts of security against any claims that might arise against the LLP. (Sec. 12189, Gov't. Code; Sec. 16953, Corp. Code)

Special rules often apply to a professional LLP, such as an LLP whose partners practice public accountancy, law, or architecture. For California purposes, see Sec. 16101, Corp. Code.

For more California LLP specifics, see Sec. 16951, Corp. Code through Sec. 16959, Corp. Code.

• *Interaction of federal and state provisions*

Modifications to IRC Sec. 701.—IRC Sec. 701 provides that the partners in a partnership, not the partnership itself, are subject to tax. Unlike the general rule of nontaxability found in federal income tax law, California imposes an annual minimum tax on a limited. The particulars for these two partnership entities are discussed below.

Limited partnership.—Unlike the general non-taxation afforded the limited partnership at the federal level, every limited partnership (as defined in Sec. 17935(d), Rev. & Tax. Code) doing business and filing a partnership return in California is subject to a nondeductible annual minimum tax. (Sec. 17935(a), Rev. & Tax. Code) The tax, which is payable on the date that the limited partnership's return is due, is currently $800. (Sec. 17935(c), Rev. & Tax. Code) Every limited partnership that has executed, acknowledged, and filed a certificate of limited partnership with the Secretary of State and every foreign limited partnership that has registered with the Secretary of State, even if it is not "doing business" in the state, is also liable for the minimum tax (or part thereof), until the limited partnership files a certificate of cancellation with the Secretary of State. (Sec. 17935(b), Rev. & Tax. Code) A limited partnership required to pay the minimum tax must file a partnership return by the 15th day of the third month after the close of its tax year (15th day of fourth month following the close of its tax year for tax years prior to 2016). (Sec. 18633(a)(2), Rev. & Tax. Code)

PLANNING NOTE: Timing of change in ownership.—Taxpayers considering selling or exchanging 50% or more of the total interests in a limited partnership may want to consider the timing of making the change. If they make a change mid-year, they will have to file two short-year returns and pay for two entities. (*Tax News*, California Franchise Tax Board, February 2010)

A limited partnership is not liable for the minimum tax if it did no business during the tax year and the tax year was 15 days or less. (Sec. 17936, Rev. & Tax. Code) Also, a limited partnership that files or registers with the Secretary of State on or after January 1, 2021, and before January 1, 2024, is exempt from the annual tax for its first taxable year, with the exemption contingent for a taxable year on a state budget measure appropriating at least $1 to the FTB for its associated administrative costs. (Sec. 17935, Rev. & Tax. Code) In addition, a limited partnership is not required to pay the minimum tax if it does the following:

— files a timely final annual tax return for a taxable year with the Franchise Tax Board,

— does not do business in this state after the end of the taxable year for which the final annual tax return was filed, and

— files a certificate of cancellation with the Secretary of State's Office before the end of the 12-month period beginning with the date the final annual tax return was filed. (Sec. 17937, Rev. & Tax. Code)

The Secretary of State must include, with instructional materials related to the registration of a domestic or foreign limited partnership, a notice that registration will obligate the limited partnership to pay an annual minimum tax for that tax year. The Secretary must update this notice annually to specify the amount of the annual tax payable to the California Franchise Tax Board (FTB). (Sec. 15621(f), Corp. Code; Sec. 15692(h), Corp. Code)

A domestic limited partnership whose certificate of limited partnership has been canceled may be revived by filing with Secretary of State a certificate of revival along with confirmation from the FTB that the partnership has paid all outstanding taxes, penalties, interest, and, fees and has filed all required tax returns. (Sec. 15902.09, Corp. Code)

PLANNING NOTE: Expedited Requests for Partnership Revivor.—The fee for submitting expedited service requests for limited partnership revivor requests is $56 (Sec. 19591, Rev. & Tax. Code; Reg. 19591, 18 CCR)

Limited liability partnership (LLP).—An LLP doing business in the state and required to file a return must also pay the annual nondeductible minimum tax of $800. (Sec. 17948(a), Rev. & Tax. Code) Every LLP that has executed, acknowledged, and filed an LLP certificate with the Secretary of State and every foreign LLP that has registered with the Secretary of State, even if it is not "doing business" in the state, is also liable for the minimum tax (or part thereof), until the LLP files a certificate of dissolution or cancellation with the Secretary of State. (Sec. 17948(b) and (d), Rev. & Tax. Code) This tax is due and payable on the date that the return is due. (Sec. 17948(c), Rev. & Tax. Code) However, an LLP is not subject to the minimum tax if it did no business in California during the tax year and the tax year was 15 days or less. (Sec. 17948.2, Rev. & Tax. Code) Also, an LLP that registers with the Secretary of State on or after January 1, 2021, and before January 1, 2024, is exempt from the annual tax for its first taxable year, with the exemption contingent for a taxable year on a state budget measure appropriating at least $1 to the FTB for its associated administrative costs. (Sec. 17948, Rev. & Tax. Code)

In addition, a limited liability partnership is not required to pay the minimum tax if it does the following:

— files a timely final annual tax return for a taxable year with the Franchise Tax Board,

— does not do business in this state after the end of the taxable year for which the final annual tax return was filed, and

— files a notice of cessation, or similar document with the Secretary of State's Office before the end of the 12-month period beginning with the date the final annual tax return was filed. (Sec. 17948.3, Rev. & Tax. Code) (FTB Pub. 1038, Guide to Dissolve, Surrender or Cancel a California Business Entity, revised January 2011)

Previously, a limited liability partnership was liable for the minimum tax until the Secretary of State officially filed a certificate of cancellation, withdrawal, surrender, or similar document, which was dependent upon receiving a tax clearance certificate from the FTB. (Former Sec. 17948.1, Rev. & Tax. Code)

Despite the usual nonliability of a general partner in a registered LLP, for California tax purposes, such a partner may be held liable for the failure to pay employer and withholding taxes (Sec. 1735, Unempl. Ins. Code) and other taxes, fees, penalties, or interest as well. (Sec. 17948.1, Rev. & Tax. Code)

The Secretary of State must include, with instructional materials related to the registration of a domestic or foreign LLP, a notice that registration will obligate the LLP to pay an annual minimum tax to the FTB for the calendar year of registration. The Secretary must update this notice annually to specify the amount of this annual tax. (Sec. 16953(g), Corp. Code; Sec. 16959(g), Corp. Code)

• *Federal income tax provisions*

The state laws regulating limited liability partnerships (LLPs) vary widely. Accordingly, it is difficult to generalize about the requirements and state law consequences of obtaining LLP status.

LLPs are general partnerships in which each individual partner is liable for the partnership's general contractual obligations, his or her own individual business liability, and the tort liabilities deriving from the acts of those over whom the partner had supervisory duties. By complying with a prescribed registration requirement, the partner is otherwise insulated from the malpractice, negligence and similar liabilities of the other partners in excess of the value of the partner's interest in the partnership. The classification and tax treatment of LLPs is not affected by the check-the-box entity selection rules. The federal income tax status of an LLP depends on the provisions of the state law under which the partnership is formed.

[¶10-240] Limited Liability Companies (LLCs)

California generally adopts the federal income tax treatment of an LLC as set out in the federal "check-the-box" regulations. The regulations issued by the Franchise Tax Board (FTB) related to the classification of a business entity must be consistent with the federal regulations as in effect May 1, 2014. (Sec. 23038(b)(2)(B), Rev. & Tax. Code; Reg. 23038(b)-1, 18 CCR through Reg. 23038(b)-3, 18 CCR) Therefore, income and losses, including net operating losses (NOLs) of the LLC flow to its members. Like the federal check-the-box regulations, the applicable California regulations permit an LLC to elect classification as either a corporation, partnership, or "disregarded entity", unless the entity meets certain specifications requiring classification as a corporation. Note that classification of an LLC for California franchise and income tax purposes is dependent upon the LLC's federal income tax classification as either a corporation, partnership, or disregarded entity. The classification elected for federal tax purposes is the same for California tax purposes.

• *Interaction of federal and state provisions*

Federal Treas. Reg. Secs. 301.7701-1 through 301.7701-3 are incorporated by California without numerous amendments. These amendments are set out and discussed below. The most significant and noteworthy differences are that California imposes entity-level annual taxes and fees while federal law does not.

Classification as a partnership.—When an LLC classified as a partnership for tax purposes files its California LLC return (Form 568), it must:

— attach the agreement of each nonresident member to file a California return, make timely payment of all California income taxes imposed on the member with respect to the LLC's income, and be subject to personal jurisdiction in California for purposes of the collection of income taxes, interest, and penalties imposed with respect to the LLC's income; or

— pay to California, on behalf of each nonresident member for whom such an agreement has not been filed, a nonconsenting nonresident (NCNR) withholding tax in an amount equal to the highest marginal tax rate in effect multiplied by the member's distributive share of LLC income, reduced by the amount of any domestic nonresident withholding tax previously paid on behalf of the member (see ¶89-104).

(Sec. 18633.5(e)(1), Rev. & Tax. Code) If an LLC must pay the income tax liability of a nonresident member and fails to do so, then the LLC is subject to penalties and interest for this failure to timely pay the tax, unless the nonresident member timely files and pays the amount due. (Sec. 18633.5(e)(2) and (e)(3), Rev. & Tax. Code) For information regarding an LLC's ability to file a group return for its nonresident members, see Sec. 18535(d), Rev. & Tax. Code.

The LLC's members, and others with economic interests in the entity, are taxed under the California franchise and income tax provisions applicable to a partnership. (Sec. 17087.6, Rev. & Tax. Code) Accordingly, the LLC, like a partnership, is generally treated as a reporting entity, rather than as a taxable entity, and the LLC's members are taxed on their distributive shares of LLC income. Note that each LLC required to file a return must furnish a copy of the information required to be on that return to the LLC's members and their nominees. (Sec. 18633.5(b) and (c), Rev. & Tax Code)

PRACTICE NOTE: Filing and payment requirements for business entity members of multiple-member LLCs.—If an LLC that is classified as a partnership for tax purposes has members that are business entities and is doing business in California, then the members are themselves generally considered to be doing business in California. However, a narrow exception may apply in limited circumstances. If an LLC is only registered to do business in California or organized in California, but has no activities or factor presence in California sufficient to constitute doing business in the state, then the LLC will have a California return filing requirement and be subject to the LLC tax and fee (discussed below), but the members will not have a California return filing requirement or be subject to California tax as a result of their membership interests in the LLC. If a member's distributive share of the California sales of the LLC exceeds the statutory threshold set forth in Sec. 23101(b), then the member will be doing business in the state on that basis, as well as on the basis of its membership interest in the LLC. (*Legal Ruling 2014-01*, California Franchise Tax Board, July 22, 2014; as modified by *Legal Ruling 2018-01*, California Franchise Tax Board, October 19, 2018)

Annual tax.—However, an LLC classified as a partnership remains subject to the annual $800 tax, provided that the LLC is doing business in California, or its articles of organization have been accepted by or its certificate of registration has been issued by the Secretary of State. (Secs. 17941(a) and (b)(1), Rev. & Tax Code; and Sec. 18633.5, Rev. & Tax Code) The annual tax is due and payable on or before the 15th day of the third month of the tax year. (Sec. 17941(c), Rev. & Tax Code; and Sec. 18633.5(a), Rev. & Tax. Code) A domestic LLC has until the 15th day of the third month after filing its articles of organization with the Secretary of State to pay the first year annual tax. Existing foreign LLCs that register or begin doing business in California after the 15th day of the third month of the taxable year must pay the annual tax immediately upon commencing business in California or upon registration with the Secretary of State's Office. (FTB Pub. 3556, Limited Liability Company Filing Information) The fee is remitted along with Form FTB 3522, LLC Payment Voucher.

> **PRACTICE POINTER:** *"Doing business" broadly defined.*—The FTB has broadly construed the term "doing business". Under the FTB's interpretation, an LLC is considered to be doing business in California if any of its members, managers, or other agents conduct business in California on behalf of the LLC. The FTB has taken the position that an out-of-state LLC is doing business in California if its California-resident member(s):
>
> — has the right to hire, fire, and oversee an out-of-state property management company that manages the LLC's out-of-state property;
>
> — uses a California address for tax filing purposes and hires a California accountant to prepare the tax returns; or
>
> — maintains a California business bank account for the LLC and secures financing in California for the LLC's out-of-state investments. (FTB Pub. 3556, Limited Liability Company Filing Information, revised April 2017)

Exemptions from annual tax.—An LLC that did no business in the state during a tax year, and the tax year was 15 days or less, is not subject to the annual tax. (Sec. 17946, Rev. & Tax. Code) Also, an LLC that organizes or registers with the Secretary of State on or after January 1, 2021, and before January 1, 2024, is exempt from the annual tax for its first taxable year, with the exemption contingent for a taxable year on a state budget measure appropriating at least $1 to the FTB for its associated administrative costs. In addition, an LLC is exempt from the annual tax upon the filing of a certificate of cancellation of the LLC or a certificate of dissolution of the LLC. However, the LLC is not entitled to a refund of any taxes or fees already paid. (Sec. 17941, Rev. and Tax. Code)

In addition, an LLC is not required to pay the minimum tax if it does the following:

— files a timely final annual tax return for a taxable year with the Franchise Tax Board (FTB);

— does not do business in this state after the end of the taxable year for which the final annual tax return was filed; and

— files a notice of cessation or similar document with the Secretary of State's Office before the end of the 12-month period beginning with the date the final annual tax return was filed. Domestic LLCs organized in California must file one or more of the following forms: (1) Certificate of Dissolution (SOS Form LLC-3); (2) Certificate of Cancellation (SOS Form LLC-4/7); or (3) Short Form Certificate of Cancellation (SOS Form LLC-4/8). Foreign LLCs must file a Limited Liability Company Certificate of Cancellation (SOS Form LLC-4/7). (Sec. 17947, Rev. & Tax. Code) (FTB Pub. 1038, Guide to Dissolve, Surrender, or Cancel a California Business Entity, revised January 2011; FTB Pub. 3556, Limited Liability Company Filing Information, revised April 2017)

PRACTICE POINTER: *Short form cancellation requirements.*—A domestic LLC may use SOS Form LLC-4/8, Limited Liability Company Short Form Certificate of Cancellation, if the form is filed within 12 months from the date the LLC's articles of organization were filed with the SOS and the following requirements are met:

— the LLC has no debts or liabilities, other than for FTB taxes;

— a timely final tax return has been or will be filed with FTB;

— the LLC has not conducted any business since organizing;

— all remaining assets have been distributed to the entitled persons after payment of, or providing payment for, all debts and liabilities;

— a majority of the managers, members, or persons that signed the articles of organization have voted to dissolve the LLC; and

— all payments the LLC received for interests have been returned to the investors.

The FTB can refund the annual tax or fee only if it is paid on or after the date the LLC files the SOS Form LLC-4/8. If an LLC files SOS Form LLC-4/7, Limited Liability Company Certificate of Cancellation, or is involved in a merger or conversion, it does not qualify for the short form cancellation even if it meets all of the requirements. (Public Service Bulletin 12-24, California Franchise Tax Board, July 30, 2012)

For the 2010 through 2017 tax years and again for the 2020 through 2029 tax years, an LLC that is a small business solely owned by a deployed member of the U.S. Armed Forces will not be subject to the annual LLC tax for any taxable year that the owner is deployed and the LLC operates at a loss or ceases operation. An LLC is a "small business" for purposes of the exemption if it has total income from all sources derived from, or attributable to, the state of $250,000 or less. (Sec. 17941, Rev. & Tax. Code)

PRACTICAL ANALYSIS: The FTB has issued a legal ruling addressing when an LLC "ceases operation" for purposes of the tax exemption. (Legal Ruling 2011-03, California Franchise Tax Board, May 27, 2011) The LLC may still be considered to have ceased operations if:

— it is winding up its business operations beyond the close of its taxable year, but is otherwise not engaged in any active business operations;

— files final tax returns with the IRS and the FTB and delivers a Certificate of Cancellation to the California Secretary of State within 12 months of the filing date of the final return;

— has zero gross income and zero gross expenses for the taxable year; or

— discontinues all business operations during the taxable year, but during the following year must defend itself in a lawsuit in state or federal court.

In addition, if the LLC discontinues all business operations during the taxable year, but resumes operations during the following taxable year, the LLC may still be considered to have ceased operations during the year in which it discontinues operations, provided the LLC:

— ceases operations contemporaneously with the deployment;

— ceases operations for at least one month during the taxable year;

— does not resume operations during the taxable year; and

— ceases operations for at least three months, even if this period extends into the following taxable year.

Currently, the Secretary of State must include, with the instructional materials related to the registration of a domestic or foreign LLC, a notice that such registration obligates the LLC to pay the annual $800 tax to the California Franchise Tax Board (FTB) for the calendar year of registration. The Secretary must update this notice yearly to specify the annual amount payable to the FTB. (Sec. 17702.01, Corp. Code, and Sec. 17708.02, Corp. Code)

Annual fee.—An annual fee based on an LLC's "total income from all sources derived from or attributable to the state" (as defined below) for the tax year is also imposed on an LLC classified as a partnership for California tax purposes. (Sec. 17942, Rev. & Tax. Code) The annual fee applies to an LLC doing business in California, an LLC not doing business in California but whose articles of organization have been accepted, or an LLC whose certificate of registration has been issued by the Secretary of State. The annual LLC fee varies according to the LLC's total income derived from or attributable to California. The current applicable fees are as follows:

(1) $900, for total California-sourced income of $250,000 or more, but less than $500,000;

(2) $2,500, for total California-sourced income of $500,000 or more, but less than $1 million;

(3) $6,000, for total California-sourced income of $1 million or more, but less than $5 million; or

(4) $11,790, for total California-sourced income of $5 million or more.

(Sec. 17942(a), Rev. & Tax. Code)

PLANNING NOTE: *Constitutionality of pre-2007 taxable year LLC fee scheme.*— A California Court of Appeal has ruled that California's pre-2007 taxable year LLC fee scheme as applied to an out-of-state LLC that had registered as an LLC with the California Secretary of State's office but that had no income from activities in California amounted to an unfairly apportioned tax in violation of the U.S. Constitution's Commerce and Due Process Clauses. The court ordered a refund of all LLC fees paid by the out-of-state LLC, plus interest and penalties. (*Northwest Energetic Services, LLC v. California Franchise Tax Board,* (2008) 159 Cal.App. 4th 841) Another California Court of Appeal also found that the LLC fee was an unconstitutional unapportioned tax, but held that in the case of a taxpayer with income from both inside and outside California, the proper remedy to be applied to the unapportioned tax was to refund the difference between the amount of the fee paid by the taxpayer and the amount of the fee that would have been required had the fee been fairly apportioned. (*Ventas Finance I, LLC v. California Franchise Tax Board*, (2008) 165 Cal.App.4th 1207, petition for review denied, California Supreme Court, No. S166870, November 13, 2008). Another case that challenges the constitutionality of the LLC fee as applied to an LLC that conducted all of its activities in California is pending in the San Francisco Superior Court (*Bakersfield Mall, LLC v. Franchise Tax Board*, San Francisco Superior Court, No. CGC-07-462728).

Legislation enacted in 2007 (Ch. 381 (A.B. 198), Laws 2007), revised the basis of the fee from one based on the LLC's total income to the LLC's total income apportionable to California, but only on a prospective basis. The Legislature stated its intent that no inference be drawn in connection with the legislative amendments for any taxable year beginning before 2007. However, for refund actions filed after October 10, 2007, or for refund actions filed prior to such date that are not final as of October 10, 2007, if the LLC fee as imposed prior to the 2007 taxable year is finally adjudged to be discriminatory or unfairly apportioned under California or federal law, the fee of any disfavored taxpayer that files a timely claim for refund asserting discrimination or unfair apportionment will be recomputed, but only to the extent necessary to remedy the discrimination or unfair apportionment. Such refunds will be limited to the amount by which the fee paid, plus any interest assessed, exceeds the amount of the fee that would have been assessed if the fee had been determined pursuant to the new provisions. (Sec. 19394, Rev. & Tax. Code)

> **CCH PRACTICE TIP:** *Claiming refunds of unconstitutional fee.*—The FTB has outlined the procedures that taxpayers with no income from activities in California should follow to have their refunds processed in light of the California Court of Appeal's final decision in *Northwest Energetic Services*, see FTB Notice 2008-2, April 14, 2008.

LLCs with income attributable solely to California or with income attributable to sources both inside and outside California should follow the protective claim procedures outlined by the FTB. (LLCs Filing Protective Claims—LLC Fee, California Franchise Tax Board, March 17, 2006)

For annual fee purposes, "total income from all sources derived from or attributable to this state" means gross income (as defined in Sec. 24271, Rev. & Tax. Code), plus the cost of goods sold that are connected with the LLC's trade or business, determined by applying the existing allocation and apportionment rules for assigning the sales of an entity doing business within and outside the state, other than those provisions under California's alternative apportionment provision and implementing regulations that exclude receipts from the sales factor (see ¶ 11-525). Thus, gains from sales of assets may not be offset by losses (which are defined in IRC Section 62, not IRC Section 61). However, allocations or attributions of income, gain, or distributions to one LLC in its capacity as a member of, or holder of an economic interest in, another LLC are not included in total income derived from or attributable to California if the allocations or attributions are directly or indirectly attributable to income that is included in determining the annual fee payable by the other LLC. (Sec. 17942(b)(1), Rev. & Tax. Code) A regulation has interpreted this to mean that income or gain or distributions paid to one LLC in its capacity as a member or holder of an economic interest in another LLC is not counted in the total California source income if the LLC that earned the income was itself subject to the LLC fee. (Reg. 17942, 18 CCR)

PRACTICE POINTER: When is an LLC subject to the fee?—An LLC that does not actually pay the LLC fee because it did not have enough total California-source income to be liable for the fee is still considered to be "subject to the fee."(Reg. 17942(b), 18 CCR)

For purposes of determining its total California-source income, an LLC that has activities both inside and outside California must:

— Adjust a distribution made to it from a pass-through entity that is not an LLC to include the cost of goods sold, if applicable.

— Utilize the sales factor numerator assignment rules under Rev. & Tax Code §§ 25135, 25136, or, if applicable, § 25137, other than those rules that exclude specified receipts such as those receipts derived from the passive holding of intangible personal property or from an occasional or isolated sale.

— Assign income from its passive holding of intangible personal property to the location from which the intangible personal property is managed by the LLC.

— Use the same sourcing rules (e.g., cost of performance, market-based sourcing) that the LLC used to assign sales for purposes of the sales factor numerator to determine its total California-source income.

In the alternative, an LLC with a sales factor numerator of $5 million or more may simply use the sales factor numerator without adjustment, because the sales factor amount exceeds the top bracket for calculating the fee amount. An LLC with a sales factor numerator of less than $5 million may use the sales factor numerator amount as the starting point for the calculation of the fee and then:

— Assign all items of total income from all sources that were previously assigned as nonbusiness income for apportionment purposes, using the assignment rules outlined above.

— Assign all items of total income from all sources that were excluded from the sales factor numerator pursuant to Rev. & Tax. Code § 25137.

— Remove all items of total income that were derived from or attributable to other LLCs that were subject to the LLC fee.

If the sales factor numerator amount is over $5 million for the taxable year, but the LLC has included an amount received from another LLC in the numerator amount such that the removal of that amount will result in the remaining sales factor numerator falling below $5 million, the LLC may remove the amount and then make the other adjustments described immediately above. (Reg. 17942(b), 18 CCR)

PRACTICE TIP: Deductibility of fee: The FTB notes that the LLC fee is generally considered an ordinary and necessary expense paid or incurred in carrying on the LLC's trade or business and is deductible on the LLC's Form 568 as an "other deduction." (Tax News, California Franchise Tax Board, August 2011)

LLCs with an ownership interest in a pass-through entity must report their distributive share of the pass-through entity's total income derived from or attributable to California (that has not already been included in the calculation of an LLC fee).

Their distributive share cannot include any deductions that are subtracted from gross ordinary income to obtain net ordinary income. (Instructions, Form 568, Limited Liability Company Return of Income)

With respect to a commonly controlled LLC, the "total income from all sources derived from or attributable to this state," accounting for any water's-edge election made under Sec. 25110, Rev. & Tax. Code, may be determined by the FTB to be the total income of all the commonly controlled LLC members if the FTB also determines that multiple LLCs were formed for the primary purpose of reducing annual LLC fees. (Sec. 17942(b)(2), Rev. & Tax. Code) An FTB determination may be made only with respect to one LLC in a commonly controlled group. However, each commonly controlled LLC is jointly and severally liable for the fee. For these fee provision purposes, "commonly controlled LLCs" include the taxpayer and any other partnership or LLC doing business in California that must file a return under Sec. 18633, Rev. & Tax. Code, or Sec. 18633.5, Rev. & Tax. Code, and in which the same persons own, directly or indirectly, more than 50% of the capital interests or profits interests. (Sec. 17942(b)(2), Rev. & Tax. Code)

PRACTICE TIP: Treatment of Series LLC: Although California law does not allow for a series LLC to be formed in California, it does recognize them. A series LLC that is formed under the laws of another state may register as a foreign LLC with the California Secretary of State and transact business in California. A series LLC, that registers to do business or conducts business in California each series in the series LLC must files its own Form 568 and pay its own separate LLC tax and fee if it is registered or doing business in California if the following conditions are met:

— the holder of interests in each series are limited to the assets of that series upon redemption, liquidation, or termination, and may share in the income only of that series; and

— under state law the payment of the expenses, charges, and liabilities of each series is limited to the assets of that series. (*Tax News*, California Franchise Tax Board, October 2011; Instructions, Form 568, Limited Liability Company Return of Income)

If the series LLC registered in California, the first LLC in the series uses the Secretary of State number as the identification number on its initial payment voucher. All other LLCs in the series must leave the identification numbers blank on their first payment vouchers. Write "Series LLC #_____" in red ink on the top of all payment vouchers, tax returns, and correspondence. The FTB will assign an identification number to the rest of the LLCs in the series LLC and will notify each series of its assigned number after the initial payment voucher is received. For example, if ABC LLC is a series LLC registered in Delaware that contains three series and files in California, it would use the names: ABC LLC, ABC LLC Series 1, and ABC LLC Series 2. (FTB Pub. 3556, Limited Liability Company Filing Information)

The annual LLC fee is due and payable on the same date as an LLC's return is due. LLCs are required to make estimated fee payments (see ¶89-104). The fee, if unpaid, is subject to the applicable interest and penalties. (Sec. 17942(c), Rev. & Tax. Code) However, an LLC is not required to pay the annual fee provided that it did no business in California during the tax year and the tax year was 15 days or less. (Sec. 17946, Rev. & Tax. Code)

CCH PRACTICE TIP: LLC fee forms.—Form 3536, Estimated Fee for LLCs, must be used to remit the estimated fee. LLCs must also use form FTB 3536 (or FTB 3588 for an e-filed return) to pay by the due date of the LLC's return, any amount of the LLC fee due that was not paid as an estimated fee payment. (*Tax News*, California Franchise Tax Board, May 4, 2009)

Classification as a disregarded entity.—An LLC with a single owner may elect to (1) be classified as an association and corporation taxation, or (2) disregard its status as an entity separate from the owner and be subject to taxation as a sole proprietorship. However, under California law, an LLC that elects sole proprietorship status for tax purposes is still (1) subject to the minimum tax and LLC fees; (2) required to file an LLC return; and (3) subject to the limitations imposed on LLCs with respect to credit amount available. (Sec. 23038(B)(iii), Rev. & Tax. Code)

An LLC classified as a disregarded entity remains subject to the annual tax, provided that the LLC is doing business in California, or its articles of organization have been accepted by or its certificate of registration has been issued by the Secretary of State. (Secs. 17941(a) and (b)(1), Rev. & Tax Code; and Sec. 18633.5(i)(1), Rev. & Tax Code) The annual tax is due and payable on or before the 15th day of the fourth month of the tax year. (Sec. 17941(c), Rev. & Tax Code; and Sec. 18633.5(i)(3), Rev. & Tax. Code) However, if the LLC did no business in the state during the tax year, and the tax year was 15 days or less, then the LLC is not subject to the annual tax. (Sec. 17946, Rev. & Tax. Code) Also, an LLC is exempt from the annual tax upon the filing of a certificate of cancellation of the LLC or a certificate of dissolution of the LLC. However, the LLC will not be entitled to a refund of any taxes or fees already paid. (Sec. 17941, Rev. and Tax. Code)

An annual fee based on the LLC's total income from all sources derived from or attributable to the state for the tax year is also imposed on an LLC classified as a disregarded entity for California tax purposes. (Sec. 17942, Rev. & Tax. Code) The annual fee applies to an LLC doing business in California, an LLC not doing business in California but whose articles of organization have been accepted, or an LLC whose certificate of registration has been issued by the Secretary of State. The annual LLC fee varies according to the LLC's total income. The annual LLC fee is due and payable with the LLC's return. The fee, if unpaid, is subject to the applicable interest and penalties. (Sec. 17942(c), Rev. & Tax. Code) However, an LLC need not pay the annual fee provided that it did no business in California during the tax year and the tax year was 15 days or less. (Sec. 17946, Rev. & Tax. Code)

With respect to an LLC organized or doing business in California, or that is registered with the Secretary of State, an individual LLC owner electing to have the business entity disregarded for tax purposes must file Form 568 by the 15th day of the fourth month following the close of the owner's tax year. The form, in addition to setting forth the annual tax and applicable LLC fee computations (Sec. 18633.5(i), Rev. & Tax. Code), must include the owner's name, taxpayer identification number, and the owner's consent to be subject to California taxation. If the consent is not included, the LLC must pay to California, on behalf of the owner, an amount equal to the highest marginal tax rate times the owner's LLC income. If an LLC must pay the income tax liability of the owner and fails to do so, then the LLC is subject to penalties and interest for the failure to timely pay the tax, unless the owner timely files and pays the amount due.

¶10-240

COMPLIANCE NOTE: Change from a disregarded entity to a partnership.—An LLC with at least two members is classified as a partnership for federal tax purposes. Therefore, if a single-member LLC classified as a disregarded entity for federal tax purposes acquires an additional member, it becomes a partnership for federal tax purposes by default, unless it affirmatively elects to be classified as a corporation. If an LLC with two or more members chooses the default rule of being classified as a partnership for federal purposes, it must also follow the federal partnerships rules (to which California conforms) for California tax purposes as well. For federal tax purposes, a disregarded single-member LLC continues to be treated as a disregarded entity until the date of the admission of an additional new member. Accordingly, the activities of the disregarded LLC will be reflected on the single-member's federal tax return until the date the new additional member is acquired. Then, from the date of the admission of the new additional member, and for subsequent years, the multiple-member LLC will file as a partnership for federal tax purposes (unless it makes an affirmative election to be classified as a corporation) using federal Form 1065. For California tax purposes, the activities of the disregarded LLC will also be reflected on the single-member's California tax return until the date of the admission of the new additional member. However, unless the admission of the new additional member occurs on the last day of the LLC's tax year, the LLC must file two short-period Form 568 returns. The first tax return will be as a single-member LLC, where the single-member completes the Single Member LLC Information and Consent section. The second short-period return will report the LLC's income and expenses following partnership tax law (unless the LLC makes an affirmative election to be classified as a corporation). The LLCs should write "short period" in red at the top of both Form 568 tax returns. (*Tax News*, California Franchise Tax Board, May 2015)

PLANNING NOTE: Timing of change in ownership.—Taxpayers considering selling or exchanging 50% or more of the total interests in an LLC may want to consider the timing of making the change. If they make a change mid-year, they will have to file two short-year returns and pay for two entities. (*Tax News*, California Franchise Tax Board, February 2010)

A California-only limitation applies to the ability to use credits generated by LLCs classified as disregarded entities. The credit allowable is limited to the excess of (1) the regular tax liability of the single owner computed with the items of income, deductions, etc., attributable to the disregarded entity over (2) the regular tax liability of the single owner computed without items of income, deductions, etc., attributable to the disregarded entity. The disregarded entity is effectively treated as if it were a separately apportioning subsidiary, and its California-source income is determined by apportioning a share of combined unitary income to it by reference to the ratio of its numerators to the unitary group's denominators. This limits the owner's use of any credit generated by a disregarded entity that flows to its owner to the amount of tax attributable to the income of the disregarded entity. (Sec. 23036(i), Rev. & Tax. Code)

EXAMPLE: Taxpayer has $10 million in income. It has total sales of $100 million, $30 million of which are assigned to the numerator of its California sales factor. It has total property of $45 million, and total payroll of $15 million, none of which are assigned to California. The taxpayer has an LLC whose sole activity is conducting research and development activities in California. The LLC is treated as a disregarded entity. Disregarded Entity has $5 million in property and $3 million in payroll, a net loss of $(500,000), and generated a research and development credit of $2 million. The taxpayer and the disregarded entity are engaged in a single, unitary business.

Taxpayer's tax with disregarded entity included:

Taxpayer's income—$10 million

Disregarded entity's income—($500,000)

Total income—$9.5 million

Apportionment percentage—22%

Apportionment income—$2,090,000

Tax rate—8.84%

Tax—$184,756

Taxpayer's tax without disregarded entity included

Taxpayer's income—$10 million

Disregarded entity's income—0

Total income—$10 million

Apportionment percentage—15%

Apportionment income—$1.5 million

Tax rate—8.84%

Tax—$132,600

Taxpayer can use $52,156 ($184,756 - $132,600) of the credit, resulting in net California tax liability of $132,600. The remaining credit can be carried forward to future years.

Classification as a corporation.—An LLC classified as a corporation must file an annual California corporation franchise or income tax return (Form 100) and pay the applicable tax, as well as the annual minimum tax on corporations. (Sec. 18633.5(h), Rev. & Tax. Code; Sec. 23038, Rev. & Tax. Code; Sec. 23151, Rev. & Tax. Code; Sec. 23221, Rev. & Tax. Code; and Sec. 23305.5, Rev. & Tax. Code) However, the annual LLC fee does not apply to an LLC classified as a corporation. (Sec. 17941, Rev. & Tax. Code; Sec. 17942, Rev. & Tax. Code; and Sec. 18633.5, Rev. & Tax Code) Rules similar to the exemptions from the annual LLC fee and annual minimum tax discussed above under "Classification as a partnership" also apply to LLCs classified as a corporation. (Sec. 23332, Rev. & Tax. Code)

Currently, the Secretary of State must include, with the instructional materials related to the registration of a domestic or foreign LLC, a notice that such registration obligates an LLC to pay an annual minimum tax to the FTB for the calendar year of registration. The Secretary must update this notice yearly to specify the minimum tax payable. (Sec. 17050, Corp. Code, and Sec. 17451(d), Corp. Code; effective January 1, 2014, changed to Sec. 17702.01, Corp. Code, and Sec. 17708.02, Corp. Code)

PRACTICE TIP: *Treatment of Delaware Series LLCs.*—The FTB has taken the position that each series within a Series LLC is a separate business entity and, if it is registered or doing business in California, each series must file its own Form 568 Liability Company Return of Income and pay its own separate LLC annual tax and fee.

CCH COMMENT: *Suspension/forfeiture process.*—Beginning in early 2009, the FTB began implementing a process of suspending/forfeiting the rights, powers, and privileges of LLCs for nonpayment of taxes, penalties, or interest, and/or failure to file a return. The FTB will send notification to all entities at their last known addresses, 60 days before imposing the suspension/forfeiture. Suspended/forfeited LLCs are subject to contract voidability. (*Tax News*, California Franchise Tax Board)

Effective September 15, 2014, foreign nonqualified LLCs are included within the definition of a "taxpayer" for purposes of the suspension/revivor provisions, and are made subject to the same provisions relating to contract voidability that apply to all other LLCs and corporations. A foreign nonqualified LLC without an FTB-assigned account number that fails to file a required tax return will be subject to contract voidability during the period beginning on the later of January 1, 2014, or the first day of the taxable year for which the taxpayer has failed to file a return, and ending when the LLC qualifies with the Secretary of State or obtains an FTB account number. A foreign nonqualified LLC with an FTB-assigned account number that fails to file a tax return or fails to pay delinquent taxes, penalties, fees, or interest within 60 days of the FTB's mailing a written demand therefor will be subject to contract voidability during the period beginning with the end of the 60-day demand period and ending on the earlier of the date relief from contract voidability is granted or the date the LLC qualifies with the Secretary of State. (Sec. 23304.1, Rev. & Tax. Code; Sec. 23305.5, Rev. & Tax. Code)

Voluntary administrative dissolution procedures.—Effective January 1, 2019, procedures are established for voluntary dissolution of domestic corporations and LLCs. Involuntary dissolution procedures are discussed at ¶ 89-206, Civil Penalties.

A voluntary dissolution option is available to businesses that (1) have never done business or have ceased doing business in California; (2) have paid all taxes due for years when it was in operation; and (3) filed all required returns before stopping business operations. Businesses applying for administrative dissolution must:

— request abatement of any unpaid minimum franchise or annual tax, interest, and penalties;

— file dissolution paperwork with the Secretary of State before abatement of the unpaid tax, interest, and penalties; and

— show that it has stopped all business activity and has no remaining assets when it files the request for abatement.

The abatement of unpaid tax, interest, and penalties is conditioned on the prior dissolution of the business. (Sec. 23310, Rev. & Tax. Code) However, the total tax, interest, and penalties that are abated will immediately be due and payable if the business continues to do business or has any remaining assets that were not disclosed with the request for abatement. In addition, a penalty equal to 50% of the total tax abated, plus interest, will be imposed. This penalty is in addition to any other penalty imposed. (Sec. 23311, Rev. & Tax. Code)

• *Federal income tax provisions*

A limited liability company (LLC) is a business entity created under state law. Every state and the District of Columbia have LLC statutes that govern the formation and operation of LLCs. An LLC has the characteristics of both a corporation and a partnership. Like a corporation, the owners (referred to as members) are usually not personally liable for the debts and other obligations of the LLC. Like a partnership or sole proprietorship, an LLC has great flexibility in the way it operates and does not need to follow corporate formalities, such as holding special and annual meetings with shareholders and directors.

An LLC has the flexibility to decide whether to be taxed as a partnership, S corporation, or C corporation. A single-member LLC is a disregarded entity, unless it elects to be taxed as a corporation for federal tax purposes. If an LLC chooses to be taxed as a partnership or S corporation, or if a single-member LLC elects to be disregarded as an entity, the LLC profits and losses are reported on the member's personal federal income tax return. Special check-the-box election timing requirements apply to LLCs.

[¶10-245] Exempt Organizations

Organizations seeking exemption from federal taxation are governed by Subchapter F (Exempt Organizations) of the Internal Revenue Code. California's corporation franchise and income tax provisions regarding exempt organizations are generally similar, but not identical, to the federal income tax provisions, IRC Sec. 501—IRC Sec. 530.

California incorporates the federal provisions regarding taxation of unrelated business income, IRC Sec. 512—IRC Sec. 514, with modifications. (Rev. & Tax. Code Sec. 23732)

California does not specifically incorporate IRC Sec. 521, relating to farmers' cooperatives.

• *Interaction of federal and state provisions*

As stated above, California does not specifically incorporate IRC Sec. 501—IRC Sec. 530, the federal corporate income tax provisions addressing exempt organizations. Nonetheless, the scope and effect of California's franchise and corporate income tax provisions applicable to exempt organizations generally follow federal tax law.

Unmodified IRC sections.—The following organizations are exempt under California and federal law:

— amateur sports organizations organized and operated exclusively to foster national and international amateur sports competition (Sec. 23701(d), Rev. & Tax. Code);

— child care organizations (Sec. 23704.4, Rev. & Tax. Code);

— cooperative hospital service organizations (Sec. 23704, Rev. & Tax. Code);

— Coverdell education savings accounts (Sec. 23712, Rev. & Tax. Code);

— credit unions (Sec. 23701y, Rev. & Tax. Code);

— employee pension, profit-sharing and stock bonus plans (these and other employee trusts are covered currently by the personal income tax rather than the bank and corporation tax) (Sec. 23701s, Rev. & Tax. Code; Sec. 23705, Rev. & Tax. Code);

— employee-funded pension plans (Sec. 23701s, Rev. & Tax. Code);

— fraternal organizations providing insurance benefits to members and families (Sec. 23701b, Rev. & Tax. Code);

— fraternal societies (Sec. 23701l, Rev. & Tax. Code);

— individual retirement account trusts (Sec. 23701p, Rev. & Tax. Code);

— nonprofit cemetery or crematory companies (Sec. 23701c, Rev. & Tax. Code);

— nonprofit recreational clubs (Sec. 23701g, Rev. & Tax. Code);

— property management corporations holding title to property for the benefit of exempt organizations (Sec. 23701h, Rev. & Tax. Code);

— religious organizations (Sec. 23701k, Rev. & Tax. Code), including the expanded definition of convention or association of churches applicable for California purposes beginning with the 2010 tax year and for federal purposes, August 17, 2006 (Sec. 23046.5, Rev. & Tax. Code);

— supplemental unemployment compensation trusts (Sec. 23701n, Rev. & Tax. Code);

— teachers' retirement associations (Sec. 23701j, Rev. & Tax. Code);

— veterans' organizations (Sec. 23701w, Rev. & Tax. Code); and

— voluntary employees' beneficiary associations. (Sec. 23701i, Rev. & Tax. Code)

Feeder organizations.—The payment of profits to one or more tax-exempt organizations by a donor organization that is operated primarily to carry on a business for profit does not confer tax-exempt status on the donor organization. (Sec. 23702, Rev. & Tax. Code) Likewise, an organization's use of profits for purposes which would otherwise be exempt from tax if conducted by a separate organization does not yield tax-exempt status. These provisions follow IRC Sec. 502, relating to feeder organizations. The provisions do not apply to trades and businesses:

— that derive rents that would be excluded under Sec. 23732, taxation of unrelated business income;

— substantially carried on without compensation; or

— by which substantially all merchandise sold is acquired from donations.

A federal regulation applicable to the interpretation of California law pertains to "feeder organizations." (Sec. 23051.5, Rev. & Tax. Code)

Modifications to IRC sections.—Federal exemptions adopted by California with minor modifications:

— Agricultural cooperatives are exempt if the organization is determined by the IRS to be a labor, agricultural, or horticultural organization. California permits such cooperatives a deduction for income allocated to members. (Sec. 23704, Rev. & Tax. Code)

— California requires an irrevocable dedication of assets to exempt purposes as a condition of qualification as a charitable organization, while IRC Sec. 501(c)(3), relating to exempt federal organizations, contains no such requirement. (Sec. 23701d, Rev. & Tax. Code)

— Both California and federal law tax homeowners' association income in excess of exempt function income, less attributable deductions and minus a $100 deduction. (Sec. 23701t, Rev. & Tax. Code) IRC Sec. 528(c)(1)(E) permits condominium management associations or residential real estate management associations to elect to be treated as homeowners associations if they meet the requirements. California specifically includes such organizations as well as cooperative housing corporations within the definition of "homeowners' associations." Both state and federal law restrict the property managed to residential use. Under California law, but not under federal law, amounts not expended for association purposes during a taxable year must be held in trust for future association needs. FTB Pub. 1028, Guidelines for Homeowners' Associations, revised November 2017, provides detailed information regarding the treatment of homeowners' associations.

— California does not include professional football leagues, as does IRC Sec. 501(c)(6). (Sec. 23701e, Rev. & Tax. Code)

— California imposes an additional qualification requirement that assets of nonprofit civic leagues, social welfare organization, or local organizations of employees exempt under IRC Sec. 501(c)(4) be irrevocably dedicated to exempt purposes. (Sec. 23701f, Rev. & Tax. Code)

— California incorporates the tightened eligibility requirements for credit counseling organizations to qualify as exempt social welfare organizations or charitable or educational organizations, but modifies the federal provision to substitute internal cross references (Sec. 23703.7, Rev. & Tax. Code);

— California grants tax-exempt status to any organization established pursuant to the Nonprofit Corporation Law (specifically, pursuant to Sec. 5005.1, Corp. Code) by three or more corporations to pool self-insurance claims or losses of those corporations. IRC Sec. 501(n) provides a similar exemption to "qualified charitable risk pools" organized under state law. (Sec. 23701z, Rev. & Tax. Code)

— Both California and the federal government classify political organizations as tax-exempt organizations but tax income from investments minus a $100 deduction. California includes the trusts of individual candidates within the definition of political organizations, whereas IRC Sec. 527 does not. California has not adopted IRC Sec. 527(f), which taxes other exempt organizations engaging in political activity in part as if they were political organizations by taxing the lesser of political expenditures or net investment income. (Sec. 23701r, Rev. & Tax. Code) (FTB Pub. 1075, Exempt Organization—Guide for Political Organizations)

— Both California (Sec. 23711, Rev. & Tax. Code) and federal law (IRC Sec. 529, Qualified Tuition Programs) exempt from taxation qualified tuition programs. In addition, California specifically grants tax-exempt status to the Golden State Scholarshare Trust as a qualified tuition program. (Sec. 24328, Rev. & Tax. Code)

— Both California (Sec. 23701h and Sec. 23701x) and federal law (IRC Sec. 501(c)(2) and IRC Sec. 501(c)(25)) exempt from taxation certain title-holding companies. For purposes of this exemption, the term "corporation" includes a limited liability company (LLC) classified as a partnership or as a disregarded entity.

— Churches and small charities must apply for a state exemption. California does not provide an exception for applying for an exemption for these organizations. (FTB Pub. 927, Overview of Exempt Organizations)

— Homeowners' associations must apply for and receive an exemption from state taxation. Under federal law, homeowners' associations may make an election to be treated as an exempt organization. (FTB Pub. 927, Overview of Exempt Organizations)

California-only exemptions.—The following organizations are designated exempt under California law, but not federal income tax law:

— civic leagues or organizations organized under the nonprofit public benefit corporation law with the specific and primary purpose of rendering financial assistance to government by financing, refinancing, acquiring, constructing, improving, leasing, selling, or otherwise conveying property of any kind to a government, and operated for the exempt purposes listed at Rev. & Tax. Code Sec. 23701f, are exempt. For purposes of this exemption, "government" means California, a city, county, city and county, school district, board of education, public corporation, hospital district, or any other special district (Sec. 23701u, Rev. & Tax. Code);

— an organization of owners of manufactured homes or mobile homes, who are tenants in a mobile home park, is exempt if formed for the purpose of purchasing that mobile home park. The organization may also manage, maintain, or care for the mobile home park (Sec. 23701v, Rev. & Tax. Code);

— effective January 1, 2020, public banks (Sec. 23701aa, Rev. & Tax. Code).

Federal-only exemptions.—The following organizations are exempt from federal income taxation, but not exempt under California law:

— benevolent life insurance companies or associations; mutual ditch, irrigation, or telephone companies;

— black lung trusts;

— cooperative service organizations of educational organizations;

— farmers' cooperatives (California permits such cooperatives a deduction for income allocated to members Cooperatives (IRC Sec. 1381 —IRC Sec. 1388));

— instrumentalities of the United States;

— multiemployer plans;

— mutual insurance companies;

— state health insurance organizations that insure high-risk individuals;

— state insurance organizations formed before June 1, 1996, to reinsure workmen's compensation.

Terrorist organizations.—California law is similar to federal law (IRC Sec. 501(p)), which suspends the tax-exempt status of organizations designated or identified at any time as terrorist organizations and disallows deductions for contributions made to such organizations. (Sec. 23703.5, Rev. & Tax. Code)

Private foundations.—California has adopted the federal category of exempt organizations classified as private foundations (Sec. 23707, Rev. & Tax. Code—Sec. 23709, Rev. & Tax. Code), but has not adopted the federal excise taxes on self-dealing, lobbying, and prohibited investment, or the special taxes on investment income. (IRC Secs. 4940—4948) Sec. 23701 charitable organizations (IRC Sec. 501(c)(3)) are presumed to be private foundations unless they have notified the FTB to the contrary. Such organizations are required to submit annual information reports and such other information as the FTB may require. (Sec. 23772, Rev. & Tax. Code) The private foundation prohibitions are enforced by the California Attorney General. The California provisions parallel IRC Secs. 507—509, incorporating the same definitions and restrictions. Termination of a private foundation under federal law is a valid termination under state law, notice of which should be forwarded to the FTB within 60 days (Reg. 23707, 18 CCR), termination by distribution of assets should be reported on the final information return.

Private foundations may not engage in those activities which result in imposition of federal excise tax. (IRC Secs. 4940—4946) These taxes are imposed upon the following: (1) the net investment income of a private foundation; (2) acts of self-dealing between the foundation and its donor or related parties; (3) foundation's failure to distribute its income for exempt purposes; (4) excessive foundation holdings in unrelated business enterprises; (5) investments which jeopardize the foundation's exempt purposes; and (6) lobbying and other foundation activities which tend to influence elections and legislation. California excludes years before 1972 from applicability of these limitations; the equivalent federal provision (IRC Sec. 508(e)(2)), which was repealed in 1976, also excluded years before 1972.

Enforcement of the restrictions discussed above is the responsibility of the Attorney General and violators discovered by the FTB will be called to the attention of the Attorney General. (Reg. 23708, 18 CCR) Notification of the Attorney General is in lieu of revoking the exemption, according to the regulation.

Private foundations are defined as IRC Sec. 501(c)(3) organizations, except for the following:

— an organization to which the 50% contributions deduction limitation applies, except those private foundations qualifying for maximum deduction and described in IRC Sec. 170(b)(1)(A)(vii) and (viii);

— an organization normally receiving more than $1/3$ of its annual support from members and the general public and not more than $1/3$ of its annual support from investment income;

— an organization organized and operated exclusively for the benefit of one or more type (1) or (2) organizations and controlled by one or more organizations, or operated in connection with one organization (or more than one, in the case of an educational organization), described in (1) or (2); or

— an organization organized and operated exclusively for the purpose of testing for public safety.

Exemption applications.—Incorporation under the Nonprofit Corporation Law does not mean that an organization is exempt from California corporate franchise and income taxes. Except as noted below, all organizations must file for exemption in California, whether or not they are exempt from federal tax. Until January 1, 2021, a $25 fee must accompany the application, which is submitted on Form FTB 3500 by all exempt organizations except political organizations. Effective January 1, 2021, California eliminated the fee. (Sec. 23701, Rev. & Tax. Code; FTB Form 3500, Exemption Application Booklet)

A central organization that has one or more California subordinates under its general supervision or control may apply for a group exemption on behalf of itself and its subordinates (e.g., chapter, local, post or unit). The organization applying for a group exemption letter must establish its own exempt status and must also establish that the subordinates to be included in the group are affiliated with it, subject to its general supervision and control, and exempt under the same lettered section under Revenue and Taxation Code section 23701. (.Reg. 23701(i), 18 CCR)

CCH PRACTICE TIP: Simplified exemption process: IRC Sec. 501(c)(3) organizations that are granted tax-exempt status under federal law may submit FTB 3500A, Affirmation of Internal Revenue Code 501(c)(3), along with a copy of their IRS issued tax-exempt status notice to the FTB to establish their California tax-exempt status. The effective date of an organization's California tax-exempt status will be no later than the effective date of that organization's federal tax-exempt status. An organization that incorporated prior to receiving its federal exempt status and that wants to receive state-exempt status retroactively in order to avoid the imposition of the minimum franchise or annual tax should file FTB 3500, Exemption Application, and not Form FTB 3500A, to request exemption retroactive to its date of incorporation.

IRC Sec. 501(c)(3) organizations must still fulfill California's exemption law requirements to receive the FTB's affirmation of federal tax exemption. This includes California's filing requirements for FTB Form 199, California Exempt Organization Annual Information Return; FTB Form 109, California Exempt Organization Business Income Tax Return; or FTB Form 100, Corporation Tax Return. Furthermore, an inactive organization is not entitled to exemption. Organizations seeking to obtain and retain California exempt status must meet requirements that they are organized and operating for nonprofit purposes within the provisions of their exempt code section. (Sec. 23701, Rev. & Tax. Code; Sec. 23701d, Rev. & Tax. Code) (FTB Notice 2008-3, May 30, 2008; Tax News, FTB, December 2007) The FTB may grant a tax exemption retroactively to years in which an organization has no financial records available. (*FTB Technical Advice Memorandum 2011-4*, May 31, 2011)

Effective January 1, 2014, organizations that are federally tax-exempt under IRC Sec. 501(c)(4), (5), (6), and (7), and effective January 1, 2018, veterans' organizations that are federally tax-exempt under IRC Sec. 501(c)(19), are also allowed to submit a copy of their federal tax-exempt determination letter or ruling to the FTB to establish their exemption from state income tax (similar to how IRC Sec. 501(c)(3) organizations may do so). As a result, these organizations will no longer need to file an exemption application with the FTB or submit a $25 filing fee. An organization that is not issued a federal determination letter may still file an application to obtain California tax-exempt status. (Sec. 23701, Rev. & Tax. Code)

PLANNING NOTE: *Expedited Request for Tax Exempt Status.*—The fee for expedited service requests for tax-exempt status is $50. The fees must be paid by certified checks, money orders, or cash. Personal checks will not be accepted. Qualified entities requesting tax exempt status must submit Form FTB 3500 (Exemption Application), along with all necessary documentation, to the Sacramento or Los Angeles FTB district office. (Reg. 19591; *FTB Notice 2004-09*, FTB, December 17, 2004)

Corporations must furnish a copy of endorsed articles of incorporation and all subsequent endorsed amendments. Foreign corporations that are qualified through the Secretary of State must submit a copy of the endorsed articles of incorporation and all subsequent endorsed amendments from the state or country in which incorporated. Unincorporated organizations should furnish a copy of their constitution, articles of association, bylaws, or other document that contains the required language and is signed by the board of directors or other governing body. Trusts should submit a copy of their trust document and any subsequent modifications to it. A California LLC should submit a copy of the endorsed articles of organization. An LLC formed in another state and qualified in California should submit a copy of the endorsed application for registration, a copy of the certificate of good standing from the home state, and a copy of the articles of organization from the home state. All organizations must submit:

— bylaws (or proposed bylaws, operating agreement, or other code of regulations);

— financial documents and accounting statements for each accounting period that the organization was in existence and for which exemption is requested (or proposed budget, if a new organization);

— a statement outlining specific funding sources, activities, and business enterprises;

— statements of purpose, of programs and activities, and of discontinued activities;

— copies of leases to which the organization is a party; and

— summaries of any literature sold or distributed by the organization and any organizational advertising. (FTB Form 3500, Exemption Application Booklet)

The information disclosed in an exemption application, together with papers submitted to support the application, and letters and documents issued by the FTB with respect to the application, is public information. (Sec. 19542, Rev. & Tax. Code) This exception to the general rules requiring confidentiality is the same under federal law. (IRC Sec. 6104(a)(1))

On request, the supporting papers may be withheld from public inspection if they contain information about a trade secret, patent process, style of work, or apparatus of the organization. The FTB may also withhold information in the papers if disclosure would adversely affect the national defense. (Sec. 19542, Rev. & Tax. Code) A similar rule applies under federal law. (IRC Sec. 6104(a)(1)(b), Publicity of Information Required From Certain Exempt Organizations and Certain Trusts)

All charitable organizations and trustees holding property for charitable purposes are required to register with the Registrar of Charitable Trusts, in the office of the Attorney General in Sacramento, California, within six months after the receipt of assets for charitable purposes. (Sec. 12581, Govt. Code; Sec. 12585, Govt. Code; Reg. 23703, 18 CCR) Such organizations must file an annual report (Form RRF-1) with the Registry of Charitable Trusts. (Sec. 12586, Govt. Code) These requirements apply in addition to the information returns that must be filed with the Franchise Tax Board (FTB).

Lobbying restrictions.—California law regarding restrictions on the amount a charitable organization may spend to influence legislation is the same as IRC Sec. 501(h), except for titles and internal references. (Sec. 23704.5, Rev. & Tax. Code)

Other exempt organizations, except churches, may elect to be treated under the provision as engaging in limited political activity without losing their exemptions. Organizations that forfeit their exempt status as a result of excessive lobbying activities or as a result of participating or intervening in any political campaign on behalf of (or in opposition to) any candidate for public office may not at a later date qualify for exemption as a civic organization, similar to provisions at IRC Sec. 504. (Sec. 23704.6, Rev. & Tax. Code; Sec. 23701f, Rev. & Tax. Code)

Permitted spending limits are the same as those in IRC Sec. 4911, except that California has not adopted the 25% tax on excess expenditures imposed by the federal provision. (Sec. 23740, Rev. & Tax. Code—Sec. 23741, Rev. & Tax. Code)

The determination of whether an electing organization is subject to loss of exemption for excess lobbying is made by comparing the amount of the lobbying expenditures with the organization's "exempt purpose expenditures" for the taxable year. Exempt purpose expenditures include the total of the amounts paid by the organization for exempt religious, charitable, educational, etc., purposes. Amounts properly chargeable to capital account must be capitalized. If the capital item is depreciable, then a reasonable allowance for depreciation, computed on the straight-line basis, is treated as an exempt purpose expenditure. Also included are administrative expenses incurred with respect to any exempt purpose, as well as all amounts paid or incurred for the purpose of influencing legislation, whether or not for exempt purposes.

Exempt purpose expenditures do not include amounts paid or incurred to or for a separate fund-raising unit of an organization (or an affiliated organization's fund-raising unit) along with amounts paid or incurred to or for any other organization, if those amounts are paid or incurred primarily for fund-raising.

The lobbying nontaxable amount for any tax year is the lesser of $1 million or, 20% of the first $500,000 of the organization's exempt-purpose expenditures for the year, plus 15% of the second $500,000, plus 10% of the third $500,000, plus 5% of any additional expenditures. The grass roots nontaxable amount for any tax year is 25% of the lobbying nontaxable amount for the organization for that year.

Exempt status will be denied if a substantial part of an organization's activities consist of attempting to influence legislation and if the organization normally (1) makes lobbying expenditures in excess of its lobbying ceiling amount for each taxable year or (2) makes grass roots expenditures in excess of its grass roots ceiling amount for each taxable year. The ceiling amount applicable is 150% of an organization's lobbying nontaxable amount for the taxable year; the grass roots ceiling amount is 150% of an organization's grass roots nontaxable amount for the taxable year. Affiliated groups are generally treated as one organization. However, member organizations of groups whose governing instruments do not require one member to be bound by the decisions of another are treated individually. (Sec. 23704.5, Rev. & Tax. Code)

Unrelated business income.—IRC Sec. 512—IRC Sec. 514, concerning unrelated business income of exempt organizations, are incorporated, with modifications, by reference into California law as of the current California conformity date (see ¶ 10-515). (Sec. 23732, Rev. & Tax. Code—Sec. 23735, Rev. & Tax. Code) Exempt organizations are taxable under both California (Sec. 23731, Rev. & Tax. Code) and federal law (IRC Sec. 511, which is not incorporated by California) on unrelated business income. Under both California law (Sec. 23731, Rev. & Tax. Code and federal law IRC Sec. 511), the rate of tax imposed on such income is the same as would be imposed on the income of a nonexempt corporation. Similarly, the alternative minimum tax is also applied at the same rate applied to other corporations. (Sec. 23455(a)(3), Rev. & Tax. Code)

California tax law modifies special rules under IRC Sec. 512(a)(3), affecting clubs organized for pleasure or recreation, voluntary employees' beneficiary associations, and trusts providing for payment of supplemental unemployment compensation benefits. Special rules under IRC Sec. 512(a)(2) affecting foreign organizations do not apply for California tax purposes. (Sec. 23732, Rev. & Tax. Code—Sec. 23735, Rev. & Tax. Code) Also, IRC Sec. 513(g), providing that pole rentals of mutual or cooperative telephone or electric companies do not qualify as an "unrelated trade or business," does not apply for California tax purposes. (Sec. 23734, Rev. & Tax. Code)

Both California and federal law (IRC Sec. 512(b)) generally exclude from unrelated business income investment income (dividends, interest, annuities, royalties, and real property rents), as well as deductions directly connected with such income. However, rent, royalty, and interest payments received or accrued by a tax-exempt organization are subject to the unrelated business income tax if they are received from a taxable or tax-exempt subsidiary that is 50% controlled by the parent (either directly or indirectly). (IRC Sec. 512(b)(13); Sec. 23732, Rev. & Tax. Code)

Because of California's federal conformity date (see ¶ 10-515), California does not conform to federal amendments increasing "unrelated business taxable income" by the amount of certain fringe benefit expenses paid or incurred after December 31, 2017, for which a deduction is disallowed. Nor does California conform to the federal requirement that "unrelated business taxable income" be separately computed for each trade or business activity for taxable years beginning after December 31, 2017. (*2017 Summary of Federal Income Tax Changes*, California Franchise Tax Board, May 16, 2018)

Prohibited transactions.—Charitable corporations and unemployment compensation trusts that engage in prohibited transactions are denied exemption. (Sec. 23736.2, Rev. & Tax. Code) However, this provision does not apply to churches and church-controlled organizations, schools, publicly supported charities, and medical institutions. (Sec. 23736, Rev. & Tax. Code) This provision follows IRC Sec. 503(a)(1), however, the federal provision applies only to (1) pension, profit-sharing and stock options plans established and maintained by the federal or a state government for the benefit of government employees; and (2) supplemental unemployment benefit trusts. Under federal law, other exempt organizations are subject to the private foundation rules and excise taxes. California has adopted the federal private foundation definition and restrictions, but not the excise tax.

California defines "prohibited transaction" for purposes of charitable organizations and unemployment compensation trusts in the same manner as former IRC Sec. 503(b), before it was repealed by the 1969 Tax Reform Act. (Sec. 23736, Rev. & Tax. Code) Although California adopted the 1969 Tax Reform Act's definition of "private foundation" and its list of prohibited transactions, it did not narrow the scope of its provisions allowing denial of exemption as the federal law did; therefore, some organizations that are subject to the California charitable organization prohibited transactions rules are also subject to the California private foundation prohibited transaction rules. Furthermore, California retained a prohibition against unreasonable accumulations applicable to all exempt charitable corporations, which the federal government repealed in 1969.

Proscribed activities include making loans without adequate security, excessive compensation, preferential services, purchases in excess of value received or sales for less than adequate compensation, or other diversion of income from its exempt purpose. (Sec. 23736.1, Rev. & Tax. Code) This provision is the same as IRC Sec. 503(b), IRC Sec. 503(e), and IRC Sec. 503(f). There is no federal provision comparable to the California transitional provision, which excepts unemployment trust indebtedness on real property incurred before 1961. (Sec. 23736.1, Rev. & Tax. Code)

Notice of denial of an organization's exemption is issued by the FTB and is effective only for taxable years after notification, unless the organization has diverted a substantial part of corpus or income through the prohibited transaction. (Sec. 23736.3, Rev. & Tax. Code)

¶10-245

An organization denied an exemption may reapply for exempt status, complying with regulations of the FTB. Exempt status, if received, becomes effective for the year after application. (Sec. 23736.4, Rev. & Tax. Code)

A regulation is applicable to the interpretation of these provisions. (Reg. 23737, 18 CCR) Federal regulations applicable to the interpretation of California law discuss the status of exempt organizations engaged in prohibited transactions. (Sec. 23051.5, Rev. & Tax. Code)

Unreasonable accumulations of income.—Charitable organizations are denied exemption for an income year, if amounts accumulated out of income and not paid out are unreasonable in amount or duration in order to carry out exempt purposes, are used to a substantial degree for nonexempt activities, or are invested in a manner which jeopardizes the execution of exempt purposes. (Sec. 23737, Rev. & Tax. Code) There is a California regulation applicable to the provision. (Reg. 23737, 18 CCR)

Dissolution.—FTB Pub. 1038, Guide to Dissolve, Surrender, or Cancel a California Business Entity, provides information on dissolving, surrendering, or cancelling a business entity, including a tax-exempt organization.

Revocation or suspension.—Exemption status may be revoked if an organization: (1) fails to file required statements or returns and payment of amounts due within one year following close of the income year; (2) fails to furnish required records to the FTB; or (3) fails to restrict activities to those permitted by the exemption. (Sec. 23777, Rev. & Tax. Code)

The FTB may revoke an organization's exempt status, even if the organization's state exemption was based on the organization's federal exempt status. Such organizations are required to notify the FTB of any federal tax-exempt status suspension or revocation. Upon receipt of such notice, the FTB may suspend or revoke the organization's state tax-exempt status. (Sec. 23701d, Rev. & Tax. Code)

Organizations that fail to elect an accounting period, to file timely returns or statements, or to pay amounts due on time may be suspended under the provisions of Sec. 23775, Rev. & Tax Code or have their exemption revoked under Sec. 23777. (Sec. 23777, Rev. & Tax. Code; Sec. 23775, Rev. & Tax. Code) When unincorporated associations or trusts become inactive and so notify the FTB prior to the date of revocation, the organizations will normally be made inactive on the FTB files rather than being revoked. An organization whose exemption is revoked for the conduct of improper activities is taxable until exempt status is reestablished. (Reg. 23777, 18 CCR)

The minimum tax will not be assessed solely because of the failure to comply with registration and reporting requirements with the Attorney General's office. Instead, when the Attorney General notifies the FTB that a corporation is out of compliance with the registration and reporting requirements, the FTB must mail a notice to the corporation indicating that the corporation has 120 days to get back into compliance, otherwise the FTB will revoke the corporation's tax-exempt status. The applicable period will be 120 days after the FTB mails notification of the intent to revoke the corporation's tax-exempt status. (Sec. 23703, Rev. & Tax. Code)

Exemption under California law may be reestablished by completion of the following steps: (1) filing new application (and prior to January 1, 2021, with payment of $25 fee); (2) submission of returns, statements, or amounts due, the delinquency of which resulted in revocation; and (3) submission of proof of correction if the exemption was revoked for nonexempt activities. Proof of correction includes evidence that future operations will be exempt and verification of payment of tax for periods of nonexemption. (Sec. 23778, Rev. & Tax. Code; Reg. 23778, 18 CCR)

To be reinstated, the organization must satisfy the requirements of the Attorney General, file an application for revivor, pay the taxes assessed, and may be required by the FTB to file a new application for exemption. (Sec. 23776, Rev. & Tax. Code)

CCH POINTER: Revivor applications and procedures.—The FTB may consider a request for exemption and a revivor application simultaneously to determine the correct amount of tax, penalty, interest, and fees due for the suspension period that must be paid to revive the corporation. In addition, the FTB may revive the corporation without receiving full payment of the amount due, if the FTB determines that revivor will improve the prospects for collection of the full amount due. (*FTB Technical Advice Memorandum 2011-4*, May 31, 2011)

• *Federal income tax provisions*

Organizations may qualify for tax-exempt status if they are organized and operated exclusively for religious, charitable, scientific, testing for public safety, literary, or educational purposes, promotion of amateur sports, or the prevention of cruelty to animals or children (Section 501(c)(3) organizations). Any corporation, community chest, fund, trust, or foundation may qualify for this exemption. Private foundations and organizations that are not public charities are exempt from tax if they are not organized for profit and their earnings do not benefit any individual. Each type of organization must meet specific requirements for exemption. Organizations that are granted exemption will still be taxed on their unrelated business income. In general, an organization must apply for exemption.

[¶ 10-325]

REGULATED INDUSTRIES

[¶ 10-335] Insurance Companies

Since California does not generally subject insurance companies doing business in the state to its corporation franchise (income) tax, there is nothing comparable in state tax law to IRC Sec. 801 through IRC Sec. 848, the federal income tax provisions addressing the treatment of insurance companies. Instead, California applies a tax on the gross premiums of insurance companies operating in the state.

• *Interaction of federal and state provisions*

Under the California Constitution, an insurance company doing insurance business in California is not subject to the state's corporation franchise (income) tax. Instead, such an entity is subject to a tax on its gross premiums. (Sec. 28, Art. XIII, Cal. Const.) Since California does not generally subject an insurance company doing business in the state to its corporation franchise (income) tax, there is nothing comparable in state tax law to IRC Secs. 801 through 848 (the federal provisions addressing insurance companies) the federal corporate income tax provisions applicable to the treatment of an insurance company. Accordingly, California does not incorporate any of these federal IRC provisions, with or without modification, for state corporation franchise (income) tax purposes.

California does have some case law and several insurance provisions that bear on this discussion. The California Supreme Court, for instance, has ruled that the *in-*

lieu provision of the California Constitution also prohibits local governments from imposing any tax on investment income earned by an insurance company selling insurance premiums in California. (*Mutual Life Insurance Company of New York v. City of Los Angeles*(1990, SCt), 50 Cal3d 402)

Furthermore, a corporation in the business of acting as an agent for one or more insurance companies is subject to the state's corporation franchise (income) tax, since the effect that the payment of this franchise tax by an agent has on the insurance company, which pays a gross premiums tax in lieu of all other taxes, is indirect. (*Brown & Sons v. McColgan*, 53 CalApp2d 504, 128 P2d 186 (1942))

Finally, even though a corporate attorney-in-fact for an interinsurance exchange remains taxable in the same manner as a stock or mutual insurance company under the gross premiums tax provisions, rather than under the corporation franchise (income) tax provisions (see Sec. 1283, Ins. Code; *Farmers Underwriters Assn. v. Franchise Tax Board*, 242 CalApp2d 589, 51 CalRptr 686 (1966); and *Agricultural Exchange Corp.*, SBE, 66-SBE-058, October 6, 1966), a corporate attorney-in-fact remains subject to the minimum franchise tax or to a franchise tax based solely on noninsurance income. (Sec. 1530, Ins. Code)

• *Federal income tax provisions*

Insurance companies are generally subject to income tax computed at the normal corporate tax rates. However, the taxable income of insurance companies is determined under special rules. A company qualifies as an insurance company if more than half of its business during the tax year is the issuing of insurance or annuity contracts, or the reinsuring of risks underwritten by insurance companies. If an insurance company's net written premiums or direct written premiums (whichever is greater) for the tax year do not exceed a specified amount, the company may elect to be taxed only on its taxable investment income. Very small property and casualty (non-life) insurance companies may be exempt from tax if they meet certain requirements.

[¶10-340] Banks--Financial Corporations

While California does not specifically incorporate IRC Sec. 581 through IRC Sec. 597 (the federal income tax provisions addressing the treatment of banks, mutual savings banks, other financial institutions, and their bad debt and loss reserves), many of California's statutory and regulatory provisions mirror these federal laws.

Furthermore, California has its own provisions addressing the taxation of a bank or a "financial corporation." Subject to the minimum tax provisions (see Sec. 23153, Rev. & Tax. Code), the annual tax imposed on every bank or financial corporation doing business in California (other than a public bank) is currently 10.84% of its annual net income, if the institution is not an S corporation. (Sec. 23186, Rev. & Tax. Code) For a bank or financial corporation that is an S corporation, the current rate is 3.5%. (Sec. 23802, Rev. & Tax. Code) This annual tax is generally in lieu of all other state, county, and municipal taxes and license fees upon a bank or a financial corporation. (Sec. 23182, Rev. & Tax. Code) Effective January 1, 2020, public banks are exempt from California franchise and income taxes and all other state and local taxes and fees except for local utility user taxes, sales and use taxes, state energy resources surcharges, state emergency telephone users surcharges, and any other tax or license fee imposed by the state upon vehicles or their operation. (Sec. 23701aa, Rev. & Tax. Code)

A financial corporation is basically a corporation that predominantly deals in money or moneyed capital in substantial competition with the business of a national bank. (Sec. 23183, Rev. & Tax. Code; Reg. 23183, 18 CCR) Examples of a financial corporation include a small loan company, a savings and loan association, a building and loan association, or a loan broker.

• *Interaction of federal and state provisions*

While California generally mirrors the federal income tax provisions applicable to banks, mutual savings banks, other financial institutions, and their bad debt and loss reserves, it has modified the federal approach for state corporation franchise (income) tax purposes. The IRC sections specifically incorporated by California without amendment, the various state modifications to the applicable IRC sections, and the California tax provisions that generally mirror the IRC are discussed below.

Unmodified IRC sections.—California specifically incorporates IRC Sec. 582, which addresses bad debts, losses, and gains with respect to securities held by financial institutions. However, with respect to a foreign bank that has in effect a water's-edge election, the California provision applies only to a gain or loss in connection with the conduct of its domestic banking business. (Sec. 24347, Rev. & Tax. Code)

California also incorporates former IRC Sec. 595, which addressed foreclosure on property securing loans (repealed by P.L. 104-188 and applicable to federal tax years after 1995). (Sec. 24348.5, Rev. & Tax. Code) Accordingly, for state tax purposes, a state or federal savings and loan association in California recognizes no gain or loss, and may not take a bad debt deduction, as a result of the acquisition of property, by foreclosure bid or otherwise, that was security for any indebtedness. Sec. 24348.5, Rev. & Tax. Code, is the same as IRC Sec. 595, prior to its repeal, except for the title, various internal references, and the organizations to which the provision applies. Any amount realized by the financial institution from a resale of the property is considered to be a payment on account of the original indebtedness, and any loss resulting from such a sale is treated as a bad debt loss to which Sec. 24348, Rev. & Tax. Code, applies.

Modifications to IRC sections.—California does not specifically modify any of the remaining federal income tax provisions addressing banks, mutual savings banks, other financial institutions, and their bad debt and loss reserves for state corporation franchise (income) tax purposes.

State provisions that mirror the IRC.—Although California's corporation franchise (income) tax provisions do not explicitly address a number of the applicable IRC sections, several state tax provisions addressing the treatment of banks, mutual savings banks, etc. mirror the federal statutes.

For instance, California generally provides for a bad debt deduction for:

— debts that become worthless within the tax year in an amount not in excess of the part charged off within that tax year (*i.e.,* the "specific charge-off method"); and

— in the case of a bank, a savings and loan association, or other financial institution (as defined by IRC Sec. 581), a reasonable addition to a reserve for bad debts as determined in accordance with IRC Sec. 585, which addresses reserves for losses on loans of banks, in lieu of any worthless debt deduction, and in the discretion of the California Franchise Tax Board (FTB).

(Sec. 24348(a), Rev. & Tax. Code)

If the FTB is satisfied that a debt is recoverable only in part, it may allow a bad debt deduction in an amount not to exceed the part charged off within the tax year.

However, if a portion of a debt is claimed and allowed as a deduction in any year, no deduction is allowed in any subsequent year for any portion of that debt that was previously charged off, regardless of whether claimed as a deduction in that prior year. (Sec. 24348(b), Rev. & Tax. Code)

In the case of any bank, savings and loan association, or financial corporation (whether a taxpayer or a member of a combined reporting group) that maintained a reserve for bad debts for the last tax year beginning before 2002, and that had to change its method of computing the reserves for bad debts, the change is treated as initiated by the institution and is characterized as an accounting method change made with FTB consent. (Sec. 24348(c), Rev. & Tax. Code)

Furthermore, the requisite adjustments taken into account by the institution (see Sec. 24721 et seq., Rev. & Tax. Code):

— are determined by taking into account only 50% of the "applicable excess reserves" (see below);

— are taken into account on the last day of the first tax year beginning after 2001; and

— the amount of "applicable excess reserves" in excess of the amount taken into account above is reduced to zero and is not taken into account for these purposes.

(Sec. 24348(c), Rev. & Tax. Code)

In the case of a large bank (as defined in IRC Sec. 585(c)(2) (that is, a bank that has more than $500 million in assets)), or a financial corporation that is not allowed to use the reserve for bad debts under IRC Sec. 585, the term "applicable excess reserves" means the balance of the bad debt reserves as of the close of the last tax year beginning before 2002. Thus, a large bank must recognize 50% of its excess bad debt reserve balance as income at the end of the first tax year beginning after 2001. In all other cases, the "applicable excess reserves" are zero and will not be taken into account for these purposes. (Sec. 24348(d), Rev. & Tax. Code)

COMMENT: *Changing to or from a water's-edge election.*—A FTB legal ruling clarifies how a bad debt reserve (see IRC Sec. 585) should be calculated when a foreign bank makes or terminates a water's-edge election. The ruling provides that a foreign bank that has U.S. (California) branch operations and makes a water's-edge election must recalculate its beginning bad debt reserve as if the water's-edge election had been in place for prior years, and then restate the beginning balance to reflect only the loss history of the branch operations. Furthermore, a foreign bank that terminates its water's-edge election must compute its beginning worldwide bad debt reserve for income years beginning after the last year of the water's-edge election as if the water's-edge election had not been in effect. The experience of the worldwide combined group must be aggregated and used to calculate the bad debt reserve. (*LR 96-6*, FTB, September 12, 1996)

Although California's tax provisions also do not explicitly address IRC Sec. 591, the state tax treatment of a mutual savings bank, or of a building and loan or a federal savings and loan association organized wholly or partly on the mutual plan, also mirrors the federal tax treatment. (See Sec. 24370, Rev. & Tax. Code and Sec. 24403, Rev. & Tax. Code.) Accordingly, a mutual savings bank may deduct the entire amount of interest paid to a depositor having no proprietary interest in the institution or in its surplus. Such a bank may also deduct an amount of interest allocable to a member with a proprietary interest in the bank or its surplus, but this deductible interest is limited to the "going rate" of interest upon state savings deposits during the calendar year preceding the applicable tax year. The Commissioner of Financial Institutions must certify this "going rate" to the FTB by March 1 of each year. (Sec. 24370, Rev. & Tax. Code)

Likewise, a building and loan association, or a federal savings and loan association, organized wholly or partly on the mutual plan, may deduct amounts paid, credited, or apportioned to the withdrawable shares of the depositors or holders of accounts. (Sec. 24403, Rev. & Tax. Code)

Furthermore, although California has no tax provision directly comparable to IRC Sec. 593, which addresses reserves for losses on loans, that is applicable to a mutual savings bank or a savings and loan association, the state does have bad debt provisions that are applicable to all financial institutions. (See above.)

Prior to 1989, California did have tax provisions that mirrored IRC Sec. 597, which addresses the treatment of transactions in which federal financial assistance is provided. Accordingly, the gross income of a bank or domestic building and loan association did not include any amount of money or other property received from the Federal Savings and Loan Insurance Corporation (FSLIC) pursuant to Section 406(f) of the National Housing Act (12 U.S.C. Section 1729(f)), regardless of whether any note or other instrument was issued in exchange. Nor was there any reduction in the basis of the institution's assets on account of any money or other property received under these circumstances. (Sec. 24322, Rev. & Tax. Code)

California has no provisions comparable to IRC Sec. 584, which addresses common trust funds, or IRC Sec. 594, which addresses the alternative tax for mutual savings banks conducting life insurance business.

• *Taxation of banks and financial corporations*

The California Constitution provides that a tax may be imposed on state and national banks and their franchises measured by net income in lieu of all other taxes imposed on these institutions, except real property taxes and motor vehicle registration and license fees. (Sec. 27, Art. XIII, Cal. Const.)

Accordingly, an annual tax is imposed on every bank or "financial corporation" doing business in California, computed at the rate provided under Sec. 23186, Rev. & Tax. Code, upon the net income for that tax year, but not less than the minimum tax specified in Sec. 23153, Rev. & Tax. Code. Special rules apply to a bank or financial corporation that operates only for a brief time or that ceases doing business during the tax year. (Sec. 23181, Rev. & Tax. Code; Sec. 23183, Rev. & Tax. Code; Sec. 23183.1, Rev. & Tax. Code; and Sec. 23183.2, Rev. & Tax. Code) Thus, the tax rate applicable to a bank or financial corporation is equal to the franchise (income) tax rate imposed on a general corporation, plus 2%. (Sec. 23186, Rev. & Tax. Code) The applicable current tax rate is therefore 10.84% (*i.e.*, 8.84% plus 2%) for a bank or financial corporation that is not an S corporation. For a bank or financial corporation that is an S corporation, the current rate is 3.5%. (Sec. 23802, Rev. & Tax. Code)

This tax is in lieu of all other state, county, and municipal taxes and license fees upon a bank or a financial corporation, except for taxes upon their real property, local utility user taxes, sales and use taxes, state energy resources surcharge, state emergency telephone users surcharge, and motor vehicle and other vehicle registration license fees and any other tax or license fee imposed by the state upon vehicles, motor vehicles, or the operation thereof. (Sec. 23182, Rev. & Tax. Code)

Financial corporation definitions.—The purpose in having a class of corporations designated as "financial" is to fulfill the federal requirement authorizing a state to impose a tax on a national bank at a rate no different from that imposed on a "financial corporation." A financial corporation is basically a corporation that predominantly deals in money or moneyed capital in substantial competition with the business of a national bank. For these purposes, a financial corporation does not include any corporation, including a wholly owned subsidiary of a bank or bank holding company, if the principal business activity of such entity consists of leasing tangible personal property. (Sec. 23183, Rev. & Tax. Code; Reg. 23183, 18 CCR) Examples of a financial corporation include a small loan company, a savings and loan association, a building and loan association, and a loan broker.

"Predominantly" means that over 50% of the corporation's total gross income is attributable to dealings in money or moneyed capital in substantial competition with a national bank. However, for a corporation to be classified as a financial corporation, the predominant character of the corporation's gross income for two consecutive years must be attributable to dealings in money or moneyed capital, and the average of the corporation's gross income in the current year, and the immediately preceding two years, must satisfy the predominance test. (Reg. 23183(b)(1), 18 CCR)

"Deals in" means conducting transactions in the course of a trade or business on the corporation's own account, rather than acting as a broker for the accounts of others. (Reg. 23183(b)(2), 18 CCR)

"Money or moneyed capital" includes coin, cash, currency, mortgages, deeds of trust, conditional sales contracts, loans, commercial paper, installment notes, credit cards, and accounts receivable. (Reg. 23183(b)(3), 18 CCR)

"In substantial competition" with a national bank means that the corporation and national banks both engage in seeking and securing, in the same locality, substantial amounts of capital investments of the same class. The activities of the corporation need not be identical to those of a national bank in order to constitute substantial competition; it is sufficient if there is competition with some phases of the business of a national bank. (Reg. 23183(b)(4), 18 CCR)

The "business of a national bank" is defined as a business in which a national bank is permitted to operate. (Reg. 23183(b)(5), 18 CCR)

• *Federal income tax provisions*

A "bank" for federal tax purposes is a corporation that receives deposits and makes loans or that exercises fiduciary powers as a trust company, and that is subject to banking regulatory supervision by a state or federal government. Banks are subject to the same federal income tax rates that apply to other corporations. Banking institutions are categorized as either commercial or non-commercial institutions. Non-commercial banking institutions include mutual savings banks, savings and loan associations, and credit unions. While similar in many respects to commercial banks, they are controlled by different sets of organizational, operational and regulatory rules, as well as by different sections of the Internal Revenue Code (IRC). Special tax treatment applies to insolvent banks and common trust funds. The definition of "bank" applies specifically under the IRC to bad debts, losses and securities gains, common trust funds, and bad debt reserves.

[¶10-375]
RATES

[¶10-380] Rates of Tax

What is the California corporate income tax rate?

The California corporation franchise and income taxes are imposed on C corporations at the rate of 8.84%. (Sec. 23151(e), Rev. & Tax. Code)

A corporation is not subject to the corporation franchise or income tax if it did not do business in California during the taxable year and its taxable year was 15 days or less. (Sec. 23114, Rev. & Tax. Code)

Tax rate changes apply to taxable years beginning after December 31 of the year before enactment, unless otherwise specified by statute. (Sec. 23058, Rev. & Tax. Code)

Banks and financial corporations. Banks and financial corporations are taxed at a rate of 10.84% (the general corporation franchise and income tax rate plus 2%). (Sec. 23186, Rev. & Tax. Code)

S corporations. S corporations, other than financial corporations, pay tax at a special rate of 1.5%. Financial corporations that are S corporations are taxed at a rate of 3.5% (the general S corporation tax rate plus 2%). (Sec. 23802, Rev. & Tax. Code; Sec. 23186, Rev. & Tax. Code)

Minimum tax. A minimum franchise tax of $800 is imposed on all corporations, including banks and financial corporations, not exempt from the corporation franchise tax. Liability for the tax begins with the earlier of the date of incorporation, qualification, or commencing to do business in California, and ends on the effective date of dissolution or withdrawal or, if later, the date the corporation ceases to do business in California. (Sec. 23153, Rev. & Tax. Code; Sec. 23151, Rev. & Tax. Code) Corporations subject to the corporation income tax (rather than the corporation franchise tax) are not subject to the minimum franchise tax.

COMPLIANCE ALERT: In *Swart Enterprises, Inc. v. Franchise Tax Board*, Court of Appeal of California, Fifth District, No. F070922, January 12, 2017, the court held that an Iowa corporation was not "doing business" in California and, therefore, was not subject to the $800 minimum franchise tax that the California Franchise Tax Board (FTB) had assessed. The Iowa corporation held a 0.2% membership interest in a manager-managed California limited liability company (LLC) that was doing business in California. The Iowa corporation acquired its membership interest in the California LLC after the original members made the decision for the California LLC to be manager-managed. The original members delegated to a sole manager full, exclusive, and complete authority to manage and control the California LLC. The Iowa corporation's sole connection to California was its ownership interest in the California LLC. After the *Swart* decision was issued, the FTB informed taxpayers that it will not appeal the decision and will follow it in situations with the same facts. Therefore, to the extent taxpayers believe their situation has the same facts as in *Swart*, they should take that into consideration in determining if they have a return filing obligation and/or if they should file a claim for refund. In addition, among other things, in any claim for refund, taxpayers should cite the holding in *Swart* and explain how their factual situation is the same as the facts in *Swart*. (*FTB Notice 2017-01*, California Franchise Tax Board, February 28, 2017; Tax News, California Franchise Tax Board, March 2018)

First-year. A corporation that incorporates or qualifies to do business in California is exempt from the minimum franchise tax for its first taxable year. (Sec. 23153, Rev. & Tax. Code)

PRACTICAL ANALYSIS: Out-of-state corporations that are doing business in California, referred to as nonqualified corporations, do not generally qualify for the waiver of the minimum tax. A nonqualified corporation may be able to receive first year relief if it subsequently qualifies with the Secretary of State's Office. A nonqualified corporation may be eligible to file a refund claim to recover the minimum tax after it qualifies. (Tax News, California Franchise Tax Board, August 2011)

Taxable years of 15 days or less. A corporation is not subject to the minimum franchise tax if it did not do business in California during the taxable year and its taxable year was 15 days or less. An inactive corporation's first taxable year of 15 days or less between the date of incorporation and its next annual accounting period is not considered the corporation's first taxable year for purposes of the minimum franchise tax. (Sec. 23114, Rev. & Tax. Code)

Final year. A corporation is not required to pay the minimum franchise tax if it files a timely final franchise tax return for a taxable year with the FTB, does not do business in California after the end of the taxable year for which the final return was filed, and files a certificate of dissolution or surrender with the Secretary of State's Office before the end of the 12-month period beginning with the date the final return was filed. (Sec. 23332, Rev. & Tax. Code)

Limited liability companies. Limited liability companies (LLCs) that are classified as partnerships or that are disregarded and treated as sole proprietorships for California tax purposes are subject to an $800 annual tax plus an annual fee. (Sec. 17941, Rev. & Tax. Code) An LLC is not subject to the annual tax if it did not do business in California during the taxable year and its taxable year was 15 days or less. (Sec. 17946, Rev. & Tax. Code) Also, an LLC that organizes or registers with the Secretary of State on or after January 1, 2021, and before January 1, 2024, is exempt from the annual tax for its first taxable year, with the exemption contingent for a taxable year on a state budget measure appropriating at least $1 to the FTB for its associated administrative costs. In addition, an LLC is exempt from the annual tax upon the filing of a certificate of cancellation or dissolution of the LLC. However, an LLC will not be entitled to a refund of any taxes or fees already paid. (Sec. 17941, Rev. and Tax. Code)

In addition, an LLC is not required to pay the annual tax if it files a timely final return for the preceding taxable year with the FTB, does not do business in California after the end of the taxable year for which the final return was filed, and files a certificate of cancellation with the Secretary of State's Office before the end of the 12-month period beginning with the date the final return was filed. (Sec. 17947, Rev. & Tax. Code; Sec. 23332, Rev. & Tax. Code)

Limited liability partnerships and limited partnerships. Limited liability partnerships (LLPs) and limited partnerships (LPs) are also subject to an $800 annual tax. (Sec. 17948, Rev. & Tax. Code; Sec. 17935, Rev. & Tax. Code) An LLP or LP is not subject to the annual tax if it did not do business in California during the taxable year and its taxable year was 15 days or less. (Sec. 17936, Rev. & Tax. Code; Sec. 17948.2 Rev. & Tax. Code)Also, an LP or LLP that files or registers with the Secretary of State on or after January 1, 2021, and before January 1, 2024, is exempt from the annual tax for its first taxable year, with the exemption contingent for a taxable year on a state budget measure appropriating at least $1 to the FTB for its associated administrative costs. (Sec. 17948, Rev. & Tax. Code; Sec. 17935, Rev. & Tax. Code)

In addition, an LLP or LP is not required to pay the annual tax if it files a timely final return for a taxable year with the FTB, does not do business in California after the end of the taxable year for which the final return was filed, and files a certificate of cancellation or notice of cessation with the Secretary of State's Office before the end of the 12-month period beginning with the date the final return was filed. (Sec. 17937, Rev. & Tax. Code; Sec. 17948.3, Rev. & Tax. Code)

Credit unions. Credit unions are exempt from the minimum franchise tax. (Sec. 23153, Rev. & Tax. Code) However, a credit union must prepay a tax of $25 when it incorporates under the California laws or when it qualifies to transact business in California.

Nonprofit cooperative associations. Qualifying nonprofit cooperative associations are exempt from the minimum franchise tax for five consecutive taxable years, beginning in the taxable year of their certification. A qualifying association must have been organized after 1993 and must receive a certificate from the board of supervisors of the county in which the association's principal place of business is located. (Sec. 23221, Rev. & Tax. Code) To be eligible for a certificate, the association must request certification in its first taxable year, be located in an economically distressed area, and have at least 90% of its members that are, or have been within the last 12 months, unemployed or receiving public assistance. (Sec. 23153, Rev. & Tax. Code)

Gold or quicksilver mining corporations. Certain inactive California corporations organized for the purpose of mining gold or quicksilver pay a minimum tax of $25. (Sec. 23153, Rev. & Tax. Code)

Professional athletic teams. An entity that operates a professional athletic team is treated as a corporation subject to the minimum franchise tax. Payment of the minimum tax by the entity satisfies liability for the minimum tax of any corporation owning any portion or share of the entity and not otherwise doing business in California. (Sec. 25141(e), Rev. & Tax. Code)

Small businesses owned by deployed service members. For the 2010 through 2017 tax years and again for the 2020 through 2029 tax years, a corporation or an LLC that is a small business solely owned by a deployed member of the U.S. Armed Forces will not be subject to the minimum franchise tax or the annual LLC tax for any taxable year that the owner is deployed and the corporation or the LLC operates at a loss or ceases operation. A "small business" for purposes of the exemption is a corporation or an LLC with total income from all California sources of $250,000 or less. (Sec. 17941, Rev. & Tax. Code; Sec. 23151, Rev. & Tax. Code)

PRACTICAL ANALYSIS: The FTB has issued a legal ruling addressing when a corporation or an LLC "ceases operation" for purposes of the exemption for small businesses owned by deployed service members. In situations where the entity is winding up its business operations beyond the close of its taxable year, but is otherwise not engaged in any active business operations, the entity may be considered to have ceased operations for tax purposes. If the entity files final tax returns with the IRS and the FTB and delivers a Certificate of Dissolution or a Certificate of Cancellation to the California Secretary of State within 12 months of the filing date of the final return, it may also be considered to have ceased operations. If the entity has zero gross income and zero gross expenses for the taxable year, it may be considered to have ceased operations for the taxable year. If the entity discontinues all business operations during the taxable year, but during the following year must defend itself in a lawsuit in state or federal court, the entity may still be considered to have ceased operations. If the entity discontinues all business operations during the taxable year, but resumes operations during the following taxable year, the entity may still be considered to have ceased operations during the year in which it discontinues operations, provided that it ceases operations at the same time as the deployment; ceases operations for at least one month during the taxable year; does not resume operations during the taxable year; and ceases operations for at least three months, even if this period extends into the following taxable year. (Legal Ruling 2011-03, California Franchise Tax Board, May 27, 2011)

CCH PRACTICE TIP: Corporations or LLCs exempt from the minimum franchise or annual tax should write "Deployed Military" in red ink in the top margin of their return. (FTB Pub. 1032, Tax Information for Military Personnel)

[¶10-500]

TAXABLE INCOME COMPUTATION

[¶10-505] Overview of Taxable Income Computation

Corporations compute their franchise or income tax on the basis of net income. (Sec. 23151, Rev. & Tax. Code; Rev. & Tax. Code Sec. 23501) "Net income" is defined as federal gross income with certain modifications less specified California deductions. (Sec. 24271, Rev. & Tax. Code; Sec. 24341, Rev. & Tax. Code)

As a practical matter, in computing its net income a corporation begins with federal taxable income (see ¶10-510), modifies it to account for differences between California and federal law (see ¶10-600 and ¶10-800), and, if the corporation also does business in other states, allocates and apportions the modified amount (see ¶11-505) to determine the portion taxable by California. An alternate computation method is discussed at ¶10-530. California's conformity to the Internal Revenue Code is discussed at ¶10-515. For rules applicable to special industries and entities, see ¶10-525. For financial institutions, see ¶10-340; for S corporations, see ¶10-215; and for limited liability companies (LLCs), see ¶10-240.

[¶10-510] Starting Point for Computation

What is the starting point for computation of the California corporate income tax?

For corporations using the federal reconciliation method to figure net income, the starting point for computation of the California corporation franchise or income tax is federal taxable income reported on Line 28 of the federal tax return. (Instructions, Form 100, California Corporation Franchise or Income Tax Return) This amount reflects the taxpayer's federal taxable income before federal net operating loss and special deductions.

Instead of using the federal reconciliation method, corporations that are not required to file a federal return or that maintain separate records for state purposes may figure their net income using a California computation method. Under the California computation method, the starting point for computation of tax is total income computed under California laws. (Instructions, Form 100, California Corporation Franchise or Income Tax Return)

[¶10-515] Federal Conformity

California incorporates many Internal Revenue Code (IRC) provisions dealing with gross income, deductions, and accounting periods and methods. Numerous IRC provisions are either incorporated directly, with or without modification, while others are simply mirrored in California's own provisions (see the discussion below under "Incorporated and mirrored provisions" for a list of these provisions). With the exception of the California provisions incorporating Part I of Subchapter D of Chapter 1 of Subtitle A of the Internal Revenue Code, relating to pension, profit-sharing, stock bonus plans, etc., which are generally incorporated as currently amended and effective for federal purposes (Sec. 24601, Rev. & Tax. Code) and the provisions governing the qualification criteria, elections, and terminations of S corporations, the provisions incorporated directly by California refer to the IRC provisions as amended through January 1, 2015 (see discussion below for California's incorporation history over the last 20 years).

Conversely, numerous IRC provisions, such as the federal adoption of the accelerated cost recovery system (ACRS) and the modified accelerated costs recovery system (MACRs) are not followed at all by California for corporation franchise or income tax purposes (see ¶10-670 Additions—Depreciation).

CCH COMMENT: Incorporation of federal exclusions and deductions.—California's corporation tax law is structured differently than California's personal income tax law as it relates to items of income, exclusions, and deductions. Under California's personal income tax law, Revenue and Taxation Code Sections 17081, 17131, and 17201 incorporate entire subchapters of the IRC that govern the treatment of items of gross income, exclusions, and deductions. The California Revenue and Taxation Code sections that follow these specific provisions then modify or specifically decouple from the IRC provisions within those subchapters. Thus, Sec. 17201 specifically incorporates the part of the IRC that contains all of the provisions governing deductions for individual and corporate taxpayers, including the IRC Sec. 193 deduction for expenses incurred for tertiary injectants. However, California personal income tax law contains another provision, Rev. & Tax. Code Sec. 17201.6, that specifically decouples from the IRC Sec. 193 deduction. Thus, California does not allow a current expense deduction for expenses incurred for tertiary injectants for personal income tax purposes, and an addition adjustment is required.

In contrast, the corporation tax law governing items of gross income and net income, does not have general provisions analogous to Rev. & Tax. Code Secs. 17081, 17131, and 17201 in the personal income tax law. Consequently, unless the corporate income tax law specifically incorporates a federal provision governing items of income, exclusions, or deductions, California does not incorporate the federal law. Using the example above, because there is no specific corporation tax law provision either directly incorporating IRC Sec. 193, nor mirroring its provisions, California does not follow federal law concerning the deduction for expenses incurred for tertiary injectants and an addition adjustment will be required on the corporation tax return for those taxpayers utilizing the federal reconciliation method (see ¶ 10-510).

In addition, unless specifically stated otherwise, California does not follow federal tax provisions concerning domestic international sales corporations (DISCs), foreign sales corporations (FSCs), personal holding companies, foreign investment companies, foreign trusts, foreign income taxes and foreign income tax credits, and federal tax credits and carryovers of federal tax credits. (Sec. 23051.5(b), Rev. & Tax. Code) Furthermore, California law does not incorporate certain repatriation provisions of the federal Tax Cuts and Jobs Act (TCJA) of 2017, such as provisions that:

— allow a 100% deduction for the foreign-source portion of dividends received from a specified 10% owned foreign corporation by a domestic corporation that is a U.S. shareholder of the foreign corporation (i.e., a participation dividends-received deduction) (IRC Sec. 245A);

— impose a one-time transition (repatriation) tax, without requiring an actual distribution, on accumulated foreign earnings of controlled foreign corporations (CFCs) or foreign corporations that are at least 10% owned by a domestic corporation (IRC Sec. 965); and

— require inclusion of "global intangible low-taxed income" (GILTI) by a person who is a U.S. shareholder of a CFC (IRC Sec. 951A).

(*Preliminary Report on Specific Provisions of the Federal Tax Cuts and Jobs Act*, California Franchise Tax Board, March 20, 2018)

PRACTICE NOTE: *Adjustments for IRC Sec. 965 amounts.*—Taxpayers that reported IRC Sec. 965 amounts on their 2017 federal return must adjust their 2017 California return. Taxpayers who filed a 2017 California return and included IRC Sec. 965 amounts should file an amended return to remove those amounts. They should write "IRC 965" on the top of their California return. Businesses can make adjustments on Schedule K (100S), Schedule K (565), or Schedule K (568). They should not include federal transition tax statement amounts on Form 100, Form 100W, or Form 109 and related schedules. (*California Guidance – Taxable Year 2017 IRC Section 965 Reporting*, California Franchise Tax Board, May 2018)

An overview of California's taxable income computation is located at ¶ 10-505.

• *Year-to-year effect of incorporating IRC provisions by reference*

When an IRC provision is incorporated by reference by California, Rev. & Tax. Code Sec. 23051.5 provides guidance in determining which federal amendments are incorporated by California. Under this provision, references to the Internal Revenue Code mean the Internal Revenue Code in effect on the following specified date:

IRC provisions as amended through:	Are applicable to California taxable years beginning:
Jan. 15, 1983	During calendar year 1983
Jan. 1, 1984	During calendar year 1984
Jan. 1, 1985	During calendar year 1985
Jan. 1, 1986	During calendar year 1986
Jan. 1, 1987	During calendar years 1987 and 1988
Jan. 1, 1989	During calendar year 1989
Jan. 1, 1990	During calendar year 1990
Jan. 1, 1991	On or after January 1, 1991
Jan. 1, 1992	On or after January 1, 1992

IRC provisions as amended through:	Are applicable to California taxable years beginning:
Jan. 1, 1993	On or after January 1, 1993
Jan. 1, 1997	On or after January 1, 1997
Jan. 1, 1998	On or after January 1, 1998
Jan. 1, 2001	On or after January 1, 2002
Jan. 1, 2005	On or after January 1, 2005
Jan. 1, 2009	On or after January 1, 2010
Jan. 1, 2015	On or after January 1, 2015

(Sec. 23051.5(a), Rev. & Tax. Code)

Any IRC provision that is incorporated as of the specified date, but that becomes operative for federal tax purposes after the specified date, also becomes operative on the same date for California franchise and income tax purposes. Likewise, any incorporated provision that becomes *inoperative* on or after the specified date also becomes inoperative on the same date for California franchise and income tax purposes. (Sec. 23051.5(h), Rev. & Tax. Code)

PLANNING NOTE: EGTRRA sunset provisions incorporated.—California incorporates the federal provision of the Economic Growth and Tax Relief and Reconciliation Act of 2001 (P.L. 107-134) that provides that all provisions of, and amendments made by, the 2001 Act shall not apply to taxable, plan, or limitation years beginning after 2010. To the extent that these EGTRRA amendments impact provisions that are incorporated by California corporation franchise and income tax laws, they will apply to in the same manner and to the same taxable years as they apply for federal income tax purposes. (Sec. 23051.5(a)(2), Rev. & Tax. Code) However, it should be noted that the FTB has taken the position that California adopts the two-year extension provided by Section 101 of the federal Tax Relief Act of 2010, which extended many of the provisions adopted by the Economic Growth and Tax Relief and Reconciliation Act of 2001 through the 2012 tax year. (*E-mail*, California Franchise Tax Board, January 26, 2011)

As a result of the January 1, 2015, incorporation date, California does not adopt most of the amendments made by the following acts to the federal provisions incorporated by California:

— Slain Officer Family Support Act of 2015 (P.L. 114-7);

— Medicare Access and CHIP Reauthorization Act of 2015 (P.L. 114-10);

— Don't Tax Our Fallen Public Safety Heroes Act (P.L. 114-14);

— Highway and Transportation Funding Act of 2015 (P.L. 114-21);

— Defending Public Safety Employees' Retirement Act (P.L. 114-26);

— Trade Preferences Extension Act of 2015 (P.L. 114-27);

— Surface Transportation and Veterans Health Care Choice Improvement Act of 2015 (P.L. 114-41); and

— Protecting Americans From Tax Hikes Act of 2015 (P.L. 114-113);

— 21st Century Cures Act (P.L. 114-255);

— Disaster Tax Relief and Airport and Airway Extension Act of 2017 (P.L. 115-63);

— Tax Cuts and Jobs Act of 2017 (P.L. 115-97);

— Bipartisan Budget Act of 2018 (P.L. 115-123);

— Taxpayer First Act (P.L. 116-25); and

— Coronavirus Aid, Relief, and Economic Security (CARES) Act (P.L. 116-136).

Prior to the 2015 tax year, California did not adopt most of the amendments made by the following acts to the federal provisions incorporated by California:

— Worker, Homeownership, and Business Assistance Act of 2009 (P.L. 111-92);

— Hiring Incentives to Restore Employment (HIRE) Act (P.L. 111-147);

— Patient Protection and Affordable Care Act (the Patient Protection Act) (P.L. 111-148);

— Dodd-Frank Wall Street Reform and Consumer Protection Act (P.L. 111-203);

— Education Jobs and Medicaid Assistance Act (P.L. 111-226);

— Small Business Jobs Act (P.L. 111-240) (2010 Jobs Act);

— FAA Modernization and Reform Act of 2012 (P.L. 112-95);

— Moving Ahead for Progress in the 21st Century Act (P.L. 112-141);

— American Taxpayer Relief Act of 2012 (P.L. 112-240);

— Tribal General Welfare Act of 2014 (P.L. 113-168);

— Tax Increase Prevention Act of 2014 (P.L. 113-295);

— Tax Technical Corrections Act of 2014 (P.L. 113-295); and

— Achieving a Better Life Experience Act of 2014 (P.L. 113-295).

Required modifications and adjustments to gross income, gross income exclusions, deductions, and credits as a result of California's nonconformity to these federal amendments are discussed in the following compilation paragraphs and are analyzed in annual summaries prepared by the FTB.

• *Elections, consents, and applications*

Whenever the California Corporation Tax Law allows a taxpayer to make an election, a proper federal election filed pursuant to the IRC or regulations issued by the Secretary of the Treasury is deemed to be a proper California election, unless a Corporation Tax Law provision or a regulation of the California Franchise Tax Board (FTB) provides otherwise. A separate election is required to secure treatment for state tax purposes that deviates from treatment applicable under a federal tax election. (Sec. 23051.5(e), Rev. & Tax. Code) The same rules apply for purposes of consents and applications. (Sec. 23051.5(f), Rev. & Tax. Code)

PRACTICE NOTE: *Doctrine of election*—2012 legislation clarified that the doctrine of election applies to any election affecting the computation of California franchise or income tax, meaning that the election must be made on an original timely filed return for the taxable period for which the election is to apply, and once made is binding. (Sec. 4, Ch. 37 (S.B. 1015), Laws 2012)

Separate elections not allowed.—In addition to those listed above, separate elections are not allowed, and a federal election, or lack thereof, is binding for California purposes for the following elections:

— an election under IRC Sec. 108(c) to exclude from gross income income from qualified real property business indebtedness (see ¶ 10-701 Additions—Discharge of Indebtedness) (Sec. 24307(f), Rev. & Tax. Code)

— an election under IRC Sec. 197 to amortize all property acquired after July 25, 1991, or to have pre-IRC Sec. 197 law apply to certain property acquired under a binding written contract in effect on August 10, 1993 (see ¶ 10-905 Subtractions—Amortization) (Sec. 24355.5(c), Rev. & Tax Code)

A federal income tax election (or lack of election) made before becoming a California taxpayer is binding for California purposes, and the taxpayer may not make a separate election for California purposes, unless that separate election is expressly authorized in a California statute or regulation. (Sec. 23051.5(e), Rev. & Tax. Code)

• *General modifications*

Under California law, if an IRC provision is incorporated, due account must be made for differences in federal and state terminology and other obvious differences, thus "Franchise Tax Board" may be substituted for "Secretary". (Sec. 23051.5(h), Rev. & Tax. Code) California law also provides that when applying the IRC for purposes of determining a statute of limitations under the Corporation Tax Law, any reference to a period of three years must be modified to refer to a period of four years. (Sec. 23051.5(g), Rev. & Tax. Code) Finally, references to IRC Sec. 501 are to be interpreted to also refer to Rev. & Tax. Code Sec. 23701. (Sec. 23051.5(h)(9), Rev. & Tax. Code)

• *Incorporated and mirrored provisions*

Below is a list of the IRC provisions that California incorporates directly, without modification, or that California law mirrors. Consequently, no adjustments to federal adjusted gross income is required for these areas when completing the California Corporation Franchise or Income Tax Return.

Incorporated IRC provisions

IRC Section	CA Revenue And Taxation Section	Purpose of provision
Definition of "Gross Income", "Adjusted Gross Income", "Taxable Income", etc.		
IRC Sec. 61	Sec. 24271	Defines "gross income"
IRC Sec. 64	Sec. 23049.1	Defines "ordinary income"
IRC Sec. 65	Sec. 23049.2	Defines "ordinary loss"
Items Specifically Included in Gross Income		
IRC Sec. 72(u)	Sec. 24272.2	Treats income received by a corporation from an annuity as ordinary income
IRC Sec. 77	Sec. 24273	Allows taxpayers to include loans from the Commodity Credit corporation as ordinary income in the year received (mirrors rather than incorporates federal law)
IRC Sec. 83	Sec. 24379	Specifies the tax treatment of stock or other property transferred in connection with the performance of services (because of federal conformity date, California not conform to federal modifications made by the Tax Cuts and Jobs Act of 2017 regarding the treatment of qualified equity grants)
IRC Sec. 88	Sec. 24275	Requires certain nuclear decommissioning costs to be included in gross income
IRC Sec. 90	Sec. 24276	Requires illegal federal irrigation subsidies to be included in gross income
Items Specifically Excluded From Gross Income		

Incorporated IRC provisions

IRC Section	CA Revenue And Taxation Section	Purpose of provision
IRC Sec. 109	Sec. 24309	Excludes from gross income a lessor's income/gain from lessee improvements upon the termination of the lease
IRC Sec. 110	Sec. 24309.5	Excludes qualified lessee construction allowances from a lessee's gross income (modifies internal cross-references)
IRC Sec. 118	Sec. 24325	Excludes contributions to capital from a corporation's gross income (because of federal conformity date, California does not conform to federal modifications related to certain contributions in aid of construction made by customers, potential customers, or governmental entities after December 22, 2017, that are not treated as contributions to capital)
IRC Sec. 136	Sec. 24326	Provides gross income exclusion for qualified energy conservation subsidies received from a public utility
IRC Sec. 139	Sec. 24329	Provides gross income exclusion for disaster relief payments
Uncodified Sec. 1078 (P.L. 98-369)	Sec. 24308	Excludes from gross income certain payments from U.S. Forest Service

Itemized Deductions for Individuals and Corporations

IRC Section	CA Revenue And Taxation Section	Purpose of provision
IRC Sec. 164(d)	Sec. 24346	Provides rules to apportion taxes on real property between seller and purchaser for purposes of determining which party may claim deduction for real property taxes
IRC Sec. 164(e)	Reg. 24345-6	Allows corporation to claim deduction for taxes paid on behalf of shareholder
IRC Sec. 166	Sec. 24347	Allows taxpayers to deduct bad debts (see ¶ 10-875 Subtractions—Bad Debts)
IRC Sec. 167(e)	Sec. 24368.1	Provides special rules governing the deductibility of payments made in connection with the transfer of a trademaker, trade name, or franchise
IRC Sec. 167(f)	Sec. 24355	Allows certain intangible property to be depreciated rather than amortized (also see ¶ 10-905 Subtractions—Amortization)
IRC Sec. 173	Sec. 24364 Reg. 24364	Allows current expense deduction, rather than depreciation or amortization, of circulation expenses
IRC Sec. 174	Sec. 24365	Allows current expensing of qualified research and experimental expenditures (changes internal cross-references) (see ¶ 10-905 Subtractions—Amortization for more details)
IRC Sec. 175	Sec. 24369	Allows farmers to currently expense, rather than depreciate costs associated with soil and water conservation and endangered species recovery expenditures.
IRC Sec. 178	Sec. 24373	Allows amortization of the cost of acquiring a lease over the period of the lease
IRC Sec. 180	Sec. 24377 Reg. 24377(a) Reg. 24377(b)	Allows farmers to currently expense, rather than depreciate, farm fertilizer expenditures (mirrors rather than incorporates federal law)
IRC Sec. 195	Sec. 24414	Allows taxpayers to currently deduct up to $5,000 in start-up expenses and amortize any remainder over a 15-year period (see ¶ 10-905 Subtractions—Amortization)
IRC Sec. 197	Sec. 24355.5	Allows goodwill and other intangibles to be amortized (see ¶ 10-905 Subtractions—Amortization)
IRC Sec. 216	Sec. 24382	Allows tenant-stockholders of housing co-ops to deduct taxes, interest, and depreciation paid on co-op's land and buildings

Special Deductions for Corporations

IRC Section	CA Revenue And Taxation Section	Purpose of provision
IRC Sec. 248	Sec. 24407	Allows taxpayers to currently deduct up to $5,000 in organizational expenses and amortize any remainder over a 15-year period (see ¶ 10-905 Subtractions—Amortization) (California mirrors rather than incorporates federal law)

Incorporated IRC provisions

IRC Section	CA Revenue And Taxation Section	Purpose of provision
IRC Sec. 249	Sec. 24439	Limits deduction of bond premiums on repurchase of bonds convertible into a corporation's own stock to amount of a normal call premium (mirrors rather than incorporates federal law, changes internal cross-references)

Items Not Deductible

IRC Section	CA Revenue And Taxation Section	Purpose of provision
IRC Sec. 263A	Sec. 24422.3	Provides uniform capitalization rules for costs associated with property produced by a taxpayer or property acquired for resale by a taxpayer (however, California has not conformed to provisions modifying the uniform capitalization rules as they relate to the expensing of certain costs of replanting citrus plants lost by reason of casualty, effective for costs paid or incurred after December 22, 2017, or excluding the aging periods for beer, wine, and distilled spirits from the production period for purposes of the uniform capitalization interest capitalization rules for interest paid or accrued during the 2018 and 2019 calendar years)
IRC Sec. 264	Sec. 24424	Prohibits deductions for (1) interest paid on debt incurred to purchase or carry insurance, endowments or annuities and (2) insurance premiums paid on most life insurance policy, annuity or endowment contract on which the taxpayer is, directly or indirectly, the beneficiary
IRC Sec. 266	Sec. 24426 Reg. 24426(a)	Allows taxpayers to elect either to deduct currently or to capitalize taxes and carrying charges not subject to the uniform capitalization rules under IRC Sec. 263A but that are chargeable to a capital account with respect to property (mirrors, rather than incorporates, federal law)
IRC Sec. 267	Sec. 24427	Disallows or defers deductions for losses, expenses, and interest with respect to transactions between related taxpayers (because of federal conformity date, California has not conformed to provision preventing transfer of loss from tax indifferent parties, which applies to sales and other dispositions of property acquired after 2015)
IRC Sec. 269	Sec. 24431	Disallows deductions, credits, or other allowances associated with stock or property acquired from another corporation if the principal purpose of the acquisition was to claim the benefit of a deduction, credit, or other allowance that would not be otherwise available (mirrors, rather than incorporates federal law, changes internal cross-references and substitutes FTB for IRS)
IRC Sec. 271	Sec. 24434	Disallows a bad debt deduction for debts issued by political parties, however banks and specified businesses may still claim deduction (mirrors rather than incorporates federal law)
IRC Sec. 274	Sec. 24443	Disallows deductions for certain entertainment expenses, listed property, etc. unless adequate substantiation is provided (because of federal conformity date, California does not conform to changes relating to the deductibility of post-2017 expenses for entertainment, amusement, or recreation, employer-provided meals, and qualified transportation fringe or commuting benefits)
IRC Sec. 276	Sec. 24429	Disallows deductions for indirect contributions to political parties
IRC Sec. 277	Sec. 24437	Limits deductions claimed by nonexempt social clubs or other membership organizations operated primarily to furnish services or goods to members to specified income received from members
IRC Sec. 279	Sec. 24438	Limits deduction for interest incurred for corporate indebtedness (mirrors, rather than incorporates, federal law)
IRC Sec. 280B	Sec. 24442	Requires that demolition expenses be depreciated rather than currently deducted
IRC Sec. 280G	Sec. 24349.2	Limits the amount of deductions that may be claimed for certain golden-parachute payments
IRC Sec. 280H	Sec. 24442.5	Limits the amount of deductions that certain personal service corporations may take for payments to employee-owners unless certain minimum distributions are made to the employee-owners

Incorporated IRC provisions

IRC Section	CA Revenue And Taxation Section	Purpose of provision
		Special Rules Relating to Corporate Preference Items
IRC Sec. 291	Sec. 24449	Modifies and/or reduces the tax treatment of the following tax preference items (1) IRC Sec. 1250 capital gains, (2) iron ore and coal depletion deductions, (3) certain financial institution preference times, (4) amortization of pollution control facilities, (5) intangible drilling costs, and (6) mineral exploration and development costs
		Deferred Compensation, Etc.
IRC Sec. 401 - IRC Sec. 436	Sec. 24601 Sec. 24611	Governs tax treatment and qualification requirements of pension, profit sharing, stock bonus plans, etc. (incorporates IRC Sec. 401 through IRC Sec. 420 and IRC Sec. 430 through IRC Sec. 436 as amended to date rather than as of a fixed-date) (also see ¶ 10-890 Job Programs and Employee Benefits)
IRC Secs. 529(c) IRC Secs. 529(e)	Sec. 24306	Governs treatment of qualified distributions from qualified tuition programs. Adopts Golden State Scholarshare Program to implement California's version of the federally-authorized Qualified Tuition Programs under IRC Sec. 529
		Natural Resources
IRC Sec. 611 - IRC Sec. 638	Sec. 24831	Governs the depletion deductions allowed for the exhaustion of natural resources. However, see ¶ 10-850 for modifications.
		Foreign-Source Income
IRC Sec. 892	Sec. 24327	Excludes from gross income a foreign government's U.S.-source investment income
		Miscellaneous Provisions
IRC Sec. 7518	Sec. 24272.5	Allows deductions for amounts deposited into a Merchant Marine capital construction fund and exempts from income tax earnings from fund from income tax (CA modifies federal law to reflect California cross-references, the dividend deduction percentage requirements, and California's tax rate)

CCH PRACTICE TIP: *Renewable energy grants.*—California law also mirrors federal law (IRC Sec. 48(d)(3)), which allows taxpayers to exclude from gross income and alternative minimum taxable income federal energy grants provided in lieu of federal energy credits and alternative minimum taxable income of individuals and business. However, the basis of the property purchased with the grant is reduced by 50% of the amount of the grant. (Sec. 24303, Rev. & Tax. Code)

IRC provisions that are directly incorporated or mirrored by California law also involve accounting methods and periods, alternative minimum tax, corporate distributions, liquidations, and reorganizations, and gains and losses (see ¶ 10-640).

• *Incorporation of IRC cross-references*

Numerous IRC sections that have been incorporated by reference into California law contain cross-references to other IRC or United States Code (USC) provisions that are not themselves incorporated by reference. The statute does not specify whether these cross-referenced IRC or USC provisions are indirectly incorporated into California law by operation of the IRC cross-references. However, according to FTB practice, such cross-referenced provisions apply in California only for purposes of applying the provisions in which the cross-references appear.

[¶10-525] Special Industries or Entities

In general, corporations compute their California net income from a statutorily-defined starting point (see ¶10-510 Starting Point for Computation), modified by specified additions (see ¶10-600 Additions to Taxable Income Base) and subtractions (see ¶10-800 Subtractions from Taxable Income Base). However, some industries or entities are subject to special rules. Below is a brief summary of the rules and the references to more detailed discussions elsewhere.

• *Exempt organizations with unrelated business taxable income*

Under both California and federal law, exempt organizations are subject to tax on their unrelated taxable income from any regularly carried on unrelated trade or business less deductions that are directly connected with the carrying on of the unrelated trade or business. California differs from federal law in the rate of tax applied, California subjects unrelated business income to the alternative minimum tax, and California subjects qualified pole rentals by telephone and electric companies to the tax on unrelated business income, see ¶10-245 Exempt Organizations for more details.

Political organizations.—Political organizations are subject to California corporate income tax on their political organization taxable income. (Sec. 23701r, Rev. & Tax. Code) California law is similar to IRC Sec. 527, however, differences arise concerning the treatment of (1) exempt organizations that are not political organizations but that engage in political activities (2) newsletter funds. California, unlike federal law subjects bingo game proceeds to the tax on unrelated business income. See ¶10-245 Exempt Organizations for more details.

• *S corporations*

For purposes of computing corporation franchise and income taxes at the reduced S corporation tax rate level (see ¶10-380 Tax Rates), an S corporation's deduction for amortization and depreciation is computed under the Personal Income Tax Law. Also, S corporations are subject to at-risk and passive activity rules in the same manner as they are applied to individuals. However, for purposes of determining whether passive activity limitations apply, S corporations are subject to a slightly modified version of the material participation standard applicable to closely held C corporations and personal service corporations (see the discussion of "Losses and credits from passive activities" at ¶10-635 Losses). In addition, the gross income exclusion allowed to individuals for gain on the sale of specified small business stock is not allowed to an S corporation. (Rev. & Tax. Code Sec. 23802) The tax treatment of S corporations is discussed in more detail at ¶10-220 S Corporations.

• *Regulated investment companies, real estate investment trusts, real estate mortgage investment companies, financial asset securitization investment trusts*

California generally follows federal law concerning the taxation of regulated investment companies (RICs), real estate investment trusts (REITs), real estate mortgage investment companies (REMICs), and financial asset securitization investment trusts (FASITs), allowing such entities to invest on behalf of their shareholders and pass on both the income from the investments and the associated tax liability to their shareholders, provided that certain conditions are satisfied.

• *Domestic international sales corporations (DISCs), interest charge DISCs, and foreign sales corporations (FSCs)*

California has no provisions comparable to former IRC Sec. 921 through IRC Sec. 927, relating to foreign sales corporations, nor to IRC Sec. 991 through IRC Sec. 997, the provisions for DISCs, interest charge DISCs, and former FSCs. Consequently, these corporations are treated under California law in the same manner as other corporations. Affected taxpayers may want to consider computing their California tax liability using the California computation method discussed at ¶ 10-530 Alternate Computation Methods.

• *Banks, savings and loans, and financial corporations*

Banks may elect to compute their bad debt deduction (see ¶ 10-875 Subtractions—Bad Debts) under the reserve method rather than the usual specific charge-off method. Under the reserve method, the amount of the bad debt deduction is based on the expected ratio of bad debt losses to outstanding loans at the end of the taxable year. (Sec. 24348, Rev. & Tax. Code) See ¶ 10-340 Banks—Financial Corporations for a detailed discussion.

• *Cooperatives*

Generally, deductions attributable to services, insurance, goods, or other items of value furnished by a cooperative association to its membership are allowed only to the extent of income derived from membership dues and transactions. (Sec. 24437, Rev. & Tax. Code) Special rules apply to farmers' and fruit growers' cooperatives, gas producers' cooperative associations, and mutual and cooperative associations.

[¶ 10-530] Alternate Taxable Income Computation Methods

In lieu of the federal reconciliation method (see ¶ 10-510), corporations that are not required to file a federal return or that maintain separate records for state purposes may compute their net income using the California computation method on California Form 100, Schedule F, Computation of Net Income. Generally, if ordinary income is computed under California law, no state adjustments are necessary (see ¶ 10-600 Additions to Taxable Income Base, and ¶ 10-800 Subtractions from Taxable Income Base). (Instructions, Form 100, California Corporation Franchise or Income Tax Return)

Corporations using the California computation method to compute net income must transfer the amount from Schedule F, line 30, to Form 100, Side 1, line 1. Corporations should complete Form 100, Side 1, line 2 through line 17, only if applicable. (Instructions, Form 100, California Corporation Franchise or Income Tax Return)

For an overview of the taxable income computation, see ¶ 10-505, Overview of Taxable Income Computation.

[¶ 10-600] Additions to Taxable Income Base

Under the federal reconciliation method of computing taxable income (¶ 10-510 Starting Point for Computation), the computation of California net income requires that the following items be added to the federal taxable amount used as the starting point for the net income calculation.

— Amortization . . . . ¶ 10-680
— Annuities . . . . ¶ 10-708

¶ 10-600

Additions to income are reported on Form 100, California Corporation Franchise or Income Tax Return.

Subtractions from the taxable income base are discussed beginning at ¶10-800 Subtractions From Taxable Income, and an overview of the taxable income computation is provided at ¶10-505 Overview of Taxable Income Computation.

[¶10-605] Additions--Net Operating Loss

Because California's taxable income computation begins with federal taxable income listed on Line 28, Federal Form 1120, before claiming the federal net operating loss deduction (see ¶10-510 Starting Point for Computation), no addition adjustment is required. See ¶10-805 Subtractions—Net Operating Loss for the subtraction modification.

Other additions to the taxable income base are listed at ¶10-600.

[¶10-610] Additions--Federally Exempt Interest

Additions are required for interest earned on specified government obligations and for interest income from loans to employee stock ownership plans. The additions required to be made for interest earned on federal, state, and local obligations is dependent upon (1) whether the taxpayer is subject to the corporation franchise tax or the corporate income tax and (2) whether the obligation is issued by the federal government, the state of California or one of its municipalities, or by another state or one if its political subdivisions. For a discussion of the subtraction required for interest on specified California obligations for California corporate income tax purposes, see ¶10-815 Subtractions—Interest.

Corporation franchise taxpayers.—Federal law prohibits states and municipalities from taxing obligations issued by the U.S. Government, unless the tax imposed is a nondiscriminatory corporate franchise tax. (Sec. 3124, U.S.C.) California imposes its corporation franchise tax on interest earned from federal obligations. Therefore, corporation franchise taxpayers must add back to federal taxable income interest received from federal obligations. Also, under California law, but not federal law, interest income from state, municipal, or other bonds, must be included in gross income for corporation franchise tax purposes, thereby necessitating an addition to federal taxable income for such interest. An addition applies to interest earned on California bonds as well as non-California state and local bonds. (Sec. 24272, Rev. & Tax. Code; Reg. 24271(e), 18 CCR) All interest from government obligations not included in federal ordinary income (loss) must be entered on Line 4, Form 100, California Corporation Franchise or Income Tax Return. (Instructions, Form 100, California Corporation Franchise or Income Tax Return)

Corporate income taxpayers.—California corporate income taxpayers must also add back to federal taxable income interest received from bonds issued by other states and their political subdivisions for purposes of computing California corporate income tax. (Reg. 24271(e), 18 CCR) Under federal law (IRC Sec. 103), which is not incorporated by California, such income is exempt from federal taxation. The amounts to be added back to federal taxable income are entered on Line 4, Form 100, California Corporation Franchise or Income Tax Return. Taxpayers are also required to add back interest received from federal and California obligations on Line 4, Form 100, however, such amounts may be subtracted by corporate income taxpayers on Line 16, see ¶10-815 Subtractions—Interest. (Instructions, Form 100, California Corporation Franchise or Income Tax Return)

The FTB has taken a position similar to federal law, allowing exempt interest income passed through as dividends to an investment company's shareholders to qualify for exemption in the shareholders' hands for corporate income tax purposes. (*Letter to CCH*, FTB, August 10, 1988 (incorporating *Letter*, FTB, July 29, 1988); *Letter*, FTB, September 14, 1988)

• *Amortization of bond premium*

A corporate taxpayer may elect to deduct amortized bond premium if the interest of the bond is taxable. The elective deduction is applicable only to bonds that pay fully taxable interest. (Sec. 24362, Rev. & Tax. Code) "Bond premium" is the difference between the bond's basis and the amount payable on maturity or on an earlier call date.

The amortization deduction is computed on FTB 3885, Corporation Depreciation and Amortization for C corporations or for S corporations on Schedule B (100S), S Corporation Depreciation and Amortization.

The California provisions are generally the same as IRC Sec. 171 as, amended by the Tax Reform Act of 1986 (the Tax Reform Act amendments are discussed below). (Sec. 24360, Rev. & Tax. Code—Sec. 24363.5, Rev. & Tax. Code) However, a rule in the California provision for computing the amount of amortizable bond premium for the year in which a bond having a call date is actually called differs from the federal rule (IRC Sec. 171(b)(2)) in two respects: (1) the issue and acquisition dates of the bonds covered by the California and federal rules differ and (2) the California rule pertains only to a bond that has a call date not more than three years after the date on which it was issued. (Sec. 24361(b), Rev. & Tax. Code) In addition, as discussed above, the bonds on which interest is taxable differs under California law.

California regulations discuss the determination of bond premiums, callable bonds, methods of amortization, taxable years in which interest is not received or accruable, and an election with respect to taxable and partially taxable bonds. (Reg. 24360-24363(a), 18 CCR—Reg. 24360-1, 18 CCR)

Dealers in tax-exempt securities.—California Corporation Tax Law does not incorporate nor have any provision similar to IRC Sec. 75, which requires a dealer in municipal bonds to amortize any premiums on them just as if the interest on the bonds had been taxable. Consequently, taxpayers required to amortize these premiums for federal purposes must make an adjustment on their California return. If the taxpayer's gross income is computed by the use of inventories and the inventories are valued on any basis other than cost, then for California purposes, the cost of the securities must be increased by the amount IRC Sec. 75 decreases the cost of the securities sold. If the taxpayer's gross income is computed without the use of inventories or by use of inventories valued at cost, then for California purposes, the adjusted basis of the bond must be increased by the amount IRC Sec. 75 decreases it.

• *Interest income from loans to ESOPs*

An addition is required for 50% of interest income received by banks, insurance companies, other commercial lenders, and regulated investment companies to the extent the income is excluded on these entities' federal return under the transitional provisions repealing former IRC Sec. 133. The IRC Sec. 133 exclusion for 50% of interest income on loans made to an employee stock ownership plan (ESOP) or to an employer corporation, the proceeds of which were used by the plan to acquire employer securities, is generally repealed for loans made after August 20, 1996. However, the exclusion continues to apply to (1) such loans made under a written binding contract in effect before June 10, 1996, and (2) to certain loans made after August 20, 1996, to refinance loans made before August 21, 1996.

¶10-610

Amounts excluded under these transitional provisions on a taxpayer's federal return must be included as an "other addition" on line 8, Form 100, California Corporate Franchise or Income Tax Return, and a schedule must be attached to itemize amounts. (Instructions, Form 100, California Corporation Franchise or Income Tax Return)

• *Original issue discount income*

As a result of California's current IRC conformity date (see ¶ 10-515), California does not adopt IRC § 163(e)(5)(F), which was enacted by the American Recovery and Reinvestment Tax Act of 2009 (Recovery Act) (P.L. 111-5), and suspends the rules limiting corporate deductions of original issue discount (OID) on high-yield discount obligations for certain obligations issued in a debt-for-debt exchange, including an exchange resulting from a significant modification of a debt instrument, after August 31, 2008, and before January 1, 2010. Consequently, an addition adjustment is required for the amount allowed as a deduction under IRC § 163(e)(5)(F) for an original issue discount (OID) on an applicable high yield discount obligation.

Other additions to the taxable income base are listed at ¶ 10-600 Additions to Taxable Income Base.

[¶10-615] Additions--Taxes

California's treatment of taxes is similar to IRC Sec. 164, which governs the deductibility of various federal, state, and local taxes. However, unlike federal law, California does not allow a deduction for California corporation franchise or income tax, or other taxes on or measured by income imposed by any taxing jurisdiction, including foreign countries. Consequently, any such amounts deducted in computing a taxpayer's federal tax liability must be added back to federal taxable income for purposes of computing a taxpayer's California corporation franchise or income tax liability. In addition, California does not permit deductions for (1) environmental taxes imposed by IRC Sec. 59A Environmental Tax, and (2) federal stamp taxes. Therefore, such amounts must also be added back to federal taxable income. However, it should be noted that federal stamp taxes may still be deducted elsewhere as a general business expense. (Sec. 24345, Rev. & Tax. Code; Reg. 24345-3, 18 CCR) See ¶ 10-840 Subtractions—Taxes for a discussion of taxes that may be subtracted for California, but not federal, corporation franchise or income tax purposes.

CCH COMMENT: *Minimum Taxes and LLC fees.*—The annual minimum tax (see ¶ 10-380) applied to limited liability partnerships cannot be deducted by the partnership or deducted from the partner's distributive share of income. (Instructions, Form 565, Partnership Return of Income) To the extent the tax was deducted on the federal return, an addition adjustment would be required.

Although the LLC fee (see ¶ 10-240) has been declared a "tax" by two California appellate courts, the FTB is still allowing the fee to be deducted. Because these fees are also deducted on the federal income tax return, no adjustment is required. (Instructions, Form 100, California Corporation Franchise or Income Tax Return; *E-mail*, Franchise Tax Board, July 1, 2008)

Taxes required to be added back to federal taxable income must be listed on Schedule A, Taxes Deducted, on Form 100, California Corporation Franchise or Income Tax Return. (Instructions, Form 100, California Corporation Franchise or Income Tax Return)

• *Income taxes*

California law specifically prohibits deductions of state, federal, or foreign taxes "on or according to or measured by income or profits," including taxes imposed on intercompany dividends paid by one member of a unitary group to another member of the unitary group and eliminated from the income of the recipient. (Sec. 24345(b), Rev. & Tax. Code) Nor does California corporate income tax law allow a credit against California tax for tax paid to other states or countries, inasmuch as income from outside California is not subject to California tax. (For details about allocation and apportionment of income, see the discussion beginning at ¶ 11-505 Allocation and Apportionment.)

The California Supreme Court has ruled that, for purposes of determining whether a tax is imposed on or measured by income, "income" means "gross income" under general tax laws. Consequently, the court held that a tax on royalties received from Texas oil well owners from oil producers was a deductible tax on *gross receipts*, as opposed to a nondeductible tax on *gross income*, because the lifting costs incurred in production could not be deducted from gross sales in computing the occupation tax as they could under a federal Revenue Ruling defining "gross income" from oil and gas producing properties. (*Beamer v. Franchise Tax Board*, 19 Cal3d 467, 563 P2d 238 (1977)) In applying the reasoning in *Beamer*, a California appellate court reached the opposite conclusion that a Canadian tax imposed against film and record distributors on rents and royalties from the films and records was a nondeductible tax because the tax was measured by income. Under California law, "gross income" was defined as income received from rents and royalties from personal income. It was irrelevant that deductions for depreciation could not be claimed, because depreciation is not taken into account in determining "gross income" under California law. (*MCA, Inc. v. Franchise Tax Board* (1981) 115 CA3d 185, 171 CRptr 242)

CCH PRACTICE TIP: *Treatment of various taxes.*—The following outlines the treatment of various state, federal, and foreign taxes. Addition requirements are only necessary for those taxes that are nondeductible under California law.

Canadian mining taxes.—Nondeductible (*Alloys, Inc.*, SBE, 84-SBE-129, September 12, 1984);

Federal minimum tax.—Nondeductible (*Coachella Valley Savings and Loan Assn.*, SBE, 87-SBE-012, March 3, 1987);

Federal social security taxes paid by employers.—Deductible (Reg. 24345-5, 18 CCR);

Foreign income taxes.—Nondeductible (California Response to CCH Multistate Corporate Income Tax Survey, California Franchise Tax Board, July 21, 2003);

Illinois personal property tax replacement (PPTR) income tax.—Nondeductible (*E-mail Response*, California Franchise Tax Board, August 20, 2015);

Kentucky license tax.—Deductible (California Response to CCH Multistate Corporate Income Tax Survey, California Franchise Tax Board, July 21, 2003);

Libyan petroleum tax surcharge.—Deductible (*Occidental Petroleum Corp.*, SBE, 83-SBE-119, March 3, 1982, op on reh'g June 21, 1983);

Michigan single business tax (MSBT).—Deductible (*Kelly Service, Inc.*, SBE, 97-SBE-010, May 8, 1997; *Dayton Hudson Corp.*, SBE, 94-SBE-003, February 3,

1994; California Response to CCH Multistate Corporate Income Tax Survey, California Franchise Tax Board, July 21, 2003);

New Hampshire business profits tax.—Nondeductible (California Response to CCH Multistate Corporate Income Tax Survey, July 21, 200);

New York franchise taxes.—Nondeductible (*Coro, Inc.*, SBE, 55-SBE-001, March 30, 1955);

Ohio franchise tax—net worth portion.—Deductible (California Response to CCH Multistate Corporate Income Tax Survey, California Franchise Tax Board, July 21, 2003);

Revised Texas franchise (margin) tax.—Deductible (*FTB Legal Ruling 2017-01*, California Franchise Tax Board, February 22, 2017);

Texas franchise tax—net worth portion.—Deductible (California Response to CCH Multistate Corporate Income Tax Survey, California Franchise Tax Board, July 21, 2003);

Unemployment insurance tax contributions paid by employers.—Deductible (Reg. 24345-5, 18 CCR);

Washington business and occupation tax.—Deductible (California Response to CCH Multistate Corporate Income Tax Survey, California Franchise Tax Board, July 21, 2003); and

West Virginia business and occupation tax.—Deductible (California Response to CCH Multistate Corporate Income Tax Survey, California Franchise Tax Board, July 21, 2003).

Foreign taxes.—A regulation governs the deductibility of foreign taxes that are partly income taxes and partly direct payments for specific economic benefits. For example, a foreign country might prohibit all petroleum operations except on the part of companies paying a special petroleum profits tax. Such a tax would be considered a "dual capacity tax," containing both a nondeductible income tax element and a deductible element consisting of a direct payment for the concession to engage in petroleum operations. A taxpayer claiming a deduction for a dual capacity tax is required to show (1) that payment of the tax is directly related to the receipt of a specific economic benefit not available to others on the same terms and (2) the exact amount that constitutes a payment for the benefit rather than a tax on income. The taxpayer may satisfy the latter requirement by demonstrating that under the facts and circumstances the tax is not an income tax or by electing to use the safe harbor method. The safe harbor method allows a taxpayer to use a standard formula that takes into account the taxpayer's gross receipts, cost of goods sold, and all operating expenses relating to the activity taxed by the foreign country for purposes of determining the amount of the tax that is not an income tax. The regulation outlines the procedures a taxpayer must follow for purposes of making the election. (Reg. 24345-7, 18 CCR)

Other additions to the taxable income base are listed at ¶ 10-600.

[¶10-620] Additions--Corporate Transactions

California follows federal law involving the treatment of most corporation transactions so no specific adjustments are required for California corporation franchise (income) tax purposes.

Other additions to the taxable income base are listed at ¶ 10-600.

[¶10-625] Additions--Depletion

California incorporates IRC Sec. 611—IRC Sec. 638 concerning deductions for depletion and natural resource expenses, as of the current California conformity date (see ¶10-515), with modifications. (Sec. 24831, Rev. & Tax. Code) California, unlike federal law, did not provide a temporary suspension of the taxable income limit on percentage depletion deductions for oil and gas production from marginal properties for tax years prior to 2012. (Sec. 24831.6, Rev. & Tax. Code) Consequently, for California corporation franchise and income tax purposes, taxpayers with income from such marginal properties were required to recompute the depletion deduction and enter the difference as an "other addition" on Line 8, Form 100, California Corporation Franchise or Income Tax Return.

In addition, California does not incorporate the federal amendment that increased the refinery limitation on independent producers, effective for federal purposes in tax years ending after August 8, 2005. (Sec. 24831.3, Rev. & Tax. Code) Taxpayers who are allowed to claim the percentage depletion deduction as a result of the increase of the refinery limitation from 50,000 to 75,000 barrels per day, are required to make an addition adjustment on their California return.

Other additions to the taxable income base are listed at ¶10-600.

[¶10-630] Additions--Dividends

As discussed at ¶10-515 Federal Conformity, California incorporates IRC Sec. 61, which includes dividends in gross income subject to tax.

The Franchise Tax Board may include a deemed dividend from an insurance company subsidiary in the gross income of the parent corporation (or a member of the corporation's combined reporting group), if all insurance companies in the commonly controlled group have a capitalization percentage (see ¶10-810 for a discussion of capitalization percentages) not exceeding 15% and the earnings and profits of the insurance company subsidiary have been accumulated with a substantial purpose of avoiding income taxes of any state. The deemed dividend is equal to the corporation's pro rata share (or the combined reporting group member's pro rata share) of the insurance companies' earnings and profits for the taxable year. However, the amount of the deemed dividend is limited to a particular insurance company's net income attributable to investment income less that insurance company's net written premiums received for the year. The amount included will be treated as a dividend received from an insurance company during the taxable year, which may be deductible under Sec. 24410 (see ¶10-810 Subtractions—Dividends). (Sec. 24900, Rev. & Tax. Code)

See ¶10-810 Subtractions—Dividends for a discussion of the subtractions from federal taxable income relating to dividends.

Other additions to the taxable income base are listed at ¶10-600.

[¶10-635] Additions--Losses

See ¶10-640 Additions—Gains for a discussion concerning California's modifications to the federal treatment of gains and losses. Casualty losses are discussed at ¶10-820 Subtractions—Losses and net operating losses are discussed at ¶10-805 Subtractions—Net Operating Loss.

¶10-625

• *Losses and credits from passive activities*

Under IRC Sec. 469, as incorporated by California as of a specified date (see ¶10-515 Federal Conformity), closely held C corporations and personal service corporations must generally limit the amount of losses from passive trade or business activities claimed as a deduction to the amount of income derived from such activities. However, California law differs from federal treatment in the following areas:

— California does not incorporate IRC Sec. 469(c)(7), which excepts certain rental real estate activities engaged in by qualified real estate businesses from the passive activity rules. These activities are treated as nonpassive for federal purposes only. Consequently, taxpayers will have to recompute the amount of loss that may be claimed for California corporation franchise and income tax purposes by limiting the amount of loss that may be claimed to the amount of income from the qualified real estate business.

— California modifies IRC Sec. 469(d)(2), concerning the passive activity unused credits that are eligible to be carried over to be claimed against passive activity income in future years to substitute for California purposes, the credits for research expenses and low-income housing and the former credits for targeted jobs and clinical testing. Consequently these amounts must be recomputed for California corporation franchise and income tax purposes.

— A clarifying amendment made to IRC Sec. 469(g)(1)(A) by the Small Business Job Protection Act of 1996 (P.L. 104-188) requires a taxpayer disposing of a passive activity in a taxable transaction to apply any net passive loss from the activity first against income or gain from the taxpayer's other passive activities. Any remaining loss from the activity is then classified as nonpassive and may be used to offset income from nonpassive activities. California modifies this provision to provide that a taxpayer must apply any net passive loss from the activity *plus* any loss realized on that disposition against any income or gain from the taxpayer's other passive activities, prior to offseting the income from nonpassive activities. The amendment applies for federal purposes to tax years beginning after 1986 and for California purposes to taxable years beginning after 1996.

— For purposes of IRC Sec. 469(i), relating to the offset for rental real estate activities, California modifies the dollar limitation for the low-income housing credit to equal $75,000 for tax years beginning before 2020 and removes that dollar limitation for tax years beginning on or after January 1, 2020.

(Sec. 24692, Rev. & Tax. Code)

California's passive activity losses and credits from passive activities are computed on California FTB 3802, Corporate Passive Activity Loss and Credit Limitations, unless the taxpayer is an S corporation. S corporations compute their passive activity losses California FTB 3801, Passive Activity Losses, and their credit limitations on California FTB 3801-CR, Passive Activity Credit Limitations. Taxpayers that dispose of an entire interest in a passive activity through a taxable transaction that make an election to increase the basis of the credit property immediately before the transaction under IRC Sec. 469(j)(9), as incorporated by California, should also use the previously mentioned forms, because frequently the amount of credit involved will likely be different under California than federal law.

Other additions to the taxable income base are listed at ¶10-600.

[¶10-640] Additions--Gains

California, like federal law (IRC Sec. 1001), defines a taxable "gain" as the excess of the amount realized on a sale, exchange, or other disposition of property over the property's adjusted basis (see ¶10-690). The "amount realized" is the sum of any money received plus the fair market value of the property, however reimbursements for real property taxes imposed on the purchaser are not taken into account, whereas real property taxes paid by the corporation are included if under California law such amounts are to be paid by the purchaser. A "loss" is defined as the excess of the property's adjusted basis over the amount realized. (Sec. 24901, Rev. & Tax Code)

Whenever a determination of a taxpayer's gain or loss with respect to a particular item of property subject to nonrecourse indebtedness requires the determination of the fair market value of the property, the fair market value of the property must be treated as being not less than the amount of the nonrecourse indebtedness. (Sec. 23043.5, Rev. & Tax. Code; IRC Sec. 7701(g))

California, unlike federal law, provides no special tax rate for sales of capital assets or assets used in a trade or business. Under California law, capital gains or losses are treated as ordinary gain or loss and the entire gain or loss is recognized, unless specifically exempt. (Sec. 24902, Rev. & Tax. Code) Although the definitions of "gain" and "loss" are the same for California and federal purposes, the actual amount of gain and loss will more likely than not differ because the adjusted basis will be different for California and federal purposes as a result of different depreciation deductions (see ¶10-900) and different basis adjustment items are allowed to increase and reduce the property's basis under California and federal law (see ¶10-690). Consequently, the amount of gain claimed on the federal return is subtracted from federal taxable income (see ¶10-825) and a separate addition computation is made to determine the amount of gain that will be recognized for California purposes. (Instructions, Form 100, California Corporation Franchise or Income Tax Return)

For California corporation franchise and income tax purposes, a taxpayer's gain or loss is computed on Schedule D (100), California Capital Gains and Losses, and Schedule D-1, Sales of Business Property. The actual amount of net capital gain recognized is entered on Line 5, Form 100, California Corporation Franchise or Income Tax Return and ordinary gain is entered on Line 8, Form 100. (Instructions, Form 100, California Corporation Franchise or Income Tax Return) As discussed below, losses are carried over to subsequent tax years and taken into account in the amount of gain recognized in the subsequent years. Special rules apply to the treatment of gains on transactions involving installment payments and basis adjustments (see ¶10-690).

• *Foreign currency transactions*

California incorporates by reference IRC Sec. 988, concerning tax treatment of certain foreign currency transactions, except that IRC Sec. 988(a)(3), relating to the source of income or loss, is inapplicable for California purposes. (Sec. 24905, Rev. & Tax. Code) Under IRC Sec. 988, a foreign currency gain or loss attributable to a "Sec. 988 transaction" receives separate treatment from that given to gain or loss on the underlying transaction and is taxable as ordinary gain or loss.

• *Basis of property*

Except as noted below and in the discussion of corporate distributions, reorganizations, and liquidations, the basis of property is generally its cost (subject to certain statutory exceptions), and excludes from the definition of "cost" real property taxes

¶10-640

imposed on the taxpayer. Except for titles and internal references, the provision is the same as IRC Sec. 1012. (Sec. 24912, Rev. & Tax. Code)

Basis of inventory.—The basis of property included in inventory is the last inventory value. (Sec. 24913, Rev. & Tax. Code) The provision is the same as IRC Sec. 1013.

Basis of property acquired by gift or transfer by trust.—The basis of property acquired by gift after 1920 is the basis of the property in the hands of the donor or the last preceding owner by whom it was not acquired by gift, limited to the fair market value of the property at the time of the gift. If the facts necessary to determine the basis in the hands of the donor or the last preceding owner are unknown to the donee, the California Franchise Tax Board (FTB) will obtain the information from the donee or determine the property's fair market value as of the date of the property's acquisition by the donor. For both California and federal purposes, if property is acquired by a transfer in trust after 1920 (other than as a gift, bequest or devise), the basis is the same as it would be in the hands of the grantor increased in the amount of gain or decreased in the amount of loss recognized by the grantor under the law applicable to the year in which the transfer in trust is made. (Sec. 24914, Rev. & Tax. Code) With the exception of the reference to the FTB rather than the IRS, the provision is the same as IRC Sec. 1015.

The basis of property acquired by gift is increased by the full amount of gift tax paid (limited to a total basis that does not exceed fair market value). (Sec. 24915, Rev. & Tax. Code) For gifts acquired after 1976, federal law (IRC Sec. 1015(d)(6)), but not California law, limits the amount of the basis increase to the portion of the gift tax attributable to the gift's net appreciation in value (excess of fair market value over adjusted basis immediately before the gift). The increase in basis is the amount of gift tax on the gift multiplied by the ratio of the net appreciation in value to the total value of the gift:

$$\frac{\text{Appreciation in value}}{\text{fair market value}} \times \text{gift tax} = \text{basis increase}$$

For gifts made prior to 1977 (before IRC Sec. 1015(d)(6) was added), the full amount of the gift tax paid was added to basis (limited so that total basis did not exceed fair market value).

Where the donor has made several gifts, California law provides that for purposes of determining basis, the amount of federal gift tax paid on a particular gift is an amount that bears the same ratio to the total amount of gift taxes paid on all gifts made by the donor during the calendar year, as the amount of the gift bears to the total amount of taxable gifts made during the calendar year. (Sec. 24915, Rev. & Tax. Code) For gifts acquired after 1981, IRC Sec. 1015(d)(2), is the same as the California provision (Sec. 24915(b)) except for internal references. Prior to its amendment in 1981, IRC Sec. 1015(d)(2) was the same as the California provision, except that under the federal law the computation of the amount of federal gift tax paid was based on a calendar quarter for gifts acquired after 1970, and on the calendar year for gifts acquired before 1971.

Where the donor and his or her spouse elect to have the gift considered as made one-half by each spouse, the amount of gift tax paid is the total of the gift taxes paid on each half of the gift. (Sec. 24915, Rev. & Tax. Code; IRC Sec. 1015(d)(3))

Basis of term interest.—Under both California and federal law (IRC Sec. 1001(e)), the basis of a term interest acquired from a decedent or by gift or transfer in trust is zero, unless the disposition is a part of a transaction in which the entire interest in property is transferred. (Sec. 24901(e), Rev. & Tax. Code)

Special basis rules.—With the following exceptions, California law mirrors federal law concerning special basis rules relating to:

— property acquired during affiliation (Sec. 24961, Rev. & Tax. Code; IRC Sec. 1051);

— carryover of prior basis laws (Sec. 24962, Rev. & Tax. Code; IRC Sec. 1052);

— basis of property acquired prior to March 1, 1913 (Sec. 24963, Rev. & Tax Code);

— basis of stock of Federal National Mortgage Association (Sec. 24965, Rev. & Tax. Code; IRC Sec. 1054);

— basis limitations for player contracts (Sec. 24989, Rev. & Tax. Code; IRC Sec. 1056);

— a corporate shareholder's basis in stock reduced by nontaxed portion of extraordinary dividends, although California's provision refers to California internal cross references (Sec. 24966, Rev. & Tax. Code; IRC Sec. 1059);

— the limitation on taxpayer's basis or inventory cost in property imported from related persons (Sec. 24966.1, Rev. & Tax. Code; IRC Sec. 1059A); and

— special allocation rules for certain asset acquisitions (Sec. 24966.2, Rev. & Tax. Code; IRC Sec. 1060).

California mirrors federal law concerning special basis rules relating to property acquired during affiliation. (Sec. 24961, Rev. & Tax. Code) According to both California (Reg. 24961, 18 CCR) and federal regulations (Reg. 1.1051-1), the basis of such property in the hands of the acquiring corporation is the same as it would be in the hands of the corporation from which it was acquired. However, California and federal regulations and law differ in their definition of "period of affiliation". For California purposes, the term "period of affiliation" is defined to exclude income years beginning on or after 1935, unless consolidated returns were made. After 1934, generally only certain affiliated railroads may file a consolidated return for California franchise tax purposes. (Reg. 24961, 18 CCR) (The California provision does not apply to controlled corporations required by the Franchise Tax Board to file a consolidated report under Rev. & Tax. Code Sec. 25104. Under federal law, the term "period of affiliation" excludes taxable years beginning after 1922, unless consolidated returns were made, and excludes taxable years after 1928.)

Federal provision inapplicable.—California has no comparable Corporation Tax Law provision to IRC Sec. 1014, concerning the basis of property acquired from a decedent. Nor does California have a provision comparable to IRC Sec. 1055, which treats redeemable ground rents as being in the nature of a mortgage. Presumably, California would treat redeemable ground rents as a regular lease. Finally, California neither incorporates nor mirrors IRC Sec. 1058 Transfer of Securities Under Certain Agreements, which allows tax-free transfers of securities under an agreement that (1) provides for the return to the transferor of identical securities; (2) requires that payments be made to the transferor in amounts equivalent to the interest, dividends, and other distributions that the owner of the securities is entitled to receive because of ownership during the period that the loan is outstanding; and (3) does not reduce the transferor's risk of loss or opportunity for gain as to the transferred securities. Presumably, California would subject such transfers to tax.

• *Substituted basis*

California's treatment of substituted basis is the same as federal law (IRC Sec. 1016(b)) Under the substituted basis rules basis is determined by reference to property formerly held by the person for whom the basis is to be determined. For example, property acquired by a parent corporation on the liquidation of a subsidiary has the same basis in the hands of the parent as it had in the hands of the subsidiary. Similarly, property acquired in a tax-free exchange may have the same basis as that of property transferred. Any adjustments to substituted basis must be made after first having made similar adjustments for the period during which the property was held by the transferor, etc., or during which the property exchanged was held by the person for whom the basis is to be determined. (Sec. 24917, Rev. & Tax. Code; Sec. 24964, Rev. & Tax. Code)

• *Nontaxable exchanges*

As under federal law, California allows the nonrecognition of gain on specified transactions. Like federal law, California allows the deferral of gain recognition for the following transactions:

— like-kind exchanges of property held for productive use or investment (Sec. 24941, Rev. & Tax. Code; IRC Sec. 1031; Sec. 24941.5, Rev. & Tax. Code) In addition, California law, unlike federal law, has an information return reporting requirement if the replacement property is purchased outside California. For tax years beginning after 2018, and for exchanges completed after January 10, 2019, California will generally conform to the TCJA amendments to IRC Sec. 1031 limiting nonrecognition of gain or loss on like-kind exchanges to real property. (Sec. 24941.5, Rev. & Tax. Code)

— nontaxable exchanges of stock for property (Sec. 24942, Rev. & Tax. Code) California, unlike federal law, treats membership fees in nonstock, retail corporations as equivalent to nontaxable stock (*Federal Employees Distributing Co. v. Franchise Tax Board*, 260 CalApp2d 937, 67 CalRptr 696 (1968); *Affiliated Government Employees' Distributing Co.*, SBE, 68-SBE-037, September 12, 1968)

— involuntary conversions (Sec. 24943, Rev. & Tax. Code—Sec. 24949.5, Rev. & Tax. Code)

— exchanges of insurance policies (Sec. 24950, Rev. & Tax. Code; IRC Sec. 1035)

— exchanges of stock for stock of same corporation (Sec. 24951, Rev. & Tax. Code; IRC Sec. 1036)

— reacquisitions of real property secured by debt (Sec. 24952, Rev. & Tax. Code; IRC Sec. 1038)

— stock sales to ESOPS (Sec. 24954, Rev. & Tax. Code; IRC Sec. 1042), however, California does not incorporate IRC Sec. 1042(g), which allows a taxpayer to defer the recognition of gain from the sale of stock of a qualified agricultural refiner or processor to an eligible farm cooperative (Sec. 24954.1, Rev. & Tax. Code)

— rollover of publicly traded securities gain into specialized small business investment companies (SBICs) for sales prior to 2018. Because the federal election to roll over tax-free capital gain realized on the sale of publicly-traded securities not apply for California purposes to any taxable year in which those provisions are inapplicable for federal purposes, California effectively conforms to the federal repeal of the rollover election provision for sales after December

31, 2017. (Sec. 24956, Rev. & Tax. Code; IRC Sec. 1044; *2017 Summary of Federal Income Tax Changes*, California Franchise Tax Board, May 16, 2018)

CCH POINTER: Common audit issues involving like-kind exchanges.—One of the FTB's top audit issues continues to be like-kind exchanges. The FTB has identified the following most common audit issues involving like kind exchanges:

— taxpayer fails to source gains to California upon disposition of replacement property received in a California deferred exchange when the replacement property was not located in California;

— taxpayer receives other property (boot) in the exchange but does not report the boot on its return;

— taxpayers do not meet identification or other technical requirements of IRC § 1031;

— relinquished and/or replacement property are not held for investment or for productive use in a trade or business (i.e., property is used for personal purposes or is held primarily for sale); and

— the taxpayer who transfers relinquished property is a different taxpayer than the party who acquires replacement property.

The FTB continues to review certain "drop and swap" or "swap and drop" transactions. Where the form does not support the economic realities or substance of the transaction, the FTB will recharacterize the taxpayer's transaction as appropriate.

The State Board of Equalization has upheld the FTB's recharacterization of transactions involving 1031 exchanges in the following appeals:

— Appeal of Aries, No. 464475 (swap and drop);

— Appeal of Marcil, No. 458832 (different taxpayer acquired replacement property, rehearing granted); and

— Appeal of Brief, Appeal No. 5308782 (deemed contribution to a partnership).

(*Tax News*, Franchise Tax Board, January 2012)

PRACTICE NOTE: Impact of filing extension on technical requirements for like-kind exchange.—IRC Sec. 1031(a)(3)(B) requires that property received by a taxpayer be treated as property that is not like-kind property if the property is received after the earlier of 180 days from the transfer of the relinquished property or the due date (determined with regard to extensions) of the taxpayer's federal tax return. Thus, the federal extended due date should be used in determining whether the property is disqualified under IRC Sec. 1031(a)(3)(B). California incorporates the provisions of IRC Sec. 1031 by reference in Rev. and Tax. Code Sec. 24941, including the provisions of IRC Sec. 1031(a)(3)(B). Thus, California will follow the federal treatment, regardless of whether or not the California return was filed under extension. Specifically, the federal extended due date should be used in determining whether the property is disqualified for like-kind treatment. (*Tax News*, Franchise Tax Board, October 2012)

Low-income housing.—California but not federal law, does not recognize gain from certain sales of low-income housing developments if the proceeds are reinvested in a qualified residential real property within two years. The following types of sales qualify for nonrecognition treatment:

(i) The sale of an assisted housing development (or a majority of the units in an assisted housing development converted to condominium units) to a tenant association, nonprofit organization, public agency, or profit-motivated individual or corporation that will commit itself and its successors in interest to keeping the housing development (or the development's condominium units) affordable for individuals or families qualifying as "lower income" or "very low income" under Health and Safety Code definitions. The buyer's commitment must be for a period of at least 30 years from the date of sale, or for the remaining term of any existing federal government assistance, whichever is greater.

(ii) The sale of real property to a majority of the current "lower income" or "very low income" residents of the property.

(iii) In the case of property converted to condominium units, the sale of a majority of the units to current "lower income" or "very low income" residents.

(Sec. 24955, Rev. & Tax. Code)

Gain from the sale of low-income housing property qualifies for nonrecognition treatment only if, within two years of the date of sale, the seller reinvests all of the proceeds in residential real property located in California. The seller may reinvest in any kind of residential property, not just low-income housing property; however, if the seller reinvests in a principal residence, the transaction does not qualify. The adjusted basis of the reinvestment property must be reduced by the amount of any gain that was not recognized on the original low-income housing sale. Federal law had a similar, but more restrictive provision prior to November 1990. (Former IRC Sec. 1039)

Involuntary conversions.—As discussed above, California mirrors federal law as of the current California conformity date (see ¶10-515), concerning the nonrecognition of gain in qualified transactions involving involuntary conversions. (Sec. 24943, Rev. & Tax. Code, *et seq.*) However, California differs from federal law by specifying that in the case of a nonprofit water utility corporation, replacement property "similar or related in service or use" includes personal property used for the transmission or storage of water. (Sec. 24944(c), Rev. & Tax. Code) In addition, the statute of limitations for making a deficiency assessment associated with an involuntary conversion election is four years from the time an election is made verses the three years authorized under federal law. (Sec. 24945, Rev. & Tax. Code; IRC Sec. 1033(a)(2)(C)) Finally, although California mirrors federal law allowing taxpayers to treat outdoor advertising displays as real property for purposes of the nonrecognition of gain for real property that is condemned and replaced with "like-kind" property, California limits the election to outdoor advertising displays located in economic development areas for which a current expense deduction may be claimed, see ¶10-845 Subtractions—Targeted Business Activities or Zones.

California has adopted amendments similar to federal amendments that (1) expand the events that may precipitate the involuntary conversion of livestock to include not only soil contamination or other environmental contamination but also drought, flood, or other weather-related conditions and (2) that ease the involuntary conversion rules as applied to livestock. (Sec. 24949.1, Rev. & Tax. Code; Sec. 24949.3, Rev. & Tax. Code)

Exchanges of U.S. obligations.—California Corporation Tax Law has no provision comparable to IRC Sec. 1037, which allows nonrecognition of gain or loss on the surrender to the U.S. of U.S. obligations issued under the Second Liberty Bond Act in exchange solely for other obligations issued under the Act. Consequently, gain must be recognized on such exchanges for California corporation franchise and tax purposes.

• *Qualified electric transmission transactions*

California does not incorporate federal law (IRC Sec. 451(i)), allowing taxpayers to elect to recognize qualified gain from a qualifying electric transmission transaction over an eight-year period. (Sec. 24661.6, Rev. & Tax. Code)

• *Wash sales; straddles*

California incorporates IRC Sec. 1091 and IRC Sec. 1092, relating to loss from wash sales of stock or securities, and straddles (Sec. 24998, Rev. & Tax. Code)

• *Capital gains and losses*

California incorporates IRC Sec. 1201—IRC Sec. 1288, concerning capital gains and losses as of the current California conformity date (see ¶10-515), with the exceptions noted below. (Sec. 24990, Rev. & Tax. Code) However, unlike federal law, California treats capital gains as ordinary income and does not apply a different tax rate to capital gains. (Sec. 24990.5, Rev. & Tax. Code) Conversely, California does follow federal law concerning the netting rules applied to short-term and long-term capital gains for purposes of determining the overall amount of capital gains and losses and does provide special rules for claiming capital losses, although capital loss carrybacks are not allowed under California law (see discussion below).

CCH POINTER: RIC net capital loss carryovers.—California follows federal law that allows RICs to treat net capital loss carryovers in a manner that is similar to such carryovers by individuals. (Sec. 24990.5, Rev. & Tax. Code)

California also incorporates IRC Sec. 7872 as of California's current federal conformity date (see ¶10-515), which provides special rules for the treatment of loans with below-market interest rates. (Sec. 24993, Rev. & Tax. Code)

Differences between California and federal law.—As discussed above, the federal alternative tax on corporations under IRC Sec. 1201 is inapplicable for California corporation franchise and income tax purposes. (Sec. 24990.5(a), Rev. & Tax. Code) California also modifies federal law as follows:

— California does not allow capital loss carrybacks allowed for federal purposes under IRC Sec. 1212(a)(1)(A), but does follow federal capital loss carryover treatment (Sec. 24990.5(b), Rev. & Tax. Code);

— California does not incorporate IRC Sec. 1248, which treats part or all of the gain from the sale or exchange of stock in certain foreign corporations by a U.S. 10-percent shareholder as ordinary dividend income and limits the dividend income to the earnings and profits of the corporation attributable to the stock sold or exchanged. Under federal law, the gain exceeding such earnings and profits is treated as capital gain. (Sec. 24990.7, Rev. & Tax. Code)

— IRC Sec. 1291—IRC Sec. 1298, which provides special treatment for certain passive foreign investment companies, is inapplicable for California corporation franchise (income) tax purposes. Consequently for California corporation franchise and income tax purposes, gains or losses realized by these companies are determined in the same manner used for any other entity (Sec. 24495, Rev. & Tax. Code)

— In addition to the property listed in IRC Sec. 1245(a)(2)(C), California also requires an increase in the adjusted basis for property located in economic development areas for which a current expense deduction was claimed, thereby increasing the amount recognized as ordinary income versus capital gain on the disposition of the property (see ¶10-845 Subtractions—Targeted Business Activity or Zones) (Sec. 24990.6, Rev. & Tax. Code)

— The definition of "tax-exempt obligations" under IRC Sec. 1275, is inapplicable for California corporation franchise (income) tax purposes, and replaced with the definition of an obligation, the interest on which is exempt under California Corporation Tax Law (Sec. 24991, Rev. & Tax. Code) Consequently, the exceptions to the special rules for bonds and other debt instruments under IRC Sec. 1271—IRC Sec. 1286, which generally require that discounts and interest on such instruments be imputed to the debt instrument holder, apply to California tax-exempt obligations rather than federally exempt tax-obligations for California corporation franchise (income) tax purposes.

— California does not follow the federal provision that allows certain financial institutions to receive ordinary income or loss treatment, rather than capital gain or loss treatment, on the sale or exchange of preferred stock in the Federal National Mortgage Association ("Fannie Mae") or the Federal Home Loan Mortgage Corporation ("Freddie Mac"). (Sec. 24990.2, Rev. & Tax. Code)

— References to IRC Sec. 1223(4) through (16) in California's corporation tax law are treated as references to IRC Sec. 1223(3) to (15).

Due to California's IRC conformity date history (see ¶10-515), for taxable years beginning on or after January 1, 2015, California incorporates the federal provision under which any interest rate swap, currency swap, basis swap, interest rate cap, interest rate floor, commodity swap, equity swap, equity index swap, or similar agreement is not treated as a Sec. 1256 contract. For federal purposes, the provision applies to taxable years beginning after July 22, 2010.

Other additions to the taxable income base are listed at ¶10-600 Additions to Taxable Income Base.

[¶10-645] Additions--Expense Items

Although California generally conforms to federal law concerning the treatment of trade and business expenses (see ¶10-830 Subtractions—Expense Items for details), California prohibits deductions for expenses associated with the activities discussed below. To the extent such items were deducted on the taxpayer's federal return, these items must be added back for California corporation franchise and income tax purposes as an "other addition" on Line 8, Form 100, California Corporation Franchise or Income Tax Return and a supporting statement must be attached.

• *Expenses incurred at discriminatory clubs*

Deductions for expenses incurred at private clubs that discriminate on the basis of sex, race, color, religion, ancestry, national origin, ethnic group identification, age, mental disability, physical disability, medical condition, genetic information, marital status, or sexual orientation are disallowed, unless the expenses are incurred at the local unit of certain American national fraternal organizations. Examples of disallowed expenses include, but are not limited to, club membership dues and assessments, food and beverage expenses, expenses for services furnished by the club, and reimbursements or salary adjustments to officers or employees for any of the preceding expenses. (Sec. 24343.2, Rev. & Tax. Code; Sec. 11135, Govt. Code)

Any alcoholic beverage club licensee that discriminates must include, on all expense receipts, a statement that the expenses covered by the receipt are not deductible for state franchise and income tax purposes. (Sec. 23438, Bus. & Prof. Code; Sec. 24343.2, Rev. & Tax. Code)

• *Illegal business expense deductions disallowed*

In addition to incorporating IRC Sec. 162(c), which prohibits the deduction as a business expense of specified illegal bribes or kickbacks (Sec. 24343, Rev. & Tax. Code), California prohibits taxpayers from claiming deductions for any income received directly derived from any act or omission of criminal profiteering activity (as defined in Calif. Penal Code § 186.2 or as defined in Chapter 6 (commencing with Section 11350) of Division 10 of the Health and Safety Code, or Article 5 (commencing with Section 750) of Chapter 1 of Part 2 of Division 1 of the Insurance Code), which includes, but is not limited to illegal activities associated with lotteries, gaming, horseracing, prostitution, pornography, burglary, larceny, embezzlement, drug trafficking, and insurance fraud. Federal law also disallows a deduction for expenses related to illegal drug trafficking. (IRC Sec. 280E) (Sec. 24436, Rev. & Tax. Code; Sec. 24436.1, Rev. & Tax. Code) Every business activity that is carried on by any taxpayer, or by another under its direction or control, on the same premises where the illegal activities are conducted, tends to promote or further such illegal activities. (Reg. 24436, 18 CCR)

The deductions may only be disallowed if the taxpayer is found guilty of the specified illegal activities in a criminal proceeding before a California state court or any proceeding in which the state, county, city and county, city, or other political subdivision was a party. (Sec. 24436.1, Rev. & Tax. Code)

• *Fines or penalties paid by sports franchise owners*

California also prohibits deductions for the amount of any fine or penalty paid or incurred by an owner of all or part of a professional sports franchise if that fine or penalty is assessed or imposed by the professional sports league that includes that franchise. (Sec. 24343.8, Rev. & Tax. Code)

• *Film and television production expenses*

California corporation tax law does not incorporate and has no provision similar to IRC Sec. 181, which allows taxpayers to currently deduct expenses associated with qualified film and television productions. Taxpayers that currently expense these items on their federal return must add such amounts back on their California return, but may increase their depreciation deduction on their California return for any depreciable expenses.

• *Foreign affiliate employee compensation*

California corporate tax law does not incorporate nor have a provision similar to IRC Sec. 176, which allows domestic corporations to deduct amounts paid or incurred to compensate U.S. citizens employed by foreign subsidiary corporations under an agreement with the Secretary of the Treasury that allows such amounts contributed to be counted toward the employee's future Social Security insurance benefits. To the extent these amounts are not otherwise deductible on the taxpayer's California return (e.g., deductible as an "ordinary" and "necessary" under Sec. 24343, Rev. & Tax. Code), such amounts must be added back to federal taxable income. The amount is claimed as an "other addition" on Line 8, Form 100, California Corporation Franchise or Income Tax Return and a supporting statement should be attached.

- *Gulf Opportunity Zone demolition and clean-up costs*

California does not incorporation nor have a provision similar to IRC Sec. 1400N(f), which allows a taxpayer to claim a current deduction for 50% of any qualified Gulf Opportunity Zone clean-up costs paid or incurred on or after August 28, 2005, and before January 1, 2014. To the extent these amounts are not otherwise currently deductible on the taxpayer's California return, such amounts must be added back to federal taxable income. The amount is claimed as an "other addition" on Line 8, Form 100, California Corporation Franchise or Income Tax Return and a supporting statement should be attached.

- *Start-up expenses*

California did not incorporate the increase in the federal start-up expense deduction under IRC Sec. 195 from $5,000 to $10,000 nor the increase in the threshold amount for reducing the limit from $50,000 to $60,000 for the 2010 tax year. Consequently, amounts claimed above the pre-2010 limits had to be added back for purposes of determining California taxable income for the 2010 tax year. The amount was claimed as an "other addition" on Line 8, Form 100, California Corporation Franchise or Income Tax Return.

- *Stock reacquisition expenses*

Although California generally conforms to IRC Sec. 162(k), which prohibits taxpayers from claiming deductions for expenses associated with stock redemption transactions other than specified expenses, California does not incorporate IRC Sec. 162(k)(2)(A)(ii), which allows a corporation that is reacquiring its stock to claim a deduction for amounts that are properly allocable to indebtedness and amortized over the term of such indebtedness. (Sec. 24343.7, Rev. & Tax. Code) Consequently, any such amount deducted from federal taxable income on a taxpayer's federal tax return, must be included as an "other addition" on Line 8, Form 100, California Corporation Franchise or Income Tax Return, and a supporting schedule must be attached.

- *California qualified stock options*

Although California incorporates IRC Sec. 421, which generally prohibits an employer from claiming a trade or business expense deduction with respect to incentive stock options or employee stock purchase plans as defined under IRC Sec. 422 and IRC Sec. 423, California also prohibits employers from claiming a business expense deduction for the granting or exercising of a California qualified stock option unless the employee makes an election under IRC Sec. 83(b) to include the gain from the option in his or her gross income in the year of transfer. (IRC Sec. 24602, Rev. & Tax. Code) Consequently, taxpayers that excluded such amounts as a trade or business expense on their federal returns, will need to add such amounts as an "other addition" on line 8, Form 100, California Corporation Franchise or Income Tax Return and include a supporting schedule.

"California qualified stock options" are stock options (1) designed by the corporation issuing the option as a California qualified stock option at the time the option is granted, (2) issued by a corporation to its employees after 1996 and before 2002, and (3) exercised by a taxpayer either while employed by the issuing corporation or within three months after leaving the employ of the issuing corporation. A taxpayer who becomes permanently and totally disabled as defined in IRC Sec. 22(e)(3) may exercise the option within one year of leaving the employ of the issuing corporation. The favorable tax treatment of California qualified stock options is available only to a taxpayer whose earned income from the corporation granting the option does not exceed $40,000 for the taxable year in which the option is exercised, and only to the extent that the number of shares transferable by the exercise by the taxpayer of qualified options does not exceed a total of 1,000 and those shares have a combined fair market value of less than $100,000. (Sec. 24602, Rev. & Tax. Code)

- *Railroad rolling stock and ties*

California corporate tax law neither incorporates nor mirrors IRC Sec. 263(d), which allows railroads to deduct currently rehabilitation expenses in connection with any unit of rolling stock (except locomotives) if the total of those costs in any 12-month period does not exceed 20% of its unadjusted basis. Nor does California follow IRC Sec. 263(f), which permits railroads to currently deduct the costs of acquiring and installing replacement ties of any material and fastenings related to such ties. Consequently, if a taxpayer makes such an election on their federal return and is unable to currently expense such items under another provision, an addition adjustment must be made on the California return. The adjustment is claimed as an "other addition" on Line 8, Form 100, California Corporation Franchise or Income Tax Return. In addition, the depreciation deduction claimed for the property must be increased for California purposes to reflect the increased value of the property as a result of California's nonrecognition of the current expense deduction.

Other additions to the taxable income base are listed at ¶ 10-600.

[¶10-650] Additions--Charitable Contributions

California corporate tax law does not incorporate the federal charitable contributions deduction governed by IRC Sec. 170, but instead provides for its own California contributions deduction, which is similar to the federal deduction. Consequently, taxpayers must add back to federal taxable income any federal contribution deduction claimed by claiming the amount as an "other addition" on Line 8, Form 100, California Corporation Franchise or Income Tax Return, and calculate a California charitable contributions deduction (see ¶ 10-880). (Instructions, Form 100, California Corporation Franchise or Income Tax Return)

Other additions to the taxable income base are listed at ¶ 10-600 Additions to Taxable Income Base.

[¶10-655] Additions--Research and Development Expenses

No addition modification is required. As discussed at ¶ 10-905 Subtractions—Amortization, California incorporates IRC Sec. 174 Research and Experimental Expenditures, which allows taxpayers to currently expense or amortize qualified research and experimental expenditures.

Other additions to the taxable income base are listed at ¶ 10-600.

[¶10-660] Additions--Items Related to Federal Deductions or Credits

There is no California provision comparable to IRC Sec. 196, which allows taxpayers to deduct on their federal returns, certain unused business credits for the first taxable year following the last taxable year in which such credits were allowed. To the extent such amounts are deducted from federal taxable income, and are not eligible for deduction under other California corporation franchise and income tax provisions, taxpayers must add such amounts to federal taxable income as an "other addition" on Line 8, Form 100, California Corporation Franchise or Income Tax Return and attach a supporting schedule.

There is similarly no California provision comparable to IRC Sec. 198A, which allows taxpayers allows costs incurred after 2007 for disasters that are federally declared after that date to be expensed rather than capitalized. To the extent such amounts are deducted from federal taxable income, and are not eligible for deduction under other California corporation franchise and income tax provisions, taxpayers must add such amounts to federal taxable income as an "other addition" on Line 8, Form 100, California Corporation Franchise or Income Tax Return and attach a supporting schedule.

In addition, there is no California provision comparable to IRC Sec. 199, which allows a deduction for qualified production activities for taxable years beginning before 2018. IRC Sec. 199 allows taxpayers to deduct up 9% (phased-in over a five-year period) of taxable income or qualified production activities income. The deduction amount is 3% for 2005 and 2006; 6% for 2007, 2008, and 2009; and 9% for 2010 through 2017. To the extent such amounts were deducted from federal taxable income, and were not eligible for deduction under other California corporation franchise or income tax provisions, taxpayers were required to add such amounts to federal taxable income as an "other addition" on Line 8, Form 100, California Corporation Franchise or Income Tax Return and attach a supporting schedule.

See ¶ 10-855 Subtractions—Items Related to Federal Deductions or Credits, for the subtraction modifications allowed for expenses associated with certain federal credits.

Other additions to the taxable income base are listed at ¶ 10-600.

[¶ 10-665] Additions--Environmental or Pollution Control

Unlike federal law, California does not allow deductions for various environmental protection cost-share payments, energy efficient commercial buildings, environmental remediation costs, nor for tertiary injectant expenses. In addition California disallows deductions for open-space easement abandonment fees and timberland tax recoupment fees. See the discussions below. Special rules apply to amortization of reforestation expenses (see ¶ 10-680 Additions—Amortization).

• *Cost-share payments*

California does not incorporate IRC Sec. 126, which excludes all or a portion of payments received under the following programs:

— the rural clean water program under the Federal Water Pollution Control Act

— the rural abandoned mine program under the Surface Mining Control and Reclamation Act

— the water bank program under the Water Bank Act

— the emergency conservation measure sunder the Agricultural Credit Act of 1978

— the agricultural conservation program authorized by the Soil Conservation and Domestic Allotment Act

— the great plains conservation program under the Soil Conservation and Domestic Policy Act

— the resource conservation and development program under the Bankhead-Jones Farm Tenant Act and the Soil Conservation and Domestic Allotment Act

— the forestry incentives program under the Cooperative Forestry Assistance Act of 1978

— any small watershed program administered by the Secretary of Agriculture that is determined by the Secretary of the Treasury to be substantially similar to the programs described above

— any program of a State, U.S. possession, or any political subdivision thereof, under which payments are made to individuals primarily for the purpose of conserving soil, protecting or restoring the environment, improving forests, or providing a habitat for wildlife.

Consequently, corporation franchise and income taxpayers must add these amounts to federal taxable income when computing a corporation's net taxable income. These amounts should be included as an "other addition" on Line 8, Other Additions, on Form 100, California Corporation Franchise or Income Tax Return, and a supporting schedule should be attached. A special rules apply for certain forest protection related cost-share payments (see ¶ 10-860).

- *Energy efficient commercial buildings deduction*

California corporate tax law neither incorporates nor has a provision similar to IRC Sec. 179D, which allowed qualified taxpayers to claim a deduction for energy efficiency improvements installed on U.S. commercial property, applicable to qualified improvements placed in service after 2005 and before 2018. Consequently taxpayers that claimed the federal deduction had to add these amounts to federal taxable income when computing their net taxable income on their California return. These amounts were includible as an "other addition" on Line 8 of Form 100, California Corporation Franchise or Income Tax Return, with a supporting schedule attached. The expenses added back to federal taxable income could then be depreciated on the California corporation franchise and income tax return. The increased depreciation deduction is computed on FTB 3885, Corporation Depreciation and Amortization, and claimed on Line 12 of Form 100, California Corporation Franchise or Income Tax Return.

- *Easement abandonment and tax recoupment fees*

California law disallows deductions for abandonment fees paid by California property owners on termination of open-space easements under Government Code Sec. 51061 or Sec. 51093, and for tax recoupment fees specified under Government Code Sec. 51142 when property is removed from zoning as timberland production property. (Sec. 24441, Rev. & Tax. Code) The provision has no federal counterpart. Consequently, to the extent these fees are deducted from federal taxable income on the federal return, taxpayers must claim these as an "other addition" on Line 8, Form 100, California Corporation Franchise or Income Tax Return, and attach a supporting schedule.

- *Environmental remediation costs*

California does not currently conform to IRC Sec. 198, which allows taxpayers to currently expense certain environmental remediation costs that would otherwise be chargeable to a capital account. (Sec. 24369.4, Rev. & Tax. Code) However, prior to 2004, California did conform to federal law in this area.

Taxpayers that currently expense qualified environmental remediation costs on their federal return must make an addition adjustment and enter such amounts as an "other addition" on Line 8, Form 100, California Corporation Franchise or Income Tax Return. Such expenses may then be depreciated on Form 3885 California Depreciation and Amortization.

• *Reforestation expenses*

Although California incorporates IRC Sec. 194, which allows taxpayers to elect currently deduct up to $10,000 of qualified reforestation expenses and to amortize any remaining amount over a seven-year period, California limits the deduction to qualified timber property located in California. (Sec. 24372.5, Rev. & Tax. Code)

• *Tertiary injectants*

California corporate tax law does not incorporate nor have a provision similar to IRC Sec. 193, which allows a taxpayer to currently deduct expenses associated with tertiary injectants injected during the taxable year. Consequently, to the extent such amounts were currently deducted on the federal return such amounts must be added to federal taxable income as an "other addition" on Line 8, Form 100, California Corporation Franchise or Income Tax Return. Although these amounts may not be currently deducted, they are treated as capital expenses for which a depreciation deduction or amortization deduction may be claimed (see ¶ 10-900 Subtractions—Depreciation).

Other additions to the taxable income base are listed at ¶ 10-600.

[¶ 10-670] Additions--Depreciation

Does California require an addback of federal bonus depreciation deductions?

California requires an addback of the amount by which depreciation claimed for federal purposes exceeds the allowable California depreciation deduction, which is computed without regard to federal bonus depreciation. (Instructions, Form 100, California Corporation Franchise or Income Tax Return; Instructions, Form 100S, California S Corporation Franchise or Income Tax Return)

Does California require an addback of federal deductions taken for depreciation other than bonus depreciation?

California requires an addback of the amount by which depreciation claimed for federal purposes exceeds the allowable state depreciation due to differences between federal and California laws. Because the corporate depreciation deduction is different for California and federal income tax purposes, California corporation franchise and income taxpayers must separately compute their California depreciation deduction. For a discussion of the California depreciation deduction, see Subtractions—Depreciation. If the depreciation amount claimed for federal purposes exceeds the amount calculated for California purposes, the excess must be entered as an addition adjustment on the return. If the depreciation amount calculated for California purposes exceeds the amount claimed for federal purposes, the excess may be entered as a subtraction adjustment on the return. C corporations and limited liability companies classified as corporations compute their California depreciation deduction on FTB Form 3885, Corporation Depreciation and Amortization. S corporations use Schedule B, Form 100S, California S Corporation Return to compute their depreciation deduction. (Instructions, Form 100, California Corporation Franchise or Income Tax Return;

FTB Form 3885, Corporation Depreciation and Amortization; Instructions, Form 100S, California S Corporation Franchise or Income Tax Return)

Does California require an addback of Sec. 179 asset expense deduction amounts?

California requires an addback of enhanced IRC Sec. 179 asset expense deduction amounts that exceed $25,000, as reduced by the $200,000 investment phaseout threshold, or that are claimed for off-the-shelf computer software. (Sec. 24356(b), Rev. & Tax. Code; Instructions, Form 100, California Corporation Franchise or Income Tax Return; Instructions, Form 100S, California S Corporation Franchise or Income Tax Return)

[¶10-675] Additions--Natural Resource Exploration

As discussed at ¶10-515 Federal Conformity, California adopts, with modifications, IRC Sec. 611 through IRC Sec. 638, concerning the depletion deduction allowed for the exhaustion of natural resources. No addition adjustment is required. However, see ¶10-850 Subtractions—Depletion for a discussion of subtraction deductions that may be allowed.

Other additions to the taxable income base are listed at ¶10-600.

[¶10-680] Additions--Amortization

Because the corporate amortization deduction is so different for California and federal income tax purposes, California corporation franchise and income taxpayers must separately compute their amortization deduction for California tax purposes. C corporations and limited liability companies classified as corporations compute their California amortization deduction on FTB Form 3885, Corporation Depreciation and Amortization. To the extent the amortization amount claimed for federal purposes exceeds the amount calculated on FTB Form 3885 for California purposes, the excess is treated as an addition adjustment and is entered on Line 6, Form 100, California Corporation Franchise or Income Tax Return. Conversely, if the amortization amount computed on FTB Form 3885 for California corporation franchise and income tax purposes exceeds the federal depreciation deduction claimed on the taxpayer's federal return, the excess is claimed as a subtraction adjustment and is entered on Line 12, Form 100. (Instructions, Form 100, California Corporation Franchise or Income Tax Return) S corporations use Schedule B, Form 100S, California S Corporation Return to compute their depreciation deduction.

Below, are some of the current differences between California and federal law concerning allowable amortization deductions. See ¶10-905 Subtractions—Amortization, for further differences between California law and federal law's treatment of amortization.

• *Pollution control facilities*

Although California incorporates IRC Sec. 169, which allows corporations to elect accelerated amortization of a "certified pollution control facility" over a period of 60 months, California limits the accelerated amortization deduction to those facilities located in California and requires that the certification be issued by the California State Air Resources Board, in the case of air pollution facilities, or the California State Water Resources Control Board, in the case of water pollution facilities. (Sec. 24372.3, Rev. & Tax. Code) In addition, because of California's current federal conformity date (see ¶10-515), California has not incorporated amendments made to IRC Sec. 169(d) by the Energy Tax Incentives Act of 2005 (ETIA) (P.L. 109-58), which allow atmospheric (coal-fired) pollution control facilities placed in service after April 11, 2005, to be amortized over an 84-month period.

The amortization deduction is in lieu of the depreciation deduction normally taken for such property (see ¶ 10-900 Subtractions—Depreciation). (Sec. 24372.3, Rev. & Tax. Code)

Taxpayer's claim this amortization deduction on FTB 3580, Application to Amortize Certified Pollution Control Facility.

• *Reforestation expenses*

Although California incorporates IRC Sec. 194, which allows taxpayers to elect to currently deduct up to $10,000 of qualified reforestation expenses and to amortize any remaining amount over a seven-year period, California limits the deduction to qualified timber property located in California. (Sec. 24372.5, Rev. & Tax. Code)

• *Musical compositions*

Because of California's current IRC conformity date (see ¶ 10-515), California does not incorporate amendments made to IRC Sec. 167(g) by the Tax Increase Prevention and Reconciliation Act of 2005 (TIPRA) (P.L. 109-222) that allow amortization of expenses paid or incurred in creating or acquiring a musical composition or a copyright to a musical composition over five-years, effective for property placed in service in tax years beginning after December 31, 2005, and before January 1, 2011.

Other additions to the taxable income base are listed at ¶ 10-600 Additions to Taxable Income Base.

[¶ 10-685] Additions--Bad Debts

California incorporates IRC Sec. 166 concerning bad debts, without modification, as of a specified. date. (Sec. 24347, Rev. & Tax. Code) Under IRC Sec. 166 a taxpayer may take a deduction for debts that become wholly or partially worthless within the taxable year. Because California does not modify federal law, no addition or subtraction adjustments should be required. However, bear in mind that the California Franchise Tax Board may apply different interpretations than the Internal Revenue Service as to when or if a debt becomes worthless. See the annotations at ¶ 10-875 Subtractions—Bad Debts for a summary of the California State Board of Equalization and California court decisions in this area.

Other additions to the taxable income base are listed at ¶ 10-600.

[¶ 10-690] Additions--Basis Adjustments

The adjusted basis for determining gain or loss on the sale of property is the basis of the property, as adjusted by Sec. 24916, Rev. & Tax. Code and Sec. 24917, Rev. & Tax. Code. (Sec. 24911, Rev. & Tax. Code) The provision is the same as IRC Sec. 1011, as of the current California conformity date (see ¶ 10-515), except that, as discussed below, the federal basis adjustments are in some cases different from those provided by California law. Special rules apply to California's treatment of gains and losses and its general basis rules (see ¶ 10-515).

In computing gain or loss on the sale or exchange of assets, adjustments to basis must be made for depreciation allowed or allowable, for various deferred expenses taken as deductions, and for many other factors, which are discussed below. (Sec. 24916, Rev. & Tax. Code)

• *Identical federal and California treatment*

The treatment of the following basis adjustments is identical for both California and federal law:

— tax free stock distributions (Sec. 24916(c), Rev. & Tax. Code; IRC Sec. 1016(a)(4))

— property pledged to the Commodity Credit Corporation (Sec. 24916(d)(3), Rev. & Tax. Code; IRC Sec. 1016(a)(8))

— deferred mine development expense (Sec. 24916(e), Rev. & Tax. Code; IRC Sec. 1016(a)(9))

— deferred research and experimental expenses (Sec. 24916(g), Rev. & Tax. Code; IRC Sec. 1016(a)(14))

— rollover of gain into a specialized small business investment company (SSBIC) (Sec. 24916(j), Rev. & Tax. Code; IRC Sec. 1016(a)(23))

— lessee-made improvements to real property (Sec. 24919, Rev. & Tax. Code; IRC Sec. 1019)

— the former deduction for clean-fuel vehicles and certain refueling property allowed under IRC Sec. 179A (Sec. 24916(l), Rev. & Tax. Code)

[*CCH Note:* California incorporates the federal basis adjustment for clean fuel vehicles and refueling property even though California did not incorporate the IRC Sec. 179A deduction.]

Although California does not include the following adjustments in its provision requiring basis adjustments, California does incorporate the underlying federal provision that requires a taxpayer to make a basis adjustment. Thus, like federal law, taxpayers must also make adjustments for the following: (1) a shareholder of an S corporation must make the adjustments to the basis of its stock in the S corporation that are required by IRC Sec. 1367, to reflect the shareholder's portion of various items of income, nontaxable return-of-capital distributions by the S corporation, etc. (Sec. 23800, Rev. & Tax. Code); and (2) a reduction in basis in qualified employer securities to employee stock ownership plans (ESOPs) or qualified worker-owned cooperatives purchased by the taxpayer for which nonrecognition of gain is available under IRC Sec. 1042. (Sec. 24954, Rev. & Tax. Code)

• *Federal basis adjustments not followed under California law*

Under IRC Sec. 1016, but not under California law, basis adjustments must be made for the following items discussed below:

— disallowed deductions on the disposal of coal or domestic iron ore (IRC Sec. 1016(a)(15));

— amounts related to a shareholder's stock in a controlled foreign corporation (IRC Sec. 1016(a)(18));

— the amount of gas guzzler tax on an automobile (IRC Sec. 1016(d));

— for pre-2005 tax years, certain amounts that must be included in the gross income of a United States shareholder in a foreign personal holding company (IRC Sec. 1016(a)(13));

— municipal bond premiums required to be amortized under IRC Sec. 75(a)(2) (IRC Sec. 1016(a)(6));

— property for which a federal investment tax credit is claimed (IRC Sec. 1016(a)(19));

— amounts specified in a shareholder's consent made under IRC Sec. 28 of the 1939 Internal Revenue Code (IRC Sec. 1016(a)(12));

— disallowed deductions on the sale of unharvested crops (IRC Sec. 1016(a)(11));

— amortization of premium and accrual of discount on bonds and notes held by a life insurance company (IRC Sec. 1016(a)(16));

— certain amounts deducted under IRC Sec. 59(e) that are not treated as tax preference items if so deducted (IRC Sec. 1016(a)(20));

— property for which a federal credit for qualified electric vehicles was claimed under IRC Sec. 30 Credit for Qualified Electric Vehicles (IRC Sec. 1016(a)(25));

— property for which a federal credit for plug-in electric motor vehicles under IRC Sec. 30D New Qualified Plug-In Electric Drive Motor Vehicles (IRC Sec. 1016(a)(25));

— facilities for which a federal employer-provided child care credit was claimed under IRC Sec. 45F (IRC Sec. 1016(a)(28)); and

— railroad track for which a credit was claimed under IRC Sec. 45G (IRC Sec. 1016(a)(29)).

In addition, California has not incorporated amendments made the Energy Tax Incentives Act of 2005 (P.L. 109-58) that require adjustments for expenses for which an IRC Sec. 179D energy efficient commercial buildings deduction was claimed. Other adjustments required under amendments made by ETIA relating to expenses for which federal credits were claimed are inapplicable for California purposes. (Sec. 23051.5(b)(8), Rev. & Tax. Code)

• *Prior law provisions applied currently*

Both California and federal laws adopt basis rules in the Revenue Acts of 1932 and 1934 for the following types of property acquired after February 1913: property acquired in a tax-free exchange; corporate property acquired in reorganization; property acquired by issuance of stock or paid-in surplus; and stock received in a corporate spin-off. (Sec. 24962(a), (b), Rev. & Tax. Code) The California provisions are the same as IRC Sec. 1052(a) and IRC Sec. 1052(b), except that the federal basis rules adopted from the Revenue Act of 1934 apply to property acquired after February 1913 and prior to 1936, whereas the California rules apply to property acquired after February 1913 and prior to 1937.

Federal and California law both carry over some basis provisions from the Internal Revenue Code of 1939. Under California law (Sec. 24962(c), (d), Rev. & Tax. Code), provisions from the Bank and Corporation Tax Law of 1954 relating to basis of property acquired in a tax free exchange, reorganization, or by issuance of stock and to the basis of stock rights remain applicable to the property to which they applied. (Sec. 24962(c), (d), Rev. & Tax. Code) Under federal law (IRC Sec. 1052(c)), eight enumerated provisions of former IRC Sec. 113 of the Internal Revenue Code of 1939 remain applicable to pre-1954 code acquisitions.

California also follows federal law (IRC Sec. 1053), requiring that fair market value be used to determine gains if the basis of property acquired before March 1, 1913, determined under ordinary basis rules, is less than fair market value as of March 1, 1913. (Sec. 24963, Rev. & Tax. Code)

Chapter 1139, Laws 1987, made numerous amendments to provisions of the Bank and Corporation Tax Law concerning tax credits, contributions, losses, and basis adjustments. However, it also added a provision that preserves the carryover of tax credits, excess contributions, losses, and basis adjustments that were in effect before 1987, but were modified or repealed by Chapter 1139. With respect to computing the basis of assets, the California provision states as follows: (1) for purposes of applying the provisions of Chapter 1139, Laws 1987, the basis or recomputed basis of any asset acquired prior to 1987, must be determined under the law at the time the asset was acquired; (2) any adjustments to basis for income years beginning prior to 1987, must be computed under applicable provisions of the Bank and Corporation Tax Law, including amendments enacted prior to 1987; and (3) any adjustments to basis for income years beginning after 1986, must be computed under the applicable provisions of Chapter 1139, Laws 1987. (Sec. 23051.7, Rev. & Tax. Code)

• *Amortizable bond premium*

Under California law, if a taxable bond is purchased at more than its face value, the buyer may elect to amortize the bond premium and deduct the amortizable amount (see ¶ 10-610 Additions—Federally-Exempt Income). For franchise tax purposes, the interest received from federal, state, or other bonds is taxable (see ¶ 10-610 Additions—Federally-Exempt Income), and the taxpayer who purchases any of these bonds at a premium is entitled to the election to amortize the premium. If the election was made, when computing gain or loss upon sale or exchange, the basis of the bonds must be reduced for franchise tax purposes by the deduction allowable for the amortizable bond premium. (Sec. 24916(d)(1), Rev. & Tax. Code)

Under California law, an amortization deduction is not allowed for the premium paid on a tax-exempt bond (¶ 10-610 Additions—Federally-Exempt Income), but the basis of a tax-exempt bond nonetheless must be reduced by the amount of the amortizable bond premium not allowed as a deduction. For California corporation income tax purposes, but not for California franchise tax purposes, bonds issued by the State of California or a local government within the State and federal bonds are tax-exempt (¶ 10-815 Subtractions—Interest), and the basis of these bonds is reduced by the disallowed bond premium deduction. Likewise, the basis of any bonds that are taxed for corporation income tax purposes is reduced by the deduction allowable as amortized bond premium. (Sec. 24916(d)(2), Rev. & Tax. Code)

California's general rules concerning the deductibility of amortizable bond premiums are generally similar to federal law (IRC Sec. 171); also, IRC Sec. 1016(a)(5), concerning the basis of bonds, is the same as California Sec. 24916(d)(2), Rev. & Tax. Code, except for titles and internal references. However, the basis adjustment under federal law as compared with the California law may be different because of the differences in computing the bond premium amortization deduction; see ¶ 10-610 Additions—Federally-Exempt Interest.

• *Bargain sales to a charity*

The adjusted basis for determining the gain from a bargain sale of property to a charity is an amount that is in the same ratio to the adjusted basis as the amount realized is to the fair market value of the property. (Sec. 24911, Rev. & Tax. Code) There is no comparable federal provision.

• *Capital expenditures*

Under both California and federal law (IRC Sec. 1016(a)(1)), capital expenditures, excluding taxes or other carrying charges and circulation expenditures for which deductions have been taken, are added to basis unless such expenses were otherwise

¶10-690

currently deducted. However, California differs from federal law in that California also prohibits basis adjustments for (1) sales or use tax paid or incurred in connection with the acquisition of property for use in an enterprise zone for which a pre-2014 tax year tax credit is claimed under Sec. 23612.2, Rev. & Tax. Code and (2) farming expenses for which a deduction has been taken under Sec. 24369, Rev. & Tax. Code. (Sec. 24916(a), Rev. & Tax. Code)

• *Deferred mine exploration expenses*

A basis adjustment is made under California law for deferred mine exploration expenses that the taxpayer deducts under IRC Sec. 617, relating to the deduction and recapture of certain mining exploration expenditures. The adjustment is required to the extent that the deductions result in a reduction of the taxpayer's tax, but must not be less than the amounts allowable as a deduction for the taxable year and prior years. Although both California and federal law allow the deduction, only California law (Sec. 24916(f), Rev. & Tax. Code) specifies that the basis adjustment is required.

• *Depreciation and depletion*

For California taxpayers subject to the franchise tax, basis is decreased by depreciation and depletion to the extent allowed for periods after 1927, but not less than the amount allowable; the same is true for taxpayers subject to corporation income tax for depreciation taken after 1936. However, for franchise tax purposes, no deduction from basis need be made for the excess of depreciation taken based on a 1928 valuation, over the amount allowable if depreciation were not based on a 1928 valuation. There is a similar provision for depletion taken prior to 1932. The basis of property is further reduced by depreciation and depletion sustained prior to 1928 for franchise tax purposes, and prior to 1937 for corporation income tax purposes. (Sec. 24916(b), Rev. & Tax. Code)

Federal law (IRC Sec. 1016(a)(2)) refers to basis adjustments for depreciation and depletion sustained before and after February 28, 1913. Generally, basis is reduced by the greater of (1) the amount of depreciation and depletion allowable or (2) depreciation and depletion deductions claimed that resulted in a tax benefit.

CCH COMMENT: *Differences between federal and California basis adjustment.*— Although both federal and California law require taxpayers to make basis adjustments for depreciation, the amount of the adjustments will differ as a result of the differences between California and federal law with regard to how the depreciation deduction is computed, see ¶10-900 Subtractions—Depreciation.

• *Discharges of indebtedness*

Although California incorporates federal law concerning basis adjustments required as the result of specified discharges of indebtedness, California modifies federal law by substituting references to affiliated groups that file a consolidated return with references to members of the same unitary group that file a combined report for California corporation franchise or income tax purposes. (Sec. 24918, Rev. & Tax. Code)

• *Economic development area current expenses*

California law requires basis adjustments for the pre-2014 tax year deductions claimed for expenses incurred acquiring certain depreciable business assets that are used by businesses operating in enterprise zones or the former Los Angeles Revitalization Zone. (Sec. 24916(h), Rev. & Tax. Code) The deduction of such expenses incurred by enterprise zone businesses, the former Los Angeles Revitalization Zone businesses, targeted tax area businesses, and businesses located in local agency military base recovery areas are discussed at ¶ 10-845 Subtractions—Targeted Business Activity or Zones. No comparable basis adjustments are required under federal law.

[*CCH Note:* Sec. 24916(h), Rev. & Tax. Code, refers to former provisions dealing with enterprise zones and the former LARZ. Presumably, basis requirements should be required for all the pre-2014 provisions allowing current expense items in economic development areas.]

• *Lessor-made improvements*

Under both IRC Sec. 168(i)(8) and California law, a lessor that disposes of or abandons a leasehold improvement that was made by the lessor for the lessee, may use the adjusted basis of the improvement in determining gain or loss upon termination of the lease. Thus, for purposes of determining gain or loss by the lessor, the adjusted basis of leasehold improvements disposed of or abandoned may be recovered at the end of the lease to which the improvements relate, even if there is no disposition of the underlying building. (Sec. 24349, Rev. & Tax. Code)

California specifies that the law does not apply to any property covered under IRC Sec. 168(f), which includes public utility property, and property depreciated during the first tax year under the unit-of-production method or certain depreciation methods not expressed in terms of years. In addition, for taxable years beginning after 1997, California law provides that in determining a lease term, (1) the term of any option to renew must be taken into account, unless the option is for renewal of a lease of nonresidential real property or residential rental property at fair market value determined at the time of the renewal, and (2) two or more successive leases that are part of the same or related transactions with respect to the same or substantially similar property must be treated as one lease. (Sec. 24349(e), Rev. & Tax. Code)

• *Incentives for production of low sulfur diesel fuel*

Although California does not directly incorporate federal provisions that require basis adjustments for capital costs currently deducted by small business refiners under IRC Sec. 179Bc and facilities for which a production of low sulfur diesel fuel credit was claimed under IRC Sec. 45H, California requires basis adjustments for the equivalent California deduction and credit available to small business refiners (see ¶ 10-860). (Sec. 23662(d), Rev. & Tax. Code; Sec. 24356.4(b), Rev. & Tax. Code)

• *Open-space easement abandonment fees and timberland tax recoupment fees*

California prohibits any basis adjustments for abandonment fees paid upon the termination of an open-space easement or for tax recoupment fees paid on timberland. (Sec. 24916.2, Rev. & Tax. Code) There is no comparable federal provision.

• *Stock in subsidiary member of combined group*

Because California does not incorporate the federal consolidated return regulations, there is no authority for applying to California combined groups the federal rule (Treas. Regs. Sec. 1.1502-32) allowing a parent corporation to make investment adjustments to the stock basis of its subsidiaries. Consequently, neither the stock basis of such a subsidiary nor the parent's gain from the sale of such stock will necessarily be the same for California purposes as for federal purposes. In particular, if the subsidiary has earnings that are included in the group's combined return but not distributed to the parent, they will be added to the stock's basis for federal purposes, but not for California purposes. Upon the sale of the subsidiary stock, the parent will thus be exposed to double taxation under the California rules because a portion of the taxable gain will be attributable to retained—and previously taxed—subsidiary earnings. (*Rapid-American Corporation*, SBE, 97-SBE-019-A, May 8, 1997)

Similarly, a taxpayer's adjustment to its basis in the stock of its subsidiaries that was based on a consent dividend properly declared on a taxpayer's federal return will not be allowed on the taxpayer's California return. Under IRC Sec. 565, a taxpayer is allowed to declare a "consent dividend," which, even though no money is actually transferred, is treated as though a dividend was paid by the subsidiary and contributed back by the parent to the subsidiary as capital, thereby increasing the parent's basis in the subsidiary's stock. However, California has never adopted IRC Sec. 565 and, therefore, no basis adjustment is allowed for California income tax purposes. (*CRG Holdings, Inc.*, SBE, 97-SBE-009, May 8, 1997)

Other additions to the taxable income base are listed at ¶ 10-600.

[¶ 10-701] Additions--Discharges of Indebtedness

California generally conforms to IRC Sec. 108 (Income from Discharge of Indebtedness), which excludes from gross income discharges (or cancellations) of indebtedness (also known as "COD" or "DOI" income) if: (1) the discharge occurs in a title 11 bankruptcy case, (2) the discharge occurs when the taxpayer is insolvent, (3) the indebtedness is "qualified farm indebtedness", or (4) in the case of non-C corporation taxpayers, the indebtedness is "qualified real property business indebtedness."

CCH COMMENT: Interaction of laws.—The Franchise Tax Board has released a document clarifying how the California Civil Procedure Code sections interact with IRC Sec. 108, in view of the large number of foreclosures in the state. (*Tax News*, California Franchise Tax Board, February 2010)

Generally, taxpayers must reduce specified tax attributes to the extent income from discharge of indebtedness is excluded from gross income under IRC Sec. 108. Reduced tax attributes include the adjusted bases of properties, net operating losses, and passive activity loss and credit carryovers. Effectively then, IRC Sec. 108, as incorporated, operates to defer, rather than eliminate, income from discharges of indebtedness. (Sec. 24307, Rev. & Tax. Code) California modifies the amount by which these attributes must be reduced.

Under IRC Sec. 108(b)(2), as modified by California, unless the taxpayer elects to reduce the basis of depreciable assets, tax attributes are reduced in the following order.

(1) net operating losses or net operating loss carryovers (see ¶ 10-805 Subtractions—Net Operating Loss), reduced dollar for dollar;

(2) California corporation franchise (income) tax credit carryovers (see ¶ 12-001 Overview of Credits), reduced 11.1 cents (33.3 cents for federal purposes) for each dollar excluded;

(3) minimum tax credit carryovers, reduced 11.1 cents (33.3 cents for federal purposes) for each dollar excluded;

(4) net capital losses or capital loss carryovers (see ¶ 10-640 Additions—Gains), reduced dollar for dollar;

(5) basis of the taxpayer's depreciable and nondepreciable property (see ¶ 10-640 Additions—Gains), reduced dollar for dollar;

(6) passive activity loss and credit carryovers, reduced 11.1 cents (33.3 cents for federal purposes) for each dollar excluded.

(Secs. 24307(b), (c), (d), Rev. & Tax. Code)

Items 3 and 6 are applicable for California purposes for post-1995 discharges in taxable years beginning after 1995 and for federal purposes to discharges of indebtedness in tax years beginning after 1993. (Sec. 24307(g), Rev. & Tax. Code) If more than one credit carryover can be claimed, the credits must be reduced on a pro-rata basis. (Sec. 24307(d), Rev. & Tax. Code) These reductions are made after the determination of tax for the year of discharge. In other words, tax attributes arising in or carried to the year of discharge reduce tax for the year of discharge before they are reduced by reason of the discharge. (IRC Sec. 108(b)(4)(A); Sec. 24307, Rev. & Tax. Code)

> **CCH EXAMPLE:** *Application of tax attribute reductions.*—In 2004, an insolvent corporation is discharged of $100 of debt. For that year, the corporation has taxable income of $30 and a research and development credit carryover equal to $40. In calculating tax for the year of discharge, the credit is applied to eliminate the $30 taxable income. Then the $100 discharge is applied against the remaining $10 credit (which is reduced by 11.1 cents for each dollar), and the insolvent corporation is left with $90 of discharge of indebtedness income to reduce other tax attributes.

• *Discharges of qualified farming indebtedness*

IRC Sec. 108(g), as incorporated by California, generally allows farmers who are not bankrupt or insolvent to apply qualified farm discharged indebtedness to reduce tax attributes and/or to reduce the basis of property used in farming rather than recognizing discharge of indebtedness income. However, amounts excluded due to cancellation of qualified farm indebtedness may not be greater than the sum of: (1) a taxpayer's adjusted tax attributes (other than basis) for the year that the debt was canceled and, (2) the total adjusted bases of qualified property (any property that is used or held for use in a trade or business or for the production of income) held by the taxpayer at the beginning of the tax year following the tax year in which the discharge occurs. To the extent the amount attributable to the discharge of qualified indebtedness exceeds this limitation, income is recognized. For purposes of applying this limitation, the taxpayer's adjusted tax attributes for the tax year of the discharge are equal to: (1) the sum of the taxpayer's net operating losses or NOL carryovers and net capital losses and capital loss carryovers, plus (2) the adjusted dollar amounts of the corporation franchise (income) tax credit carryovers, the minimum tax credit, and the passive activity loss and credit carryovers. The adjusted dollar amounts are determined by taking into account nine dollars (three dollars for federal purposes) for each one dollar of these attributes. (Sec. 24307(e), Rev. & Tax. Code)

• *Discharges of real property business indebtedness*

California incorporates IRC Sec. 108(a)(1)(D), allowing taxpayers other than C corporations to elect to exclude from gross income income from qualified real property business indebtedness. The A taxpayer's federal election, or lack thereof, is binding for California purposes. (Sec. 24307(f), Rev. & Tax. Code)

• *Special rules for S corporations*

California incorporates federal law (IRC Sec. 108(d)(8)) that precludes S corporation shareholders from treating cancellation of indebtedness (COD) income as an item of income that may be passed through from the S corporation to increase the shareholders' basis in their S corporation stock. However, this prohibition does not apply to any discharge of indebtedness made before March 1, 2002, pursuant to a plan of reorganization filed with a bankruptcy court before October 12, 2001. (Sec. 24307(h), Rev. & Tax. Code) Because California's treatment is the same as federal no adjustments are required, unless the discharge occurred between October 11, 2001 (the federal effective date) and January 1, 2002 (the California effective date).

• *Deferral of discharge of indebtedness income from reacquisition of debt instruments*

California does not adopt the federal provision in IRC Sec. 108(i) allowing taxpayers to defer the recognition of discharge of indebtedness income arising from a qualified reacquisition of business debt instruments issued by the taxpayer or a related person ratably over a five-year period. Consequently, taxpayers are required to make an addition adjustment in the first year the income is deferred equal to the difference between the amount of deferred income included on the federal return and the full amount of the income discharged. (Sec. 24307(i), Rev. & Tax. Code; *E-mail*, California Franchise Tax Board, February 7, 2011) Subtraction adjustments will be allowed in the subsequent years in which taxpayers include the deferred income in their federal taxable income (see ¶ 10-918).

Other additions to the taxable income base are listed at ¶ 10-600.

[¶ 10-702] Additions--Substandard Housing

California law denies a corporate lessor of substandard housing any deduction for interest (¶ 10-815 Subtractions—Interest), taxes (¶ 10-840 Subtractions—Taxes), depreciation (¶ 10-900 Subtractions—Depreciation), or amortization (¶ 10-905 Subtractions—Amortization) relating to such housing. (Sec. 24436.5, Rev. & Tax. Code) Federal law has no comparable provision. Consequently, taxpayers that claim the previously listed deductions for the substandard housing on their federal returns must include these amounts as "other additions" on Line 8, Form 100, California Corporation Franchise or Income Tax Return, and attach a supporting schedule.

"Substandard housing" means occupied dwellings from which a taxpayer derives rental income, or unoccupied or abandoned dwellings, for which either of the following apply:

— For occupied dwellings from which a taxpayer derives rental income, a governmental regulatory agency has found the housing to be in violation of local health, safety, or building codes; or

— For dwellings that are unoccupied or abandoned for at least 90 days, a governmental regulatory agency has cited the housing for conditions that constitute a serious violation of state law or local codes dealing with health, safety, or building, and that constitute a threat to public health and safety.

And either of the following occur:

— The housing has not been repaired within six months after the later of the date of a notice of violation or the time prescribed in the notice; or

— Good faith efforts for compliance have not been commenced.

(Sec. 24436.5(b), Rev. & Tax. Code)

"Substandard housing" also includes employee housing that has not been brought into compliance with the conditions stated in a notice of violation issued under the Employee Housing Act within 30 days of the date of the notice. (Sec. 24436.5(b), Rev. & Tax. Code)

However, deductions may be claimed for a period of three years for properties that have been rendered substandard as a result of a natural disaster. Deductions may also be claimed for properties for which financing cannot be obtained under certain circumstances and for housing that is found to be substandard because of a change in the local housing standards, unless the occupants are in danger. Also exempt from the prohibition against claiming deductions are lenders engaged in a "federally related transaction", as defined by statute, that acquire title to abandoned or unoccupied substandard housing through judicial or nonjudicial foreclosure, or that accept a deed in lieu of foreclosure. (24436.5(d), (e), and (h), Rev. & Tax. Code)

Owners of noncomplying units are required to notify the local regulatory agency when the property is sold or transferred, supplying the name of the new owner and the date of transfer. Extensive notification and reporting rules are provided. (Sec. 24436.5(c) and (f), Rev. & Tax. Code)

Other additions to the taxable income base are listed at ¶ 10-600.

[¶ 10-703] Additions--Recovery of Tax Benefit Items

Although California incorporates IRC Sec. 111, concerning the recovery of tax benefit items, California substitutes references to federal credits and credit carryovers with references to California corporation franchise (income) tax credits and credit carryovers. (Sec. 24310, Rev. & Tax Code) Under IRC Sec. 111 any income attributable to the recovery during the taxable year of any amount deducted in a prior taxable year is excludable from gross income in the year of the recovery to the extent that the amount did not reduce income subject to tax in the prior year. If a tax credit was allowable for a prior income year and during the current income year there is a downward price adjustment or similar adjustment, the tax for the current year must be increased by the amount of the prior credit attributable to the adjustment; however, no increase in the current year's tax is required to the extent that the credit allowable for the recovered amount did not reduce the prior year's tax.

Because California substitutes references to federal credits and credit carryovers with references to California corporation franchise and income tax credits and credit carryovers, differences may arise in the amount that must be added back. An additional amount required to be included on the California return is reported as an "other addition" on Line 8, Form 100, California Corporation Franchise or Income Tax Return and a supporting schedule must be attached.

Other additions to the taxable income base are listed at ¶ 10-600.

[¶ 10-704] Additions--Foreign Aircraft/Ships

Income derived from the operation of aircraft or ships by a foreign corporation is exempt from taxation if (1) the aircraft are registered or the vessels are documented in a foreign country, (2) the income of the corporation is exempt from national income taxation under a treaty which provides an equivalent exemption for U.S. corporations, and (3) local units of the foreign government do not tax U.S. corporations on income from operation of U.S. registered or documented aircraft or vessels. (Sec. 24320, Rev. & Tax. Code) Local governmental units are prohibited from directly taxing income excluded from taxation by Sec. 24320 and from levying any tax measured by income or profits from operation of foreign-registered vessels. (Sec. 24321, Rev. & Tax. Code)

IRC Sec. 883 contains a similar exemption but does not include the provision regarding taxation by local governments. Also, the federal provision generally does not apply to a foreign corporation that is not publicly traded if 50% or more of the value of the corporation's stock is owned by individuals who are not residents of any foreign country meeting the requirements described in the previous paragraph; California has not adopted any such exception. If as a result of the prohibition against local governments taxing such income, the income is not excludable for California corporation franchise or income tax return, but is excludable for federal purposes, such amount must be added to federal taxable income as an "other addition" on Line 8, Form 100, California Corporation Franchise or Income Tax Return, and a supporting schedule must be attached. Conversely, to the extent such income is included in federal taxable income, taxpayers may claim such amount as a deduction. (see ¶ 10-913 Subtractions—Foreign Aircraft/Ships)

Other additions to the taxable income base are listed at ¶ 10-600.

[¶ 10-705] Additions--Contributions to Certain Trusts

California corporate tax law does not incorporate or have any provision similar to IRC Sec. 192, which allows a taxpayer to claim a deduction for amounts contributed to a Black Lung Benefit Trust under IRC Sec. 501(c)(21). Consequently, such amounts must be claimed as an "other addition" on Line 8, Form 100, California Corporation Franchise or Income Tax Return, unless the trust is set up as a charitable organization the donations to which qualify for California's contribution deduction under Sec. 24357, Rev. & Tax. Code *et seq.* as discussed at ¶ 10-880 Subtractions—Charitable Items.

In addition. California corporate tax law does not incorporate or have any provision similar to IRC Sec. 194A Contributions to Employer Liability Trusts, which allows a taxpayer to claim a deduction for amounts contributed to an Employer Liability Trust under IRC Sec. 501(c)(22). Consequently, such amounts must be claimed as an "other addition" on Line 8, Form 100, California Corporation Franchise or Income Tax Return.

Other additions to the taxable income base are listed at ¶ 10-600.

[¶ 10-706] Additions--Damage Awards

In lieu of the federal deduction allowable under IRC Sec. 186 for recovery of certain damage awards, California law provides for "spreadback" relief in the taxation of income attributable to awards of compensatory damages for patent infringements, damages received for breach of contract or fiduciary relationship, and lump sum antitrust awards. For purposes of the provisions discussed below, California law disregards a fractional part of the month unless it amounts to more than half a month, in which case it is considered to be a month. (Sec. 24679, Rev. & Tax. Code) Consequently, taxpayers that received such awards must determine the amounts deductible under IRC Sec. 186 (the compensatory amount or the amount of the unrecovered losses sustained as a result of such compensable injury) for federal purposes and the amount deductible for California purposes (as described below) and make the appropriate addition or subtraction modification on Line 8 or Line 16, respectively, of Form 100, California Corporation Franchise or Income Tax Return.

• *Patent infringement damages*

The tax attributable to an award of compensatory damages for infringement of a patent may not exceed the increase in taxes that would have resulted had the amount of the award been included in gross income in equal installments for each month of the infringement. (Sec. 24675, Rev. & Tax. Code)

• *Breach of contract award*

When a corporation receives an award of $3,000 or more for breach of contract or fiduciary relationship, the tax on the award may not exceed the total amount of tax increases that would have resulted had the award been allocated to the income of the previous taxable year or years to reflect the amount of income that would have been received in each year but for the breach of contract. (Sec. 24677, Rev. & Tax. Code)

Regardless of the amount of the award, the corporation may deduct all credits and deductions for depletion, depreciation, etc., to which it would have been entitled had the income been received during the year in which it would have been received but for the breach of contract. However, these credits and deductions are allowed only with respect to that part of the award that represents the corporation's share of income from the actual operation of the property.

• *Damages from Clayton Act*

Tax attributable to a damages award under the Clayton Act may not exceed the total increases in taxes that would have resulted if the amount of the award had been included in equal installments for each month during the period in which the corporation sustained injuries resulting from antitrust violations. (Sec. 24678, Rev. & Tax. Code)

Other additions to the taxable income base are listed at ¶ 10-600 Additions to Taxable Income Base.

[¶ 10-707] Additions--Extraterritorial Income

California did not incorporate and had no provision similar to IRC Sec. 114, which provided an exclusion for extraterritorial income. Consequently, any such amounts excluded under federal law, to the extent not otherwise deductible, had to be added back for California purposes. IRC Sec. 114 was repealed by the American Jobs Creation Act of 2004 (AJCA) (P.L. 108-357), effective for tax years after 2006.

Other additions to the taxable income base are listed at ¶ 10-600.

[¶ 10-708] Additions--Life Insurance Payments

As to payments received other than those paid on death of the insured, gross income does not include amounts received under life insurance, endowment, or annuity contracts to the extent that the amounts received are equal to the premiums that were paid on the contracts. (Sec. 24302, Rev. & Tax. Code) This provision differs from IRC Sec. 72, dealing with annuities, which requires computation of an exclusion rate to determine the taxable portion of each payment received. To the extent the amount excludable under California law is less than that excludable under federal law, the amount should be listed as an "other addition" on Line 8, Form 100, California Corporation Franchise or Income Tax Return. Although California does not incorporate the other provisions of IRC Sec. 72, it does incorporate IRC Sec. 72(u), which specifies the tax treatment accorded annuities that are not held by natural persons. (Sec. 24272.2, Rev. & Tax. Code) Consequently no adjustment is required for such amounts.

Other additions to the taxable income base are listed at ¶ 10-600.

[¶ 10-709] Additions--Federal Drug Subsidies

California corporate tax law does not incorporate and does not have any provision similar to IRC Sec. 139A, which allows taxpayers to exclude special federal subsidies for prescription drug plans received under Sec. 1860D-22 of the Social Security Act. To the extent such amounts are excluded from federal taxable income, they must be added back for California corporation franchise and income tax purposes as an "other addition" on Line 8, Form 100, California Corporation Franchise or Income Tax Return.

[¶10-800] Subtractions from Taxable Income Base

The following items, to the extent included in federal adjusted gross income, may be subtracted for purposes of computing California net income:

Subtractions from income are reported on Form 100, California Corporation Franchise or Income Tax Return.

• *Disallowance of capital expenditures*

Amounts treated as capital expenditures may not be deducted. (Sec. 24421, Rev. & Tax. Code; Sec. 24422, Rev. & Tax. Code) The provision is the same as IRC 263(a), except for titles, internal references, and the following differences.

CCH COMMENT: *Federal "repair regulations."*— California follows the federal "repair regulations," which provide rules for distinguishing capital expenditures from deductible supply, repair, and maintenance costs. (*Tax News*, California Franchise Tax Board, March 2015)

Under both federal and California law, exceptions to the general prohibition against currently deducting depreciable expenses are provided for expenditures for certain business assets (see ¶10-900), the development of mines, research and experimental expenditures, soil and water conservation expenditures, expenditures by farmers for fertilizer, and expenditures for removal of architectural adaptations for seniors and the disabled (see ¶10-515 Federal Conformity and ¶10-830 Subtractions—Expense Items, for more details concerning these deductions). (Sec. 24422, Rev. & Tax. Code)

¶10-800

Federal, but not California law, also provides current expense deductions for expenditures for tertiary injectants under IRC Sec. 193 (see ¶10-665 Additions— Environmental or Pollution Control).

Conversely, California, but not federal law, previously allowed businesses located in enterprise zones or the former Los Angeles Revitalization Zone to currently expense a portion of the expenditures associated with the zone(s). (see ¶10-845 Subtractions—Targeted Business Activity or Zones) (Sec. 24422, Rev. & Tax. Code)

See ¶10-830 Subtractions—Depletion, for a discussion of the current expense deduction allowed for intangible drilling and development costs of oil, gas, and geothermal units. Once a taxpayer elects to currently expense such items, the election is binding.

California neither incorporates nor has provisions similar to IRC Sec. 263(d), IRC Sec. 263(f), or IRC Sec. 263(g), which provide special treatment for expenditures in connection with certain railroad stock, railroad ties, or certain interest and carrying costs in the case of straddles. Because California does not incorporate IRC Sec. 263(g), which prohibits a deduction for taxes and carrying charges for straddles, a deduction may be claimed on a taxpayer's California corporation franchise or income tax return for such amounts as long as the charges are qualified carrying charges under Sec. 24426, Rev. & Tax. Code. See ¶10-645 Additions—Expense Items for a discussion of expenditures in connection with certain railroad stock and railroad ties.

• *Deductions allocable to tax-exempt income*

Like federal law (IRC Sec. 265(a)), deduction of expenses allocable to tax-exempt income is not allowed. (Sec. 24425, Rev. & Tax. Code) Under the allocation and apportionment provisions of Sec. 25101*et seq.*, if some income is not included within a corporation's measure of tax, any deductions in connection with the production of such income may not be deducted from income attributable to such sources.

Also, under California law, no deduction is allowed for specified interest and other expenses paid or incurred to an insurer, if the insurer is a member of the taxpayer's commonly controlled group and the amount paid or incurred would constitute income to the insurer if the insurer were subject to California corporation franchise or income tax. The expenses to which this provision applies include:

— interest paid or incurred to an insurer in the taxpayer's commonly controlled group with respect to indebtedness (other than qualified marketable debt instruments), the principal amount of which is attributable to a contribution of money by a noninsurer member of the taxpayer's commonly controlled group to the capital of an insurer member of that group, including the principal amount of a loan arising from a direct or indirect transfer of money from that contribution to capital from one insurer to another insurer of the same commonly controlled group;

— interest paid or incurred to an insurer with respect to a note or other debt instrument (other than qualified marketable debt instruments) contributed to the capital of an insurer with respect to its stock by a noninsurer member of the commonly controlled group;

— interest paid or incurred within five years after the direct or indirect acquisition of the insurer by a member of the commonly controlled group (other than interest on qualified marketable debt instruments);

— interest paid or incurred during the taxable year to any insurer in the commonly controlled group multiplied by a disqualifying percentage;

¶10-800

— interest determined by multiplying the amount of interest paid or incurred to an insurer in the commonly controlled group by the ratio of the commonly controlled group determined under Sec. 24410(1)(d) for the taxable year (whether or not a dividend was paid or accrued in that year);

— an expense other than interest that is attributable to property formerly held by the taxpayer or a member of the taxpayer's commonly controlled group that was acquired by the insurer in a transaction in which gain was realized but not recognized by the taxpayer or a member of its commonly controlled group; and

— an expense other than interest that is attributable to property purchased with the proceeds attributable to a contribution by a noninsurer member of the taxpayers' commonly controlled group to the capital of an insurer member of that group, including amounts attributable to a direct or indirect transfer of money from that contribution from one insurer to another insurer in the same group.

Amounts that are described under more than one category will be included only in the category that will result in the highest disallowance amount. (Sec. 24425, Rev. & Tax. Code)

Additions to the taxable income base are discussed beginning at ¶10-600, and an overview of the taxable income computation is provided at ¶10-505.

[¶10-805] Subtractions--Net Operating Loss

Does California allow a net operating loss (NOL) deduction?

California allows a state NOL deduction. (Sec. 24416, Rev. & Tax. Code) Because the starting point for computing California corporation franchise and income tax liability is Line 28 of federal Form 1120, before the federal NOL and special deduction, taxpayers must calculate the California NOL deduction independently of the federal NOL deduction.

Computation of NOL. The California NOL is computed according to the provisions of IRC § 172 as of the current federal conformity date, but with significant modifications. (Sec. 24416, Rev. & Tax. Code)

Under IRC § 172(c) and § 172(d) as incorporated, "net operating loss" means the amount by which deductions for a taxable year exceed gross income, calculated without any NOL deduction. Under IRC § 172(b) as incorporated, an NOL that exceeds taxable income from the current year is carried over to the earliest taxable years to which it may be carried. (Sec. 24416, Rev. & Tax. Code)

California does not conform to the federal provision generally limiting the NOL deduction to 80% of taxable income for losses arising in taxable years beginning after December 31, 2017. (*2017 Summary of Federal Income Tax Changes*, California Franchise Tax Board, May 16, 2018)

Prior to 2004, the general California NOL deduction was limited to a percentage of the amount allowed under federal law. The deductible percentage was:

— 100% for NOLs incurred after 2003;

— 60% for NOLs incurred during 2002 and 2003;

— 55% for NOLs incurred in 2000 and 2001; and

— 50% for NOLs incurred prior to 2000.

The limitations on NOLs incurred prior to 2004 did not apply to NOLs incurred by businesses operating in an enterprise zone, former Los Angeles Revitalization Zone, local agency military base recovery area, or former program area; certain new or small businesses; and farming businesses affected by Pierce's disease. (Sec. 24416(b), Rev. & Tax. Code)

Multistate businesses. Corporations whose income is subject to allocation and apportionment must compute the amount of their NOL deduction by subtracting their "net loss for state purposes" from "net income for state purposes." "Net income (loss) for state purposes" is the sum of the net income or loss apportionable to California and the income or loss allocable to California as nonbusiness income. (Sec. 24416(h), Rev. & Tax. Code; Sec. 25108, Rev. & Tax. Code) Special rules also apply to NOLs incurred by members of a combined reporting group.

Suspension of NOL deduction. California has suspended the use of NOL deductions for the 2020—2022 taxable years, except for taxpayers with taxable income of less than $1 million for the taxable year. However, the carryover period for any NOL that is not deductible during those years as a result of the suspension provisions is extended by:

— one year for losses incurred during 2021;

— two years for losses incurred during 2020; and

— three years for losses incurred before 2020.

(Sec. 24416.23, Rev. & Tax. Code)

An NOL deduction also could not be claimed during the 2008—2011 taxable years, unless a taxpayer met specified income thresholds. However, the carryover period for any NOL that was not deductible during those years as a result of the suspension provisions was extended by:

— one year for losses incurred during 2010;

— two years for losses incurred during 2009;

— three years for losses incurred during 2008; and

— four years for losses incurred before 2008.

(Sec. 24416.21, Rev. & Tax. Code)

CCH PRACTICE TIP: Small business exemption from 2008—2011 NOL suspension. Qualified small businesses were exempt from the 2008—2011 NOL suspension. Different qualifying thresholds applied, depending on when the NOL was incurred or a carryover was claimed. For 2008 or 2009, an NOL deduction or carryover could be claimed by taxpayers with less than $500,000 of taxable income. For 2010 or 2011, only businesses with preapportioned income of less than $300,000 for the taxable year could claim the NOL deduction. "Preapportioned income" means net income, including business and nonbusiness income, after state adjustments and before the application of California's apportionment and allocation provisions. For taxpayers included or includable in a combined report, preapportioned income is determined at the aggregate level for all members included in a combined report, and not at the individual group member level. (Sec. 24416.21(d) and (e), Rev. & Tax. Code)

The California NOL deduction (including any of the enhanced NOL deductions available for special taxpayers) was also suspended for NOLs incurred during or carried over to the 2002 and 2003 taxable years. The carryover period for any NOL that was not deductible as a result of the suspension was extended by one year for losses incurred during 2002, and by two years for losses incurred prior to 2002. (Sec. 24416.3, Rev. & Tax. Code)

CCH PRACTICE TIP: Exception for certain disaster victims. Any NOL deduction attributable to the severe storms that occurred in March 2011 in Santa Cruz County, the severe winds that occurred in November 2011 in Los Angeles and San Bernardino Counties, or the wildfires that occurred in May 2014 in San Diego County may not be suspended, deferred, reduced, or otherwise diminished unless specifically provided for in enacted legislation. (Sec. 24347.11, Rev. & Tax. Code; Sec. 24347.12, Rev. & Tax. Code; Sec. 24347.13, Rev. & Tax. Code)

Mergers and acquisitions. California generally follows, as of California's current IRC conformity date, the IRC § 269 anti-abuse rules, the IRC § 381 carryover rules, and the IRC § 382 and § 384 loss limitation rules that govern the use of NOLs following corporate mergers and acquisitions. (Sec. 24451, Rev. & Tax. Code) However, California does not follow Internal Revenue Service Notice 2008-83, 2008-42 I.R.B. 905, issued on October 20, 2008, relating to the treatment of deductions under IRC § 382(h) following an ownership change. (Sec. 24458, Rev. & Tax. Code) Also, IRC § 382(n), which provides an exception from the application of the IRC § 382 limitations for certain ownership changes, does not apply for California purposes. (Sec. 24459, Rev. & Tax. Code) In addition, although California incorporates IRC § 381, California law substitutes references to the federal general business credit and credit for prior year minimum tax liability that may be carried over to the acquiring corporation with references to the allowable California credits. (Sec. 24471, Rev. & Tax. Code)

Apportionment. For California tax purposes:

— the limitation provided for in IRC § 382(b)(1) is applied on a pre-apportionment basis;

— the recognized built-in gains and losses provided for in IRC § 382(h)(2) are determined on a post-apportionment basis;

— the net unrealized built-in gains and losses provided for in IRC § 382(h)(3) are determined on a post-apportionment basis;

— the limitation of the use of excess credits provided for in IRC § 383(a)(1), which references the limitation provided for in IRC § 382, is applied on a pre-apportionment basis; and

— the recognized built-in gains provided for in IRC § 384(a)(2) are determined on a post-apportionment basis when considered for purposes relating to pre-acquisition losses, as also provided for in IRC § 384(a)(2).

In addition, when utilizing the examples contained in federal Treasury Regulation § 1.383-1(f), which illustrate the application of IRC § 383, the California corporate franchise tax rate provided in Sec. 23151, Rev. & Tax. Code and Sec. 23186, Rev. & Tax. Code should be substituted for the applicable federal corporate income tax referenced in the examples. (*Technical Advice Memorandum 2017-03*, California Franchise Tax Board, April 6, 2017)

S corporations. S corporations that incur an NOL during C corporation years cannot carry those losses forward to their S corporation years. S corporations may, however, deduct an NOL incurred during a year in which they elect to be treated as an S corporation. The NOL is also passed through to the S corporation's shareholders in the year in which the loss is incurred, and is taken into account in determining each shareholder's available NOL carryover. (Sec. 23802(d), Rev. & Tax. Code)

CCH PRACTICE TIP: Built-in gains tax. Although an S corporation generally may not apply an NOL incurred prior to its becoming an S corporation to offset income subject to the 1.5% tax on S corporations, losses incurred while the corporation was a C corporation may be applied against the S corporation's built-in gains tax. If the corporation incurred losses while it was a C corporation and an S corporation, and the S corporation is using C corporation losses to offset its built-in gains, the S corporation must complete two forms FTB 3805Q and attach them to Form 100S, California S Corporation Franchise or Income Tax Return.

Unused losses incurred while an S corporation was a C corporation are "unavailable" except as noted above, unless the S corporation reverts back to a C corporation or the carryover period expires. However, if an S corporation changes to a C corporation, any S corporation NOLs are lost. (Instructions, FTB 3805Q, Net Operating Loss (NOL) Computation and NOL and Disaster Loss Limitations—Corporations)

Forms. The following forms are used to claim California NOLs:

— FTB 3805Q, Net Operating Loss (NOL) Computation and NOL and Disaster Loss Limitations—Corporations

— FTB 3805Z, Enterprise Zone Deduction and Credit Summary

— FTB 3806, Los Angeles Revitalization Zone Net Operating Loss (NOL) Carryover Deduction

— FTB 3807, Local Agency Military Base Recovery Area Deduction and Credit Summary

— FTB 3809, Targeted Tax Area Deduction and Credit Summary

— FTB 3805D, Net Operating Loss (NOL) Computation and Limitation - Pierce's Disease

Does California allow NOL carryback and/or carryforward adjustments?

California NOLs may be carried forward for up to 20 years if incurred after 2007, 10 years if incurred after 1999 and before 2008, or five years if incurred before 2000. (Sec. 24416(e), Rev. & Tax. Code)

NOL carrybacks are eliminated for tax years after 2018. (Sec. 24416(d), Rev. & Tax. Code) However, for tax years 2013 through 2018, a two-year carryback is allowed, but it was phased in and limited to:

• 50% of the loss for NOLs incurred in 2013;

• 75% for NOLs incurred in 2014; and

• fully allowed for NOLs incurred thereafter.

(Sec. 24416(d), Rev. & Tax. Code; Sec. 24416.05, Rev. & Tax. Code; Sec. 24416.21(c), Rev. & Tax. Code) Different NOL carryover periods may apply for economic development area businesses, new or small businesses, and farming business affected by Pierce's disease.

California does not conform to the federal provision allowing indefinite NOL carryovers for losses arising in taxable years ending after December 31, 2017. (*2017 Summary of Federal Income Tax Changes*, California Franchise Tax Board, May 16, 2018)

CCH PRACTICE TIP: Suspension period inapplicable. An NOL incurred in 2013 may be carried back and be claimed on an amended return for the 2011 tax year, even though NOLs were suspended during the 2011 tax year. (Legal Ruling 2011-04, California Franchise Tax Board, September 23, 2011)

CCH POINTER: Interplay between the suspension and carryover/carryback provisions. The interplay between California's NOL suspension provisions, NOL limitations, and carryover/carryback provisions is extremely complex. Although California law allows an extended carryover period for NOLs that could not be claimed as a result of the suspension, the extended carryover periods do not apply to NOLs that could not be claimed because there was insufficient income to offset the NOL. Thus, when determining whether NOLs incurred in multiple tax years may be carried over or be carried back, taxpayers must claim the earliest-incurred NOL. If there is insufficient income to offset an NOL during a suspension year, the extended NOL carryover provisions will not apply, because the NOL deduction was not disallowed as a result of the suspension provisions. The FTB has issued Legal Ruling 2011-04 to explain these complex rules and illustrate how they are applied in hypothetical situations.

EXAMPLE: Example 1: W Corporation has a $20 million NOL from the 2006 taxable year and a $20 million NOL from the 2007 taxable year. W has $500,000 of income subject to tax in 2008, and $500,000 of income subject to tax in 2009. W does not have any income or loss in either the 2010 or 2011 taxable years.

W's 2006 NOL deduction is suspended for both the 2008 and 2009 taxable years, but W's 2007 NOL is not suspended for either 2008 or 2009. Because W's 2006 NOL must be taken into account first, $500,000 of W's 2006 NOL deduction for 2008 is suspended, and an additional $500,000 of W's 2006 NOL deduction is suspended for 2009. The small business exception to the suspension does not apply, because W did not have less than $500,000 in income. W's 2007 NOL is not affected by the suspension provisions in either 2008 or 2009 because the 2007 NOL could not be used until the 2006 NOL is fully absorbed.

Under the general NOL carryover provisions in effect for the 2006 tax year, W would be able to carry forward the NOL for 10 years through the 2016 taxable year. However, because the 2006 NOL could not be claimed in 2008 and 2009 due to the suspension provisions, W may carry over the 2006 NOL for an additional four years, until the end of the 2020 taxable year. Conversely, the 10-year carryover period that applies to the 2007 NOL is not extended, because none of W's 2007 NOL deduction was denied by operation of the suspension provisions.

EXAMPLE: Example 2: X Corporation has a $2,727,272.73 NOL from the 2001 taxable year, $500,000 of income subject to tax in 2002, and a $1,666,666.67 NOL from 2003. X does not have any income or loss from 2004 through 2007. X has $500,000 of income subject to tax in 2008. X does not have any income or loss from 2009 through 2012. In 2013, X has $1 million of income subject to tax.

Question: As of the first day of X's 2014 taxable year, what is the remaining carryover amount and carryover period for X's 2001 and 2003 NOLs?

Answer: On the first day of X's 2014 taxable year, X has a 2001 NOL carryover of $500,000, but does not have a 2003 NOL carryover, which expired unused.

X may only carryover $1.5 million of the NOL incurred in 2001, because under the NOL limitation provisions in effect during 2001, X's 2001 NOL is limited to 55% of its entire amount. The applicable carryover period for NOLs incurred in 2001 is 10 years. However, in 2002, $500,000 of X's 2001 NOL deduction is suspended under the 2002 suspension provision. Therefore, the carryover period for X's 2001 NOL carryover is extended by two taxable years. In 2008, $500,000 of X's 2001 NOL deduction is again denied because of the suspension in effect during 2008. So, the carryover period for X's 2001 NOL carryover is extended by an additional four taxable years. Thus, the 2001 NOL would expire at the end of X's 2017 taxable year, rather than the 2011 taxable year.

X may only carryover $1 million of the NOL incurred during 2003 due to the 60% limitation in effect during that year. The carryover period in effect during 2003 was 10 years. So, X's 2003 NOL would normally expire at the end of the 2013 taxable year. X's 2003 NOL is not suspended in 2008, because it could not be used until the 2001 NOL is fully absorbed. X must first use its 2001 NOL for X's 2013 taxable year. Thus, X would deduct $1 million of its $1.5 million 2001 NOL carryover at the end of the 2013 taxable year, leaving X with a $500,000 2001 NOL carryover remaining for use in the 2014 taxable year. As a result, X's 2003 NOL would expire unused at the end of X's 2013 taxable year because the 2001 NOL had not yet been fully absorbed and the 2003 NOL was thus not claimed, but not as a result of the suspension provisions. Thus, the carryover period for the 2003 NOL was not eligible for extension.

EXAMPLE: **Example 3:** Y Corporation has $300,000 of pre-apportionment income and $100,000 of income subject to tax in California for the 2011 taxable year. Y has a $100,000 NOL for each of the 2012 and 2013 taxable years, and has no NOL carryovers from any prior taxable years. Y has $75,000 of income subject to tax for the 2014 taxable year. Y does not waive its 2013 California NOL carryback.

Question: As of the first day of Y's 2015 taxable year, what are the carryover amounts and carryover periods of Y's 2012 and 2013 NOLs?

Answer: On the first day of Y's 2015 taxable year, Y's remaining 2012 NOL carryover is $25,000, and Y's remaining 2013 NOL carryover is $50,000.

Y cannot carry back its 2012 NOL, because it was incurred prior to the 2013 taxable year. Because Y did not elect to waive its 2013 carryback, it is required to carryback 50% of its NOL incurred in 2013. Although Y would not have been allowed to claim an NOL carryover in 2011 because it had $300,000 of income subject to tax, it is allowed an NOL deduction for its 2013 NOL carryback.

On the first day of Y's 2014 taxable year, Y's remaining 2012 NOL carryover is $100,000, and Y's remaining 2013 NOL carryover is $50,000. Y must first use its 2012 NOL for the 2014 taxable year. Y deducts $75,000 of its 2012 NOL in the 2014 taxable year, so that at the start of the 2015 taxable year, Y's remaining 2012 NOL carryover is $25,000.

New businesses. A new business, as defined in Sec. 24416(f) and (g), Rev. & Tax. Code and FTB Legal Ruling 96-5, that incurs NOLs after 1993 may claim a 100% NOL deduction for its first three years of business, but only to the extent of its net loss. The portion of the NOL deduction that exceeds the new business's net loss is carried over as a general NOL, and was subject to the applicable percentage limits for general NOLs incurred prior to the 2004 taxable year. "Net loss" means the amount of net loss after application of IRC § 465, which limits deductions to the amount at risk, and IRC § 469, which limits the amount of passive activity losses and credits. The NOL deduction for new businesses is subject to the same suspension periods that apply to other NOL deductions.

The carryover period for the new business NOL is currently the same as the general NOL carryover period. Previously, the carryover period was:

— eight years for NOLs incurred in the new business's first taxable year;

— seven years for NOLs incurred in the new business's second taxable year; and

— six years for NOLs incurred in the new business's third taxable year.

The amount of the NOL that exceeds the new business's net loss and was subject to the applicable percentage limits for computing the general NOL must be carried over and be exhausted prior to carrying over the enhanced portion of the NOL. (Sec. 24416(b) and (e), Rev. & Tax. Code)

> **CCH POINTER: *Relationship to general NOL.*** Because the NOL for both new and existing businesses is equal to 100% for taxable years beginning after 2003, and the carryover period for both is the same for taxable years beginning after 2007, unless new legislation is enacted there is no "enhanced" NOL deduction amount for new businesses or small businesses for NOLs incurred after the 2003 taxable year and no extended carryover period for new businesses for NOLs incurred after the 2007 taxable year. (*Legal Division Guidance 2011-10-01*, Franchise Tax Board, October 2011)

Small businesses. A small business, as defined in Sec. 24416(f), Rev. & Tax. Code and FTB Legal Ruling 96-5, may claim a 100% NOL deduction, but only to the extent that the NOL exceeds the small business's net loss. The portion of the NOL deduction that exceeds the small business's net loss is carried over as a general NOL, and was subject to the applicable percentage limits for general NOLs incurred prior to the 2004 taxable year. The NOL carryover period is the same as the general NOL carryover period. The NOL deduction for small businesses is subject to the same suspension periods that apply to other NOL deductions. The amount of the NOL that exceeds the new business's net loss and was subject to the applicable percentage limits for computing the general NOL must be carried over and be exhausted prior to carrying over the enhanced portion of the NOL. (Sec. 24416(b) and (e), Rev. & Tax. Code)

CCH CAUTION: Reclassification of NOL. The FTB may reclassify any new business NOL or small business NOL as a general NOL to prevent tax evasion. (Sec. 24416(k), Rev. & Tax. Code)

Farming businesses. Because California has its own NOL carryback provisions, the extended federal carryback provisions for farm losses do not apply. However, special NOL treatment is available for farming businesses whose crops were impacted by Pierce's disease and its carriers. For NOLs attributable to a farming business affected by Pierce's disease and its carriers in the 2001 and 2002 taxable years, the entire amount of the NOL may be carried forward to the nine taxable years following the taxable year of loss. The loss is apportioned to the area affected by Pierce's disease and its carriers by multiplying the total loss from the farming business by a fraction. The numerator of the fraction is the property factor plus the payroll factor, and the denominator of the fraction is two. An NOL carryover will be allowed only for the taxpayer's farming business income that is attributable to the area affected by Pierce's disease and its carriers. A taxpayer may use the special NOL carryover provision only if the California Department of Food and Agriculture determines that Pierce's disease and its carriers caused the NOL. (Sec. 24416.1, Rev. & Tax. Code; Sec. 24416.7, Rev. & Tax. Code)

Economic development area businesses. Special provisions authorize businesses in designated enterprise zones (EZs), local agency military base recovery areas (LAMBRAs), targeted tax areas (TTAs), and the former Los Angeles Revitalization Zone (LARZ), to carry forward 100% of an NOL generated in the zone or area in a taxable year beginning before 2008 for up to 15 years following the year of loss. For NOLs incurred in taxable years beginning after 2007, the general 20-year NOL carryover period applies. Taxpayers can no longer generate EZ or LAMBRA NOLs for taxable years beginning after 2013, TTA NOLs for taxable years beginning after 2012, or LARZ NOLs for taxable years beginning after 1997. However, taxpayers may carry over NOL deductions from prior years. (Sec. 24416.2(a)(1) and (a)(2)(D), Rev. & Tax. Code; Sec. 24416.4(a)(1) and (a)(7), Rev. & Tax. Code; Sec. 24416.5(a)(1) and (a)(8), Rev. & Tax. Code; Sec. 24416.6(b), Rev. & Tax. Code) The carryover period is limited to five years for financial institutions subject to special federal provisions governing the treatment reserves for financial institutions and investment companies (and located in the former LARZ or a LAMBRA). (Sec. 24416.4(a), Rev. & Tax. Code; Sec. 24416.5(a), Rev. & Tax. Code)

The NOL deductions for economic development area businesses are subject to the same suspension periods that apply to other NOL deductions. (Sec. 24416.3, Rev. & Tax. Code)

The loss attributable to a zone or area is computed by first determining the business income attributable to California sources using the standard allocation and apportionment procedures. That figure is further apportioned to the area or zone using a modified UDITPA formula, comprised of a payroll factor and a property factor. The numerators of the factors are limited to the property and payroll associated with the area or zone, and the denominators include the taxpayer's payroll and property paid in or located in California. (Sec. 24416.2(a)(2), Rev. & Tax. Code; Sec. 24416.4(a)(3), Rev. & Tax. Code; Sec. 24416.5(a)(5)—(7), Rev. & Tax. Code; Sec. 24416.6(b), Rev. & Tax. Code)

If a taxpayer elects to claim one of the enhanced NOL deductions, the provisions of IRC § 172(b)(1)(B) and § 172(b)(1)(C), providing special rules for real estate investment trusts and specified liability losses, do not apply. (Sec. 24416.1(a)(3), Rev. & Tax. Code)

Taxpayers wishing to claim an enhanced NOL deduction for a business located in an EZ, LAMBRA, TTA, or the former LARZ, had to make an irrevocable election specifying under which provisions the NOL was being claimed. The amount of the loss determined for that taxable year under the elected NOL provision is the only NOL allowed to be carried over from that taxable year. (Sec. 24416.1(c), Rev. & Tax. Code; Sec. 24416.2(b)-(d), Rev. & Tax. Code; Sec. 24416.4(c)-(e), Rev. & Tax. Code; Sec. 24416.5(b)-(d), Rev. & Tax. Code; Sec. 24416.6(c)-(e)) The following special rules apply:

EZs. Any carryover of an NOL sustained by a qualified EZ taxpayer under Sec. 24416.2, Rev. & Tax. Code, as that section read prior to 1997, was required to be computed under the pre-1997 rules. (Sec. 24416.1(d), Rev. & Tax. Code)

LAMBRAs. Only qualified taxpayers operating within a LAMBRA could claim the enhanced LAMBRA NOL deduction. To qualify, a taxpayer had to conduct a trade or business within the LAMBRA and for the first two taxable years after commencing operations in the LAMBRA have a net increase in jobs (defined as 2,000 paid hours per employee per year) of one or more employees in the LAMBRA and in California. Only taxpayers with a net increase in jobs in California and with one or more full-time employees employed within the LAMBRA could claim the deduction. (Sec. 24416.5(a)(4), Rev. & Tax. Code) Taxpayers could claim the enhanced NOL deduction in their first year of operation even if they had not fulfilled the net increase in jobs requirement. However, if after the second taxable year of operation they did not satisfy the requirement, the enhanced NOL deduction claimed during the prior year could be recaptured. (FTB 3807 Booklet, Local Agency Military Base Recovery Area Businesses)

TTAs. Only taxpayers located in a TTA and involved in the following business activities described in the federal Standard Industry Classification Manual or North American Industry Classification System Manual were eligible to claim the enhanced TTA NOL deduction: manufacturing; transportation; communications; electric, gas, and sanitary services; and wholesale trade. (Sec. 24416.6(a), Rev. & Tax. Code)

Waiver of carryback period. Because California follows the federal NOL treatment prior to its amendment by the Tax Cuts and Jobs Act of 2017, except as specifically modified, California follows the federal waiver provisions. (Sec. 24416(d), Rev. & Tax. Code; Sec. 24416.21(c), Rev. & Tax. Code)

CCH PRACTICE TIP: Separate California election. California law allows taxpayers to make separate elections for California purposes, unless specifically prohibited by statute or regulation. There are currently no statutes or regulations prohibiting a taxpayer from making a separate election to waive the carryback period for California corporation franchise and income tax purposes. (Sec. 23051.5(e), Rev. & Tax. Code)

Other subtractions from the taxable income base are listed at ¶10-800 Subtractions From Taxable Income Base.

Nonconformity to certain IRC Sec. 172 special rules

For tax years after 2018, California does not conform to the following federal provisions:

- IRC Sec. 172(b)(1)(B), relating to special rules for REITs
- IRC Sec. 172(b)(1)(E), relating to excess interest loss; and
- IRC Sec. 172(h), relating to corporate equity reduction interest losses.

(Sec. 24416(d), Rev. & Tax. Code)

[¶10-810] Subtractions--Dividends

Because California begins with Line 28, Federal Form 1120, before claiming the net operating loss and special deductions, including the federal dividends received deduction, California's deductions are calculated independently of the federal dividends received deduction. California law authorizes an intercompany dividend deduction for unitary businesses, a deduction for IRC Sec. 78 gross-up of dividends, a deduction for dividends received from corporations taxed by California, and a deduction for dividends received from an insurance company subsidiary. The latter two deductions have been the subject of intensive litigation (see discussions below), however, California enacted a new deduction for dividends received from an insurance company subsidiary applicable to post-2003 taxable years. Water's-edge taxpayer's may also deduct dividends received from foreign corporations (see ¶11-550).

The elimination of intercompany dividends and the deduction for dividends received from insurance company subsidiaries are computed on Schedule H (100), Dividend Income Deduction. The IRC Sec. 78 gross-up of dividends deduction is treated as an "other deduction" claimed on Line 16, Form 100, California Corporation Franchise or Income Tax Return.

• *Intercompany dividend deduction*

Dividends received from a unitary subsidiary are deducted but only to the extent that the dividends are paid from unitary earnings and profits accumulated while both the payee and the payer corporation were members of a combined report (see ¶11-550). (Sec. 25106, Rev. & Tax. Code; Instructions, Schedule H (100), Dividend Income Deduction)

Dividend elimination is available whether or not the members of the group are California taxpayers. Dividends paid by a group member may be eliminated even if no group members were subject to California taxation at the time the income was earned as long as the income would have been included in a California combined report had any of the group members been subject to California taxation at the time that the income was earned. (Sec. 25106(a), Rev. & Tax. Code)

Intercompany dividends may also be eliminated if paid from the unitary group's income to a newly formed corporation if the recipient corporation was part of the unitary group from the time it was formed until the time the dividends were received.

Tax evasion.—The FTB may deny the elimination of intercompany dividends available to members of a unitary combined reporting group if the FTB determines that the transaction is entered into or structured with a principal purpose of evading California corporation franchise or income taxes. (Sec. 25106(a)(2)(B), Rev. & Tax. Code)

• *IRC Sec. 78 gross-up of dividends*

The California Corporation Tax Law has no provision comparable to IRC Sec. 78, which requires a domestic corporation that elects the foreign tax credit for a proportionate part of foreign taxes paid by a foreign corporation from which the domestic corporation has received dividends to include in gross income not only the actual dividends received from such foreign corporation, but also the foreign taxes it is deemed to have paid. Consequently, California corporations, which must use their federal taxable income as a starting point in computing California taxes may deduct from gross income the amount of their IRC Sec. 78 gross-up of dividends. (*Letter to CCH*, FTB, March 25, 1987) The deduction is claimed as an "other deduction" on Line 16, Form 100, California Corporation Franchise or Income Tax Return.

• *Dividends received from corporations taxed by California*

Prior to its being struck down as unconstitutional in *Farmer Bros. Co. v. Franchise Tax Board*, California Court of Appeal, Second Appellate District, 108 Cal.App.4th 936, 134 Cal.Rptr.2d 390 (2003), U.S. Supreme Court, Dkt. 03-776, petition for certiorari denied February 23, 2004, Sec. 24402, Rev. & Tax. Code, allowed a corporation to deduct from gross income all or part of a dividend received from another corporation if it was paid out of income that was "included in the measure" of California franchise tax or corporation income tax and met the holding periods discussed below. A corporate taxpayer could deduct 100% of a dividend received from a bank or corporation in which the taxpayer owned more than 50% of the stock; 80% of a dividend received from a corporation in which the taxpayer owned between 20% and 50% of the stock; and 70% of a dividend received from a corporation in which the taxpayer owned less than 20% of the stock. The California provision was generally similar to IRC Sec. 243—IRC Sec. 247, under which a corporation may deduct 70% (80% in the case of a 20% owned corporation) of the amount of dividends received from another domestic corporation, 100% of the amount of dividends received from a small business investment company, and 100% of qualifying dividends received from an affiliated corporation. (Sec. 24402, Rev. & Tax. Code; Reg. 24402, 18 CCR)

CCH COMMENT: *Constitutionality and remedy.*—Following the reasoning of the U.S. Supreme Court in *Fulton Corp. v. Faulkner* (1996) 516 U.S. 325, 331 [116 S.Ct. 848, 854, 133 L.Ed.2d 796] and a California court of appeal in *Ceridian Corp. v. Franchise Tax Board*, CtApp, No. A084298, 85 Cal.App. 4th 875, 102 Cal.Rptr. 2d 611 (2000), a California court of appeal struck down California's dividends received deduction as facially discriminatory under the U.S. Constitution's Commerce Clause. (*Farmer Bros. Co. v. Franchise Tax Board*, 108 Cal.App.4th 936, 134 Cal.Rptr.2d 390 (2003))

The appellate court in *Farmer Bros.* did not address the remedy issue as the FTB failed to appeal this issue. The California Legislative Counsel has taken the position that under Rev. & Tax. Code Sec. 19393, the FTB has the authority to recompute a taxpayer's tax liability if a statute has been declared invalid. (*Legislative Counsel Opinion*, No. 24420, March 21, 2002) Following this reasoning, the FTB has issued a resolution stating its intention to retroactively deny all dividend deductions under Sec. 24402 for all taxpayers for all open tax years. This approach was upheld in an unpublished appellate court decision in *Abbott Laboratories v. Franchise Tax Board*, California Court of Appeal, Second Appellate District, No. B204210, July 21, 2009, modified August 6, 2009.

In an internal memorandum sent to the FTB's audit staff, the FTB has outlined its post-*Farmer Bros.* decision policies for dealing with returns in which a dividends received deduction was claimed. For tax years ending after November 30, 1999, the FTB will disallow all Sec. 24402 deductions. Expenses associated with the dividend income that were previously added back because the dividend income was not included in the measure of tax, should be subtracted. For tax years ending prior to December 1, 1999, all dividends received from non-insurance corporations are deductible, subject to the statutory ownership limitations. However, expenses associated with the dividend income must be added back to federal taxable income for purposes of computing California taxable income. (*Memorandum*, FTB, Multistate Audit Program Bureau, May 17, 2004)

In *General Motors Corp. v. Franchise Tax Board*, (2004) 120 Cal.App.4th 114, the California court of appeal upheld the lower court's granting of a refund resulting from the court's granting of a deduction for dividends received from an insurance company subsidiary. Following the reasoning of the appellate court in *Farmers Bros. Co. v. FTB*, (2003) 108 Cal.App.4th 936, 134 Cal.Rptr.2d 390, the court determined that California's dividends received deduction under Rev. and Tax Code Sec. 24402 was facially discriminatory, and therefore unconstitutional, because it only allowed taxpayers to claim a dividends received deduction if the dividends were paid from a California corporation. Therefore, the court allowed the taxpayer to claim the deduction for dividends received by its insurance company subsidiary. The decision did not address whether the deduction could be claimed for a dividend paid by a corporation subject to an insurance premiums tax rather than the corporation franchise tax.

COMMENT: *Implementation of Farmer Bros. decision.*—A California court of appeal has upheld the FTB's denial of a taxpayer's deductions for dividends received in 1999 and 2000 from corporations taxed by California, following the California court of appeal's decision in *Farmer Bros.* (*River Garden Retirement Home v. Franchise Tax Board*, CalCtApp, No. A123316, July 15, 2010) Contrary to the taxpayer's assertions on appeal, Sec. 24402 could not be saved by severance of the offending language or by reformation. Such action would have been inconsistent with the Legislature's intent. Also, the FTB had the authority to remedy the Commerce Clause violation infecting Sec. 24402, and the remedy of disallowing the dividends received deductions for the years at issue did not violate the due process prohibition against excessively retroactive tax increases. Deductions are a matter of legislative grace, and the taxpayer had no vested right in the dividends received deduction. Furthermore, the period of retroactivity embedded in the FTB's remedy coincided squarely with the four-year statute of limitations for issuing a deficiency assessment, adding reasonableness to the remedy. The FTB's decision to recoup the deductions for the years at issue also did not run afoul of Art. XIII A, Sec. 3, of the California Constitution, which requires a two-thirds vote of the Legislature to enact revenue increasing tax laws. The FTB's disallowance of the dividends received deduction was a policy directive undertaken under the authority of state and federal law. The FTB did not enact anything within the meaning of the law. Moreover, the purpose of the policy directive was to rectify the Commerce Clause inequities caused by Sec. 24402, and not to increase revenues.

As noted above, the denial of deductions for open tax years was also upheld by an appellate court in *Abbott Laboratories v. Franchise Tax Board*, California Court of Appeal, Second Appellate District, No. B204210, July 21, 2009, modified August 6, 2009.

Holding periods.—Under both California law and federal law (IRC Sec. 246(c)), a deduction for dividends received may not be claimed if the dividend paying stock is held less than 46 days during the 90-day period that begins 45 days before the stock becomes ex-dividend with respect to the dividend. The holding period for dividends on preferred stock attributable to a period or periods in excess of 366 days is increased to 91 days during the 180-day period that begins 90 days before the stock becomes ex-dividend with respect to the dividend.

The day of disposition, but not the day of acquisition, is accounted for in determining the period of time a taxpayer has held a share of stock. Also, IRC Sec. 1223(4) does not apply to this determination for state tax purposes. Finally, the holding period is reduced when the risk of loss on stock held by a taxpayer is diminished because the taxpayer has (a) an option to sell, is under an obligation to sell, or has made (and not closed) a short sale of substantially identical stock or securities; (b) granted an option to purchase substantially identical stock or securities; or (c) reduced the risk by holding one or more other positions with respect to substantially similar or related property. (Sec. 24402, Rev. & Tax. Code)

- *Dividends received from subsidiary insurance company*

A deduction is allowed for a portion of the qualified dividends received by a corporation or by members of the corporation's commonly controlled group (if any) from an insurance company subsidiary, regardless of whether the insurance company is engaged in business in California, if at the time of each dividend payment at least 80% of each class of stock of the insurer was owned by the corporation receiving the dividend. The deduction is equal to 85% of the qualified dividends received. (Sec. 24410, Rev. & Tax. Code) The deduction is computed on Sch. H (Form 100), Dividend Income Deduction.

Disincentives to overcapitalization of insurance company subsidiaries.—Dividends qualifying for the deduction must be reduced on the basis of an overcapitalization percentage. The overcapitalization percentage is calculated by dividing the five-year average of net written premiums for all insurance companies in the insurance company's commonly controlled group by the five-year average of total income for all insurance companies in the insurance company's commonly controlled group. If the overcapitalization percentage is 70% or greater, the dividends qualifying for the deduction will not be reduced. If the overcapitalization percentage is greater than 10% and less than 70%, the dividends qualifying for the deduction will be ratably reduced for each percentage point by which the overcapitalization percentage falls below 70%. If the overcapitalization percentage is 10% or less, the dividends qualifying for the deduction will be reduced to zero. (Sec. 24410, Rev. & Tax. Code)

Special rules for dividends from self-insurance companies.—Special rules apply to dividends received from an insurance company that insures risks of a member of its commonly controlled group. Premiums received or accrued from another member of the insurance company's commonly controlled group will not be included in the overcapitalization ratio calculation. Furthermore, dividends attributable to premiums received or accrued by the insurance company from a member of the insurance company's commonly controlled group will not qualify for the dividends-received deduction. (Sec. 24410, Rev. & Tax. Code)

- *Expenses allocable to tax-exempt income*

Taxpayers are prohibited from deducting expenses allocable to earning tax-exempt income (see ¶10-800). (Sec. 24425, Rev. & Tax. Code) Consequently, the California Supreme Court disallowed deductions claimed for expenses attributable to exempt dividend income received by a foreign corporation from a California corporation because dividends were not included in the measure of tax. (*Great Western Financial Corp. v. Franchise Tax Board*, 4 Cal3d 1, 479 P2d 993 (1971))

Other subtractions from the taxable income base are listed at ¶ 10-800 Subtractions From Taxable Income Base.

[¶10-815] Subtractions--Interest

Taxpayers may subtract interest from specified government obligations and interest paid or accrued for the production of income. California taxpayers are prohibited from claiming an interest expense deduction for interest expenses allocable to earning tax-exempt income (see ¶ 10-800 Subtractions from Taxable Income Base).

• *Interest from government obligations*

In contrast to the corporation franchise tax, the corporate income tax is subject to the federal prohibition against states taxing interest from federal obligations. (Sec. 3124, U.S.C.) In addition, California law exempts from California corporate income tax income from bonds issued by the state of California or by a local government within the state. (Sec. 26(b), Art. XIII, Cal. Const.) Because interest from all federal and California obligations is added back to federal taxable income on Line 4, Form 100, California Corporation Franchise or Income Tax Return (see ¶ 10-840 Subtractions—Taxes), interest received from exempt federal and California obligations must be subtracted for purposes of computing California net income. The subtraction amount is entered as an "other deduction" on Line 16, Form 100, California Corporation Franchise or Income Tax Return. (Instructions, Form 100, California Corporation Franchise or Income Tax Return)

• *Interest expense deduction*

IRC Sec. 163, incorporated as of the California conformity date (see ¶ 10-515), concerning the deduction of interest paid or accrued, is incorporated by reference into California law with modifications concerning (1) taxpayers who are required to allocate or apportion income under the Uniform Division of Income for Tax Purposes Act or that make a water's edge election and (2) taxpayers with interest expense incurred for purposes of foreign investments. (Sec. 24344(a), Rev. & Tax. Code; Reg. 24344(a), 18 CCR) Because of California's conformity date, California has not conformed to the federal limitations on deductions of business interest, as enacted by the Tax Cuts and Jobs Act of 2017 applicable to taxable years beginning after December 31, 2017. (*2017 Summary of Federal Income Tax Changes*, California Franchise Tax Board, May 16, 2018)

Interest offset rule (pre-Hunt-Wesson).—One area of intense litigation centered on California's Sec. 24344(b), Rev. & Tax. Code, the interest offset rule, whereby corporations subject to allocation and apportionment or to water's-edge treatment are limited in the amount of interest expense they may deduct depending on the amount of income attributable to "business income" taxable by California or "nonbusiness income" attributable to another state and not taxable by California. Unlike most other deductions, which treat all of a taxpayer's income the same, whether or not attributable to business or nonbusiness income, by differentiating between business and nonbusiness income for purposes of determining the amount of interest expense that may be deducted, the interest off-set rule determines the amount of the deduction on the basis of the taxpayer's source of income.

For taxpayers subject to apportionment the interest deductible under Sec. 24344(b), Rev. & Tax. Code, as written, is equal to the interest income subject to apportionment ("business income" as discussed at ¶ 11-510 Income Subject to Allocation and Apportionment), plus the amount, if any, by which the remaining interest expense exceeds interest and dividend income (except dividends deductible under Sec. 24402, Rev. & Tax Code and dividends subject to the deductions provided for in Sec. 24411, Rev. & Tax. Code to the extent of those deductions) not subject to formula apportionment ("nonbusiness income", see ¶ 11-510 for details). Interest not included in the preceding sentence is directly offset against nonbusiness interest and dividend income (except dividends deductible under Sec. 24402, Rev. & Tax. Code and dividends subject to the deductions provided for in Sec. 24411, Rev. & Tax. Code to the extent of those deductions as discussed at ¶ 10-810 Subtractions—Dividends).

The U.S. Supreme Court has held that the offset provision in Sec. 24344(b) violates the Due Process Clause and the Commerce Clause of the U.S. Constitution because it imposes tax on income outside California's jurisdictional reach (see *Hunt-Wesson, Inc. v. Franchise Tax Board*, 538 U.S. 458 (2000)). Under Sec. 24344(b), the nondomiciliary taxpayer's interest expense deduction in excess of business interest income was reduced dollar for dollar by the amount of nonbusiness interest and dividend income. Although the offset provision does not directly tax nonunitary income, it does in effect constitute indirect taxation of such income, the Court said. The Court noted that offset provisions reasonably reflecting the proper allocation of interest expenses to unitary and nonunitary income would be constitutionally acceptable. However, by reducing a nondomiciliary's interest expense deduction in the precise amount of nonunitary income, the California offset scheme does not reasonably allocate the portion of interest expenses incurred to the generation of actual nonunitary income related to such expenses. The Court therefore held that inclusion of nontaxable income in California's existing offset computation scheme constitutes impermissible taxation of a nondomiciliary's nonunitary income.

Interest offset rule (post-Hunt-Wesson).—The FTB issued *FTB Notice 2000-9* to explain the deductibility of interest expense in light of the U.S. Supreme Court decision in *Hunt-Wesson*. The FTB policy, discussed below, is that the interest-offset provision invalidated in *Hunt-Wesson* will not be applied to nondomiciliary corporations, but that all other provisions in the interest-offset rules will continue to apply.

Based on the notice, domestic and foreign corporations must compute their allowable interest expense deduction differently. Foreign (*i.e.,* non-California) corporations allocate their interest expense between apportionable and nonapportionable income as follows:

(1) A deduction for interest expense equal to business interest income may be claimed in computing income subject to apportionment.

(2) A deduction for interest expense in excess of business interest income may be claimed in computing income subject to apportionment in an amount equal to the amount of nonbusiness interest and dividend income.

(3) Any interest expense in excess of interest income and nonbusiness dividend income may be assigned to other types of nonbusiness income, such as rents and royalties, under authority of Reg. 25120(d). Interest expense assigned to such nonbusiness income items would not be deductible in determining apportionable income. Note, however, that the FTB will not apply Regulation Section 25120(d) to assign interest expense to assets that have the potential to generate interest and dividend income. In other words, the FTB will not use the regulation to assign interest expense to capital gains or losses from sales or other exchanges of stocks, bonds, and similar instruments.

¶ 10-815

(4) Any remaining interest expense (after applying steps 1 through 3) is deductible against apportionable income.

For domestic (*i.e.*, California) corporations, interest expense is allocated in the same manner, except that step 2 is modified to provide that interest expense in excess of business interest income may reduce nonbusiness interest and dividend income allocable to California in an amount equal to the amount of nonbusiness interest and dividend income. In other words, California corporations continue to enjoy a full offset of interest expense against nonbusiness interest and dividend income.

The above steps are illustrated in examples provided by the FTB in *FTB Notice 2000-9*.

Assumptions:
$400 Total Interest Expense
$200 Interest expense directly traceable to nonbusiness stock
$ 50 Interest expense directly traceable to a nonbusiness mortgage assigned to California
$100 Business interest income
$100 Nonbusiness dividend income
The only nonbusiness items are the nonbusiness stock and property securing the mortgage.

California Apportionment Percentage — 50%
Non-California Domiciliary

Interest Assignment	Business Assigned	Nonbusiness Assigned	Unassigned Interest
Total Interest Expense			$400
Business Interest Income	$100		$300
Nonbusiness Dividends & Interest	$100		$200
Mortgage 25120(d)		$50 (California)	$150
Residue	$150		0
Total	$350	$50 (California)	

Total Deduction attributable to California ($350 × 50%) + 50 = $225

California Domiciliary

Interest Assignment	Business Assigned	Nonbusiness Assigned	Unassigned Interest
Total Interest Expense			$400
Business Interest Income	$100		$300
Nonbusiness Dividends & Interest		$100 (California)	$200
Mortgage 25120(d)		$50 (California)	$150
Residue	$150		0
Total	$250	$150 (California)	

Total Deduction Attributable to California ($250 × 50%) + $150 = $275

Interest on foreign investments.—Interest expense allowable under IRC Sec. 163 that is incurred for purposes of foreign investments may be offset against foreign dividends deductible under Sec. 24411, Rev. & Tax. Code (see ¶ 10-810 Subtractions—Dividends). The amount of interest that may be offset against foreign dividends is determined by multiplying the interest deductible under IRC Sec. 163 by the same percentage used to determine the dividend deduction under Sec. 24411, Rev. & Tax. Code. (Sec. 24344(c), Rev. & Tax. Code) To the extent this interest expense was already deducted in computing federal taxable income, taxpayers should add such amounts back to federal taxable income as an "other addition" on Line 8, Form 100, California Corporation Franchise or Income Tax Return, recompute the deductible amount under California law, and subtract the recomputed amount as an "other deduction" on Line 16, Form 100, California Corporation Franchise or Income Tax Return.

Original issue discount (OID).—California incorporates IRC Sec. 163(e), concerning the deduction of original issue discount (OID) on certain debt instruments, as of the current California federal conformity date (see ¶10-515), with certain modifications that are discussed below. (Sec. 24344(a), Rev. & Tax. Code) For any taxable year beginning after 1986 and before the taxable year in which the obligation-bearing OID matures or is sold, exchanged, or otherwise disposed of, the amount of OID deductible for California purposes is the same as the amount deductible on the federal tax return. Consequently, no adjustment is required. For obligations issued after 1984, any difference between the amount deductible on the federal return and the amount deductible for California purposes for any taxable year that began before 1987 is deductible in the taxable year in which the debt instrument ultimately matures or is sold, exchanged, or otherwise disposed of. (Sec. 24344.5, Rev. & Tax. Code) If differences exist, the federal deduction should be added back to federal taxable income as an "other addition" on Line 8, Form 100, California Corporation Franchise or Income Tax Return and the California amount should be subtracted from federal taxable income as an "other deduction" on Line 16, Form 100, California Corporation Franchise or Income Tax Return. The inclusion of original issue discount in the income of the holder of the debt instrument is discussed at ¶10-640 Additions—Gains.

Disqualified interest.—Under the earnings stripping rules of IRC Sec. 163(j), incorporated as of the current California conformity date (see ¶10-515), a corporation that has excess interest expense for the tax year and that has a debt-to-equity ratio at the close of the taxable year of greater than 1.5 to 1 may not deduct interest paid or accrued to a related tax-exempt entity. (Sec. 24344, Rev. & Tax. Code) IRC Sec. 163(j), as incorporated, also applies to interest paid or accrued with respect to an indebtedness to a nonrelated entity if the indebtedness is guaranteed by a related entity and no gross basis tax is imposed with respect to such interest.

For purposes of IRC Sec. 163(j), as incorporated by California, all members of the same combined report (affiliated group for federal purposes) are treated as one taxpayer; see ¶11-550 for a discussion of combined reports. (Sec. 24344(e), Rev. & Tax. Code)

Other subtractions from the taxable income base are listed at ¶10-800 Subtractions From Taxable Income Base.

[¶10-820] Subtractions--Losses

California incorporates IRC Sec. 165, under which deductions are allowed for any uncompensated losses sustained during the taxable year. (Sec. 24347, Rev. & Tax. Code) Losses from thefts are treated as sustained during the taxable year the loss is discovered by the taxpayer. If a security becomes worthless during the taxable year, the loss is treated as a loss from its sale or exchange on the last day of the taxable year. The basis for determining the loss deduction is the adjusted basis for determining the loss from sale or other disposition of property, see ¶10-690 Additions—Basis Adjustments.

To the extent that taxpayers treat their losses the same for federal and California corporation franchise or income tax purposes, no adjustments are required. Below is a discussion of the areas where California law differs from federal law.

For a discussion of ordinary gains and losses, see ¶10-635 Additions—Losses and ¶10-640 Additions—Gains. Net operating losses are discussed at ¶10-805 Subtractions—Net Operating Loss. Adjustments required as a result of California's modification of the federal limitations on passive losses and credits are discussed in detail at ¶10-635 Additions—Losses.

• *Disaster losses*

California incorporates, with modifications, IRC Sec. 165(i), which allows taxpayers who sustain disaster losses in a Presidentially-declared disaster area to elect to take a deduction for those losses in the taxable year preceding the year of the loss. (Sec. 24347, Rev. & Tax. Code) For the 2014 to 2023 taxable years, the California deduction may be claimed for the immediately preceding taxable year **or** the taxable year in which the disaster occurred for any loss sustained as a result of a disaster occurring in any city, county, or city and county in the state that is proclaimed by the Governor to be in a state of emergency (without requiring separate legislative action). (Sec. 24347.14, Rev. & Tax. Code)

COMPLIANCE NOTE: Any law, other than Sec. 24416.20, Rev. & Tax. Code, that suspends, defers, reduces, or otherwise diminishes a net operating loss (NOL) deduction does not apply for the 2014 to 2023 taxable years to an NOL attributable to a loss sustained as a result of any disaster occurring in any city, county, or city and county in this state that is proclaimed by the Governor to be in a state of emergency. (Sec. 24347.14(c), Rev. & Tax. Code) If a taxpayer has both disaster loss carryovers and NOL carryovers, they must be used in the order that the taxpayer incurred them. There is no requirement to deduct NOL carryovers before disaster loss carryovers. (FTB Publication 1034, Disaster Loss - How to Claim a State Tax Deduction)

In 2020, at the time this book went to press, the President and/or Governor declared a state of emergency for the following disasters:

— Wildfires - Fresno, Los Angeles, Madera, Mendocino, Napa, San Bernardino, San Diego, Shasta, Siskiyou, and Sonoma (September 2020)

— Fires and Extreme Weather Conditions - Butte, Lake, Monterey, Napa, San Mateo, Santa Clara, Santa Cruz, Solano, Sonoma, and Yolo (August and September 2020); and

— Fires and Extreme Weather Conditions - All other California counties not listed above (August and September 2020).

In 2019, the President and/or Governor declared a state of emergency for the following disasters:

— Extreme Wind and Fire Weather Conditions - All California counties (October 2019);

— Kincade and Tick Fires - Los Angeles, Sonoma (October 2019);

— Eagle, Reche, Saddleridge, Sandalwood, and Wolf Fires in - Los Angeles and Riverside counties (October 2019);

— Earthquake - Kern and San Bernardino counties (July 2019);

— Atmospheric River Storm System - Amador, Glenn, Lake, Mendocino, and Sonoma counties (February 2019); and

— Atmospheric River Storm System - Calaveras, El Dorado, Humboldt, Los Angeles, Marin, Mendocino, Modoc, Mono, Monterey, Orange, Riverside, San Bernardino, San Diego, San Mateo, Santa Barbara, Santa Clara, Shasta, Tehama, Trinity, Ventura, and Yolo counties (January and February 2019).

In 2018, the President and/or Governor declared a state of emergency for the following disasters:

— Fire - Orange and Riverside counties (August 2018);

— Fires - Lake, Mariposa, Mendocino, Napa, Riverside, San Diego, Santa Barbara, Shasta, and Siskiyou counties (July 2018);

— Rainstorm - San Bernardino county (July 2018);

— Fire - Lake county (June 2018);

— Storms in - Amador, Fresno, Kern, Mariposa, Merced, Stanislaus, Tulare, and Tuolumne counties (March 2018); and

— Mudslides - Santa Barbara and Ventura Counties (January 2018).

In 2017, the President and/or Governor declared a state of emergency for the following disasters:

— Wildfires - Los Angeles, San Diego, Santa Barbara, and Ventura Counties (December 2017);

— Winter Storms - Inyo and Mono Counties (October 2017);

— Wildfires - Butte, Lake, Mendocino, Napa, Nevada, Orange, Solano, Sonoma, and Yuba Counties (October 2017);

— Wildfires - Los Angeles County (September 2017);

— Wildfires - Madera, Mariposa, and Tulare Counties (August and September 2017);

— Wildfires - Butte and Trinity Counties (August 2017);

— Rainstorms - San Bernardino County (July 2017);

— Wildfires - Butte, Mariposa, Modoc, and Santa Barbara Counties (July 2017);

— Winter Storms - Alameda, Amador, Butte, Calaveras, El Dorado, Humboldt, Lake, Lassen, Marin, Mendocino, Merced, Mono, Monterey, Napa, Nevada, Placer, Plumas, Sacramento, San Benito, San Luis Obispo, Santa Clara, Santa Cruz, Shasta, Sierra, Siskiyou, Sonoma, Sutter, Trinity, Tuolumne, Yolo, and Yuba Counties declared by President and Governor (Alpine, Colusa, Del Norte, Fresno, Glenn, Kern, Kings, Los Angeles, Mariposa, Modoc, San Bernardino, San Diego, San Joaquin, San Mateo, Santa Barbara, Stanislaus, Tehama, and Ventura declared by Governor only) (February 2017); and

— Winter Storms - Alameda, Butte, Calaveras, Contra Costa, El Dorado, Humboldt, Inyo, Lake, Lassen, Marin, Mendocino, Merced, Mono, Monterey, Napa, Nevada, Placer, Plumas, Sacramento, San Benito, San Luis Obispo, Santa Clara, Santa Cruz, Shasta, Sierra, Siskiyou, Solano, Sonoma, Sutter, Trinity, Tuolumne, Yolo, and Yuba Counties declared by President and Governor (Alpine, Fresno, Kern, Kings, Los Angeles, Madera, Modoc, Orange, Riverside, San Bernardino, San Diego, San Francisco, San Mateo, Santa Barbara, Stanislaus, Tehama, Tulare, and Ventura declared by Governor only) (January 2017).

In 2016, the President and/or Governor declared a state of emergency for the following disasters:

— Winter Storms - Del Norte, Humboldt, Mendocino, Shasta, Santa Cruz, and Trinity Counties (December 2016);

— Rainstorms - Siskiyou County (December 2016);

— Wildfires - Lake, San Bernardino, San Luis Obispo Counties (August 2016);

— Wildfires - Los Angeles and Monterey Counties (July 2016); and

— Wildfires - Kern County (June 2016).

In 2015, the President and/or Governor declared a state of emergency for the following disasters:

— Rainstorms - San Diego county (city of Carlsbad) (December 2015);

— Rainstorms - Inyo, Kern, and Los Angeles counties (October 2015);

— Wildfires - Amador and Calaveras Counties (September 2015);

— Wildfires - Lake and Napa Counties (September 2015);

— Rainstorms - Imperial, Kern, Los Angeles, Riverside, San Bernardino and San Diego Counties (July 2015);

— Wildfires - Lake and Trinity Counties (July 2015);

— Wildfires - Butte, El Dorado, Humboldt, Lake, Madera, Napa, Nevada, Sacramento, San Bernardino, San Diego, Shasta, Solano, Tulare, Tuolumne and Yolo Counties (June 2015);

— Oil Spill - Santa Barbara County (May 2015);

— Rainstorms - Humboldt, Mendocino and Siskiyou Counties (February 2015); and

— Wildfires - Mono County (February 2015).

(*List of Disasters*, California Franchise Tax Board, October 2020)

For a list of the most current California disasters declared by the President and/or the Governor, go to http://ftb.ca.gov and search for "disaster loss for individuals and businesses."

In addition, California also allows taxpayers to may make an election to declare a disaster loss in the taxable year preceding the year of the loss, whether or not the President declares the area a disaster, if (1) the loss is listed by the legislature in Rev. & Tax. Code Sec. 24347.5(a) (see listing *below* of disasters with loss carryovers or carrybacks allowed), and (2) the loss is sustained in an area declared a disaster area by the Governor. (Sec. 24347.5(d), Rev. & Tax. Code) California has also extended the election to claim the loss on a prior year's return to taxpayers who suffered disaster losses as the result of the severe storms that occurred in March 2011 in Santa Cruz County, the severe winds that occurred in November 2011 in Los Angeles and San Bernardino Counties, and the wildfires that occurred in May 2014 in San Diego County, even though those areas did not receive designation as federal or state disaster areas. However, these taxpayers may not claim an extended loss carryover for such losses as discussed below. (Sec. 24347.11, Rev. & Tax. Code; Sec. 24347.12, Rev. & Tax. Code; Sec. 24347.13, Rev. & Tax. Code)

CCH PRACTICE TIP: Separate elections allowed.—As there is nothing in California law prohibiting a taxpayer from making a separate election for California corporation franchise and income taxpayers, taxpayers may elect to carryback the disaster loss to the preceding taxable year for federal purposes and not for California purposes, or vice versa. If separate elections are made, taxpayers must make the requisite addition/subtraction modifications on Line 8 and/or Line 15, Form 100, California Corporation Franchise or Income Tax Return.

Under IRC Sec. 165(i)(4), which California follows, an appraisal used to secure a disaster loan or loan guarantee from the federal government may be used to establish the amount of the disaster loss, to the extent provided in regulations or other guidance issued by the Secretary of the Treasury. (Sec. 24347.4, Rev. & Tax. Code)

In addition to allowing taxpayers to elect to claim the loss in the year preceding the loss year, California, but not federal law, allows 100% of any excess loss resulting from specified disasters to be carried forward to the next succeeding five years. Also, prior to the September 2000 disaster, 50% of any such loss remaining after the five-year period may be carried forward to the next succeeding 10 years. Beginning with the September 2000 disaster, the percentage of any loss remaining after the five-year period that may be carried forward to the next succeeding 10 years is tied to NOL deduction percentages (see ¶10-805 Net Operating Loss). (Sec. 24347.5, Rev. & Tax. Code; Sec. 24347.7, Rev. & Tax. Code) The disaster loss carryover is claimed on Line 21, Form 100, California Corporation Franchise or Income Tax Return.

A corporation whose income is subject to apportionment (see ¶11-520 Apportionment) must compute its excess loss by following the principles that such corporations are required to use in computing NOLs. (Sec. 24347.5(e), Rev. & Tax. Code) However, disaster losses may not be taken into account in computing an NOL deduction (see ¶10-805 Net Operating Loss). (Sec. 24347.5(f), Rev. & Tax. Code)

Losses incurred as a result of the following disasters qualify for purposes of the California excess disaster loss carryover or the optional California carryback provisions to the extent they are sustained in an area determined by either the President or the Governor to be in a state of disaster (Sec. 24347.5(a), Rev. & Tax. Code):

(1) fire or any other related casualty occurring in 1990 in California;

(2) the Oakland/Berkeley Fire of 1991, or any other related casualty;

(3) storm, flooding, or any other related casualty occurring in February 1992 in California;

(4) earthquake, aftershock, or any other related casualty occurring in April 1992 in the County of Humboldt;

(5) riots, arson, or any other related casualty occurring in April or May 1992 in California;

(6) earthquakes that occurred in the County of San Bernardino in June and July of 1992, or any other related casualty;

(7) the Fountain Fire that occurred in the County of Shasta or the fires that occurred in the Counties of Calaveras and Trinity in August 1992, or any other related casualty;

(8) storm, flooding, or any other related casualty that occurred in the Counties of Alpine, Contra Costa, Fresno, Humboldt, Imperial, Lassen, Los Angeles, Madera, Mendocino, Modoc, Monterey, Napa, Orange, Plumas, Riverside, San Bernardino, San Diego, Santa Barbara, Sierra, Siskiyou, Sonoma, Tehama, Trinity, and Tulare, and the City of Fillmore in January 1993;

(9) fire that occurred in the Counties of Los Angeles, Orange, Riverside, San Bernardino, San Diego, and Ventura during October or November of 1993, or any other related casualty;

(10) the earthquake, aftershocks, or any other related casualty that occurred in the Counties of Los Angeles, Orange, and Ventura on or after January 17, 1994;

(11) fire that occurred in the County of San Luis Obispo during August of 1994, or any other related casualty;

(12) storms or flooding occurring in 1995, or any other related casualty, sustained in any county of this state subject to a disaster declaration with respect to the storms and flooding;

(13) storms or flooding occurring in December 1996 or January 1997, or any related casualty, sustained in any county of this state subject to a disaster declaration with respect to the storms or flooding;

(14) storms or flooding occurring in February 1998, or any related casualty, sustained in any county of this state subject to a disaster declaration with respect to the storms or flooding;

(15) a freeze occurring in the winter of 1998-99, or any related casualty, sustained in any California county subject to a disaster declaration with respect to the freeze;

(16) an earthquake occurring in September 2000, that was included in the Governor's proclamation of a state emergency for Napa County;

(17) the Middle River levee break in San Joaquin County occurring in June 2004;

(18) the fires occurring in Los Angeles, San Bernardino, Riverside, San Diego, and Ventura Counties in October and November 2003, or any floods, mudflows, and debris flows directly related to those fires;

(19) the San Simeon earthquake, aftershocks, or any other related casualty occurring in Santa Barbara and San Luis Obispo Counties in December 2003;

(20) the wildfires that occurred in Shasta County, beginning August 11, 2004, and any other related casualty;

(21) the severe rainstorms, related flooding and slides, and any other related casualties that occurred in the counties of Kern, Los Angeles, Orange, Riverside, San Bernardino, San Diego, Santa Barbara, and Ventura in December 2004, January 2005, February 2005, March 2005, or June 2005;

(22) the severe rainstorms, related flooding and landslides, and any other related casualties that occurred in Alameda, Alpine, Amador, Butte, Calaveras, Colusa, Contra Costa, Del Norte, El Dorado, Fresno, Humboldt, Kings, Lake, Lassen, Madera, Marin, Mariposa, Mendocino, Merced, Monterey, Napa, Nevada, Placer, Plumas, Sacramento, San Joaquin, San Luis Obispo, San Mateo, Santa Cruz, Shasta, Sierra, Siskiyou, Solano, Sonoma, Stanislaus, Sutter, Trinity, Tulare, Tuolumne, Yolo, and Yuba counties in December 2005, and January, March, and April 2006 (FTB Pub. 1034A-8, California Disaster Relief Tax Provisions—Northern California Storms, December 2005 & January 2006, revised March 2007; FTB Pub. 1034A-9, California Disaster Relief Tax Provisions—California Severe Storms, Flooding, Mudslides, and Landslides: Northern California, March-April 2006, revised March 2007);

(23) the wildfires in San Bernardino County in July 2006 (FTB Pub. 1034A-11, California Disaster Relief Tax Provisions—San Bernardino County Wildfires: San Bernardino County California, July 2006, revised December 2006);

(24) the wildfires in Riverside and Ventura counties durng the 2006 calendar year;

(25) the freeze in El Dorado, Fresno, Imperial, Kern, Kings, Madera, Merced, Monterey, Riverside, San Bernardino, San Diego, San Luis Obispo, Santa Barbara, Santa Clara, Stanislaus, Tulare, Ventura, and Yuba counties in January 2007 (FTB Pub. 1034A-12, California Disaster Relief Tax Provisions—California Severe Freeze: January 2007, revised May 2007);

(26) the wildfires in El Dorado County in June 2007;

(27) the Zaca Fire in Santa Barbara and Ventura counties during the 2007 calendar year;

(28) the wildfires in Inyo County that started in July 2007;

(29) the wildfires in Los Angeles, Orange, Riverside, San Bernardino, San Diego, Santa Barbara, and Ventura counties that were the subject of the Governor's disaster proclamations of September 15, 2007, and October 21, 2007;

(30) the wind storms in Riverside County in October 2007;

(31) the wildfires in Butte, Kern, Mariposa, Mendocino, Monterey, Plumas, Santa Clara, Santa Cruz, Shasta, and Trinity counties in May or June 2008 that were the subject of the Governor's proclamations of a state of emergency;

(32) the wildfires in Santa Barbara County in July 2008;

(33) the severe rainstorms, related flooding and landslides, and any other related casualties in Inyo County during July 2008;

(34) the wildfires in Humboldt County that started in May 2008;

(35) the wildfires in Santa Barbara County in November 2008;

(36) the wildfires in Los Angeles and Ventura Counties in October or November 2008 that were the subject of the Governor's proclamations of a state of emergency;

(37) the wildfires in Orange, Riverside, and San Bernardino Counties in November 2008;

(38) the wildfires in Santa Barbara County in May 2009;

(39) the earthquake in Humboldt County in January 2010 (Sec. 24347.7, Rev. & Tax. Code);

(40) the wildfires that occurred in Placer, Los Angeles, and Monterey counties in August 2009 and in Kern County in July 2010 (Sec. 24347.9, Rev. & Tax. Code);

(41) the winter storms that occurred in Calaveras, Imperial, Los Angeles, Orange, Riverside, San Bernardino, San Francisco, and Siskiyou counties in January and February 2010 (Sec. 24347.9, Rev. & Tax. Code);

(42) the earthquake that occurred in Imperial County in April 2010 (Sec. 24347.8, Rev. & Tax. Code); and

(43) the fire and explosion that occurred in San Mateo County in September 2010 (Sec. 24347.10, Rev. & Tax. Code).

Losses sustained as a result of the firestorms that occurred beginning on October 21, 1996, in Los Angeles, Orange, and San Diego counties may be deducted in the prior income year because the President designated those counties as disaster areas. (FTB Pub. 1026M, California Disaster Relief Tax Provisions, Fire Damaged Locations—California, 1996) However, losses resulting from the firestorms do not qualify for carryover treatment under Sec. 24347.5, Rev. & Tax. Code, because legislation was never enacted that added this disaster to the list of disasters for which the special disaster loss carryover treatment is available.

For most of disasters in the list above, the election under IRC Sec. 165(i), which allows taxpayers to claim a refund for losses incurred, may be made for California purposes on a return or amended return filed on or before the due date of the return (determined with regard to extension) for the taxable year in which the disaster occurred. Generally, the election to deduct a loss on a prior year return must be made on a return filed on or before the original due date of the return for the taxable year in which the disaster occurred. (Sec. 24347.5(g), Rev. & Tax. Code; Sec. 24347.7(g), Rev. & Tax. Code)

For federal income tax purposes, IRC Sec. 165(i) applies only to any loss attributable to a disaster occurring in an area determined by the President to warrant federal assistance under the Disaster Relief and Emergency Assistance Act, but is not restricted to losses occurring in any particular year or to losses resulting from forest fires, storms, flooding, earthquake, or related casualties as under the California carryover provision.

Taxpayers can find additional information on disaster losses in FTB Publication 1034, Disaster Loss - How to Claim a State Tax Deduction.

[¶10-825] Subtractions--Gains

California, like federal law (IRC Sec. 1001), defines a taxable "gain" as the excess of the amount realized on a sale, exchange, or other disposition of property over the property's adjusted basis (see ¶10-690 Additions—Basis Adjustments). The "amount realized" is the sum of any money received plus the fair market value of the property, however reimbursements for real property taxes imposed on the purchaser are not taken into account, whereas real property taxes paid by the corporation are included if under California law such amounts are to be paid by the purchaser. A "loss" is defined as the excess of the property's adjusted basis over the amount realized. (Sec. 24901, Rev. & Tax Code)

Whenever a determination of a taxpayer's gain or loss with respect to a particular item of property subject to nonrecourse indebtedness requires the determination of the fair market value of the property, the fair market value of the property must be treated as being not less than the amount of the nonrecourse indebtedness. (Sec. 23043.5, Rev. & Tax. Code; IRC Sec. 7701(g))

California, unlike federal law, provides no special tax treatment for sales of capital assets or assets used in a trade or business. Under California law, capital gains or losses are treated as ordinary gain or loss and the entire gain or loss is recognized, unless specifically exempt. (Sec. 24902, Rev. & Tax. Code) Although the definitions of "gain" and "loss" are the same for California and federal purposes, as discussed at ¶10-640 Additions—Gains, the actual amount of gain and loss will more likely than not differ because the adjusted basis will be different for California and federal purposes as a result of different depreciation deductions (see ¶10-670 Additions—Depreciation and ¶10-900 Subtractions—Depreciation) and, as discussed at ¶10-690 Additions—Basis Adjustments, different items are allowed to increase and reduce the property's basis under California and federal law. Consequently, the amount of gain claimed on the federal return is subtracted federal taxable income (see ¶10-825 Subtractions—Gains) and a separate addition computation is made to determine the amount of gain that will be recognized for California purposes.

For California corporation franchise and income tax purposes, a taxpayer's gain or loss is computed on Schedule D (100), California Capital Gains and Losses, and Schedule D-1, Sales of Business Property. The actual amount of gain recognized is entered on Line 5, Form 100, California Corporation Franchise or Income Tax Deduction. (Instructions, Form 100, California Corporation Franchise or Income Tax Deduction) As discussed at ¶10-640 Additions—Gains, losses are carried over to subsequent tax years and taken into account in the amount of gain recognized in the subsequent years.

See ¶10-640 Additions—Gains for a detailed discussion of California's treatment of gains and losses.

Other subtractions from the taxable income base are listed at ¶10-800 Subtractions From Taxable Income Base.

[¶10-830] Subtractions--Expense Items

California generally incorporates IRC Sec. 162 as of the state's federal conformity date (see ¶10-515), concerning deductible business expenses, although differences arose in prior taxable years. Other differences are discussed below.

> **CCH CAUTION:** *"Ordinary" and "necessary" expenses.*—It should not be assumed that an item of expense that is allowed under federal law will always be allowed by California, because the interpretations of different taxing authorities concerning what are "ordinary" and "necessary" business expenses are not always uniform. Also, expenses that would normally be deductible under federal law are not allowed by California when they are attributable to income that is not taxed by California. See ¶10-800 Subtractions From Taxable Income Base.

Issues frequently arise concerning the following:

— whether an expense should be classified as a personal or business expense;

— whether payments made to executives are deductible compensation or dividend distributions; and

— whether an item is currently deductible or is a capitalizable expense.

> **OBSERVATION:** *Federal "repair regulations."*— California follows the federal "repair regulations," which provide rules for distinguishing capital expenditures from deductible supply, repair, and maintenance costs. (*Tax News*, California Franchise Tax Board, March 2015)

Because of California's federal conformity date, California does not conform to provisions enacted by the Tax Cuts and Jobs Act of 2017 that specifically disallow deductions for:

— any disqualified related party amount paid or accrued in a hybrid transaction or by, or to, a hybrid entity in taxable years beginning after 2017 (IRC Sec. 267A);

— cash, gift cards, and other nontangible personal property given as employee achievement awards after 2017 (IRC Sec. 274(j));

— amounts paid on or after December 22, 2017, for local lobbying expenses (IRC Sec. 162(e));

— amounts paid on or after December 22, 2017, to a government for a violation of the law (IRC Sec. 162(f)); and

— amounts paid on or after December 22, 2017, as a settlement subject to a nondisclosure agreement in connection with sexual harassment or abuse (IRC Sec. 162(q)).

(2017 Summary of Federal Income Tax Changes, California Franchise Tax Board, May 16, 2018)

For tax years beginning after 2018, California conforms to modifications made by the Tax Cuts and Jobs Act of 2017 to the federal limitations on excessive employee remuneration (IRC Sec. 162(m)). However, under federal law, a transition rule applies to changes made by the TCJA. The federal grandfathering period applies to compensation provided pursuant to a written binding contract which was in effect on November 2, 2017, that has not been modified in any material respect. The relevant date for California purposes is March 31, 2019. (Sec. 24343.1, Rev. & Tax. Code)

For tax years after 2018, California also generally conforms to the federal limitation on the FDIC premium deduction enacted by the Tax Cuts and Jobs Act. Under this provision, the deduction of the applicable percentage of FDIC premiums for banks and other financial institutions with over $10 billion in consolidated assets is limited. However, Article 9 (beginning with Section 23361) of Chapter 2 of Part 11 of the Revenue and Taxation Code does not apply for the purposes of the FDIC premium deduction limitation. (Sec. 24343.1, Rev. & Tax. Code)

• *Automobile expenses*

Federal and California law both allow taxpayers to claim a deduction based on mileage driven during the taxable year, in lieu of actual auto expenses. California uses the same federal mileage deduction rates, so no adjustment is required. (*Information Letter 90-110*, FTB, February 23, 1990)

• *Golden parachute payments*

California incorporates IRC Sec. 280G for corporation franchise and income tax purposes. (Sec. 24349.2, Rev. & Tax. Code)

• *Ridesharing subsidies*

California gives employers a business deduction for expenses incurred in promoting and subsidizing a variety of employee ridesharing arrangements. Nongovernmental employers with employees that provide services for more than eight hours per week in exchange for pay may claim the deduction. Post-secondary private or public educational institutions may also claim the deduction for subsidies provided to a registered, full-time student at a postsecondary educational institution who lives off-campus and commutes to school on a regular (though not necessarily a daily) basis. (Sec. 24343.5, Rev. & Tax. Code) There is no federal counterpart. Consequently, to the extent included in federal taxable income, taxpayers may deduct such amounts incurred by claiming an "other deduction" on Line 16, Form 100, California Corporation Franchise or Income Tax Return, and attaching a supporting schedule.

Deductible expenses include those incurred in the following:

— subsidizing employee commuting in vanpools, carpools, private commuter buses or buspools, and subscription taxipools;

— paying for monthly transit passes for employees and their dependents (except for dependents in elementary and secondary schools);

— providing free or preferential parking to vehicles used in any kind of ridesharing arrangement and giving cash equivalents to employees who do not need parking;

— making facility improvements designed to encourage ridesharing, bicycling, or walking to work;

— providing company commuter van or bus service to employees and other commuters; and

— providing employees with certain business-related transportation services.

(Sec. 24343.5, Rev. & Tax. Code)

Facility improvements.—Facility improvements for which an employer may deduct expenses include, but are not limited to, the construction of bus shelters; the installation of bicycle racks and other facilities, such as showers and locker rooms, intended to encourage bicycle commuting; and parking lot modifications giving preferential treatment to carpools, vanpools, or buspools. The cost of these improvements may be claimed as a depreciation deduction, allowable over a 36-month period. (Sec. 24343.5, Rev. & Tax. Code)

Direct provision of transportation services.—An employer may deduct the noncapital cost of providing employees and other commuters with commuter van or bus services. However, this category does not include the cost of providing employees with transportation required as part of the employer's business activities. Instead, the noncapital cost of providing employees with such work-related transportation is deductible only to the extent that the transportation would be provided by employees without reimbursement in the absence of an employer-sponsored ridesharing incentive program. (Sec. 24343.5, Rev. & Tax. Code)

Parking cash-out programs.—Employers may also claim a business expense deduction, under California law only, for cash payments they make to employees under "parking cash-out programs". (Sec. 24343.5, Rev. & Tax. Code) Payments are to be equivalent to the difference between (1) the amount an employer would pay to provide an employee with a parking space not owned by the employer and (2) the amount, if any, that the employee would pay for the space. (Sec. 65088.1, Govt. Code)

Other definitions.—The statute provides specific definitions for a "company commuter bus or van," "third-party vanpool," "private commuter bus," "monthly transit pass," "transit," "subscription taxipool," "carpool," and "buspool." (Sec. 24343.5, Rev. & Tax. Code)

• *Architectural adaptations for seniors and the handicapped; Emergency exit systems*

California, like federal law (IRC Sec. 190), allows taxpayers to elect to deduct a portion of the cost of architectural adaptation for the handicapped and elderly, up to a maximum of $15,000 per taxable year. However, the California deduction appears to cover modifications to a transportation vehicle used in the taxpayer's trade or business regardless of whether the vehicle is used by the taxpayer or by the general public, whereas only a "public transportation vehicle" is covered by the federal deduction. Also, under California law, the deduction is extended to cover the costs of installing a qualified emergency exit/safe area refuge system. (Sec. 24383, Rev. & Tax. Code) The federal deduction contains no specific provisions concerning such systems. To the extent that such amounts are not deducted from federal taxable income, taxpayers may claim such amounts as an "other deduction" on Line 16, Form 100, California Corporation Franchise or Income Tax Returns.

CCH PRACTICE TIP: Federal and California elections likely to differ.—Because federal law allows taxpayers to claim a credit for expenses incurred to improve access for the disabled and precludes a taxpayer from claiming an IRC Sec. 190

deduction for expenses for which a credit is claimed, taxpayers may forego the federal deduction but elect to claim the deduction for California corporation franchise or income tax purposes. In such instances, the full amount is claimed as an "other deduction" on Line 16, Form 100.

• *Interindemnity arrangement for medical malpractice insurance*

California allows a deduction for payments made to a cooperative corporation by its members for malpractice coverage, but only if a similar federal deduction is available. (Sec. 24415, Rev. & Tax. Code; Sec. 5, Ch. 1276, Laws 1984) Like federal law (Sec. 1031, P.L. 99-514), the deduction may be taken only to the extent that the payment does not exceed the amount that would otherwise be payable to an independent insurance company for similar medical malpractice coverage. Excess payments may be carried forward five years. Refunded payments must be included in the taxpayer's income in the year received. However, federal, but not California law, prohibits taxpayers from claiming the deduction if the association to which the payments are made: (1) was operative and was providing such protection, or had received a permit for the offer and sale of memberships, under the laws of any State before January 1, 1984, (2) is not subject to regulation by any State insurance department, (3) has a right to make unlimited assessments against all members to cover current claims and losses, and (4) is not a member of, nor subject to protection by, any insurance guaranty plan or association of any State. (Sec. 1031, P.L. 99-514)

Other subtractions from the taxable income base are listed at ¶ 10-800.

[¶ 10-835] Subtractions--Corporate Transactions

As discussed at ¶ 10-515 Federal Conformity, California follows federal law disallowing deductions, credits, and allowances associated with stock or property acquired from another corporation if the purpose of the transaction was to benefit from such tax incentives. (Sec. 24431, Rev. & Tax. Code) Although California law mirrors federal law, the FTB may view a transaction differently than the IRS, or vice versa, thereby necessitating an addition to, or subtraction from, federal adjusted gross income. If an adjustment is required, the adjustment should be reported as either an "other addition" on Line 8 or as an "other deduction" on Line 16, Form 100, California Corporation Franchise or Income Tax Return.

Other subtractions from the taxable income base are listed at ¶ 10-800.

[¶ 10-840] Subtractions--Taxes

California, like federal law (IRC Sec. 164) allows taxpayers to deduct most taxes paid during the taxable year. However, under both California and federal law, taxes assessed for local benefits tending to increase the value of the property assessed, other than that portion that is properly allocable to maintenance or interest charges, may not be deducted. California, unlike federal law, makes an exception for irrigation or water district assessments for the payment of the principal of any improvement or other bonds for which a general assessment on all lands within the district is levied. Consequently, taxpayers may subtract such payments from federal taxable income when computing California corporation franchise (income) tax. (Sec. 24345(c), Rev. & Tax. Code; Reg. 24345-2, 18 CCR; *Legal Ruling 2017-01*, California Franchise Tax Board, February 22, 2017) The subtraction amount is entered as an "other deduction" on Line 16, Form 100, California Corporation Franchise or Income Tax Return. See ¶ 10-615 Additions—Taxes for a discussion of the addition adjustments required as a result of differences between California and federal law.

> *CCH COMMENT: Treatment of licenses.*—Although California's law (Sec. 24345, Rev. & Tax. Code) and a regulation (Reg. 24345-1, 18 CCR) specify that "licenses" are also deductible, whereas IRC Sec. 164 does not specifically address this issue, federal case law makes it clear that license fees may be deducted as either a deductible tax or as a deductible business expense. If the license is deducted for federal purposes, a California adjustment is not required. A double deduction is not allowed. Therefore, taxes deducted as a business expense or that are added to the cost of the property with respect to which they are imposed, may not be deducted separately as taxes. (Reg. 24345-1, 18 CCR)

For taxable years beginning on or after January 1, 2015, California conforms to the federal provision that denies deductions for the annual fee imposed by Section 9008 of the Patient Protection and Affordable Care Act (P.L. 111-148) on branded prescription manufacturers and importers. (Sec. 24345.5, Rev. & Tax. Code)

• *Sales and use taxes; gasoline taxes*

Under both California and federal law IRC Sec. 164(a) a deduction of state or local general sales or use taxes is allowed if incurred in a trade or business or for-profit activity. Under both California and federal law, however, taxes paid upon acquisition of depreciable property used in business may be added to the basis of the property and capitalized; when such taxes are incurred on the disposition of property, they are treated as a reduction in the amount realized. (Sec. 24345(e), Rev. & Tax. Code)

Unlike federal law, California also allows a deduction for gasoline and sales taxes paid by a purchaser of services or tangible personal property, provided they are not paid in connection with its trade or business. (Reg. 24345-4, 18 CCR) For example, gasoline taxes paid by a traveling salesperson would be deductible. To the extent that these taxes are not otherwise deducted in computing federal taxable income, such amounts may be claimed as an "other deduction" on Line 16, Form 100, California Corporation Franchise or Income Tax Return.

Other subtractions from the taxable income base are listed at ¶ 10-800.

[¶ 10-845] Subtractions--Targeted Business Activity or Zones

Prior to the 2014 taxable year, businesses located in an enterprise zone, a targeted tax area, or a local agency military base recovery area, may elect to deduct the cost of certain property and used exclusively in the zone or area. In addition, a taxpayer that receives qualified interest from a business located in an enterprise zone may deduct the interest received.

Enterprise zone (EZ) deductions are computed on FTB 3805Z, Enterprise Zone Credit and Deduction Summary. The deductions associated with the targeted tax area (TTA) are computed on FTB 3809, Targeted Tax Area Deduction and Credit Summary, and local agency military base recovery area (LAMBRA) businesses compute the deduction on FTB 3807, Local Agency Military Base Recovery Area Deduction and Credit Summary. The deductions computed on the foregoing forms are then entered on Line 15, Form 100, California Corporation Franchise or Income Tax Return. The form on which the deduction is computed (FTB 3805Z, 3807, or 3809) must be attached to the corporation's Form 100. Failure to attach the form may result in a disallowance of the deduction. (Instructions, Form 100, California Corporation Franchise or Income Tax Return)

See ¶ 10-805 Subtractions—Net Operating Loss for a discussion of the enhanced net operating loss deduction for businesses located in these economic development areas.

• *Election to expense certain property located in economic development areas*

For pre-2014 taxable years, a taxpayer that conducts a trade or business in an EZ, TTA, or LAMBRA, may elect to deduct the cost of certain property and used exclusively in the zone or area for the taxable year during which the property is placed in service. The deduction is available for property placed in service after 1996 for businesses located in an EZ (Sec. 24356.7, Rev. & Tax. Code), for property placed in service after 1997 for businesses located in a TTA (Sec. 24356.6, Rev. & Tax. Code), and for property placed in service after 1998 for businesses located in a LAMBRA. (Sec. 24356.8, Rev. & Tax. Code) A similar deduction was available for qualified property purchased after August 31, 1992, and prior to December 1, 1998, by a business located in former Los Angeles Revitalization Zone (LARZ). (Former 24356.4, Rev. & Tax. Code)

Amount of deduction.—Taxpayers may elect to expense (currently deduct) 40% of the cost of qualified property purchased for exclusive use in a trade or business conducted in an EZ, TTA, or LAMBRA. The cost that may be taken into account is limited to $100,000 for the taxable year that an area is designated as an enterprise zone, $100,000 for the first taxable year thereafter, $75,000 for the second and third taxable years after the year of designation, and $50,000 for each taxable year after that. (Sec. 24356.6, Rev. & Tax. Code; Sec. 24356.7, Rev. & Tax. Code; Sec. 24356.8, Rev. & Tax. Code) The cost of property does not include that portion of the basis of that property that is determined by reference to the basis of other property held at any time by the person acquiring that property.

CCH CAUTION: *Businesses located in expansion area of EZ.*—For businesses located in an expansion area of an EZ, the amount of the deduction is determined using the original EZ designation date. (FTB 3805Z Booklet, Enterprise Zone Business Booklet)

For income years beginning before 1999, the maximum allowable deduction for LAMBRA businesses was $5,000 for the income year during which a LAMBRA designation was made and for the income year following the year of designation, $7,500 for the second and third income years following the year of designation, and $10,000 for income years thereafter. (Sec. 24356.8, Rev. & Tax. Code; prior to amendment by Ch. 1012 (A.B. 3), Laws 1998) LARZ businesses were allowed to fully deduct the cost of the qualified property purchased for exclusive use in the LARZ. (Former 24356.4, Rev. & Tax. Code)

S corporations in LAMBRAs.—For purposes of S corporations claiming the LAMBRA deduction, the dollar limitation described above is applied both at the entity level and at the shareholder level. (Sec. 24356.8(c)(8), Rev. & Tax. Code)

"Qualified property" defined.—For purposes of these deductions, "qualified property" is property that (1) meets the eligibility requirements set forth in IRC Sec. 1245(a)(3); (2) is purchased and placed in service by the taxpayer for exclusive use in an EZ, TTA, or LAMBRA trade or business; and (3) is purchased and placed in service before the date the EZ, TTA, or LAMBRA designation expires, is no longer binding, or becomes inoperative. (Sec. 24356.6, Rev. & Tax. Code; Sec. 24356.7, Rev. & Tax. Code; Sec. 24356.8, Rev. & Tax. Code)

Property does not qualify for the EZ, TTA, or LAMBRA expense deduction under the following circumstances:

— The property was acquired from parties treated as related under federal law. In applying the federal rules governing constructive ownership of stock by related parties, a taxpayer's family is treated as including only spouses, ancestors, and lineal descendants;

— The property was acquired by an affiliated group member from another member of the same affiliated group. For this purpose, the federal definition of affiliated group is adopted, except that a more-than-50-percent test is used instead of the federal 80 percent voting and value tests to determine if a taxpayer is a member of an affiliated group;

— The property was received as a gift or from a decedent;

— The property was exchanged for other property; and

— The property cannot be depreciated under MACRS, including property the taxpayer elects to depreciate under the unit-of-production or similar methods, certain public utility property, films, video tape, sound recordings and certain property placed in service in churning transactions

The enterprise zone expense deduction also does not apply to property for which the taxpayer, because of the provisions of IRC Section 179(d) is prohibited from claiming an expense deduction for federal income tax purposes. (Sec. 24356.6, Rev. & Tax. Code; Sec. 24356.7, Rev. & Tax. Code; Sec. 24356.8, Rev. & Tax. Code)

Eligible taxpayers.—Taxpayers located in an enterprise zone who purchase the property for exclusive use within the EZ may claim the deduction. Only those taxpayers involved in the following business activities described in the federal Standard Industrial Classification (SIC) Manual (or North American Industry Classification System Manual) are eligible to claim the TTA deduction: manufacturing; transportation; communications; electric, gas, and sanitary services; and wholesale trade. For pass-through entities, eligibility is determined at the entity level. (Sec. 24356.6, Rev. & Tax. Code) Only those LAMBRA businesses that have a net increase of one or more employees in the first two taxable years are eligible to claim the deduction. (Sec. 24356.8, Rev. & Tax. Code)

Members of an affiliated group are treated as one qualified taxpayer. The taxpayer must apportion the deduction among the members of the affiliated group in whatever manner prescribed by the FTB.

Election.—An expense deduction election must be made on a taxpayer's original return for the taxable year during which qualified property is placed in service, and must specify the items of property to which the election applies. Once an election has been made, it may be revoked only with the consent of the FTB. (Sec. 24356.7, Rev. & Tax. Code)

Taxpayers make the election by showing a separate item on Form FTB 3885. The amount of the deduction is then reported on Schedule B of Franchise Tax Board Form 100. The property for which the election is made and the amount of the deduction must also be reported on Form FTB 3805Z.

Interaction with other deductions.—A taxpayer that elects to claim a current expense deduction for the qualified property may not also claim the additional first-year bonus depreciation discussed at ¶10-900 Subtractions—Depreciation. However, a depreciation deduction may be claimed for the cost of the property not currently expensed, beginning with the taxable year following the taxable year in which the property is placed in service.

¶10-845

CCH CAUTION: State depreciation deduction will differ from federal deduction.—Because there is no comparable federal election to currently expense property purchased for use in an EZ, TTA, or LAMBRA, the depreciation deduction will differ for federal and state purposes. See ¶10-900 Subtractions—Depreciation, for a discussion of how to report the difference.

Recapture of income.—Any amounts deducted under the first-year enterprise zone business expense provision must be recaptured as income if the property for which the deduction is claimed ceases to be used in a trade or business within an enterprise zone, TTA, or LAMBRA before the close of the second taxable year after the property is placed in service. The income must be reported in the year in which the property ceases to be used in the zone or area. However, a taxpayer then can increase the depreciable basis of the qualified property by the amount required to be included in the taxpayer's gross income as a result of the recapture event. (Sec. 24356.6, Rev. & Tax. Code; Sec. 24356.7, Rev. & Tax. Code; Sec. 24356.8, Rev. & Tax. Code)

Recordkeeping requirements.—There are no special statutory record-keeping requirements for substantiating the deduction. A taxpayer's records should, however, do the following:

— identify items for which the election is made and their purchase price;

— specify the date the property is placed in service in an enterprise zone and the date of the enterprise zone designation; and

— show the location where the property is used.

• *Interest received from enterprise zone and former Los Angeles Revitalization Zone businesses*

A taxpayer that receives interest prior to January 1, 2014, on indebtedness from a qualified trade or business located in an enterprise zone may subtract from federal taxable income the amount of net interest from the trade or business if

— the trade or business is located solely within an enterprise zone,

— the indebtedness is incurred solely in connection with activity within the enterprise zone, and

— the taxpayer has no equity or other ownership interest in the debtor. (Sec. 24384.5, Rev. & Tax. Code)

The subtraction is claimed on Line 15, Form 100, California Corporation Franchise or Income Tax Return, and a supporting schedule must be attached. The deduction is inoperative for post-2013 taxable years. A similar deduction was available for qualified interest received from businesses located in the former Los Angeles Revitalization Zone for pre-1999 taxable years.

Other subtractions from the taxable income base are listed at ¶10-800 Subtractions From Taxable Income Base.

[¶10-850] Subtractions--Depletion

California generally incorporates IRC Sec. 611—IRC Sec. 638 concerning deductions for depletion and natural resource expenses, as of the current California conformity date (see ¶10-515), with modifications as discussed at ¶10-625. (Sec. 24831, Rev. & Tax. Code)

[¶ 10-855] Subtractions--Items Related to Federal Deductions or Credits

Although California incorporates the portions of IRC Sec. 280C, which disallow a deduction or credit for (1) qualified clinical testing expenses that were otherwise available to the extent that such expenses were claimed for the federal clinical testing tax credit purposes and (2) that portion of qualified research expenses or basic research expenses that equals the credit amount allowed for such expenses under IRC Sec. 41, California does not incorporate the other provisions of IRC Sec. 280C, which disallow a deduction for expenses for which a federal Indian employment credit, the employer wage credit for employees who are active duty members of the uniformed services, work opportunity credit, empowerment zone employment credit, employer credit for housing employees affected by Hurricane Katrina, or employee retention credit is allowed. (Sec. 24440, Rev. & Tax. Code) Consequently, taxpayers may deduct from federal taxable income expenses for which the latter credits were claimed on the federal return by claiming such amounts as an "other deduction" on Line 16, Form 100, California Corporation Franchise or Income Tax Return and attaching a supporting schedule.

California law does not incorporate federal law disallowing a deduction for the portion of expenses for which the federal low sulfur diesel fuel production credit was claimed under IRC Sec. 45H. However, California does deny a deduction for expenses for which the California ultra-low sulfur diesel fuel production credit is claimed. (Sec. 23662(e), Rev. & Tax. Code) In addition, California does not incorporate or follow federal law (IRC Sec. 280C (e) and (f)) that disallows deductions for expenses for which the federal mine rescue team training credit or the credit for security of agricultural chemicals was claimed.

Also, because of California's federal conformity date (see ¶ 10-515), California does not conform to the federal provision (IRC Sec. 267A) that disallows deductions for any disqualified related party amount paid or accrued in a hybrid transaction or by, or to, a hybrid entity. The federal provision applies to taxable years beginning after December 31, 2017. (*Summary of Federal Income Tax Changes – 2017*, California Franchise Tax Board, May 16, 2018)

Other subtractions from the taxable income base are listed at ¶ 10-800.

[¶ 10-860] Subtractions--Environmental or Pollution Control

California allows subtraction modifications for income associated with the following conservation and environmental and pollution control activities. These subtractions are generally claimed as an "other deduction" on Line 16, Form 100, California Corporation Franchise or Income Tax, and a supporting schedule must be attached. See ¶ 10-830 Subtractions—Expense Items, for the deduction available for employers' costs associated with promoting and subsidizing a variety of employee ridesharing arrangements.

• *Beverage container recycling income*

Gross income does not include redemption money received from returning empty beverage containers to recycling centers. (Sec. 24315, Rev. & Tax. Code)

• *Carousel Housing Tract cleanup*

Gross income does not include certain amounts received as a result of the Carousel Housing Tract cleanup in Carson, California. Taxpayers can exclude amounts received:

— from the Shell Oil Company for temporary accommodations and relocation;

— under the Optional Real Estate Program of the Revised Remedial Action Plan; or

— from a settlement arising out of the investigation, cleanup, or abatement of waste discharged at the former Kast Property Tank Farm facility.

(Sec. 24308.8, Rev. & Tax. Code)

Taxpayers must receive the amounts pursuant to California Regional Water Quality Control Board, Los Angeles Region, Order R4-2011-046, and they must currently own or have previously owned property in the Carousel Housing Tract. (Sec. 24308.8, Rev. & Tax. Code)

The exclusion applies to all tax years. If a taxpayer previously paid tax on these amounts, the taxpayer has until September 28, 2019, to file for a credit or refund. The regular limitations period for claiming a credit or refund from the overpayment will not apply. (Sec. 24308.8, Rev. & Tax. Code)

• *Forest protection cost-share payments*

California law provides an exclusion from gross income for cost-share payments received by forest landowners from the Department of Forestry and Fire Protection pursuant to the California Forest Improvement Act of 1978 or from the United States Department of Agriculture, Forest Service, under the Forest Stewardship Program and the Stewardship Incentives Program, pursuant to the federal Cooperative Forestry Assistance Act. The amount of any cost-share payment so excluded may not be considered when (1) determining the basis of property acquired or improved or (2) computing any deduction to which the taxpayer may otherwise be entitled. (Sec. 24308.5, Rev. & Tax. Code) See ¶10-701 Additions—Environmental or Pollution Control, for a discussion of the addition adjustment required by California's nonconformity with the federal exclusion for certain cost-share payments under IRC Sec. 126 Certain Cost-Share Payments.

• *Water and energy conservation rebates*

Certain water conservation rebates received by taxpayers from local water agencies or suppliers are treated as refunds or price adjustments rather than as income for California corporation franchise (income) tax purposes. There is no comparable federal provision. To qualify, a rebate must be for expenses incurred by the taxpayer to purchase or install a water conservation toilet that meets specified performance standards and uses no more than 1.6 gallons per flush. (Sec. 24323, Rev. & Tax. Code)

Similarly, any amount received as a rebate, voucher, or other financial incentive issued by the California Energy Commission, the California Public Utilities Commission, or a local public utility for the purchase or installation of certain energy conservation devices is excluded from gross income. Qualifying devices are any of the following: (1) thermal energy systems, (2) solar energy systems, (3) wind energy systems that produce electricity, and (4) fuel cell generating systems that produce electricity. (Sec. 24308.1, Rev. & Tax. Code)

For taxable years beginning on or after January 1, 2014, and before January 1, 2019, California also excludes from gross income any amount received as a rebate, voucher, or other financial incentive issued by a local water agency or supplier for participation in a turf removal water conservation program. (Sec. 24308.2, Rev. & Tax. Code)

Other subtractions from the taxable income base are listed at ¶10-800.

[¶10-865] Subtractions--Income Taxed to Another Entity

California law does not have a subtraction modification relating to income taxed to another entity.

Other subtractions from the taxable income base are listed at ¶10-800.

[¶10-870] Subtractions--Income Taxed in Another Federal Tax Year

California does not have a subtraction modification relating to income taxed in another federal tax year.

Other subtractions from the taxable income base are listed at ¶10-800.

[¶10-875] Subtractions--Bad Debts

California incorporates IRC Sec. 166, concerning the bad debt deduction, without modification, as of a specified date. (Sec. 24347, Rev. & Tax. Code) Under IRC Sec. 166 a taxpayer may take a deduction for debts that become wholly or partially worthless within the taxable year. However, when satisfied that a debt is recoverable in part only, the California Franchise Tax Board (FTB) may allow that debt in an amount not in excess of the part charged off within the taxable year as a deduction; provided however, that if a portion of a debt is claimed and allowed as a deduction in any year, no deduction is allowed in any subsequent year for any portion of the debt that was charged off in a prior year, regardless of whether claimed as a deduction in that prior year. (Sec. 24348(b), Rev. & Tax. Code) California also requires special treatment of bad debts incurred by banks, savings and loan associations, or financial corporations, see ¶10-340 Banks—Financial Institutions, for more details.

Because California does not modify federal law for nonfinancial institutions, no addition or subtraction adjustments should be required. However, bear in mind that the FTB may apply different interpretations than the Internal Revenue Service as to when or if a debt becomes worthless.

Other subtractions from the taxable income base are listed at ¶10-800.

[¶10-880] Subtractions--Charitable Items

Corporate contributions to nonprofit charitable organizations and cemeteries, governmental entities, and war veterans organizations are deductible. The California and federal laws are generally parallel. However, there are differences in the (1) income from which the contributions are deducted, (2) types of contributions eligible for the deduction, (3) substantiation requirements, and (4) treatment of appreciated property and scientific property as well as other types of property discussed below. (Sec. 24359, Rev. & Tax. Code)

Because the contribution deduction is limited to the adjusted basis of the assets being contributed and the income from which the contributions are deducted, taxpayers must add back the federal contributions deduction and recalculate the amount that may be deducted for California corporation franchise and income tax purposes. The computation is completed on a separate worksheet, using the Form 100, California Corporation Franchise or Income Tax Return as a format and adding in any federal contribution deduction on Line 8, Form 100 (see ¶10-650). An additional worksheet is also provided in the Form 100, Instructions to Line 14 to complete the computation. (Instructions, Form 100, California Corporation Franchise or Income Tax Return)

Following is a list of the California provisions and comparable federal provisions:

California	Federal	Subject
24357	IRC Sec. 170(a)	Charitable contributions
- - -	IRC Sec. 170(b)(1)	Limitations for individuals
24358	IRC Sec. 170(b)(2)	Limitations on corporate contributions
24359	IRC Sec. 170(c)	Charitable contribution defined
- - -	IRC Sec. 170(d)(1)	Carryovers for individuals
24358	IRC Sec. 170(d)(2)	Carryovers for corporations
24357.1	IRC Sec. 170(e)(1)	Contributions of ordinary income and capital gain property
- - -	IRC Sec. 170(e)(3)	Certain contributions of inventory and other property
24357.8	IRC Sec. 170(e)(4)	Scientific property used for research
- - -	IRC Sec. 170(e)(5)	Appreciated property to private foundations
24357.9	IRC Sec. 170(e)(6)	Computer technology and equipment
24357.1(c)	IRC Sec. 170(e)(7)	Dispositions of exempt use property (applicable for California purposes to contributions made after 2009)
24359.1	- - -	Benefit to donor of donated equipment
24357.5	IRC Sec. 170(f)(1)	Disallowance of deduction
24357.2	IRC Sec. 170(f)(3)	Partial interest in property
24357.3	IRC Sec. 170(f)(4)	Valuation of remainder interest in real property
24357.4	IRC Sec. 170(f)(5)	Reduction for certain interest
24357.6	IRC Sec. 170(f)(6)	Out-of-pocket expenditures
24357	IRC Sec. 170(f)(8)	Substantiation of contributions
24357	IRC Sec. 170(f)(9)	Contributions for lobbying activities
- - -	IRC Sec. 170(f)(10)	Split dollar insurance arrangements
- - -	IRC Sec. 170(f)(11)	Qualified appraisals and substantiation requirements
24357(h)	IRC Sec. 170(f)(11)(E)	Qualified appraisals and appraisers defined (applicable for California purposes to contributions made after 2009)
24357.1(e)	IRC Sec. 170(f)(15)	Valuation of taxidermy property donations (applicable for California purposes to contributions made after 2009)
24357(i)	IRC Sec. 170(f)(16)	Contributions of clothing and household items (applicable for California purposes to contributions made after 2009)
24357(j)	IRC Sec. 170(f)(17)	Recordkeeping requirements (applicable for California purposes to contributions made after 2009)
- - -	IRC Sec. 170(g)	Students maintained in household
24357.7	IRC Sec. 170(h)	Conservation contributions
- - -	IRC Sec. 170(i)	Standard mileage rate
24357	IRC Sec. 170(j)	Denial of deduction for certain travel expenses
- - -	IRC Sec. 170(k)	Disallowance of deductions in certain cases
24357.10	IRC Sec. 170(l)	Donations to colleges and universities
- - -	IRC Sec. 170(m)	Donations of intellectual property
24357(k)	IRC Sec. 170(o)	Special rules for fractional gifts (applicable for California purposes to contributions made after 2009)

California regulations are applicable. (Reg. 24357-1, 18 CCR; Reg. 24357-2, 18 CCR)

Only those areas where California law differs from federal law are discussed below.

• *Limitation on amount*

Under California law, a corporation's deduction for charitable contributions may not exceed 10% of its *net* income. (Sec. 24358, Rev. & Tax. Code) Under IRC Sec. 170(b)(2) a corporation may take a federal charitable contribution deduction of up to 10% of its *taxable* income. Like federal law (IRC Sec. 162(b)), California prohibits taxpayers from claiming as ordinary business expenses, amounts contributed in excess of the percentage limitations or dollar limitations, or that may not be claimed as a result of time constraints. (Sec. 24343, Rev. & Tax. Code) California has not adopted provisions similar to the federal enhanced deductions for book inventory (prior to 2012) and food inventory donations. In addition, California does not follow federal provisions that allow increased deductions for contributions of real property for conservation purposes for tax years after 2011, or that extend the deduction to native corporations under the Alaska Native Claims Settlement Act after 2015.

The 10% federal limitation applies to taxable income, excluding:

— charitable contributions;

— special deductions for corporations allowed under Part VIII (other than the deduction for certain organizational expenditures under IRC Sec. 248);

— net operating loss carrybacks; and

— capital loss carrybacks.

In computing the 10% California limitation, the following deductions are excluded from net income:

— S corporation's previously taxed built-in gains and passive investment income;

— charitable contributions deduction;

— special deductions for corporations allowed under Art. 2 of Chapter 7 (other than the deduction for specified deferred organizational expenses deduction), which includes the dividends received deductions and net operating losses. (Sec. 24358, Rev. & Tax. Code; Instructions, Form 100, California Corporation Franchise or Income Tax Return) See ¶ 10-505 Overview of Taxable Income computation for the definition of "net income."

• *Substantiation of contributions*

California incorporates IRC Sec. 170(f)(8) as of a fixed conformity date, which generally disallows deductions for charitable contributions of $250 or more (both cash and noncash contributions) unless the contribution is substantiated by a contemporaneous written acknowledgment from the donee organization. The FTB may not deny the deduction for lack of substantiation, if a taxpayer demonstrates that the substantiation requirements were met with respect to that contribution for federal purposes. (Sec. 24357(e), Rev. & Tax. Code) Because of California's federal conformity date, California does not conform to the repeal of the exception to the contemporaneous written acknowledgment requirement for contributions made in tax years beginning after 2016. (2017 Summary of Federal Income Tax Changes, California Franchise Tax Board, May 16, 2018)

Taxpayers who sell land to the state for conservation purposes and claim a charitable contribution deduction in excess of $5,000 for the value of the land in excess of the price paid must attach an appraisal for the property to their tax return for the year the deduction is claimed in order to substantiate the amount of the charitable contribution deduction, and the appraisal must be prepared by an appraiser licensed by the Office of Real Estate Appraisers. (Sec. 5096.518, Pub. Res. Code) California incorporates the federal definitions of a "qualified appraisal" and a "qualified appraiser." (Sec. 24357(h), Rev. & Tax. Code)

California law, unlike federal law, does not impose increased substantiation requirements for deductions claimed for donations of motor vehicles, vessels, and aircraft with a claimed value of $500 or other noncash donations of $500 or more. Nor does California law require the submission of a qualified appraisal for donations of $500,000 or authorize the requirement of a qualified appraisal of donations of between $5,000 and $500,000.

- *Appreciated property*

Under California law, the amount of any charitable contribution of property is reduced by the amount of gain that would have resulted had the property been sold at its fair market value. Therefore, the deduction allowed for the contribution of appreciated property is generally equal to the taxpayer's cost basis in the property. (Sec. 24357.1, Rev. & Tax. Code)

Under federal law, a contribution of "ordinary income property" (property whose sale at fair market value would result in ordinary income or short-term capital gain) must be reduced by the amount of gain that would have resulted from the property's sale at fair market value (IRC Sec. 170(e)(1)), and is generally equal to its cost basis. However, for federal purposes, if a contribution of tangible personal property is put to an unrelated use by the donee, or if property other than appreciated stock is donated to certain private foundations, the allowable deduction is reduced by the long term capital gain that would have been realized if the property had been sold at fair market value. A federal deduction is allowed for the fair market value of qualified appreciated stock donated to private foundations. (IRC Sec. 170(e)(5))

- *Disallowance of deductions for certain donations*

Charitable contribution deductions are denied under both California and federal law (IRC Sec. 170(f)(1)) for contributions to certain foreign organizations engaged in prohibited transactions. However, California does not conform to the disallowance under federal law (IRC Sec. 170(f)(1)) of a deduction for any donation to a foundation whose status as a private foundation has been terminated or to certain taxable trusts and private foundations. Nor does California conform to the disallowance under federal law (IRC Sec. 170(f)(2)) of a deduction for the donation of (1) a remainder interest in trust where there is a noncharitable income beneficiary, unless the trust is a "charitable remainder annuity trust," a "charitable remainder unitrust," or a pooled income fund or (2) an income interest in trust, unless the grantor is taxed on the income interest and the trust interest is payable in the form of a guaranteed annuity, or the trust instrument requires that the charity annually receive a fixed percentage of the fair market value of the trust property. (Sec. 24357.5, Rev. & Tax. Code)

Also, California does not conform to the federal repeal of the deduction for amounts paid in exchange for college athletic event seating rights in tax years beginning after December 31, 2017. For California purposes, under Sec. 24357.10, if an amount is paid to or for the benefit of a school or university and the amount would be deductible as a charitable contribution except for the fact that the taxpayer is given the right to buy tickets for seating at an athletic event in the institution's stadium, 80% of the contribution will be allowed as charitable contribution. The deductible amount does not include the portion of the contribution representing the actual cost of the tickets. (2017 Summary of Federal Income Tax Changes, California Franchise Tax Board, May 16, 2018)

- *Scientific property*

California does not conform to IRC Sec. 170(e)(4), under which corporate contributions of scientific equipment or apparatus to colleges or universities are deductible if the property is (1) tangible personal property and (2) stock in trade or property includable in inventory of the corporation. Under federal law, a corporation may deduct its basis in the property plus one-half of the unrealized appreciation, up to a limit of twice its basis for the property. (Sec. 24357.8, Rev. & Tax. Code)

- *Intellectual property*

California has not adopted and has no provisions similar to the federal provision that limits the charitable contributions deduction for patents and most other intellectual property donated to a charitable organization after June 3, 2004, to the lesser of the donor's basis in the property or its fair market value, but allow limited additional deductions for such contributions if the donee has income attributable to the donation during the 12 years after the property is donated. (IRC Sec. 170(m))

- *Hurricane Harvey, Irma, and Maria disaster relief*

For qualifying charitable contributions associated with qualified hurricane relief, the federal Disaster Tax Relief and Airport and Airway Extension Act of 2017 (P.L. 115-63):

— temporarily suspends the majority of the AGI limitations on charitable contributions;

— provides that contributions will not be taken into account for purposes of applying AGI and carryover period limitations to other contributions; and

— provides eased rules governing the federal treatment of excess contributions.

California does not conform to IRC Sec. 170, but instead has stand-alone law that is generally similar to federal law allowing corporations a deduction for charitable contributions. There are no similar California provisions for hurricane relief suspension of AGI limitations, exclusion of carryover period limitations to other contributions, and eased rules governing the treatment of excess contributions. (2017 Summary of Federal Income Tax Changes, California Franchise Tax Board, May 16, 2018)

- *Disclosure related to quid pro quo contributions*

Under both California and federal law (IRC Sec. 6115), charitable organizations must inform donors that *quid pro quo* contributions in excess of $75 are deductible only to the extent that the contributions exceed the value of goods or services provided by the organization. The requirement is met for California purposes upon a showing that the requirement was met with respect to the contribution for federal purposes. (Sec. 18648.5, Rev. & Tax. Code)

A penalty will be imposed for failure to satisfy the disclosure requirement. For both California and federal purposes, the penalty amount is determined in accordance with IRC Sec. 6714. (Sec. 19182.5, Rev. & Tax. Code)

Other subtractions from the taxable income base are listed at ¶ 10-800.

[¶ 10-885] Subtractions--Research and Development Expenses

California has no subtraction modifications for research and development expenses. See ¶ 10-905 Subtractions—Amortization for subtraction modifications required by California.

Other subtractions from the taxable income base are listed at ¶ 10-800.

[¶10-890] Subtractions--Job Programs or Employee Benefits

Other than the deductions allowed for golden parachute payments and ridesharing subsidies discussed at ¶10-830 Subtractions—Expense Items, California has no separate provisions governing subtraction modifications relating to job programs or employee benefits.

Other subtractions from the taxable income base are listed at ¶10-800.

[¶10-895] Subtractions--Agriculture

California does not have separate provisions governing subtraction modifications relating to agriculture.

Other subtractions from the taxable income base are listed at ¶10-800.

[¶10-900] Subtractions--Depreciation

A taxpayer may claim a depreciation deduction for the exhaustion, wear, and tear of real or personal property used in a trade or business or held for the production of income. (Sec. 24349, Rev. & Tax. Code) The California corporation franchise and income tax depreciation provisions are generally the same as those contained in the pre-1981 federal asset depreciation range deduction of IRC Sec. 167. Except as discussed below, the federal Accelerated Cost Recovery System (ACRS) for post-1980 assets and the federal modified ACRS (MACRS) for post-1986 assets have not been incorporated into the California Corporation Tax Law. However, MACRS depreciation is recognized by S corporations (discussed below) and is also recognized by C corporations to the extent the depreciation deduction is passed through from a partnership or limited liability company treated as a partnership. (Instructions, FTB Form 3885, Corporation Depreciation and Amortization)

Otherwise, as a result of California's general nonconformity to IRC Sec. 168 for corporation franchise and income tax purposes, California does not follow numerous federal depreciation provisions, such as the federal bonus depreciation, accelerated writeoffs of Indian reservation property authorized by IRC Sec. 168(j), and the federal provisions that make the following changes:

— place limits on sales-in lease-out (SILO transactions), applicable generally for federal purposes to lease transactions entered into after March 12, 2004, unless specified exceptions apply;

— set a 15-year recovery period for qualified improvement property;

— increase the recovery periods for land-clearing costs and electric utility property, applicable for federal purposes to property placed in service after October 22, 2004;

— allow a 50% additional depreciation allowance for (1) qualified cellulosic biomass ethanol plant property acquired and placed in service after December 20, 2006, and before January 1, 2014, (2) reuse and recycling property acquired and placed in service after August 31, 2008, and (3) disaster assistance property placed in service after 2007, with respect to disasters declared after 2007 and declared prior to 2010;

— authorize the IRC Sec. 168(k) bonus depreciation deduction for assets placed in service in 2008—2026 (2008—2027 in the case of property with a long production period and certain noncommercial aircraft);

— raise the cap under IRC Sec. 280F for luxury autos to $8,000 of bonus depreciation in addition to the regular limitation for vehicles placed in service in tax years 2008—2010;

— reduce the recovery period for race horses two years or younger from seven to three years for horses placed in service after 2008 and before 2017; and

— authorize in lieu accelerated alternative minimum tax credit or research and development credit for qualified IRC Sec. 168(k)(2) property acquired after March 31, 2008, and placed in service before 2020 (2021 for property with a long production period and certain noncommercial aircraft).

CCH CAUTION: California allows only a limited IRC Sec. 179 asset expense election and does not allow the additional 30%/50% first-year bonus depreciation deduction.—California allows only a limited IRC Sec. 179 asset expense election for post-2004 taxable years. In addition, California law has not conformed to IRC Sec. 168(k), which (1) allows taxpayers to claim on their federal returns additional bonus depreciation deduction for qualified property placed in service in 2008 to 2026 (2008—2027 in the case of property with a long production period and certain noncommercial aircraft), and (2) allowed taxpayers to claim an additional 30% or 50% bonus depreciation for qualified property purchased after September 10, 2001, and before 2005. However, California does allow a limited 20% first-year bonus depreciation deduction (see below). California also does not allow the in lieu accelerated alternative minimum tax credit or research and development credit for qualified IRC Sec. 168(k)(2) property acquired after March 31, 2008, and placed in service before 2020. Nor did California incorporate (1) the additional 30% first-year bonus depreciation deduction allowed for qualified New York Liberty Zone property, or (2) the 50% additional bonus depreciation deduction allowed for qualified Gulf Opportunity Zone property placed in service in the Gulf Opportunity Zone after August 27, 2005, and before 2008 (2009 for property located in specified GO Zone areas).

See discussion below for a detailed discussion of all the differences between California and federal law concerning depreciation. Special rules also apply to amortization of intangibles and other specified property (see ¶ 10-905).

Because the corporate depreciation deduction is so different for California and federal income tax purposes, California corporation franchise and income taxpayers must separately compute their depreciation deduction for California tax purposes. C corporations and limited liability companies classified as corporations compute their California depreciation deduction on FTB Form 3885, Corporation Depreciation and Amortization. To the extent the depreciation amount claimed for federal purposes exceeds the amount calculated on FTB Form 3885 for California purposes, the excess is treated as an addition adjustment and is entered on Line 6, Form 100, California Corporation Franchise or Income Tax Return. Conversely, if the depreciation amount computed on FTB Form 3885 for California corporation franchise (income) tax purposes exceeds the federal depreciation deduction claimed on the taxpayer's federal return, the excess is claimed as a subtraction adjustment and is entered on Line 12, Form 100. (Instructions, Form 100, California Corporation Franchise or Income Tax Return; Form FTB 3885, Corporation Depreciation and Amortization) S corporations use Schedule B, Form 100S, California S Corporation Return to compute their depreciation deduction.

• *IRC Sec. 179 asset expense election*

C corporations may elect to claim an IRC Sec. 179 asset expense election for corporation income and franchise purposes in lieu of the first-year additional bonus depreciation deduction discussed below. California's asset expense election is limited to $25,000 per taxable year. For federal purposes, the limit is $1 million for tax years after 2017; $500,000 for tax years 2010 through 2017 (adjusted annually for inflation beginning with the 2016 tax year); $250,000 for the 2008 and 2009 tax years; $125,000 for the 2007 tax year; and $100,000 for the 2003 through 2006 tax years. (Sec. 24356(b), Rev. & Tax. Code) California also does not incorporate the increased IRC Sec. 179 limitations available for qualified enterprise zone property under IRC Sec. 1397A, Gulf Opportunity Zone property under IRC Sec. 1400N, or qualified disaster property under IRC Sec. 179(e).

However, for both federal and California tax purposes, if the cost of qualified property placed in service during the taxable year exceeds a specified amount, then the applicable ceiling amount is reduced by the amount of the excess. For California purposes, the phase-out threshold amount is $200,000. For federal purposes, the phase-out threshold amount is $2.5 million for tax years after 2017; $2 million for tax years after 2010 through 2017 (adjusted annually for inflation beginning with the 2016 tax year); $800,000 for the 2008 and 2009 tax years; $500,000 for the 2007 tax year; and $400,000 for the 2003 through 2006 tax years (subject to inflation adjustment). Also, for both federal and California tax purposes, the aggregate cost of property taken into account in any taxable year may not exceed the taxpayer's taxable income derived from a trade or business for that taxable year, although any amount that would otherwise have been deductible for the taxable year may be carried over to the succeeding year and then deducted. (Sec. 24356(b), Rev. & Tax. Code)

California also differs from federal law in that taxpayers may not make the election for purchases of off-the-shelf computer software. (Sec. 24356(b), Rev. & Tax. Code) In addition, due to California's IRC conformity date, California does not conform to the federal provisions that allow expensing of air conditioning and heating units (see IRC Sec. 179(d)(1), as amended by the Protecting Americans from Tax Hikes (PATH) Act of 2015 (P.L. 114-113)), or eliminated the limitation on the amount of Sec. 179 property that can be attributable to qualified improvement property and the corresponding provision on carryforwards of disallowed amounts attributable to qualified improvement property (see IRC Sec. 179(f), as amended by the PATH Act of 2015). Also, because of California's IRC conformity date, California does not conform to the provisions in the Tax Cuts and Jobs Act of 1027 that expanded the definition of "qualified property" for taxable years beginning after 2017 to include (1) certain depreciable tangible personal property used predominantly to furnish lodging or in connection with furnishing lodging, and (2) roofing, heating, ventilation, air-conditioning property, fire protection, alarm systems, and security system improvements to nonresidential real property placed in service after the date the property was first placed in service. (*2017 Summary of Federal Income Tax Changes*, California Franchise Tax Board, May 16, 2018)

The election must be made by the return filing due date, including extensions, for the taxable year. Once the election is made for California franchise or income tax purposes, it can only be revoked with the consent of the Franchise Tax Board. (Sec. 24356(b), Rev. & Tax. Code)

• *MACRS depreciation allowed for S corporations*

For purposes of computing corporation franchise and income taxes, an S corporation's deduction for depreciation and amortization (including the IRC Sec. 179

election) is computed under the Personal Income Tax Law. (Instructions, Form 100S) For tax years beginning after 1986, the Personal Income Tax Law has incorporated IRC Sec. 168, concerning the MACRS method of depreciation, with modifications. (Sec. 17201, Rev. & Tax. Code) See ¶15-670 Federal Base—Depreciation in the Personal Income Tax Division for more information.

COMMENT: *Depreciation for assets placed in service while taxable as a C corporation.*—California does not allow depreciation under MACRS for assets placed in service while a corporation was taxable as a C corporation. This is a change in accounting method for which the taxpayer must request the FTB's consent. (Instructions, Schedule B (100S), S Corporation Depreciation and Amortization)

• *Methods of computing depreciation*

Taxpayers may choose between the following methods of depreciating personal property: straight-line, declining balance, sum-of-the-years method, or any other consistent method as long as the total accumulated depreciation at the end of any taxable year during the first 2/3 of the useful life of the property is not more than the amount that would have resulted from using the declining balance method. (Sec. 24349, Rev. & Tax. Code) The latter three methods may only be used for tangible property with a useful life of three years or more. (Sec. 24350, Rev. & Tax. Code)

Regardless of the method used in computing depreciation, deductions for depreciation may not exceed such amounts as may be necessary to recover the unrecovered cost or other basis less salvage during the remaining useful life of the property. The reasonableness of any claim for depreciation is determined upon the basis of conditions known to exist at the end of the period for which the return is made. It is the responsibility of the taxpayer to establish the reasonableness of the deduction for depreciation claimed. Generally, depreciation deductions will be changed only where there is a clear and convincing basis for a change. (Sec. 24349(b), Rev. & Tax. Code; Reg. 24349(k), 18 CCR) Detailed explanations and examples of each of the depreciation methods are provided in Reg. 24349(k), 18 CCR.

General methods of depreciating personal property.—A California regulation adopts by reference the Federal Asset Depreciation Range (ADR) System for property placed in service after 1970 (federal regulation 1.167(a)-11) (Reg. 24349(l), 18 CCR) However, California does not permit the use of the 20% ADR variances given for each asset guideline period and excludes federal rules for depreciation of public utility property that conflict with the California Code. As under pre-1981 federal law, California taxpayers using the ADR system may elect double declining balance, sum-of-the-years digits, or the straight-line methods for eligible new property, and 150% declining balance and the straight-line method for eligible used assets. (Reg. 24349(l), 18 CCR)

Under CA Reg. 24349 (I), California conforms to the federal useful lives of property.

Use the following information as a guide to determine reasonable periods of useful life for purposes of calculating depreciation. Actual facts and circumstances will determine useful life. Note, however, that the figures listed below represent the normal periods of useful life for the types of property listed as shown in IRS Rev. Proc. 83-35.

¶10-900

Office furniture, fixtures, machines, and equipment . . . . 10 yrs.
This category includes furniture and fixtures (that are not structural components of a building) and machines and equipment used in the preparation of paper or data.
Examples include: desks; files; safes; typewriters, accounting, calculating, and data processing machines; communications equipment; and duplicating and copying equipment.
Computers and peripheral equipment (printers, etc.) . . . . 6 yrs.
Transportation equipment and automobiles (including taxis) . . . . 3 yrs.
General-purpose trucks:
Light (unloaded weight less than 13,000 lbs.) . . . . 4 yrs.
Heavy (unloaded weight 13,000 lbs. or more) . . . . 6 yrs.
Buildings
This category includes the structural shell of a building and all of its integral parts that service normal heating, plumbing, air conditioning, fire prevention and power requirements, and equipment such as elevators and escalators.
Type of building:
Apartments . . . . 40 yrs.
Dwellings (including rental residences) . . . . 45 yrs.
Office buildings . . . . 45 yrs.
Warehouses . . . . 60 yrs.

A useful life of seven years applies to Alaska natural gas pipelines. (Sec. 24355.3, Rev. & Tax. Code) However, due to California's IRC conformity date, California does not allow the seven-year useful life for motorsports entertainment complexes for property placed in service after 2014 (see IRC Sec. 168(e)(3)(C)(ii), as amended by the PATH Act of 2015).

Corporations may use the straight-line method for any depreciable property. Before using other methods, consider the kind of property, its useful life, whether it is new or used, and the date it was acquired. Use the following chart as a general guide to determine which method to use:

Property description	Maximum depreciation method
Real estate acquired 12/31/70 or earlier	
New (useful life 3 yrs. or more)	200% Declining balance
Used (useful life 3 yrs. or more)	150% Declining balance
Real estate acquired 1/1/71 or later	
Residential Rental:	
New	200% Declining balance
Used (useful life 20 yrs. or more)	125% Declining balance
Used (useful life less than 20 yrs.)	Straight-line
Commercial and industrial:	
New (useful life 3 yrs. or more)	150% Declining balance
Used	Straight-line
Personal property	
New (useful life 3 yrs. or more)	200% Declining balance
Used (useful life 3 yrs. or more)	150% Declining balance

Other depreciation methods may be used as long as the total accumulated depreciation at the end of any taxable year during the first 2/3 of the useful life of the property is not more than the amount that would have resulted from using the declining balance method.
The Guideline Class Life System of depreciation may be used for certain classes of assets placed in service before 1971.
The Class Life ADR System of depreciation may be used for designated classes of assets placed in service after 1970.

Income forecast method.—California incorporates, with modifications, IRC Sec. 167(g) as of the current California conformity date (see ¶ 10-515), which clarifies the computation of depreciation using the income forecast method for specified property, with modifications to change internal references. (Sec. 24349(f), Rev. & Tax. Code) Under IRC Sec. 167(g) as incorporated by California, a taxpayer may elect to use the income forecast method to compute depreciation for film, video tape, sound recordings, copyrights, books, patents, and other property to be specified by federal regulations. However, the income forecast method is not available for intangible property amortizable under IRC Sec. 197 (see ¶ 10-905) or for consumer durable property subject to rent to own contracts as defined by IRC Sec. 168(i)(14). (Sec. 24349(f), Rev. & Tax. Code; Sec. 24355.4, Rev. & Tax. Code)

Unlike federal law, California does not prohibit taking distribution costs into account for purposes of determining the depreciation deduction using the income forecast method. (Sec. 24349(f)(2), Rev. & Tax. Code) Nor does California incorporate the federal provision providing special rules for depreciating participations and residuals, allowing taxpayers to currently deduct participations and residuals rather than depreciate them using the income forecast method. (Sec. 24349(f)(5), Rev. & Tax. Code)

- *Agreement as to useful life; Changes in method*

A taxpayer may enter into a written agreement with the FTB as to the useful life and depreciation rate of a particular property. (Sec. 24351, Rev. & Tax. Code; Sec. 24352, Rev. & Tax. Code)

Any change in the agreement must be approved by the FTB and be based on facts or circumstances not taken into consideration in the adoption of the agreement. The burden of proof is on the party initiating the modification. However, a taxpayer may elect to change from the declining balance method to the straight-line method if there is no provision in a written agreement with the FTB prohibiting such a change. (Sec. 24351, Rev. & Tax. Code; Sec. 24352, Rev. & Tax. Code; Reg. 24352, 18 CCR)

- *Salvage value reduction*

The amount of salvage value to be taken into consideration in computing the amount of qualified personal property subject to depreciation may be reduced by up to 10% of the depreciable basis of the property, before an adjustment for additional first-year depreciation is taken (see discussion below). The salvage value reduction applies only to personal property other than livestock with a useful life of three years or more. However, in the limited circumstances when California allows the use of ACRS depreciation (e.g., S corporations), no salvage value reduction is allowed. (Sec. 24352.5, Rev. & Tax. Code) The California provision is similar to former IRC Sec. 167(f).

- *Additional ("bonus") first-year depreciation*

A taxpayer that does not make the IRC Sec. 179 election discussed above, may make an irrevocable election to take an additional 20% first-year depreciation deduction on tangible personal property, including fixtures, used in business or held for production of income. The additional first-year depreciation bonus is limited to 20% of up to $10,000 of the cost of new or used personal property having a useful life of at least six years. The limitations are applied to each taxpayer, and not to each taxpayer's trade or business. (Sec. 24356, Rev. & Tax. Code; Reg. 24356(a), 18 CCR; Reg. 24356-1, 18 CCR; Reg. 24356(d), 18 CCR) The provision is the same as IRC Sec. 179 as it existed before it was repealed by the Economic Recovery Tax Act of 1981.

To qualify for the bonus depreciation under California law, the property must have been acquired from an unrelated person and may not be acquired by an affiliated group member from another member of the group. In addition, property does not qualify when the taxpayer's basis is determined by reference to the transferor's basis. (Sec. 24356(d), Rev. & Tax. Code; Reg. 24356(c), 18 CCR)

In determining the allowable first-year depreciation bonus, all members of an affiliated group (as defined in IRC Sec. 1504 but substituting the phrase "more than 50 percent" for "at least 80 percent") are treated as one taxpayer. (Sec. 24356(d), Rev. & Tax. Code; Reg. 24356-1, 18 CCR) The allowance may be taken by any one member or allocated among the several members in any manner in accordance with a group agreement, however, the amount allocated to any one member, may not exceed 20% of the cost of qualifying property actually purchased by the member in the taxable year. (Reg. 24356-1, 18 CCR)

¶10-900

The additional first-year depreciation bonus may not be claimed with respect to any property for which the taxpayer claims:

— the special expense deduction allowed for enterprise zone businesses prior to the 2014 taxable year;

— the special expense deduction allowed for local agency military base recovery areas prior to the 2014 taxable year; or

— the special expense deduction allowed for a targeted tax area prior to the 2014 taxable year.

See ¶ 10-845 Subtractions—Targeted Business Activity or Zones. (Sec. 24356.6(e), Rev. & Tax. Code; Sec. 24356.7(e), Rev. & Tax. Code; Sec. 24356.8(e), Rev. & Tax. Code)

Making/revoking the election.—A separate election must be made for each taxable year in which an additional first-year depreciation allowance is claimed and must be made on the taxpayer's tax return for the income year to which the election applies. For the election to be valid, the return must be filed by the due date for filing the return, including extensions, for the taxable year. The election is made by showing as a separate item on the taxpayer's tax return the total additional first-year depreciation claimed with respect to Section 24356 property selected. The taxpayer must maintain records that permit specific identification of each piece of property for which the election was made and reflect how and from whom such property was acquired.

The election is irrevocable, unless the California Franchise Tax Board gives its consent to revoke the election. Taxpayers wishing to revoke the election or to change the property selected for the additional first-year depreciation allowance must submit a written request to the FTB within six months of the due date for filing the tax return for the year (without regard to extensions) in which the additional first-year bonus depreciation was claimed, stating the year and property involved, and the reasons for the request to revoke the election or to change the selection of property. Ordinarily, a request for consent to revoke the election or to change the selection of property will not be granted if it appears from all the facts and circumstances that the only reason for the desired change is to obtain a tax advantage. (Reg. 24356(d), 18 CCR)

• *Basis for depreciation*

The basis of an asset for the purpose of computing the depreciation deduction is the same as the adjusted basis for determining gain on the sale or other disposition of the property (see ¶ 10-690 Additions—Basis Adjustments). (Sec. 24353, Rev. & Tax. Code) The federal provision is identical (IRC Sec. 167(c)); however, it is applicable only to assets acquired before 1981. On the federal level, the Accelerated Cost Recovery System, applicable to assets acquired after 1980, applies depreciation percentages to the unadjusted basis.

• *Luxury automobiles and personal use property*

California incorporates a modified version of IRC Sec. 280F, as of the current California conformity date (see ¶ 10-515), concerning limitations on depreciation for luxury automobiles and certain "listed" property used for personal purposes. IRC Sec. 280F is modified for California tax purposes to substitute the depreciation deduction amounts allowed for state purposes for references to "deduction" or "recovery deduction under IRC Sec. 168," terms that relate to the federal modified accelerated cost recovery system used for federal purposes. Also, "recovery period" in the federal provision means the class life depreciation range for California tax purposes. California has not adopted IRC Sec. 280F provisions related to the federal investment tax credit, because California does not allow an investment tax credit. (Sec. 24349.1, Rev. & Tax. Code) California follows the federal amendment enacted by the Small Business Jobs Act of 2010 that deletes cell phones and similar telecommunications equipment from the definition of "listed property," thereby making it easier for expenses incurred for such equipment eligible to be currently expensed or depreciated on the return. However, different effective dates apply. For California purposes, the amendments apply to taxable years beginning on or after January 1, 2015, while for federal purposes the amendments are effective for taxable years ending after December 31, 2009.

COMMENT: *Federal regulations.*—California conforms to temporary federal regulations issued under IRC Sec. 280F to the extent that California conforms to the underlying IRC provisions and the regulations do not conflict with California statutes and regulations. Because California modifies IRC Sec. 280F for corporation franchise and income tax purposes by requiring that the depreciation deduction be determined by using Sec. 24349, Rev. & Tax. Code, instead of IRC Sec. 168, if the temporary regulations issued under IRC Sec. 280F modify the treatment of depreciation determined under IRC Sec. 168, the modification will have no effect for California corporation franchise and income tax purposes. *E-mail*, California Franchise Tax Board, November 13, 2003.

The depreciation limitations for passenger automobiles (that are not trucks or vans) placed in service in calendar year 2020 for which the IRC Sec. 168(k) additional first year depreciation deduction does not apply are:

— 1st Tax Year: $3,304

— 2nd Tax Year: $5,227

— 3rd Tax Year: $3,084

— Each Succeeding Year: $1,856

(*Memorandum*, California Franchise Tax Board, September 1, 2020)

The depreciation limitations for trucks and vans placed in service in calendar year 2020 for which the IRC Sec. 168(k) additional first year depreciation deduction does not apply are:

— 1st Tax Year: $3,721

— 2nd Tax Year: $5,959

— 3rd Tax Year: $3,502

— Each Succeeding Year: $2,169

(*Memorandum*, California Franchise Tax Board, September 1, 2020)

• *Environmental remediation expenses*

Environmental remediation expenses that are capitalized costs that were currently expensed under IRC Sec. 198 on the federal return, but added back for purposes of computing California taxable income (see ¶ 10-665), may be depreciated for California franchise and corporation income tax purposes.

• *Qualified disaster expenses*

Qualified disaster expenses that are capitalized costs that were currently expensed under IRC Sec. 198A on the federal return (see ¶ 10-660), but added back for purposes of computing California taxable income, may be depreciated for California franchise and corporation income tax purposes.

• *Film and production expenses*

Film and television production expenses that are capitalized costs that were currently expensed under IRC Sec. 181 on the federal return, but added back for purposes of computing California taxable income (see ¶ 10-645), may be depreciated for California franchise and corporation income tax purposes.

• *Conditional sale vs. operating lease*

For purposes of determining whether the lessor or the lessee may claim the depreciation deduction, it must first be determined whether the terms of the lease are such that the transaction is considered a conditional sale (in which case the lessee is eligible to claim the deduction) or an operating lease (in which case the lessor is eligible to claim the deduction). The determination is made on the basis of which party bears most of the benefits and burdens of ownership. (*Alameda Bancorporation, Inc., et al.*, SBE, 95-SBE-001, March 9, 1995)

• *Rent-to-own property*

Qualified rent-to-own property, as defined by IRC Sec. 168(i)(14), is depreciated using a class-life of four years. (Sec. 24355.5, Rev. & Tax. Code) This mirrors the federal depreciation treatment mandated by IRC Sec. 168(g).

• *Tax exempt use property*

The deduction for property leased to governments and other tax-exempt entities, as defined in IRC § 168(h), is limited to the amount determined IRC § 168(g), relating to alternative depreciation system for certain property. (Sec. 24349(g), Rev. & Tax. Code) This mirrors the federal depreciation treatment mandated by IRC Sec. 168(g), under which a pre-1987 ACRS deduction (or any other depreciation or amortization deduction) must be computed by using the straight-line method (without regard to salvage value) and special longer recovery periods.

• *Phylloxera-infested vineyards*

The useful life for any grapevine replaced in a California vineyard in a taxable year beginning after 1991 as a direct result of phylloxera infestation is five years under the ADR system. The five-year depreciation life under the ADR system also applies to any grapevine replaced in a California vineyard in a taxable year beginning after 1996 as a direct result of Pierce Disease infestation. If a taxpayer elects under IRC Sec. 168 to use the Alternative Depreciation System and also elects under IRC Sec. 263A not to capitalize costs of the infested vineyard, then any phylloxera-infested grapevines replaced in a taxable year beginning after 1991 or any Pierce Disease-infested grapevine replaced in a taxable year beginning after 1996 have a class life of 10 years.

Taxpayers claiming a special depreciation deduction for infected grapevines must obtain and retain a written certification from an independent state-certified integrated pest management adviser, or a state agricultural commissioner or adviser, that specifies that the replanting was necessary to restore a vineyard infested with phylloxera or Pierce's Disease. (Sec. 24349(c), Rev. & Tax. Code)

• *Depreciation of real property*

The depreciation of new commercial real estate bought or constructed after 1970, is restricted to the straight-line method, 150% declining balance method, or any other consistent method that does not give greater allowances in the first two-thirds of useful life than the 150% declining balance method. As to new residential property acquired after 1970, the 200% declining balance may be used for new property, the 125% declining balance may be used for used property with a useful life of 20 years or more, and the straight-line method may be used for used property with a useful life of less than 20 years. (Sec. 24354.1, Rev. & Tax. Code; Instructions, FTB 3885, Corporation Depreciation and Amortization) The California provision, except for titles, internal references, and a subsection excluding public utility property, is the same as former IRC Sec. 167(j).

Foreign residential rentals.—Under both California law and prior federal law applicable to pre-1981 acquisitions, foreign residential rental property may be depreciated under the 200% declining balance method only if the laws of the foreign country provide a comparable method. If foreign law allows a less accelerated method, that law applies, unless the amount allowed is less than it would be under the 150% declining balance method. "Residential rental property" is defined as property from which 80% or more of the gross rental income is derived from dwelling units. (Sec. 24354.1, Rev. & Tax. Code)

Used real property.—With regard to used real property acquired after 1970, accelerated depreciation is prohibited, except for used residential rental property having a useful life of 20 years or more, which may be depreciated using a 125% declining balance method. (Sec. 24354.1, Rev. & Tax. Code; Instructions, FTB 3885, Corporation Depreciation and Amortization)

New property.—For new real property acquired or constructed before 1971, California allowed use of the 200% declining balance method and sum-of-the-year's-digits methods. For used real property acquired before 1971, California allowed the 150% declining balance method.

• *Safe-harbor leases*

California recognizes safe harbor leases under former IRC Sec. 168(f). (California Response to CCH Corporate Income Tax Multistate Survey, California Franchise Tax Board, July 21, 2003)

• *Property of life tenants and trust beneficiaries*

The depreciation of property held by a life tenant is computed as if the life tenant were the absolute owner of the property and is not apportioned with a remainder-man. In the case of property held by a trust, the deduction is apportioned between the beneficiaries and the trustee according to the provisions of the trust or on the basis of the trust income allocable to each. (Sec. 24354, Rev. & Tax. Code) The identical provisions are contained in IRC Sec. 167(d), except for the exclusion (in California law) of the treatment of estate property.

• *Prior law*

Residential rental property.—Under prior California law, taxpayers were allowed to use the accelerated cost recovery system (ACRS) of IRC Sec. 168 in determining depreciation for certain California residential rental property on which construction began after June 30, 1985, and before July 1, 1988. (Former Sec. 24349.5, Rev. & Tax. Code) For taxable years beginning before 1987, California apparently applied IRC Sec. 168 as it read prior to an amendment made by P.L. 99-121 that changed the 18-year recovery period for certain real property to 19 years and prior to the amendments made by the Tax Reform Act of 1986, that enacted the modified ACRS (MACRS) method of depreciation. However, a problem of interpretation arises because the former California provision referred to the provisions of IRC Sec. 168 as they read on January 1, 1984; IRC Sec. 168 made no provision for "18-year real property" until the section was amended by the Tax Reform Act of 1984, which was not enacted until July 18, 1984. The problem is further complicated by the amendments made to IRC Sec. 168 by the Tax Reform Act of 1986. Under federal law, for taxable years beginning after 1986, residential rental property must be depreciated under MACRS using the straight-line method over a recovery period of 27.5 years. According to the Franchise Tax Board (FTB), this conflict must be resolved by treating residential rental property on which construction began before 1987, in California (other than low-income housing) as "18-year real property." With respect to residential rental property on which construction began between January 1, 1987, and July 1, 1988, taxpayers could treat such property as either 18-year real property, 27.5-year residential rental property, or Asset Depreciation Range (ADR) property. (*Letter*, FTB, September 13, 1988)

Boilers fueled by oil or gas.—Under prior California law, no accelerated depreciation was allowed for oil- or gas-fueled boilers placed in service after September 30, 1978, that were not eligible for the investment credit under IRC Sec. 38. Straight-line method depreciation was required, using the class life prescribed by the FTB. (Former Sec. 24354.3, Rev. & Tax. Code) Except for titles and internal references, the California provision was the same as former IRC Sec. 167(p).

Under another repealed California provision, boilers or combustors in use on October 1, 1978, and fueled by petroleum or natural gas, could be written off (straight line) over a shortened useful life established by the taxpayer. However, if retirement did not occur on the expected date, interest applied to the tax benefit amount derived. (Former Sec. 24354.4, Rev. & Tax. Code) The California provision corresponded to former IRC Sec. 167(q).

The repeal of subsections (p) and (q) of IRC Sec. 167 by the Revenue Reconciliation Act of 1990 was generally effective with respect to property placed in service after November 5, 1991. The repeal of the corresponding California provisions was effective for income years beginning after 1990.

Railroad grading and tunnel bores.—California Corporation Tax Law has no provision comparable to former IRC Sec. 185, which allowed a domestic common carrier railroad to elect to depreciate grading and tunnel bore costs over a 50-year useful life. IRC Sec. 185 was repealed for taxable years beginning after 1986.

Other subtractions from the taxable income base are listed at ¶ 10-800 Subtractions From Taxable Income Base.

[¶ 10-905] Subtractions--Amortization

Because the corporate amortization deduction is different for California and federal income tax purposes, California corporation franchise and income taxpayers must separately compute their amortization deduction for California tax purposes. C corporations and limited liability companies classified as corporations compute their California amortization deduction on FTB Form 3885, Corporation Depreciation and Amortization. To the extent the amortization amount claimed for federal purposes exceeds the amount calculated on FTB Form 3885 for California purposes, the excess is treated as an addition adjustment and is entered on Line 6, Form 100, California Corporation Franchise or Income Tax Return. Conversely, if the amortization amount computed on FTB Form 3885 for California corporation franchise or income tax purposes exceeds the federal amortization deduction claimed on the taxpayer's federal return, the excess is claimed as a subtraction adjustment and is entered on

Line 12, Form 100. (*Instructions, Form 100, California Corporation Franchise or Income Tax Return*) S corporations use Schedule B (100S), S Corporation Depreciation and Amortization to compute their depreciation deduction.

Other differences are discussed at ¶10-680. Special rules apply to amortization of bond interest (see ¶10-610).

- *Goodwill and certain other intangibles*

California incorporates IRC Sec. 197, which provides for the amortization, over a 15-year period, of goodwill and other intangibles used in a trade or business or for the production of income as of California's current federal conformity date (see ¶10-515). California also incorporates IRC Sec. 167(f), which allows a depreciation deduction in lieu of an amortization deduction for specified intangibles. (Sec. 24355.5, Rev. & Tax. Code) Although California incorporates IRC Sec. 197(f)(10), which requires certain intangible property to be amortized over an extended recover period of not less than 125% of the lease term if it is leased to a tax-exempt entity and would otherwise be considered tax-exempt use property, different effective dates apply. The provision is generally effective for federal purposes to leases entered into after October 3, 2004, and is applicable for California purposes to taxable years beginning after 2004.

Under IRC Sec. 197, amortization of intangibles is available for acquisitions made after August 10, 1993, or, on an elective basis, for all property acquired after July 25, 1991. However, no amortization deduction is allowed under California law for any taxable year beginning before 1994. For property acquired in a taxable year beginning before 1994, the amount that may be amortized may not exceed the adjusted basis of that intangible as of the first day of the first tax year beginning in 1994 and that amount is amortized ratably from that day until 15 years after the month in which the intangible was acquired. (Sec. 24355.5, Rev. & Tax Code)

A federal election, or lack thereof, to amortize all property acquired after July 25, 1991, or to have pre-IRC Sec. 197 law apply to certain property acquired under a binding written contract in effect on August 10, 1993, is binding for California purposes and a separate election is not allowed. (Sec. 24355.5(c), Rev. & Tax Code)

- *Research and experimental expenditures*

California incorporates IRC Sec. 174, as of California's current federal conformity date (see ¶10-515), with modifications that substitute federal references to California's provisions concerning adjusted basis and depreciation. IRC Sec. 174 allows taxpayers to either treat research and experimental expenditures (other than those specifically excluded) as currently deductible expenses or, at the election of the taxpayer, to amortize the expenditures over a period of not less than 60 months, beginning with the month in which the taxpayer first realizes benefits from the expenditures. (Sec. 24365, Rev. & Tax. Code; Reg. 24365-24368(a), 18 CCR—Reg. 24365-24368(d), 18 CCR) Because of California's current federal conformity date (see ¶10-515), California does not conform to the federal requirement that research and experimental expenditures paid or incurred in taxable years beginning after 2021 be amortized ratably over five years (15 years for foreign research). (2017 Summary of Federal Income Tax Changes, California Franchise Tax Board, May 16, 2018)

The election to amortize must be made before the date for filing the return (including extensions) for the taxable year for which the election is made. The election to deduct or amortize research expenditures is binding until the FTB approves a change.

¶10-905

CCH PRACTICE TIP: Separate election allowed.—The California Franchise Tax Board will consider each taxpayer request to change the method of reporting research and development expenditures on its own merits without requiring the taxpayer to first obtain approval by the Internal Revenue Service to change the federal method of reporting. (*FTB Notice 92-6*, August 27, 1992)

• *Organizational expenditures*

California law currently mirrors federal law (IRC Sec. 248) regarding the treatment of organizational expenditures. (Sec. 24407, Rev. & Tax. Code) However, different effective dates apply for purposes of the amendments made by the American Jobs Creation Act of 2004 (AJCA) (P.L. 108-357), to which California now conforms. These amendments allow taxpayers to currently deduct up to $5,000 in start-up expenses and amortize any remainder over a 15-year period. The amendments apply for federal purposes to expenses incurred after October 22, 2004, and for California purposes, to taxable years beginning after 2004. Consequently, for taxpayers that paid or incurred start-up expenses after October 22, 2004, but before January 1, 2005, adjustments may be required. For California purposes prior to the 2005 taxable year, taxpayers could elect to amortize such expenses for up to a 60 month period.

• *Prior law*

Child development services facilities.—For taxable years beginning before 1997, capital expenditures made after June 30, 1970, and before 1977, for certified child development facilities established by owners of places of employment for their employees could be amortized over a 60-month period. (Former 24371.5, Rev. & Tax. Code) Former IRC Sec. 188 also permitted employers a five-year write-off of expenditures for similar facilities, but only for expenditures made between 1972 and 1981. Because of the differences between federal and state law, the basis of the facilities may differ for federal and California income tax purposes.

Reforestation expenses.—For pre-1998 taxable years, a California taxpayer could amortize the cost of forest land improvements over a five-year, rather than a seven year, period. Amortizable expenses included labor costs, and the cost of materials and equipment required to reestablish commercial tree species and accomplish forest improvement work pursuant to Secs. 4561 and 4793 of the California Public Resources Code. Current laws address the current amortization deduction available for reforestation expenses (see ¶ 10-680).

Pre-1987 amortization of construction-period interest and taxes.—The Tax Reform Act of 1986 repealed IRC Sec. 189 and enacted the uniform capitalization rules embodied in IRC Sec. 263A (see ¶ 10-800), which is incorporated by California for post-1986 taxable years. Thus, the treatment of construction period interest and taxes will be determined under the uniform capitalization rules of IRC Sec. 263A for both federal and California purposes, with one exception. Federal transition rules (which are incorporated with the adoption of IRC Sec. 263A for California purposes) provide that the rules of former IRC Sec. 189 will continue to apply to self-constructed assets if substantial construction occurred before March 1, 1986. If an asset is part of an integrated facility and construction began on the facility before March 1, 1986, then the former rules will continue to apply to each component of the integrated facility, even if construction is not commenced before March 1, 1986. An asset generally is considered an integral part of a facility only if the asset will be placed in service at essentially the same time as the other assets comprising the facility.

Under former IRC Sec. 189, as incorporated by former Sec. 24373.5, real property construction period interest and taxes had to be capitalized in the income year in which the obligations were paid or accrued. The expenses were then amortized over a term of income years that depended on the kind of property involved and the years in which the obligations were paid or incurred. The capitalization-amortization requirement did not apply to construction period interest and taxes relating to low-income housing or real property that could not reasonably be expected to be used in a trade or business or in an activity engaged in for profit. If property was sold during an amortization year, a taxpayer was allowed a partial amortization deduction for the year of sale. The deduction was based either on the depreciation convention or recovery period used for the building or on the proportion of the year held before the sale. However, a sale or transfer after which the property received had a basis determined, in whole or in part, by reference to the property given up was not treated as an exchange. In such cases, the transferor continued to deduct the amortization allowable over the amortization period remaining after the transfer.

Other subtractions from the taxable income base are listed at ¶10-800 Subtractions From Taxable Income Base.

[¶10-910] Subtractions--Basis Adjustments

See ¶10-690 for California's modifications to federal basis adjustments.

Other subtractions from the taxable income base are listed at ¶10-800.

[¶10-911] Subtractions--Recovery of Tax Benefit Items

Although California incorporates IRC Sec. 111 Recovery of Tax Benefit Items, California substitutes references to federal credits and credit carryovers with references to California corporation franchise and income tax credits and credit carryovers. (Sec. 24310, Rev. & Tax Code) Under IRC Sec. 111 any income attributable to the recovery during the taxable year of any amount deducted in a prior taxable year is excludable from gross income in the year of the recovery to the extent that the amount did not reduce income subject to tax in the prior year. If a tax credit was allowable for a prior income year and during the current income year there is a downward price adjustment or similar adjustment, under the tax benefit rule, the tax for the current year must be increased by the amount of the prior credit attributable to the adjustment; however, no increase in the current year's tax is required to the extent that the credit allowable for the recovered amount did not reduce the prior year's tax.

Because California substitutes references to federal credits and credit carryovers with references to California corporation franchise and income tax credits and credit carryovers, a subtraction may be taken to reflect amounts that were required to be included as a result of a price adjustment for which a federal credit was claimed. Such amounts may be reported as "other deductions" on Line 16, Form 100, California Corporation Franchise or Income Tax Return, and a schedule itemizing the amounts must be attached. See ¶10-703 Additions—Recovery of Tax Benefit Items, for a discussion of related additions.

• *Restoration of value of certain securities*

California does not incorporate nor have a provision similar to IRC Sec. 80 Restoration of Value of Certain Securities, which subjects to tax the restoration in value of securities of a corporation whose properties were previously expropriated if a taxpayer that held such securities previously claimed a tax deduction as a result of the expropriation. However, the same results can be achieved by applying the tax benefit rule. Consequently, although California corporate tax law does not directly incorporate the IRC Sec. 80 inclusion in gross income, taxpayers may want to think twice before claiming an adjustment on their California corporation franchise (income) tax return.

Other subtractions from the taxable income base are listed at ¶ 10-800.

[¶10-912] Subtractions--Relocation Assistance

To the extent included in federal taxable income, a taxpayer may claim an exclusion from gross income for relocation assistance (including tenant relocation assistance), mandated by state law or local ordinance to compensate taxpayers displaced by the state's or local government's acquisition of real property for public purposes. (Sec. 7269, Govt. Code) The excluded amount is claimed as an "other deduction" on Line 16, Form 100, California Corporation Franchise or Income Tax Return.

Other subtractions from the taxable income base are listed at ¶ 10-800.

[¶10-913] Subtractions--Foreign Aircraft/Ships

Income derived from the operation of aircraft or ships by a foreign corporation is exempt from taxation if (1) the aircraft are registered or the vessels are documented in a foreign country, (2) the income of the corporation is exempt from national income taxation under a treaty which provides an equivalent exemption for U.S. corporations, and (3) local units of the foreign government do not tax U.S. corporations on income from operation of U.S. registered or documented aircraft or vessels. (Sec. 24320, Rev. & Tax. Code) Local governmental units are prohibited from directly taxing income excluded from taxation by Sec. 24320 and from levying any tax measured by income or profits from operation of foreign-registered vessels. (Sec. 24321, Rev. & Tax. Code)

IRC Sec. 883 contains a similar exemption but does not include the provision regarding taxation by local governments. Also, the federal provision generally does not apply to a foreign corporation that is not publicly traded if 50% or more of the value of the corporation's stock is owned by individuals who are not residents of any foreign country meeting the requirements described in the previous paragraph; California has not adopted any such exception. To the extent such income is included in federal taxable income, taxpayers may claim such amount as an "other deduction" on Line 16, Form 100, California Corporation Franchise or Income Tax Return. A supporting schedule must be attached. Conversely, if as a result of the prohibition against local governments taxing such income, the income is not excludable for California corporation franchise (income) tax return, but is excludable for federal purposes, such amount must be added to federal taxable income as an "other addition" on Line 8, Form 100, and a supporting schedule must be attached.

Other subtractions from the taxable income base are listed at ¶ 10-800.

[¶10-914] Subtractions--Transfers to Political Parties

California corporate tax law does not incorporate nor have any provision similar to IRC Sec. 84, which treats transfers of appreciated property to political organizations as a sale, the gain on which is subject to tax. Consequently, it appears that California would treat such a transaction as a gift and taxpayers that are required to include gain from such transfers in their federal taxable income, may subtract such amounts for purposes of computing their California taxable income. Such amounts would be claimed as an "other deduction" on Line 16, Form 100, California Corporation Franchise or Income Tax Return.

Other subtractions from the taxable income base are listed at ¶ 10-800.

[¶10-915] Subtractions--Damage Awards

In lieu of the federal deduction allowable under IRC Sec. 186 Recoveries of Damages for Antitrust Violations, Etc., California law provides for "spreadback" relief in the taxation of income attributable to awards of compensatory damages for patent infringements, damages received for breach of contract or fiduciary relationship, and lump sum antitrust awards. For purposes of the provisions discussed below, California law disregards a fractional part of the month unless it amounts to more than half a month, in which case it is considered to be a month. (Sec. 24679, Rev. & Tax. Code) Consequently, taxpayers that received such awards must determine the amounts deductible under IRC Sec. 186 (the compensatory amount or the amount of the unrecovered losses sustained as a result of such compensable injury) for federal purposes and the amount deductible for California purposes (as described below) and make the appropriate addition or subtraction modification on Line 8 or Line 16, respectively, of Form 100, California Corporation Franchise or Income Tax Return.

• *Patent infringement damages*

The tax attributable to an award of compensatory damages for infringement of a patent may not exceed the increase in taxes that would have resulted had the amount of the award been included in gross income in equal installments for each month of the infringement. (Sec. 24675, Rev. & Tax. Code)

• *Breach of contract award*

When a corporation receives an award of $3,000 or more for breach of contract or fiduciary relationship, the tax on the award may not exceed the total amount of tax increases that would have resulted had the award been allocated to the income of the previous taxable year or years to reflect the amount of income that would have been received in each year but for the breach of contract. (Sec. 24677, Rev. & Tax. Code)

Regardless of the amount of the award, the corporation may deduct all credits and deductions for depletion, depreciation, etc., to which it would have been entitled had the income been received during the year in which it would have been received but for the breach of contract. However, these credits and deductions are allowed only with respect to that part of the award that represents the corporation's share of income from the actual operation of the property.

• *Damages from Clayton Act*

Tax attributable to a damages award under the Clayton Act may not exceed the total increases in taxes that would have resulted if the amount of the award had been included in equal installments for each month during the period in which the corporation sustained injuries resulting from antitrust violations. (Sec. 24678, Rev. & Tax. Code)

Other subtractions from the taxable income base are listed at ¶ 10-800 Subtractions From Taxable Income Base.

[¶10-916] Subtractions--Life Insurance Payments

As to payments received other than those paid on death of the insured, gross income does not include amounts received under life insurance, endowment, or annuity contracts to the extent that the amounts received are equal to the premiums that were paid on the contracts. (Sec. 24302, Rev. & Tax. Code) This provision differs from IRC Sec. 72, dealing with annuities, which requires computation of an exclusion rate to determine the taxable portion of each payment received. To the extent the amount excludable under California law is more than that excludable under federal law, the amount should be listed as an "other deduction" on Line 16, Form 100, California Corporation Franchise or Income Tax Return. Although California does not incorporate the other provisions of IRC Sec. 72, it does incorporate IRC Sec. 72(u), which specifies the tax treatment accorded annuities that are not held by natural persons. (Sec. 24272.2, Rev. & Tax. Code) Consequently no adjustment is required for such amounts.

Other subtractions from the taxable income base are listed at ¶ 10-800.

[¶10-917] Subtractions--Death Benefits

Although California law mirrors federal law (IRC Sec. 101) concerning the exclusion from gross income of life insurance benefits paid upon the death of an insured, other than certain interest, differences may arise as regards the treatment of benefits from a life insurance policy held by an employer. Although California incorporates IRC Sec. 101(j), which limits the exclusion for employers holding a life insurance policy as a beneficiary that covers the life of an employee, different effective dates apply. California incorporates the limits applicable generally to life insurance contracts issued after January 1, 2010, whereas the limits generally apply for federal purposes to life insurance contracts issued after August 17, 2006 (Sec. 24305, Rev. & Tax. Code; Reg. 24305, 18 CCR) To the extent the exclusion is limited for federal income tax purposes, but not California income tax purposes for contracts issued prior to 2010, taxpayers may subtract the difference between the full amount of the benefits paid, less certain interest, and the amount of the federal exclusion. Prior taxpayers may subtract the difference between the full amount of the benefits paid, less certain interest, and the amount of the federal exclusion.

Other subtractions from the taxable income base are listed at ¶ 10-800.

[¶10-918] Subtractions--Discharge of Indebtedness

• *Forgiven PPP loan amounts*

For tax years beginning on and after January 1, 2020, California follows federal law excluding from income any covered loan amount forgiven pursuant to:

— Section 1106 of the Coronavirus Aid, Relief, and Economic Security (CARES) Act (P.L. 116-136);

— the Paycheck Protection Program and Health Care Enhancement Act (P.L. 116-139); or

— the Paycheck Protection Program Flexibility Act of 2020 (P.L. 116-142).

For California purposes, "covered loan" has the same meaning as in the CARES Act. (Sec. 24308.6, Rev. & Tax. Code)

California will not allow a credit or deduction for any expenses paid for using forgiven PPP funds. Taxpayers must reduce any credit or deduction otherwise allowed for those expenses by the amount of the forgiven loan excluded from income. (Sec. 24308.6, Rev. & Tax. Code)

• *Discharge of indebtedness from qualified reacquisition*

California does not adopt the federal provision in IRC Sec. 108(i) allowing taxpayers to defer the recognition of discharge of indebtedness income arising from a qualified reacquisition after December 31, 2008, and before January 1, 2011, of business debt instruments ratably over a five-year period. Consequently, taxpayers are required to make an addition adjustment in the year that the indebtedness is discharged. Subtraction adjustments may be made in subsequent years when the deferred income is reported on the federal return. (Sec. 24307, Rev. & Tax. Code; *E-mail*, California Franchise Tax Board, February 7, 2011)

Other subtractions from the taxable income base are listed at ¶10-800.

[¶10-919] Subtractions--Earthquake Loss Mitigation Incentives

For taxable years beginning on or after July 1, 2015, California gross income does not include an amount received as a loan forgiveness, grant, credit, rebate, voucher, or other financial incentive issued by the California Residential Mitigation Program or the California Earthquake Authority to assist a residential property owner or occupant with expenses paid, or obligations incurred, for earthquake loss mitigation. (Sec. 24308.7(a), Rev. & Tax. Code)

"Earthquake loss mitigation" means an activity that reduces seismic risks to a residential structure or its contents, or both. For purposes of structural seismic risk mitigation, a residential structure is either of the following:

— a structure described in Section 10087(a) of the Insurance Code; or

— a residential building of not fewer than two, but not more than 10, dwelling units.

(Sec. 24308.7(b), Rev. & Tax. Code)

Other subtractions from the taxable income base are listed at ¶10-800.

[¶10-920] Subtractions--Qualified Health Care Service Plan Income

Effective July 1, 2016, California gross income does not include qualified health care service plan income that is accrued with respect to enrollment or services that occur on or after July 1, 2016, and on or before June 30, 2019, by a health care service plan that is subject to the managed care organization provider tax imposed under Sec. 14199.54 of the Welfare and Institutions Code. Also, a qualified health care service plan with no income for a taxable year other than qualified health care service plan income that is excluded from gross income pursuant to this provision will be exempt from the minimum franchise tax (see ¶10-380) for that year. (Sec. 24330, Rev. & Tax. Code)

"Qualified health care service plan income" means any of the following revenue that is associated with the operation of a qualified health care service plan and that is required to be reported to the Department of Managed Health Care:

— premiums (commercial);

— copayments, COB, subrogation;

— Title XIX Medicaid;

— point-of-service premiums;

— risk pool revenue;

- capitation payments;
- Title XVIII Medicare;
- fee-for-service;
- interest; and
- aggregate write-ins for other revenues, including capital gains and other investment income.

(Sec. 24330, Rev. & Tax. Code)

Other subtractions from the taxable income base are listed at ¶ 10-800.

[¶ 11-500]

ALLOCATION AND APPORTIONMENT

[¶11-505] Allocation and Apportionment

The tax liability of multistate and multinational corporations doing business in more than one state or country is problematic. For such corporations, it is difficult to determine with precision the amount of income that is properly taxable in a state because corporate activities both inside the taxing state and elsewhere may contribute to the production of total income.

Most states that impose franchise and/or corporation income taxes have adopted the Uniform Division of Income for Tax Purposes Act (UDITPA) or have enacted legislation substantially similar to UDITPA. A number of states have also signed the Multistate Tax Compact. These two enactments specify how the income of a corporation doing business in, and deriving income from, more than one state or country is divided and assigned to a state or country for tax purposes.

California has enacted its own UDITPA provisions (Sec. 25120, Rev. & Tax. Code through Sec. 25139, Rev. & Tax. Code) as the statutory base for determining the extent to which the income of multistate and multinational corporations may be attributed to the state for corporation franchise and income tax purposes. Generally, such a determination is made by *allocating* nonbusiness income in its entirety to the state of origin or to the commercial domicile of the taxpayer and by *apportioning* business income among the states that are the sources of the income.

Prior to June 27, 2012, California also adopted provisions of the Multistate Tax Compact. (Sec. 38001—38021, Rev. & Tax. Code) Effective June 27, 2012, the state's Multistate Tax Compact provisions are repealed. However, the repeal is not to be construed to create any inference that a change in interpretation with respect to that part, or any reference to that part, prior to its repeal is implied. (Sec. 4, Ch. 37 (S.B. 1015), Laws 2012)

For allocation and apportionment purposes, "business income" is derived from transactions and activity conducted in the regular course of a taxpayer's trade or business; income from the acquisition, management, and disposition of property that constitutes an integral part of the taxpayer's regular trade or business qualifies as business income. Conversely, "nonbusiness income" is derived from sources that are not a part of, or conducted in the course of, a taxpayer's usual trade or business (see ¶ 11-510 Income Subject to Allocation and Apportionment).

Under federal constitutional principles, a corporation's income is not subject to allocation or apportionment unless the corporation engages in an income-producing activity that has a relationship (*i.e.*, "nexus") with the taxing state. A corporation is subject to corporation franchise or income tax in California if it is "doing business" in the state (see ¶ 10-075 Nexus—Doing Business in California).

With the exception of (1) provisions excluding from taxation income derived from foreign operation of foreign aircraft or ships (¶ 10-704 Additions—Foreign Aircraft/Ships) and (2) provisions concerning gain or loss treatment of certain foreign currency transactions (¶ 10-825 Subtractions—Gains), California has no provisions comparable to IRC Subchapter N, which concerns tax on income from sources within or without the United States.

• *Allocation*

A corporation commercially domiciled in California is subject to tax in California on all income derived from sources not apportionable to another state (see ¶ 11-515 Allocation).

• *Apportionment*

Business income is apportioned among the states that are the sources of the income. If one or more corporations engage in business both within and without the state and act as a unitary business, then UDITPA requires that the entire income of the business be considered in apportioning income to the taxing state. Generally, the existence of a unitary business may be established if there is unity of ownership, operation, and use, or if the business in the state contributes to or is dependent on the business outside the state (see ¶ 11-520 Apportionment).

Beginning with the 2013 tax year, the use of a single-sales factor apportionment formula is required (*i.e.*, only the sales factor (see ¶ 11-525) is used), except for taxpayers primarily engaged in an agricultural, extractive, savings and loan, or banking or financial business activity. (Sec. 25128.7, Rev. & Tax. Code) Prior to the 2013 tax year, a double-weighted sales factor apportionment formula was generally required (*i.e.*, property factor plus payroll factor plus *twice* the sales factor, dividing by four). (Sec. 25128, Rev. & Tax. Code) However, for the 2011 and 2012 tax years, taxpayers (other than those primarily engaged in an agricultural, extractive, savings and loan, or banking or financial business activity) were allowed to make an irrevocable election to apportion their business income utilizing a single-sales factor apportionment formula. (Sec. 25128.5, Rev. & Tax. Code)

• *Alternative apportionment methods*

If formula apportionment does not fairly reflect the extent of a corporation's business activity in California, then the corporation may petition the California Franchise Tax Board (FTB), or the FTB may require a taxpayer, to use a modified formula or to use separate accounting. In addition, there are special rules for allocating and apportioning the income of taxpayers engaged in specific industries (see ¶ 11-540 Apportionment Factors for Specific Industries).

• *Consolidated returns*

California generally does not allow the filing of consolidated returns by affiliated corporations, except in the case of an affiliated group of railroad corporations connected through stock ownership with a common parent corporation. However, the FTB may require affiliated corporations to file a consolidated return in certain cases to prevent tax evasion or to clearly reflect income.

• *Combined reporting*

When a group of corporations conducts a unitary business, members of the group must file a combined report if the group's unitary activities are conducted partly within and partly outside California. Unitary group members that derive income solely from California sources may elect to file a combined report, but are not required to do so (see ¶ 11-550 Combined Reports).

• *Water's-edge election*

Multinational corporations that are subject to unitary tax on their worldwide operations may compute their California apportionable tax base on a water's-edge basis, rather than on a worldwide basis. Corporations making a water's-edge election may generally exclude from the combined report some or all of the income and apportionment factors of certain foreign affiliates (see ¶ 11-550 Combined Reports).

[¶11-510] Income Subject to Allocation and Apportionment

Business income is apportioned among multiple states using an apportionment formula (see ¶ 11-520). Nonbusiness income is allocated in its entirety to the state of origin or to the commercial domicile of the taxpayer (see ¶ 11-515).

• *"Business income" defined*

"Business income" is derived from transactions and activity in the regular course of a taxpayer's trade or business, and includes income from tangible and intangible property, the acquisition, management, and disposition of which constitute integral parts of the taxpayer's regular trade or business. In effect, all income that arises from the conduct of a taxpayer's trade or business operations is business income. Income is presumed to be business income for allocation and apportionment purposes unless it is clearly classifiable as nonbusiness income. (Sec. 25120, Rev. & Tax. Code; Reg. 25120, 18 CCR)

• *"Nonbusiness income" defined*

"Nonbusiness income" is all income other than business income. (Sec. 25120, Rev. & Tax. Code; Reg. 25120, 18 CCR)

• *Classification of income*

Analyses under two tests, transactional and functional, determine whether income is business income or nonbusiness income (see *CTS Keene, Inc., and CTS Corporation*, 93-SBE-005, February 10, 1993). The California Supreme Court has held that analysis under both tests is required to determine the correct classification of income (see *Hoechst Celanese Corporation v. Franchise Tax Board*, 25 Cal. 4th 508 (2001)). If either test is satisfied, then the income is apportionable as business income among California and the other states from which it is derived. If neither test is satisfied, then the income is fully allocable to the state of commercial domicile as nonbusiness income. (Sec. 4010, *Multistate Audit Technique Manual*, FTB, December 2002)

Transactional test.—The transactional test identifies income as apportionable business income if the transaction or activity from which the income was derived occurred in the regular course of the taxpayer's trade or business. (Sec. 4010, *Multistate Audit Technique Manual*, FTB, December 2002)

Functional test.—The functional test identifies income as apportionable business income if the acquisition, management, and disposition of the income-producing property was an integral part of the taxpayer's trade or business operations. (Sec. 4010, *Multistate Audit Technique Manual*, FTB, December 2002)

> **COMMENT:** *Income earned with respect to repatriated dividends:* The California Franchise Tax Board has stated that income from the interim investment of proceeds from cash dividends repatriated to the United States pursuant to IRC Sec. 965 (allowing a temporary dividends received deduction), which is earned pending reinvestment of those dividends pursuant to a domestic reinvestment plan, will constitute apportionable business income for California purposes if the dividends are earmarked (as evidenced by the reinvestment plan) for a business use. On the other hand, income from the interim investment of those funds will not be apportionable business income if the repatriated dividends are earmarked for a nonbusiness function or are earmarked for a line of business separate from the taxpayer's unitary trade or business. (*Legal Ruling 2005-02*, California Franchise Tax Board, July 8, 2005)

> **COMMENT:** *Sale of stock:* In *Appeal of Occidental Petroleum*, 83-SBE-119, the State Board of Equalization held that the classification of income from intangibles under the functional test of business income must be made on the basis of the relationships between the intangible and the taxpayer's unitary business. Sales of stock in entities that were fully integrated and functioning parts of the taxpayer's existing unitary business gave rise to apportionable income. Sales of stock in corporations that were intended to be integrated into the taxpayer's business, but at the time of the sales were not yet integrated, generated nonbusiness income. This distinction—between the intent and potential for integration, on the one hand, versus actual integration, on the other—has led to confusion as to what the result should be where the two corporations have had a preexisting business relationship beyond that involved in the mere acquisition of stock, yet the purpose for the acquisition of the stock is based on intent to integrate the target into the taxpayer's unitary business operations. If the integration does not occur, and the intent of the taxpayer is frustrated, questions have arisen as to whether a sale of the stock should properly give rise to nonbusiness income even though there are preexisting operational ties unrelated to the acquisition of the stock. The California Franchise Tax Board has issued a legal ruling that addresses this issue and provides examples of the application of the law to various situations. In making the determination of business or nonbusiness income, it is the actual operational ties and the significance of such ties that are most important. While the taxpayer's intent, along with other factors, may support a determination that an operational relationship did or did not exist, the frustration of the taxpayer's intended purpose for the acquisition of the stock is not a determining factor. (*Legal Ruling 2012-01*, California Franchise Tax Board, August 29, 2012)

- *Distributive partnership income*

The standard functional and transactional tests discussed above are used to determine whether distributive partnership income is classified as business or nonbusiness income. The classification of business/nonbusiness income is made at the partnership level if an apportioning trade or business is conducted by a partner or member that is unitary with the apportioning trade or business of the partnership or

LLC. If the partner and corporate owner are nonunitary, the classification is made at the partner level. (Reg. 25137-1(a), 18 CCR; Instructions, Schedule R, Apportionment and Allocation of Income)

• *Proration of deductions*

If an allowable deduction applies to the business incomes of more than one trade or business and/or to several items of nonbusiness income, then the deduction must be prorated among such trades or businesses and/or items of nonbusiness income in a manner that fairly distributes the deduction among the classes of income to which it applies. (Reg. 25120, 18 CCR)

[¶11-515] Allocation

Nonbusiness income is generally allocated in its entirety to the state of origin or to the commercial domicile of the taxpayer. (Sec. 25123, Rev. & Tax. Code through Sec. 25127, Rev. & Tax. Code) See ¶11-510 Income Subject to Allocation and Apportionment for definitions of "business income" and "nonbusiness income."

Allocated income is reported on Form 100, California Corporation Franchise or Income Tax Return.

Interest, dividends, rents and royalties from real and personal property, patent and copyright royalties, and gains and losses are specifically allocated as discussed below.

• *Commercial domicile*

A corporation's commercial domicile may be established by the activity that a corporation does in the state and by the absence of a commercial domicile elsewhere. (*Simon, Inc.*, SBE, 72-SBE-008, March 28, 1972) It may also be established by a showing of a principal place of business in the state. (Sec. 25120(b), Rev. & Tax. Code) A commercial domicile is the principal place from which a trade or business is directed or managed. (Sec. 25120, Rev. & Tax. Code)

CCH COMMENT: *Commercial domicile distinguished from legal domicile.*—A commercial domicile is different from a legal domicile, the latter being the state of incorporation. (Sec. 1500, *Multistate Audit Technique Manual*, FTB, December 2002)

• *Interest*

Interest derived from nonbusiness activities, such as investments not related to the trade or business of a corporation, is taxable in the commercial domicile of the corporation. (Sec. 25126, Rev. & Tax. Code) Interest derived from the trade or business, such as interest earned by a retailer using conditional sales or installment sales contracts, is apportionable income (see ¶11-520 Apportionment).

• *Dividends*

Dividends received by a corporation are generally nonbusiness income allocated to, and taxable by, the state of commercial domicile. (Sec. 25126, Rev. & Tax. Code) However, dividends received by a corporation constitute apportionable business income if they are derived from stock arising out of, or acquired in the regular course of, the taxpayer's trade or business or if the purpose for acquiring and holding the stock is related or incidental to the taxpayer's trade or business. (Reg. 25120, 18 CCR)

A special provision applies to dividends from subsidiaries whose income is included in total income subject to apportionment (see ¶11-520 Apportionment).

• *Interest expense deduction*

California law limits the California interest expense deduction by corporations whose income is subject to apportionment. (Sec. 24344, Rev. & Tax. Code) There is no comparable federal limitation. The U.S. Supreme Court has held that a statutory offset provision in Sec. 24344(b) limiting the deductibility of interest expenses for income apportionment purposes violates the Due Process Clause and the Commerce Clause of the U.S. Constitution because it imposes tax on income outside California's jurisdictional reach (see *Hunt-Wesson, Inc. v. Franchise Tax Board*, 538 U.S. 458 (2000)). Under Sec. 24344(b), the taxpayer's interest expense deduction in excess of business interest income was reduced by the amount of nonbusiness interest and dividend income not subject to apportionment by formula. Although the offset provision does not directly tax nonunitary income, it does in effect constitute indirect taxation of such income, the Court said. The Court noted that offset provisions reasonably reflecting the proper allocation of interest expenses to unitary and nonunitary income would be constitutionally acceptable. However, by reducing an interest expense deduction in the precise amount of nonunitary income, the California offset scheme does not reasonably allocate the portion of interest expenses incurred to the generation of actual nonunitary income related to such expenses. The Court therefore held that inclusion of nontaxable income in California's existing offset computation scheme constitutes impermissible taxation of nonunitary income.

The California Franchise Tax Board (FTB) issued *FTB Notice 2000-9* to explain the deductibility of interest expense in light of the U.S. Supreme Court decision in *Hunt-Wesson*. The FTB policy is that the interest-offset provision invalidated in *Hunt-Wesson* will not be applied to nondomiciliary corporations, but that all other provisions in the interest-offset rules will continue to apply.

Based on *FTB Notice 2000-9*, domestic and foreign corporations must compute their allowable interest expense deduction differently. Foreign (*i.e.*, non-California) corporations allocate their interest expense between apportionable and nonapportionable income as follows:

(1) A deduction for interest expense equal to business interest income may be claimed in computing income subject to apportionment.

(2) A deduction for interest expense in excess of business interest income may be claimed in computing income subject to apportionment in an amount equal to the amount of nonbusiness interest and dividend income.

(3) Any interest expense in excess of interest income and nonbusiness dividend income may be assigned to other types of nonbusiness income, such as rents and royalties, under authority of Reg. 25120(d), 18 CCR. Interest expense assigned to such nonbusiness income items would not be a deductible in determining apportionable income. Note, however, that the FTB will not apply Reg. 25120(d), 18 CCR, to assign interest expense to assets that have the potential to generate interest and dividend income. In other words, the FTB will not use the regulation to assign interest expense to capital gains or losses from sales or other exchanges of stocks, bonds, and similar instruments.

(4) Any remaining interest expense (after applying steps 1 through 3) is deductible against apportionable income.

For domestic (*i.e.*, California) corporations, interest expense is allocated in the same manner, except that step 2 is modified to provide that interest expense in excess of business interest income may reduce nonbusiness interest and dividend income allocable to California in an amount equal to the amount of nonbusiness interest and dividend income. In other words, California corporations continue to enjoy a full offset of interest expense against nonbusiness interest and dividend income. (*FTB Notice 2000-9*, California Franchise Tax Board, December 19, 2000)

Under statutory provisions not directly affected by *Hunt-Wesson*, dividends received from California corporations that are otherwise excludable from taxable income as income already subject to tax (Sec. 25106, Rev. & Tax. Code; Sec. 25140, Rev. & Tax. Code) are not accounted for in computing the interest expense deduction or in determining the tax of the recipient, except for tax deduction computation purposes under Sec. 24345, Rev. & Tax. Code (see ¶ 10-840 Subtractions—Taxes). For water's-edge election purposes, dividends from foreign corporations that are deductible under Sec. 24411, Rev. & Tax. Code (see ¶ 11-550 Combined Reports) are not accounted for in computing the interest expense deduction. (Sec. 24344, Rev. & Tax. Code)

All other interest expense generally must be offset against interest and dividend income not subject to apportionment (except the excludable dividends noted above). However, interest expense incurred for foreign investment purposes may be offset against the foreign dividends deductible under Sec. 24411, Rev. & Tax. Code. The interest expense amount incurred for foreign investment purposes that may be offset against deductible dividends must be computed by multiplying the interest expense amount by the same percentage used to determine the taxpayer's dividend deduction under Sec. 24411, Rev. & Tax. Code (Sec. 24344, Rev. & Tax. Code) See also the discussion of interest as a deductible expense at ¶ 10-815 Subtractions—Interest.

Under Sec. 24402, Rev. & Tax. Code, the percentage of dividends excludable as derived from sources in California that have already been subject to tax is adjusted to reflect the extent of nonunitary and nontaxable income. However, a California court of appeal has struck down Sec. 24402, Rev. & Tax. Code, as facially discriminatory under the Commerce Clause of the U.S. Constitution. (*Farmer Bros. Co. v. Franchise Tax Board*, Cal. Ct. App., No. B160061, May 21, 2003) See ¶ 10-810 Subtractions—Dividends for a full discussion of the dividends received deduction and the issues relating to the deduction being held invalid.

• *Rents and royalties from real and personal property*

Real property.—Rents and royalties from real property are allocated to California if the real property is located in California. (Sec. 25124, Rev. & Tax. Code)

Personal property.—Rents and royalties received from tangible personal property are allocated to California if the tangible personal property is used in California or if the taxpayer has its commercial domicile in California and the taxpayer is not organized under or taxable in the state in which the property is used. If rents and royalties are derived from tangible personal property used in a unitary business, then they are apportioned to California by formula (see ¶ 11-520 Apportionment). If the property is only partially used in California, then the extent to which the property is used in California is determined by applying to total rents and royalties a ratio computed by dividing the number of days that the property is used in California by the number of days that it is used everywhere. (Sec. 25124, Rev. & Tax. Code)

• *Patent and copyright royalties*

If a patent or copyright is used by a licensee in California, then the royalties paid to the licensor for such use are allocated to California. If a patent or copyright is used in a place other than California, then the royalties are allocated, to the extent that it was used in another state, to that other state. (Sec. 25127, Rev. & Tax. Code) A patent or other royalty received is apportionable if the patent is used in, or the management of patents is part of, the unitary business of the taxpayer (see ¶11-520 Apportionment).

A patent is used in another state if it is employed in fabrication, manufacture, or other processing of a product, or if a product embodying the patent is produced in the other state. If the place of use cannot be determined, then all royalties are allocated to the commercial domicile of the taxpayer. (Sec. 25127, Rev. & Tax. Code)

A copyright is used in another state if printing or publishing a work protected by a copyright occurs in that state. To the extent that it cannot be determined where the printing or publishing occurs, the royalties are allocated to the taxpayer's commercial domicile. (Sec. 25127, Rev. & Tax. Code)

• *Gains and losses*

Sale of real property.—Gains and losses realized from sales of real property located in California are allocated to California. (Sec. 25125, Rev. & Tax. Code)

Sale of tangible personal property.—Gains and losses realized from sales of tangible personal property are allocated to California if the property's "situs" is in California at the time of the sale, or if the taxpayer's commercial domicile is in California and the taxpayer is not subject to tax in the state of the property's situs. (Sec. 25125, Rev. & Tax. Code) Gains or losses resulting from ownership of or transactions in nonbusiness personal property, tangible or intangible, are apportioned to California if the property is used in a unitary business (see ¶11-520 Apportionment).

Sale of qualifying investment securities.—The distributive share of interest, dividends, and gains from the sale or exchange of qualifying investment securities derived by a corporate partner in a qualified investment partnership is exempt from tax, provided such income is the taxpayer's only income derived from or attributable to sources within California. However, such income is taxable by California if the taxpayer participates in the management of the investment partnership's investment activities. California tax also applies if the taxpayer is engaged in a unitary business with another corporation or partnership that either participates in the management of the investment partnership's investment activities or has income derived from, or attributable to, sources within the state other than income from qualifying investment securities. (Sec. 23040.1, Rev. & Tax. Code)

CCH PRACTICE TIP: *Treatment of master fund's investment in commodity-linked derivative securities.*—In response to a taxpayer's inquiry, the California Franchise Tax Board's chief counsel has determined that investments in commodity-linked derivative securities are qualified investment securities for California personal income and corporation franchise and income tax purposes. Consequently, a fund that invests in the commodity-linked derivative securities would be a qualified investment partnership and the income from the investments would be exempt from corporation franchise and income taxes provided all other conditions are satisfied. (*Chief Counsel Ruling 2010-01*, California Franchise Tax Board, March 25, 2010)

Receipt of stock or securities by alien corporation.—Income, gains, and losses from stock or securities received by an alien corporation are also exempt, provided that trading in such stock or securities on the corporation's own account constitutes its sole activity in California, and provided that trading is not conducted by dealers in stock or securities. (Sec. 23040.1, Rev. & Tax. Code)

Sale of intangible personal property.—Except in the case of a sale of a partnership interest, capital gains and losses from the sale of intangible personal property are otherwise allocated to California if the taxpayer's commercial domicile is in California. When a partnership interest is sold, allocation depends upon the extent to which partnership assets consist of tangible property. If tangible property constitutes 50% or more of the value of partnership assets at the time of sale, then gain or loss is allocated to California in the ratio that the partnership's in-state tangible property's original cost bears to the total original cost of all tangible property, wherever located. However, if intangible property constitutes greater than half the value of partnership assets, gain or loss on the sale of a partnership interest is allocated according to the partnership's sales factor for the first full tax period immediately preceding the tax period during which the sale occurred. (Sec. 25125, Rev. & Tax. Code)

CCH CAUTION: Passive pass-through entity owners.—As discussed immediately above, a taxpayer taxable as a corporation may have to pay California taxes on a gain from the sales of a partnership interest even if the taxpayer is a passive investor and the partnership interest was a nonbusiness asset. S corporations. S corporations and their shareholders should be aware that the income from the sale is sourced differently for corporation tax purposes than for the shareholders. Regulation 17951-4(f) states the source of an S corporation's items of nonbusiness income for purposes of tax on the S corporation has no relevance in determining the source of the item for purposes of taxing a nonresident shareholder. In contrast, for purposes of determining the LLC fee, taxpayers must follow the rules for assigning sales under Rev. & Tax Code § 25135 (i.e. tangible personal property) and § 25136 (i.e. market-based rules for services and intangibles). Regulation 17951-4(c), (d), and (g) rules do not apply. (*Tax News*, California Franchise Tax Board, September 2013)

[¶11-520] Apportionment

What is the standard California apportionment formula?

Beginning with the 2013 taxable year, California requires most multistate corporations to apportion their business income using a single-factor apportionment formula that consists of only a sales factor. (Sec. 25128.7, Rev. & Tax. Code)

Prior to the 2013 taxable year, most multistate corporations were required to apportion their business income using a double-weighted sales factor apportionment formula. The formula was a fraction consisting of, a property factor plus a payroll factor plus a double-weighted sales factor, divided by four. (Sec. 25128, Rev. & Tax. Code) However, for the 2011 and 2012 taxable years, taxpayers could make an election to apportion their business income using a single-sales factor apportionment formula. (Sec. 25128.5, Rev. & Tax. Code)

Businesses involved in agricultural, extractive, savings and loans, or banking or financial business activities must use an equally-weighted three-factor apportionment formula. (Sec. 25128, Rev. & Tax. Code)

California also has adopted special apportionment formulas and rules for other specific industries.

A taxpayer is subject to allocation and apportionment of its income only if it has business income that is taxable both in and outside California. A taxpayer's business income is considered to be taxable in another state if:

— the taxpayer is subject to a net income tax, franchise tax measured by net income, franchise tax for the privilege of doing business, or corporate stock tax in the other state; or

— the other state has jurisdiction to impose a net income tax, regardless of whether it imposes the tax.

A taxpayer is not taxable in another state if its only activity there is the production of nonbusiness income or its business activities there relate to a nonunitary trade or business. A taxpayer that claims it is subject to tax in a state may be required to submit proof of taxability. The FTB may request that the taxpayer provide proof that it has filed a tax return with the other state and has paid tax to the other state. A taxpayer's failure to produce this material may be used as evidence of nontaxability in the other state. (Sec. 25122, Rev. & Tax. Code; Reg. 25122, 18 CCR)

PRACTICE NOTE: The State Board of Equalization (BOE) has held that taxability in a foreign country is established only by reference to U.S. constitutional limitations, without regard to any limitations imposed by Public Law 86-272. The BOE held that the immunity provided by Public Law 86-272 is expressly limited to interstate commerce. So, while Reg. 25122(c) states that U.S. jurisdictional standards must be applied to determine whether a foreign country has jurisdiction to tax an entity, for foreign commerce transactions this language refers to U.S. constitutional nexus. Jurisdictional limitations of Public Law 86-272 are not considered. Thus, if goods are shipped from California to a foreign destination, the relevant question is whether the taxpayer has constitutional nexus in the foreign country. If nexus is present, the taxpayer is considered to have a taxable presence in that country, even if its activities in that country do not go beyond solicitation of orders for sales. *Dresser Industries, Inc.,* BOE, 82-SBE-307, June 29, 1982; opinion denying reh'g, October 26, 1983.

If an allowable deduction applies to the apportionable business income of more than one trade or business and/or to several items of allocable nonbusiness income, then the taxpayer must prorate the deduction among the trades or businesses and the items of nonbusiness income in a manner that fairly distributes the deduction among the types of income to which it applies. (Reg. 25120(d), 18 CCR)

Elective single-sales factor formula for 2011 and 2012. The single-sales factor election for the 2011 and 2012 taxable years could be made by any of the following:

— a corporation;

— a corporation that was a member of a combined reporting group;

— a division of a corporation engaged in a separate trade or business not unitary with the other trades or businesses of the corporation;

— a partnership owned by a corporate partner that was not unitary with the partnership, whether the corporation stood alone or was a member of a combined reporting group;

— a partnership owned by a nonresident individual partner; or

— a sole proprietorship operated by a nonresident individual.

(Reg. 25128.5, 18 CCR)

¶11-520

A taxpayer was required to make the election on a timely filed (including extensions) original return for the year of the election. (Reg. 25128.5(b)(8), 18 CCR) A taxpayer that was engaged in more than one apportioning trade or business could make a separate election for each apportioning trade or business. (Reg. 25128.5(b)(6), 18 CCR) Timely filings that only supplemented a previously filed return, or corrected mathematical or other errors, were treated as incorporating the previously filed return, to the extent not inconsistent, and were treated as the original return for election purposes. Timely filings that clearly reflected an intent to withdraw an election made on a previously filed return were also treated as original returns. (Reg. 25128.5(b)(8), 18 CCR)

An election was valid if the tax was computed consistent with the election, and written notification of the election was made on Part B of Schedule R-1 attached to the taxpayer's return. (Reg. 25128.5(b)(7), 18 CCR)

An apportioning trade or business could make the election even if it included one or more business activities that would normally require the use of an equally-weighted three factor apportionment formula, as long as not more than 50% of the gross business receipts were derived from those business activities. (Reg. 25128.5(b)(3), 18 CCR)

EXAMPLE: Partnership P conducted an apportioning trade or business and was owned 65% by Corp. W and 35% by Corp. T. Partnership P derived less than 50% of its gross business receipts from extractive business activity. Partnership P, Corp. T, and Corp. W were not unitary with each other. As a result, Corp. W and Corp. T could not independently decide whether to make a single-sales factor method election for their distributive share items of income from the nonunitary Partnership P. However, Partnership P could use the single-sales factor formula to determine California source income for Corp. W and Corp. T on Part B of Schedule R-1 of Form 565 using the Partnership P factor(s) because Partnership P's separate apportioning trade or business derived less than 50% of its gross business receipts from extractive business activities. (Reg. 25128.5(b)(3), 18 CCR)

In the case of a combined reporting group, all California taxpayer members of the group had to make the election in order for the election to be valid. For instance, if a parent corporation included in a combined report made the election on its separately filed return but its subsidiary did not, then neither was treated as having made the election. (Reg. 25128.5(b), 18 CCR)

An election made on a group return was an election by each taxpayer member included in that group return. However, the election made on a group return did not have any effect if a member of the group filed a separate return in which no election was made, unless the business assets held by the electing group members were greater than the business assets held by the non-electing members. (Reg. 25128.5(b)(2), 18 CCR)

Corporations that were non-electing taxpayers, but that were subsequently found to be members of a combined reporting group as the result of a Franchise Tax Board (FTB) audit determination, were considered to have made the election if the value of the total business assets of the electing taxpayers was greater than those of the non-electing taxpayers. Business assets of members who were not California taxpayers were not included. The starting date of the deemed election was the same as the commencement date of the electing taxpayers. Conversely, if the value of the total business assets of the electing taxpayers did not exceed the value of the total business assets of the non-electing taxpayers, then the single-sales factor formula election of each electing taxpayer was terminated as of the date the non-electing taxpayers were, as the result of an audit determination, properly included in the same combined reporting group as the electing taxpayers. However, the deemed election did not apply if the FTB audit determination was withdrawn or overturned. (Reg. 25128.5(b)(4)(A), 18 CCR)

A taxpayer that was subsequently found not to be a member of the combined reporting group during an FTB audit could make the election on an amended return within 60 days (or up to 180 days for good cause) after the date of the applicable FTB notice. Separate elections could be made for each taxable year included in the audit. In the case of a refund claim made by an entity that was erroneously included in a combined reporting group, a request to make the election had to be made in the claim itself or be presented before the notice of action on the claim was issued. (Reg. 25128.5(b)(5)(A), 18 CCR)

Elections were made at the end of each taxable year when changes in affiliation were known. When a corporation was acquired by a combined reporting group and became unitary mid-year, then the members of the combined reporting group had the option of electing to use the single-sales factor formula at the end of that taxable year. The income and factors of the acquired entity were not included in the combined report for the portion of the year before acquisition, and the acquired entity had to file a return reflecting its income from California sources and could make its own separate election for that time period. When a combined reporting group sold a corporation, at the end of the year the taxpayer members of the combined reporting group could make a group election. However, the sold entity's income and factors were not included for the time period after the sale. The divested entity had to file its own tax return for the post-sale time period and could make its own separate election for that portion of the year. (Reg. 25128.5(c)(3), 18 CCR)

CCH POINTER: A taxpayer could not make a single-sales factor election and then pay California corporation franchise and income tax computed as though no election was made in order to avoid the large corporate understatement penalty (LCUP) in the event that the taxpayer was later determined to be ineligible to use the single-sales factor formula. Both the single-sales factor election and the tax for purposes of measuring the LCUP understatement had to be reported on the last return filed on or before the extended due date of the return. So, a taxpayer could not, for the same taxable year, make the single-sales factor election and report tax based on income apportioned using a three-factor formula. (*Legal Division Guidance 2012-03-02*, California Franchise Tax Board, March 2012)

Multistate Tax Compact's equally-weighted three-factor formula (*Gillette*). California was a member of, and adopted the text of, the Multistate Tax Compact from 1974 to 2012 (repealed effective June 27, 2012). (Sec. 38006, Rev. & Tax. Code) During that time, the Compact contained an election provision that allowed taxpayers to use *either* an equally-weighted three-factor apportionment formula or an alternative apportionment formula adopted by the state. On July 29, 2015, the Compact was amended to delete the equally-weighted three-factor formula and allow adopting member states to replace it with any state apportionment formula. (Sec. 38006, Art. III(1), Art. IV(9), Rev. & Tax. Code) In 1993, California enacted Sec. 25128, Rev. & Tax. Code, which *required* most taxpayers to apportion business income using a double-weighted sales-factor formula, "notwithstanding Section 38006." In

2015, the California Supreme Court held that, despite the Compact's apportionment formula election provision, taxpayers could not use the Compact's equally-weighted three-factor formula to apportion net income for California corporation franchise and income tax purposes. Instead, the court said taxpayers must use the apportionment formula required under California law (*i.e.,* a double-weighted sales factor formula for tax years beginning before 2013, or a single-sales factor formula for tax years beginning after 2012). (*The Gillette Company v. Franchise Tax Board*, California Supreme Court, No. S206587, December 31, 2015) The court determined that (1) the Compact constitutes state law (without the force of federal law), (2) the Compact was not a binding contract between the signatory states, (3) the California Legislature had the authority to repeal the Compact's election provision, (4) the California Legislature intended to repeal the election provision, and (5) the legislation repealing the election provision did not violate the state's "reenactment rule."

Equally-weighted three-factor formula for qualified businesses. Apportioning trades or businesses that derive more than 50% of their gross business receipts from one or more qualified business activities must apportion business income to California using an equally-weighted three-factor apportionment formula. The formula is a fraction consisting of a property factor plus a payroll factor plus a sales factor, divided by three. (Sec. 25128, Rev. & Tax. Code; Reg. 25128, 18 CCR) A "qualified business activity" is any of the following:

— agricultural business activity (as defined in Reg. 25128-2, 18 CCR);

— extractive business activity (as defined in Reg. 25128-1, 18 CCR);

— savings and loan activity; or

— banking or financial business activity.

(Sec. 25128, Rev. & Tax. Code; Reg. 25137-4.2, 18 CCR)

In determining whether apportioning trades or businesses derive more than 50% of their gross business receipts from one or more of these business activities, "gross business receipts" means all gross receipts not allocated to a state, whether the receipts are excluded from the sales factor by any adjustments. In the case of entities required to be included in a combined report, "gross business receipts" includes the gross business receipts of the entire apportioning trade or business of the group, excluding gross receipts from sales or other transactions among members of the group. (Sec. 25128, Rev. & Tax. Code)

PRACTICE NOTE: If an activity generates both income that is included in the tax base and excluded income, only factors related to the production of income should be used to apportion that income. For example, for payroll factor purposes, this may be accomplished through a time ratio for the employees engaged in activities that generate taxable income and exempt income. The property factor can be divided in a manner similar to that provided for business income and nonbusiness income. In the case of the sales factor, it can be accomplished by eliminating sales from the sales factor to the extent they relate to exempt income not subject to apportionment. (*Legal Ruling 2006-01,* California Franchise Tax Board, April 28, 2006) The Legislature has stated its intent that *Legal Ruling 2006-01* applies to apportionment factors attributable to the income of qualified health care service plans that is excluded from gross income by Rev. & Tax. Code Sec. 24330. (Sec. 2, Ch. 2 (S.B. 2), Laws 2016, 2nd Extra. Session)

Apportionment of pass-through entity income. S corporations, partnerships, and limited liability companies (LLCs) treated as partnerships for tax purposes must use the same apportionment formula as C corporations to apportion their business income. (Instructions, Schedule R, Apportionment and Allocation of Income)

Distributive income of nonresident corporate owners. If the activities of a partnership and a nonresident corporate partner constitute a unitary business, the partner must add its share of the partnership's property, payroll, and sales in and outside California to its own property, payroll, and sales in and outside California to determine the income apportionable to California on its tax return. Adjustments are required to eliminate the effect of intercompany uses of property and intercompany sales. If the activities of a partnership and a nonresident corporate partner are nonunitary, the partner's share of the partnership's trade or business must be treated as a separate trade or business of the partner. In that case, the partner's share of the partnership's business income is added to the partner's other business income apportioned to California and nonbusiness income allocable to California to determine the partner's tax for the year. The rules applicable to partnerships and partners also apply to LLCs treated as partnerships and their members. (Reg. 25137-1, 18 CCR; Instructions, Schedule R, Apportionment and Allocation of Income; *Instructions, Schedule K-1 (565)*, Partner's Share of Income, Deductions, Credits, etc.)

Distributive income of nonresident individual owners. A nonresident individual partner's factors must be combined with the partner's distributive share of the partnership's factors if: the partner owns at least a 20% interest, or if the FTB determines combination is necessary to properly reflect income or loss of the partnership or its partners. Partnership-level apportionment factors are applied to the partner's distributive business income, including guaranteed payments, if the partner and partnership are not engaged in a unitary business. (Reg. 17951-4(d), 18 CCR; Reg. 25137-1, 18 CCR; Instructions, Schedule R, Apportionment and Allocation of Income)

Built-in gains for S corporations. When an apportioning S corporation sells property generating net recognized built-in gain under IRC § 1374, the income should be apportioned for California income tax purposes according to the factors in the year of the sale, rather than according to the factors in the year of the S corporation conversion. (*Technical Advice Memorandum 2017-02*, California Franchise Tax Board, April 3, 2017)

Does California allow alternative apportionment methods?

If the standard allocation and apportionment provisions do not fairly represent the extent of a taxpayer's business activity in California, then the corporation may petition for, or the FTB may require, the use of any of the following, if reasonable:

— separate accounting;

— exclusion of any one or more of the factors;

— inclusion of one or more additional factors; or

— employment of any other method to fairly allocate and apportion the taxpayer's income.

Departure from the standard allocation and apportionment provisions is permitted only in limited cases where unique and nonrecurring fact situations produce improper results under the standard provisions. (Sec. 25137, Rev. & Tax. Code; Reg. 25137, CCR)

¶11-520

PRACTICE TIP: Start-up businesses.—For businesses (mostly start-ups) that have organized in California, registered to do business in California, or otherwise meet the legal definition of "doing business" in California, but have no current year sales, the FTB recommends filing a petition for use of an alternative apportionment methodology since there will be no sales factor. (*Tax News,* California Franchise Tax Board, October 2016)

Application procedures. Petitions to use an alternative apportionment method need not take any particular form, but usually are contained in letters mailed to the FTB's Legal Division. Petitions must include:

— a detailed description of the taxpayer's activities in the state;

— identification of the standard apportionment formula;

— an analysis of how the standard formula does not fairly reflect the extent of the taxpayer's activity in California; and

— a proposed alternative method, with an analysis of how and why the proposed alternative is reasonable.

Petitions may be submitted in advance of the filing of a return or at any time when the statute of limitations for a particular tax year remains open. If granted, petitions apply to specified tax years, and may include years in the future. Open-ended petitions are not granted. The application of petitions to future years is conditioned on the factual underpinnings of the petitions continuing into those years. (*E-mail*, California Franchise Tax Board, May 1, 2014)

Burden of proof. The party seeking to use an alternative apportionment method has the burden of proving by clear and convincing evidence that the standard apportionment formula fails to fairly reflect the extent of a taxpayer's activity in California and that the proposed alternative is reasonable. (*Microsoft Corp. v. Franchise Tax Board*, 39 Cal. 4th 750 (2006))

[¶11-525] Sales Factor

What is the California sales factor?

The sales factor of the California apportionment formula (Sec. 25134, Rev. & Tax. Code; Reg. 25134, 18 CCR) (see ¶11-520) for multistate taxpayers that derive business income (Sec. 25120, Rev. & Tax. Code; Reg. 25120, 18 CCR) (see ¶11-510) from California is a fraction. The numerator of the fraction is the taxpayer's total sales in California during the taxable year, and the denominator is the taxpayer's total sales everywhere during the taxable year. (Sec. 25134, Rev. & Tax. Code; Reg. 25134, 18 CCR)

The sales factor is computed on Sch. R, Apportionment and Allocation of Income, and used to apportion net income on Form 100, California Corporation Franchise or Income Tax Return.

Sales or receipts included in the California sales factor. "Sales" means all gross receipts of the taxpayer that are not allocated (Sec. 25120(e), Rev. & Tax. Code). This includes all gross receipts derived from a taxpayer's business activities, even if the income is not from usual business sources. It does not include receipts from nonbusiness activities. (Sec. 25134, Rev. & Tax. Code; Reg. 25134, 18 CCR)

"Gross receipts" is the amount received from:

— the sale or exchange of property;

— the performance of services; or

— the use of property or capital in a transaction that produces business income, and in which the income, gain, or loss is recognized under federal law, as applied for California purposes (or would be recognized if the transaction were in the United States).

CCH PRACTICE TIP: Amounts realized on the sale or exchange of property are not reduced by the cost of goods sold or the basis of property sold.

(Sec. 25120(f)(2), Rev. & Tax. Code)

"Sales" includes gross receipts from the following:

— sales of manufactured goods or products, less returns and allowances, that the taxpayer sells or purchases and resells, including interest income, service charges, carrying charges, or time-price differential charges incidental to those sales (Reg. 25134(a)(1)(A), 18 CCR);

— federal and state excise taxes from sales of manufactured goods or products, if the taxes are passed on to the buyer or included as part of the product's selling price (Reg. 25134(a)(1)(A), 18 CCR);

— contract fees and expense reimbursements relating to cost plus fixed fee contracts, like certain contracts for the operation of government-owned plants (Reg. 25134(a)(1)(B), 18 CCR);

— performance of services, including fees, commissions, and similar items (Reg. 25134(a)(1)(C), 18 CCR);

— renting, leasing, or licensing the use of real or tangible personal property (Reg. 25134(a)(1)(D), 18 CCR);

— sales, assignment, or licensing of intangible personal property, like patents and copyrights (Reg. 25134(a)(1)(E), 18 CCR); and

— sales of equipment used in the taxpayer's business. For instance, a truck express company that owns a fleet of trucks and sells its trucks under a regular replacement program would include the receipts from the program in its sales factor. (Reg. 25134(a)(1)(F), 18 CCR)

Sales or receipts excluded from the California sales factor. The following items are excluded from gross receipts, even if considered business income:

— repayment, maturity, or redemption of the principal of a loan, bond, mutual fund, certificate of deposit, or similar marketable instrument;

— principal received under a repurchase agreement or other transaction properly characterized as a loan;

— proceeds from the issuance of the taxpayer's own stock or the sale of treasury stock;

— damages and other amounts received as the result of litigation;

— property an agent acquires on behalf of another;

— tax refunds and other tax benefit recoveries;

— pension reversions;

— contributions to capital (except sales of securities by securities dealers);

— income from discharge of indebtedness;

— amounts realized from exchanges of inventory that are not recognized under the Internal Revenue Code;

— amounts received from transactions in intangible assets held in connection with a treasury function of the taxpayer's unitary business, and gross receipts and overall net gains from the maturity, redemption, sale, exchange, or other disposition of those intangible assets; and

— amounts received from hedging transactions involving intangible assets.

(Sec. 25120(f)(2), Rev. & Tax. Code)

Also, for taxable years beginning on or after January 1, 2013, a member of a combined reporting group engaged in the cable network business that makes a minimum investment in the state of $250 million for the taxable year may exclude 50% of the gross business receipts from providing network services (other than gross business receipts from the sale or rental of customer premises equipment) that would otherwise be assigned to California. (Sec. 25136.1, Rev. & Tax. Code)

CCH POINTER: The exclusion of an item from the definition of gross receipts does not determine its character as business income or nonbusiness income. (Sec. 25120(f), Rev. & Tax. Code)

CCH COMMENT: Under Treasury Regulation 26 CFR §1.482-7(b), a cost sharing arrangement (CSA) is an arrangement under which controlled participants share the costs and risks of developing cost shared intangibles in proportion to their share of reasonably anticipated benefits. Payments received from controlled participants under a CSA for current operational research and development costs reduce the expense deductions for the recipient and, thus, are not gross receipts for California sales factor purposes. On the other hand, payments in excess of the deductions available for the costs being reimbursed to the payee are payments for the use of property or services made available to the CSA and, thus, are gross receipts for sales factor purposes. Also, payments from controlled participants for resources or capabilities developed, maintained, or acquired externally to the CSA (whether before or during the course of the CSA) that are reasonably anticipated to benefit the development of cost shared intangibles in the CSA are not reimbursements of costs under the CSA, but are consideration for use of the intangible property or resource and, thus, are gross receipts for sales factor purposes. Also, while Treasury Regulation 26 CFR §1.482-7 allows platform contribution transaction (PCT) payments to be reduced by amounts owed to the payer, under *General Mills v. Franchise Tax Board*, 208 Cal.App.4th 1290 (2012), these offset amounts owed to the payee, which constitute PCT payments, are included at gross in the sales factor, subject to potential distortion analysis. (*Technical Advice Memorandum 2015-01*, California Franchise Tax Board, March 18, 2015)

Treasury function income and receipts. Treasury function income and receipts are excluded from the sales factor. This includes interest and dividends from intangible assets held in connection with a treasury function of the taxpayer's unitary business, as well as gross receipts and net gains from the maturity, redemption, sale, exchange or other disposition of these assets. It also includes foreign currency hedging activity, but not hedging related to the price risk for products the taxpayer consumes, produces, or sells. "Treasury function" means the pooling, management, and investment of intangible assets to satisfy a business's cash flow needs. Taxpayers principally engaged in purchasing and selling intangible assets of the type typically held in a taxpayer's treasury function, like registered broker-dealers, are not performing a treasury function regarding the income produced. (Reg. Sec. 25137(c)(1)(D), 18 CCR)

Exception for incidental or occasional sales. Substantial amounts of gross receipts arising from an occasional sale of a taxpayer's fixed asset or other business property are excluded from the sales factor. For example, the gross receipts from the sale of a factory, patent, or affiliate's stock are excluded if the receipts are substantial. Sales of assets to the same purchaser in a single year are aggregated to determine if the combined receipts are substantial. A sale is considered occasional if the transaction is outside the taxpayer's normal course of business and occurs infrequently. A sale is considered substantial if its exclusion results in a 5% or greater decrease in the taxpayer's sales factor denominator or the sales factor denominator of the taxpayer's combined reporting group as a whole. (Reg. 25137(c)(1)(A), 18 CCR)

In (*Appeal of Imperial, Inc.*, Nos. 472648 and 477927, July 13, 2010), the BOE ruled that the gross proceeds from goodwill on the sale of a corporation's assets were properly excluded from the sales factor because substantial amounts of the gross receipts arose from an infrequent, occasional sale of property used in the business. Also, it was improper to source the gains solely to Wisconsin, the location of the corporation's headquarters, because the goodwill was inseparable from the corporation's business activities in all of the states where it had operations.

Insubstantial amounts of gross receipts arising from incidental or occasional transactions or activities may be excluded from the sales factor, unless that exclusion would materially affect the amount of income apportioned to California. (Reg. 25137(c)(1)(B), 18 CCR)

What are the California sourcing rules for sales of tangible property?

Sales of tangible personal property are sourced to California if the property is delivered or shipped to a purchaser, other than the U.S. government, in California, regardless of the F.O.B. point or other conditions of the sale. Property is considered delivered or shipped to a purchaser in California if:

— the recipient is located in California, even if the property is ordered from outside the state;

— the shipment terminates in California, even though the purchaser transfers the property afterward to another state; or

— a seller is shipping the property from the state of origin to a consignee in another state and it is diverted while en route to a purchaser in California

A "purchaser within California" includes the ultimate recipient of the property if the taxpayer in California, at the designation of the purchaser, delivers to or has the property shipped to the ultimate recipient in California. (Sec. 25135, Rev. & Tax. Code; Reg. 25135, 18 CCR)

EXAMPLE: A taxpayer with inventory in Washington sold $100,000 of its products to a purchaser having branch stores in several states, including California. The order was placed by the purchaser's central purchasing department located in Arizona. $25,000 of the products was shipped directly to the purchaser's branch store in California. The branch store in California is the purchaser in California with respect to $25,000 of the taxpayer's sales.

CCH POINTER: A presumption exists that the state where the purchaser first took actual or constructive possession of goods is the ultimate destination. This presumption may be rebutted if the taxpayer can demonstrate that the purchaser immediately transported the property to another state. (*Legal Ruling 95-3*, California Franchise Tax Board) However, if goods are shipped to a purchaser's location in California, or if a purchaser takes possession (or constructive possession through an agent or bailor) in California for purposes like warehousing, repackaging, adding accessories, etc., the property is "delivered to a purchaser in the state," and the sale is a California sale. Any subsequent transportation of the goods to another state will not affect the California assignment of the sale. (*Legal Ruling 95-3*, California Franchise Tax Board) This ruling reflects the holdings in both *McDonnell Douglas Corp. v. Franchise Tax Board*, 26 CalApp4th 808 (1994), and *Mazda Motors of America, Inc.*, 94-SBE-009, November 29, 1994.

What are the sourcing rules in California for sales of other than tangible property?

Beginning with the 2013 tax year for all taxpayers, and beginning with the 2011 tax year for taxpayers that elected to use the single-sales factor apportionment formula (Sec. 25128.5, Rev. & Tax. Code; Reg. 25128.5, 18 CCR) (see ¶ 11-520), sales of other than tangible personal property are sourced to California if the taxpayer's market for the sale is in the state. (Sec. 25136, Rev. & Tax. Code)

COMPLIANCE NOTE: Penalty relief.—For late payment penalties (Sec. 19132, Rev. & Tax. Code) imposed with respect to tax liabilities shown on timely filed returns for taxable years beginning in 2015, penalty relief is available to the extent the payment is attributable to compliance with amendments to the California market-based sourcing regulations effective on January 1, 2017, and applicable retroactively to taxable years beginning on or after January 1, 2015. The regulatory amendments added definitions, assignment rules, and examples relating to marketable securities, dividends, goodwill, and interest. Compliance with the amendments may require some taxpayers to file an original or amended return to report new or revised tax liabilities for taxable years beginning on or after January 1, 2015. The Franchise Tax Board (FTB) is required to impose a late payment penalty when a taxpayer fails to pay the amount shown as tax on a return on or before the return's due date, unless the late payment was due to reasonable cause and not willful neglect. Because the amendments apply to taxable years beginning on or after January 1, 2015, but became final on September 15, 2016, the FTB will presume reasonable cause and not willful neglect in the case of a late payment attributable to the amendments and waive the associated penalty. The FTB will also consider both prepayment requests for relief, as well as claims for refund of amounts paid in satisfaction of the penalty. Business entities or individual taxpayers, including nonresident individuals properly included in a group return, are eligible to request this penalty relief. Taxpayers seeking this penalty relief should submit Form FTB 2924 or Form FTB 2917. When submitting these forms, taxpayers should (1) write "25136-2 Penalty Relief" on the top of the form, (2) compute and explain the amount of the late payment attributable to compliance with the regulatory amendments for taxable years beginning in 2015 on Part 3, (3) identify the amount of the late payment penalty imposed and attach a copy of the notice received showing the amount of the penalty imposed, and (4) enter "zero" for the refund amount if the form is being filed for prepayment relief of the late payment penalty. (*FTB Notice 2017-02*, California Franchise Tax Board, March 29, 2017)

Complete sale/transfer of intangible property. Receipts from the complete sale/transfer of intangible property (Reg. 25136-2(b)(3), 18 CCR) are sourced to California to the extent the property is used in California, determined under the following cascading rules:

(1) use will be presumed to be in California to the extent the contract between the taxpayer and the purchaser or the taxpayer's records indicate that the property is used in the state at the time of the sale;

(2) if the extent of use in the state cannot be determined under (1), or the presumption is overcome, the location of use will be reasonably approximated; or

(3) if the extent of use in the state cannot be determined under either (1) or (2), the location of use will be in the state if the purchaser's billing address is in the state.

Special rules apply for purposes of determining the location of use in (1) above if the sale/transfer involves a corporate stock sale or the sale of an ownership interest in a pass-through entity, other than a sales of marketable securities, or where the gross receipts from intangible property are dividends or goodwill. If 50% or more of the assets sold consist of real and/or tangible personal property, the sale of the stock or ownership interest will be assigned by averaging the entity's California payroll and property factors for the previous 12-month taxable year (or for the current year taxable year if the sale occurs more than six months into the current taxable year). If 50% or more of the assets sold consist of intangible property, the sale of the stock or ownership interest will be assigned using the entity's California sales factor for the previous 12-month taxable year (or for the current year if the sale occurs more than six months into the current taxable year). (Reg. 25136-2(d)(1), 18 CCR) Examples for applying these rules are provided in Reg. 25136-2(d)(1)(D), 18 CCR.

If the gross receipts from intangible property is interest, the interest is assigned as follows:

— Interest from investments, other than certain loans from a bank for financial institution, is assigned to California if the investment is managed in the state;

— Interest from certain loans from a bank for financial institution that are secured by real property is assigned to California to the extent the real property is located in the state; and

— Interest from certain loans from a bank for financial institution that are not secured by real property is assigned to California if the borrower is located in the state.

(Reg. 25136-2(d)(1)(A)(2), 18 CCR)

Licensing/leasing/renting of marketing intangible property. Receipts from the licensing/leasing/renting of marketing intangibles (Reg. 25136-2(b)(4)(A), 18 CCR) are sourced to California to the extent the property is used in California, determined as follows:

(1) the contract between the taxpayer and the licensee or the taxpayer's records will be presumed to provide a method for determining if the ultimate customers are in California (i.e., the property is used in the state); or

(2) if the location where the property is used cannot be determined under (1), or if the presumption is overcome, then the location will be reasonably approximated.

When making a reasonable approximation, factors that may be considered include:

— the number of licensed sites in each state;

— the volume of property manufactured, produced, or sold under the arrangement at locations in California; or

— other data that reflects the relative use of the property in California.

When the licensing of marketing intangible property is for the right to use the intangible property in connection with wholesale sales, rather than directly to retail customers, the taxpayer may lack information to determine where the property is ultimately used. In this case, the taxpayer may attribute receipts to the state based on a percentage of the state's total population, as compared to the total population of the geographic area where the licensee uses the property. If the taxpayer can show that the property is being used materially in other parts of the world, then the populations of those other countries where the intangible is being materially used will be added to the total population. (Reg. 25136-2(d)(2)(A), 18 CCR)

Licensing/leasing/renting of non-marketing or manufacturing intangible property. Receipts from the licensing/leasing/renting of non-marketing or manufacturing intangible property (Reg. 25136-2(b)(4)(B), 18 CCR), like a patent, copyright, or trade secret used in a manufacturing or other non-marketing process, are sourced to California to the extent the property is used in California, determined as follows:

(1) the contract between the taxpayer and the licensee or the taxpayer's books and records will be presumed to provide a method for determining the extent of use in the state;

(2) if the location where the property is used cannot be determined under (1), or if the presumption is overcome, then the location will be reasonably approximated; or

(3) if the location cannot be determined under either of the above provisions, the property will be presumed to be in the state if the licensee's billing address is in the state.

Special rules also apply when the intangible property licensed/leased/rented involves a mixture of marketing and non-marketing intangibles. If the fees to be paid are separately stated in the licensing contract, the FTB will accept that separate statement if it reasonably allocates the fees. If the FTB determine that the allocation is not reasonable, the FTB may assign the fees using a reasonable method that accurately reflects the licensing of a marketing intangible and the licensing of a non-marketing or manufacturing intangible. If the fees to be paid are not separately stated, the fees will be presumed to be paid entirely for the license of a marketing intangible, unless the taxpayer or the FTB can reasonably establish otherwise. (Reg. 25136-2, 18 CCR)

Marketable securities. In the case of marketable securities, sales are in California if the customer is in the state. (Sec. 25136(a)(2), Rev. & Tax. Code)

For an individual customer, the sale is assigned to California if the customer's billing address is in the state. (Reg. 25136-2(e)(1), 18 CCR)

If the customer is a corporation or other business entity, the sale is assigned to California if the customer's commercial domicile is in the state. A customer's commercial domicile is determined from the taxpayer's books and records at the end of the taxable year. However, the customer's commercial domicile can be based on something other than the taxpayer's books and records if, based on a preponderance of the evidence, other credible documentation shows that the customer's commercial domicile is in another state. (Reg. 25136-2(e)(2), 18 CCR)

If the customer's billing address or commercial domicile cannot be determined, then the customer's location will be reasonably approximated. (Reg. 25136-2(e)(3), 18 CCR)

Tax years before 2013. Prior to the 2013 tax year, except for taxpayers that elected in 2011 or 2012 to use the single-sales factor apportionment formula (Sec. 25128.5, Rev. & Tax. Code; Reg. 25128.5, 18 CCR) (see ¶11-520), sales of other than tangible personal property were attributable to California if the activity that produced the sale was performed in California. Sales of other than tangible personal property were sourced to California if:

— the income-producing activity was performed entirely in California; or

— the income-producing activity was performed both in and outside California, but a greater proportion of the income producing activity was performed in California based on costs of performance.

(Sec. 25136, Rev. & Tax. Code; Reg. 25136, 18 CCR)

The term "income producing activity" applied to each separate item of income and meant the transactions and activity the taxpayer directly engaged in during the regular course of its trade or business for the ultimate purpose of gains or profit. Activities performed for a taxpayer by an independent contractor were treated the same as activities performed directly by the taxpayer. (Reg. 25136, 18 CCR)

"Income-producing activity" included, but was not limited to, the following:

— employees, or agents or independent contractors acting for the taxpayer, rendering personal services, or the taxpayer's, or an independent contractor's, use of tangible and intangible property in performing a service;

— selling, renting, leasing, licensing or otherwise using real property;

— renting, leasing, licensing or otherwise using tangible personal property; and

— selling, licensing, or otherwise using intangible personal property.

The mere holding of intangible personal property was not an income producing activity. (Reg. 25136, 18 CCR)

"Costs of performance" meant direct costs determined in a manner consistent with generally accepted accounting principles and according to accepted conditions or practices in the taxpayer's trade or business. It included the taxpayer's payments to an agent or independent contractor for performing personal services and using tangible and intangible property that generated the particular item of income. (Reg. 25136(c), 18 CCR)

¶11-525

What are the California sourcing rules for the rental, leasing, or licensing of property?

Receipts from the sale, lease, rental, or licensing of real property are in California if the real property is in California. (Sec. 25136(a)(3), Rev. & Tax. Code; Reg. 25136(d)(2)(A), 18 CCR)

Receipts from the rental, lease, or licensing of tangible personal property are also in California if the property is located in California. Renting, leasing, licensing, or other use of tangible personal property in California is a separate income producing activity from renting, leasing, licensing, or other use of the same property in another state. Thus, if the property is in and outside California during the rental, lease, or licensing period, gross receipts attributable to California are measured by the ratio of time the property was physically present or used in California compared to the total time or use of the property everywhere during that period. (Sec. 25136(a)(4), Rev. & Tax. Code; Reg. 25136(d)(2)(B), 18 CCR)

What are the California sourcing rules for services?

Beginning with the 2013 tax year for all taxpayers, and beginning with the 2011 tax year for taxpayers that elected to use the single-sales factor apportionment formula (Sec. 25128.5, Rev. & Tax. Code; Reg. 25128.5, 18 CCR) (see ¶ 11-520), market-based sourcing is required for sourcing sales of services. Sales of services are sourced to California to the extent the purchaser received the benefit of the service in California.

CCH POINTER: *Activities not treated as a service.*—"Service" does not include activities performed by a person who is not in a regular trade or business offering its services to the public, and does not include services rendered to another member of the taxpayer's combined reporting group. (Reg. 25136-2(b)(8), 18 CCR)

If the purchaser of the service is a business entity, other than another combined reporting group member (Sec. 25102, Rev. & Tax. Code; Sec. 25110, Rev. & Tax. Code), then the location where the purchaser received the benefit of the service is determined as follows:

(1) it will be presumed to be in California if the contract between the taxpayer and the customer or the taxpayer's records indicate that the benefit of the service is in the state;

(2) if the location cannot be determined under (1), or the presumption is overcome, then it will be reasonably approximated;

(3) if the location cannot be determined or reasonably approximated under (1) or (2), then it will be presumed to be in the state if the customer placed the order from the state; or

(4) if the location cannot be determined under any of the above provisions, then it will be in the state if the customer's billing address is in the state.

(Reg. 25136-2(c)(2), 18 CCR) Examples are provided in (Reg. 25136-2(c)(2)(E), 18 CCR)

If the purchaser of the service is an individual, then the location where the purchaser received the benefit of the service will be determined as follows:

(1) it will be presumed to be in California if the customer's billing address is in California, unless the contract or the taxpayer's and records show otherwise; or

(2) if the presumption is overcome, but an alternative method of assigning the sales cannot be determined from the contract or the records, then the location will be reasonable approximated.

(Reg. 25136-2(c)(1), 18 CCR)

CCH PRACTICE TIP: *Rebutting the presumption*: To overcome the presumption that the benefit of the service was received at the customer's billing address, the taxpayer must prove by a preponderance of the evidence that either the contract between the taxpayer and the customer, or records kept in the normal course of the taxpayer's business, demonstrate the extent to which the benefit of the service was received at a location other than the customer's billing address. If the taxpayer uses the customer's billing address as the method of assigning sales to this state, the FTB must accept this method of assignment. The reasonable approximation method may be used only if the taxpayer demonstrates that the benefit was not received at the customer's billing address and the FTB determines that neither the contract nor the taxpayer's books and records provides a reasonable alternative for determining where the benefit was received. (Reg. 25136-2(c)(1)(C), 18 CCR)

Tax years before 2013. Prior to the 2013 tax year, except for taxpayers that elected in 2011 or 2012 to use the single-sales factor apportionment formula (Sec. 25128.5, Rev. & Tax. Code; Reg. 25128.5, 18 CCR) (see ¶ 11-520), if personal services constituting a separate income producing activity were performed partly in and partly outside California, the gross receipts from the services that were attributable to the state were measured by the ratio of time spent performing the services in the state compared to the total time spent performing the services everywhere. Time spent performing services included the amount of time spent performing a contract or other obligation generating the gross receipts. Time spent performing personal services not directly connected with the performance of the contract or obligation, like time spent negotiating the contract, was excluded from the computations. (Reg. 25136(d)(2)(C), 18 CCR)

If an agent or independent contractor performed an income producing activity for a taxpayer, the activity was attributed to California if it was in California. The income producing activity was in California if the taxpayer could reasonably determine, at the time of filing its return, that the agent or independent contractor actually performed all of the activity in California. In determining whether an income producing activity was in California, the following cascading rules applied:

— if the contract between the taxpayer and the agent/independent contractor or the taxpayer's records indicated that the services were to be performed in California and the portion of the payment to the agent/independent contractor associated with the performance in California could be determined under the contract, the income producing activity was in California;

— if the location of the income producing activity could not by determined under (1), but the terms of the contract between the taxpayer and the taxpayer's customer or the taxpayer's records indicated that the activity was to be performed in California and the portion of the taxpayer's payment to the agent or independent contractor associated with the performance in California could be determined under the contract, the income producing activity was in California;

— if the location of the income producing activity could not by determined under (1) or (2), it was in California if the customer's domicile was in California;

— if the location of the income producing activity could not by determined under any of the above provisions, or the income-producing activity was in a state where the taxpayer was not taxable, then the income producing activity was disregarded in determining the taxpayer's income producing activity.

(Reg. 25136(d)(3), 18 CCR)

Does California have a throwback or throwout rule?

California has sales factor throwback and throwout rules.

Throwback rule. California has an exception to the destination test for the sourcing of tangible personal property, otherwise known as a "throwback rule." Under the rule, sales of tangible personal property are sourced to California if the property is shipped from an office, store, warehouse, factory, or other place of storage in California and:

— the purchaser is the U.S. government; or

— the taxpayer is not taxable in the purchaser's state.

(Sec. 25135(a), Rev. & Tax. Code)

Sales by a subcontractor to a prime contractor (the party to the contract with the U.S. Government) do not qualify as sales to the U.S. government and are not treated as California sales. (Reg. 25135, 18 CCR)

A taxpayer is taxable in another state if:

— it is subject to a net income tax, a franchise tax measured by net income, a franchise tax for the privilege of doing business, or a corporate stock tax in that state ("subject-to-tax" test); or

— that state has jurisdiction to subject the taxpayer to a net income tax, regardless of whether the state actually imposes the tax on the taxpayer ("jurisdiction-to-tax" test).

(Sec. 25122, Rev. & Tax. Code; Reg. 25122(b), 18 CCR)

OBSERVATION: The FTB noted that the Georgia corporate net worth tax, Ohio commercial activity tax, Tennessee franchise tax, Texas franchise (margins) tax, and Washington business and occupation tax each constitute one of the four enumerated taxes that satisfy the "subject-to-tax" test. (*Tax News*, California Franchise Tax Board, December 2017)

Upon request by the FTB, a taxpayer must provide proof that it is subject to one of the enumerated taxes in another state. A taxpayer is not considered subject to one of the enumerated taxes if it voluntary files and pays one of the taxes or pays a minimal fee for qualifying to do business in that state, but:

— does not actually engage in business activity in that state, or

— engages in some business activity in that state, but not sufficient activity for nexus, and the minimum tax paid bears no relation to the taxpayer's business activity in the state.

(Reg. 25122(b), 18 CCR)

Jurisdiction to tax is not present if the state is prohibited from imposing the tax because of P.L. 86-272. Special rules for determining whether a taxpayer is subject to tax in another state apply to combined reporting group members. (Sec. 25102, Rev. & Tax. Code; Sec. 25110, Rev. & Tax. Code)

> **CCH POINTER:** A taxpayer is subject to tax in a foreign jurisdiction if the taxpayer's business activity would be sufficient for the jurisdiction to impose a net income tax under the U.S. Constitution or statutes as those provisions are applied to the states. (Reg. 25122(c), 18 CCR; *Chief Counsel Ruling 2012-01*, California Franchise Tax Board, August 28, 2012)

Throwout rule. If business income from intangible property cannot easily be attributed to a particular income producing activity of the taxpayer, the income is excluded from the sales factor. For example, income from the mere holding of intangible personal property, like bonds, government securities, and royalties on patents and copyrights, is excluded. (Reg. 25137(c)(1)(C), 18 CCR) Similarly, dividends received from a taxpayer's passive investment in a company are excluded. (*FTB Legal Ruling 2003-3* (2003)) In addition, the FTB ruled that investment activities performed by unrelated third parties for a taxpayer were not income producing activities of the taxpayer, so the receipts from these activities could be excluded from the sales factor. (*Chief Counsel Ruling 2007-2*, California Franchise Tax Board, June 4, 2007)

[¶11-530] Property Factor

California has moved to singles sales factor apportionment formula (see ¶11-520) for most taxpayers, beginning with the 2013 tax year. For pre-2013 tax years and for taxpayers still required to use a three factor apportionment formula, the property factor is a fraction, the numerator of which is the average value of the taxpayer's real and tangible personal property owned or rented and used in California during the tax period, and the denominator of which is the average value of the taxpayer's real and tangible personal property owned or rented and used. (Sec. 25129, Rev. & Tax. Code)

The property factor is determined on Sch. R, Apportionment and Allocation of Income. Property and rent are reported on Form 100, California Corporation Franchise or Income Tax Return.

Property used in the production of nonbusiness income is not included in the property factor, unless the property is also used in the production of business income. Property held as reserves or standby facilities or property held as a reserve source of materials is included in the factor. Property or equipment under construction during the taxable year (except inventoriable goods in process) is excluded from the property factor until the property is actually used in the regular course of the taxpayer's trade or business. Property used in the regular course of a taxpayer's trade or business will remain in the property factor until its permanent withdrawal is established by an identifiable event, such as its conversion to the production of nonbusiness income, its sale, or the lapse of an extended period of time (normally, five years) during which the property is held for sale. (Reg. 25129, 18 CCR)

> **CCH PRACTICE TIP:** *Property under development.*—Real property constituting "construction in progress" (CIP) of a homebuilder/developer is excluded from the property factor because it is not regarded as property owned or rented and used in California during the taxable year under the plain language of the controlling regulation. Conversely, specified items such as land that has not yet

become CIP or that may be treated as CIP at some point in the future, or that is not CIP because it has been completed and is held for sale or other disposition is included in the property factor because it is treated as reserve property that is available for or capable of being used in the taxpayer's regular trade or business or property. Such property is valued for property tax purposes by the averaging of monthly values during the taxable year if reasonably required to reflect properly the average value of the taxpayer's property, particularly in circumstances where substantial fluctuations in the values of the property exist during the taxable year or where property is acquired after the beginning of the taxable year or disposed of before the end of the taxable year.

If the FTB wants to include CIP property in the property factor it has to prove distortion and an unfair reflection of the taxpayer's business activity in California, a showing that cannot be satisfied by merely establishing that including CIP in the property factor would result in a different tax burden from one that would be imposed if the CIP is excluded from the property factor. Different rules apply in cases in which the taxpayer is a contractor using the percentage of completion method of accounting, or the completed contract method of accounting for long-term contracts. (*Technical Advice Memorandum 2011-1*, California Franchise Tax Board, January 6, 2011)

Intangible property.—To include intangible property in the factor, a taxpayer must demonstrate by clear and convincing evidence that the absence of its intangible property from the standard formula actually results in an unfair reflection of the level of its business activity in the state (*Microsoft Corporation v. Franchise Tax Board*, California Superior Court for San Francisco County, No. CGC08-471260, February 17, 2011)

Property in transit.—Property in transit between a taxpayer's own locations is considered to be at the destination state for purposes of the property factor. Property in transit between a buyer and a seller that is included by the taxpayer in the denominator of its property factor in accordance with its regular accounting practices is included in the numerator of the property factor on the basis of the destination state. The value of mobile or movable property located within and without the state during the taxable year is determined for purposes of the property factor numerator on the basis of total time within the state during the taxable year. An automobile assigned to a traveling employee will be included in the property factor numerator of the state to which the employee's compensation is assigned under the payroll factor or will be included in the property factor numerator of the state in which the automobile is licensed. (Reg. 25129, 18 CCR)

Mobile property.—The value of mobile or movable property located within and without the state during the taxable year is determined for purposes of the property factor numerator on the basis of total time within the state during the taxable year. An automobile assigned to a traveling employee will be included in the property factor numerator of the state to which the employee's compensation is assigned under the payroll factor or will be included in the property factor numerator of the state in which the automobile is licensed. (Reg. 25129, 18 CCR)

• *Value of property*

Owned property.—Property owned by a taxpayer is generally valued for property factor purposes at its original cost, including the cost of improvements, without allowance for depreciation If the original cost is unascertainable, then the property is valued at its fair market value as of the date of acquisition by the taxpayer. (Sec. 25130, Rev. & Tax. Code; Reg. 25130, 18 CCR)

> *EXAMPLE: Determination of value.*—A taxpayer acquired a factory building in California at a cost of $500,000 and 18 months later expended $100,000 for major remodeling of the building. The taxpayer files its return for the current taxable year on a calendar-year basis. A depreciation deduction in the amount of $22,000 is claimed for the building on the taxpayer's return for the current taxable year. The value of the building includible in the numerator and denominator of the property factor is $600,000 because, unlike the cost of property improvements, the depreciation deduction is not taken into account in determining the value of the building for purposes of the property factor.

Inventory of stock of goods is included in the property factor in accordance with the valuation method used for federal income tax purposes. Property acquired by gift or inheritance is included in the property factor at its basis for determining depreciation for federal income tax purposes. (Reg. 25130, 18 CCR)

The average value of property will generally be determined by averaging the values at the beginning and ending of the taxable year. However, the Franchise Tax Board may require the averaging of monthly values during the taxable year if reasonably required to reflect properly the average value of the taxpayer's property. Monthly averaging will be deemed appropriate if the amount of property owned by the taxpayer during the year fluctuates greatly or if a substantial piece of property is acquired and disposed of during the same taxable year. (Sec. 25131, Rev. & Tax. Code; Reg. 25131, 18 CCR)

Rented or leased property.—Rented property is valued at eight times its annual rent. Subrents received by the taxpayer must be deducted from rental value prior to determining property value unless the property that produces the subrents is used in the regular course of the taxpayer's trade or business and the property produces business income. (Sec. 25130, Rev. & Tax. Code; Reg. 25131, 18 CCR)

> *EXAMPLE: Subrents.*—A taxpayer rents a 20-story office building and uses the lower two stories for its general corporation headquarters. The remaining 18 floors are subleased to others. The rental of the 18 floors is not incidental to, but is separate from, the operation of the taxpayer's trade or business. Thus, the subrents are nonbusiness income and must be deducted from the rent paid by the taxpayer in determining the value of the building for purposes of the property factor.

If the subrents taken into account in determining the net annual rental rate produce a negative or clearly inaccurate value for any item of property, then the California Franchise Tax Board (FTB) may require, or the taxpayer may request, that another valuation method be used to properly reflect the value of the rented property. However, the net annual rental rate must not be less than an amount that bears the same ratio to the annual rental rate paid by the taxpayer for such property as the fair market value of that portion of the property used by the taxpayer bears to the total fair market value of the rented property. (Reg. 25137, 18 CCR)

> *EXAMPLE: Net annual rental rate.*—A taxpayer rents a 10-story building at an annual rental rate of $1 million. The taxpayer occupies two stories and sublets eight stories for $1 million a year. The net annual rental rate of the taxpayer must not be less than two-tenths of the taxpayer's annual rental rate for the entire year, or $200,000.

If property owned by others is used by the taxpayer at no charge or rented by the taxpayer for a nominal rate, then the net annual rental rate for such property must be determined on the basis of a reasonable market rental rate for such property. (Reg. 25137, 18 CCR)

If a taxpayer enters upon property owned by others for the purpose of extracting natural resources such as timber, oil, gas, or hard minerals, regardless of whether such entry or extraction is pursuant to an agreement between the holder of the interest in the property and the taxpayer and also regardless of whether such relationship is characterized as a profit á prendre or some other relationship, consideration actually paid by the taxpayer to the holder of the interest in the property that constitutes a sharing of current or future production or extraction of the timber, oil, gas, or hard minerals from such property (regardless of the method of payment or how such consideration is characterized, whether as a royalty, advance royalty, rental, or otherwise) and consideration actually paid by the taxpayer for the right to enter the property and extract the timber, oil, gas, or hard minerals (such as forest management fees, fire protection fees, reforestation or reclamation fees, road maintenance fees, etc.) for the taxable year at issue will constitute the net annual rental rate. (Reg. 25137, 18 CCR)

Leasehold improvements are treated as owned by the taxpayer and are included in the value of the property, even though the taxpayer may remove the improvements at the end of the rental term or lease. The improvements are valued at their original cost. (Reg. 25130, 18 CCR)

[¶11-535] Payroll Factor

California has moved to singles sales factor apportionment formula (see ¶11-520) for most taxpayers, beginning with the 2013 tax year. For pre-2013 tax years and for taxpayers still required to use a three factor apportionment formula, the payroll factor of the apportionment formula is a fraction, the numerator of which is the total amount paid in California during the tax period by the taxpayer for compensation, and the denominator of which is the total compensation paid everywhere during the tax period. (Sec. 25132, Rev. & Tax. Code)

Compensation in any form, including wages, salaries, commissions, board, rent, housing, lodging, and other benefits or services (such as nonqualified stock options) provided to employees in return for personal services, is included in the payroll factor. Generally, if such items would constitute income to the employee under the federal Internal Revenue Code, then they must be included in computing the payroll factor. (Sec. 25132, Rev. & Tax. Code; Reg. 25132, 18 CCR)

The payroll factor is computed on Sch. R, Apportionment and Allocation of Income. Payroll is reported on Form 100, California Corporation Franchise or Income Tax Return.

Compensation related to the production of nonbusiness income is excluded from the payroll factor. (Reg. 25132, 18 CCR)

Officer compensation.—California does not exclude officer compensation from the payroll factor. Nor is compensation paid to any individual who, under common law rules, is an employee. Generally, a person will be considered an employee if the person must be reported by the employer as an employee under the Federal Insurance Contributions Act, unless the person is not an employee under common law rules. (Reg. 25132, 18 CCR)

Director compensation.—Compensation paid to a director not acting in the capacity of an employee is excluded from the payroll factor. (Reg. 25132(a)(3) and (4), 18 CCR)

Leased employee compensation.—Payments made as compensation to leased employees musts be examined under the facts and circumstances of each case to determine whether or not those payments may be included in a particular corporation's payroll factor. (*Unofficial guidance,* California Franchise Tax Board, May 2014)

Compensation paid in states where taxpayer is immune under P.L. 86-272.—If the services of an employee are performed in a state in which the taxpayer is not subject to income tax, then the compensation of the employee is included in total payroll (*i.e.,* the denominator of the payroll factor). (Reg. 25132, 18 CCR)

> *EXAMPLE: Computation of payroll factor.*—A taxpayer has employees in its state of legal domicile, State A, and is taxable in State B. In addition, the taxpayer has other employees whose services are performed entirely in State C where the taxpayer is immune from taxation by P.L. 86-272. For the latter employees, the compensation will be assigned to State C where their services are performed and will be included in the denominator, but not the numerator, of the payroll factor, even though the taxpayer is not taxable in State C.

Method of accounting.—Total compensation paid during the year is determined on the basis of the taxpayer's accounting method. If the taxpayer has adopted the accrual method of accounting, all accrued compensation is deemed paid. Notwithstanding the taxpayer's method of accounting, the taxpayer may elect to include compensation paid to employees in the payroll factor using the cash method if the taxpayer reports compensation by the cash method for unemployment compensation purposes. (Reg. 25132, 18 CCR)

• *Sourcing rules*

The numerator of the payroll factor is the total amount paid by the taxpayer for compensation in California during the taxable year. Compensation paid to employees is attributed to California when:

> — the employee's services are performed entirely in the state;

> — the employee's services are performed both within and without the state, but the work done outside the state is incidental to the work in the state;

> — some of the employee's services are performed in California and the employee's base of operations is within California or, if there is no base of operations, the employee is controlled or directed by the taxpayer from a place within California; or

> — some of the employee's services are performed in California and the employee's base of operations or the place from which the employee is directed or controlled is not in any state in which some part of the employee's services is performed, but the employee resides in California.

(Sec. 25133, Rev. & Tax. Code; Reg. 25133, 18 CCR)

[¶11-540] Apportionment Factors for Specific Industries

What special industry apportionment formulas does California use?

California has special apportionment formula provisions for air transportation companies, banks and financial corporations, commercial fishing businesses, contractors, franchisors, motion picture and television film producers, mutual fund service providers, print media, professional athletic teams, railroads, sea transportation companies, space transportation companies, and trucking companies, which differ from the standard apportionment formula provisions that apply to other taxpayers.

PRACTICE NOTE: Beginning with the 2013 tax year, most taxpayers must use a single sales factor apportionment formula, unless they derive more than 50% of their gross business receipts from qualified business activities (agricultural, extractive, savings and loan, and bank and financial activities). (Sec. 25128, Rev. & Tax. Code; Sec. 25128.7, Rev. & Tax. Code) Thus, for most taxpayers, only the sales/receipts factor modifications in the special apportionment rules will apply, and the property and payroll factor rules in the regulations will now be disregarded. However, businesses that derive more than 50% of their gross business receipts from qualified business activities continue to use an equally-weighted three factor apportionment formula under Rev. & Tax. Code Sec. 25128(b), with any required modifications set forth in the special apportionment rules.

Air transportation companies. Air transportation companies, including scheduled airlines, supplemental airlines, and air taxis, must apportion their business income under a special regulation. Beginning with the 2013 tax year, these businesses generally must use a single sales factor apportionment formula. In determining the sales factor numerator, revenue from hauling passengers, freight, mail, and excess baggage is attributed to California based on (1) the ratio that the air time of the taxpayer's aircraft in California bears to the total air time of the taxpayer's aircraft everywhere, by model of aircraft, weighted at 80%; and (2) the ratio of arrivals and departures in California to total arrivals and departures everywhere, by type of aircraft, weighted at 20%. (Reg. 25137-7, 18 CCR)

Prior law and exceptions. For tax years prior to 2013 or if a business qualifies under Sec. 25128(b) to use a three-factor apportionment formula, property and payroll modifications also apply. In determining the property factor numerator, the time in state is the proportionate amount of time, both in the air and on the ground, that certificated aircraft have spent in the state during the taxable year as compared to the total time spent everywhere during the taxable year. This factor is multiplied by 75%. Arrivals and departures in state is the number of arrivals in and departures of certificated aircraft from in-state airports during the taxable year as compared to the total number of arrivals in and departures from airports both in the state and elsewhere during the taxable year. This factor is multiplied by 25%. The time in state factor is then added to the arrivals and departures factor. The total figure is applied to the original cost of property owned or rented by the taxpayer. In determining the payroll factor numerator, compensation paid to flight personnel is attributed to California based on the ratio that air and ground time spent in performing services in California bears to the total air and ground time spent in performing services everywhere by type of aircraft. (Sec. 25101.3, Rev. & Tax. Code; Reg. 25137-7, 18 CCR)

Other special rules. The factors are determined using the taxpayer's annual statistics, if available. Otherwise, statistics for a representative period are used. (Sec. 25101.3, Rev. & Tax. Code)

Banks and financial corporations. Banks and financial corporations must apportion their business income under a special regulation. (Reg. 25137-4.2, 18 CCR)

Businesses that derive more than 50% of their gross business receipts from savings and loan or bank and financial activities must use an equally-weighted three factor apportionment formula consisting of property, payroll, and receipts factors. (Sec. 25128, Rev. & Tax. Code)

An international banking facility maintained by a bank in California is considered to be located outside the state. Intangible personal property and sales reflected on the segregated books attributable to the international banking facility must be attributed to the international banking facility in determining the bank's property, payroll, and sales factors. (Sec. 25107, Rev. & Tax. Code)

Property factor. The property factor includes, in addition to all real or tangible personal property owned by or rented to the taxpayer, the average value of the taxpayer's loans and credit card receivables located or used in and outside California during the income year, without regard to any reserve for bad debts. Real or tangible personal property is included in the property factor numerator under the standard property factor rules, while loans and credit card receivables are included in the property factor numerator if they are assigned to the taxpayer's regular place of business in California. (Reg. 25137-4.2, 18 CCR)

Payroll factor. The payroll factor for banks and financial corporations is computed the same as a general business corporation's payroll factor. (Reg. 25137-4.2, 18 CCR)

Receipts factor. The receipts factor for banks and financial corporations includes the following items:

— interest, dividends, net gains, and other income from investment and trading assets and activities;

— the amount by which interest on federal funds sold and securities purchased under resale agreements exceeds interest expense on federal funds purchased and securities sold under repurchase agreements;

— the amount by which interest, dividends, gains, and other income from trading assets and activities exceeds payments in lieu of interest or dividends and losses from the assets and activities; and

— net gains from the sale of loans, including income recorded under the IRC § 1268 rules relating to coupon stripping.

(Reg. 25137-4.2, 18 CCR)

The receipts factor numerator includes the following items:

— receipts from leases or rentals of real or tangible personal property, other than transportation property, that is owned by the taxpayer if the property is located in California;

— receipts from leases or rentals of transportation property to the extent the property is used in California;

— interest from loans secured by real property located in California;

— interest from loans not secured by real property if the borrower is located in California;

— the California amount of net gains from the sale of loans;

— credit card receivables if the card holder's billing address is in California;

— the California amount of net gains from the sale of credit card receivables;

— the California amount of all credit card issuer's reimbursement fees;

— receipts from merchant discounts if the merchant's commercial domicile is in California;

— the California amount of loan servicing fees;

— receipts from other services performed in California;

— interest, dividends, net gains, and other income from investment and trading assets and activities that are attributable to California;

— other receipts assignable to California under the standard sales factor rules; and

— all receipts assignable to California under the throwback rule, when the taxpayer's commercial domicile is in California and the receipts would otherwise be assigned to a state in which the taxpayer is not taxable.

(Reg. 25137-4.2, 18 CCR)

Mixed general (non-financial) and financial group. Unitary business groups that contain a combination of banks or financial corporations and general corporations, but that are predominantly engaged in activities that are not financial, must apportion their business income under a special regulation. Typically, the regulation covers groups engaged in a mining, manufacturing, mercantile, or service business, but with one or more subsidiaries performing ancillary financial functions. Examples of ancillary financial functions include providing financing to product distributors, holding title to receivables arising from extending credit to customers, and holding title to headquarters buildings and branch locations. (Reg. 25137-10, 18 CCR) (Reg. 25137-10(g), 18 CCR) Beginning with the 2013 tax year, these groups must use a single sales factor apportionment formula, unless they derive more than 50% of their gross business receipts from agricultural, extractive, savings and loan, or bank and financial activities, in which case they must use an equally-weighted three factor apportionment formula consisting of property, payroll, and sales factors. (Sec. 25128, Rev. & Tax. Code; Sec. 25128.7, Rev. & Tax. Code)

Property factor. The property factor denominator for a mixed general/financial unitary group includes, in addition to the property required to be included under the statutes and regulations for general corporations or for banks and financial corporations, a general corporation's receivables from financial activities, to the extent not otherwise included. For a general corporation, the property factor numerator includes, in addition to property that would ordinarily be assigned to California under the general regulations, receivables from the corporation's financial activities, to the extent they arise from an in-state retail sale or a non-retail sale made to a California customer. The numerator also includes receivables from a general corporation's financial activities if the taxpayer is not taxable in the state where the sale is made, but the office at which the credit is first applied for is in California. For a bank or financial corporation, the property factor numerator includes:

— assets, other than transferred receivables, that would be assigned to California under the regulation for banks and financial corporations (Reg. 25137-4.2);

— if the bank or financial corporation is taxable in California, transferred receivables that would have been assigned to California if held by a general corporation; and

— if the bank or financial corporation has a California commercial domicile, transferred receivables that, if held by a general corporation, would have been assigned to a state in which the bank or financial corporation is not taxable.

(Reg. 25137-10, 18 CCR)

Intangible personal property, coin, and currency included in the property factor must be valued at 20% of their tax basis for federal income tax purposes. (Reg. 25137-10, 18 CCR)

Payroll factor. The payroll factor for these groups is computed the same as a general business corporation's payroll factor. (Reg. 25137-10, 18 CCR)

Sales factor. For a general corporation, the sales factor numerator includes, in addition to the items that would be assigned to California under the general statutes and regulations, any other amounts realized on receivables from financial activity assigned to California. For a bank or financial corporation, the sales factor numerator includes, in addition to receipts that would otherwise be assigned to California under the regulation for banks and financial corporations (Reg. 25137-4.2), receipts, other than receipts from transferred receivables, assigned to California and any other amounts realized on receivables transferred from a general corporation in the same group and assigned to California. (Reg. 25137-10, 18 CCR)

Commercial fishing businesses. Beginning with the 2013 tax year, commercial fishing businesses must use a single sales factor apportionment formula. (Sec. 25128.7, Rev. & Tax. Code) The apportionment formula factors are computed on the basis of a ratio of port days spent in the state to the total port days spent everywhere. A "port day" is a day or part of a day spent in port or on the seas while the ship is in operation. "In operation" means that a ship is searching for fish, fishing, transporting fish, or engaged in pre-voyage or post-voyage activities like loading, unloading, refueling, or provisioning the ship. (Reg. 25137-5, 18 CCR)

Contractors. When a taxpayer elects to use the percentage-of-completion method of accounting or the completed contract method of accounting for long-term construction, manufacturing, or fabrication contracts, and the taxpayer has income from sources both in and outside California, the taxpayer's business income derived from California sources is determined under a special regulation. Beginning with the 2013 tax year, contractors generally must use a single sales factor apportionment formula. (Reg. 25137-2, 18 CCR)

Under the percentage-of-completion method of accounting, the taxpayer either receives or accrues income on the basis of the percentage of the contract that has been completed. The amount of business income is determined by multiplying the gross contract price by the percentage of the entire contract that has been completed during the taxable year, then subtracting expenses. Under the completed contract method of accounting, the taxpayer does not account for any income until the contract has been completed. A special rule is used to calculate the apportionment percentage, in order to account for the absence of income during years in which the contract was being performed. Under this rule, a fraction is determined for each year that the contract was in progress on the basis of the costs of the contract that were paid or accrued during that year compared to the total costs. The regular apportionment percentage for each year that the contract was in progress is then multiplied by the costs fraction for each year, and the products are totaled. This total is then multiplied by the net income (or loss) from the project. The result is the amount of business income (or loss) apportioned to California in the year of completion. (Reg. 25137-2, 18 CCR)

Gross receipts derived from the performance of a contract are included in the sales factor numerator if the project is located in California. If the project is located partly in and partly outside California, then the gross receipts included in the sales factor numerator are based on the ratio that costs for the project in California incurred during the taxable year bears to the total costs for the entire project during the taxable year. Any other method, like engineering cost estimates, may be used if it will provide a reasonable apportionment. If the percentage-of-completion method of accounting is used, then the sales factor denominator includes only that portion of the gross contract price that corresponds to the percentage of the entire contract that was completed during the taxable year. If the completed contract method of accounting is used, then the sales factor denominator includes the portion of the gross receipts received or accrued during the taxable year that is attributable to each contract. (Reg. 25137-2, 18 CCR)

— **Prior law and exceptions.** For tax years prior to 2013 or if a business qualifies under Sec. 25128(b) to use a three-factor apportionment formula, property and payroll modifications also apply. When either the percentage-of-completion method or the completed contract method of accounting is used, the property factor denominator must include the average value of the taxpayer's costs (including materials and labor) of works in progress that exceed progress billings. The numerator must include the value of these costs attributable to projects in California. Rent paid for equipment use is included at eight times the net annual rental, even though the rent value may be included in the project's cost. Also, when either the percentage-of-completion method or the completed contract method of accounting is used, the payroll factor denominator must include all compensation paid to employees that is attributable to a particular project, even though the compensation is included in the project's cost. Compensation paid to employees at a project site is assigned to the sales factor numerator where the services are performed. (Reg. 25137-2, 18 CCR)

— **Other special rules.** Other special rules are provided for apportioning the income of a taxpayer that has elected the percentage-of-completion method of accounting or the completed contract method of accounting for long-term contracts and that ceases to do business, dissolves, or withdraws from California during the taxable year. (Reg. 25137-2, 18 CCR)

Franchisors. Franchisors must apportion their business income under a special regulation. Beginning with the 2013 tax year, franchisors generally must use a single sales factor apportionment formula. (Reg. 25137-3, 18 CCR)

For purposes of determining the sales factor numerator, the following receipts are attributed to the state where the franchisee's place of business is located, provided the taxpayer is taxable in that state:

— fees received for advertising, advisory, administrative, and other specified services provided to the franchisee; and

— fees or royalties received to use the franchisor's trademark, trade name, service mark, or right to market a product or service.

If the taxpayer is not taxable in the state where the franchisee's place of business is located, then the receipts are attributed to the state of the taxpayer's commercial domicile. (Reg. 25137-3, 18 CCR)

CCH POINTER: The Franchise Tax Board (FTB) Chief Counsel's office has advised a taxpayer that receives license fees and royalties from foreign affiliates that manufacture, distribute, and/or sell products bearing the taxpayer's licensed trademarks that the taxpayer is a franchisor subject to the special apportionment regulation. (*Chief Counsel Ruling 2010-2*, California Franchise Tax Board, May 11, 2010)

Prior law and exceptions. For tax years prior to 2013 or if a business qualifies under Sec. 25128(b) to use a three-factor apportionment formula, payroll modifications also apply. The payroll factor is computed the same as a general business corporation's payroll factor, except that for purposes of determining the payroll factor numerator, compensation paid to traveling employees regularly providing administrative or advisory services at the franchisee's place of business must be determined on the basis of the ratio that the time spent performing the services in California bears to the total time spent performing the services everywhere. (Reg. 25137-3, 18 CCR)

Motion picture and television film producers. A business entity with income from sources both in and outside California that is in the business of producing or distributing motion picture, film, or television programming, or television commercials, whether broadcast or telecast through the public airwaves, cable, direct or indirect satellite transmission, or any other means of communication, either through a network (including owned and affiliated stations) or through an affiliated, unaffiliated, or independent television broadcasting station must apportion its business income under a special regulation. Income from new technologies, including, but not limited to, video streaming and online websites, to the extent they are used by motion picture and television film producers, television commercial producers, and television networks to produce business income, is also covered by the regulation. Beginning with the 2013 tax year, businesses with income from these sources generally must use a single sales factor apportionment formula. The sales factor is computed the same as a general business corporation's sales factor, except that in computing the sales factor numerator, California gross receipts specifically include:

— gross receipts, including advertising revenue, from films in release to theaters and television stations in California;

— for films in release to or by a television network for network telecast, the portion of gross receipts representing the ratio that the audience for network stations in California bears to the audience for all network stations; and

— for films in release to subscription television telecasters, the portion of gross receipts represented by the ratio that California subscribers bear to all subscribers.

Receipts from the sale, rental, licensing, or other disposition of video cassettes and discs or any other format or medium intended for personal use are included in the sales factor numerator. (Reg. 25137-8.2, 18 CCR)

"Film" means the physical embodiment of a play, story, or other literary, commercial, educational, or artistic work, produced for telecast, as a motion picture, video tape, disc, or any other type of format or medium (except if intended for personal use). Each episode of a series of films produced for television is considered a separate film, even if the series relates to the same principal subject and is produced during one or more television seasons. (Reg. 25137-8.2, 18 CCR)

Prior law and exceptions. For tax years prior to 2013 or if a business qualifies under Sec. 25128(b) to use a three-factor apportionment formula, property and payroll modifications also apply. The factors are computed the same as for general business corporation, except for purposes of computing the property factor, the value of a film is not included until its release date. The value of a film is the original production cost as determined for federal income tax purposes, before any adjustment for federal credits not claimed for state purposes, and including talent salaries. Videocassettes and discs are included at their inventory cost, as shown in the taxpayer's books and records. Films, other than films for which the cost is expensed for California tax purposes at the time of production, are included in the property factor at original cost for 12 years beginning with the release date. All other films must be aggregated and included in the property factor as a single film property, valued at eight times the gross receipts generated during the income year from theater distribution, network television, television syndication, cable or satellite television, subscription and marketing of video cassettes and discs through licensing or direct selling, or similar receipts, but in an amount not greater than the total original cost of the aggregated film property. Films of a topical nature, including news or current event programs, sporting events, or interview shows, the cost of which is expensed for California tax purposes at the time of production, are included in the property factor at original cost for one year beginning with the release date. In computing the property factor numerator, the value of films is attributed to California in the ratio that the total California receipts from the films, as determined for sales factor purposes, bears to the total receipts everywhere. If tangible property other than films is located or used in California for part of the income year, its value attributed to California is determined by applying the ratio of the number of days the property is located or used in California to the total number of days the property is owned or rented during the income year. Also, for purposes of computing the payroll factor, substantial compensation paid to a corporation for providing the services of an actor or director who is the corporation's employee, or who is under contract with the corporation, is treated as compensation paid to the producer's employee. In computing the payroll factor numerator, compensation paid to employees engaged in producing a film on location is attributed to the state where the services are or were performed. (Reg. 25137-8.2, 18 CCR)

Mutual fund service providers. Mutual fund service providers must apportion their business income under a special regulation. Beginning with the 2013 tax year, mutual fund service providers must use a single sales factor apportionment formula. (Reg. 25137-14, 18 CCR)

Receipts from performing services for regulated investment companies (RICs). Receipts from the direct or indirect provision of management, distribution, or administration services to or on behalf of a RIC are assigned to the sales factor numerator using a shareholder ratio. The ratio is calculated by multiplying total receipts for the taxable year from each separate RIC for which the mutual fund service provider performs management, distribution, or administration services by a fraction. The fraction numerator is the average of the number of shares owned by the RIC's California-domiciled shareholders at the beginning of and at the end of the RIC's taxable year, and the denominator is the average of the number of shares owned by the RIC's shareholders everywhere at the beginning of and at the end of the RIC's taxable year. However, if a shareholder's domicile cannot be reasonably determined, then all shares held by the shareholder will be disregarded in computing the shareholder ratio.

The RIC's taxable year for computing the shareholder ratio is either the taxable year that ends during the taxable year of the principal member of the mutual fund service provider's combined reporting group or the taxable year of the principal member of the mutual fund service provider's combined reporting group. Once a method for computing the shareholder ratio is chosen, that methodology must be applied consistently in later years. (Reg. 25137-14(b)(1)(A), 18 CCR)

Receipts from asset management services. A mutual fund service provider's receipts from performing asset management services are assigned to California if the asset's beneficial owner's domicile is located in California. In the case of asset management services directly or indirectly provided to a pension plan, retirement account, or institutional investor, like private banks, national and international private investors, international traders, or insurance companies, receipts are assigned to California to the extent the domicile of the beneficiaries of the plan, account, or similar pool of assets held by the institutional investor is in California. If a beneficiary's domicile cannot be reasonably determined, the receipts must be disregarded in computing the sales factor. (Reg. 25137-14(b)(1)(B), 18 CCR)

Receipts from services performed by non-taxpayer members. If a mutual fund service provider has non-taxpayer members that provide management, distribution, or administration services to or on behalf of a RIC with California shareholders, or that provide asset management services directly or indirectly for California-domiciled beneficiaries, the receipts from these activities that are assigned to the sales factor numerator must be included in the sales factor numerator in determining the unitary group's business income apportionable to California, even though the specific entity that performed the services is not a California taxpayer. (Reg. 25137-14(b)(1)(C), 18 CCR)

Throwback provision. If the shareholder ratio or asset management assignment provisions assign receipts to a state where no member of the mutual fund service provider's unitary group is taxable, the receipts must be thrown back to the location of the income-producing activity that gave rise to the receipts. (Reg. 25137-14(b)(1)(D), 18 CCR)

Print media. Taxpayers in the business of publishing, selling, licensing, or distributing newspapers, magazines, periodicals, trade journals, or other printed material and that have income from both in and outside California must apportion their business income using a special regulation Beginning with the 2013 tax year, these businesses must use a single sales factor apportionment formula. When calculating the sales factor numerator, a business must include all gross receipts from California sources, including, but not limited to, gross receipts from:

— the sale of tangible personal property delivered or shipped to a purchaser or subscriber in California;

— advertising and the sale, rental, or other use of the taxpayer's customer lists, attributed to California as determined by the taxpayer's circulation factor during the taxable year; and

— all sources, including receipts from the sale of printed material, advertising, and the sale, rental, or other use of the taxpayer's customer lists, if the purchaser or subscriber is the U.S. government or the taxpayer is not taxable in another state and the printed material or other property is shipped from an office, store, warehouse, factory, or other storage or business place in California. (Reg. 25137-12, 18 CCR)

A publication's "circulation factor" is equal to the ratio that the publication's circulation to purchasers and subscribers in California bears to its total circulation to purchasers and subscribers everywhere. Publishers of printed material containing advertising must determine a California circulation factor for each of their publications. (Reg. 25137-12, 18 CCR)

If specific items of advertisement can be shown to be distributed solely to a limited regional or local geographic area, then the taxpayer may petition, or the FTB may require, that the corresponding receipts be attributed on the basis of a regional or local geographic area circulation factor. (Reg. 25137-12, 18 CCR)

Professional athletic teams. Beginning with the 2013 tax year, a professional athletic team must apportion its business income derived directly or indirectly from its operations as a professional athletic team using a single sales factor apportionment formula. (Sec. 25128.7, Rev. & Tax. Code) The sales factor is computed the same as a general business corporation's sales factor, except that if the team's operations are based in California, then the team's total sales anywhere during the taxable year are treated as made in California. If the team's operations are based outside California, then its sales everywhere are treated as out-of-state sales. (Sec. 25141, Rev. & Tax. Code)

A "professional athletic team" is any entity that, during the taxable year:

— employs five or more persons concurrently as participating members of an athletic team participating in public contests;

— is a member of a league composed of five or more entities engaged in operating athletic teams;

— has total paid attendance for all contests played anywhere aggregating at least 40,000 persons; and

— has gross income of at least $100,000.

(Sec. 25141, Rev. & Tax. Code)

If any team based in California must allocate or apportion part of its business income to another state or country and pay income or franchise tax to the other state or country as a result of that allocation or apportionment, then the team's business income otherwise assigned to California is reduced by the amount of its business income allocated or apportioned to, and taxed by, the other state or country. Other teams in the same league that are based in the other state or country allocate and apportion their business income to California using the other state or country's formula, rather than using California's special provisions for professional athletic teams. (Sec. 25141, Rev. & Tax. Code)

Prior law and exceptions. For tax years prior to 2013 or if a business qualifies under Sec. 25128(b) to use a three-factor apportionment formula, property and payroll modifications also apply. If the team's operations are based in California, then the average value of all of its real and tangible personal property, wherever located, that it owned or rented and used during the taxable year must be treated as California property. If the team's operations are based outside California, then the average value of all of its real and tangible personal property, wherever located, that it owned or rented and used during the taxable year is treated as out-of-state property. If the team's operations are based in California, then the total compensation paid anywhere during the taxable year is treated as paid in California. If the team's operations are based outside California, then the total compensation paid everywhere during the taxable year is treated as paid outside California. (Sec. 25141, Rev. & Tax. Code)

Railroads. Railroads must apportion their business income using a special regulation. Beginning with the 2013 tax year, railroads generally must use a single sales factor apportionment formula. The sales factor is computed the same as a general business corporation's sales factor, except all *per diem* and mileage charges collected by the taxpayer are excluded. Also, the sales factor numerator includes the sum of all receipts from shipments that both originate and terminate in California and that portion of the receipts from each interstate shipment in the ratio of the miles traveled on the taxpayer's lines in California to the total miles traveled on the taxpayer's lines from the point of origin to destination. Both freight and passenger receipts are determined in this manner. (Reg. 25137-9, 18 CCR)

Prior law and exceptions. For tax years prior to 2013 or if a business qualifies under Sec. 25128(b) to use a three-factor apportionment formula, property and payroll modifications also apply. Railroad cars owned and operated by other railroads and temporarily used by a taxpayer that pays a *per diem* or mileage charge are not included in the property factor as rented property. Cars owned and operated by the taxpayer that are temporarily used by other railroads and for which a per diem charge is made by the taxpayer are included in the taxpayer's property factor. The property factor numerator includes all stationary property in California. It also includes mobile or moveable property, like passenger or freight cars, locomotives, and freight containers in the ratio that locomotive miles and car miles in California bear to the total miles everywhere. Compensation paid to enginemen, trainmen, or individuals engaged in similar activities on interstate trains is included in the payroll factor numerator in the ratio that the compensation required to be reported to California for withholding purposes bears to the total compensation required to be reported to the Internal Revenue Service. (Reg. 25137-9, 18 CCR)

Sea transportation companies. Taxpayers carrying on the business of transporting passengers, mail, freight, and other cargo at sea must apportion their business income using a special regulation. Beginning with the 2013 tax year, they must use a single sales factor apportionment formula. The factors are computed on the basis of in-state voyage days to total voyage days. A "voyage day" is any day or part of a day that a ship is in operation for purposes of transporting cargo, including all sailing days, days spent in port while loading and unloading, and days laid up for ordinary repairs, refueling, or provisioning. A ship is not in operation when it is out of service, in drydock, or laid up for extended repairs, overhaul, or modification. (Reg. 25101, 18 CCR)

Space transportation companies. For taxable years beginning on or after January 1, 2016, space transportation companies must apportion their business income using a special regulation. In determining the numerator of the sales factor, gross receipts must be attributed to California based upon a mileage factor, weighted at 80%, and a departure factor, weighted at 20%. The **mileage factor** must be determined by computing the mileage ratio applicable to each launch contract for which the taxpayer recognizes revenue in the taxable year. (Reg. 25137-15, 18 CCR)

The **numerator of the mileage ratio** for each launch contract will be the total projected mileage that all launch vehicles launched or planned to be launched pursuant to that launch contract will travel within California. If a launch occurs or is planned to occur in California, the contribution of that launch to the numerator of the mileage ratio will be 62 statute miles. If a launch occurs or is planned to occur outside of California, the contribution of that launch to the numerator of the mileage ratio will be zero. The **denominator of the mileage ratio** for each launch contract will be the total mileage that all launch vehicles launched pursuant to that contract are projected at the time of the execution of the contract to travel from launch to separation. If the Internal Revenue Service or the FTB is prevented by reasons of secrecy or confidentiality imposed by governmental authorities from determining the projected mileage of any launch contract, the mileage ratio denominator of those contracts will be conclusively presumed to be 310 statute miles multiplied by the number of launches pursuant to that contract. (Reg. 25137-15, 18 CCR)

For each launch contract under which revenue is recognized in a taxable year, the mileage ratio for that contract must be multiplied by the revenue recognized from that contract in the taxable year. The product must be added to the products for each launch contract for which the taxpayer recognizes revenue in the taxable year, the sum of which will be the **numerator of the mileage factor**. The **denominator of the mileage factor** will be the total revenue recognized from all launch contracts during the taxable year. (Reg. 25137-15, 18 CCR)

For each launch contract under which the taxpayer recognizes revenue in a taxable year, the contribution to the **numerator of the departure factor** will be the number of launches in California as specified in the contract at the time of execution of the contract. The numerator of the departure factor will include all launches in California specified in the contract regardless of the taxable year in which the launches occur or are planned to occur. The numerator of the departure factor will be the sum of the contributions to the numerator factor for all launch contracts under which the taxpayer recognizes revenue. For each launch contract under which the taxpayer recognizes revenue in a taxable year, the contribution to the **denominator of the departure factor** will be the number of launches everywhere as specified in the contract at the time of execution of the contract. The denominator of the departure factor will include all launches specified in the contract regardless of the taxable year in which the launches occur or are planned to occur. The denominator of the departure factor will be the sum of the contributions to the departure factor for all launch contracts under which the taxpayer recognizes revenue. (Reg. 25137-15, 18 CCR)

Trucking companies. Trucking companies that have income from sources both in and outside California must apportion their business income under a special regulation. Beginning with the 2013 tax year, they generally must use a single sales factor apportionment formula. The sales factor is computed the same as a general business corporation's sales factor, except the total revenue attributable to California from hauling freight, mail, and express that must be included in the sales factor numerator is equal to the sum of all receipts from any shipment that both originates and terminates in California and that portion of the receipts from movements or shipments that originate in one state and terminate in another state in the ratio that mobile property miles traveled in the state during the year bear to mobile property miles traveled everywhere during the year. (Reg. 25137-11, 18 CCR)

— **Prior law and exceptions.** For tax years prior to 2013 or if a business qualifies under Sec. 25128(b) to use a three-factor apportionment formula, property and payroll modifications also apply. The factors are computed the same as for a general business corporation, except mobile property is included in the property factor numerator in the ratio that mobile property miles traveled in the state during the year bear to mobile property miles traveled everywhere during the year. When a trucking company employs property other than mobile property to transport goods between states, that property will be included in the property factor numerator. Compensation paid to personnel who operate or maintain mobile property is included in the payroll factor numerator in the ratio that mobile property miles traveled in the state during the year bear to mobile property miles traveled everywhere during the year. When a trucking company employs property other than mobile property to transport goods between states, the compensation paid to personnel who operate or maintain it during transportation are included in the payroll factor numerator. (Reg. 25137-11, 18 CCR)

— **De minimis nexus requirement.** Trucking company income is not subject to the regulation unless during the taxable year the company engaged in at least one of the following activities:

　　— owned or rented real or personal property in the state, other than mobile property operated in and outside California;

　　— made pick-ups or deliveries in California;

　　— traveled more than 25,000 mobile property miles in California;

　　— traveled more than 3% of its total property miles in California; or

　　— made more than 12 trips into California.

(Reg. 25137-11, 18 CCR)

Other industries. Certain industries and activities are covered by special apportionment guidelines that have not been adopted as regulations. Generally, the only FTB publication that explains these guidelines is an internal manual entitled the "Multistate Audit Technique Manual." These non-regulatory guidelines provide special apportionment rules for the following industries and activities:

　　— bus transportation (Sec. 7765)

　　— pipeline companies (Sec. 7797)

　　— stockbrokers (Sec. 7800)

　　— telecommunications companies (Sec. 7805)

(*Multistate Audit Technique Manual*, California FTB, revised December 2013)

Subscribers to *CCH Tax Research NetWork* can view these guidelines.

The guidelines do not have the force and effect of regulations that have been approved and adopted by the California Office of Administrative Law. Historically, the FTB has allowed taxpayers to follow these guidelines without requiring them to prove that the standard formula does not fairly reflect the taxpayer's business activity in California. However, a taxpayer is not legally bound to follow guidelines that are only set forth in the FTB's Multistate Audit Technique Manual. If a taxpayer disagrees with the application of these guidelines to a specific fact pattern, the FTB may not cite the guidelines as authority for modifying the standard apportionment factor computation. Instead, the FTB bears the burden of demonstrating, under the authority of Rev. & Tax. Code Sec. 25137, that the standard formula does not fairly represent the extent of the taxpayer's activities in California.

[¶11-550] Combined Reports

Does California allow elective combined reporting?

If a unitary group derives its income wholly from California sources, then its members may elect to report their income on a combined report basis. (Sec. 25101.15, Rev. & Tax. Code)

Does California require combined reporting for unitary business groups?

If two or more C corporations are engaged in a unitary business and derive income from sources in and outside California, then the members of the unitary group that are subject to California franchise or income tax must allocate and apportion their income on a worldwide combined basis, unless they elect to exclude some or all of the income and apportionment factors of certain foreign affiliates by making a water's-edge election. A single corporation engaged in one or several businesses or a group of affiliated corporations may make a water's-edge election. (Sec. 25102, Rev. & Tax. Code; Sec. 25110, Rev. & Tax. Code)

Worldwide combined reporting is a method of reporting that includes the income and apportionment factors of all members of a unitary group, wherever located. (Sec. 25102, Rev. & Tax. Code) Water's-edge combined reporting is a method of reporting that includes the income and apportionment factors of only unitary group members that are incorporated in the United States and other entities that have sufficient connections to the United States. (Sec. 25110, Rev. & Tax. Code)

COMMENT: Except as otherwise provided in the statutory provisions governing water's-edge elections, when any of the statutory provisions governing water's-edge elections refers to a provision of the Internal Revenue Code (IRC), the reference is to the IRC including all amendments in effect for federal purposes for the taxable period. (Sec. 25116, Rev. & Tax. Code) This overrides the general incorporation date for IRC provisions (see ¶10-515 Federal Conformity) so that relevant changes to federal law will be applied in computing the income and deductions of a water's-edge group for California purposes.

An S corporation generally may not be included in a combined report. However, in some cases, the Franchise Tax Board (FTB) may require the use of combined reporting methods to clearly reflect the income of an S corporation. (Sec. 23801, Rev. & Tax. Code)

If a corporation becomes a member or ceases to be a member of a unitary group after the beginning of the taxable year and is required to file two short period returns for the taxable year, then the income for the period in which the member was unitary with the group must be determined on a combined basis. The income for the remaining short period must be determined on a separate basis (or on a combined basis with a different group, if the taxpayer had a unitary relationship with one or more corporations in that short period). If the part-year member is not required to file short period returns, then it must file a single return for the entire year. The income reported on that return must be determined by combined reporting procedures for any period in which the part-year member was part of a unitary group, and by separate accounting for any period in which it was not part of a unitary group. (Reg. 25106.5-9, 18 CCR; Publication 1061, Guidelines for Corporations Filing a Combined Report)

Unitary business group. There are three general tests for determining whether a business is unitary:

— the *Butler Brothers v. McColgan*, 62 SCt 701 (1942), 315 US 501, three unities test;

— the *Edison California Stores v. McColgan*, 30 Cal2d 472, 183 P2d 16 (1947) contribution and dependency test; and

— the *Container Corp. of America v. Franchise Tax Board*, 463 US 159, 103 SCt 2933 (1983), functional integration test.

The existence of a unitary business is established if any of these tests is met.

If a taxpayer has two or more businesses that are not engaged in the same trade or business, then the businesses are considered separate businesses for allocation and apportionment purposes, and they are not treated as unitary. (Reg. 25120, 18 CCR)

When a business is acquired, questions arise not only about whether, but about when, a unitary relationship arises. Although difficult to prove, some companies are deemed instantly unitary, beginning on the date of acquisition. In some cases, the taxpayer acquires a supplier or marketer with whom it would have been unitary in the past, but for lack of controlling ownership. (See, e.g., *Dr. Pepper Bottling Co. of Southern California*, BOE, 90-SBE-015, December 5, 1990) In other situations, an existing business is acquired and integrated into another business over a period of time, and a unitary relationship is not immediately formed. (See, e.g., *The Signal Cos., Inc.*, BOE, 90-SBE-003, January 24, 1990)

Three unities test. In *Butler Brothers v. McColgan*, the U.S. Supreme Court held that the existence of a unitary business was established by the presence of unity of ownership; unity of operation, as evidenced by central purchasing, advertising, accounting, and management divisions; and unity of use in a centralized executive force and general system of operation. (*Butler Brothers v. McColgan*, 315 US 501, 62 SCt 701 (1942))

EXAMPLE: D is a California corporation engaged both in and outside California in the business of providing review and advice to insurance companies regarding dental insurance claims. D forms F, a wholly owned Nevada subsidiary that operates small farms in California. F's bookkeeping, accounting, check writing, legal, and insurance requirements are all performed or paid for by D's personnel at D's California headquarters. D advances over $1 million to F and also issues loan guarantees for several of F's obligations. The majority of F's directors and officers are G (D's president and majority shareholder) and K (D's secretary and treasurer, as well as D's attorney). F has only one employee, its president and remaining director, who investigates business opportunities and presents them to F's board for approval. F's board has responsibility for ultimate policy decisions, especially regarding investments and other financial matters. Management firms unrelated to D conduct F's daily operations under agreements negotiated and executed by G and K. However, G approves all checks F issues as well as the farm managers' decisions regarding deepening a well, repairing wind machines, and establishing the mix of a product. G decides to plant table grapes at one ranch, install a drip irrigation system, sell one ranch, and acquire three other ranches. G applies for water delivery for F and executes an agreement with the irrigation district for the installation of a pump. G telephones the various farm managers weekly and more frequently during harvest time. D, which enjoys significant profits, and F, which reports significant losses, file combined reports as a unitary business. D and F are entitled to do so because they meet the three unities test. Substantial intercompany loans and the centralization of all administrative functions of both companies are evidence of unity of operation. Strong centralized management, including significant overlap of directors and officers and the management role D generally and G in particular play is evidence of unity of use. This type of management is far more than the occasional oversight any parent routinely gives to an investment in a subsidiary. (*Dental Insurance Consultants v. FTB*, 1 CalApp4th 343, pet. for review denied January 30, 1992)

The State Board of Equalization (BOE) has held that unity of ownership may exist when a group of shareholders act together to operate two or more corporations as a single economic unit. (*AMP Inc.*, BOE, 96-SBE-017, October 10, 1997)

The FTB has issued a detailed legal ruling outlining the proper method for determining whether multiple corporations share unity of ownership for corporation franchise or income tax purposes. Generally, more than 50% of the voting stock of all members of the group must be owned or controlled, directly or indirectly, by the same interests. (*LR 91-1*, FTB, November 1, 1991)

The unity of ownership requirement is satisfied if two or more corporations are members of a commonly controlled group. A "commonly controlled group" is any of the following:

— a group of corporations that is connected through stock ownership (or constructive ownership) if the parent corporation owns stock having more than 50% of the voting power of at least one corporation, and the parent or one or more of the other corporations owns stock cumulatively representing more than 50% of the voting power of each of the corporations (other than the parent);

— any two or more corporations if stock representing more than 50% of the voting power of the corporations is owned (or constructively owned) by one person;

— any two or more corporations if more than 50% of the ownership or beneficial ownership of the stock having voting power in each corporation consists of stapled interests; or

— any two or more corporations if stock representing more than 50% of the voting power of the corporations is cumulatively owned (without regard to the rules of constructive ownership) by, or for the benefit of, members of the same family.

(Sec. 25105, Rev. & Tax. Code)

If a corporation is eligible to be a member of more than one commonly controlled group, then it must elect to be a member of a single group. The election will remain in effect unless revoked with FTB approval. Membership in a commonly controlled group will be terminated when a corporation's stock is sold, exchanged, or otherwise disposed of, except that the FTB may treat membership as continuing if the corporation requalifies as a member of the same commonly controlled group within a two-year period. (Sec. 25105, Rev. & Tax. Code)

Contribution and dependency test. In *Edison California Stores v. McColgan*, the California Supreme Court stated that businesses are unitary if the operation of the portion of the business done in California depends on or contributes to the operation of the business outside California. (*Edison California Stores v. McColgan*, 30 Cal2d 472, 183 P2d 16 (1947))

Functional integration test. In *Container Corp. of America v. Franchise Tax Board*, the U.S. Supreme Court found that a domestic parent and several foreign subsidiaries were unitary because their contributions to income resulted from functional integration, centralized management, and economies of scale. (*Container Corp. of America v. Franchise Tax Board*, 463 US 159; 103 SCt 2933 (1983))

Computation of income. In a combined report, the entire amount of unitary business income of all corporations in the unitary group (including unitary members with no property, payroll, or sales in California) is aggregated. The combined business income of the unitary group is then apportioned to California and to the unitary members subject to tax in California. The California net income of each member is then computed, taking into account its apportioned share of the unitary group business income or loss plus any income from a business wholly conducted in California, California source nonbusiness income or loss, and allowable California source net operating loss. (Reg. 25106.5, 18 CCR; Publication 1061, Guidelines for Corporations Filing a Combined Report)

Intercompany transactions. Most intercompany transactions between members of a combined reporting group are eliminated. A regulation provides guidance for reporting intercompany transactions in order to clearly reflect the taxable income of the group members that is allocated or apportioned to California. California generally conforms to the provisions of Treasury Regulation § 1.1502-13. If members of a combined reporting group make a federal election to recognize income or loss from intercompany transactions on a separate entity basis under Treasury Regulation § 1.1502-13(e)(3), then the members will be treated as having made a similar election for California purposes, unless a different election is made. (Reg. 25106.5-1, 18 CCR)

PRACTICE NOTE: Combined reporting group members must make annual disclosures regarding deferred intercompany stock account (DISA) transactions. The balance of each DISA must be disclosed annually on a taxpayer's return. (Reg. 25106.5-1(j)(7), 18 CCR) If a taxpayer fails to disclose its DISA balance on its annual return, FTB staff may require the amounts in the undisclosed DISA account to be taken into account in part or in whole in any year of the failure. (Reg. 25106.5-1(j)(7), 18 CCR) This could result in additional tax liability and the imposition of various penalties, including the accuracy-related penalty and the large corporate underpayment penalty.

Taxpayers use Form 3726, DISA and Capital Gain Information, to satisfy the annual disclosure requirement. In addition, taxpayers should respond to the question contained on Form 100, Corporation Franchise or Income Tax Return, and Form 100W, Corporation Franchise or Income Tax Return—Water's-Edge Filers, asking whether taxpayers have a DISA balance and, if so, the amount of that balance. An appropriately completed Form 3726 must be included with a taxpayer's original return if a member of the combined group has a DISA balance. (*FTB Notice 2009-01*, California Franchise Tax Board, February 20, 2009; *FTB Notice 2009-05*, California Franchise Tax Board, July 17, 2009)

In addition to being required to disclose all DISA balances, taxpayers must also disclose all DISA balances that have been previously reduced and/or eliminated as the result of any subsequent capital contributions. (Reg. 25106.5-1(j)(7), 18 CCR)

Gains and losses. In a combined reporting group, gains and losses from capital assets, IRC § 1231 assets, and involuntary conversion are combined, and each taxpayer member determines its share of the business gain/loss items in each class based on its apportionment percentage. Then, each taxpayer member applies the federal netting rules to its post-apportioned share of business gain/loss items and its California-source nonbusiness gain/loss items. If a net loss results for any taxpayer member, it may be carried forward by that member for up to five years. (Reg. 25106.5-2, 18 CCR; Publication 1061, Guidelines for Corporations Filing a Combined Report)

Net operating losses. Corporations that are members of a unitary group filing a combined report must separately compute net operating loss (NOL) carryovers for each corporation in the group using their individual apportionment factors. (Reg. 25106.5, 18 CCR) Each corporation included in the combined report must complete a separate Form FTB 3805Q, Net Operating Loss (NOL) Computation and NOL Disaster Loss Limitations—Corporation, and attach it behind the combined Form 3805Q for all members. Unlike the NOL treatment on a federal consolidated return, a loss carryover for one member included in a combined report may not be applied to the intrastate apportioned income of another member included in a combined report. (Instructions, FTB 3805Q Booklet, Net Operating Loss (NOL) Computation and NOL Disaster Loss Limitations—Corporation) Below is an example of how an NOL is applied in combined report.

Applying an NOL in a Combined Report

YEAR 1:	Corp. X	Corp. Y	Corp. Z	Combined
Unitary business income (loss) subject to apportionment	(400,000)	(10,000)	60,000	(350,000)
Apportionment percentages	5 %	1 %	3 %	9 %
Loss apportioned to California (Combined loss × apportionment %)	(17,500)	(3,500)	(10,500)	(31,500)
Nonbusiness items wholly attributable to California	50,000	(2,500)	0	
California net income (loss)	32,500	(6,000)	(10,500)	
NOL available to be carried forward (100% of loss)	0	(6,000)	(10,500)	

YEAR 2:	Corp. X	Corp. Y	Corp. Z	Combined
Unitary business income (loss) subject to apportionment	50,000	80,000	(5,000)	125,000
Apportionment percentages	6 %	4 %	4 %	14 %
Income apportioned to California (Combined income × apportionment %)	7,500	5,000	5,000	17,500
Nonbusiness items wholly attributable to California	2,500	(10,000)	0	
California net income (loss)	10,000	(5,000)	5,000	
Application of NOL carryover from Year 1	0	0	(5,000)	
California net income (loss)	10,000	(5,000)	0	
NOL available to be carried forward (100% of loss)	0	(5,000)	0	

	Corp. X	Corp. Y	Corp. Z
Remaining NOL from Year 1	0	(6,000)	(5,500)
Loss in Year 2	0	(5,000)	0
NOL available to be carried forward	0	(11,000)	(5,500)

For water's-edge taxpayers, an NOL carryover generated during a non-water's-edge tax year is limited to the lesser amount redetermined by computing the income and factors of the original worldwide combined reporting group as if the water's-edge election had been in force for the year of the loss. (Sec.

24416.20(c), Rev. & Tax. Code) If a recomputation is required, the NOL carryover for each corporation may be decreased, but not increased. (Instructions, FTB 3805Q, Net Operating Loss (NOL) Computation and NOL Disaster Loss Limitations—Corporation)

Accounting methods. Members of the combined reporting group may determine a group member's net income under accounting methods and other elections authorized by California law independently of the net income of other members of the combined reporting group. (Reg. 25106.5-3, 18 CCR) If the accounting periods of the principal member and one or more of the other members of the group do not begin and end on the same dates, adjustments must be made to fiscalize the other members' combined report business income and apportionment data and assign an appropriate amount of those values to the accounting period of the principal member. (Reg. 25106.5-4, 18 CCR)

Apportionment. Total group combined report business income for the principal member's accounting period is multiplied by the California apportionment percentage of the combined reporting group to arrive at the group's California source combined report business income. The resulting California source total group combined report business income is apportioned between the taxpayer members of the group by multiplying the group's California source combined report business income by each member's intrastate apportionment percentage to arrive at each taxpayer member's California source combined report business income. (Reg. 25106.5(c)(7), 18 CCR)

California law adopts the *Finnigan* approach applying the throwback rule to sales made by a combined unitary group member. Thus, all sales are considered California sales if the transaction otherwise qualifies as a California sale and one of the unitary group members is taxable by California, even if the group member that makes the sale is not subject to California taxation. An out-of-state sale will not be thrown back to California and be included in the California sales factor numerator if a member of the taxpayer's combined reporting group is taxable in the purchaser's state. (Sec. 25135(b), Rev. & Tax. Code; *Chief Counsel Ruling 2012-01*, California Franchise Tax Board, August 28, 2012)

PRACTICE NOTE: The California sales of each corporation included in a combined reporting group must be taken into account in the apportionment of business income to California, including amounts attributable to entities exempt from California taxation, like entities protected by P.L. 86-272. (Instructions, Schedule R, Apportionment and Allocation of Income)

CCH POINTER: The income received from foreign affiliates of a unitary group that elects water's-edge treatment are not excluded from the apportionment formula. Rather, these payments are treated as payments received by a unitary group from any other third-party. For example, royalty and franchise payments received from a taxpayer's foreign subsidiaries are treated as payments by third-party licensees for combined reporting purposes. (*Chief Counsel Ruling 2010-2*, California Franchise Tax Board, May 11, 2010)

Credits. Unless otherwise provided by statute, credits are applied against tax on a separate entity basis and are available only to the taxpayer that incurred the expenses that generated the credits. (Publication 1061, Guidelines for Corporations Filing a Combined Report) However, members of a combined reporting group may assign credits to other eligible members of the group. To be eligible to receive the credit, the assignee must have been a member of the assigning taxpayer's unitary combined group on (1) the last day of the first taxable year in which the credit was allowed to the taxpayer, and (2) the last day of the assigning taxpayer's taxable year in which the credit is assigned. The taxpayer must make an irrevocable election on its original return for the taxable year in which the assignment is made. Any credit limitations that would apply to the assigning taxpayer in the absence of an assignment also apply to the assignee. An assignee may pay the assigning taxpayer for the credit transfer. However, the assignee may not claim any deduction for the amount paid, and the assigning taxpayer may not include in its gross income the amount received. (Sec. 23663, Rev. & Tax. Code)

PRACTICE NOTE: The FTB adopted regulations clarifying the assignment of credits to combined group members. Regs. 23663-1 through 23663-5 provide guidance for when a defective assignment occurs. A defective assignment is one that does not meet the strict requirements of Sec. 23663. For instance, a defective assignment can occur when the amount of credits assigned is greater than the amount available following an audit. It can also occur if the FTB determines that an assignee was not a member of the same combined reporting group as the assignor on the dates required under the statute. The regulations provide default allocation rules for defective assignments, procedures for correcting errors, and a way for taxpayers to request an alternative allocation. For cases involving an overlap between the various rules, the regulations specify an order in which the rules apply.

If a taxpayer over-assigns credits, the default allocation will generally be in the ratio of credits assigned in the original defective assignment. If an assignment is defective for another reason (e.g., an ineligible assignee), then the assignment will generally be treated as if it had not been made. Special rules apply to scenarios involving credits claimed in a closed tax year.

An assignor may correct a defective assignment if all parties to the assignment agree in writing to the correction. Generally, the assignor must request the correction by the earlier of the filing date or the extended due date of its, or any assignee's, return for the year after the year of the original assignment. However, for one year from September 18, 2018 (when the regulations took effect), assignors may request corrections without regard to the normal limitations period.

Water's-edge combined reporting requirements.

Eligible group members. A water's-edge combined report must include only the income and apportionment factors of members of the unitary group that are any of the following:

— a corporation, other than a bank, regardless of where it is incorporated, if the average of its property, payroll, and sales factors in the United States is 20% or more;

— a corporation incorporated in the United States, if more than 50% of its stock is controlled, directly or indirectly, by the same interests (except a corporation electing "possession corporation" treatment under IRC §§ 931 to 936);

— a domestic international sales corporations (DISC) or foreign sales corporation (FSC), as defined in IRC § 992;

— an export trade corporation, as defined in IRC § 971;

— a "controlled foreign corporation" (CFC), as defined in IRC § 957, that has "Subpart F income", as defined in IRC § 952, in which case the income and apportionment factors of the corporation are included in the combined report based on the ratio of the corporation's total Subpart F income for the year to its current year earnings and profits; and

— any other corporation not described above, or any foreign organized bank that has income attributable to sources in the United States, to the extent of its U.S. located income (*i.e.*, income that is effectively connected, or treated as effectively connected, with a U.S. trade or business) and apportionment factors. Any income satisfying the federal definition of "effectively connected income" that is excluded from federally taxable income due to a tax treaty is included for California income tax purposes. (Reg. 25110, 18 CCR; Instructions, Form 100W, California Corporation Franchise or Income Tax Return—Water's-Edge Filers)

For purposes of these provisions, a CFC is treated as having no Subpart F income if the income is less than $1 million and represents less than 5% of the CFC's earnings and profits. (Sec. 25110, Rev. & Tax. Code; Reg. 25110, 18 CCR)

U.S. source income of a foreign corporation is excluded from the definition of "United States income" for water's-edge reporting purposes if the income is not effectively connected with a U.S. business, unless the income arises from a contract or agreement that has a principal purpose of avoiding federal income tax or California franchise or income tax. Nothing prevents the FTB from making adjustments to related party transactions to reflect arm's length terms. (Reg. 25110, 18 CCR)

If an entity is described by a statute as one whose income and apportionment factors are taken into account under a water's-edge election, that affiliate must be included in the water's-edge group even if it is described as excluded elsewhere in the statute. (Sec. 25110, Rev. & Tax. Code; Reg. 25110, 18 CCR)

EXAMPLE: "Possession corporations" (*i.e.*, corporations that meet certain requirements concerning income derived from U.S. possessions and that have elected to exclude income under IRC § 936, the Puerto Rico and possession tax credit provisions) are generally excluded from the water's-edge group by one paragraph of the statute. However, under another paragraph, a corporation must be included if the average of its payroll, property, and sales factors in the United States reaches 20% or more. Thus, a possession corporation could be included if the average of its payroll, property, and sales factors within the United States is 20% or more.

PRACTICE NOTE: All affiliated entities (*i.e.*, members of a commonly controlled group) are considered in determining the existence of a unitary business relationship, not just those whose income and apportionment factors are required to be considered under a water's-edge election. Thus, an entity outside the water's-edge group may provide the unitary link that places other entities within the group. (Reg. 25110, 18 CCR)

Deduction of foreign dividends. A water's-edge taxpayer may deduct from its apportionable income a specified portion of dividends from any corporation in which it owns more than 50% of the total combined voting power of all classes of voting stock, if the average of that corporation's property, payroll, and sales factors in the United States is less than 20%. The deductible portion of these dividends is 75% (except for certain dividends from construction projects). Dividends received from these corporations are termed "qualifying dividends." The term does not include amounts that are deemed to be dividends under federal law, unless there is an actual or constructive distribution of those amounts or a California provision under which the amounts are considered dividends. (Sec. 24411, Rev. & Tax. Code; Reg. 24411, 18 CCR)

This deduction will not be allowed for any dividends for which another deduction has been allowed or that have been eliminated from income. Dividends are considered to have been paid first out of the current year's earnings and profits, and then from the most recently accumulated earnings and profits by year. (Reg. 24411, 18 CCR)

In *Fujitsu IT Holdings Inc. v. Franchise Tax Bd.,* Cal.Ct.App., (2004) 120 Cal. App. 4th, the court held that United Kingdom (U.K.) advance corporation tax (ACT) refunds received by a U.S. corporation from its U.K. subsidiaries were dividends for California tax purposes and were therefore subject to elimination under Rev. & Tax. Code Sec. 25106 or a partial deduction under Rev. & Tax. Code Sec. 24411. Dividends received by first-tier subsidiaries out of the unitary income of lower-tier subsidiaries were excludable in determining the portion of controlled foreign corporation Subpart F income includable in the corporation's water's-edge combined report. To the extent the dividends were from subsidiaries with both Subpart F income and other income, the dividends were deemed as paid first out of income eligible for elimination from the combined report. Finally, a 75% deduction limitation for foreign source dividends did not discriminate against foreign commerce in violation of the Commerce Clause of the U.S. Constitution.

Qualifying dividends from certain foreign construction projects, when the location is not subject to the taxpayer's control, are 100% deductible by water's-edge taxpayers. The construction project must be undertaken for an entity that is not affiliated with the taxpayer, and the majority of the cost of performance must be attributable to an addition to real property or an alteration of land or an improvement to land. Construction projects do not include the operation, rental, leasing, or depletion of land or improvements to land. (Sec. 24411, Rev. & Tax. Code)

The location of a project is not subject to the taxpayer's control if the majority of the construction, measured by cost of performance, must be performed at the location because of the nature and character of the project, and not because of the terms of the construction contract. (Sec. 24411, Rev. & Tax. Code; Reg. 24411, 18 CCR) For example, when building a dam or a skyscraper, the location is not subject to the taxpayer's control, because the dam or skyscraper must be built at a specific site. On the other hand, when erecting prefabricated buildings, the location is normally under the taxpayer's control, because the majority of the cost involves prefabrication of components, which can occur anywhere.

The deductible amount of qualifying foreign dividends for water's-edge taxpayers is reduced by the amount of any "interest expense incurred for purposes of foreign investments." The amount of interest expense incurred for purposes of foreign investments that may be offset against deductible dividends must be multiplied by the same percentage used to determine the taxpayer's foreign dividend deduction. (Sec. 24344(c), Rev. & Tax. Code)

A regulation describes how interest expense attributable to foreign investment must be calculated for purposes of offsetting the interest expense against deductible foreign dividends. Generally, the interest is apportioned on a worldwide basis, rather than being allocated to specific investments. Interest expense will be directly traced to specific property only if:

— the indebtedness on which the interest was paid was specifically incurred to purchase, maintain, or improve specific property;

— the proceeds of the borrowing were actually applied to the specified purpose;

— only the specific property is security for payment of principal and interest on the loan; and

— the motive for structuring the transaction has some economic significance.

If an interest deduction is directly traceable to specific property, then both the interest and the property to which it relates are eliminated from the formula used to assign other interest expense, even if the specifically assigned interest expense relates to foreign investment. (Reg. 24344(c), 18 CCR)

The calculation of foreign investment interest expense that is not assigned to specific property begins by deducting specifically assigned interest from total interest. The result is multiplied by the ratio of the value of foreign investment to the total value of all assets. The product is the amount of otherwise unassigned interest expense attributable to foreign investment. (Reg. 24344(c), 18 CCR)

Interest expense paid with respect to debt incurred after 1987 can be eliminated from the calculation if the proceeds of the debt are paid into an account that is restricted to preclude its use for foreign investment. However, the proceeds of debt used to refinance pre-1988 debt and the proceeds of a line of credit or similar account are not eligible for the restricted account treatment. (Reg. 24344(c), 18 CCR)

Required consents. A corporation making a water's-edge election must agree with the FTB that dividends received by any of the following entities are both functionally related dividends and presumptively business income:

— a corporation engaged in the same general line of business that is more than 50% owned by members of the unitary business; or

— a corporation that is a significant purchaser from or source of supply to the unitary business.

"Significant" means 15% or more of either input or output. (Sec. 25110, Rev. & Tax. Code; Reg. 25110, 18 CCR)

In addition, an electing taxpayer must consent to the taking of depositions from key officers or employees and to the acceptance of subpoenas requiring that documents be produced for the FTB, the BOE, or state courts for use in reviewing and adjusting income or deductions and for conducting an investigation of a unitary business in which the taxpayer may be involved. A key officer or employee is one whom the taxpayer would designate as among its three most knowledgeable individuals in response to a discovery request in a court proceeding. The individuals may be employees or former employees that maintain an office in the United States, whose activities are directed from the United States or who direct the activities of an office in the United States. (Sec. 25110, Rev. & Tax. Code; Reg. 25110, 18 CCR)

Election method. A corporation must do the following to make a water's-edge election:

— compute its income on a water's-edge basis;

— complete Form 100W, Corporation Franchise or Income Tax Return—Water's-Edge Filers; and

— attach Form 100WE, Water's-Edge Election, to its timely filed original return for the year of the election.

(Sec. 25113, Rev. & Tax. Code; Instructions, Form 100W, Corporation Franchise or Income Tax Return—Water's-Edge Filers)

In lieu of Form 100WE, the FTB may consider other objective evidence of making a water's-edge election such as (1) a statement attached to a timely-filed, original return indicating a water's-edge election is being made or (2) the inclusion of one or more substantially completed forms associated with water's-edge combined reporting with the taxpayer's timely filed-original return. Examples of such forms include FTB Form 1115, Request for Consent for a Water's-Edge Re-Election; Form 2416, Schedule of Included Controlled Foreign Corporations (CFC); or Form 2424, Water's-Edge Foreign Investment Interest Offset. (Reg. 25113, 18 CCR) The filing of federal informational returns, likes federal Forms 5471 and 5472, is not considered to be other objective evidence for purposes of making a water's-edge election. (*Tax News*, California Franchise Tax Board, June 2015)

Generally, an election will be effective only if made by every member of the self-assessed combined reporting group that is subject to California corporation franchise or income tax. An election on a group return will constitute an election by each member included in the group return, unless one of the members files a separate return in which no election is made and the nonelecting member is not otherwise considered to have elected water's-edge treatment. A group member that does not make a water's-edge election on its own return will be considered to have made an election if either of the following applies:

— the nonelecting member's income and apportionment factors are included in the self-assessed combined reporting group on an electing parent corporation's original, timely-filed return, including a group return; or

— the nonelecting member's income and apportionment factors are reflected in the self-assessed combined reporting group on an electing taxpayer's original, timely-filed return, and the written notification of election filed with the return is signed by an officer or other authorized agent of a parent corporation or another corporation with authority to bind the nonelecting member to an election.

(Sec. 25113, Rev. & Tax. Code; Reg. 25113, 18 CCR)

If a corporation that is a water's-edge group member is not itself subject to California corporation franchise or income tax in the year for which the water's-edge election is made, but it subsequently becomes subject to tax, then it will be considered to have made a water's-edge election with the other members of the combined reporting group. (Sec. 25113, Rev. & Tax. Code)

Also, for taxable years beginning on or after January 1, 2021, if a unitary foreign affiliate becomes a California taxpayer solely due to California's "doing business" statute (Sec. 23101(b), Rev. & Tax. Code), California will treat that corporation as having made a water's-edge election with other members of the unitary group. (Sec. 25113, Rev. & Tax. Code) The FTB previously issued notices indicating it would not terminate an otherwise-valid water's-edge election when a unitary foreign affiliate became a California taxpayer in a taxable year beginning on or before December 31, 2020, solely by application of the amended "doing business" statute. (*FTB Notice 2016-02*, California Franchise Tax Board, September 9, 2016; *FTB Notice 2017-04*, California Franchise Tax Board, October 16, 2017; *FTB Notice 2019-02*, California Franchise Tax Board, June 26, 2019)

A corporation engaged in more than one apportioning trade or business may make a separate election for each apportioning trade or business. (Sec. 25113, Rev. & Tax. Code)

If an electing member and a nonelecting member become members of a new unitary group, then the nonelecting taxpayer will be considered to have elected water's-edge status if the value of the total business assets of the electing taxpayer and its component unitary group is larger than the value of the total business assets of the nonelecting taxpayer and its component unitary group, if any. (Sec. 25113, Rev. & Tax. Code) Goodwill recorded as a result of a corporation's acquisition of another corporation is included as a business asset of the target corporation for this purpose. (*Chief Counsel Ruling 2017-02*, California Franchise Tax Board, September 8, 2017)

In cases involving taxpayers with different fiscal years, each member of the water's-edge group must make the election on its timely filed original return for the taxable year for which the election is being made. The election becomes effective as of the beginning of the taxable year of the last member of the water's-edge group to file its return and election. Each taxpayer in the group must file on a worldwide basis for that portion of the taxable year between the beginning of its taxable year and the date the election becomes effective. A return based on a water's-edge basis is filed for the remaining portion of the taxable year. (*FTB Notice 2004-2*, California Franchise Tax Board, May 3, 2004)

Election period. A water's-edge election on an original, timely filed return will remain in effect until it is terminated. Except as otherwise provided, if one or more electing members becomes disaffiliated or otherwise is no longer included in the combined reporting group, the water's-edge election will remain in effect for both the departing members and any remaining members. (Sec. 25113, Rev. & Tax. Code; Reg. 25113, 18 CCR)

If water's-edge group members with different water's-edge election commencement dates become members of a new unitary group, the earliest election date will be considered to apply to all electing members if the total business assets of the earliest electing member and its component unitary group is larger than the value of the total business assets of the later electing member and its component unitary group. On the other hand, if the total business assets of the later electing member and its component unitary group, is larger than the value of the total business assets of the earlier electing member and its component unitary group, the later election commencement date will apply to all electing taxpayers. (Sec. 25113, Rev. & Tax. Code)

Termination. A water's-edge election may be terminated on an original, timely filed return without the consent of the FTB after it has been in effect for at least 84 months. To be effective, the termination must be made by every member of the water's-edge group in the same manner as a water's-edge election. (Sec. 25113, Rev. & Tax. Code)

Termination is accomplished by filing a return on a worldwide basis. Once an election is terminated, a taxpayer is precluded from filing on a water's-edge basis for 84 months. (*FTB Notice 2004-2*, California Franchise Tax Board, May 3, 2004) The FTB may consider objective factors similar to those for determining whether a valid election was made when determining whether a taxpayer has terminated its water's-edge election after the initial 84-month election period has expired. A request for termination before the expiration of the 84-month period may be granted by the FTB for good cause. (Reg. 25113, 18 CCR)

CCH PRACTICE TIP: To request termination of a water's-edge election, a taxpayer must timely file Form FTB 1117, Request to Terminate Water's-Edge Election, with the FTB no later than the 120th day prior to the due date, including extensions, of the return for which the termination would be effective. Form FTB 1117 must be filed separately from any return or any other form. If the FTB takes no action or requests no additional information within 90 days of the filing of the request to terminate the election, the request is considered to be disallowed. The FTB will send a notification of the termination if the request is granted. (Sec. 25113, Rev. & Tax. Code; Reg. 25113, 18 CCR; Instructions, Form 100W, Corporation Tax Booklet, Water's-Edge Filer; *FTB Notice 2004-2*, California Franchise Tax Board, May 3, 2004)

CCH COMMENT: The FTB must consent to a termination requested by all members of a water's-edge group if the purpose of the request is to permit the state to contract with an expatriate corporation or its subsidiary. A water's-edge election terminated for this reason will, however, be effective for the year in which the expatriate corporation, or its subsidiary, enters into the contract with the state. (Sec. 25113, Rev. & Tax. Code)

If an electing member and a nonelecting member become members of a new unitary group and the value of the total business assets of the electing taxpayer and its component unitary group, is smaller than the value of the total business assets of the nonelecting taxpayer and its component unitary group, the water's-edge election will be deemed automatically terminated. (Sec. 25113, Rev. & Tax. Code)

If a taxpayer with a terminated election is subject to the 84-month limit on making a new election and becomes a member of a new unitary group with another taxpayer that is not subject to the prohibition, any water's-edge election of the other taxpayer will terminate, and any restrictions on making a new election will apply to all members of the new unitary group, if the total business assets of the taxpayer subject to the prohibition and its component unitary group, is larger than the total business assets of the other taxpayer and its component unitary group. If two taxpayers with terminated water's-edge elections are subject to the 84-month prohibition and become members of a new unitary group, the termination date of the taxpayer whose total business assets are the largest will be the termination date of the new group. (Sec. 25113, Rev. & Tax. Code; Reg. 25113, 18 CCR)

A request to reelect water's-edge reporting before the 84-month period following a water's-edge termination must be filed with the FTB no later than the 90th day before the due date, including extensions, of the return for which the reelection would be effective. If the FTB takes no action or requests no additional information within 60 days of the filing of the request to reelect water's-edge reporting, the request is deemed to be disallowed. A taxpayer may withdraw its request at any time prior to the FTB's granting permission. Consent to reelect water's-edge reporting may not be granted retroactively. (Reg. 25113, 18 CCR)

Reelection. After termination, a taxpayer must obtain the FTB's consent to reelect water's-edge filing for any taxable year that begins before the 84-month period following the last day of the terminated election. A taxpayer must demonstrate good cause to obtain the FTB's consent, and the request must be in writing and must clearly state the reason. A taxpayer seeking consent to reelect for good cause must use Form FTB 1115, Request for Consent for a Water's-Edge Re-Election. (*FTB Notice 2004-2*, California Franchise Tax Board, May 3, 2004)

Recordkeeping requirements. A taxpayer electing water's-edge treatment must maintain, and provide to the FTB, upon request, information or documents that are material to a determination of the taxpayer's tax. This includes:

— audit questionnaires;

— identification of officers or employees with access to records of pricing, profit or cost centers, and methods of allocating income and expenses;

— ruling requests;

— correspondence and documents affecting either the assignment of income to the United States or a foreign tax liability;

— forms filed with the Internal Revenue Service regarding foreign and foreign-owned corporations;

— state tax returns; and

— other information necessary to determine or verify net income, apportionment factors, or the geographic source of income pursuant to the IRC.

The information or documents must be retained for as long as they are relevant to open taxable years or pending appeals. (Sec. 25112, Rev. & Tax. Code)

A penalty of $1,000 is imposed for each taxable year in which requested information is not provided. An additional $1,000 penalty is imposed for each 30-day period during which requested information is not provided, up to a maximum $24,000 penalty, starting 90 days after the mailing of a formal FTB document request. The penalties may be excused if there is reasonable cause for failing to furnish the information. However, the possibility of incurring foreign civil or criminal penalties for disclosure of the requested information is not reasonable cause for failing to furnish the information unless the court finds otherwise. (Sec. 25112, Rev. & Tax. Code)

Repatriation provisions of the federal Tax Cuts and Jobs Act (TCJA) of 2017. The California water's-edge provisions do not specifically refer to certain repatriation provisions enacted by the federal Tax Cuts and Jobs Act (TCJA) of 2017. As a result, California water's-edge combined reporting requirements do not conform to federal provisions that:

— allow a 100% deduction for the foreign-source portion of dividends received from a specified 10% owned foreign corporation by a domestic corporation that is a U.S. shareholder of the foreign corporation (i.e., a participation dividends-received deduction) (IRC Sec. 245A);

— impose a one-time transition (repatriation) tax, without requiring an actual distribution, on accumulated foreign earnings of controlled foreign corporations (CFCs) or foreign corporations that are at least 10% owned by a domestic corporation (IRC Sec. 965); and

— require inclusion of "global intangible low-taxed income" (GILTI) by a person who is a U.S. shareholder of a CFC (IRC Sec. 951A).

(Sec. 25116, Rev. & Tax. Code; *Preliminary Report on Specific Provisions of the Federal Tax Cuts and Jobs Act*, California Franchise Tax Board, March 20, 2018)

Filing requirements. There is no combined report form. The resulting tax due is calculated on an attachment to Form 100, Corporation Franchise or Income Tax Return, or Form 100W, Corporation Franchise or Income Tax Return—Water's-Edge Filers. (Publication 1061, Guidelines for Corporations Filing a Combined Report)

Corporations that are members of the same combined reporting group may elect to file a single group return. The election applies only to those unitary group members that are subject to California franchise or income tax. Corporations may file a group return if more than one unitary business is being conducted by any one taxpayer. To qualify to file a group return, one of the group members must be designated as the "key corporation" for the group and agree to act as agent and surety for the remaining taxpayers included in the combined report. The designation of the key corporation and identification of the remaining members of the group is made by completing Schedule R-7 of Schedule R, Apportionment and Allocation of Income, and attaching it to the Form 100 filed by the key corporation. The group must also attach a copy of its combined report showing how the business income of the group is apportioned among the various states. (Reg. 25106.5, 18 CCR to Reg. 25106.5-11, 18 CCR; Instructions, Schedule R, Apportionment and Allocation of Income)

Unitary group members accept the election's terms and conditions by the key corporation's filing of the election form and the failure of the other members to file their own separate returns. Payments are made using the key corporation's California corporation identification number, and any subsequent adjustments to the member's liabilities are assessed, billed, or paid to that corporation. (Reg. 25106.5, 18 CCR to Reg. 25106.5-11, 18 CCR; *Legal Ruling 95-2*, California Franchise Tax Board, July 7, 1995; Instructions, Schedule R, Apportionment and Allocation of Income)

Does California allow or require affiliated group combined reporting?

California does not allow or require affiliated corporations to report income on a combined basis, except to the extent they are engaged in a unitary business. (Sec. 25101.15, Rev. & Tax. Code; Sec. 25102, Rev. & Tax. Code; Sec. 25110, Rev. & Tax. Code)

[¶12-000]

CREDITS

[¶12-001] Overview of Credits

California allows the following credits against corporation franchise (income) tax for the following purchases, activities, and practices:

• *Enterprise zone credits*

   Employer's credit for qualified wages

   Credit for sales and use tax paid on certain machinery

• *Targeted tax area credits*

   Employer's credit for qualified wages

   Credit for sales and use tax paid on certain machinery

• *Local Agency Military Base Recovery Area (LAMBRA) credits*

   Employer's credit for qualified wages

   Credit for sales and use tax paid on certain machinery

• *Manufacturing enhancement area credits*

   Employer's credit for qualified wages

• *Research credits*

   Research expenditures

- *Job creation/hiring credits*

    Disabled access expenditures

    Prison inmate labor

    New jobs credit (Pre-2014 tax years)

    New employment credit (Post-2013 tax years)

    Wages paid by manufacturers of property for new advanced strategic aircraft

    Small business hiring credit

- *Environmental credits*

    Utra-low sulfur diesel fuel credit

- *Economic development credits*

    Economic development areas

    Motion picture production credits

    California competes credit

- *Land conservation/preservation credits*

    Natural heritage

- *Capital investment credits*

    Community development investment

- *Housing credits*

    Low-income housing

- *Other credits*

    Donated agricultural products transportation

    Enhanced oil recovery

    Donated agricultural products

    College access tax credit

Credits may be claimed on Form 100, California Corporation Franchise or Income Tax Return.

- *Estimated tax and tax overpayments*

Tax liability is reduced by amounts previously paid as estimated taxes at the time the return is filed. (Sec. 19002, Rev. & Tax. Code) In addition, the state may credit overpayments against taxes owed. (Form 100, California Corporation Franchise or Income Tax Return)

- *Credit for first-year tax*

A corporation that commenced doing business before 1972 and dissolved after 1972 is entitled to a credit for the franchise tax paid during its first full year of doing business (see ¶ 10-210 C Corporations).

¶12-001

• *Credit for payment of another state's tax*

California does not allow a credit for taxes paid to a foreign country (see ¶ 10-055 Comparison of Federal/State Key Features), but instead allows a deduction from gross income for the amount of dividend gross-up under IRC Sec. 78, relating to dividends received from certain foreign corporations by domestic corporations choosing foreign tax credit (see ¶ 10-855 Subtractions—Items Related to Federal Deductions or Credits).

• *Credit carryforwards*

When the amount of a credit exceeds a taxpayer's tax liability for a taxable year, the excess may sometimes be carried over beyond the expiration date to succeeding taxable years. In some instances, the remaining carryover from a repealed or inoperative credit may be carried over and applied to tax until the credit is exhausted, unless the law specifically provides otherwise. (Sec. 23036, Rev. & Tax. Code) Excess credit amounts may not be carried back and applied to previous taxable years. (Instructions, Form FTB 3540, Credit Carryover Summary)

• *Credit limitations*

CCH PRACTICE TIP: 2020, 2021, and 2022 limitation on credit amounts.— For the 2020, 2021, and 2022 tax years, the amount of credits and credit carryovers (other than low-income housing credits and carryovers) that may reduce a taxpayer's tax (as defined by Sec. 23036) is limited to $5 million per year. Taxpayers required to be included in a combined report are subject to a combined $5 million limit. Any unused credit may be carried over. The carryover period is extended by the number of taxable years the credit, or any portion thereof, was not allowed as a result of the limitation. (Sec. 23036.3, Rev. & Tax. Code)

CCH PRACTICE TIP: *2008 and 2009 limitation on credit amounts.*—The amount of credits and credit carryovers that could be claimed by taxpayers on a corporation franchise and income tax return were limited to 50% of a taxpayer's tax (as defined by Sec. 23036) during the 2008 and 2009 tax years. Any unused credit could be carried over. The carryover period was extended by the number of taxable years the credit, or any portion thereof, was not allowed as a result of the 50% limitation. A taxpayer with net business income of less than $500,000 for the taxable year was exempt from the 50% limitation. (Sec. 23036.2, Rev. & Tax. Code)

The 50% limitation did not apply to the full-time employment hiring credit. (Sec. 23036.2(b), Rev. & Tax. Code)

Although many of California's credits correspond to credits allowed under federal law, California does not have credits comparable to IRC Sec. 38, the federal general business credit, or IRC Sec. 34, the federal credit for excise tax on gas and oil.

Credits may not be applied against the minimum tax and, with limited exceptions, may not be used to reduce regular tax below the tentative minimum tax (see ¶ 10-380 Rates of Tax). For federal purposes, IRC Sec. 26, which specifies limitations based on tax liability, provides that the total amount of certain specified credits may not exceed the amount by which the regular tax exceeds the tentative minimum tax. A separate California provision generally prohibits the use of credits to reduce the regular tax below the tentative minimum tax, but certain credits are excepted. The credits excepted (which are allowed only after the allowance of the minimum tax credit under Rev. & Tax. Code Sec. 23453) include:

— carryovers from the former solar energy credits (former Rev. & Tax. Code Sec. 23601, former Rev. & Tax. Code Sec. 23601.4, and former Rev. & Tax. Code Sec. 23601.5);

— the low-income housing credit (Rev. & Tax. Code Sec. 23610.5);

— the credit for research expenditures (Rev. & Tax. Code Sec. 23609);

— carryovers from the former credit for clinical testing expenses (former Rev. & Tax. Code Sec. 23609.5);

— the pre-2014 taxable year credits for sales and use taxes paid or incurred in connection with the purchase of qualified property used in an enterprise zone, the former Los Angeles Revitalization Zone, or a targeted tax area business (Rev. & Tax. Code Sec. 23612.2, former Rev. & Tax. Code Sec. 23612.6, and Rev. & Tax. Code Sec. 23633);

— the enterprise zone, former Los Angeles Revitalization Zone, and targeted tax area wage credits (generally inoperative for post-2013 tax years) (Rev. & Tax. Code Sec. 23622.7, former Rev. & Tax. Code Sec. 23623.5, Rev. & Tax. Code Sec. 23625, and Rev. & Tax. Code Sec. 23634);

— carryovers from the former program area sales and use tax and wage credits (former Rev. & Tax. Code Sec. 23612 and former Rev. & Tax. Code Sec. 23623);

— the former manufacturer's investment credit (Rev. & Tax. Code Sec. 23649);

— the natural heritage credit (Rev. & Tax. Code Sec. 23036.1);

— the motion picture production credit (Rev. & Tax. Code Sec. 23685);

— for taxable years beginning on or after January 1, 2014, the California Competes credit (Rev. & Tax. Code Sec. 23689);

— for taxable years beginning on or after January 1, 2016, the new motion picture production credit (Rev. & Tax. Code Sec. 23695);

— for taxable years beginning on or after January 1, 2014, the college access tax credit allowed under Rev. & Tax. Code Sec. 23686;

— for taxable years beginning on or after January 1, 2017, the college access tax credit allowed under Rev. & Tax. Code Sec. 23687; and

— for taxable years beginning on or after January 1, 2020, and before January 1, 2026, the new advanced strategic aircraft credit allowed under Rev. & Tax. Code Sec. 23636.

A credit that is partially or wholly denied as a result of this provision may be carried over to succeeding taxable years if the credit is one that may otherwise be carried over when the amount of the credit exceeds the tax. (Sec. 23036, Rev. & Tax. Code)

S corporations and limited liability companies (LLCs).—In the case of an S corporation, credits are generally computed at the S corporation level, and any limitation on the expenses qualifying for the credit or limitation upon the amount of the credit is applied to the S corporation as well as to each shareholder. The amount of credit claimed may also be limited for taxpayers that own a direct or indirect interest in an LLC that is disregarded as a business entity and treated as a sole proprietorship for income tax purposes (see ¶10-240 Limited Liability Companies (LLCs)). The amount of any credit attributable to the disregarded business entity (including credit carryovers) that may be applied against such a taxpayer's net tax is limited to the excess of the taxpayer's regular tax determined by including income attributable to the disregarded business entity less the taxpayer's regular tax determined by excluding the income attributable to the disregarded business entity. However, as discussed above, in some cases excess credit that may not be claimed against the net tax during the current taxable year may be carried forward to subsequent taxable years. (Sec. 23036, Rev. & Tax. Code)

• *Repealed and expired credits*

California has several credits that were repealed or have expired, but for which the audit or carryforward period has not expired.

Credits that become inoperative after 2001 and that are passed through (in the first year after the credit becomes inoperative) to a taxpayer who is a partner or shareholder of an eligible pass-through entity may be claimed in the year of pass-through. An eligible pass-through entity is any partnership or S corporation that files a fiscal year return and is entitled to a credit in the last year that the credit is operative. (Sec. 23036, Rev. & Tax. Code)

PERSONAL INCOME

[¶15-050]

FEDERAL/MULTISTATE ISSUES

[¶15-055] Comparison of Federal/State Key Features

The following is a comparison of key features of federal income tax laws that have been enacted as of March 27, 2020, and California personal income tax laws. California adjusted gross income is based on federal adjusted gross income. The California personal income tax combines unique state provisions with subchapters and individual provisions of the Internal Revenue Code (IRC) that are incorporated by reference as amended through a specified date (see ¶15-515) and modified for California purposes. State modifications to federal adjusted gross income required by law differences are discussed beginning at ¶16-005 for additions and ¶16-205 for subtractions. Special attention should be paid to adjustments required for same-sex married individuals and registered domestic partners who are required to use the joint or married filing separately filing status.

Nonresidents and part-year residents.—California taxes its residents on their entire income, regardless of its source (see ¶15-110), while nonresidents are taxed only on income derived from California (see ¶15-115). A part-year resident must include in California adjusted gross income all income from any source for the part of the tax year when he or she resided in the state and income received from California sources during the portion of the year he or she was a nonresident (see ¶15-120). A nonresident's or part-year resident's tax liability is determined by first computing tax on total taxable income, as though the taxpayer were a full-year California resident for the taxable year and for all prior taxable years for any carryover items, deferred income, suspended losses, or suspended deductions, and dividing that tax by the income that the tax was calculated upon, to arrive at the tax rate. This rate is then applied to the California source taxable income of the nonresident or part-year resident to determine the nonresident's or part-year resident's tax liability (see ¶15-115 and ¶15-120).

• *Alternative Minimum Tax (IRC Sec. 55 — IRC Sec. 59)*

California imposes an alternative minimum tax (AMT) that is a modified version of the federal AMT (IRC Sec. 55—IRC Sec. 59).

• *Asset Expense Election (IRC Sec. 179)*

California allows a limited asset expense election (IRC Sec. 179) for personal income tax purposes that is limited to $25,000, and reduced if the cost of all IRC Sec. 179 property placed in service during the taxable year is more than $200,000. California does not allow an expanded asset expense election for disaster assistance property, nor does it permit revocation of an election without approval. California also does not allow the expensing of off-the-shelf computer software or of air conditioning and heating units. In addition, California has not conformed to federal changes that repealed the limitation on the amount of Sec. 179 property that can be attributable to qualified real property and the corresponding provision on carryforwards of disallowed amounts attributable to qualified real property. Furthermore, California has not adopted the redefinition of "qualified real property" eligible for expensing to include improvements to the interior of any nonresidential real property; roofs, heating, ventilation, and air-conditioning property; fire protection and alarm systems; and security systems. Finally, California does not conform to the elimination of the exclusion for tangible personal property used in connection with lodging facilities and the post-2018 inflation adjustment of the $25,000 expensing limit on certain heavy vehicles (see ¶ 15-670 and ¶ 16-040).

- *Bad Debts (IRC Sec. 166)*

California's treatment of bad debts is the same as federal because IRC Sec. 166 is incorporated by reference (see ¶ 15-515).

- *Capital Gains and Capital Losses (IRC Secs. 1(h), 1202, 1211, 1212, and 1221)*

California generally determines capital gains and losses in the same manner as federal law (IRC Sec. 1(h), IRC Sec. 1211, IRC Sec. 1212, and IRC Sec. 1221). However, unlike federal law, (1) California law treats capital gains as ordinary income and the amount of tax is not dependent on the holding period, (2) California does not permit capital loss carrybacks, and (3) California law does not provide for any special tax rates for capital gains. California no longer allows the deferral or exclusion of gain from the sale of qualified small business stock. Also, California has not adopted federal provisions that (1) exclude certain self-created property (e.g., patents, inventions, models, designs, or secret formulas or process) from the definition of a "capital asset" for dispositions after 2017 (see ¶ 16-070).

- *Charitable Contributions (IRC Sec. 170)*

The California charitable contribution deduction is generally the same as the federal (IRC Sec. 170). However, California does not conform to federal provisions that provide an enhanced deduction for contributions of real property for conservation purposes and donations by businesses of food inventory, or disallow the deduction for contributions made to certain donor-advised funds (see ¶ 15-625, ¶ 16-025).

California offers a credit for donations of real property for conservation purposes and a credit for the costs of transporting donated agricultural products to nonprofit charitable organizations. However, California does not adopt amendments allowing individuals to claim a maximum 50% charitable deduction for contributions to certain agricultural research organizations applicable to contributions made on and after December 18, 2015. Also, California has not conformed to federal amendments (1) increasing the percentage limitation on the charitable deduction contribution base to 60% of an individual's adjusted gross income for cash donations to public charities in 2018 through 2025 (100% of contribution base in 2020 with a 5 year carryforward for qualified cash contributions that exceed the individual's contribution base); (2) repealing the deduction for amounts paid for college athletic seating rights; or (3) repealing the exception to the contemporaneous written acknowledgment requirement for contributions of $250 or more.

California also has not conformed to the federal above-the-line deduction of up to $300 that is allowed for tax years beginning in 2020 for an individual who does not itemize deductions for charitable contributions made to churches, nonprofit schools, nonprofit medical institutions, and other organizations in calculating adjusted gross income (AGI).

- *Child Care Credit (IRC Sec. 45F)*

California has no equivalent to the federal employer-provided child care credit (IRC Sec. 45F).

¶15-055

• *Civil Rights Deduction (IRC Sec. 62)*

California incorporates the federal civil rights deduction (IRC Sec. 62) (see ¶15-650).

• *Dependents (IRC Sec. 152)*

California conforms to the federal definition of "dependent" (IRC Sec. 152).

• *Depreciation (IRC Secs. 167, 168, and 1400N)*

California adopts federal depreciation provisions (IRC Sec. 167 and IRC Sec. 168) for personal income tax purposes (see ¶15-670). However, California does not adopt "bonus" depreciation allowed under IRC Sec. 168(k) or IRC Sec. 1400N. In addition, California does not incorporate the shortened recovery periods for qualified improvement property and motorsports entertainment complexes; the accelerated MACRS recovery periods for Indian reservation property; the special depreciation treatment for participations and residuals; the shortened recovery period for young racehorses placed in service after 2007 and before 2021; the requirement that certain major integrated oil companies amortize geological and geophysical expenditures over a five-year period instead of a 24-month period; or the 50% additional depreciation allowance for qualified cellulosic biomass ethanol plant property (see ¶16-040).

• *Earned Income Credit (IRC Sec. 32)*

For taxable years beginning on or after January 1, 2015, California provides an earned income tax credit in modified conformity with the federal earned income tax credit.

• *Educational Assistance Benefits and Deductions (IRC Secs. 62(a)(2)(D), 127, 221, 222, and 529)*

California law is generally the same as federal law concerning employee educational assistance benefits (IRC Sec. 127) and the above-the-line deduction for interest on student loans (IRC Sec. 221) (see ¶15-685). However, California does not allow the federal above-the-line deduction for qualified tuition and related expenses (IRC Sec. 222). Nor does California allow the above-the-line deduction for teacher's expenses (IRC Sec. 62(a)(2)(D)) (see ¶16-050). Although California adopts the federal treatment of qualified tuition programs (IRC Sec. 529), California does not conform to federal provisions modifying IRC Sec. 529 qualified tuition plans to allow the plans to distribute no more than $10,000 in tuition expenses incurred during the tax year for designated beneficiaries enrolled at a public, private, or religious elementary or secondary school. However, for tax years beginning after 2018, California conforms to the federal provision allowing rollover of a Sec. 529 account to an ABLE account without penalty.

California has not yet adopted federal provisions effective after December 31, 2018, allowing distributions from 529 plans to be excluded from gross income of the designated beneficiary if used to cover: 1) up to $10,000 of student loan payments, or 2) the costs associated with registered apprenticeship programs.

Because of its federal conformity date, California also has not yet conformed to federal amendments to IRC Sec. 127 allowing payments made before January 1, 2021, by an employer to either an employee or a lender to be applied toward an employee's student loans to be excluded from the employee's income.

• *Foreign Earned Income (IRC Secs. 911 and 912)*

The federal provision allowing an exemption for income earned by U.S. citizens living abroad (IRC Sec. 911), is not applicable in California; therefore, amounts excluded from federal adjusted gross income must be added back for California personal income tax purposes. Presumably, amounts excluded under IRC Sec. 912, providing an exemption for certain allowances paid to civilian employees of the U.S. working abroad, also have to be added back (see ¶16-060).

• *Health Insurance and Medical Expenses; Health Savings Accounts (HSAs) (IRC Secs. 105(b), 106(e), 139D, 162(l), 213(a), and 223)*

Generally, treated the same as federal because IRC Sec. 105(b), IRC Sec. 106(e), IRC Sec. 139D, and IRC Sec. 162(l) are incorporated by reference (see ¶15-755, ¶15-805). Self-employed individuals may also claim a deduction for health insurance costs paid for a registered domestic partner and the domestic partner's dependents.

California, like federal law (IRC Sec. 213(a)), allows taxpayers to claim an itemized deduction for unreimbursed medical expenses. However, unlike federal law, California has not increased the medical expense itemized deduction threshold from 7.5% to 10% for post-2012 tax years (temporarily reduced back to 7.5% for federal purposes for the 2017 through 2020 tax years) (see ¶15-755).

California does not recognize health savings accounts (HSAs). Consequently, an addition adjustment is required for contributions to and earnings on HSAs (see ¶16-100). However, California personal income taxpayers may subtract any nonqualified distributions from an HSA included in federal taxable income (see ¶16-307).

California has not yet issued guidance on whether it will follow federal law (1) eliminating the requirement that individuals obtain a prescription in order to be reimbursed for over-the-counter medicines and drugs under Archer medical savings accounts (MSAs), health flexible spending accounts (FSAs), and health reimbursement arrangements (HRAs) for amounts paid or incurred after December 31, 2019, and (2) allowing menstrual care products paid for or incurred after December 31, 2019, as eligible medical care expenses for purposes of Archer MSAs, health FSAs, and HRAs.

• *Indebtedness (IRC Secs. 108 and 163)*

Generally, California incorporates IRC Sec. 108 by reference, with some modifications, including modifications for the discharge of student loans when the borrower is unable to complete a program of study because the school closes or did something wrong (applies to discharges from 2015 to 2019) (see ¶15-685). California only partially conformed to federal provisions allowing an exclusion from gross income for income from the discharge of an individual's qualified principal residence indebtedness, and only allowed the exclusion through 2013 (see ¶15-680). In addition, California does not adopt the federal provision allowing taxpayers to defer the recognition of discharge of indebtedness income arising from a qualified reacquisition of business debt instruments issued by the taxpayer or a related person. For tax years after 2018, California conforms to the federal treatment of student loan cancellation that are discharged on account of death or total and permanent disability of the student (IRC Sec. 108(f)(5)). Unlike the federal provision, the exclusion from gross income is permitted indefinitely (see ¶15-680).

California's treatment of interest on indebtedness is the generally the same as federal because IRC Sec. 163 is incorporated by reference (see ¶15-720); however, certain modifications regarding OID instruments, mortgage interest, investment interest, and interest from loans made to enterprise zone businesses apply with the exception of certain OID instruments and investment interest (see ¶16-075 and ¶16-280). California has not adopted the repeal of the exception from the registration requirements for foreign targeted obligations under IRC Sec. 163(f). Also, California has not conformed to federal amendments that (1) limit the itemized deduction for home mortgage interest for tax years 2018 through 2025 to interest paid or accrued on acquisition debt during those years; (2) suspend the deduction of interest on home equity debt; and (3) reduce the maximum amount that may be treated as acquisition debt to $750,000 ($375,000 if married filing separately) for any acquisition debt incurred after December 15, 2017.

- *Interest on Federal Obligations (IRC Sec. 61)*

Generally, California does not tax interest received from obligations of the United States and its political subdivisions. (IRC Sec. 61). The interest from these bonds is subtracted from federal adjusted gross income in computing California adjusted gross income (see ¶16-280).

The California Franchise Tax Board has ruled that interest from certain specified federal agency obligations is not taxable, whereas the interest from other federal agency obligations is taxable (see ¶16-280).

- *Interest on State and Local Obligations (IRC Sec. 103)*

Interest on obligations of state and local governments, other than from obligations of California and its political subdivisions, must be added to federal adjusted gross income in determining California taxable income (see ¶16-075).

- *Losses Not Otherwise Compensated (IRC Sec. 165)*

The California deduction for business losses, casualty and disaster losses, and theft losses is generally the same as the federal deduction for such losses (IRC Sec. 165) (see ¶15-745). California, but not federal, law also allows 100% of any excess loss resulting from specified disasters to be carried forward to the next succeeding 15 years (see ¶16-300) (see ¶16-095).

California has not conformed to federal provisions clarifying that the limitation on losses from wagering transactions applies not only to the actual costs of wagers incurred by an individual, but to other expenses incurred by the individual in connection with the conduct of that individual's gambling activities, effective for tax years 2018 through 2025. Nor has California adopted the federal provision limiting (in tax years beginning after 2017 and before 2026) the itemized deduction for personal casualty losses to losses attributable to federally declared disasters or the federal provision providing temporary relief from the casualty loss rules is provided for net disaster losses occurring in 2016 and 2017 in a 2016 disaster area.

- *Net Operating Loss (IRC Secs. 172 and 1400N)*

California allows a deduction for net operating losses (NOLs) that is patterned on the federal net operating loss (IRC Sec. 172), except that (1) NOLs may be carried forward for 20 years (10 years if incurred between 2000 and 2007, or five years if incurred before 2000); (2) a two-year carryback is allowed for tax years 2013-2018; (3) California suspended NOL deductions for the 2008—2011 and 2020—2022 taxable years; (4) California does not follow the federal expanded NOL (IRC Sec. 1400N) for qualified hurricane and tornado disaster victims or federal disaster victims; and (5) only a specified percentage of pre-2004 NOLs could be carried over (an exception was provided for losses of businesses located in economic incentive areas and certain new businesses and small businesses)(6) the extended federal carryback for farm losses does not apply (although special NOL treatment is available for farming businesses whose crops were impacted by Pierce's disease); and (7) California does not conform to the limitation of NOL deductions to 80% of taxable income (see ¶16-310). Special rules apply to taxpayers residing in California for less than the entire tax year in which a net operating loss is incurred (see ¶15-120).

California also does not conform to the NOL modifications allowing a five-year carryback period and an unlimited carryforward period for NOLs arising in tax years beginning in 2018, 2019, and 2020.

- *Excess Business Loss Limitation (IRC Sec. 461(l))*

California generally conforms to the excess business loss limitation (IRC Sec. 461(l)). However, California decouples from the federal expiration of the limitation and NOL carry forward. The disallowed excess business loss is treated as a carryover that may be included in the following year's excess business loss computation rather than being treated as an NOL. California has not conformed to the federal suspension of the excess business loss limitation for tax years beginning in 2018, 2019, and 2020.

- *Pass-Through Deduction (IRC Sec. 199A)*

California has not adopted the federal pass-through deduction (IRC Sec. 199A). California uses federal adjusted gross income as its starting point. Since the federal pass-through deduction is a deduction from adjusted gross income to arrive at taxable income (i.e., a "below-the-line" deduction), no California adjustment is required.

- *Personal Residence (IRC Secs. 121, 132(n), 163, and 1033)*

California incorporates, with modifications, the federal provision regarding the gross income exclusion of income from the sale of a personal residence (IRC Sec. 121) and the federal provision regarding nonrecognition of gain when property is involuntarily converted (IRC Sec. 1033) (see ¶15-710, ¶16-070, and ¶16-270). California does not allow a deduction for mortgage insurance premiums (see ¶16-075).

Also, California has not conformed to federal amendments that (1) limit the itemized deduction for home mortgage interest for tax years 2018 through 2025 to interest paid or accrued on acquisition debt during those years; (2) suspend the deduction of interest on home equity debt; and (3) reduce the maximum amount that may be treated as acquisition debt to $750,000 ($375,000 if married filing separately) for any acquisition debt incurred after December 15, 2017.

- *Retirement Plans (IRC Secs. 401 — 424 and IRC Sec. 1400Q)*

California generally conforms to federal provisions, as amended to date, regarding retirement plans (IRC Sec. 401—IRC Sec. 424) (see ¶15-800). The favorable treatment provided by federal law to incentive and employee stock options applies for California purposes to California qualified stock options (see ¶16-345). Although California generally conforms to federal deferred compensation provisions as amended to date, because California does not recognize health savings accounts (HSAs) it does not conform to an amendment made to IRC Sec. 408 that authorizes a one-time tax-free distribution from an IRA to an HSA. Consequently, a California taxpayer who makes such a distribution is required to include the distribution in his or her gross income and is subject to California's penalty on premature withdrawals (see ¶16-135). California also has not conformed to a federal provision allowing certain employees who are granted stock options to elect to defer recognition of income for up to five years.

¶15-055

Also, because of its federal conformity date, California has not automatically conformed to federal law increasing the limit on loans from an employer-sponsored retirement plan for a qualified individual affected by the coronavirus (COVID-19).

• *Start-Up Expenses (IRC Sec. 195)*

California's treatment of start-up expenditures is the same as IRC Sec. 195, because IRC Sec. 195 is incorporated by reference (see ¶15-615).

• *Taxes Paid (IRC Sec. 164)*

Although California incorporates IRC Sec. 164 (see ¶15-820), California does not allow the federal deductions for state, local, and foreign income taxes; state disability insurance; foreign real property taxes (no federal deduction is available for 2018 to 2025 tax years); or sales and use taxes. These disallowed federal tax deductions must be subtracted from federal itemized deductions in computing California itemized deductions. In addition, California does not conform to the federal $10,000 limit ($5,000 for married taxpayer filing a separate return) on state and local tax deductions for the 2018 to 2025 tax years (see ¶16-145). California permits credits for net income taxes paid to other states, the District of Columbia, or U.S. possessions (but not to the United States or to foreign countries) on income that is also taxed by California. Such credits are available to residents, nonresidents, estates and trusts, partners, S corporation shareholders, limited liability company members, and estate and trust beneficiaries.

• *Unemployment Compensation (IRC Sec. 85)*

California does not tax unemployment compensation (see ¶16-370).

[¶15-100]

TAXPAYERS

[¶15-105] Taxation of Part-Year Residents and Nonresidents

Nonresidents are taxed only on income received from California sources. Part-year residents are taxed on all income received while a resident plus income received from California sources during the portion of the year the taxpayer was a nonresident. (Sec. 17041, Rev. & Tax. Code) Below is an overview of the taxation of nonresidents and part-year residents. Additional discussion concerning the taxation of nonresidents and part-year residents can be found at ¶15-115 and ¶15-120, respectively.

A nonresident's or part-year resident's tax liability is determined by first computing tax on total taxable income, as though the taxpayer were a full-year California resident for the taxable year and for all prior taxable years for any carryover items, deferred income, suspended losses, or suspended deductions, and dividing that tax by the income that the tax was calculated upon, to arrive at the tax rate. This rate is then applied to the California taxable income of the nonresident or part-year resident to determine the California tax due. (Sec. 17041(b), Rev. & Tax Code)

In determining the California taxable income of a nonresident or part-year resident, the calculation of any carryover items, deferred income, or suspended losses or deductions is made as if the nonresident or part-year resident, for the period of nonresidency, was a nonresident for all prior years. (Sec. 17041(i)(3), Rev. & Tax. Code)

Furthermore, for purposes of determining taxable income during any period of nonresidence, gross income includes only California source gross income (see ¶16-505).

A part-year resident or nonresident must report income on Form 540NR, California Nonresident or Part-Year Resident Income Tax Return.

• *Itemized or standard deductions*

Nonresidents and part-year residents can claim a portion of the standardized deduction or itemized deductions, determined by the ratio of California adjusted gross income to total adjusted gross income. (Sec. 17301, Rev. & Tax. Code; FTB Pub. 1100, Taxation of Nonresidents and Individuals Who Change Residency)

• *Net operating losses*

If a net operating loss is sustained during a taxable year in which the taxpayer is a nonresident or part-year California resident, then only a portion of the net operating loss may be claimed. The amount that may be claimed is the sum of:

— the portion of the net operating loss attributable to the part of the year in which the taxpayer is a resident; plus

— the portion of the net operating loss that, during the portion of the year when the taxpayer is not a resident, is attributable to California source income and deductions (see ¶16-560).

(Sec. 17041(i)(2), Rev. & Tax. Code)

• *Credits*

Tax credits are generally allowed to nonresident taxpayers in the same proportion as the ratio that California source taxable income bears to total taxable income. Credits that are conditional upon a transaction occurring wholly within California are granted in full without proration. (Sec. 17055, Rev. & Tax Code)

Other state tax credit.—Nonresidents are allowed a credit for net income taxes imposed by and paid to their states of residence if those states do not allow their residents a credit for net income taxes paid to California. Part-year residents follow the other state tax credit instructions for residents for the part of the year that they were California residents and for nonresidents for the part of the year that they were nonresidents.

Renter's credit.—Nonresidents may not claim the renter's credit, but part-year residents may claim a prorated renter's credit.

[¶15-110] Residents

California taxes its residents on their entire income, regardless of its source. (Sec. 17014, Rev. & Tax. Code)

California residents file on Form 540, 540A (pre-2013 tax years only), or 5402 EZ, California Resident Income Tax Returns.

• *"Resident" and "domicile" defined*

A "resident" is defined as:

— every individual who is in the state for other than a temporary or transitory purpose; and

— every individual who is domiciled in California who is outside the state for a temporary or transitory purpose.

(Sec. 17014, Rev. & Tax. Code)

Domicile is defined as the place where the taxpayer has his or her permanent home, and to which he or she intends to return whenever he or she is absent. (Reg. 17014(c), 18 CCR)

"Residency" is not the same as "domicile." (*Whittell v. Franchise Tax Board* (1964) 231 CA2d 278, 41 CRptr 673) One may be a resident although not domiciled in the state, and conversely, may be domiciled in the state without being a resident. (Reg. 17014(a), 18 CCR)

FTB Pub. 1031, Guidelines for Determining Resident Status, provides the following partial list of factors to be considered when determining whether a taxpayer is a California resident:

— the amount of time the taxpayer spends in California versus amount of time the taxpayer spends outside California;

— the location(s) of the taxpayer's spouse and children;

— the location of the taxpayer's principal residence;

— where the taxpayer was issued a driver's license;

— where the taxpayer's vehicles are registered;

— where the taxpayer maintains professional licenses;

— where the taxpayer is registered to vote;

— the locations of banks where the taxpayer maintains accounts;

— the origination point of the taxpayer's financial transactions;

— the locations of the taxpayer's doctors, dentists, accountants, and attorneys;

— the location of the taxpayer's social ties, such as place of worship, professional associations, or social and country clubs of which the taxpayer is a member;

— the locations of the taxpayer's real property and investments; and

— the permanence of the taxpayer's work assignments in California.

• *Temporary or transitory purpose*

Whether an individual is present in California for a "temporary or transitory purpose" so as to be taxable as a nonresident depends on the facts and circumstances of each case. (Reg. 17014(b), 18 CCR)

Where a taxpayer was president of a California corporation and maintained a home in the state with his minor son, he was not in California for a temporary or transitory purpose and was a California resident, despite his business interest in Vietnam. (*Yaron*, SBE, 76-SBE-119, December 15, 1976) In another case, a wife who was living with her husband in Mexico and who visited their California home occasionally did not become a California resident. The California home was maintained as a convenience for her two sons in the armed forces and was used merely as a mailing address. The California location of the wife's checking account and safe deposit box was not sufficient to establish residency. (*Lyon*, SBE, 50-SBE-009, May 17, 1950) But in *Appeal of Schermer*, the taxpayer became a California resident because he opened a bank account in the state, filed a credit application with a California store, and stated his residence as California on his federal tax returns. (*Schermer*, SBE, 61-SBE-065, November 6, 1961)

A stay in California to improve one's health or recover from an illness is not "temporary or transitory" if a relatively long or indefinite stay is anticipated. (Reg. 17014(b), 18 CCR) Where a taxpayer spent 90% of his time in California during a five-year period in order to improve his health, he was a California resident even though he had property and business interests in Illinois. (*Joslyn*, SBE, 58-SBE-026, September 15, 1958) A Massachusetts resident who came to California for a short period, but became ill and remained for eight years also became a California resident. (*Loyal*, SBE, 66-SBE-043, August 1, 1966)

Retiring from business and moving to California for other than a short and definite stay will make one a resident; however, if a person is passing through the state on the way to another state, or is in California for a short period to take a vacation, that person is in the state for a temporary purpose and is not a resident. An individual may be a seasonal visitor, tourist, or guest even though the individual owns or maintains an abode in California, or has a bank account here for the purpose of paying personal expenses, or joins local social clubs. (Reg. 17014(b), 18 CCR)

California domiciliaries remain taxable as residents until they leave the state for other than temporary or transitory purposes. (Sec. 17014, Rev. & Tax. Code) A California resident who left the state to lead a migratory existence, dividing his time among several states, remained a California resident. (*Tarola*, SBE, 65-SBE-001, January 5, 1965) Employment outside the state is regarded as temporary unless steps are taken to establish connections in a new state or country that are more significant than the old connections in California. Thus, for example, a California resident who had minimal connections with a foreign country while employed overseas, and who maintained a family, personal belongings, and bank accounts in California, remained a California resident. (*Simpson*, SBE, 75-SBE-060, August 19, 1975) Another taxpayer, a California motion picture director who was in Europe for three years on film-making contracts, also retained his California residency because of his California home and business connections. (*Juran*, SBE, 68-SBE-004, January 8, 1968) Although he was on an indeterminate job assignment in the Orient, another taxpayer remained a California resident because his contacts with California, including membership in a local labor union, a California driver's license, and a home and bank accounts in the state, were more substantial than his contacts with the Orient. (*Salton*, SBE, 77-SBE-114, August 16, 1977)

Some cases emphasize the taxpayer's intentions when the taxpayer left the state. In *Appeal of Rand*, SBE, 76-SBE-042, April 5, 1976, a California domiciliary who was employed in Libya under a contract that required a commitment of at least 18 months, but that had no definite termination date, was outside the state for other than a temporary purpose. Despite his business contacts with California, including bank accounts and rental property, he did not intend to return to California upon completion of the minimum employment commitment. In *Appeal of Hardman*, SBE, 75-SBE-052, August 19, 1975, a professional writer domiciled in California went to England to write a screenplay. His one-way ticket to England, use of professional services in the country, and enrollment of his daughter in an English school, indicated that he intended to remain in England indefinitely and he lost his California residency for income tax purposes.

PRACTICE NOTE: *Residency during COVID-19 pandemic.*—When determining filing requirements and residency status for 2020 California returns, individuals should weigh actions taken related to COVID-19 and Executive Order No. 33-20. Actions taken based on COVID-19 may support a determination of individuals being in or out of California for other than a temporary or transitory purpose. In addition to the non-exhaustive factors identified for determining residency in *Appeal of Stephen Bragg*, 2003-SBE-002 (May 28, 2003), the following non-exhaustive factors might be relevant:

- when the individual entered California;

- whether the individual remained in California after the COVID-19 period (and if so, how long);

- whether the individual remained in California throughout the COVID-19 period;

- whether the individual provided COVID-19-related services in California; and

- whether the individual cared for an at-risk family member or friend.

(COVID-19 Frequently Asked Questions for Tax Relief and Assistance, California Franchise Tax Board, October 2020)

• *Presumption of abandonment of domicile*

Any California domiciliary who is absent from the state for an uninterrupted period of at least 546 days under an employment-related contract and any spouse who accompanies such an individual will be considered to be outside the state for other than a temporary or transitory purpose, except as discussed below. Return visits to California totaling not more than 45 days during a taxable year will be disregarded for purposes of such a determination. The 546-day rule will not apply to any individual, including any accompanying spouse, who has income from stocks, bonds, notes, or other intangible personal property in excess of $200,000 in any taxable year in which the employment-related contract is in effect. In the case of married individuals, the test concerning intangible income must be applied separately to the income of each spouse. The 546-day rule also will not apply to an individual whose absence from California is for the purpose of avoiding personal income tax. (Sec. 17014, Rev. & Tax. Code)

• *Presumption of residence*

Anyone who spends more than nine months of the tax year in California is presumed to be a resident. The nine-month presumption may be overcome by satisfactory evidence that presence in the state is for a temporary or transitory purpose. (Sec. 17016, Rev. & Tax. Code) A taxpayer who spent more than nine months in California during the tax year, but lived in a hotel on a weekly basis and maintained a permanent home outside the state, overcame the presumption of residency, the SBE ruled. However, a taxpayer failed to overcome the presumption when he purchased a home in California and learned that the foreign employment he desired was no longer available. (*Woolley*, SBE, 51-SBE-005, July 19, 1951)

COMMENT: *Overcoming presumption of residency.*—If an individual is presumed to be a resident for any tax year, or if any question as to the individual's status exists, the individual should file a return to avoid the possibility of penalties, even though the individual believes that he or she was a nonresident and even if the individual has received no income from California. The return should be accompanied by a signed statement setting forth why the individual believes he or she was a nonresident and any other supporting evidence such as certificates and affidavits. If the Franchise Tax Board is not satisfied with the evidence and statement, the individual may submit additional evidence either in writing or at a hearing before the Franchise Tax Board. Generally, affidavits or testimony of friends, employers, or business associates that the taxpayer was in California to take a vacation, complete a particular transaction, or work for a limited time will overcome a presumption of residency. Affidavits stating that the individual votes in or files income tax returns as a resident of some other state or country, although relevant in determining domicile, are otherwise of little value in determining residency. (Reg. 17014(d), 18 CCR)

There is no presumption of nonresidence if the taxpayer spends less than nine months in California; a person may be a resident even though not in the state during any portion of the year. (Reg. 17016, 18 CCR; *Jones,* SBE, 72-SBE-033, October 24, 1972) The nine-month presumption does not apply to a California domiciliary's absence from the state.

• *Commercial pilots*

A commercial pilot who was transferred from Dallas to California to make flights to Vietnam became a California resident because his contacts with California were more substantial than his contacts with Texas. Although he continued to maintain a business in Texas, he built a home in California and spent a large portion of his time in that state. (*Leggett,* SBE, 84-SBE-021 January 31, 1984) A pilot who was domiciled in Florida became a California resident based on his ties with California, which included an apartment, a California driver's license and auto registration, and a wife living in the state. (*Berger,* SBE, 73-SBE-029, May 8, 1973)

• *Merchant seamen*

A merchant seaman domiciled in California remained a resident even though he spent part of his time at sea, because he retained his California property, auto registration, driver's license and voting privileges. (*Dayton,* SBE, 73-SBE-008, February 6, 1973) Another seaman who held a Hawaii driver's license and an Ohio bank account remained a California resident while away at sea because his family home was in California, and he voted and registered his car in the state. (*Duckworth,* SBE, 76-SBE-067, June 22, 1976) Another seaman lacked ties with California, such as a business that required his active participation, a home, or dependents, and thus lost his California residency status upon leaving the state. (*Vohs,* SBE, 73-SBE-055, September 17, 1973. Aff'd on reh'g, 75-SBE-045, June 3, 1975) In another case, although a seaman did not have a family or home in California, his storage of personal property in the state, local union membership, and California bank accounts were sufficient to show residency. (*Miller,* SBE, 75-SBE-067, September 17, 1975)

• *Athletes*

A baseball player who was domiciled in California but went to Pennsylvania during the baseball season remained a California resident because his absence was to fulfill a particular baseball contract, which was a temporary or transitory purpose. (*Brucker,* SBE, 61-SBE-045, July 18, 1961) A person who spent part of the year bartending in California and the remainder of the year as a baseball player in Pennsylvania also remained a California resident. He had closer connections with California than with Pennsylvania because he maintained a home, bank accounts, and business interests in California. (*Selma,* SBE, 77-SBE-124, September 28, 1977) In another case, a football player residing in California, did not lose his California residency even though he went to Canada to play football. His ties to California were established by his California driver's license, and the storage of his car and the maintenance of a bank account in the state. (*Berry*, SBE, 71-SBE-007, March 22, 1971)

• *Students and teachers*

A student who attended college in California for more than nine months every year rebutted the presumption that she was a resident since she paid nonresident tuition fees, remained in California only as long as was necessary for her education, and returned to the state of her domicile immediately on achieving this purpose. (FTB Legal Ruling 122, December 5, 1958) A California teacher who was absent from the state on a sabbatical leave from the school district remained a resident, since she was absent for a temporary or transitory purpose. (*Meacham*, SBE, 75-SBE-055, August 19, 1975) But a California professor who went to Pennsylvania as a visiting professor for the full academic year with the understanding that a permanent position would become available in Pennsylvania lost his California residency. (*Massy*, SBE, 72-SBE-012, April 27, 1972)

• *Estates, trusts, and beneficiaries*

Special residency provisions apply to estates, trusts, and their beneficiaries (see ¶ 15-205).

Appeals of deficiency assessments based on the residency issue are specially treated (see ¶ 89-236).

[¶ 15-115] Nonresidents

Nonresidents are taxed only on income received from California sources. (Sec. 17041, Rev. & Tax. Code) A "nonresident" means any individual other than a resident. (Sec. 17015, Rev. & Tax. Code)

Rules for determining the California source income of a nonresident are discussed under Income Attributable to State Sources (¶ 16-505) and the paragraphs that follow.

Nonresidents calculate their California income tax by multiplying their California source taxable income by an effective tax rate. The effective tax rate is the tax on their total taxable income as if they were California residents for the entire tax year and for all prior years for purposes of any carryover items, deferred income, or suspended losses or deductions, divided by their total taxable income. (Sec. 17041(b), Rev. & Tax. Code)

Nonresidents file on Form 540NR, California Nonresident or Part-Year Resident Income Tax Return.

For purposes of computing the taxable income of a nonresident, any carryover item, deferred income, or suspended loss or deduction is includable or allowable only to the extent the carryover item, deferred income, or suspended loss or deduction was derived from California sources, computed as if the taxpayer, for the portion of the year that the taxpayer was a nonresident, had been a nonresident for all prior years. (Sec. 17041(i)(3), Rev. & Tax. Code)

If a net operating loss (NOL) is sustained during a taxable year in which the taxpayer is a nonresident, then the amount of NOL that may be claimed is limited to the portion of the NOL that is attributable to California source income and deductions. (Sec. 17041(i)(2), Rev. & Tax. Code) For further details concerning NOLs, see Additions--Net Operating Losses at ¶ 16-105 and Subtractions--Net Operating Losses (see ¶ 16-310).

Nonresidents may either itemize deductions (see ¶15-545) or take the standard deduction (see ¶15-540). California itemized deductions are figured on Sch. CA (540NR), California Adjustments—Nonresident or Part-Year Resident.

Special rules apply to alimony deductions for nonresidents (see ¶15-610).

• *Credits*

Tax credits are generally allowed to nonresident taxpayers in the same proportion as the ratio that California source taxable income bears to total taxable income. Credits that are conditional upon a transaction occurring wholly within California are granted in full without proration. (Sec. 17055, Rev. & Tax Code)

Other state tax credit.—In some instances, nonresidents are entitled to a tax credit for double-taxed income.

Renter's credit.—Nonresidents may not claim the renter's credit.

• *Limitations on taxation of nonresidents*

California expressly conforms to federal statutes that limit or preempt California's ability to tax the California source income of the following nonresidents:

— a nonresident who performs regularly-assigned duties while engaged as a pilot, master, officer, or crewman on a vessel operating on the navigable waters of more than one state;

— a nonresident employee of an airline, if 50% or less of the pay received by the employee is earned in California;

— a nonresident employee of a railroad, if the employee performs services in two or more states;

— a nonresident employee of an interstate motor carrier, if the employee performs services in two or more states; and

— a nonresident member of the armed forces who is stationed in California.

(Sec. 17951, Rev. & Tax. Code)

• *Proof of nonresidency*

A regulation discusses how an individual may establish his or her status as a nonresident. If the individual is presumed to be a resident for any tax year, or if any question as to the individual's status exists, the individual should file a return to avoid the possibility of penalties, even though the individual believes that he or she was a nonresident and even if the individual has received no income from California. The return should be accompanied by a signed statement setting forth why the individual believes he or she was a nonresident and any other supporting evidence such as certificates and affidavits. If the Franchise Tax Board is not satisfied with the evidence and statement, the individual may submit additional evidence either in writing or at a hearing before the Franchise Tax Board. Generally, affidavits or testimony of friends, employers, or business associates that the taxpayer was in California to take a vacation, complete a particular transaction, or work for a limited time will overcome a presumption of residency. Affidavits stating that the individual votes in or files income tax returns as a resident of some other state or country, although relevant in determining domicile, are otherwise of little value in determining residency. (Reg. 17014(d), 18 CCR)

¶15-115

• *Nonresident aliens*

Some provisions of IRC Sec. 871 through IRC Sec. 879, concerning nonresident aliens, are comparable to California law on income of nonresidents. However, a California provision makes federal law relating to nonresident aliens inapplicable. (Sec. 17024.5(b)(11), Rev. & Tax. Code)

PRACTICAL ANALYSIS: *California adjustment.*—Federal law requires nonresident aliens to report only U.S. source income. California requires nonresident aliens to report adjusted gross income from all sources. Federal income must be adjusted on Sch. CA (540NR), California Adjustments—Nonresident or Part-Year Resident, to reflect worldwide income computed under California statutes. Losses from foreign sources are entered on line 21f, column B, and foreign source income is entered on line 21f, column C. (FTB Pub. 1001, Supplemental Guidelines to California Adjustments)

For taxable years beginning on or after January 1, 2021, and until January 1, 2026, a nonresident alien's gross income does not include any payment of tax, additions to tax, interest, or penalties by an entity filing a nonresident group return on the nonresident alien's behalf. (Sec. 17132.1, Rev. & Tax. Code)

[¶15-120] Part-Year Residents

Part-year residents are taxed on all income received while a resident plus income received from California sources during the portion of the year the taxpayer was a nonresident. (Sec. 17041, Rev. & Tax. Code) A "part-year resident" is an individual who is both a resident and a nonresident during a taxable year, see ¶15-110 and ¶15-115, respectively. (Sec. 17015.5, Rev. & Tax. Code)

Part-year residents file on Form 540NR, California Nonresident or Part-Year Resident Income Tax Return.

For purposes of computing the taxable income of a part-year resident, any carryover item, deferred income, or suspended loss or deduction is includable or allowable only to the extent the carryover item, deferred income, or suspended loss or deduction was derived from California sources, computed as if the taxpayer, for the portion of the year that the taxpayer was a nonresident, had been a nonresident for all prior years. (Sec. 17041(i)(3), Rev. & Tax. Code)

If a net operating loss (NOL) is sustained during a taxable year in which the taxpayer is a part-year California resident, then the amount of NOL that may be claimed is limited to the sum of:

— the portion of the net operating loss attributable to the part of the year in which the taxpayer is a resident; plus

— the portion of the net operating loss that, during the portion of the year when the taxpayer is not a resident, is attributable to California source income and deductions.

(Sec. 17041(i)(2), Rev. & Tax. Code) For further details concerning NOLs, see Additions--Net Operating Losses at ¶16-105 and Subtractions--Net Operating Losses (see ¶16-310).

Rules for determining the California source income of a part-year resident are discussed under Income Attributable to State Sources (¶16-505) and the paragraphs that follow.

Part-year residents may either itemize deductions (see ¶ 15-545) or take the standard deduction (see ¶ 15-540). California itemized deductions are figured on Sch. CA (540NR), California Adjustments—Nonresident or Part-Year Resident.

• *Credits*

Tax credits of part-year residents are generally allowable in the ratio of their California taxable income to total taxable income. (Sec. 17041, Rev. & Tax Code) Credits that are conditional upon a transaction occurring wholly within California are granted in full with no proration. In some instances, part-year residents are entitled to a tax credit for double-taxed income. Although nonresidents may not claim the renter's credit, part-year residents may claim a prorated renter's credit.

[¶15-150]

SPECIAL TAXPAYERS

[¶15-175] Military Personnel

California law incorporates federal law concerning:

— the determination of residency for military personnel and their spouses (see below);

— the treatment of military compensation, pensions, retirement pay, and benefits and income earned by spouses who change residency as a result of their spouse's military orders (see below);

— the tax exemption for military personnel who die while on activity duty (see below),

— the filing extensions available to military personnel serving in combat zones or outside the United States (see ¶ 89-102);

— the early distribution penalty waiver for distributions from Coverdell education savings accounts if the distribution is used for the beneficiary's attendance at a U.S. armed forces related academy (Sec. 23712(c)(3)(D), Rev. & Tax. Code) (see ¶ 15-685);

— the increased contribution limits for Coverdell education savings accounts for contributions paid with military death benefits or gratuities (see ¶ 15-685) (Sec. 23712(f), Rev. & Tax. Code);

— the exclusion of disability income attributable to injuries incurred as a direct result of a terrorist or military action (IRC Sec. 104) (Sec. 17131, Rev. & Tax. Code);

— the easing of eligibility requirements to qualify for the nonrecognition of gain on sale of a personal residence (see ¶ 15-710);

— eligibility of military reserve personnel to claim away-from-home traveling expenses (see ¶ 15-805);

— the inclusion of military income excluded under IRC Sec. 112 in a military servicemember's compensation for purposes of determining the contribution limits for the military servicemember's individual retirement account (IRA). (Sec. 17203, Rev. & Tax. Code) (FTB Publication 1032, *Tax Information for Military Personnel*); and

— the waiver of the premature withdrawal penalty for certain withdrawals from retirement accounts by qualified members of the National Guard or the Reserve who are called to active duty, applicable for federal purposes retroactively to September 11, 2001 (see ¶ 15-800).

> *CCH CAUTION: Military disability income exclusion.*—The FTB has found that numerous taxpayers have been erroneously filing amended returns to reduce taxable income based on calculations that used the taxpayer's disability rating from the Veterans Administration based on Treasury Regulation Section 1.122-1. This calculation appears to be erroneous because the excluded income had already been excluded from the taxpayer's Form 1099-R used to report taxable income. Tax preparers should ensure that the income has not already been excluded from gross income prior to filing an amended return. (*Public Service Bulletin 2012-12*, California Franchise Tax Board, April 20, 2012)

Collection activities and the accrual of interest on assessments are also suspended during a military service person's period of service.

In addition, California provides an exclusion for the $10,000 in death benefits paid by the state to the surviving spouse of, or a beneficiary designated by, any member of the California National Guard, military reserve, or naval militia who dies or is killed in the performance of duty (see below). (Sec. 17731, Rev. & Tax. Code)

Military personnel report their income on Form 540, California Resident Income Tax Return.

• *Servicemembers Civil Relief Act*

California law conforms to the federal Servicemembers Civil Relief Act (SCRA) (P.L. 108-189) for California personal income tax purposes. Among the provisions of this legislation are the following:

— the military compensation of a servicemember not domiciled in California may not be used to increase the tax liability imposed on other income earned by that servicemember or that servicemember's spouse;

— the running of the statute of limitations is suspended for the period of a servicemember's military service;

— the interest rate is limited to a maximum of 6% per year on any underpayment incurred before the servicemember enters military service;

— a servicemember not domiciled in California does not become a resident by reason of being present in the state solely in compliance with military orders;

— military compensation of a servicemember not domiciled in California is not income for services performed or from sources within the state; and

— Native American servicemembers whose legal residence or domicile is a federal Indian reservation are treated as living on the federal Indian reservation and the compensation for military service is deemed to be income derived wholly from federal Indian reservation sources. The term "Native American" for purposes of this legislation has the same meaning as the term "Indian" has for federal purposes.

(Sec. 17140.5, Rev. & Tax. Code)

• *Nonresident military personnel*

The federal Servicemembers Civil Relief Act (Sec. 574, Tit. 50, U.S.C.), provides that a member of the armed forces does not acquire a new residence or domicile in a state solely by reason of being there pursuant to military orders. Military pay received while in a state under military orders is not deemed to be income from services performed within the state and may not be included in gross income for purposes of determining the tax rate to be applied to nonmilitary California-source income. A non-California domiciliary may subtract his or her military income from federal adjusted gross income by entering the military pay on Schedule CA (540NR) Part II, line 7, column B. Write "MPA" on the dotted line to the left of column A. Do not include military pay in column E. (FTB Publication 1032, *Tax Information for Military Personnel*)

Military personnel assigned to California.—Military personnel assigned to California are not taxable by California on their military income, unless they have established a California domicile. However, just as any nonresident, they are subject to California tax on all other income derived from California sources. (FTB Publication 1032, *Tax Information for Military Personnel*)

Income used to calculate deductions and credits.—Military pay of personnel domiciled outside California may not be used to determine whether federal adjusted gross income limits have been reached for purposes of determining whether the full amount of specified California credits or deductions may be claimed. The deductions and credits that may be affected are listed in FTB Publication 1032, *Tax Information for Military Personnel.*

Credit for child and dependent care expenses.—For purposes of claiming the child and dependent care credit, earned income includes compensation, other than pensions or retirement pay, received by a member of the Armed Forces for active services as a member of the Armed Forces, whether or not the member is domiciled in California. However, income for services performed in California by a servicemember's spouse that is not subject to state tax under the Military Spouses Residency Relief Act of 2009 (MSRRA) (discussed below) is not considered earned income from California sources. California domiciliaries stationed outside California qualify for the credit if the care was provided for in California. Non-California domiciliaries on active duty in California also qualify for the credit. For taxable years beginning before 2004, the California credit was limited to taxpayers who maintained a household in California during the taxable year. (Sec. 17052.6, Rev. & Tax. Code) (FTB Publication 1032, *Tax Information for Military Personnel*)

Military spouses.—The Military Spouses Residency Relief Act of 2009 (P.L. 111-97) prohibits a servicemember's spouse from either losing or acquiring a residence or domicile for purposes of taxation because he or she is absent or present in any U.S. tax jurisdiction solely to be with the servicemember in compliance with the servicemember's military orders, if the residence or domicile is the same for the servicemember and the spouse. P.L. 111-97 also prohibits a spouse's income from being considered income earned in a tax jurisdiction if the spouse is not a resident or domiciliary of such jurisdiction when the spouse is in that jurisdiction solely to be with a servicemember serving under military orders. (FTB Publication 1032, *Tax Information for Military Personnel*)

The federal Veterans Benefits and Transition Act of 2018 (P.L. 115-407) amended the Servicemembers Civil Relief Act to allow spouses of a service member to elect to use the same residence as the service member for tax purposes on any taxable year of the marriage, regardless of the date on which the marriage occurred. The provision is effective for California tax returns filed beginning with the 2018 taxable year. To make the election, taxpayers must write "VBTA" in red ink at the top of their tax return, or follow their software's instructions.

EXAMPLE: Henry, a military service member, is a Florida resident. He married Elita in 2016. Elita grew up in Oklahoma and she is domiciled there. Henry has PCS orders at Camp Pendleton, California dated January 15, 2018. Elita is also living in California solely to be with Henry, who is serving in compliance with military orders. Elita has a job working at a local hardware store in nearby Oceanside. Prior to the passage of the Veterans Benefits and Transition Act of 2018, Elita could not elect to claim Henry's state of residence, Florida, because they did not share the same state of domicile. Now, she can elect to have the same residence outside of California as her military spouse, and she is considered a nonresident for tax purposes. And since she is in California solely to be with the service member, who is serving in compliance with military orders, her income from the local hardware store is not considered to be from sources within California. (*Tax News*, California Franchise Tax Board)

Military pay may not be characterized as community property if the military member is a nonresident who is domiciled outside California, unless the nonresident military personnel is domiciled in another community property state. (Sec. 17140.5, Rev. & Tax. Code)

Permanent change of status.—California domiciliaries are considered nonresidents when stationed outside of California on Permanent Change of Status (PCS) orders. (*Legal Ruling 300*, Franchise Tax Board April 23, 1965) However, nonresident domiciliaries stationed in California on PCS orders are not considered California residents. (FTB Publication 1032, *Tax Information for Military Personnel*)

COMMENT: Native Americans serving in the U.S. Military.—Native American servicemembers whose legal residence or domicile is a federal Indian reservation are treated as living on the federal Indian reservation and the compensation for military service is deemed to be exempt income derived wholly from federal Indian reservation sources. (FTB Pub. 674, *Frequently Asked Questions About the Income Taxation of Native American Indians*)

•*Military compensation, pensions, retirement pay, and benefits*

California incorporates federal law (IRC Sec. 112, IRC Sec. 122, and IRC Sec. 134), concerning military combat zone compensation, certain reductions of military retirement pay, and certain fringe benefits, as of California's current federal conformity date (see ¶15-515). (Sec. 17131, Rev. & Tax. Code) California has not conformed to the federal provision enacted by the Tax Cut and Jobs Act of 2017 (P.L. 115-97) that grants combat zone tax benefits to members of the Armed Forces serving in the Sinai Peninsula of Egypt. (*2017 Summary of Federal Income Tax Changes*, California Franchise Tax Board, May 16, 2018)

PRACTICE NOTE: The federal Combat-Injured Veterans Tax Fairness Act of 2016 (P.L. 114-292) gives veterans who retired from the Armed Forces for medical reasons additional time to claim a federal tax refund if they had taxes improperly withheld from their severance pay. Severance pay received for a combat-related injury may be excluded from gross income. While California does not conform to the federal legislation establishing the extended statute of limitations, claims for refund may still be filed under California law. If the regular California statute of limitations is still open, a claim for refund may be filed independent of the corresponding federal claim. However, if the California statute of limitations has expired, the California claim for refund should not be filed until the IRS has allowed the corresponding federal claim. Generally, the

FTB allows two years from the date of a federal change to file a claim for refund resulting from the federal change. (*Tax News*, California Franchise Tax Board)

• *California National Guard, State Military Reserve, or Naval Militia*

The entire amount of a $10,000 death benefit paid by the state to the surviving spouse of, or a beneficiary designated by, any member of the California National Guard, State Guard (formerly known as State Military Reserve), or Naval Militia, who dies or is killed after March 1, 2003, in the performance of duty is excluded from gross income. (Sec. 17132.4, Rev. & Tax. Code) The subtraction may be taken on Sch. CA (540), line 21(f), column B.

• *Exemption for military personnel who die on duty and terrorist victims*

California incorporates federal law (IRC Sec. 692), as of California's current federal conformity date (see ¶15-515), relating to the abatement of income taxes for members of the Armed Services who die while serving on active duty. However, California does not incorporate the $10,000 minimum federal death benefit (see ¶16-036). (Sec. 17731, Rev. & Tax. Code)

[¶15-185] Owners of Pass-Through Entities

California generally follows the federal treatment of pass-through entities and their owners. Consequently, with the exception of S corporations, pass-through entities are treated as reporting, but not taxable, entities for California income tax purposes. The income of the entity is passed through to the owners and each owner is taxed on his or her distributive share. The income retains the same character as it had at the entity level. (Sec. 17087.5, Rev. & Tax. Code; Sec. 17851, Rev. & Tax. Code; Sec. 18633.5, Rev. & Tax. Code)

Owners of pass-through entities report their personal income on Form 540, California Resident Income Tax Return. The additions and subtractions applied to individual taxpayer's income also apply to pass-through entity income (see ¶16-005 and ¶16-205, respectively)

Unlike federal law, California treats S corporations as a hybrid-type entity, imposing a reduced corporation tax rate at the entity level and also taxing the distributive share of the owners' income at the owners' level (see ¶10-215).

In addition, limited partnerships, limited liability partnerships, and limited liability companies (LLCs) are subject to an annual minimum tax of $800 (see ¶10-225 and ¶10-240, respectively). (Sec. 17935, Rev. & Tax. Code; Sec. 17936, Rev. & Tax. Code; Sec. 17941, Rev. & Tax. Code; Sec. 17948, Rev. & Tax. Code) This tax may not be claimed as a deduction by either the entity or the owners. (*FTB Notice 89-129*, March 22, 1989; Instructions, Form 565, Partnership Return of Income) LLCs are also subject to an LLC fee (see ¶10-240). The classification of an LLC as a corporation, partnership, or disregarded entity elected for federal tax purposes is the same for California tax purposes. (Sec. 23038(b), Rev. & Tax. Code)

S corporations incorporated in California or doing business in California are also subject to the $800 minimum tax. S corporations are exempt from the minimum tax during their first year of incorporation or qualification to do business in California. (Sec. 23153, Rev. & Tax. Code) (Instructions, Form 100S, California S Corporation Franchise or Income Tax Return)

Special withholding provisions apply to S corporations, partnerships, and LLCs (see ¶89-104).

¶15-185

• *Limitations on pass through of losses and deductions*

For purposes of determining the amount of the owner's distributive income subject to tax, owners of pass-through entities begin with the figures provided by the entity on California Schedule K-1(100S) for S corporations, Schedule K-1(565) for partnerships, or Schedule K-1(568) for LLCs. The owners transfer the amounts reported on the K-1 to the appropriate California form (e.g., Sch. CA (540), line 17, for income and losses, Sch. D, for depreciation adjustments, etc).

> **CCH POINTER:** *How to avoid erroneous contacts from the FTB.*—Pass-through entities who have income from both inside and outside California are reminded to attach copies of the California Schedule K-1s rather than attaching schedules to the federal Schedule K-1s. According to the FTB, he California Schedule K-1 form reflects the accurate California sourced income in a format that the FTB systems recognize. If the FTB systems do not recognize the attached schedule reporting the partner's, member's, or shareholder's income, or lack thereof, the FTB will send a letter communicating a filing requirement even when there is none. Pass-through entity owners should ensure that the entity attaches a California Schedule K-1 to their return to avoid these erroneous contacts. (*Tax News*, California Franchise Tax Board, March 1, 2011)

Partners must first determine if the items of income and losses are subject to any limitations. The three primary limitations relate to the owner's adjusted basis of the ownership interest, the at-risk rules, and passive activity loss limitations.

> **COMMENT:** *Other limitations.*—According to the Franchise Tax Board (FTB), other limitations may apply to specific deductions, such as the investment interest expense deduction. These limitations on specific deductions generally apply before the basis, at-risk, and passive loss limitations. (Instructions, Sch. K-1 (565), Partner's Share of Income, Deductions, Credits, etc.)

Adjusted basis.—An owner may not claim losses (including capital losses) in excess of the California adjusted basis of the owner's interest in the entity (see ¶16-020). Because of California's current federal conformity date (see ¶10-515), California does not conform to federal law (IRC Sec. 704(d)(3)) providing that charitable contributions and foreign taxes are taken into account in determining the basis limitation on partner losses. (*2017 Summary of Federal Income Tax Changes*, California Franchise Tax Board, May 16, 2018)

> **COMMENT:** *Partnership's and LLCs records are not controlling.*—The partnership/LLC is not responsible for keeping the information needed to compute the basis of the partner's or member's interest. Although the partnership/LLC does provide partners/members with an analysis of the changes to their capital accounts, that information is based on the partnership's/LLC's books and records and should not be used to compute the partner's/member's basis. (Instructions, California Sch. K-1 (565), Partner's Share of Income, Deductions, Credits, etc., and California Sch. K-1 (568), Member's Share of Income, Deductions, Credits, etc.)

At-risk limitation.—Owners may also not claim losses (including losses on asset dispositions) and other deductions (the IRC Sec. 179 or enterprise zone asset expense election) in excess of the amount the owner has at-risk. The at-risk limitation (see

¶15-745) is computed on federal Form 6198 using California amounts. (Instructions, California Sch. K-1(565), Partner's Share of Income, Deductions, Credits, etc., and Instructions, California Sch. K-1(100S), Shareholder's Share of Income, Deductions, Credits, etc.)

Passive activity loss limitation.—Finally, any losses or deductions remaining after the limitations discussed above are subject to the passive activity loss limitations (see ¶15-745). Even though the passive loss rules do not apply to grantor trusts, partnerships, or LLCs, they do apply to owners of these entities. (Instructions, California Sch. K-1(565), Partner's Share of Income, Deductions, Credits, etc.) Only amounts from a rental activity or a trade or business activity in which the owner does not materially participate are subject to the passive activity loss limitation. Limited partners are generally subject to the passive activity loss limitations unless they materially participate in a partnership activity.

Individuals, estates, and trusts complete form FTB 3801, Passive Activity Loss Limitations, to calculate the allowable passive losses, and form FTB 3801-CR, Passive Activity Credit Limitations, to calculate the allowable passive credits.

> *COMMENT: Carryover of prior year's limitations.*—Losses, deductions, credits, etc. from a prior year that were not deductible or usable because of the limitations described above may be carried forward for purposes of determining the taxpayer's net income, loss, etc. for the current taxable year. However, taxpayers should not combine the prior year amounts with any amounts shown on the K-1 for the current year to get a net figure to report on any supporting schedules, statements, or forms attached to the tax return. Instead, report the amounts on an attached schedule, statement, or form on a year-by-year basis. (Instructions, California Sch. K-1(565), Partner's Share of Income, Deductions, Credits, etc., and Sch. K-1(568), Member's Share of Income, Deductions, Credits, etc.)

• *Partners*

Although California generally follows the treatment of a partner's income as of California's current federal conformity date (see ¶15-515), the following outlines the differences between California and federal law. (Sec. 17851, Rev. & Tax. Code)

Unrealized receivables.—Stock in certain foreign corporations, the right to payment for stock in a domestic international sales corporation, and oil, gas, or geothermal property are considered "unrealized receivables" for federal purposes, but not for California purposes. (Sec. 17024.5(b)(2), Rev. & Tax. Code; Sec. 17855, Rev. & Tax. Code)

Partnership returns.—The federal partnership return provisions have not been incorporated into California law. Instead, California has adopted its own partnership return provisions (see ¶89-102).

Elections.—IRC Sec. 703(b), as incorporated, requires that elections affecting the computation of taxable income be made by the partnership. (Sec. 17851, Rev. & Tax. Code; Sec. 17024.5(e), Rev. & Tax. Code) In addition, for California purposes, when the partnership makes an election relating to the computation of depreciation, each partner must take into account that partner's distributive share of the amount computed under such an election. (Sec. 17858, Rev. & Tax. Code)

Discharge of indebtedness.—Although California conforms to an amendment made to IRC Sec. 108(e) by the American Jobs Creation Act of 2004 (P.L. 108-357), which provides that a debtor partnership that satisfies an indebtedness by a capital or profits interest in itself must recognize cancellation of indebtedness income from the transfer in an amount equal to the fair market value of the partnership interest transferred, different effective dates apply. The amendment is applicable for California purposes beginning with the 2005 taxable year and is effective for federal purposes for cancellations of indebtedness occurring after October 21, 2004. Any discharge of indebtedness income of a partnership must be included in the distributive share of taxpayers who were partners in the partnership immediately before the debt. (Sec. 17024.5, Rev. & Tax. Code; Sec. 17851, Rev. & Tax. Code)

• *S corporation shareholders*

An S corporation item must be treated on the shareholder's return in a manner that is consistent with the treatment of the item on the S corporate return unless:

— the S corporation has not filed a return or, if the S corporation has filed a return, the shareholder's treatment of the item on the shareholder's return is, or may be, inconsistent with the treatment of the item on the corporate return; and

— the shareholder files a statement with the FTB identifying the inconsistency.

(Sec. 18601(e)(2), Rev. & Tax. Code)

Distributions in excess of an S corporation's accumulated adjustments account (AAA) may be taxable to S corporation shareholders. Differences may exist between the AAA balance for California and federal income tax purposes because California did not recognize S corporations until 1987 and, until 2002, California allowed federal S corporations to remain C corporations for California purposes. Taxpayers that have distributions for pre-1987 earnings or earnings in any later year that the corporation was a federal S corporation and a California C corporation must be entered on Sch. CA (540 or 540NR), line 9, column C. (FTB Pub. 1001, Supplemental Guidelines to California Adjustments)

The FTB has issued a technical advise memorandum (TAM) that addresses how a shareholder's basis in an S corporation is calculated when some years are closed by the statute of limitations. The TAM concludes that in situations when an S corporation has both items of income and deduction for the closed years and the shareholder failed to report these items on the shareholder's personal income tax return for the closed years, the shareholder's basis is not increased for items of income but basis is decreased for items of deduction but not below zero. Because the shareholder has not reported the items of loss or deduction, the shareholder may carry over any items of loss or deduction in excess of basis to future years. In instances when an S corporation has both items of income and deduction for the closed years and the shareholder reports all of these items on the shareholder's personal income tax return, basis is increased for items of income and basis decreased for items of loss and deduction but not below zero. Because the shareholder has reported and received the benefit of claiming these items of loss or deduction, the shareholder may not carry over any items of loss or deduction in excess of basis to future years. (Technical Advice Memorandum 2003-305, FTB, June 4, 2005)

The FTB has also taken the position that IRC Sec. 1016, the duty of consistency and/or the tax benefit rule does not require a shareholder that reported items of loss and deduction in excess of the shareholder's basis in a closed year to increase the shareholder's income in an open year by the amount of the erroneous items of income and loss reported. In addition, a worthless loss deduction claimed in an open tax year generated from income items in an open tax year is not a double deduction even if a shareholder reported losses in excess of basis in a closed year. The worthless loss deduction is not a double deduction with respect to the previous loss deductions. The basis that permits the taxpayer to take a deduction was generated from the income items in the open year. It is not attributable to any basis that was previously used. (Technical Advice Memorandum 2003-305, FTB, June 4, 2005)

• *Nonresident and part-year resident shareholders, partners, and members*

Nonresident owners are taxed on the portion of their distributive shares of a pass-through entity's income or loss, as modified for California purposes, that is attributable to California sources (see ¶ 16-565). (Sec. 17951, Rev. & Tax. Code)

Other than certain nonresident withholding requirements (see ¶ 89-104), there is no provision requiring S corporations, partnerships, or limited liability companies (LLCs) to remit California income tax on behalf of their nonresidents owners. However, pass-through entities are allowed to file group (composite) returns and to make composite tax payments on behalf of electing nonresident shareholders. a composite return may be filed on behalf of a single nonresident individual. Prior to the 2009 taxable year, a minimum of two nonresident individuals had to be included in a composite return. (Sec. 18535, Rev. & Tax. Code) Nonresident owners must make an annual irrevocable election as to whether or not to be included in the group return. The election is also available to a single 100% nonresident S corporation shareholder. Prior to the 2009 taxable year, nonresident individuals with California taxable income in excess of $1 million who were subject to the mental health services tax (see ¶ 15-355) could not be included in the nonresident group return. FTB Pub. 1067, Guidelines for Filing a Group Form 540NR, provides detailed information concerning nonresident group returns.

PRACTICAL ANALYSIS: *Pros and Cons of Nonresident Group Returns:* Nonresident owners should carefully consider whether it makes sense to file a group return. The group return is much less cumbersome. However, because taxpayers are precluded from claiming the personal exemption credit and a net operating loss on the group return and are also limited to claiming only those credits generated by the pass-through entity, the tax is often higher on the group return than if the nonresident owner completes Form 540NR, California Nonresident or Part-Year Resident Income Tax Return.

Special sourcing rules apply to a part-year resident owner's distributive share of pass-through entity income (see ¶ 16-565).

The FTB may adjust the income of a nonresident owner included in a group return if the FTB has reason to believe that the income attributable to that shareholder does not properly reflect the shareholder's taxable income. (Sec. 18535(e), Rev. & Tax. Code)

• *Allocation and apportionment*

The pass-through entity is required to show on the California Schedule K-1, the items of income and expenses attributable to each partner that is reported on the federal Schedule K-1. California additions (see ¶ 16-005) and subtractions (see ¶ 16-205) are then made for purposes of determining the amount of the partner's income subject to California taxation.

All of an owners' distributive shares of the entity's income must be included in the owner's California taxable income if the owner is a resident. If the owner is a nonresident, all of the entity's income is considered California income if all of the entity's business is conducted within California. In addition, if the entity's trade or business is conducted inside and outside California, but the part within California is so separate that the income can be separately accounted for, then the separately accounted for California income is treated as California taxable income. All other business income from an entity that is conducted both inside and outside California is subject to allocation and apportionment, see ¶ 11-520. (Limited Liability Company Tax Booklet; Partnership Tax Booklet) Apportionment of investment partnerships is also discussed at ¶ 11-520.

Nonbusiness income attributable to real or tangible personal property located in California is sourced to California (see ¶ 16-550). The source of nonbusiness income attributable to intangible personal property is generally sourced to the owner's state or residence or commercial domicile (see ¶ 16-530) (Limited Liability Company Tax Booklet; Partnership Tax Booklet)

• *Credits*

Partners, members of LLCs treated as partnerships, and S corporation shareholders may claim a credit for taxes paid to another state by the pass-through entity. Special rules also apply to eligibility for and computation of other credits earned by a pass-through entity.

• *Deduction for qualified business income*

California does not conform to the federal 20% deduction for "qualified business income" from a pass-through entity (see IRC Sec. 199A). (*2017 Summary of Federal Income Tax Changes*, California Franchise Tax Board, May 16, 2018)

• *Regulated investment company shareholders*

California incorporates the provisions of IRC Sec. 852, concerning the taxation of shareholders of a regulated investment company (RIC) (commonly known as a mutual fund), as amended by the Regulated Investment Company Modernization Act of 2010 (Public Law 111-325), with the exception of provisions concerning exempt-interest dividends and undistributed capital gains. (Sec. 17088, Rev. & Tax. Code; Sec. 17321, Rev. & Tax. Code) Under IRC Sec. 852(b), as incorporated, a RIC that meets the strict requirements of the law generally is not taxed on income it distributes to its shareholders; such income is "passed through" to the shareholders and taxed at personal income tax rates.

Pass through of exempt income.—Both California and federal law have provisions that allow RICs to pass through to their shareholders income that is designated as tax-exempt. The California provision is similar to IRC Sec. 852(b)(5), which California does not incorporate. (Sec. 17145, Rev. & Tax. Code; Sec. 17088, Rev. & Tax. Code)

For California purposes, a management company may pay exempt-interest dividends if, as of the close of each quarter, at least 50% of the value of its assets consists of obligations that, when they are held by individuals, pay interest that is exempt from tax under California law. (Sec. 17145, Rev. & Tax. Code) State and federal tax-exempt obligations may be combined for purposes of meeting the 50% test.

The amount that may be designated by a RIC as an exempt-interest dividend is subject to a special limitation. (Sec. 17145, Rev. & Tax. Code) The limitation applies if the aggregate amount designated for a taxable year is greater than the excess of:

— the amount of interest received by the company during the taxable year on obligations that, if held by an individual, would pay tax-exempt interest under California or federal law, over

— amounts that, if the company were treated as an individual, would be considered expenses related to exempt income and thus would not be deductible under California or federal law.

If the limitation applies, the portion of the designated amount that will be allowed as an exempt-interest dividend is only the proportion that the above excess bears to the designated amount.

Capital gains dividends.—California does not incorporate IRC Sec. 852(b)(3)(D), which allows shareholders a credit for federal tax paid on undistributed capital gains and requires the inclusion in income of the retained gain. (Sec. 17088, Rev. & Tax. Code) Such dividends are not recognized for California purposes unless the shareholder has the option of receiving cash or additional shares. Taxpayers should not enter the amount of undistributed capital gains on California Sch. D (540).

If capital gain from a RIC is earned in one year and distributed in a later year, enter the dividends included in federal income for the year earned on Sch. CA (540 or 540NR), line 9, column B and enter the dividends for the year distributed on Sch. CA (540 or 504NR), line 9, column C. (FTB Pub. 1001, Supplemental Guidelines to California Adjustments)

[¶15-200]

ESTATES AND TRUSTS

[¶15-205] Estates and Trusts--Residency

California law contains provisions dealing with residence as a factor in the taxability of estates, trusts, and their beneficiaries. (Sec. 17742, Rev. & Tax. Code) These provisions have no federal counterparts.

• *Estates*

Residents.—The entire income of an estate is taxable to the estate if the decedent was a resident, regardless of the residence of the fiduciary or beneficiary and regardless of the source of the income. (Sec. 17742, Rev. & Tax. Code)

Nonresidents.—If the decedent was a nonresident (see ¶15-115) at the time of death, the estate is taxable only on California source income. (Reg. 17742, 18 CCR; Fiduciary Income Tax Booklet)

Beneficiaries.—Resident estate beneficiaries are taxable on all income, whether from resident or nonresident estates. Nonresident estate beneficiaries are taxable only on California source income (see ¶15-235).

• *Trusts*

Residents.—The entire income of a trust is taxable by California if either all the fiduciaries or all the beneficiaries are residents, regardless of the residence of the settlor. Contingent beneficiaries are not considered for purposes of determining taxability of a trust. The residence of a corporate fiduciary is the place where the corporation transacts the major portion of its administration of the trust. (Sec. 17742, Rev. & Tax. Code)

Nonresidents.—If the fiduciaries and noncontingent beneficiaries of a trust are all nonresidents, only California source income is taxable. A noncontingent beneficiary is one whose interest in the trust does not require that something happen (e.g., survivorship) before some right accrues or some act is performed. (Reg. 17742, 18 CCR; Fiduciary Income Tax Booklet)

Mixed resident and nonresident fiduciaries.—If there are two or more fiduciaries of a trust, some of whom are residents and some of whom are nonresidents, the taxable income is apportioned according to the number of fiduciaries who are residents. If a trust has both resident and nonresident fiduciaries, and nonresident beneficiaries, the trust is taxable on all net income from California sources, and on that portion of the net income from all other sources which reflects the proportion of resident fiduciaries to the total number of fiduciaries. (Sec. 17743, Rev. & Tax. Code; Reg. 17743, 18 CCR)

Mixed resident and nonresident beneficiaries.—Taxable income is apportioned when the taxability of a trust depends on the residence of the beneficiary and there are two or more beneficiaries, some of whom are residents and some of whom are not. If all of the fiduciaries are nonresidents, and if at least one noncontingent beneficiary is a resident and at least one noncontingent beneficiary is a nonresident, the trust is taxable on all income from California sources and on that portion of the net income from all other sources that eventually is to be distributed to the noncontingent resident beneficiaries. (Sec. 17744, Rev. & Tax. Code; Reg. 17744, 18 CCR)

Mixed resident and nonresident fiduciaries and beneficiaries.—The California law and regulations do not address the situation where a trust has resident and nonresident fiduciaries and resident and nonresident noncontingent beneficiaries. However, the Franchise Tax Board (FTB) has ruled that the above provisions for taxing trusts with mixtures of resident and nonresident fiduciaries or mixtures of resident and nonresident beneficiaries should be applied consecutively. (*FTB Legal Ruling 238*, October 27, 1959)

> **EXAMPLE:** *Calculation.*—A trust has $90,000 total taxable income that is not sourced to California. There are three trustees, one of whom is a California resident, and two noncontingent beneficiaries, one of whom is a California resident. Taxable income is first allocated to California by the ratio of California trustees to total trustees, multiplying $90,000 x 1/3 = $30,000. This amount is subtracted from total taxable income ($90,000 - $30,000 = $60,000), and the remainder is then allocated to California by the ratio of the number of California noncontingent beneficiaries to total noncontingent beneficiaries, multiplying $60,000 x 1/2 - $30,000. The sum of the fiduciary calculation ($30,000) and the noncontingent beneficiary calculation ($30,000) is the amount of non-California source income taxable by California ($60,000).

[¶15-215] Estates and Trusts--Computation of Income

Under IRC Sec. 641(b), as incorporated by California as of California's federal conformity date (see ¶15-515), the taxable income of an estate or trust is computed in the same manner as for an individual, except as provided by law, as discussed below. (Sec. 17731, Rev. & Tax. Code)

In the case of a trust that is otherwise exempt from tax under Rev. & Tax. Code Sec. 17631, the taxable income of the trust is its unrelated business taxable income. (Sec. 17651, Rev. & Tax. Code)

Charitable trusts are defined as corporations by California law. (Sec. 17009, Rev. & Tax. Code) The corporate provisions are discussed in the Corporation Franchise (Income) division of the Reporter (see ¶ 10-245).

• *Deductions*

California incorporates IRC Sec. 642, as amended as of California's federal conformity date (see ¶ 15-515), providing special rules for deductions and credits allowed to estates and trusts (Sec. 17731, Rev. & Tax. Code), with the modifications discussed below and at special credit rules.

Personal exemption.—California allows a personal exemption credit instead of the personal exemption deduction allowed under IRC Sec. 642(b).

Charitable contributions.—California conforms to the provisions of IRC Sec. 642(c), allowing certain trusts and estates an unlimited charitable contributions deduction for amounts that have been paid or permanently set aside during the tax year for charitable purposes under the terms of the instrument creating the trust or estate, except that California modifies the federal provision to:

— substitute December 31, 1970, for the October 9, 1969, federal date by which a complex trust must have been created in order to qualify for a deduction for amounts permanently set aside for charitable purposes; and

— require an adjustment if the amount allowable as a deduction under this provision consists of gain for which a small business stock exclusion is allowed under Rev. & Tax. Code Sec. 18152.5 (rather than the small business stock exclusion allowed under IRC Sec. 1202(a) for federal purposes).

(Sec. 17736, Rev. & Tax. Code)

Also, under IRC Sec. 681 as incorporated by California as of California's federal conformity date (see ¶ 15-515), a complex trust may not claim a charitable contribution deduction that is allocable to its unrelated business income. (Sec. 17731, Rev. & Tax. Code)

Simple trusts are not allowed a deduction for charitable contributions, because under IRC Sec. 651(a), as incorporated by California as of California's federal conformity date (see ¶ 15-515), a "simple trust" by definition cannot contain charitable contribution provisions. (Sec. 17731, Rev. & Tax. Code)

Net operating losses.—IRC Sec. 642(d), which allows a net operating loss deduction, is applicable for California purposes. (Sec. 17731, Rev. & Tax. Code) However, the net operating loss deduction allowed under California law differs from that allowed under federal law; see Additions—Net Operating Losses (see ¶ 16-105) and Subtractions—Net Operating Losses (see ¶ 16-310).

Depreciation and depletion.—Under IRC Sec. 642(e), as incorporated by California, estates and trusts are allowed deductions for depreciation (see ¶ 15-670) and depletion (see ¶ 15-665) only to the extent not allowable to beneficiaries under IRC Sec. 167(d) and IRC Sec. 611(b). (Sec. 17731, Rev. & Tax. Code) Under IRC Sec. 167(d) and IRC Sec. 611(b), as incorporated by California as of California's federal conformity date (see ¶ 15-515), in the case of property held in trust, the allowable depreciation deduction and/or depletion deduction must be apportioned between the income beneficiaries and the trustee pursuant to the provisions of the instrument creating the trust or, in the absence of such provisions, on the basis of the trust income allocable to each. Also, in the case of an estate, the allowable depreciation deduction and/or depletion deduction must be apportioned between the estate and the heirs, legatees, and devisees on the basis of the income of the estate allocable to each. (Sec. 17201, Rev. & Tax. Code; Sec. 17681, Rev. & Tax. Code)

Amortization.—Under IRC Sec. 642(f), as incorporated by California, estates and trusts are allowed the amortization deductions under IRC Sec. 169 for pollution control facilities (see ¶16-210) and IRC Sec. 197 for goodwill and certain other intangibles (see ¶16-210). (Sec. 17731, Rev. & Tax. Code) However, the allowable deduction must be apportioned between the income beneficiaries and the fiduciary under prescribed regulations.

Disallowance of double deductions.—IRC Sec. 642(g) disallows an income tax deduction for certain expenses, indebtedness, taxes, and losses of an estate of a decedent if such amounts may be claimed by the estate as deductions for federal estate tax purposes. A California provision (Sec. 17024.5(b), Rev. & Tax. Code) states that in applying an Internal Revenue Code provision for California income tax purposes, any provision relating to the federal estate tax generally is not applicable for California personal income tax purposes. However, the Franchise Tax Board (FTB) has indicated that despite the California provision, the correct interpretation in regard to IRC Sec. 642(g) is that the provision *does* apply for California personal income tax purposes. Thus, the FTB has stated that estate administration expenses may be deducted for California personal income tax purposes or California estate pickup tax purposes, but not both. (*Tax News*, FTB, May 1988)

Loss carryovers and excess deductions on termination.—Under IRC Sec. 642(h) as incorporated into California law, deductions in excess of gross income in the termination year of a trust or estate, as well as unused net operating loss carryovers and capital loss carryovers, may be carried over to the succeeding beneficiaries. However, the amount will differ for California and federal purposes because the state income tax is deductible on the federal income tax return for the estate, but not on the California return (see ¶16-145), and because the California provisions relating to net operating losses contain modifications to the federal provisions; see Additions—Net Operating Losses (see ¶16-105) and Subtractions—Net Operating Losses (see ¶16-310)

Simple trust deduction for income distributions.—California incorporates, without change, IRC Sec. 651 as amended as of California's federal conformity date (see ¶15-515), allowing simple trusts a deduction for income distributions, up to the amount of distributable net income. (Sec. 17731, Rev. & Tax. Code) As a result, the beneficiary, not the trust, is taxable on the income.

Deduction for estates and trusts accumulating income or distributing corpus.— IRC Sec. 661, allowing a deduction to estates and trusts that accumulate income or distribute corpus, and IRC Sec. 663, excluding certain items from eligibility for the deduction under IRC Sec. 661, are incorporated by reference into California law as amended as of California's federal conformity date (see ¶15-515). (Sec. 17731, Rev. & Tax. Code) However, a California provision states that for taxable years beginning before January 1, 2014, an estate cannot take a deduction under IRC Sec. 661(a) for income distributed during the year with respect to amounts attributable and taxable to nonresident beneficiaries unless the fiduciary has obtained a certificate stating that all California personal income taxes due, or to become due, from the decedent or estate have been paid or accrued. (Sec. 17735, Rev. & Tax. Code)

California law also specifically provides that the federal elections under IRC Sec. 663(b) (distributions in first 65 days of taxable year) and IRC Sec. 663(c) (separate shares treated as separate estates or trusts), or the failure to make those elections for federal purposes, are binding for California purposes, and no separate California elections will be allowed. (Sec. 17752, Rev. & Tax. Code)

• *Distributable net income*

California conforms to the federal definition of "distributable net income" in IRC Sec. 643, as amended as of California's federal conformity date (see ¶ 15-515) (Sec. 17731, Rev. & Tax. Code), except as follows:

— California modifies IRC Sec. 643(a) to provide that the exclusion for gain on the sale of small business stock (see ¶ 16-270) shall not be taken into account (Sec. 17750, Rev. & Tax. Code)

— California does not follow the federal rule requiring the addback of the personal exemption, because California provides a credit in lieu of a deduction. A California provision specifically makes the federal provisions relating to personal exemptions deductions inapplicable for California purposes. (Sec. 17024.5(b)(12), Rev. & Tax. Code)

• *Community income*

The estate of a deceased spouse is taxable on the income from his or her half of community property that is properly subject to administration in the hands of his or her estate under the California Probate Code. Income received by the estate, but derived from the surviving spouse's share of the community property, is taxable to the surviving spouse. (Reg. 17742, 18 CCR) Under the Probate Code, community property that is subject to administration is property not passing directly to the surviving spouse, or property passing directly to the surviving spouse but which the surviving spouse elects to have administered. (Secs. 13500—13506, Prob. Code)

• *Taxable year of trusts*

California incorporates by reference IRC Sec. 644 as amended as of California's federal conformity date (see ¶ 15-515), providing that the taxable year of any trust generally must be the calendar year. However, this rule does not apply to a trust that is exempt from taxation under IRC Sec. 501(a) or IRC Sec. 4947(a)(1). (Sec. 17731, Rev. & Tax. Code)

• *Change in accounting period*

An estate may change its annual accounting period one time without prior approval of the FTB. (Sec. 17556, Rev. & Tax. Code) This election is similar to that allowed under IRC Sec. 1398(j) (not incorporated into California law), permitting estates in bankruptcy and subject to tax under 11 U.S.C. 346(b)(2) to change accounting periods once without IRS approval.

• *Certain revocable trusts treated as part of estate*

Under IRC Sec. 645, as incorporated by California as of California's federal conformity date (see ¶ 15-515), a qualified revocable trust may elect to be treated as part of a decedent's estate for income tax purposes. (Sec. 17731, Rev. & Tax. Code) A federal election, or lack thereof, is binding for California purposes. (Sec. 17751, Rev. & Tax. Code)

• *Grantor trusts*

IRC Sec. 671—IRC Sec. 678 as amended as of California's federal conformity date (see ¶ 15-515), concerning grantors and others treated as substantial owners, are incorporated by reference into California law (Sec. 17731, Rev. & Tax. Code) without change, except for modifications making federal provisions relating to foreign trusts

¶15-215

inapplicable to California. (Sec. 17024.5(b)(6), Rev. & Tax. Code) Under IRC Sec. 671—IRC Sec. 678 as incorporated, the income of a grantor trust is taxed to the grantor if the grantor retains substantial elements of control over the trust.

IRC Sec. 679, which applies grantor trust rules to a U.S. person who transfers property to a foreign trust (other than an employee trust) that has a U.S. beneficiary, does not apply for California purposes because of a provision that specifically makes inapplicable to California all federal provisions relating to foreign trusts. (Sec. 17024.5(b)(6), Rev. & Tax. Code)

• *Trusts as exchange funds*

IRC Sec. 683 as amended as of California's federal conformity date (see ¶15-515), relating to the use of trusts as exchange funds, is incorporated into California law (Sec. 17731, Rev. & Tax. Code) without change. Under IRC Sec. 683, trusts may not be used as vehicles for transfer of appreciated stock without payment of the capital gains tax. Pooled income funds are excepted from the provisions.

• *Transfers to foreign trusts and estates*

California does not incorporate IRC Sec. 684, which provides special gain recognition rules for certain transfers to foreign trusts and estates. (Sec. 17760, Rev. & Tax. Code)

• *Pre-need funeral trusts*

IRC Sec. 685, under which a trustee may elect special tax treatment for qualified pre-need funeral trusts, is incorporated into California law as amended as of California's federal conformity date (see ¶15-515) Sec. 17731, Rev. & Tax. Code, with California modifications that:

— disallow a personal exemption credit under California law (rather than a personal exemption deduction under federal law);

— change internal cross-references to refer to California provisions; and

— specify that a federal election, or lack thereof, is binding for California purposes.

If the election is made, the trust is not treated as a grantor trust (see above) and the tax on the annual earnings of the trust is payable by the trustee, utilizing the tax rate schedule generally applicable to estates and trusts and treating each beneficiary's interest in the trust as a separate interest. (Sec. 17760.5, Rev. & Tax. Code)

• *Alaska Native Settlement Trusts*

California does not incorporate IRC Sec. 646, relating to the tax treatment of electing Alaska Native Settlement Trusts. (Sec. 17734.6, Rev. & Tax. Code)

• *Filing requirements*

Form 541, California Fiduciary Income Tax Return, is used to file a return for an estate or trust.

COMMENT: *When form not required.*—Form 541 need not be filed if there are no California fiduciaries, noncontingent beneficiaries, or California sourced income. (Instructions, Form 541, California Fiduciary Income Tax Return)

[¶15-220] Estates and Trusts--Exemptions

Under IRC Sec. 664(c) as incorporated by California as of California's federal conformity date (see ¶15-515), a charitable remainder annuity trust or unitrust is exempt from taxation, unless it has unrelated business income. (Sec. 17731, Rev. & Tax. Code)

California also provides personal exemption credits to estates and trusts.

[¶15-225] Estates and Trusts--Rates of Tax

The taxable income of estates and trusts is subject to tax at the tax rates imposed on single taxpayers (see ¶15-355). (Sec. 17041(e), Rev. & Tax. Code)

If certain types of deductions, exclusions, and credits are claimed, estates and trusts may also be subject to California's alternative minimum tax. (Instructions, Form 541, Fiduciary Income Tax Return)

For taxable years beginning on or after January 1, 2014, California law generally conforms to the federal tax treatment of charitable remainder trusts that have unrelated business taxable income, except that instead of the excise tax imposed on unrelated business taxable income under federal law, tax will be imposed on unrelated business taxable income for California purposes at the graduated rates (see ¶15-355) set forth in Rev. and Tax. Code Sec. 17651. This allows charitable remainder trusts that have unrelated business taxable income in any taxable year to retain their tax-exempt status on other trust income for that year. Previously, if a charitable remainder trust had unrelated business taxable income in any taxable year, then for California purposes it lost its tax-exempt status for that taxable year. (Sec. 17755, Rev. & Tax. Code)

[¶15-235] Estates and Trusts--Beneficiaries

Income from a trust or estate is taxable to a resident beneficiary when distributed or distributable to the beneficiary if, for any reason, the income taxes were not paid by the estate or trust when due. If the beneficiary is a nonresident, only income derived from sources within the state is taxable. (Sec. 17745(a), Rev. & Tax. Code)

When taxes have not been paid on trust income because a resident beneficiary's interest was contingent, the income is taxable to the beneficiary when distributed or distributable. The beneficiary is taxed as though the income were ratably received in the year of receipt and five previous years, or over the period of accumulation, whichever is shorter. (Sec. 17745(b), Rev. & Tax. Code)

• *"Beneficiaries" defined*

Under IRC Sec. 643(c), as incorporated by California as of California's federal conformity date (see ¶15-515), the term "beneficiaries" for purposes of the taxation of estates and trusts includes heirs, legatees, and devisees. (Sec. 17731, Rev. & Tax. Code)

• *Simple trust beneficiaries*

California incorporates IRC Sec. 652 as amended as of California's federal conformity date (see ¶15-515), under which beneficiaries of simple trusts that are required to distribute all income currently are taxable on their proportion of income, whether or not it is distributed. (Sec. 17731, Rev. & Tax. Code) The federal provision is modified for California purposes so that nonresident beneficiaries are taxed only on income derived from sources within the state. (Sec. 17734, Rev. & Tax. Code)

• *Complex trust and estate beneficiaries*

California also incorporates IRC Sec. 662 as amended as of California's federal conformity date (see ¶15-515), under which beneficiaries of complex trusts or estates must include in their taxable income the income that is required to be distributed to them, whether or not it is actually distributed during the taxable year, plus any other amounts that are properly paid or required to be distributed for that year. (Sec. 17731, Rev. & Tax. Code) The federal provision is modified for California purposes so that nonresident beneficiaries are taxed only on income derived from sources within the state. (Sec. 17734, Rev. & Tax. Code)

• *Charitable remainder trust beneficiaries*

California also incorporates the provisions of IRC Sec. 664 as amended as of California's federal conformity date (see ¶15-515), under which amounts paid by a charitable remainder annuity trust or charitable remainder unitrust have specified characteristics in the beneficiary's hands. (Sec. 17731, Rev. & Tax. Code)

• *Accumulation distributions*

IRC Sec. 665—IRC Sec. 668 as amended as of California's federal conformity date (see ¶15-515), which impose tax on beneficiaries for distributions of accumulated income of a trust that are in excess of the taxable income for the year in which distributed, are incorporated by reference into California law (Sec. 17731, Rev. & Tax. Code) with the modifications noted below. For California purposes, the federal provisions on foreign trusts and distributions to nonresident aliens and foreign corporations do not apply. (Sec. 17024.5(b), Rev. & Tax. Code)

PRACTICAL ANALYSIS: *California adjustment.*—If a trust has a California resident trustee or beneficiary, the beneficiary is noncontingent, and the trust has not filed a California return and paid California tax as the income was accumulated, then the full amount of the accumulation distribution is taxable to the beneficiary in the year the accumulation distribution is received. If the beneficiary received a federal Schedule J (1041), Accumulation Distribution for Certain Complex Trusts, but did not receive a California Schedule J (541), Trust Allocation of an Accumulation Distribution, an adjustment is required on Sch. CA (540), California Adjustments—Residents. (FTB Pub. 1001, Supplemental Guidelines to California Adjustments)

The provisions of IRC Sec. 665—IRC Sec. 668 do not apply to distributions made to beneficiaries under Rev. & Tax. Code Sec. 17745(b) and (d) (i.e., distributions where taxes have not been paid on trust income because a resident beneficiary's interest was contingent). (Sec. 17779, Rev. & Tax. Code) Under Rev. & Tax. Code Sec. 17745(b) and (d), the tax attributable to the inclusion of accumulated income in the gross income of a beneficiary for the year that the income is distributed or distributable will be the aggregate of the taxes that would have been attributable to that income had it been included in the gross income of that beneficiary ratably for the year of distribution and the five preceding taxable years, or for the period that the trust accumulated or acquired income for that contingent beneficiary, whichever period is shorter. (Sec. 17745(b) and (d), Rev. & Tax. Code)

PRACTICAL ANALYSIS: *California computation.*—If a trust has a California resident trustee or beneficiary, the beneficiary is contingent, and the trust has not filed a California return and paid California tax as the income was accumulated, then the beneficiary is entitled to the benefit of income averaging under the provisions of Rev. & Tax. Code Secs. 17745(b) and (d) and must use California form FTB 5870A, Tax on Accumulation Distribution of Trusts, to compute the part of the accumulation distribution that is includable in California adjusted gross income. (FTB Pub. 1001, Supplemental Guidelines to California Adjustments)

A resident beneficiary who leaves the state within 12 months before the date of distribution of accumulated income and who returns within 12 months after distribution is considered to be a resident throughout the distribution period. (Sec. 17745(e), Rev. & Tax. Code)

• *Alimony trusts*

IRC Sec. 682, relating to alimony trusts, is incorporated into California law as of California's federal conformity date (see ¶ 15-515). (Sec. 17731, Rev. & Tax. Code) Payments of trust income that constitute alimony or separate maintenance are taxed to the spouse receiving the payments.

Under both IRC Sec. 682 and California law (Sec. 17737, Rev. & Tax. Code), a spouse receiving alimony payments is considered the trust beneficiary for purposes of computing trust income. Child support is taxed to the grantor. These rules apply to an estate or trust that was created at the time of a divorce pursuant to a decree or to a trust that was created before the divorce and not in contemplation of the divorce.

[¶ 15-250]

FILING THRESHOLDS

[¶ 15-255] Residency and Filing Thresholds

The determination of residency is important for California personal income tax purposes because a taxpayer's residence, part-year residence, and/or nonresidence determines what portion of income is subject to California income tax. (Sec. 17041, Rev. & Tax. Code) See specific discussions for residents (see ¶ 15-110), nonresidents (see ¶ 15-115), and part-year residents (see ¶ 15-120)

• *Filing thresholds*

Taxpayers are required to file a personal income tax return if their gross income or adjusted gross income exceeds specified dollar amounts for their filing status, age, and number of dependents. Specific filing thresholds for residents and nonresidents, are discussed in the paragraphs that follow (see ¶ 15-260 and ¶ 15-265).

Resident individuals must file on Form 540, Form 5402 EZ, or, for pre 2013 tax years, Form 540A (California Resident Income Tax Returns). Nonresident individuals must file on Form 540NR (California Nonresident or Part-Year Resident Income Tax Return). Estates and trusts must file on Form 541 (California Fiduciary Income Tax Return).

[¶ 15-260] Filing Thresholds--Residents

Individuals must file personal income tax returns if their adjusted gross income (AGI) or their gross income exceeds specified levels that are adjusted annually, based on changes in the California Consumer Price Index. California AGI or gross income threshold levels requiring unmarried individuals or married couples to file returns are adjusted upward to reflect any dependency credit or credit for old age that may be claimed against California personal income tax. There are no AGI or gross income threshold amounts applicable to qualifying widows or widowers if they have no dependents. Individuals for whom a federal dependent exemption may be claimed must file a separate state income tax return if the individual's gross income from all sources exceeds the basic standard deduction amount allowed under IRC Sec. 63(c)(5). (Sec. 18501, Rev. & Tax. Code)

> **CCH PRACTICE TIP:** *Gain from sale of personal residence.*—California follows federal treatment that, for purposes of determining whether an individual is required to file a return, excludes the gain from the sale of a personal residence from the calculation of gross income. (*Senate Floor Analysis* of Ch. 164 (A.B. 816), Laws 2001)

Even if a taxpayer's income does not exceed the filing thresholds, a taxpayer should still file a return to get a refund if California state income tax was withheld from the taxpayer's pay or if the taxpayer made California estimated tax payments or had real estate withholding.

The filing thresholds for resident individuals are shown in the charts below.

•*Filing thresholds*

2020 Filing Thresholds

On 12/31/20, the taxpayer's filing status was:	and on 12/31/20, the taxpayer's age was[6]:	California Gross Income[1]			California Adjusted Gross Income[2]		
		Dependents			Dependents		
		0	1	2 or more	0	1	2 or more
Single or Head of household[3]	Under 65	18,496	31,263	40,838	14,797	27,564	37,139
	65 or older	24,696	34,271	41,931	20,997	30,572	38,232
Married/RDP filing jointly or filing separately[4]	Under 65 (both spouses/RDPs)	36,996	49,763	59,338	29,599	42,366	51,941
	65 or older (one spouse/RDP)	43,196	52,771	60,431	35,799	45,374	53,034
	65 or older (both spouses/RDPs)	49,396	58,971	66,631	41,999	51,574	59,234
Qualifying widow(er)[3]	Under 65	N/A	31,263	40,838	N/A	27,564	37,139
	65 or older	N/A	34,271	41,931	N/A	30,572	38,232
Dependent of another person Any filing status	Any age	More than your standard deduction[5]					

[1] **California gross income** is all income received from all sources in the form of money, goods, property, and services that are not exempt from tax. Gross income does not include any adjustments or deductions.

[2] **California adjusted gross income** is federal adjusted gross income from all sources reduced or increased by all California income adjustments.

[3] See ¶ 114.

[4] The income of both spouses or registered domestic partners (RDPs) must be combined; both spouses or RDPs may be required to file a return even if only one spouse or RDP had income over the amounts listed.

[5] Use the California Standard Deduction Worksheet for Dependents in the 2020 California Resident Booklet to compute the standard deduction.

[6] If the taxpayer's 65th birthday is on January 1, 2021, she or he is considered to be age 65 on December 31, 2020.

> **COMMENT:** *Tax liability threshold distinguished.*—Tax liability is incurred at lower income levels than the thresholds requiring taxpayers to file returns. (Sec. 18501, Rev. & Tax. Code) For the 2020 tax year, tax liability is incurred if the AGI of single or married, filing separate taxpayers is $15,235 or more, or if the AGI of joint filer, surviving spouse, or unmarried head of household taxpayers is $30,471 or more. (*Memorandum,* California Franchise Tax Board, September 1, 2020)

The FTB has taken the position that a taxpayer is still required to file a tax return and pay tax if he or she is liable for tax even if his or her income is below the filing threshold for his or her filing status. (*Technical Advice Memorandum 2008-1*, California Franchise Tax Board, November 20, 2008) The California State Board of Equalization upheld this position in a nonprecidential letter decision (*Appeal of Martinez*, No. 479960, February 23, 2010)

• *Related provisions*

Special rules apply to joint filers (see ¶ 15-310) and married taxpayers filing separate returns (see ¶ 15-315). Different filing requirements apply to estates and trusts and fiduciaries. Partnership return requirements are discussed under Owners of Pass-Through Entities (see ¶ 15-185). Federal return filing requirements are contained in IRC Sec. 6012.

[¶ 15-265] Filing Thresholds--Nonresidents and Part-Year Residents

The filing thresholds for nonresidents are the same as for residents (see ¶ 15-260).

Even if a taxpayer's income does not exceed the filing thresholds, a taxpayer should still file a return to get a refund if California state income tax was withheld from the taxpayer's pay or if the taxpayer made California estimated tax payments or has earned income and qualified for the child care credit. (Nonresident or Part-Year Resident Booklet)

Whether the income of married persons who are nonresidents must be reported by either spouse if separate returns are filed depends on whether, under the laws of the state of residence, the income belongs to the husband or wife. (Reg. 18501, 18 CCR)

[¶ 15-300]

FILING STATUS

[¶ 15-305] Filing Status

With the exception of same-sex married individuals, registered domestic partners, and the exceptions noted below, an individual is required to use the same filing status for California as that used on his or her federal income tax return. If no federal return is required, the taxpayer must choose the filing status that would have been chosen on a federal return. Filing status is reported on Form 540, California Resident Income Tax Return. (Sec. 18521, Rev. & Tax. Code)

In addition to the exceptions noted above, there are two exceptions to the rule requiring California taxpayers to use the same filing status as that used on the federal return. A couple who files a joint federal income tax return may file either separate returns or a single joint return in California if:

— either spouse was an active member of the military during the taxable year; or

— either spouse was a nonresident of California for the entire taxable year and had no income from a California source during the taxable year.

(Sec. 18521, Rev. & Tax. Code) Detailed rules apply to these exceptions to the federal filing status requirements (see ¶ 15-310).

Detailed rules are also provided for the following filing status categories:

— Married, filing joint return (see ¶ 15-310)

— Married, filing separately (see ¶ 15-315)

— Head of household(see ¶ 15-320)

— Qualifying Widow(er) with Dependent Child (¶ 15-325)

— Single (see ¶ 15-330)

In addition, the Franchise Tax Board may revise a taxpayer's filing status for a California personal income tax return if the taxpayer's federal filing status was incorrect. (Sec. 18521, Rev. & Tax. Code)

[¶ 15-310] Joint Filers

An individual must generally use the same filing status for California personal income tax purposes as that used on his or her federal personal income tax return. If no federal return is required, then the taxpayer must choose the filing status that would have been chosen on a federal return. The Franchise Tax Board may revise a taxpayer's filing status for a California personal income tax return if the taxpayer's federal filing status was incorrect. (Sec. 18521, Rev. & Tax. Code)

• *Registered domestic partners and same-sex married individuals*

Taxpayers who are registered as domestic partners by the close of the taxable year may file personal income tax returns jointly or separately by applying the same standards as are applied to married taxpayers under federal income tax law. (Sec. 18521, Rev. & Tax. Code) Special rules apply for purposes of determining limitations based on adjusted gross income.

Similarly, same-sex married individuals must file their tax returns and are required to recompute many of their deductions using a federal adjusted gross income recomputed on the basis of their filing status for their state tax return. Same-sex married individuals are treated as "spouses" for purposes of the California Revenue and Taxation Code. (FTB Notice 2008-5, June 20, 2008)

• *Different taxable years*

If spouses or registered domestic partners have different taxable years, they generally may not file a joint return. However, there is an exception to this rule if:

— their taxable years begin on the same day and end on different days as a result of the death of either or both;

— the surviving spouse or registered domestic partner does not remarry before the close of his or her taxable year; and

— neither spouse's or registered domestic partner's tax year is a "short period" under IRC Sec. 443(a).

(Sec. 18521, Rev. & Tax. Code)

• *Surviving spouse*

A joint return may be filed by a surviving spouse or beginning with the 2007 taxable year, a surviving registered domestic partner, provided that no return has been made by the decedent for the same year and no executor or administrator has been appointed or is appointed before the last day for filing the return of the surviving spouse. An administrator appointed after the joint return is filed may disaffirm the joint return by filing a separate return for the decedent within one year of the due date for the return of the surviving spouse or registered domestic partner. (Sec. 18521, Rev. & Tax. Code) IRC Sec. 6013(a) contains the same provisions. See the discussion of Qualifying Widow(er) with Dependent Child (¶ 15-325) for more information on the filing of returns by surviving spouses.

• *Marital status*

Marital status is determined at the close of the taxable year or at the time of one spouse's death. (Sec. 18532(a), Rev. & Tax. Code, and IRC Sec. 7703) If spouses have different taxable years because of the death of either spouse, their joint return will be treated as if the taxable years of both spouses ended on the date of closing of the surviving spouse's taxable year. (Sec. 18531.5, Rev. & Tax. Code)

An individual who is legally separated from his or her spouse under a decree of divorce, termination of registered domestic partnership, or of separate maintenance is not considered married or in a registered domestic partnership. (Sec. 18532(b), Rev. & Tax. Code)

• *Liability for tax*

If a joint return is made, the tax is computed on the aggregate income and the liability with respect to the tax is joint and several. (Sec. 18532(c), Rev. & Tax. Code) However, this liability may be revised by a court in a dissolution proceeding (in some instances) or by the FTB in the case of an innocent spouse (see ¶ 89-210). (Sec. 19006, Rev. & Tax. Code) The same is true for federal law under IRC Sec. 6013(c) and IRC Sec. 6013(d).

In a proceeding for a dissolution of marriage, a court may not revise the joint and several California personal income tax liabilities of spouses if their reported joint gross income exceeds $150,000, or if the liability of the relieved spouse exceeds $7,500. (Sec. 19006(b), Rev. & Tax. Code)

PRACTICE NOTE: *Revision of joint liability.*—Taxpayers entering into a written agreement during a divorce proceeding providing for one of the taxpayers to be responsible for payment of their joint tax liabilities often mistakenly believe that the FTB must automatically follow their agreement and revise their joint tax liabilities. This is not the case if the agreement is not in compliance with the specific statutory requirements set out in Sec. 19006(b) for court-ordered relief. Sec. 19006(b) provides that a joint liability may be revised by the court during a divorce proceeding provided that the court order does not relieve a spouse of a tax liability on income earned by or subject to the exclusive management and control of that spouse; separately states the income tax liabilities for the tax years for which the revision is being granted; and does not revise a tax liability that has been paid prior to the effective date of the order. If the gross income reported on the joint return exceeds $150,000 or the tax liability for which relief is sought exceeds $7,500, a tax revision clearance certificate must be obtained from the FTB and be filed with the court. (*Tax News*, Franchise Tax Board, October 2013)

• *Nonresidents and part-year residents*

If spouses or registered domestic partners file a joint federal income tax return and one of the spouses or partners was a California resident for the entire taxable year and the other spouse or partner was a nonresident for all or any portion of the year, a joint nonresident return (Form 540NR, California Nonresident or Part-year Resident Income Tax Return) is generally required to be filed. There are two exceptions to this rule. A couple or a registered domestic partnership who files a joint federal income tax return may file either separate returns (¶ 15-315) or a single joint return in California if:

— either spouse or partner was an active member of the military during the taxable year, or

— either spouse or partner was a nonresident of California for the entire taxable year and had no income from a California source during the taxable year.

(Sec. 18521, Rev. & Tax. Code) See Married, Filing Separately (see ¶ 15-315) for a discussion of married taxpayers filing separate returns.

• *Military personnel*

California incorporates by reference IRC Sec. 2(a)(3), which allows spouses of military personnel who are missing in action (within the meaning of IRC Sec. 6013(f)) from service in a combat zone or a qualified hazardous duty area to file a joint return for up to two years after the termination of combat activities or hazardous duties. (Sec. 17142.5, Rev. & Tax. Code) See Military Personnel (¶ 15-175) for a general discussion of provisions affecting service members.

• *Election to file joint return after separate returns are filed*

Spouses may elect to file a joint return after they have filed separate returns even though the time required for filing a return has expired. This option is available only if a joint federal return is also made available under IRC Sec. 6013(b). (Sec. 18522, Rev. & Tax. Code)

California law does not permit a joint return after separate returns are filed if:

— the four-year statute of limitations has expired;

— either spouse has filed a protest or appeal in response to a deficiency assessment;

— either spouse has initiated a suit for recovery of tax for the year in question; or

— either spouse has entered into a closing agreement with respect to the year.

(Sec. 18526, Rev. & Tax. Code) IRC Sec. 6013(b)(2) contains the same limitations, except that the federal statute of limitations is three years.

An election made by either spouse on his or her separate return for the year (other than the election to file a separate return) with respect to any income, deduction, or credit applies to the joint return when the election would have been irrevocable if the joint return had not been made. (Sec. 18523, Rev. & Tax. Code) If a joint return is filed after the death of a spouse, the decedent's return must be made by his or her executor or administrator. (Sec. 18524, Rev. & Tax. Code) IRC Sec. 6013(b)(1) contains the same provisions.

If the tax due on a joint return made after separate returns were filed exceeds the aggregate amount of tax paid by the spouses on their separate returns, and if any part of the excess is the result of negligence, 20% of the total amount of the excess must be paid in addition to the tax due. If any part of the excess is attributable to fraud, 75% of the amount of excess is added to the tax due. (Sec. 18530, Rev. & Tax. Code)

For purposes of assessment and collection limitations and provisions governing delinquent returns, a joint return made after separate returns were filed is deemed to have been filed on:

— the date that the last separate return was filed if both spouses previously filed separate returns;

— the date that the separate return was filed if one spouse filed a separate return and the other had $8,000 or less in adjusted gross income from all sources and $10,000 or less in gross income from all sources; or

— the date that the joint return was filed if only one spouse previously filed a separate return and the other had income over the limits stated above.

(Sec. 18528, Rev. & Tax. Code)

The period of limitations on the making of assessments and collection of taxes includes one year immediately after the date of the filing of the joint return, computed without regard to the provisions of Sec. 18528 explained above. (Sec. 18529, Rev. & Tax. Code) IRC Sec. 6013(b)(3) and (4) are generally the same.

For purposes of refunds and credits, a joint return filed after separate returns were filed is deemed to have been filed on the later of the last date for filing a return for the taxable year in question (determined without regard to any extension of time granted to either spouse) or the date the later timely filed separate return was filed. (Sec. 18527, Rev. & Tax. Code) IRC Sec. 6013(b)(3)(B) is generally the same.

The term "return" as used in provisions relating to fraudulent returns includes a separate return filed by a spouse for a taxable year for which a joint return is later filed. (Sec. 18531, Rev. & Tax. Code) IRC Sec. 6013(b)(5) contains the same provision.

A regulation discusses the filing of a joint return after filing separate returns. (Reg. 18522, 18 CCR)

[¶15-315] Married, Filing Separately

An individual is generally required to use the same filing status for California as that used on his or her federal income tax return. If no federal return is required, the taxpayer must choose the filing status that would have been chosen on a federal return. The Franchise Tax Board (FTB) may revise a taxpayer's filing status for a California personal income tax return, if the taxpayer's federal filing status was incorrect. (Sec. 18521, Rev. & Tax. Code)

> **PLANNING NOTE:** *Registered domestic partnerships and same-sex married individuals.*—Taxpayers who are registered as domestic partners by the close of the taxable year may file personal income tax returns jointly or separately by applying the same standards as are applied to married taxpayers under federal income tax law. (Sec. 18521, Rev. & Tax. Code) Special rules apply for purposes of determining limitations based on adjusted gross income (AGI). Same-sex married individuals are treated as "spouses" for purposes of the California Revenue and Taxation Code. (*FTB Notice 2008-5*, June 20, 2008)
>
> California's community property tax laws apply to registered domestic partners as well. Consequently, registered domestic partners who file separate income tax returns each must report one-half of the combined income earned by both domestic partners, as spouses do, rather than their respective individual incomes for the taxable year. (Uncodified Sec. 1, Ch. 802 (S.B. 1827), Laws 2006)

Married persons or domestic partners who file a joint federal income tax return may file either separate returns or a joint return in California if:

— either spouse or partner was an active member of the military during the taxable year; or

— either spouse or partner was a nonresident of California for the entire taxable year and had no income from a California source during the taxable year.

(Sec. 18521, Rev. & Tax. Code) For a discussion of joint returns, see Joint Filers (¶ 15-310).

• *Different taxable years*

For both federal and California purposes, a couple or partnership must file separate returns if the spouses or registered domestic partners have different taxable years, unless:

— the difference is caused by the death of one or both of the spouses or partners during the taxable year;

— the surviving spouse or partner does not remarry during the same taxable year; and

— neither spouse's or partner's tax year is a "short period" under IRC Sec. 443(a).

(Sec. 18521, Rev. & Tax. Code) The California provision is similar to IRC Sec. 6013.

• *Liability for tax*

When separate returns are filed, the spouse who controls the disposition of or who receives or spends community income, as well as the spouse who is taxable on the income, is liable for the payment of California personal income taxes imposed on that income. (Sec. 19006(a), Rev. & Tax. Code) The FTB may allocate income between spouses filing separate returns when necessary to reflect income properly. (Sec. 17555, Rev. & Tax. Code)

[¶ 15-320] Head of Household

With specified exceptions (see ¶ 15-305), an individual is required to use the same filing status for California as that used on his or her federal income tax return. If no federal return is required, the taxpayer must choose the filing status that would have been chosen on a federal return. The Franchise Tax Board (FTB) may revise a taxpayer's filing status for a California personal income tax return, if the taxpayer's federal filing status was incorrect. (Sec. 18521, Rev. & Tax. Code)

CCH PRACTICE TIP: *Electronic filers.*—Taxpayers who file electronically should file Form 4803e with their electronic return. By filing Form 4803e, (an electronic version of the HOH Audit Letter) with their electronic return, most electronic filers who provide complete and accurate information can avoid later receiving a paper copy of the HOH Audit Letter in the mail asking them to provide information about their qualifications for head of household filing status. (*Tax News*, California Franchise Tax Board, March 1, 2011)

Head-of-household filing status is granted to unmarried taxpayers maintaining a household for qualifying persons, and to married persons who are living apart from their spouse and who are maintaining a household for their child. The tax rates are higher than those for married filing joint and lower than those for single persons. California incorporates by reference IRC Sec. 2(b) and IRC Sec. 2(c) as amended through California's current federal conformity date (see ¶ 15-515) to define "head-of-household." (Sec. 17042, Rev. & Tax. Code)

COMPLIANCE ALERT: For taxable years beginning on or after January 1, 2015, California requires taxpayers who use the head of household filing status to file Form FTB 3532, *Head of Household Filing Status Schedule*, to report how the filing status was determined. (Instructions, Form FTB 3532, Head of Household Filing Status Schedule)

PRACTICE TIP: Guidelines.—The legal requirements for head of household filing status under state and federal tax laws are more complicated than simply being the head of the house. Individuals who use the head of household filing status, but who are not qualified to do so, may be subject to additional tax, interest, and penalties. The FTB has issued a publication that provides general rules and self-tests for determining eligibility for the head of household filing status. (*FTB Pub. 1540, Tax Information for Head of Household Filing Status- Tax Year 2010*) In addition, the FTB provides a self-test on its website for determining eligibility for the filing status. (*Tax News*, California Franchise Tax Board, February 2012)

• *Missing child*

Under federal law as incorporated by California, a taxpayer's child who is presumed by law authorities to have been kidnapped by a nonrelative and who qualified as the taxpayer's dependent for the portion of the year prior to the kidnapping will be treated as the taxpayer's dependent for purposes of determining eligibility for head of household status under IRC Sec. 2. (Sec. 17042, Rev. & Tax. Code) A taxpayer who met the principal place of abode requirement of IRC Sec. 2 for head of household filing status with respect to his or her dependent child immediately before the kidnapping of the child will continue to meet that requirement during the period that the child is kidnapped. This special treatment ends with the first tax year of the taxpayer that begins after the year in which the kidnapped child is determined to be deceased or in which the child would have reached age 18, whichever occurs earlier.

Because of California's current federal conformity date, California does not conform to the federal penalty for failure to be diligent in determining eligibility for the head of household filing status, which is authorized by IRC Sec. 6695(g), as amended by the Tax Cuts and Jobs Act of 2017 (P.L. 115-97). (*2017 Summary of Federal Income Tax Changes*, California Franchise Tax Board, May 16, 2018)

• *Married child or descendant*

Generally, a taxpayer's married child or descendant will qualify the taxpayer as head of household only if the taxpayer may claim that person as a dependent for the tax year. (Sec. 17042, Rev. & Tax. Code) However, head-of-household status is permitted even if the taxpayer is not eligible to claim the married child as a dependent, provided the ineligibility results because:

— the taxpayer was the custodial parent in a divorce agreement and signed a waiver of the right to claim the child as a dependent; or

— the provisions of a pre-1985 divorce or separation agreement provide that the custodial parent will not claim the child as a dependent.

• *Tax return preparer penalties*

Because of California's current federal conformity date (see ¶ 15-515), California does not conform to the federal tax return preparer penalty for failure to be diligent in determining eligibility for the head of household filing status, which is authorized by IRC Sec. 6695(g), as amended by the Tax Cuts and Jobs Act of 2017 (P.L. 115-97). (*2017 Summary of Federal Income Tax Changes*, California Franchise Tax Board, May 16, 2018)

[¶ 15-325] Qualifying Widow(er) with Dependent Child

A joint return (see ¶ 15-310), under California and federal law, may be filed by a qualifying widow or widower (a "surviving spouse") with a dependent child. With specified exceptions (see ¶ 15-305), an individual is generally required to use the same filing status for California purposes as that used on his or her federal income tax return. If no federal return is required, the taxpayer must choose the filing status that would have been chosen on a federal return. The California Franchise Tax Board (FTB) may revise a taxpayer's filing status for a California personal income tax return, if the taxpayer's federal filing status was incorrect. (Sec. 18521, Rev. & Tax. Code)

California incorporates by reference IRC Sec. 2(a) as amended through a California's federal conformity date (see ¶ 15-515) to provide that a qualifying widow or widower with a dependent child may obtain joint return rates for two years following the year of the spouse's death. (Sec. 17046, Rev. & Tax. Code)

In order to qualify for surviving spouse status for both federal and California purposes, the taxpayer must not remarry within the taxable year, must maintain a home as the principal residence for one or more dependent children, and must furnish more than half the cost of maintaining the household. (Sec. 17046, Rev. & Tax. Code)

Under IRC Sec. 2(a)(3) as incorporated by California, a spouse of a person who is missing in action from military service in a combat zone or a qualified hazardous duty area may qualify to file as a surviving spouse for up to two years after termination of the combat activities or hazardous duties. (Sec. 17142.5, Rev. & Tax. Code) See Military Personnel (¶ 15-175) for a general discussion of provisions affecting service members.

• *Missing child*

Under federal law as incorporated by California, a taxpayer's child who is presumed by law authorities to have been kidnapped by a nonrelative and who qualified as the taxpayer's dependent for the portion of the year prior to the kidnapping will be treated as the taxpayer's dependent for purposes of determining eligibility for surviving spouse status under IRC Sec. 2. (Sec. 17046, Rev. & Tax. Code) A taxpayer who met the principal place of abode requirement of IRC Sec. 2 for surviving spouse status with respect to his or her dependent child immediately before the kidnapping of the child will continue to meet that requirement during the period that the child is kidnapped. This special treatment ends with the first tax year of the taxpayer that begins after the year in which the kidnapped child is determined to be deceased or in which the child would have reached age 18, whichever occurs earlier.

[¶15-330] Single

With specified exceptions (see ¶15-305), an individual is required to use the same filing status for California as that used on his or her federal income tax return. If no federal return is required, the taxpayer must choose the filing status that would have been chosen on a federal return. The Franchise Tax Board may revise a taxpayer's filing status for a California personal income tax return, if the taxpayer's federal filing status was incorrect. (Sec. 18521, Rev. & Tax. Code)

The requirements for the "single" filing status are the same for California as for federal purposes. (compare Rev. & Tax. Code Sec. 18501 and IRC Sec. 6012). In order to file as single, the taxpayer must be unmarried or separated under a legal decree of divorce or separate maintenance. The marital status of an individual is determined as of the last day of the tax year.

[¶15-350]

RATES

[¶15-355] Rates of Tax

The tax imposed on California residents and nonresidents whose income is derived from California sources is in six brackets, ranging from 1.0% to 12.3% (1% to 9.3% for post-2030 tax years). (Sec. 17041(a)(1), Rev. & Tax. Code; Sec. 36(f), Title XIII, Calif. Const.)

Separate rate schedules apply to taxpayers who are:

— single (see ¶15-330) or married filing separately;

— heads of households; and

— married filing jointly (see ¶15-310) or surviving spouses (see ¶15-325).

The California Franchise Tax Board (FTB) recomputes tax brackets annually to reflect changes in the California Consumer Price Index (see discussion below). (Sec. 17041, Rev. & Tax. Code)

Generally, taxpayers must use either the California tax tables or tax schedules to compute the amount of California personal income tax due.

Special tax rate provisions apply to the unearned income of minor children.

Estates and trusts are taxed at the tax rate imposed on single taxpayers, with certain electing small business trusts taxed at the highest rate applicable to individuals (see ¶15-225).

• *Additional tax on millionaires*

An additional 1% personal income tax is imposed on the portion of a taxpayer's income in excess of $1 million. Revenues raised from the additional tax will be used to support the provision of local government mental health services. Personal income tax credits may not be applied against this additional tax. (Sec. 17043, Rev. & Tax. Code)

• *Limited partnerships, limited liability partnerships, and limited liability companies*

Limited partnerships, limited liability partnerships (see ¶10-225), and limited liability companies (LLCs) that are not taxable as a corporation (see ¶10-240) are required to pay a minimum franchise tax of $800 for the privilege of doing business in the state. (Sec. 17935, Rev. & Tax. Code; Sec. 17941, Rev. & Tax. Code; Sec. 17948, Rev. & Tax. Code) LLCs are also required to pay annual fees (see ¶10-240). (Sec. 17942, Rev. & Tax. Code)

• *Tax on accumulation distributions of trusts*

California incorporates the federal tax on accumulation distributions of trusts, with modifications to account for residency issues (see ¶15-235 for details). (Sec. 17731, Rev. & Tax. Code; Sec. 17745, Rev. & Tax. Code)

The tax on accumulation distributions is calculated on FTB Form 5870A, Tax on Accumulation Distribution of Trusts.

• *Tax on lump sum distributions*

California incorporates the federal tax on lump sum distributions (IRC Sec. 402(e)(4)(d)), but applies the California tax rate and brackets in lieu of the federal rates. Taxpayers must elect the same special lump-sum distribution averaging method that is elected for federal purposes. In addition, California modifies the federal transitional rules applicable to lump-sum distributions made after 1986 that are partly attributable to pre-1974 participation in a qualified plan. Qualified taxpayers may choose to have the distributions taxed at a special capital gains tax rate or taxed as ordinary income. California applies a 5.5% tax rate rather than the federal rate of 20% to the portion of a lump-sum distribution to which capital gains treatment continues to apply. Taxpayers make the election on Part II of Schedule G-1, Tax on Lump Sum Distributions. Finally, the amount subject to the tax on lump sum distributions may be different because of differing basis amounts stemming from different deductions available for contributions. (Sec. 17504, Rev. & Tax. Code) See FTB Pub. 1005, Pension and Annuity Guidelines, for more information.

The tax on lump sump distributions is calculated on Schedule G-1, Tax on Lump Sum Distributions.

• *Publicly traded partnerships*

Certain grandfathered publicly traded partnerships that elect to continue to be treated as partnerships rather than corporations must pay a special tax on gross income from the active conduct of any trades or businesses (see the discussion of Electing Large Partnerships at ¶10-245).

• *Consumer Price Index*

Tax brackets are fully indexed to the percentage change in the California Consumer Price Index (CCPI) from June of each year to the following June. The Department of Industrial Relations is required to transmit the annual CCPI change to the FTB by August 1 of each year. The FTB then computes an inflation adjustment factor by adding 100% to the CCPI percentage change, and dividing the result by 100. The inflation adjustment factor is then applied to each prior year tax bracket, and the result is rounded off to the nearest dollar. (Sec. 17041, Rev. & Tax. Code)

[¶15-360] Unearned Income of Minors

California incorporates IRC Sec. 1(g), as of California's current federal conformity date (see ¶15-515), which applies tax to certain unearned income of a minor child at the highest marginal tax rate of the child's parents, provided that the child is:

— under age 18 at the end of the taxable year;

— 18 years old and does not provide half of his or her own support costs with earned income; or

— 19 to 23 years-old and is a full-time students who does not provide half of his or her own support costs with earned income.

In addition, either parent of the child must be living at the close of the taxable year and the parents must not have taken a special election (discussed below) to include the child's income on the parent's return.

(Sec. 17041(g), Rev. & Tax. Code) This tax is commonly referred to as the "kiddie tax."

PRACTICE NOTE: Tax Cut and Jobs Act of 2017.—Because of the state's current federal conformity date history (see ¶15-515), California does not conform to the simplification of the "kiddie tax" by the federal Tax Cuts and Jobs Act of 2017 (P.L. 115-97), which effectively applies ordinary and capital gains rates applicable to trusts and estates to the net unearned income of a child. (*2017 Summary of Federal Income Tax Changes*, California Franchise Tax Board, May 16, 2018)

A qualifying child's net unearned income in excess of a prescribed amount (adjusted annually for inflation), reduced by the child's standard or itemized deductions allocated to such income, is taxed at the parents' top marginal tax rate. For this purpose, the federal standard deduction is incorporated by California. (Sec. 17073.5, Rev. & Tax. Code) For the 2019 and 2020 taxable years, a child's net unearned income that exceeds $1,100 ($1,050 for 2015 to 2018) is subject to tax at the parents' top marginal rate. If the parents can claim the child as a dependent on their return, the child is not allowed a personal exemption. However, up to $1,100 for 2019 and 2020 ($1,050 for 2015 to 2018) of the child's standard deduction can be used to offset unearned income. Therefore, only unearned income of a minor child that exceeds $2,200 for 2019 and 2020 ($2,100 for 2015 to 2018) is taxed at the parents' rate.

If the parents are not married, the tax on the child's unearned income is computed using the custodial parent's income. With respect to married persons filing separately, the tax on the child's unearned income is computed using the income of the parent with the greater taxable income.

The source of the child's unearned income is not a factor. The child's unearned income is used in calculating a parent's "allocable parental tax." Tax that would be imposed on the parent's taxable income if such income included the net unearned income of all children of the parent to which the requirement applies, less the tax that would otherwise be imposed on the parent without regard to the children's unearned income, constitutes "allocable parental tax." The parental tax is then allocated to the children on a *pro rata* basis. The tax normally imposed, disregarding this requirement, or the sum of the child's tax payable without unearned income and the child's share of parental tax, whichever is greater, constitutes the child's tax liability.

Form FTB 3800, Tax Computation for Children Under Age 14 with Investment Income, is used to compute the "kiddie tax."

• *Special filing election*

Parents may elect to include on their return a child's unearned income if the child's unearned income is between prescribed amounts, subject to annual adjustment for inflation ($1,100 to $11,000 for 2019 and 2020; $1,050 to $10,500 for 2015 to 2018), provided that such income consists solely of interest, dividends, or Alaska Permanent Fund dividends. (Sec. 17041(g), Rev. & Tax. Code) This election eliminates the requirement for the child to file a tax return, as the child is treated as having no gross income. The election is not available if estimated tax is paid for the tax year in the child's name, using the child's taxpayer identification number, or if the child is subject to backup withholding.

In electing to include a child's unearned income on the parents' return, the child's gross income exceeding an adjusted amount ($2,200 for 2019 and 2020; $2,100 for 2015 to 2018) is taxed at the parents' highest marginal rate. An additional tax is also imposed, equal to 1% (10% for federal purposes) of the lesser of $1,100 for 2019 and 2020 ($1,050 for 2015 to 2018) or the child's income exceeding $1,100 for 2019 and 2020 ($1,050 for 2015 to 2018).

The election is made on Form FTB 3803, Parent's Election to Report Child's Interest and Dividends.

[¶15-500]

TAXABLE INCOME COMPUTATION

[¶15-505] Determination of Income

California uses federal adjusted gross income as the starting point for determining California taxable income (see ¶15-110). Specified additions (see ¶16-005) and subtractions (see ¶16-205) are then made to federal adjusted gross income to determine California adjusted gross income. Taxpayers then subtract the larger of their standard deduction (see ¶15-540) or itemized deductions (see ¶15-545) to arrive at California taxable income. Personal income is reported on Form 540, California Resident Income Tax Return.

Unlike federal law, California does not allow a subtraction for personal and dependent exemptions (see ¶15-535), but instead allows taxpayers to claim personal exemption credits against California adjusted gross income to arrive at California taxable income. (Sec. 17073, Rev. & Tax. Code)

The California Franchise Tax Board releases an annual publication that outlines the major adjustments required to be made when computing California taxable income. (2010 FTB Pub. 1001, Supplemental Guidelines to California Adjustments)

Computation of California taxable income of individuals is discussed in the paragraphs that follow. For a discussion of the taxable income of estates and trusts, see ¶15-205 *et seq.* For tax rates applied to taxable income, see Rates of Tax (¶15-355).

[¶15-510] Starting Point for Computation

California uses federal adjusted gross income as the starting point for computing California taxable income. (Instructions, Form 540, California Resident Income Tax Return; Instructions, Form 540NR, California Nonresident or Part-Year Resident Income Tax Return)

• *Federal definitions of "gross income" and "adjusted gross income" incorporated*

IRC Sec. 61, which defines "gross income," is incorporated by reference without modification into California law as of California's current federal conformity date (see ¶15-515). (Sec. 17071, Rev. & Tax. Code) IRC Sec. 61 defines "gross income" as all income from whatever source derived, including but not limited to:

— compensation for services;

— gross income derived from business;

— gains from dealings in property;

— interest and dividends;

— rents and royalties;

— alimony and separate maintenance payments;

— annuities;

— income from life insurance and endowment contracts;

— pensions;

— income from discharge of indebtedness;

— distributive shares of partnership gross income;

— income in respect of a decedent; and

— income from an interest in an estate or trust.

(Sec. 17071, Rev. & Tax. Code)

IRC Sec. 62, defining adjusted gross income, is incorporated by reference into California law as of California's current federal conformity date (see ¶15-515), with a modification that disallows the above-the-line deductions for qualified expenses incurred by elementary and secondary school teachers during the 2002 through 2011 tax years (see ¶16-050) and for attorney's fees and court costs paid by or on behalf of the taxpayer in connection with any whistleblower award for providing information about violations of the tax laws. (Sec. 17072, Rev. & Tax. Code)

The IRC Sec. 62 definition of "adjusted gross income" does not apply if a California provision provides otherwise. However, if an Internal Revenue Code refers to "adjusted gross income" for purposes of computing a limitation that is based on a percentage of adjusted gross income, "adjusted gross income" means the amount required to be shown as adjusted gross income on the federal income tax return for the same taxable year. (Sec. 17024.5(h), Rev. & Tax. Code)

PLANNING NOTE: Treatment of registered domestic partners.—Registered domestic partners (RDPs) may file returns jointly or separately by applying the same standards as are applied to married taxpayers under federal income tax law. (Sec. 18521, Rev. & Tax. Code) For purposes of computing an RDP's and former RDP's personal income tax liability, AGI means the AGI on a federal tax return computed as if the RDP or former RDP was treated as a spouse or former spouse, respectively, for federal income tax purposes, and using the same filing status that was used on the state tax return for the same taxable year. (Sec. 17024.5(h), Rev. & Tax. Code)

[¶15-515] Federal Conformity

California incorporates most of the federal Internal Revenue Code (IRC) provisions governing the computation of federal adjusted gross income as of a specified conformity date, currently January 1, 2015, but has its own unique provisions regarding tax rates, credits, taxation of nonresidents, administration, etc. The following table shows those Internal Revenue Code provisions that are incorporated by reference into California law, and the California provisions that incorporate them:

Subject	IRC Sections	Incorporated by Cal. Rev. & Tax. Code Sections
Alternative minimum tax	55-59	17062-17063
Definitions of gross income, etc.	61-68	17071-17077
	988	
Items specifically included in gross income	71-84,	17081
	88-90	
Exclusions	101-102,	17131, 17131.8
	104-140	
Determination of marital status	7703	17021.5
Deductions	161-192,	17201
	194-195,	
	197,	
	211-221,	
	261-280H,	
Corporate distributions	301-385	17321
Deferred compensation	401-409	17501
	410-424	
Accounting	441-469	17551
	471-483	
Qualified tuition programs	529	17140.3
Common trust funds	584	17671
Natural resources	611-638	17681
Estates & trusts, etc.	641-692	17731
Partnerships	701-761	17851
RICs, REITS, and REMICS	851-860G	17088
Gain or loss on dispositions of property	1001-1021,	18031, 18038
	1031-1038,	
	1041-1044,	
	1046-1060,	
	1091-1092	
Capital gains & losses	1201-1245,	18151
	1250-1297	
S corporation shareholders	1366-1368,	17087.5
Merchant Marine construction fund deposits	7518	17088.3

COMMENT: *Federal treaties.*—Treaties between the U.S. and foreign governments that refer to federal taxes and not to state taxes, have no impact on California personal income taxation. Taxpayers should pay careful attention to items impacted by federal treaties, to see if they apply to state taxes. If not, an adjustment will likely be required; see *de Mey van Streefkerk*, SBE, 85-SBE-135, November 6, 1985.

• *Conformity date*

California's incorporation of federal amendments has been sporadic. Consequently, in those years in which California does not provide for a general IRC incorporation update, federal amendments made to the IRC provisions that California incorporates by reference that are adopted after California's last general incorporation date update will not be followed for California personal income tax purposes, unless specifically allowed by California law. (Rev. & Tax. Code Sec. 17024.5(a)(1))

Sec. 17024.5(a)(1) specifies the cutoff date of IRC provisions for purposes of determining the effective date of their incorporation into the respective tax years for California taxation purposes:

IRC provisions as amended through:	Are applicable to California tax years beginning:
Jan. 1, 1984	Within calendar year 1984
Jan. 1, 1985	Within calendar year 1985
Jan. 1, 1986	Within calendar year 1986
Jan. 1, 1987	Within calendar years 1987 or 1988
Jan. 1, 1989	On or after January 1, 1989
Jan. 1, 1990	On or after January 1, 1990
Jan. 1, 1991	On or after January 1, 1991
Jan. 1, 1992	On or after January 1, 1992
Jan. 1, 1993	On or after January 1, 1993
Jan. 1, 1997	On or after January 1, 1997
Jan. 1, 1998	On or after January 1, 1998

IRC provisions as amended through:	Are applicable to California tax years beginning:
Jan. 1, 2001	On or after January 1, 2002
Jan. 1, 2005	On or after January 1, 2005
Jan. 1, 2009	On or after January 1, 2010
Jan. 1, 2015	On or after January 1, 2015

PLANNING NOTE: EGTRRA sunset provisions incorporated.—California incorporates the federal provision of the Economic Growth and Tax Relief and Reconciliation Act of 2001 (P.L. 107-134) that provides that all provisions of, and amendments made by, the 2001 Act shall not apply to taxable, plan, or limitation years beginning after 2010. Pursuant to Rev. & Tax. Code Section 17024.5(a)(2), California also adopts the two-year extension provided by Section 101 of the Tax Relief Act of 2010. The Internal Revenue Code (IRC) and California Revenue and Taxation Code will thereafter be applied and administered as if these provisions and amendments had not been enacted. (Sec. 17024.5(a)(2), Rev. & Tax. Code) (*E-mail*, California Franchise Tax Board, January 26, 2011)

As a result of the January 1, 2015 incorporation date, California does not adopt most of the amendments made by the following acts to the federal provisions incorporated by California:

— Slain Officer Family Support Act of 2015 (P.L. 114-7);

— Medicare Access and CHIP Reauthorization Act of 2015 (P.L. 114-10);

— Don't Tax Our Fallen Public Safety Heroes Act (P.L. 114-14);

— Highway and Transportation Funding Act of 2015 (P.L. 114-21);

— Defending Public Safety Employees' Retirement Act (P.L. 114-26);

— Trade Preferences Extension Act of 2015 (P.L. 114-27);

— Surface Transportation and Veterans Health Care Choice Improvement Act of 2015 (P.L. 114-41);

— Protecting Americans From Tax Hikes Act of 2015 (P.L. 114-113);

— United States Appreciation for Olympians and Paralympians Act of 2016 (P.L. 114-239);

— 21st Century Cures Act (P.L. 114-255);

— Disaster Tax Relief and Airport and Airway Extension Act of 2017 (P.L. 115-63);

— Tax Cuts and Jobs Act of 2017 (P.L. 115-97);

— Bipartisan Budget Act of 2018 (P.L. 115-123);

— Taxpayer First Act (P.L. 116-25); and

— Coronavirus Aid, Relief, and Economic Security (CARES) Act (P.L. 116-136).

PRACTICE NOTE: Adjustments for IRC Sec. 965 amounts.—The federal Tax Cuts and Jobs Act of 2017 (P.L. 115-97) imposes a one-time transition (repatriation) tax on untaxed earnings and profits of certain foreign corporations (IRC Sec. 965). California does not conform to IRC Sec. 965. Taxpayers that reported IRC Sec. 965 amounts on their 2017 federal return must adjust their 2017 California return. Taxpayers who filed a 2017 California return and included IRC Sec. 965 amounts should file an amended return to remove those amounts. They should write "IRC 965" on the top of their California return. Individuals can make adjustments on Schedule CA (540) or Schedule CA (540NR). They should not include federal transition tax statement amounts on Form 541 and related schedules. (*California Guidance – Taxable Year 2017 IRC Section 965 Reporting*, California Franchise Tax Board, May 2018)

Prior to the 2015 tax year, California did not adopt most of the amendments made by the following acts to the federal provisions incorporated by California:

— Worker, Homeownership, and Business Assistance Act of 2009 (P.L. 111-92);

— Hiring Incentives to Restore Employment (HIRE) Act (P.L. 111-147);

— Patient Protection and Affordable Care Act (the Patient Protection Act) (P.L. 111-148);

— Dodd-Frank Wall Street Reform and Consumer Protection Act (P.L. 111-203);

— Education Jobs and Medicaid Assistance Act (P.L. 111-226);

— Small Business Jobs Act (P.L. 111-240) (2010 Jobs Act);

— FAA Modernization and Reform Act of 2012 (P.L. 112-95);

— Moving Ahead for Progress in the 21st Century Act (P.L. 112-141);

— American Taxpayer Relief Act of 2012 (P.L. 112-240);

— Tribal General Welfare Act of 2014 (P.L. 113-168);

— Tax Increase Prevention Act of 2014 (P.L. 113-295);

— Tax Technical Corrections Act of 2014 (P.L. 113-295); and

— Achieving a Better Life Experience Act of 2014 (P.L. 113-295).

Any federal provisions that have not been incorporated, will generally require an addition or subtraction modification to federal adjusted gross income for purposes of computing California adjusted gross income.

Required modifications and adjustments to gross income, gross income exclusions, deductions, and credits as a result of California's nonconformity to these federal amendments are discussed in the following compilation paragraphs and are analyzed in annual summaries prepared by the FTB.

• *Interpretation of effective dates of federal conformity legislation*

An IRC provision incorporated by California that becomes operative or inoperative for federal purposes on or after the latest California federal conformity date becomes operative or inoperative for California purposes on the same date as for federal purposes. (Sec. 17024.5(h)(5), Rev. & Tax. Code)

• *Internal Revenue Code provisions inapplicable in California*

Although California incorporates by reference most of the IRC provisions applicable to the computation of taxable income (see above), many of these IRC provisions incorporated by reference are modified or made inapplicable in California in order to reflect California taxing policies that differ from federal policies. There are two kinds of these "modifying-type" California provisions:

— those that provide specific California provisions that replace counterpart federal provisions or modify particular IRC sections despite their incorporation, e.g. California provisions concerning credits, taxation of part-year and nonresidents, exempt trusts, and administrative matters; and

— those that cut across the entire IRC and are applicable to scores of IRC provisions.

References to the following IRC sections incorporated by reference into California law are not applicable in California. (Sec. 17024.5(b), Rev. & Tax. Code)

— **Electing small business corporations (except as otherwise provided):** IRC provisions relating to electing small business corporations, as defined in IRC Sec. 1361(b), are inapplicable in California, except as provided by Chapter 4.5 of Part 11 of Division 2 of the Revenue and Taxation Code. Chapter 4.5 generally provides recognition of S corporations for California personal income tax purposes by adopting most of the federal S corporation provisions, although some of the federal S corporation provisions are not adopted by California.

— **Foreign trusts:** IRC provisions relating to foreign trusts, as defined in IRC Sec. 679, are inapplicable in California. (Sec. 17024.5(b)(6), Rev. & Tax. Code) California has no provisions comparable to IRC Sec. 679 concerning foreign trusts with U.S. beneficiaries (see ¶15-215).

— **Foreign income taxes and foreign credits:** IRC provisions relating to foreign income taxes and foreign tax credits are inapplicable in California because the state does not allow a foreign tax credit. (Sec. 17024.5(b)(7), Rev. & Tax. Code) (see ¶16-145)

— **U.S. citizens living abroad:** IRC Sec. 911, relating to U.S. citizens living abroad, is not applicable in California. (Sec. 17024.5(b)(8), Rev. & Tax. Code)

— **Credits and credit carryovers:** IRC provisions relating to federal credits and credit carryovers are generally not applicable in California, because the state maintains its own system of credits under Rev. & Tax. Code Sec. 17001—Sec. 17063. (Sec. 17024.5(b)(10), Rev. & Tax. Code) However, IRC Sec. 111(b) and IRC Sec. 111(c), which relate to the recovery of credits and credit carryovers from which a taxpayer derived a tax benefit in a prior taxable year, is applicable to credits for California purposes (see ¶15-810). (Sec. 17142, Rev. & Tax. Code)

— **Nonresident aliens:** Internal Revenue Code provisions relating to nonresident aliens are not applicable in California (see ¶15-115). (Sec. 17024.5(b)(11), Rev. & Tax. Code)

— **Personal exemptions:** Internal Revenue Code provisions relating to the deduction for personal exemptions provided in IRC Sec. 151 are not applicable in California (see ¶15-535). (Sec. 17024.5(b)(12), Rev. & Tax. Code)

— **Generation-skipping transfers:** Federal provisions relating to the tax on generation-skipping transfers imposed under IRC Sec. 2601 et seq. are inapplicable in California. (Sec. 17024.5(b)(13), Rev. & Tax. Code)

— **Estate tax:** IRC provisions relating to the tax on estates imposed under IRC Secs. 2001 or 2101 are inapplicable in California (see ¶15-225). (Sec. 17024.5(b)(14), Rev. & Tax. Code)

California law provides that when applying the IRC or any applicable regulation thereunder for California personal income tax purposes, any reference to the "Secretary" (i.e., the IRS) must be substituted with the "Franchise Tax Board" (FTB) when appropriate. (Sec. 17024.5(h), Rev. & Tax. Code)

California law also provides that when an IRC provision is applicable for determining a statute of limitations for California personal income tax purposes, any reference in the IRC provision to a period of three years must be modified to read four years. (Sec. 17024.5(g), Rev. & Tax. Code) Finally, California law requires that all references to IRC Sec. 501 be interpreted to also apply to Rev. & Tax. Code Sec. 23701. (Sec. 17024.5(h)(8), Rev. & Tax. Code)

• *Federal elections and consents*

If a proper federal election is filed pursuant to an IRC provision that California incorporates by reference into its personal income tax law, the election is deemed to be a proper election for California income tax purposes, unless a California provision or regulation provides otherwise, or unless a different election is timely filed with the FTB. (Sec. 17024.5(e), Rev. & Tax. Code) Although a proper federal election under a federal provision is generally deemed to be a proper election for California purposes, a taxpayer may wish to elect different tax treatment for California purposes. Conversely, a taxpayer may wish to utilize an election for California purposes while deciding *not* to make a similar election for federal purposes. Similar rules apply to federal consents. (Sec. 17024.5(f), Rev. & Tax. Code) (*FTB Notice 95-1*, FTB, March 15, 1995)

To obtain treatment other than that elected for federal purposes, the taxpayer must file a separate proper election with the FTB. (Sec. 17024.5(e), Rev. & Tax. Code) Such statements or elections are required by California either to avoid the application of a federal election or to utilize an election not adopted for federal purposes.

PRACTICE NOTE: *Doctrine of election*—2012 legislation clarified that the doctrine of election applies to any election affecting the computation of California income tax, meaning that the election must be made on an original timely filed return for the taxable period for which the election is to apply, and once made is binding. (Sec. 4, Ch. 37 (S.B. 1015), Laws 2012)

If the rules that make a proper federal election, or a federal application, or the seeking of federal consent sufficient for California purposes are applicable to an IRC provision incorporated by reference in California, then another rule providing that references to the "Secretary" are deemed to mean the "Franchise Tax Board" (Sec. 17024.5(h)(7), Rev. & Tax. Code) is not applicable. The former rules are specific, but the latter rule is general and applies only when the specific rules do not apply.

A federal income tax election (or lack of election) made before becoming a California taxpayer is binding for California purposes, and the taxpayer may not make a separate election for California purposes, unless that separate election is expressly authorized in a California statute or regulation. (Sec. 17024.5(e), Rev. & Tax. Code)

COMMENT: *California incorporation of IRC cross-references.*—Numerous IRC sections incorporated by reference into California law contain cross-references to other IRC or United States Code (USC) provisions that are not themselves incorporated by reference. Such cross-referenced provisions apply in California only for purposes of applying the provisions in which the cross-references appear.

For example, California incorporates by reference IRC Sec. 408 (concerning individual retirement accounts), which contains a reference in subsection (e)(2)(A) to IRC Sec. 4975 (concerning tax on prohibited transactions), which California has not otherwise incorporated by reference. According to the FTB, IRC Sec. 4975 is applicable for purposes of applying IRC Sec. 408, but is not otherwise incorporated into California law.

Also, whenever an IRC provision that California has incorporated by reference contains a cross-reference to another IRC provision that California has incorporated with modifications, the modified version must be applied.

[¶15-535] Personal Exemptions

Unlike federal law, California does not allow personal and dependency exemptions, but does allow personal and dependency exemption credits. The personal and dependency exemption credits are reported on Form 540, California Resident Income Tax Return.

[¶15-540] Standard Deduction

Taxpayers who do not itemize deductions are allowed a standard deduction in computing taxable income. (Sec. 17073, Rev. & Tax. Code) California standard deduction amounts are as follows: (Sec. 17073.5, Rev. & Tax. Code)

Calendar Year 2020

Filing Status	Standard Deduction Amount
Married individuals filing jointly, surviving spouses, and heads of households	$9,202
Single individuals and married individuals filing separately	$4,601

(*Memorandum*, California Franchise Tax Board, September 1, 2020)

The standard deduction is limited with respect to individuals claimed as dependents by other persons. Under IRC Sec. 63(c)(5), as incorporated by California, the standard deduction limitation amount is (1) $500 (adjusted for inflation to $1,100 for 2020), or (2) the dependent's earned income plus $250 (adjusted for inflation to $350 for 2020), whichever is greater. (Sec. 17073.5, Rev. & Tax. Code)

California also incorporates IRC Sec. 63(c)(6), which provides that the standard deduction for the following taxpayers is zero:

— a married individual filing a separate return when either spouse itemizes deductions;

— an individual filing a short-period return due to a change in his or her annual accounting period; and

— an estate, trust, common trust fund, or partnership.

IRC Sec. 63(c)(6) also denies the standard deduction to nonresident aliens, but California does not incorporate that part of the provision. (Sec. 17024.5(b)(11), Rev. & Tax. Code)

• *Indexing the standard deduction*

The Franchise Tax Board annually adjusts the amount of the standard deduction according to an inflation adjustment factor that is computed on the basis of the percentage change in the California Consumer Price Index. The amount allowed to a head of household, surviving spouse, or married couple filing jointly must always be twice the amount allowed to all other taxpayers. (Sec. 17073.5, Rev. & Tax. Code)

[¶15-545] Itemized Deductions

A taxpayer may claim a standard deduction (see ¶15-540) or may elect to itemize deductions. (Sec. 17073(c), Rev. & Tax. Code) As under federal law, a taxpayer whose itemized deductions exceed the amount of the standard deduction can reduce tax liability by electing to itemize deductions. California and federal standard deduction amounts differ, and itemized deductions allowed under California and federal law also vary. Taxpayers should therefore reach separate decisions about the relative merits of standard and itemized deductions for California and federal tax purposes.

California's itemized deductions are computed on Sch. CA (540), California Adjustments—Residents, and reported on Form 540, California Resident Income Tax Return.

A taxpayer that itemizes deductions on his or her California return, but not on his or her federal return, must complete federal Schedule A prior to computing the amount of California itemized deductions that may be claimed. (Instructions, Sch. CA (540), California Adjustments—Residents)

• *Itemized deductions*

The California definition of "itemized deductions" conforms to federal law (IRC Sec. 63(d)), relating to itemized deductions, with certain modifications. (Sec. 17201, Rev. & Tax. Code; Sec. 17024.5(b)(12), Rev. & Tax. Code;Sec. 17024.5(i), Rev. & Tax. Code)

Under California law, "itemized deductions" means the deductions allowed under personal income tax provisions of the Internal Revenue Code, as incorporated and modified by California (Sec. 17024.5(i), Rev. & Tax. Code), other than deductions allowed from California gross income. Under federal law, "itemized deductions" means all federal deductions, other than the deductions allowable as adjustments to federal gross income and the deduction for personal exemptions provided in IRC Sec. 151. California has not adopted the deduction for personal exemptions, however California does allow credits for personal and dependency exemptions.

Although California allows most of the federal itemized deductions for purposes of computing California personal income tax liability, California modifies many of the deductions allowed, see the addition and subtraction adjustment discussions (see ¶16-005 and ¶16-205, respectively). Following are some of the major differences between California and federal itemized deductions:

— **Taxes.**—State, local, and foreign income taxes, state disability insurance tax (SDI), qualified sales and use taxes, federal estate taxes, and generation skipping transfer taxes may be deducted for federal, but not California, purposes. In addition, California does not conform to the federal limit on state and local tax deductions for the 2018 to 2025 tax years (see ¶16-145).

— **Mortgage interest.**—California, unlike federal law, does not reduce the mortgage interest expense deduction by the amount claimed for the federal mortgage interest credit (see ¶16-280).

— **Medical expenses.**—California has not adopted the federal increase of the deduction threshold for unreimbursed medical expenses from 7.5% of adjusted gross income (AGI) to 10% of AGI (temporarily reduced back to 7.5% for federal purposes for the 2017 and 2018 tax years). In addition, unlike federal law, California allows a deduction for medical expenses and health insurance costs incurred on behalf of a registered domestic partner. Adjustments must be made on Sch. CA (540).

— **Employee business.**—Differences in California and federal law concerning depreciation and the IRC Sec. 179 asset expense election may require adjustments (see ¶16-040).

— **Health savings accounts.**—Because California does not recognize health savings accounts (HSAs), taxpayers may add medical expenses paid with feder-ally-exempt HSA withdrawals to the deduction for medical expenses for Califor-nia personal income tax purposes (see ¶16-307).

• *Two percent floor for certain miscellaneous itemized deductions*

California incorporates federal law (IRC Sec. 67) as of the state's IRC tie-in date (see ¶15-515), allowing certain "miscellaneous itemized deductions" only to the extent that, in the aggregate, these deductions exceed 2% of the taxpayer's federal adjusted gross income (AGI). (Sec. 17076, Rev. & Tax. Code; Sec. 17201, Rev. & Tax. Code) Because of California's current IRC tie-in date, California does not conform to the federal provision enacted by the Tax Cuts and Jobs Act of 2017 that suspends all miscellaneous itemized deductions for federal purposes for taxable years 2018 through 2025. (*2017 Summary of Federal Income Tax Changes*, California Franchise Tax Board, May 16, 2018)

• *Limitation on itemized deductions for high-income taxpayers*

California incorporates with modifications to IRC Sec. 68 as of the state's IRC tie-in date (see ¶15-515), which imposes limits on the total amount of itemized deduc-tions of high income taxpayers. (Sec. 17077, Rev. & Tax. Code) For California personal income tax purposes, if adjusted gross income exceeds a statutory threshold amount, the itemized deduction amount allowed is reduced by the lesser of:

— 6% (3% under federal law) of the excess of adjusted gross income over the threshold amount, or

— 80% of the amount of the itemized deductions otherwise allowed for the tax year.

Statutory threshold amounts are adjusted annually for inflation.

Because of California's current IRC tie-in date, California does not conform to the temporary federal repeal of the overall limitation on itemized deductions, which applies for federal purposes to taxable years 2018 through 2025. (*2017 Summary of Federal Income Tax Changes*, California Franchise Tax Board, May 16, 2018)

California threshold amounts.—The indexed threshold amounts for 2020 are:

— $203,341 for single taxpayers or married taxpayers filing separate returns,

— $305,016 for heads of household, and

— $406,687 for married taxpayers filing joint returns and surviving spouses.
(*Memorandum*, California Franchise Tax Board, September 1, 2020)

(Sec. 17077, Rev. & Tax. Code)

With respect to both California personal income tax and federal personal income tax, the itemized deduction limitations do not apply to medical expenses, casualty and theft losses, or investment interest expenses. Also, the limitations do not apply for alternative minimum tax purposes.

California did not incorporate the federal phaseout and repeal of the limitation on itemized deductions for high-income individuals. (Sec. 17077, Rev. & Tax. Code) The federal phase-out began in the 2006 tax year, with a complete repeal of the limitation for tax years beginning after 2009. However, the federal phaseout of itemized deductions for higher-income individuals was reinstated for tax years beginning after December 31, 2012.

¶15-545

• *Amendment of itemization*

Under both California and federal law (IRC Sec. 63) taxpayers who do not itemize deductions for a tax year may amend their returns for the year to reflect itemized deductions. Likewise, taxpayers who itemize deductions may file amended returns to reflect the available standard deduction. However, if spouses file separate returns for a tax year, neither spouse may amend their return unless both spouses do so. Each spouse must also consent in writing to an extension of the period of assessment for the year. (Sec. 17076, Rev. & Tax. Code)

[¶15-600]

TAXABLE INCOME COMPUTATION--FEDERAL BASE

[¶15-605] Federal Base--Adoption Assistance Programs

California incorporates federal law (IRC Sec. 137), concerning the exclusion of employer-provided adoption expenses. (Sec. 17131, Rev. & Tax. Code) However, because of California's Internal Revenue Code conformity date (see ¶15-515), California does not incorporate an increase in the federal exclusion for the 2010 tax year. Consequently, an addition adjustment may be required (see ¶16-010).

CCH PRACTICE TIP: As a result of California's general IRC conformity date, California does not incorporate an amendment made by the Patient Protection and Affordable Care Act of 2010 (PPACA) to IRC Sec. 137 that increased the exclusion by $1,000 for the 2010 tax year (see ¶16-010). However, because California does incorporate the extension of the Economic Growth and Tax Relief Reconciliation Act of 2001 (EGTRRA) sunset date, it follows the federal extension of the original increase in the exclusion from $5,000 ($6,000 for special needs children) to $10,000, adjusted for inflation, that was originally enacted by EGTRRA. (E-mail, California Franchise Tax Board, January 26, 2011)

A general discussion of California's conformity to federal law is provided at ¶15-515.

[¶15-610] Federal Base--Alimony

As a result of California's general incorporation of federal law governing gross income as of California's federal conformity date (see ¶15-515), alimony and separate maintenance payments are included in gross income for California tax purposes to the same extent as under federal law prior to its amendment by the Tax Cuts and Jobs Act of 2017. (IRC Sec. 71; Sec. 17081, Rev. & Tax. Code) Under IRC Sec. 71 as incorporated, such payments are includable if they are made in cash under a divorce or separation agreement, and received by or on behalf of a spouse or former spouse of the payor, who does not file a joint return with the payor. The obligation to make the payments must terminate absolutely with the payee-spouse's death, although the decree need not specifically state this. California does not conform to the federal repeal of the inclusion of such amounts in income. For federal purposes, the repeal of the income inclusion is effective for any divorce or separation instrument executed after December 31, 2018, or for any divorce or separation instrument executed on or before December 31, 2018, and modified after that date, if the modification expressly provides that the federal amendments apply to the modification. (*2017 Summary of Federal Income Tax Changes*, California Franchise Tax Board, May 16, 2018)

California also follows federal law (IRC Sec. 215) as of the state's IRC conformity date (see ¶15-515) allowing a deduction for alimony, separate maintenance, and spousal support payments that are includable in the gross income of the recipient. Special California rules apply to the treatment of the deduction claimed by nonresidents and part-year residents (see ¶16-012). California does not conform to the federal repeal of the deduction for alimony payments. For federal purposes, the repeal of the deduction is effective for any divorce or separation instrument executed after December 31, 2018, or for any divorce or separation instrument executed on or before December 31, 2018, and modified after that date, if the modification expressly provides that the federal amendments apply to the modification. (*2017 Summary of Federal Income Tax Changes*, California Franchise Tax Board, May 16, 2018)

A general discussion of California's conformity to federal law is provided at ¶15-515.

[¶15-615] Federal Base--Amortization

Except as noted, California follows the federal provisions governing the amortization of the items discussed below. Certain reforestation expenses may also be amortized (see ¶15-690).

California generally incorporates the federal provisions governing amortization of the following items:

— goodwill and other intangibles (IRC Sec. 197) (Sec. 17279, Rev. & Tax. Code)

— lease acquisition costs (IRC Sec. 178) (Sec. 17201, Rev. & Tax. Code)

— pollution control facilities (IRC Sec. 169) (Sec. 17250, Rev. & Tax. Code), however, an addition adjustment is required for non-California facilities and may also be required prior to the 2010 tax year as a result of federal amendments that expanded the amortization deduction for atmospheric pollution control facilities (see ¶16-015)

— start-up expenditures (IRC Sec. 195), although an addition adjustment is required for the 2010 tax year and effective date differences applied in previous tax years (see below). (Sec. 17201, Rev. & Tax. Code)

Effective date differences.—Although California incorporates the federal provision (IRC Sec. 197(f)(10)) requiring certain intangible property, including copyright or patent interests, intangible property, and computer software, to be amortized over an extended recovery period of not less than 125% of the lease term if it is leased to an exempt entity and would otherwise be considered tax-exempt user property, different effective dates apply. The provision is applicable for California purposes beginning with the 2005 taxable year, and is generally effective for federal purposes to leases entered into after October 3, 2004.

Finally, although California incorporates the latest version of IRC Sec. 195, which allows taxpayers to currently deduct specified amounts of start-up expenditures and amortize the remainder over a 15-year period, different effective dates apply. The provision is applicable for California purposes to taxable years beginning after 2004, and is effective for federal purposes for expenditures paid or incurred after October 22, 2005.

• *Bond premiums*

California follows federal law (IRC Sec. 171) concerning the amortization of bond premiums, as of California's current federal conformity date (see ¶15-515). (Sec.

17201, Rev. & Tax. Code) Under IRC Sec. 171 as incorporated, a taxpayer who acquires a bond bearing tax-exempt interest is required to amortize the bond premium, but may not deduct the amortizable premium, in figuring taxable income. If the taxpayer acquires taxable bonds, he or she has the option of amortizing the premium. If the election is made to amortize the bond premium paid for a taxable bond, the amount of the amortizable bond premium for the taxable year is allowed as a deduction. For bonds acquired after 1987, bond premium amortization is an offset against interest income from the bond. Thus, the deduction for amortized premium is limited to the taxpayer's investment income from the bond for the year.

Although California incorporates IRC Sec. 171, California and federal law differ as to which bonds produce tax-exempt interest income (see ¶ 15-720). Consequently, addition and subtraction adjustments may be required (see ¶ 16-005 and ¶ 16-205, respectively).

• *Pollution control facilities*

California incorporates federal law (IRC Sec. 169), as of California's current federal conformity date (see ¶ 15-515), which allows a taxpayer to elect accelerated amortization of a "certified pollution control facility" over a period of 60 months. (Sec. 17250, Rev. & Tax. Code) However, an addition adjustment is required for accelerated amortization claimed for non-California facilities and may also be required prior to the 2010 tax year as a result of different effective dates for amendments that expand the amortization deduction for atmospheric pollution control facilities (see ¶ 16-015).

A general discussion of California's conformity to federal law is provided at ¶ 15-515.

[¶ 15-617] Federal Base--Bad Debts

California incorporates federal law (IRC Sec. 166), as of California's current federal conformity date (see ¶ 15-515), relating to the deduction for bad debts. (Sec. 17201, Rev. & Tax. Code) Under IRC Sec. 166, as incorporated, a California taxpayer may deduct bad debts that are business related as well as those that are not. In general, a bad debt deduction is allowed only in the year in which the debt actually becomes wholly or partially worthless.

Under IRC Sec. 166(d)(1)(B), as incorporated, bad debts that are not related to business are deductible only when wholly worthless and only as short-term capital losses.

A general discussion of California's conformity to federal law is provided at ¶ 15-515.

[¶ 15-620] Federal Base--Capital Gains and Losses

Although California does not incorporate the federal capital gains tax rate, California law does incorporate IRC Sec. 1201—IRC Sec. 1288, as of California's current federal conformity date (see ¶ 15-515), relating to capital gains and losses (Sec. 18151, Rev. & Tax. Code), with modifications. In addition, California follows federal law that allows regulated investment companies to treat net capital loss carryovers similar to the treatment available to individuals Among the incorporated provisions. (Sec. 18155, Rev. & Tax. Code) California conforms to federal law concerning the following:

— the definition of capital assets (IRC Sec. 1221);

— the limitation on capital losses (IRC Sec. 1211(b));

— capital loss carryovers (IRC Sec. 1212(c));

— losses on small business investment company stock (IRC Sec. 1242 and IRC Sec. 1243);

— losses on small business stock (IRC Sec. 1244);

— recapture of depreciation on certain depreciable property (IRC Sec. 1245), however, adjustments may be required because California does not incorporate all the federal amortization and depreciation deductions (see ¶16-070); and

— recapture of depreciation on real property (IRC Sec. 1250), with certain exceptions (see ¶16-040).

(Sec. 18151, Rev. & Tax. Code)

• *Treatment of capital gain or loss*

A taxpayer who has only gains or only losses on sales or exchanges of capital assets during the year, combines the gains or losses regardless of the holding period. If a taxpayer has both gains and losses on sales or exchanges of capital assets, the taxpayer must net all his or her long-term capital gains with long-term capital losses, net his or her short-term capital gains with short-term capital losses, and determine the excess of net long-term capital gain or loss against net short-term capital gain or loss, or vice versa. With the exception of the ordinary loss deduction allowed for losses incurred from the sale, exchange, or worthlessness of small business stock (IRC Sec. 1244 as incorporated by California), the combined capital gain or loss, or the excess net capital gain or loss, is treated as follows:

Gains: the gains are taxed as ordinary income for California income tax purposes.

Losses: the losses may be used to offset up to $3,000 of ordinary income ($1,500 in the case of a married individual filing separately). (IRC Sec. 1211(b))

• *Federal-California differences*

1. California does not incorporate IRC Sec. 1202, which provides a 50% exclusion of gain from the sale of certain small business stock, but prior to being struck down as unconstitutional, adopted a substantially similar provision. (Sec. 18152, Rev. & Tax. Code; Sec. 18152.5, Rev. & Tax. Code) (see ¶16-070.)

2. California does not permit capital loss carrybacks. (Sec. 18155, Rev. & Tax. Code) (see ¶16-095.)

3. California renders inoperative for specified periods certain federal rules relating to recapture of excess depreciation of pollution control facilities and certain residential property, and of pre-1983 amortization of trademarks, and provides for some exceptions to federal rules concerning low-income rental housing and certified historic structures. (Sec. 18171, Rev. & Tax. Code)

4. The amount of original issue discounts reported on California returns is different from the amount reported on federal returns for debt instruments issued in 1985 and 1986, because California did not conform to federal tax rules for tax-exempt stripped bonds during these two years. Such differences are reported for California purposes in the tax year of the disposal or maturation of the instrument. (Sec. 18178, Rev. & Tax. Code)

5. California does not adopt the special federal tax rates imposed on long-term capital gains.

¶15-620

6. California does not incorporate IRC Sec. 1291 through IRC Sec. 1298, relating to the treatment of certain passive foreign investment companies. (Sec. 18181, Rev. & Tax. Code)

7. Because of California's IRC conformity date history (see ¶15-515), for taxable years beginning on or after January 1, 2015, California incorporates the federal provision under which any interest rate swap, currency swap, basis swap, interest rate cap, interest rate floor, commodity swap, equity swap, equity index swap, or similar agreement is not treated as a Sec. 1256 contract. For federal purposes, the provision applies to taxable years beginning after July 22, 2010.

Except as otherwise noted taxpayers must make addition or subtraction adjustments to account for these differences (see ¶16-070 and ¶16-270, respectively).

• *Gain on small business stock*

California law provides an exclusion from gross income of up to 50% of the gain realized on the disposition of qualified small business stock sold prior to 2013, provided the stock was originally issued after August 10, 1993, was held for more than five years, and met other specified criteria, see ¶16-070 for details.

A general discussion of California's conformity to federal law is provided at ¶15-515.

[¶15-625] Federal Base--Charitable Contributions

California incorporates federal law (IRC Sec. 170), as of California's current federal conformity date (see ¶15-515), relating to the charitable contribution deduction. (Sec. 17201, Rev. & Tax. Code; Sec. 17275.5, Rev. & Tax. Code) Under IRC Sec. 170, as incorporated, contributions to qualified nonprofit charitable organizations, governmental entities, and conservation projects are deductible from adjusted gross income, subject to specified limitations, including the limitation on the charitable mileage deduction amount. (Sec. 17275.5, Rev. & Tax. Code)

CCH PRACTICE TIP: Substantiation requirements.—California conforms to federal law requiring taxpayers to retain specified forms of documentation to substantiate charitable contributions. All cash contributions, regardless of amount, require either a bank statement, receipt from the charity, or a payroll deduction record. For cash donations of $250 or more, a written acknowledgment from the charitable organization is also required. Noncash contributions require additional documentation that varies depending on the value of the donation as follows:

— Less than $250: . Receipt from charity with name, date, and donation description.

— Greater than $250 but less than $500: . . . . Contemporaneous written acknowledgment from charity.

— Greater than $500 but less than $5,000: . . . . Written acknowledgment plus file IRS Form 8283, Noncash Charitable Contributions.

— Greater than $5,000 (not including stock, art, and autos): . . Qualified appraisal and IRS Form 8283.

However, because of California's federal conformity date (see ¶15-515), California does not conform to the repeal of the exception to the contemporaneous written acknowledgment requirement for contributions made in tax years beginning after 2016. (*2017 Summary of Federal Income Tax Changes*, California Franchise Tax Board, May 16, 2018)

Substantiation requirements for stock, art, and autos are outlined in IRS Publication 526, Charitable Contributions. Taxpayers who donate clothing and household items and receive only a receipt from the charity with a date should keep detailed descriptions of items donated as well as the condition of the items in order to substantiate the value of the donation. Taxpayers may want to take pictures of the items so they will be able to prove "good used condition or better" if need be during an audit. (*Tax News*, California Franchise Tax Board, March 2012)

California generally follows federal law (IRC Sec. 170(f)(10)), relating to split dollar insurance arrangements. Under both California and federal law a charitable deduction is disallowed for a transfer of money to a charitable organization if, in connection with the transfer, (1) the charitable organization directly or indirectly pays a premium on a life insurance, annuity, or endowment contract and (2) the transferor, any member of the transferor's family, or any other person (other than a charity) chosen by the transferor is a direct or indirect beneficiary under the contract. However, a federal provision requiring payment of an excise equal to the amount of nondeductible premiums, does not apply for California purposes. (Sec. 17275.5, Rev. & Tax. Code)

Subtraction adjustments may be allowed as a result of (1) differences in the federal and California carryover amounts from prior year deductions, and (2) California's nonconformity to the federal provision limiting deductions for contributions to donor advised funds and the fee requirement for contributions of certain interests in buildings located in registered historic districts (see ¶ 16-220). Addition adjustments (see ¶ 16-025) may be required as a result of California's nonconformity to provisions governing contributions of food and book inventory, contributions of real property for conservation purposes, and contributions to agricultural research organizations. California also does not conform to the increase (from 50% to 60%) of the income-based percentage limit for certain charitable contributions of cash to public charities and certain other organizations for the 2018 to 2025 tax years (see IRC Sec. 170(b)(1)(A)) or the repeal of the deduction for amounts paid for college athletic seating rights in tax years beginning after December 31, 2017 (see IRC Sec. 170(*l*)). (*2017 Summary of Federal Income Tax Changes*, California Franchise Tax Board, May 16, 2018) Also, California prohibits certain charitable contribution deductions by taxpayers found guilty in the college admissions cheating scandal (see ¶ 16-025).

Taxpayers who sell land to the state for conservation purposes and claim a charitable contribution deduction in excess of $5,000 for the value of the land in excess of the price paid must attach an appraisal for the property to their tax return for the year the deduction is claimed in order to substantiate the amount of the charitable contribution deduction, and the appraisal must be prepared by an appraiser licensed by the Office of Real Estate Appraisers (Sec. 5096.518, Pub. Res. Code)

California law also allows a deduction for a taxpayer's check-off contributions to specified funds listed on the taxpayer's personal income tax return. (see ¶ 89-224)

• *Disaster-related donations*

Hurricane Harvey, Irma, and Maria disaster relief.—For qualifying charitable contributions, the federal Disaster Tax Relief and Airport and Airway Extension Act of 2017 (P.L. 115-63):

¶ 15-625

— temporarily suspended the majority of the AGI limitations on charitable contributions;

— provides that contributions will not be taken into account for purposes of applying AGI and carryover period limitations to other contributions;

— provides eased rules governing the treatment of excess contributions; and

— provides an exception from the overall limitation on itemized deductions for certain qualified contributions.

The changes are intended to provide relief to taxpayers affected by Hurricanes Harvey, Irma, and Maria.

Since California generally conforms to the federal charitable contribution rules under IRC Sec. 170 as of the federal conformity date (see ¶ 15-515), state law does not conform to the these federal hurricane relief provisions. (*2017 Summary of Federal Income Tax Changes,* California Franchise Tax Board, May 16, 2018)

• *Charitable gifts made on behalf of U.S. House members, others*

California also specifically incorporates IRC Sec. 7701(k), concerning the tax treatment of contributions made to charitable organizations on behalf of members of the U.S. House of Representatives and certain other officers and employees of the federal government who are prohibited by federal ethics laws from directly accepting honoraria. (Sec. 17020.13, Rev. & Tax. Code) Under Sec. 7701(k) as incorporated, such individuals are not required to include such charitable contributions in their gross income for state or federal income tax purposes and are not entitled to claim charitable deductions for such contributions.

A general discussion of California's conformity to federal law is provided at ¶ 15-515.

[¶ 15-630] Federal Base--Child Care Expenses

There is no California or federal provision that specifically provides an employer with a deduction for payments to employees for child care. However, under the federal trade and business expense provision (IRC Sec. 162(a)), incorporated by California (see ¶ 15-805), a deduction may be taken for salaries or other compensation for personal services actually rendered. Employer payments for employee child care are presumably deductible by the employer as salary or other compensation. For example, a Revenue Ruling provides that an employer's payments to a day care center to provide care for children of its employees while the parents are at work are deductible as business expenses. (Rev. Rul. 73-348, 1973-2 C.B. 31)

Both federal law (IRC Sec. 45F) and California law allow credits for qualified child care expenses. California allows employers to claim credits for qualified child care programs and for qualified child care contributions.

• *Employee's expenses for child care*

Both California and federal law allow a credit for household and dependent care expenses necessary for gainful employment.

A general discussion of California's conformity to federal law is provided at ¶ 15-515.

[¶15-635] Federal Base--Claim of Right Adjustment

California allows a claim of right adjustment similar to the adjustment allowed under federal law (IRC Sec. 1341). (Sec. 17049, Rev. & Tax. Code) Depending on whether a federal credit is taken in lieu of a deduction, an addition or subtraction adjustment may be required for California personal income tax purposes (see ¶16-027 or ¶16-225, respectively).

A general discussion of California's conformity to federal law is provided at ¶15-515.

[¶15-640] Federal Base--Compensation and Remuneration

California generally follows federal law (IRC Sec. 162) allowing taxpayers to deduct compensation and remuneration paid as trade or business expenses (see ¶15-805). In addition, California incorporates federal law as of the current federal conformity date (see ¶15-515), concerning the tax treatment of the following forms of compensation:

— the inclusion of certain employer contributions to employee group life-insurance in employees' gross income (IRC Sec. 79) (Sec. 17081, Rev. & Tax. Code);

— transfers of property in connection with the performance of services (IRC Sec. 83) (Sec. 17081, Rev. & Tax. Code); and

— compensation for injuries or sickness (IRC Sec. 104) (Sec. 17131, Rev. & Tax. Code).

For tax years beginning after 2018, California conforms to modifications made by the Tax Cuts and Jobs Act of 2017 to the federal limitations on excessive employee remuneration (IRC Sec. 162(m)). However, under federal law, a transition rule applies to changes made by the TCJA. The federal grandfathering period applies to compensation provided pursuant to a written binding contract which was in effect on November 2, 2017, that has not been modified in any material respect. The relevant date for California purposes is March 31, 2019. (Sec. 17271, Rev. & Tax. Code)

Because of California's federal conformity date (see ¶15-515), California conforms for taxable years beginning on or after January 1, 2015, to the enactment by the Moving Ahead for Progress in the 21st Century Act of IRC Sec. 79(f), which provides an exception for life insurance purchased in connection with qualified transfers of excess pension assets. The provision is effective for federal purposes for transfers made after July 6, 2012.

Under IRC Sec. 83, as incorporated by California, the value of restricted stock or other property transferred to an employee in connection with the performance of services is not taxable until the interest in the property becomes transferable or no longer subject to a substantial risk of forfeiture, whichever comes first. The amount includable in gross income is the difference between the consideration paid and the fair market value when transferable or not subject to forfeiture. Because of California's federal conformity date (see ¶15-515), California does not conform to federal amendments made by the Tax Cuts and Jobs Act of 2017 that allow a qualified employee to elect to defer income inclusion for certain income attributable to qualified stock transferred to the employee by the employer. (2017 Summary of Federal Income Tax Changes, California Franchise Tax Board, May 16, 2018)

¶15-635

311

An exclusion from gross income for California personal income tax purposes is provided for supplementary payments received by in-home supportive service providers (see ¶16-295).

A general discussion of California's conformity to federal law is provided at ¶15-515.

[¶15-645] Federal Base--Corporate Distributions and Adjustments

Although California personal income tax law and federal law (IRC Secs. 301—385) regarding dividends and other corporate distributions are generally the same as of California's current federal conformity date (see ¶15-515), California has not completely conformed to current federal law. (Sec. 17321, Rev. & Tax. Code) In addition, prior differences in California and federal law may still affect the cost basis of property.

> *CAUTION NOTE: Basis differences.*—The 1983 recodification of the personal income tax law did not eliminate the effect of the pre-1983 provisions governing the basis of stock the rights to which were acquired before 1935 and 1941, contained in former Rev. & Tax. Code Secs. 17347 and 17348. Former Sec. 17347 provided that if a stock right acquired prior to 1935 constituted income, the basis of the related stock is unaffected. Former Sec. 17348 governs the basis of the stock acquired through rights acquired before 1941.

The principal provisions of federal law to which California conforms may be summarized very briefly as follows:

— any distribution out of earnings and profits of the current year or out of earnings and profits accumulated after February 28, 1913, is a dividend (IRC Sec. 316)

— Certain liquidating distributions are treated as payments in exchange for stock (IRC Sec. 302, IRC Sec. 303)

— A redemption of stock that is "essentially equivalent to the distribution of a taxable dividend" is to be treated as such. Detailed rules are provided for some situations. Certain types of redemptions are not to be treated as taxable dividends. These include disproportionate distributions, termination of a shareholder's interest, and redemption of stock to pay death taxes. (IRC Sec. 305)

— Certain stock dividends may be nontaxable (IRC Sec. 305).

— Detailed rules are provided for the computation of earnings and profits so that a determination can be made regarding the taxability of a corporate distribution in the hands of shareholders (IRC Sec. 312).

• *Distributions from mutual funds*

California adopts the federal tax treatment of regulated investment companies (RICs) and their shareholders (IRC Sec. 852) as amended by the Regulated Investment Company Modernization Act of 2010. Consequently, California incorporates federal law that treats certain redemptions of stock of publicly offered RICs as exchanges (IRC Sec. 302) and allows losses on certain redemptions of stock by fund-of-funds RICs (IRC Sec. 316). (Sec. 17321, Rev. & Tax. Code; Former Sec. 17322.1, Rev. & Tax. Code)

• *Constructive dividends*

Following federal cases involving the same issue, the California State Board of Equalization held in *Gilmore*, SBE, 61-SBE-071, November 7, 1961, that unsupported travel and entertainment expenses disallowed to a closely-held corporation were taxable as constructive dividends to the individual shareholders. Later cases have held to the same effect.

• *Current California-federal differences*

Current differences between California and federal law are summarized as follows:

— Federal law provides for consent dividends (applicable to personal holding companies, etc.). There is no comparable California provision.

— Federal limitations periods for waivers of stock attribution are modified to refer to California provisions. (Sec. 17132, Rev. & Tax. Code)

— California has not adopted a special federal rule (IRC Sec. 303(d)) governing generation-skipping transfers. (Sec. 17024.5(b), Rev. & Tax. Code)

— The federal provision (IRC Sec. 316(b)(2)), relating to distributions by personal holding companies is not incorporated into California law. (Sec. 17024.5(b)(3), Rev. & Tax. Code)

— The federal provision (IRC Sec. 312(m)) relating to distributions by foreign corporations is not applicable for California purposes. (Sec. 17024.5(b), Rev. & Tax. Code)

— Under both California and federal law, a corporate distribution may be a nontaxable return of capital if there are no earnings and profits out of which the distribution is made. However, the amount of a corporation's earnings and profits may be different for California tax purposes than it is for federal tax purposes. Such a difference may result in a particular distribution being nontaxable under one law, but a taxable dividend under the other.

— California does not incorporate the special federal provisions for Domestic International Sales Corporations (DISCs). (Sec. 17024.5(b), Rev. & Tax. Code) Accordingly, a DISC is taxed under California law in the same manner as other corporations, and the special federal treatment of its dividends has no effect for California tax purposes.

— California, unlike federal law, does not apply a lower tax rate to qualified dividend distributions.

— Because of California's current federal conformity date (see ¶ 15-515), California has not conformed to federal amendments that authorize the Secretary to specify the method to be used to determine the value of intangible property in the context of an IRC Sec. 367(d) transfer in tax years beginning after December 31, 2017. (*Summary of Federal Income Tax Changes – 2017*, California Franchise Tax Board, May 16, 2018)

• *Prior-year differences*

In addition to the differences listed above, there were prior-year differences that may continue to affect computations of basis. These prior year differences concert the following:

¶ 15-645

— federal rules for distributions by World War I "personal service corporations";

— rules for corporate liquidations in 1954, 1955, and 1956;

— special California provisions for 1935 or 1936 distributions by a personal holding company;

— effective dates (all before 1972) of provisions regarding redemption of stock through an affiliate, and collapsible corporations;

— various amendments, in 1981 and before, relating to special rules for redemption of stock to pay death taxes;

— 1958 federal amendments to special rules for 12-month liquidations;

— 1964-1978 difference in rules for "sidewise attribution" in stock ownership rules;

— 1954-1961 difference in special rules regarding distributions of property with a government-secured loan; and

— 1969-1971 differences in rules for taxation of stock dividends.

A general discussion of California's conformity to federal law is provided at ¶15-515.

[¶15-650] Federal Base--Damage Awards

California incorporates federal law (IRC Sec. 104(a)(2)), as of the current California conformity date (see ¶15-515), concerning compensation for injuries or sickness. (Sec. 17131, Rev. & Tax. Code) A payment under Section 103(c)(10) of the Ricky Ray Hemophilia Relief Fund Act of 1998 to an individual is treated as damages received for personal injuries or sickness, for both California and federal tax purposes. (Sec. 17132.7, Rev. & Tax. Code)

Under both California and federal law, compensation, other than from employer or employer-financed accident and insurance plans, for items directly related to personal injuries or sickness are excluded from taxable income. In addition, California also allows a subtraction for compensation paid for wrongful incarceration (see ¶16-235).

• *Recoveries of antitrust, breach of contract, patent infringement damages*

California incorporates federal law (IRC Sec. 186), without modification, relating to the deduction of amounts recovered for certain compensable injuries. (Sec. 17201, Rev. & Tax. Code). Under Sec. 186, as incorporated, amounts received from awards or settlements of civil actions as compensation for injuries from

— patent infringement,

— breach of contract or fiduciary duty or relationship, or

— antitrust violations under the Clayton Act, which are includable in the recipient's gross income, are deductible to the extent of the lesser of (a) the compensatory amount or (b) the amount of unrecovered loss sustained as a result of the injury.

• *Exclusion for Virginia Tech victims*

California law, like federal law, excludes from gross income amounts received from the Hokie Spirit Memorial Fund established by Virginia Tech Foundation that were paid as a result of the tragic shooting on April 16, 2007. The California exclusion was enacted as part of the California 2010 Conformity Act (Ch. 14, (S.B. 401), Laws 2010), and applies retroactively without regard to tax year. (Sec. 17132.8, Rev. & Tax. Code)

Other additions to the taxable income base are listed at ¶16-005.

A general discussion of California's conformity to federal law is provided at ¶15-515.

[¶15-655] Federal Base--Death Benefits

California incorporates federal law (IRC Sec. 101), as of California's current federal conformity date (see ¶15-515), relating to the exclusion of death benefits. (Sec. 17131, Rev. & Tax. Code; Sec. 17132.5, Rev. & Tax. Code)

However, an adjustment is required because California has not incorporated the provision that provides a minimum $10,000 federal tax benefit to victims of a terrorist attack and does not incorporate a federal provision that excludes certain death benefits received by survivors of public safety officers killed in the line of duty (see ¶16-036). (Sec. 17132.5, Rev. & Tax. Code; Sec. 17731, Rev. & Tax. Code)

California also allows a subtraction for death benefits paid by the state of California on behalf of California National Guard, State Military Reserve or Naval Militia killed in the line of duty (see ¶15-175).

Because of California's current federal conformity date (see ¶15-515), California does not conform to federal amendments providing that the exceptions to the transfer for value rules are inapplicable in the case of a post-2017 transfer of a life insurance contract, or any interest in a life insurance contract, in a reportable policy sale. (*2017 Summary of Federal Income Tax Changes*, California Franchise Tax Board, May 16, 2018)

A general discussion of California's conformity to federal law is provided at ¶15-515.

[¶15-660] Federal Base--Dependent Care Assistance Payments

California incorporates federal law (IRC Sec. 129), as of California's current federal conformity date (see ¶15-515), concerning dependent care assistance programs. Under both California and federal law, payments of up to $5,000 ($2,500 in the case of a married person filing separately) to an employee for dependent care assistance, when made under an employer's written nondiscriminatory plan, are excludable from the employee's gross income. (Sec. 17131, Rev. & Tax Code)

A general discussion of California's conformity to federal law is provided at ¶15-515.

[¶15-665] Federal Base--Depletion

California incorporates federal law (IRC Sec. 611—IRC Sec. 638), as of California's current federal conformity date (see ¶15-515), relating to the deduction for depletion of natural resources. (Sec. 17681, Rev. & Tax. Code) However, California does not incorporate the IRC Sec. 613A suspension of the 100% taxable income limit on percentage depletion deductions for oil and gas production from marginal properties and does not increase the barrel limitation for small refiners to qualify to use the percentage depletion method. Consequently an addition adjustment may be required (see ¶16-037).

A general discussion of California's conformity to federal law is provided at ¶15-515.

¶15-655

[¶15-670] Federal Base--Depreciation

California conforms to federal law (IRC Sec. 167 and IRC Sec. 168), as of California's current federal conformity date (see ¶15-515), allowing taxpayers to depreciate assets utilizing the modified accelerated cost recovery system (MACRs) for assets placed in service after 1986. (Sec. 17201, Rev. & Tax. Code) However, California does not incorporate the federal bonus depreciation deduction and other special allowances available to specified properties, nor does California allow small film producers to elect to currently deduct costs associated with qualified film and television productions (see ¶16-040). Additional areas of nonconformity require adjustments as well (see ¶16-040).

For assets placed in service before 1987, California permitted the use of ACRS depreciation only for residential rental property. All other property that was placed in service before 1987, must continue to be depreciated using the asset depreciation range (ADR) system. Consequently, basis adjustments may be required (see ¶16-020). Basis adjustments are also required for expenses for which a variety of state tax credits were claimed (see ¶16-020).

• *IRC Sec. 179 asset expense election*

Except as noted below, California incorporates federal law (IRC Sec. 179), as of California's current federal conformity date (see ¶15-515), granting taxpayers an election to currently expense certain depreciable business assets. (Sec. 17201, Rev. & Tax. Code) Under both California and federal law, the excess of the deduction over the otherwise allowable depreciation is recaptured if the property ceases to be used predominantly in the taxpayer's trade or business before the end of its recovery period (see ¶15-620). The deduction cannot exceed the taxable income derived from the trade or business during the tax year.

Differences between California law and federal law exist concerning the amount that may be deducted and the limitations placed on the deduction. In addition, California allows additional expense deductions for the cost of qualified property used in a trade or business within a targeted tax area, an enterprise zone, the Los Angeles Revitalization Zone, or a local agency military base recovery area. Consequently, addition and subtraction adjustments may be required (see ¶16-040 and ¶16-245, respectively).

• *Luxury automobiles and certain personal use property*

California generally incorporates IRC 280F, as of California's current federal conformity date (see ¶15-515), which limits the depreciation of luxury automobiles and "listed property". (Sec. 17201, Rev. & Tax. Code) Limits also apply to trucks and vans, including sport utility vehicles (SUVs) and minivans that are built on a truck chassis. However, because California does not allow the federal bonus depreciation provisions, the amount that may be depreciated for automobiles first placed into service after September 10, 2001 and before 2011 will differ. In addition, although California follows the federal amendment enacted by the Small Business Jobs Act of 2010 that deletes cell phones and similar telecommunications equipment from the definition of "listed property," different effective dates apply. Consequently, addition adjustments may be required for such expenses on California returns for tax years prior to 2015 (see ¶16-040).

The depreciation limitations for passenger automobiles (that are not trucks or vans) placed in service in calendar year 2020 for which the IRC Sec. 168(k) additional first year depreciation deduction does not apply are:

— 1st Tax Year: $3,304

— 2nd Tax Year: $5,227

— 3rd Tax Year: $3,084

— Each Succeeding Year: $1,856

(*Memorandum*, California Franchise Tax Board, September 1, 2020)

The depreciation limitations for trucks and vans placed in service in calendar year 2020 for which the IRC Sec. 168(k) additional first year depreciation deduction does not apply are:

— 1st Tax Year: $3,721

— 2nd Tax Year: $5,959

— 3rd Tax Year: $3,502

— Each Succeeding Year: $2,169

(*Memorandum*, California Franchise Tax Board, September 1, 2020)

• *Leasehold and other improvements*

California has not incorporated the shortened recovery period for qualified leasehold and other types of property and an adjustment is required (see ¶ 16-040). For both California and federal purposes, leasehold improvements placed in service after 1986, are depreciated under the modified ACRS method. Before 1987, the cost of such improvements could be amortized over the term of the lease, as defined by IRC Sec. 178, prior to its amendment by the Tax Reform Act of 1986. IRC Sec. 178, as amended, allows for the amortization of the cost of acquiring a lease.

• *Motion picture films, books, copyrights, etc.*

Under both California and federal law (IRC Sec. 167(g)), taxpayers may elect to compute depreciation using the income forecast method for property such as film, video tape, sound recordings, copyrights, books, patents, and other property of a similar character approved by federal regulation. (Sec. 17250, Rev. & Tax. Code; Sec. 17250.5, Rev. & Tax. Code) However, California has not conformed to all the income forecast method provisions, thereby requiring California adjustments (see ¶ 16-040).

The income forecast method may not be used to compute depreciation for intangible property amortizable under IRC Sec. 197 or for consumer durables subject to rent-to-own contracts.

• *Safe harbor sale-leasebacks*

For purposes of both federal and California law, the "safe harbor lease rules" that were in effect before the Economic Recovery Tax Act of 1984 was enacted continue to apply to real property leases. These rules consist of judicially formulated standards as supplemented by IRS ruling and procedures (FTB, LR 419, December 3, 1981).

• *Effective date differences*

Although California incorporates many of the pre-2005 federal amendments that impact the depreciation deduction, different effective dates apply. (Sec. 17024.5(a), Rev. & Tax. Code) The effective date differences relate to the following amendments.

— The requirement that certain intangible property, including copyright or patent interests, intangible property, and computer software, be amortized over an extended recovery period of not less than 125% of the lease term if it is leased to an exempt entity and would otherwise be considered tax-exempt user property under IRC Sec. 168(h), applies for California purposes to taxable years beginning after 2004 and is generally effective for federal purposes to leases entered into after October 3, 2004;

— The establishment of a seven-year depreciation period for motorsports entertainment complexes applies for California purposes beginning with the 2005 through 2007 taxable years and is applicable for federal purposes to property placed in service after October 22, 2004, and before 2015.

— The increase in the cost recovery period from seven to 20 years for initial land clearing and grading costs incurred by electric utilities and from seven to 15 years for costs incurred by gas utilities, applies for California purposes to taxable years beginning after 2004, and is generally effective for federal purposes for property placed in service after October 22, 2004.

— The limits placed on depreciation deductions associated with sale-in, lease-out transactions (SILOs) involving purchases of municipal property and the denial of the deduction of tax-exempt use losses if the lessor does not have sufficient ownership rights in the property are applicable for California purposes beginning with the 2005 taxable year and are generally effective for federal purposes for property placed in service after October 22, 2004.

A general discussion of California's conformity to federal law is provided at ¶15-515.

[¶15-673] Federal Base--Disability Expenses and Savings Accounts

Under the Achieve a Better Living Experience (ABLE) Act of 2014, states are authorized to establish a tax-favored savings account program that may accept contributions and make distributions to pay for the expenses of individuals who are blind or disabled on or before the date the individual turnes 26 years of age. A qualified ABLE program is generally exempt from taxation under IRC Sec. 529A.

Effective January 1, 2016, California generally conforms to IRC Sec. 529A. However, the additional tax on ABLE distributions that are includible in income (see below), unless the distribution is made after the death of the designated beneficiary, is equal to 2.5% tax for California purposes (instead of 10% for federal purposes). (Sec. 17140.4, Rev. & Tax. Code)

Contributions.—Contributions must be in cash, and the aggregate annual contribution amount cannot exceed the annual federal gift tax exclusion amount. The limit does not apply to rollover contributions. Aggregate total contributions, including contributions from any prior ABLE program on behalf of a designated beneficiary, may not exceed the limits established by the state for its qualified college savings plan with respect to the amount necessary to provide for a beneficiary's qualified higher education expenses.

For tax years after 2018, California conforms to the increased limitation on contributions made by the designated beneficiary of an ABLE account before 2026. This increase was enacted by the federal Tax Cut and Jobs Act of 2017 (P.L. 115-97). (Sec. 17140.4(e), Rev. & Tax. Code)

Distributions.—Distributions from an ABLE account for a tax year are not includible in federal gross income unless they exceed the amount of qualified disability expenses incurred during the tax year. If the distribution is in excess of qualified disability expenses, the amount includible in gross income is the excess amount reduced by an amount in the same ratio as the expenses bear to the distributions.

Qualified disability expenses.—Qualified disability expenses include any expenses related to the blindness or disability of the individual with a disability which are made for the benefit of an individual who is the designated beneficiary. These include expenses for:

— education;

— housing;

— transportation;

— employment training and support;

— assistive technology and personal support services;

— health, prevention and wellness;

— financial management and administrative services;

— legal fees;

— oversight and monitoring; and

— funeral and burial.

[¶15-675] Federal Base--Disaster Relief Payments

California incorporates federal law concerning the following items:

— the exclusion from gross income of insurance payments for living expenses made to a taxpayer whose principal residence is damaged by fire, storm, or other casualty or who is denied access to the residence by government authorities because of such casualty (IRC Sec. 123);

— the exclusion from gross income of any amount received by an individual as a qualified disaster relief payment (IRC Sec. 139). In addition, California treats the 2010 San Bruno explosion and fire as a federally-recognized disaster, even though the disaster was not recognized at the federal level. See ¶16-290 for details.

(Sec. 17131, Rev. & Tax. Code)

A general discussion of California's conformity to federal law is provided at ¶15-515.

[¶15-680] Federal Base--Discharge of Indebtedness

California personal income tax law incorporates federal law (IRC Sec. 108), as of California's current federal conformity date, relating to income from the discharge of indebtedness (Sec. 17131, Rev. & Tax. Code), with certain modifications. California also conforms to IRC Sec. 108(f)(4), which excludes from gross income repayments made under state loan repayment or forgiveness programs that are intended to provide for the increased availability of health care services in underserved or health professional shortage areas. (Sec. 17131, Rev. & Tax. Code; Former Sec. 17134.1 Rev. & Tax. Code)

For tax years after 2018, California generally conforms to the federal treatment of student loan cancellation that are discharged on account of death or total and permanent disability of the student (IRC Sec. 108(f)(5)). Unlike the federal provision enacted by the federal Tax Cut and Jobs Act of 2017 (P.L. 115-97), the exclusion from gross income is permitted indefinitely. (Sec. 17144.8, Rev. & Tax. Code)

California partially conforms to federal law allowing an exclusion from gross income for discharge of an individual's qualified principal residence indebtedness, but addition adjustments are required to account for differences between the California law and federal law. Special rules apply to the discharge of qualified farm indebtedness. (Sec. 17144, Rev. & Tax. Code)

CCH POINTER: *Short sales.*—In a letter issued on September 19, 2013, the IRS had stated that under California Code of Civil Procedure § 580e a taxpayer will not have cancellation of debt (COD) income arising from a short sale of specified property. However, upon further examination the IRS has determined that its initial interpretation was overly broad and has now based its reasoning on a different section of the California Code for its analysis than that relied upon in its previous letter. The IRS has now taken the position that pursuant to California Code of Civil Procedure § 580b(a)(3) a purchase money loan between a lender and a mortgagor is from its inception a nonrecourse loan and, thus, a short sale involving such a loan does not result in cancellation of debt income. Under § 580b(a)(3) a purchase money loan is a loan that is used to pay part or all of the purchase price of an owner-occupied dwelling for not more than four families and that is secured by that property. (*Letter,* Internal Revenue Service, April 29, 2014)

CCH PRACTICE TIP: *Compliance issues for cancellation of debt (COD) income exclusion.*—Taxpayers should make sure that the 1099-Cs and 1099-As are reflecting the proper amount of income. The FTB has found that more than 50% of the taxpayers reporting COD income had received inaccurate information from their lenders on the 1099-Cs. Taxpayers claiming a COD income exclusion must attach federal Form 982, Reduction of Tax Attributes Due to Discharge of Indebtedness, to their California return rather than reporting the income/exclusion on other statements within the return. Similarly, Form 982 must be attached by taxpayers claiming insolvency. Those who claim insolvency must also reduce tax attributes as required by IRC § § 108 and 1017 due to the potential impact of basis in remaining real property holdings. Finally, taxpayers must report COD income, gain, or loss from foreclosed property on the return and include a copy of their federal return, including Form 982 and Section 1082 Basis Adjustment, with their original California tax return. (*Tax News,* California Franchise Tax Board, October 2011)

IRC Sec. 108(i), which allows taxpayers to elect to defer the recognition of cancellation of indebtedness income arising from a qualified reacquisition of certain business debt instruments in 2009 and 2010 that were issued by the taxpayer or a related person, does not apply for California purposes. (Sec. 17144(f), Rev. & Tax. Code) Addition (¶ 16-017) and subtraction (¶ 16-213) adjustments are therefore required.

CCH COMMENT: *Interaction of laws.*—The Franchise Tax Board has released a document clarifying how the California Civil Procedure Code sections interact with IRC Sec. 108, in view of the large number of foreclosures in the state. (*Tax News,* California Franchise Tax Board, February 2010)

Under both California and federal law, an exclusion also applies to the discharge of a student loan (see ¶ 15-685) (including when the borrower is unable to complete a program of study because a school closes or does something wrong). However, because of California's federal conformity date, California does not conform to the federal exclusion from gross income for student loan discharges due to the death or disability of the debtor. The federal provision was enacted by the Tax Cuts and Jobs Act of 2017 (P.L. 115-97) and applies to the discharge of debt income due to the discharge of an eligible loan after 2017 and before 2026. (*2017 Summary of Federal Income Tax Changes*, California Franchise Tax Board, May 16, 2018)

• *Reduction of tax attributes required*

Under IRC Sec. 108(b), a taxpayer who does not elect to reduce the basis of depreciable assets or inventory realty by the amount of a discharged obligation must use the excluded amount of discharged indebtedness to reduce the following seven items ("tax attributes") in the following order:

(1) net operating losses and carryovers;

(2) general business credit carryovers, subject to certain limitations;

(3) the minimum tax credit;

(4) capital losses and carryovers;

(5) the basis of the taxpayer's property;

(6) passive activity loss and credit carryovers; and

(7) foreign tax credit carryovers.

For California tax purposes, foreign tax credit carryovers are not subject to reduction because California does not incorporate federal foreign tax credit provisions. (Sec. 17024.5(b), Rev. & Tax. Code) In addition, rather than the reduction of general business credit carryovers required under federal law, excluded indebtedness must be used to reduce any carryover to or from the discharge year of California personal income tax credits. (Sec. 17144, Rev. & Tax. Code)

Tax attributes other than the general business credit carryovers, the minimum tax credit, passive activity credit carryovers, and, for federal purposes only, foreign tax credit carryovers are reduced one dollar for each dollar of debt discharge excluded. For federal tax purposes, the remaining tax attributes are reduced at the rate of $33^{1}/_{3}¢$ for each dollar excluded. California modifies the federal law to require reduction of only 11.1¢ for each dollar excluded. (Sec. 17144, Rev. & Tax. Code)

Instead of applying excluded amounts against the items listed above, a taxpayer may elect under IRC Sec. 108(b)(5), for both California and federal tax purposes, to apply amounts discharged to reduce the basis of depreciable property (see ¶ 15-710).

• *Discharge of indebtedness of an S corporation*

California incorporates IRC Sec. 108(d)(7)(A), which provides that income from the discharge of indebtedness of an S corporation that is excluded from the corporation's income under IRC Sec. 108(a) is not taken into account as an item of income that flows through to any shareholder. (Sec. 17144, Rev. & Tax. Code)

• *Basis adjustments*

California also follows federal law (IRC Sec. 1017), providing operative rules for adjusting or reducing the basis of property to reflect a discharge of indebtedness when the discharge is excluded from gross income under IRC Sec. 108. (Sec. 18031, Rev. & Tax. Code)

¶15-680

A general discussion of California's conformity to federal law is provided at ¶ 15-515.

• *Forgiven PPP loan amounts*

For tax years beginning on and after January 1, 2020, California follows federal law excluding from income any covered loan amount forgiven pursuant to:

— Section 1106 of the Coronavirus Aid, Relief, and Economic Security (CARES) Act (P.L. 116-136);

— the Paycheck Protection Program and Health Care Enhancement Act (P.L. 116-139); or

— the Paycheck Protection Program Flexibility Act of 2020 (P.L. 116-142).

For California purposes, "covered loan" has the same meaning as in the CARES Act. (Sec. 17131.8, Rev. & Tax. Code)

California will not allow a credit or deduction for any expenses paid for using forgiven PPP funds. Taxpayers must reduce any credit or deduction otherwise allowed for those expenses by the amount of the forgiven loan excluded from income. (Sec. 17131.8, Rev. & Tax. Code)

[¶ 15-682] Federal Base--Domestic Production Activities Deduction

California does not incorporate federal law (IRC Sec. 199) allowing manufacturers to deduct a portion of their domestic production activities income for taxable years beginning before 2018. (Sec. 17201.6, Rev. & Tax. Code) Consequently, taxpayers claiming the deduction on their federal return must make an addition adjustment on their California personal income tax return (see ¶ 16-085).

A general discussion of California's conformity to federal law is provided at ¶ 15-515.

[¶ 15-685] Federal Base--Educational Benefits, Expenses, and Savings Plans

California conforms to federal law as of California's current Internal Revenue Code conformity date, concerning the treatment of the following items:

— discharge of student loans (IRC Sec. 108(f)) (Sec. 17131, Rev. & Tax. Code; Sec. 17134, Rev. & Tax. Code; Sec. 17144.7, Rev. & Tax. Code);

— the exclusion of qualified scholarships and fellowship grants (IRC Sec. 117) (Sec. 17131, Rev. & Tax. Code);

— the exclusion of employer-provided educational assistance benefits for graduate and under graduate level courses (IRC Sec. 127) (Sec. 17151, Rev. & Tax. Code);

— the above-the-line deduction for interest paid on qualified student loans, however an addition adjustment may be required (Sec. 17201, Rev. & Tax. Code, Sec. 17204, Rev. & Tax. Code);

— Coverdell education savings accounts (formerly Education IRAs) (IRC Sec. 530) (Sec. 23712, Rev. & Tax. Code), however California applies a lower penalty rate on nonqualified distributions; and

— except as noted below, qualified tuition programs (IRC Sec. 529) (Sec. 17140.3, Rev. & Tax. Code).

In addition, for taxable years beginning on or after January 1, 2014, California allows an exclusion from gross income for any loan amount repaid by the U.S. Secretary of Education or canceled pursuant to Section 1098e of Title 20 of the U.S. Code (income-based repayment plans). For taxable years beginning on or after January 1, 2017, and before January 1, 2022, the exclusion also applies to any loan amount canceled or repaid by the U.S. Secretary of Education pursuant to Sec. 1087e(e) of Title 20 of the U.S. Code (income contingent repayment plans, pay-as-you-earn repayment plans, and revised pay-as-you-earn repayment plans). (Sec. 17132.11, Rev. & Tax. Code)

• *Additional exclusions for discharge of student loans*

For discharges of indebtedness occurring on or after January 1, 2015, and before January 1, 2020, IRC Sec. 108(f)(1) is modified for California personal income tax purposes to provide an additional exclusion for income that would otherwise result from a forgiven student loan if the taxpayer:

— is granted a discharge of his or her student loan pursuant to the agreement between ECMC Group, Inc., Zenith Education Group, and the Consumer Financial Protection Bureau concerning the purchase of certain assets of Corinthian Colleges, Inc., dated February 2, 2015;

— is granted a discharge of his or her student loan pursuant to federal regulations because (1) the individual could not complete a program of study because the school closed, or (2) the individual successfully asserts that the school did something wrong or failed to do something that it should have done; or

— attended a Corinthian Colleges, Inc., school on or before May 1, 2015, is granted a discharge of any student loan made in connection with attending that school, and that discharge is not excludable from gross income as a result of the reasons listed above.

(Sec. 17144.7, Rev. & Tax. Code)

In addition, IRC Sec. 108(f)(2) is modified to additionally provide that a "student loan" means a student obligation note or other debt evidencing a loan to any individual for the purpose of attending a for-profit higher education company or for the purpose of consolidating or refinancing a loan used to attend a for-profit higher education company, which is either a guaranteed student loan, an educational loan, or a loan eligible for consolidation or refinancing under Part B of Title IV of the Higher Education Act of 1965 (20 U.S.C. Sec. 1071 et seq.). (Sec. 17144.7(b), Rev. & Tax. Code) This modification also applies to discharges of indebtedness occurring on or after January 1, 2015, and before January 1, 2020. (Sec. 17144.7(e), Rev. & Tax. Code)

Furthermore, any loan made pursuant to the Forgivable Loan Program of the California State University is deemed to be a "student loan" within the meaning of IRC Sec. 108(f)(2), and IRC Sec. 108(f)(1) applies to any discharge of the loan that is made in connection with the borrower's performance of services for the California State University. (Sec. 17134, Rev. & Tax. Code)

For tax years after 2018, California generally conforms to the federal treatment of student loan cancellation that are discharged on account of death or total and permanent disability of the student (IRC Sec. 108(f)(5)). Unlike the federal provision enacted by the federal Tax Cut and Jobs Act of 2017 (P.L. 115-97), the exclusion from gross income is permitted indefinitely. (Sec. 17144.8, Rev. & Tax. Code)

• *Contributions to Coverdell education savings account*

As a part of California's 2010 conformity act, California retroactively incorporated federal amendments made to IRC Sec. 530 by the Heroes Earnings Assistance and Relief Tax Act of 2008 (P.L. 110-245), that allow an individual to contribute a military death gratuity or payment under the Servicemembers' Group Life Insurance (SGLI) program to a Coverdell education savings account (Coverdell ESA), notwithstanding the $2,000 annual contribution limit and the income phase-out of the limit that would otherwise apply. The amendments are generally effective for both California federal purposes with respect to deaths from injuries occurring after June 16, 2008, although the amendments also apply to contributions from gratuities or payments made with respect for deaths from injuries occurring after October 6, 2001, and before June 17, 2008, if such contribution is made not later than one year after June 17, 2008. (Sec. 23712(f), Rev. & Tax. Code) Because California did not incorporate these amendments until 2010, taxpayers may have to file amended returns if they contributed more than $2,000 to their Coverdell education savings plans prior to the 2010 tax year.

• *Qualified tuition programs*

California conforms to federal law (IRC Sec. 529), relating to qualified tuition programs, as of the current IRC conformity date. (Sec. 17140.3, Rev. & Tax. Code) Under IRC Sec. 529, taxpayers may invest in either a college savings plan or a prepaid tuition program. Although contributions to the programs are subject to tax, earnings on the accounts set up under these programs are exempt from tax and qualified withdrawals from the accounts are also exempt. However, California does not conform to federal provisions modifying Sec. 529 plans to allow the plans to distribute no more than $10,000 in tuition expenses incurred during the tax year for designated beneficiaries enrolled at a public, private, or religious elementary or secondary school

For tax years after 2018, California conforms to the federal provision enacted by the federal Tax Cut and Jobs Act of 2017 (P.L. 115-97) allowing the rollover of certain amounts from a Sec. 529 plan to an ABLE account without penalty. (Sec. 17140.3, Rev. & Tax. Code) Prior to 2019, an addition adjustment was required on the California return to reconcile differences between federal law and California law.

COMMENT: *EGTRRA amendments made permanent?.*—The Pension Protection Act of 2006 (PPA) (P.L. 109-28) made permanent the amendments enacted by the Economic Growth and Tax Relief and Reconciliation Act (EGTRRA) that affect qualified tuition programs. (Uncodified Sec. 1304 of the PPA) These amendments were originally scheduled to expire at the end of 2010. California incorporates the EGTRRA's sunset date provision "in the same manner and to the same taxable years as it applies for federal income tax purposes." (Sec. 17024.5(a)(2)(B), Rev. & Tax. Code) As the PPA made the sunset provision inapplicable to the EGTRRA amendments that impacted qualified tuition programs, it appears as though California would similarly disregard the sunset provision and make these amendments permanent for California income tax purposes as well.

California's qualified tuition program is the Golden State ScholarShare Trust program. California law, unlike federal law, specifically states that contributions by a for-profit, nonprofit, or state or local governmental entity for the benefit of an owner or employee (or a beneficiary designated by the employee) are included in the gross income of the owner or employee in the year the contribution is made. (Sec. 17140, Rev. & Tax. Code)

[¶15-690] Federal Base--Environmental Expenses and Conservation Payments

California incorporates, as of the current California federal conformity date (see ¶15-515), the federal treatment of the following items:

— the exclusion of cost-share payments received under specified conservation and environmental production programs (IRC Sec. 126) (Sec. 17131, Rev. & Tax. Code) (California also allows a subtraction adjustment (see ¶16-260) for cost-share payments from California agencies);

— the exclusion from a customer's gross income of the value of a subsidy provided (directly or indirectly) by a public utility to a customer for the purchase or installation of an energy conservation measure for a dwelling unit is excluded (IRC Sec. 136) (Sec. 17131, Rev. & Tax. Code); and

— the exclusion from gross income of US. Forest Service payments made as a result of restricting motorized traffic in the Boundary Waters Canoe Area that are reinvested within a two-year period in depreciable property used by the taxpayer in a trade or business (Sec. 1078, Tax Reform Act of 1984) (Sec. 17136, Rev. & Tax. Code)

In addition, like federal law, California excludes from gross income and alternative minimum taxable income federal energy grants provided in lieu of federal energy credits and alternative minimum taxable income of individuals and business. However, the basis of the property purchased with the grant is reduced by 50% of the amount of the grant. (Sec. 17131.3, Rev. & Tax. Code)

CCH PRACTICE TIP: Retroactive application.—Although the exclusion was not enacted until 2010, it applies to any taxable year in which the grant was received, and is thus retroactive in its application. (*Tax News Alert*, California Franchise Tax Board, April 13, 2010)

Addition adjustments (see ¶16-055) are required as a result of California's nonconformity with federal law concerning:

— environmental remediation costs; and

— environmental protection agency sulfur regulation compliance costs.

However, California has its own deduction for EPA or California Air Regulation Board sulfur regulation compliance costs (see ¶16-260). Alternatively, taxpayers may claim a credit for such costs.

Amortization of reforestation expenses.—California incorporates federal law (IRC Sec. 194) as of California's current federal conformity date (see ¶15-515), relating to the amortization of reforestation expenses, with one modification. Under Sec. 194, as incorporated, a taxpayer may elect to amortize up to $10,000 of expenditures that relate to the reforestation or forestation of qualified timber property.

However, California limits the deduction to expenses associated with qualified timber property located in California (see ¶16-055). (Sec. 17278.5, Rev. & Tax. Code)

A general discussion of California's conformity to federal law is provided at ¶15-515.

[¶15-695] Federal Base--Exempt Income Expenses

Although California mirrors federal law (IRC Sec. 265), which denies deductions for expenses and interest relating to tax-exempt income, because the same items of income are not exempt under both California and federal law, interest and expenses denied under federal law may be allowed for California personal income tax purposes, and expenses allowed under federal law may not be allowed for California personal income tax purposes. Consequently, addition and subtraction adjustments may be required (see ¶16-110 and ¶16-315, respectively). (Sec. 17280, Rev. & Tax. Code)

A general discussion of California's conformity to federal law is provided at ¶15-515.

[¶15-700] Federal Base--Foreign Source Income and Expenses

California incorporates federal law (IRC Sec. 893), which excludes from gross income a foreign government employee's compensation provided certain conditions are satisfied. (Sec. 17146, Rev. & Tax. Code) With the exception of the sourcing rules, California also incorporates federal law (IRC Sec. 988), concerning the tax treatment of certain foreign currency transactions. (Sec. 17078, Rev. & Tax. Code) Under IRC Sec. 988, a foreign currency gain or loss attributable to a "Sec. 988 transaction" receives separate treatment from that given to gain or loss on the underlying transaction, and is taxable as ordinary gain or loss.

However, addition or subtraction adjustments may be required for income exempt under foreign treaties and for foreign income received by nonresident aliens (see ¶16-060 and ¶16-263, respectively).

A general discussion of California's conformity to federal law is provided at ¶15-515.

[¶15-705] Federal Base--Fringe Benefits

California incorporates federal law concerning the exclusion from an employee's gross income of specified employer-provided fringe benefits (IRC Sec. 132) as of California's current federal conformity date (see ¶15-515), but has not conformed to federal amendments that expand the definition of a qualified child as applies to many of these benefits, thereby addition adjustments may be required (see ¶16-065). Specifically, California excludes the following from an employee's gross income:

— accident and health benefits provided under employer-financed plans, including amounts paid under qualified long-term care insurance contracts (IRC Sec. 105, IRC Sec. 7702B) (Sec. 17131, Rev. & Tax. Code; Sec. 17020.6, Rev. & Tax. Code);

— de minimis fringes (IRC Sec. 132);

— coverage under an accident or health plan (IRC Sec. 106) (Sec. 17131, Rev. & Tax Code);

— meals and lodging provided to an employee for the convenience of the employer (IRC Sec. 119);

— contributions to, and benefits received under a cafeteria plan (IRC Sec. 125);

— dependent care assistance (IRC Sec. 129);

— employer-provided qualified retirement planning services (IRC Sec. 132);

— moving expense reimbursements (IRC Sec. 132);

— no-additional cost services (IRC Sec. 132);

— qualified employee discounts (IRC Sec. 132);

— qualified transportation fringe benefits (IRC Sec. 132) (although California allows additional benefits (see ¶ 16-265)); and

— working condition fringes (IRC Sec. 132).

(Sec. 17131, Rev. & Tax Code)

Addition adjustments are required for employer contributions to health savings accounts as well as for health insurance costs (see ¶ 16-100). Subtraction adjustments are required for sick-pay benefits paid to railroad employees (see ¶ 16-265). Subtraction adjustments are available for health and health-related benefits provided to registered domestic partners and same-sex married couples (see ¶ 15-705 and ¶ 16-265).

Because of California's federal conformity date, California does not conform to the federal suspension for tax years 2018 through 2025 of the exclusion from gross income for (a) qualified moving expense reimbursements, except in the case of a member of the U.S. Armed Forces on active duty who moves pursuant to a military order, and (b) qualified bicycle commuting reimbursements. (*2017 Summary of Federal Income Tax Changes*, California Franchise Tax Board, May 16, 2018)

A general discussion of California's conformity to federal law is provided at ¶ 15-515.

[¶ 15-710] Federal Base--Gains

California follows federal law (IRC Sec. 1001—1092) as of California's current federal conformity date (see ¶ 15-515), concerning the treatment of gains and losses on the disposition of property and capital gains and losses (see ¶ 15-620). (Sec. 18031, Rev. & Tax. Code) Under both California and federal law (IRC Sec. 1001) gain or loss on the sale or other disposition of property is the generally the difference between the amount realized and the adjusted basis. However, differences may arise between the amount of gain or loss recognized for California and federal purposes as a result of differences in a property's adjusted basis for federal and California income tax purposes (see ¶ 16-020).

Special federal rules that California incorporates govern the following areas:

— basis adjustments (IRC Sec. 1016), however California law makes additional adjustments (see ¶ 16-020);

— basis of property acquired from a decedent for deaths occurring after 1984 (Sec. 18031, Rev. & Tax. Code);

— like-kind exchanges (IRC Sec. 1031 and IRC Sec. 1035), although adjustments may be required in like-kind exchanges involving long-term care insurance contracts. In addition, California law, unlike federal law, has an information return reporting requirement if the replacement property is purchased outside California (see ¶ 89-104). For tax years beginning after 2018, and for exchanges completed after January 10, 2019, California will generally conform to the TCJA amendments to IRC Sec. 1031 limiting nonrecognition of gain or loss on like-kind exchanges to real property. However, the conformity provision only applies to individuals with adjusted gross incomes of over $250,000, for single filers and $500,000, for joint filers (Sec. 18031.5, Rev. & Tax. Code);

— involuntary conversions (IRC Sec. 1033), although subtraction and addition adjustments may be required in transactions involving San Bruno explosion and fire victims, outdoor advertising displays, and Hurricane Katrina victims (see ¶ 16-070 and 16-270);

— nonrecognition of gain on sales of qualified securities to an employee stock ownership plan (ESOP) or to an eligible worker-owned cooperative (IRC Sec. 1042), however an adjustment may be required because California does not incorporate the federal provision relating to the sale of stock of a qualified agricultural refiner or processor (see ¶ 16-070) (Sec. 18042, Rev. & Tax. Code);

— rollover of publicly traded securities gain into specialized small business investment companies (SSBICs) (IRC Sec. 1044) for sales prior to 2018. Because the federal election to roll over tax-free capital gain realized on the sale of publicly-traded securities not apply for California purposes to any taxable year in which those provisions are inapplicable for federal purposes, California effectively conforms to the federal repeal of the rollover election provision for sales after December 31, 2017. (Sec. 18044, Rev. & Tax. Code; *2017 Summary of Federal Income Tax Changes*, California Franchise Tax Board, May 16, 2018)

— wash sales of stock or securities (IRC Sec. 1091);

— limitation of straddle losses (IRC Sec. 1092);

— nonrecognition of gain or loss on transfers of property to a corporation solely in exchange for stock if the transferors are in control after the exchange (IRC Sec. 351) (Sec. 17321, Rev. & Tax. Code);

— nonrecognition of gain in stock and securities sales and exchanges involved in corporate reorganizations and spin-offs, split-offs, and split-ups (IRC Sec. 351, IRC Sec. 354, IRC Sec. 355) (Sec. 17321, Rev. & Tax. Code);

— basis of property to distributees in tax-free exchange (IRC Sec. 358).

(Sec. 18031, Rev. & Tax. Code)

CCH POINTER: *Common audit issues involving like-kind exchanges.*—One of the FTB's top audit issues continues to be like-kind exchanges. The FTB has identified the following most common audit issues involving like kind exchanges:

— taxpayer fails to source gains to California upon disposition of replacement property received in a California deferred exchange when the replacement property was not located in California;

— taxpayer receives other property (boot) in the exchange but does not report the boot on its return;

— taxpayers do not meet identification or other technical requirements of IRC § 1031;

— relinquished and/or replacement property are not held for investment or for productive use in a trade or business (i.e., property is used for personal purposes or is held primarily for sale); and

— the taxpayer who transfers relinquished property is a different taxpayer than the party who acquires replacement property.

The FTB continues to review certain "drop and swap" or "swap and drop" transactions. Where the form does not support the economic realities or substance of the transaction, the FTB will recharacterize the taxpayer's transaction as appropriate.

The State Board of Equalization has upheld the FTB's recharacterization of transactions involving 1031 exchanges in the following appeals:

— Appeal of Aries, No. 464475 (swap and drop);

— Appeal of Marcil, No. 458832 (different taxpayer acquired replacement property, rehearing granted); and

— Appeal of Brief, Appeal No. 5308782 (deemed contribution to a partnership).

(*Tax News*, Franchise Tax Board, January 2012)

PRACTICE NOTE: *Impact of filing extension on technical requirements for like-kind exchange.*—IRC Sec. 1031(a)(3)(B) requires that property received by a taxpayer be treated as property that is not like-kind property if the property is received after the earlier of 180 days from the transfer of the relinquished property or the due date (determined with regard to extensions) of the taxpayer's federal tax return. Thus, the federal extended due date should be used in determining whether the property is disqualified under IRC Sec. 1031(a)(3)(B). California incorporates the provisions of IRC Sec. 1031 by reference in Rev. and Tax. Code Sec. 24941, including the provisions of IRC Sec. 1031(a)(3)(B). Thus, California will follow the federal treatment, regardless of whether or not the California return was filed under extension. Specifically, the federal extended due date should be used in determining whether the property is disqualified for like-kind treatment. (*Tax News*, Franchise Tax Board, October 2012)

Because of California's current federal conformity date (see ¶ 15-515), California has not conformed to the federal provision (IRC Sec. 1061) recharacterizing certain gains in the case of partnership profits interests held in connection with the performance of investment services for taxable years beginning after December 31, 2017. (*2017 Summary of Federal Income Tax Changes*, California Franchise Tax Board, May 16, 2018)

• *Rollover of gain from sale of small business stock sale*

California law mirrors with modifications, rather than incorporates, federal law (IRC Sec. 1045), concerning the rollover of gain from the sale of small business stock sold prior to 2013. (Sec. 18038.5, Rev. & Tax. Code; Sec. 18038.4, Rev. & Tax. Code) Gain from such a sale is recognized only to the extent that the amount realized on the sale exceeds the cost of the replacement small business stock, as reduced by any portion of the cost previously taken into account.

The California definition of "qualified small business stock" is the same as that used for purposes of the 50% exclusion for gain on the sale of qualified small business stock (see ¶ 15-620) (Sec. 18038.5, Rev. & Tax. Code)

¶15-710

> *PRACTICE NOTE:* One requirement for deferring recognition of gain from the sale of qualified small business stock is that the taxpayer must replace the qualified small business stock within 60 days of the sale of the relinquished stock. For transactions on or after August 14, 2007, a taxpayer may use a partnership other than the one selling the qualified small business stock to acquire the replacement stock, and an individual may use a partnership to acquire replacement stock on his or her behalf. This position is based on final federal Reg. 1.1045-1, which took effect August 14, 2007, clarifying some issues regarding partnerships and qualified small business stock. For transactions prior to August 14, 2007, a taxpayer could not use a partnership other than the one selling the qualified small business stock to acquire the replacement stock, and an individual could not use a partnership to acquire replacement stock on his or her behalf. This FTB position was based on proposed federal Reg. 150562-03 concerning the application of IRC Sec. 1045 to partnerships and their partners. (*Tax News*, California Franchise Tax Board, October 2007)

• *Determining fair market value of property subject to nonrecourse indebtedness*

California incorporates federal law (IRC Sec. 7701(g)), which provides that in the calculation of gain or loss (or deemed gain or loss) with respect to any property, whenever it is necessary to determine the fair market value of any property that is subject to nonrecourse indebtedness, the fair market value of the property cannot be less than the amount of the nonrecourse indebtedness. (Sec. 17020.5, Rev. & Tax. Code)

• *Sale of primary residence*

California incorporates federal law (IRC Sec. 121), as of California's current federal conformity date (see ¶ 15-515), concerning the exclusion of gain from the sale of a personal residence. (Sec. 17131, Rev. & Tax. Code; Sec. 17152, Rev. & Tax. Code) Under both California and federal law, an individual taxpayer may exclude up to $250,000 ($500,000 for married taxpayers filing jointly) of gain realized on the sale or exchange of his or her residence if the taxpayer owned and occupied the residence as a principal residence for an aggregate period of at least two of the five years prior to the sale or exchange. (Sec. 17152, Rev. & Tax. Code)

Under both California and federal law, uniformed or foreign service personnel called to active duty away from home may elect to suspend the five-year test period for a period of up to ten years. A federal election, or lack thereof, is binding for California purposes. (Sec. 17152(e), Rev. & Tax. Code)

However, California does not incorporate IRC Sec. 121(d)(11), which extends the principal residence exclusion to a decedent's principal residence that is sold by the estate, an heir, or a qualified revocable trust, applicable to decedents dying after 2009. (Sec. 17152(f), Rev. & Tax. Code)

An addition (see ¶ 16-070) or subtraction (see ¶ 16-270) adjustment may be required as a result of California's nonconformity to federal amendments until the 2010 tax year as well as California's special treatment of Peace Corps volunteers.

• *Basis of property acquired from a decedent*

Although California generally follows federal law (IRC Sec. 1014), concerning basis of property of a decedent for decedents who die after 1984, the basis rules for property acquired from a decedent are very complex, and the basis value is dependent on the date of death and whether the property was separate property, community property, or joint tenancy. FTB Pub. 1039, Basis of Property Decedent and Surviving Spouse provides a detailed explanation of how to compute the basis of property of a decedent and surviving spouse.

For taxable years beginning after 1986, California incorporates by reference the provisions of IRC Sec. 1014(b)(6) and (7) concerning the basis of community property acquired from a decedent. (Sec. 18031, Rev. & Tax. Code) However, California does not incorporate federal provisions that replace the stepped-up basis rules of IRC Sec. 1014 with carryover basis rules under IRC Sec. 1022 beginning in 2010. (Sec. 18035.6, Rev. & Tax Code; Sec. 18036.6, Rev. & Tax. Code)

• *Basis of property acquired by gift or transfer in trust*

California incorporates federal law (IRC Sec. 1015) as of California's current federal conformity date (see ¶ 15-515), concerning the basis of property acquired by gifts or transfers in trust. (Sec. 18031, Rev. & Tax. Code) Under IRC Sec. 1015(a), and for property acquired by gift after 1920, the basis for gain is generally the donor's basis, and the basis for loss is the lesser of the donor's basis or the fair market value at the time of the gift.

The basis of property acquired by gift must be adjusted for the amount of federal gift tax paid (IRC Sec. 1015(d)), as incorporated by California). For California purposes, if the gift is acquired in a tax year beginning on or after January 1, 1985, then, under IRC Sec. 1015(d)(6) as incorporated, the increase in basis is equal to the amount of gift tax multiplied by the ratio of the net appreciation in value to the total value of the gift. Net appreciation in value is the excess of fair market value over adjusted basis immediately before the gift. The same adjustment must be made for federal purposes if the gift is acquired after 1976. For gifts received in tax years beginning prior to 1985, California requires that the full amount of gift tax paid be added to the basis of the gift (former Sec. 18034). The same adjustment applies for federal purposes if the gift is acquired prior to 1977. (IRC Sec. 1015(d)(1))

• *Effective date differences*

IRC Sec. 1033 amendments.—Although California currently incorporates federal provisions that (1) ease the involuntary conversion rules for livestock sold on account of weather-related conditions and expand the replacement period in such situations from two years to four years, and (2) allow the Secretary to extend on a regional basis the replacement period if the weather-related conditions continue for more than 3 years, different effective dates apply. These provisions are applicable for California purposes beginning with the 2005 taxable year (Sec. 17024.5, Rev. & Tax. Code), and are effective for federal purposes in any tax year with respect to which the original due date for the return is after 2002.

IRC Sec. 1091 amendments.—Although California incorporates IRC Sec. 1091, as of California's current federal conformity date (see ¶ 15-515), which disallows losses on stock or securities that are replaced with substantially identical stock or securities within 30 days before or after a sale (a 61-day period) unless specified exceptions apply (Sec. 18031, Rev. & Tax. Code), different effective dates apply concerning federal amendments to the provision. Under an amendment made to IRC Sec. 1091 by the Community Renewal Tax Relief Act of 2000, the wash sale rule applies to a contract, or an option to acquire such property, even though the contract or option is, or could be, settled in cash or property other than stock or securities. The amendment is effective for federal purposes on December 21, 2000, and applies for California purposes in taxable years beginning after 2001. (Sec. 17024.5, Rev. & Tax. Code)

¶15-710

IRC Sec. 1092 amendments.—Although California incorporates IRC Sec. 1092, as of California's current federal conformity date (see ¶15-515), which provides rules relating to the recognition of gain or loss on transactions involving straddles, different effective dates for amendments to the provision apply. (Sec. 18031, Rev. & Tax. Code) A "straddle" means offsetting positions with respect to personal property. Straddle rules deal with "contracts," "options," or "rights" involving possible price fluctuations as the result of future events and a taxpayer's attempts to reduce the risk of loss on such investments. California has not incorporated amendments made to IRC Sec. 1092 by the Tax Technical Corrections Act of 2007 (P.L. that amended the basis adjustment provisions of the straddle rules effective for federal purposes after October 21, 2004, and the straddle identification rules, effective for federal purposes to straddles acquired after December 29, 2007.

Under both California and federal law, the following types of stock are considered personal property and part of a straddle: (1) stock of a corporation formed or utilized to take positions in personal property that offset positions taken by any of its shareholders; and (2) any stock if at least one of the offsetting positions is either:

— (a) an option with respect to such stock or substantially identical stock or securities,

— (b) a position with respect to substantially similar or related property other than stock, or

— (c) a securities futures contract with respect to such stock or substantially identical stock or securities.

The category of personal property in (2)(c) above was added by the Community Renewal Tax Relief Act of 2000, effective for federal purposes on December 21, 2000, and applicable for California purposes in taxable years beginning after 2001. (Sec. 17024.5, Rev. & Tax. Code)

Additional amendments made to IRC Sec. 1092 by the American Jobs Creation Act of 2004 (P.L. 108 -37), are applicable for California purposes beginning with the 2005 taxable year (Sec. 17024.5, Rev. & Tax. Code), and effective for federal purposes for positions established after October 21, 2004.

AJCA amendments to IRC Sec. 351 et seq.—Although California incorporates an amendment made by the AJCA that clarifies the definition of nonqualified preferred stock, the amendment applies for California purposes beginning with the 2005 taxable year (Sec. 17024.5, Rev. & Tax. Code) and is effective for federal purposes for transactions after May 14, 2003.

Other amendments made by the AJCA to IRC Sec. 362 limit the transfer or importation of built-in losses in tax-free transactions. The amendment applies for California purposes beginning with the 2005 taxable year (Sec. 17024.5, Rev. & Tax. Code), and to transactions after October 22, 2005, for federal purposes.

IRC Sec. 362(d) amendment.—Although California incorporates an amendment made by the Miscellaneous Trade and Technical Corrections Act (MTTCA) of 1999, which enacted IRC Sec. 362(d), the amendment applies for federal purposes to transfers after October 18, 1998, and for California purposes to transfers after 2001. (Sec. 68, Ch. 35 (A.B. 1122), Laws 2002) Under IRC Sec. 358(d), for purposes of determining the basis of property received in tax free exchanges or distributions, the assumption of a taxpayer's liability by another party to the exchange as part of the consideration paid for the exchange is treated as money received by the taxpayer on the exchange. The MTTCA modified IRC Sec. 358(d) by excluding the acquisition of property from a taxpayer subject to a liability from this assumption of liability treatment.

IRC Sec. 358 amendment.—Under IRC Sec. 358(h), as enacted by the Community Renewal Tax Relief Act (CRTRA) of 2000, if the basis of the stock received by the transferor as part of a tax-free exchange with a controlled corporation exceeds the fair market value of the stock, then the basis of the stock received is reduced, but not below fair market value, by any liability that is assumed in exchange for the stock and that did not otherwise reduce the company's basis by reason of the assumption. IRC Sec. 358(h) applies for federal purposes to assumptions of liability after October 18, 1999. California incorporates this provision for taxable years beginning after 2001. (Sec. 17024.5, Rev. & Tax. Code) An amendment made to IRC Sec. 358(h) by the Job Creation Worker Assistance Act of 2002, which California incorporates, clarifies that this provision only applies to the amount of any liability that is assumed by another person (i.e., a party other than the person transferring the property in exchange for stock). This amendment is effective as if included in IRC Sec. 358(h) as enacted by the CRTRA.

[¶15-715] Federal Base--Gifts and Inheritances

California incorporates federal law (IRC Sec. 102), concerning the tax treatment of gifts and inheritances, as of California's current federal conformity date (see ¶15-515). (Sec. 17131, Rev. & Tax. Code) Under both California and federal law, the value of property received as a gift, bequest, devise, or inheritance is excludable from gross income. However, income from property received as a gift, bequest, devise, or inheritance must be included in gross income.

A general discussion of California's conformity to federal law is provided at ¶15-515.

[¶15-720] Federal Base--Interest

Except as noted below, California conforms to federal law concerning the treatment of the interest expense deduction, interest on government obligations, and amortization of bond premiums.

• *Interest expenses*

California incorporates federal law (IRC Sec. 163), as of California's current federal conformity date (see ¶15-515), relating to the deduction of interest expense (Sec. 17201, Rev. & Tax. Code) with certain modifications. Although the general rule of IRC Sec. 163(a) is that interest paid or accrued during a taxable year is allowed as a deduction, IRC Sec. 163(h) disallows all deductions for personal interest. Special rules apply for deducting "qualified residence interest," investment interest, redeemable ground rents, and original issue discount.

If interest that is otherwise deductible under IRC Sec. 163 is a business expense, it is deductible from gross income. If the interest is incurred other than as a business expense, it is an itemized deduction from adjusted gross income; in that case, the interest deduction under IRC Sec. 163 is not one of the miscellaneous itemized deductions that are allowable only to the extent that, when aggregated, they exceed 2% of adjusted gross income. However, an itemized interest expense deduction is subject to the 6% overall limitation for high-income taxpayers (see ¶15-545).

Adjustments.—Addition or subtraction adjustments may be taken for investment interest, original issue discount for debt instruments issued (and loans made) in 1985 and 1986, payments made to the California Housing Finance Agency by first-time homeowners, interest on income exempt from California taxation, and private mortgage insurance treated as deductible interest on a federal return (see ¶ 16-075 and ¶ 16-280, respectively).

Also, adjustments may be required because California has not conformed to federal amendments made by the Tax Cuts and Jobs Act of 2017 that:

— limit deductions of business interest for taxable years beginning after December 31, 2017; and

— limit the itemized deduction for home mortgage interest, suspend the deduction of interest on home equity debt, and reduce the maximum amount that may be treated as acquisition debt for tax years 2018 through 2025.

(*2017 Summary of Federal Income Tax Changes*, California Franchise Tax Board, May 16, 2018)

• *Exclusion of interest on government obligations*

California does not incorporate by reference IRC Sec. 103 and IRC Sec. 141—IRC Sec. 150, which provide federal exclusions of interest earned on state and local bonds (Sec. 17143, Rev. & Tax. Code) Instead, California excludes from gross income interest on bonds issued by California or local governments within California (Sec. 26(b), Art. XIII, Cal. Const.) and interest on bonds and other obligations issued by the United States or its territories. California allows a subtraction adjustment for federal obligation interest and specified California bond interest and requires an addition adjustment for non-California state and local bond interest (see ¶ 16-280 and ¶ 16-075, respectively).

Because California state and local bond interest is generally excludable from federal taxable income, no adjustment is generally required for interest income on California state and local bonds. However, a subtraction modification may be allowed for certain California bond interest included in federal taxable income (see ¶ 16-280). The determination of whether a bond is issued by California or by a local government in California must be made without regard to (1) the source of payment of the bond or the security for the bond, whether public or private, and (2) whether public improvements are financed by the bond. (Sec. 17133, Rev. & Tax. Code)

The California State Board of Equalization has ruled that a promissory note issued by a California municipality constitutes a "bond", excludable from California taxable income. (*Odenheimer*, SBE, 64-SBE-064, June 29, 1964) The California Attorney General has also issued opinions that interest from bond anticipation notes and interest on improvement district warrants are excludable from California personal income tax. (*Opinion of the Attorney General, No. 53/169*, January 28, 1954, 23 Ops Cal Atty Gen 59; *Opinion of the Attorney General, No. 63/182*, November 13, 1963, 42 Ops Cal Atty Gen 133)

• *Amortization of bond premium*

California incorporates federal law (IRC Sec. 171) as of California's current federal conformity date (see ¶ 15-515), relating to the deduction of amortized bond premium. (Sec. 17201, Rev. & Tax. Code) Under IRC Sec. 171 as incorporated, a taxpayer who acquires a bond bearing tax-exempt interest is required to amortize the bond premium but may not deduct the amortizable premium, in figuring taxable income. If the taxpayer acquires taxable bonds, he or she has the option of amortizing the premium. If the election is made to amortize the bond premium paid for a taxable bond, the amount of the amortizable bond premium for the taxable year is allowed as a deduction. Under IRC Sec. 171(e), providing that for obligations acquired after

October 22, 1986, the deduction for an amortizable bond premium must be treated as interest, except as otherwise provided by regulations. Thus, for example, a bond premium is treated as interest for purposes of applying the investment interest limitations of IRC Sec. 163(d).

A general discussion of California's conformity to federal law is provided at ¶ 15-515.

[¶ 15-725] Federal Base--Inventory Costs

California follows the federal treatment of inventories.

A general discussion of California's conformity to federal law is provided at ¶ 15-515.

[¶ 15-730] Federal Base--Investment Expenses

California incorporates federal law (IRC Sec. 212), relating to the deduction of expenses for the production of income (Sec. 17201, Rev. & Tax. Code) without modification. IRC Sec. 212, as incorporated, provides that a taxpayer may take a deduction for ordinary and necessary expenses incurred for

— the production and collection of income,

— the management and maintenance of income-producing property, or

— in connection with the determination, collection, or refund of any tax.

CCH PRACTICE TIP: Tax payment credit and debit card convenience fees.— California conforms to the IRS conclusion that a deduction may be claimed for credit card fees paid in connection with the payment of federal income taxes. Consequently, taxpayers that claim these credit card fees on their federal return and report their itemized deductions for California purposes do not need to make an adjustment on Schedule CA. The recent IRS conclusion also applies to credit card fees paid in connection with the payment of state income taxes. (*Tax News*, California Franchise Tax Board, March 2010)

However, California applies a modified federal passive activity loss limitations for real estate rental activities (see ¶ 16-095).

In line with federal law, the California State Board of Equalization (SBE) frequently looks to the taxpayer's intent in determining whether an expense is incurred "for the production of income;" if a profit motive is established, the expense is deductible (*Newland*, SBE, 75-SBE-068, September 17, 1975). The SBE looks to factors such as investigation of profit potential, and personal use of the property (*Sherbondy*, SBE, 79-SBE-081, April 10, 1979).

• *2% floor on miscellaneous itemized deductions*

The 2% floor on miscellaneous itemized deductions (see ¶ 15-545) generally applies to deductions claimed under IRC Sec. 212. Under federal law, taxpayers are entitled to miscellaneous itemized deductions only to the extent that the aggregate amount of those deductions exceeds 2% of the taxpayer's adjusted gross income. However, deductions attributable to property held for the production of rents and royalties are deductible from gross income in arriving at adjusted gross income and thus are not subject to the 2% floor.

Expenses related to investment income or property (such as investment counsel fees), as well as tax return preparation costs and related expenditures under IRC Sec. 212(3), are subject to the 2% floor and the overall limitation on itemized deductions for high-income taxpayers.

A general discussion of California's conformity to federal law is provided at ¶ 15-515.

[¶ 15-735] Federal Base--Items Related to Federal Deductions or Credits

California incorporates federal law (IRC Sec. 280C) that disallows a deduction for that portion of the qualified clinical testing expenses otherwise available as a deduction that is equal to the amount of the clinical testing tax credit allowed under IRC Sec. 28. California also incorporates the IRC Sec. 280C provision that disallows a deduction for that portion of qualified research expenses or basic research expenses that equals the amount of the credit allowed for such expenses under IRC Sec. 41 (which California incorporates with modifications). (Sec. 17201, Rev. & Tax. Code) However, a subtraction adjustment is allowed for wage and benefit expenses disallowed as a result of a taxpayer claiming federal employment credits and for other expenses for which a federal credit is claimed (see ¶ 16-290).

California does not conform to the federal 20% deduction for "qualified business income" from a pass-through entity (see IRC Sec. 199A). (2017 Summary of Federal Income Tax Changes, California Franchise Tax Board, May 16, 2018)

A general discussion of California's conformity to federal law is provided at ¶ 15-515.

[¶ 15-740] Federal Base--Lessee Expenses

California incorporates federal law IRC Sec. 109, concerning improvements made by a lessee, as of the California's current federal conformity date (see ¶ 15-515). (Sec. 17131, Rev. & Tax. Code) IRC Sec. 109 allows lessors of real property an exclusion from gross income for the income, other than rent, that is derived by reason of the acquisition, upon termination of a lease, of buildings or other improvements made by a lessee. California also follows federal law (IRC Sec. 1019), prohibiting the lessor from adjusting the basis in the property for improvements for which the lessor claimed the exclusion. (Sec. 18031, Rev. & Tax. Code)

In addition California incorporates IRC Sec. 110, which allows a retail tenant to exclude from gross income cash or rent reductions received from the lessor of the retail space if the cash or rent reduction is used for qualified construction or improvement to the space. (Sec. 17131, Rev. & Tax. Code) California does not allow the federal shortened recovery period for depreciation of qualified leasehold improvements (see ¶ 16-040).

A general discussion of California's conformity to federal law is provided at ¶ 15-515.

[¶ 15-745] Federal Base--Losses

In addition to the federal provisions governing gain and losses, including trade and business losses, and capital gains and losses (see ¶ 15-710 and ¶ 15-620, respectively), California incorporates federal law (IRC Sec. 165) as of California's current federal conformity date (see ¶ 15-515), relating to the deduction of losses. (Sec. 17201, Rev. & Tax. Code) Although California does not incorporate the expanded federal casualty loss deduction available for federal disasters (see ¶16-095), California provides its own expanded disaster loss deduction (see ¶16-300).

Because of California's current federal conformity date (see ¶15-515), California does not conform to a federal provision enacted by the Tax Cuts and Jobs Act of 2017 indicating for tax years 2018 through 2025 that the limitation on losses from wagering transactions applies not only to the actual costs of wagers incurred by an individual, but also to other expenses incurred by the individual in connection with the conduct of that individual's gambling activity (for instance, an individual's otherwise deductible expenses in traveling to or from a casino). (*2017 Summary of Federal Income Tax Changes*, California Franchise Tax Board, May 16, 2018)

• *Limitation of deductions to amount at risk*

California incorporates federal law (IRC Sec. 465) as amended as of California's current federal conformity date (see ¶15-515) to limit the deduction of losses from activities that are part of any trade or business, or for the production of income, to the amount at risk. (Sec. 17551, Rev. & Tax. Code) California makes no modification to the federal provision, except that references in IRC Sec. 465 to personal holding companies are inapplicable for California purposes. (Sec. 17024.5(b)(3), Rev. & Tax. Code)

• *Passive activity losses and credits*

California incorporates IRC Sec. 469, as of California's current federal conformity date (see ¶15-515), concerning passive activity losses and credits, with the modifications discussed below. (Sec. 17551, Rev. & Tax. Code; Sec. 17561, Rev. and Tax Code) IRC Sec. 469 limits the deductibility of losses from passive trade or business activities to the amount of income derived from such activities.

Publicly traded partnerships.—Publicly traded partnerships that are not treated as corporations are required to apply the passive loss rules of IRC Sec. 469 separately for the items attributable to each publicly traded partnership. (Sec. 17561, Rev. and Tax Code)

Rental real estate activities.—Under IRC Sec. 469 as incorporated and modified by California, passive losses from rental real estate are deductible from nonpassive income only if a taxpayer actively participates in a rental real estate activity of which that person is at least a 10% owner. However, California still treats such losses as passive losses, subject to the passive loss limitations. Consequently, an addition adjustment may be required (see ¶16-095). Additional adjustments may be required for taxpayers claiming the low-income housing credit. (Sec. 17561, Rev. and Tax Code)

Carryovers.—California modifies IRC Sec. 469(d)(2), concerning passive activity credits that may be carried over, to refer to the following California credits:

— the credit for research expenses;

— the low-income housing credit;

— the former targeted jobs credit (former Sec. 17053.7, Rev. and Tax. Code); and

— the former credit for clinical testing expenses (former Sec. 17057, Rev. and Tax. Code).

(Sec. 17561, Rev. and Tax Code)

¶15-745

Filing requirements—Forms.—Form FTB 3801, Passive Activity Loss Limitations, is used to determine the amount of any passive activity loss allowed and the adjustments required to be made to account for differences between California passive activity losses and federal passive activity losses for the current taxable year. Form FTB 3801-CR, Passive Activity Credit Limitations, is used to determine the amount of any passive activity credit allowed for the current taxable year.

• *Tax-exempt use loss limitation*

Although California incorporates IRC Sec. 470, which places limits on the amount of deductions that may be claimed for property leased to tax exempt entities, different effective dates apply. The provision is applicable for California purposes beginning with the 2005 taxable year, and is effective for federal purposes to leases entered into after March 12, 2004.

A general discussion of California's conformity to federal law is provided at ¶ 15-515.

[¶ 15-755] Federal Base--Medical Expenses and Savings Accounts

California incorporates federal law (IRC Sec. 213), relating to the deduction for medical expenses (including travel and mileage expenses), as of California's current IRC conformity date(see ¶ 15-515). However, California has not incorporated the increase from 7.5% to 10% in the adjusted gross income floor that applies for federal tax purposes beginning with the 2013 tax year (temporarily reduced back to 7.5% for federal purposes for the 2017 and 2018 tax years). To be deductible, the medical expenses must be paid during the taxable year (and not compensated for by insurance or otherwise) for medical care of the taxpayer, his or her spouse, or a dependent. (Sec. 17201, Rev. & Tax. Code; Sec. 17241, Rev. & Tax. Code; *Preliminary Report on Specific Provisions of the Federal Tax Cuts and Jobs Act*, California Franchise Tax Board, March 20, 2018) However, California law, unlike federal law, allows taxpayers to claim a deduction for medical expenses paid or on behalf of a registered domestic partner. The adjusted gross income used for this purpose is that on the federal income tax return for the same taxable year, and not that on the California return. (Sec. 17024.5(h), Rev. & Tax. Code)

PRACTICE NOTE: Employer-provided accident and health insurance plan reimbursements.—California also conforms to federal amendments extending the exclusion for employer-provided accident and health insurance plan reimbursements (IRC Sec. 105) to reimbursements for expenses incurred on or after March 30, 2010, for medical care for any child of the employee who is under age 27 at the end of the tax year, even if the child is not a dependent. (Sec. 17131, Rev. & Tax. Code; Former Sec. 17131.7, Rev. & Tax. Code) (*California Excludes From Taxes Health Care Coverage for Adult Children Up to Age 27*, California Franchise Tax Board, April 12, 2011)

Under both California and federal law, the deduction of medical expenses under IRC Sec. 213 is not subject to the 2% floor imposed on certain itemized deductions or the overall limitation on itemized deductions for high-income taxpayers (see ¶ 15-545).

• *Medical savings accounts*

Generally, California incorporates federal law concerning the tax treatment of medical savings accounts, otherwise known as Archer MSAs (IRC Sec. 220) as of California's current IRC conformity date(see, ¶ 15-515). The amount allowed as a deduction for California purposes is equal to the amount allowed as a deduction under IRC Sec. 220 on the federal income tax return filed by the individual for the same tax year. (Sec. 17201, Rev. & Tax. Code; Sec. 17215, Rev. & Tax Code)

Penalty on nonqualified withdrawal.—Although California follows the federal provisions applicable to nonqualified withdrawals from MSAs, the amount of the penalty is 10% (increased to 12.5% for disbursements made during taxable years beginning on or after January 1, 2016) for California personal income tax purposes, rather than the 20% imposed at the federal level. (Sec. 17215, Rev. & Tax Code)

PRACTICAL ANALYSIS: *Relationship to health savings accounts.*—Because California does not recognize health savings accounts (see discussion below), amounts withdrawn from an MSA and rolled over into a health savings account are not considered qualified withdrawals for California personal income tax purposes and are therefore subject to the California penalty. (Instructions, Form 3805P, Additional Taxes on Qualified Plans (Including IRAs) and Other Tax-Favored Accounts)

Compliance issues.—The penalties are reported on FTB Form 3805P, Additional Taxes on Qualified Plans (Including IRAs) and Other Tax-Favored Accounts. Taxpayers required to file California Form 540, California Resident Income Tax Return, or Long Form 540NR, California Nonresident of Part-Year Resident Income Tax Return, must attach FTB Form 3805P to their returns. Taxpayers not required to file Form 540 or Long Form 540NR must file Form 3805P and pay the accompanying tax by the due date for filing Form 540 or 540NR. (Instructions, Form 3805P)

Taxpayers filing Form 3805P for a prior year, should use the Form 3805P for that tax year and, if appropriate, attach it to a completed Form 540-X, Amended Individual Income Tax Return. (Instructions, Form 3805P, Additional Taxes on Qualified Plans (Including IRAs) and Other Tax-Favored Accounts)

Form 3805P must be signed if not attached to Form 540, Long Form 540NR, or Form 540X. (Instructions, Form 3805P, Additional Taxes on Qualified Plans (Including IRAs) and Other Tax-Favored Accounts)

• *Health savings accounts and prescription drug subsidies*

California has not incorporated federal provisions concerning health savings accounts, and did not incorporate the prescription drug subsidy exclusion until the 2010 tax year. Consequently, addition adjustments may be required (see ¶ 16-100).

A general discussion of California's conformity to federal law is provided at ¶ 15-515.

• *Indian health care benefits*

California incorporates the federal exclusion for qualified health care benefits provided to the member of an Indian tribe, the member's spouse, or the member's dependents (IRC Sec. 139D), applicable to benefits and coverage provided after March 23, 2010. (Sec. 17131, Rev. & Tax. Code; Former Sec. 17131.12, Rev. & Tax Code)

¶15-755

•*COBRA premium assistance*

California incorporates the federal exclusion of COBRA premium reduction assistance (IRC Sec. 139C). (Sec. 17131, Rev. & Tax. Code)

[¶15-760] Federal Base--Moving Expenses

California incorporates federal law (IRC Sec. 82), as of California's current federal conformity date (see ¶15-515), relating to reimbursements for moving expenses. (Sec. 17081, Rev. & Tax. Code) Under IRC Sec. 82, taxpayers are required to include in their gross income, reimbursements of moving expenses that are attributable to the taxpayer's employment, unless the expenses are excludable as a qualified fringe benefit.

California also incorporates federal law (IRC Sec. 217, prior to amendment by the Tax Cuts and Jobs Act of 2017) relating to the above-the-line deduction for employees and self-employed individuals for moving expenses incurred in connection with the commencement of work at a new principal place of work. (Sec. 17201, Rev. & Tax. Code) Because of California's current federal conformity date (see ¶15-515), California does not conform to the federal suspension of the deduction for tax years 2018 through 2025. (*2017 Summary of Federal Income Tax Changes*, California Franchise Tax Board, May 16, 2018)

The source of reimbursed moving expenses is the state to which the taxpayer moves, regardless of the taxpayer's place of residence when the reimbursement is made (see ¶16-535). (FTB Pub. 1031, Guidelines for Determining Resident Status)

A general discussion of California's conformity to federal law is provided at ¶15-515.

[¶15-765] Federal Base--Net Operating Losses

Although California's net operating loss deduction is similar to federal law (IRC Sec. 172), significant differences do exist. (Sec. 17276, Rev. & Tax. Code) Consequently, addition and subtraction adjustments are required (see ¶16-105 and ¶16-310, respectively).

A general discussion of California's conformity to federal law is provided at ¶15-515.

[¶15-770] Federal Base--Net Profits

Because the computation of California adjusted gross income begins with federal adjusted gross income, California's treatment of net profits is similar to federal law. However, California modifies federal law concerning deductible trade or business expenses, so some differences may arise (see ¶15-805).

A general discussion of California's conformity to federal law is provided at ¶15-515.

[¶15-775] Federal Base--Nondeductible Expenses

California incorporates federal law as of California's federal conformity date (see ¶15-515) disallowing or limiting deductions for the following:

— capital expenditures (IRC Sec. 263), however, taxpayers may claim a depreciation deduction over a period of years on both their federal and California returns for qualified assets (see ¶15-670);

— credits, deductions, or other allowances resulting from a taxpayers' acquisition of control of a corporation in order to evade or avoid tax by taking the credit or deduction (IRC Sec. 269);

— credits, deductions, exclusions, or income allocation resulting from the taxpayers' utilization of a personal service corporation to avoid or evade income tax (IRC Sec. 269A);

— drug trafficking expenditures (IRC Sec. 280E);

— employer-provided health insurance if the employer is the beneficiary (IRC Sec. 264);

— entertainment and gift expenses not directly related to a trade or business (IRC Sec. 274) (see ¶15-805);

— hobby losses to the extent the losses exceed hobby income (IRC Sec. 183);

— losses, interest, and expenses arising from transactions between related taxpayers (IRC Sec. 267); and

— personal and family living expenses (IRC Sec. 262).

(Sec. 17201, Rev. & Tax. Code)

Because of California's IRC conformity date, California does not conform to federal amendments made by the Tax Cuts and Jobs Act of 2017 that:

— repeal the exception to the deduction disallowance for entertainment, amusement, or recreation that is directly related to the active conduct of a trade or business, applicable to amounts paid or incurred after 2017;

— eliminate business expense deductions for certain employer-provided meal expenses after 2025;

— eliminate certain business expense deductions associated with providing qualified transportation fringe or commuting benefits to employees (except as necessary to ensure employee safety) after 2017;

— prohibit deductions for cash, gift cards, and other nontangible personal property as employee achievement awards after 2017;

— deny deductions for amounts paid after 2017 for local lobbying expenses, to a government for a violation of the law, or as a settlement subject to a nondisclosure agreement in connection with sexual harassment or abuse;

— prohibit members of Congress from deducting up to $3,000 in living expenses when they are away from home for taxable years beginning after December 22, 2017; and

— disallow deductions for any disqualified related party amount paid or accrued in a hybrid transaction or by, or to, a hybrid entity in taxable years beginning after 2017.

(2017 Summary of Federal Income Tax Changes, California Franchise Tax Board, May 16, 2018)

A general discussion of California's conformity to federal law is provided at ¶15-515.

¶15-775

[¶15-780] Federal Base--Prizes and Awards

California incorporates federal law (IRC Sec. 74), under which amounts received as prizes and awards, other than qualified achievement awards, are includable in gross income. (Sec. 17081, Rev. & Tax. Code)

California subtraction adjustments are allowed for specified prizes, awards, and rewards (see ¶16-325).

Because of California's federal conformity date (¶15-515), California has not conformed to an amendment made by the United States Appreciation for Olympians and Paralympians Act of 2016 (P.L. 114-239) that allows prize money awarded to a U.S. athlete by the U.S. Olympic Committee (USOC), as well as the value of any medal awarded in the Olympic Games or the Paralympic Games, to be excluded from the athlete's gross income, provided the athlete's adjusted gross income for the taxable year does not exceed $1 million ($500,000 for a married individual filing separately). The provision is effective for federal purposes for prizes and awards received after December 31, 2015.

A general discussion of California's conformity to federal law is provided at ¶15-515.

[¶15-785] Federal Base--Related Party Transactions

California incorporates federal law (IRC Sec. 267), as of California's current federal conformity date (see ¶15-515), relating to transactions between related tax-payers. (Sec. 17201, Rev. & Tax. Code) IRC Sec. 267, as incorporated, contains two general rules that limit the deduction of losses, interest, and expenses arising from transactions between "related taxpayers". The first general rule prohibits the deduction of any loss from the sale or exchange of property, directly or indirectly, between related taxpayers, except for a loss in the case of a distribution in corporate liquidation. The second general rule denies any deduction for payments of interest or other expenses made to a related taxpayer if, by reason of the accounting method of the payee, the amount of the payment is not includable in the payee's gross income in the same taxable year in which it is otherwise deductible by the payor. However, the deduction of the payment is allowable as of the day on which the payment is includable in the payee's gross income. Because of California's federal conformity date (see ¶15-515), California has not conformed to a federal provision preventing the transfer of loss from tax indifferent parties. The federal provision applies to sales and other dispositions of property acquired after December 31, 2015.

Additionally, California follows federal law that makes the loss disallowance and loss deferral rules inapplicable to any redemption of stock of a fund-of-funds regulated investment compan (RIC) if the RIC issues only stock that is redeemable upon the demand of the stockholder and the redemption is upon the demand of another RIC. (Sec. 17201, Rev. & Tax. Code; Former Sec. 17280.1, Rev. & Tax. Code)

California also incorporates federal law (IRC Sec. 1239), as of California's current federal conformity date (see ¶15-515), relating to gain on depreciable property transferred between related taxpayers. (Sec. 18151, Rev. & Tax. Code) Under IRC Sec. 1239, as incorporated, gain on the sale of depreciable property is not eligible for capital gains treatment when the property is sold or exchanged between related persons.

Finally, IRC Sec. 1059A, defining a limitation on the taxpayer's basis or inventory cost in property imported into the U.S. between related persons, is incorporated by reference into California law without modification. (Sec. 18031, Rev. & Tax. Code)

A general discussion of California's conformity to federal law is provided at ¶15-515.

[¶15-790] Federal Base--Rents, Royalties, Patents, and Copyrights

In determining the amount of income subject to California personal income taxation, California includes the amount of income from rental real estate, royalties, partnerships, S corporations, trusts that is reported on IRS Form 1040, line 17, which is taken from the federal Schedule E. However, adjustments may be required as a result of differences in California's passive activity loss limitations for rental real estate activities and the depreciation deduction (see ¶16-095 and ¶16-040, respectively). Additional adjustments are also required for owners of pass-through entities and for trust beneficiaries (see ¶15-185 and ¶15-235, respectively). (Sch. CA (540 or 540NR), California Adjustments)

A general discussion of California's conformity to federal law is provided at ¶15-515.

[¶15-795] Federal Base--Research and Development Expenses

California incorporates federal law (IRC Sec. 174), as of California's current federal conformity date (see ¶15-515), relating to the deduction of research and experimental expenditures. (Sec. 17201, Rev. & Tax. Code) Under IRC Sec. 174, as incorporated without modification, research and experimental expenditures may be treated as expenses and deducted currently or, at the election of the taxpayer, may be amortized over a period of not less than 60 months, beginning with the month in which the taxpayer first realizes benefits from the expenditures. Because of California's current federal conformity date (see ¶15-515), California does not conform to the federal requirement that research and experimental expenditures paid or incurred in taxable years beginning after 2021 be amortized ratably over five years (15 years for foreign research). (*2017 Summary of Federal Income Tax Changes*, California Franchise Tax Board, May 16, 2018)

California also allows a research and development credit.

A general discussion of California's conformity to federal law is provided at ¶15-515.

[¶15-800] Federal Base--Retirement Plans and Benefits

California's personal income tax treatment of retirement benefits and annuities is generally the same as federal law (IRC Sec. 401—IRC Sec. 436, IRC Sec. 457). Unlike California's incorporation of most IRC provisions, which are tied to a specified federal conformity date (see ¶15-515), the incorporated federal provisions concerning retirement benefits and deferred compensation plans (IRC Sec. 401—IRC Sec. 420), minimum funding standards and benefit limitations (IRC Sec. 430—IRC Sec. 436), and governmental deferred compensation plans (IRC Sec. 457) are incorporated into California law without regard to the taxable year, to the same extent as applicable for federal purposes. Consequently, California incorporates the amendments made to IRC Sec. 401 through IRC Sec. 420, IRC Sec. 430—IRC Sec. 436, and IRC Sec. 457 by the Patient Protection and 2010 Reconciliation Acts (P.L. 111-148 and P.L. 111-152). However, California will not automatically conform to any post-2009 federal elective deferral increases. (Sec. 17501, Rev. & Tax. Code; Sec. 17551(c), Rev. & Tax. Code)

Although California incorporates Part I (IRC Sec. 401 through IRC Sec. 420), which relates to pension, profit-sharing, stock bonus plans, etc, and Part III (IRC Sec. 430 through IRC Sec. 436), which relates to rules relating to minimum funding standards and benefit limitations, of Subchapter D of Chapter 1 of Subtitle A of the Internal Revenue Code, California does not automatically incorporate federal amendments made to Part II of Subchapter D of Chapter 1 of Subtitle A of the Internal Revenue Code. Consequently, the federal provisions governing certain stock options (IRC Sec. 421—IRC Sec. 424) are incorporated by California, but only as of California's current federal conformity date (see ¶ 15-515).

California follows federal law concerning:

— the deduction for contributions to employer liability trusts (IRC Sec. 194A);

— the deduction for an individual's qualified retirement contribution (IRC Sec. 219);

— 401(k) (Keogh) plans;

— Employee stock ownership plans (ESOPs) (a subtraction adjustment is also available for California qualified stock options) (see ¶ 16-345);

— Individual retirement accounts (IRAs), Roth IRAs, and Roth contribution programs;

— Qualified and nonqualified plans;

— Public and nonprofit employee plans (IRC Sec. 457) (Sec. 17551, Rev. & Tax. Code);

— Retiree health care accounts, however, California did not incorporate this provision during the 2001 taxable year;

— Rollovers from qualified pension, profit-sharing, stock bonus, annuity plan, and governmental IRC Sec. 457 deferred compensation plans;

— Savings incentive match plans for employees (SIMPLE plans);

— Simplified employee pensions (SEPs); and

— Welfare benefit plans.

(Sec. 17201, Rev. & Tax. Code; Sec. 17203, Rev. & Tax. Code; Sec. 17501, Rev. & Tax. Code) As a result of California's federal conformity date history, addition adjustments (see ¶ 16-135) may be required because California did not incorporate amendments concerning IRA contribution limits made to IRC Sec. 219 at the same time as adopted for federal purposes.

CCH COMMENT: *Tax on lump-sum distributions.*—Although California incorporates the federal tax on lump sum distributions (IRC Sec. 402(e)(4)(d)), California applies its own tax rate and brackets in lieu of the federal rates (see ¶ 15-355).

CAUTION: *IRA distributions to health savings accounts.*—Although California generally conforms to federal provisions as amended to date, because California does not recognize health savings accounts (HSAs) it does not conform to an amendment made to IRC Sec. 408(d)(9), which authorizes a one-time tax-free distribution from an IRA to an HSA, effective for tax years beginning after 2006. A California taxpayer who makes such a distribution is required to include the distribution in his or her gross income and is subject to California's penalty on premature withdrawals (see discussion below).

California also incorporates IRC Sec. 7701(j), which provides that the federal Thrift Savings Fund is to be treated as a qualified trust under IRC Sec. 401(a), allowing federal employees to make tax-deferred contributions into the plan, and as a tax-exempt organization under IRC Sec. 501(a). (Sec. 17510, Rev. & Tax. Code)

Although California generally follows federal law in this area, subtraction adjustments may be required as a result of basis differences arising from prior year contribution limits, and California's exclusion of Social Security and railroad retirement benefits (see ¶ 16-345).

For the sourcing of retirement benefits earned prior to the establishment of California residency, see ¶ 16-545.

• *Nonqualified deferred compensation*

California generally conforms to federal law for income received under IRC Sec. 409A on a nonqualified deferred compensation (NQDC) plan and discounted stock options and stock appreciation rights. Income received under IRC Sec. 409A is subject to an additional tax plus interest for federal and California purposes. (Sec. 17501, Rev. & Tax. Code) For taxable years beginning after 2012, California modifies its conformity to IRC Sec. 409A by reducing the rate of additional tax to 5% on any amount deferred under a nonqualified deferred compensation plan that is includible in income because it is not subject to a substantial risk of forfeiture and does not meet the requirements of IRC Sec. 409A. (Sec. 17508.2, Rev. & Tax. Code) For taxable years beginning prior to 2013, California conformed to the 20% additional tax rate in IRC Sec. 409A. Additional California tax, if any, is reported on Form 540, line 63. Write "NQDC" on the dotted line to the left of the amount. (Instructions, Form 540, California Individual Income Tax Return)

California does not incorporate IRC Sec. 457A, which requires that any compensation that is deferred under a nonqualified deferred compensation plan of a nonqualified entity be included in gross income when there is no substantial risk of forfeiture of the rights to the compensation (Sec. 17551(g), Rev. & Tax. Code)

• *Annuities*

California incorporates IRC Sec. 72 concerning the tax treatment of annuities, as of the current California conformity date (see ¶ 15-515). (Sec. 17081, Rev. & Tax. Code; Sec. 17085, Rev. & Tax. Code) However, subtraction adjustments may be required as a result of different effective date's for the repeal of the three-year basis recovery rule, the treatment of employer contributions for citizens living abroad, and different basis rules (see ¶ 16-345). The amount of the penalty on early distribution rules is also reduced for California personal income tax purposes.

Addition adjustments may also be required as a result of California's nonconformity with federal law (1) concerning the treatment of the long-term care insurance coverage rider costs and (2) allowing contract holders to annuitize a portion of an annuity, endowment, or life insurance contract, while the balance is not annuitized, provided that the annuitization period is for 10 years or more, or for the lives of one or more individuals (see ¶ 16-135). California, unlike federal law, does not exclude from taxable distributions from annuity and life insurance contracts the cost of a qualified long-term care insurance coverage rider that is charged against the cash or cash surrender value of the contract. The amendments are effective for federal purposes for contracts issued after 1996, but only with respect to tax years beginning after 2009.

• *Penalties on nonqualified and premature withdrawals*

California law modifies the federal penalties imposed under IRC Sec. 72(m), IRC Sec. 72(o), IRC Sec. 72(q), and IRC Sec. 72(t) so that they are imposed at a reduced rate of 2.5% for California income tax purposes instead of the 10% rate generally applicable for federal purposes. (Sec. 17085(c)(1), Rev. & Tax. Code) These penalties are imposed for distributions from qualified trusts to 5% owners of the employers involved (IRC Sec. 72(m)) and for certain premature distributions (IRC Sec. 72(o), IRC Sec. 72(q), and IRC Sec. 72(t)). California does not have taxes similar to the federal tax on excess accumulations, tax on excess contributions, or tax on excess distributions. (FTB Pub. 1005, Pension and Annuity Guidelines)

> **CAUTION NOTE:** *Tax Base May Be Different.*—Not only is the amount of the tax imposed on premature distributions from qualified plans different for federal and California law, the amount of the withdrawal subject to tax may be different as a result of different basis rules (see ¶16-345).

The penalty is increased for early withdrawals from a SIMPLE plan that are made during the two-year period beginning on the date that the employee first began participating in the plan (IRC Sec. 72(t)(6)). The federal penalty is 25% and the California penalty is 6%. (Sec. 17085(c)(2), Rev. & Tax. Code)

Also, for taxable years beginning after 2012, California modifies its conformity to IRC Sec. 409A by reducing the rate of additional tax on certain amounts deferred under a nonqualified deferred compensation plan (discussed above).

Under both federal law (IRC Sec. 72(t)(2)(A)(vii)) and California law (Sec. 17085.7, Rev. & Tax. Code), a post-1999 distribution from a qualified retirement plan that is made on account of a FTB notice to withhold from the plan is not subject to the penalty for early withdrawals from a qualified retirement plan.

> **CCH PRACTICE TIP:** *Withdrawals made by active duty reservists and emergency service personnel.*—In 2010, California retroactively incorporated IRC Sec. 72(t)(10), which waives the early withdrawal penalty for certain distributions to qualified public safety employees who separate from service after age 50, applicable for federal purposes to distributions made after August 17, 2006, and IRC Sec. 72(t)(2)(G), which waives the premature withdrawal penalty for certain withdrawals by qualified members of the National Guard or the Reserve who are called to active duty, applicable for federal purposes retroactively to September 11, 2001. These provisions apply in the same manner and in the same periods for California purposes as they apply for federal purposes. (Sec. 88, Ch. 14 (S.B. 401), Laws 2009)

Compliance issues.—The penalties are reported on FTB Form 3805P, Additional Taxes on Qualified Plans (Including IRAs) and Other Tax-Favored Accounts. Taxpayers required to file California Form 540, California Resident Income Tax Return, or Long Form 540NR, California Nonresident of Part-Year Resident Income Tax Return, must attach FTB Form 3805P with their returns. Taxpayers not required to file Form 540 or Long Form 540NR must file Form 3805P and pay the accompanying tax by the due date for filing Form 540 or 540NR. (Instructions, Form 3805P, Additional Taxes on Qualified Plans (Including IRAs) and Other Tax-Favored Accounts)

Taxpayers filing Form 3805P for a prior year, should use the Form 3805P for that tax year and, if appropriate, attach it to a completed Form 540-X, Amended Individual Income Tax Return. (Instructions, Form 3805P, Additional Taxes on Qualified Plans (Including IRAs) and Other Tax-Favored Accounts)

Joint returns.—A separate Form 3805P must be completed for each spouse or registered domestic partner (RDP) that has a premature withdrawal from a qualified plan. If both spouses or RDPs are required to file Form 3805P, the combined tax must be entered on Form 540, line 33 or Long Form 540NR, line 41. (Instructions, Form 3805P, Additional Taxes on Qualified Plans (Including IRAs) and Other Tax-Favored Accounts)

A general discussion of California's conformity to federal law is provided at ¶ 15-515.

•*Loans from retirement plans*

Under IRC Sec. 72(p) as it existed prior to September 29, 2017, a loan from a qualified employer plan to a participant or beneficiary was generally treated as a plan distribution for federal income tax purposes unless, among other things:

— the loan amount does not exceed the lesser of $50,000, or half of the present value of the employee's nonforfeitable accrued benefit under the plan; and

— the loan is required to be repaid within five years, except that a longer repayment period can be used for a principal residence plan loan.

Effective September 29, 2017, the federal Disaster Tax Relief and Airport and Airway Extension Act of 2017 (P.L. 115-63):

— increased the maximum amount that a participant or beneficiary can borrow from a qualified employer plan from $50,000 to $100,000;

— removed the one half of present value limitation; and

— allows a longer repayment term, if the due date for any repayment with respect to the loan occurs during a qualified beginning date that is Hurricane-specific and ends on December 31, 2018, by delaying the due date of the first repayment by one year and adjusting the due dates of subsequent repayments accordingly.

These changes were intended to help taxpayers affected by Hurricanes Harvey, Irma, and Maria.

Since California incorporates IRC Sec. 72 as of the current California conformity date (see ¶ 15-515), state law does not conform to the federal loan provision modifications made by the Disaster Tax Relief and Airport and Airway Extension Act of 2017. (Sec. 17081, Rev. & Tax. Code; Sec. 17085, Rev. & Tax. Code; *2017 Summary of Federal Income Tax Changes*, California Franchise Tax Board, May 16, 2018)

[¶ 15-805] Federal Base--Trade or Business Expenses

California generally conforms to federal law (IRC Sec. 162), as of California's current federal conformity date (¶ 15-515), relating to deductible trade or business expenses. (Sec. 17201, Rev. & Tax. Code; Sec. 17273, Rev. & Tax. Code; Sec. 17072, Rev. & Tax. Code)

Under IRC Sec. 162, as incorporated into California law (Sec. 17201, Rev. & Tax. Code), ordinary and necessary business expenses include a reasonable allowance for salaries or other compensation for personal services; travel expenses incurred in the pursuit of a trade or business; rental for the use of property used in a business; management expenses; the costs of supplies, commissions, incidental repairs, advertising, and expenses of operating automobiles used in a trade or business; and traveling expenses while away from home solely in the pursuit of a trade or business. (Fed. Reg. 1.162-1). Deductions may not be claimed for hobby expenses or expenses associated with non-profit making activities (see ¶ 15-775).

As a result of California's incorporation of federal law (IRC Sec. 162), California's treatment of the following expenses is the same as federal law:

— automobile and mileage expenses

— bonuses

— compensation

— disabled access expenditures (IRC Sec. 190)

— employee business expenses

— golden parachute payments

— health insurance costs of self-employed individuals

— home office expenses (IRC Sec. 280A)

— illegal activities (however, an addition adjustment may be required, see ¶ 16-110)

— insurance premiums

— legal and litigation expenses

— life insurance contracts (see also the discussion on nondeductible expenses at ¶ 15-775)

— listed property

— lobbying and political expenses (see prior law rules)

— meals and entertainment expenses

— start-up expenditures (IRC Sec. 195), however, an adjustment may be required in certain tax years, see ¶ 16-150

— travel expenses (however, adjustments may be required for state legislator's travel expenditures, see ¶ 16-135)

— vacation rental expenses (IRC Sec. 280A)

PRACTICAL ANALYSIS: Home office expenses.—The deduction for home office expenses was allowed to a teacher where he substantiated the amount of allowable expenses by showing that part of his home had been especially constructed for an office and was used in connection with his profession as a teacher. The taxpayer was not provided with an office for his teaching duties at the school, and the area used as an office was specially designed and included many features not ordinarily found in the typical home. (*Roy,* SBE, 76-SBE-028, March 8, 1976)

CAUTION NOTE: Ordinary and necessary expenses: It should not be assumed that an item of expense that is allowed under federal law will always be allowed by California, because the interpretations of different taxing authorities concerning what are "ordinary" and "necessary" business expenses are not always uniform. Also, expenses that would normally be deductible under federal law are not allowed by California when they are attributable to income that is not taxed by California, see ¶16-110.

• *Physicians' interindemnity arrangements*

California law, like federal law (Sec. 1031, P.L. 99-514), allows a deduction for payments made to a cooperative corporation by its members for malpractice coverage. (Sec. 17278, Rev. & Tax. Code; Uncodified Sec. 5, Ch. 1276, Laws 1984)

Deductions for such payments are valid only to the extent that the payment does not exceed the amount that would otherwise be payable to an independent insurance company for similar medical malpractice coverage. Excess payments may be carried forward five years. The deductible payment may be made either as a contribution to, or in response to an assessment by, the interindemnity arrangement. (Sec. 17278, Rev. & Tax. Code; Uncodified Sec. 5, Ch. 1276, Laws 1984)

Refunded payments must be included in the taxpayer's income in the year received. Such payments must be reported by the trust to the FTB in the year made. The FTB may require, by regulation, the trust to withhold a specified amount of any refund made to a nonresident. (Sec. 17278, Rev. & Tax. Code; Uncodified Sec. 5, Ch. 1276, Laws 1984)

The comparable federal provision does not provide for the carryover of excess payments. Instead, the federal provision allows an initial contribution in a lump-sum payment or in substantially equal payments over a period not to exceed six years. (Sec. 1031, P.L. 99-514) To the extent the amount that may be claimed on the federal and California returns, an addition or subtraction adjustment is required (see ¶16-110 and ¶16-365, respectively).

• *Accrued vacation or severance pay*

Although California incorporates federal law (IRC Sec. 404(a)(11)) allowing an employer to deduct accrued vacation or severance pay in a particular year only if the pay is actually received by the employee within 2.5 months after the end of the tax year, different effective dates apply. The provision applies generally for federal purposes to tax years ending after July 22, 1998, and for California purposes to taxable years beginning after 2001. Any change in a taxpayer's method of accounting required by this provision will be treated as initiated by the taxpayer with the consent of the Franchise Tax Board (FTB), and any California adjustment required as a result of this change will be taken into account ratably over the three taxable year period beginning with that taxpayer's first taxable year beginning after 2001. (Sec. 17563.5, Rev. & Tax. Code)

• *College admissions cheating scheme payments*

Applicable retroactively for taxable years beginning on or after January 1, 2014, California specifically prohibits certain business expense deductions by taxpayers found guilty in the college admissions cheating scandal (see ¶16-150).

A general discussion of California's conformity to federal law is provided at ¶15-515.

[¶15-810] Federal Base--Tax Benefit Rule

California incorporates federal law (IRC Sec. 111), as of California's current federal conformity date (see ¶15-515), concerning the recovery of tax benefit items (Sec. 17131, Rev. & Tax. Code) with modifications. (Sec. 17142, Rev. & Tax. Code) As a result of these modifications, addition or subtraction adjustments may be required (see ¶16-120 and ¶16-327, respectively).

A general discussion of California's conformity to federal law is provided at ¶15-515.

[¶15-815] Federal Base--Tax Evasion and Tax Shelter Activities

California incorporates federal law (IRC Sec. 269A), as of California's current federal conformity date (see ¶15-515), concerning the use of personal service corporations to avoid or evade income tax. (Sec. 17201, Rev. & Tax. Code) California modifies federal law by substituting "California Personal Income Tax" for "Federal Income Tax." (Sec. 17287, Rev. & Tax. Code)

Under IRC Sec. 269A as modified by California, if a personal service corporation is being utilized to avoid or evade personal income taxation, the Franchise Tax Board (FTB) may allocate income, deductions, credits, exclusions, and other allowances between the personal service corporation and its employee-owners to prevent such tax avoidance or evasion or to clearly reflect the income of the corporation and its employee-owners.

California also incorporates IRC Sec. 482, allowing the FTB to allocate income, deductions, and credits between or among businesses controlled by the same interests if such action is necessary to prevent tax evasion or clearly reflect income (see ¶15-480). (Sec. 17551, Rev. & Tax. Code)

As part of California's crack down on abusive tax shelters, increased penalties may be applied to taxpayers involved in reportable transactions and listed transactions (see ¶89-206). These penalties may be abated or rescinded if certain conditions are satisfied (see ¶89-210).

A general discussion of California's conformity to federal law is provided at ¶15-515.

[¶15-820] Federal Base--Taxes

California generally incorporates federal law (IRC Sec. 164), with modifications, as of California's current federal conformity date (see ¶15-515), relating to the deduction of taxes. (Sec. 17201, Rev. & Tax. Code) IRC Sec. 164, as incorporated, provides for the deduction of:

— state and local real property taxes;

— state and local personal property taxes;

— state and local taxes related to a trade or business or property held for income production; and

— one-half of the federal self-employment taxes imposed under IRC Sec. 1401.

COMMENT: California does not limit the deduction for real property taxes to ad valorem (assessed value) taxes. (*Understanding the Real Estate Tax Deduction*, California Franchise Tax Board, April 13, 2012)

California modifies federal law by disallowing the deduction for state, local, and foreign income, war profits, and excess profits taxes and the deduction of foreign real property taxes (no federal deduction is available for foreign real property taxes for the 2018 to 2025 tax years). In addition, unlike federal law, California does not allow taxpayers to elect to deduct specified sales and use taxes in lieu of personal income taxes. Taxpayers are also precluded from claiming a deduction of the environmental tax or qualified motor vehicle taxes on their California returns. Addition adjustments are required as a result of these modifications (see ¶16-145).

Because of California's IRC conformity date, California also does not conform to the federal $10,000 limit ($5,000 for married taxpayer filing a separate return) on state and local tax deductions for the 2018 to 2025 tax years. (*Preliminary Report on Specific Provisions of the Federal Tax Cuts and Jobs Act*, California Franchise Tax Board, March 20, 2018)

However, for tax years beginning after 2014, California conforms to the federal provision that denies deductions for the annual fee imposed by Section 9008 of the Patient Protection and Affordable Care Act (P.L. 111-148) on branded prescription manufacturers and importers. (Sec. 17240, Rev. & Tax. Code)

• *Federal windfall profits tax*

The federal windfall profits tax on domestic crude oil is deductible as a tax under IRC Sec. 164, as incorporated into California law, or as a trade or business expense, or as an expense for the production of income (*Letter to CCH*, FTB, October 5, 1981).

A general discussion of California's conformity to federal law is provided at ¶15-515.

[¶15-825] Federal Base--Unemployment Compensation

Unlike federal law (IRC Sec. 85), California does not tax unemployment compensation. (Sec. 17083, Rev. & Tax. Code) Consequently, a subtraction adjustment may be allowed (see ¶16-370).

A general discussion of California's conformity to federal law is provided at ¶15-515.

[¶15-830] Federal Base--Payments to Wrongfully Incarcerated Individuals

California incorporates federal law (IRC Sec. 139F), as of California's current federal conformity date (see ¶15-515), relating to the exclusion from gross income for civil damages, restitution, or other monetary awards received by wrongly incarcerated individuals. (Sec. 17156.1(a), Rev. & Tax. Code)

A general discussion of California's conformity to federal law is provided at ¶15-515.

[¶16-000]

TAXABLE INCOME COMPUTATION--ADDITIONS

[¶16-005] Additions to Taxable Income Base

The computation of California taxable income requires that the items listed below be added to federal adjusted gross income.

— Abandonment or tax recoupment fees (see ¶16-150)

— Adoption assistance programs (see ¶16-010)

— Alaska natural gas pipelines (see ¶ 16-040)

— Alimony payments made by nonresidents and part-year residents (see ¶ 16-012)

— Amortization of pollution control facilities (see ¶ 16-015)

— Annuities (see ¶ 16-135)

— Asset expense (IRC Sec. 179) election (see ¶ 16-040)

— Basis adjustments (see ¶ 16-020)

— Bonus depreciation (see ¶ 16-040)

— Canadian registered retirement savings plans (see ¶ 16-135)

— Capital loss carryback (see ¶ 16-095)

— Casualty losses incurred in federal disaster areas (see ¶ 16-095)

— Charitable contributions of real property for conservation purposes (see ¶ 16-025)

— Claim of right adjustment (see ¶ 16-027)

— Clean fuel vehicle and clean fuel vehicle refueling property (see ¶ 16-055)

— Clergy housing allowances

— Death benefits (see ¶ 16-036)

— Discharge of indebtedness (see ¶ 16-017)

— Discriminatory club expenses (see ¶ 16-150)

— Distributions from IRAs, employees' trusts and employee annuities (see ¶ 16-135)

— Dividends from other state's obligations and controlled foreign corporations (see ¶ 16-045)

— Enterprise zone property (see ¶ 16-040)

— EPA sulfur regulations compliance costs (see ¶ 16-055)

— Environmental remediation costs (see ¶ 16-040)

— Exempt income expenses (see ¶ 16-110)

— Extraterritorial income (see ¶ 16-060)

— Federal business credit carryover deduction (see ¶ 16-085)

— Federal estate tax deduction

— Film and production property expenses (see ¶ 16-150)

— Foreign earned income and housing exclusion (see ¶ 16-060)

— Foreign social security benefits (see ¶ 16-135)

— Generation skipping transfer tax deduction

— Grapevines, diseased (see ¶ 16-040)

— Health savings accounts (see ¶ 16-100)

— Illegal business expenses (see ¶ 16-110)

— Illegal payments (see ¶ 16-150)

— Individual retirement accounts (IRAs) (see ¶ 16-135)

— Investment interest (see ¶ 16-075)

— Involuntarily converted advertising displays (see ¶ 16-070)

— Leasehold improvements (see ¶ 16-040)

— Los Angeles revitalization zone (LARZ) property (see ¶16-040)

— Lottery losses (see ¶16-095)

— Low-income housing rehabilitation expenditures (see ¶16-040)

— Manufacturing enhancement area property (see ¶16-040)

— Native American reservation property (see ¶16-040)

— Net operating losses (see ¶16-105)

— Nonresidential real property depreciation deduction (see ¶16-040)

— Original issue discount (see ¶16-075)

— Parking cash-out program payments (see ¶16-065)

— Participations and residuals (see ¶16-040)

— Passive activity losses (see ¶16-095)

— Personal residence sales (see ¶16-070)

— Physician interindemnity payments (see ¶16-150)

— Prescription drug subsidies (see ¶16-100)

— Qualified tuition program nonqualified withdrawals (see ¶16-050)

— Recapture of depreciation (see ¶16-070)

— Recovery of tax benefit items (see ¶16-120)

— Reforestation expenses for non-California qualified timber property (see ¶16-055)

— Regulated investment company (RIC) undistributed gain (see ¶16-045)

— Research and development expenses (see ¶16-130)

— Restaurant property (see ¶16-040)

— Small business stock sales (see ¶16-070)

— Targeted tax area property (see ¶16-040)

— Teachers' expenses (see ¶16-050)

— Vehicle license fee refund (see ¶16-120)

These adjustments must be made on Sch. CA (540), California Adjustments. Major adjustments are also outlined in the FTB Pub. 1001, Supplemental Guidelines to California Adjustments.

[¶16-010] Additions--Adoption Assistance Programs

Although California incorporates the federal exclusion of employer-provided adoption expenses (see ¶15-605), as a result of California's current federal conformity date history (see ¶15-515), California did not adopt the increase to the dollar limitation for the income exclusion by $1,000 to $13,360 per eligible child (including a special needs child) that was in effect during the 2010 and 2011 tax years. Consequently, the amounts excluded above the $12,360 on the 2011 federal return ($12,170 for 2010), had to be added back to federal adjusted gross income. (2011 FTB Pub. 1001, and 2010 FTB Pub. 1001)

Other additions to the taxable income base are listed at ¶16-005.

¶16-010

[¶16-012] Additions--Alimony

A nonresident or part-year resident may only deduct a portion of alimony payments made. The portion is calculated by multiplying the payments made while a nonresident by a fraction, the numerator of which is the taxpayer's California adjusted gross income, computed without regard to the alimony deduction, and the denominator of which is total adjusted gross income, likewise computed without regard to the alimony deduction. (Sec. 17302, Rev. & Tax. Code) The adjustments are made on Sch. CA (540NR), line 31a. (Instructions, Sch. CA (540NR), California Adjustments—Nonresidents and Part-Year Residents)

A nonresident alien that did not include alimony payments received on his or her federal income tax return, must make an addition adjustment on Sch. CA (540 or 540NR), line 11, column C. (FTB Pub. 1001, Supplemental Guidelines to California Adjustments) A corresponding subtraction adjustment may be made by nonresident alien alimony payors (see ¶16-207).

Other additions to the taxable income base are listed at ¶16-005.

[¶16-015] Additions--Amortization

Except as noted below, California generally conforms to federal amortization deductions (see ¶15-615). Taxpayers who have amortization differences resulting from the items discussed below, should determine their California amortization deduction on FTB Form 3885A and make the appropriate addition or subtraction adjustment on Sch. CA (540), line 12, column B or C.

An amortization adjustment is also required for reforestation expenses related to non-California qualified timber properties (see ¶16-055).

• *Pollution control facilities*

California does not allow the accelerated amortization deduction for pollution control facilities available under both California and federal law (IRC Sec. 169) for facilities located outside of California. (Sec. 17250, Rev. & Tax. Code) Consequently, adjustments must be made for accelerated write-offs claimed for non-California facilities. (*FTB Pub. 1001, Supplemental Guidelines to California Adjustments*)

In addition, under both California and federal law, the pollution control facility must be certified by both federal and state certifying agencies. California modifies IRC Sec. 169 to provide that the state certifying agency in cases involving air pollution is the State Air Resources Board, and in cases involving water pollution is the State Water Resources Control Board. (Sec. 17250, Rev. & Tax. Code) The federal certifying agency is the Secretary of the Interior or the Secretary of Health and Human Services.

Also, California did not conform to federal amendments that expanded the amortization deduction for atmospheric pollution control facilities until the 2010 tax year. The amendments allow the amortization deduction to be claimed for qualified air pollution control facilities placed in service after April 11, 2005, even if not used in connection with a plant that was in operation before January 1, 1976. However, the amortization period applicable to taxpayers eligible under the expanded criteria is extended from 60 months to 84 months. To the extent taxpayers only qualified for the amortization deduction on their pre-2010 federal tax return under the expanded eligibility criteria, the taxpayer was required to make an addition adjustment on their pre-2010 tax year California tax return.

Other additions to the taxable income base are listed at ¶ 16-005.

[¶ 16-017] Additions--Discharge of Indebtedness

Although California generally conforms to federal law concerning the treatment of income from the discharge of indebtedness, addition adjustments may be required for differences between California law and federal law.

● *Mortgage debt relief*

California partially conformed to the federal exclusion for mortgage debt forgiveness occurring after 2008 and before 2014. However, for California personal income tax purposes, the maximum exclusion was capped at $500,000 ($250,000 for married taxpayers filing separately) and the qualified principal residence indebtedness was limited to $800,000 ($400,000 for married taxpayers filing separately). There was no cap on the federal exclusion, and the qualified principal residence indebtedness was limited federally to $2 million ($1 million for married taxpayers filing separately). Also, for federal purposes, but not California purposes, the exclusion was extended through 2016. (Sec. 17144.5, Rev. & Tax. Code)

CCH PRACTICE TIP: *Short sales involving out-of-state property.*—Additional complications may arise when the short sale involves out-of-state property. The issue of how to report a short sale of property located in another state is dependent on whether the other state classifies the loan as a recourse or nonrecourse loan. If under the other state's law the lender is able to pursue the borrower for payment of the remaining balance of the debt after the property is sold, the loan is recourse. If the lender's only remedy is to repossess the property used as collateral, the loan is nonrecourse. Forgiveness of a nonrecourse loan resulting from either a foreclosure or a short sale will not generate cancellation of debt income (COD). Rather, the foreclosure or short sale is considered a deemed sale, and the full amount of debt is treated as part of the amount realized and treated as a capital gain or loss. Upon the deemed sale, a Form 1099A is issued.

If the loan is a recourse loan, a taxpayer is required to report the difference in the property's fair market value and the outstanding balance that is forgiven as COD income in the year in which the lender forgives the deficiency. Generally, a 1099C is issued. Taxpayers must determine if one of the federal COD exclusions applies, such as the federal mortgage debt forgiveness exclusion to which California law partially conforms.

Issues also arise as to how the income from the short sale/foreclosure should be sourced. California residents are taxed on all income received. So, if the taxpayer has established a California domicile by the time the out-of-state property is sold, he or she is subject to tax on the income, including COD income, associated with the sale. (*Tax News*, California Franchise Tax Board, May 31, 2010)

● *Deferral of discharge of indebtedness income from reacquisition of debt instruments*

California does not adopt the federal provision (IRC Sec. 108(i)) allowing taxpayers to defer the recognition of discharge of indebtedness income arising from a qualified reacquisition of business debt instruments in 2009 or 2010 that were issued by the taxpayer or a related person ratably over a five-year period. (Sec. 17144(f), Rev.

& Tax. Code) Taxpayers were required to make an addition adjustment in the first year the income was deferred equal to the difference between the amount of deferred income included on the federal return and the full amount of the income discharged. (2011 FTB Pub. 1001; *E-mail*, California Franchise Tax Board, February 7, 2011) Subtraction adjustments are allowed in the subsequent years in which taxpayers include the deferred income in their federal taxable income (see ¶ 16-213).

[¶ 16-020] Additions--Basis Adjustments

Although California generally incorporates federal law (IRC Sec. 1016) as of California's current federal conformity date (see ¶ 15-515), concerning adjustments to basis, many of the federal adjustments are inapplicable for California because California does not incorporate the federal credits or deductions that require the basis adjustments. In addition, when applying the incorporated provisions of IRC Sec. 1016(a) to make California basis adjustments, any references in IRC Sec. 1016 to other IRC provisions must be treated as including California modifications to those other IRC provisions. (Sec. 17024.5(i), Rev. & Tax. Code)

The following federal basis adjustments, although contained in IRC Sec. 1016(a), are inapplicable under California law (Sec. 18036(b), Rev. & Tax. Code):

— adjustments for amounts related to a shareholder's stock in a controlled foreign corporation (made inapplicable by Sec. 17024.5(b)(9));

— adjustments for certain federal investment tax credits (made inapplicable by Sec. 17024.5(b)(10)); and

— adjustments to the basis of a U.S. taxpayer's stock in a foreign personal holding company to reflect certain undistributed income of the company (made inapplicable by Sec. 17024.5(b)(4)).

The following basis adjustments required by IRC Sec. 1016(a) and IRC Sec. 1016(d) are technically incorporated by California but have no practical effect because California does not incorporate the underlying credit or deduction. Thus, for California personal income tax purposes, no adjustments are required for the following:

— adjustments for amounts specified in a shareholder's consent made under IRC Sec. 28 of the 1939 Internal Revenue Code;

— adjustment for amortization under IRC Sec. 811(b) of premium and accrual of discount on bonds and notes held by a life insurance company;

— adjustment for certain carryover basis property acquired from a decedent under IRC Sec. 1023;

— the adjustments to the basis of stock required by IRC Sec. 1059, concerning a basis reduction for extraordinary dividends;

— an adjustment for adoption costs for which a taxpayer has claimed a federal credit under IRC Sec. 23;

— the adjustment with respect to property the acquisition of which resulted in the nonrecognition of gain on the rollover of empowerment zone investments under IRC Sec. 1397B;

— the adjustment required with respect to property for which a federal employer-provided child care credit was claimed under IRC Sec. 45F, although California requires a similar basis adjustment for taxpayers who claimed the California employer's credit for child care programs (see ¶ 16-090);

— the adjustment required under IRC Sec. 1016(d) for certain automobiles for which a taxpayer is required to pay the federal "gas guzzler tax";

— the adjustment required under IRC Sec. 179D for energy efficient commercial buildings; and

— adjustments for expenses for which taxpayers claimed credits for new energy efficient homes (IRC Sec. 45L), nonbusiness energy property (IRC Sec. 25C), residential energy efficient property (IRC Sec. 25D), alternative motor vehicles (IRC Sec. 30B), alternative fuel vehicle refueling property (IRC Sec. 30C), and new qualified plug-in electric drive motor vehicles (IRC Sec. 30D).

Adjustments must also be made for certain deducted enterprise zone, former Los Angeles Revitalization Zone, and local military base recovery area business expenses (see ¶16-040). No comparable basis adjustments are required under federal law.

Finally, in addition to the adjustments required under IRC Sec. 1016, proper adjustments must be made for

— upon the sale of depreciable property for amounts for which the federal bonus depreciation deduction or increased federal IRC Sec. 179 asset expense election was claimed (see ¶16-040);

— amounts that were formerly allowed as deductions as deferred expenses under former Rev. & Tax Code Secs. 17689(b) or 17689.5, relating to certain exploration expenditures, and that resulted in a reduction of the taxpayer's California personal income taxes; and

— amounts deducted under former Sec. 17252.5 (replaced by Sec. 17267.2), which allowed a deduction for a portion of the cost of certain property used in an enterprise-zone business, former Sec. 17265 (also replaced by Sec. 17267.2), which allowed a deduction of 40% of the cost of certain property used in a program-area business, or Sec. 17266, which allows a deduction for the cost of certain property used in the Los Angeles Revitalization Zone. (Sec. 18036(a), Rev. & Tax. Code)

Because of California's current federal conformity date (see ¶15-515), California does not conform to federal law that provides that in determining the basis of a life insurance or annuity contract, no adjustment is made for mortality, expense, or other reasonable charges incurred under the contract. (*2017 Summary of Federal Income Tax Changes*, California Franchise Tax Board, May 16, 2018)

• *Business property moves into California*

Depreciation methods and useful lives of trade or business property must be acceptable to California. If an unacceptable method was used before the move into California, taxpayers must use the straight-line method to compute the basis in the property. (*FTB Pub. 1001, Supplemental Guidelines to California Adjustments*)

• *Amortizable bond premium*

Under IRC Sec. 171 as incorporated by California, if a taxable bond is purchased at more than its face value, the buyer may elect to amortize the bond premium and deduct the amortizable amount (see ¶15-720). California incorporates by reference IRC Sec. 1016(a)(5), which provides that the basis of the bond must be reduced by the deduction allowable for the amortizable bond premium. (Sec. 18031, Rev. & Tax. Code) Under both California and federal law, an amortization deduction is not allowed for the premium paid on a tax-exempt bond, but the basis of a tax-exempt bond nonetheless must be reduced by the amount of the amortizable bond premium not allowed as a deduction.

The general rules concerning the deductibility of amortizable bond premiums are the same under federal law (IRC Sec. 171) as under California law. However, the basis adjustment under federal law as compared with the California law may be different because of the differences in tax exemptions for bonds (see ¶16-280).

• *Unrecognized gain on the sale of qualified small business stock*

California law follows federal law (IRC Sec. 1016(a)), requiring an adjustment in basis for unrecognized gain on the sale of qualified small business stock rolled over into replacement small business stock. (Sec. 18036.5, Rev. & Tax. Code) However, California previously had its own definition of qualified small business stock (see ¶16-070). To the extent gain is not recognized, the unrecognized amount is applied to reduce the basis of the replacement stock in the order in which such stock is acquired. Differences in the basis adjustments may be required if the gain is not recognized for federal, but not California, income tax purposes.

• *Basis adjustments under prior law*

With respect to changes in California's Personal Income Tax Law enacted by Ch. 1138, Laws 1987, a California provision (Sec. 17029.5(c), Rev. & Tax. Code) added by that Act specifies that for purposes of applying the provisions of that Act, the basis or recomputed basis of any asset acquired prior to 1987, must be determined under the law at the time the asset was acquired, and any adjustments to basis must be computed using the following rules:

— any adjustments to basis for taxable years beginning prior to 1987, must be computed under applicable provisions of the Personal Income Tax Law, including all amendments enacted prior to 1987; and

— any adjustments to basis for taxable years beginning after 1986, must be computed under the applicable provisions of Ch. 1138.

Other additions to the taxable income base are listed at ¶16-005.

[¶16-025] Additions--Charitable Contributions

California generally conforms to IRC Sec. 170 for personal income tax purposes. However, California does not conform to federal provisions that allow enhanced charitable contributions of wholesome food inventories and of book inventory contributions made to public schools prior to the 2012 tax year. (Sec. 17275.2, Rev. & Tax. Code); Sec. 17275.3, Rev. & Tax. Code Also, because of California's federal conformity date (see ¶15-515), California does not conform to federal provisions that allow increased deductions for contributions of real property for conservation purposes, nor does California conform to the special treatment for certain agricultural research organizations for contributions made on or after December 18, 2015. Likewise, California does not conform to the increased percentage limitation on the charitable deduction contribution base to 60% (from 50%) of an individual's adjusted gross income for cash donations to public charities in 2018 through 2025. Nor does California conform to the federal repeal of the deduction for amounts paid for college athletic seating rights in tax years beginning after December 31, 2017. (*2017 Summary of Federal Income Tax Changes*, California Franchise Tax Board, May 16, 2018)

Applicable retroactively for taxable years beginning on or after January 1, 2014, California specifically prohibits charitable contribution deductions for payments to postsecondary institutions or the Key Worldwide Foundation by taxpayers that:

— are charged as defendants in certain criminal complaints (relating to the federal college admissions cheating investigation);

— are found guilty with regard to an offense arising out of such a complaint; and

— took the deduction unlawfully pursuant to the final determination of guilt or pursuant to a determination by the FTB.

(Sec. 17275.4, Rev. & Tax. Code)

Subtraction adjustments may also be required.

Other additions to the taxable income base are listed at ¶ 16-005.

[¶ 16-027] Additions--Claim of Right Adjustment

California has its own unique claim of right adjustment (see ¶ 16-225), similar to the federal provision. A taxpayer that claims a deduction on the federal return, but claims a credit in lieu of the deduction on the California return, must make an adjustment on the California return. The adjustment is made by entering the federal deduction as a negative amount on Sch. CA (540), line 41. The credit amount is added on Form 540, line 44, the total payment line. Taxpayers should write "IRC 1341" and the amount of the credit to the left of the total. (Instructions, Sch. CA (540), California Adjustments—Residents)

A related subtraction adjustment is also allowed. Other additions to the taxable income base are listed at ¶ 16-005.

[¶ 16-036] Additions--Death Benefits

Although California incorporates IRC Sec. 692(d), which provides a personal income tax exemption for individuals who died as a result of specified terrorist attacks, California does not incorporate the $10,000 minimum federal death benefit. Consequently, to the extent the minimum benefit is claimed, an adjustment must be made on the California personal income tax return. (Sec. 17731, Rev. & Tax. Code)

California law does not allow the federal exclusion of survivor annuities paid on the death of a public safety officer killed in the line of duty for amounts received in post-2001 tax years with respect to individuals dying prior to 1997. (Sec. 17132.5, Rev. & Tax. Code) Consequently, taxpayers that excluded such amounts on their federal returns were required to make an addition adjustment on their California personal income tax returns.

The addition adjustment for public safety officer survivor annuities is made on Sch. CA (540 or 540NR), line 21(f), column B. (FTB Pub. 1001, Supplemental Guidelines to California Adjustments)

Other additions to the taxable income base are listed at ¶ 16-005.

[¶ 16-037] Additions--Depletion

California does not incorporate the federal extension of the temporary suspension of the taxable income limit with respect to the percentage depletion deduction for oil and natural gas marginal production to include the 2004—2007 and 2009—2011 tax years under IRC Sec. 613A(c)(6)(H). (Sec. 17681.6, Rev. & Tax. Code). Consequently, personal income taxpayers that claim the percentage depletion deduction in excess of the 100-percent-of-net-income limitation on percentage depletion deductions for those years must make an adjustment on their California personal income tax return.

California also does not incorporate the IRC Sec. 613A(d)(4) increase in the barrel limitation from 50,000 to 75,000 for purposes of small refiners qualifying as independent producers eligible to use the percentage depletion method. (Sec. 17681.3, Rev. & Tax. Code) Therefore, small refiners that produce more than 50,000 barrels may have to make an addition adjustment on their California return.

Other additions to the taxable income base are listed at ¶16-005.

[¶16-040] Additions--Depreciation

Except as noted below, for personal income tax purposes, California generally conforms to the federal depreciation deduction (see ¶15-670) for assets placed in service after 1987. Taxpayers who have depreciation differences resulting from the items discussed below, should determine their California depreciation deduction on FTB Form 3885A and make the appropriate addition or subtraction adjustment on Sch. CA (540), line 12, column B or C. It should be noted that items that require an addition adjustment in one year, may result in a smaller California depreciation deduction in later years, thereby requiring a subtraction adjustment. Other differences between California and federal law may also result in subtraction adjustments (see ¶16-245).

• *Election to currently expense depreciable property (IRC Sec. 179)*

Although California incorporates IRC Sec. 179 for assets placed in service after 1986 (Sec. 17201, Rev. & Tax. Code), California does not incorporate the federal amendments that

— increase the maximum federal deduction for post-2011 tax years as listed below;

— increase the investment phase-out amount for post-2011 tax years as listed below;

— allow the deduction to be claimed for off-the-shelf computer software or qualified improvement property;

— allow the deduction to be claimed for air conditioning and heating units for tax years beginning after 2015;

— expand the definition of "qualified property" for taxable years beginning after 2017 include (1) certain depreciable tangible personal property used predominantly to furnish lodging, and (2) roofing, heating, ventilation, air-conditioning property, fire protection, alarm systems, and security system improvements to nonresidential real property placed in service after the date the property was first placed in service (*2017 Summary of Federal Income Tax Changes*, California Franchise Tax Board, May 16, 2018); and

— index the deduction and investment limits.

(Sec. 17255, Rev. & Tax. Code)

California's maximum current expense deduction is $25,000 for property placed in service after 2002, as opposed to the federal maximums listed below. (Sec. 17255(a), Rev. & Tax. Code)

California also does not incorporate the enhanced IRC Sec. 179(e) deduction available for qualified disaster assistance property. (Sec. 17255(g), Rev. & Tax. Code) In addition, as a result of California's federal conformity date history (see ¶15-515), California did not incorporate the federal provisions that allowed enhanced IRC Sec.

179 deductions for Gulf Opportunity Zone property or for qualified Code Sec. 179 recovery assistance property purchased by victims of the 2007 Kansas tornadoes.

Currently, there are no California and federal differences on maximum deduction limits for sports utility vehicles. Federal provisions limit the federal asset expense deduction to $25,000 for SUVs with loaded weights between 6,000 and 14,000 pounds, applicable to vehicles placed in service after October 22, 2004. SUVs placed in service after 2002 and before October 23, 2004, qualified for the higher deduction on a taxpayer's federal, but not California, return.

The following chart lists the maximum IRC Sec. 179 expense deductions for both California and federal purposes for various years:

MAXIMUM CURRENT EXPENSE DEDUCTION

Property placed in service in:	California Law	Federal Law
		$1,000,000 adjusted for
2019 and later tax years	$25,000	inflation
2018	$25,000	$1,000,000
2017	$25,000	$510,000
2016	$25,000	$500,000
2015	$25,000	$500,000
2014	$25,000	$500,000
2013	$25,000	$500,000
2012	$25,000	$500,000
2011	$25,000	$500,000
2010	$25,000	$500,000
2009	$25,000	$250,000
2008	$25,000	$250,000
2007	$25,000	$125,000
2006	$25,000	$108,000
2005	$25,000	$105,000
2004	$25,000	$102,000
2003	$25,000	$100,000
2001-2002	$24,000	$24,000
2000	$20,000	$20,000
1999	$19,000	$19,000
1998	$16,000	$18,500
1997	$13,000	$18,000
After 1992 and before 1997	$10,000	$17,500

Because depreciable basis must be reduced by any IRC Sec. 179 deduction, the depreciable basis of property may differ for federal and state purposes.

For both California purposes and pre-2003 federal law purposes, the deduction is reduced, but not below zero, by the excess of the total investment in qualified property over $200,000 in the tax year. (Sec. 17255(b), Rev. & Tax. Code) The $200,000 limit was increased to $400,000 for federal purposes for property placed in service after 2002 and before 2007 (adjusted to $410,000 for the 2004 tax year, $420,000 for the 2005 tax year, and $430,000 for the 2006 tax year), to $500,000 for property placed in service in 2007, to $800,000 during the 2008 and 2009 tax years, $2 million for the 2010 through 2017 tax years (adjusted to $2,010,000 for 2016, $2,030,000 for 2017), $2.5 million for 2018, and subject to adjustment for inflation thereafter.

In addition, California does not incorporate the federal provision that allows taxpayers to revoke or modify an IRC Sec. 179 election without IRS permission on an amended return, with respect to property placed in service after 2002. Presumably, a taxpayer is required to obtain the California Franchise Tax Board's permission to revoke or amend an election on the California return. (Sec. 17255(e), Rev. & Tax. Code)

• *Bonus depreciation*

California does not allow the federal IRC Sec. 168(k) 50% bonus depreciation for property placed in service in 2008—2026 (2008—2027 in the case of property with a long production period and certain noncommercial aircraft) or the provisions that allow taxpayers to elect to claim an accelerated alternative minimum tax credit or research credit in lieu of claiming bonus depreciation. California also did not allow the federal IRC Sec. 168(k) 30% bonus depreciation deduction for property purchased after September 10, 2001, and placed in service prior to 2005; the optional 50% first-year bonus depreciation deduction for property purchased after May 5, 2003, and placed in service before 2005; or the 30%/50% first-year depreciation allowance for purchases of qualified New York Liberty Zone property. (Sec. 17250(a)(4), Rev. & Tax. Code) Taxpayers that claim the bonus depreciation on their federal returns must recalculate their depreciation deduction on FTB Form 3885A, Depreciation and Amortization Adjustments.

Because California does not incorporate the first-year bonus depreciation deduction, California also does not incorporate the increased limits applied to luxury automobiles (IRC Sec. 280F) to which the bonus depreciation deductions apply. Consequently, taxpayers are also required to adjust the depreciation deduction for such luxury automobiles. (Instructions, FTB Form 3885A, Depreciation and Amortization Adjustments)

• *Bonus depreciation for disaster-related property*

Unlike federal law (IRC Sec. 168(n)), California does not allow a 50% depreciation deduction for the first year that qualified disaster assistance property is placed in service. (Sec. 17250(a)(11), Rev. & Tax. Code)

• *Business property moves into California*

Depreciation methods and useful lives of trade or business property must be acceptable to California. If an unacceptable method was used before the move into California, taxpayers must use the straight-line method to compute the basis in the property. (FTB Pub. 1001, Supplemental Guidelines to California Adjustments)

• *Income forecast method*

Although California conforms to federal law concerning the income forecast method, unlike federal law, California does not prohibit taking distribution costs into account for purposes of determining the depreciation deduction using the income forecast method. (Sec. 17250.5(c), Rev. & Tax. Code) Nor does California incorporate the federal provision providing special rules for depreciating participations and residuals, allowing taxpayers to currently deduct participations and residuals rather than depreciate them using the income forecast method. (Sec. 17250.5(d), Rev. & Tax. Code)

• *Qualified improvement property*

California does not incorporate federal law that classifies "qualified improvement property" as 15-year MACRS property with a 15-year recovery period using the straight-line method unless the MACRS alternative depreciation system (ADS) is elected or otherwise applies. (Sec. 17250(a)(5), (6), and (7), Rev. & Tax. Code) Consequently, such property must be depreciated using the standard MACRS recovery periods for California personal income tax purposes.

• *Film and television production costs*

Because California does not incorporate the federal deduction for film and television production costs (IRC Sec. 181) (see ¶ 16-150), taxpayers may claim an increased California depreciation deduction for the cost of depreciable property that was currently expensed. (Sec. 17201.5, Rev. & Tax. Code)

¶16-040

• *Farm machinery and equipment*

Unlike federal law, California law does not provide a shortened recovery period for farm machinery or equipment, the original use of which begins with the taxpayer in 2009, and that is placed in service by the taxpayer in a farming business in 2009. (Sec. 17250(a)(12), Rev. & Tax. Code) Presumably, the recovery period applicable for California income tax purposes would remain 10 years for such property, rather than the 5-year period allowed under federal law.

• *Cellulosic biofuel plant property; reuse and recycling property; refinery property*

California does not incorporate the 50% first-year depreciation deduction for cellulosic biofuel plant property or for certain reuse and recycling property that is available under federal law. (IRC Sec. 168(m) and (n)) (see ¶ 16-150). (Sec. 17250(a)(8) and (9), Rev. & Tax. Code) Consequently, California's depreciation deduction may be greater than that claimed on the federal return.

Similarly, California did not incorporate

— IRC Sec. 179C, which allowed taxpayers to elect up to 50% qualified refinery property, effective for federal purposes for properties placed in service after August 8, 2005, and before 2014 (Sec. 17257, Rev. & Tax. Code);

— IRC Sec. 179D, which allowed taxpayers to deduct the cost of energy efficient commercial building property placed in service after 2005 and before 2018 (Sec. 17257.2, Rev. & Tax. Code);

— IRC Sec. 179E, which allowed taxpayers to expense up to 50% of the cost of any qualified advanced mine safety equipment property purchased after December 20, 2006, and placed in service prior to 2018.

Because taxpayers will be able to deduct a larger amount of the property costs associated with refineries, energy efficient commercial building property, and advanced mine safety equipment property on their federal returns in the year the property is placed in service, the depreciation deductions for this property will differ on the federal and state returns.

• *Listed property*

As a result of California's current IRC conformity date (see ¶ 15-515), California follows the federal amendment enacted by the Small Business Jobs Act of 2010 that deletes cell phones and similar telecommunications equipment from the definition of "listed property," thereby making it easier for expenses incurred for such equipment eligible to be currently expensed or depreciated on the return. However, different effective dates apply. For California purposes, the amendments apply to taxable years beginning on or after January 1, 2015, while for federal purposes the amendments are effective for taxable years ending after December 31, 2009. Consequently, addition adjustments may be required for such expenses on California returns for tax years prior to 2015.

• *Motorsports entertainment complex*

California incorporates the federal shortened 7-year recovery period for motorsports entertainment complexes beginning with the 2005 tax year and applicable to property placed in service prior to 2008. Federal law allows the shortened recovery period for property placed in service after October 22, 2004, and before 2017. (Sec. 17250(a)(11), Rev. & Tax. Code)

¶16-040

• *Other nonconformity issues*

Because of California's federal conformity date history (see ¶ 15-515), California did not incorporate the following federal provisions until the 2010 tax year:

— the 75% deduction of qualified capital costs paid or incurred during the tax year for the purpose of complying with the Highway Diesel Fuel Sulfur Control Requirements of the EPA that is available to a small business refiner, effective for federal purposes for expenses incurred after 2002 in tax years ending after 2002; and

— the 5-year amortization period for expenses paid or incurred in creating or acquiring a musical composition or a copyright to a musical composition over five-years, effective for property placed in service in tax years beginning after December 31, 2005 for federal purposes; and

— the shortened recovery period for young racehorses placed in service after 2008 and before 2015 (from seven to three years).

Consequently, adjustments will be required for such property placed in service prior to the 2010 tax year.

Also, because of California's current federal conformity date (see ¶ 15-515), California has not conformed to the federal extension of the three-year recovery period for racehorses. California also does not conform to federal amendments made by the Tax Cuts and Jobs Act of 2017 that:

— shorten the alternative depreciation system recovery period for residential rental property from 40 years to 30 years for property placed in service after December 31, 2017; and

— require an electing farming business to use the alternative depreciation system to depreciate certain recovery property for taxable years beginning after December 31, 2017.

(*2017 Summary of Federal Income Tax Changes*, California Franchise Tax Board, May 16, 2018)

• *Accelerated write-offs in economic development areas*

Prior to the 2014 taxable year, taxpayers, other than estates or trusts, may elect to currently deduct 40% (20% in the case of spouses filing separate returns) of the cost of qualified property purchased for exclusive use in a trade or business conducted in an enterprise zone (EZ), targeted tax area (TTA), or local agency military base recovery area (LAMBRA) for the taxable year during which the property is placed in service. (Sec. 17267.2(a) and (d)(4), Rev. & Tax. Code; Sec. 17267.6(a) and (d)(4), Rev. & Tax. Code; Sec. 17268(a), Rev. & Tax. Code) A similar deduction was available for qualified property purchased after August 31, 1992, and prior to December 1, 1998, by a business located in former Los Angeles Revitalization Zone (LARZ). (Former 17266, Rev. & Tax. Code)

The cost that may be taken into account is limited to

— $100,000 for the taxable year that an area is designated as an enterprise zone, TTA, or LAMBRA

— $100,000 for the first taxable year thereafter,

— $75,000 for the second and third taxable years after the year of designation, and

— $50,000 for each taxable year after that.

(Sec. 17267.2(g), Rev. & Tax. Code; Sec. 17267.6(g), Rev. & Tax. Code; Sec. 17268(f), Rev. & Tax. Code) The cost of property does not include that portion of the basis of that property that is determined by reference to the basis of other property held at any time by the person acquiring that property.

"Qualified property" defined.—For purposes of these deductions, "qualified property" is property that

— meets the eligibility requirements set forth in IRC Sec. 1245(a)(3);

— is purchased and placed in service by the taxpayer for exclusive use in an EZ, TTA, or LAMBRA trade or business; and

— is purchased and placed in service before the date the EZ, TTA, or LAMBRA designation expires, is no longer binding, or becomes inoperative. (Sec. 17267.2(d), Rev. & Tax. Code; Sec. 17267.6(d), Rev. & Tax. Code; Sec. 17268(d), Rev. & Tax. Code) These economic development programs were repealed effective January 1, 2014.

The deductions do not apply to property for which the taxpayer, because of the provisions of IRC Sec. 179(d), is prohibited from claiming an expense deduction for federal income tax purposes. (Sec. 17267.2(d)(5), Rev. & Tax. Code; Sec. 17267.6(d)(5), Rev. & Tax. Code; Sec. 17268(i), Rev. & Tax. Code)

Property does not qualify for the EZ, TTA, or LAMBRA expense deduction if

— it was acquired from a related person (as defined by statute),

— it was acquired by one member of an affiliated group from another member of the same group, or

— the taxpayer's basis in the property is determined, in whole or in part, by reference to the adjusted basis of the property in the hands of the person from whom it was acquired.

(Sec. 17267.2(d), Rev. & Tax. Code; Sec. 17267.6(d), Rev. & Tax. Code; Sec. 17268(d), Rev. & Tax. Code) In addition, the deduction is unavailable for property described in IRC Sec. 168(f). The latter exception is listed in the Instructions to the FTB 3805Z (Enterprise Zone Booklet) and FTB 3809 (Targeted Tax Area Booklet), but is only specifically mentioned in the statute governing the current expense deduction for LAMBRAs. (Sec. 17268(d)(7), Rev. & Tax. Code)

Eligible taxpayers.—Taxpayers located in an enterprise zone who purchase the property for exclusive use within the EZ may claim the deduction. (Sec. 17267.2(e), Rev. & Tax. Code) Only those taxpayers involved in the following business activities described in the federal Standard Industrial Classification (SIC) Manual (or North American Industry Classification System Manual) are eligible to claim the TTA deduction: manufacturing; transportation; communications; electric, gas, and sanitary services; and wholesale trade. For pass-through entities, eligibility is determined at the entity level. (Sec. 17267.6(e), Rev. & Tax. Code) Only those LAMBRA businesses that have a net increase of one or more employees in the first two taxable years are eligible to claim the deduction. (Sec. 17268(e), Rev. & Tax. Code)

Election.—An expense deduction election must be made on a taxpayer's original return for the taxable year during which the qualified property is placed in service, and must specify the items of property to which the election applies. Once an election has been made, it may be revoked only with the consent of the FTB. (Sec. 17267.2(c), Rev. & Tax. Code; Sec. 17267.6(c), Rev. & Tax. Code; Sec. 17268(c), Rev. & Tax. Code)

Interaction with other deductions.—A taxpayer that elects to claim a current expense deduction for the qualified property may not also claim an IRC Sec. 179 deduction for California personal income tax purposes. (Sec. 17267.2(f), Rev. & Tax. Code; Sec. 17267.6(f), Rev. & Tax. Code; Sec. 17268(i), Rev. & Tax. Code)

• *Nonresidential real property*

For both federal and California purposes beginning with the 1997 taxable year, nonresidential real property is depreciated over a 39-year recovery period. Nonresidential real property is property that is neither residential rental property nor property with a class life of less than 27.5 years. The Revenue Reconciliation Act of 1993 increased the federal recovery period for nonresidential real property to 39 years, generally applicable to property placed in service after May 12, 1993. California's recovery period for property placed in service after May 12, 1993, and before 1997 is 31.5 years. (Sec. 17250, Rev. & Tax. Code) (FTB Pub. 1001, Supplemental Guidelines to California Adjustments)

• *Property on Native American reservations*

California does not incorporate IRC Sec. 168(j), which provides special rules for depreciation of qualified Indian reservation property, generally applicable for federal purposes to property placed in service after 1993 and before 2017. (Sec. 17250, Rev. & Tax. Code) Under federal law, special MACRS recovery periods are provided for qualified Indian reservation property to allow accelerated write-offs of such property.

• *Environmental remediation costs*

Because California does not allow the federal expensing of environmental remediation costs after 2003 and during the 2001 taxable years (see ¶16-055), these costs must be capitalized for California personal income tax purposes. The adjustment is made on FTB 3885A, to enter on Sch. CA (540 or 540NR).

• *Disaster costs*

California does not incorporate IRC Sec. 198A, which allows costs incurred after 2007 for disasters that are federally declared after that date and before 2010 to be expensed rather than capitalized. (Sec. 17279.6, Rev. & Tax. Code) To the extent such amounts are deducted from federal taxable income, and are not eligible for deduction under other California personal income tax provisions, taxpayers must add such amounts to federal taxable income. Amounts that are added back are eligible for increased depreciation deductions in subsequent tax years.

• *Grapevines*

The capitalization of expenditures incurred in planting and developing fruit and nut groves or orchards is determined in accordance with IRC Sec. 263A. Federal law generally requires a 10-year recovery period for fruit bearing vines for purposes of ACRS and a 20-year recovery period for those vines under an alternative depreciation system

However, a five-year depreciation period under the ACRS method is used for any grapevine replaced in a California vineyard (1) in a taxable year beginning after 1991, as a direct result of phylloxera infestation or (2) in a taxable year beginning after 1996, as a direct result of Pierce's Disease. If a taxpayer elects under IRC Sec. 168 to use the Alternative Depreciation System, then any phylloxera-infested grapevines replaced in a taxable year beginning after 1991 or Pierce's Disease-infested grapevines replaced in a taxable year beginning after 1996, have a class life of 10 years. (Sec. 17250, Rev. & Tax. Code)

• *Tertiary injectants*

For federal purposes, the cost of certain tertiary injectants may be currently deducted as an expense in the year incurred under IRC Sec. 193. Taxpayers claiming the addition on their federal return must make an addition adjustment on their California return. The addition adjustment is made on Sch. CA (540 or 540NR), line 12, column C. Although such cost may not be currently deducted, it may be depreciated for California purposes. (Sec. 17260(a), Rev. & Tax. Code) (FTB Pub. 1001, Supplemental Guidelines to California Adjustments)

• *Electric transmission property and natural gas lines*

Because of California's federal conformity date history (see ¶ 15-515), California did not incorporate until the 2010 tax year federal provisions that provide the following recovery periods under IRC Sec. 168:

— for certain electric transmission property, 15 years;

— for new natural gas gathering lines, seven years; and

— for new natural gas distribution lines, 15 years.

The changes are effective for federal purposes for property placed in service after April 11, 2005.

• *Pre-1987 methods of depreciation*

IRC Sec. 167, relating to the depreciation of property, is incorporated by reference into California law (Sec. 17201, Rev. & Tax. Code) with modifications. Under IRC Sec. 167 as incorporated, a taxpayer is permitted a deduction for depreciation of property used in a trade or business or held for the production of income. (Sec. 17201, Rev. & Tax. Code) Under both California law applicable to assets placed in service before 1987 in taxable years beginning before 1987, and federal law applicable to assets placed in service before 1981, depreciation may be computed under the straight-line method, the double declining balance method, the sum-of-the-years-digits method, and other "consistent" methods, with the latter three methods applicable only to tangible property with a useful life of three or more years.

Under federal law, the pre-ACRS methods found in IRC Sec. 167 are applicable to property completed or acquired after 1953, and before December 31, 1980; while under California law they are applicable to property completed or acquired after 1958, and placed in service before 1987 in taxable years beginning before 1987.

Useful life.—Under federal regulations applicable for California purposes in interpreting IRC Sec. 167 (Sec. 17024.5(c), Rev. & Tax. Code), personal property had to be depreciated over its useful life (Fed. Reg. 1.167(a)-1(b)). The useful life, for this purpose, is not necessarily the useful life inherent in the asset. It is the period over which the asset may reasonably be expected to be useful to the taxpayer in his trade or business or in the production of his income. The period may be determined either by reference to the taxpayer's experience or general experience in the industry with similar property taking into account present conditions and probable future developments (Fed. Reg. 1.167(a)-1(b)), or it may be determined under the Asset Depreciation Range system discussed below (Fed. Reg. 1.167(a)-11).

Buildings, unlike personal property, may not be depreciated over a period determined under the Asset Depreciation Range System (ADR), because there are no ADR classes (except for some special purpose buildings). Taxpayers may use the federal guideline lives under Revenue Procedure 62-21 as a guide in determining the useful life of buildings; however, the SBE has ruled that Rev. Proc. 62-21 (1962-2 CB 418) is only a guide, and may not be arbitrarily applied with no objective standard.

The guideline lives for new buildings under Rev. Proc. 62-21 are:

Apartment buildings, hotels, theaters . . . . 40 years

Factories, garages, machine shops, office buildings, dwellings . . . . 45 years

Loft buildings, banks . . . . 50 years

Wholesale and retail business buildings, warehouses, grain elevators . . 60 years

The guideline lives measure the useful lives of assets acquired new because it is not possible to prescribe guidelines for used assets. The useful life of any used asset depends upon its age at the time acquired (answer to question 18, Rev. Proc. 62-21, 1962-2 CB 418). However, the fact that a taxpayer has a substantial amount of used assets in a guideline class would be taken into account by the Internal Revenue Service as a factor demonstrating that a shorter life than the guideline life may be justified for that class.

Asset depreciation range (ADR) system.—California adopted the provisions of Federal Revenue Procedure 62-21, for assets placed in service before 1971. Former California Regulation 17208 adopted by reference federal regulation 1.167(a)-11, which provided for the Federal ADR System for property placed in service after 1970, and before 1987. The federal ADR provision was effective, beginning in 1971, for assets placed in service after 1970 and before 1981. From 1971 to years ending before March 21, 1977, rates established by Federal Revenue Procedure 72-10 were applicable in California; the rates for years ending on and after March 21, 1977, were originally stated in Revenue Procedure 77-10 and have been restated and to some extent modified in Revenue Procedure 83-35. The ADR rates were used for federal tax purposes until replaced by ACRS.

Former Reg. 17208 did not permit use of the 20% ADR variances given for each asset guideline period for California purposes, and excluded federal rules for depreciation of public utility property which conflicted with the California code. As under pre-1981 federal law, California taxpayers using ADR could elect double declining balance, sum-of-the-years-digits or the straight-line methods for eligible new property, and 150% declining balance and the straight-line method for eligible used assets.

As under pre-1981 federal law, depreciation rates for real estate were treated separately. Under former subsection (j) of IRC Sec. 167, which was incorporated by California prior to its repeal by the Revenue Reconciliation Act of 1990, the depreciation of new commercial real estate bought or constructed after 1970, and before 1987, was restricted to the straight-line method, 150% declining balance method, or any other consistent method that did not give greater allowances in the first two-thirds of useful life than the 150% declining balance method; as to new residential property acquired after 1970 and before 1987, the 200% declining balance and sum-of-the-years digits methods could be used.

For federal purposes, the provision was applicable only to property acquired in tax years ending after July 24, 1969, and before 1981.

First year allowance (bonus depreciation).—Prior to its repeal for tax years beginning after 1986, former Rev. & Tax. Code Sec. 17252 allowed the deduction of 20% of the cost of certain depreciable property in the first year of use as depreciation in addition to the depreciation otherwise allowed. A basis adjustment of the property for which first-year bonus depreciation was taken was required.

¶16-040

Salvage value reduction.—For assets placed in service before 1987, and depreciated under the ADR system, California allowed an amount of salvage value to be taken into account in computing the amount subject to depreciation. Assets placed in service after 1986, are depreciated using the federal modified ACRS method, under which salvage value is not taken into account. Also, salvage value is not taken into account in depreciating assets for which the taxpayer elects to use the straight-line method. For assets placed in service before 1987, a salvage value reduction required a basis adjustment. Salvage value was determined under former subsection (f) of IRC Sec. 167.

Child care facilities.—For taxable years beginning before 1987, certain child care facilities could be depreciated over a period of 60 months for California purposes (see ¶ 15-585). Federal law permitted a similar write-off for tax years between 1972 and 1981.

Energy conservation measures.—For California purposes, for taxable years beginning before 1987, the cost of certain energy conservation measures could have been credited or deducted as depreciation expense over a 36-month period. There was no equivalent federal provision.

Residential rental property.—Prior to 1987, when California adopted MACRS, IRC Sec. 168, concerning ACRS, could only be used in determining depreciation for certain California residential rental property on which construction was begun after June 30, 1985 (former Rev. & Tax. Code Sec. 17250.5). California generally adopted the use of modified ACRS to depreciate property placed in service after 1986, in taxable years after 1986; previously, ACRS could be used only for residential rental property.

Former Rev. & Tax. Code Sec. 17250.5 provided that qualified residential rental property except low-income housing was considered "18-year real property" for purposes of depreciation using former subsection (b) of IRC Sec. 168. For federal purposes, residential rental property placed in service after May 8, 1985, was treated as "19-year real property" rather than 18-year real property.

Foreign residential rental property.—Under former subsection (j) of IRC Sec. 167, which was incorporated by California prior to its repeal by the Revenue Reconciliation Act of 1990, foreign residential rental property placed in service before 1987, could be depreciated under the 200% declining balance method only if the laws of the foreign country provided a comparable method. If foreign law allowed a less accelerated method, that law applied unless the amount allowed was less than under the 150% declining balance method. "Residential rental property" was defined as property from which 80% or more of the gross rental income is derived from dwelling units.

Used real property.—Under former subsection (j) of IRC Sec. 167, which was incorporated by California prior to its repeal by the Revenue Reconciliation Act of 1990, accelerated depreciation was prohibited, except for used residential rental property having a useful life of 20 years or more, which could be depreciated using a 125% declining balance method.

Safe-harbor sale-leasebacks.—California did not incorporate the safe-harbor leasing rules under former IRC Sec. 168(f).

Currently, for purposes of both federal and California law, the "pre-safe harbor lease rules" that were in effect before the Economic Recovery Tax Act of 1984 was enacted continue to apply to real property leases. These rules are comprised of judicially formulated standards as supplemented by IRS ruling and procedures.

Other additions to the taxable income base are listed at ¶ 16-005.

¶16-040

[¶16-045] Additions--Dividends

An addition adjustment is required for federally exempt interest dividends from other states, or their municipal obligations from mutual funds that do not meet the 50% rule (see ¶15-185). (Sec. 17088, Rev. & Tax. Code; Sec. 17145, Rev. & Tax. Code)

In addition, California taxes controlled foreign corporation (CFC) dividends in the year distributed rather than the year earned. If CFC dividends are earned in one year and distributed in a later year, an addition adjustment is required for the dividends included in federal income for the year earned. The adjustment is made on Sch. CA (540 or 540NR), line 9, column B. A corresponding subtraction adjustment is made in the year the dividend is distributed (see ¶16-250). (FTB Pub. 1001, Supplemental Guidelines to California Adjustments)

Similar treatment is applied to undistributed capital gain from a regulated investment company (RIC). (Sec. 17088(c), Rev. & Tax. Code) California taxes undistributed capital gain from a RIC in the year distributed rather than the year earned. If capital gain from a RIC is earned in one year and distributed in a later year, an addition adjustment is required for the capital gain included in federal income for the year earned. The adjustment is made on Sch. CA (540 or 540NR), line 9, column B. A corresponding subtraction adjustment is made in the year the capital gain is distributed (see ¶16-250). (FTB Pub. 1001, Supplemental Guidelines to California Adjustments)

Dividends received from a Health Savings Account must also be added back to federal adjusted gross income (see ¶16-100). The adjustment is made on Sch. CA (540), line 9, column C. (FTB Pub. 1001, Supplemental Guidelines to California Adjustments)

Other additions to the taxable income base are listed at ¶16-005.

[¶16-050] Additions--Education Expenses

Addition adjustments may be required for taxpayers that claim the above-the-line deductions for (1) qualified tuition and related expenses and (2) elementary or secondary school teachers expenses and for taxpayers who make nonqualified withdrawals from a qualified tuition program.

• *Qualified tuition and related expenses*

Unlike federal law (IRC Sec. 222), California does not allow a deduction for qualified tuition and related expenses incurred by individual taxpayers. (Sec. 17204.7, Rev. & Tax. Code)

The addition adjustment required as a result of California's nonconformity with the federal deduction is made on Sch. CA (540 or 540NR), line 34, column B. (FTB Pub. 1001, Supplemental Guidelines to California Adjustments)

• *Teachers' expenses*

California does not incorporate federal law authorizing an above-the-line deduction for qualified expenses incurred by elementary and secondary school teachers, instructors, counselors, principals, or aides. (Sec. 17072, Rev. & Tax. Code) Taxpayers that claim the deduction on the federal return must make an adjustment on Sch. CA (540 or 540NR), line 23, column B. (FTB Pub. 1001, Supplemental Guidelines to California Adjustments)

• *Nonqualified withdrawals from qualified tuition program*

California does not conform to federal provisions modifying Sec. 529 plans to allow the plans to distribute after December 31, 2017, no more than $10,000 in tuition expenses incurred during the tax year for designated beneficiaries enrolled at a public, private, or religious elementary or secondary school. (Sec. 17140.3, Rev. & Tax. Code) Prior to 2019, California also did not conform to an amendment made to Sec. 529 that allows the rollover of certain amounts from a Sec. 529 plan to an ABLE account after December 22, 2017, and before January 1, 2026, without penalty. The federal changes to IRC Sec. 529 were enacted by the Tax Cut and Jobs Act of 2017 (P.L. 115-97). (*2017 Summary of Federal Income Tax Changes*, California Franchise Tax Board, May 16, 2018)

Taxpayers who make nonqualified withdrawals for California purposes will have to make an addition adjustment on their California return, and may be subject to a penalty for premature withdrawal.

[¶16-055] Additions--Environmental or Pollution Control

California requires addition adjustments for the following environmental-related federal deductions. Also, see the discussion of prior law computation rules (see ¶15-530) for adjustments relating to clean-fuel vehicles and clean fuel vehicle refueling property and environmental remediation costs.

•*Reforestation expenses*

California, unlike federal law (IRC Sec. 194), does not allow a current expense deduction or amortization deduction for qualified reforestation expenses associated with qualified timber located outside California. (Sec. 17278.5, Rev. & Tax. Code) Consequently, taxpayers that claim the deduction on their federal return for timber located outside California, must make adjustments on Sch. CA (540 or 540NR), lines 12, 17, or 18, as appropriate, column B. Amortization adjustments are reflected on FTB Form 3885A, Depreciation and Amortization Adjustments.

•*EPA sulfur regulations compliance costs*

California does not incorporate the federal deduction (IRC Sec. 179B) of capital costs incurred in complying with Environmental Protection Agency sulfur regulations. (Sec. 17201.4, Rev. & Tax. Code) Consequently, an addition adjustment is required.

Other additions to the taxable income base are listed at ¶16-005.

[¶16-060] Additions--Foreign Source Income/Expenses

Other than the exclusion of foreign employee compensation and the treatment of foreign currency transactions (see ¶15-700), California does not incorporate federal law (IRC Secs. 891 through 999), concerning income from sources outside the United States. Residents are taxable on all income and nonresidents are taxed on all income attributable to California sources. Federal foreign earned income and the housing exclusion deducted from federal income under IRC Sec. 911 on Form 1040, line 21, are added back for California personal income tax purposes on Sch. CA (540), line 21(f), column C. (Instructions, Sch. CA (540), California Adjustments—Residents)

In addition, income exempted by treaty under federal law may be excluded for California only if the treaty specifically excludes the income for state purposes. If a state-exemption is not provided, the income excluded on the federal return must be added back to federal income on Sch. CA (540 or 540NR), line 7, column C. (FTB Pub.

1001, Supplemental Guidelines to California Adjustments) An adjustment may also be required for foreign losses (see ¶ 16-263).

Other additions to the taxable income base are listed at ¶ 16-005. For a discussion of the former adjustment required for taxpayers who claimed the former IRC Sec. 114 extraterritorial income exclusion see the discussion regarding prior law computation rules (¶ 15-530).

[¶ 16-065] Additions--Fringe Benefits

Cash paid to employees by employers under a California "parking cash-out program" must be included in the employee's gross income, except any portion treated as an excludable ridesharing benefit (see ¶ 16-265). (Sec. 17090, Rev. & Tax. Code) A parking cash-out program is an employer-funded program under which an employer offers to provide a cash allowance to an employee equivalent to the parking subsidy that the employer would otherwise pay to provide the employee with a parking space. (Sec. 65088.1, Govt. Code)

To the extent excluded from federal taxable income, an addition adjustment is required for parking cash-out payments that are not treated as an excludable California ridesharing benefit. The adjustment is made on Sch. CA (540), line 21(f), column C.

An addition adjustment is also required for employer contributions to health savings accounts (see ¶ 16-100).

Other additions to the taxable income base are listed at ¶ 16-005.

[¶ 16-070] Additions--Gains

Adjustments may be required for the gain recognized on the transactions discussed below.

• *Sale of personal residence*

California law (but not federal law) provides that if a taxpayer serves in the Peace Corps during the five years preceding the sale of the taxpayer's principal residence, the IRC Sec. 121 two-year ownership and use requirement incorporated by California, may be reduced by the amount of time served in the Peace Corps, but by no more than 18 months. (Sec. 17152, Rev. & Tax. Code)

Although California currently conforms to the IRC Sec. 121 exclusion of gain on the sale of a principal residence, different effective dates apply concerning post-2004 federal amendments as follows:

— the suspension of the five-year test period for certain employees of the intelligence community serving on qualified extended duty outside the U.S, is effective for sales or exchanges after December 31, 2010 for California purposes, and to sales and exchanges occurring after December 20, 2006 for federal purposes;

— that suspension of the five-year test period for taxpayers or their spouses serving outside the United States in the Peace Corps during the period of their service, applies for California purposes beginning with the 2010 tax year and for federal purposes beginning with the 2008 tax year;

— the extension of the requirement that a personal residence acquired in a like-kind exchange be held for at least five years in order to be eligible for the exclusion to transferees of the property applies for California purposes beginning with the 2010 tax year and for federal purposes to sales or exchanges occurring after October 22, 2004; and

— the provision allowing an unmarried surviving spouse to claim the $500,000 exclusion available to joint filers if the principal residence is sold or exchanged within two years of the spouse's death applies for California purposes to sales or exchanges after 2009 and to for sales or exchanges after 2007 for federal purposes.

If there are differences in the amounts excluded under federal and California law, taxpayers should complete Schedule D (540 or 540NR). Transfer the amount from California Schedule D, line 12a to Sch. CA (540 or 540NR), line 13, column C if the California gain is more than the federal. (FTB Pub. 1001, Supplemental Guidelines to California Adjustments) See ¶16-270 for the corresponding subtraction adjustment.

• *Gain on sale of small business stock*

Legislation enacted in 2013 (Ch. 546 (A.B. 1412)), retroactively reinstated a modified version of California's qualified small business stock gain deferral and exclusion provisions for the 2008—2012 tax years. (Sec. 18038.5, Rev. & Tax. Code; Sec. 18152.5, Rev. & Tax. Code) California's original QSBS gain deferral provision, which was based on the QSBS exclusion eligibility provision, was struck down in *Cutler v. Franchise Tax Board* (2012) 146 Cal.Rptr.3d 244, 208 Cal.App.4th 1247, as an unconstitutional violation of the dormant Commerce Clause because it was only available to taxpayers that invested in corporations that had a significant presence in California. In response to the court's decision in *Cutler*, which did not address the remedy issue, the Franchise Tax Board (FTB) issued FTB Notice 2012-03, which retroactively denied the deferral and exclusion provisions for all taxpayers for all open tax years.

California's QSBS provisions were generally identical to the federal provisions. However, unlike federal law, to qualify for the California exclusion in effect prior to the *Cutler* decision, California also required that:

— at least 80% of the corporation's payroll measured by total dollar value, has to be attributable to employment located within California and

— at least 80 percent (by value) of the assets of the corporation used by the corporation must be in the active conduct of one or more qualified trades or businesses in California. (Sec. 18152.5(c)(2)(A), Rev. & Tax. Code)

The modified provisions enacted by A.B. 1412 in 2013, and effective retroactively to the 2008—2012 tax years, eliminated the previous requirement that 80% percent of business activity occur in California during the holding period. However, the QSBS still had to meet the 80% California payroll requirement at the time of the stock's acquisition to claim the gain exclusion or deferral, but the 80% California-employment level no longer needed to be maintained for all periods for which the exclusion was claimed. The reinstatement of the 50% gain exclusion applied to sales, including installment sales, occurring in each taxable year beginning after 2007 and before 2013, and to installment payments received in taxable years beginning after 2007, for sales of QSBS made in taxable years beginning before 2013.

Prior to being struck down as unconstitutional in the *Cutler* decision, California's exclusion of 50% of the gain on qualified small business stock was almost identical to the federal exclusion prior to its amendment by the American Recovery and Reinvestment Tax Act of 2009 (Recovery Act) (P.L. 111-5) and Small Business Jobs Act (P.L. 111-240) (2010 Jobs Act) (IRC Sec. 1202). However, California did not incorporate federal amendments that increased the IRC Sec. 1202 federal exclusion from income on the gain of small business stock from 50% to 75% for stock acquired after February 17, 2009 and before January 1, 2011, and that further increased the exclusion to 100% for stock acquired after September 27, 2010, and before 2014 (2017 for empowerment zone businesses), and held for more than five years.

CCH COMMENT: Interest/penalty waivers.—No penalties or interest will accrue with respect to any addition to tax that may result from the A.B. 1412 amendments described above or, if the provisions discussed above are struck down by an appellate court, to any addition to tax to the extent that the increase is attributable to the implementation of the appellate court's decision invalidating the provisions as amended, coupled with the implementation of the appellate court's decision in *Cutler*. (Sec. 18153, Rev. & Tax. Code)

• *Involuntary conversions*

Although California generally incorporates the federal involuntary conversion provisions (IRC Sec. 1033) as of California's current federal conformity date (see ¶15-515), California differs from federal law concerning the treatment of transactions involving outdoor advertising displays.

Under both California and federal law involuntarily converted real property held for productive use or investment may be replaced with similar property without recognition of gain. Federal law will only treat outdoor advertising displays as real property eligible for involuntary conversion gain nonrecognition if the taxpayer has not elected to expense it as a depreciable asset under IRC Sec. 179, the asset expense election. However, California does not incorporate this limitation. Thus, for purposes of involuntary conversions, advertising displays that have been expensed on the taxpayer's federal return may be treated as real property. (Sec. 18037, Rev. & Tax. Code)

• *Like-kind exchanges*

Although California generally incorporates the federal rules governing like-kind exchanges under IRC Sec. 1031, California does not conform to federal amendments that extend like-kind exchange tax deferred treatment to an exchange of certain mutual ditch, reservoir, or irrigation company stock completed after May 22, 2008. (Former Sec. 18031.5, Rev. & Tax. Code) However, according to the FTB's Summary of 2008 Federal Legislative Changes, under California law mutual water companies that were formed before September 26, 1977, are allowed to transfer assets to community services districts tax-free. Thus, changes to IRC Sec. 1031, relating to special rules for mutual ditch, reservoir, or irrigation company stock does not apply.

NEW DEVELOPMENTS: Under the federal Tax Cuts and Jobs Act of 2017 (P.L. 115–97), the special rules under IRC Sec. 1031(i), relating to mutual ditch, reservoir, or irrigation company stock, were repealed.

In addition, California law, unlike federal law, has an information return reporting requirement if the replacement property is purchased outside California (see ¶89-104).

Finally, California does not conform to the federal amendments that extend the like-kind exchange exemption applicable to qualified exchanges of insurance contracts to apply to exchanges of an annuity, endowment, or life insurance contract for a qualified long-term care insurance contract or to exchanges of one qualified long-term care insurance contract for another long-term care insurance contract. (Sec. 18037.5, Rev. & Tax. Code)

For tax years beginning after 2018, and for exchanges completed after January 10, 2019, California will generally conform to the TCJA amendments to IRC Sec. 1031 limiting nonrecognition of gain or loss on like-kind exchanges to real property. However, the conformity provision only applies to individuals with adjusted gross incomes of over $250,000, for single filers and $500,000, for joint filers. Taxpayers that do not fall into the categories noted above are subject to the pre-TCJA IRC Sec. 1031 like-kind exchange rules. (Sec. 18031.5, Rev. & Tax. Code)

• *Recapture of depreciation on certain depreciable property*

Although California incorporates federal law (IRC Sec. 1245) that treats the gain on the sale of Sec. 1245 property as ordinary income rather than as capital gain to the extent of all previously allowed or allowable depreciation or amortization, differences may arise because California does not recognize the same amortization and depreciation deductions allowed under federal law. IRC Sec. 1245(a)(2) as incorporated by California, treats the following deductions as amortization for purposes of this recapture treatment:

— the current expense deduction available under IRC Sec. 179;

— the deduction for clean-fuel vehicles under IRC Sec. 179A;

— expenses deducted to provide access to the handicapped and the elderly under IRC Sec. 190; and

— tertiary injectant expenses deducted under IRC Sec. 193.

However, because California does not incorporate the tertiary injectant expense deduction (see ¶16-150) and allows a lower amount to be currently expensed under IRC Sec. 179 (see ¶16-040), these expenses are not subject to recapture for California income tax purposes. Furthermore, California also treats the current expense deductions available for enterprise zone property and the Los Angeles Revitalization Zone property (see ¶16-040) as amortization for purposes of IRC Sec. 1245 recapture. (Sec. 18165, Rev. & Tax. Code) Presumably, these differences should be reflected on Sch. D (540 or 540NR).

In addition, California's the effective date for the provision that requires recapture as ordinary income on disposal of multiple IRC Sec. 197 assets (intangibles) to the extent amortization deductions were claimed on any one or all of the assets differs for California and federal purposes. The recapture provision applies for California purposes to dispositions of property after 2009 and for federal purposes to dispositions after August 8, 2005. (Sec. 18165, Rev. & Tax. Code)

• *Recapture of depreciation on real property*

Although California generally incorporates the federal rules governing the recapture of depreciation on real property, differences may arise as a result of the different current depreciation rules (see ¶16-040) and as a result of historical differences. (Sec. 18171, Rev. & Tax. Code; Sec. 18171.5, Rev. & Tax. Code) Presumably, these differences should be reflected on Sch. D (540 or 540NR).

• *Special rules on foreign investment company stock*

California does not incorporate IRC Sec. 1248, providing special rules for gain from certain sales or exchanges of stock in certain foreign corporations, and IRC Sec. 1249, which denies capital gains treatment on the sale or exchange of a patent, invention, copyright, formula or similar property right to a foreign corporation controlled by the transferor. Nor did California incorporate former IRC Sec. 1246 and IRC Sec. 1247, which provided special rules for gain on foreign investment company stock. (Sec. 17024.5(b)(5), (9), Rev. & Tax. Code) These latter provisions were repealed for foreign corporations were repealed for federal purposes beginning after 2004, and for tax years of U.S. shareholders with or within which such tax years of foreign corporations end. California does not provide special treatment for foreign-source income (see ¶ 15-700). Any necessary adjustments would presumably be reported on Sch. D (540 or 540NR).

• *Gain or loss from sale or exchange of Fannie Mae or Freddie Mac preferred stock*

California does not incorporate the federal provision that provides ordinary gain or loss treatment to the sale or exchange of Fannie Mae or Freddie Mac preferred stock by certain financial institutions. (Sec. 18151.5, Rev. & Tax. Code) Consequently, a transaction in Fannie Mae or Freddie Mac preferred stock receives treatment as capital gain or loss for California tax purposes and would be subject to the capital loss limitation rules. Consequently, and addition and subsequent subtraction modifications may be required.

• *Gains from electric transmission transactions*

California does not incorporate federal law (IRC Sec. 451(i)), which allows taxpayers to recognize qualified gain from a qualifying electric transmission transaction over an eight-year period. (Sec. 17551(f), Rev. & Tax. Code) Consequently, taxpayers must recognize the entire gain for California purposes in the year of the transaction. Presumably, this difference is reflected on Sch. D (540 or 540NR)

• *Loans with below market interest rates*

California also incorporates IRC Sec. 7872 as of California's current federal conformity date, which provides special rules for the treatment of loans with below-market interest rates. (Sec. 18180(b), Rev. & Tax. Code) Under IRC Sec. 7872, when certain types of loans are made at below-market interest rates, the lender is treated as transferring, and the borrower is treated as receiving, the excess of the amount loaned over the present value of all payments that are required to be made under the terms of the loan. However, the provision that relaxes the requirements of exemption from the below-market interest loan rules for loans to continuing care facilities for a five-year period is applicable for California purposes beginning after 2009, with respect to loans made before, on or after January 1, 2010, but is applicable for federal purposes in calendar years beginning after 2005, with respect to loans made before, on, or after December 31, 2005. (Sec. 18180(b), Rev. & Tax. Code) Consequently, modifications may be required for loans made after 2004 and before 2010.

• *Agricultural refiner/processors stock sales to farm cooperatives*

California does not incorporate federal law (IRC Sec. 1042(g)), which allows a taxpayer to defer the recognition of gain from the sale of stock of a qualified agricultural refiner or processor to an eligible cooperative. (Sec. 18042, Rev. & Tax. Code) Taxpayers that elect gain nonrecognition on their federal return, must recompute the amount of reportable gain for California income tax purposes on Sch. D (540 or 540NR).

• *Basis of certain property acquired under prior codes*

Although California incorporates by reference IRC Sec. 1052(a) and (b), prescribing the method for determining the basis of certain property acquired after February 28, 1913, under the basis rules of the Revenue Acts of 1932 and 1934 (property acquired in a tax-free exchange, corporate property acquired in reorganization, property acquired by issuance of stock or paid-in surplus, and stock received in a corporate spin-off) (Sec. 18031, Rev. & Tax. Code), California does not incorporate IRC Sec. 1052(c), which retains eight enumerated basis provisions of former IRC Sec. 113 of the 1939 code, applicable for pre-1954-code acquisitions (relating to tax-free exchanges, certain transfers to corporations, property acquired by issuing stock or as paid-in surplus, partnership property, property acquired by a corporation upon complete liquidation of another, property received in certain corporate liquidations, certain stock dividends and stock rights, and stock on certain spin-off distributions). However, California retains seven basis provisions from the Personal Income Tax Law of 1954, applicable for property to which they applied (concerning property acquired in certain tax-free exchanges, property acquired by partnerships, certain stock-acquisition rights, property acquired in certain corporate liquidation redemptions, and certain tax-free distributions) (see ¶16-070). (Sec. 18039, Rev. & Tax. Code)

Other additions to the taxable income base are listed at ¶16-005.

[¶16-075] Additions--Interest

California requires addition adjustments for interest earned on non-California state and municipal obligations, investment interest, and original issue discount (OID) for debt instruments issued in 1985 and 1986. Interest received from a health savings account must also be added back to federal adjusted gross income (see ¶16-100).

• *Interest on non-California state and municipal obligations*

Unlike federal law, California does not allow an exclusion for interest earned on non-California state and local bonds. (Sec. 17143, Rev. & Tax. Code) The addition adjustment is made on Sch. CA (540 or 540NR), line 8, column C. In addition to non-California state and municipal bond interest, interest from the following obligations must also be included:

— obligations of the District of Columbia issued after December 27, 1973;

— non-California bonds if interest was passed through from S corporations, trusts, partnerships, or LLCs; and

— bonds or other obligations issued by the Government of American Samoa.

(Instructions, Sch. CA (540), California Adjustments—Residents)

California does allow an exclusion for interest earned on California state and local bonds and obligations (see ¶16-280).

• *Investment interest*

Under federal law (IRC Sec. 163(d)), as incorporated by California, a deduction is allowed for interest up to the amount of net investment income. (Sec. 17201, Rev. & Tax. Code) Because the amount of net investment income reported on the federal return may be different than that reported on the California return because of differences in the classifications of exempt income, depreciation, capital gains, etc., the amount of the deduction may likewise be different. The California deduction is calculated on FTB 3526, Investment Interest Expense Deduction.

Net capital gain from the disposition of investment property is generally excluded from investment income. However taxpayers may elect to include as much of their net capital gain as they choose in calculating the investment interest limitation for federal purposes if they also reduce the amount of net capital gain eligible for the special federal capital gains tax. Taxpayers are allowed to make a similar election for California purposes; however, California treats capital gains as ordinary income.

Any amount not allowed as a deduction for any taxable year because of this limitation may be carried over and treated as deductible investment interest in the succeeding taxable year. The limitation on itemized deductions for high-income taxpayers (see ¶15-545) does not apply to investment interest expenses.

• *Original issue discount*

Although California generally conforms to the federal interest deduction allowed under IRC Sec. 163, an addition adjustment may be required by issuers of original issue discount (OID) for debt instruments issued in 1985 and 1986. Unlike federal law, an issuer is required to deduct the amount of OID attributable to the instrument each year. However, different rules applied in California for debt instruments issued in 1985 or 1986 and California law requires that any differences between state and federal law concerning the OID for these instruments be taken into account in the year that the debt instrument matures, is sold, exchanged, or otherwise disposed of. (Sec. 17224, Rev. & Tax. Code) Consequently, issuers of the debt instruments must make an addition adjustment to the extent that the amount eligible for deduction for California personal income tax purposes exceeds the amount reported on the federal return. The addition adjustment is made on Sch. CA (540), line 21(f), column B. (FTB Pub. 1001, Supplemental Guidelines to California Adjustments) A subtraction adjustment is allowed (see ¶16-280) if the federal deduction exceeds the California deduction.

• *Private mortgage insurance*

California does not incorporate IRC Sec. 163(h)(3)(E), which treats qualified premiums paid for mortgage insurance in 2007 through 2016 as deductible interest. (Sec. 17225, Rev. & Tax. Code) Consequently, taxpayers must make an adjustment on Schedule CA (540), line 41.

Other additions to the taxable income base are listed at ¶16-005.

[¶16-085] Additions--Items Related to Federal Deductions or Credits

Adjustments are required on the California return as a result of the federal treatment of the following federal credits, exclusions, and deductions.

• *Qualified business credits*

IRC Sec. 196, which allows a deduction for certain "qualified business credits" that do not result in a tax benefit because they remain unused at the end of the applicable 20 year carryforward period (15 years for credits arising in tax years beginning before 1998) is inapplicable for California personal income tax purposes. (Sec. 17024.5(b)(10), Rev. & Tax. Code) Consequently, an addition adjustment must be made for amounts deducted on the federal tax return.

• *Domestic production activities deduction*

California does not incorporate federal law (IRC Sec. 199) allowing taxpayers to claim a deduction for domestic production activities for taxable years beginning before 2018. (Sec. 17201.6, Rev. & Tax. Code) Taxpayers that claim this deduction on their federal return, must make an addition adjustment by subtracting the amount from the federal business income or loss figure on Sch. CA (540), line 35, column B.

[¶ 16-090] Additions--Items Related to State Credits

To prevent taxpayers from receiving double tax benefits, California requires that addition adjustments be made for deductions claimed on a taxpayer's federal return for expenses for which the following California personal income tax credits are claimed. The adjustment is made on Sch. CA (540 or 540NR), line 12, line 17, or line 18, column C.

— Donated agricultural products transportation credit (Sec. 17053.12(b), Rev. & Tax. Code)

— Employer-paid child care program and child care contribution credits (repealed beginning with the 2012 tax year) (Sec. 17052.17(f), Rev. & Tax. Code; Sec. 17052.18(i), Rev. & Tax. Code)

— Enterprise zone, local agency military base recovery area, and manufacturing enhancement area hiring credits (generally repealed for post-2013 tax years) (Sec. 17053.74(h), Rev. & Tax Code; Sec. 17053.46(g), Rev. & Tax. Code; Sec. 17053.47(f), Rev. & Tax. Code)

— Farmworker housing credit (repealed for post-2008 tax years) (Sec. 17053.14(g), Rev. & Tax. Code)

— Rice straw credit (Sec. 17052.10(d), Rev. & Tax. Code)

(FTB Pub. 1001, Supplemental Guidelines to California Adjustments)

Other additions to the taxable income base are listed at ¶ 16-005.

[¶ 16-095] Additions--Losses

Adjustments may be required for passive activity losses, capital loss carrybacks, casualty losses, and lottery losses.

• *Passive activity losses*

California incorporates, with the changes noted below, federal law (IRC Sec. 469), that generally prohibits the use of passive losses to reduce nonpassive income. (Sec. 17551, Rev. & Tax. Code; Sec. 17561, Rev. & Tax. Code)

California makes the following modifications to the federal rule as incorporated:

— California has not conformed to federal amendments that ease application of the passive activity loss rules for qualified real estate professionals. Federal law (IRC Sec. 469(c)(7)) treats rental real estate losses incurred by qualified real estate professionals as nonpassive losses, whereas California still treats these activities as passive losses.

— Under IRC Sec. 469(d)(2), certain federal passive income credits may be carried over to later tax years if they exceed the tax attributable to the passive activity; for California purposes, credits that may be carried over are the research expenses credit, the low-income housing credit, and the former credits for targeted jobs and orphan drug research.

— A clarifying amendment made to IRC Sec. 469(g)(1)(A) by the Small Business Job Protection Act of 1996 (P.L. 104-188) requires a taxpayer disposing of a passive activity in a taxable transaction to apply any net passive loss from the activity first against income or gain from the taxpayer's other passive activities. Any remaining loss from the activity is then classified as nonpassive and may be used to offset income from nonpassive activities. California modifies this provision to provide that a taxpayer must apply any net passive loss from the activity *plus* any loss realized on that disposition against any income or gain from the taxpayer's other passive activities, prior to offseting the income from nonpassive activities. The amendment applies for federal purposes to tax years beginning after 1986 and for California purposes to taxable years beginning after 1996.

— For purposes of IRC Sec. 469(i), relating to the offset for rental real estate activities, California modifies the dollar limitation for the low-income housing credit to equal $75,000 for tax years beginning before 2020 and removes that dollar limitation for tax years beginning on or after January 1, 2020.

(Sec. 17561, Rev. & Tax. Code)

Computation.—All California taxpayers who engage in passive activities must segregate California adjustments that relate to passive activities from California adjustments that relate to nonpassive activities.

On FTB 3801, the taxpayer first adjusts passive activity losses to reflect any California/federal differences (as in depreciation) and then subjects the modified figure to the passive activity loss limitation rules. The resultant figure, which is the California passive activity loss, is transferred to the form or schedule normally used to report the California adjustment amount. The adjustment is computed and then entered on the appropriate line of Schedule CA (540) or Schedule CA (540NR). If there is no California schedule or form to compute the passive activity loss adjustment ("e.g." for rental real estate losses), the adjustment is computed on a special worksheet on FTB 3801 and then transferred directly to the corresponding line in either the subtraction or addition section of Schedule CA (540) or Schedule CA (540NR). To compute passive activity loss adjustment amounts for Schedule CA (540) or Schedule CA (540NR), the taxpayer should use total adjusted gross income amounts and should not start with federal income amounts.

Taxpayers should consult FTB Pub. 1100, Taxation of Nonresidents and Individuals Who Change Residency, for detailed explanations and examples of how the passive activity loss limitations impact nonresidents and part-year residents.

Excess passive activity losses and credits may be carried forward and subtracted from passive activity income in succeeding tax years.

• *Capital loss carrybacks*

Unlike federal law, California does not allow carrybacks of capital losses on mark-to-market contracts. (Sec. 18155, Rev. & Tax. Code) Taxpayers claiming a capital loss carryback of such losses on their federal return, must complete a Schedule D (540 or 540NR), for California personal income tax purposes.

• *Casualty losses*

California does not follow the federal special rules applicable to casualty losses in federally declared disasters. (Sec. 17204, Rev. & Tax. Code) Also, because of California's federal conformity date (see ¶15-515), California has not adopted federal provisions enacted by Tax Cuts and Jobs Act of 2017 (P.L. 115-97) that (1) provide temporary relief from the casualty loss rules for net disaster losses occurring in 2016 and 2017 in a 2016 disaster area and (2) clarify that the limitation on losses from wagering transactions applies not only to the actual costs of wagers incurred by an individual, but to other expenses incurred by the individual in connection with the conduct of that individual's gambling activities, effective for tax years 2018 through 2025. (*2017 Summary of Federal Income Tax Changes*, California Franchise Tax Board, May 16, 2018)

In addition, because of the state's federal conformity date history (see ¶15-515), California does not incorporate federal amendments that eliminated the 10% of AGI and $100 floor limitations for casualty losses that arose in a Hurricane Harvey, Irma, or Maria disaster area and that were attributable to those hurricanes in 2017. (*2017 Summary of Federal Income Tax Changes*, California Franchise Tax Board, May 16, 2018)

Furthermore, California does not conform to uncodified federal provisions in the federal Disaster Tax Relief and Airport and Airway Extension Act of 2017 (P.L. 115-63) that defined a net disaster loss as the excess of qualified disaster-related personal casualty losses over personal casualty gains. Under these federal provisions, qualified disaster-related personal casualty losses are losses that arose in the:

— Hurricane Harvey disaster area on or after August 23, 2017, and that were attributable to Hurricane Harvey;

— Hurricane Irma disaster area on or after September 4, 2017, and that were attributable to Hurricane Irma; or

— Hurricane Maria disaster area on or after September 16, 2017, and that were attributable to Hurricane Maria.

(*2017 Summary of Federal Income Tax Changes*, California Franchise Tax Board, May 16, 2018)

• *Lottery losses*

Losses associated with lottery winnings are not deductible for California personal income tax purposes. (*Letter*, FTB, February 26, 1986) Consequently, any losses associated with lottery winnings that are deducted on the federal return must be added back for purposes of computing California taxable income. The adjustment is made on Sch. CA (540), line 14, column C.

Other additions to the taxable income base are listed at ¶16-005.

[¶16-100] Additions--Medical Expenses and Savings Accounts

California does not incorporate federal law concerning health savings accounts (HSAs) (IRC Sec. 223) and the exclusion for qualified prescription drug subsidies (IRC Sec. 139A).

• *Employer-provided accident and health insurance plan reimbursements and self-employed health care premiums*

California conforms to the federal exclusion from gross income for reimbursements made under an employer-provided accident or health insurance plan for medical care expenses of an employee, employee's spouse, or employee's dependents (IRC Sec. 105), including the federal amendments that extend the exclusion to reimbursements for expenses incurred on or after March 30, 2010, for medical care for any child of the employee who is under age 27 at the end of the tax year, even if the child is not a dependent. (Sec. 17131, Rev. & Tax. Code; Former Sec. 17131.7, Rev. & Tax. Code)

California also conforms to federal law allowing a deduction for health insurance costs of self-employed individuals (IRC Sec. 162(*l*)), including the federal amendments extending the deduction to costs incurred on or after March 30, 2010, for health insurance for any child of the employee who is under age 27 at the end of the tax year, even if the child is not a dependent. (Sec. 17201, Rev. & Tax. Code; Former Sec. 17201.1, Rev. & Tax. Code)

• *Health savings accounts*

California does not incorporate the federal gross income exclusion of employer contributions to HSAs. (Sec. 17131.4, Rev. & Tax. Code; Sec. 17131.5, Rev. & Tax. Code)

> **COMMENT:** *Employer contributions excluded from W-2 wages:* Because employers are required to exclude HSA contributions made to eligible employees from their W-2 wages, employers must reflect California and federal wage differences on their employees' Form W-2s.

In addition, an individual's contributions to HSAs that were deducted on the federal tax return must be added back for California personal income tax purposes. (Sec. 17215.4, Rev. & Tax. Code) The addition is made by entering the amount deducted on the federal return on Sch. CA (540 or 540NR), line 25, column B. The amount of any employer contribution from federal Form W-2, line 12, code W is entered on on Schedule CA (540 or 540NR), line 7, column C. (FTB Pub. 1001, Supplemental Guidelines to California Adjustments)

As a result of California's nonconformity to federal law, interest and dividends earned on HSAs are also subject to California personal income tax. Because such amounts are excluded from federal adjusted gross income, an addition adjustment is required for the excluded interest and dividends. Interest earned on the account is entered on Sch. CA (540), line 8, column C. Current year dividends are entered on Sch. CA (540), line 9, column C. (FTB Pub. 1001, Supplemental Guidelines to California Adjustments)

Finally, amounts rolled over from a medical savings account into an HSA are excluded from federal income tax, but subject to California personal income tax. (Sec. 17215.1, Rev. & Tax. Code) The addition adjustment is entered on Sch. CA (540), line 21f, column C. (FTB Pub. 1001, Supplemental Guidelines to California Adjustments) The amount withdrawn from the MSA is subject to California's penalty on nonqualified withdrawals (see ¶ 15-755).

Corresponding subtraction adjustments may also be required for distributions from health savings accounts (see ¶ 16-307).

• *Prescription drug subsidies*

An addition adjustment is required for the federal government subsidies provided to employers to compensate them for costs incurred in a qualified retiree prescription drug plan that are excluded from the employer's federal taxable income under IRC Sec. 139A(a). (Sec. 17139.6, Rev. & Tax. Code) Taxpayers claiming the exclusion on their federal return claim the adjustment on Sch. CA (540 or 540NR), line 21f, column C. (FTB Pub. 1001, Supplemental Guidelines to California Adjustments)

Other additions to the taxable income base are listed at ¶ 16-005.

[¶ 16-105] Additions--Net Operating Losses

Taxpayers that claim a federal net operating loss (NOL) must add the federal NOL back to federal income and recompute a California NOL deduction (see ¶ 16-310). The federal NOL is added as a positive number on Sch. CA (540), line 21(c), column C. (Instructions, Sch. CA (540), California Adjustments—Residents).

Other additions to the taxable income base are listed at ¶ 16-005.

[¶16-110] Additions--Nondeductible Expenses

Although California law mirrors federal law (IRC Sec. 265), denying deductions for expenses and interest incurred in producing income that is wholly exempt from tax, an addition adjustment is required when expenses and/or interest is incurred to produce income that is exempt from California, but not federal, taxation (e.g. income from U.S. bonds). (Sec. 17280, Rev. & Tax. Code) In such instances, taxpayers should enter the amount as a negative number on Sch. CA (540), line 41. (Instructions, Sch. CA (540), California Adjustments—Residents)

A corresponding subtraction adjustment is allowed for expenses and interest incurred in producing income that is exempt from federal, but not California, taxation (see ¶16-315).

• *Illegal business expenses*

In addition to incorporating federal law disallowing deductions for illegal drug trafficking expenditures (see ¶15-775), California prohibits taxpayers from claiming deductions for any income received directly derived from any act or omission of criminal profiteering activity (as defined in Calif. Penal Code § 186.2 or as defined in Chapter 6 (commencing with Section 11350) of Division 10 of the Health and Safety Code, or Article 5 (commencing with Section 750) of Chapter 1 of Part 2 of Division 1 of the Insurance Code), which includes, but is not limited to illegal activities associated with lotteries, gaming, horseracing, prostitution, pornography, burglary, larceny, embezzlement, drug trafficking, and insurance fraud. (Sec. 17282, Rev. & Tax. Code)

The deductions may only be disallowed if the taxpayer is found guilty of the specified illegal activities in a criminal proceeding before a California state court or any proceeding in which the state, county, city and county, city, or other political subdivision was a party. (Sec. 17282, Rev. & Tax. Code)

To the extent these expenses were deducted on the federal return, taxpayers must make an addition adjustment on Sch. CA (540 or 540NR), line 12.

However, for tax years 2021 through 2024, California licensees engaged in commercial cannabis activity are permitted to deduct expenses and claim tax credits related to that trade or business. In doing so, the state decouples from the federal disallowance of tax expenditures related to the illegal sale of drugs. (Sec. 17209, Rev. & Tax. Code)

California taxpayers deriving income from the specified illegal activities are taxed on gross income without allowance of any business deductions, including cost of goods sold. Although California law provides that wagering losses may be allowed to the extent of gains (see ¶15-745), the California State Board of Equalization (BOE) has ruled, under former Sec. 17297, that wagers lost by a bookmaker are deductions connected with illegal activity that are not allowed, rather than exclusions. (*Van Cleave*, SBE, May 11, 1955)

Reconstruction of income.—To ensure compliance, the BOE has ruled under former Sec. 17297, that the Franchise Tax Board may reconstruct the taxpayer's gross income by adding to his reported net receipts the money he has returned to winning players. (*John*, SBE, 61-SBE-050, July 19, 1961) Thus, a bookmaker is taxed on the total amount of bets placed with him rather than on the portion of his "handle", which he retains. By using the percentage paid out by California's parimutuel racetracks, 86%, the SBE has ruled under former Sec. 17297, that the bookmaker's net receipts are said to represent only 14% of his taxable income. (*Brownell*, SBE, 59-SBE-033, October 13,

1959) The SBE has also ruled under former Sec. 17297, that the gross income of an operator of illegal pinball machines is the total amount deposited by players, without regard to how much is paid out in winnings. After estimating the percentage that was paid out—as high as 60% and as low as 20% in individual cases—the operator's reported net receipts are said to represent only 40% to 80% of his taxable income, as the case may be. (*Anderson,* SBE, 62-SBE-076, November 27, 1962)

Legal and illegal businesses.—If a taxpayer operates a legitimate business in close connection and association with illegal activities, it has been held under former Rev. & Tax. Code Sec. 17297, that all regular business deductions for the legitimate business, except cost of goods sold, are also disallowed. (*Moses, Banks, and Thornburg,* SBE, 63-SBE-121, October 21, 1963) A bookmaker's tavern (*Sorsoli,* SBE, 61-SBE-046, July 18, 1961) and an illegal pinball machine operator's music and amusement machines (*Felkins and Leerskov,* SBE, 61-SBE-049, July 19, 1961) serve as examples of the application of former Rev. & Tax. Code Sec. 17297 to associated businesses.

• *Fines or penalties paid by sports franchise owners*

For taxable years beginning on or after January 1, 2014, California also prohibits deductions for the amount of any fine or penalty paid or incurred by an owner of all or part of a professional sports franchise if that fine or penalty is assessed or imposed by the professional sports league that includes that franchise. (Sec. 17228, Rev. & Tax. Code)

Other additions to the taxable income base are listed at ¶ 16-005.

[¶ 16-120] Additions--Recovery of Tax Benefit Items

Although California incorporates IRC Sec. 111, concerning the recovery of tax benefit items, California substitutes references to federal credits and credit carryovers with references to California personal income tax credits and credit carryovers. (Sec. 17131, Rev. & Tax Code) Under IRC Sec. 111 any income attributable to the recovery during the taxable year of any amount deducted in a prior taxable year from which the taxpayer derived a tax benefit is included in gross income. If the amount did not reduce income subject to tax in the prior year, the recovery amount may be excluded. If a tax credit was allowable for a prior taxable year and during the current taxable year there is a downward price adjustment or similar adjustment, the tax for the current year must be increased by the amount of the prior credit attributable to the adjustment; however, no increase in the current year's tax is required to the extent that the credit allowable for the recovered amount did not reduce the prior year's tax.

Because California substitutes references to federal credits and credit carryovers with references to California personal income tax credits and credit carryovers, amounts related to the federal credits and credit carryovers must be included on the California return and are reported on Sch. CA (540), line 21(f), column C. A related subtraction adjustment may also be allowed (see ¶ 16-327).

For a discussion of the adjustments required for vehicle license fee refunds prior to the 2005 taxable year, see ¶ 15-530 Prior Law Computation Rules.

Other additions to the taxable income base are listed at ¶ 16-005.

[¶ 16-130] Additions--Research and Development Expenses

A deduction of research and development expenses must be reduced by the expenses for which the California research credit was claimed. (Sec. 17201, Rev. & Tax Code) Taxpayers first enter the amount of expenses disallowed on the federal return then enter the amount of California research expenses after reduction for the California research credit on Sch. CA (540 or 540NR), line 12, line 17, or line 18, column B. (FTB Pub. 1001, Supplemental Guidelines to California Adjustments)

Other additions to the taxable income base are listed at ¶ 16-005.

[¶ 16-135] Additions--Retirement Plans and Retirement Benefits

California generally conforms to the federal treatment of retirement plans and benefits (see ¶ 15-800). However an addition may be required for the items discussed below. Subtraction adjustments may also be allowed (see ¶ 16-345).

• *Foreign social security benefits*

Foreign social security benefits are taxable by California. A tax treaty between the United States and a foreign country that excludes foreign social security benefits from federal taxable income or that treats foreign social security as U.S. Social Security does not apply for California personal income tax purposes. (FTB Pub. 1005, Pension and Annuity Guidelines) Consequently, taxpayers that exclude such amounts on their federal returns, must add such amounts back on Sch. CA (540), line 7 or line 20, Column C.

Canadian registered retirement savings plans.—A federal treaty with Canada allows taxpayers to treat Canadian registered retirement savings plans (RRSPs) like IRAs and defer taxation on their RRSP earnings until the time of distribution. However, the treaty does not apply for California personal income tax purposes. Consequently, taxpayers must include the RRSP earnings in their taxable income in the year earned. The adjustment is made on Sch. CA (540 or 540NR), line 8, line, 9, or line 13, column C. (FTB Pub. 1001, Supplemental Guidelines to California Adjustments)

• *Distributions from IRAs, employees' trusts and employee annuities*

Generally, the treatment of distributions is the same for federal and California purposes. However, the amount of a distribution that is subject to California taxation may be less than the amount subject to federal taxation as a result of different basis rules for federal and California income tax purposes. Although California and federal law have allowed the same amount of deductible contributions to IRAs since 1987, differences in basis may arise as a result of:

— different contribution rules applied during 1982 through 1986 and prior to 1976,

— a taxpayer's election to treat contributions differently on the California return than on the federal return, or

— the taxpayer's previous nonresidency.

Roth IRA basis differences may arise as a result of a conversion from a regular IRA to a Roth IRA in 1998. The basis in a Self-Employed Pension (SEP) plan and Self-Employed Retirement plan (Keogh) may be different as a result of differences in the amount of deductible contributions prior to 1996 and differences in the determination of the amount of federal self-employment income and California self-employment income prior to 1996. (Sec. 17081, Rev. & Tax. Code; Sec. 17085, Rev. & Tax. Code) (FTB Pub. 1005, Pension and Annuity Guidelines)

CAUTION: IRA distributions to health savings accounts.—Although California generally conforms to federal provisions as amended to date, because California does not recognize health savings accounts (HSAs) it does not conform to an amendment made to IRC Sec. 408 by the Tax Relief and Health Care Act of 2006 (TRHCA) (P.L. 109-432) that authorizes a one-time tax-free distribution from an IRA to an HSA, effective for tax years beginning after 2006. A California taxpayer who makes such a distribution is required to include the distribution in his or her gross income and is subject to California's penalty on premature withdrawals.

CAUTION: Loans from retirement plans.—Under IRC Sec. 72(p) as it existed prior to September 29, 2017, a loan from a qualified employer plan to a participant or beneficiary was generally treated as a plan distribution for federal income tax purposes unless, among other things, (1) the loan amount does not exceed the lesser of $50,000, or half of the present value of the employee's nonforfeitable accrued benefit under the plan; and (2) the loan is required to be repaid within five years, except that a longer repayment period can be used for a principal residence plan loan. Effective September 29, 2017, the federal Disaster Tax Relief and Airport and Airway Extension Act of 2017 (P.L. 115-63) (1) increased the maximum amount that a participant or beneficiary can borrow from a qualified employer plan from $50,000 to $100,000; (2) removed the one half of present value limitation; and (3) allow a longer repayment term, if the due date for any repayment with respect to the loan occurs during a qualified beginning date that is Hurricane-specific and ends on December 31, 2018, by delaying the due date of the first repayment by one year and adjusting the due dates of subsequent repayments accordingly. The changes were intended to help taxpayers affected by Hurricanes Harvey, Irma, and Maria. Because of the state's conformity date, California does not follow these federal changes. (Sec. 17081, Rev. & Tax. Code; Sec. 17085, Rev. & Tax. Code; *2017 Summary of Federal Income Tax Changes*, California Franchise Tax Board, May 16, 2018)

Detailed explanations of these differences, and how to compute the California addition or subtraction adjustment arising as a result of these differences are discussed in detail in FTB Pub. 1005, Pension and Annuity Guidelines. The actual addition adjustment is made on Sch. CA (540), line 15, column B. (Instructions, Sch. CA (540), California Adjustments)

• *IRA contribution limits*

Because of California's federal conformity date history (see ¶ 15-515), California did not incorporate amendments made to IRC Sec. 219(b) that allowed qualifying individuals who participated in a bankrupt employer's 401(k) plan to make additional IRA contributions of up to $3,000 for 2007 through 2009. Nor did California incorporate until the 2010 tax year the indexing for inflation of the income limits for:

— deductible contributions to a traditional IRA for active participants in an employer-sponsored retirement plan or whose spouse is an active participant in an employer-sponsored plan; and

— Roth IRA contributions.

Federal law allows the indexing of these limits beginning in 2007.

Taxpayers that claim these increased contribution deductions on their federal return must make an addition adjustment on their California personal income tax return. The adjustment is made on Sch. CA (540), line 32, column B. (Instructions, Sch. CA (540), California Adjustments).

In addition, beginning with the 2010 tax year California follows the federal provisions that include differential wages in compensation for purposes of determining the annual limitations on contributions to traditional individual retirement arrangements (IRAs) and Roth IRAs, effective for federal purposes beginning with the 2009 taxable year. A differential wage payment is any payment made by an employer to an employee for any period during which the employee is performing qualified military service to compensate the employee for the difference between the employee's military pay and the amount the employee would have received as wages from the employer.

Other additions to the taxable income base are listed at ¶ 16-005.

• *Annuities*

Beginning with the 2010 tax year, addition adjustments may be required as a result of California's nonconformity with federal law concerning the treatment of the long-term care insurance coverage rider costs. California, unlike federal law, does not exclude from taxable distributions from annuity and life insurance contracts the cost of a qualified long-term care insurance coverage rider that is charged against the cash or cash surrender value of the contract. (Sec. 17085(e), Rev. & Tax. Code)

Also, because of California's federal conformity date history (see ¶ 15-515), California did not incorporate until the 2015 tax year the federal amendment to IRC Sec. 72 that allows contract holders to annuitize a portion of an annuity, endowment, or life insurance contract, while the balance is not annuitized, provided that the annuitization period is for 10 years or more, or for the lives of one or more individuals. For federal purposes, the provision applies to amounts received in tax years beginning after 2010. Differences may arise regarding the exclusion ratio, the determination of the investment in the contract, the expected return, the annuity starting date, and amounts not received as an annuity. Further, the amount of taxable distribution of the annuity may differ for federal and state purposes, thereby necessitating an adjustment.

[¶ 16-145] Additions--Taxes

Although California generally conforms to the federal treatment of the deduction for taxes (see ¶ 15-820), California modifies federal law by disallowing the deduction for the following taxes:

— state, local, or foreign income, war profits, or excess profit taxes;

— state and local sales taxes;

— foreign real property taxes (no federal deduction is available for 2018 to 2025 tax years);

— state disability insurance or voluntary plan disability insurance;

— California franchise tax; and

— the annual tax imposed on limited partnerships, limited liability partnerships, and limited liability companies treated as partnerships or that are disregarded and taxed as sole proprietorships.

(Sec. 17024.5(b)(7), Rev. & Tax. Code; Sec. 17220, Rev. & Tax. Code; Sec. 17222, Rev. & Tax. Code) Taxpayers that deducted these taxes on their federal tax returns must subtract them from federal itemized deductions in computing California itemized deductions on Schdedule CA (540 or 540NR). (FTB Pub. 1001, Supplemental Guidelines to California Adjustments)

In addition, because of California's IRC conformity date, California does not conform to the federal $10,000 limit ($5,000 for married taxpayer filing a separate return) on state and local tax deductions for the 2018 to 2025 tax years. (*Preliminary Report on Specific Provisions of the Federal Tax Cuts and Jobs Act*, California Franchise Tax Board, March 20, 2018)

> **COMMENT:** In the case of state and local real property and personal property taxes, a federal deduction is still allowed with no dollar limit if the taxes are paid or accrued in carrying on a trade or business, or on property held for the production of income (e.g., an individual may deduct property taxes if the taxes are imposed on business or income producing assets such as residential rental property). (IRC Sec. 164(b)(6))

When the taxpayer has paid tax on the same income in another state, in most cases the tax may be taken as a credit for taxes paid to another state. The California State Board of Equalization (SBE) and the California Supreme Court have ruled that a tax on production or gross receipts that is not based on income may be deductible as a business tax. (*Knudsen*, SBE, 53-SBE-004, April 1, 1953; *Beamer v. FTB*, 19 Cal3d 467, 563 P2d 238 (1977))

A subtraction adjustment is available for state income tax refunds (see ¶ 16-360).

Other additions to the taxable income base are listed at ¶ 16-005.

[¶ 16-150] Additions--Trade or Business Expenses

Adjustments must be made for the following trade or business expenses.

• *Abandonment or tax recoupment fees for open-space easements and timberland preserves*

California law disallows any deduction for fees paid by California property owners on termination of open-space easements or timberland preserve status. (Sec. 17275, Rev. & Tax. Code) Taxpayers are allowed to claim these fees paid as a trade or business expense on their federal return. Consequently, taxpayers must make an addition adjustment for California personal income tax purposes. The addition is made by entering the amount of fees incurred and deducted on the federal return on Sch. CA (540 or 540NR), line 12, line 17, or line 18, column C. (FTB Pub. 1001, Supplemental Guidelines to California Adjustments)

• *Expenses incurred at discriminatory clubs*

California prohibits taxpayers from claiming a business expense deduction for expenses incurred at private clubs that discriminate on the basis of sex, race, color, religion, ancestry, national origin, ethnic group identification, age, mental disability, physical disability, medical condition, genetic information, marital status, or sexual orientation. However, an exemption is available for any local unit of certain American national fraternal organizations. (Sec. 17269, Rev. & Tax. Code; Sec. 11135, Govt. Code)

Also, any alcoholic beverage club licensee that discriminates must include, on all expense receipts, a statement that the expenses covered by the receipt are not deductible for state income tax purposes. (Sec. 23438, Bus. & Prof. Code)

Taxpayers that claim these expenses on their federal return, must add these expenses back on Sch. CA (540 or 540NR), line 12, line 17, or line 18, column C. (FTB Pub. 1001, Supplemental Guidelines to California Adjustments)

• *Film and television production costs*

California does not incorporate the federal current expense deduction available for costs incurred in qualified film and television productions. (Sec. 17201.5, Rev. & Tax. Code) Consequently, taxpayers that claim the deduction on their federal return must make an addition adjustment on their California return.

• *Illegal payments*

Although California incorporates IRC Sec. 162(c), which prohibits the deduction of any payment made directly or indirectly to an official or employee of any government, or of any agency or instrumentality of any government, if (1) the payment constitutes an illegal bribe or kickback, or (2) the payment is to an official or employee of a foreign government and the payment is unlawful under the federal Foreign Corrupt Practices Act of 1987, California requires additional adjustments. With respect to payments to officials or employees of foreign governments, California disallows deductions for any payment that would be unlawful under federal law if those laws were applicable to the payment and to the official or employee. (Sec. 17286, Rev. & Tax. Code)

To the extent California law increases the amount subject to taxation, an addition adjustment must be made on Sch. CA (540), line 12, column C.

Special rules apply to illegal business expenses as well (see ¶ 16-110).

• *Physician's interindemnity arrangements*

California allows a deduction for payments made to a cooperative corporation by its members for malpractice coverage. (Sec. 17278, Rev. & Tax. Code; Uncodified Sec. 5, Ch. 1276, Laws 1984)

Deductions for such payments are valid only to the extent that the payment does not exceed the amount that would otherwise be payable to an independent insurance company for similar medical malpractice coverage. Excess payments may be carried forward five years. The deductible payment may be made either as a contribution to, or in response to an assessment by, the interindemnity arrangement. (Sec. 17278, Rev. & Tax. Code; Uncodified Sec. 5, Ch. 1276, Laws 1984)

Refunded payments must be included in the taxpayer's income in the year received. (Sec. 17278, Rev. & Tax. Code; Uncodified Sec. 5, Ch. 1276, Laws 1984) Such payments must be reported by the trust to the Franchise Tax Board (FTB) in the year made. The FTB may require, by regulation, the trust to withhold a specified amount of any refund made to a nonresident.

The comparable federal provision does not provide for the carryover of excess payments. Instead, the federal provision allows an initial contribution in a lump-sum payment or in substantially equal payments over a period not to exceed six years (Sec. 1031, P.L. 99-514.). To the extent that the California deduction is less than that claimed on the federal return, an addition adjustment is required. Conversely, a subtraction adjustment may be required (see ¶ 16-365).

• *Self-employed health insurance deduction*

California conforms to federal law allowing a deduction for health insurance costs of self-employed individuals (IRC Sec. 162(l)), including the federal amendments extending the deduction to costs incurred on or after March 30, 2010, for health insurance for any child of the employee who is under age 27 at the end of the tax year, even if the child is not a dependent. (Sec. 17201, Rev. & Tax. Code; Former Sec. 17201.1, Rev. & Tax. Code)

• *State legislator's expenses*

California does not incorporate IRC Sec. 162(h), which allows state legislators living more than 50 miles away from the state capital an election to define the home located within the district represented as the "tax home". Rather, California deems the legislator's residence within his or her district to be the tax home. (Sec. 17270(a), Rev. & Tax. Code) To the extent the federal deduction exceeds the California allowable deduction, an addition adjustment is required. The adjustment is made on Sch. CA (540), line 12, column C. If the federal deduction exceeds the California deduction, a subtraction adjustment is allowed (see ¶ 16-365).

• *Substandard housing deductions*

California law denies a lessor of substandard housing any deduction for interest, taxes, depreciation, or amortization relating to the substandard housing. (Sec. 17274, Rev. & Tax. Code) Federal law has no comparable provision.

"Substandard housing" means occupied dwellings from which a taxpayer derives rental income or unoccupied or abandoned dwellings for which both of the following apply:

(1) For occupied dwellings from which a taxpayer derives rental income, a governmental regulatory agency has found the housing to be in violation of local health, safety, or building codes; and

(2) For dwellings that are unoccupied or abandoned for at least 90 days, a government regulatory agency has cited the housing for conditions that constitute a serious violation of state law or local codes dealing with health, safety, or building, and that constitute a threat to public health and safety.

And either of the following occur:

(1) The housing has not been repaired within six months after the date of a notice of violation; or

(2) Good faith efforts for compliance have not been commenced. (Sec. 17274, Rev. & Tax. Code)

"Substandard housing" also includes employee housing that has not been brought into compliance with the conditions stated in a notice of violation issued under the Employee Housing Act within 30 days of the date of the notice. (Sec. 17274, Rev. & Tax. Code)

Deductions may still be claimed for a period of three years if the properties were rendered substandard as a result of a natural disaster. Deductions may also be claimed for substandard housing if the taxpayer was unable to obtain financing solely because the housing is located in a neighborhood or geographical area in which financial institutions do not provide financing for rehabilitation of that type of housing. (Sec. 17274, Rev. & Tax. Code) In addition, housing that is found to be substandard because of a change in the local housing standards is not included in the provisions, unless the occupants are in danger.

Owners of noncomplying units are required to notify the local regulatory agency when the property is sold or transferred, supplying the name of the new owner and the date of transfer. Extensive notification and reporting rules that apply to the regulatory agencies are provided.

• *Tertiary injectants*

California does not incorporate, nor does it have a provision similar to, IRC Sec. 193, which allows a taxpayer to currently deduct expenses associated with tertiary injectants injected during the taxable year. Consequently, to the extent such amounts were currently deducted on the federal return such amounts must be added back. The addition adjustment is made on Sch. CA (540 or 540NR), line 12, column C. (FTB Pub. 1001, Supplemental Guidelines to California Adjustments) Although these amounts may not be currently deducted, they are treated as capital expenses for which a depreciation deduction may be claimed (see ¶16-245).

• *College admissions cheating scheme payments*

Applicable retroactively for taxable years beginning on or after January 1, 2014, California specifically prohibits business expense deductions for payments to Edge College and Career Network, LLC, by taxpayers that:

— are charged as defendants in certain criminal complaints (relating to the federal college admissions cheating investigation);

— are found guilty with regard to an offense arising out of such a complaint; and

— took the deduction unlawfully pursuant to the final determination of guilt or pursuant to a determination by the FTB.

(Sec. 17275.4, Rev. & Tax. Code)

Other additions to the taxable income base are listed at ¶16-005.

[¶16-200]

TAXABLE INCOME COMPUTATION--SUBTRACTIONS

[¶16-205] Subtractions from Taxable Income Base

The computation of California taxable income allows the items listed below to be subtracted from federal adjusted gross income.

— Alimony paid by nonresident alien (see ¶16-207)

— Amortization of bond premiums (see ¶16-210)

— Annuity distributions for which the three-year recovery basis rule was elected (see ¶16-345)

— Armenian genocide payments (see ¶16-335)

— Beverage container redemption income (see ¶16-260)

— California death benefits paid on behalf of California National Guard, State Military Reserve, or Naval Militia personnel (see ¶15-175)

— California qualified stock options (see ¶16-345)

— Canadian government Japanese internment reparation payments (see ¶16-335)

— Charitable contributions (see ¶16-220)

— Claim of right adjustments (see ¶16-225)

— Clergy housing allowances (see ¶15-155)

— Controlled foreign corporation dividends (see ¶16-250)

— Controlled foreign corporation income (see ¶16-280)

— Cost-share payments received by forest landowners (see ¶16-260)

— Crime hotline rewards (see ¶16-325)

— Death benefits from employer-provided life insurance (see ¶16-240)

— Depreciation (see ¶16-245)

— Disaster losses (see ¶16-300)

— Discharge of indebtedness deferral amounts (see ¶16-213)

— Distributions from IRAs, employees' trusts and employee annuities; Basis recovery (see ¶16-345)

— Earthquake loss mitigation incentives (see ¶16-255)

— Employer's parking cash-out payments (see ¶16-365)

— Empowerment zone employment credit expenses (see ¶16-290)

— Energy conservation rebates and vouchers (see ¶16-260)

— Energy resource conservation grants received by low-income individuals (see ¶16-260)

— Erroneous incarceration compensation (see ¶16-235)

— Federal credit expenses (see ¶16-290)

— Federally exempt treaty income (see ¶16-263)

— Health savings account nonqualified distributions (see ¶16-307)

— In-home support service supplementary payments (see ¶16-295)

— Indian employment credit wages (see ¶16-290)

— Interest from enterprise zone business loans (see ¶16-280)

— Interest on California obligations subject to federal taxation (see ¶16-280)

— Interest on energy efficient product loans (see ¶16-260)

— Interest on federal obligations (see ¶16-280)

— Investment interest (see ¶16-280)

— Lottery winnings from California State Lottery (see ¶16-305)

— Low-income housing project sales (see ¶16-270)

— Low-sulfur diesel fuel production credit expenses (see ¶16-290)

— Mortgage interest (see ¶16-280)

— Net operating loss (see ¶16-310)

— Noncash patronage allocations from farmer's cooperatives (see ¶15-170)

— Paid family leave insurance (see ¶16-370)

— Personal residence sale (see ¶ 16-270)

— Railroad retirement benefits (see ¶ 16-345)

— Recovery of tax benefit items (see ¶ 16-327)

— Regulated investment company (RIC) undistributed capital gain (see ¶ 16-250)

— Relocation assistance payments (see ¶ 16-332)

— Reparation payments for Holocaust and Armenian genocide survivors and Japanese internment victims (see ¶ 16-335)

— Retirement benefit contributions made by an employer on behalf of citizens living abroad (see ¶ 16-345)

— Ridesharing arrangement benefits (see ¶ 16-265)

— Social Security benefits (see ¶ 16-345)

— State income tax refunds (see ¶ 16-360)

— State legislator's expenses (see ¶ 16-365)

— Ultra-low sulfur diesel fuel environmental compliance costs (see ¶ 16-260)

— Unemployment compensation (see ¶ 16-370)

— U.S. Forestry service reimbursement payments (see ¶ 16-260)

— Vehicle license fee refunds (see ¶ 16-327)

— Water conservation rebates and vouchers (see ¶ 16-260)

These adjustments must be made on Sch. CA (540), California Adjustments. Major adjustments are also outlined in the FTB Pub. 1001, Supplemental Guidelines to California Adjustments.

Additions to the taxable income base are listed at ¶ 16-005.

[¶16-207] Subtractions--Alimony

A nonresident alien that did not deduct alimony expenses on his or her federal return, may claim a deduction on the California personal income tax return. The deduction is claimed on Sch. CA (540 or 540NR), line 31a, column C. (FTB Pub. 1001, Supplemental Guidelines to California Adjustments) An addition adjustment is required for nonresident alien alimony recipients (see ¶ 16-012).

Other subtractions to the taxable income base are listed at ¶ 16-205.

[¶16-210] Subtractions--Amortization

Differences between California and federal law may result in either addition or subtraction adjustments to the amortization deduction claimed on the federal return (see ¶ 16-015).

[¶16-213] Subtractions--Discharge of Indebtedness

California does not incorporate IRC Sec. 108(i), which allows taxpayers to elect to defer the inclusion of income from the discharge of indebtedness in connection with the reacquisition after December 31, 2008, and before January 1, 2011, of certain business debt instruments ratably over a five-tax-year period. (Sec. 17144(f), Rev. & Tax. Code) Taxpayers were required to make an addition adjustment in the year that the indebtedness was discharged. (2011 FTB Pub. 1001) Subtraction adjustments may be made in subsequent years when the deferred income is reported on the federal return. (*E-mail*, California Franchise Tax Board, February 7, 2011)

• *Student loans*

California conforms to IRC Sec. 108(f), which provides an exclusion from gross income for the discharge of certain student loans. However, IRC Sec. 108(f) is also modified for California personal income tax purposes to provide an additional exclusion for discharged student loan amounts when the borrower is unable to complete a program of study because the school closes or did something wrong. The additional exclusion applies to discharges of indebtedness occurring on or after January 1, 2015, and before January 1, 2020. (Sec. 17144.7, Rev. & Tax. Code)

For tax years after 2018, California also conforms to the federal treatment of student loan cancellation that are discharged on account of death or total and permanent disability of the student (IRC Sec. 108(f)(5)). Unlike the federal provision enacted by the federal Tax Cut and Jobs Act of 2017 (P.L. 115-97), the exclusion from gross income is permitted indefinitely. (Sec. 17144.8, Rev. & Tax. Code)

[¶16-215] Subtractions--Basis Adjustments

Although California generally incorporates federal law (IRC Sec. 1016) as of California's current federal conformity date (see ¶15-515), concerning adjustments to basis, many of the federal adjustments are inapplicable for California because California does not incorporate the federal credit or deduction that requires the basis adjustments. In addition, when applying the incorporated provisions of IRC Sec. 1016(a) to make California basis adjustments, any references in IRC Sec. 1016 to other IRC provisions must be treated as including California modifications to those other IRC provisions. (Sec. 17024.5(i), Rev. & Tax. Code) Detailed rules are provided (see ¶16-020).

Other subtractions to the taxable income base are listed at ¶16-205.

[¶16-220] Subtractions--Charitable Contributions

California generally conforms to the federal charitable contributions deduction (see ¶15-625). However, an adjustment is also allowed if a taxpayer has a larger charitable contribution carryover than that allowed on the federal return. Taxpayers may make an adjustment on Sch. CA (540), line 41 by entering a positive number. (Instructions, Sch. CA (540), California Adjustments—Residents)

Subtraction adjustments may also be required as a result of California's nonconformity with the federal provisions limiting deductions for contributions to donor advised funds and disallowing the deduction for contributions of certain interests in buildings located in registered historic districts unless the requisite filing fee is paid. (Sec. 17275(d) and (e), Rev. & Tax. Code)

In addition, as a result of California's federal conformity date (see ¶15-515), California does not conform to the federal repeal of the deduction for amounts paid for college athletic seating rights in tax years beginning after December 31, 2017. (*2017 Summary of Federal Income Tax Changes*, California Franchise Tax Board, May 16, 2018)

Other subtractions to the taxable income base are listed at ¶16-205.

[¶16-225] Subtractions--Claim of Right Adjustment

California allows a claim of right adjustment similar to the adjustment allowed under federal law (IRC Sec. 1341). Under the claim of right provision, an individual may recompute his or her personal income tax liability if an individual includes in his or her California adjusted gross income for a preceding taxable year(s) income in excess of $3,000 that he or she appeared to have an unrestricted right to, but had to repay that amount during the taxable year because he or she was not entitled to such income. The tax is recomputed by subtracting from the amount of tax otherwise due for the taxable year the decrease in personal income tax for the preceding taxable year(s) that would result solely from the exclusion of the item from the taxpayer's adjusted gross income for the preceding taxable year(s). This adjustment may not be claimed if the taxpayer takes a claim of right deduction for the income on his or her federal return. (Sec. 17049, Rev. & Tax. Code) Prior to the 2004 taxable year, California did not have a statutory provision relating to the claim of right doctrine, but it did recognize a claim of right under common law and in case law.

Deductions of repaid amounts that were previously included in income under a claim of right are exempt from the 2% floor for miscellaneous itemized deductions (see ¶15-545). (Sec. 17076, Rev. & Tax. Code) An individual eligible to claim the adjustment who included the income in prior taxable years when he or she was a nonresident may make the claim of right adjustment only for income that was attributable to California during the preceding years. (Sec. 17049, Rev. & Tax. Code)

A taxpayer that claims a credit in lieu of the deduction on the federal return, but claims a deduction on the California return, must make an adjustment on the California return. The adjustment is made by entering the allowable deduction as a positive number on Sch. CA (540), line 41. The Franchise Tax Board advises taxpayers to examine the Repayment section of federal Pub 525, Taxable and Nontaxable Income, to help determine whether to take a credit or deduction. Taxpayers should remember to use the California tax rate in their computations. (Instructions, Sch. CA (540), California Adjustments—Residents)

A related addition adjustment is required. Other subtractions to the taxable income base are listed at ¶16-205.

[¶16-235] Subtractions--Damage Awards

California allows an exclusion for payments received as the result of a determination of wrongful incarceration. (Sec. 17157, Rev. & Tax. Code) To the extent included in federal adjusted gross income, a subtraction adjustment may be taken on Sch. CA (540 or 540NR), line 21(f), column B. (Instructions, Sch. CA (540), California Adjustments—Residents)

Other subtractions to the taxable income base are listed at ¶16-205.

[¶16-240] Subtractions--Death Benefits

Although California incorporates the limit on the death benefit exclusion for employers holding a life insurance policy as a beneficiary that covers the life of an employee (IRC Sec. 101(j)), different effective dates apply. Under both California and federal law, the employer's exclusion is limited to an amount equal to the amount paid for the policy as premiums or other payments unless the employer satisfies several requirements, including notice and consent requirements. The limitation is applicable generally for federal purposes to life insurance contracts issued after August 17, 2006, but only applies for California purposes to contracts issued after

January 1, 2010, with some limited exceptions. Consequently, to the extent the exclusion is limited for federal income tax purposes but not California purposes for contracts issued prior to 2010, taxpayers may subtract the difference between the full amount of the benefits paid, less certain interest, and the amount of the federal exclusion.

Other subtractions to the taxable income base are listed at ¶16-205.

[¶16-245] Subtractions--Depreciation

California does not incorporate federal law (IRC Sec. 193), allowing a deduction for tertiary expenditures. Consequently, an addition adjustment is required for such amounts (see ¶16-150). However, California does allow such expenditures to be depreciated for California purposes, if the injectants qualify as property used in a trade or business or property held for the production of income. If so, taxpayers should attach a schedule reflecting the depreciation computation of tertiary injectants placed in service during the taxable year, then complete form FTB 3885A, Depreciation and Amortization Adjustments. (FTB Pub. 1001, Supplemental Guidelines to California Adjustments).

Numerous other differences exist between California and federal law (see ¶16-040). To the extent these differences result in a greater deprecation deduction than allowed for federal purposes, a subtraction adjustment may be made. Use FTB Form 3885A to determine the California depreciation deduction.

Other subtractions to the taxable income base are listed at ¶16-205.

[¶16-250] Subtractions--Dividends

California taxes controlled foreign corporation (CFC) dividends in the year distributed rather than the year earned. If CFC dividends are earned in one year and distributed in a later year, a subtraction adjustment is made during the year the dividends are distributed. The adjustment is made on Sch. CA (540 or 540NR), line 9, column C. A corresponding addition adjustment is made in the year the dividend is earned (see ¶16-045). (FTB Pub. 1001, Supplemental Guidelines to California Adjustments)

Similar treatment is applied to undistributed capital gain from a regulated investment company (RIC). (Sec. 17088(c), Rev. & Tax. Code) California taxes undistributed capital gain from a RIC in the year distributed rather than the year earned. If capital gain from a RIC is earned in one year and distributed in a later year, a subtraction adjustment is made during the year the capital gains is distributed. The adjustment is made on Sch. CA (540 or 540NR), line 9, column C. A corresponding addition adjustment is made in the year the dividend is earned (see ¶16-045). (FTB Pub. 1001, Supplemental Guidelines to California Adjustments)

Other subtractions to the taxable income base are listed at ¶16-205.

[¶16-255] Subtractions--Earthquake Loss Mitigation Incentives

For taxable years beginning on or after July 1, 2015, California gross income does not include an amount received as a loan forgiveness, grant, credit, rebate, voucher, or other financial incentive issued by the California Residential Mitigation Program or the California Earthquake Authority to assist a residential property owner or occupant with expenses paid, or obligations incurred, for earthquake loss mitigation. (Sec. 17138.3(a), Rev. & Tax. Code)

"Earthquake loss mitigation" means an activity that reduces seismic risks to a residential structure or its contents, or both. For purposes of structural seismic risk mitigation, a residential structure is either of the following:

— a structure described in Section 10087(a) of the Insurance Code; or

— a residential building of not fewer than two, but not more than 10, dwelling units.

(Sec. 17138.3(b), Rev. & Tax. Code)

Other subtractions to the taxable income base are listed at ¶16-205.

[¶16-260] Subtractions--Environmental or Pollution Control

California allows subtraction modifications for income associated with the following conservation and environmental and pollution control activities.

• *Beverage container recycling income*

Gross income does not include redemption money received by consumers who return empty beverage containers to recycling centers. (Sec. 17153.5, Rev. & Tax. Code) To the extent such income was included in federal taxable income, taxpayers may claim a subtraction adjustment on Sch. CA (540), line 21(f), column B. (Instructions, Sch. CA (540), California Residents—Adjustments)

• *Carousel Housing Tract cleanup*

Gross income does not include certain amounts received as a result of the Carousel Housing Tract cleanup in Carson, California. Taxpayers can exclude amounts received:

— from the Shell Oil Company for temporary accommodations and relocation;

— under the Optional Real Estate Program of the Revised Remedial Action Plan; or

— from a settlement arising out of the investigation, cleanup, or abatement of waste discharged at the former Kast Property Tank Farm facility.

(Sec. 17138.4, Rev. & Tax. Code)

Taxpayers must receive the amounts pursuant to California Regional Water Quality Control Board, Los Angeles Region, Order R4-2011-046, and they must:

— currently own or previously owned property in the Carousel Housing Tract; or

— reside or previously resided in the Carousel Housing Tract.

(Sec. 17138.4, Rev. & Tax. Code)

The exclusion applies to all tax years. If a taxpayer previously paid tax on these amounts, the taxpayer has until September 28, 2019, to file for a credit or refund. The regular limitations period for claiming a credit or refund from the overpayment will not apply. (Sec. 17138.4, Rev. & Tax. Code)

• *Conservation grants paid to low-income individuals*

Grants awarded under the State Energy Resources Conservation and Development Commission's grant program to residential property owners with gross annual income equal to or less than 200% of the federal poverty level are excluded from the computation of their gross income. (Sec. 25433.5, Public Resources Code)

The amounts excluded are entered as a subtraction on Sch. CA (540), line 21(f), column B. (Instructions, Sch. CA (540), California Residents—Adjustments)

• *Forest protection cost-share payments*

California law provides a specific exclusion from gross income for cost-share payments received by forest landowners from the Department of Forestry and Fire Protection pursuant to the California Forest Improvement Act of 1978 or from the U.S. Department for Agriculture, Forest Service, under the Forest Stewardship Program and the Stewardship Incentives Program, pursuant to the federal Cooperative Forestry Assistance Act. Like the federal exclusion (see ¶ 15-690), the amount of any cost-share payment excluded under the California provision must not be considered when determining the basis of property acquired or improved or when computing any deduction to which the taxpayer may otherwise be entitled. (Sec. 17135.5, Rev. & Tax. Code)

The amounts excluded are entered as a subtraction on Sch. CA (540), line 21(f), column B. (Instructions, Sch. CA (540), California Residents—Adjustments)

• *Interest on loans to buy energy efficient products*

California law allows an itemized deduction from personal income tax for the amount of interest paid or incurred by a taxpayer on a public utility-financed loan or indebtedness obtained to acquire any energy-efficient product or equipment for installation in a qualified residence located in California. (Sec. 17208.1, Rev. & Tax. Code)

For California tax purposes, the deduction is not subject to the 2% floor imposed on miscellaneous itemized deductions (see ¶ 15-545). (Sec. 17073, Rev. & Tax. Code)

No other deduction may be claimed for the same amount of interest. Also, the deduction allowed will be in lieu of any credit otherwise available for interest paid or incurred in connection with the purchase of the energy-efficient product or equipment. (Sec. 17208.1, Rev. & Tax. Code)

The deduction is made by entering a positive number on Sch. CA (540), line 41. (Instructions, Sch. CA (540), California Adjustments—Residents)

• *Water and energy conservation rebates and vouchers*

California excludes from gross income any amount received as a rebate or voucher from a local water or energy agency or supplier for any expenses the taxpayer paid or incurred for the purchase or installation of any of qualified water conservation toilet, a water and energy efficient clothes washer, and/or a plumbing device necessary to serve specified recycled water uses. (Sec. 17138, Rev. & Tax. Code)

California also excludes any amount received as a rebate, voucher, or other financial incentive issued by the California Energy Commission, the California Public Utilities Commission, or a local public utility for the purchase or installation of certain energy conservation devices. Qualifying devices are any of the following:

— thermal energy systems,

— solar energy systems,

— wind energy systems that produce electricity, and

— fuel cell generating systems that produce electricity. (Sec. 17138.1, Rev. & Tax. Code)

For taxable years beginning on or after January 1, 2014, and before January 1, 2019, California also excludes from gross income any amount received as a rebate, voucher, or other financial incentive issued by a local water agency or supplier for participation in a turf removal water conservation program. (Sec. 17138.2, Rev. & Tax. Code)

To the extent such amounts are included in federal income, taxpayers may claim a subtraction adjustment on Sch. CA (540 or 540NR), line 21(f), column B. (Instructions, Sch. CA (540), California Adjustments—Residents)

Other subtractions to the taxable income base are listed at ¶ 16-205.

[¶16-263] Subtractions--Foreign Source Income/Expenses

Income exempted by treaty under federal law may be excluded for California personal income tax purposes only if the treaty specifically excludes the income for state purposes. If a state-exemption is not provided, losses disallowed on the federal return because they are associated with tax exempt income may be subtracted from federal income on Sch. CA (540 or 540NR), line 21f, column B. (FTB Pub. 1001, Supplemental Guidelines to California Adjustments) An addition adjustment may also be required for foreign income (see ¶ 16-060).

Under federal law (IRC Sec. 951), U.S. shareholders who own stock in a controlled foreign corporation (CFC) on the last day of the taxable year in which it was a CFC must include in gross income their pro-rata share of income, if the foreign corporation is a CFC for an uninterrupted period of at least 30 days during any taxable year. The pro rata shares are included in the U.S. shareholders' income even though there may be intervening entities in a chain between a CFC and such shareholders. Because California does not incorporate federal provisions involving foreign corporations (Sec. 17024.5(b)(9), Rev. & Tax. Code), California does not incorporate this provision and such amounts may be subtracted on Sch. CA (540 or 540NR), line 17, column B. (FTB Pub. 1001, Supplemental Guidelines to California Adjustments)

Other subtractions to the taxable income base are listed at ¶ 16-205.

[¶16-265] Subtractions--Fringe Benefits

California allows additional deductions for specified ridesharing benefits and for health care benefit compensation provided to employees with registered domestic partners and same-sex spouses.

Also, because of California's federal conformity date, California does not conform to the federal suspension for tax years 2018 through 2025 of the exclusion from gross income for (a) qualified moving expense reimbursements, except in the case of a member of the U.S. Armed Forces on active duty who moves pursuant to a military order, and (b) qualified bicycle commuting reimbursements. (*2017 Summary of Federal Income Tax Changes*, California Franchise Tax Board, May 16, 2018)

• *Ridesharing benefits*

California provides a more expansive exclusion than the federal exclusion from the gross income of an employee for compensation for, or the fair market value of, certain employer-provided ridesharing arrangements that are described below. (Sec. 17149, Rev. & Tax. Code)

The term "ridesharing arrangement" means the transportation of persons in a motor vehicle when such transportation is incidental to another purpose of the driver. The term includes commuting by carpool, buspool, vanpool, private commuter bus, subscription taxipool, bus, ferry, or any other alternative method of transportation that reduces the use of a motor vehicle by a single occupant to or from his or her place of employment. The value of monthly transit passes provided to employees and their dependents (other than transit passes for use by elementary and secondary school students who are dependents of the employee) is specifically covered by the ridesharing exclusion, as is the value of free or subsidized parking provided to ridesharing participants. Detailed definitions of these ridesharing arrangements are provided in the governing statute. (Sec. 17149, Rev. & Tax. Code)

Unlike federal law, California does not cap the amount of the benefits that may be excluded and California's definitions of "qualifying ridesharing arrangements" are more expansive than the federal definitions. To the extent California's exclusion is greater than that allowed under federal law, enter the difference on Sch. CA (540), line 7, column B. (Instructions, Sch. CA (540), California Adjustments—Residents)

• *Health care compensation*

An exclusion from gross income was available during the 2013—2018 tax years for employer-provided reimbursements paid to compensate an employee for additional federal income taxes that were incurred by the employee on employer-provided health-care benefits because the employee's same-sex spouse or domestic partner was not considered the employee's spouse for federal income tax purposes. The exclusion from gross income also applied to any amount of the health-care compensation paid to an employee that represented the "grossed-up" amount that an employer included to offset additional federal income taxes incurred on such compensation. (Sec. 17141, Rev. & Tax. Code)

Other subtractions to the taxable income base are listed at ¶ 16-205.

[¶ 16-270] Subtractions--Gains

California allows adjustments for the sale of a personal residence, the sale of low-income housing projects, and for gain on involuntary conversions received by San Bruno explosion and fire victims.

• *Sale of personal residence*

California law, unlike federal law, provides that if a taxpayer serves in the Peace Corps during the five years preceding the sale of the taxpayer's principal residence, the two-year ownership and use requirement (see ¶ 15-710) may be reduced by the amount of time served in the Peace Corps, but by no more than 18 months. (Sec. 17152, Rev. & Tax. Code)

Although California otherwise currently conforms to the IRC Sec. 121 exclusion of gain on the sale of a principal residence, different effective dates apply concerning post-2004 federal amendments as follows:

— the extension of the requirement that a personal residence acquired in a like-kind exchange be held for at least five years in order to be eligible for the exclusion to transferees of the property applies for California purposes beginning with the 2010 tax year and for federal purposes to sales or exchanges occurring after October 22, 2004; and

— the limitation of the to gain from the periods of qualified use applies for California purposes to tax years beginning after 2009 and for federal purposes to sales and exchanges after 2008.

If there are differences in the amounts excluded under federal and California law, taxpayers should complete Schedule D (540 or 540NR). Transfer the amount from California Schedule D, line 12a to Sch. CA (540 or 540NR), line 13, column B if the California gain is less than the federal. (FTB Pub. 1001, Supplemental Guidelines to California Adjustments) For the corresponding subtraction adjustment, see ¶16-070.

• *Sales of low-income housing projects*

California does not recognize gain on certain types of low-income housing sales if the proceeds are reinvested in qualified residential real property within two years. (Sec. 18041.5, Rev. & Tax. Code)

Qualified low-income housing sales.—The following types of sales qualify for nonrecognition treatment under California law (Sec. 18041.5, Rev. & Tax. Code):

(1) The sale of an assisted housing development (or a majority of the units in an assisted housing development converted to condominium units) to a tenant association, nonprofit organization, public agency, or profit-motivated individual or corporation that will commit itself and its successors in interest to keeping the housing development (or the development's condominium units) affordable for individuals or families qualifying as "lower income" or "very low income" under Health and Safety Code definitions. The buyer's commitment must be for a period of at least 30 years from the date of sale or for the remaining term of any existing federal government assistance, whichever is greater;

(2) The sale of real property to a majority of the current "lower income" or "very low income" residents of the property; or

(3) In the case of property converted to condominium units, the sale of a majority of the units to current "lower income" or "very low income" residents.

Reinvestment requirement; basis adjustment.—Gain from the sale of low-income housing property qualifies for nonrecognition treatment only if, within two years of the date of sale, the seller reinvests all of the proceeds in residential real property located in California. (Sec. 18041.5, Rev. & Tax. Code) The seller may reinvest in any kind of residential property, not just low-income housing property. However reinvestments in a principal residence do not qualify. The adjusted basis of the reinvestment property must be reduced by the amount of any gain that was not recognized on the original low-income housing sale.

Special rules for assessment of deficiency on gain.—If a qualified low-income housing sale results in gain, a special provision extends the statutory period for the assessment of any deficiency attributable to such gain. (Sec. 18041.5, Rev. & Tax. Code) Such a deficiency may be assessed at any time up to four years after the Franchise Tax Board is notified of

— the cost of the replacement property;

— the seller's intention not to reinvest the sales proceeds within the required two-year period; or

— the seller's failure to reinvest the sales proceeds within the required two-year period.

• *San Bruno explosion and fire victims*

California treats the natural gas transmission line explosion and fire that occurred in San Bruno, California, on September 9, 2010, as a federally declared disaster even though it was never formally declared a disaster at the federal level. Consequently, any gain from an involuntary conversion that is related to the disaster is excluded from California gross income and taxpayers may claim a subtraction adjustment on their California personal income tax return. (Sec. 18154, Rev. & Tax. Code)

Other subtractions to the taxable income base are listed at ¶ 16-205.

[¶ 16-280] Subtractions--Interest

A subtraction adjustment to federal income and deductions is available for the items discussed below. A subtraction is also allowed for interest on loans to buy energy efficient products (see ¶ 16-260). For a discussion of the subtraction adjustment allowed for parents who claim their children's investment income on their federal return, but not their California return, or vice versa, see the discussion of unearned income of minors.

• *Investment interest*

Under federal law (IRC Sec. 163(d)), as incorporated by California, a deduction is allowed for interest up to the amount of net investment income. (Sec. 17201, Rev. & Tax. Code) Because the amount of net investment income reported on the federal return may be different than that reported on the California return as a result of differences in the classifications of exempt income, depreciation, capital gains, etc., the amount of the deduction may likewise be different. The California deduction is calculated on FTB 3526, Investment Interest Expense Deduction.

Net capital gain from the disposition of investment property is generally excluded from investment income. However taxpayers may elect to include as much of their net capital gain as they choose in calculating the investment interest limitation for federal purposes, if they also reduce the amount of net capital gain eligible for the special federal capital gain tax. Taxpayers are allowed to make a similar election for California purposes; however, California treats capital gains as ordinary income.

Any amount not allowed as a deduction for any taxable year because of this limitation may be carried over and treated as deductible investment interest in the succeeding taxable year. The limitation on itemized deductions for high-income taxpayers (see ¶ 15-545) does not apply to investment interest expenses.

• *Interest on U.S. obligations*

California and its political subdivisions generally are prohibited from taxing obligations issued by the U.S. Government. (31 U.S.C. Sec. 3124) Generally, interest on federal obligations is taxable for federal income tax purposes. Because of the U.S. Constitution's Supremacy clause, California tax treatment ultimately depends on application of federal law.

Interest income from the following sources are exempt from California personal income taxation:

— U.S. savings bonds (except for interest from series EE U.S. savings bonds issued after 1989 that qualified for the Education Savings Bond Program exclusion);

— U.S. Treasury bills, notes, and bonds; and

— other bonds or obligations of the United States and its territories. (Instructions, Sch. CA (540), California Adjustments—Residents)

Issues frequently arise as to whether or not an instrument is a bond or obligation of the United States or U.S. territories. Obligations from the following have been held to be U.S. obligations, the interest on which is exempt:

— Federal Farm Credit and Federal Home Loan Banks (Letter, FTB, June 15, 1988)

— Student Loan Marketing Association (SLMA), the Resolution Funding Corporation, the Production Credit Association, and the Commodity, Credit Corporation.

— CATS (Certificates of Accrual on Treasury Securities) and TIGRS (Treasury Investment Growth Receipts) (31 U.S.C. Sec. 3124).

A subtraction adjustment for interest on these and other exempt U.S. obligations is taken on Sch. CA (540 or 540NR), line 8, column B. (FTB Pub. 1001, Supplemental Guidelines to California Adjustments)

Conversely, a subtraction adjustment is not allowed for interest on obligations issued from the following sources:

— Federal National Mortgage Association (Fannie Mae)

— Government National Mortgage Association (Ginnie Mae)

— Federal Home Loan Mortgage Corporation (Freddie Mac) (FTB Pub. 1001, Supplemental Guidelines to California Adjustments

— obligations issued by the District of Columbia after December 24, 1973 (*Letter of Advice*, FTB, June 15, 1988)

COMMENT: *Interest on Repurchase Agreements Subject to Tax:* The U.S. Supreme Court has held that a state's income tax on interest that a taxpayer received from owning shares in mutual funds that entered into repurchase agreements involving federal obligations was a valid tax on interest derived from loans in which a mutual fund loaned cash to a seller-borrower who delivered a federal obligation to the mutual fund as collateral for the loan. Because the tax was not imposed on interest from the obligations themselves, the tax did not violate 31 U.S.C. Sec. 3124(a), which exempts U.S. government obligations and interest from such obligations from state taxation. (*Nebraska Department of Revenue v. Loewenstein*, Dkt. 93-823, (US SCt December 12, 1994) The California State Board of Equalization has reached a similar conclusion in relation to California's taxation of such interest. *Bewley v. FTB*, 9 Cal4th 526, 37 CalRptr2d 298 (1995)),

---

Special rules apply to dividends from regulated investment companies dealing in federal obligations (see ¶ 15-185).

• *Interest on California obligations*

IRC Secs. 103 and 141—150, which California does not incorporate (Sec. 17143, Rev. & Tax. Code), contain a number of complex restrictions on the exclusion of state and municipal bond interest; generally, they provide that bond interest is not tax-free if it is derived from unregistered bonds, "arbitrage" bonds (the proceeds of which are invested in high-yield securities), or, with a number of codified exceptions, bonds used to fund private business activities. California has no similar provisions, and exempts interest on all California state and local government bonds. (Sec. 26(b), Art. XIII, Cal. Const.) Accordingly, a subtraction adjustment is allowed for interest on California bonds that are subject to federal taxation under these provisions. Although not listed in the subtractions on the Sch. CA (540), presumably such amounts would be subtracted on Sch. CA (540), line 8, column B.

• *Original issue discount*

Although California generally conforms to the federal interest deduction allowed under IRC Sec. 163, an addition adjustment may be required by holders of original issue discount (OID) for debt instruments issued in 1985 and 1986. Unlike federal law, a holder of a debt instrument is required to include in taxable income the amount of OID attributable to the instrument each year. However, different rules applied in California for debt instruments issued in 1985 or 1986 and California law requires that any differences between state and federal law concerning the OID for these instruments be taken into account in the year that the debt instrument matures, is sold, exchanged, or otherwise disposed of. (Sec. 17224, Rev. & Tax. Code) Consequently, holders of the debt instruments may make a subtraction adjustment to the extent that the amount reported on the federal return exceeds the amount eligible for deduction for California personal income tax purposes. The subtraction adjustment is made on Sch. CA (540), line 21(f), column C. (FTB Pub. 1001, Supplemental Guidelines to California Adjustments)

• *Mortgage interest*

Although California generally conforms to the federal mortgage interest deduction, because of California's current federal conformity date (see ¶ 15-515), California has not conformed to federal amendments made by the Tax Cuts and Jobs Act of 2017 that for tax years 2018 through 2025:

— limit the itemized deduction for home mortgage interest to interest paid or accrued on acquisition debt during those years;

— suspend the deduction of interest on home equity debt; and

— reduce the maximum amount that may be treated as acquisition debt to $750,000 ($375,000 if married filing separately).

(*2017 Summary of Federal Income Tax Changes*, California Franchise Tax Board, May 16, 2018)

Also, under a unique California provision, payments made to the California Housing Finance Agency by first-time home buyers under a "buy-down mortgage plan" are considered payments of mortgage interest and are deductible for California purposes. (Sec. 17230, Rev. & Tax. Code) Under the plan, the state agency contracts with qualified mortgage lenders and pays to those lenders an amount of money in order to reduce the effective interest cost on loans made by those lenders to first-time home buyers. The home buyer is required to repay the amount advanced with interest to the agency at the end of the sixth year, or on an amortized basis beginning with the seventh year through the thirtieth year, or some other term.

COMMENT: *Treatment on federal return:* Although there is no comparable provision in the federal law, it might be argued that the payments are made in lieu of interest and therefore should be treated as interest for federal as well as California purposes. However, to the extent these payments are not deducted from federal income, taxpayers may make a subtraction adjustment by increasing the amount of the federal mortgage interest deduction. The amount should be entered as a positive number on Sch. CA (540), line 41.

In addition, taxpayers that reduced their federal mortgage interest deduction by the amount of their mortgage interest credit (from federal Form 8396), may increase their California itemized deductions by the same amount. The amount should be entered as a positive number on Sch. CA (540), line 41. (Instructions, Sch. CA (540), California Adjustments—Residents)

• *Interest on smog impact fee refund*

California, unlike federal law, provides an exclusion for interest received from the State of California in conjunction with the refund of the smog impact fee for individuals who were not allowed to deduct the smog impact fee when it was paid. (Sec. 17139.5, Rev. & Tax. Code)

Other subtractions to the taxable income base are listed at ¶ 16-205.

[¶ 16-290] Subtractions--Items Related to Federal Credits or Deductions

California does not incorporate federal law (IRC Sec. 280C(a)), which disallows a deduction for expenses for which the federal employment credits are allowed. (Sec. 17270(b), Rev. & Tax. Code) Consequently, taxpayers that claimed the federal Indian employment credit (IRC Sec. 45A), the employer wage credit for employees who are active duty members of the uniformed services (IRC Sec. 45P), the work opportunity credit (IRC Sec. 51), or the empowerment zone employment credit (IRC Sec. 1396), may claim a subtraction adjustment for wage expenses disallowed on their federal returns as a result of claiming these credits. The adjustment is made on Sch. CA (540 or 540NR), line 12, 17, or 18, column B. (FTB Pub. 1001, Supplemental Guidelines to California Adjustments)

A similar subtraction adjustment is made for expenses for which the federal small business tax credit for new retirement plan expenses were claimed. However, this adjustment is made on Sch. CA (540 or 540NR), line 16, column B. (FTB Pub. 1001, Supplemental Guidelines to California Adjustments)

Under California's general conformity provision, all IRC provisions incorporated into federal law that are related to federal credits and carryovers are inapplicable for California personal income tax purposes. (Sec. 17024.5(b)(10), Rev. & Tax. Code) Consequently, other federal provisions that disallow deductions for which federal credits are claimed are also inapplicable for California personal income tax purposes, and taxpayers are allowed to take a subtraction adjustment for amounts disallowed on the federal return.

Also, because of California's federal conformity date (see ¶ 15-515), California does not conform to the federal provision (IRC Sec. 267A) that disallows deductions for any disqualified related party amount paid or accrued in a hybrid transaction or by, or to, a hybrid entity. The federal provision applies to taxable years beginning after December 31, 2017. (*Summary of Federal Income Tax Changes – 2017*, California Franchise Tax Board, May 16, 2018)

• *Disaster related payments*

California treats the natural gas transmission line explosion and fire that occurred in San Bruno, California, on September 9, 2010, as a federally declared disaster even though the explosion and fire were never declared an official federal disaster.

Consequently, taxpayers may exclude disaster relief payments related to the explosion or fire to the extent such payments would have been excluded under federal law if the disaster had been declared a federal disaster. (Sec. 17131.10, Rev. & Tax. Code)

Other subtractions to the taxable income base are listed at ¶ 16-205.

[¶ 16-295] Subtractions--Job Programs or Employee Benefits

An exclusion from gross income for California personal income tax purposes is provided for supplementary payments received by a provider of in-home supportive services. (Sec. 17131.9, Rev. & Tax. Code) The supplementary payments are equal to the sales tax on the gross receipts of the provider for the sale of the services, plus an amount equal to the amount of any increased payroll withholding required for federal income tax, Social Security, and Medicare purposes due to the supplementary payment. (Sec. 12306.6, Welf. & Inst. Code)

[¶ 16-300] Subtractions--Losses

• *Disaster losses*

California incorporates, with modifications, IRC Sec. 165(i), which allows taxpayers who sustain disaster losses in a Presidentially-declared disaster area to elect to take a deduction for those losses in the taxable year preceding the year of the loss. (Sec. 17201, Rev. & Tax. Code) For the 2014 to 2023 taxable years, the California deduction also may be claimed for the immediately preceding taxable year **or** the taxable year in which the disaster occurred for any loss sustained as a result of a disaster occurring in any city, county, or city and county in the state that is proclaimed by the Governor to be in a state of emergency (without requiring separate legislative action). Excess disaster losses can currently be carried forward for up to 20 years. (Sec. 17207.14, Rev. & Tax. Code)

California does not conform to the temporary federal provision enacted by Tax Cuts and Jobs Act of 2017 (P.L. 115-97) that limits (in tax years beginning after 2017 and before 2026) the itemized deduction for personal casualty losses to losses attributable to federally declared disasters. (*2017 Summary of Federal Income Tax Changes*, California Franchise Tax Board, May 16, 2018)

> **COMPLIANCE NOTE:** Any law, other than Sec. 17276.20, Rev. & Tax. Code, that suspends, defers, reduces, or otherwise diminishes a net operating loss (NOL) deduction does not apply for the 2014 to 2023 taxable years to an NOL attributable to a loss sustained as a result of any disaster occurring in any city, county, or city and county in this state that is proclaimed by the Governor to be in a state of emergency. (Sec. 17207.14(c), Rev. & Tax. Code) If a taxpayer has both disaster loss carryovers and NOL carryovers, they must be used in the order that the taxpayer incurred them. There is no requirement to deduct NOL carryovers before disaster loss carryovers. (FTB Publication 1034, Disaster Loss - How to Claim a State Tax Deduction)

In 2020, at the time this book went to press, the President and/or Governor had a state of emergency for the following disasters:

— Wildfires - Fresno, Los Angeles, Madera, Mendocino, Napa, San Bernardino, San Diego, Shasta, Siskiyou, and Sonoma (September 2020)

— Fires and Extreme Weather Conditions - Butte, Lake, Monterey, Napa, San Mateo, Santa Clara, Santa Cruz, Solano, Sonoma, and Yolo (August and September 2020); and

— Fires and Extreme Weather Conditions - All other California counties not listed above (August 2020).

In 2019, the President and/or Governor declared a state of emergency for the following disasters:

— Extreme Wind and Fire Weather Conditions - All California counties (October 2019);

— Kincade and Tick Fires - Los Angeles, Sonoma (October 2019);

— Eagle, Reche, Saddleridge, Sandalwood, and Wolf Fires in - Los Angeles and Riverside counties (October 2019);

— Earthquake - Kern and San Bernardino counties (July 2019);

— Atmospheric River Storm System - Amador, Glenn, Lake, Mendocino, and Sonoma counties (February 2019); and

— Atmospheric River Storm System - Calaveras, El Dorado, Humboldt, Los Angeles, Marin, Mendocino, Modoc, Mono, Monterey, Orange, Riverside, San Bernardino, San Diego, San Mateo, Santa Barbara, Santa Clara, Shasta, Tehama, Trinity, Ventura, and Yolo counties (January and February 2019).

In 2018, the President and/or Governor declared a state of emergency for the following disasters:

— Fire - Orange and Riverside counties in August 2018;

— Fires - Lake, Mariposa, Mendocino, Napa, Riverside, San Diego, Santa Barbara, Shasta, and Siskiyou counties (July 2018);

— Rainstorm - San Bernardino county (July 2018);

— Fire - Lake county (June 2018);

— Storms in - Amador, Fresno, Kern, Mariposa, Merced, Stanislaus, Tulare, and Tuolumne counties (March 2018); and

— Mudslides - Santa Barbara and Ventura Counties (January 2018).

In 2017, the President and/or Governor declared a state of emergency for the following disasters:

— Fires - Los Angeles, San Diego, Santa Barbara, and Ventura Counties (December 2017);

— Storms - Inyo and Mono Counties (October 2017);

— Fires - Butte, Lake, Mendocino, Napa, Nevada, Orange, Solano, Sonoma, and Yuba Counties (October 2017);

— Fires - Los Angeles County (September 2017);

— Fires - Madera, Mariposa, and Tulare Counties (August and September 2017);

— Fires - Butte and Trinity Counties (August 2017);

— Rainstorms - San Bernardino County (July 2017);

— Fires - Butte, Mariposa, Modoc, and Santa Barbara Counties (July 2017);

— Winter Storms - Alameda, Amador, Butte, Calaveras, El Dorado, Humboldt, Lake, Lassen, Marin, Mendocino, Merced, Mono, Monterey, Napa, Nevada, Placer, Plumas, Sacramento, San Benito, San Luis Obispo, Santa Clara, Santa Cruz, Shasta, Sierra, Siskiyou, Sonoma, Sutter, Trinity, Tuolumne, Yolo, and Yuba Counties declared by President and Governor (Alpine, Colusa, Del Norte, Fresno, Glenn, Kern, Kings, Los Angeles, Mariposa, Modoc, San Bernardino, San Diego, San Joaquin, San Mateo, Santa Barbara, Stanislaus, Tehama, and Ventura declared by Governor only) (February 2017); and

— Winter Storms - Alameda, Butte, Calaveras, Contra Costa, El Dorado, Humboldt, Inyo, Lake, Lassen, Marin, Mendocino, Merced, Mono, Monterey, Napa, Nevada, Placer, Plumas, Sacramento, San Benito, San Luis Obispo, Santa Clara, Santa Cruz, Shasta, Sierra, Siskiyou, Solano, Sonoma, Sutter, Trinity, Tuolumne, Yolo, and Yuba Counties declared by President and Governor (Alpine, Fresno, Kern, Kings, Los Angeles, Madera, Modoc, Orange, Riverside, San Bernardino, San Diego, San Francisco, San Mateo, Santa Barbara, Stanislaus, Tehama, Tulare, and Ventura declared by Governor only) (January 2017).

For 2016, the President and/or Governor declared a state of emergency for the following disasters:

— Winter Storms - Del Norte, Humboldt, Mendocino, Shasta, Santa Cruz, and Trinity Counties (December 2016);

— Rainstorms - Siskiyou County (December 2016);

— Wildfires - Lake, San Bernardino, San Luis Obispo Counties (August 2016);

— Wildfires - Los Angeles and Monterey Counties (July 2016); and

— Wildfires - Kern County (June 2016).

For 2015, the President and/or Governor declared a state of emergency for the following disasters:

— Rainstorms - San Diego county (city of Carlsbad) (December 2015);

— Rainstorms - Inyo, Kern, and Los Angeles counties (October 2015);

— Wildfires - Amador and Calaveras Counties (September 2015);

— Wildfires - Lake and Napa Counties (September 2015);

— Rainstorms - Imperial, Kern, Los Angeles, Riverside, San Bernardino and San Diego Counties (July 2015);

— Wildfires - Lake and Trinity Counties (July 2015);

— Wildfires - Butte, El Dorado, Humboldt, Lake, Madera, Napa, Nevada, Sacramento, San Bernardino, San Diego, Shasta, Solano, Tulare, Tuolumne and Yolo Counties (June 2015);

— Oil Spill - Santa Barbara County (May 2015);

— Rainstorms - Humboldt, Mendocino and Siskiyou Counties (February 2015); and

— Wildfires - Mono County (February 2015).

(*List of Disasters*, California Franchise Tax Board, October 2020)

For a list of the most current California disasters declared by the President and/or the Governor, go to http://ftb.ca.gov and search for "disaster loss for individuals and businesses."

In addition, California personal income taxpayers may elect to declare the loss in the taxable year preceding the year of the loss, whether or not the President declares the area a disaster, if (1) the loss is listed by the legislature in Rev. & Tax. Code Sec.

17207(a) (see listing *below* of disasters with loss carryovers or carrybacks allowed), and (2) the loss is sustained in an area declared a disaster area by the Governor. California has also extended the election to claim the loss on a prior year's return to taxpayers who suffered disaster losses as the result of the severe storms that occurred in March 2011 in Santa Cruz County, the severe winds that occurred in November 2011 in Los Angeles and San Bernardino Counties, and the wildfires that occurred in May 2014 in San Diego County, even though the areas did not receive designation as a federal or state disaster areas. However, these taxpayers may not claim an extended loss carryover for such losses as discussed below (Sec. 17207.11, Rev. & Tax. Code; Sec. 17207.12, Rev. & Tax. Code; Sec. 17207.13, Rev. & Tax. Code)

For disaster losses incurred in taxable years 2004 through 2011, taxpayers are generally allowed to carryover 100% of the excess loss for up to 15 years. For disaster losses incurred in taxable years 2000 through 2003, taxpayers can deduct any excess loss that remains after the initial five-year carryover period for up to 10 more years at the following percentage rates:

— 60% for disasters incurred in taxable years 2002 and 2003; and

— 55% for disasters incurred in taxable years 2000 and 2001.

(FTB Publication 1034, Disaster Loss - How to Claim a State Tax Deduction)

For purposes of the disaster loss carryovers allowed under California law, "excess losses" that may be carried forward are those that exceed the taxpayer's "adjusted taxable income," as defined in IRC Sec. 1212(b), in the year in which the loss is claimed. (Sec. 17207, Rev. & Tax. Code) Adjusted taxable income under IRC Sec. 1212(b) is taxable income increased by the sum of (1) the personal exemption deduction or any deduction allowed in lieu thereof, and (2) the lower of (a) $3,000 ($1,500 in the case of a married taxpayer filing a separate return) or (b) the excess of the taxpayer's losses from sales or exchanges of capital assets over gains from such sales or exchanges.

Under IRC Sec. 165(i)(4), which California follows (Sec. 17207.4, Rev. & Tax. Code), an appraisal used to secure a disaster loan or loan guarantee from the federal government may be used to establish the amount of the disaster loss, to the extent provided in regulations or other guidance issued by the Secretary of the Treasury.

California's disaster loss deduction may not be taken into account in computing a net operating loss deduction under IRC Sec. 172 (see ¶ 16-310). (Sec. 17207(e), Rev. & Tax. Code)

The California loss is computed on Form FTB 3805V, Net Operating Loss (NOL) Computation and NOL and Disaster Loss Limitations—Individuals, Estates, and Trusts, and transferred to Sch. CA (540 or 54NR), line 21b, column B. (FTB Pub. 1001, Supplemental Guidelines to California Adjustments)

Losses incurred as a result of the following disasters qualify for purposes of the California excess disaster loss carryover provision to the extent they are sustained in an area determined by the President or the Governor to be in a state of disaster (Sec. 17207, Rev. & Tax. Code):

(1) fire or any other related casualty occurring in 1990 in California;

(2) the Oakland/Berkeley Fire of 1991, or any other related casualty;

(3) storm, flooding, or any other related casualty occurring in February 1992 in California;

(4) earthquake, aftershock, or any other related casualty occurring in April 1992 in the County of Humboldt;

(5) riots, arson, or any other related casualty occurring in April or May 1992 in California;

(6) earthquakes that occurred in the County of San Bernardino in June and July of 1992, or any other related casualty;

(7) the Fountain Fire that occurred in the County of Shasta or the fires that occurred in the Counties of Calaveras and Trinity in August 1992, or any other related casualty;

(8) storm, flooding, or any other related casualty that occurred in the Counties of Alpine, Contra Costa, Fresno, Humboldt, Imperial, Lassen, Los Angeles, Madera, Mendocino, Modoc, Monterey, Napa, Orange, Plumas, Riverside, San Bernardino, San Diego, Santa Barbara, Sierra, Siskiyou, Sonoma, Tehama, Trinity, and Tulare, and the City of Fillmore in January 1993;

(9) fire that occurred in the Counties of Los Angeles, Orange, Riverside, San Bernardino, San Diego, and Ventura during October or November of 1993, or any other related casualty;

(10) the earthquake, aftershocks, or any other related casualty that occurred in the Counties of Los Angeles, Orange, and Ventura on or after January 17, 1994;

(11) fire that occurred in the County of San Luis Obispo during August of 1994, or any other related casualty;

(12) storms or flooding occurring in 1995, or any other related casualty, sustained in any county of this state subject to a disaster declaration with respect to the storms and flooding;

(13) storms or flooding occurring in December 1996 or January 1997, or any related casualty, sustained in any county of this state subject to a disaster declaration with respect to the storms or flooding;

(14) storms or flooding occurring in February 1998, or any related casualty, sustained in any county of this state subject to a disaster declaration with respect to the storms or flooding;

(15) a freeze occurring in the winter of 1998-99, or any related casualty, sustained in any California county subject to a disaster declaration with respect to the freeze;

(16) an earthquake occurring in September 2000, that was included in the Governor's proclamation of a state emergency for Napa County;

(17) the Middle River levee break in San Joaquin County occurring in June 2004;

(18) the fires occurring in Los Angeles, San Bernardino, Riverside, San Diego, and Ventura Counties in October and November 2003, or any floods, mudflows, and debris flows directly related to those fires;

(19) the San Simeon earthquake, aftershocks, or any other related casualty occurring in Santa Barbara and San Luis Obispo Counties in December 2003;

(20) the wildfires that occurred in Shasta County, beginning August 11, 2004, and any other related casualty;

(21) the severe rainstorms, related flooding and slides, and any other related casualties in the counties of Kern, Los Angeles, Orange, Riverside, San Bernardino,

San Diego, Santa Barbara, and Ventura as a result of that occurred in December 2004, January 2005, February 2005, March 2005, or June 2005;

(22) the severe rainstorms, related flooding and landslides, and any other related casualties that occurred in Alameda, Alpine, Amador, Butte, Calaveras, Colusa, Contra Costa, Del Norte, El Dorado, Fresno, Humboldt, Kings, Lake, Lassen, Madera, Marin, Mariposa, Mendocino, Merced, Monterey, Napa, Nevada, Placer, Plumas, Sacramento, San Joaquin, San Luis Obispo, San Mateo, Santa Cruz, Shasta, Sierra, Siskiyou, Solano, Sonoma, Stanislaus, Sutter, Trinity, Tulare, Tuolumne, Yolo, and Yuba Counties in December 2005, and January, March, and April 2006 (FTB Pub. 1034A-8, California Disaster Relief Tax Provisions --Northern California Storms, December 2005 & January 2006, revised March 2007; FTB Pub. 1034A-9, California Disaster Relief Tax Provisions - California Severe Storms, Flooding, Mudslides, and Landslides: Northern California, March-April 2006, revised March 2007);

(23) the wildfires in San Bernardino County in July 2006 (FTB Pub. 1034A-11, California Disaster Relief Tax Provisions --San Bernardino County Wildfires: San Bernardino County California, July 2006, revised December 2006);

(24) the wildfires in Riverside and Ventura Counties during the 2006 calendar year;

(25) the freeze in El Dorado, Fresno, Imperial, Kern, Kings, Madera, Merced, Monterey, Riverside, San Bernardino, San Diego, San Luis Obispo, Santa Barbara, Santa Clara, Stanislaus, Tulare, Ventura, and Yuba counties in January 2007 (FTB Pub. 1034A-12, California Disaster Relief Tax Provisions --California Severe Freeze: January 2007, revised May 2007);

(26) the wildfires in El Dorado County in June 2007;

(27) the Zaca Fire in Santa Barbara and Ventura Counties during the 2007 calendar year;

(28) the wildfires in Inyo County that started in July 2007;

(29) the wildfires in Los Angeles, Orange, Riverside, San Bernardino, San Diego, Santa Barbara, and Ventura Counties that were the subject of the Governor's disaster proclamations of September 15, 2007, and October 21, 2007;

(30) the wind storms in Riverside County in October 2007;

(31) the wildfires in Butte, Kern, Mariposa, Mendocino, Monterey, Plumas, Santa Clara, Santa Cruz, Shasta, and Trinity Counties in May or June 2008 that were the subject of the Governor's proclamations of a state of emergency;

(32) the wildfires in Santa Barbara County in July 2008;

(33) the severe rainstorms, related flooding and landslides, and any other related casualties in Inyo County during July 2008;

(34) the wildfires in Humboldt County that started in May 2008;

(35) the wildfires in Santa Barbara County in November 2008;

(36) the wildfires in Los Angeles and Ventura Counties in October or November 2008 that were the subject of the Governor's proclamations of a state of emergency;

(37) the wildfires in Orange, Riverside, and San Bernardino Counties in November 2008;

(38) the wildfires in Santa Barbara County in May 2009; and

(39) the earthquake in Humboldt County in January 2010 (Sec. 17207, Rev. & Tax. Code; Sec. 17207.2, Rev. & Tax. Code);

(40) the wildfires that occurred in Placer, Los Angeles, and Monterey Counties in August 2009 and in Kern County in July 2010 (Sec. 17207.6, Rev. & Tax. Code);

(41) the winter storms that occurred in Calaveras, Imperial, Los Angeles, Orange, Riverside, San Bernardino, San Francisco, and Siskiyou counties in January and February 2010 (Sec. 17207.6, Rev. & Tax. Code);

(42) the earthquake that occurred in Imperial County in April 2010 (Sec. 17207.3, Rev. & Tax. Code); and

(43) the fire and explosion that occurred in San Mateo County in September 2010 (Sec. 17207.8, Rev. & Tax. Code).

Losses sustained as a result of the firestorms that occurred beginning on October 21, 1996, in Los Angeles, Orange, and San Diego Counties may be deducted in the prior tax year because the President designated those counties as disaster areas. (FTB Pub. 1026M, California Disaster Relief Tax Provisions, Fire Damaged Locations—California, 1996) However, losses resulting from the firestorms do not qualify for treatment under the California carryover provision (Sec. 17207, Rev. & Tax. Code), because legislation was never enacted that added this disaster to the list of disasters for which the special disaster loss carryover treatment is available.

The election under IRC Sec. 165(i), which allows taxpayers to claim a refund for losses incurred, may be made for California purposes on a return or amended return filed on or before the due date of the return (determined with regard to extension) for the taxable year in which the disaster occurred. (Sec. 17207, Rev. & Tax. Code; Sec. 17207.2, Rev. & Tax. Code) Generally, the election to deduct a loss on a prior year return must be made on a return filed on or before the original due date of the return for the taxable year in which the disaster occurred.

Taxpayers can find additional information on disaster losses in FTB Publication 1034, Disaster Loss - How to Claim a State Tax Deduction.

• *Federal tax relief for Hurricanes Harvey, Irma, and Maria*

Because of the state's federal conformity date history (see ¶ 15-515), California does not incorporate federal amendments that eliminated the 10% of AGI and $100 floor limitations for casualty losses that arose in a Hurricane Harvey, Irma, or Maria disaster area and that were attributable to those hurricanes in 2017. (*2017 Summary of Federal Income Tax Changes*, California Franchise Tax Board, May 16, 2018)

In addition, uncodified provisions in the federal Disaster Tax Relief and Airport and Airway Extension Act of 2017 (P.L. 115-63) defined a net disaster loss as the excess of qualified disaster-related personal casualty losses over personal casualty gains. Under these federal provisions, qualified disaster-related personal casualty losses are losses that arose in the:

— Hurricane Harvey disaster area on or after August 23, 2017, and that were attributable to Hurricane Harvey;

— Hurricane Irma disaster area on or after September 4, 2017, and that were attributable to Hurricane Irma; or

— Hurricane Maria disaster area on or after September 16, 2017, and that were attributable to Hurricane Maria.

California does not conform to these uncodified federal provisions. (*2017 Summary of Federal Income Tax Changes*, California Franchise Tax Board, May 16, 2018)

• *Farm losses*

California does not incorporate IRC Sec. 461(j), which limits the amount of net Schedule F losses from farming activities that may be claimed by taxpayers, other than C corporations, who receive Commodity Credit Corporation loans or certain other farm subsidies, beginning with the 2010 tax year. (Sec. 17560.5, Rev. & Tax. Code) Consequently, taxpayers whose losses were limited on the federal return as a result of this provision may be able to claim a greater loss on their California return.

Other subtractions to the taxable income base are listed at ¶ 16-205.

[¶16-305] Subtractions--Lottery Winnings

California law prohibits the imposition of any state or local tax on the sale of lottery tickets or shares of the lottery, any prize awarded by the California State lottery, or any amount received by a prizewinner pursuant to a validly executed or judicially ordered assignment. (Sec. 8880.68, Govt. Code) A subtraction adjustment for any California lottery winnings included in federal taxable income may be made on Sch. CA (540), line 21(a), column B. (Instructions, Sch. CA (540), California Adjustments—Residents)

PLANNING NOTE: Interaction With Gambling Losses: Under both California and federal law, gambling losses may only be claimed to the extent of gambling income. Taxpayers that reduce their gambling income for California lottery income may need to reduce the losses included in the federal itemized deductions on line 37. These losses are entered on line 41 as a negative number. (Instructions, Sch. CA (540), California Adjustments—Residents)

Other subtractions to the taxable income base are listed at ¶ 16-205.

[¶16-307] Subtractions--Medical Expenses and Savings Accounts

Nonqualified distributions from health savings accounts (HSAs) are subject to federal taxable income. However, because contributions to and earnings on HSAs are subject to California personal income tax (see ¶ 16-100), such distributions are not subject to California personal income taxation. The adjustment is made on Sch. CA (540), line 21f, column B. (Instructions, Sch. CA (540), California Adjustments—Residents)

Also, for taxable years beginning on or after January 1, 2020, any amount received as a premium assistance subsidy under the Individual Market Assistance program is excludable from gross income. (Sec. 17141.1, Rev. & Tax. Code)

Other subtractions to the taxable income base are listed at ¶ 16-205.

[¶16-310] Subtractions--Net Operating Loss

Although California generally conforms to federal law (IRC Sec. 172), concerning the net operating loss (NOL) deduction, significant differences do exist. Consequently, taxpayers are required to add back the federal NOL(see ¶ 16-105) and recompute the California NOL.

The California NOL is computed in accordance with the federal NOL under IRC Sec. 172 as of California's current federal conformity date (see ¶15-515), but with significant modifications relating to suspension periods, the pre-2004 NOL percentage, carrybacks, the pre-2008 carryover period, and allocation and apportionment for California purposes. (Sec. 17276.20, Rev. & Tax. Code) Special rules also apply to new and small businesses; businesses operating in enterprise zones, the former Los Angeles Revitalization Zone (LARZ), local agency military base recovery areas (LAMBRAs), and the targeted tax area (TTA); and farming businesses impacted by Pierce's Disease.

•*Forms*

Taxpayers claiming a general NOL compute the NOL on Form 3805V, Net Operating Loss (NOL) Computation and NOL and Disaster Loss Limitations—Individuals, Estates, and Trust. The NOL amount is then entered as a positive number on Sch. CA (540 or 540NR),. (FTB Pub. 1001, Supplemental Guidelines to California Adjustments)

The NOL deduction for enterprise zone taxpayers is claimed on FTB 3805Z, Enterprise Zone Deduction and Credit Summary. LARZ businesses claim the NOL carryover deduction on FTB 3806, Los Angeles Revitalization Zone Deduction and Credit Summary. LAMBRA businesses claim the NOL on FTB 3807, Local Agency Military Base Recovery Area Deduction and Credit Summary, and TTA businesses claim the NOL on FTB 3809, Targeted Tax Area Deduction and Credit Summary. Farming businesses impacted by Pierce's disease claim the NOL carryover deduction on FTB 3805D, Net Operating Loss (NOL) Computation and Limitation - Pierce's Disease.

•*"Net operating loss" defined*

Under IRC Sec. 172(c) and IRC Sec. 172(d) as incorporated and modified by California, "net operating loss" means the amount by which deductions for a taxable year exceed gross income, calculated without any NOL deduction. Under IRC Sec. 172(b), an NOL that exceeds taxable income from the current year is carried over to the earliest taxable years to which it may be carried. In determining the amount of an NOL carryover, the law in effect during the year to which the NOL is carried over is applied. (IRC Sec. 172(c))

•*Significant California modifications to federal NOL deduction*

Deductible losses.—For NOLs incurred in tax years beginning after 2017, federal law, but not California law, limits the NOL deduction to 80% of taxable income. (*2017 Summary of Federal Income Tax Changes*, California Franchise Tax Board, May 16, 2018) For NOLs incurred after 2003 and prior to 2018, the amount of the general NOL allowed under California law is the same as under federal law. For NOLs incurred prior to 2004, the amount of the general NOL under Sec. 17276.20, Rev. & Tax. Code is limited to a specified percentage of the amount allowed under federal law. The deductible percentage for California purposes is 60% for NOLs incurred during 2002 and 2003, 55% for NOLs incurred in 2000 and 2001, and 50% for NOLs incurred prior to 2000. (Sec. 17276.20(b), Rev. & Tax. Code) The limitations on NOLs incurred prior to 2004 do not apply to NOLs incurred by businesses operating in an enterprise zone, former Los Angeles Revitalization Zone, local agency military base recovery area, and former program area businesses, or to certain new or small businesses and farming businesses affected by Pierce's disease (see below).

Suspension of NOL deductions.—California has suspended the use of NOL deductions for the 2020—2022 taxable years, except for taxpayers with taxable income of less than $1 million for the taxable year. However, the carryover period for any NOL that is not deductible during those years as a result of the suspension provisions is extended by:

— one year for losses incurred during 2021;

— two years for losses incurred during 2020; and

— three years for losses incurred before 2020.

(Sec. 17276.23, Rev. & Tax. Code)

An NOL deduction also was not allowed for California purposes for taxable years beginning in 2008—2011 unless the small business exemption applied (see below); however, the carryover period for which a NOL deduction was not allowed during those years was extended by one year for losses incurred during the 2010 tax year, two years for losses incurred during the 2009 tax year, three years for losses incurred during the 2008 tax year, and four years for NOLs incurred prior to 2008. (Sec. 17276.21, Rev. & Tax. Code) There was no comparable suspension of the NOL deduction for federal purposes.

CCH PRACTICE TIP: Exception for certain disaster victims.—Any NOL deduction attributable to the severe storms that occurred in March 2011 in Santa Cruz County, the severe winds that occurred in November 2011 in Los Angeles and San Bernardino Counties, or the wildfires that occurred in May 2014 in San Diego County could not be suspended, deferred, reduced, or otherwise diminished unless otherwise specified in later enacted legislation. (Sec. 17207.11, Rev. & Tax. Code(c); Sec. 17207.12, Rev. & Tax. Code(c); Sec. 17207.13, Rev. & Tax. Code(c))

CCH PRACTICE TIP: Small business exemption from 2008—2011 NOL suspension,—Qualified small businesses were exempt from the 2008—2011 NOL suspension. Different qualifying thresholds applied, depending on when the NOL was incurred or carryover claimed. For the 2008 or 2009 tax years, an NOL deduction or carryover could be claimed by taxpayers with less than $500,000 of net business income. Whereas for the 2010 and 2011 suspension period, only taxpayers with modified adjusted gross income (MAGI) of less than $300,000 for the taxable year could still claim the NOL deduction. (Sec. 17276.21(d), Rev. & Tax. Code)

For purposes of the NOL suspension exemption, "MAGI" means adjusted gross income claimed on the taxpayer's return, determined without regard to the NOL deduction. "Business income" means:

— Income from a trade or business, whether conducted by the taxpayer or by a passthrough entity owned directly or indirectly by the taxpayer.

— Income from rental activity.

— Income attributable to a farming business.

(Sec. 17276.21(d), Rev. & Tax. Code)

CCH POINTER: Exemption from 2008—2011 suspension clarified for S corporations and their shareholders.—For purposes of determining eligibility for the 2008—2011 NOL suspension exemption for S corporations and their shareholders, the $500,000 limit was applied at both the entity and shareholder levels. Consequently, the S corporation might be subject to the limitation and the shareholder might not be, and vice versa. The NOL suspension rules applied to the shareholder's business income regardless of the source of the income. (*E-mail*, California Franchise Tax Board, December 12, 2008)

An NOL deduction (including any of the enhanced NOL deductions discussed below) also was not allowed for taxable years beginning in 2002 and 2003 for California personal income tax purposes; however, the NOL carryover period for which a deduction was not allowed during those years wais extended by one year for losses incurred during 2002, and by two years for losses incurred before January 1, 2002. (Sec. 17276.3, Rev. & Tax. Code) There was no comparable suspension of the NOL deduction for federal purposes.

Carrybacks.—NOL carrybacks are eliminated for tax years after 2018. (Sec. 17276, Rev. & Tax. Code)

Additionally, for California purposes, a taxpayer may not carry back NOLs incurred prior to 2013, but may carry back:

- 50% for NOLs incurred in 2013;

- 75% for NOLs incurred in 2014; and

- 100% for NOLs incurred in 2015 through 2018.

This differs from the general federal carryback period of two years for NOLs incurred prior to 2018 (except five years for NOLs incurred during 2001, 2002, 2008, and 2009) and the federal disallowance of carrybacks for NOLs incurred after 2017. (Sec. 17276.05, Rev. & Tax. Code; Sec. 17276.20(c), Rev. & Tax. Code; Sec. 17276.22, Rev. & Tax. Code; *2017 Summary of Federal Income Tax Changes*, California Franchise Tax Board, May 16, 2018);

Carryovers.—California allows a 20 year carryover period for NOLs incurred after 2007, 10 years for NOLs incurred after 1999 and prior to 2008, and five years for NOLs incurred prior to 2000. Federal law, on the other hand, allows indefinite carryovers for NOLs incurred after 2017, and 20 years for NOLs incurred prior to 2018. (Sec. 17276.20(d), Rev. & Tax. CodeSec. 17276.22, Rev. & Tax. Code; *2017 Summary of Federal Income Tax Changes*, California Franchise Tax Board, May 16, 2018). Also, special California NOL carryover periods apply for economic development area businesses (applicable to pre-2014 taxable years), certain new or small businesses, and farming business affected by Pierce's disease (see below).

•*Nonresidents and part-year residents*

If a net operating loss is sustained during a taxable year in which the taxpayer is a nonresident or part-year California resident, then only a portion of the net operating loss may be claimed. The amount that may be claimed is the sum of (1) the portion of the net operating loss attributable to the part of the year in which the taxpayer is a resident, plus (2) the portion of the net operating loss that, during the portion of the year when the taxpayer is not a resident, is attributable to California source income and deductions.

Net operating loss carryovers are only allowable to the extent that the carryover item or suspended loss was derived from California sources (see ¶16-560), calculated as if the nonresident or part-year resident, for the portion of the year he or she was a nonresident, had been a nonresident for all prior years. (Sec. 17041(i), Rev. & Tax. Code) Taxpayers should consult FTB Pub. 1100, Taxation of Nonresidents and Individuals Who Change Residency, for detailed explanations and examples of how the NOL is computed for nonresidents and part-year residents.

• *Enhanced NOL deduction for new businesses*

Eligible new businesses that incur NOLs after 1993 may claim a 100% NOL deduction, but only to the extent of the new business's net loss. The portion of the taxpayer's NOL that exceeds the new business's net loss is carried over as a general NOL, subject to the applicable percentages discussed above for losses incurred prior to the 2004 taxable year. (Sec. 17276.20(b)(2), Rev. & Tax. Code) "Net loss" means the amount of net loss after application of IRC Sec. 465, which limits deductions to the amount at risk, and IRC Sec. 469, which limits the amount of passive activity losses and credits (see ¶ 15-745). (Sec. 17276.20(b)(6), Rev. & Tax. Code) The NOL deduction for new businesses was also suspended for the 2002 and 2003 taxable years. (Sec. 17276.3, Rev. & Tax. Code)

For NOLs incurred by a new business prior to 2000, the carryover period was dependent on the year in which the NOL was incurred, as follows: eight years for NOLs incurred in the new business's first taxable year; seven years for NOLs incurred in the new business's second taxable year, and six years for NOLs incurred in the new business's third taxable year. For NOLs incurred after 1999 by a new business, the carryover period is the same as the general NOL carryover period discussed above. The amount of the NOL that exceeds the new business's net loss and is subject to the applicable percentages applied for computing the general NOL (discussed above) must be carried over and exhausted prior to carrying over the enhanced portion of the NOL. (Sec. 17276.20(b) and (d), Rev. & Tax. Code)

> **COMMENT: Relationship to general NOL.**—Because the NOL for both new and existing businesses is equal to 100% for taxable years beginning after 2003 and the carryover period for both is 20 years for taxable years beginning after 2007, unless new legislation is enacted there is no "enhanced" NOL deduction amount for new businesses for NOLs incurred after the 2003 taxable year and no extended carryover period for new businesses for NOLs incurred after the 2007 taxable year. (*Legal Division Guidance 2011-10-01*, Franchise Tax Board, October 2011)

"New business" defined.—A "new business" is any trade or business activity that is first commenced in California after 1993, excluding:

—a business that is created when an existing business undergoes a change in legal form or when any of the assets of an existing business are acquired by a taxpayer, partnership, or related person (as defined under IRC Sec. 267 or IRC Sec. 318), if the aggregate fair market value of the assets of the business that has undergone the change in form or whose assets have been acquired exceeds 20% of the total business assets of the taxpayer, partnership, or related person (the 20% asset test). This determination is made as of the last day of the first taxable year in which the taxpayer first uses any of the acquired trade or business assets in its business activity. Only those assets that continue to be used in the same division classification listed in the Standard Industrial Classification (SIC) manual as were used immediately prior to the acquisition are used to determine whether the 20% asset test is satisfied; and

—an additional business activity commenced by a taxpayer, partnership, or related person who is currently engaged in business in this state or who has been engaged in business in this state within the preceding 36 months, unless the additional business activity is classified under a different division of the SIC than any of the current or prior business activities of the taxpayer, partnership, or related person. The FTB has taken the position that the "different division" requirement applies only to those activities being conducted or that had previously been conducted during the preceding 36-month period by the taxpayer (or any related party) within California, or within and without California, but not to those activities wholly outside California.

(Sec. 17276.20(e) and (f), Rev. & Tax. Code; Legal Ruling 96-5, FTB, August 1996, as modified by Legal Ruling 99-2, FTB, March 2, 1999)

California law still uses the SIC for purposes of determining eligibility for the new business and eligible small business NOL. (Instructions, Form FTB 3805V, Net Operating Loss (NOL) Computation and NOL and Disaster Loss Limitations - Individuals, Estates, and Trusts)

Legal Ruling 96-5, FTB, August 1996, provides numerous examples of whether a variety of types of purchases by both in-state and out-of-state taxpayers qualify as new businesses for purposes of claiming the enhanced NOL deduction.

In addition, a "new business" includes any taxpayer that is engaged in biopharmaceutical or other biotechnology activities described in SIC Codes 2833 to 2836 and that has not received regulatory approval for any product from the U.S. Food and Drug Administration. "Biopharmaceutical activities" and "other biotechnology activities" are defined by statute, see Sec. 17276.20(f)(7), Rev. & Tax. Code.

CCH COMMENT: *Businesses that qualify as both "new" and "small" businesses.*—In the case of a taxpayer who operates a business that qualifies as both a new and an eligible small business (discussed below), the business will be treated as a new business for the first three taxable years of the new business. This distinction is important only for NOLs incurred prior to 2000, as these NOLs were eligible for an extended carryover period of up to eight years, while the NOL carryover period for small businesses was limited to five years. As discussed above, NOLs incurred after 1999 by both new and small businesses may be carried over for 10 years.

Taxpayers that operate one or more new businesses and one or more eligible small businesses must determine the amount of the loss attributable to its various businesses in the following manner:

(1) the NOL is first treated as a new business NOL to the extent of the loss from the new business;

(2) any remaining NOL is then treated as an eligible small business NOL to the extent of the loss from the eligible small business; and

(3) any further remaining NOL is treated as a general NOL.

• *Enhanced NOL deduction for small businesses*

An eligible small business may claim a 100% NOL deduction, but only to the extent that the taxpayer's NOL exceeds the small business's net loss; see the discussion above of net loss under "Enhanced NOL deduction for new businesses". The portion of a taxpayer's NOL deduction that exceeds the small business's net loss is subject to the applicable percentages as outlined under the general NOL deduction discussion above. The NOL may be carried over for 20 years (10 years for NOLs incurred after 1999 and prior to 2008, five years for NOLs incurred prior to 2000). The

NOL deduction for small businesses was also suspended for the 2002 and 2003 taxable years. The amount of the NOL that exceeds the new business's net loss and is subject to the applicable percentages discussed above must be carried over and exhausted prior to carrying over the enhanced portion of the NOL.

> **COMMENT: Relationship to general NOL.**—Because the NOL for both eligible small businesses and regular businesses is equal to 100% for taxable years beginning after 2003, unless new legislation is enacted there is no "enhanced" NOL deduction amount for small businesses for NOLs incurred after the 2003 taxable year. (*Legal Division Guidance 2011-10-01*, Franchise Tax Board, October 2011)

"Eligible small business" defined.—For purposes of this enhanced NOL deduction, a "small business" is one that has gross receipts of less than $1 million dollars during the taxable year. (Sec. 17276.20(e)(1), Rev. & Tax. Code) Each of a business's trades or activities will be treated as a separate business for purposes of determining whether a business qualifies as a small business for NOL purposes, if the activities are classified in different SIC divisions. (*Legal Ruling 96-5*, FTB, August 1996)

> **CCH CAUTION: Reclassification of NOL.**—The FTB may reclassify any new business NOL or small business NOL as a general NOL to prevent tax evasion. (Sec. 17276.20(j), Rev. & Tax. Code)

• *Enhanced NOL deductions for businesses operating in economic development areas*

Businesses located in enterprise zones (EZs), local agency military base recover areas (LAMBRAs), targeted tax areas (TTAs), and the former Los Angeles Revitalization Zone (LARZ), may claim 100% of an NOL deduction incurred in the zone or area after the zone or area's designation date and prior to the zone or area's expiration or repeal date. (Sec. 17276.1, Rev. & Tax. Code) An EZ, LAMBRA, TTA, or LARZ "expiration date" is the date the zone or area designation expires, is no longer binding, becomes inoperative, or in the case of a TTA, the date the designation is revoked. The special economic development area NOLs for EZ and LAMBRA businesses are inoperative for post-2013 taxable years and repealed December 1, 2014. For designation of the TTA expired on December 31, 2012. (Sec.17276.2(a)(2)(D) and (e), Rev. & Tax. Code; Sec. 17276.5(a)(7) and (f), Rev. & Tax. Code; Sec. 17276.6(b)(5), Rev. & Tax. Code; Sec. 17276.4(a)(6) and (g), Rev. & Tax. Code)

> **CCH PRACTICE TIP:** *Impact of EZ/LAMBRA NOL deduction for fiscal year taxpayers.*—The EZ or LAMBRA net operating loss (NOL) is allowed for losses attributable to the taxpayer's business activities within the EZ and LAMBRA through December 31, 2013, without regard to the ending date of the taxpayer's taxable year. For a taxpayer with a taxable year on a fiscal year basis, this loss is calculated by computing the EZ or LAMBRA NOL as if the EZ or LAMBRA had remained in existence the entire year. This full year loss is then prorated by the number of days the taxpayer operated in an EZ for the taxable year over the total number of days in the taxable year. The TTA NOL expired on December 31, 2012, and is therefore not impacted by the legislation.

NOLs attributable to these zones or areas may be carried over for 15 taxable years following the taxable year of loss. (Sec. 17276.1(a)(1), Rev. & Tax. Code;

Sec.17276.2(a)(1), Rev. & Tax. Code; Sec. 17276.5(a)(1), Rev. & Tax. Code; Sec. 17276.6(b)(1), Rev. & Tax. Code; Sec. 17276.4(a)(1), Rev. & Tax. Code)

A net operating loss deduction was not allowed for taxable years beginning in 2002 and 2003 for California personal income tax purposes; however, the net operating loss carryover period for which a deduction was not allowed during these years is extended by one year for losses incurred during 2002, and by two years for losses incurred before January 1, 2002. (Sec. 17276.3, Rev. & Tax. Code)

The loss attributable to a zone or area is computed by first determining the business income attributable to sources in California using the standard allocation and apportionment procedures (see ¶11-505). That figure is further apportioned to the area or zone using a modified UDITPA formula (see ¶11-505), comprised of a two factor apportionment formula comprised of a payroll and a property factor. The numerators of the factors are limited to the property and payroll associated with the area or zone and the denominators encompass the taxpayer's payroll and property paid in or located in California. (Sec. 17276.2(a)(2)(C), Rev. & Tax. Code; Sec. 17276.5(a), Rev. & Tax. Code; Sec. 17276.6(1), Rev. & Tax. Code; Sec. 17276.4(a), Rev. & Tax. Code)

Special rules for EZ taxpayers.—Any carryover of an NOL sustained by a qualified EZ taxpayer under pre-1997 California law, is computed under the pre-1997 rules. (Sec. 17276.1(c), Rev.& Tax. Code)

Special rules for LARZ taxpayers.—Because the provisions governing the designation of the LARZ were repealed effective December 1, 1998, qualified taxpayers may claim NOL carryovers only for losses sustained after 1991 but prior to the 1998 taxable year. (Sec. 17276.4(f), Rev. & Tax. Code) However, according to the Franchise Tax Board, a taxpayer could receive a LARZ NOL in 1998 as a pass-through NOL from a 1997 fiscal-year partnership, S corporation, or limited liability company. (Telephone conversation, California FTB, December 3, 1998)

Special rules for LAMBRA taxpayers.—Only qualified taxpayers operating within a LAMBRA are eligible to claim the enhanced NOL deduction. To qualify, a taxpayer must conduct a trade or business within the LAMBRA and for the first two taxable years after commencing operations in the LAMBRA have a net increase in jobs (defined as 2,000 paid hours per employee per year) of one or more employees in the LAMBRA. Only those taxpayers that have a net increase in jobs in California and with one or more full-time employees employed within the LAMBRA may claim the deduction. (Sec. 17276.5(a)(3), Rev. & Tax. Code) Taxpayers may claim the enhanced NOL deduction in their first year of operation even if they have not fulfilled the net increase in jobs requirement. However, if after the second taxable year of operation the taxpayer does not satisfy the requirement, the enhanced NOL deduction claimed during the prior year is subject to recapture. (FTB 3807 Booklet, Local Agency Military Base Recovery Area Businesses)

Special rules for TTA taxpayers.—Only those taxpayers located in a TTA that are involved in the following business activities, described in the federal SIC Manual or NAICS Manual, are eligible to claim the enhanced TTA NOL deduction: manufacturing; transportation; communications; electric, gas, and sanitary services; and wholesale trade. (Sec. 17276.6(a), Rev. & Tax. Code)

• *Enhanced NOL for farming businesses affected by Pierce's disease*

Applicable to net operating losses attributable to the 2001 and 2002 taxable years, a qualified farming business may carry forward the entire amount of an NOL to the nine taxable years following the taxable year of loss if the loss is attributable to farming business activities affected by Pierce's disease and its vectors. A loss will be apportioned to the area affected by Pierce's disease and its vectors by multiplying the total loss from the farming business by a fraction, the numerator of which is the property factor plus the payroll factor and the denominator of which is two. An NOL carryover will be allowed only with respect to the taxpayer's farming business income attributable to the area affected by Pierce's disease and its vectors. Furthermore, a taxpayer may utilize the special NOL carryover provision only if the California Department of Food and Agriculture determines that Pierce's disease and its vectors caused the NOL. (Sec. 17276.1, Rev. & Tax. Code; Sec. 17276.7, Rev. & Tax. Code)

• *Elections*

Taxpayers wishing to claim an enhanced NOL deduction for a business located in an EZ, LAMBRA, TTA, or the former LARZ, or for a business that was impacted by Pierce's disease must make an irrevocable election specifying under which provision the NOL is being claimed. A taxpayer is limited to claiming one type of NOL for a taxable year and must attach a statement specifying which NOL the taxpayer is electing on the original return timely filed for the tax year in which the NOL is incurred. The amount of the loss determined for that taxable year under the elected NOL provision is the only NOL allowed to be carried over from that taxable year. (Sec. 17276.1(b), Rev. & Tax. Code; Sec.17276.2(b) and (d), Rev. & Tax. Code; Sec. 17276.5(b) and (d), Rev. & Tax. Code; Sec. 17276.6(b) and (d), Rev. & Tax. Code; Sec. 17276.4(c) and (e), Rev. & Tax. Code)

> **PLANNING NOTE: Determining which NOL to use.**—A worksheet is provided in the FTB 3805Z, FTB 3806, FTB 3807, and FTB 3809 booklets to assist taxpayers in determining the most advantageous NOL.

Other subtractions to the taxable income base are listed at ¶ 16-205.

• *Nonconformity to special IRC Sec. 172 rules*

For tax years after 2018, California also does not conform to the following federal provisions:

- IRC Sec. 172(b)(1)(B), relating to special rules for REITs
- IRC Sec. 172(b)(1)(E), relating to excess interest loss; and
- IRC Sec. 172(h), relating to corporate equity reduction interest losses.

(Sec. 17276, Rev. & Tax. Code)

[¶16-315] Subtractions--Nondeductible Expenses

Although California law mirrors federal law (IRC Sec. 265), denying deductions for expenses and interest incurred in producing income that is wholly exempt from tax, a subtraction adjustment is allowed when expenses and/or interest are incurred to produce income that is exempt from federal, but not California, taxation (e.g., non-California state and municipal bonds). (Sec. 17280, Rev. & Tax. Code) In such instances, taxpayers should enter the amount as a negative number on Sch. CA (540), line 41. (Instructions, Sch. CA (540), California Adjustments—Residents)

A corresponding addition adjustment is allowed for expenses and interest incurred in producing income that is exempt from California, but not federal, taxation (see ¶ 16-110).

Other subtractions to the taxable income base are listed at ¶ 16-205.

[¶ 16-325] Subtractions--Prizes, Awards, and Rewards

California excludes from gross income rewards received by a taxpayer from any crime hotline that is authorized by a government entity. Employees of a government agency or nonprofit charitable organization that contributes reward funds to the crime hotline are ineligible to claim this exclusion. (Sec. 17147.7, Rev. & Tax Code)

To the extent the amount is included in federal adjusted gross income, a subtraction adjustment may be claimed on Sch. CA (540), line 21(f), column B. (Instructions, Sch. CA (540), California Adjustments—Residents)

Other subtractions to the taxable income base are listed at ¶ 16-205.

[¶ 16-327] Subtractions--Recovery of Tax Benefit Items

Although California incorporates IRC Sec. 111 Recovery of Tax Benefit Items, California substitutes references to federal credits and credit carryovers with references to California personal income tax credits and credit carryovers. (Sec. 17142, Rev. & Tax. Code) Under IRC Sec. 111 any income attributable to the recovery during the taxable year of any amount deducted in a prior taxable year from which the taxpayer derived a tax benefit is included in gross income. If the amount did not reduce income subject to tax in the prior year, the recovery amount may be excluded. If a tax credit was allowable for a prior taxable year and during the current taxable year there is a downward price adjustment or similar adjustment, the tax for the current year must be increased by the amount of the prior credit attributable to the adjustment; however, no increase in the current year's tax is required to the extent that the credit allowable for the recovered amount did not reduce the prior year's tax.

Because California substitutes references to federal credits and credit carryovers with references to California personal income tax credits and credit carryovers, a subtraction may be taken to reflect amounts that were required to be included as a result of a price adjustment for which a federal credit was claimed. The subtraction is claimed on Sch. CA (540), line 21(f), column B. A related addition adjustment may also be required (see ¶ 16-120).

For a discussion of the adjustments allowed for pre-2005 vehicle license fee refunds, see ¶ 15-530.

Other subtractions to the taxable income base are listed at ¶ 16-205.

[¶ 16-332] Subtractions--Relocation Assistance Payments

State payments for moving and related expenses of taxpayers displaced as a result of the acquisition of real property by the state for public use are excludable from state gross income. (Sec. 7269, Govt. Code) Also excluded from gross income are tenant relocation assistance payments that are mandated by state statute or local ordinance. (Sec. 7269, Govt. Code) To the extent these payments are included in federal taxable income, taxpayers should make a subtraction adjustment on Sch. CA (540), line 21(f), column B.

Other subtractions to the taxable income base are listed at ¶ 16-205.

[¶ 16-335] Subtractions--Reparation Payments

California law mirrors federal law (Uncodified Sec. 803 of the Economic Growth and Tax Relief Reconciliation Act of 2001, P.L. 107-16) that excludes from gross income any Holocaust restitution payments and related interest received by an eligible individual or the individual's heirs or estate. (Sec. 17131.1, Rev. & Tax. Code), California also excludes from gross income any amount, including any interest or property, received as compensation pursuant to the German Act Regulating Unresolved Property Claims. The basis of any property received pursuant to the German Act will be the fair market value of the property at the time of receipt by the taxpayer. (Sec. 17155, Rev. & Tax. Code) In addition, California excludes from gross income any humanitarian reparation payments made to persons required to perform slave or forced labor during World War II. (Sec. 17155.5, Rev. & Tax. Code) To the extent any of these amounts are included in federal taxable income, taxpayers may claim a subtraction adjustment on Sch. CA (540), line 21(f), column B.

• *Armenian genocide settlement payments*

Settlement payments and related interest received after 2004 by eligible individuals (or by the heirs or estates of eligible individuals) who were persecuted on the basis of race or religion by the regime that was in control of the Ottoman Turkish Empire from 1915 through 1923 (during the Armenian genocide) are excludable from gross income for California personal income tax purposes. (Sec. 17131.2, Rev. & Tax. Code) To the extent any of these amounts are included in federal taxable income, taxpayers may claim a subtraction adjustment on Sch. CA (540), line 21(f), column B.

The basis of any property received by an eligible individual or by the individual's heirs or estates will be the fair market value of the property at the time of receipt. (Sec. 17131.2, Rev. & Tax. Code)

• *Reparation payments to Canada's Japanese internment victims*

Gross income does not include reparation payments made by the Canadian government for the purpose of redressing the injustice done to persons of Japanese ancestry who were interned in Canada during World War II. (Sec. 17156.5, Rev. & Tax. Code) To the extent any of these amounts are included in federal taxable income, taxpayers may claim a subtraction adjustment on Sch. CA (540), line 21(f), column B.

Other subtractions to the taxable income base are listed at ¶ 16-205.

[¶ 16-340] Subtractions--Research and Development Expenses

California, requires that the deduction of research and trade expenses be reduced by the portion of the expenses for which the California credit was claimed. (Sec. 17270, Rev. & Tax. Code) The subtraction is made on Sch. CA (540 or 540NR), line 12, 17, or 18, column B. (FTB Pub. 1001, Supplemental Guidelines to California Adjustments)

[¶ 16-345] Subtractions--Retirement Plans and Benefits

California generally conforms to the federal treatment of retirement plans and benefits (see ¶ 15-800). However subtractions may be allowed for the items discussed below. Addition adjustments may also be required (see ¶ 16-135).

• *Nonresidents*

California does not tax retirement income received by a nonresident. An extensive list of the retirement income to which this rule applies is provided in FTB Pub. 1005, Pension and Annuity Guidelines. Nonresidents make an adjustment on Sch. CA (540NR), line 16, column E (Instructions, Sch. CA (540NR), California Adjustments—Nonresidents and Part-Year Residents)

• *Social Security and railroad retirement benefits*

California law does not incorporate IRC Sec. 86, which requires that Social Security benefits and Tier 1 Railroad Retirement Benefits be included in income to the extent that the benefits exceed certain limits. (Sec. 17087(a), Rev. & Tax. Code)

The subtraction of Railroad Retirement Tier 1 benefits applies to:

— the social security equivalent benefit (SSEB) and non-SSEB portion of the tier one railroad retirement benefits;

— Tier 2 railroad retirement benefits reported on federal Form 1099-R; and

— sick pay benefits under the Railroad Unemployment Insurance Act.

Railroad retirement benefits paid by individual railroads are taxable by California and may not be subtracted. (FTB Pub. 1005, Pension and Annuity Guidelines)

Taxpayers that include these benefits in their federal taxable income may claim a subtraction adjustment on Sch. CA (540), line 20, column B. (Instructions, Sch. CA (540), California Adjustments—Residents. Nonresidents claim the subtraction on Sch. CA (540NR)),

---

CAUTION NOTE: Foreign social security benefits are taxable by California, including amounts excluded from federal taxable income under a treaty between the United States and a foreign country (see ¶ 16-135).

• *Distributions from IRAs, employees' trusts and employee annuities*

Generally, the treatment of distributions is the same for federal and California purposes. However, the amount of a distribution that is subject to California taxation may be less than the amount subject to federal taxation as a result of different basis rules for federal and California income tax purposes. Until 2008, California and federal law have allowed the same amount of deductible contributions to IRAs since 1987.

As a result of California's IRC conformity date history, California did not conform to federal law that indexes the adjusted gross income (AGI) phase-out limits for traditional IRAs for taxpayers who are active participants in their or their spouses' employer-sponsored retirement plan for the 2008 and 2009 tax years. Therefore, taxpayers participating in their or their spouses' employer-sponsored retirement plan could potentially have a different federal basis than state basis if they fall between the phase-out limits, and were contributing to a traditional IRA beginning in the 2008 taxable year. For 2008, the phase-out range for federal purposes for single taxpayers is between $52,000 and $62,000, whereas the range for California personal income tax purposes remains between $50,000 and $60,000. The AGI phase-out range for joint federal returns is $83,000 to $103,000, as compared to the California phase-out range of between $75,000 and $85,000. Finally, for individuals who are not an active participant, but whose spouse is an active participant, the phase-out range is between $156,000 and $166,000 on the federal return and between $150,000 and $160,000 on the California return. (*Tax News*, FTB, December 2007)

Differences in basis may also arise as a result of:

— different contribution rules applied during 1982 through 1986 and prior to 1976;

— a taxpayer's election to treat contributions differently on the California return than on the federal return; or

— the taxpayer's previous nonresidency.

(Sec. 17507, Rev. & Tax. Code)

Roth IRA basis differences may arise as a result of a conversion from a regular IRA to a Roth IRA in 1998. The basis in a Self-Employed Pension (SEP) plan and Self-Employed Retirement plan (Keogh) may be different as a result of differences in the amount of deductible contributions prior to 1996. (Sec. 17081, Rev. & Tax. Code; Sec. 17085, Rev. & Tax. Code) (FTB Pub. 1005, Pension and Annuity Guidelines)

Detailed explanations of these differences, and how to compute the California subtraction adjustment arising as a result of these differences are discussed in detail in FTB Pub. 1005, Pension and Annuity Guidelines. The actual subtraction adjustment is claimed on Sch. CA (540), line 15, column C. (Instructions, Sch. CA (540), California Adjustments)

• *California qualified stock options*

The favorable tax treatment afforded by federal law to incentive and employee stock options applies for California purposes to California qualified stock options. (Sec. 17502, Rev. & Tax. Code) Accordingly, taxpayers may postpone paying personal income taxes on qualifying options until disposing of the options or the underlying stock. "California qualified stock options" are stock options:

— designed by the corporation issuing the option as a California qualified stock option at the time the option is granted;

— issued by a corporation to its employees after 1996 and before 2002; and

— exercised by a taxpayer either while employed by the issuing corporation or within three months after leaving the employ of the issuing corporation.

A taxpayer who becomes permanently and totally disabled as defined in IRC Sec. 22(e)(3) may exercise the option within one year of leaving the employ of the issuing corporation.

The favorable tax treatment of California qualified stock options is available only to a taxpayer whose earned income from the corporation granting the option does not exceed $40,000 for the taxable year in which the option is exercised, and only to the extent that the number of shares transferable by the taxpayer by the exercise of qualified options does not exceed a total of 1,000 and those shares have a combined fair market value of less than $100,000. The combined fair market value of stock is determined as of the time an option is granted, and options are taken into account in the order in which they were granted. The postponement of tax on a California qualified stock option does not apply to any stock option for which an election to include gain in gross income in the year of transfer has been made under IRC Sec. 83(b).

The exclusion is made on Sch. CA (540 or 540NR), line 7, column B. (FTB Pub. 1001, Supplemental Guidelines to California Adjustments)

• *Annuities—Three-year basis recovery rule*

Taxpayers whose annuity starting date was after July 1, 1986, and before January 1, 1987, who elected to have the three-year basis recovery rule apply for California personal income tax purposes, must make an adjustment on their California Sch. CA (540). For annuities starting prior to 1987, a payment received by an employee generally was treated, in part, as a return of the employee's contribution and, in part, as taxable income. Under the former three-year basis recovery rule, the first three years of annuity payments after the annuity starting date would equal or exceed the individual's aggregate employee contributions, all distributions were treated as a return of employee contributions (and thus were nontaxable) until all of the individual's employee contributions were recovered. Thereafter, all distributions were fully taxable. Taxpayers that elected the three-year basis recovery rule after July 1, 1986, and before 1987 for California purposes and used the pre-1987 annuity rules for federal purposes, must subtract the federal taxable amount from the California taxable amount on Sch. CA (540), Line 16, Column C. (Sec. 17085(a), Rev. & Tax. Code; FTB Pub. 1005, Pension and Annuity Guidelines) (Instructions, Schedule CA(540), California Adjustments)

• *Citizens living abroad*

Under both California and federal law (IRC Sec. 72(f)(2)) contributions to a retirement plan by an employer are included in an employee's basis if, had they been paid directly to the employee instead of contributed to the plan, they would not have been included in the employee's gross income (Code Sec. 72(f)(2)) However, federal law, but not California law, does not include contributions paid on behalf of a citizen living abroad whose income is excludable under IRC Sec. 911. Consequently, such contributions would be included in basis for purposes of calculating the amount of taxable distribution and would be entered as a subtraction.

Other subtractions to the taxable income base are listed at ¶16-205.

[¶16-350] Subtractions--Targeted Business Activity or Zones

Businesses located in an enterprise zone, local agency military base recovery area (LAMBRA), targeted tax area, manufacturing enhancement area, or former Los Angeles revitalization zone (LARZ) may be eligible for accelerated depreciation deductions (see ¶16-040), enhanced net operating loss deductions (see ¶16-310), and employer wage credits. In addition, interest earned on loans made to enterprise zone businesses may be deducted (see ¶16-280).

Other subtractions to the taxable income base are listed at ¶16-205.

[¶16-360] Subtractions--Taxes

California excludes state income tax refunds from gross income. The amount of state income tax refunds included in federal taxable may be subtracted on Sch. CA (540 or 540NR), line 10, column B. (FTB Pub. 1001, Supplemental Guidelines to California Adjustments)

An addition adjustment is required for state income taxes paid and deducted on the federal return (see ¶16-145).

Other subtractions to the taxable income base are listed at ¶16-205.

[¶16-365] Subtractions--Trade or Business Expenses

Adjustments are available for the following items.

• *Employer's parking cash-out payments*

Employers may claim a business expense deduction, under California law only, for cash payments that they make to employees under "parking cash-out programs". (Sec. 17202, Rev. & Tax. Code) Payments are to be equivalent to the difference between (1) the amount that an employer would pay to provide an employee with a parking space not owned by the employer and (2) the amount, if any, that an employee would pay for the space. (Sec. 65088.1, Govt. Code) Presumably, the adjustment would be made on Sch. CA (540), line 12, column B.

• *State legislator's expenses*

California does not incorporate IRC Sec. 162(h), which allows state legislators living more than 50 miles away from the state capital an election to define the home located within the district represented as the "tax home". Rather, California deems the legislator's residence within his or her district to be the tax home. (Sec. 17270(a), Rev. & Tax. Code) To the extent the California deduction exceeds the federal deduction, a subtraction adjustment is allowed. The adjustment is made on Sch. CA (540), line 12, column B. If the federal deduction exceeds the California deduction, an addition adjustment is required (see ¶ 16-150).

Other subtractions to the taxable income base are listed at ¶ 16-205.

• *Physician's interindemnity arrangements*

California allows a deduction for payments made to a cooperative corporation by its members for malpractice coverage. (Sec. 17278, Rev. & Tax. Code; Uncodified Sec. 5, Ch. 1276, Laws 1984)

Deductions for such payments are valid only to the extent that the payment does not exceed the amount that would otherwise be payable to an independent insurance company for similar medical malpractice coverage. Excess payments may be carried forward five years. The deductible payment may be made either as a contribution to, or in response to an assessment by, the interindemnity arrangement. (Sec. 17278, Rev. & Tax. Code; Uncodified Sec. 5, Ch. 1276, Laws 1984)

Refunded payments must be included in the taxpayer's income in the year received. (Sec. 17278, Rev. & Tax. Code; Uncodified Sec. 5, Ch. 1276, Laws 1984) Such payments must be reported by the trust to the Franchise Tax Board (FTB) in the year made. The FTB may require, by regulation, the trust to withhold a specified amount of any refund made to a nonresident.

The comparable federal provision does not provide for the carryover of excess payments. Instead, the federal provision allows an initial contribution in a lump-sum payment or in substantially equal payments over a period not to exceed six years. (Sec. 1031, P.L. 99-514) To the extent that the California deduction is more than that claimed on the federal return, a subtraction adjustment is allowed. Conversely, an addition adjustment may be required (see ¶ 16-150).

[¶ 16-370] Subtractions--Unemployment Compensation

California does not incorporate IRC Sec. 85, which subjects unemployment compensation to federal income tax. (Sec. 17083, Rev. & Tax. Code) California does not tax unemployment compensation.

Taxpayers who receive unemployment compensation or paid family leave insurance, should claim a subtraction from federal taxable income in the amounts reported on federal Forms 1099-G. Residents claim the subtraction on Sch. CA (540), line 19, Column B. (Instructions, Form 540, Sch. CA (540), California Adjustments—Residents) Nonresidents claim the subtraction on Sch. CA (540NR), line 13, column B (Instructions, Form 540NR (Long), Sch. CA (540NR), California Adjustments—Nonresidents or Part-Year Residents)

Other subtractions to the taxable income base are listed at ¶ 16-205.

[¶16-500]

SOURCING RULES

[¶16-505] Income Attributable to State Sources

For purposes of determining taxable income during any period of nonresidence, gross income includes only California source gross income, which includes:

— income from real or tangible personal property located in the state;

— income from a business, trade, or profession carried on within the state;

— compensation for personal services performed within the state;

— income from stocks, bonds, and other intangible personal property having a business or taxable situs in the state; and

— income from rentals or royalties for the use of patents, copyrights, good will, franchises and other like property having a taxable or business situs in the state.

(Sec. 17951, Rev. & Tax. Code; Reg. 17951-2, 18 CCR)

COMMENT: *Taxpayers' Rights Advocate observations.*—The Franchise Tax Board's Taxpayers' Rights Advocate notes that some states are taking more aggressive positions in determining what is or is not income sourced to their states. Most of the time it involves sourcing income where "services provided" is not clearly defined. Clear rules for sourcing income in some of the gray areas may not be available until some current cases are litigated. In the meantime, taxpayers who receive income from within and outside of California are provided guidance in the form of a table for sourcing different types of income. (*Tax News*, Franchise Tax Board, June 2011)

[¶16-515] Sourcing of Business Income

A nonresident's income from California sources includes income from a business, trade, or profession carried on in California. If the nonresident's business, trade, or profession is carried on partly within California and partly outside California, and the part within the state is so separate and distinct from the part outside the state such that the respective business activities are not part of a unitary business, trade, or profession, only income from the part conducted within the state is considered California source income. (Reg. 17951-4, 18 CCR)

• *Unitary business income*

If a nonresident sole proprietor carries on a unitary multistate business, trade, or profession, then the nonresident's business income from sources within the state is determined by the apportionment formula provided in the Uniform Division of Income for Tax Purposes Act (UDITPA), Sec. 25120, Rev. & Tax. Code through Sec. 25129, Rev. & Tax. Code, and the regulations thereunder (see ¶11-520), except as provided for professional service organizations. (Reg. 17951-4, 18 CCR) If a nonresident is a partner in a partnership, sole member of a limited liability company (LLC) whose separate existence is disregarded for tax purposes, member of an LLC that is classified as a partnership for tax purposes, or shareholder of an S corporation, and the business entity carries on a unitary multistate business, then the same formula is used to determine the nonresident partner's, member's, or shareholder's distributive share of partnership, LLC, or S corporation business income apportioned to California. (Reg. 17951-4, 18 CCR) If the partnership and the business activity of the partner are part of one unitary business, then the rules of Reg. 25137-1(f), 18 CCR apply and the apportionment of the partnership business income is done at the partner level for the unitary partner or partners. (Reg. 17951-4, 18 CCR)

The source of net income from a business, trade, or profession that is not business income must be determined in accordance with the sourcing rules of Sec. 17951, Rev. & Tax. Code through Sec. 17955, Rev. & Tax. Code and the regulations thereunder, and not by reference to the nonbusiness allocation rules of UDITPA, Sec. 25120, Rev. & Tax. Code through Sec. 25129, Rev. & Tax. Code, and the regulations thereunder. (Reg. 17951-4, 18 CCR)

CCH PRACTICE TIP: Single sales factor apportionment formula.—Beginning with the 2011 tax year, a nonresident individual who is a sole proprietor of a business that engages in activities both inside and outside California may also determine California-source income using the single-sales factor formula. Similarly, a nonresident individual who is a partner in a partnership that engages in activities inside and outside California may determine California-source income using the single-sales factor formula on Part B of schedule R-1 of Form 565. If the partnership elects to use the single factor formula, the partnership must use the single-sales factor formula to determine California-source income for all nonunitary nonresident partners. (Reg. 25128.5(c)(2), 18 CCR) Beginning with the 2013 tax year, an apportioning trade or business, regardless of the form of ownership (e.g., sole proprietorship, partnership, limited liability company, or corporation) that carries on within and out of California is required to use the single sales factor apportionment formula, unless one of the specified exceptions applies. (*Tax News*, California Franchise Tax Board, April 2013)

Also, for the above purposes, the business activity of a partnership, LLC, or S corporation will not ordinarily be considered part of a unitary business with another business activity unless the partner, member, or shareholder owns, directly or indirectly, a 20% or more capital or profits interest in a partnership, LLC, or S corporation. In addition, the FTB will have discretion to treat business activities as part of a unitary business if it determines such combination is appropriate after conducting a comparable uncontrolled price examination. (Reg. 17951-4, 18 CCR)

[¶16-530] Sourcing of Income from Intangibles

A nonresident's income from intangible personal property generally is not California source income. However, if the property has acquired a business situs in California, the nonresident's income from the property will constitute California source income. In addition, if a nonresident buys or sells intangible property (such as stocks and bonds) in California or places orders with brokers in California to buy or sell such property, and does so on such a regular, systematic, and continuous basis as to constitute doing business in California, the nonresident's profit or gain derived from such activity constitutes California source income regardless of the situs of the property. (Sec. 17952, Rev. & Tax. Code)

The source of gains and losses from the sale or other disposition of intangible personal property is determined at the time of the sale or disposition of that property. Consequently, gain from an installment sale of intangible property made by a California resident taxpayer continues to be sourced to California even if the taxpayer subsequently becomes a nonresident. In addition, a California nonresident who sells intangible personal property that had a business situs in California at the time of the sale would be taxed by California on gain as it is recognized upon receipt of future installment payments. (Reg. 17952, 18 CCR)

A nonresident's income from qualifying investment securities is not taxable by California if the nonresident receives the income as:

— an individual whose only contact with the state with respect to the securities is through a broker, dealer, or investment adviser located in California;

— a partner in an investment partnership;

— a beneficiary of a qualifying estate or trust whose only contact with the state with respect to the securities is through an investment account managed by a corporate fiduciary located in California; or

— a unit holder in a regulated investment company, as defined in IRC Sec. 851.

However, income from qualifying investment securities is taxable by California if the income is from investment activity that is interrelated with a California trade or business in which the nonresident owns an interest and the primary activities of the trade or business are separate and distinct from the acts of acquiring, managing, or disposing of qualified investment securities. Likewise, income from qualifying investment securities that are acquired with the working capital of a California trade or business in which the nonresident owns an interest is taxable by California. (Sec. 17955, Rev. & Tax. Code)

• *"Qualifying investment securities" defined*

"Qualifying investment securities" include:

— preferred stock and common stock, including preferred or debt securities convertible into common stock;

— bonds, debentures, and other debt securities;

— foreign and domestic currency deposits or equivalents;

— securities convertible into foreign securities;

— mortgage- or asset-backed securities secured by federal, state, or local governmental agencies;

— repurchase agreements and loan participations;

— foreign currency exchange contracts and forward and futures contracts on foreign currencies;

— stock and bond index securities and futures contracts and other similar financial securities and futures contracts on those securities;

— options for the purchase or sale of any of the securities, currencies, contracts, or financial instruments specified above; and

— regulated futures contracts.

(Sec. 17955, Rev. & Tax. Code)

CCH PRACTICE TIP: *Treatment of income from investment in commodity-linked derivative securities.*—In response to a taxpayer's inquiry, the California Franchise Tax Board's chief counsel has determined that investments in commodity-linked derivative securities are qualified investment securities for California personal income and corporation franchise and income tax purposes. Consequently, a fund that invests in the commodity-linked derivative securities would be a qualified investment partnership and its U.S. individual investors who are not California residents would not be subject to California personal income tax or reporting requirements on such income. Such income would be exempt from corporation franchise and income taxes provided certain conditions are satisfied. (*Chief Counsel Ruling 2010-01*, California Franchise Tax Board, March 25, 2010)

• *"Investment partnership" and "qualifying estate or trust" defined*

A partnership is an "investment partnership," and an estate or trust is a "qualifying estate or trust" if:

— at least 90% of the cost of its total assets is from qualifying investment securities, deposits at banks or other financial institutions, and office space and equipment reasonably needed to carry on investment activities; and

— at least 90% of its gross income consists of interest, dividends, and gains from the sale or exchange of qualifying investment securities.

(Sec. 17955, Rev. & Tax. Code)

• *Related discussions*

Sourcing rules for nonresident beneficiary income from intangible personal property held by a trust or estate are discussed under Nonresident Beneficiary Income at ¶16-540. Sourcing rules for installment gains received by a nonresident from the sale of intangible property are discussed under Property-Related Income at ¶16-550.

[¶16-540] Sourcing of Nonresident Beneficiary Income

Estate and trust income distributed or distributable to nonresident beneficiaries is California source income to the beneficiary only if such income is derived by the estate or trust from a source within the state. (Sec. 17953, Rev. & Tax. Code) For purposes of computing taxable income, deductions are included in that computation only to the extent that the deduction is derived from sources within the state. (Sec. 17041, Rev. & Tax. Code)

• *Income from intangible personal property*

A nonresident beneficiary will be treated as the owner of intangible personal property from which estate or trust income is derived. (Sec. 17953, Rev. & Tax. Code) Thus, stocks, bonds, and similar intangible assets held by a California trust or estate are regarded as having a situs at the domicile of the nonresident beneficiary, and generally do not give rise to California source income.

A California regulation provides that income from such intangible personal property is not California source income to the nonresident beneficiary unless:

— the property is so used by the estate as to acquire a business situs in the state; or

— in the case of royalties, patents, copyrights, secret processes and formulas, good will, trademarks, trade brands, franchises, and other like property, the estate or trust permits or licenses the property to be used as an asset of a business, trade, or profession in the state.

(Reg. 17951-3, 18 CCR)

• *Income and losses from trusts required to distribute income currently*

The Franchise Tax Board (FTB) has issued a legal ruling providing guidance on the inclusion and sourcing of income and losses from certain trusts required to distribute income currently when the beneficiary is a part-year resident during any part of its own or the trust's taxable year. Beneficiaries realize income and losses throughout the trust year as the income is realized by the trust. All items of income and loss realized by the trust during the trust year when the beneficiary was a resident are included in the beneficiary's California taxable income. Also, all California-source items of income and loss realized by the trust during the trust year when the beneficiary was a nonresident are included in the beneficiary's California taxable income. In the absence of information that reflects the actual date of realization of items of income and loss, the taxpayer must allocate an annual amount on a proportional basis between the periods of residency and nonresidency using a daily pro-rata methodology prescribed by the FTB. These provisions are consistent with federal law dealing with a dual-status taxpayer. (*Legal Ruling 2003-1*, FTB, April 7, 2003)

For additional details regarding nonresident beneficiaries, see ¶ 15-235.

[¶16-545] Sourcing of Retirement Income

Sourcing rules for retirement income are discussed below.

• *Retirement income received by nonresidents*

Under both federal and state law, qualified retirement income received after 1995 by former California residents is not taxable by California. (Sec. 114, Tit. 4, U.S.C.; Sec. 17952.5, Rev. & Tax. Code) Such income will either escape taxation altogether or be taxable in the person's new state of residence.

The exclusion from California gross income applies to income received from the following plans:

— qualified IRC Sec. 401(a) trusts exempt from taxation under IRC Sec. 501(a);

— IRC Sec. 408(k) simplified employee pensions;

— IRC Sec. 403(a) annuity plans;

— IRC Sec. 403(b) annuity contracts;

— IRC Sec. 7701(a)(37) individual retirement plans;

— IRC Sec. 457 deferred compensation plans;

— IRC Sec. 414(d) government plans; and

— IRC Sec. 501(c)(18) trusts.

The exclusion also applies to distributions from nonqualified plans described in IRC Sec. 3121(v)(2)(c), or any written plan, program, or arrangement that provides for retirement payments in recognition of prior service to be made to a retired partner and that is in effect immediately before retirement begins, if payments are made at least annually and spread over the actuarial life expectancy of the beneficiaries or spread over at least a 10-year period, or if payments are made after termination of employment and under a plan maintained solely to provide retirement benefits to employees in excess of those that may be provided under qualified plans. The fact that payments may be adjusted from time to time pursuant to a plan, program, or arrangement to limit total disbursements under a predetermined formula or to provide cost-of-living or similar adjustments, will not cause the periodic payments provided to fail the "substantially-equal-periodic-payments" test. The exclusion also applies to any retired or retainer pay of a member or former member of the armed forces that is computed under Chapter 71 (commencing with Sec. 1401) of Title 10 of the U.S. Code. California's gross income exclusion will remain in effect as long as the federal prohibition against a state's taxation of a former resident's qualified retirement income remains in effect. (Sec. 114, Tit. 4, U.S.C.; Sec. 17952.5, Rev. & Tax. Code)

• *Employer-sponsored retirement plan income received by residents*

Because California residents are taxed on all income, including income from sources outside California (see ¶ 15-110), qualified pension, profit-sharing, and stock bonus plan income attributable to services performed outside California, but received after becoming a California resident, is taxable. (FTB Pub. 1005, Pension and Annuity Guidelines; FTB Pub. 1100, Taxation of Nonresidents and Individuals Who Change Residency)

> **EXAMPLE:** *Move-in to California.*—A taxpayer permanently moved from Florida to California on January 1, 2012. The taxpayer received pension income during 2012 through a qualified plan from her former Florida employer. The taxpayer's qualified pension income is taxable by California because the taxpayer was a California resident when she received the income. The taxpayer does not make any adjustment on Sch. CA (540), California Adjustments—Residents, to exclude any of the retirement income.

• *Individual retirement account (IRA) income received by residents*

A resident taxpayer no longer receives a stepped-up basis for annual contributions and earnings on IRAs simply because the taxpayer was a nonresident when he or she made the contributions. The taxpayer is treated as a resident for all prior years for all items of deferred income, which includes IRA income. Accordingly, the taxpayer is allowed a basis for contributions the taxpayer actually made that would not have been allowed under California law had the taxpayer been a California resident. California did not conform to the $2,000 or 100% of compensation annual contribution limit permitted under federal law from 1982 through 1986. During these years, California limited the deduction to the lesser of 15% of compensation or $1,500 and denied a deduction altogether to individuals who were active participants in qualified or government plans. Any amounts an individual contributed in excess of California deduction limits during these years create a basis in the IRA. (FTB Pub. 1005, Pension and Annuity Guidelines; FTB Pub. 1100, Taxation of Nonresidents and Individuals Who Change Residency)

• *Related discussion*

See the discussion of Pass-Through Entity Income and Deductions (¶ 16-565) for information on the allocation of deductions for contributions to a qualified retirement plan on behalf of nonresident partners.

[¶ 16-550] Sourcing of Property-Related Income

All of the following are included in the California source income of a nonresident:

> — rent from real or tangible personal property located in California;

> — gains from the sale or transfer of real or tangible personal property located in California, regardless of where the sale or transfer is consummated; and

— any other type of income derived from the ownership, control, or management of real or tangible personal property located in California, regardless of whether a trade, business, or profession is carried on in California.

(Reg. 17951-3, 18 CCR)

• *Installment sales*

California taxes installment gains received by a nonresident from the sale of tangible or intangible property on a source basis. Gains on the sale of real property are generally sourced to where the property is located. Gains on the sale of intangible property are generally sourced to the recipient's state of residence at the time of the sale. A California resident who sells property located outside California on an installment basis while a nonresident, is subject to tax on any installment proceeds received while a California resident. On the other hand, a former California resident who sells property located outside California on an installment basis while a California resident is not subject to tax on any installment proceeds received while a nonresident. (FTB Pub. 1100, Taxation of Nonresidents and Individuals Who Change Residency)

> **EXAMPLE:** *Move out of California.*—In January 2012, while a California resident, a taxpayer sold a parcel of real property located in Washington in an installment sale. On March 1, 2012, the taxpayer became an Ohio resident. On June 1, 2012, the taxpayer received installment proceeds comprised of capital gain income and interest income. The capital gain income is not taxable by California because the property was not located in California. The interest income is not taxable by California because the taxpayer was a nonresident of California when the taxpayer received the proceeds.

• *Deferred gains and losses (like-kind exchanges)*

When a taxpayer exchanges one kind of property for the same kind of property under the requirements of IRC Sec. 1031 (see ¶ 15-710), the taxpayer realizes a gain or loss on the transaction and defers paying tax on the gain or claiming the loss until the property is sold or otherwise disposed of. A gain or loss from the sale or exchange of real or tangible personal property located in California is sourced to California at the time the gain or loss is realized. (FTB Pub. 1100, Taxation of Nonresidents and Individuals Who Change Residency)

California property exchanged for out-of-state property.—If a taxpayer is a nonresident and exchanges real or tangible property located within California for real or tangible property located outside California, the realized gain or loss will be sourced to California. Taxation will not occur until the gain or loss is recognized. This requires the taxpayer to keep track of deferred California sourced gains and losses to report them to California in the year the taxpayer sells or otherwise disposes of the property received in the exchange. (FTB Pub. 1100, Taxation of Nonresidents and Individuals Who Change Residency)

> **EXAMPLE:** *Sourcing of gain.*—As a resident of Texas, a taxpayer exchanged a condominium located in California for like-kind property located in Texas. The taxpayer realized a gain of $15,000 on the exchange that was properly deferred under IRC Sec. 1031. The taxpayer then sold the Texas property in a non-deferred transaction and recognized a gain of $20,000. The $15,000 deferred gain (the lesser of the deferred gain or the gain recognized at the time the taxpayer disposed of the Texas property) has a source in California and is taxable by California.

Out-of-state property exchanged for California property.—If a taxpayer exchanges real or tangible property located outside California for real or tangible property located within California, the gain recognized when the taxpayer sells or otherwise disposes of the California property in a non-deferred transaction has a California source and is taxable by California. (FTB Pub. 1100, Taxation of Nonresidents and Individuals Who Change Residency)

> **EXAMPLE:** *Sourcing of gain.*—While a resident of Kansas, a taxpayer exchanged real property located in Kansas for like-kind real property located in California. The taxpayer realized a $12,000 gain on the exchange that was properly deferred under IRC Sec. 1031. The taxpayer then became a California resident and, while a resident, sold the California property in a non-deferred transaction and recognized a gain of $40,000. California taxes the $40,000 gain because the taxpayer was a California resident at the time of the sale. If the taxpayer paid tax to Kansas on the $12,000 deferred gain, the taxpayer is allowed a credit for taxes paid.

• *Gains and losses from sale of trade or business property*

Upon the sale, exchange, or involuntary conversion of property used in a trade or business (IRC Sec. 1231 property), losses are netted against gains. If Sec. 1231 losses exceed Sec. 1231 gains, the losses receive ordinary tax treatment. If Sec. 1231 gains exceed Sec. 1231 losses, the gains receive capital gain tax treatment. Sec. 1231 gains and losses retain this characterization regardless of whether the taxpayer changes residency status. For purposes of computing California taxable income, the taxpayer nets only California source Sec. 1231 gains and losses. (FTB Pub. 1100, Taxation of Nonresidents and Individuals Who Change Residency)

> **EXAMPLE:** *Computation.*—The taxpayer is a resident of Washington. In 2010, the taxpayer's California and non-California source Sec. 1231 gains and losses included a $3,000 California gain, a $2,000 California loss, a $4,000 Washington gain, and a $5,000 Washington loss. Based upon the netting of the taxpayer's total and California source Sec. 1231 gains and losses, the taxpayer's capital gain or ordinary loss is determined as follows:

Taxable year 2010:	Total taxable income	CA taxable income
CA section 1231 gain	$ 3,000	$ 3,000
CA section 1231 loss	(2,000)	(2,000)
WA section 1231 gain	4,000	
WA section 1231 loss	(5,000)	
Capital gain	$ 0	$ 1,000

• *Related discussion*

See the discussion of Nonresident Beneficiary Income (¶ 16-540) for sourcing provisions applicable to nonresident beneficiary owners of intangible personal property from which estate or trust income is derived.

[¶ 16-555] Sourcing of Gains and Losses

Special rules are provided for determining capital loss carryovers and passive activity losses for nonresidents and those who change their residency status.

• *Capital gains and losses*

Always a nonresident.—If a taxpayer has always been a nonresident of California, the taxpayer determines capital loss carryovers and capital loss limitations based only upon California source income and loss items in order to compute California taxable income. (FTB Pub. 1100, Taxation of Nonresidents and Individuals Who Change Residency)

> **EXAMPLE:** *Computation:* The taxpayer has always been a New York resident. In 2011, the taxpayer's California and non-California source capital gains and losses included California capital gains of $2,000, California capital losses of $6,000, New York capital gains of $5,000, and New York capital losses of $2,000. The taxpayer had no capital loss carryovers prior to 2011. The taxpayer nets capital gains and losses to determine the capital losses allowed in 2011 (the $3,000 limitation applies) and the capital loss carryover to 2012.

Taxable year 2011:	Total taxable income	CA taxable income
CA capital gain	$ 2,000	$ 2,000
CA capital loss	(6,000)	(6,000)
NY capital gain	5,000	
NY capital loss	(2,000)	
Total	$ (1,000)	$ (4,000)
Capital loss allowed in 2011	1,000	3,000
Capital loss carryover to 2012	$ 0	$ (1,000)

Move-in to California.—If a taxpayer has capital loss carryovers and was a nonresident of California in prior years, the capital loss carryovers need to be restated as if the taxpayer had been a California resident for all prior years. (FTB Pub. 1100, Taxation of Nonresidents and Individuals Who Change Residency)

> **EXAMPLE:** *Computation.*—Assume the same facts as in the prior example. Then, on January 1, 2012, the taxpayer becomes a California resident. During 2012, the taxpayer sells property located in Wyoming for a capital gain of $5,000 and incurs a $4,000 capital loss from the sale of property located in California. The taxpayer must restate the 2011 capital loss carryover as if the taxpayer had been a California resident for all prior years and then net capital gains and losses to determine the amount of capital gain to include in total taxable income as follows:

Step 1: Restate 2011 capital loss carryover as if the taxpayer had been a California resident for all prior years.

2011 Restatement:	Total taxable income
CA capital gain	$ 2,000
CA capital loss	(6,000)
NY capital gain	5,000
NY capital loss	(2,000)
Total	$ (1,000)
Capital loss allowed in 2011	1,000
Capital loss carryover to 2012	$ 0

Step 2: Net capital gains and losses to determine the amount of capital gain income to include in total taxable income.

Taxable year 2012:	Total taxable income
CA capital loss	$ (4,000)
WY capital gain	5,000
Capital loss carryover	0
Capital gain income	$ 1,000

Move-out of California.—If a taxpayer has capital loss carryovers and becomes a nonresident of California, the taxpayer's capital loss carryovers need to be restated as if the taxpayer had been a nonresident of California for all prior years. (FTB Pub. 1100, Taxation of Nonresidents and Individuals Who Change Residency)

> **EXAMPLE:** Assume the same facts as in the prior two examples. Then, on January 1, 2013, the taxpayer becomes a nonresident of California again. During 2013, the taxpayer sells property located in Texas for a capital gain of $8,000, sells property located in California for a $9,000 capital gain, and incurs a $5,000 capital loss from the sale of property located in California. The taxpayer restates

capital loss carryovers as if the taxpayer had been a nonresident of California for all prior years by netting capital gains and losses from California sources only, and then nets capital gains and losses to determine the amount of capital gain income to include in total taxable income and California taxable income.

Step 1: Restate capital loss carryovers as if the taxpayer had been a nonresident of California for all prior years by netting capital gains and losses from California sources only.

2011 Restatement:	Total taxable income	CA taxable income
CA capital gain	$ 2,000	$ 2,000
CA capital loss	(6,000)	(6,000)
NY capital gain	5,000	
NY capital loss	(2,000)	
Total	$ (1,000)	$ (4,000)
Capital loss allowed in 2011	1,000	3,000
Capital loss carryover to 2012	$ 0	$ (1,000)

2012 Restatement:	Total taxable income	CA taxable income
CA capital loss, 2012	$ (4,000)	$ (4,000)
WY capital gain	5,000	
Capital loss carryover from 2011		(1,000)
Capital gain or loss	$ 1,000	$ (5,000)
Capital loss allowed in 2012		3,000
Capital loss carryover to 2013	$ 0	$ (2,000)

Step 2: Net capital gains and losses to determine the amount of capital gain income to include in total taxable income and California taxable income.

Taxable year 2013:	Total taxable income	CA taxable income
CA capital gain	$ 9,000	$ 9,000
CA capital loss	(5,000)	(5,000)
TX capital gain	8,000	
Total	$ 12,000	$ 4,000
Capital loss carryover from 2012	0	(2,000)
Capital gain income	$ 12,000	$ 2,000

Part-year resident.—If a taxpayer changes residency during a year, the taxpayer must compute income and deductions using resident rules for the period of the year that the taxpayer was a California resident and using nonresident rules for the period of the year that the taxpayer was a nonresident. The taxpayer must compute any prior year carryover loss as if the taxpayer was a California resident for all prior years *and* as if the taxpayer was a nonresident for all prior years. The taxpayer must then prorate both capital loss carryover amounts based upon the period of California residency and the period of nonresidency during the year. (FTB Pub. 1100, Taxation of Nonresidents and Individuals Who Change Residency)

• *Passive activity losses*

Always a nonresident.—If a taxpayer has always been a nonresident of California, the taxpayer must determine allowed passive activity losses (see ¶ 15-745) and suspended losses based only upon California source passive income and loss items to compute California taxable income. Only California source passive losses carry forward into the following year. (FTB Pub. 1100, Taxation of Nonresidents and Individuals Who Change Residency)

EXAMPLE: *Computation.*—The taxpayer has always been a resident of Texas. Prior to 2011, the taxpayer was not engaged in any passive activities. During 2011, the taxpayer purchased rental properties in both California and Texas. In 2011, the taxpayer's California and non-California source passive income and losses included California rental income of $2,000, California rental losses of $30,000, and Texas rental income of $4,000. Based upon the netting of the taxpayer's passive income and losses and the allowance of up to $25,000 for rental losses, the taxpayer's passive losses allowed in 2011 and suspended to 2012 are as follows:

Taxable year 2011:	Total taxable income	CA taxable income
CA rental income	$ 2,000	$ 2,000
CA rental losses	(30,000)	(30,000)
TX rental income	4,000	
Total	$ (24,000)	$ (28,000)
Allowed rental losses	24,000	25,000
Suspended loss to 2012	$ 0	$ (3,000)

Move-in to California.—If a taxpayer had suspended passive losses and was a nonresident of California in prior years, the suspended passive losses need to be restated as if the taxpayer had been a California resident for all prior years. (FTB Pub. 1100, Taxation of Nonresidents and Individuals Who Change Residency)

EXAMPLE: *Computation.*—Assume the same facts as in the prior example. Then, on January 1, 2012, the taxpayer became a California resident. In 2012, the taxpayer's passive income and losses include California source partnership income of $3,000, California source S corporation losses of $1,000, and New York source partnership income of $7,000. The taxpayer must restate 2011 suspended passive loss as if the taxpayer had been a California resident for 2011, and then net passive income and losses to determine the amount of passive income to include in total taxable income as follows:

Step 1: Restate 2011 suspended passive loss as if the taxpayer had been a California resident for 2011.

2011 Restatement:	Total taxable income
CA partnership income	$ 2,000
CA S corporation loss	(8,000)
NY partnership income	3,000
Suspended passive loss	
to 2012	$ (3,000)

Step 2: Net passive income and losses to determine the amount of passive income to include in total taxable income.

Taxable year 2012:	Total taxable income
CA partnership income	$ 3,000
CA S corporation loss	(1,000)
NY partnership income	7,000
Total	$ 9,000
Suspended passive loss, 2011	(3,000)
Passive income, 2012	$ 6,000

Move-out of California.—If a taxpayer has suspended passive losses and becomes a nonresident of California, the taxpayer's suspended passive losses need to be restated as if the taxpayer had been a nonresident of California for all prior years. (FTB Pub. 1100, Taxation of Nonresidents and Individuals Who Change Residency)

EXAMPLE: *Computation:* Assume the same facts as in the prior two examples. Then, on January 1, 2012, the taxpayer became a nonresident of California again. During 2013, the taxpayer's passive income and losses include California source partnership income of $15,000, California source S corporation losses of $7,000, and New York source partnership income of $2,000. The taxpayer must restate suspended passive losses as if the taxpayer had been a nonresident of

California for all prior years by netting passive income and passive losses from California sources only, then must net passive income and losses to determine the amount of passive income to include in total taxable income and California taxable income as follows:

Step 1: Restate suspended passive losses as if the taxpayer had been a nonresident of California for all prior years by netting passive income and passive losses from California sources only.

2011 Restatement:	Total taxable income	CA taxable income
CA partnership income	$ 2,000	$ 2,000
CA S corporation loss	(8,000)	(8,000)
NY partnership income	3,000	
Suspended passive loss to 2012	$ (3,000)	$ (6,000)

2012 Restatement:	Total taxable income	CA taxable income
CA partnership income	$ 3,000	$ 3,000
CA S corporation loss	(1,000)	(1,000)
NY partnership income	7,000	
Total	$ 9,000	$ 2,000
Suspended loss from 2011	(3,000)	(6,000)
Income or suspended loss, 2012	$ 6,000	$ (4,000)

Step 2: Net passive income and losses to determine the amount of passive income to include in total taxable income and California taxable income.

Taxable year 2013:	Total taxable income	CA taxable income
CA partnership income	$ 15,000	$ 15,000
CA S corporation loss	(7,000)	(7,000)
NY partnership income	2,000	
Total	$ 10,000	$ 8,000
Suspended loss from 2012	0	(4,000)
Passive income, 2013	$ 10,000	$ 4,000

Part-year resident.—If a taxpayer changes residency during the year, the taxpayer must compute income and deductions using resident rules for the period of the year that the taxpayer was a California resident and using nonresident rules for the period of the year that the taxpayer was a nonresident. The taxpayer must compute any suspended passive losses as if the taxpayer was a California resident for all prior years *and* as if the taxpayer was a nonresident for all prior years. Then, the taxpayer must prorate both suspended passive loss amounts based upon the period of California residency and the period of nonresidency during the year. (FTB Pub. 1100, Taxation of Nonresidents and Individuals Who Change Residency)

• *Related discussions*

See also the following related discussions:

— Property-Related Income (¶ 16-550) for sourcing rules for gains on installment sales of property, deferred gains and losses on like-kind exchanges of property, and gains and losses on sales of property used in a trade or business (including involuntary conversions);

— Net Operating Losses (¶ 16-560) for sourcing rules for net operating losses; and

— Compensation for Personal Services (¶ 16-570) for sourcing rules for capital gains from the sale of stock in a qualifying disposition of statutory stock options.

[¶16-565] Sourcing of Pass-Through Entity Income and Deductions

Sourcing rules for pass-through entity income and deductions are discussed below.

Residents.—A resident must include his or her entire distributive share of partnership, limited liability company (LLC), or S corporation income and loss in his or her California income. (California Partnership Tax Booklet; Limited Liability Company Tax Booklet; S Corporation Tax Booklet)

Nonresidents.—A nonresident is taxed on his or her distributive share of partnership, LLC, or S corporation income and loss derived from California sources. In determining the source of pass-through entity's income, the following rules apply:

— if all of the entity's trade or business is conducted within California, then all of the entity's income is considered California source income;

— if the entity's trade or business is conducted within and outside California, but the part within California is so separate that the income can be separately accounted for, then the separately accounted for California income is treated as California source income; and

— if the entity conducts a single trade or business within and outside California, then California source business income of that trade or business is determined by apportionment (see ¶11-520).

Nonbusiness income attributable to real or tangible personal property located in California is sourced to California. Nonbusiness income attributable to intangible personal property is sourced to the owner's state of residence or commercial domicile. (California Partnership Tax Booklet; Limited Liability Company Tax Booklet; S Corporation Tax Booklet)

COMMENT: *Contributions by personal-service partnerships to retirement plans.*—The Franchise Tax Board (FTB) has ruled that when a personal-service partnership that derives income from both within and without California makes contributions to a qualified retirement plan on behalf of a nonresident partner, the nonresident partner's deduction for the contributions is calculated on the basis of the ratio of the partnership's earned income derived from California sources to the partnership's total earned income. In calculating this ratio, the apportionment principles of the Uniform Division of Income for Tax Purposes Act (UDITPA) are used. (*FTB Legal Ruling 431*, November 2, 1988) If the partnership elects to file a single group return, it may deduct contributions made on behalf of electing nonresident partners. (FTB Notice 89-659, October 23, 1989)

Part-year residents.—The FTB has issued a legal ruling providing guidance on the inclusion and sourcing of income and losses from partnerships (including LLCs classified as partnerships) and S corporations, when the partner or shareholder is a part-year resident during any part of its own or the partnership's or S corporation's taxable year. Partners and shareholders realize income and losses throughout the partnership or S corporation year as the income is realized by the partnership or S corporation. All items of income and loss realized by the partnership or S corporation during the partnership or S corporation year when the partner or shareholder was a resident are included in the partner's or shareholder's California taxable income. Also, all California-source items of income and loss realized by the partnership or S corporation during the partnership or S corporation year when the partner or shareholder was a nonresident are included in the partner's or shareholder's California taxable income. In the absence of information that reflects the actual date of realization of items of income and loss, the taxpayer must allocate an annual amount on a proportional basis between the periods of residency and nonresidency using a daily pro-rata methodology prescribed by the FTB. These provisions are consistent with federal law dealing with a dual-status taxpayer. (*Legal Ruling 2003-1*, FTB, April 7, 2003)

FTB Pub. 1100, Taxation of Nonresidents and Individuals Who Change Residency, contains several examples of the computation for part-year residents.

• *Basis in pass-through entities*

The FTB has provided the following guidance on how to compute basis in a pass-through entity.

Always a nonresident.—A nonresident partner's, member's, or shareholder's basis in a partnership, limited liability company (LLC) that elects to be treated as a partnership, or S corporation is equal to the partner's, member's, or shareholder's contributions to capital, adjusted by California sourced items only. (FTB Pub. 1100, Taxation of Nonresidents and Individuals Who Change Residency)

> **EXAMPLE:** *Computation.*—The taxpayer is a resident of Nevada. In 2012, the taxpayer invested $10,000 in a partnership and became a 50% partner. At the close of 2012, the partnership generated a $4,000 loss. 30% of the loss has a California source. The taxpayer's year-end basis in the partnership is computed as follows:

Taxable year 2012:		Basis
Contribution to capital		$10,000
Partnership loss	$ (4,000)	
California source loss percentage	× 30 %	
Partnership source loss	$ (1,200)	
Partner's percentage of loss	× 50 %	
Partner's loss		$ (600)
Partner's basis, December 31, 2012		$ 9,400

Move-in to California.—If a taxpayer becomes a resident of California, the taxpayer's basis in a pass-through entity needs to be restated under California law as if the taxpayer had been a California resident for all prior years. Basis is adjusted for the taxpayer's share of flow-through items, regardless of source, generated during the taxpayer's period of nonresidency. (FTB Pub. 1100, Taxation of Nonresidents and Individuals Who Change Residency)

Move-out of California.—If a taxpayer becomes a nonresident of California, the taxpayer's basis in a pass-through entity needs to be restated as if the taxpayer had been a nonresident of California for all prior years. (FTB Pub. 1100, Taxation of Nonresidents and Individuals Who Change Residency)

[¶16-570] Sourcing of Compensation for Personal Services

Nonresidents who are employed within and without California and who are paid on a daily, weekly, or monthly basis must allocate their compensation between California and out-of-state locations according to the number of working days spent within and without the state. Employees who are paid on some other basis must apportion their income in such a manner as to allocate to California that portion of the total compensation that is reasonably attributable to personal services performed in the state. (Reg. 17951-5, 18 CCR) However, gross income from California sources does not include qualified retirement income received by a nonresident (see ¶ 16-545).

> *EXAMPLE: Nonresident employed within and without California.*—The taxpayer is a nonresident of California and lives and works in Wyoming. The taxpayer's Wyoming employer temporarily assigns the taxpayer to California for four months to complete a project. The taxpayer continues to receive paychecks from the employer's Wyoming headquarters. The taxpayer earns $5,000 per month. Because the taxpayer performed four months of services in California, $20,000 ($5,000 x 4 months) of the taxpayer's compensation has a source in California and is taxable by California.

Also, if a taxpayer changes from resident to nonresident during the year, California taxes any compensation received for the performance of services on a source basis. However, if a taxpayer changes from nonresident to resident during the year, any compensation received by the taxpayer while a California resident that accrued before the taxpayer became a California resident is taxable by California. (FTB Pub. 1100, Taxation of Nonresidents and Individuals Who Change Residency)

> *EXAMPLE: Move-in to California.*—The taxpayer lived and worked in New York until April 30, 2012. The taxpayer permanently moved to California on May 1, 2012. The taxpayer's former New York employer pays its employees on the 5th of every month. On May 8, 2012, the taxpayer received in the mail a final paycheck of $3,000 from the taxpayer's former New York employer. The $3,000 of compensation is taxable by California because the taxpayer was a California resident when the taxpayer received the income. If the taxpayer also paid tax to New York on this compensation, the taxpayer is allowed a credit for New York taxes paid.

> *CCH COMMENT: Sourcing of wages for telecommuting employees.*—As more employers utilize employees who telecommute from their homes in another state, either on a full-time or part-time basis, issues relating to which state may tax what portion of these employees' wages become more prevalent. Absent a compact between states regarding the sourcing of wages of each other's residents, the states use one of two tests to source wages of telecommuting employees: the physical presence test or the convenience/necessity test.

> Under the physical presence test, employee income is allocated to the employee's location at the time the work was performed. For example, an employee who works from his home in State A two days a week, and from his employer's office in State B three days a week, would have 40% of his income sourced to State A and 60% of his income sourced to State B.

> Under the convenience/necessity test, all employee income is allocated to the employer's location unless the employee is able to prove that she performed her work away from the employer's location due to employer necessity, rather than employee convenience.

> Only four states (New York, New Jersey, Nebraska, and Pennsylvania) utilize the convenience/necessity test.

> *PRACTICE NOTE: Income sourcing during COVID-19.*—The Franchise Tax Board (FTB) has addressed income sourcing during the COVID-19 pandemic.

For nonresidents temporarily relocated to California, the FTB has addressed factual scenarios involving:

- an individual who works for an out-of-state employer and temporarily relocates to California;

- an individual who works for a California employer and temporarily relocates to California; and

- an independent contractor who temporarily relocates to California.

(COVID-19 Frequently Asked Questions for Tax Relief and Assistance, California Franchise Tax Board, October 2020)

• *Stock options*

Nonstatutory stock options.—California taxes the wage income received by a nonresident taxpayer from nonstatutory stock options on a source basis, whether the taxpayer was always a nonresident or was formerly a California resident. On the other hand, if a taxpayer is granted nonstatutory stock options while a nonresident and later exercises the options while a California resident, the resulting compensation is taxable by California because the wage income is recognized while the taxpayer is a California resident. The taxable wage income is the difference between the fair market value of the stock on the exercise date and the option price. (FTB Pub. 1004, Stock Option Guidelines; FTB Pub. 1100, Taxation of Nonresidents and Individuals Who Change Residency)

> **EXAMPLE:** *Nonresident.*—On February 1, 2007, while a California resident, the taxpayer was granted nonstatutory stock options. The taxpayer performed all of his services in California from February 1, 2007, to May 1, 2012, the date he left the company and permanently moved to Texas. On June 1, 2012, he exercised his nonstatutory stock options. The income resulting from the exercise of his nonstatutory stock options is taxable by California because the income is compensation for services having a source in California, the state where he performed all of his services.

> **EXAMPLE:** *Move-in to California.*—On March 1, 2006, while a Nevada resident, the taxpayer was granted nonstatutory stock options. On April 1, 2012, the taxpayer retired and permanently moved to California. On May 1, 2012, the taxpayer exercised her options. The compensation resulting from the exercise of her nonstatutory stock options is taxable by California because she was a California resident when the income was recognized.

Statutory stock options.—California taxes the capital gain income received by a former nonresident from the sale of stock in a qualifying disposition of statutory stock options because the stock is sold while the taxpayer is a resident. (FTB Pub. 1004, Stock Option Guidelines FTB Pub. 1100, Taxation of Nonresidents and Individuals Who Change Residency)

> **EXAMPLE:** *Move-in to California.*—On February 1, 2006, while a Texas resident, the taxpayer was granted incentive stock options. On February 1, 2012, the taxpayer exercised his options. On December 1, 2012, the taxpayer permanently moved to California, and on March 1, 2013, the taxpayer sold his stock for a gain. The resulting capital gain is taxable by California because the taxpayer was a California resident when he sold the stock.

In the reverse situation, if statutory stock options are granted to a taxpayer while he or she works in California, but are exercised and sold in a qualifying disposition after the taxpayer moves out of California, the capital gain on the sale of the stock would not be taxed by California. (Question 14, California Society of CPAs 2001 Liaison Meeting with FTB, November 14, 2001; FTB Pub. 1004, Stock Option Guidelines)

•*Interstate transportation workers*

The federal Amtrak Reauthorization and Improvement Act of 1990 (P.L. 101-322) prevents double taxation of compensation paid by interstate rail and motor carriers to their employees who regularly perform duties in more than one state. The federal law applies to employees of:

— rail, rail-water, express, pipeline, and motor carriers operating under the jurisdiction of the Interstate Commerce Commission; and

— private motor carriers.

Compensation paid by these carriers to any of their employees who regularly perform duties in more than one state is subject to the income tax laws of the state (or its subdivision) that is the employee's residence.

[¶16-600]

WITHHOLDING

[¶16-605] Withholding Introduction

California requires the withholding of personal income taxes from wages of resident employees for services performed either within or outside California and of nonresident employees for services performed in California (see ¶16-615), to the extent not otherwise exempt from withholding (see ¶16-660).

California also requires withholding on:

— payments to nonresidents for services performed within the state (see ¶16-635).

— deferred compensation payments to California residents (see ¶16-645);

— amounts paid to foreign partners;

— sales of California realty;

— dissolutions or transfers of businesses;

— rents and royalties paid to nonresidents (see ¶16-650); and

— other nonwage income paid to nonresidents (see ¶16-655).

The Employment Development Department (EDD) is authorized to require information necessary for the identification of individuals subject to wage withholding (Sec. 13015, Unempl. Ins. Code), and an employee is obligated to furnish his or her employer with his or her name and address for withholding purposes. (Sec. 13016, Unempl. Ins. Code)

Also, the Franchise Tax Board (FTB) may require a payor of income to furnish the name, address, and effective October 23, 2009, Social Security number, or other taxpayer identification of the recipient of such income for withholding purposes. (Sec. 18661, Rev. & Tax. Code)

The issuance by the FTB of orders to withhold to collect unpaid income taxes is discussed under Other Collection Methods (see ¶ 89-176) in the Practice and Procedure division.

• *Law changes*

The provisions of any law that change any withholding requirements will be applied to withholding in the calendar year succeeding the year the provision was chaptered or operative, whichever is later. (Sec. 18665, Rev. & Tax. Code)

• *Federal backup withholding*

For information concerning California incorporation of the federal backup withholding requirements under IRC Sec. 3406, see ¶ 16-655.

[¶ 16-615] Withholding on Wages

Employers are required to deduct and withhold personal income tax from wages paid to employees for each payroll period. (Sec. 13020, Unempl. Ins. Code) The same requirement for federal purposes is found in IRC Sec. 3402(a).

An employer is not required to withhold any tax from wages unless the wages fall within the definition of "wages" in Sec. 13009, Unempl. Ins. Code. (Sec. 13009.5, Unempl. Ins. Code)

The California withholding provision applies to wages of California employees for services performed either within or outside the state and to wages of nonresidents for services performed in the state. The tax is to be computed in such a manner as to produce an amount "substantially equivalent" to the amount of personal income tax estimated to be due under the Personal Income Tax Law when the employee's wages are included in gross income. (Sec. 13006, Unempl. Ins. Code; Sec. 13020, Unempl. Ins. Code) In fact, the California methods of calculating withholding do not require the employer to take into account any income other than the wages paid to the employee (see ¶ 16-620).

An employer who pays a nonresident for services performed both within and outside the state must withhold tax only from the portion attributable to services within the state. (Reg. 18805-2, 18 CCR) This portion is determined in accordance with allocation rules found in Reg. 17951-5 (see ¶ 16-570).

CAUTION: An employer or withholding agent is liable for personal income tax required to be deducted and withheld, or withheld and not timely remitted. (Sec. 13070, Unempl. Ins. Code; Sec. 18668, Rev. & Tax. Code) The employer or withholding agent is generally liable whether or not the tax was collected and withheld. (Reg. 4370-1, 22 CCR; Sec. 18668, Rev. & Tax. Code) If the tax for which an employer is liable is paid or if the employee reports the wages to the Franchise Tax Board, the employer is relieved of liability for the tax itself but not for penalties or additions to the tax arising out of the failure to withhold. (Sec. 13071, Unempl. Ins. Code)

• *"Employer" defined*

An employer is "any person for whom an individual performs or performed any service" as the employee of such a person. (Reg. 4305-1, 22 CCR) It is not necessary that the services be continuing at the time the wages are paid for the status of employer to exist. An employer is any individual, corporation, association, partnership, or limited liability company doing business in the state, deriving income from state sources, or an entity that is in any way subject to state law. This includes the Regents of the University of California, the state, and its agencies and political subdivisions. (Sec. 13005, Unempl. Ins. Code) If the person for whom the individual performs services does not have control of the payment of wages, the "employer" is the person who does control payment, whether or not the controlling person is subject to state law. (Sec. 13010, Unempl. Ins. Code) The same is true under IRC Sec. 3401(d).

A withholding agent is any person required to deduct and withhold tax under the state wage withholding system. (Sec. 13010, Unempl. Ins. Code)

• *"Employee" defined*

"Employee" is defined as a resident individual who receives remuneration for services performed within or without the state or a nonresident individual who receives remuneration for services performed within the state. (Sec. 13004, Unempl. Ins. Code) The state definition includes officers and employees of the United States, a state, a territory, or any of their political subdivisions, as does IRC Sec. 3401(c), except that the federal definition does not mention officers and employees of a territory. Corporate officers are also employees. Under California law, whether an individual provides equipment is not a consideration in determining whether he or she is an employee.

The term "employee" includes any individual who is an employee (under Labor Code Sec. 2750.5) of a person who holds, or is required by law to obtain, a valid state contractor's license. (Sec. 13004.5, Unempl. Ins. Code) A licensed real estate broker performing services in the capacity of a broker and individuals performing in-home demonstration services of consumer products, including services or other intangibles, are excluded from the definition of an "employee" for withholding purposes. (Sec. 13004.1, Unempl. Ins. Code) Also, effective January 1, 2015, the term "employee" specifically excludes any member of a limited liability company that is treated as a partnership for federal income tax purposes. (Sec. 13004.6, Unempl. Ins. Code)

PRACTICE NOTE: Impact of A.B. 5.—A.B. 5, Laws 2019, which went into effect on January 1, 2020, may impact whether workers are treated as employees or as independent contractors under California law. There are different tax reporting and filing requirements for workers classified as employees or independent contractors. The Franchise Tax Board (FTB) has answered some frequently asked questions (FAQs) about A.B. 5 to help workers achieve tax compliance. A.B. 5 addresses employment status when a hiring entity claims that a person was hired as an independent contractor. It codifies a portion of the California Supreme Court's decision in *Dynamex Operations West, Inc. v. Superior Court*, 4 Cal.5th 903 (2018). It requires application of a 3-part test, commonly known as the "ABC test" to determine if workers in California are employees or independent contractors for purposes of the Labor Code, the Unemployment Insurance Code, and Industrial Welfare Commission (IWC) wage orders. The FTB's FAQs address the tax reporting and filing requirements when a worker is classified as:

- an employee for both federal and California purposes;

- an independent contractor for both federal and California purposes; and

- an independent contractor for federal purposes and employee for California purposes.

(*Worker Classification and AB 5 Frequently Asked Questions*, California Franchise Tax Board, January 29, 2020)

Subsequent legislation made clear that these provisions will determine whether an individual is an employee or an independent contractor for state income tax purposes. (Rev. & Tax. Code Sec. 17020.12; Rev. & Tax. Code Sec. 23045.6)

In *The People v. Uber Technologies, Inc., et al.*, a California court of appeal affirmed a trial court's injunctive order restraining rideshare companies Uber and Lyft from classifying their drivers as independent contractors rather than employees. The California Attorney General and several city attorneys sued the companies on behalf of the People, alleging that the companies improperly classified their drivers in violation A.B. 5. The court of appeal concluded, based on prong B of the ABC test, that there was more than a reasonable probability that the People would prevail on the merits at trial. Also, the trial court properly weighed the substantial harm to the public in the absence of an injunction against the potential harm to the rideshare companies from the issuance of the injunction. (*The People v. Uber Technologies, Inc., et al.*, Court of Appeal of California, First District, Nos. A160701, A160706, October 22, 2020) However, California voters at the November 3, 2020, general election approved a measure (Proposition 22) which overrides the provisions of A.B. 5 with respect to app-based rideshare and delivery drivers. Under the measure, app-based rideshare and delivery drivers are independent contractors, rather than employees or agents, of the company that hires them, as long as the company does not:

- unilaterally set their hours;

- require acceptance of specific ride and delivery requests; or

- restrict them from working for other companies.

Proposition 22 added new provisions to the Business and Professions Code, but also made the provisions applicable to the Personal Income Tax Law. Rev. & Tax. Code Sec. 17037

Special rules for certain industries.—Special rules are applicable to determine whether an individual is an employee or an independent contractor in specific industries. Under common law rules, to determine whether an employer-employee relationship exists, the most important factor is the right of the principal to control the manner and means of accomplishing a desired result. If the principal has the right to control the manner and means of accomplishing a desired result, regardless of whether that right is exercised, an employer-employee relationship exists. Strong evidence of that right to control is the principal's right to discharge at will, without cause. (Reg. 4304-1, 22 CCR)

Although determinations of whether an individual is an employee or an independent contractor in each specific industry will generally be determined by the provisions of Reg. 4304-1, information on the application of those provisions to the following industries is contained in additional rules:

— real estate industry (Reg. 4304-2, 22 CCR);

— home health care industry (Reg. 4304-3, 22 CCR);

— computer services industry (Reg. 4304-4, 22 CCR);

— artists (Reg. 4304-5, 22 CCR);

— newspaper distribution industry (Reg. 4304-6, 22 CCR);

— product demonstrators (Reg. 4304-7, 22 CCR);

— security dealers (Reg. 4304-8, 22 CCR);

— language interpreters (Reg. 4304-9, 22 CCR);

— amateur athletic officials (Reg. 4304-10, 22 CCR);

— process servers (Reg. 4304-11, 22 CCR); and

— barbering and cosmetology industries (Reg. 4304-12, 22 CCR).

• *Wages subject to withholding*

Wages subject to withholding are defined as "all remuneration (other than fees paid to a public official) for services performed by an employee for his employer," including the cash value of remuneration paid in any medium other than cash. It includes tips received by an employee and compensation paid to a limited liability company member filing a federal corporate income tax return. (Sec. 13009, Unempl. Ins. Code) The name by which the remuneration is designated, the basis on which it is paid, and the medium in which it is paid is immaterial as long as it is paid as compensation for services performed by the employee for his or her employer. (Reg. 4309-1, 22 CCR) Payments of pensions, annuities, and other deferred income are also "wages" subject to withholding (see ¶16-645). The following types of payments are covered by regulation:

— travel and other expenses;

— vacation allowances;

— dismissal payments;

— employer deductions;

— payments of employee's tax by employer and employee;

— remuneration for services as employee of nonresident alien individual or foreign entity;

— amounts paid under wage continuation plans;

— cost of meals and lodging;

— facilities or privileges;

— annual benefits paid under the Teachers' Replacement Benefits Program (Sec. 24260, Education Code); and

— tips or gratuities.

(Reg. 4309-1, 22 CCR)

Exclusions.—"Wages" subject to withholding does not include remuneration paid:

— for agricultural labor;

— for domestic service;

— for services not in the course of the employer's trade or business, unless the amount earned in a calendar quarter is $50 or more and the individual is regularly employed by the employer during that calendar quarter to perform such services;

— for services performed for foreign governments or international organizations;

— for services performed by nonresident aliens;

— for services performed by a minister;

— for delivery of newspapers and magazines by persons under 18;

— for services not in the course of the employer's trade or business, to the extent paid in any medium other than cash;

— to, or on behalf of an employee, or his or her beneficiary, from or to an exempt trust under Rev. & Tax. Code Sec. 17631 (unless the payment is made to the employee as remuneration for services rendered as an employee and not as a trust beneficiary);

— to, or on behalf of an employee, or his or her beneficiary, under or to an annuity plan that, at the time of payment, is a qualified plan;

— to, or on behalf of an employee, or his or her beneficiary, under or to a bond purchase plan that, at the time of payment, is a qualified bond purchase plan;

— to, or on behalf of an employee, or his or her beneficiary, for a payment that is expected to qualify for a individual retirement account deduction;

— to, or on behalf of an employee, or his or her beneficiary, under a cafeteria plan;

— to crew members on vessels engaged in foreign, coastwise, intercoastal, interstate, or noncontiguous trade;

— for services performed by Peace Corps volunteers or volunteer leaders;

— in the form of group term life insurance;

— to the extent that the payment is expected to be deducted as moving expenses;

— as cash tips amounting to less than $20 per month or as noncash tips (see below);

— for services performed by an individual on a boat engaged in catching fish or other forms of aquatic animal life under a specific type of arrangement with the owner or operator of the boat;

— for medical care reimbursement made to, or for the benefit of, an employee under a self-insured medical reimbursement plan described in IRC Sec. 105(h)(6);

— to, or on behalf of an employee, to the extent not includable in gross income; and

— for private postsecondary school intermittent and adjunct instructor services under Unempl. Ins. Code Sec. 633.

(Sec. 13009, Unempl. Ins. Code; Reg. 4309-2, 22 CCR) IRC Sec. 3401 is similar. IRC Sec. 3401 also excludes remuneration for specified categories of foreign service. IRC Sec. 3402(q) requires withholding from certain types of gambling winnings. There is no comparable state provision.

Corporations are not required to withhold income taxes from wages, salaries, fees, or other compensation paid to nonresident corporate directors for director services performed in California for that corporation. (Sec. 13020, Unempl. Ins. Code)

Withholding requirements do not apply to payments of interest. (Sec. 13014, Unempl. Ins. Code)

¶16-615

> **PRACTICAL ANALYSIS:** *Employer's Guide.*—Publication DE 44, California Employer's Guide, identifies specific types of payments, such as educational assistance, fringe benefits, gifts, etc., and indicates whether those payments are subject to personal income tax withholding.

Domestic service employee wages.—Although state law requires an employer of household workers to report payments of cash wages of $750 or more in a calendar quarter, they are not required to withhold personal income taxes from those wages. (Publication DE 231L - Rev. 17 (12-04), Household Employment) However, an employer and an employee may enter into a voluntary agreement to have personal income tax withheld from the employee's wages (see discussion below relating to Voluntary Withholding Agreements).

Wages and other payments received from same employer during payroll period.—The law governing situations in which an employee receives from the same employer both wages and other payments during a payroll period of 31 days or less is as follows:

— if the remuneration for one-half or more of the period constitutes wages, then all payments by the employer during that period are treated as wages; or

— if the payments for more than one-half the period are not wages, none of the remuneration paid during the period is considered wages.

(Sec. 13031, Unempl. Ins. Code) IRC Sec. 3402(e) is identical. These rules do not apply, however, if there is no period that constitutes a payroll period within the meaning of Sec. 13008, Unempl. Ins. Code, or Reg. 4308-1, or if the payroll period exceeds 31 consecutive days. In such cases, withholding is required from that portion of the remuneration that constitutes wages. (Reg. 4331-1, 22 CCR)

• *Payroll period*

A "payroll period" is the period of service for which wages are ordinarily paid to an employee, whether it be daily, weekly, biweekly, semimonthly, monthly, quarterly, semiannually or annually. (Sec. 13008, Unempl. Ins. Code) Any payroll period other than these is considered a "miscellaneous payroll period." (Sec. 13007, Unempl. Ins. Code) The same is true under IRC Sec. 3401(b). An employee can have only one payroll period with respect to wages paid by any one employer. (Reg. 4308-1, 22 CCR)

A California provision, for which there is no federal counterpart, provides rules for determining the number of days in a miscellaneous payroll period or in a period that does not constitute a payroll period. In the former, the payroll period includes the number of days, including Sundays and holidays, equal to the number of days for which wages are paid. In the latter, the period includes the number of days, including Sundays and holidays, that have elapsed since the date of the last payment of wages during the calendar year. (Sec. 13030, Unempl. Ins. Code)

In computing the amount of withholding from wages when the payroll period is less than one week, an employer may use the excess of the total wages paid during the calendar week over the withholding exemption allowed by Sec. 13020 for a weekly payroll period. (Sec. 13030, Unempl. Ins. Code; Reg. 4330-1, 22 CCR)

Taxes are to be deducted from wages paid for a payroll period of more than one year. (Sec. 13043, Unempl. Ins. Code) IRC Sec. 3402(g)(3) is comparable to the California provision.

• *Tips*

Cash tips of more than $20 per month received by an employee in the course of employment are to be included in wages. Tips amounting to less than $20 per month and noncash tips are excluded. (Sec. 13009, Unempl. Ins. Code) IRC Sec. 3401(a)(16) and IRC Sec. 3401(f) contain the same requirements.

An employee who receives cash tips amounting to more than $20 a month must report such tips to the employer monthly in writing. (Sec. 13055, Unempl. Ins. Code) Reporting requirements and procedures, which are the same as the federal (IRC Sec. 6053(a)), are discussed in a regulation. (Reg. 4355-1, 22 CCR) Federal Form 4070, Report of Tips to Employers, is used to report tips to an employer.

Tips are deemed to be paid to an employee at the time they are reported in a written statement to the employer. If they are not reported, they are deemed to have been paid when they were actually received by the employee. (Reg. 4309-3, 22 CCR)

Tips reported to employers under these provisions are not subject to the federal reporting requirements of IRC Sec. 6041 or the state reporting requirements of Sec. 18631(c)(4), Rev. & Tax. Code (see ¶ 89-104 in the "Practice and Procedure" division) when employers file information returns reporting wages on which tax was not deducted and withheld.

Withholding obligation.—Employers are required to deduct and withhold tax only on tips that are reported by the employee and only to the extent that the employer can collect the tax by deducting it from the employee's wages (exclusive of tips). (Sec. 13027, Unempl. Ins. Code) Under both California law and a comparable federal provision (IRC Sec. 3402(k)), an employer may withhold tax on tips reported under Sec. 13055, even if at the time the reports are received, the tips total less than $20. An employee may furnish to the employer funds to cover deductions and withholding of tax on tips if the amount of tax on reported tips exceeds wages exclusive of tips. Priorities governing tax deduction from employees' wages are established by regulation. (Reg. 4327-1, 22 CCR)

• *Supplemental wage payments*

Special rules determine the amount of tax to be withheld from supplemental wages, including the following types of payments, whether they are paid according to the employee's regular pay period, a different pay period, or without regard to a pay period:

— overtime pay,

— bonuses,

— commissions,

— sales awards,

— back pay (including retroactive wage increases), and

— reimbursements for nondeductible moving expenses,

(Sec. 13043, Unempl. Ins. Code; Sec. 18663, Rev. & Tax. Code)

When supplemental wages are paid after the payment of regular wages, the employer may determine the withholding tax by using a percentage rate of 6.6% (6.0% for supplemental wages paid before November 1, 2009), without allowance for exemptions or credits and without reference to the regular wages, or by adding the supplemental wages to the regular wages and computing tax on the whole amount. The computed tax, minus the tax withheld from regular wages, is the amount withheld from the supplemental wages. A withholding rate of 10.23% (9.3% effective for options and bonus payments paid prior to November 1, 2009) is applied to stock options and bonus payments that constitute wages paid, in lieu of using the withholding tables or the withholding rate specified for other supplemental wages. (Sec. 18663, Rev. & Tax. Code; Sec. 13043, Unempl. Ins. Code)

When supplemental wages are paid at the same time as regular wages, tax is computed on the total of both types of wages as if they constituted a single wage payment for the regular payroll period. (Sec. 13043, Unempl. Ins. Code)

IRC Sec. 3402(g) is identical to the California law except for internal references.

• *Supplemental unemployment compensation benefits and sick pay*

A supplemental unemployment compensation benefit paid to an individual is treated as if it were a payment of wages made by an employer to an employee for the payroll period and, therefore, is subject to withholding. For withholding purposes, "supplemental unemployment compensation benefits" refers to amounts paid to an employee, pursuant to a plan to which the employee's employer is a party, because of the employee's involuntary separation from employment resulting directly from a reduction in force, the discontinuance of a plant or operation, or other similar conditions, but only to the extent that the payments are includable in the employee's gross income for personal income tax purposes. (Sec. 13028.5, Unempl. Ins. Code)

Any payment of sick pay that does not constitute "wages" generally will not be subject to withholding. However, such payments will be subject to withholding if at the time the payments are made there is a request in effect from the payee that the sick pay be subject to withholding. For withholding purposes, "sick pay" means any amount that is paid to an employee pursuant to a plan to which the employer is a party and that constitutes remuneration, or a payment in lieu of remuneration, for any period during which the employee is temporarily absent from work on account of sickness or personal injury. An employee's request that sick pay be subject to tax withholding must be in writing, be made to the person making the payments, contain the employee's social security number, and specify the amount the employee wishes withheld. A request is not required if sick pay is being paid pursuant to a collective bargaining agreement that specifies that tax will be withheld from the payments and that contains a provision for determining the amount to be withheld. (Sec. 13028.6, Unempl. Ins. Code)

The federal provisions concerning withholding on supplemental unemployment compensation benefits and sick pay are in IRC Sec. 3402(o).

• *Noncash remuneration paid to retail commission salespersons*

An employer who makes an occasional noncash award to a retail commission salesperson may elect not to withhold tax on the fair market value of the award, provided the noncash award is paid specifically for services performed by the employee as a retail commission salesperson and the employee is ordinarily paid only in cash commissions. (Sec. 13025, Unempl. Ins. Code; IRC Sec. 3402(j) permits the same election. Whether or not the employer withholds tax on the value of the noncash award, the employer must include the value of the remuneration in the employee's total wages on Form W-2.)

Noncash remuneration includes payment in any medium other than cash, such as goods or commodities, stocks, bonds, or other forms of property. Noncash remuneration may not be disregarded for withholding purposes where the employee is paid both a salary and cash commissions on sales. (Reg. 4325-1, 22 CCR)

The term "retail commission salesperson" includes an employee who solicits orders at retail. The term does not include an employee who solicits orders from wholesalers, retailers, or others, for merchandise for resale. An individual may be employed as a retail commission salesperson by one employer at the same time the individual is employed to solicit orders from wholesalers for a different employer. (Reg. 4325-1, 22 CCR)

• *Income taxes of other states*

An employer required to withhold income taxes for other states or the District of Columbia must subtract from the applicable California tax the amount required to be deducted and withheld by the other state. (Reg. 4320-1, 22 CCR) Thus, where the other state's withholding amount is greater than the California amount, there is no California income tax withholding.

• *Additional withholding from wages*

In addition to the tax required to be deducted and withheld in accordance with Sec. 13020, an employer and employee may agree that an additional amount be withheld from the employee's wages. (Sec. 13025, Unempl. Ins. Code) IRC Sec. 3402(i) authorizes the same type of agreement for federal withholding purposes. The agreement must be in writing in a form prescribed by the employer and may be made effective for any definite or indefinite period of time. Either the employer or the employee may terminate the agreement by furnishing a written notice to the other. (Reg. 4325-1, 22 CCR)

The amount deducted and withheld under the agreement is considered a tax, and all provisions of law and regulations applicable to taxes withheld apply to the withholding of the additional tax. (Reg. 4325-1, 22 CCR)

• *Voluntary withholding agreements*

An employee and employer may make an agreement to provide for the withholding of tax on remuneration that does not constitute wages, such as payments for agricultural labor or domestic service. (Sec. 13029, Unempl. Ins. Code) The same type of agreement may be made under IRC Sec. 3402(p) for federal tax purposes.

A California regulation allows such an agreement for state purposes only if a similar agreement is made for the withholding of federal income tax and only with respect to amounts that are includable in the employee's gross income. The agreement must apply to all similar remuneration paid by the employer, and the amount to be withheld is determined in the same way as other withholding. Payments that are not subject to withholding, such as payments from or to certain tax-exempt trusts, moving expenses, and noncash tips, may not be covered by voluntary withholding agreements. (Reg. 4329-1, 22 CCR)

Information that must be included in an employee's request for withholding is specified by regulation. (Reg. 4329-1, 22 CCR) The agreement is not effective until the employer begins to withhold as requested.

• *Wages paid by agent on behalf of two or more employers*

Taxes must be deducted from wages paid through an agent, fiduciary, or other person who also controls or pays wages payable by another employer. (Sec. 13043, Unempl. Ins. Code) IRC Sec. 3402(g)(4) is identical to the California law, except for internal references

¶16-615

• *Deferred compensation payments*

Certain payments of pensions, annuities, and other deferred income are also considered wages subject to withholding (see ¶ 16-645).

• *Forms*

Form DE 9, *Quarterly Contribution Return and Report of Wages*, is used to report quarterly personal income tax withholding, unemployment insurance, employment training tax, and state disability insurance contributions. Form DE 9C, *Quarterly Contribution Return and Report of Wages (Continuation)*, is used to report detailed wage items for each worker. Form DE 88ALL, *Payroll Tax Deposit*, is used to make deposits of personal income tax withholding. Beginning January 1, 2017, a requirement is phased in to file all withholding returns and reports electronically (see ¶ 89-106). (Sec. 13021, Unempl. Ins. Code; Sec. 13050, Unempl. Ins. Code)

[¶ 16-620] Withholding Tables and Schedules

California provides two methods for determining the amount of wages and salaries to be withheld for state personal income tax:

- Method A - Wage Bracket Table Method (limited to employees with wages and salaries less than $1 million)

- Method B - Exact Calculation Method

Method A provides a quick and easy way to select the appropriate withholding amount, based on the payroll period, filing status, and number of withholding allowances (regular and additional) if claimed. The standard deduction and exemption allowance credit are already included in the wage bracket tables. Even though this method involves fewer computations than Method B, it cannot be used with a computer in determining amounts to be withheld.

Method B may be used to calculate withholding amounts either manually or by computer. This method will give an exact amount of tax to withhold. To use this method, an employer must enter the payroll period, filing status, number of withholding allowances, standard deduction, and exemption allowance credit amounts. These amounts are included in Tables 1 through 5 of the exact calculation section.

[¶ 16-635] Withholding from Nonresident Personal Service Income

The California Franchise Tax Board (FTB) requires the withholding of tax from payments made to nonresidents performing personal services in California. (Sec. 18662, Rev. & Tax. Code; FTB Pub. 1017, Resident and Nonresident Withholding Guidelines) Taxes must be withheld from payments for personal services if the total payments made to a nonresident during the calendar year exceed $1,500 or the payor is directed to withhold by the FTB. (Reg. 18662-4, 18 CCR) The following types of payments are specifically subject to withholding:

— payments for personal services performed in California;

— payments to nonresident entertainers for services rendered in California;

— payments for a covenant not to compete in California;

— payments releasing a contractual obligation to perform services in California;

— income from options received as a result of performing personal services in California;

— bonuses for services performed in California.

(FTB Pub. 1017, Resident and Nonresident Withholding Guidelines)

PRACTICAL ANALYSIS: Source of income from personal services.—Where the nonresident lives, the location where the contract for services is entered into, and the place of payment do not determine the source of income for personal services. Instead, the source of income from personal services is the location where the services are performed.

Compensation for personal services includes fees for professional services and payments to entertainers and to independent contractors. (Reg. 18662-5, 18 CCR)

Withholding of tax is not required from wages, fees, salaries, or other compensation paid by a corporation to nonresident corporate directors for director services performed in California for that corporation, including attendance at a board of directors' meeting. However, corporations are required to supply informational returns to the FTB and statements to any nonresident directors whenever such compensation is paid. (Sec. 18662, Rev. & Tax. Code)

CCH PRACTICE TIP: Withholding tool.—FTB 1018, Small Business Withholding Tool, helps to determine when withholding on payments of California source income is required. The tool helps identify the steps and required forms at three different stages (before making a payment, at the time of making a payment, and after making a payment). (*Tax News*, California Franchise Tax Board, February 2012)

• *Entertainers*

The types of payments made to nonresident entertainers for services rendered in California that are subject to withholding include, but are not limited to:

— guaranteed payments;

— overages;

— royalties; and

— residual payments.

Withholding is required even if the payment is not made directly to the nonresident entertainer, but is made directly to a California agent or promoter. (FTB Pub. 1017, Resident and Nonresident Withholding Guidelines)

• *Rate of withholding*

The amount of tax to be withheld from such income is computed by applying a rate of 7%, or a lesser rate as authorized by the FTB. (Reg. 18662-4, 18 CCR)

• *Certificates of residence, nonresidence*

If a payee claims an exemption from withholding based on his or her California residency, then he or she must fill out a Certificate of Residence found on Form 590, Withholding Exemption Certificate, and file the original and a copy of the form with the payor. The payor transmits the original certificate to the FTB before making any payments to the payee. If the payee's resident status continues, the retained certificate relieves the payor from the duty of withholding for the calendar year or until otherwise directed by the FTB. (Reg. 18662-4, 18 CCR)

• *Withholding on wages*

See Withholding on Wages (see ¶16-615) for a discussion of withholding from wages of employees.

• *Form*

For domestic nonresident withholding, the payor must file Form 592, Resident and Nonresident Withholding Statement.

[¶16-645] Withholding from Pensions, Annuities, and Other Deferred Compensation

Payments of pensions, annuities, and other deferred income (as described in IRC Sec. 3405) to California residents are considered wages and are subject to income tax withholding under California law. Amounts withheld from pensions, annuities, and other deferred income will be treated as if the amounts are withheld by an employer, and only amounts withheld must be reported in quarterly reports filed by the employer. (Sec. 13028, Unempl. Ins. Code; Reg. 4328-1, 22 CCR)

If a payee makes an election under IRC Sec. 3405 not to have federal income tax withheld from such payments, that election will also apply for California purposes, unless the payee elects, with the consent of the payer, to have the payments subject to California income tax withholding. (Sec. 13028, Unempl. Ins. Code; Reg. 4328-1, 22 CCR) Conversely, if a payee has not made a federal election to exclude his or her payments of pensions, annuities, or deferred compensation from federal income tax withholding requirements, the payee nevertheless may file a California election to exclude those payments from the California withholding requirements. (Sec. 13028, Unempl. Ins. Code)

Under the California provision, a payer of a pension, annuity, or other deferred compensation is not required to withhold tax if the amount to be withheld would total less than $10 per month. (Sec. 13028, Unempl. Ins. Code)

• *Amount of withholding*

For California personal income tax purposes, the payer may elect to withhold tax from a designated distribution, whether periodic or nonperiodic in nature, in one of the following amounts:

— that which would be withheld if the distribution constituted "wages;"

— a dollar amount requested by the payee; or

— 10% of the amount withheld for federal tax purposes under IRC Sec. 3405.

(Sec. 13028, Unempl. Ins. Code) (As discussed above, the taxpayer may also elect not to have tax withheld from a distribution.)

• *Nonresidents*

The California withholding provision does not apply to pensions, annuities, and other deferred income payable to payees with addresses outside the state, as shown on the most current records of the payer. (Sec. 13028, Unempl. Ins. Code) However, if the Director of the Employment Development Department determines that nonpayment of California income tax by a nonresident may occur, the Director must notify the payer of any pensions, annuities, or other deferred income payments due the nonresident that withholding is required from those payments. Upon receiving notice from the Director, the payer must withhold from those payments the same amount that would be withheld if the payments were wages. The Director must also notify the nonresident payee that withholding has been ordered and the reason for the Director's determination that nonpayment of tax might otherwise occur. (Sec. 13028.1, Unempl. Ins. Code)

• *Forms*

Form DE 9, *Quarterly Contribution Return and Report of Wages*, is used to report quarterly personal income tax withholding, unemployment insurance, employment training tax, and state disability insurance contributions. Form DE 9C, *Quarterly Contribution Return and Report of Wages (Continuation)*, is used to report detailed wage items for each worker. Form DE 88ALL, *Payroll Tax Deposit*, is used to make deposits of personal income tax withholding. Beginning January 1, 2017, a requirement is phased in to file all withholding returns and reports electronically (see ¶ 89-106). (Sec. 13021, Unempl. Ins. Code; Sec. 13050, Unempl. Ins. Code)

[¶ 16-650] Withholding from Rents and Royalties Paid to Nonresidents

The California Franchise Tax Board (FTB) requires the withholding of tax from payments of rents and royalties for the use of property (real or personal) located in California. (Sec. 18662, Rev. & Tax. Code; FTB Pub. 1017, Resident and Nonresident Withholding Guidelines) Taxes must be withheld if the total payments made to a nonresident during the calendar year exceed $1,500 or the payor is directed to withhold by the FTB. (Reg. 18662-4, 18 CCR)

• *Rate of withholding*

The amount of tax to be withheld from such income is computed by applying a rate of 7%, or a lesser rate as authorized by the FTB. (Reg. 18662-4, 18 CCR)

• *Certificates of residence, nonresidence*

If a payee claims an exemption from withholding based on his or her California residency, then he or she must fill out a Certificate of Residence found on Form 590, Withholding Exemption Certificate, and file the original and a copy of the form with the payor. The payor transmits the original certificate to the FTB before making any payments to the payee. If the payee's resident status continues, the retained certificate relieves the payor from the duty of withholding for the calendar year or until otherwise directed by the FTB. (Reg. 18662-4, 18 CCR)

• *Form*

Form 592, Resident and Nonresident Withholding Statement, is used to report the income and withholding amount for each nonresident payee.

[¶ 16-655] Withholding at Source from Nonwage Income

California requires payors to withhold 7% from specified reportable payments, California's provision is similar to the federal backup withholding provisions under IRC Sec. 3406. However, California's requirements apply to rents, prizes and winnings, compensation for services, including bonuses, and other fixed or determinable annual or periodic gains, profits, and income, but do not apply to payments of interest and dividends or any release of loan funds made by a financial institution in the normal course of business. (Sec. 18664, Rev. & Tax. Code) In instances where both backup withholding and other types of withholding apply, backup withholding replaces all other types of withholding. (FTB Pub. 1017, Resident and Nonresident Withholding Guidelines)

Backup withholding is remitted using Form 592, Resident and Nonresident Withholding Statement.

In addition, the California Franchise Tax Board (FTB) may, by regulation, require withholding at the source from certain items of fixed or determinable income in order to ensure the collection of tax. (Sec. 18662, Rev. & Tax. Code) However, the FTB has required withholding at the source only from income derived by nonresidents and corporations not having a permanent place of business in California. (Reg. 18662-1, 18 CCR; Reg. 26131-1, 18 CCR)

The items of income subject to withholding at the source are interest, dividends, rent, prizes and winnings, premiums, annuities, emoluments, compensation for personal services, and other fixed or determinable annual or periodical gains, profits, and income. A withholding agent who fails to withhold, underwithholds, or fails to remit withholding from payments or distributions of California source income to a nonresident payee when required is liable for the greater of (a) the amount actually withheld; or (b) the amount of taxes due from the nonresident, but not more than the amount required to be withheld. The FTB may also assess a civil penalty for each information return not filed (see ¶89-206). (Sec. 18662, Rev. & Tax. Code; Reg. 18662-2, 18 CCR; Reg. 26131-2, 18 CCR; *Tax News*, California Franchise Tax Board, May 2010) Withholding from nonresident compensation for personal services is discussed separately under Withholding from Nonresident Personal Service Income (see ¶16-635).

Withholding is not required unless the income payments to a payee by the same payor exceed $1,500 during the calendar year or the payor is directed to withhold by the FTB. (Reg. 18662-4, 18 CCR; Reg. 26131-2, 18 CCR) The amount of tax to be withheld is computed by applying a rate of 7%, or any lesser rate authorized in writing by the FTB. (Reg. 18662-4, 18 CCR; Reg. 26131-2, 18 CCR)

PRACTICE TIP: Withholding tool.—FTB 1018, Small Business Withholding Tool, helps to determine when withholding on payments of California source income is required. The tool helps identify the steps and required forms at three different stages (before making a payment, at the time of making a payment, and after making a payment). (*Tax News*, California Franchise Tax Board, February 2012)

Regulations specify the time and place for filing returns of tax withheld and for remitting withheld amounts. (Reg. 18662-8, 18 CCR; Reg. 26131-5, 18 CCR)

• *Form*

For domestic nonresident withholding, the payor must file Form 592, Nonresident Withholding Annual Return.

[¶16-660] Withholding Exemptions

The number of withholding exemptions allowed in computing the amount of an employee's personal income tax withholding is determined by the exemption certificate filed by the employee. (Sec. 13040, Unempl. Ins. Code; Sec. 13041, Unempl. Ins. Code) The federal Form W-4 or California Form DE 4, Employee's Withholding Allowance Certificate, or substantially similar forms devised by the employer, may be used. (Reg. 4340-1, 22 CCR)

PRACTICAL ANALYSIS: Completion of both state and federal forms.—An employee should complete both state and federal forms if the employee claims a different marital status, number of regular allowances, or additional dollar amount to be withheld for state purposes than for federal purposes, or if the employee claims additional allowances for estimated deductions. (Instructions, Form DE 4 Rev. 33 (1-07), Employee's Withholding Allowance Certificate)

The number of withholding exemptions is considered to be zero if no withholding certificate has been filed. (Sec. 13041, Unempl. Ins. Code) The same provision is contained in IRC Sec. 3401(e).

The Franchise Tax Board may require an employer to submit copies of income tax withholding exemption certificates. (Sec. 18667, Rev. & Tax. Code)

The personal and dependent exemptions available under state law are generally the same as those available under IRC Sec. 3402(f), except that the federal exemptions result in tax deductions, while the state exemptions result in tax credits. California provides additional exemptions to the blind and to taxpayers 65 years or older, which are no longer provided under federal law. Also, the state certificate recognizes the "head of household" status; under the federal system, a head of household is considered single for withholding purposes.

If an individual's marital status cannot be determined from the certificate, the employee must be treated as a single person. (Sec. 13040, Unempl. Ins. Code) The same provision is contained in IRC Secs. 3401(l).

Federal regulations governing withholding exemption certificates apply for California withholding purposes. (Reg. 4340-1, 22 CCR)

If an employee has filed both a federal Form W-4 and a California Form DE 4 and the federal form is not reportable to the IRS but the state form is reportable under the applicable federal regulation, the employer must file the Form DE 4 with the Employment Development Department as part of the employer's next Quarterly Wage and Withholding Report (Form DE 6). (Reg. 4340-1, 22 CCR) Additional information is provided in Publication DE 44, California Employer's Guide.

• *Additional allowances*

Both the California and federal withholding systems allow an individual to claim additional withholding allowances if itemized deductions (see ¶ 15-545) and tax credits are expected to result in overwithholding. (Reg. 4340-1, 22 CCR) The state allows one additional allowance for each $1,000 by which the employee expects itemized deductions to exceed the standard deduction. For federal purposes, one additional allowance is permitted for each $2,500 of excess itemized deductions.

PLANNING NOTE: Worksheet.—Form DE 4, Employee's Withholding Allowance Certificate, provides a worksheet for determining whether an employee's expected estimated deductions may entitle the employee to claim one or more additional withholding allowances for state purposes.

• *Effective date of exemption certificate*

A new withholding exemption certificate, filed to replace an existing certificate, is effective for the first payment of wages on or after the first "status determination date" occurring at least 30 days from the date the certificate is furnished. (Sec. 13042, Unempl. Ins. Code) However, the employer may elect to make the certificate effective for any payment of wages on or after the date the certificate is furnished. The status determination dates are January 1, May 1, July 1, and October 1, of each year. A similar provision is contained in IRC Sec. 3402(f)(3)(B).

Exemption certificates expire on February 15 of the next year. (Form DE 4, Employee's Withholding Allowance Certificate)

• *Requirements for complete exemption*

An employer need not withhold any tax on the wages of an employee who files a federal withholding allowance certificate stating that the employee was not liable for federal income tax for the preceding taxable year and anticipates no liability for the current year. (Sec. 13026, Unempl. Ins. Code; Reg. 4340-1, 22 CCR) The provision is the same as IRC Sec. 3402(n) except for title and internal references.

[¶16-800]

CREDITS

[¶16-805] Credits Against Tax

In addition to the personal and dependency exemption credits, the following credits may be claimed against California taxable income for purposes of determining a taxpayers' personal income tax liability:

• *Credits for other taxes paid*

Taxes Paid Another State

Excess State Disability Insurance Payments Credit

• *Investment credits*

Community Development Investment Credit

• *Enterprise zone credits*

Employee's credit for qualified wages

Employer's credit for qualified wages

Credit for sales and use tax paid on certain machinery

• *Targeted tax area credits*

Employer's credit for qualified wages

Credit for sales and use tax paid on certain machinery

• *Local Agency Military Base Recovery Area (LAMBRA) credits*

Employer's credit for qualified wages

Credit for sales and use tax paid on certain machinery

• *Manufacturing enhancement area credits (pre-2014 tax years)*

Employer's credit for qualified wages

- *Research credits*
    - Research Expenditures Credit
- *Job creation/hiring credits*
    - Prison Inmate Labor Credit
    - New Jobs Credit (pre-2014 tax years)
    - New Employment Credit (post-2013 tax years)
    - Small Business Hiring Credit
- *Environmental credits*
    - Ultra-Low Sulfur Diesel Fuel Credit
- *Economic development credits*
    - Economic Development Areas
    - Motion Picture Production Credit
    - New Motion Picture Production (Post-2015 Tax Years)
    - California Competes Credit
    - New Motion Picture Production (Post-2019 Tax Years)
- *Land conservation/preservation credits*
    - Natural Heritage Credit
- *Housing credits*
    - Low-Income Housing Credit
    - Renter's Credit
    - 2010 New Home and First-Time Home Buyers Credits
- *Family credits*
    - Senior Head of Household Credit
    - Adoption Costs Credit
    - Household and Dependent Care Credit
    - Joint Custody Head of Household Credit
    - Credit for Maintaining a Dependent Parent in the Household
    - Young Child Credit
- *Other credits*
    - Donated Agricultural Products Transportation Credit
    - Enhanced Oil Recovery Credit
    - Disabled Access Credit
    - Donated Agricultural Products Credit
    - College Access Tax Credit

• *Withheld tax*

The amount of any tax withheld during the year is allowed as a credit against the tax for the taxable year with respect to which the amount was withheld. (Sec. 19002, Rev. & Tax. Code)

In the case of a nonresident alien electing to file in a nonresident group return , the amount withheld during any calendar year will be allowed to the recipient of the income as a credit against the tax for the taxable year with respect to which the amount was withheld. (Sec. 19002, Rev. & Tax. Code)

• *Estimated tax*

Tax liability is reduced by amounts previously paid as estimated taxes at the time the return is filed. (Sec. 19002, Rev. & Tax. Code)

• *Forms*

Tax credits may be claimed on Form 540, California Resident Income Tax Return, or Form 540NR, California Nonresident or Part-Year Resident Income Tax Return.

• *Credit carryforwards*

When the amount of a credit exceeds a taxpayer's tax liability for a taxable year, the excess may sometimes be carried over beyond the expiration date to succeeding taxable years. In some instances, the remaining carryover from a repealed or inoperative credit may be carried over and applied to tax until the credit is exhausted, unless the law specifically provides otherwise. (Sec. 17039(d), Rev. & Tax. Code) Excess credit amounts may not be carried back and applied to previous taxable years. (Instructions, Form FTB 3540, Credit Carryover Summary)

• *Credit limitations*

Personal income tax credits may not be applied against the additional tax on millionaires (see ¶ 15-355). (Sec. 17043, Rev. & Tax. Code)

CCH PRACTICE TIP: 2020, 2021, and 2022 limitation on credit amounts.— For the 2020, 2021, and 2022 tax years, the amount of business credits and business credit carryovers that may reduce a taxpayer's tax (as defined by Sec. 17039, Rev. & Tax. Code) is limited to $5 million per year. Any unused credit may be carried over and the carryover period is extended by the number of taxable years the credit, or any portion thereof, was not allowed as a result of the limitation. Sec. 17039.3, Rev. & Tax. Code

Nonbusiness credits must be applied before any business credits. (Sec. 17039.3, Rev. & Tax. Code)

The low-income housing credit is considered a nonbusiness credit. (Sec. 17039.3, Rev. & Tax. Code)

CCH PRACTICE TIP: 2008 and 2009 limitation on credit amounts.—The amount of business credits and business credit carryovers that could be claimed by taxpayers was limited to 50% of a taxpayer's tax (as defined by Sec. 17039, Rev. & Tax. Code) during the 2008 and 2009 tax years. Any unused credit could be carried over. The carryover period was extended by the number of taxable years the credit, or any portion thereof, was not allowed as a result of the 50% limitation. A taxpayer with net business income of less than $500,000 for the taxable year was exempt from the 50% limitation. (Sec. 17039.2, Rev. & Tax. Code)

For purposes of determining the amount of business credits that could be claimed, nonbusiness credits had to be applied before any business credits. (Sec. 17039.2, Rev. & Tax. Code)

The full-time employment hiring credit and the credits for new home purchases and first-time home-buyers were considered nonbusiness credits. (Sec. 17039.2(b)(4), Rev. & Tax. Code; Sec. 17059.1, Rev. & Tax. Code)

Also, special limitations apply to credits arising from passive activities (see ¶ 15-745).

Furthermore, except as noted below, credits may not be used to reduce the sum of a taxpayer's regular tax plus the tax imposed on lump-sum distributions from employee's trusts below the taxpayer's tentative minimum tax. (Sec. 17041, Rev. & Tax. Code; Sec. 17048, Rev. & Tax. Code; Sec. 17504, Rev. & Tax. Code) The following credits are excepted from the tentative minimum tax restriction:

— solar energy credit and carryovers from the former solar energy credit;

— the research expenditures credit;

— credits for sales and use taxes related to the purchase of qualified property used in an enterprise zone, a targeted tax area, or the former Los Angeles Revitalization Zone;

— carryovers from the former program area sales and use tax and hiring credits;

— the renter's credit;

— enterprise zone, targeted tax area, and former Los Angeles Revitalization Zone hiring credits;

— the former manufacturers' investment credit;

— carryovers from the former credit for clinical testing expenses;

— the low-income housing credit;

— the excess state disability insurance contributions credit;

— credits for taxes paid to other states;

— the withholding credit (discussed above);

— personal exemption credits;

— the natural heritage credit;

— the former credentialed teacher retention credit;

— the adoption costs credit;

— the senior head of household credit;

— the joint custody head of household and dependent parent credits;

— for taxable years beginning on or after January 1, 2014, the California Competes credit;

— for taxable years beginning on or after January 1, 2014, the college access tax credit allowed under Rev. & Tax. Code Sec. 17053.86; and

— for taxable years beginning on or after January 1, 2017, the college access tax credit allowed under Rev. & Tax. Code Sec. 17053.87.

(Sec. 17039(c), Rev. & Tax. Code; Sec. 17039.1, Rev. & Tax. Code)

• *Repealed and expired credits*

Unless otherwise provided, taxpayers may continue to carry over the balance of any credit effective immediately before the credit was repealed or became inoperative. (Sec. 17039, Rev. & Tax. Code)

• *Credit sharing*

The law provides general rules governing the sharing of tax credits. Unless a credit provision specifies some other sharing arrangement, two or more taxpayers (other than spouses) may share a tax credit in proportion to their respective shares of creditable costs. With regard to spouses filing separately, either may claim the whole of the credit or they may divide it equally between them. Partners may divide a credit in accordance with a written partnership agreement. (Sec. 17039(e), Rev. & Tax. Code)

With respect to partnerships, credits are generally computed at the partnership level; any limitation on expenses qualifying for the credit or limitation on the credit amount is applied to the partnership and to each partner. The credit amount claimed may also be limited for taxpayers that own a direct or indirect interest in a business entity that is disregarded and treated as a sole proprietorship (see the discussion of Limited Liability Companies at ¶ 10-240). Credit amounts attributable to the disregarded business entity, including credit carryovers, that may be applied against net tax are limited to the excess of regular tax, determined by including income attributable to the disregarded business entity, less regular tax, determined by excluding the income attributable to the disregarded business entity. As discussed above, any credit amount that may not be claimed against net tax during the current taxable year may be carried forward to subsequent taxable years. (Sec. 17039, Rev. & Tax. Code)

Allocation of credits for S corporation shareholders is discussed in the "Corporation Franchise (Income)" division (see ¶ 10-215).

• *Nonresidents and part-year residents*

Certain credits for nonresidents and part-year residents, including the personal exemption credit and the credit for child and dependent care, are prorated on the basis of California source taxable income to total taxable income. Credits based on transactions occurring wholly within California—e.g., installation of a solar energy device in California—are granted in full. Additional details are provided in the discussions of Nonresidents (see ¶ 15-115) and Part-Year Residents (see ¶ 15-120).

PROPERTY

[¶20-100]

TAXABILITY OF PROPERTY AND PERSONS

[¶20-105] Classification of Property

Property is classified for assessment purposes as real property (Sec. 104, Rev. & Tax. Code; Sec. 105, Rev. & Tax. Code; Reg. 121, 18 CCR; Reg. 122, 18 CCR; Reg. 122.5, 18 CCR) or tangible personal property. (Sec. 106, Rev. & Tax. Code; Reg. 123, 18 CCR) The tax treatment of real property and tangible personal property is discussed at ¶20-310 and ¶20-295, respectively. Real property is further classified as land, improvements, or fixtures. (Sec. 104, Rev. & Tax. Code; Sec. 105, Rev. & Tax. Code) Intangible personal property is exempt from tax. (see ¶20-230) Real property is defined at ¶20-310, and tangible personal property is defined below. Assessments made on a property may be classified as either a secured assessment or an unsecured assessment.

• *Land and improvements distinguished*

When land is reshaped or expanded, the affected portion is land. However, when a substantial amount of other materials, such as concrete, is added to an excavation, both the excavation and the added materials are improvements. Materials added solely for drainage purposes qualify as land. With respect to property owned by a county, municipal corporation, or public district, fill added to taxable land constitutes an improvement. (Reg. 121, 18 CCR)

A State Board of Equalization (SBE) regulation lists examples of property classified as land and property classified as improvements. (Reg. 124, 18 CCR)

• *Fixtures*

The manner of annexation, the adaptability of the item to the purpose for which the realty is used, and the intent with which the annexation is made are important elements in deciding whether an item has become a fixture or remains personal property. Classification of an item as a fixture or as personal property is determined by applying SBE regulations. (Reg. 122.5, 18 CCR) "Fixture" is defined at ¶20-310.

• *Tangible personal property distinguished from real property*

Property that may be seen, weighed, measured, felt, or touched, or that is in any other manner perceptible to the senses, except land and improvements, is tangible personal property. (Reg. 123, 18 CCR) See ¶20-295 for further discussion of tangible personal property.

The California Constitution authorizes the legislature to classify personal property for differential taxation or for exemption. (Sec. 2, Art. XIII, Cal. Const.)

• *Secured and unsecured assessments*

A "secured" assessment for taxes on real property creates a lien against real estate (land and improvements) where the real estate is of sufficient value to guarantee satisfaction for unpaid taxes. An "unsecured" assessment of property is made in cases where the assessor believes that the value of real property owned by the assessee on which the subject property is located is insufficient to ensure payment of the tax, or where the assessee owns no rights to land. (AH 201, Assessment Roll Procedures, (06-85))

[¶20-115] Agriculture

Implements of husbandry, which include tools, machines, equipment, appliances, devices, or apparatus used in agricultural operations, are assessed uniformly throughout the state at full cash value. "Implements of husbandry" includes implements listed in the California Vehicle Code but does not include implements intended for sale in the ordinary course of business. A county assessor may require the owner of implements of husbandry to file a statement of the make, model, and year of manufacture of the implements. (Sec. 411, Rev. & Tax. Code; Sec. 412, Rev. & Tax. Code; Sec. 413, Rev. & Tax. Code; Sec. 410, Rev. & Tax. Code; Sec. 414, Rev. & Tax. Code)

The Board of Equalization *Assessors' Handbook* includes two manuals pertaining to agricultural property. (AH 521, Assessment of Agricultural and Open-Space Properties, (10-03) and AH 534, Rural Building Costs, (Revised Annually—2018 version linked))

• *Urban agriculture incentive zones*

Until January 1, 2029 (2019, prior to January 1, 2018), California cities, counties or cities and counties can establish by ordinance urban agriculture incentive zones that, among other things, will be subject to favorable property tax assessment provisions. (Sec. 51040, Govt. Code) An "urban agriculture incentive zone" is an area within a county or city and county that is comprised of individual properties designated as urban agriculture preserves for farming purposes. (Sec. 51040.3(b), Govt. Code)

Following adoption of an ordinance, the county or city and county may enter into contracts with landowners to enforeably restrict the use of the land subject to the contract to uses consistent with urban agriculture. (Sec. 51042(a)(1)(A), Govt. Code) Any contract entered into must contain at least the following provisions:

— an initial term of at least five years;

— a restriction on property (property, or combination of contiguous properties, after 2017) of at least 0.10 acres and not more than three acres;

— a requirement that the entire property subject to the contract shall be dedicated toward commercial or noncommercial agriculture use;

— a prohibition again any dwellings on the property while under contract; and

— a notification that a landowner that cancels a contract is subject to a cancellation fee.

(Sec. 51042(b), Govt. Code)

No new contracts can be entered into and no existing contract can be renewed after January 1, 2029. However, any contract entered into before that date will be valid and enforceable for the duration of the contract. (Sec. 51042(e), Govt. Code)

Assessment.—For assessment purposes, the term "open-space land" includes land subject to contract for an urban agricultural incentive zone. Open-space land subject to contract for an urban agricultural incentive zone shall be valued for assessment at the rate based on the average per-acre value of irrigated cropland in the state, with certain adjustments. (Sec. 422.7, Rev. & Tax. Code)

Irrigated cropland per-acre value for 2020.—The average per-acre value for irrigated cropland in California to be used for the 2020 lien date is $15,100. (*Letter to County Assessors, No. 2019/028*, California State Board of Equalization, September 12, 2019)

¶20-115

•*Growing crops*

Growing crops are exempt from property taxation. (Sec. 3(h), Art. XIII, Cal. Const.; Sec. 202(a)(1), Rev. & Tax. Code)

•*Fruit and nut trees, grape vines, and date palms*

Fruit- and nut-bearing trees that are not planted on land subject to enforceable restrictions are exempt from property taxes for the first four years after the season in which they were planted in an orchard. Grapevines are similarly exempt for a period of three years after the season in which they were planted in a vineyard. Fruit-and nut-bearing trees and grape vines older than four and three years, respectively, are taxed as improvements to the land. (Sec. 3(i), Art. XIII, Cal. Const.; Sec. 211(a), Rev. & Tax. Code; Sec. 105(b), Rev. & Tax. Code; Reg. 131, 18 CCR)

Any fruit- and nut-bearing tree or grapevine severely damaged during specified natural disasters so as to require pruning to the trunk or bud union to establish a new shoot as a replacement for the damaged tree or grapevine is considered a new planting for purposes of the exemption. Qualifying "natural disaster" includes:

    (1) a December 1990 freeze;

    (2) a December 1998 freeze;

    (3) a January 2007 freeze;

    (4) strong, damaging winds commencing on October 20, 2007; and

    (5) wildfires commencing on October 21, 2007.

(Sec. 211(a), Rev. & Tax. Code)

Fruit and nut trees and grapevines held by a grower for planting on the lien date and planted at some time during the assessment year are exempt from property taxation. Fruit and nut trees and grapevines growing in plant nurseries are not exempt. (Sec. 223, Rev. & Tax. Code)

Fruit and nut trees and vines when first assessed are valued at full cash value on the lien date for that year. However, county boards of supervisors may adopt local ordinances that specify that the initial base year value of grapevines planted to replace grapevines that were less than 15 years old and that were removed solely because of phylloxera or Pierce's Disease infestation, is the base year value of the removed vines factored to the lien date of the first taxable year of the replacement vines. The assignment of base year replacement value is limited to that portion of the replacement grapevines that are substantially equivalent to the grapevines that were replaced, if the replacement grapevines are planted at a greater density. (Sec. 53, Rev. & Tax. Code)

If exempt fruit and nut trees and grapevines are planted on land otherwise subject to an enforceable restriction, they are valued as if they are not exempt from taxation by reason of age. The income derived from such plantings is to be used in valuing the land, and no other value can then be ascribed to the trees or vines. (Sec. 429, Rev. & Tax. Code)

The regulations applicable to fruit and nut trees apply to date palms as well. Date palms are valued with the land from the lien date that they become taxable until they reach the age of eight years, after which they are valued separately as improvements. (Sec. 105(b), Rev. & Tax. Code; Reg. 131, 18 CCR)

Stakes, trellises, fences, and other structural orchard and vineyard improvements are taxable both during and after the exemption period for trees and vines. (Reg. 131, 18 CCR)

• *Seed potatoes*

Seed potatoes held by a grower for planting on the lien date and planted in the field at some time during the assessment year are exempt from property taxation. This exemption does not apply to plant nurseries. (Sec. 234, Rev. & Tax. Code)

• *Agricultural enterprises—Business inventories*

Crops (as distinguished from growing crops), animals, and feed held primarily for sale or lease in the ordinary course of business are considered part of exempt business inventory. Animals used in the production of food and fiber and the feed for such animals are also treated as exempt business inventory. (Sec. 129, Rev. & Tax. Code; Reg. 133, 18 CCR)

"Crops" means products grown, harvested, and held primarily for sale, including seeds held for sale or seeds to be used in the production of a crop that is to be held primarily for sale. The term "crops" does not include exempt growing crops, fruit and nut trees, and grapevines. (Reg. 133, 18 CCR)

"Animals used in the production of food and fiber" includes animals customarily employed in the raising of crops; for the feeding, breeding, and management of livestock; and for dairying. The term also includes all other confined animals whose products are normally used as food for human consumption or for the production of fiber useful to man, but excludes animals held principally for sport, recreation, or pleasure, such as show animals, racehorses, and pets. (Reg. 133, 18 CCR)

"Feed for animals" includes every type of natural-grown or commercial product fed to animals, except medicinal commodities intended to prevent or cure disease unless purchased as a component part of feed. (Reg. 133, 18 CCR)

• *Open space land*

Certain "open space" land that includes land dedicated to agricultural use is partially exempt from taxation. Included in the lands entitled to be classified as enforceably restricted "open space" land is land used for the production of food or fiber and land subject to an agricultural conservation easement. (Sec. 422.5, Rev. & Tax. Code; Sec. 8, Art. XIII, Cal. Const.)

• *Homesteads*

See ¶ 20-205 for a discussion of the exemption for homesteads on agricultural land.

[¶20-135] Computer Hardware and Software

The taxability of computer system components depends on whether the components are hardware, software, or storage media.

COMMENT: If funding is available, the California State Board of Equalization (SBE) must conduct a study to obtain and analyze data to update information used to develop property tax valuation factors annually published by the SBE that are applied to nonproduction computers, semiconductor manufacturing equipment, and biopharmaceutical equipment and fixtures. The agency must conduct the study in consultation with the California Assessors' Association and representatives of the "high technology focused" computer, semiconductor, and biopharmaceutical industries. (Sec. 401.20, Rev. & Tax. Code)

The SBE can conduct the study only if funds are appropriated by the Legislature to the Board for that purpose during the 2005-06 Regular Session. Values determined by using valuation factors resulting from the study shall be rebuttably presumed to be the full cash value of the equipment. The presumption will not apply to a tax year if the information upon which the factors are based was last reviewed more than six years before the lien date for that tax year.

●*Hardware*

Computer hardware and equipment (processors, disk drives, printers, etc.) are taxable as tangible personal property unless they qualify for a specific exemption from personal property tax. (see ¶20-295) Alternatively, computer hardware and equipment qualify as "fixtures" to real property and are therefore taxable as real property. (Reg. 122.5(e)(7), 18 CCR) However, banks enjoy a constitutional exemption on computer equipment that would otherwise be subject to personal property tax. (Sec. 27, Art XIII, Cal. Const.)

Computer hardware components are fixtures if extensive improvements, such as a specific physical space, air conditioning, emergency power supply, or fire suppression systems, are constructed specifically to accommodate the components, provided that such improvements are otherwise not useful or are otherwise only marginally useful. A computer is constructively annexed to a fixture if it is dedicated to controlling or monitoring the fixture. A computer is personal property if it can be moved without material damage or expense, and if it is not essential to the intended use of the real estate. (Reg. 122.5(e)(7), 18 CCR)

Bank-owned computers.—Computers owned by banks qualify for the constitutional exemption from property tax as bank personal property. (Sec. 27, Art XIII, Cal. Const.; Sec. 23182, Rev. & Tax. Code) The California Constitution provides that the income tax on state and national banks applies in lieu of other taxes, except for taxes upon their real property and vehicle registration and license fees.

Single-price sale or lease.—Valuation of computer equipment sold or leased at a single price without segregating taxable and nontaxable programs may account for the total amount as the property's value. A claim that a single-price sale or lease includes charges for nontaxable programs must be supported by facts, identifying the nontaxable property and supply sales prices, costs, or other information to enable the assessor to reach an informed decision about the proper value of such equipment. (Reg. 152, 18 CCR)

San Diego Supercomputer Center.—Computer equipment of the San Diego Supercomputer Center located on the campus of the University of California, San Diego, is exempt from property taxes. (Sec. 226, Rev. & Tax. Code; Sec. 2, Ch. 1559, Laws 1988) Such computer equipment includes any supercomputer and all peripheral computers and other equipment related to the system.

●*Software*

Computer software or programs usually comprise written instructions, magnetic imprints, required documentation, or other processes designed to enable the user to communicate with or operate a computer. (Sec. 995, Rev. & Tax. Code) They are exempt from property taxes.

CCH COMMENT: SBE staff is directed to deduct the value of embedded software, including processing programs, service programs, data management systems, and application programs, in the valuation of centrally assessed, computerized telephone switching equipment. (*Reporter's Transcript*, California State Board of Equalization Motion on Valuation of Microprocessor-Controlled Telephone Switch Software, February 23, 2000) The premise underlying this directive is based on legislative and regulatory intent. The Legislature did not consider commercial use of microprocessor-controlled telephone switches containing embedded systems because the use of such systems was not widespread in the 1970s when the controlling statute (Sec. 995, Rev. & Tax. Code) was enacted. Nor did the SBE consider the issue when the related regulation (Reg. 152, 18 CCR) was adopted and subsequently amended. No courts have ruled on this issue. (*Internal Memorandum*, California State Board of Equalization Legal Division, January 13, 2000)

The control program elements of an operating system, including supervisors, monitors, executives, and control or master programs, constitute a "basic operational program" that is fundamental and necessary to the operation of a computer. (Sec. 995.2, Rev. & Tax. Code) A "basic operational program" is a "control program" that is included in the computer equipment's sale or lease price. (Reg. 152, 18 CCR) Such programs regulate a computer's input/output operations, allocate memory locations, and generally regulate the computer's processing activities. However, such programs are not equivalent to "applications" programs that process particular sets of data to yield specified results.

A program is included in the sale or lease price of equipment if the equipment and the program are sold or leased at a single price. Alternatively, the sale or lease price of computer equipment includes a control program, even if the purchase or lease documents set forth separate prices for the equipment and the program, provided that the equipment may not be purchased without the program. The relevant regulation describes examples of taxable basic operational programs. (Reg. 152, 18 CCR)

• *Storage media*

Computer storage media are the physical components on which data are stored, and usually are in the form of tapes, discs, drums, CD-ROMs, or punched cards. Valuation of storage media for tax purposes is determined as if there were no computer program stored thereon, except for basic operational programs. (Sec. 995, Rev. & Tax. Code; Reg. 152, 18 CCR)

Tax on storage media may be assessed only against the taxpayer who actually owns, claims, possesses, or controls such media on the lien date. Program licensers who do not own, claim, possess, or control the storage media on which the program is stored may not be assessed. (Reg. 152, 18 CCR)

The constitutional personal property tax exemption for banks applies to storage media, as well as computer hardware. (Sec. 27, Art XIII, Cal. Const.)

[¶20-145] Construction Work in Progress

Property under construction that is not completed on the lien date is subject to taxation as real property. (Sec. 71, Rev. & Tax. Code) When incomplete construction is valued for tax purposes, the value of the construction on the lien date is added to the 1975 value of the real property without the construction. (Reg. 463, 18 CCR) When the construction is completed, the newly constructed property is reappraised in total under the provisions of Art. XIII A, California Constitution (Proposition 13). (Sec. 71, Rev. & Tax. Code; Sec. 2, Art. XIIIA, Cal. Const.)

AH 410, Assessment of Newly Constructed Property, (05-14) discusses the statutes, regulations, and the various statutory exclusions that pertain to, in addition to newly constructed property, construction work in progress.

• *School district levies*

A school district is authorized to levy a fee, charge, dedication, or other requirement against any construction within its boundaries for the purpose of funding the construction or reconstruction of school facilities. The authority extends to:

— new commercial and industrial construction;

— new residential construction; and

— other residential construction if the resulting increase in assessable space exceeds 500 square feet.

Construction, installation, or modification of a dwelling to provide accessibility for a severely and permanently disabled resident of the dwelling is exempt from such charges. (Sec. 17620, Ed. Code)

[¶20-165] Energy Systems or Facilities

Through 2023-2024 fiscal year property tax lien dates, active solar energy system construction or additions do not constitute "new construction" requiring valuation reassessment for property tax purposes. For purposes of supplemental assessment, Sec. 73, Rev. & Tax. Code applies only to qualifying construction or additions completed on or after January 1, 1999. (Sec. 73, Rev. & Tax. Code)

The term "newly constructed," as used in Section 2(a) of Article XIIIA of the California Constitution, does not include the construction or addition of any active solar energy system for California property tax purposes. Moreover, wind machines and turbines are excluded from new construction under Sec. 73, Rev. & Tax. Code only if installed between January 1, 1981 and July 19, 1981. Wind machines and turbines installed before or after these dates are subject to property tax. (Sec. 2(a), Art. XIIIA, Cal. Const.; *Letter to County Assessors, No. 2004/051*, BOE, September 20, 2004)

An "active solar energy system" is defined as a system that uses solar devices that, upon completion of the construction of a system as part of a new property or the addition of a system to an existing property, are thermally isolated from living space or any other area where the energy is used, to provide for the collection, storage, or distribution of solar energy. The term does not include solar swimming pool heaters or hot tub heaters. (Sec. 73(b), Rev. & Tax. Code)

Active solar energy systems may be used for domestic, recreational, therapeutic, or service water heating, space conditioning, the production of electricity, the processing of heat, or solar mechanical energy. (Sec. 73(b)(3), Rev. & Tax. Code)

An active solar energy system that uses solar energy in the production of electricity includes storage devices, power conditioning equipment, transfer equipment, and related parts. The use of solar energy in the production of electricity involves the transformation of sunlight into electricity through the use of devices such as solar cells or other collectors. However, an active solar energy system used in the production of electricity includes only equipment used up to, but not including, the stage of the transmission or use of the electricity. (Sec. 73(d)(1)(B), Rev. & Tax. Code)

The term "parts" includes spare parts that are owned by the owner of, or the maintenance contractor for, an active solar energy system for which the parts were specifically purchased, designed, or fabricated by or for that owner or maintenance contractor for installation in that system. (Sec. 73(d)(1)(B), Rev. & Tax. Code; *Letter to County Assessors, No. 2004/051*, California State Board of Equalization, September 20, 2004)

A reassessment exemption applies to 75% of the value of pipes and ducts that carry solar or non-solar energy, and to 75% of dual-use equipment, such as ducts and hot water tanks used in auxiliary and solar energy equipment. (Sec. 73(d)(2) and (3), Rev. & Tax. Code)

Any solar energy system that has qualified for this exclusion will continue to receive the benefit until that property changes ownership. (Sec. 73(f), Rev. & Tax. Code)

This exclusion is repealed effective January 1, 2025. (Sec. 73(i)(1), Rev. & Tax. Code) However, systems that qualify for the newly constructed exclusion prior to that date shall continue to be excluded until there is a subsequent change in ownership. (Sec. 73(i)(2), Rev. & Tax. Code)

• *Sale-leaseback arrangements*

The California legislature expressed its intent to extend the exclusion from property tax reassessment requirements for purchases of new active solar energy systems to systems that are sold in qualifying sale-leaseback arrangements. As long as the system is newly constructed or added and another taxpayer has not received an exclusion for the same system, the exclusion would apply to systems sold or transferred in sale-leaseback arrangements, partnership flip structures, or other transactions to purchasers that may also be eligible for federal tax benefits. (Sec. 1(b) of Ch. 3 (A.B. 15), Laws 2011 (First Extraordinary Session), effective June 28, 2011)

Further, newly constructed systems that are constructed freestanding or parking lot canopies or that are constructed as installations on existing buildings qualify for the exclusion, including such systems sold in sale-leaseback transactions. (Sec. 1(c) of Ch. 3 (A.B. 15), Laws 2011 (First Extraordinary Session), effective June 28, 2011)

• *Initial building purchase*

The exclusion for active solar energy systems also applies that portion of the value of an initial purchase of a California building attributable to an active solar energy system incorporated by the owner-builder in the initial construction, provided the owner-builder did not intend to occupy or use the building or receive the exclusion and the purchase occurred prior to the building becoming subject to reassessment to the owner-builder. If the purchaser files an appropriate claim with the county property tax assessor, the value of the system minus the amount of any qualifying rebates will be deducted from the new base year value of the building established as a result of the change in ownership. Extension of the exclusion to the purchaser will remain in effect until there is a subsequent change in ownership of the building. (Sec. 73(e), Rev. & Tax. Code)

[¶20-170] Enterprise Zones and Other Redevelopment Areas

California does not provide special property tax treatment for property located in an enterprise zone. However, local governments and districts are authorized to grant rebates for economic revitalization manufacturing property and for property owned by large manufacturers in areas that have established a capital investment incentive program. These rebates are discussed in detail at ¶20-265 Manufacturing and Industrial Property.

[¶20-195] Health Care Facilities and Equipment

Human whole blood, plasma, blood products, and blood derivatives, or any human body part held in a bank for medical purposes, are exempt from taxation.

(Sec. 33, Rev. & Tax. Code) Personal property used to collect, store, and process human blood is not exempt. (*Alpha Therapeutic Corp. v. County of Los Angeles*, 179 CalApp3d 265 (1986))

The tax treatment of nonprofit hospitals and charitable health facilities is discussed at ¶ 20-285.

[¶ 20-205] Homestead

An owner-occupied single-family dwelling and the land required for the convenient occupation and use of the dwelling may not be valued at an amount greater than would reflect the use of the land as a site for a single-family dwelling, if the dwelling is on land that is zoned exclusively for single-family home use or on land zoned for agricultural use on which single-family homes are permitted. (Sec. 9, Art. XIII, Cal. Const; Sec. 401.4, Rev. & Tax. Code)

Also, special provisions prevent the levy or state lien upon the principal residence of an innocent investor. (see below)

The California State Board of Equalization (BOE) *Assessors Handbook* includes a manual on residential building costs. (AH 531, Residential Building Costs, (Revised Annually—2018 version linked))

• *Homeowners' exemption*

The first $7,000 of the full value of a homeowner's dwelling is exempt from property taxes. (Sec. 3, Art. XIII, Cal. Const.; Sec. 218, Rev. & Tax. Code; Reg. 149, 18 CCR) The Constitution authorizes an increase in the exemption or a denial of the exemption if the owner received state or local aid to pay taxes on the dwelling. (Sec. 3, Art. XIII, Cal. Const.)

Extent of exemption.—The exemption is available for single-family dwellings, multiple-family dwellings if the owner occupies one unit, condominiums, and cooperative housing shares. Two-dwelling units are to be considered as two single-family dwellings. The taxpayer must reside in the dwelling, and it must be his or her principal residence. Persons purchasing homes under a contract of sale are eligible. The exemption is first applied to the building, structure, or other shelter; the excess, if any, is applied to land on which the building, structure, or shelter is located. (Sec. 218, Rev. & Tax. Code)

The homeowners' exemption does not extend to property that is rented, vacant, under construction on the lien date, or a vacation or secondary home, and does not apply to property on which the owner receives the veteran's exemption.

Disaster relief.—There are cases in which a dwelling will not be disqualified as a "dwelling" or be denied an exemption solely on the basis that the dwelling was temporarily damaged or destroyed or was being reconstructed by the owner following a specified disaster. Currently, this exception applies to any dwelling that qualified for the homeowners' exemption prior to:

— October 15, 2003, that was damaged or destroyed by fire or earthquake during October, November, or December 2003 and has not changed ownership since October 15, 2003;

— June 3, 2004, that was damaged or destroyed by flood during June 2004, and that has not changed ownership since June 3, 2004;

— August 11, 2004, that was damaged or destroyed by the wildfires that occurred in Shasta County during August 2004, and that has not changed ownership since August 11, 2004;

— December 28, 2004, that was damaged or destroyed by severe rainstorms, floods, mudslides, or the accumulation of debris in a disaster during December

2004, January 2005, February 2005, March 2005, or June 2005, and that has not changed ownership since December 28, 2004 (including a dwelling that was temporarily uninhabited as a result of restricted access to the property due to floods, mudslides, the accumulation of debris, or washed out or damaged roads);

— December 19, 2005, that was damaged or destroyed by severe rainstorms, floods, mudslides, or the accumulation of debris in a disaster during January 2006, April 2006, May 2006, or June 2006, and that has not changed ownership since December 19, 2005 (including a dwelling that was temporarily uninhabited as a result of restricted access to the property due to floods, mudslides, the accumulation of debris, or washed-out or damaged roads);

— July 9, 2006, that was damaged or destroyed by the wildfires that occurred in the County of San Bernardino in July 2006, and that has not changed ownership since July 9, 2006 (including a dwelling that was temporarily uninhabited as a result of restricted access to the property due to the wildfires);

— the commencement dates of the wildfires of 2006 that was damaged or destroyed by the wildfires that occurred in the counties of Riverside and Ventura, and that has not changed ownership since the commencement dates;

— January 11, 2007, that was damaged or destroyed by severe freezing conditions, commencing on January 11, 2007, that occurred in the counties of El Dorado, Fresno, Imperial, Kern, Kings, Madera, Merced, Monterey, Riverside, San Bernardino, San Diego, San Luis Obispo, Santa Barbara, Santa Clara, Stanislaus, Tulare, Ventura, and Yuba as a result of a disaster, and that has not changed ownership since January 11, 2007;

— June 24, 2007, that was damaged or destroyed by the wildfires that occurred in the county of El Dorado, and that has not changed ownership since June 24, 2007;

— July 4, 2007, that was damaged or destroyed by the Zaca Fire that occurred as a result of this disaster in the counties of Santa Barbara and Ventura, and that has not changed ownership since July 4, 2007.

— July 6, 2007, that was damaged or destroyed by the wildfires that occurred as a result of this disaster in Inyo County, and that has not changed ownership since July 6, 2007;

— September 15, 2007, or October 21, 2007, that was damaged or destroyed by the wildfires that occurred in the counties of Los Angeles, Orange, Riverside, San Bernardino, San Diego, Santa Barbara, and Ventura, and that has not changed ownership since the commencement date of those disasters;

— October 27, 2007, that was damaged or destroyed by the extremely strong and damaging winds that occurred as a result of this disaster in the County of Riverside, and that has not changed ownership since October 20, 2007;

— May, June or July 2008, that was damaged or destroyed by the wildfires that occurred in the counties of Butte, Kern, Mariposa, Mendocino, Monterey, Plumas, Santa Clara, Santa Cruz, Shasta, and Trinity, and that has not changed ownership since the commencement date of those disasters;

— July 1, 2008, that was damaged or destroyed by wildfires that occurred as a result of this disaster in Santa Barbara County, and that has not changed ownership since July 1, 2008;

— July 12, 2008, that was damaged or destroyed by severe rainstorms, floods, landslides, or the accumulation of debris in July 2008, and that has not changed ownership since July 12, 2008;

— May 22, 2008, that was damaged or destroyed by the wildfires that occurred in Humboldt County, and that has not changed ownership since May 22, 2008;

— October 13, 2008, or November 15, 2008, that was damaged or destroyed by the wildfires that occurred in the Counties of Los Angeles and Ventura, and that has not changed ownership since the commencement dates of the wildfires;

— November 13, 2008, that was damaged or destroyed by the wildfires that occurred in the County of Santa Barbara, and that has not changed ownership since November 13, 2008;

— November 15, 2008, or November 17, 2008, that was damaged or destroyed by the wildfires that occurred in the Counties of Orange, Riverside, and San Bernardino, and that has not changed ownership since the commencement dates of these disasters;

— May 5, 2009, that was damaged or destroyed by the wildfires in the County of Santa Barbara, and that has not changed ownership since May 5, 2009;

— August 2009, that was damaged or destroyed by the wildfires in the Counties of Los Angeles and Monterey, and that has not changed ownership since the commencement dates of these disasters as listed in the Governor's disaster proclamations;

— August 30, 2009, that was damaged or destroyed by the wildfires in Placer County and that has not changed ownership since August 30, 2009; (Sec. 218(e)-(y), Rev. & Tax. Code)

— January 9, 2010, that was damaged or destroyed by the earthquake and any other related casualty that occurred as a result of the disaster in the County of Humboldt, that has not changed ownership since January 9, 2010; (Sec. 218.2, Rev. & Tax. Code)

— January 2010, that was damaged or destroyed by the severe winter storms or the severe rainstorms, heavy snows, floods, or mudslides that occurred as a result of these disasters in Calaveras, Imperial, Los Angeles, Orange, Riverside, San Bernardino, San Francisco, and Siskiyou counties as declared by the Governor in January 2010, and that has not changed ownership since the commencement dates of these disasters; (Sec. 218.4, Rev. & Tax. Code);

— April 4, 2010, that was damaged or destroyed by the earthquake in Imperial County, and that has not changed ownership since April 4, 2010 (Sec. 218.3, Rev. & Tax. Code); and

— September 9, 2010, that was damaged or destroyed by the explosion and fire that occurred in San Mateo County, and that has not changed ownership since September 9, 2010.

(Sec. 218.6, Rev. & Tax. Code)

Exemption claim.—Homeowners must file a claim for the exemption with the county assessor. (Sec. 275, Rev. & Tax. Code) A claim remains in effect until such time as title to the property changes, the owner does not occupy the home as his or her principal residence on the lien date, or the property is otherwise ineligible. (Sec. 253.5, Rev. & Tax. Code) The county recorder is responsible for advising the county assessor of any changes in the ownership of the property. (Sec. 255.7, Rev. & Tax. Code) The county assessor is responsible for verifying the eligibility of each claimant to continue receiving the exemption. (Sec. 255.6, Rev. & Tax. Code)

Affidavits for exemption must be filed with the county assessor no later than 5 p.m. on February 15 of the tax year. (Sec. 253.5, Rev. & Tax. Code; Sec. 255, Rev. & Tax. Code; Sec. 254, Rev. & Tax. Code) Failure to receive a form does not excuse a person from timely filing of the required affidavit. (Sec. 255.3, Rev. & Tax. Code; Sec. 255.8, Rev. & Tax. Code; Reg. 135, 18 CCR)

Extensions of time for filing a correct claim may be granted by the assessor to a claimant who has filed a defective claim on time. If a claim is erroneous, the claimant is allowed a six-month extension of time to correct the claim. If the claimant is notified by the assessor of an error in the claim, the assessor may extend the filing period for no more than three months from the date notice is given to the taxpayer. (Sec. 255.1, Rev. & Tax. Code)

A homeowner is allowed 15 days after denial of a claim for the veterans' exemption within which to file a homeowners' exemption claim. (Sec. 255.2, Rev. & Tax. Code)

A late filing may result in a reduction in the amount of the exemption allowed. If an original claim for the homeowners' exemption is not filed on time, but is filed prior to December 10 of the year to which it is to apply, the exemption allowed is the lesser of $5,600 or 80% of the full value of the dwelling. If the filing is made after November 15, the exemption will apply only to the second installment of taxes due on April 10, and the first installment due on December 10 must be paid in full to avoid delinquency. (Sec. 275, Rev. & Tax. Code; Reg. 135, 18 CCR)

• *Residence of innocent investor*

A levy or state lien cannot be made on the principal residence of an innocent investor when notice has been given to the Franchise Tax Board (FTB) that (1) the levy or lien is due to an underpayment of personal income taxes with respect to an abusive tax shelter for tax years ending before 2001 and (2) the principal residence is owned by the innocent investor. In addition, a levy cannot be made on the proceeds from the sale of the principal residence of an innocent investor, and a state tax lien on such a residence must be released without satisfaction. An innocent investor is any individual who:

    — was liable for the underpayment of tax;

    — had no responsibility for the creation, promotion, operation, management, or control of the abusive tax shelter; and

    — in the tax years to which the underpayment applies, reasonably believed that the tax treatment of an abusive tax shelter item was proper.

(Sec. 21015.6, Rev. & Tax Code)

Once it receives the required written notification, the FTB must return any proceeds from the sale of a residence that it receives after January 1, 2002, in excess of the amount due, including interest, with respect to a levy or satisfaction of a lien. (Sec. 21015.6, Rev. & Tax Code)

The owner of the residence may file an action within one year of the FTB's receipt of the proceeds or within 90 days after the FTB's notification of its denial of the request to return the proceeds. The owner may consider the request denied for purposes of bringing an action if the FTB fails to mail this notification within six months of receiving the request. (Sec. 21015.6, Rev. & Tax Code)

[¶20-215] Housing

Property used exclusively for housing and related facilities for elderly or handicapped families of low or moderate income, as rental housing for low-income persons, and as temporary or emergency shelter facilities for homeless people, may qualify for the welfare exemption if the property is owned and operated by a religious, hospital, scientific, charitable, or veteran's organization. (see ¶ 20-285 Nonprofit, Religious, Charitable, Scientific, and Educational Organizations)

Also, an exemption is allowed for homes of certain disabled or blinded veterans who, as a result of a service-connected injury or disease, died while on active duty in military service.

• *Low-cost housing*

The welfare exemption applies to property that is owned and operated by a qualifying nonprofit corporation that is organized and operated for the purpose of building and rehabilitating single-family or multi-family residences for sale at cost to low-income families. In the case of property not previously designated as open space, this exemption may not be denied on the basis that the subject property does not currently include a residence or a residence under construction. (Sec. 214.15, Rev. & Tax. Code)

Restrictions in a contract between the nonprofit corporation organization and low-income families who participate in a special no-interest loan program must be considered by an assessor during assessment. Under the terms of the contract:

— use of the land is restricted for at least 30 years to owner-occupied housing available at affordable cost;

— a deed of trust on the property in favor of the nonprofit corporation is included to ensure compliance with the terms of the program;

— a finding that the long-term deed restrictions serve a public purpose must be made by a local housing authority or official; and

— the contract must be recorded and provided to the assessor.

(Sec. 402.1(a)(10), Rev. & Tax. Code)

Similarly, during assessment the assessor must consider, among other things, restrictions in a contract that is a renewable 99-year ground lease between a community land trust and the qualified owner of an owner-occupied single-family dwelling or an owner-occupied unit in a multifamily dwelling. The contract must subject the dwelling and the land on which it is situated to affordability restrictions. One of several enumerated public agencies or officials must make a finding that the restrictions serve the public interest to create and preserve the affordability of residential housing for persons and families of low or moderate income.

PILOT *agreement prohibition.*—Local governments are prohibited from entering into a payment in lieu of taxes (PILOT) agreement with a property owner of a low-income housing project. An escape or supplemental assessment will not be levied on the basis that payments made under a PILOT agreement were used in a manner incompatible with certain certification requirements for low-income housing projects. (Sec. 214.08, Rev. & Tax. Code)

• *Rental housing*

Both the possessory and fee interests in property leased to a tax-exempt organization for a term of 35 years or more and used exclusively for rental housing and related facilities for low-income tenants as defined by Sec. 50093 of the Health and Safety Code are exempt even though the lessor does not otherwise qualify for the welfare exemption. The exemption also applies to transfers of such leased property when the remaining term is 35 years or more. The property must be leased to, and operated by, religious, hospital, scientific, or charitable funds, foundations, or corporations, as well as public housing authorities, public agencies, or a limited partnership in which the managing general partner has received a determination that it is a charitable organization under IRC Sec. 501(c)(3). In addition, the charitable organization must operate the property in accordance with its exempt purpose. (Sec. 236, Rev. & Tax. Code)

• *Residential real property for auction*

A city, county, or nonprofit organization may request that a tax collector bring to the next scheduled public auction residential real property that meets the following requirements:

— the property taxes have been delinquent for at least three years;

— the real property will serve the public benefit of providing housing directly related to low-income persons; and

— the real property is not occupied by the owner as his or her principal residence.

The deed for a single-family home that is sold by a low-income owner/occupant who purchased the property from a nonprofit organization, which originally purchased the property at a California property tax sale, may provide for equity sharing between the nonprofit organization and the low-income owner. (Sec. 3692.4, Rev. & Tax. Code)

[¶20-230] Intangible Property

Although the California Constitution specifically authorizes the taxation of intangible property albeit at a lower tax rate than other property, intangible property is statutorily exempt from property taxation. (Sec. 2, Art. XIII, Cal. Const.)

The value of intangible assets and rights may not enhance or be reflected in the value of taxable property, except that taxable property may be assessed and valued by assuming the presence of intangible assets or rights necessary to put the taxable property to beneficial or productive use. (Sec. 212, Rev. & Tax. Code; Sec. 3(n), Art. XIII, Cal. Const.)

"Intangible property" includes notes, debentures, shares of stock, solvent credits, bonds, deeds of trust, mortgages, and any interests in such property. Bonds issued by the U.S., state, or local governments are also exempt. (Sec. 3(c), Art. XIII, Cal. Const.; Sec. 208, Rev. & Tax. Code; 31 U.S.C. § 3124)

Money kept on hand in the regular course of a trade, business, or profession is specifically exempt from property taxes. (Sec. 212, Rev. & Tax. Code)

[¶20-245] Leased Property

Recorded leases of real property for periods of 15 years or longer under which the lessee is required to pay or to reimburse the lessor for the real property taxes may be separately assessed. (Sec. 2188.4, Rev. & Tax. Code) This does not apply to land used for grazing or other agricultural purposes or to property assessed by the State Board of Equalization (discussed at ¶20-330 Utilities). Either the lessor or the lessee may request a separate assessment prior to the lien date. Separate assessments will continue to be made for the duration of the lease or until one of the parties to the lease requests that they be discontinued.

The assessor may elect to assess the leased property to either the lessor or the lessee but must mail all assessment notices and tax bills to the lessor in care of the lessee or mail copies of such documents to the lessee. (Sec. 2188.4, Rev. & Tax. Code) Special valuation procedures for leased personal property are discussed further at ¶20-610.

Separate assessment of a leasehold may be obtained only if the property has frontage access on a dedicated street and the boundaries of the leased parcel do not pass through any improvement except along a bearing partition. (Sec. 2188.4, Rev. & Tax. Code)

See also the discussions of leased property used for educational purposes at ¶20-285, leasehold interests for the production of gas and petroleum at ¶20-270, leased property used for rental housing for low-income persons at ¶20-215, and leased church property at ¶20-285.

• *Heavy equipment rental tax reimbursement*

For purposes of California personal property tax, whether a qualified heavy equipment renter may add estimated tax reimbursement to the rental price of heavy equipment to a lessee depends solely on the terms of the rental agreement. Beginning January 1, 2018, agreement to the addition will be rebuttably presumed if:

— the agreement expressly provides for the addition of estimated reimbursement;

— estimated reimbursement is separately stated and charged on the agreement; and

— the estimated tax amount does not exceed 0.75% of the rental price.

(Sec. 31201, Rev. & Tax. Code)

• *Welfare exemption*

Property owned by a nonprofit corporation and leased to the state or a county, city, public corporation, or hospital district for such lessees' exclusive use may qualify for the welfare exemption. The exemption is not available for leases of possessory interests to a nonexempt entity. (Sec. 231, Rev. & Tax. Code)

Real property that is leased for 35 years or more and used exclusively by the lessee for the operation of a public park of a governmental character, qualifies for the welfare exemption if:

— the lessee is a charitable foundation;

— the operation of the public park is within the lessee's tax exempt activities;

— the lessee acquired the leasehold in the property through a charitable donation; and

— the lessee, under the terms of the lease, acquires all ownership interest in the property by the end of the lease period.

(Sec. 236.5, Rev. & Tax. Code)

Also exempt is property leased to a community college, state college, or state university for educational purposes or leased to an exempt governmental entity for the purpose of conducting an activity that if conducted by the organization owning the property would qualify for the exemption. However, the total income received by the organization in the form of rents, fees, or charges from the lease must not exceed the ordinary and usual expenses in maintaining the leased property. (Sec. 214.6, Rev. & Tax. Code)

When property is used jointly by a church and a public school, community college, state college, or state university, including the University of California, the church need only annually file claim form BOE-263-C, Church Lessor's Exemption Claim, with the county assessor where the property is located. The claim form was adopted by the California State Board of Equalization on November 19, 2009, and was developed specifically for use under these circumstances. (*Letter to County Assessors No. 2009/055*, California State Board of Equalization, November 20, 2009)

[¶20-260] Manufactured and Mobile Homes

There are three categories of manufactured homes subject to property taxation:

— those first sold new after June 30, 1980, which are taxed as personal property;

— those that have been made subject to property taxation as personal property at the request of the owner; and

— those that have become real property by being affixed to land on a permanent foundation.

(Sec. 5801, Rev. & Tax. Code; Sec. 5810, Rev. & Tax. Code)

All other manufactured homes are subject, in lieu of property taxes, to an annual vehicle license fee of 0.65% of the market value of the manufactured home, payable to the Department of Housing and Community Development. (Sec. 10758, Rev. & Tax. Code; Sec. 18115, Hlth. & Sfty. Code)

The California State Board of Equalization *Assessors' Handbook* contains a manual pertaining to manufactured and mobile homes. (AH 511, Assessment of Manufactured Homes and Parks, (11-01))

When a manufactured home that is located in a resident-owned mobile home park or a rental park in the process of being changed to resident ownership is converted to property that is taxed to the registered owner pursuant to Health and Safety Code Sec. 18555, the assessor must determine the home's base-year value such that the property taxes levied are of the same amount as the vehicle license fee that was imposed for the year in which the home was converted to property taxation. Supplemental assessments, however, are not to be made upon conversion from the vehicle license fee to the local property tax, and must be made upon a change in ownership or completion of new construction. (Sec. 5802, Rev. & Tax. Code)

The base year value of a manufactured home that is subject to local property tax pursuant to Health and Safety Code Sec. 18119 (governing transfers from the vehicle license fee to local property taxation) is its full cash value on the lien date for the fiscal year in which it is first enrolled. (Sec. 5802, Rev. & Tax. Code)

A manufactured home that has been affixed to land on a permanent foundation system loses its characterization as a "manufactured home" for property tax purposes and is taxed as real property. (Sec. 5801, Rev. & Tax. Code) Manufactured homes that have not become real property by being affixed to land are taxed in the same manner as any other personal property on the assessment roll. (Sec. 5810, Rev. & Tax. Code)

A manufactured home that has been removed from its situs and returned to a dealer's place of business for purposes of resale is not subject to property taxation while it is held in the dealer's inventory if it remains personal property. (Sec. 5815, Rev. & Tax. Code) A mobile home used primarily for residential purposes and located on rental spaces within a mobile home park is not subject to property taxes for debt service of any water district or any improvement district in a water district. (Sec. 20220, Water Code)

Taxes levied on manufactured homes taxed as personal property are placed on the secured roll, but may be collected as unsecured taxes in the case of delinquency. (Sec. 5830, Rev. & Tax. Code) Upon or prior to completion of the roll, the assessor must notify each assessee whose manufactured home's taxable value has increased. (Sec. 5831, Rev. & Tax. Code)

A blind or disabled individual may qualify for postponement of California property tax on a mobile home that he or she occupies as a principal residence.

• *"Manufactured home" and "mobile home" defined*

For property tax purposes, a manufactured home may be a "manufactured home" or a "mobile home," as defined in the Health and Safety Code. (Sec. 5801, Rev. & Tax. Code) A "manufactured home" is a structure transportable in one or more sections that is built on a permanent chassis and designed to be used as a dwelling unit, with or without a permanent foundation, when connected to utilities. (Sec. 18007, Hlth. & Sfty. Code) A "mobile home" is a structure that meets the requirements for classification as a "manufactured home" and is not a recreational vehicle, a commercial coach, or factory-built housing. (Sec. 18008, Hlth. & Sfty. Code)

• *Valuation of manufactured homes taxed as personal property*

For a manufactured home taxed as personal property, a base-year value is determined according to the full cash value of the manufactured home on the date that it was purchased or changed ownership. (Sec. 5812, Rev. & Tax. Code; Sec. 5814, Rev. & Tax. Code) The Department of Housing and Community Development must furnish to each county assessor a monthly listing of all new registrations and titles to manufactured homes sited or to be sited in that county. (Sec. 5841, Rev. & Tax. Code)

If the manufactured home undergoes any new construction after it is purchased or changes ownership, the base-year value of the new construction is its full cash value on the date on which the new construction is completed and, if not completed, on the lien date. New construction that will trigger reassessment includes:

— an addition to the manufactured home;

— an alteration that constitutes major rehabilitation or converts the property to another use; or

— an activity that results in a substantial equivalent of a new manufactured home.

Revaluation occurs only to the part of the manufactured home affected by the new construction. Reconstruction or replacement of a manufactured home following a misfortune or calamity does not trigger reassessment. (Sec. 5825, Rev. & Tax. Code)

The "full cash value" of a manufactured home, used to establish the "base year value," is the amount at which a manufactured home would sell on the open market. However, if the manufactured home is located on rented or leased land, then the "full cash value" of the manufactured home does not include any value attributable to the particular site. (Sec. 5803, Rev. & Tax. Code)

The taxable value of a manufactured home is the lesser of the:

(1) base year value subject to the annually compounded adjustment of up to 2% to reflect an inflation factor, or

(2) full cash value on the lien date as modified by any reductions in value due to damage, depreciation, obsolescence, destruction, or other factors causing a decline in value.

(Sec. 5804, Rev. & Tax. Code; Sec. 5813, Rev. & Tax. Code)

The amount of tax on a manufactured home is determined by applying the appropriate assessment ratio and tax rate to the taxable value of the manufactured home. (Sec. 5811, Rev. & Tax. Code)

• *Base-year value transfers*

There are guidelines for base year value transfers for manufactured homes. Relief may be available if the original property, or the replacement dwelling, or both include a manufactured home, or a manufactured home and any land owned by the claimant on which the manufactured home is situated. "Land owned by the claimant" includes a pro rata interest in a resident-owned mobile home park that is assessed pursuant to Section 62.1(b). (Sec. 69.5, Rev. & Tax. Code; Sec. 62.1(b), Rev. & Tax. Code)

Persons over age 55 and the disabled can transfer a base year value of land as well as the improvement to and from manufactured home parks owned by resident entities, to address situations in which certain persons own their manufactured home as individuals, but the land on which the manufactured home is situated is owned by a legal entity in which they hold pro rata ownership interests. (Sec. 69.5, Rev. & Tax. Code)

• *Accessories for manufactured homes sold before 1977*

Manufactured home accessories that were subject to vehicle license fees and installed on a rented or leased lot with a manufactured home first sold prior to 1977 are exempt from property taxation unless the manufactured home itself is subject to property taxation or the accessory is permanently affixed to the land. Manufactured home accessories installed on a rented or leased lot with a manufactured home first sold prior to 1977 are presumed to be subject to the state vehicle license fee, unless the accessories were not included in the vehicle license fee base for the manufactured home. (Sec. 5805, Rev. & Tax. Code)

• *Floating homes*

Floating homes are assessed in the same manner as real property. (Sec. 229, Rev. & Tax. Code) See ¶ 20-310 for a discussion of real property. For purposes of determining valuation under Proposition 13 rules, however, the 1979 lien date is substituted for the 1975 lien date.

A "floating home" is defined as a floating structure, not a vessel, that is designed and built to be used as a stationary, waterborne residential dwelling. A floating home has no mode of power of its own and is dependent on a continuous shore hookup for utilities and sewage service. (Sec. 229, Rev. & Tax. Code)

• *Destruction or condemnation of manufactured homes*

The owner of a manufactured home destroyed as a result of a disaster declared by the Governor is entitled to relief from property taxation. (Sec. 172, Rev. & Tax. Code) Any replacement manufactured home purchased by the taxpayer of comparable size, utility, and location to the one destroyed must, on application of the taxpayer, be enrolled at the same taxable value as the destroyed manufactured home at the time of its destruction. (Sec. 172.1, Rev. & Tax. Code) In addition, reconstruction or replacement of any manufactured home damaged or destroyed by a misfortune or calamity does not qualify as "new construction" for reassessment purposes, unless the replaced or reconstructed manufactured home is not substantially equivalent to the damaged or destroyed manufactured home; in the latter case, the manufactured home is considered to be new construction and is subject to reassessment and a new base year value. (Sec. 5825, Rev. & Tax. Code)

A special rule applies to manufactured homes that are subject to vehicle license and registration fees, rather than property taxes. If, after having been destroyed or damaged by misfortune or calamity, taken by eminent domain, acquired by a public entity, or adjudged to be inversely condemned, such a manufactured home is replaced by a substantially equivalent manufactured home subject to property taxation, then the base value of the replacement manufactured home must be determined so that property taxes levied on it, after adjustment for any applicable exemption, are the same amount as the vehicle license and registration fees imposed on the previous manufactured home, either for the year prior to the misfortune or calamity or for the year in which the manufactured home was taken, acquired, or adjudged to be inversely condemned. (Sec. 5825, Rev. & Tax. Code)

[¶20-265] Manufacturing and Industrial Property

Valuation procedures for manufacturing and industrial property are discussed at ¶20-610. Local governments and districts may establish special rebate programs to encourage the creation and expansion of manufacturing and industrial employment within their jurisdictions. (see discussion below)

The California State Board of Equalization (BOE) Assessors' Handbook includes a manual on the technical explanation of the mathematical origin of the percent good factors. (AH 582, Explanation of the Derivation of Equipment Percent Good Factors, (02-81))

• *Employee-owned hand tools exemption*

Up to $50,000 worth of employee-owned hand tools required for employment is exempt from property taxation. (Sec. 241, Rev. & Tax. Code)

• *Capital investment incentive programs*

The governing body of any county, city and county, or city, is authorized to adopt a local ordinance establishing a capital investment incentive program (CIIP), under which the local government may "rebate" to certain large manufacturers an amount up to the amount of California property tax revenues derived from the taxation of the assessed value in excess of $150 million of any qualified manufacturing facility that a manufacturer has elected to locate in the local government's jurisdiction. (Sec. 51298, Govt. Code)

Qualified manufacturing facility.—To be a "qualified manufacturing facility," each of the following criteria must be met:

— the manufacturer must have made an initial investment in the facility, in real and personal property, that exceeds $150 million; and

— the facility must be located within the jurisdiction of the local government authorizing the rebate; and either

— the facility must be operated either by a business described in Codes 3500 to 3899 of the federal Standard Industrial Classification Manual, or by a business engaged in the recovery of minerals from geothermal resources, including the proportional amount of geothermal electric generating plants providing electricity as an integral of the recovery process, or by a business engaged in the manufacturing of parts or components related to the production of electricity using solar, wind, biomass, hydropower, or geothermal resources; and

— the manufacturer must be currently engaged in commercial production, or in the perfection of a manufacturing process or product with intent to manufacture.

(Sec. 51298, Govt. Code)

Incentive payments.—Capital investment incentive payments are issued beginning with the first fiscal year after the date a qualified facility is certified for occupancy, or in the absence of such certification, the first fiscal year after the date such a facility commences operations. Also, the manufacturer of the facility must enter into a community services agreement with the local government, under which the manufacturer agrees to pay a community services fee equal to 25% of the rebate, but not to exceed $2 million annually, and sets forth a job creation plan. (Sec. 51298, Govt. Code)

Sunset date.—The sunset date of the capital investment incentive program is January 1, 2024, although a program established prior to that date may remain in effect for the full term of that program. (Sec. 51298.5, Govt. Code)

• *Oil refining property*

There is a property tax rule defining "petroleum refining property" and establishing, for purposes of recognizing declines in value, a rebuttable presumption that fixtures (and machinery and equipment classified as improvements) for petroleum refining properties are part of the same appraisal unit as the land and improvements. The presumption must be overcome before fixtures are treated as a separate appraisal unit for declines in value, except when measuring declines in value caused by disaster, in which case land constitutes a separate appraisal unit. (Reg. 474, 18 CCR)

[¶20-270] Mining, Oil, and Gas Properties

Mines, minerals, and quarries and all rights and privileges pertaining to them are included in the definition of "real property". (Sec. 104, Rev. & Tax. Code) and are taxed as real property. (see ¶20-310) When land and the rights and privileges pertaining to mines or minerals are assessed separately, the words "mining rights" or "mineral rights" on the assessment roll include the right to enter the land for the exploration, development, and production of minerals, including oil, gas, and other hydrocarbons (Sec. 607.5, Rev. & Tax. Code), as well as geothermal resources. (*Phillips Petroleum Company v. County of Lake*, 15 CalApp4th 180, 18 CalRptr2d 765, (1993)) The right to explore for minerals is taxable to the extent it has value separate from the right to develop and produce any discovered minerals. (Reg. 469, 18 CCR) Although the right to develop and the right to produce minerals are separate rights, their separate values are virtually unascertainable and, therefore, no separate value need be established for the right to develop unless there is an intervening change in ownership, at which time the right to develop may have an assessable value as reflected in the purchase price.

The California *Assessors' Handbook* includes manuals that cover assessment of mining and petroleum properties. (AH 560, Assessment of Mining Properties, (03-97); AH 566, Assessment of Petroleum Properties, (01-99))

Mineral rights associated with producing mineral properties are assigned a 1975 base year value, unless there is a change in ownership or production commences. The market value of mineral rights is determined by valuing the estimated quantity of proved reserves that can reasonably be expected to be produced during the time period the rights are exercisable. The valuation of proved reserves is based on present and reasonably projected economic conditions. The assessor may select an appropriate appraisal method, but the income approach is generally the most relevant appraisal method employed. (Reg. 469, 18 CCR)

Increases in proved reserves that occur following commencement of production constitute additions to the mineral rights that have not been assessed and that will be assessed on the regular roll as of the lien date following the date they become proved reserves. Reductions in the recoverable amount of minerals caused by production or by changed conditions or a change in the expectation of future production capabilities constitute reductions in the measure of the mineral rights and will correspondingly reduce value on the subsequent lien date. (Reg. 469, 18 CCR)

The value of the right to produce minerals is established as of the date that the production of minerals commences. When the value of the right to produce minerals is enrolled, the roll value of the exploration or development rights for the same reserves is reduced to zero. (Reg. 469, 18 CCR)

The existence of mines, minerals, and quarries on open-space land is taken into consideration in the valuation of such land. (Sec. 427, Rev. & Tax. Code)

• *Oil and gas producing properties*

The right to remove petroleum and natural gas from the earth is a taxable real property interest. (Reg. 468, 18 CCR) The market value of an oil and gas mineral property interest is determined by estimating the value of the volumes of proved reserves. "Proved reserves" are reserves that may be recoverable in the future, taking into consideration reasonably projected physical and economic operating conditions.

Under Article XIII A of the California Constitution (Proposition 13), oil and gas property interests are assigned a 1975 base year value. (Sec. 2, Art. XIII A, Cal. Const.) Newly constructed improvements and additions to reserves are valued as of the lien date of the year for which the roll is being prepared. Improvements removed from the site are deducted from taxable value. Once determined, a base year value may be increased no more than 2% per year. Base year reserve values must be adjusted annually to reflect changes in the oil and gas reserves on the property. The use of a modified capitalization of income system to value oil and gas property interests is constitutionally valid.

CCH CAUTION: *Value of oil remaining in ground.*—The value of oil remaining in the ground may not be increased on the basis of an increase in the selling price for oil. (*Opinion of the Attorney General, No. 80-322*, 63 OpsCalAttyGen 491)

• *Geothermal properties*

The rights to explore for, develop, and produce geothermal energy are taxable real property interests to the extent they have value separate and apart from the value of the physical quantity of the geothermal resources. The valuation of the rights to explore and develop geothermal resources is governed by substantially the same rules as apply to the valuation of the rights to explore and develop other minerals. However, the roll value of exploration rights of proved reserves must be reduced to zero when the value of the right to produce such proved reserves is enrolled. (Reg. 473, 18 CCR)

Absent a change of ownership, the base year value of the right to produce geothermal energy is established as of the date production commences after completion of construction and initial testing. The market value of such a right is determined by valuing the estimated quantity of proved reserves that can reasonably be expected to be produced during the time period these rights are exercisable. While the assessor is given full discretion to select the appropriate appraisal method, the income approach is considered the most relevant method for establishing the value for the total property. (Reg. 473, 18 CCR)

As with the valuation of oil and gas properties, once a base year value is assigned, the base year value of the geothermal properties may not be increased more than 2% per year. However, the value of new construction and demonstrable additions or subtractions to the proved reserves will be reflected on the next subsequent roll. (Reg. 473, 18 CCR)

• *Oil and gas leases*

Oil and gas leases, as temporary interests in land and profits a prendre (right to make some use of the soil to another), are taxable (Sec. 107, Rev. & Tax. Code), but not as possessory interests. The taxes due on an interest in an oil and gas lease are secured by the leasehold estate, but if the taxes are delinquent, they may be collected as though they were on the unsecured tax roll.

After the decision in *DeLuz Homes* (see ¶20-310 Real Property), some, but not all, counties began assessing oil and gas leasehold interests by including the value of royalties reserved to tax-exempt lessors. Because this created an inequity throughout the state, the legislature enacted remedial sections (Sec. 107.2, Rev. & Tax. Code; Sec. 107.3, Rev. & Tax. Code) that permitted the exclusion from the income used to capitalize the value of an oil and gas lease those royalties paid to tax-exempt entities. The exclusion was permitted for leases entered into before July 27, 1963, and for leases renewed thereafter if the renewal was pursuant to a provision of local law or a contract provision requiring retention of the prerenewal royalty rate. (Sec. 107.3, Rev. & Tax. Code) Subsequent to July 26, 1963, and the excepted renewals, all leases for oil and gas entered into thereafter are valued in the same manner as possessory interests without any exclusion of royalties payable to the tax-exempt lessor.

Regulations issued by the State Board of Equalization to the county assessors require that the value be determined through the use of either the comparative sales or the income capitalization approach used for possessory interests. (Reg. 27, 18 CCR)

• *Oil and gas machinery and equipment*

The California Constitution authorizes the taxation of all tangible personal property not otherwise constitutionally exempt. (Sec. 2, Art. XIII, Cal. Const.) A California regulation provides specific examples to illustrate how specific items may be classified. (Reg. 124, 18 CCR)

Oil refining property.—There is a property tax rule defining "petroleum refining property" and establishing, for purposes of recognizing declines in value, a rebuttable presumption that fixtures (and machinery and equipment classified as improvements) for petroleum refining properties are part of the same appraisal unit as the land and improvements. The presumption must be overcome before fixtures are treated as a separate appraisal unit for declines in value, except when measuring declines in value caused by disaster, in which case land constitutes a separate appraisal unit. (Reg. 474, 18 CCR)

For a discussion of the valuation of oil and gas property, see ¶20-610, Valuation Procedures

[¶20-275] Motor Vehicles

Discussed here is property taxation of motor vehicles, as well as payments and the state motor vehicle license fee, which is a payment in lieu of property taxes. Taxation of mobile and manufactured homes is covered at ¶20-260.

• *Property tax*

Steel-wheeled and track-laying equipment that is not subject to motor vehicle licensing is subject to the property tax in the county in which it has a tax situs on the lien date. Licensed rubber-tired equipment, except commercial vehicles and cranes registered under the Vehicle Code, is also subject to the property tax in the county in which it has a tax situs on the lien date; however, any license fee paid prior to the lien date may be deducted from the property tax due. (Sec. 994, Rev. & Tax. Code)

Implements of husbandry are assessed at full cash value in the county they are located. (Sec. 412, Rev. & Tax. Code; Sec. 413, Rev. & Tax. Code) "Implements of husbandry" are tools, machines, equipment, appliances, devices, or apparatus used in the conduct of agricultural operations (see ¶20-115), as well as vehicles used exclusively in the conduct of agricultural operations, as defined in the Vehicle Code. (Sec. 411, Rev. & Tax. Code)

A logging dolly, pole or pipe dolly, or trailer bus having a valid identification plate, or any auxiliary dolly or tow dolly is exempt from California personal property taxes. The exemption does not apply to a logging dolly that is used exclusively off-highway. (Sec. 225, Rev. & Tax. Code)

• *Vehicle license fee—payment in lieu of taxes*

The state vehicle license fee is a payment in lieu of taxes, including property tax. Vehicles subject to registration under the Vehicle Code and on which an "in lieu" license tax is paid to the Department of Motor Vehicles are not subject to any property taxes, whether or not such vehicles are registered. Such vehicles include motor vehicles and unoccupied trailer coaches in the inventory of vehicles held for sale by a manufacturer, remanufacturer, distributor, or dealer, as well as vehicles of historical value. (Sec. 10758, Rev. & Tax. Code)

For any vehicle other than a trailer or semitrailer, an annual license fee is due in an amount equal to 0.65% of vehicle market value, as determined by the Director of Motor Vehicles. (Sec. 10752, Rev. & Tax. Code; Sec. 10752.1, Rev. & Tax. Code) The fee is payable even for vehicles awarded as prizes in the state lottery. (Sec. 8880.68, Govt. Code) When the registration year for a vehicle is less than or more than 12 months, the fee for the vehicle is decreased or increased by $1/12$ of the annual fee for each month of such period less than or in excess of 12 months. (Sec. 10755, Rev. & Tax. Code) The fee is in lieu of all other state, county, and municipal ad valorem taxes (Sec. 10758, Rev. & Tax. Code), and is due annually on or before the expiration date assigned by the Director. (Sec. 10851, Rev. & Tax. Code) Special fee provisions are made for mobile homes, see ¶ 20-260. (Sec. 18115, Hlth. & Sfty. Code)

Only vehicles of historic value that have been issued special identification license plates are eligible for the $2 California motor vehicle license fee. (Sec. 10753.5, Rev. & Tax. Code)

Exemptions.—Disabled persons' modification costs are excluded in determining the value of the vehicle. (Sec. 10753.6, Rev. & Tax. Code) The fee does not apply to:

— any mobile home which is sold and installed on a foundation system (Sec. 10784, Rev. & Tax Code);

— any new mobile home which is sold and installed for occupancy after June 30, 1980 (Sec. 10785, Rev. & Tax. Code); or

— any mobile home or trailer coach owned by and constituting the principal place of residence of a disabled veteran who is blind in both eyes, has lost the use of two or more limbs, or is totally disabled as a result of injury or disease incurred in military service, or the unremarried surviving spouse, to the extent of the first $20,000 of market value ($30,000 in the case of a veteran coming within the income limitations of the senior citizens property tax postponement provisions). (Sec. 10788, Rev. & Tax. Code)

Specialized transportation service vehicles serving the handicapped and senior citizens are exempt from the license fee if purchased with specified federal funds. (Sec. 10789, Rev. & Tax. Code)

A qualifying surviving spouse of a former American prisoner of war is exempt for one vehicle. (Sec. 10783.2, Rev. & Tax. Code)

A vehicle owned by a federally recognized Indian tribe is exempt if the vehicle is used exclusively within the boundaries of lands under the jurisdiction of the tribe, including the incidental use of the vehicle on highways within those boundaries. (Sec. 10781.1, Rev. & Tax Code)

[¶20-285] Nonprofit, Religious, Charitable, Scientific, and Educational Organizations

Property owned or held in trust by nonprofit organizations and exclusively used for religious, hospital, scientific, or charitable purposes may be eligible for the "welfare exemption." (Sec. 4, Art. XIII, Cal. Const.; Sec. 214, Rev. & Tax. Code) This exemption also extends to buildings under construction, land required for their convenient use, and equipment in the buildings if its intended use meets exemption qualification requirements. (Sec. 5, Art. XIII, Cal. Const.; Sec. 214.1, Rev. & Tax. Code) Special valuation provisions also apply to nonprofit golf courses (see discussion below). (Sec. 10, Art. XIII, Cal. Const.; Sec. 52, Rev. & Tax. Code)

The California State Board of Equalization (BOE) *Assessors' Handbook* contains a manual on the welfare exemption and one on assessment of golf courses. (AH 267, Welfare, Church, and Religious Exemptions, (10-04) and AH 515, Assessment of Golf Courses, (01-83))

In addition, the BOE provides a periodically updated publication on the topic. (*Publication 149, Property Tax Welfare Exemption*, BOE)

> **CCH CAUTION:** The "welfare exemption" does not exempt property from special assessments. (*Cedars of Lebanon Hospital v. Los Angeles County*, 35 Cal2d 729, 221 P2d 31 (1950))

> **CCH CAUTION:** Because tax-exempt status under the Internal Revenue Code includes organizations operated for a wider scope of purpose than what is allowed under California tax laws, not every 501(c)(3) exempt organization will qualify for the welfare exemption. For chambers of commerce or other business leagues, literary societies, scientific societies, college fraternities or sororities, lodges, or mutual benefit societies generally do not qualify for the welfare exemption even though they may be exempt for income tax purposes as these organizations are usually not organized and operated exclusively for charitable purposes, nor are their properties used exclusively for charitable activities. (Publication 149, Property Tax Welfare Exemption, BOE)

• *Welfare exemption process*

An organization seeking a welfare exemption must go through a two-step process. First, the BOE must determine whether the organization qualifies under Sec. 214, and then the local county assessor must determine whether the organization's property qualifies for the exemption. Both the BOE and the assessor can monitor exempt organization's to ensure their continuing eligibility.

> **COMMENT: Transfer of BOE powers.**—Beginning July 1, 2017, all California State Board of Equalization (BOE) administrative powers, duties, and responsibilities that are not constitutionally mandated to the BOE, with certain exceptions in the short term, were transferred to the California Department of Tax and Fee Administration (CDTFA). The Timber Yield Tax Program was transferred to the CDTFA.
>
> The following programs, however, return to the BOE Property Tax Division effective February 1, 2018, because the duties of staff in these programs are intertwined with the constitutional duties that remain with the BOE:

— Tax Area Services Section (TASS);

— Legal Entity Ownership Program (LEOP); and

— Welfare Exemption Program.

(Ch. 6 (A.B. 102), Laws 2017; Ch. 37 (A.B. 1817), Laws 2018, effective June 27, 2018)

Certificate of clearance.—The BOE determines whether an organization is eligible for the welfare exemption. The organization must file the first filing documents, which include Form BOE-277, Claim for Organizational Clearance Certificate—Welfare Exemption, along with its articles of incorporation, tax letters, and (if requested) financial statements, one time with the BOE, and need not file in duplicate in each county in which the organization has property. The Form BOE-277 may be filed at any time during the year. Once the BOE determines that an organization has qualified, the BOE will issue an "organizational clearance certificate" that the organization/claimant must file with the assessor in any of California's 58 counties. (Sec. 254.5(a), Rev. & Tax. Code; Reg. 140.2, 18 CCR; *Publication 149, Property Tax Welfare Exemption*, BOE)

If the BOE staff determines that a claimant is not eligible for an organizational clearance certificate, the BOE must notify the claimant. The claimant then has 60 days from the date of the notice to file an appeal of the BOE's finding of ineligibility. The appeal must be in writing and must state specific grounds. (Sec. 254.6, Rev. & Tax. Code)

Once granted, an organizational certificate of clearance remains valid until BOE staff determines that the organization no longer meets statutory requirements for the exemption. (Sec. 254.6(e)(1), Rev. & Tax. Code)

Property eligibility.—The county assessor determines whether a qualifying organization's property is eligible for the exemption based on the property's use. Such a determination is made without BOE review. However, the assessor may not grant a claim unless the organization holds a valid organizational clearance certificate issued by the BOE. (Sec. 254.6, Rev. & Tax. Code; Reg. 140.2, 18 CCR; Reg. 143, 18 CCR)

Continuing qualification.—The BOE and the assessor may audit organizations to verify continuing qualification for the exemption. (Sec. 254.5(c)(2), Rev. & Tax. Code; Sec. 254.6(f), Rev. & Tax. Code) The BOE is required to review the assessors' administration of the welfare exemption as part of the assessment standards surveys conducted by BOE staff to ensure proper administration of these exemptions. (Sec. 254.5(g), Rev. & Tax. Code)

An applicant who is granted an exemption is not required to reapply in any subsequent year in which there has been no transfer of, or other change in title to, the property and the property is used exclusively by a governmental entity or nonprofit corporation for its interest and benefit. The assessor must annually mail a notice to every applicant relieved of the requirement of filing an annual application. (Sec. 254.5(d), Rev. & Tax. Code)

Claims for the welfare exemption must be filed annually with the assessor by February 15. Form BOE-267, Claim for Welfare Exemption, must be filed if the claimant is a new filer in a county or is seeking exemption on a new location in the county. Form BOE 267-A, Claim for Welfare Exemption, is filed if the claimant is requesting exemption on an annual basis after initial exemption was granted for that property location. The assessor may not approve a property tax exemption claim until the claimant has been issued a valid organizational clearance certificate. (Sec. 254.5, Rev. & Tax. Code) A welfare exemption claim must show that the property use requirements entitling the property to the exemption are met, and that the claimant has a valid organizational clearance certificate. (Sec. 259.5, Rev. & Tax. Code)

Property for which the claim for exemption is filed after February 15 may qualify for a partial exemption. if a claim is filed with the county assessor between February 16 of the current calendar year and January 1 of the following calendar year, 90 percent of any tax, penalty, or interest may be canceled or refunded. If a claim is filed with the county assessor after January 1 of the next calendar year, 85 percent of any tax, penalty, or interest may be canceled or refunded. If a claim is not filed timely, the combined tax, penalty, and interest may not exceed $250. (Sec. 270(a), Rev. & Tax. Code)

Separate exemptions for educational institutions and religious organizations are discussed further below.

For welfare exemption purposes, construction includes the demolition or razing of a building with the intent to replace it with facilities to be used for exempt purposes and on-site physical activity connected with the construction or rehabilitation of a building to be used for exempt purposes. (Sec. 214.2, Rev. & Tax. Code; Sec. 4, Ch. 897, Laws 1991)

The welfare exemption applies to eligible property in addition to other available exemptions. (Sec. 214, Rev. & Tax. Code) Consequently, the exemption for property used for free public libraries and museums (Sec. 202, Rev. & Tax. Code) does not preclude the welfare exemption for such property.

To qualify for the exemption, the property must be used for the actual operation of the exempt activity, may not exceed an amount of property reasonably necessary to the accomplishment of the exempt purpose, and must be irrevocably dedicated to the exempt purpose. (Sec. 214, Rev. & Tax. Code; Sec. 214.01, Rev. & Tax. Code; Reg. 143, 18 CCR) An organization is eligible for the exemption only if net earnings from its exempt activity do not benefit any of the organization's private shareholders, individuals, officers, employees, directors, trustees, contributors, or bondholders. In addition, excepting volunteer fire departments discussed below, the exemption may not be granted unless the organization qualifies as an exempt organization under either Sec. 23701d, Rev. & Tax. Code, or Sec. 501(c)(3) of the Internal Revenue Code and files with the county assessor duplicate copies of a valid, unrevoked letter or ruling from the Franchise Tax Board (FTB) or the Internal Revenue Service (IRS) certifying the organization's tax-exempt status. (Sec. 214.8, Rev. & Tax. Code) The nonprofit organization must be a community chest, fund, foundation, corporation, or eligible limited liability company. (*Publication 149, Property Tax Welfare Exemption*, BOE)

To qualify for the welfare exemption from real property taxes, the claimant's interest in the property must be on record on the lien date in the office of the recorder of the county in which the property is located. A claimant that on the lien date has a possessory interest in publicly-owned land, owns water rights, or owns improvements on land owned by another may, in lieu of the recordation requirement, file a copy of the document giving rise to the possessory interest or water rights or file a written statement attesting to the separate ownership of the improvements. The document or statement remains in effect until the possessory interest terminates or ownership is transferred. (Sec. 261, Rev. & Tax. Code)

The exemption does not require ownership and operation of the property by the same entity, but does require that both entities separately qualify as a religious, hospital, scientific, or charitable organization to claim the exemption. (*Assessors' Handbook*, AH 267, Welfare, Church, and Religious Exemptions, (10-04), California State Board of Equalization) Consequently, if the owner of real property is not a qualifying organization, the lessee may claim the exemption only for its personal property. If the owner does qualify, but the lessee does not, the owner is precluded from claiming the exemption for the portion of the property leased to a nonqualifying organization. Although the State Board of Equalization's (BOE) Assessor's Handbook states that any leasing arrangement should not be intentionally profit-making or commercial in nature, court decisions have granted exemptions in cases when rents charged exceeded the lessor's costs as long as the lessee operated the property consistent with the qualifying activities. (*Christ The Good Shepherd Lutheran Church v. Mathiesen*, 81 CalApp3d 355, 146 CalRptr 321 (1978); *Y.M.C.A. v. Los Angeles County*, 35 Cal2d 760, 221 P2d 47 (1950))

The use of the property for occasional fundraising activities also does not preclude tax exemption if the organization files with the county assessor copies of the organization's federal exemption determination and most recent federal income tax return. Also, the use of the property as a meeting place for *other* tax-exempt organizations will not disqualify it for exemption as long as the meetings are incidental to the other organization's primary activities, are unrelated to fundraising, and do not occur more than once per week. The other organization and its use of the property must also satisfy exemption requirements, and copies of the other organization's federal tax-exempt determination and most recent federal tax return must also be filed with the assessor. The property may not be used for social purposes unless such use is clearly incidental to its exempt purpose. (Sec. 214, Rev. & Tax. Code)

The exemption applies to property used for a charitable or hospital purpose for at least 30 years, even though there may be a provision for reversion of the property to a person or entity not qualifying for the exemption after liquidation, dissolution, or abandonment of the exempt entity if the ownership, operation, use, and dedication of the property are within the exemption provisions. (Sec. 214.3, Rev. & Tax. Code)

The welfare exemption also applies to property being constructed pursuant to the Community Redevelopment Law if the property is both dedicated to religious, charitable, scientific, or hospital purposes in the redevelopment plan, and required by the redevelopment plan to be conveyed to the state, a county, a city, or a nonprofit entity entitled to the welfare exemption. However, if the property is not conveyed to the state, a county, a city, or a nonprofit entity entitled to the welfare exemption within three years of the completion of construction, the property owner is liable for all taxes that otherwise would have been imposed on the property during construction plus a 25% penalty. (Sec. 214.13, Rev. & Tax. Code)

A nonprofit organization organized and operated for the advancement of education, improvement of social conditions, and improvement of the job opportunities of low-income, unemployed, or underemployed persons may not be disqualified from receiving the exemption solely because it receives all its funds from governmental agencies. (Sec. 214.10, Rev. & Tax. Code)

Property used as residential accommodations to house an exempt organization's employees or constituents may also be exempt, provided the residential use of such property is incidental to and reasonably necessary, or institutionally necessary for the operation of the organization. A property's use by the organization owner, rather than its use by occupants, is relevant to determining exemption eligibility; the occupant's use for personal or residential purposes is subsidiary to the organization's primary purpose. A property's remote location is not necessarily relevant, inasmuch as the organization owner's use of the property is the primary determining factor. (Sec. 214, Rev. & Tax. Code; Reg. 137, 18 CCR)

An affidavit for claiming the welfare exemption must be filed with the county assessor between the lien date and 5:00 p.m. on February 15 of each year. (Sec. 255, Rev. & Tax. Code; Sec. 254, Rev. & Tax. Code) However, an organization that is denied the church or religious exemption (discussed further below) may file an affidavit for the welfare exemption within 15 days of the date of notification of ineligibility for the church or religious exemption. A nonprofit corporation that receives the welfare exemption and leases its property for exclusive governmental use is not required to reapply for the welfare exemption in any subsequent year in which there has been no transfer of, or change in title to, the property. (Sec. 254.5, Rev. & Tax. Code)

When a timely welfare exemption application is not filed for qualifying property, 90% of any tax, penalty, or interest paid on such property may be cancelled or refunded when an appropriate application for exemption is filed within 90 days of the lien date in the next succeeding calendar year, or 85% of the tax, penalty, or interest paid may be cancelled or refunded when the application is filed thereafter. (Sec. 270, Rev. & Tax. Code) However, when the total amount of any tax, penalty, or interest exceeds $250, the total amount may be cancelled or refunded provided an appropriate claim for exemption has been filed. Similar provisions apply to property acquired after the lien date. (Sec. 271, Rev. & Tax. Code)

Welfare exemption claims are subject to review by the BOE. The BOE must schedule an oral hearing on a welfare exemption petition and must give the petitioner 75 days notice of the hearing date and time. (Reg. 5522.6(a)(1), 18 CCR) The petitioner may waive the oral hearing and have the matter decided on the basis of the written petition. (Reg. 5522.6(c)(2), 18 CCR)

The welfare exemption will expire upon the property's being sold to a third party that is not eligible for the exemption. (Sec. 271.5, Rev. & Tax. Code)

• *Hospitals*

Property owned and operated by a nonprofit organization that qualifies for the welfare exemption will be deemed to be exclusively used for hospital purposes as long as it is exclusively used to meet the needs of hospitals that qualify for property tax exemption under the welfare exemption or any other law of the United States or California. (Sec. 214.11, Rev. & Tax. Code) The term "needs of hospitals" includes any use incidental to, and reasonably necessary for, the functioning of a full hospital operation. Although a nonprofit gift shop that is operated by a hospital or hospital auxiliary, and that serves only hospital patients, visitors, and employees may qualify for the welfare exemption, a hospital thrift shop does not qualify. (*Assessors' Handbook*, AH 267, Welfare, Church, and Religious Exemptions, (10-04), California State Board of Equalization) A hospital is operated on a nonprofit basis if its operating revenues, excluding gifts, endowments, or grants, do not exceed operating expenses by more than 10%. (Sec. 214, Rev. & Tax. Code)

The use of hospital property by a licensed physician who is compensated for services does not disqualify the hospital for the welfare exemption, but those portions of the hospital leased or rented to a physician for an office for the general practice of medicine are not included within the exemption. (Sec. 214.7, Rev. & Tax. Code; Sec. 214.9, Rev. & Tax. Code)

Outpatient clinics that furnish psychiatric services for emotionally disturbed children and certain nonprofit multispecialty clinics, as described in Sec. 1206 of the Health and Safety Code, can qualify for the welfare exemption as hospitals. (Sec. 214.9, Rev. & Tax. Code) Although other clinics do not fit the definition of "hospital," they may qualify as a charitable organization if their services benefit the community at large. (*Assessors' Handbook*, AH 267, Welfare, Church, and Religious Exemptions, (10-04) California State Board of Equalization; *Christ The Good Shepherd Lutheran Church v. Mathiesen*, 81 CalApp3d 355, 146 CalRptr 321 (1978))

• *Volunteer fire departments*

Property used exclusively for volunteer fire department purposes qualifies for the "welfare exemption." For the exemption to apply, a volunteer fire department must own the property and qualify for income tax exemption under IRC Sec. 501(c) subsection (3) or (4) or under Sec. 23701d or Sec. 23701f of the Rev. & Tax. Code and must have official recognition and support from its local governmental agency. The organization must file with the assessor a valid organizational clearance certificate. (Sec. 213.7, Rev. & Tax. Code; Sec. 254.6, Rev & Tax. Code)

• *Zoological societies*

Personal property used exclusively in operating a zoo or displaying horticultural exhibits on publicly owned land owned by a nonprofit zoological society may qualify for the welfare exemption if exemption requirements are met. (Sec. 222, Rev. & Tax. Code) Possessory interests in such property may also qualify for exemption. (Sec. 222.5, Rev. & Tax. Code)

• *Nonprofit golf courses*

Under Sec. 10, Art. XIII, of the California Constitution, golf courses of more than 10 acres used for nonprofit purposes on the lien date, and for two years immediately preceding the lien date, must be assessed on the basis of such use, plus any value in the land attributable to mines, quarries, hydrocarbon substances, or other minerals, and the rights to extract those minerals. A California court of appeal found no conflict between this provision and Sec. 2, Art. XIIIA, Cal. Const. (Proposition 13), which requires that real property be assessed at its full cash value as shown on the 1975-1976 tax bill. (*Los Angeles County Club, Bel-Air Country Club v. Pope*, 220 CalRptr 584 (CtApp 1985)) Under Art. XIIIA, nonprofit golf course property must be assessed at its full cash value shown on its 1975-1976 tax bill, but such value may not reflect any other factors than the property's use as a golf course, as provided under Art. XIII. (Sec. 10, Art. XIII, Cal. Const.; Sec. 52, Rev. & Tax. Code)

• *Scientific organizations*

Scientific organizations are entitled to the welfare exemption, provided they are nonprofit organizations chartered by Congress and/or are engaged in medical research. An institutional purpose to encourage or conduct scientific investigation, research, and discovery for the benefit of the community at large is also requisite to exempt status. (Sec. 214, Rev. & Tax. Code)

CCH CAUTION: According to the BOE, the exemption for the scientific organization's real property (land, buildings, and fixtures) used for scientific purposes is exempt only if it is also used for religious, hospital, or charitable purposes. The California Constitution gives the power to the Legislature to exempt, in whole or in part, tangible personal property. However, only the constitution can exempt real property (land, buildings, and fixtures). Because the Constitution only exempts real property used for religious, hospital, or charitable purposes, a scientific organization can only have its real property exempt from property taxation if the real property is also used for a religious, hospital, or charitable purpose. Personal property used for scientific purposes does not need to qualify under religious, hospital, or charitable purposes. It is sufficient that personal property is used exclusively for scientific purposes. (*Publication 149, Property Tax Welfare Exemption*, BOE)

• *Educational institutions*

Property used exclusively for public schools, community colleges, state colleges, and state universities, including the University of California, is exempt from property taxation. (Sec. 3(d), Art. XIII, Cal. Const.; Sec. 202(a), Rev. & Tax. Code; Sec. 203(a), Rev. & Tax. Code) The exemption also applies to off-campus facilities owned or leased by an apprenticeship program sponsor if the facilities are used exclusively by public schools for classes or related and supplemental instruction for apprentices or trainees that are conducted by the schools under Chapter 4 of the Labor Code. Beginning January 1, 2018, it also applies to an interest in property, including a possessory interest, belonging to the state, a county, a city, a school district a community college district, or any combination thereof, that is used to provide certain rental housing for public school districts or community college districts. (Sec. 202(b), Rev. & Tax. Code) Personal property used in conjunction with educational activities of state colleges (Sec. 202.5, Rev. & Tax. Code), with public school student body organization activities (Sec. 202.6, Rev. & Tax. Code), and with the University of California student government activities (Sec. 202.7, Rev. & Tax. Code) is exempt from property taxation.

Buildings, land, equipment, and securities used exclusively for educational purposes by a nonprofit institution of higher education are also exempt from property taxation. (Sec. 3(e), Art. XIII, Cal. Const.) The exemption extends to buildings under construction, land required for their convenient use, and equipment in the buildings, if the intended use would qualify the property for exemption. (Sec. 5, Art. XIII, Cal. Const.)

Property owned by the California School of Mechanical Arts, California Academy of Sciences, or Cogswell Polytechnical College, or held in trust for the Huntington Library and Art Gallery is exempt from property taxation. (Sec. 4, Art. XIII, Cal. Const.; Sec. 203.5, Rev. & Tax. Code)

For exempt computer equipment of the San Diego Supercomputer Center at the University of California, San Diego, see ¶ 20-135 Computer Hardware and Software.

Welfare exemption.—The "welfare exemption" for property used exclusively for religious, charitable, scientific, or hospital purposes may be applied to property owned and operated by educational institutions of collegiate grade. (Sec. 214(e), Rev. & Tax. Code; Sec. 214.5, Rev. & Tax. Code) Such property qualifies for the welfare exemption if the educational institution meets all the requirements for the welfare exemption, including the requirement that property be irrevocably dedicated to religious, charitable, scientific, or hospital purposes. (Sec. 214(e), Rev. & Tax. Code) An educational institution is deemed to have met this requirement if (1) the institution's articles of incorporation irrevocably dedicate the property to either charitable and educational purposes, to religious and educational purposes, or to educational purposes and (2) the articles of incorporation provide for distribution of the property on its liquidation, dissolution, or abandonment to a fund, foundation, or corporation organized and operated for religious, hospital, scientific, charitable, or educational purposes that meets the requirement for property tax exemption under either the college exemption (Sec. 203(b), Rev. & Tax. Code) or the welfare exemption.

Property used exclusively for school purposes of less than collegiate grade (including nursery schools) and owned and operated by nonprofit religious, hospital, or charitable funds, foundations, or corporations is included within the "welfare exemption." (Sec. 214(b), Rev. & Tax. Code; Sec. 214(c), Rev. & Tax. Code)

Any nonprofit corporation organized and operated for the advancement of education, improvement of social conditions, and improvement of job opportunities of low-income, unemployed, and underemployed persons of communities in which it operates qualifies for the welfare exemption, regardless of whether it receives all its funds from governmental agencies, if it meets all the requirements of the welfare exemption. (Sec. 214.10, Rev. & Tax. Code)

An educational institution of collegiate grade is an institution incorporated as a college or seminary that confers academic or professional degrees based on a course of at least two years in liberal arts or sciences, or at least three years in professional studies, such as law, theology, education, medicine, dentistry, engineering, veterinary medicine, pharmacy, architecture, fine arts, commerce, or journalism. (Sec. 203(b), Rev. & Tax. Code) No part of the income of such a nonprofit institution may benefit any private person. (Sec. 203(c), Rev. & Tax. Code) Schools offering a degree in flight test technology or flight test science are also eligible for a California property tax exemption. (Sec. 203(b), Rev. & Tax. Code) The degree must be based on a course of study lasting for at least one year. The Master's Degree program at the school must have been approved by the California Council for Private Post Secondary and Vocational Education or by the Bureau for Private Post Secondary and Vocational Education.

A school of "less than collegiate grade" is:

(1) an institution of learning, the attendance at which exempts a student from attendance at a public full-time elementary or secondary day school or

(2) an institution of learning, a majority of whose students are persons that have been excused from attendance at a full-time elementary or secondary day school.

(Sec. 214.4, Rev. & Tax. Code)

A nursery school is a group facility for minors that has obtained a written license or permit to operate as such from the State Department of Social Services, or from an inspection service approved or accredited by the State Department of Social Services, and that is owned and operated to provide:

— day care for minors whose parents are employed;

— training and education for minors of preschool age; or

— instruction to parents on the subject of raising minors and training and education for minors.

(Sec. 221, Rev. & Tax. Code)

College bookstores.—Bookstore property that is either owned by an educational institution of collegiate grade or used by a nonprofit corporation affiliated with the educational institution is subject to property tax to the extent that the bookstore generates unrelated "business taxable income," as defined in IRC Sec. 512. (Sec. 202(c), Rev. & Tax. Code) (For a discussion of unrelated business taxable income, see ¶ 10-245 Exempt Organizations in the "Corporation Franchise" division of the Reporter.) The property tax imposed on the bookstore property is without prejudice to the educational institution's right to assert an exemption otherwise available under Sec. 3(d) or (e), Article XIII, of the California Constitution. The portion of the bookstore subject to property tax is determined by the ratio of unrelated business taxable income to the total gross income of the bookstore.

Personal property owned or used by nonprofit corporations operating student bookstores of colleges affiliated with the University of California (Sec. 202.7, Rev. & Tax. Code) or affiliated with educational institutions of collegiate grade (Sec. 203(b), Rev. & Tax. Code) is exempt from property taxation. (Sec. 203.1, Rev. & Tax. Code)

Public radio and television stations.—Personal property owned or leased by a nonprofit educational television or radio station is exempt from property taxation if no earnings inure to the benefit of a private shareholder or individual. (Sec. 215.5, Rev. & Tax. Code)

Property of noncommercial educational television or FM radio stations owned and operated by religious, hospital, scientific, or charitable funds, foundations, or corporations is exempt under the welfare exemption if the organizations meet all the specified exemption requirements. (Sec. 214(d), Rev. & Tax. Code)

An "educational television station" is a facility that transmits television programs and does not accept advertising for a consideration. (Sec. 225.5, Rev. & Tax. Code) At least 25% of such station's operating expenses are covered by contributions from the general public or by membership dues. A "noncommercial educational FM broadcast station" is a facility that is licensed and operates under Subpart (C) of Part 73 of Title 47 of the Code of Federal Regulations.

Leased property.—Any reduction in the taxes on property leased to exempt schools, colleges, or universities inures to the benefit of the exempt lessee. If the lessor claims the exemption and the lease or rental agreement does not specifically provide that the exemption for educational property is taken into account in setting the terms, the lessee must receive a reduction in payments or a refund in an amount equal to the reduction in taxes. If the lessor fails to claim the exemption, the lessee may do so. (Sec. 202.2, Rev. & Tax. Code)

Exhibits.—Educational exhibits brought into the state for temporary public showing, which are subject to taxation in another state or country, are exempt from California property taxes. (Sec. 213, Rev. & Tax. Code)

Exemption affidavits.—Affidavits for claiming the educational institutions exemption must be filed with the county assessor annually between the lien date and 5 p.m. on February 15. (Sec. 254, Rev. & Tax. Code; Sec. 255, Rev. & Tax. Code) The affidavit for the college exemption must show that the claimant is a nonprofit collegiate level educational institution, that the land for which the exemption is claimed is that on which the college is located, and that the property is used exclusively for educational purposes. (Sec. 258, Rev. & Tax. Code) The affidavit for the public schools exemption must show the owner's name, the name of the public school that is using the exempt property exclusively for its purposes, and the terms of the agreement by which the school obtained the property. (Sec. 259.10, Rev. & Tax. Code) The affidavit for the welfare exemption is discussed above.

Untimely exemption applications.—When a timely exemption application is not filed for property that qualifies for the exemption, 90% of any tax, penalty, or interest paid on such property may be cancelled or refunded when an appropriate application for exemption is filed on or before the lien date in the next succeeding calendar year, or 85% of the tax, penalty, or interest paid may be cancelled or refunded when the application is filed thereafter. (Sec. 270, Rev. & Tax. Code) However, when the total amount of any tax, penalty, or interest exceeds $250, the total amount may be cancelled or refunded provided an appropriate claim for exemption has been filed. Similar provisions apply to property acquired after the lien date. (Sec. 271, Rev. & Tax. Code)

• *Religious organizations*

Property used exclusively for religious purposes is exempt from property taxation. (Sec. 207, Rev. & Tax. Code) Property owned and operated by a church and used for religious worship and school purposes, except property used solely for schools of collegiate grade, is deemed used exclusively for religious purposes and is entitled to the exemption. Also, personal property leased to a church and used as provided is deemed to be used exclusively for religious purposes. (Sec. 207.1, Rev. & Tax. Code) The State Board of Equalization publishes guidance specifically for religious organizations. (*Publication 48, Property Tax Exemptions for Religious Organizations*, California State Board of Equalization, June 2017)

CCH PRACTICE TIP: Churches that lease property to schools that are operated on their properties must file for the welfare exemption for those portions of the properties used by the schools. In addition, the school must also file for the welfare exemption as the operator of the property. The welfare exemption must also be claimed for uses of the property beyond the scope of religious worship and schools, or if the property also is used regularly by a charitable organization. If a property qualifies under both the religious exemption and the welfare exemption, the religious exemption is more advantageous in that in only requires a one-time filing. (*Publication 149, Property Tax Welfare Exemption*, BOE)

Buildings, land on which they are situated, and equipment used exclusively for religious worship are exempt. (Sec. 3, Art. XIII, Cal. Const.; Sec. 206, Rev. & Tax. Code) The exemption extends to buildings or facilities under construction, the land required for their convenient use, and the equipment in them if the use qualifies for exemption. (Sec. 206, Rev. & Tax. Code; Sec. 5, Art. XIII, Cal. Const.; Sec. 214.1, Rev. & Tax. Code) The term "facilities in the course of construction" includes (1) the demolition or razing of a building for the purpose of constructing a facility to be used for religious purposes and (2) onsite physical activity connected with the construction or rehabilitation of a new or existing building to be used for religious purposes. (Sec. 214.2, Rev. & Tax. Code)

Parking lots.—All real property that is necessary and reasonably required for the parking of automobiles of persons who are attending religious services, or are engaged in religious services or worship or any religious activity, is exempt from taxation. The exemption includes land and improvements leased by a religious organization if the leased real property is exclusively used for parking the members' automobiles and the following requirements are met:

— the religious organization's congregation must not be greater than 500 members;

— the religious organization must pay the property taxes levied on the land and improvements, including any reimbursement of taxes paid by the owner; and

— the county and the owner of the real property must agree that the owner will pay the total amount of taxes that would be levied on the real property for a current fiscal year and the first two subsequent fiscal years in the absence of a grant of exemption for the current year, if the real property is not used exclusively for the aforementioned parking purposes during either of those two subsequent fiscal years.

(Sec. 206.1, Rev. & Tax. Code; Sec. 4, Art. XIII, Cal. Const.)

Welfare exemption.—If property is not used for religious worship it may still qualify for the "welfare exemption" if it:

— is used exclusively for religious purposes;

— owned by community chests, funds, foundations, or corporations organized and operated for religious purposes; and

— the owner is not organized or operated for profit.

(Sec. 4, Art. XIII, Cal. Const.; Sec. 214, Rev. & Tax. Code; Sec. 214.01, Rev. & Tax. Code; Sec. 214.5, Rev. & Tax. Code)

Property used to generate unrelated business taxable income, as defined in IRC Sec. 512, is entitled to only a partial exemption. (Sec. 214.05, Rev. & Tax. Code)

If, while in the process of reviewing each claim for an organizational clearance certificate, the BOE finds that an applicant for the welfare exemption is ineligible for an organizational clearance certificate, because at the time of the filing of the claim, the applicant's articles of incorporation, bylaws, articles of association, constitution, or regulations (as the case may be), did not include a statement of irrevocable dedication to only religious, charitable, scientific, or hospital purposes, the BOE must notify the applicant in writing. The applicant has until the next succeeding lien date to amend its documents and file a certified copy of such amendments with the BOE. The BOE shall make a finding that the applicant, if otherwise qualified, is eligible for an organizational clearance certificate and forward that finding to the assessor. (Sec. 214.01, Rev. & Tax. Code)

Property under development pursuant to the Community Redevelopment Law that is dedicated to religious purposes and that is required to be conveyed to a governmental entity entitled to a welfare exemption is exempt from taxation during construction if the title to the property is to be conveyed to the governmental entity within three years of the construction's completion. (Sec. 214.13, Rev. & Tax. Code)

Property used exclusively for charitable purposes of museums and owned and operated by a religious fund, foundation, or corporation that meets all the requirements of the welfare exemption is also exempt from taxation. (Sec. 214.14, Rev. & Tax. Code)

Leased property.—If an exemption is claimed by a property owner who leases property to a religious institution, the exemption will be allowed only if the reduction in taxes results in a benefit to the lessee. (Sec. 206.2, Rev. & Tax. Code)

Exemption affidavits.—Claimants for the religious exemption must submit an affidavit showing that the property is owned and operated by a nonprofit organization devoted exclusively to religious purposes; the building, equipment, and land are used exclusively for religious purposes; and the land is required for the convenient use of the building. (Sec. 257, Rev. & Tax. Code; Sec. 256, Rev. & Tax. Code) The affidavit must be filed with the assessor annually between the lien date and February 15. (Sec. 255, Rev. & Tax. Code)

The religious exemption, once granted, remains in effect until the property is transferred or is no longer used for a religious purpose. A request for confirmation of the continued religious exemption will be mailed out each year prior to the lien date by the assessor. Any person who has been granted a religious exemption must notify the assessor by June 30th if the property becomes ineligible for the exemption. (Sec. 257, Rev. & Tax. Code; Sec. 257.1, Rev. & Tax. Code)

CCH COMMENT: A claimant who has been found ineligible for the religious exemption may file an affidavit for the welfare exemption within 15 days after notification of ineligibility. (Sec. 255, Rev. & Tax. Code)

Untimely exemption claim.—When a timely exemption application is not filed for property that qualifies for the exemption, 90% of any tax, penalty, or interest paid on such property may be cancelled or refunded when an appropriate application for exemption is filed on or before the lien date of the next succeeding calendar year, or 85% of the tax, penalty, or interest paid may be cancelled or refunded when the application is filed thereafter. (Sec. 270, Rev. & Tax. Code) However, when the total amount of any tax, penalty, or interest exceeds $250, the total amount may be cancelled or refunded, provided an appropriate claim for exemption has been filed.

Property acquired after lien date.—If an organization that qualifies for the religious exemption acquires property after the lien date for a given calendar year and files an application for the exemption within 90 days from the first day of the month following the date on which the property was acquired (prior to January 1, 2004, by the lien date of the following year), taxes due on the property after its acquisition by the organization will be refunded or cancelled. (Sec. 271, Rev. & Tax. Code)

• *Limited liability companies*

Limited liability companies (LLCs) that otherwise meet the eligibility criteria are authorized to claim the welfare exemption available to qualified nonprofit organizations for property used exclusively for religious, hospital, scientific, or charitable purposes. (Sec. Rev. & Tax. Code 214; Sec. Rev. & Tax. Code 214.01; Sec. Rev. & Tax. Code 214.02; Sec. Rev. & Tax. Code 214.5; Sec. Rev. & Tax. Code 214.14) An LLC wholly owned by one or more qualifying organizations, which may include governmental entities and nonprofit organizations, that are exempt under specified provisions of California or federal law qualify as an exempt organization for purposes of the welfare exemption. An LLC that does not have a valid, unrevoked letter from the FTN or the IRS will not be allowed to claim the exemption unless each nonprofit tax-exempt LLC member files with the BOE a copy of a valid, unrevoked letter or ruling from either the FTB or the IRS that states that the organization qualifies as an exempt organization. (Sec. 214.8, Rev. & Tax. Code)

Organizations eligible for the welfare exemption from California property tax include certain nonprofit exempt limited liability companies (LLCs) wholly owned by qualified organizations. A "qualifying organization" is an organization that is:

(1) exempt under IRC Sec. 501(c)(3) or a specific section of the California Revenue and Taxation Code, and

(2) qualified for exemption.

An LLC is a qualifying organization if all of its members are so exempt and qualify for the exemption. Moreover, the term "qualifying organization" also includes an exempt government entity and an LLC if one or more of its members is a government entity, as specified, and all other members are likewise exempt and qualify for exemption. (Sec. 214.8, Rev. & Tax. Code; Reg. 136, 18 CCR)

• *Unrelated business taxable income*

Property that is used to generate unrelated business taxable income, as defined in IRC Sec. 512, qualifies only for a partial welfare exemption. Organizations that have unrelated business taxable income must file with the assessor specific information concerning the property. (Sec. 214.05, Rev. & Tax. Code)

The partial exemption is calculated under the following rules: (Sec. 214.05, Rev. & Tax. Code)

First, if the tax-exempt activities are attributable to a reasonably ascertainable portion of the entire property, then the partial exemption will be calculated by multiplying the total value of that portion of the property by the ratio of:

(1) the organization's income attributable to that portion of the property that is exempt from corporation franchise and income taxation over

(2) the organization's total income attributable to that portion.

(Sec. 214.05, Rev. & Tax. Code)

Second, if the property is used for both exempt non-income-producing activities and unrelated business income-producing activities, and those activities are attributable to a reasonably ascertainable portion of the entire property, then the partial exemption for that portion of the property will be calculated by multiplying the value of that portion by the ratio of:

(1) the amount of time actually devoted to those exempt non-income-producing activities of the organization attributable to that portion over

(2) the total amount of time actually devoted to all of the activities of the organization attributable to that portion.

(Sec. 214.05, Rev. & Tax. Code)

Third, if the activities described in the first two rules above cannot be attributed to a reasonably ascertainable portion of the entire property, the *entire property* is entitled only to a partial exemption. If the activities are described in the first rule, the partial exemption is calculated by multiplying the value of the entire property by the ratio of:

(1) the amount of the organization's income attributable to the entire property that is exempt from income or franchise taxation over

(2) the organization's total income attributable to the entire property.

If the activities are described in the second rule, the partial exemption is calculated by multiplying the value of the entire property by the ratio of:

(1) the amount of time actually devoted to exempt non-income-producing activities of the organization attributable to the entire property over

(2) the total amount of time actually devoted to all of the organization's activities attributable to the entire property.

(Sec. 214.05, Rev. & Tax. Code)

Fourth, the first three rules must be disregarded if more than 75% of the organization's income is attributable to property that has qualified for the welfare exemption under Section 214 but is not specifically related to the organization's use of the particular property. In that case, the property will be entitled only to a partial exemption calculated by multiplying the property's total value by the ratio of:

(1) the organization's income that is attributable to activities in California and that is exempt from income or franchise taxation over

(2) the organization's total income attributable to activities in California.

(Sec. 214.05, Rev. & Tax. Code)

[¶ 20-295] Personal Property

The California Constitution authorizes the taxation of all tangible personal property not otherwise constitutionally exempt. (Sec. 2, Art. XIII, Cal. Const.) Personal property subject to tax is all property that is not real property or improvements to real property. (Sec. 106, Rev. & Tax. Code; Sec. 104, Rev. & Tax. Code; Reg. 123, 18 CCR) The legislature may classify personal property for differential taxation or for exemption purposes. (Sec. 2, Art. XIII, Cal. Const.) Substantial portions of personal property, such as business inventories, property used at an exhibition (see below), household goods and personal effects, intangibles (see ¶ 20-230), and qualifying space flight property (see below) are statutorily or constitutionally exempt from property taxation.

The California State Board of Equalization (BOE) *Assessors' Handbook* includes a manual relating to personal property and fixtures. (AH 504, Assessment of Personal Property and Fixtures, (10-02))

A county board of supervisors may exempt from taxation personal property with a full value so low that the total taxes, special assessments, and applicable subventions on the property would amount to less than the cost of assessing and collecting them. (Sec. 155.20, Rev. & Tax. Code)

• *Space flight*

Until July 1, 2025, qualified property for use in space flight is exempt from California property tax. "Qualified property" is "[t]angible personal property, whether raw materials, work in process or finished goods, that has, or upon manu-facture, assembly, or installation has, space flight capacity, including, but not limited to, an orbital space facility, space propulsion system, space vehicle, launch vehicle, satellite, or space station of any kind, and any component thereof, regardless of whether that property is to be ultimately returned to this state." The definition also includes fuel produced, sold, and used exclusively for space flight. "Space flight" means any flight designed for suborbital, orbital, or interplanetary travel by a space vehicle, satellite, space facility, or space station of any kind. (Sec. 242, Rev. & Tax. Code)

The exemption:

— cannot be denied due to the failure, postponement, or cancellation of any qualifying launch or the destruction of any launch vehicle or launch vehicle component;

— does not apply to any material that is not intended to be launched into space; and

— is limited to taxpayers that have a primary business purpose in space flight activities.

(Sec. 242, Rev. & Tax. Code)

The exemption is operative only from the January 1, 2014, lien date to, and including, the January 1, 2024, lien date. Effective July 1, 2025, the exemption provision is repealed. (Sec. 242, Rev. & Tax. Code) Space flight property also is exempt as business inventory.

• *Exhibits*

Personal property brought to California exclusively for use at any exposition, fair, carnival, or public exhibit of literary, scientific, educational, religious, or artistic works, is exempt from tax, provided it is used only for such purposes while in the state. (Sec. 213, Rev. & Tax. Code) Only property removed from the state after its use or exhibition, and that is subject to tax in another jurisdiction, qualifies for the exemption; all taxes due the other jurisdiction must have been paid. Exemption claimants must file an affidavit with the county assessor. (Sec. 254, Rev. & Tax. Code; Sec. 259, Rev. & Tax. Code)

If an exemption application for exhibits is not timely filed, 90% of any tax, penalty, or interest paid on such property may be cancelled or refunded, provided that an appropriate application is filed on or before the lien date in the next succeeding calendar year. Likewise, 85% of any tax, penalty, or interest paid may be cancelled or refunded if an application is filed after the next succeeding calendar year. (Sec. 270, Rev. & Tax. Code) If the total amount of any tax, penalty, or interest exceeds $250, however, the total amount may be cancelled or refunded, provided an appropriate claim for exemption has been filed. Similar provisions apply to property acquired after the lien date. (Sec. 271, Rev. & Tax. Code)

Classification of property as tangible personal property is discussed at ¶20-105. Valuation rules applicable to tangible personal property are discussed at ¶20-645. Manufacturing and industrial property is discussed at ¶20-265.

[¶20-310] Real Property

The California Constitution provides for the taxation of all real property, not specifically exempted, in proportion to its full value. (Sec. 1, Art. XIII, Cal. Const.) However, county boards of supervisors are authorized to exempt real property with a base year value, as adjusted by an annual inflation factor, of $10,000 ($5,000 prior to 2010) or less. (Sec. 7, Art. XIII, Cal. Const.; Sec. 155.20, Rev. & Tax. Code) This exemption is inapplicable to property that is enforceably restricted and a higher threshold is applicable to certain possessory interests (see below).

The Board of Equalization Assessors' Handbook contains manuals related to personal property and fixtures, possessory interests, and golf courses. (AH 504, Assessment of Personal Property and Fixtures, (10-02), AH 510, Assessment of Taxable Possessory Interests, (12-02), and AH 515, Assessment of Golf Courses, (01-83))

Real property includes the land; any right to possession of land; ownership or claim to ownership of land; all standing timber, whether planted or of natural growth and whether or not owned by the owner of the land; all mines, minerals, and quarries on the land; and any rights or privileges that are appurtenant to standing timber, mines, minerals, and quarries. (Sec. 104, Rev. & Tax. Code; Reg. 121, 18 CCR) Real property also includes any improvements on the land.

Classification of property as real property is discussed at ¶20-105. Valuation of real property is discussed at ¶20-640.

• *Improvements*

Improvements include buildings, structures, fixtures, and fences erected on or affixed to land. (Sec. 105, Rev. & Tax. Code; Reg. 122, 18 CCR) Also defined as improvements are fruit and nut-bearing trees, ornamental trees, and vines that are not naturally growing on the land and not specifically exempt from taxation. (see ¶20-115 Agriculture)

Fixtures.—Fixtures are items of tangible property that were originally personalty but that are classified as realty for property tax purposes because they are indefinitely physically or constructively annexed to realty. A three-pronged test determines whether fixtures are classified as real or personal property:

— actual annexation; (the manner in which an item is affixed to realty)

— appropriation or adaptation; (the manner in which the item is used) and

— intention. (whether the property is intended to be permanently or temporarily affixed to the realty)

An item is intended to remain "annexed indefinitely" if it is intended to remain annexed until it is worn out or superseded by a more suitable replacement, or until the purpose to which the realty is devoted has been accomplished or materially altered. Property that is not physically annexed to realty is constructively annexed if it is a necessary, integral, or working part of the realty. (Reg. 122.5, 18 CCR)

A California regulation provides specific examples to illustrate how specific items may be classified. (Reg. 124, 18 CCR)

Fixtures added to or removed from real property must be included in the annual property statement. (Sec. 75.15, Rev. & Tax. Code)

• *Possessory interests*

Possessory interests are included in the definition of "taxable real property." (Sec. 104, Rev. & Tax. Code) A possessory interest is an independent, durable, and exclusive right to possess or use land or the improvements on land without ownership of the land or the improvements (Sec. 107, Rev. & Tax. Code; Reg. 20, 18 CCR) "Taxable possessory interests" are possessory interests in publicly-owned real property, excluding possessory interests in real property located in federal enclaves. (Reg. 20, 18 CCR) Possessory interests are assessed to lessees or other users on the same basis or percentage used to assess other tangible property. (Sec. 107.1, Rev. & Tax. Code)

Taxable possessory interests include employee housing (other than military housing) owned by a public agency, a right to cut standing timber on public lands, a right to graze livestock on public lands, and rights of possession of public property at such places as harbors, marinas factories, airports, golf courses, recreation areas, parks, and stadiums. (Reg. 28, 18 CCR)

Possessory interests in taxable property owned by local governments are assessed and taxed California property taxes in the same manner as any other taxable possessory interest, excluding those that result from the possessor having a lease for agricultural purposes. A lease is a lease for agricultural purposes if it is for the purpose of the production or husbandry of plants or animals, including:

— gardening;

— horticulture;

— fruit growing; and

— the storage and marketing of agricultural products.

(Reg. 29, 18 CCR)

If, on the lien date, the total assessed value of all possessory interests in an appraisal unit of taxable government-owned real property exceeds the constitutional limitation amount, the assessed values are either reduced or ratably reduced, depending on the number of possessory interests in the appraisal unit, until the assessed value no longer exceeds the limitation amount. (Reg. 29, 18 CCR)

"Independent," "durable," and "exclusive" defined.—Possession or use is "independent" if the holder has the ability to exercise authority and control over the management or operation of the property and is sufficiently autonomous to constitute more than a mere agent of the owner. (Sec. 107, Rev. & Tax. Code; Reg. 20, 18 CCR) In order to be "sufficiently autonomous," the holder's authority and control over the management or operation of the property must be separate and apart from the policies, statutes, ordinances, rules, and regulations of the public owner of the real property. (Reg. 20, 18 CCR) Possession or use is "durable" if it applies to a determinable period and there is a reasonable certainty that the possession or use will continue for that period. (Sec. 107, Rev. & Tax. Code; Reg. 20, 18 CCR)

Finally, a possessory interest is "exclusive" if the holder enjoys exclusive use of the property, together with the ability to legally exclude from possession any others who may interfere with that enjoyment. The presence of occasional trespassers or occasional interfering users will not be sufficient in itself to make a use nonexclusive. (Reg. 20, 18 CCR)

For taxable possessory interests, "possession" of real property means actual physical occupation of the property pursuant to rights not granted to the general public. (Reg. 20, 18 CCR) It requires more than incidental benefit from the public property. Continuity of possession or use of the land or improvement is required to establish a taxable possessory interest (Reg. 22, 18 CCR), but such use or possession may be by multiple users for only certain portions of the time (as by professional sports teams) or by concurrent users that do not interfere with each other (as grazing cattle on the same land). (Reg. 20, 18 CCR)

Exemption for specified low value interests.—County boards of supervisors are authorized to exempt possessory interests in real property with a base year value, as adjusted by an annual inflation factor, of $10,000 ($5,000 prior to 2010) or less. (Sec. 7, Art. XIII, Cal. Const.; Sec. 155.20, Rev. & Tax. Code) However, the $10,000 threshold is increased to $50,000 in the case of a possessory interest, for a temporary and transitory use, in a publicly owned convention, cultural facility, or publicly owned fairground or fairground facility. (Sec. 155.20, Rev. & Tax. Code)

Effective July 12, 2019, the $50,000 limit that a county board of supervisors may exempt from property tax is changed as follows:

- for lien dates January 1, 2020 through January 1, 2024, the $50,000 limit applies to any possessory interest; and

- beginning with the January 1, 2025 lien date, the $50,000 level reverts back to the prior language and will be limited to possessory interests for a temporary and transitory use in a publicly owned fairground, fairground facility, convention facility, or cultural facility.

(Sec. 155.20, Rev. & Tax. Code; *Letter to County Assessors, No. 2019/023*, California State Board of Equalization, August 19, 2019)

As a result, for the period beginning July 12, 2019 and ending December 31, 2024, a county board of supervisors may change its low value ordinance or resolution to apply the $50,000 limit to all possessory interests. (Sec. 155.20, Rev. & Tax. Code; *Letter to County Assessors, No. 2019/023*, California State Board of Equalization, August 19, 2019)

A "publicly owned convention or cultural facility" for purposes of this exemption is a publicly owned convention center, civic auditorium, theater, assembly hall, museum, or other civic building that is used primarily for staging:

— conventions, trade and consumer shows, or civic and community events;

— live theater, dance, or musical productions;

— artistic, historic, technological, or educational exhibits.

Valuation of possessory interests in tax-exempt property.—A possessory interest in tax-exempt property, except one created by an oil and gas lease, is valued by deducting from annual future gross income the annual estimated expenses for operation and maintenance, as well as amounts deposited in a replacement reserve and capitalizing the resulting amount at a rate that considers risk, interest, and taxes for the remaining life of the interest under the rules set forth in *DeLuz Homes v. San Diego*, 45 Cal2d 546, 290 P2d 544 (1955). The entire period remaining for the interest is used despite the possibility that the interest may be terminated by the tax-exempt remainderman.

The *DeLuz* decision caused some assessors to reassess possessory interests and to apply the formula of the California Supreme Court. This resulted in inequities among the counties that the legislature sought to remedy by ratifying the assessment actions taken prior to the 1955 decision and making the *DeLuz* formula applicable only to subsequent years. (Sec. 107.1, Rev. & Tax. Code)

The State Board of Equalization has issued a comprehensive regulation that set forth the manner in which assessments of pre- and post-*DeLuz* possessory interests are to be made. The regulation authorizes the use, in determining the present value of the future interest of a possessory interest, of either an income capitalization, comparative value, or cost approach, suitably adjusted to reflect the term of the interest. A regulation defines the taxable value of a possessory interest as the sum of the value of all property rights in land and improvements held by the possessor, undiminished by any obligation to pay rent or to retire debt secured by the possessory interest. (Reg. 21, 18 CCR)

The *DeLuz* decision also has implications for the valuation of oil and gas leases on land owned by exempt entities. See ¶ 20-270 Mining, Oil, and Gas Properties.

Governmental entities that are owners of real property or improvements in which possessory interests are created are required to notify their lessees or users of any potential tax liability. (Sec. 107.6, Rev. & Tax. Code)

Possessory interests renewed, extended, subleased, or assigned for any term must be appraised at their full value as of the date of renewal or extension or as of the date the sublessee or assignee obtains the right to occupancy or use of the property. An interest is considered renewed or extended when the term of possession originally agreed upon is lengthened by mutual consent or by the exercise of an option by either party to the agreement. The term of possession for valuation purposes is defined as the "reasonably anticipated (stated) term of possession," unless there is clear and convincing evidence that the public owner and private possessor have modified the stated term based on a mutual understanding or agreement that the term of possession is shorter or longer than that stated. In addition, when there is no stated term of possession, the reasonably anticipated term of possession is determined using certain specified criteria based on the intent of the public owner and private possessor and the intent of similarly situated parties. Finally, a month-to-month taxable possessory interest, a taxable interest without fixed term, or a taxable possessory interest of unspecified duration are taxable possessory interests with no stated term of possession. (Reg. 21, 18 CCR)

Cable franchise or video service systems.—The right of a cable operator or a video service provider to place wires, conduits, and appurtenances along or across public streets, rights-of-way, or public easements is a taxable possessory interest. (Sec. 107.7, Rev. & Tax. Code) Although the operator's or provider's intangible rights or assets, including franchises or licenses to construct, operate, and maintain a cable television system, are not subject to property taxation, an assumption of their value may be made to facilitate valuing the possessory interest. (*County of Stanislaus v. County of Stanislaus Assessment Appeals Board and Post-Newsweek Cable, Inc.*, 206 CalApp3d 482 (1988); op on reh'g, 213 CalApp3d 1445 (1989))

The preferred method of valuation of either a cable possessory interest or a video possessory interest is to capitalize the annual economic rent, which is that portion of the franchise fee that is determined to be payment for the remaining or anticipated term of the franchise or license, using an appropriate capitalization rate. (Sec. 107.7, Rev. & Tax. Code)

Lease-leaseback of public property.—In a situation involving the lease-leaseback of publicly-owned real property, the interests possessed by the lessee (such as the possession of, claim to, or right to the possession of land) pursuant to the lease are not "independent" rights if certain lease terms exist. (Sec. 107.8, Rev. & Tax. Code) Accordingly, such interests are not possessory interests and are not treated as taxable real property.

The interests are not independent if the lessee:

— is obligated simultaneously to sublease the property to the public owner for all or substantially all of the lease period;

— may not control the management or operation of the property separately and apart from the policies, statutes, ordinances, rules and regulations of the public owner;

— provides as part of the sublease that the public owner has the right to repurchase all of the lessee's rights in the lease; and

— cannot receive rent or other amounts from the public owner under the sublease in which the present value of such amounts, at the time the lease is entered into, exceeds the present value of the rent or other amounts payable by the lessee under the lease.

(Sec. 107.8, Rev. & Tax. Code)

Privatized military housing.—A possession or use of land or improvements is not independent and, therefore, does not give rise to a taxable possessory interest for California property tax purposes if the possession or use is pursuant to a contract, including, but not limited to, a long-term lease, for the private construction, renovation, rehabilitation, replacement, management, or maintenance of housing for active duty military personnel and their dependents, and all of the following requirements are met:

— the housing is on a military facility under military control (i.e., a military base that restricts public access to the military base);

— all services normally provided by a municipality are required to be purchased from the military facility or a provider designated by the military;

— the contractor is not given the right and ability to exercise any significant authority and control over the management or operation of the military family housing, separate and apart from the rules and regulations of the military;

— the military controls the distribution of revenues from the project to the contractor;

— the military sets the rents charged to military personnel or their dependents for the housing units;

— the military prescribes rules and regulations governing the use and occupancy of the property;

— tenants are designated by a military housing agency;

— evictions from the housing units are subject to the military justice system;

— the military has the authority to remove or bar persons from the property;

— the military may impose access restrictions on the contractor and its tenants;

— the number of units, the number of bedrooms per unit, and the unit mix are set by the military, and may not be changed by the contractor without prior approval by the military;

— the private contractor is allowed only a predetermined profit or fee for constructing the military family housing;

— the military approves the financing for the project selected by the contractor/developer;

— the construction is performed under military guidelines in the same manner as construction that is performed by the military;

— the housing is constructed, renovated, rehabilitated, remodeled, replaced, or managed under the federal Military Housing Privatization Initiative (MHPI), or any successor law; and

— any property tax savings resulting from this provision inure to the benefit of the residents of the military housing through improvements such as a child care center provided by the contractor.

(Sec. 107.4(c), Rev. & Tax. Code)

However, this section does not apply to any military housing unit managed by a private contractor that is rented to a tenant who is an unaffiliated member of the general public (not a current member of the military). The contractor must notify the assessor by February 15 each year of any housing units rented to unaffiliated members of the general public as of the immediately preceding lien date, and the contractor is responsible for any property taxes on those units. (Sec. 107.4(b), Rev. & Tax. Code)

Placement on secured roll.—Any possessory interest may, in the discretion of the county board of supervisors, be considered as sufficient security for the payment of any taxes levied on such interest and may be placed on the secured roll. (Sec. 107, Rev. & Tax. Code)

Oil and gas leases are classified as a special kind of possessory interest and are placed on the secured roll, but the tax may be collected using the procedures available for collecting unsecured taxes. (see ¶20-270 Mining, Oil, and Gas Properties)

[¶20-330] Utilities

The State Board of Equalization (BOE) assesses property owned by public utilities in the same manner as other property. (Sec. 19, Art. XIII, Cal. Const.) The Constitution defines a public utility as a line, plant, or system for the transportation of people or property, for the transmission of telephone or telegraph messages, for the production, generation, transmission, or distribution of electricity, water, heat, and light, or for the provision of wharfages directly or indirectly to common carriers. (Sec. 3, Art. XII, Cal. Const.) An electric generation facility is state assessed if the facility was constructed pursuant to a certificate of public convenience and necessity issued by the California Public Utilities Commission to the company that presently owns the facility or the company owning the facility is a state assessee for reasons other than its ownership of the generation facility or its ownership of pipelines, flumes, canals, ditches, or aqueducts lying within two or more counties. (Reg. 905, 18 CCR)

The Board of Equalization *Assessors' Handbook* includes a manual relating to state-assessed property, including utility properties, and a manual relating to water companies. (State Assessment Manual, (03-03) and AH 542, Assessment Of Water Companies And Water Rights, (12-00))

Beginning with the California property tax assessment lien date for the 2003 tax year, the California State Board of Equalization (BOE) is required to assess an electric generation facility if the facility has a generating capacity of 50 megawatts or more and is owned or used by an electrical corporation as defined by Sec. 218 of the Public Utilities Code. (Reg. 905, 18 CCR;Sec. 721.5, Rev. & Tax. Code) The BOE may assess a company that is a state assessee for reasons other than ownership of pipelines, flumes, canals, ditches, or aqueducts lying within two or more counties. (Reg. 905, 18 CCR)

An "electric generation facility" does not include a qualifying small power production facility, a qualifying cogeneration facility, or, beginning January 1, 2018. a facility producing power from other than a conventional power source that is an exempt wholesale generator, as defined under federal law. (Sec. 721.5, Rev. & Tax. Code; Reg. 905, 18 CCR)

Property tax revenues from these facilities are allocated entirely to the county in which the facility is located. These revenues are allocated in the same percentage shares as revenues derived from locally assessed property among the jurisdictions in which the property is located. (Sec. 100.9, Rev. & Tax. Code) However, beginning with that fiscal year for plant and associated equipment placed in service by a public utility after 2006 (qualified property), the assessed value shall be allocated entirely to the county in which the qualified property is located. Revenues from the qualified property will be allocated among the county, certain special districts, and school entities in the same shares as derived from the utility in the prior fiscal year. Of the remaining revenues, the city in which the qualified property is located will receive 90% and the citty or the water district that provides water service to the property will receive the remaining 10%. All other entities that formerly would have received a share of the utility's property tax will no longer do so. (Sec. 100.95, Rev. & Tax. Code)

The legislature may prescribe additional classes of public utilities. Certain one-way paging companies are assessed by county assessors, not the BOE. (*Letter to County Assessors, No. 96/25*, BOE, March 28, 1996)

• *Assessment*

In assessing the property of a public utility, the BOE may use the principle of unit valuation in valuing properties that are operated as a unit in a primary function of the assessee. When so valued, such properties are known as "unitary property." (Sec. 723, Rev. & Tax. Code)

Besides unitary property, there are two other classes of public utility property: "nonunitary properties," which are properties that are not valued by the use of the principle of unit valuation (Sec. 723, Rev. & Tax. Code), and "operating nonunitary properties," which are properties that the assessee and its regulatory agency consider to be operating as a unit, but that the BOE considers not part of a unit in the primary function of the assessee. (Sec. 723.1, Rev. & Tax. Code) State-assessed property of regulated railway companies is classified into unitary and nonunitary. When valuing nonunitary property of a public utility, the BOE must consider current market value information of comparable properties provided by the assessor immediately prior to the BOE's appraisal of the public utility property. (Sec. 723, Rev. & Tax. Code)

The BOE gives notice prior to June 1 for unitary property assessments and prior to the last day of June for assessments made of nonunitary property assessments. (Sec. 731, Rev. & Tax. Code; Sec. 732, Rev. & Tax. Code; Reg. 904, 18 CCR) Each such notice must state the date and place where a petition for reassessment must be filed. (Sec. 731, Rev. & Tax. Code; Sec. 732, Rev. & Tax. Code; Sec. 733, Rev. & Tax. Code) Assessments of state-assessed property are made as of 12:01 a.m. on January 1 of each year. The property is assessed at its fair market or full value. (Sec. 722, Rev. & Tax. Code)

The assessed values determined by the BOE are allocated among the taxing jurisdictions in which the properties of the taxpayer are located and the tax rate for the taxing jurisdiction applied to the assessed value allocated to it. (Sec. 745, Rev. & Tax. Code) A single countywide tax rate area is required in each county for the assignment of the assessed value of unitary and operating nonunitary property of state assessees other than railroads. (Sec. 100, Rev. & Tax. Code)

Property of utilities not assessed initially may be the subject of an escape assessment by the BOE. (Sec. 861 Rev. & Tax. Code—Sec. 868, Rev. & Tax. Code)

• *Property tax statements*

State assessees must file property tax statements by March 1 if the BOE's request is mailed before January 1 or else within 60 days after the request is mailed if the request is mailed on or after January 1. (Sec. 830, Rev. & Tax. Code; Sec. 826 Rev. & Tax. Code—Sec. 829, Rev. & Tax. Code; Reg. 901, 18 CCR) The BOE may extend the time for filing portions of the property statement on a showing of good cause. For any part of the statement relating to the development of the unit value of the operating property, an extension not exceeding 45 days may be granted by the BOE, and for any part of the statement that lists or describes specific operating property or describes specific nonunitary property, an extension not exceeding 30 days may be granted by the BOE. If a 45- or 30-day extension is granted, an additional 15-day extension may be granted on the showing of extraordinary circumstances that prevented the filing of the statement within the first extension. (Sec. 830.1, Rev. & Tax. Code)

A special rule applies to the filing of corrected statements because of changes in tax rates. The BOE provides a service, to which taxpayers may subscribe, that advises assessees of any changes in tax rates throughout the state. Corrected statements must be filed by May 30 if the assessee receives notice from the BOE before May 1 of a tax rate change. If information is received by the taxpayer after May 1, the corrected property statement must be filed no later than 60 days after the notice of change has been mailed. (Sec. 830, Rev. & Tax. Code)

Penalties.—A penalty of 10% of the value of the property is imposed for failure to file a property statement, plus an additional penalty of 25% of the assessed value of the estimated assessment if there is a fraudulent or willful attempt to evade a tax. A willful failure to file a property statement is deemed a willful attempt to evade the tax. Penalties may not exceed $20 million. (Sec. 830, Rev. & Tax. Code)

A limitation is placed on the imposition of further penalties if a claim for refund of the penalty is filed within three months after the due date of the second installment of taxes and the assessee initiates a superior court action for refund of the penalty within one year of the filing of the claim for refund. In such case, the BOE must not, until the year after a final decision of the court, add any further penalties to any subsequent assessments for failure to comply with any subsequent request seeking information or data with respect to the same issues set forth in the claim for refund. The "same issue" is defined to mean the type of information that was the subject of the disputed request for information the state assessee failed to answer and therefore suffered the penalty he or she seeks refunded for his failure to answer. (Sec. 830, Rev. & Tax. Code)

Even after a final decision of the court on the suit for refund, a penalty may be imposed for a failure to comply with a request for information on the same issue only if the request deals with assessments made after the final decision of the court. (Sec. 830, Rev. & Tax. Code)

• *Franchises*

Real property interests not otherwise exempt from taxation or assessment that are created by special franchises issued by state and local governments to public utilities are taxable to the same extent as other public utility property. (Sec. 23154, Rev. & Tax. Code) Utility franchises, although a form of intangible personal property, are not included in the definition of exempt intangible property. (Sec. 2, Art. XIII, Cal. Const.; Sec. 212, Rev. & Tax. Code) The value of intangible assets or rights must not enhance or be reflected in the value of a real property interest created by a special franchise, except that the real property interest may be valued by assuming the presence of intangible assets and rights necessary to put the interest to beneficial or productive use. (Sec. 23154, Rev. & Tax. Code)

See ¶ 20-310 Real Property for a discussion of the valuation of television cable companies' possessory interests rights-of-way, etc.

• *Intercounty pipeline rights-of-way*

CCH COMMENT: Land and rights-of-way through which intercounty pipelines run are subject to assessment by county assessors rather than the BOE. (*Southern Pacific Pipe Lines, Inc. v. Board of Equalization of the State of California, County of Los Angeles, et al.*, 14 CalApp4th 42, 17 CalRptr2d 345 (1993))

A county assessor must determine the assessed value in the county attributable to intercounty pipeline rights-of-way on the basis of a single, countywide parcel per taxpayer by combining the assessed values of each separate right-of-way interest, or segment thereof, of the taxpayer in the county. (Sec. 401.8, Rev. & Tax. Code) The aggregate assessed value of all locally-assessed intercounty pipeline rights-of-way must then be assigned to a single, countywide tax rate area. The tax rate to be applied must be determined in the manner provided for determining the tax rate applicable to the assessed value of unitary and operating nonunitary property of state assessees. (Sec. 100.01, Rev. & Tax. Code)

The value of an intercounty pipeline right-of-way for each tax year from 1984-85 through 2020-21 will be rebuttably presumed to be the full cash value of the right-of-way for that year, determined by using a 1975-76 base year value and annual adjustments for inflation. The 1975-76 base year value computation must comply with the following schedule:

— $20,000 per mile for high density (densely urban) property;

— $12,000 per mile for transitional density (urban) property; and

— $9,000 per mile for low density (valley-agricultural, grazing, mountain, or desert) property.

The density classifications that apply are those assigned by the BOE for the 1984-85 tax year or, if classifications were not assigned for the 1984-85 tax year, the classifications first assigned for a subsequent tax year. For valuation purposes, an "intercounty pipeline right-of-way" is an interest in publicly or privately owned real property through which or over which an intercounty pipeline is placed. However, any parcel or facility that was originally separately assessed by the BOE using a valuation method other than that discussed above is not an "intercounty pipeline right-of-way." (Sec. 401.10, Rev. & Tax. Code)

If a taxpayer owns multiple pipelines in the same right-of-way, an additional 50% of the value attributed to the right-of-way for the presence of the first pipeline must be added for each of the first two additional pipelines. If the BOE determines that a pipeline within a multiple pipeline right-of-way has been abandoned as a result of physical removal or blockage, the assessed value of the right-of-way that is attributable to the last pipeline will be reduced by at least 75% of the increase in assessed value that resulted from the recognition of that pipeline. If all of the pipelines within a multiple pipeline right-of-way have been abandoned as a result of physical removal or blockage, the assessed value of that right-of-way must be reduced to no more than 25% of the assessed value otherwise determined for the right-of-way for a single pipeline. (Sec. 401.10, Rev. & Tax. Code)

Notwithstanding any change in ownership, new construction, or decline in value occurring after March 1, 1975, if an assessor uses the above methodology to assign values to pipeline rights-of-way for any tax year from 1984-85 through 2020-21, the taxpayer may not challenge the right to assess the property, and the values determined by the assessor will be rebuttably presumed to be correct. (Sec. 401.10, Rev. & Tax. Code) County assessors are required to maintain for five calendar years records for each intercounty pipeline right-of-way interest, or segment thereof, located within the county and make the records with respect to any given pipeline right-of-way interest available to taxpayers upon request. (Sec. 401.8, Rev. & Tax. Code)

Appeals.—Appeals of the assessed value of intercounty pipeline right-of-way interests, or segments thereof, must be filed with respect to the assessed value of each separate right-of-way interest, or segment thereof, and not on the basis of the taxpayer's single, countywide parcel valuation. (Sec. 401.8, Rev. & Tax. Code)

Tax payments and refunds.—If taxes due with respect to an intercounty pipeline right-of-way are not paid within 45 days of billing by the tax collector, late payment penalties and interest will apply. (Sec. 401.11, Rev. & Tax. Code)

If taxes due on a local assessment of an intercounty pipeline right-of-way, calculated using the above methodology, are less than the taxes paid by the taxpayer for that year, the county must refund the difference. Simple interest at the county pool apportioned rate must be paid on any overpayment. (Sec. 401.11, Rev. & Tax. Code)

Settlement agreements.—The above provisions concerning the method of valuing intercounty pipeline rights-of-way (Sec. 401.10, Rev. & Tax. Code) and the requirements for payments and refunds of local assessments of pipeline rights-of-way (Sec. 401.11, Rev. & Tax. Code) do not abrogate, rescind, preclude, or otherwise affect any separate settlement agreement on the same subject matter that was entered into prior to June 28, 1996, between a county and a taxpayer. In the event of any conflict between a settlement agreement and the statutory provisions, the agreement will control. (Sec. 401.12, Rev. & Tax. Code)

• *Intracounty pipeline rights-of-way*

A county assessor must also determine the assessed value of pipelines and related rights-of-way that are located wholly within a county on the basis of a single, countywide parcel per taxpayer. The assessed value of each component or segment of those pipelines or rights-of-way must be combined, although the assessor is required to maintain a separate base year value for each component or segment. (Sec. 401.13, Rev. & Tax. Code)

[¶20-400]

RATES

[¶20-405] Rates of Tax

The county board of supervisors determines annually the rates of county and district taxes within the limitations imposed by the California Constitution and the statutes. (Sec. 2151, Rev. & Tax. Code; Sec. 29100, Govt. Code; Sec. 29101, Govt. Code; Sec. 29102, Govt. Code) The tax rates generally must be determined on or before October 3 of each year. (Sec. 29100, Govt. Code)

The county auditor then applies the tax rate to the assessed values shown on the assessment rolls. (Sec. 2152, Rev. & Tax. Code) The auditor may, if so ordered by the board of supervisors, round off the amount of taxes due for each installment of taxes. (Sec. 2152.5, Rev. & Tax. Code)

In computing tax rates, the exempt values for which the homeowners' property tax exemption is granted, together with the values of taxable property against which the taxes are levied, must be included in the base. (Sec. 16122, Govt. Code)

• *Average county tax rates*

The State Board of Equalization compiles average property tax rates in Table 14 of its Annual Reports. The BOE also maintains an archive of its Annual Reports.

• *Tax rate limitations*

The California Constitution (Proposition 13) limits the maximum tax on real property to 1% of the full cash value of that property. However, the Constitution provides that this limitation does not apply when a higher rate is required to pay interest and redemption charges for local government indebtedness approved by the voters prior to July 1, 1978, or, under a subsequent constitutional amendment, effective June 4, 1986, to pay for any local government bonded indebtedness incurred for the acquisition or improvement of real property when approved, on or after July 1, 1978, by at least two-thirds of the votes cast on the proposition. (Sec. 1, Art. XIII A, Cal. Const.)

The statute allows a county to levy a tax rate of $4.00 per $100 of assessed valuation when the property is assessed at 25% of its full cash value, as it was prior to and including the 1980-81 fiscal year, and at an equivalent rate when it is assessed at 100% of its full cash value, as it has been assessed since the 1981-1982 fiscal year. (Sec. 93, Rev. & Tax. Code; Sec. 135, Rev. & Tax. Code; Sec. 20, Art. XIII, Cal. Const.) For these purposes, "tax rate" means a rate expressed as a percentage of full value. (Sec. 135, Rev. & Tax. Code) A property tax rate in excess of the rate permitted by statute may be levied to produce needed revenues to make annual payments on the interest and principal on bonded indebtedness for the acquisition or improvement of real property, when approved by two-thirds of the voters on or after June 4, 1986. (Sec. 93, Rev. & Tax. Code) The county auditor, in computing tax rates on the unsecured tax roll, may add to the 1% tax rate the rate levied on the prior year's secured tax roll for indebtedness approved by the voters prior to July 1, 1978, and for bonded indebtedness for the acquisition or improvement of real property approved by two-thirds of the voters on or after June 4, 1986. (Sec. 2237.5, Rev. & Tax. Code)

Local agencies must report to the State Controller any property tax levies at a rate in excess of the 1% limitation. (Sec. 2237.2, Rev. & Tax. Code)

Prohibition against new taxes.—To increase revenue, the state may increase tax rates or change the methods of tax computation with the consent of two-thirds of the members of both houses of the legislature, except that no new *ad valorem* taxes on real property or transaction taxes on the sales of real property may be imposed. (Sec. 3, Art. XIII A, Cal. Const.) Counties, cities, and special districts may adopt special taxes, subject to approval by two-thirds of the voters, but may not impose any additional *ad valorem* taxes on real property or transaction taxes on the sales of real property. (Sec. 4, Art. XIII A, Cal. Const.)

Personal property tax rate.—Because the California Constitution provides that the tax rate on personal property cannot be higher than the rate on real property, the Proposition 13 tax rate limitation applies indirectly to personal property taxes. (Sec. 2, Art. XIII, Cal. Const.) In addition, personal property on the unsecured roll is taxed at the rate applied in the preceding tax year to property on the secured roll. (Sec. 12, Art. XIII, Cal. Const.) Therefore, since all taxable property is on either the secured roll or the unsecured roll, the Proposition 13 tax rate limitation of 1% is indirectly applicable to taxable personal property.

Any additions to the 1% tax rate to pay for local government indebtedness also apply to taxable personal property on the unsecured roll in the year after the additional rates are first applied to property on the secured roll.

¶20-405

Intangibles tax rate.—The California Constitution provides that the tax on any interest in notes, debentures, shares of capital stock, bonds, solvent credits, deeds of trust, or mortgages may not exceed 0.4% of the full value. (Sec. 2, Art. XIII, Cal. Const.)

• *Special tax rates*

The statutes provide special tax rates for certain types of property that are not directly subject to the constitutional limitation on real property tax rates.

Property on unsecured tax roll.—Personal property, possessory interests in land, and taxable improvements located on tax-exempt land for which there is inadequate security in real property are taxed at the rate in effect for the last lien date for property of the same kind on the secured tax roll. (Sec. 12, Art. XIII, Cal. Const.; Sec. 2905, Rev. & Tax. Code) The California Supreme Court has upheld the applicability of the prior year's tax rate for property on the secured tax roll to unsecured property under the provisions of Art. XIII A of the California Constitution (Proposition 13). (*Board of Supervisors of San Diego County v. Lonergan*, 27 Cal3d 855, 616 P2d 802 (1980))

Escape assessments.—Escape assessments are taxed at the rate in effect for the fiscal year for which the assessment should have been made. (Sec. 2905, Rev. & Tax. Code; Sec. 506, Rev. & Tax. Code; Sec. 531, Rev. & Tax. Code; Sec. 534, Rev. & Tax. Code)

Assessment corrections.—If a correction in the assessment of property is made, the tax rate for the year for which the original assessment was made applies. (Sec. 4836.5, Rev. & Tax. Code)

[¶20-500]
EXEMPTIONS

[¶20-505] Exemptions in General

Some exemptions, such as the homeowner's exemption, must be specifically claimed by the taxpayer, while other exemptions are allowed on the basis of the assessor's appraisal of the property. Some exemptions are lost if no claim or affidavit of eligibility is filed with the assessor. (Sec. 6, Art. XIII, Cal. Const.) Other property loses only a portion of the available exemption if a claim is filed late but within a grace period. Most exemption claims must be filed by February 15, however, see the exemption-claim provisions relating to specific property or taxpayers in the paragraphs at which such property or taxpayers are discussed.

The State Board of Equalization is responsible for prescribing procedures and forms to implement property tax exemptions. (Sec. 251, Rev. & Tax. Code; Reg. 101, 18 CCR) A person who does not comply with required procedures forfeits the exemption. (Sec. 260, Rev. & Tax. Code)

Exemption claims and affidavits are timely filed with a taxing agency if they bear a post office cancellation mark of the due date or earlier date stamped on the envelope or on the document itself. (Sec. 166, Rev. & Tax. Code)

An assessor is required to retain documents containing information obtained from taxpayers with respect to the administration of the California homeowners' property tax exemption for six years. (Reg. 135, 18 CCR)

• *Notice of change in tax-exempt real property*

Owners of tax-exempt real property must report to the assessor within 60 days any transaction by which a lease, sublease, license, use permit, or other document conveying a right to use the property is created, renewed, subleased, or assigned. (Sec. 480.5, Rev. & Tax. Code) The requirement applies, however, only in those counties that elect to be subject to its provisions.

Sale of property receiving a tax exemption.—In the event that property receiving the college, cemetery, church, religious, exhibition, veterans' organization, tribal housing, or welfare exemption is sold or otherwise transferred, the exemption will cease to apply on the date of the sale or transfer. (Sec. 271.5, Rev. & Tax. Code)

• *Appeals*

The State Board of Equalization will hear petitions for, among other things, objections to findings of ineligibility for an organizational clearance certificate, denials of claims for supplemental clearance certificates, and claims for the veteran's organization exemption. (Reg. 5310, 18 CCR) Petitions relating to organizational clearance certificates, supplemental clearance certificates, veterans' organization exemption, and local assessment procedures become final 30 days after the date notice of the BOE's decision is mailed to the petition unless the petitioner files a petition for rehearing within that period. (Reg. 5345, 18 CCR)

[¶20-600]
VALUATION, ASSESSMENT, AND EQUALIZATION

[¶20-610] Valuation Procedures

All property subject to general property taxation in California is taxed at its full value. (Sec. 401, Rev. & Tax. Code) "Full value" is the fair market value, the full cash value, or such other standard as is required by the California Constitution or statutory provisions. (Sec. 110.5, Rev. & Tax. Code)

Under Proposition 13, the taxable value of most locally-assessed real property (other than restricted property) and taxable government lands is the lesser of:

— the adjusted base year value, or

— the full cash value on the lien date, accounting for any factors causing a decline in value.

(Sec. 1, Art. XIII A, Cal. Const.; Sec. 2, Art. XIII A, Cal. Const.; Sec. 51, Rev. & Tax. Code)

Personal property and state-assessed property, which are not subject to the value limitations of Proposition 13, are taxed at current fair market value each year (Sec. 401, Rev. & Tax. Code; Sec. 722, Rev. & Tax. Code; Reg. 2, 18 CCR)

• *Assessors' Handbook*

The Board of Equalization Assessors' Handbook includes a variety of manuals on general discussions of assessment procedures:

— AH 201, Assessment Roll Procedures;

— AH 215, Assessment Map Standards for Manual Systems;

— AH 501, Basic Appraisal;

— AH 502, Advanced Appraisal; and

— AH 503, Cash Equivalent Analysis.

• *Full cash value*

"Full cash value" (or "fair market value") is the amount of cash or its equivalent that property would bring at a sale in the open market when both the buyer and seller know of all the property's potential uses and purposes, and of all enforceable restrictions on such uses and purposes, neither party being able to take advantage of the other. (Sec. 110, Rev. & Tax. Code; Reg. 2, 18 CCR)

For real property, other than possessory interests, full cash value when the property is purchased is the purchase price paid, unless a preponderance of the evidence shows that the property would not have been transferred for that price in an open market transaction. (Sec. 110, Rev. & Tax. Code; Reg. 2, 18 CCR)

There is a rebuttable presumption that the purchase price is the full cash value if transaction terms were negotiated at arm's length between a knowledgeable transferor and transferee, neither of whom could take advantage of the exigencies of the other. (Sec. 110, Rev. & Tax. Code) The presumption may be rebutted by evidence that the full cash value deviates from the purchase price by more than 5%. (Reg. 2, 18 CCR)

The presumption does not apply if:

— purchase consideration consists in whole or in part of ownership interests in a legal entity (e.g., shares of stock); or

— the taxpayer fails to provide information concerning the arm's-length nature of the transaction, as required by the State Board of Equalization in the statement of change in ownership. (Sec. 110, Rev. & Tax. Code, Reg. 2, 18 CCR)

There is an additional rebuttable presumption that the purchase price of property encumbered by an improvement bond lien reflects the value of improvements financed by bond proceeds. Assessors may overcome this presumption if a preponderance of the evidence establishes that the purchase price does not reflect all or a portion of the value of the improvements. (Sec. 110, Rev. & Tax. Code)

The value of intangible assets and rights relating to the going concern value of a business or the exclusive nature of a concession, franchise, or similar agreement must not enhance or be reflected in the full cash value of taxable property. With respect to properties operated and valued as a unit, the value of intangible assets and rights that are a part of the unit must be omitted from the unit's assessed value. However, valuation may assume the presence of intangible assets or rights necessary for beneficial or productive use of the property. Moreover, the value of real property must reflect intangible attributes directly related to the property, such as zoning and location. (Sec. 110, Rev. & Tax. Code)

• *Base year value of real property*

Under Proposition 13, the base year value of real property, including possessory interests in real property, is the full cash value of the property as shown on the assessment roll for the 1975-1976 tax year, unless the property is purchased, is newly constructed, or changes ownership after the 1975 tax lien date. (Sec. 2, Art. XIII A, Cal. Const.; Sec. 110.1, Rev. & Tax. Code; Reg. 460, 18 CCR)

The base year value of real property is subject to annual adjustments for inflation, with increases limited, under Proposition 13, to a maximum of 2% per year. (Sec. 2, Art. XIII A, Cal. Const.; Sec. 51, Rev. & Tax. Code; Sec. 110.1, Rev. & Tax. Code)

The inflation factor for the 2020 assessment roll is 1.02. (*Letter to County Assessors, No. 2019/050*, California State Board of Equalization, December 27, 2019)

The base year value may also be reduced to reflect substantial damage, destruction, or other factors causing a decline in value. (Sec. 2, Art. XIII A, Cal. Const.)

New construction.—For property constructed after the 1975 lien date, the base year value is its value on the date on which construction is completed. (Sec. 110.1, Rev. & Tax. Code; Sec. 50, Rev. & Tax. Code)

Change in ownership.—For property purchased or changing ownership after the 1975 lien date, the property's value on the date of purchase or change in ownership is its base year value.

COMPLIANCE NOTE: Approval of Proposition 19 at November 3, 2020, general election.—California voters approved Proposition 19, which was on the ballot in California on November 3, 2020, as a legislatively referred constitutional amendment. The ballot measure proposed an amendment to the California Constitution that added the "Home Protection for Seniors, Severely Disabled, Families, and Victims of Wildfire or Natural Disasters Act" to Article XIIIA.

Among other provisions and operative April 1, 2021, the approved measure allows homeowners who are over 55, severely disabled, or the victim of a wildfire or natural disaster to transfer their primary residence's property tax base year value to a replacement residence that is acquired or newly constructed within two years of the sale of the original primary residence. (Sec. 2.1(b), Art. XIII A, Cal. Const.)

In addition, the constitutional amendment:

— allows eligible homeowners to transfer their property tax assessments anywhere within California and allows tax assessments to be transferred to a more expensive home with an upward adjustment;

— increases the number of times that persons over 55 years old or with severe disabilities can transfer their tax assessments from one to three;

— operative February 16, 2021, replaces the existing property tax exclusion with a new exclusion for a transfer of a family home between parents and children and, under limited circumstances, between grandparents and grandchildren (Sec. 2.1(c), Art. XIII A, Cal. Const.); and

— allocates additional revenue or net savings resulting from the ballot measure to wildfire agencies and counties.

Proposition 19 added Sections Sec. 2.1, Art. XIII A, Cal. Const., Sec. 2.2, Art. XIII A, Cal. Const., and Sec. 2.3, Art. XIII A, Cal. Const. to Article XIII A of the California Constitution. Although Proposition 19 was approved effective November 3, 2020, it is likely that the state legislature will need to amend certain statutory code sections to reflect these changes. (*State Ballot Measures—Statewide Results*, California Secretary of State, November 4, 2020; as proposed by Ch. 31 (A.C.A. 11), Laws 2020, effective November 3, 2020, upon approval of Proposition 19 at the November 3, 2020, general election, and operative as noted)

The California State Board of Equalization (BOE) provides guidance regarding Proposition 19. (*Letter to County Assessors, No. 2020/061*, California State Board of Equalization, December 11, 2020, ¶ 407-387)

• *Transfers for value before escape assessment*

If real property that is the subject of an escape assessment has been transferred for value or has been encumbered for value after July 1 of the year in which the property escaped assessment, the escape assessment and the taxes due do not become a lien on the property, but are entered on the unsecured tax roll in the name of the person who would have been the assessee if the assessment had been properly made. The tax rate imposed on such assessee is the rate for secured property for the year in which the assessment should have been made. (Sec. 531.2, Rev. & Tax. Code)

A county's board of supervisors may adopt a resolution providing for proration of property taxes. In that case, when realty has been transferred to a bona fide purchaser for value after July 1 of either the year of escape or the year in which the property should have been assessed, taxes resulting from escape assessments must be prorated between the property's purchaser and the person who would have been the assessee if the change in ownership had not occurred. If the property has changed hands more than once during the year, each owner of record is liable for a pro rata share of the taxes assessed. (Sec. 531.2, Rev. & Tax. Code)

If real property has been incorrectly granted a homeowners' exemption and is transferred to a purchaser for value between the lien date and the next succeeding July 1 of the calendar year of the assessment year, and the claimant of the homeowners' exemption is not the purchaser, any penalty or interest imposed because of the escape assessment is forgiven. (Sec. 531.6, Rev. & Tax. Code)

• *Listing of property on assessment rolls*

After the county assessor has determined the assessed value of taxable property, the value is entered on the local assessment roll opposite the name of the assessee. (Sec. 601, Rev. & Tax. Code)

Land and improvements are listed separately on the assessment roll (Sec. 607, Rev. & Tax. Code; Sec. 608, Rev. & Tax. Code), as are personal property and possessory interests. (Sec. 602, Rev. & Tax. Code)

Taxable improvements on land that is exempt from taxation are listed on the assessment roll as any other real estate, but these improvements are not a lien against the exempt land. (Sec. 609, Rev. & Tax. Code)

When a separate assessment is made of mining and mineral rights and the land itself, the words "mining rights" or "mineral rights" on the assessment roll include the right to enter the land for exploration, development, and production of minerals. (Sec. 607.5, Rev. & Tax. Code)

After tax-defaulted property is assessed, it is entered on the assessment roll. (Sec. 614, Rev. & Tax. Code)

When land is situated in multiple revenue districts, each part in each district is separately assessed. (Sec. 606, Rev. & Tax. Code)

However, when the same person owns two or more contiguous parcels comprising a tract of land and the full value of any parcel is less than $5,000, the parcel may be combined with the contiguous parcel with the greatest assessed valuation. Also, when the same person owns two or more contiguous parcels comprising a tract of land and the tract of land is used for a single-family residence and constitutes 15,000 square feet or less, the smallest parcel may be combined with the largest contiguous parcel. The assessor may not combine parcels into a single assessment when any of the parcels has been declared to be tax-defaulted for delinquent taxes. (Sec. 455, Rev. & Tax. Code)

When a person has succeeded in requesting separate valuation of a parcel of property that has been assessed as part of a larger parcel, the new valuation is entered on the assessment roll. (Sec. 2824, Rev. & Tax. Code)

County assessors may aggregate all leased personal property located in a county that is assessed against one taxpayer and place a single assessment for such property on the tax roll even if there are different tax rates in the county. (Sec. 623, Rev. & Tax. Code; Reg. 204, 18 CCR)

Assessees.—Once described on the assessment roll, land need not be described a second time, but any person wanting to be assessed for it may have his or her name inserted along with the assessee's name. (Sec. 610, Rev. & Tax. Code)

When a person is assessed as agent, trustee, bailee, guardian, conservator, executor, or administrator, the representative designation is added to his or her name; the assessment is entered separately on the assessment roll from his or her individual assessment. (Sec. 612, Rev. & Tax. Code)

If the assessor knows the name of an absent owner or the name appears of record in the office of the county recorder, the property is assessed to such owner; otherwise, the property is assessed to unknown owners. (Sec. 611, Rev. & Tax. Code)

Mistakes in the name of the owner of property do not invalidate an assessment (Sec. 613, Rev. & Tax. Code), nor does an omission of the details of the personal property assessed. (Sec. 602, Rev. & Tax. Code)

Procedure after completion of assessment roll.—The assessment roll must be completed annually by July 1. (Sec. 616, Rev. & Tax. Code) The "assessment year" is the period beginning with a lien date and ending immediately prior to the succeeding lien date. (Sec. 118, Rev. & Tax. Code)

The assessor prepares an index to the local roll under the names of the assessees and delivers the index to the tax collector (Sec. 615, Rev. & Tax. Code) and the roll itself to the county auditor. (Sec. 617, Rev. & Tax. Code)

The auditor:

— enters on the roll the total valuation of each kind of property and the total valuation of all property (Sec. 1646, Rev. & Tax. Code);

— corrects the roll to reflect any changes made by the county board of supervisors (Sec. 1646.1, Rev. & Tax. Code); and

— transmits the unsecured roll to the tax collector.

(Sec. 1651, Rev. & Tax. Code)

The auditor also:

— prepares valuation statements from the local roll (Sec. 1647, Rev. & Tax. Code; Sec. 1648, Rev. & Tax. Code); and

— transmits one statement to the controller and one statement to the board of supervisors. (Sec. 1649, Rev. & Tax. Code)

Secured and unsecured assessment rolls.—Assessment rolls are listings of taxable properties within a taxing jurisdiction, their assessed values, and the persons to whom they are taxable. "Current roll" is the assessment roll listing the property on which current taxes are a lien. (Sec. 125, Rev. & Tax. Code)

"Secured roll" is the part of the assessment roll listing state-assessed property, other real property, and personal property attached to real property, the taxes on which constitute a lien on real property sufficient to secure payment of the taxes. (Sec. 109, Rev. & Tax. Code)

The remainder of the roll is the "unsecured roll" consisting, generally, of personal property not taxed to the owner of the land, including possessory interests in real property. (Sec. 109, Rev. & Tax. Code; Sec. 134, Rev. & Tax. Code)

The "last equalized roll" is the entire assessment roll. (Sec. 2050 Rev. & Tax. Code—Sec. 2056, Rev. & Tax. Code)

A "machine-prepared roll" is an assessment roll prepared by electronic data-processing equipment, bookkeeping machine, typewriter, or other mechanical device. (Sec. 109.5, Rev. & Tax. Code; Sec. 618, Rev. & Tax. Code)

Regulations issued by the State Board of Equalization discuss requirements for contents of an assessment roll (Reg. 252, 18 CCR; Reg. 254, 18 CCR), and entering of penalties on a roll. (Reg. 261, 18 CCR)

• *Statements of property ownership*

Persons owning personal property (other than a mobile home or manufactured home) must file a property statement in any assessment year in which the aggregate cost of the property is $100,000 or more. (Sec. 441, Rev. & Tax. Code)

The statement must show all property owned, claimed, possessed, controlled, or managed by the person making the statement, including property that is leased under a conditional sales agreement. (Sec. 442, Rev. & Tax. Code; Sec. 445, Rev. & Tax. Code)

When the owner of any property is absent or unknown, the assessor must estimate the property's value. (Sec. 460, Rev. & Tax. Code) The assessor may also request the filing of a property statement for any personal property, or any real property. (Sec. 441, Rev. & Tax. Code)

Business personal property statements may be electronically filed and authenticated by means other than a traditional signature. (Sec. 441, Rev. & Tax. Code; Sec. 441.5, Rev. & Tax. Code)

Due dates.—Property statements must show information as of 12:01 a.m. on the lien date (Sec. 448, Rev. & Tax. Code), and must be filed with the assessor of the county in which the property is located between the January 1 lien date and 5 p.m. on April 1. (Sec. 441, Rev. & Tax. Code; Sec. 443, Rev. & Tax. Code) However, the assessor may appoint another final date before which the statement must be filed, but this date cannot be earlier than April 1.

The 10% late filing penalty applies to statements not filed by May 7. Every person required to file a property statement is permitted to amend the statement until May 31 of the year in which the property statement is due for errors or omissions not the result of willful intent to erroneously report. The late filing penalty does not apply to an amended statement received prior to May 31 provided the original statement is not subject to penalty. (Sec. 441, Rev. & Tax. Code)

For purposes of the oil, gas, and mineral extraction industry only, any information necessary to file a true, correct, and complete statement must be made available by the assessor, upon request, to the taxpayer by mail or at the office of the assessor by February 28. For each business day beyond February 28 that the information is unavailable, the filing deadline for the annual property statement is extended in that county by one business day for those statements affected by the delay. However, the filing deadline is not extended beyond June 1 or the first business day after June 1. (Sec. 441, Rev. & Tax. Code)

¶20-610

The date of the postmark as affixed by the U.S. Postal Service or the date certified by a bona fide private courier service on the envelope containing the application is controlling for purposes of determining the filing date. (Sec. 441, Rev. & Tax. Code) An unsigned property statement or mineral production report does not constitute a valid filing. (Reg. 172, 18 CCR)

Forms.—The State Board of Equalization (BOE) prescribes the forms to be used for filing property statements. (Sec. 452, Rev. & Tax. Code; Reg. 171, 18 CCR) A taxpayer may furnish the required information as either:

— an attachment to the property statement;

— an authenticated electronically filed property statement; or

— a property statement substantially similar to the property statement printed by the assessor that is signed by the taxpayer.

(Sec. 441.5(a), Rev. & Tax. Code)

However, the attachment must be in a format specified by the assessor, and one copy of the printed property statement must be executed by the taxpayer and carry appropriate reference to the attached data. (Sec. 441.5(a), Rev. & Tax. Code)

In regard to business personal property statements to be filed in the 2008 assessment year and each assessment year thereafter, the California State Board of Equalization (BOE) must prescribe that the property statement also include the following:

— a brief statement that notes the obligation to pay California use tax on taxable purchases for which sales tax was inapplicable;

— information regarding payment of use tax, which information may be limited to the BOE's phone number and a Web site address at which specific information and forms for use tax payment may be obtained; and

— a statement advising the taxpayer that information provided on a property statement may be shared with the BOE.

(Sec. 452(b), Rev. & Tax. Code)

Records and information.—Records and information relating to the property for which a statement is required must be made available to the assessor for his or her examination. This includes records regarding personal property that becomes a part of new construction performed by an owner-builder or owner-developer if that new construction is sold to a third party, constructed on behalf of a third party, or constructed for the purpose of selling the property to a third party. (Sec. 441, Rev. & Tax. Code; Sec. 454, Rev. & Tax. Code)

If a taxpayer fails to provide requested records or information to the assessor and subsequently introduces any such records or information at an assessment appeals board hearing, the assessor is entitled to a reasonable continuance. The assessor may also require a property owner to furnish a legal description of the owner's land. (Sec. 456, Rev. & Tax. Code—Sec. 459.5, Rev. & Tax. Code)

Any market data in the assessor's possession, and all documents relating to the appraisal and assessment of an assessee's property, must be made available to the assessee or the assessee's designated representative for inspection or copying when requested. The assessor must be reimbursed for any reasonable costs incurred. If an assessor fails to permit the requested inspection or copying of materials or information and subsequently introduces such materials or information at an assessment appeals board hearing, the assessee is entitled to a reasonable continuance. (Sec. 408, Rev. & Tax. Code)

The assessor may request any person in the county to file an affidavit showing the person's residence or place of business. (Sec. 453, Rev. & Tax. Code)

State-assessed property.—When requested by the BOE, a property statement must be filed pertaining to state-assessed property owned, claimed, possessed, used, controlled, or managed by the taxpayer. (Sec. 826, Rev. & Tax. Code) The property statement must contain information specifically required by the BOE. (Sec. 827, Rev.

& Tax. Code) Failure of the BOE to demand or secure a property statement does not invalidate any assessment. (Sec. 829, Rev. & Tax. Code)

When the BOE's request is mailed before the lien date, the property statement must be filed with the BOE by March 1. (Sec. 830, Rev. & Tax. Code; Reg. 901, 18 CCR) When the request is mailed on or after the first day of January following the lien date, the property statement must be filed within 60 days after the request is mailed. However, the BOE may extend the time for filing portions of the property statement as follows:

— an extension not exceeding 45 days for any part relating to the development of the unit value of operating property; and

— an extension not exceeding 30 days for any part listing or describing specific operating property or specific nonunitary property.

(Sec. 830.1, Rev. & Tax. Code)

An additional 15-day extension may be granted upon showing of extraordinary circumstances that prevent the filing of the statement within the first extension.

A person who subscribes to the BOE's tax rate area change service and who receives a change mailed between April 1 and May 1 must file a corrected statement no later than May 30 with respect to those parts of the property statement that are affected by the change. (Sec. 830, Rev. & Tax. Code)

Records pertinent to the valuation of state-assessed property must be made available to the BOE on request. (Sec. 828, Rev. & Tax. Code) The BOE may require county assessors to report any information in their possession concerning the value of state-assessed property. (Sec. 831, Rev. & Tax. Code)

All information required by the BOE or furnished in the property statement is confidential and not open for public inspection. (Sec. 833, Rev. & Tax. Code; Sec. 832, Rev. & Tax. Code) The BOE is required to keep all information received and may destroy such information only when seven years have elapsed since the lien date for the taxes for which the information was obtained. (Sec. 834, Rev. & Tax. Code)

[¶20-620] Income Method of Valuation

The income method of valuing property is used when the property was purchased in anticipation of deriving income. It is the preferred valuation method for land when reliable sales data for comparable land is not available. It is also the preferred method for improved real property and personal property when reliable sales data for comparable properties is not available and the cost method is unreliable because the property has suffered considerable physical depreciation or obsolescence or is substantially overimproved or underimproved, misplaced, or subject to legal restrictions on income that are unrelated to cost. (Reg. 8, 18 CCR)

The Board of Equalization Assessors' Handbook includes a manual on capitalization tables and formulas. (AH 505, Capitalization Formulas and Tables, (06-93))

The income method of valuation consists of determining the income that will be derived from the property and applying an appropriate capitalization rate to that income to determine its present value. The capitalization rate may be developed by:

(1) comparing the anticipated income from comparable properties with their sales prices, or

(2) deriving a weighted average of the capitalization rates for debt and for equity capital appropriate to the California money markets and adding increments for expenses that are excluded from outgo because they are based on the value that is being sought or the income that is being capitalized.

(Reg. 8, 18 CCR)

In valuing property for persons of low and moderate income who have received financing under Section 236 or Section 515 of the National Housing Act, the assessor must not consider as income any interest subsidy payments made by the federal government to a lender on such property. (Sec. 402.9, Rev. & Tax. Code) Similarly, assessors must exclude from income the benefit from federal and state low-income housing tax credits allocated by the California Tax Credit Allocation Committee when they value property under the income method of appraisal. (Sec. 402.95, Rev. & Tax. Code)

[¶20-625] Sales Method of Valuation

When reliable market data is available for real property, the preferred method of valuation is the comparable sales method. (Reg. 4, 18 CCR) Under this method, the value of the property is determined by reference to the sales prices at which comparable properties have recently sold. If this method is used, the sales selected must be sufficiently near in time to the valuation date and the properties must be located fairly close to each other and be sufficiently alike in character, size, situation, usability, and zoning or other legal restrictions on use. (Sec. 402.5, Rev. & Tax. Code) "Near in time to the valuation date" excludes any sale more than 90 days after the valuation date.

When valuing an unencumbered fee interest in property, the assessor must convert the sales price of comparable property encumbered with a debt or a lease to its unencumbered fee price equivalent. Sales prices must also be adjusted to reflect any change in price level for the type of property between the time the sales prices were negotiated and the date the subject property is valued. If there are differences in the physical attributes of the properties, the location of the properties, restrictions on the properties, and the income and amenities that the properties are expected to produce, the assessor must also make adjustments to reflect the differences. (Reg. 4, 18 CCR)

[¶20-630] Cost Method of Valuation

The replacement or reproduction cost method of valuation is preferred when neither reliable sales information nor income information is available and when the income from the property is not so regulated as to make the cost irrelevant. (Reg. 6, 18 CCR) This method is particularly appropriate in valuing construction work in progress (see ¶20-145, Construction Work in Progress) and other property that has suffered little physical deterioration, is not misplaced, is not overimproved or under-improved, and is not affected by other forms of depreciation or obsolescence.

The Board of Equalization *Assessors' Handbook* includes a manual on capitalization formulas and tables and one related to percent good and valuation factors. (AH 505, Capitalization Formulas and Tables, (06-93) and AH 581, Equipment and Fixtures Index, Percent Good and Valuation Factors, (Revised Annually—2018 version linked))

The county assessor is prohibited from averaging percent good factors applied to property acquired new and property acquired used when valuing tangible personal property or trade fixtures for California property tax purposes using the reproduction or replacement cost approach. However, the assessor may average these published factors, if the taxpayer's reported information does not disclose whether the property was first acquired new or used. In addition, when using percent good factors that include a minimum percent good, the county assessor must use minimum percent good factors that are determined in a manner that is supportable. (Sec. 401.16, Rev. & Tax. Code) See *Assessors' Handbook*, California State Board of Equalization (AH 581,

Equipment and Fixtures Index, Percent Good and Valuation Factors, (Revised Annually—2013 version linked)) for several tables of equipment index, percent good, and valuation factors that will aid in the mass appraisal of various types of personal property and fixtures.

The replacement cost method involves either:

(1) adjusting the property's original cost for price level changes and abnormalities or

(2) applying current prices to the property's labor and materials components, with appropriate additions for entrepreneurial services, interest on borrowed or owner-supplied funds, and other costs typically incurred in bringing the property to the condition it is in at the time of the assessment.

If the method in (1) is used, the original cost is adjusted by the appropriate price index factor for each year since the original cost was incurred. If the property was not new when acquired by its present owner and the original cost is not known, acquisition cost may be substituted for original cost in (1) above. (Reg. 6, 18 CCR)

Replacement cost is reduced by the amount by which the cost exceeds the current value of the property because of physical deterioration, misplacement, overimprovement or underimprovement, and other forms of depreciation or obsolescence. (Reg. 6, 18 CCR)

CCH COMMENT: Depreciation.—The most difficult aspect of the cost approach is the estimation of depreciation. An accountant's approach to and calculation of depreciation is quite different from an assessor's. For accounting purposes, an asset is depreciated over a preselected life until the value of the asset reaches a salvage value. At any given time, the book value of an asset, as shown on the accounting records, is the asset's acquisition cost reduced by the amount of accumulated depreciation charges against it. By contrast, an assessor attempts to estimate the remaining value of the property (compared to its cost when new), as evidenced by the market as of the date the property is being valued. The remaining value determined by the assessor is likely to be different, either higher or lower, than the book value indicated on accounting records. (Sec. 501, Assessors' Handbook, California State Board of Equalization; http://www.boe.ca.gov/proptaxes/pdf/ah501.pdf)

In valuing special use property using the replacement cost method, the assessor must not add an increment of value to reflect entrepreneurial profit unless there is market-derived evidence that such profit exists and that it has not been fully offset by physical deterioration or economic obsolescence. (Sec. 401.6, Rev. & Tax. Code) For purposes of this limitation, "special use property" means any limited market property that requires special construction materials or that has a unique physical design or a layout that restricts its utility to the use for which it was built. "Entrepreneurial profit" is either (1) the amount that a developer would expect to recover with respect to the property over the costs of development or (2) the difference between the fair market value of the property and the total costs incurred with respect to that property.

• *Historical cost method*

If the income from property is regulated by law and the regulatory agency uses historical cost or historical cost less depreciation as a rate base, the historical amount invested in the property or the amount invested less depreciation may be an appropriate indicator of value. (Reg. 3, 18 CCR) This valuation method is frequently used to value property owned by utilities. (see ¶ 20-330 Utilities)

¶20-630

[¶20-635] Unit Method of Valuation

Unit valuation applies to property in certain highly regulated industries that cross jurisdictions. When unit valuation was first developed, the U.S. Supreme Court acknowledged that the true value of a railroad line was greater than the aggregate value of its separate parts, recognizing the added value of a network allowing railroads to combine operations as one continuous line (*Cleveland, Cincinnati, Chicago, & St. Louis Railway Co. v. Backus*, 154 U.S. 439 (1894)). The California State Board of Equalization (SBE) may use unit valuation principles in the valuation of state-assessed properties that are operated as a unit in a primary function of the assessee. (Sec. 723, Rev. & Tax. Code) The SBE has used the principle of unit valuation in valuing public utility property. (see ¶20-330 Utilities)

[¶20-640] Real Property Valuation

Real property subject to general property taxation in California is taxed at its full value. (Sec. 401, Rev. & Tax. Code)

For a discussion of valuation procedures, see ¶20-625.

[¶20-645] Personal Property Valuation

Personal property is taxed at current fair market value. (Sec. 401, Rev. & Tax. Code; Reg. 2, 18 CCR) The words "full value," "full cash value," "cash value," "actual value," and "fair market value," mean the price at which a property, if exposed for sale in the open market with a reasonable time for the seller to find a purchaser, would transfer for cash or its equivalent under prevailing market conditions between parties who have knowledge of the uses to which the property may be put, both seeking to maximize their gains and neither being in a position to take advantage of the exigencies of the other. (Reg. 2(a), 18 CCR)

• *Trade level adjustments*

In valuing tangible personal property, assessors must consider the trade level at which the property is situated and the principle that property normally increases in value as it progresses through production and distribution channels, attaining its maximum value when it reaches the consumer level. (Reg. 10(a), 18 CCR)

Property held by consumers is valued at the cash amount, or at an amount equivalent to what like property at the same trade level would command on the open market. If a cost approach is employed, the cost shall include the full economic cost of placing the property in service. "Full economic cost" (i.e., replacement or reproduction cost) included costs typicallyincurred in bringing the property to a finished state, including:

— labor and materials,

— freight or shipping cost,

— installation costs,

— sales or use taxes, and

— additions to for market supported entrepreneurial services with appropriate allowances for trade, quantity, or cash discounts.

Full economic cost does not include:

— extended service plans or extended warranties;

— supplies; or

— other assets or business services that may have been included in a purchase contract.

(Reg. 10(b), 18 CCR)

• *Leased property*

Property leased, rented, or loaned for six months or less, with a situs where the lessor normally keeps the property, is valued at the cash amount, or at an amount equivalent to what that property would transfer to other lessors or retailers of similar property. (Reg. 10(c), 18 CCR) Property leased, rented, or loaned for an unspecified and extended time, with the same situs, is valued by estimating the cash price or its equivalent that the property could command at fair market value at the same level of trade as the lessee. (Reg. 10(d), 18 CCR)

• *Other property*

Property acquired from internal sources for self-consumption or use is valued by estimating the cash price or its equivalent that the property could command at fair market value at the same trade level. (Reg. 10(e), 18 CCR) Property in the possession of a manufacturer, wholesaler, or retailer and a consumer is valued by estimating the cash price or its equivalent that the property could be sold at fair market value at the same respective levels of trade. (Reg. 10, 18 CCR)

• *Assessor audits of business property*

For any California taxpayers engaged in a profession, trade, or business that is not fully exempt from property tax, the county assessor annually must conduct a significant number of audits, including at least 50% of large businesses, as measured by fixtures and personal property, from a pool of businesses, each of which must be audited at least once in any four-year period. The express legislative intent of this provision is to provide assessors with discretion in selecting business taxpayers to audit, thus adding an element of unpredictability to the audit process. A "significant number of audits" means at least 75% of the fiscal year average of the total number of audits the assessor was required to conduct during the period from fiscal year 2002-2003 through fiscal year 2005-2006. Under the process, 50% of the audits required annually shall be performed on taxpayers selected from a pool of those taxpayers that have the largest assessments of trade fixtures and business tangible personal property in the county. Each taxpayer in the pool must be audited at least once every four years following the latest fiscal year covered by a preceding audit, and nothing precludes a taxpayer being audited more than once in four years. The selection of businesses for the other 50% of audits performed annually shall be conducted in a fair and equitable manner and may be based on evidence of underreporting. (Sec. 469, Rev. & Tax. Code; *Letter to County Assessors, No. 2009/003*, California State Board of Equalization) The Board of Equalization has released a listing by county of the minimum number of audits required for taxpayers with the largest assessments, as well as for the pool of all other taxpayers. (*Letter to County Assessors, No. 2009/049*, California State Board of Equalization) Prior to 2009, county assessors had to audit at least once every four years the books and records of each taxpayer engaged in a trade, business, or profession whose locally assessable trade fixtures and business tangible personal property had a full value of $400,000 or more.

The purpose of the audit is to collect data relating to the determination of taxability, situs, and value of the property. (Reg. 191, 18 CCR) At the completion of the audit, the auditor must give the taxpayer written findings with respect to any information that would alter any previously enrolled assessment. (Sec. 469(c)(1), Rev. & Tax. Code; Reg. 191, 18 CCR; Reg. 192, 18 CCR)

Equalization of the property of a taxpayer by a county board of equalization or an assessment appeals board does not preclude an assessment resulting from an audit subsequent to the equalization hearing, but the additional assessment is not an escape assessment. If the audit discloses an escape assessment, the original assessment is reviewed and may be equalized or otherwise adjusted by the county board of equalization or the assessment appeals board, unless it has been previously equalized. If the property was assessed in excess of its true value, the assessor must notify the taxpayer of the option to file a claim for cancellation of the tax or for a refund. (Sec. 469, Rev. & Tax. Code)

A regulation clarifies the conditions under which a taxpayer may file an application for review, equalization, and adjustment of California property taxes assessed, excepting property previously equalized for the year at issue. The taxpayer's right to file an application arises when an assessor concludes, after an audit of business property, that there exist business property subject to a retroactive escape assessment to remedy an omission or error in the original assessment. (Reg. 305.3, 18 CCR)

The regulation requires that the assessor provide the taxpayer with written notice of the audit results for all property, locations and years that were the subject of the audit, and notice for filing an application no later that 60 days after the date of mailing of the notice of the audit results. (Reg. 305.3, 18 CCR)

The notice for filing an application must disclose the audit results, including the audit's disclosure of property subject to escape assessment and must be sent by regular United States mail addressed to the taxpayer at the taxpayer's last known address, unless, prior to the mailing of the notice, the assessor receives written notice of a change in address. In addition, the notice for filing an application, depending on the conclusion of the audit, may be in the form of a tax bill based on the audit results and resulting escape assessment, or the notice of audit results, itself. If in the form of the notice of audit result, the notice must state that it is the assessor's notice of the taxpayer's right to file an application. The regulation lists several examples illustrative of these forms of notice to file an application. (Reg. 305.3, 18 CCR)

Generally, the taxpayer must make records available to the assessor at the taxpayer's principal place of business, the taxpayer's principal location or principal address in California, or a place mutually convenient so that the audit may be conducted. However, a taxpayer with a principal place of business outside California may pay the county an amount representing the reasonable and ordinary expenses incurred by the county to examine the taxpayer's records at a place outside California. (Sec. 470, Rev. & Tax. Code)

[¶20-750]

PAYMENT, COLLECTION OF TAXES

[¶20-752] Interest

For California property tax purposes, if a taxpayer does any of the following, interest at the rate of 0.75% per month is imposed on the amount of taxes determined to be delinquent:

— fails to furnish information concerning a veteran's exemption claim; (Sec. 506, Rev. & Tax. Code)

— conceals property in an effort to evade tax; (Sec. 506, Rev. & Tax. Code)

— fails to file a property statement or commits an act of fraud resulting in an escape assessment; (Sec. 531, Rev. & Tax. Code)

— provides incorrect information resulting in the improper allowance of an exemption; (Sec. 531.1, Rev. & Tax. Code)

— fails to file a change in ownership statement or a preliminary change in ownership report; (Sec. 531.2, Rev. & Tax. Code)

— fails to provide an accurate accounting of the cost of personal property; (Sec. 531.3, Rev. & Tax. Code)

— fails to accurately report business property; (Sec. 531.4, Rev. & Tax. Code)

— supplies incorrect information resulting in an erroneous classification of property as exempt business property; (Sec. 531.5, Rev. & Tax. Code) or

— erroneously claims the homeowner's exemption. (Sec. 531.6, Rev. & Tax. Code)

If a taxpayer does not pay taxes listed on the unsecured roll and instead files an application for assessment reduction, interest at the rate of 1% per month is imposed on the amount of taxes determined to be delinquent. (Sec. 2922.5, Rev. & Tax. Code)

Generally, interest at the greater of 3% per annum or the county pool apportioned rate is paid on property tax refunds, provided the amount of interest is $10 or more. Interest begins to accrue on the following dates:

— the date the tax was paid if a timely application for an assessment reduction was filed or if the refund resulted from a tax roll correction;

— the date the deed was recorded if the tax was imposed on property acquired by a public agency in eminent domain;

— 120 days after a county assessor has sent authorization to a county auditor for a reduction in the assessed value of property that was damaged or destroyed; or

— the later of the date the tax was paid or the refund claim was filed in all other cases.

(Sec. 5151, Rev. & Tax. Code)

Regardless of the date that interest begins to accrue, the computation of interest terminates within 30 days of the date the refund was mailed or personally delivered. (Sec. 5151, Rev. & Tax. Code)

The "county pool apportioned rate" is the annualized rate of interest earned on the total amount of pooled idle funds from all accounts held by the county treasurer in excess of the county treasurer's administrative costs with respect to that amount as of June 30 of the fiscal year preceding the date the refund is calculated by the auditor. (Sec. 5151(a), Rev. & Tax. Code)

No interest is payable to a taxpayer who was given written notice of overpayment by the tax collector and failed to apply for a refund within 30 days after the notice was mailed. Any interest paid on a refund at a rate provided under Sec. 5151 as it read prior to 2009 shall be deemed to be correct. (Sec. 5151(a), Rev. & Tax. Code; Sec. 2635, Rev. & Tax. Code)

Interest on refunds of amounts of tax that became due and payable before March 1, 1993, and that were not refunded as of April 6, 1995, continue to be payable at the rate provided under the law as it existed prior to January 1, 1993. (Sec. 5151, Rev. & Tax. Code)

If a refund of supplemental taxes is not made within the required 90-day period, interest is paid at the same rate for ordinary property tax refunds, provided the amount of interest is $10 or more. (Sec. 75.43, Rev. & Tax. Code)

• *Private railroad car taxes; timber yield taxes*

Interest on underpayments and overpayments of private railroad car taxes and timber yield taxes is applied at the same rate that applies to underpayments and overpayments of corporation franchise (income) and personal income taxes (see ¶ 89-204). (Sec. 11405, Rev. & Tax. Code; Sec. 11555, Rev. & Tax. Code; Sec. 38451, Rev. & Tax. Code; Sec. 38606, Rev. & Tax. Code)

[¶20-756] Payment of Tax

On or before November 1 of each year, the county tax collector mails or electronically transmits to fee owners, assessees, or their agents a county tax bill for property carried on the secured roll for taxes levied for the fiscal year beginning the previous July 1. (Sec. 2610.5, Rev. & Tax. Code; Sec. 75.6, Rev. & Tax. Code) Failure to receive a tax bill does not relieve the taxpayer of the obligation to pay the taxes or from penalties imposed on delinquencies. (Sec. 2610.5, Rev. & Tax. Code) However, penalties may be cancelled if the assessee or fee owner demonstrates that the delinquency is due to the tax collector's failure to mail the tax bill to the address provided on the tax roll or failure to electronically transmit the tax bill to the electronic address provided by the taxpayer.

When a tax bill is sent to an agent authorized to pay taxes on behalf of the assessee, the tax collector must send a copy of the tax bill to the assessee. (Sec. 2610.6, Rev. & Tax. Code) After payment of the taxes, the agent is required to either mail the original tax bill or a copy of the bill to the assessee within 30 days of receiving a written request from the assessee. (Sec. 2910.7, Rev. & Tax. Code)

Separate tax bills are issued by the tax collector for tax-defaulted property and property that is not tax delinquent. (Sec. 2612.5, Rev. & Tax. Code)

Statutory provisions specify information that must be reflected on the tax bill or on a statement accompanying the bill. (Sec. 2611.6, Rev. & Tax. Code; Sec. 2611.7, Rev. & Tax. Code; Sec. 2612, Rev. & Tax. Code; Sec. 2615.5, Rev. & Tax. Code; Sec. 2615.6, Rev. & Tax. Code)

A county tax collector must, at the request of a taxpayer, issue a single tax statement listing all of the properties on the secured roll with respect to which the taxpayer is an assessee, provided that the tax collector has adopted the consolidated property tax statement requirement in the form of a written memorandum that has been transmitted to the county board of supervisors and recorded with the county recorder. A request for a consolidated property tax statement must be in writing, must be submitted by September 1, and remains valid only for property taxes assessed during the first five fiscal years following the date of the request. Additionally, only one named assessee may request and receive a consolidated property tax statement for any one parcel. Such a statement does not take the place of a tax bill and a tax collector may not incur any legal liability with respect to any information contained in the statement. (Sec. 2611.7, Rev. & Tax. Code)

Annually on or before November 1 of each year, the tax collector must publish a notice in a newspaper or post in a public place information concerning the due and delinquency dates of taxes on the secured roll, the penalties and costs for delinquency, the time and place of payment, and the availability of early payment. (Sec. 2609, Rev. & Tax. Code; Sec. 2610, Rev. & Tax. Code) After 2017, if the notice is given in a newspaper, it also must be provided on the tax collector's regularly maintained website for the same amount of time as the it is required to be published in the newspaper. (Sec. 36.5, Rev. & Tax. Code)

• *Payment due dates and delinquency dates*

All personal property taxes and the first installment of real property taxes on the secured roll are due and payable November 1 and, if not paid, become delinquent at the later of 5 p.m. or the close of business on December 10. (Sec. 2605, Rev. & Tax. Code; Sec. 2617, Rev. & Tax. Code; Sec. 2701, Rev. & Tax. Code; Sec. 2704, Rev. & Tax. Code) The second installment of real property taxes is due and payable the following February 1 and, if not paid, becomes delinquent at the later of 5 p.m. or the close of business on April 10. (Sec. 2606, Rev. & Tax. Code; Sec. 2618, Rev. & Tax. Code; Sec. 2702, Rev. & Tax. Code; Sec. 2705, Rev. & Tax. Code)

If December 10 or April 10 falls on a Saturday, Sunday, legal holiday, or other day in which county offices are officially closed, the time of delinquency is the later of 5 p.m. or the close of business on the next business day. (Sec. 2619, Rev. & Tax. Code; Sec. 2705.5, Rev. & Tax. Code)

A county board of supervisors may authorize two equal installments for the payment of personal property taxes on the secured roll. (Sec. 2700, Rev. & Tax. Code *et seq.*)

The tax collector to whom taxes are paid may set an earlier date for payment. (Sec. 2608, Rev. & Tax. Code) However, according to the California Attorney General, this date may not be before the tax roll is actually delivered to the tax collector. (*Opinion of the Attorney General No. 85-104*, August 6, 1985)

Full payment of real property taxes may be made when the first installment is due and payable, but the second installment may be paid separately only if the first installment has been paid. (Sec. 2607, Rev. & Tax. Code) If authorized by the county board of supervisors, a county tax collector must accept payment of the second installment of real property taxes at a discounted amount if payment of that installment is made by the due date for the first installment. (Sec. 2607.1, Rev. & Tax. Code)

The tax collector must accept payment of current year taxes even though prior year real property tax delinquencies may exist. (Sec. 2607, Rev. & Tax. Code)

• *Liable parties*

Heirs, guardians, executors, or administrators of an estate of a decedent are liable for taxes assessed on the decedent's property that is not yet distributed. (Sec. 982, Rev. & Tax. Code) However, property assessed to a person in his or her representative capacity, is kept separate on the assessment rolls from the property assessed to that person in his or her individual capacity. (Sec. 612, Rev. & Tax. Code) Property of a decedent distributed to the state of California is assessed to the estate and to the state. (Sec. 982.1, Rev. & Tax. Code)

Property that is the subject of litigation and that is in the hands of an official of the county or the courts is assessed to the officer in possession. (Sec. 983, Rev. & Tax. Code) Assessors are responsible for all taxes on property that has not been assessed because of their failure or neglect. (Sec. 1361, Rev. & Tax. Code)

• *Unsecured property taxes*

Taxes on unsecured property are due on the January 1 lien date and, if not paid, become delinquent at the later of 5 p.m. or the close of business on August 31. Taxes added to the unsecured roll after July 31 become delinquent on the last day of the month after the month in which the assessment was added to the unsecured roll. (Sec. 2192, Rev. & Tax. Code; Sec. 2901, Rev. & Tax. Code; Sec. 2922, Rev. & Tax. Code)

• *Tax deferrals for disaster victims*

An owner of eligible property that has been damaged severely in a natural disaster may be able to defer payment of property taxes without penalty or interest by filing a claim for deferral with the county assessor. (Sec. 194.1, Rev. & Tax. Code) The county in which the property is located must have been proclaimed by the Governor to be in a state of emergency as a result of the disaster and must have adopted an appropriate disaster relief ordinance. (Sec. 194, Rev. & Tax. Code)

A claim for deferral of the first postdisaster installment of regular secured property taxes must be filed with the county assessor on or before the delinquency date (December 10 or April 10). A claim for disaster-related reassessment must be filed in conjunction with the claim for deferral. Payment of the installment will then be deferred until after the property has been reassessed and until 30 days after the owner receives a corrected tax bill. If the assessor determines upon reassessment that the property owner was not entitled to a tax deferral and did not file the deferral claim in good faith, the owner will be assessed a delinquency penalty. (Sec. 194, Rev. & Tax. Code; Sec. 194.1, Rev. & Tax. Code)

A county may, by ordinance, permit deferral of the second consecutive installment following the disaster until the next regular installment date. (Sec. 195.1, Rev. & Tax. Code)

A county ordinance may also permit the deferral of the unpaid nondelinquent supplemental roll taxes until the last day of the month after the month in which a corrected bill is mailed or until the delinquent date of the next installment of the regular bill, whichever is later. (Sec. 194.9, Rev. & Tax. Code)

The tax collector of a county that is designated by the governor to be in a state of emergency or disaster due to a major misfortune or calamity may defer for a period of one year tax payments under an installment plan if the assessee incurred substantial disaster damage in connection with his or her property as a result of the disaster, files an application for deferral on or before September 1 of the following fiscal year, and is not receiving any other disaster relief. (Sec. 4222.5, Rev. & Tax. Code)

Payment deferral deadlines clarified.—When a property owner has timely filed a claim for disaster relief and deferral of the next property tax bill installment, and the assessor has reassessed the property and a corrected tax bill has been sent to the property owner, the current year's taxes are to be paid on the later of either:

• December 10 for the first installment or April 10 for the second installment; or

• 30 days after the date the corrected bill is mailed or electronically submitted to the property owner.

(Sec. 194.1, Rev. & Tax. Code)

When a property owner has filed for disaster relief and deferral of the next property tax bill installment, but the assessor has determined that the real property is not eligible for disaster relief, the property tax bill must be paid on the later of either:

• December 10 for the first installment or April 10 for the second installment; or

• within 30 days of the later of the date of mailing or postmark date on the county assessor's notice.

(Sec. 194.1, Rev. & Tax. Code)

• *Partial payments*

If authorized by the board of supervisors, a county tax collector may accept a partial payment of property taxes. (Sec. 2636, Rev. & Tax. Code; Sec. 2708, Rev. & Tax. Code; Sec. 2927.6, Rev. & Tax. Code) Partial payments are applied first to any penalty, interest, or costs due as a result of previous delinquencies, with the remainder applied to the current tax. The balance due is treated as delinquent.

Partial payments of delinquent taxes on tax-defaulted property may also be accepted by the tax collector if approved by the board of supervisors. (Sec. 4143, Rev. & Tax. Code) Partial payments on tax-defaulted property are not considered redemptions, partial redemptions, or installment payments of delinquent taxes, and the tax-defaulted property remains subject to a power of sale on the original date prescribed. The taxpayer may, however, elect to pay the balance of delinquent taxes under an installment plan. (See ¶ 20-756)

A tax collector may also accept a pro rata tax payment in a case in which an assessee on the unsecured roll has a recorded, undivided interest in the assessed property. The payment must be equal to the portion of the total tax due that corresponds to the assessee's percentage interest in the assessed property. A proper pro rata payment discharges the assessee from any tax lien on the property. (Sec. 2927.7, Rev. & Tax. Code)

• *Escape assessments—installment payments*

Taxes due on an escape assessment may be paid over a four-year period at the option of the assessee regardless of any fault on the part of the assessee in causing the escape assessment. However, a written request for installment payment must be filed with the tax collector and the additional tax due must exceed $500. The request must be filed before the second installment of taxes on the secured roll becomes delinquent or by the last day of the month following the month in which the tax bill is mailed, whichever is later. For unsecured taxes, the request must be filed prior to the date on which the taxes become delinquent. (Sec. 4837.5, Rev. & Tax. Code)

At least 20% of the additional tax must be paid no later than the deadline for filing the written request for installment payment. In each succeeding fiscal year, the assessee must pay, at a minimum, a sum sufficient to reduce the outstanding balance of the taxes being paid in installments by 20% of the original amount. Such payments must be made before the delinquency date of the second installment of current taxes on the secured roll. For unsecured taxes, the required annual installment must be paid on or before August 31. (Sec. 4837.5, Rev. & Tax. Code)

If any installment is not paid on time, or if the property changes ownership, the balance of the tax remaining to be paid becomes due immediately. However, if the second or subsequent installment is not paid on time and the assessee was not at fault for the missed payment, the tax collector may reinstate the installment account if the assessee pays the installment plus interest to the date of reinstatement and the payment is received prior to the time the property becomes tax defaulted or June 30 of the current fiscal year, whichever occurs earlier. (Sec. 4837.5, Rev. & Tax. Code)

• *Railroad car tax, timber yield tax—installment payments*

The State Board of Equalization (SBE) may enter into installment payment agreements for the payment of, together with penalties and interest, for private railroad car tax (Sec. 11253, Rev. & Tax. Code) and timber yield tax. (Sec. 38504, Rev. & Tax. Code)

¶20-756

• *Payment of separate lien*

Taxes on any parcel of real property contained in an assessment and having a separate valuation on the current roll may be paid separately from the payment of other taxes or special assessments if the taxes constitute a separate lien against the property. (Sec. 2801, Rev. & Tax. Code—Sec. 2812, Rev. & Tax. Code) A taxpayer has the right to remove a lien created by a special assessment by making a payment separately from the payment of the general taxes.

• *Payment methods*

Property taxes are payable in cash, but the tax collector may also accept payments by electronic funds transfer (EFT), checks, drafts, money orders, and certificates of eligibility issued by the State Controller to senior citizens. (Sec. 2502, Rev. & Tax. Code; Sec. 2503.1, Rev. & Tax. Code; Sec. 2503.2, Rev. & Tax. Code; Sec. 2504, Rev. & Tax. Code—Sec. 2508, Rev. & Tax. Code)

Additionally, a county board of supervisors may authorize payments by credit card. (Sec. 2511.1, Rev. & Tax. Code)

A receipt is given for cash payments or on request. (Sec. 2615, Rev. & Tax. Code; Sec. 2910.5, Rev. & Tax. Code)

If a check is not good, the tax collector may, upon notifying the taxpayer and making the required cancellation on the tax roll, charge a fee to cover processing the check or draft. (Sec. 2509, Rev. & Tax. Code; Sec. 2509.1, Rev. & Tax. Code; Sec. 2510, Rev. & Tax. Code) or a credit card draft is not paid. (Sec. 2511.1, Rev. & Tax. Code)

By resolution of a county board of supervisors, a county warrant for a particular fiscal year may be received in payment of taxes for the same fiscal year if the amount of the warrant does not exceed the amount of taxes being paid. (Sec. 2511, Rev. & Tax. Code)

• *Electronic fund transfer*

When a taxpayer makes an aggregate property tax payment of $50,000 or more on the two most recent regular installments on the secured roll or on the one installment of the most recent unsecured roll, the tax collector has the discretion to require that the taxpayer make subsequent payments by EFT. (Sec. 2503.2, Rev. & Tax. Code) A county tax collector, at his or her discretion, is allowed to accept electronic funds transfers as payment for a purchase at a tax sale and for tax defaulted property and tax-defaulted property sold at public auction. (Sec. 2503.2, Rev. & Tax. Code; Sec. 3451, Rev. & Tax. Code)

A remittance made by an electronic payment option such as wire transfer, telephoned credit card, or electronic Internet means is deemed received on the date that the taxpayer completes the transaction. However, a taxpayer must present proof, in the form of a confirmation number or other convincing evidence, of the date the transaction was completed. A property tax payment is deemed received on the date the taxpayer completes an electronic payment only if the payment is made through the tax collector's authorized Web site or telephone number. (Sec. 2512, Rev. & Tax Code)

If an electronic funds transfer is not accepted by the bank designated to receive payment, the tax collector may, upon notifying the taxpayer and making the required cancellation on the tax roll, charge a fee to cover processing the transfer. (Sec. 2503.2, Rev. & Tax. Code)

• *Senior citizens postponement payments*

The property tax postponement law is reinstated, and the Controller may take applications beginning July 1, 2016.

• *Injunction or mandamus restraining tax collection*

California property tax law expressly prohibits a taxpayer from asking the courts for an injunction or writ of mandate against any county, district, municipality, or any of its officers to prevent the collection of property taxes. (Sec. 4807, Rev. & Tax. Code) For state-assessed property, the California Constitution similarly prohibits the issuance of an injunction against the state to prevent the collection of tax. (Sec. 32, Art. XIII, Cal. Const.) The federal Tax Injunction Act expressly bars federal injunctive relief from state taxes if there is a plain, speedy, and efficient remedy in the state's courts. (28 U.S.C. 1341)

A taxpayer is limited to the remedy of suing in state court for a refund of a tax improperly collected or bringing an action in state court against the assessor for declaratory relief, rather than being permitted to delay collection while the validity of an assessment is litigated. (Sec. 4808, Rev. & Tax. Code)

A writ of mandate is available to control some functions of local tax officials, such as to compel the officials to comply with the tax laws (*Hyatt v. Allen*, 54 Cal 353 (1880)), or to challenge the legality of seizing property for unsecured taxes prior to delinquency. (Sec. 2954, Rev. & Tax. Code)

A writ of review may be granted only when there is no appeal or other plain, speedy, or adequate remedy at law. (Sec. 1068, Civ. Proc. Code)

[¶20-758] Assessment of Delinquent Tax

Personal property taxes and the first installment of real property taxes on the secured roll become delinquent if not paid by December 10. (Sec. 2617, Rev. & Tax. Code; Sec. 2704, Rev. & Tax. Code) The second installment of real property taxes becomes delinquent if not paid by April 10. (Sec. 2618, Rev. & Tax. Code; Sec. 2705, Rev. & Tax. Code)

If a supplemental tax bill is mailed within the months of July through October, the first installment of the supplemental taxes becomes delinquent if not paid by December 10, and the second installment becomes delinquent if not paid by the following April 10. If the supplemental tax bill is mailed within the months of November through June, the first installment becomes delinquent if not paid by the last day of the month following the month in which the bill is mailed, and the second installment becomes delinquent if not paid by the last day of the fourth month following the date on which the first installment is delinquent. (Sec. 75.52, Rev. & Tax. Code)

Taxes on property on the unsecured roll as of July 31 become delinquent if not paid by August 31. Taxes on property added to the unsecured roll after July 31 become delinquent if not paid by the last day of the month following the month of enrollment. (Sec. 2922, Rev. & Tax. Code)

The property tax on racehorses becomes delinquent if not paid by February 15 of the tax year. (Sec. 5762, Rev. & Tax. Code)

Upon termination, dissolution, or abandonment of a business, any person who has control of, or responsibility for, filing returns or paying taxes on behalf of the business may be held personally liable for private railroad car and timber yield taxes that the person intentionally, consciously, and voluntarily failed to remit, plus interest and penalties. (Sec. 38574, Rev. & Tax. Code) In addition, personal liability may also be imposed on a purchaser for unpaid private railroad car and timber yield (Sec. 38561, Rev. & Tax. Code); Sec. 38562, Rev. & Tax. Code taxes and fees incurred by a former owner:

• *Deficiency assessments*

Property taxes are collected by the county tax collector. (Sec. 2602, Rev. & Tax. Code) However, any tax, penalty, cost, or fee of $20 or less need not be collected. (Sec. 2611.4, Rev. & Tax. Code)

Unpaid taxes on real property automatically become a lien on the property as of January 1 each year. When a taxpayer defaults in paying property taxes, the property is designated "tax-defaulted" property at the end of the fiscal year as a preliminary step in the actual enforcement of the tax lien against the land. The tax collector may sell tax certificates giving the certificate holder the right to receive the delinquent taxes, assessments, and penalties collected in connection with certain tax-defaulted property. The declaration of default by the tax collector starts the running of the five-year period, during which the taxpayer may redeem the property by payment of taxes and interest, and at the expiration of which the tax collector may sell legal title to the property to the highest bidder.

The tax collector can utilize procedures for the collection of taxes on the unsecured roll to collect any amount that becomes delinquent on the secured roll. The tax collector must send a notice of delinquency stating the intent to enforce collection at least 60 days before initiating collection procedures. (Sec. 760, Rev. & Tax. Code)

The tax collector may mail or electronically transmit a tax bill for taxes and assessments on the unsecured roll no later than 30 days prior to the date on which taxes are delinquent and as soon as reasonably possible after receipt of the extended assessment roll, unless the total amount due is too small to justify the cost of collection. (Sec. 2903, Rev. & Tax. Code; Sec. 2910.1, Rev. & Tax. Code) Failure to receive a tax bill does not relieve the tax lien or prevent the imposition of penalties. However, if the assessee convinces the tax collector that he or she did not receive the tax bill mailed to the address provided on the tax roll or the electronic address provided by the taxpayer, the penalty imposed for delinquent taxes is canceled.

Taxes on certain property such as possessory interests to which the homeowners' exemption applies, oil and gas leases secured by the leasehold estate (Sec. 2189.5, Rev. & Tax. Code), and mobile homes secured by a lien on the owner's real property, when delinquent, are collected as though they were on the unsecured tax roll.

Separately billed taxes on state-assessed personal property, when delinquent, may be collected through use of the unsecured tax collection procedures. (Sec. 2189.1, Rev. & Tax. Code) Any separately billed taxes on state-assessed personal property remaining unpaid after June 30, together with penalties and costs added to such taxes, must be transferred to the unsecured roll and become subject to the additional penalties imposed on delinquent unsecured personal property taxes. (see ¶ 20-770)

In addition to standard delinquent property tax collection procedures, a county tax collector may prevent the owner of a property-tax-delinquent vessel from transferring the vessel or renewing the vessel's registration. If the tax collector exercises this option, within 30 days after taxes on a vessel become delinquent, the tax collector must inform the owner in writing that until the delinquent taxes are paid, the Department of Motor Vehicles will not renew or transfer the vessel's registration. (Sec. 3205, Rev. & Tax. Code)

A tax collector is prohibited from selling a military serviceperson's real or personal property for property tax collection purposes unless granted permission by a court. The prohibition against the sale of real property applies only to real property owned and occupied for dwelling, professional, business, or agricultural purposes by a person in military service or his or her dependents at the commencement of military service and still occupied by his or her dependents or employees. This prohibition extends for a period not exceeding six months following termination of the serviceperson's period of service. Interest, but not penalties, may be applied to delinquent taxes and assessments. (Sec. 560, 50 U.S.C.)

Priority in bankruptcy proceedings is given to unsecured property tax assessed before the filing of a petition in bankruptcy and last payable without penalty within one year before the date of the filing of the petition. (11 U.S.C. 507(a)(7)(B)) The priorities noted in the Bankruptcy Reform Act represent the order of payment out of the bankrupt's estate. In the case of a collection of taxes pursuant to a bankruptcy proceeding, the county may request a reasonable amount of attorney's fees. (Sec. 4807, Rev. & Tax. Code)

• *Jeopardy assessments*

Taxing authorities may issue jeopardy assessments if they believe that a delay will jeopardize collection of private railroad car tax (Sec. 11351, Rev. & Tax. Code), timber yield tax (Sec. 38431, Rev. & Tax. Code), and property tax on racehorses. (Sec. 5764, Rev. & Tax. Code)

A person petitioning for redetermination or reassessment of a jeopardy determination or jeopardy assessment for private railroad car tax and timber yield tax must deposit security as the SBE deems necessary to secure compliance with the tax laws or to ensure payment of the amount due. (Sec. 38501, Rev. & Tax. Code)

• *Withhold, levy notices*

Notices to withhold may be issued for private railroad car tax and timber yield tax. (Sec. 38502, Rev. & Tax. Code) For those same taxes, notices of levy can be issued. (Sec. 38503, Rev. & Tax. Code)

• *Annual notices of delinquency*

Annually, by June 8, the tax collector must publish a notice stating that if any taxes, assessments, penalties, and costs imposed on real property are not fully paid by the close of business on June 30 (or the next business day if June 30 falls on a Saturday, Sunday, or a legal holiday), then the property will be declared in default. If the tax collector sends reminder notices prior to the close of the fiscal year and annually sends a redemption notice of the prior year taxes due, then the annual notice of impending default for failure to pay taxes on real property and the annual affidavit of tax-defaulted property that the tax collector must publish must include only those properties that have been tax-delinquent for three or more years and for which the latest reminder notice or redemption notice was returned to the tax collector as undeliverable. (Sec. 3351, Rev. & Tax. Code)

The notice must be made by publication in a newspaper of general circulation in the county one time a week for three successive weeks or, if no such newspaper is published in the county, by posting in three public places in the county. (Sec. 3353, Rev. & Tax. Code) After 2017, the notice also must be provided on the tax collector's regularly maintained website for three successive weeks. (Sec. 36.5, Rev. & Tax. Code)

By September 8 of each year, the tax collector must publish a list of tax-defaulted property, called the "published delinquent list," showing the address of the property and the assessee's name. However, in a county that mails delinquent notices to assessees before June 30, the tax collector is not required to publish the list of delinquent property until September 8 of the year after the year of default. If the tax collector sends reminder notices prior to the close of the fiscal year and annually sends a redemption notice of prior year taxes due, then the annual notice of impending default for the failure to pay taxes on real property and the annual affidavit of tax-defaulted property that the tax collector must publish must include only those properties that have been tax-delinquent for three or more years and for which the latest reminder notice or redemption notice was returned to the tax collector as undeliverable. (Sec. 3371, Rev. & Tax. Code; Sec. 3372, Rev. & Tax. Code) Unless an alternative method of publication is prescribed, the list must be published in a newspaper of general circulation in the county one time a week for three successive weeks or, if no such newspaper is published in the county, be posted in three public places in the county. (Sec. 3353, Rev. & Tax. Code) After 2017, the notice also must be provided on the tax collector's regularly maintained website for three successive weeks. (Sec. 36.5, Rev. & Tax. Code)

• *Summary judgment*

Summary judgment is a procedure that a county may use to enforce payment of unsecured property taxes. (Sec. 3103, Rev. & Tax. Code; Sec. 3106, Rev. & Tax. Code) The lien has the effect of a judgment lien and continues for at least 10 years from the date of recording; however, the lien may be extended for 10-year periods by recording the judgment in the office of the county recorder. (Sec. 3105, Rev. & Tax. Code) The judgment may be satisfied and the lien removed if the judgment amount, penalties, and the recording fee for release of the lien are paid. (Sec. 3107, Rev. & Tax. Code)

Notices of intention to use the summary judgment procedure must be mailed to the assessee by the tax collector. (Sec. 3101, Rev. & Tax. Code) If there is no payment of the back taxes within ten days of the mailing, the tax collector files the certificate in the office of the county clerk, who enters a judgment against the taxpayer. (Sec. 3102, Rev. & Tax. Code)

In the event that the judgment debtor sells personal property encumbered by the recorded judgment, the lien attached to such property cannot be enforced against the purchaser unless the purchaser had actual knowledge of the lien. (Sec. 3103, Rev. & Tax. Code)

The filing of a certificate of delinquency by the tax collector is another method for collecting unsecured property taxes. (Sec. 2191.3, Rev. & Tax. Code through Sec. 2191.6, Rev. & Tax. Code).

[¶20-762] Agreements in Compromise of Tax Due

There are no provisions for agreements in compromise of property tax due.

[¶20-768] Audits

CCH POINTER: Assessment Handbook Audit Chapter—March 2015.— The California State Board of Equalization (BOE) has adopted and authorized publication of *Assessors' Handbook Section 506 (AH 506), Property Tax Audits and Audit Program*. The handbook section, which is posted on the BOE website at www.boe.ca.gov/proptaxes/ahcont.htm, was developed to provide guidance in developing and improving property tax audits and audit programs in county assessors' offices, according to the BOE.

For any California taxpayers engaged in a profession, trade, or business that is not fully exempt from property tax, the county assessor annually must conduct a significant number of audits, including at least 50% of large businesses, as measured by fixtures and personal property, from a pool of businesses, each of which must be audited at least once in any four-year period. (Sec. 469, Rev. & Tax. Code; Reg. 191, 18 CCR; Reg. 192, 18 CCR)

Under this process, 50% of the audits required annually shall be performed on taxpayers selected from a pool of those taxpayers that have the largest assessments of trade fixtures and business tangible personal property in the county. Each taxpayer in the pool must be audited at least once every four years following the latest fiscal year covered by a preceding audit, and nothing precludes a taxpayer being audited more than once in four years. The selection of businesses for the other 50% of audits performed annually shall be conducted in a fair and equitable manner and may be based on evidence of underreporting. (Sec. 469, Rev. & Tax. Code)

Effective January 1, 2019, county assessors are provided with flexibility in meeting this annual audit requirement. Beginning with the 2019-20 fiscal year, assessors may also meet the requirements of Sec. 469 by completing the four-year total of required annual audits within that four-year period. (Sec. 469, Rev. & Tax. Code)

For example, if an assessor is required to conduct 150 audits annually for the four fiscal years beginning with 2019-20 through 2022-23, the assessor may meet this requirement either by conducting the required 150 audits for each fiscal year on an annual basis or by completing the 600 (4 x 150) total audits required for those four fiscal years at any time within the four-year period. (*Letter to County Assessors, No. 2018/067*, California State Board of Equalization, December 31, 2018)

• *Veterans' exemption*

Eligibility for the veterans' exemption is subject to an annual audit by the county auditor for both the current and prior tax years. (Sec. 280, Rev. & Tax. Code; Sec. 281, Rev. & Tax. Code) Taxpayers may be required to cooperate in the audit and may be required to produce substantiating documents. (Sec. 282, Rev. & Tax. Code) Failure to comply with requirements to produce evidence may result in the loss of the exemption, subjecting the property to full assessments. (Sec. 282.5, Rev. & Tax. Code)

• *Racehorses*

There are special provisions for audits of the books and records of owners of racehorses that are subject to the annual racehorse tax that is imposed in lieu of the regular property tax. (Sec. 5765, Rev. & Tax. Code; Reg. 1045, 18 CCR)

• *Utilities*

For regulatory and tax purposes, the Public Utilities Commission (PUC) must inspect and audit books and records as follows:

— at least once every three years in the case of every electrical, gas, heat, telegraph, telephone, and water corporation serving over 10,000 customers or in accordance with the commission authorized general rate case cycle, if that cycle provides for a rate case no less frequently than once every five years; and

— at least once every five years in the case of every electrical, gas, heat, telegraph, telephone, and water corporation serving 10,000 or fewer customers.

Reports of such inspections and audits and other pertinent information must be posted on the PUC website. (Sec. 314.5, Pub. Util. Code)

• *Maintenance of records*

Taxpayer records must be available to the assessor/auditor at the taxpayer's principal place of business, principal location, or California address, or at a location that is mutually convenient for the conduct of an audit. Alternatively, the taxpayer may pay the auditor/assessor's reasonable and ordinary expenses to examine taxpayer records at the taxpayer's principal place of business located outside California. (Sec. 470, Rev. & Tax. Code)

[¶20-770] Penalties

Delinquent property taxes are subject to a penalty of 10% of the amount due. (Sec. 2617, Rev. & Tax. Code; Sec. 2618, Rev. & Tax. Code; Sec. 2704, Rev. & Tax. Code; Sec. 2705, Rev. & Tax. Code; Sec. 2922, Rev. & Tax. Code; Sec. 75.52, Rev. & Tax. Code)

Unsecured taxes remaining unpaid on the last day of the second month after the 10% penalty attaches are subject to an additional penalty of 1.5% per month attaching on the first day of each month and continuing to attach until the earlier of the date payment is made or the date a court judgment is entered for the amount of unpaid taxes and penalties. (Sec. 2922, Rev. & Tax. Code)

The tax collector may also collect actual costs incurred by the county in collecting delinquent unsecured property taxes. (Sec. 2922, Rev. & Tax. Code)

If the delinquent taxes were imposed in part through an error of the assessor, the penalty is applicable only to the portion of the tax not erroneously levied. (Sec. 2922.5, Rev. & Tax. Code) In addition, delinquency penalties may be canceled by the auditor or tax collector if the failure to pay on time is due to reasonable cause and the underlying delinquency is paid no later than June 30 of the fourth fiscal year in which the tax became delinquent, if there is an inadvertent error in the amount of payment, or if cancellation is ordered by a local, state, or federal court. (Sec. 4985.2, Rev. & Tax. Code) Moreover, delinquent property taxes, penalties, interest, and related charges may be waived if the amount to be collected is so small that it would not cover the cost of collection or if collection enforcement is impractical. (Sec. 2611.1, Rev. & Tax. Code; Sec. 2923, Rev. & Tax. Code)

Only those delinquency penalties that apply to the difference between the county board of supervisors' final determination of value and the assessed value that was appealed may be canceled. Affected taxpayers must receive notice of these penalty relief provisions. Those taxpayers who have paid at least 80% of the final amount of tax due within 60 days of mailing or presentation of the penalty relief notice may pay the balance of the tax due without penalties or interest. (Sec. 4833.1, Rev. & Tax. Code; Sec. 4985.3, Rev. & Tax. Code)

In counties that have established the required cancellation procedure, delinquency penalties may be canceled by order of the county board of supervisors if the assessee or fee owner has demonstrated to the tax collector's satisfaction that the delinquency resulted from the county's failure to send a tax notice to the owner of property acquired after the lien date on the secured roll. (Sec. 2610.5, Rev. & Tax. Code) However, in such cases, the taxes must be paid no later than June 30 of the fiscal year in which the property owner is named as the assessee for taxes coming due.

In addition, a delinquency penalty may be canceled if the delinquency resulted from the tax collector's failure to mail or electronically transmit the tax bill to the address on the tax roll or the electronic address provided by the taxpayer. (Sec. 2610.5, Rev. & Tax. Code; Sec. 2910.1, Rev. & Tax. Code)

• *Failure to file property statement; refusal to provide information*

Persons who fail to file a required property statement are subject to a penalty of 10% of the assessed value of the unreported property placed on the current tax roll. (Sec. 463, Rev. & Tax. Code; Sec. 5367, Rev. & Tax. Code)

Persons who refuse to give information when requested are, in addition, guilty of a misdemeanor and subject to a fine of not more than $1,000 or confinement in the county jail for not more than six months. Corporations that refuse to provide information when requested by the assessor are subject to a fine of $200 per day so long as the refusal continues, up to $20,000. (Sec. 462, Rev. & Tax. Code)

Persons who willfully make false statements that form the basis for assessments for tax purposes are guilty of a misdemeanor and are subject to the same penalties as for refusal to furnish information to the assessor. (Sec. 461, Rev. & Tax. Code)

In addition to these penalties, the assessor may obtain the assistance of the superior court for an order requiring the information to be furnished to the court. (Sec. 468, Rev. & Tax. Code)

A person who fails to file a timely statement of state-assessed property is subject to a penalty of 10% of the value of the property. If the failure to timely file is due to a fraudulent or willful attempt to evade tax, a penalty of 25% of the assessed value of the estimated assessment must be added. However, no penalty may exceed $20,000,000 of full value. (Sec. 830, Rev. & Tax. Code)

• *Failure to file change of ownership statement*

A person who fails to file a notice of change of ownership of real property within 45 days of the date of a written request by the assessor is subject to a penalty equal to the greater of $100 or 10% of the taxes reflecting the new base-year value. The penalty may not exceed $2,500, if the failure to file was not willful. (Sec. 482, Rev. & Tax. Code)

If a corporation, partnership, limited liability company, or other legal entity undergoes a change in control or change in ownership and does not file notice of change of ownership of real property within 45 days of the date of the change in ownership or the date of a written request by the California State Board of Equalization (BOE), the entity is liable for a penalty of 10% of the taxes applicable to either the new base-year value of the property if the change in control or ownership occurred or the current year's taxes if no change in ownership or control occurred. (Sec. 482(b), Rev. & Tax. Code)

If a life insurance company is required to file a statement of transfer with respect to a transfer of real property to or from a separate account and fails to file that statement within 45 days from the date of the transfer, the company will be subject to a penalty of $1,000 in addition to any other penalty prescribed by law. (Sec. 480.7, Rev. & Tax. Code)

• *Escape assessments*

If a person willfully conceals, fails to disclose, removes, transfers, or misrepresents tangible personal property to evade tax and it results in an assessment lower than that required by law, a penalty of 25% of the assessed value of the escaped property is added to the assessment roll. (Sec. 502, Rev. & Tax. Code; Sec. 504, Rev. & Tax. Code)

If a person through a fraudulent act or omission causes any taxable tangible personal property to escape assessment or be underassessed, the person is subject to a penalty of 75% of the assessed value of the escaped property. (Sec. 503, Rev. & Tax. Code)

If a veteran's or homeowner's exemption was allowed incorrectly because of erroneous or incorrect information knowingly submitted by the claimant, a penalty of 25% of the assessed value of the escaped property is added to the assessment roll. (Sec. 504, Rev. & Tax. Code; Sec. 531.1, Rev. & Tax. Code; Sec. 531.6, Rev. & Tax. Code)

If business property is improperly claimed as business inventory, or an exemption is allowed for business inventory on the basis of improper or erroneous information knowingly supplied by the taxpayer, a penalty of 25% of the assessed value of the escaped property is added. (Sec. 504, Rev. & Tax. Code; Sec. 531.5, Rev. & Tax. Code)

If a failure to file a required property statement required results in either no assessment or an improperly reduced assessment, a penalty of 10% of the assessed value of the escaped property applies. (Sec. 531, Rev. & Tax. Code; Sec. 463, Rev. & Tax. Code)

If a taxpayer willfully or fraudulently fails to file an accurate business property statement or property cost statement, a penalty of 75% of the assessed value of the property escaping assessment is imposed. (Sec. 503, Rev. & Tax. Code; Sec. 531.3, Rev. & Tax. Code; Sec. 531.4, Rev. & Tax. Code)

• *Redemption*

The amount necessary to redeem tax-defaulted property includes a redemption penalty in addition to any other delinquent penalties that may already have been imposed. The redemption penalty is imposed on the declared amount of defaulted taxes at the rate of 1.5% per month beginning July 1 of the year of the declaration of tax default to the time of redemption. (Sec. 4102, Rev. & Tax. Code; Sec. 4103, Rev. & Tax. Code)

• *Private railroad cars*

Failure to file a timely private railroad car report is subject to a penalty of 10% of the assessed value. (Sec. 11273, Rev. & Tax. Code)

• *Criminal penalties*

A person who refuses to give information when requested by the assessor is guilty of a misdemeanor and subject to a fine of up to $1,000 or confinement in the county jail for up to six months. (Sec. 462, Rev. & Tax. Code)

A person who willfully makes a false statement that forms the basis for an assessment is guilty of a misdemeanor and is subject to the same penalties as for refusal to furnish information to the assessor. (Sec. 461, Rev. & Tax. Code)

A tax claim preparer who endorses or negotiates a warrant issued to a taxpayer in connection with senior citizens property tax assistance is subject to a penalty of $250 and is guilty of a misdemeanor punishable by a fine of up to $1,000, imprisonment for up to one year, or both the fine and imprisonment. (Sec. 20645.7, Rev. & Tax. Code; Sec. 20645.9, Rev. & Tax. Code)

• *Waiver*

Property tax delinquency penalties may be canceled by the auditor or tax collector if:

— the failure to timely pay is due to reasonable cause and the underlying delinquency is paid by June 30 of the fourth fiscal year following the fiscal year in which the tax became delinquent;

— there is an inadvertent error in the amount of payment; or

— cancellation is ordered by a local, state, or federal court.

(Sec. 4985.2, Rev. & Tax. Code)

Also, delinquent taxes, penalties, interest, and related charges may be waived if:

(1) the amount is too small to justify the cost of collection,

(2) the likelihood of collection does not warrant the expense involved, or

(3) the amount thereof has been otherwise lawfully compromised or adjusted.

(Sec. 2611.1, Rev. & Tax. Code; Sec. 2923, Rev. & Tax. Code)

Those taxpayers who have paid at least 80% of the final amount of tax due within 60 days of mailing or presentation of a penalty relief notice may pay the balance of the tax due without penalties or interest. (Sec. 4833.1, Rev. & Tax. Code; Sec. 4985.3, Rev. & Tax. Code)

In counties that have established the required cancellation procedure, delinquency penalties may be canceled by order of the county board of supervisors if the assessee or fee owner has demonstrated to the tax collector's satisfaction that the delinquency resulted from the county's failure to send a tax notice to the owner of property acquired after the lien date on the secured roll. In addition, a delinquency penalty may be canceled if the delinquency resulted from the tax collector's failure to mail or electronically transmit the tax bill to the address on the tax roll or to the electronic address provided by the taxpayer. (Sec. 2610.5, Rev. & Tax. Code; Sec. 2910.1, Rev. & Tax. Code)

If an assessee shows that a failure to file a required property statement was due to reasonable cause and not willful neglect, the county board of supervisors may abate the penalty. (Sec. 480.7, Rev. & Tax. Code)

If an exemption was improperly allowed as a result of an assessor's error, interest shall be forgiven. (Sec. 531.1, Rev. & Tax. Code; Sec. 531.6, Rev. & Tax. Code)

Interest may also be canceled on any delinquent tax if the interest resulted from an error of the tax collector, auditor, or assessor or from an inability to complete valid procedures initiated prior to the delinquency, provided payment of the corrected or additional amount is made within 30 days from the date the correction was entered on the roll or abstract record. (Sec. 4985, Rev. & Tax. Code)

Only those delinquency penalties that apply to the difference between the county board of supervisors' final determination of value and the assessed value that was appealed may be canceled. (Sec. 531.3, Rev. & Tax. Code) Affected taxpayers must receive notice of these penalty relief provisions. Those taxpayers who have paid at least 80% of the final amount of tax due within 60 days of mailing or presentation of the penalty relief notice may pay the balance of the tax due without penalties or interest. (Sec. 4833.1, Rev. & Tax. Code; Sec. 4985.3, Rev. & Tax. Code)

Subject to approval of the local county board of supervisors, tax collector, and auditor, where a taxpayer has failed to pay an amount of tax computed upon assessed value that is the subject of a pending informal review based upon a decline in value as a result of damage, destruction, depreciation, obsolescence, and removal of property, any relief from penalties would apply only to the difference between the assessor's final determination of value and the value on the assessment roll for the fiscal year covered by the application. For any taxpayer that, within 30 days of filing an application for reassessment, has paid at least 80% of the amount of tax finally determined due by the assessor, the tax collector must accept payment of the balance of the tax due without penalties or interest. These provisions apply only to property for which applications for an informal review based on declines in value are pending as of January 1, 2013, or are filed after that date. (Sec. 4985.5, Rev. & Tax. Code)

Private railroad cars.—The penalty for failure to file a timely private railroad car report may be abated if the failure was due to reasonable cause and occurred notwithstanding the exercise of ordinary care and in the absence of willful neglect. (Sec. 11273, Rev. & Tax. Code)

• *Collection cost recovery fee*

For purposes of the private railroad car tax and the timber yield tax, the California State Board of Equalization (BOE) can impose a collection cost recovery fee (collection fee) on any person that fails to pay an amount of fee, interest, penalty, or other amount due and payable. The collection fee is imposed only if the BOE has mailed its demand notice to that person for payment that advises that continued failure to pay the amount due may result in collection action, including the imposition of the collection fee. (Sec. 11534, Rev. & Tax. Code; Sec. 38577, Rev. & Tax. Code)

Interest shall not accrue with respect to the collection fee, which shall be collected in the same manner as the collection of any other fee imposed by the BOE for the tax, surcharge, or fee at issue. A person shall be relieved of the collection fee if the failure to pay any otherwise qualified amount:

> (1) was due to reasonable cause and circumstances beyond the person's control and

> (2) occurred notwithstanding the exercise of ordinary care and the absence of willful neglect.

Any person seeking to be relieved of the collection fee must file with the BOE a statement under penalty of perjury setting forth the facts upon which the person bases the claim for relief. (Sec. 11534, Rev. & Tax. Code; Sec. 38577, Rev. & Tax. Code)

[¶20-800]

CREDITS, ABATEMENTS, REFUNDS, INCENTIVES

[¶20-805] Credits

Taxpayers may substitute credits against future property tax liabilities for the payment of refunds and accrued interest by California cities and counties. A substituted credit is available on execution of a written settlement agreement between the taxpayer and the affected county, or city and county. Interest on a substituted credit may continue to accrue until the credit is fully offset against future tax liabilities. (Sec. 5103, Rev. & Tax. Code)

• *Rebates*

Local taxing jurisdictions are authorized to rebate property tax revenues derived from property utilized by specified taxpayers that demonstrate their success in the establishment or expansion of manufacturing jobs. These rebate programs are discussed at ¶20-265 Manufacturing and Industrial Property.

[¶20-810] Abatements

Penalties for failure to file certain property tax statements can be abated under certain circumstances. Uncollected taxes, penalties, and costs may be canceled by the county auditor on order of the board of supervisors, upon a showing that collection cannot be enforced because of errors in assessment, description, equalization, levy, or other proceeding. Additionally, delinquent property taxes, penalties, interest, and related charges may be waived if:

> (1) the amount is too small to justify the cost of collection,

> (2) the likelihood of collection does not warrant the expense involved, or

> (3) the amount thereof has been otherwise lawfully compromised or adjusted.

(Sec. 2611.1, Rev. & Tax. Code; Sec. 2923, Rev. & Tax. Code)

Relief generally is conditioned on approval by the county board of supervisors or, in cases of state assessments, the State Board of Equalization (BOE).

• *Failure to file statement*

For local assessments, if an assessee establishes to the satisfaction of the county board of equalization or the assessment appeals board that a failure to file a timely annual property statement or a timely change in ownership statement was due to reasonable cause and not due to willful neglect, the penalty may be abated in whole or in part if the assessee files a written application for abatement within the time prescribed by law for filing an application for assessment reduction. Beginning January 1, 2016, the penalty may be abated if the assessee establishes that the failure was due to reasonable cause and circumstances beyond the assessee's control and occurred notwithstanding the exercise of ordinary care in the absence of willful neglect. (Sec. 463, Rev. & Tax. Code; Sec. 483, Rev. & Tax. Code)

In the case of state assessments, if an assessee establishes to the satisfaction of the BOE that a failure to either file a timely property statement or file an accurate property statement was due to reasonable cause and occurred notwithstanding the exercise of ordinary care and the absence of willful neglect, the penalty may be abated in whole or in part if the assessee files a written application for abatement within the time prescribed by law for filing an application for assessment reduction. (Sec. 830, Rev. & Tax. Code; Sec. 862, Rev. & Tax. Code)

If an assessee fails to timely file a property statement for aircraft, as requested by the local county assessor, penalties can be abated if the assessee establishes that the failure to file the statement was due to reasonable cause and not due to willful neglect. (Sec. 4367, Rev. & Tax. Code)

• *Cancellation*

For cancellations resulting from assessment appeals, only those penalties for failure to pay tax that apply to the difference between the county board of supervisors' final determination of value and the assessed value that was appealed may be canceled. Affected taxpayers must receive notice of these new penalty relief provisions. Those taxpayers who have paid at least 80% of the final amount of tax due within 60 days of mailing or presentation of the penalty relief notice may pay the balance of the tax due without penalties or interest. (Sec. 4985.3, Rev. & Tax. Code)

If all or any portion of the property was taxable for the year of cancellation, the last assessee of the property is sent a notice of the proposed cancellation, indicating the grounds for cancellation and stating that collection of the tax for the year involved will be enforced unless cause is shown why it should not be, and that the assessee has 10 days after notice to request a hearing with the board of supervisors. (Sec. 4946, Rev. & Tax. Code; Sec. 4947, Rev. & Tax. Code) If the board orders that collection of the tax be enforced, the assessor assesses the property at its value on the lien date for the year of cancellation, the assessment is put on the current assessment roll, and collection is enforced in the same manner as other taxes on the roll. (Sec. 4948, Rev. & Tax. Code)

The county auditor may also cancel delinquent taxes, penalties, interest, and costs if they have been levied more than once, erroneously levied, levied on nonexistent property, levied on property annexed by a public entity after the lien date, levied on government-owned property, or levied in excess of assessed value. If the taxes, penalties, or costs are collected more than four years following the enrollment of the tax bill, the cancellation authorized pursuant to the aforementioned provision may be performed if the cancellation action is initiated within 120 days of the payment. (Sec. 4986, Rev. & Tax. Code; Sec. 4986.2, Rev. & Tax. Code) Taxes may also be canceled as follows:

— when property is assessed more than once by the same taxing agency; (Sec. 4990, Rev. & Tax. Code)

— on property, subject to assessment for the payment of certain bonds, acquired after the lien date by a city, county, special district, school district, joint powers authority, or other political subdivision of the state on foreclosure proceedings; (Sec. 4986.3, Rev. & Tax. Code)

— on property deeded to the Veterans Welfare Board; (Sec. 4986.4, Rev. & Tax. Code)

— on property of an estate held by the state; (Sec. 4986.5, Rev. & Tax. Code) and

— on public lands on application of the State Lands Commission. (Sec. 5026, Rev. & Tax. Code through Sec. 5029, Rev. & Tax. Code) or the property owner (Sec. 5061, Rev. & Tax Code through Sec. 5064, Rev. & Tax. Code)

The tax collector may also cancel taxes of such small amounts that collection is uneconomical. (Sec. 4986.8, Rev. & Tax. Code)

Any uncollected penalty, cost, interest, or fee attaching because of an error caused by the tax collector, auditor, or assessor, or because of the failure to complete valid proceedings prior to the delinquency date, is canceled if the payment of the correct amount is made within 30 days from the date the roll is corrected. (Sec. 4985, Rev. & Tax. Code)

There are also special provisions for the cancellation of uncollected penalties or costs upon a finding that failure to make a timely payment was due to reasonable cause and circumstances over which the taxpayer had no control. The cancellation is conditioned upon the payment of the principal amount no later than June 30 of the fourth fiscal year following the fiscal year in which the tax became delinquent. Such cancellation is also permissible if:

(1) a local, state, or federal court has ordered cancellation or

(2) the taxpayer unintentionally paid an incorrect amount and payment of the proper amount of the tax due is made within 10 days after the notice of shortage is mailed by the tax collector.

(Sec. 4985.2, Rev. & Tax. Code)

Errors of understatement of less than $5 in the amount of tax as a result of the auditor's clerical error may be canceled by the auditor. (Sec. 4832.1, Rev. & Tax. Code) Similarly, transfers of delinquent taxes, penalties, and costs to the unsecured roll that amount to less than $20 may be canceled rather than transferred. (Sec. 5089, Rev. & Tax. Code)

Taxes on exempt property may be entirely or partially canceled when a claim for exemption was available but not timely filed by an exempt organization. (Sec. 270, Rev. & Tax. Code; Sec. 4987, Rev. & Tax. Code)

Delinquency penalties may be canceled if the delinquency resulted from the county's failure to send a notice of taxes to the owner of property acquired after the lien date on the secured roll or from the tax collector's failure to mail or electronically transmit the tax bill to the address on the tax roll or the electronic address provided by the taxpayer. (Sec. 2610.5, Rev. & Tax. Code; Sec. 2910.1, Rev. & Tax. Code)

Subject to approval of the local county board of supervisors, tax collector, and auditor, where a taxpayer has failed to pay an amount of tax computed upon assessed value that is the subject of a pending informal review based upon a decline in value as a result of damage, destruction, depreciation, obsolescence, and removal of property, any relief from penalties would apply only to the difference between the assessor's final determination of value and the value on the assessment roll for the fiscal year covered by the application. For any taxpayer that, within 30 days of filing an application for reassessment, has paid at least 80% of the amount of tax finally determined due by the assessor, the tax collector must accept payment of the balance of the tax due without penalties or interest. These provisions apply only to property for which applications for an informal review based on declines in value are pending as of January 1, 2013, or are filed after that date. (Sec. 4985.5, Rev. & Tax. Code)

• *Innocent spouse, registered domestic partner relief*

The innocent spouse relief provisions administered by the State Board of Equalization (BOE) for sales and use tax also applies to—among other taxes, surcharges, and fees—private railroad car tax and timber yield tax. (Sec. 11408.5, Rev. & Tax. Code; Sec. 38454.5, Rev. & Tax. Code)

However, the relief under the miscellaneous taxes, all of which were enacted in the same law, expressly is extended to qualifying registered domestic partners. In addition, the relief provided to the taxes other than sales and use applies retroactively to liabilities arising prior to the effective date of the enacting law. According to a legislative declaration, enactment of the relief and its retroactive application are necessary for the public purpose of providing equitable relief to innocent spouses or registered domestic partners. In addition, a regulation details the relief. (Reg. 4903, 18 CCR)

[¶20-815] Refunds

Property taxes may be refunded only if:

— they were paid more than once;

— they were erroneously or illegally collected;

— they were paid as a result of the assessor's clerical error or excessive or improper assessments attributable to erroneous property information supplied by the assessee;

— they were paid on improvements that did not exist on the lien date;

— they were paid on an assessment in excess of the value of the property as determined by the county assessment appeals board;

— they were paid on an assessment in excess of the value of the property;

— the amount paid exceeds the amount due on the property as shown on the roll by an amount greater than $10;

— the amount paid exceeds the amount due on the property as the result of corrections to the roll or cancellations after the taxes were paid; or

— the amount paid exceeds the amount due on the property as a result of a reduction attributable to a hearing before an assessment appeals board or an assessment hearing officer.

(Sec. 5096, Rev. & Tax. Code; Sec. 5097.2, Rev. & Tax. Code; Sec. 533, Rev. & Tax. Code)

"Taxes" includes penalties, interest, and costs. (Sec. 5107, Rev. & Tax. Code)

Taxes collected by a local agency when the property is annexed to another local agency without being technically detached from the first are refundable. (Sec. 5096.1, Rev. & Tax. Code)

Refunds of tax (or cancellations) may also be made when an exempt organization fails to timely file a claim for exemption. (Sec. 270, Rev. & Tax. Code)

If current taxes have been paid on property acquired by a public agency through negotiation after the beginning of the fiscal year, the pro rata share that, if unpaid, would be subject to cancellation is deemed erroneously collected and is refunded to the person who paid the tax, unless the person was reimbursed for the tax by the acquiring agency. (Sec. 5096.7, Rev. & Tax. Code)

• *Refund procedures*

Refund procedures are discussed:

Refunds without the filing of a claim.—Refunds are allowed without the filing of a claim if:

• there has been no transfer of the property during or since the fiscal year for which the taxes subject to the refund have been levied; and

• the amount of the refund is less than $5,000.

(Sec. 5105, Rev. & Tax. Code)

This provision becomes operative in a county only if the county board of supervisors adopts a resolution or ordinance that approves the operation of the provision. (Sec. 5105, Rev. & Tax. Code)

Refund procedures generally.—Generally, to obtain a property tax refund, a taxpayer must file a claim in writing with the tax collector or the county auditor within the later of:

— generally four years after the date of payment;

— one year after the tax collector mails notice of overpayment;

— the assessment period agreed to between the taxpayer and the assessor; or

— within 60 days or receipt of required notice following correction of an assessment that entitles the assessee to a refund.

Claims must set forth the grounds for the refund and the portion of the assessment challenged. (Sec. 5097(a)(2), Rev. & Tax. Code; Sec. 5097.02, Rev. & Tax. Code; Sec. 5097.2, Rev. & Tax. Code)

A claim must be filed within eight years after making the payment sought to be refunded, if the claim for refund is filed on or after January 1, 2015, and relates to the disabled veterans' exemption described in Sec. 205.5, Rev. & Tax. Code. (Sec. 5097(a)(4), Rev. & Tax. Code)

If an application for either a reduction of assessment or equalization of an assessment is filed without notice that the application is intended to constitute a claim for a refund, the assessee must file a claim for refund before six months after the earlier of:

— the time the assessment board makes a final determination on the application and mails notice to the assessee that does not advise the assessee to file a claim for a refund, or

— the expiration of the time period for the county assessment appeals board to hear evidence or to make a final determination on the application for reduction and the board fails to do either.

(Sec. 5097(a)(3)(A), Rev. & Tax. Code)

Where an application is filed without notice that it is intended to constitute a claim for refund and the board makes a determination on the application and notifies the assessee advising the applicant to file a claim for refund within six months, the assessee will have six months in which to do so. (Sec. 5097(a)(3)(B), Rev. & Tax. Code)

Taxpayers may also claim a refund on an application for a reduction in property tax assessment. (Sec. 1604, Rev. & Tax. Code; Sec. 5097, Rev. & Tax. Code) These refund claims are discussed below under "Equalization proceedings."

The California Court of Appeals has determined that the property tax limitations periods also apply to refund claims for special benefit assessments; see *Special benefit assessments* below under "Other taxes and fees."

Any overpayments of tax paid prior to the reassessment of property damaged or destroyed by misfortune or calamity may be refunded to the taxpayer without the filing of a refund claim. (Sec. 170, Rev. & Tax. Code)

Generally, property tax refunds are payable to the person who paid the tax to be refunded. However, any property tax refund that results from a reduction in the value of taxable property may be paid to the latest recorded owner of the property, instead of to the individual or entity identified as having paid the tax, if:

> (1) there has been no transfer of the property during or since the fiscal year for which the taxes subject to refund were levied and

> (2) the amount of the refund is less than $5,000.

(Sec. 5104, Rev. & Tax. Code)

The tax collector may apply any refund due a taxpayer to any delinquent taxes due on the same property for which the taxpayer is liable. (Sec. 2635.5, Rev. & Tax. Code) Conversely, taxpayers may substitute credits against future property tax liabilities for the payment of refunds and accrued interest by California cities and counties. A substituted credit is available on execution of a written settlement agreement between the taxpayer and the affected county, or city and county. Interest on a substituted credit may continue to accrue until the credit is fully offset against future tax liabilities. (Sec. 5103, Rev. & Tax. Code)

• *Equalization proceedings*

An application for a reduction in a property tax assessment filed with a county board of supervisors, meeting as a county board of equalization or an assessment appeals board, pursuant to equalization proceedings under Sec. 1603, Rev. & Tax. Code constitutes a sufficient claim for refund if the applicant states in the application that the application is also intended as a claim for refund. (Sec. 1601, Rev. & Tax Code; Sec. 1604, Rev. & Tax. Code; Sec. 5097(b), Rev. & Tax. Code) If the application is also a refund claim, the claim is deemed denied on the date the final installment of the tax becomes delinquent or on the date the equalization board makes its final determination on the application, whichever is the later. (Sec. 5141, Rev. & Tax. Code)

A taxpayer that is not notified by a county assessor of an increase in the value of his or her property may pay the taxes under protest and apply to the county board of equalization for an adjustment in the valuation. (Sec. 620, Rev. & Tax. Code)

An assessee and the county assessor may file a stipulation with the county board of equalization stating that a property tax refund claim does not involve valuation issues. If the board accepts the stipulation, an assessee will be deemed to have complied with the requirement that an assessee file and prosecute an application for reduction in order to exhaust administrative remedies before bringing a civil action for a refund. However, acceptance of the stipulation does not excuse or waive the requirement of timely filing a refund claim. (Sec. 5142, Rev. & Tax. Code)

• *Supplemental assessments*

If, as a result of a supplemental assessment, a refund is due the assessee, the auditor must make the refund within 90 days of the date of enrollment of the negative assessment on the supplemental roll. (Sec. 75.43, Rev. & Tax. Code) Refunds must be made from taxes collected on assessments made on the supplemental roll.

If there is a property tax refund owed to the transferor of property that has had its base year value reduced, the portion of the refund representing taxes on the reduction in base value after the transfer must be applied to satisfy the supplemental assessment against the transferee. (Sec. 5096.8, Rev. & Tax. Code) However, this rule applies only if a county's supervisors have adopted an implementing resolution.

Refunds of supplemental taxes are limited to the difference between the tax, penalty, or interest paid on property and the tax, penalty, or interest due on the property because of its new base-year value. (Sec. 75.43, Rev. & Tax. Code)

• *Retroactive application of constitutional exemptions*

Refunds are allowed in situations in which the taxes were validly levied and collected but a constitutional amendment granting an exemption was subsequently enacted and applied retroactively. (Sec. 5096.5, Rev. & Tax. Code) Claims for refund must be filed within four years from the effective date of the amendment.

• *Return of replicated payments*

If a taxpayer submits a payment to be applied to a specific tax or tax installment that has already been paid, the county must return the second payment to the party who tendered it within 60 days, whether or not the second payment is in the same amount as the first. The second payment must be returned within 60 days of the date the payment becomes final, which is the date the original payment is no longer subject to charge-back, dishonor, or reversal. (Sec. 2781, Rev. & Tax. Code; Sec. 2780, Rev. & Tax. Code; Sec. 2780.5, Rev. & Tax. Code)

However, a California property owner of record can instruct a tax collector in writing to refund a replicated payment on a current property tax assessment to a tendering party who is not an owner of record. This law does not apply to delinquent payments. The measure is expressly intended to address problems and difficulties that arise when an adverse party attempts to pay taxes for property for which the adverse party is not the owner of record. (Sec. 2781.5, Rev. & Tax. Code)

If a replicated payment is made of any tax or tax installment already paid by a certificate of eligibility issued pursuant to the Senior Citizens' Property Tax and Assistance Law, the replicated payment must be paid by the county within 60 days to the person shown on the certificate of eligibility instead of to the party tendering the payment. (Sec. 2781, Rev. & Tax. Code) If the replicated payment is not returned within the 60 days, the county must pay interest on the amount of the replicated payment at the county pool apportioned rate from 60 days from the date the payment becomes final until the payment is refunded. Such interest is payable only if it amounts to $10 or more. (Sec. 2782, Rev. & Tax. Code)

A county tax collector may exercise his or her judgment, however, in determining how and to what tax a payment should be applied if the payor:

(1) returns the wrong payment stub in claiming the payment is a replicated payment or

(2) makes no indication as to how the payment is to be applied.

(Sec. 2783, Rev. & Tax. Code)

• *Interest*

Except as noted below, interest at the greater of 3% per annum or the county pool apportioned rate (see ¶ 20-752) begins to accrue on property tax refunds on the following dates, provided that the amount of interest is $10 or more:

— the date the tax was paid if a timely application for an assessment reduction was filed or if the refund resulted from a tax roll correction;

— the date the deed was recorded if the tax was imposed on property acquired by a public agency in eminent domain;

— 120 days after a county assessor has sent authorization to a county auditor for a reduction in the assessed value of property that was damaged or destroyed; or

— the latter of the date the tax was paid or the refund claim was filed in all other cases.

Regardless of the date that interest begins to accrue, the computation of interest terminates within 30 days of the date the refund was mailed or personally delivered. (Sec. 5151, Rev. & Tax. Code)

No interest is payable to a taxpayer who was given written notice of overpayment by the tax collector and failed to apply for a refund within 30 days after the notice was mailed. (Sec. 5151, Rev. & Tax. Code; Sec. 2635, Rev. & Tax. Code)

If a refund of supplemental property taxes is not made within the required 90-day period, interest is generally paid at the same rate for ordinary property tax refunds. (Sec. 75.43, Rev. & Tax. Code)

• *Rescission of tax sale*

When the sale of tax-defaulted property is rescinded, the purchaser is entitled to a refund of the amount paid as the purchase price. (Sec. 3731, Rev. & Tax. Code; Sec. 3731.1, Rev. & Tax. Code)

When a court holds a tax deed void, the purchaser at the sale is entitled to a refund for the amount paid as the purchase price in excess of the amount for which the purchaser has been reimbursed for taxes, penalties, and costs. (Sec. 3729, Rev. & Tax. Code) The claim for refund must be made within one year after the judgment becomes final.

However, in either of the above cases, the holder of a tax certificate who receives all or any part of the amount paid at the sale will not be obligated to make any refund or repayment of that amount to the purchaser, the delinquent taxpayer, the county, or any other person. (Sec. 3731, Rev. & Tax. Code; Sec. 3729, Rev. & Tax. Code)

• *Erroneous payment*

If property taxes have erroneously been paid on the wrong property through no fault of the assessee, the payment may be transferred to the correct property by the tax collector. If a taxpayer mistakenly pays property taxes on property the taxpayer does not own (unintended property) and the taxpayer has no property to which the payment may be applied, the taxes must be refunded within 60 days of the county verifying that the payment was paid by mistake or the credit or refund will be subject to interest. Prior to 2012, the refund had to be paid at any time before a guaranty or certificate of title issues respecting the unintended property and before two years have elapsed since the date of the payment. (Sec. 4911, Rev. & Tax. Code—Sec. 4916, Rev. & Tax. Code)

• *Private railroad car, timber yield taxes*

The claim for a refund must be filed by the later of four years from December 10 of the year in which the assessment is made or six months from the date of overpayment. (Sec. 11553, Rev. & Tax. Code) If the SBE disallows a claim for refund or credit the private railroad car tax or the timber yield tax, the claimant may bring an action to recover the whole or any part of the disallowed amount. Suits for refund of private railroad car tax or timber yield tax must be brought within 90 days after the mailing of notice of action upon the refund claim. (Sec. 11573, Rev. & Tax. Code; Sec. 38613, Rev. & Tax. Code)

• *Appeals*

Suits for property tax refunds generally must be brought within six months after rejection of the refund claim. (Sec. 5141, Rev. & Tax. Code; Sec. 5145, Rev. & Tax. Code; Sec. 5145.5, Rev. & Tax. Code)

Civil actions.—Generally, a civil action for a refund of an improper property tax payment may not be brought unless the taxpayer has exhausted his or her administrative remedies, that is, the taxpayer has filed a timely application for reduction of assessment with the county board of equalization or assessment appeals board, paid the tax, and then filed a claim for tax refund. (Sec. 1605, Rev. & Tax. Code)

A person who has paid a property tax may bring an action in superior court, but not in the small claims division of the superior court, against a county or city to recover the tax when the county or city board of supervisors has refused to refund the tax. (Sec. 5140, Rev. & Tax. Code)

No action may be brought unless a claim for refund has first been filed (see ¶20-815), except with respect to actions for refund of state-assessed taxes. (Sec. 5142, Rev. & Tax. Code; Sec. 5148, Rev. & Tax. Code) If a claim for refund relates only to the validity of a portion of an assessment, an action may be brought only as to that portion. (Sec. 5143, Rev. & Tax. Code)

Refund suits may be brought within six months of the date the refund claim is rejected. If a claim is not acted upon by the authorities within six months, the taxpayer may consider the claim disallowed and file suit. If the taxpayer designates an application for a reduction of assessment to be a claim for refund, the refund claim is deemed denied on the date the equalization board makes its final decision on the application or on the date the final installment of taxes becomes delinquent, whichever is later. (Sec. 5141, Rev. & Tax. Code)

Refund actions have priority over other civil actions, except those for which special preference is given by law and for certain state-assessed public utility property. (Sec. 5148, Rev. & Tax. Code; Sec. 5149, Rev. & Tax. Code) A summons must be served on the parties involved, and a return must be made within one year of the commencement of the action. (Sec. 5147, Rev. & Tax. Code) If the county collected a city property tax, the city must be joined in the lawsuit, as well as the State Board of Equalization if the property is state assessed. (Sec. 5146, Rev. & Tax. Code)

If an assessment is held void in part or in whole, judgment is entered for the taxes paid on the void assessment. (Sec. 5144, Rev. & Tax. Code) If the judgment is for the taxpayer, the taxpayer is entitled to interest. (Sec. 5150.5, Rev. & Tax. Code) The court may also award a refund of penalties, interest, and costs. (Sec. 5149.5, Rev. & Tax. Code)

A taxpayer who has paid the first installment under an installment plan of redemption from a tax sale and filed a claim for its recovery that has been denied may bring an action for a refund, even though the property taxes due have not been paid in full. Suits must be brought within six months of rejection of the claim. The suit, however, does not relieve the taxpayer from making payments pursuant to the agreement. If the owner defaults, he or she loses his or her right to maintain the action. The following conditions must be satisfied before an owner can bring action:

— the first installment must have been paid within six months of the delinquency of the taxes being paid by installments; and

— the taxpayer must either post bond or pledge other property as security if the tax liability remaining after the first installment, including interest and penalties, exceeds 66^2/3 of the full cash value of the property on which the taxes are a lien. If, after subsequent installment payments, the unpaid tax no longer exceeds this percentage, the requirement for security terminates.

(Sec. 5145, Rev. & Tax. Code)

Also, a court action may be brought by a person who has paid a first installment under an installment plan entered into pursuant to a written request filed after June 30, 1997, for payment of an escape assessment. If the taxpayer defaults on any obligation in the installment plan, the right to court action terminates. (Sec. 5145.5, Rev. & Tax. Code)

A special refund action must be used to challenge the valuation of state-assessed property or the allocation of value of such property for assessment purposes. The filing of a tax refund claim is not a prerequisite for bringing suit with respect to state-assessed property. However, the taxpayer must have previously filed a petition for reassessment. After payment of the taxes at issue, a single action must be brought in a county in which the California Attorney General has an office or in which the assessee has a significant presence. The State Board of Equalization (BOE) and all of the counties that collected taxes on the state-assessed property are named as defendants, but only the BOE must be served with a summons and complaint. The BOE acts as agent for service of process on the defendant counties. If a defendant county collected taxes on behalf of a city, the county must in turn notify the city of the action, giving it an opportunity to intervene. (Sec. 5142, Rev. & Tax. Code; Sec. 5148, Rev. & Tax. Code)

Any action to challenge the valuation of state-assessed property must be brought within four years after either the BOE mailed its decision or its written findings and conclusion, whichever is later. A taxpayer's petition for reassessment or correction of allocated assessment constitutes a claim for refund if the petitioner states so in the petition. (Sec. 5148, Rev. & Tax. Code)

Unlike actions concerning locally-assessed property, courts are not restricted to the record before the BOE in reviewing refund suits involving state-assessed property. Courts must consider all relevant and admissible evidence, regardless of whether the issue raised is one of fact or of law. However, review is limited to the grounds cited in taxpayer's petition. (Sec. 5170, Rev. & Tax. Code)

[¶20-820] Incentives

The governing body of any county, city and county, or city, may adopt a local ordinance establishing a capital investment incentive program (CIIP), under which the local government may "rebate" to certain large manufacturers an amount up to the amount of California property tax revenues derived from the taxation of the assessed value in excess of $150 million of any qualified manufacturing facility within the local government's jurisdiction. (Sec. 51298, Govt. Code) For a more detailed discussion, see ¶20-265, Manufacturing and Industrial Property.

[¶20-900]

TAXPAYER RIGHTS AND REMEDIES

[¶20-904] Overview of Appeal Process

The California State Board of Equalization provides guidance materials on the general topic of assessment appeals, including the following:

— Assessment Appeals Manual, (05-03);

— Publication 29, California Property Tax: an Overview;

— Publication 30, Residential Property Assessment Appeals; and

— BOE Publication 143, Your Appeal Hearing Before the Board Members.

Taxpayers generally are entitled to representation by agents during the assessment appeal process. However, there are time limits for appeals.

Taxpayers can start the appeals process informally by talking to the county assessor. Still at the local county level, a taxpayer can then appeal either to the county board of supervisors meeting as the county board of equalization or to the local appeals board, depending on the county. In some counties, the taxpayer may have the option of a hearing before a hearing officer, whose decision, in turn, could be appealed to the county board of equalization or to the local appeals board.

Assessments of state-assessed property may be appealed to the State Board of Equalization. Finally, taxpayers can appeal to courts.

CCH PLANNING NOTE: Preliminary steps to formal protests.—Prior to instituting the formal protest process, a good first step in most cases is to review the assessor's valuation records, which are public records, for neighboring and/or comparable properties to confirm whether any glaring inconsistencies are evident. For example, if the other properties have been assigned relatively higher values, that may caution against proceeding with a protest to avoid the risk of having an appraised value increased or otherwise alerting the assessor to what may essentially be a favorable appraisal. It also may be useful to directly contact the assessor to discuss what factors the assessor considered in valuing the property, as this may alert the parties to obvious valuation errors that the assessor may be willing to correct without requiring the property owner to pursue a formal protest.

[¶20-906] Protest and Appeal of Assessments

Discussed here in relation to the assessment appeals are:

— representation of taxpayers,

— limitations periods for appeals,

— informal conferences,

— local administrative hearings,

— state administrative hearings, and

— judicial appeals and remedies.

• *Representation of taxpayers*

An assessor must permit an assessee or the assessee's designated representative to inspect any information and records relating to the appraisal and the assessment of the assessee's property. (Sec. 408.2, Rev. & Tax. Code) An appeal of an assessment may be filed by the taxpayer, the taxpayer's agent, the taxpayer's spouse, or the taxpayer's children or parents. (Sec. 1603, Rev. & Tax. Code) If the application is made by an agent, the agent will be deemed to have been duly authorized if the applicant's written agent authorization is on or attached to the application at the time it is filed with the board. The agent authorization must include, among other things, the following:

— the name, address, and telephone number of the specific agent who is authorized to represent the applicant;

— the applicant's signature and title; and

— a statement that the agent will provide the applicant with a copy of the application.

(Sec. 1603, Rev. & Tax. Code; Reg. 305(a)(1), 18 CCR)

If the applicant is a corporation, limited partnership, or a limited liability company, the agent authorization must be signed by an officer or authorized employee of the business entity who has been designated in writing by the board of directors or corporate officer to represent the corporation on property tax matters. (Reg. 305(a)(3), 18 CCR)

The taxpayer or the taxpayer's representative must be notified of the time and date of the hearing at least 45 days before the hearing, unless a shorter notice period is mutually agreed upon. (Sec. 1605.6, Rev. & Tax. Code)

The applicant and the assessor may be represented by legal counsel, except that when an assessment protest is heard by a hearing officer appointed pursuant to section 1636 of the Revenue and Taxation Code, the assessor may have legal counsel only if the applicant is represented by an attorney. (Reg. 314, 18 CCR)

• *Limitations periods for appeals*

Limitations periods vary for different types of appeals.

Assessment appeals—county boards.—The assessment appeal regular filing period for all real and personal property located in a county is dependent upon when the county assessor elects to mail assessment notices to all owners of real property on the secured roll. If the notices are mailed by August 1, appeals must be filed between July 2 through September 15. If those notices are not sent out by August 1, the filing period is July 2 through November 30. (Reg. 305(d)(1), 18 CCR)

Additionally, an application appealing a base year value for the most recent lien date, where that value is not the value currently on the assessment roll, shall be filed with the clerk during the regular filing period beginning July 2 but no later than September 15 or November 30, as applicable. (Reg. 305(d)(1), 18 CCR)

Other limitations periods for assessment appeals include:

— for an escape assessment or a supplemental assessment, 60 days after the date of mailing printed on the notice of assessment or the postmark date, whichever is later, or no later than 60 days after the date of mailing printed on the tax bill or the postmark date, whichever is later, in the county of Los Angeles and in those counties where the board of supervisors has adopted a resolution to that effect, pursuant to section 1605 of the Revenue and Taxation Code; (Reg. 305(d)(2), 18 CCR)

— for a proposed reassessment for property damaged by misfortune or calamity pursuant to section 170 of the Revenue and Taxation Code an appeal must be filed with the clerk no later than six months after the date of mailing of the notice of proposed reassessment by the assessor; (Sec. 170(c), Rev. & Tax. Code; Reg. 305(d)(3), 18 CCR) and;

— for an untimely notice of assessment, within 60 days of the earlier of receipt of a notice of assessment or the mailing of a tax bill. (Reg. 305(d)(4), 18 CCR)

Furthermore, the application may be filed within 12 months following the month in which the assessee is notified of assessment if the assessee and the assessor stipulate that there is an error in the assessment. (Sec. 1603, Rev. & Tax. Code)

Except as provided in sections 1603 and 1605 of the Revenue and Taxation Code, the board has no jurisdiction to hear an application unless filed within the time periods specified above. (Sec. 1603, Rev. & Tax. Code; Reg. 305, 18 CCR)

The appeals deadline extension is a general county-wide deadline for all real and personal property on either the secured or unsecured roll if the assessor does not provide by August 1 notice to all assessees of real property on the local secured roll, so that each county has a deadline of either September 15 or November 30 for all property located in the county. Further, the assessor must notify the clerk and tax collector by April 1 if notices will be provided to taxpayers by August 1, and newspaper publications may not be substituted for personal notice to the taxpayer as a means of notice for purposes of the assessment appeal deadline extension. Moreover, the BOE must maintain a statewide listing of the assessment appeals period for each county from information provided by county clerks so that the BOE, counties, tax practitioners, and taxpayers may rely on a central source of information. (Sec. 1603, Rev. & Tax. Code; Sec. 2611.6, Rev. & Tax. Code)

The last day for filing the application is November 30 for an assessee of real property on the local secured roll if:

(1) a notice is not required to be provided to the assessee with respect to that property under Sec. 619, Rev. & Tax. Code and

(2) the county assessor does not, by August 1, provide notice to the assessee of the assessed value of the assessee's real property on the local secured roll.

(Sec. 1603, Rev. & Tax. Code)

CCH CAUTION: Application must be filed each year.—An application must be filed for each year an assessment is contested, even if an identical appeal is still pending for a prior year. (*Publication 30*, California BOE)

A county board of supervisors may by resolution allow a reduction application to be filed within 60 days of the mailing of the notice of the assessor's response to a request for reassessment to full cash value due to a decline in value, provided that:

(1) the reassessment request was submitted to the assessor in writing;

(2) the reassessment request was made on or before the preceding March 15;

(3) the assessor's response was mailed after August 31;

(4) the assessor did not reduce the assessment in the full amount requested;

(5) the assessment reduction application is filed by December 31 of the year in which the reassessment request was filed; and

(6) the assessment reduction application is accompanied by a copy of the assessor's response.

(Sec. 1603, Rev. & Tax. Code)

Valuation of state-assessed property.—An action challenging the valuation of state-assessed property or the allocation of value of such property for assessment purposes must be brought only after payment of the taxes at issue and within four years after the later of the date that the BOE:

(1) has mailed its decision or

(2) has mailed its written findings and conclusions.

(Sec. 5148, Rev. & Tax. Code) Other state-assessed property petitions must be filed by:

— July 20 for reassessmentof unitary property; (Sec. 731, Rev. & Tax. Code; Reg. 5323(a), 18 CCR)

— September 20 for reassessment of nonunitary property; (Sec. 732, Rev. & Tax. Code; Reg. 5323(c), 18 CCR)

— July 20 if a state assessee disagrees with an assessment allocation; (Reg. 5323(b), 18 CCR)

— the date stated on the notice if a state assessee disagrees with a value or penalty in a notice of escaped or excessive assessment; (Reg. 5323(d), 18 CCR)

— within 50 days following the notice of assessment for private railroad cars; (Sec. 11338, Rev. & Tax. Code; Sec. 11339, Rev. & Tax. Code; Reg. 5323(e)(3), 18 CCR) and

— July 20 for a correction of an allocated assessment. (Sec. 746, Rev. & Tax. Code)

The BOE generally must render its decision on a petition for reassessment of private railroad cars within 45 days of the date of the hearing on the petition. (Sec. 11341, Rev. & Tax. Code) An extension of 15 days may be granted to file a petition if a written request is made prior to the filing deadline. (Sec. 733, Rev. & Tax. Code)

Decisions on petitions for reassessment must be made before December 31 of the assessment year. (Sec. 744, Rev. & Tax. Code)

Clerical errors made by the BOE in its assessment or errors that the BOE discovers through an audit that had caused it to assess the property at a higher value may be corrected by the BOE within four years after assessment or within the period during which a waiver was granted by the taxpayer to extend the statute of limitations for making an escape assessment. (Sec. 4876, Rev. & Tax. Code—Sec. 4880, Rev. & Tax. Code)

Escaped assessments; underassessments.—Generally, any assessment of property that previously escaped taxation or was underassessed must be made within four years after July 1 of the assessment year at issue. (Sec. 532(a), Rev. & Tax. Code) However, there are exceptions to the four-year limitations period, as follow:

(1) any assessment involving a 25% penalty due to the taxpayer's willful concealment, failure to disclose, removal, transfer, or misrepresentation of tangible personal property must be made within eight years after July 1 of the assessment year; (Sec. 532(b)(1), Rev. & Tax. Code)

(2) any assessment resulting from an unrecorded change in ownership for which either a qualifying change in ownership statement or a qualifying preliminary change in ownership report was not timely filed must be made within eight years after July 1 of the assessment year in which the property escaped taxation or was underassessed; and (Sec. 532(b)(2), Rev. & Tax. Code)

(3) where property has escaped taxation or has been underassessed following a change in ownership or control due to collusion involving the assessor or the assessor's agent such that the property is subject to a penalty totalling 75% of the additional assessed value, an escape assessment shall be made for each year in which the property escaped taxation or was underassessed.

(Sec. 532(b)(3), Rev. & Tax. Code)

Civil actions.—The Code of Civil Procedure prescribes specific periods of time for the commencement of civil actions, depending upon the nature of the action. The prescribed period for an action on a liability created by statute other than a penalty or forfeiture is three years (Sec. 338(a), Civ. Proc. Code), and an action against an officer to recover damages for the seizure of property or against an officer in his or her official capacity as tax collector is six months. (Sec. 341, Civ. Proc. Code)

The three-year period for bringing an action upon a liability applies to suits for taxes on personal property (see *Continental Corporation v. Los Angeles County*, 113 CalApp2d 207, 248 P2d 157, (1952)), but does not apply to filing claims for property tax refunds. (see *Consolidated Liquidating Corporation v. Ford*, 131 CalApp2d 576, 281 P2d 20, (1955))

A court action brought by any government agency or officer to review a determination of a county board of equalization or an assessment appeals board must be filed within six months of the final determination. (Sec. 1615, Rev. & Tax. Code)

• *Informal conferences*

The State Board of Equalization notes that a taxpayer may challenge an assessment initially by discussing the matter informally with the assessor's office. The taxpayer should request an explanation of how the assessment was determined and inform the assessor of any facts that may affect the value of the property. (Publication 29, California Property Tax: an Overview, California State Board of Equalization; Publication 30, Residential Property Assessment Appeals, California State Board of Equalization)

A county board of supervisors also may establish procedures for prehearing conferences, which may be set at the request of the applicant or the applicant's agent, the assessor, or the appeals board. The purpose of a prehearing conference may include, but is not limited to:

— clarifying and defining the issues;

— determining the status of exchange of information requests;

— stipulating to matters on which agreement has been reached;

— combining applications into a single hearing;

— bifurcating hearing issues; and

— scheduling a date for a hearing officer or the board to consider evidence on the merits of the application.

(Reg. 305.2, 18 CCR)

• *Local administrative hearings*

A taxpayer seeking a reduction in a local property tax assessment must file a timely application with the county board of supervisors meeting as a county board of equalization or an assessment appeals board. (Sec. 1603, Rev. & Tax. Code) There are 19 counties that use boards of equalization and 39 counties that use assessment appeals boards. (Assessment Appeals Manual, (05-03))

After an application for reduction of an assessment is filed, the clerk of the county board will notify both the applicant or the applicant's agent and the assessor of the time and place for the hearing. The notice will be given no fewer than 45 days prior to the hearing. The notification will be by way of United State mail or, upon request, electronically. The notice will include a statement, among others, that the board is required to find the full value of the property from the evidence presented at the hearing and that the board can raise, under certain circumstances, as well as lower or confirm the assessment being appealed. (Sec. 1605.6, Rev. & Tax. Code; Reg. 307, 18 CCR)

An application appealing a regular assessment shall be filed with the clerk during the regular filing period. A regular assessment is one placed on the assessment roll for the most recent lien date, prior to the closing of that assessment roll. (Reg. 305(d)(4), 18 CCR) An application will be deemed to have been timely filed if the postmark of a properly mailed application or a private postage meter postmark falls within the filing period or satisfactory proof establishes that the mailing occurred within the filing period. (Sec. 166, Rev. & Tax. Code; Reg. 305, 18 CCR)

If a taxpayer files a duplicate application that seeks the same relief with respect to the same property for the same tax year, only the first application filed by or on behalf of the taxpayer will be accepted. (Sec. 1603.5, Rev. & Tax. Code)

If a county assessment appeals board fails to hear evidence and make a final determination on a timely filed application for reduction in assessment within two years of its filing, the market value claimed by the taxpayer on the application generally will prevail unless:

(1) the taxpayer and the county assessment appeals board agree in writing to extend the time for the hearing or

(2) the application is consolidated for hearing with another application for which an extension of time has been granted.

(Sec. 1604, Rev. & Tax. Code)

COMPLIANCE ALERT: Extension of two-year deadline for county boards of equalization to render final determinations. On July 31, 2020, Gov. Newsom issued Executive Order N-72-202 extending the deadline. The order provides that notwithstanding Sec. 1604 or any other law, for any pending assessment appeal filed with a County Assessment Appeals Board on or before March 4, 2020, the deadline within which the County Assessment Appeals Board must render a decision is extended until January 31, 2021. As a result, a County Board of Equalization or Assessment Appeals Board may render a final determination by January 31, 2021, for any appeal application that was timely filed prior to March 4, 2020, and with a two-year deadline that falls between, and including, July 31, 2020 and January 31, 2021. (*Letter to County Assessors, No. 2020/036,* California State Board of Equalization, August 4, 2020, ¶ 407-205)

Burden of proof.—The presumption that the duties of the assessor have been performed properly imposes on the taxpayer the burden of proving that the value on the assessment roll is not correct or that the property otherwise has not been assessed correctly. (Reg. 321, 18 CCR) However, the burden of proof shifts to the assessor when the taxpayer has supplied all information in an administrative hearing involving the imposition of tax on, or the assessment of, an owner-occupied single family dwelling. The burden of proof also shifts to the assessor when the taxpayer has supplied all information in an administrative hearing involving the appeal of an escape assessment, unless the escape assessment resulted from the taxpayer's failure to file a change in ownership statement or business property statement or to obtain a permit for new construction. The assessor also has the burden of proof with respect to establishing a basis for imposition of penalties. (Sec. 167, Rev. & Tax. Code; Reg. 321, 18 CCR)

Hearings before assessment hearing officers.—The county board of supervisors may also appoint an assessment hearing officer to conduct hearings on applications for assessment reductions. (Sec. 1636, Rev. & Tax. Code) A taxpayer may request that a hearing on an assessment protest be held before an assessment hearing officer appointed by the county board of supervisors. (Sec. 1637, Rev. & Tax. Code) The recommendation of the hearing officer is binding on the county board unless the county board by resolution makes such recommendations nonbinding. (Sec. 1640, Rev. & Tax. Code; Sec. 1640.1, Rev. & Tax. Code)

In counties that utilize an assessment hearing officer whose report is advisory, either the party protesting the assessment or the assessor may request that the county board of equalization or assessment appeals board reject the hearing officer's recommendation and set the reduction application for hearing by the local board of equalization. In lieu of making such a request, either the protesting party or the assessor may make application for a hearing before the county board or assessment appeals board. (Sec. 1641.1, Rev. & Tax. Code)

An assessee of unitary mining or mineral property located in more than one county may request a hearing before a panel composed of assessment hearing officers from each county by filing in each county a multicounty application for reduction of assessment. (Sec. 1642, Rev. & Tax. Code—Sec. 1645, Rev. & Tax. Code)

A reduction in an assessment on the local property tax assessment roll shall not be made unless the taxpayer makes and files with the county board a verified, written application showing the facts claimed to require the reduction and the applicant's opinion of the full value of the property. (Sec. 1603(a), Rev. & Tax. Code) Generally, the application must be filed between July 2 and September 15, inclusive. (Sec. 1603(b)(1), Rev. & Tax. Code) If a county assessor does not provide by August 1 a notice to all assessees of real property on the local secured roll of the assessed value of their property, the last day of the filing period in that county will be November 30. (Sec. 1603(b)(3), Rev. & Tax. Code)

The State Board of Equalization has provided guidance on the administrative appeals process for residential property assessments. (BOE Publication 30, Residential Property Assessment Appeals, March 2003)

• *State administrative hearings*

The State Board of Equalization will hear petitions regarding property tax from only designated taxpayers or for designated issues. Specifically, the BOE will hear:

— petitions for reassessment of state-assessed property and private railroad cars;

— applications for review, equalization, and adjustment of assessment of qualifying publicly owned lands and improvements;

— petitions objecting to findings of ineligibility for an organizational clearance certificate, denials of claims for supplemental clearance certificates, and claims for the veteran's organization exemption; (See ¶ 20-505) and

— petitions filed by county assessors regarding surveys of local assessment procedures.

(Reg. 5310, 18 CCR)

The BOE's decision on petitions relating to state-assessed property, private railroad cars, and qualifying publicly owned lands and improvement are final. The BOE may not grant a rehearing to reconsider a final decision and may not modify a final decision except to correct a clerical error. (Reg. 5345, 18 CCR)

State-assessed property, private railroad cars.—An owner of state-assessed property may file a petition for reassessment with the BOE to appeal the assessed value of unitary and nonunitary property. (Sec. 741, Rev. & Tax. Code; Reg. 5323, 18 CCR) A petition for reassessment of unitary property must be filed by July 20. (Sec.

731, Rev. & Tax. Code; Reg. 5323(a), 18 CCR) A petition for reassessment of nonunitary property must be filed by September 20. (Sec. 732, Rev. & Tax. Code; Reg. 5323(c), 18 CCR)

If a state assessee disagrees with an assessment allocation, the assessee must file a petition by July 20 of the year in which the assessment was made. (Reg. 5323(b), 18 CCR) If a state assessee disagrees with a value or penalty in a notice of escaped or excessive assessment, the assessee must file a petition for reassessment no later than the date stated in the notice. (Reg. 5323(d), 18 CCR)

An owner or lessee of property assessed for private railroad car tax may petition for reassessment. A petition for reassessment with respect to an assessment made outside of the regular assessment period must be filed within 50 days following the notice of assessment. (Sec. 11338, Rev. & Tax. Code; Sec. 11339, Rev. & Tax. Code; Reg. 5323(e)(3), 18 CCR)

The BOE generally must render its decision on a petition for reassessment within 45 days of the date of the hearing on the petition. (Sec. 11341, Rev. & Tax. Code) An extension of 15 days may be granted to file a petition if a written request is made prior to the filing deadline. (Sec. 733, Rev. & Tax. Code)

A public hearing will be held on a petition for reassessment of state-assessed property, and the BOE, if requested, will make a written record of the hearing and its decision. (Sec. 743, Rev. & Tax. Code)

Decisions on petitions for reassessment must be made before December 31 of the assessment year. (Sec. 744, Rev. & Tax. Code)

A petition for a correction of an allocated assessment must be filed by July 20. (Sec. 746, Rev. & Tax. Code)

Clerical errors made by the BOE in its assessment or errors that the BOE discovers through an audit that had caused it to assess the property at a higher value may be corrected by the BOE within four years after assessment or within the period during which a waiver was granted by the taxpayer to extend the statute of limitations for making an escape assessment. (Sec. 4876, Rev. & Tax. Code—Sec. 4880, Rev. & Tax. Code) Erroneous or illegal assessments by the BOE may be canceled. (Sec. 5011, Rev. & Tax. Code—Sec. 5014, Rev. & Tax. Code)

• *Judicial appeals and remedies*

A county may file a civil action against the taxpayer to enforce the collection of delinquent taxes or assessments, if the past-due taxes are not a lien on real property sufficient to secure the payment of the taxes. (Sec. 3003, Rev. & Tax. Code) Civil actions must be commenced within three years of the date the unsecured taxes became delinquent. (Sec. 3007, Rev. & Tax. Code) However, the limitation period may be tolled for any period during which collection actions are prohibited by federal bankruptcy laws or rules or by court order.

Courts may not issue an injunction or other legal or equitable process against and taxing district or taxing district officers to prevent or enjoin the collection of property taxes. (Sec. 4807, Rev. & Tax. Code)

If an assessee of property on the unsecured roll moves to another county, the tax collector in the county in which the property was assessed may likewise sue for unsecured taxes. (Sec. 3002, Rev. & Tax. Code)

In any suit for taxes, the assessment roll showing the name of the assessee, the property involved, and the amount of unpaid taxes and assessments is prima facie evidence of the county's right to recover. (Sec. 3004, Rev. & Tax. Code)

The tax collector may commence an action for the recovery of taxes prior to the date of delinquency if, in his or her opinion, it is necessary because of the taxpayer's financial position or other "appropriate reason." (Sec. 3006, Rev. & Tax. Code) Also, the collector can apply to the court for an *ex parte* writ of attachment.

The owner of the property may recover the attached property and attack the declaration of the tax collector by filing with the court a bond sufficient to pay the overdue taxes. (Sec. 3006, Rev. & Tax. Code)

Although oil and gas leases are placed on the secured roll for tax payment purposes, they are transferred to the unsecured roll for collection purposes and a suit may be brought by the county. (Sec. 2189.5, Rev. & Tax. Code)

Private railroad car tax.—The BOE may bring an action to collect delinquent private railroad car tax, penalties, and interest at any time within four years after the tax becomes due and payable or delinquent or within any period during which a lien is in force. (Sec. 11471, Rev. & Tax. Code)

MISCELLANEOUS TAXES AND FEES

[¶37-000]

ALCOHOLIC BEVERAGES

[¶37-001] Alcoholic Beverages

California's Alcoholic Beverage Tax is covered in Revenue and Taxation Code, Division 2 Other Taxes, Part 14 Alcoholic Beverage Tax. Current tax rates per gallon are:

— beer, still wines, sparkling hard cider $0.20

— champagne, sparkling wine $0.30

— distilled spirits (100 proof or less) $3.30

— Distilled spirits (more than 100 proof) $6.60

(http://www.boe.ca.gov/sptaxprog/tax_rates_stfd.htm)

Comprehensive coverage of taxation of alcohol, as well as licensing and distribution information is provided in Wolters Kluwer, CCH Liquor Control Law Reporter. For more information go to CCHGroup.com or contact an account representative at 888-CCH-REPS (888-224-7377).

[¶37-050]

DOCUMENT RECORDING TAX

[¶37-051] Document Recording Tax

The documentary transfer tax is patterned after the federal stamp tax, which was repealed in 1976. It is currently imposed by all California counties and most cities on deeds of transfer of realty. The amount of the tax is based on the value of, or consideration from, the realty transferred. The county rate is 55 cents for each $500 of value, and the noncharter city rate is one-half of the county rate. City tax paid under an ordinance in conformity with the Act is credited against the county tax due. (P.L. 94-455, Sec. 1904(a)(12))

The Documentary Transfer Tax Act (added by Stats. 1967, Ch. 1332, §1, operative January 1, 1968), provides the authority for the imposition of the tax. The Act does not impose the tax; rather, it enables counties and cities to impose the tax in conformity with its provisions. (Sec. 11901, Rev. & Tax Code)

In addition, any ordinance adopted pursuant to the documentary transfer tax authority may include an administrative appeal for resolution of disputes relating to the tax. (Sec. 11935(a), Rev. & Tax Code) Whether the amount of transfer tax is determined by an administrative appeal process or established by a court, the value of the property established for purposes of determining the amount of documentary transfer tax is not binding in the determination of the value of the property for property tax purposes. (Sec. 11935(b), Rev. & Tax Code)

Although counties and cities imposing the tax under the authority of the Act must conform their ordinances to the Act, charter cities may impose a nonconforming tax under their general power over municipal affairs. Consequently, the terms and rates of several California charter city transfer tax ordinances vary significantly from the Act, and the local ordinances must be consulted for the variances.

• *Transfers subject to tax*

The tax is imposed on every document, not specifically exempted, by which any realty with a value or purchase price over $100 in excess of existing encumbrances, sold within a county imposing the tax, is conveyed to or vested in the purchasers or any other persons by the direction of the purchasers. (Sec. 11911, Rev. & Tax. Code)

The transfer of a mobile home is subject to the tax if the mobile home is installed on a foundation system, pursuant to Sec. 18551, Health and Safety Code, and is subject to local property taxation. (Sec. 11913, Rev. & Tax. Code)

A partnership, at the time of its termination within the meaning of IRC Sec. 708, is deemed to have transferred all of its realty for purposes of the tax. The tax base is the fair market value of the realty, less the value of any lien or encumbrances on the property. Only one tax may be imposed upon the termination of a partnership and any transfer of property made pursuant to the termination. (Sec. 11925, Rev. & Tax. Code)

• *Exempt transfers*

The tax does not apply to instruments in writing given to secure a debt. (Sec. 11921, Rev. & Tax. Code) Nor does the tax apply to a deed to a beneficiary or mortgagee as a result of or in lieu of foreclosure, except to the extent that the consideration for the deed exceeds the unpaid debt, including accrued interest and the cost of foreclosure. (Sec. 11926, Rev. & Tax. Code)

To qualify for the foreclosure exemption, the consideration, the amount of the unpaid debt, and the identification of the grantee as beneficiary or mortgagee must be noted on the deed or stated in an affidavit or declaration under penalty of perjury. (Sec. 11926, Rev. & Tax. Code)

Documents under which the federal or state government or any agency, instrumentality, or political subdivision acquires title to realty are exempt from the tax. (Sec. 11922, Rev. & Tax. Code)

The tax does not apply to documents made, delivered or filed to effect a plan of reorganization or adjustment if:

(1) confirmed under the Federal Bankruptcy Act;

(2) approved in a railroad equity receivership proceeding as defined in subdivision (m) of Section 205 of Title 11 of the United States Code;

(3) approved in a corporate equity receivership proceeding as defined in subdivision (3) of Section 506 of Title 11 of the United States Code; or

(4) whereby a mere change in identity, form, or place of organization is effected.

To qualify for the exemption, the making, delivery, or filing of the document must occur within five years from the date of the confirmation, approval, or change. (Sec. 11923, Rev. & Tax. Code)

Certain conveyances made to effect orders of the Securities and Exchange Commission relating to the Public Utility Holding Company Act of 1935 are exempt from tax. (Sec. 11924, Rev. & Tax. Code)

The tax does not apply to a document which purports to transfer, divide, or allocate community, quasi-community, or quasi-marital property assets between spouses for the purpose of effecting a division of property as required by a judgment decreeing a dissolution of marriage or legal separation under the Family Code. Nor does the tax apply to a document effecting a division as required by a written agreement between the spouses, executed in contemplation of any such judgment, whether or not the agreement is incorporated as part of the judgment. To qualify for the exemption, a document effecting a division of property between spouses must include a written recital, signed by either spouse, stating that the document is entitled to the exemption. (Sec. 11927, Rev. & Tax. Code)

Any deed, instrument, or other writing that grants, assigns, transfers, conveys, divides, allocates, or vests property or any property interest is exempt from the documentary transfer tax if through such inter vivos gift or bequest or by reason of the death of a person the property or property interest is transferred outright to, or in trust for the benefit of, any person or entity. (Sec. 11930, Rev. & Tax. Code)

The tax does not apply to a transfer of an interest in realty held by a an entity treated as a partnership for federal income tax purposes due to the transfer of an interest in the partnership if the partnership is considered as continuing under Section 708 of the Internal Revenue Code, and the continuing partnership keeps the property. Also exempt is any transfer between an individual or individuals and a legal entity or between legal entities that results solely in a change in the method of holding title to the realty and in which proportional ownership interests in the realty remain the same immediately after the transfer. (Sec. 11925, Rev. & Tax. Code)

Also, existing business entities, such as partnerships and corporations, may convert into or transfer real property to limited liability companies without incurring a documentary transfer tax, provided that the direct or indirect proportionate interests in the property remain the same. (Sec. 29, Ch. 57, Laws 1996)

• *Tax rate and basis*

The basis of the tax is the consideration for, or value of, the interest transferred in excess of the amount of any lien or encumbrance on the interest at the time of transfer. The county tax rate is 55 cents for each $500 or fractional part thereof. The city tax rate under the Act is one-half of the county rate, and the city tax, if in conformity with the Act, is allowed as a credit against the county tax. (Sec. 11911, Rev. & Tax. Code)

• *Local taxes*

Any city within a county which has imposed the tax, may impose a tax on transfers at one-half of the county rate. (Sec. 11911, Rev. & Tax. Code) If the city tax conforms to the Act, the county in which the city is located must grant a credit against the county tax in the amount of the city tax. (Sec. 11931, Rev. & Tax. Code)

The county must collect both the county and the city tax, and allocate the money collected to the appropriate cities and the county. Money collected under a non-charter city tax that does not conform to the Act may not be credited against the county tax and must be allocated entirely to the county. (Sec. 11931, Rev. & Tax. Code)

Under the authority vested by California Constitution Art. XI, Section 5, to make and enforce all ordinances and regulations in respect to municipal affairs subject only to restrictions and limitations provided in their charters, charter cities may impose realty transfer taxes not in conformity with the Documentary Transfer Tax Act. (Cal. Const., Art. XI, Sec. 5) Several charter cities have exercised this power and have imposed transfer taxes with rates and tax bases significantly different from those under the Act. The current local ordinances should be consulted for details of the taxes.

• *Party liable for tax*

The transfer tax must be paid by the person who makes, signs, or issues a document subject to the tax or by the person for whose use or benefit the document is made, signed, or issued. (Sec. 11912, Rev. & Tax. Code)

• *Penalties*

An ordinance imposing the tax may require the tax roll parcel number of realty transfer to be noted on documents of transfer. The number is to be used only for administrative and procedural purposes. The number is not proof of title, nor does it prevail over the stated legal description on the document. (Sec. 11911.1, Rev. & Tax. Code)

Every document subject to the tax, when submitted for recordation, must show, on its face, the location of the realty. The amount of tax due must also appear on the face of the transfer document or, (until January 1, 2014) at the request of the party submitting the document for recordation, on a separate paper affixed to the document by the recorder after the permanent record is made and before the original is returned. (Sec. 11932, Rev. & Tax. Code)

The county recorder (Sec. 11903, Rev. & Tax. Code) may not record a transfer document, subject to the tax, until the tax is paid. In determining whether the tax has been paid, the recorder may rely upon the declaration of the amount of tax due on the face of the document or (until January 1, 2014) on a separate paper affixed thereto. (Sec. 11933, Rev. & Tax. Code)

• *Refunds*

The procedure for refunds of the transfer tax is the same as for refunds of property tax under Division 1, Part 9, Chapter 5 of the Revenue and Taxation Code, discussed at ¶20-815 Refunds. (Sec. 11934, Rev. & Tax. Code)

[¶37-100]
MOTOR VEHICLES

[¶37-101] Motor Vehicles

California imposes a variety of taxes and fees on motor vehicles. Vehicle registration fees generally are administered by the state Department of Motor Vehicles (DMV), which operates generally under the terms of the state Vehicle Code. (http://www.dmv.ca.gov/portal/dmv/)

Property taxation of motor vehicles and the vehicle license fee are discussed at ¶20-275 Motor Vehicles. Sales taxation of motor vehicles is discussed at ¶60-570 Motor Vehicles.

[¶37-150]
ENVIRONMENTAL TAXES AND FEES

[¶37-151] Environmental Taxes and Fees

California imposes a variety of taxes and fees relating to environmental issues. The California Department of Tax and Fee Administration (CDTFA) maintains a list of some of the current environmental fees reported here on its website at https://www.cdtfa.ca.gov/taxes-and-fees/tax-rates-stfd.htm.

Some environmental taxes and fees qualify for managed audit treatment.

The following are discussed here:

— fees for disposers of hazardous waste;

— facility and generator fees;

— other hazardous waste fees;

— uniform hazardous waste manifest form;

— local taxes;

— solid waste disposal facility fee;

— oil spill fees;

— tire recycling fee;

— medical waste fees;

— occupational lead poisoning fees;

— ballast water management/marine invasive species fee;

— volatile organic compounds emissions fee;

— covered electronic device recycling fee;

— propane safety inspection and enforcement fee and surcharge;

— underground storage tank fee;

— motor oil fees;

— lubricating oil fees;

— fire prevention fee; and

— managed audits.

- *Hazardous waste disposal fee*

Fees apply to hazardous waste disposed in the state. (Sec. 25174.1, Hlth. & Sfty. Code) The California Department of Toxic Substances Control may adopt regulations exempting certain disaster victims from the fee if specified conditions are satisfied. (Sec. 25205.5.1, Hlth. & Sfty. Code) Current fees are available on the CDTFA website at https://www.cdtfa.ca.gov/taxes-and-fees/tax-rates-stfd.htm.

Taxpayer remedies.—The CDTFA administers and collects disposal fees. (Sec. 25174.6, Hlth. & Sfty. Code and Sec. 43051, Rev. & Tax. Code) Monthly reporting and payments are due on or before the last day of the third calendar month following the end of the calendar month for which the fee is due. (Sec. 43151, Rev. & Tax. Code) Returns filed under the hazardous substances tax may be filed electronically. (Sec. 43152.9, Rev. & Tax. Code; Sec. 43173, Rev. & Tax. Code)

Penalties for the late payment of hazardous substances tax or the late filing of a return may be waived without a showing of reasonable cause for tardiness under criteria to be developed by the CDTFA. The goal of the criteria must be to foster efficient resolution of requests for relief from penalties. The CDTFA may not require taxpayers to file statements supporting their claims for relief under penalty of perjury, as is the case when a person seeks waiver under a claim of reasonable cause for tardiness. (Sec. 43157, Rev. & Tax. Code)

A taxpayer may be relieved of penalties for late payment of hazardous substances tax if the taxpayer enters into an installment plan for paying tax within 45 days after a notice of determination or redetermination is final. The taxpayer must comply with the agreement for the waiver to remain effective, and waiver may not be granted in cases of fraud. (Sec. 43448, Rev. & Tax. Code)

In addition, persons may be relieved from liability for the payment of the fee for disposal of hazardous waste, including any interest or penalties, when their liability resulted from a failure to timely file a return or make a payment and that failure is found by the CDTFA to be due to reasonable reliance on written advice given by the CDTFA in a manner prescribed by Reg. 4902, 18 CCR. (Reg. 3021, 18 CCR)

Taxpayers that have entered into installment agreements to pay hazardous substances tax must receive an annual statement from the CDTFA itemizing the balance of tax owed at the beginning and end of a year and the amount of tax paid during the year. (Sec. 43448.5, Rev. & Tax. Code)

The limitations period for filing refund claims for hazardous substances tax is suspended during the period that a person is unable to manage financial affairs because of a physical or mental impairment that is life threatening or that is expected to last for at least 12 months. There is no waiver for individuals who are represented in their financial matters by their spouses or other persons. (Sec. 43452.1, Rev. & Tax. Code)

Taxpayers that have been unreasonably assessed hazardous substances tax by the CDTFA are entitled to reimbursement of their fees and expenses for attending CDTFA hearings. They may be reimbursed for costs incurred as of the filing of a notice of determination, jeopardy determination, or refund claim. (Sec. 43520, Rev. & Tax. Code)

An employer that has been ordered by the CDTFA to withhold wages from an employee to satisfy the employee's debt for unpaid hazardous substances tax, but that has failed to remit the withheld amount to the CDTFA, may be held liable by the CDTFA for the unremitted amount, which may be treated as a tax deficiency of the employer. The CDTFA has seven years from the first day on which the employer withheld wages from an employee to assess the deficiency, with interest. The employee's liability for tax must be credited for the unremitted amount and no further action may be taken to collect that sum from the employee. (Sec. 43444.3, Rev. & Tax. Code)

Preparers of hazardous substances tax returns who, without a client's consent, knowingly or recklessly disclose the client's confidential tax information for any purpose other than return preparation may be convicted of a misdemeanor, fined up to $1,000, and imprisoned up to one year. A preparer also may be liable for prosecution costs. (Sec. 43506, Rev. & Tax. Code)

• *Facility and generator fees*

Facility operators are subject to an application fee and an annual facility fee based on the size and type of the facility. The fee is administered and collected by the California Department of Tax and Fee Administration (CDTFA). (Sec. 25205.2, Hlth. & Sfty. Code; Sec. 25205.4, Hlth. & Sfty. Code; Sec. 25205.12, Hlth. & Sfty. Code; Sec. 43053, 43152.6, 43152.12, and 43152.15, Rev. & Tax. Code; Sec. 25205.7, Hlth. & Sfty. Code)

Hazardous waste facility owners operating under a permit-by-rule, a grant of conditional authorization to operate without a hazardous waste permit, or a conditional exemption from hazardous waste permitting requirements, are exempt from the hazardous waste facility fee. (Sec. 25205.2, Hlth. & Sfty. Code and Sec. 25205.12, Hlth. & Sfty. Code) However, such owners are subject to other fees, as discussed below. An exemption from the permit application and facility fees also applies to facilities operated in order to:

— collect household hazardous waste;

— treat waste as part of a program supervised by local vector control agencies or agricultural commissioners;

— segregate, handle, and store hazardous waste pursuant to a load checking program;

— treat, store, dispose of, or recycle hazardous waste resulting from a public agency's (or public agency contractor's) investigation, removal, or remediation of a hazardous waste release caused by another person; or

— store hazardous waste onsite at an otherwise closed facility.

(Sec. 25205.3, Hlth. & Sfty. Code)

Operators that secure a Department of Toxic Substances Control variance from the hazardous waste facility permit requirement are also exempt from facility fees. Moreover, facilities engaged exclusively in treatment to accomplish a removal, remedial, or corrective action in accordance with a Department or Environmental Protection Agency order are fee-exempt, provided that the facility was put into operation solely for the purpose of complying with the order. (Sec. 25205.2, Hlth. & Sfty. Code)

In addition, hazardous waste facility operators operating under a standardized permit or grant of interim status are eligible for an annual facility fee credit for a time period equal to the number of years that the facility lawfully operated before September 21, 1993, and paid facility fees. (Sec. 25205.2, Hlth. & Sfty. Code)

Permit application fees.—New applicants must enter into a written agreement with the Department that provides for reimbursement of costs incurred by the Department in processing the application. The same reimbursement agreement applies to costs incurred by the Department in responding to a request for any of the following:

— a new hazardous waste facilities permit (including a standardized permit);

— a hazardous waste facilities permit for postclosure;

— renewal of an existing permit;

— a class 2 or class 3 modification of an existing permit;

— a variance; or

— a waste classification determination.

(Sec. 25205.7, Hlth. & Sfty. Code)

Alternatively, applicants for a new permit, permit for postclosure, renewal of an existing permit, or class 2 or class 3 permit modification, may instead pay a fee pursuant to a schedule. Existing permit renewal applicants must pay an amount equal to the fee assessable had the applicant requested the same changes in a modification application; but renewal application fees may not be less than one-half of the fee applicable to a new permit. Any application for a standardized permit for a transportable treatment unit that is submitted after a full hazardous waste facilities permit is issued is not considered as a new permit application. Operators of research, development, and demonstration facilities may be eligible for a two-year exemption from paying costs reimbursement and permit application fees. (Sec. 25205.7, Hlth. & Sfty. Code)

Activity fee.—Absent a reimbursement agreement, the application fee amount is based on the type and size of the facility and/or the type of permit applied for. (Sec. 25205.7, Hlth. & Sfty. Code) The CDTFA establishes these fees using base rates that are subject to annual adjustment to reflect cost of living increases or decreases during the prior fiscal year, as measured by the Consumer Price Index. Current fees are available on the CDTFA website at https://www.cdtfa.ca.gov/taxes-and-fees/tax-rates-stfd.htm.

Annual facility fees.—The CDTFA establishes facility fees using an annually adjusted base rate that reflects cost of living increases or decreases during the prior fiscal year, as measured by the Consumer Price Index. The base rate for the 2011 reporting period is $28,659. The fee and return are due annually by the last day of the second month following the end of the calendar year. Two prepayments accompanied by a prepayment return are due by the last day of February and the last day of August. The prepayment must be at least 50% of the applicable fee as stated on the hazardous waste facilities permit, interim status document, or Part A application. (Sec. 25205.4, Hlth. & Sfty. Code)

A percentage factor based on a facility's category is applied against the base rate above to determine the fee required. Current fees are available on the CDTFA website at https://www.cdtfa.ca.gov/taxes-and-fees/tax-rates-stfd.htm. Postclosure fees due are 50% of those shown if the Department of Toxic Substances Control is not the lead agency.

If more than one category applies to a facility, or if more than one category corresponds to multiple operations under a single hazardous waste facility permit or grant of interim status, the facility operator's fee is determined only by the highest rate.

Fees for permit-by-rule or conditional authorization.—Owners or operators of a hazardous waste facility or transportable treatment unit operating under a permit-by-rule are subject to an annual fee, unless a certified unified program agency (CUPA) fee has already been paid. (Sec. 25205.14, Hlth. & Sfty. Code) The fee is subject to annual cost-of-living adjustments. The permit-by-rule fee (facility and TTU) is $1,514 for 2015.

In addition, generators operating under a conditional exemption or commercial laundry permit are subject to a $38 fee in the initial year and for each year thereafter.

Generator fees.—In addition to hazardous waste disposal fees discussed at ¶ 37-151 Fee for Disposers of Hazardous Waste, hazardous waste generator fees apply to each generator site location. Such fees do not apply, however, if the generator has paid a facility fee or received a credit for each specific site for the calendar year for which the generator fee is due. (Sec. 25205.5, Hlth. & Sfty. Code) In addition, the Department of Toxic Substances Control may adopt regulations exempting certain disaster victims from the fee if specified conditions are satisfied. (Sec. 25205.5.1, Hlth. & Sfty. Code) The fee and return are due annually by the last day of the second month following the end of the calendar year. Prepayment, accompanied by a prepayment return, is due no later than the last day of August in an amount not less than

(1) the applicable fee for the site for January 1 through June 30 of the calendar year in which the prepayment is due, less any specified local fees, or

(2) 50% of the generator fee from the prior calendar year.

(Sec. 43152.9, Rev. & Tax. Code; Sec. 43152.7, Rev. & Tax. Code)

The additional generator fee is set by the CDTFA using a base rate which the CDTFA annually adjusts to reflect cost-of-living increases or decreases during the previous fiscal year, as measured by the Consumer Price Index. (Sec. 25205.5, Hlth. & Sfty. Code) The low end of the generator fee range is 5% of the base rate, applicable to generators that generate at least five tons, but less than 25 tons, of hazardous waste during the prior calendar year. The high end of the fee range is 20 times the base rate, applicable to generators that generate 2,000 tons or more of hazardous waste during the prior calendar year.

Current fees are available on the CDTFA website at https://www.cdtfa.ca.gov/taxes-and-fees/tax-rates-stfd.htm.

Hazardous materials that are not transferred offsite after recycling and used onsite are not considered to be hazardous wastes for generator fee purposes. Aqueous waste is not considered to be hazardous waste in determining the hazardous waste generator fee if the waste is treated in a treatment unit operating pursuant to a permit-by-rule, a grant of conditional authorization to operate without a hazardous waste permit, or a conditional exemption from hazardous waste permitting requirements. (Sec. 43152.9, Rev. & Tax. Code; Sec. 43152.7, Rev. & Tax. Code; Sec. 25205.5, Hlth. & Sfty. Code)

Hazardous waste generator fee refunds may be granted to generators that pay a hazardous waste generator inspection fee to a Certified Unified Program Agency (CUPA), and to generators that transfer hazardous materials to an offsite facility for recycling, provided that certain requirements are satisfied. (Sec. 25205.5, Hlth. & Sfty. Code) A refund application must be submitted by September 30 following the fiscal year during which the fee was paid. (Sec. 25205.2, Hlth. & Sfty. Code)

¶37-151

Hazardous material charge.—Except for nonprofit corporations engaged primarily in providing residential social personal care for children, the aged, and persons as described in SIC Code 8361 edition of the U.S. Office of Management and Budget's Standard Industrial Classification Manual as having limited ability to care for themselves, each corporation, limited liability company, limited partnership, limited liability partnership, general partnership, and sole proprietorship with at least 50 employees that uses, generates, or stores hazardous materials or conducts activities in California related to hazardous materials must pay an annual charge. (Sec. 25205.6, Hlth. & Sfty. Code; Sec. 1, Ch. 344 (A.B. 1813), Laws 2006) Current fees are available on the CDTFA website at https://www.cdtfa.ca.gov/taxes-and-fees/tax-rates-stfd.htm.

The CDTFA applies annual inflation adjustments to the charge amounts. (Sec. 25205.6, Hlth. & Sfty. Code)

It has been determined that this charge is a constitutional tax. In addition, a regulation promulgated to implement the statute that imposes the tax on all businesses with at least 50 employees, except for nonprofit residential health care facilities, is consistent and not in conflict with the statute. (*The Morning Star Co. v. Board of Equalization*, California Court of Appeal, Third Appellate District, C063437, May 5, 2011)

Annual returns and payments are due on the last day of February following the end of the calendar year. (Sec. 25205.6, Hlth. & Sfty. Code; Sec. 43152.9, Rev. & Tax. Code)

Consolidated statement.—The CDTFA must submit to each generator of hazardous waste a consolidated statement of all applicable facility fees, generator fees, and hazardous waste material fees. Any return or other document required to be submitted by a generator of hazardous waste to the CDTFA must be accompanied by the consolidated statement. (Sec. 43152, Rev. & Tax. Code)

Annual verification fee.—The Department of Toxic Substances Control may impose an annual verification fee on all generators, transporters, and facility operators with 50 or more employees that possess a valid identification number issued either by the Department or by the Environmental Protection Agency. The fee for each generator, transporter, and facility operator, based on number of employees, is:

— 0-49 employees, $0;

— 50-74 employees, $150;

— 75-99 employees, $175;

— 100-249 employees, $200;

— 250-499 employees, $225; and

— 500 or more employees, $250.

No generator, transporter, or facility operator will be assessed a fee that exceeds, in total, $5,000. (Sec. 25205.16, Hlth. & Sfty. Code)

The fee must be paid within 30 days of receiving a notice of assessment from the Department. (Sec. 25205.16, Hlth. & Sfty. Code)

Recordkeeping requirements.—Taxpayers that are liable for the payment of a hazardous substances tax (disposal fee, environmental fee, facility fee, generator fee, and activity fee) must maintain and make available for examination, on CDTFA request, records maintained in the manner prescribed by Reg. 4901, 18 CCR. In addition, every feepayer that is liable for payment of the hazardous substances tax must maintain the following records:

— uniform hazardous waste manifests;

— transporter billings or invoices;

— weight tickets; and

— waste profile analysis reports.

Every feepayer that is liable for payment of the environmental fee must maintain payroll reports and employment agreements or contracts. (Reg. 3020, 18 CCR)

Relief from liability.—Persons may be relieved from liability for the payment of the fees collected pursuant to the hazardous substances tax (disposal fee, environmental fee, facility fee, generator fee, and activity fee), including any interest or penalties, when their liability resulted from a failure to timely file a return or make a payment and that failure is found by the CDTFA to be due to reasonable reliance on written advice given by the CDTFA in a manner prescribed by Reg. 4902, 18 CCR. (Reg. 3021, 18 CCR)

Relief from California special tax and fee liabilities includes relief due to reasonable reliance on written advice from the California Department of Tax and Fee Administration (CDTFA) to a person who relies on advice provided in a prior audit of a related person, under specific circumstances. Written advice from the CDTFA that was received during a prior audit of the person, as provided, may be relied upon by the person audited or a person with shared accounting and common ownership with the audited person or by a legal or statutory successor to those persons. A person is considered to have shared accounting and common ownership if the person:

— is engaged in the same line of business as the audited person;

— has common verifiable controlling ownership of 50% or greater ownership or has a common majority shareholder with the audited person; and

— shares centralized accounting functions with the audited person (i.e., the audited person routinely follows the same business practices that are followed by each entity involved).

(Reg. 4902, 18 CCR)

Evidence that may indicate sharing of centralized accounting functions includes, but is not limited to:

— quantifiable control of the accounting practices of each business by the common ownership or management that dictates office policies for accounting and tax return preparation;

— shared accounting staff or an outside firm that maintains books and records and prepares returns for special tax and fee programs, as provided; and

— shared accounting policies and procedures.

(Reg. 4902, 18 CCR)

In addition, the taxpayer is required to establish that these requirements existed during the periods for which relief is sought. A subsequent written notification from the CDTFA that provides that the advice was not valid at the time it was issued, or was subsequently rendered invalid to any party with shared accounting and common ownership, including the audited party, serves as notification to all parties with shared accounting and common ownership, including the audited party, that the prior written advice may not be relied upon as of the notification date. (Reg. 4902, 18 CCR)

• *Other hazardous waste fees*

A variety of other fees apply to activities related to hazardous wastes, including potentially responsible party fees, waste classification fees, and hauler fees.

Any potentially responsible party at a site, or any person who has notified the Department of Toxic Substances Control of that person's intent to undertake removal or remediation at a site, must reimburse the Department for the Department's costs incurred for its oversight of any preliminary endangerment assessment at the site. (Sec. 25343, Hlth. & Sfty. Code)

Hazardous waste haulers are required to register with the Department of Toxic Substances Control. (Sec. 25166, Hlth. & Sfty. Code)

• *Uniform hazardous waste manifest form*

The California Department of Toxic Substances Control (Department) imposes a fee of $7.50 for each California Hazardous Waste Manifest form used in the previous calendar year. Manifests that are used solely for hazardous wastes that are recycled are exempt. A $3.50 manifest fee is charged for each form used solely for hazardous waste derived from air compliance solvents. (Sec. 25205.15, Hlth. & Sfty. Code)

• *Local taxes*

According to a general law, a city or county may impose and enforce a license tax on the operation of an existing hazardous waste facility at a rate not to exceed 10% of the annual gross receipts of the existing hazardous waste disposal facility (Sec. 25149.5, Hlth. & Sfty. Code)

Cities and counties are authorized to impose and enforce a tax or a user fee on the operation of an offsite, multiuser hazardous waste facility located within the jurisdiction of the city or county. The tax or the user fee cannot exceed 10% of the facility's annual gross receipts for the treatment, storage, or disposal of hazardous waste at the facility. No city or county can impose a tax or a user fee upon:

(1) an existing hazardous waste facility for which a city or county license tax is authorized,

(2) an offsite, multiuser hazardous waste facility that began operations before 1987 and was issued a hazardous waste facilities permit or was granted interim status before 1987, or

(3) that portion of the gross receipts of the hazardous waste facility that derives from the recycling of hazardous wastes.

(Sec. 25173.5, Hlth. & Sfty. Code)

A city, county, or city and county may impose fees in amounts sufficient to pay the costs of preparing, adopting, and implementing a countywide integrated waste management plan. (Sec. 41901, Pub. Res. Code)

A city, county, district, or regional agency may structure its solid waste management fees in a manner that requires nonprofit charitable reusers of donated goods to pay only the direct costs of handling and disposing of their residue or that exempts them from fees imposed on the handling and disposal of such residue. (Sec. 41904, Pub. Res. Code)

Bay Area greenhouse gas fee.—A fee is imposed upon each permitted facility that emits greenhouse gases (GHG). The fee is assessed on an annual basis to permitted facilities with GHG emissions at a rate of $0.044 per metric ton of carbon dioxide equivalent emissions. The GHG emissions are determined by the Bay Area Air Quality Management District based on data reported for the most recent 12 months prior to billing. The fee is assessed at the time a facility's permit to operate is renewed and is added to other applicable fees. An emissions-based fee schedule was determined based on an assessment of program activity costs and GHG emissions from permitted sources. (Regulation 3-334 and Schedule T, Bay Area Air Quality Management District; *Staff Report*, Bay Area Air Quality Management District, May 12, 2008; *Telephone Interview*, Bay Area Air Quality Management District, May 27, 2008)

The District is a regional agency created by the legislature to address air pollution. The District's jurisdiction encompasses all of seven counties (i.e., Alameda,

Contra Costa, Marin, San Francisco, San Mateo, Santa Clara and Napa) and portions of two others (i.e., southwestern Solano and southern Sonoma).

No fees are assessed for emissions of "biogenic carbon dioxide," which is defined as carbon dioxide emissions that result from materials that are derived from living cells, excluding fossil fuels, limestone and other materials that have been transformed by geological processes. Biogenic carbon dioxide contains carbon that can be released in the form of emissions and is present in materials that include but are not limited to wood, paper, vegetable oils, animal fat and food, animal and yard waste. (Regulation 3-334 and Schedule T, Bay Area Air Quality Management District, effective July 1, 2008)

Electronic funds transfer payments.—Persons whose estimated hazardous substances tax or integrated waste management fee liability averages $20,000 or more per month, as determined by the CDTFA pursuant to methods of calculation prescribed by the CDTFA, must remit amounts due by electronic funds transfer. Persons whose estimated liability averages less than $20,000 per month may elect to remit amounts due by electronic funds transfer with the approval of the CDTFA. The election is operative for a minimum of one year. (Sec. 43170, Rev. & Tax. Code)

• *Solid waste disposal facility fee*

Each operator of a solid waste disposal facility must pay a quarterly fee to the California Department of Tax and Fee Administration (CDTFA) based on the amount, by weight or volumetric equivalent, of all solid waste disposed of at each disposal site. The solid waste fee is increased to $1.40 per ton. The fee is adjusted annually by the CDTFA but may not exceed $1.40 per ton. (Sec. 48000, Pub. Res. Code)

The CDTFA may exempt any operator of a solid waste landfill that receives less than a monthly average of five tons per operating day of solid waste. (Sec. 48006, Pub. Res. Code)

The fee is to be reported and paid to the CDTFA on or before the 25th day of the month following each quarterly period. (Sec. 45151, Rev. & Tax. Code)

• *Oil spill fees*

An oil spill prevention and administration fee is imposed on marine terminal operators and pipeline operators and an oil spill response fee is imposed on marine terminal, pipeline, and refinery operators.

Oil Spill Prevention and Administration Fee.—The Administrator for Oil Spill Response will collect annually a fee in an amount determined by the Administrator to be sufficient to implement oil spill prevention programs, to study improved oil spill prevention and response, and to finance environmental and economic studies relating to the effects of oil spills. The fee must be set so that projected revenues from the fee, including any interest, will equal the expenses incurred in administering the oil spill prevention program. The annual assessment cannot exceed $0.065 per barrel of crude oil or petroleum products. (Sec. 8670.40, Govt. Code)

The fee is imposed on:

— a person owning crude oil at the time the oil is received at a marine terminal, by any mode of delivery that passed over, across, under, or through waters of the state, from within or outside the state, and upon a person who owns petroleum products at the time those products are received at a marine terminal, by any mode of delivery that passed over, across, under, or through California waters, from outside the state; and

— a person owning crude oil or petroleum products at the time the oil or products are received at a refinery within California by any mode of delivery that passed over, across, under, or through California waters, whether from within or outside the state.

(Sec. 8670.40, Govt. Code)

A rebuttable presumption is enacted that crude oil or petroleum products received at a marine terminal or a refinery have passed over, across, under, or through California waters. This presumption may be overcome by a marine terminal operator, refinery operator, or owner of the crude oil or petroleum products by showing that the crude oil or petroleum products did not pass over, across, under, or through California waters. Evidence to rebut the presumption may include, but is not limited to, documentation, including shipping documents, bills of lading, highway maps, rail maps, transportation maps, related transportation receipts, or another medium that indicates the crude oil or petroleum products did not pass over, across, under, or through waters of the state. (Sec. 8670.40, Govt. Code)

Every person who operates a refinery, a marine terminal in California waters, or a pipeline, is required to register with the California Department of Tax and Fee Administration. (Sec. 8670.40, Govt. Code)

The fee must be remitted to the California Department of Tax and Fee Administration (CDTFA) by the terminal or pipeline operator based on the number of barrels of crude oil or petroleum products received at a marine terminal or transported by pipeline during the preceding month. No fee will be imposed with respect to any crude oil or petroleum products if the person who would be liable for that fee, or responsible for its collection, establishes that the fee has been collected by a registered terminal operator or paid to the Board with respect to the crude oil or petroleum products. (Sec. 8670.40, Govt. Code) Reports and payments are due to the CDTFA on or before the 25th day of each month for the preceding month. An annual information return is due on or before each February 1 for the preceding calendar year. (Sec. 46151, Rev. & Tax. Code) Returns filed under the oil spill response, prevention, and administration fee may be filed electronically. (Sec. 45163, Rev. & Tax. Code)

For purposes of implementing the Oil Spill Response, Prevention and Administration Law, the CDTFA has adopted regulations that define the terms "petroleum products," "barrel of crude oil," and "barrel of petroleum products." In addition, the regulations provide for relief from liability, and set forth recordkeeping requirements for feepayers. (Sec. 8670.40, Govt. Code)

Oil Spill Response Fee.—This fee is not currently being collected.

The Administrator for Oil Spill Response, after consultation with the CDTFA, will set a uniform oil spill response fee in an amount not to exceed 25¢ per barrel of petroleum products upon each person owning petroleum products at the time the petroleum products are received at a marine terminal within the state by means of a vessel from a point of origin outside the state. The fee may only be set at less than 25¢ per gallon when the Administrator finds that the assessment of a lesser fee will cause the fund to reach the designated amount within four months. The fee must be remitted by the terminal operator to the CDTFA based on the number of barrels of petroleum products received during the preceding month. Every operator of a pipeline must also pay a fee not to exceed 25¢ for each barrel of petroleum products transported into the state by means of a pipeline operating across, under, or through the marine waters of the state. The fee is based on the number of barrels of petroleum products so transported into the state during the preceding month. Every operator of a refinery must pay a fee not to exceed 25¢ for each barrel of crude oil received at a refinery within the state. The fee is based on the number of barrels of crude oil received during the preceding month. The fee is not to be imposed by a refiner or person or entity acting as an agent for a refiner on crude oil produced by an independent crude oil producer. (Sec. 8670.48, Govt. Code)

Every marine terminal operator must pay a fee not to exceed 25¢ per barrel of crude oil transported from within this state by means of marine vessel to a destination outside this state. Every operator of a pipeline must pay a fee not to exceed 25¢

¶37-151

for each barrel of crude oil transported out of the state by pipeline. These two fees are to be paid in any calendar year beginning with the month following the month in which the total cumulative year-to-date amount of barrels of crude oil shipped or piped out of the state by all fee payers exceeds 6% by volume of the total barrels of crude oil and petroleum products otherwise subject to oil spill response fees for the prior calendar year. (Sec. 8670.48, Govt. Code)

The fees will not be assessed if specified statutory requirements are met. (Sec. 8670.48, Govt. Code)

The fees must be reported and paid to the CDTFA on or before the 25th day of each month for the preceding month. An annual information return is due on or before each February 1 for the preceding calendar year. (Sec. 46151, Rev. & Tax. Code; Sec. 8670.48, Govt. Code)

For purposes of implementing the Oil Spill Response, Prevention and Administration Law, the CDTFA has adopted regulations that define the terms "petroleum products," "barrel of crude oil," and "barrel of petroleum products." In addition, the regulations provide for relief of liability, and set forth recordkeeping requirements of the feepayers. (Sec. 8670.40, Govt. Code)

Electronic funds transfer payments.—Persons whose estimated oil spill prevention and administration fee or oil spill response fee liability averages $20,000 or more per month, as determined by the CDTFA pursuant to methods of calculation prescribed by the CDTFA, must remit amounts due by electronic funds transfer. Persons whose estimated liability averages less than $20,000 per month may elect to remit amounts due by electronic funds transfer with the approval of the CDTFA. The election is operative for a minimum of one year. (Sec. 45160, Rev. & Tax. Code)

Taxpayer remedies.—Penalties for the late payment of an oil spill resource, prevention, and administration fee or the late filing of a return may be waived without a showing of reasonable cause for tardiness under criteria to be developed by the CDTFA. In addition, penalties for failure to file a timely information return may be waived when the failure is due to reasonable cause. (Sec. 46156, Rev. & Tax. Code) The goal of the criteria must be to foster efficient resolution of requests for relief from penalties. The CDTFA may not require taxpayers to file statements supporting their claims for relief under penalty of perjury, as is the case when a person seeks waiver under a claim of reasonable cause for tardiness.

A taxpayer may be relieved of penalties for late payment of an oil spill resource, prevention, and administration fee if the taxpayer enters into an installment plan for paying the fee within 45 days after a notice of determination or redetermination is final. (Sec. 46464, Rev. & Tax. Code) The taxpayer must comply with the agreement for the waiver to remain effective, and waiver may not be granted in cases of fraud.

Persons may be relieved from liability for the payment of the oil spill response fee and/or the oil spill prevention and administration fee, including any interest or penalties, when their liability resulted from a failure to timely file a return or make a payment and that failure is found by the CDTFA to be due to reasonable reliance on written advice given by the CDTFA in a manner prescribed by Reg. 4902, 18 CCR. (Reg. 2250, 18 CCR; Sec. 8670.40, Govt. Code)

Taxpayers that have entered into installment agreements to pay an oil spill resource, prevention, and administration fee must receive an annual statement from the CDTFA itemizing the balance of the fee owed at the beginning and end of a year and the amount of the fee paid during the year. (Sec. 46464.5, Rev. & Tax. Code)

The limitations period for filing refund claims for oil spill resource, prevention, and administration fees is suspended during the period that a person is unable to manage financial affairs because of a physical or mental impairment that is life threatening or that is expected to last for at least 12 months. (Sec. 46502.1, Rev. & Tax. Code) There is no waiver for individuals who are represented in their financial matters by their spouses or other persons.

Taxpayers that have been unreasonably assessed an oil spill resource, prevention, and administration fee by the CDTFA are entitled to reimbursement of their fees and expenses for attending CDTFA hearings. (Sec. 46620, Rev. & Tax. Code) They may be reimbursed for costs incurred as of the filing of a notice of determination, jeopardy determination, or refund claim.

An employer that has been ordered by the CDTFA to withhold wages from an employee to satisfy the employee's debt for an unpaid oil spill resource, prevention, and administration fee, but that has failed to remit the withheld amount to the CDTFA, may be held liable by the CDTFA for the unremitted amount, which may be treated as a fee deficiency of the employer. (Sec. 46407, Rev. & Tax. Code) The CDTFA has seven years from the first day on which the employer withheld wages from an employee to assess the deficiency, with interest. The employee's liability for the fee must be credited for the unremitted amount and no further action may be taken to collect that sum from the employee.

Preparers of oil spill resource, prevention, and administration fee returns that, without a client's consent, knowingly or recklessly disclose the client's confidential fee information for any purpose other than return preparation may be convicted of a misdemeanor, fined up to $1,000, and imprisoned for up to one year. (Sec. 46606, Rev. & Tax. Code) A preparer also may be liable for prosecution costs.

An oil spill response and/or prevention and administration feepayer must maintain and make available for examination, on CDTFA request, records maintained in the manner prescribed by Reg. 4901, 18 CCR.

• *Tire recycling fee*

Purchasers of new tires from new tire retail sellers must pay the seller a fee of $1.75 per tire through January 1, 2024. On that date, the rate will be decreased to $0.75 per tire. A retailer may retain 1.5% of the fee as reimbursement for the administrative costs of collecting the fee. The remainder of the fee must be deposited quarterly with the California Tire Recycling Management Fund. (Sec. 42885, Pub. Res. Code)

Retailers must provide customers with invoices that identify the fee separately from the rest of a tire's purchase price or any other disposal or transaction fee. (Sec. 42885, Pub. Res. Code) Retailers may be penalized up to $25,000 for knowingly, or with reckless disregard, submitting documents falsifying information on the fee. Also, the California Integrated Waste Management Board may penalize a retailer up to $5,000 for violating any rule or permit regarding the collection and administration of the fee.

The California Department of Tax and Fee Administration (CDTFA) issues and updates a publication on the fee. (Publication 91, California Department of Tax and Fee Administration)

Relief from liability.—Persons may be relieved from liability for the payment of the tire fee, including any interest or penalties, when their liability resulted from a failure to timely file a return or make a payment and that failure is found by the CDTFA to be due to reasonable reliance on written advice given by the CDTFA in a manner prescribed by Reg. 4902, 18 CCR. (Reg. 3502, 18 CCR)

The California tire fee does not apply to any tire sold with, or sold separately for use on, any self-propelled wheelchair, motorized tricycle, or motorized quadricycle. (Sec. 42885, Pub. Res. Code)

• *Medical waste fees*

California imposes registration and permit fees on medical waste generators, medical waste treatment facilities, and medical waste hauling transfer stations under the Medical Waste Management Act. (Sec. 117600 et seq., Hlth. & Sfty. Code) Waste that is regulated under the Act is exempted from regulation under, and fees assessed by, the hazardous waste control laws. (Sec. 25117.5, Hlth. & Sfty. Code)

Small quantity generators are subject to an annual medical waste generator fee of $25, except for small quantity generators with on-site treatment of medical waste, which are required to pay a biennial registration and inspection fee of $100. (Sec. 117923 Hlth. & Sfty. Code; Sec. 117924, Hlth. & Sfty. Code)

For large quantity medical waste generators, registration and annual permit fees payable to the Department of Health Services under the Medical Waste Management Act are as follows (Sec. 117995, Hlth. & Sfty. Code):

Acute psychiatric hospitals, licensed clinical laboratories, veterinary clinics or hospitals, large quantity generator medical offices $200

Intermediate care facilities $300

Specialty clinics, primary care clinics, health care service plan facilities . $350

Skilled nursing facilities

1-99 beds $275

100-199 beds $350

200 or more beds $400

General acute care hospitals

1-99 beds $600

100-199 beds $860

200-250 beds $1,100

251 or more beds $1,400

An additional annual medical waste treatment facility inspection and permit fee of $300 is imposed on large quantity generators that provide on-site treatment of medical waste, except for general acute care hospitals. For general acute care hospitals, the additional fee ranges from $300 to $1,000, depending on the number of hospital beds. (Sec. 117995, Hlth. & Sfty. Code)

The annual permit fee for an offsite medical waste treatment facility is $0.002 for each pound of medical waste treated or $10,000, whichever is greater. The initial application fee for each type of treatment technology at an off-site medical waste treatment facility is $100 per hour that the Department spends processing the application, up to a maximum of $50,000. (Sec. 118210, Hlth. & Sfty. Code)

The annual permit fee for a medical waste hauling transfer station is $2,000 or as provided in regulations. Additionally, an applicant for a transfer station permit must pay a fee of $100 for each hour that the Department spends processing the application, not to exceed $10,000 or an amount set by regulation. (Sec. 118045, Hlth. & Sfty. Code)

Permit fees for large quantity medical waste generators and medical waste treatment facilities are subject to annual adjustment to reflect changes in the cost of providing services. (Sec. 117990, Hlth. & Sfty. Code; Sec. 118205, Hlth. & Sfty. Code.)

• *Occupational lead poisoning fee*

Employers in industry categories identified as hazardous for potential lead poisoning exposure are subject to occupational lead poisoning fees, provided that they employ at least 10 people. (Sec. 105190, Hlth. & Sfty. Code) The California Department of Tax and Fee Administration (CDTFA) Publication 94 provides basic information on the fee.

The fees vary based on the business category and number of employees. (Sec. 105195, Hlth. & Sfty. Code) Current fees are available on the CDTFA website at https://www.cdtfa.ca.gov/taxes-and-fees/tax-rates-stfd.htm.

The California Department of Health Services may modify the list of affected industries. Employers using or disturbing lead in *de minimis* amounts (as defined in California Department of Health Services regulations) are exempt from the occupational lead poisoning fees. (Sec. 105191, Hlth. & Sfty. Code)

Fees are due at the California Department of Tax and Fee Administration (CDTFA) on or before the last day of February following the end of the calendar year. (Sec. 43152.13, Rev. & Tax. Code) The fees are adjusted annually by the CDTFA to reflect changes in the Consumer Price Index. (Sec. 105190, Hlth. & Sfty. Code)

Recordkeeping requirements.—Every feepayer that is liable for payment of the occupational lead poisoning prevention fee must maintain payroll reports, waiver requests and Department of Health Services' responses. (Reg. 3020, 18 CCR)

Relief from liability.—Persons may be relieved from liability for the payment of the occupational lead poisoning fee and the occupational lead poisoning prevention fee, including any interest or penalties, when their liability resulted from a failure to timely file a return or make a payment and that failure is found by the CDTFA to be due to reasonable reliance on written advice given by the CDTFA in a manner prescribed by Reg. 4902, 18 CCR. (Reg. 3021, 18 CCR)

- *Marine invasive species fee*

The California marine invasive species fee (ballast water management fee) applies to all vessels that enter California ports with ballast water loaded outside a defined coastal zone (the "exclusive economic zone"). Effective April 1, 2017, the fee is $1,000 per qualifying vessel voyage (formerly, $850). (*Special Taxes and Fees*, California Department of Tax and Fee Administration, March 2017)

Recordkeeping requirements.—A feepayer must maintain and make available for examination, on CDTFA request, records maintained in the manner prescribed by Reg. 4901, 18 CCR. In addition, every feepayer that is liable for payment of the fee must maintain records that document:

    — ballast water loading and discharge;

    — ship schedules;

    — ports of call; and

    — routes taken.

(Reg. 3501, 18 CCR)

Originally set to expire January 1, 2010, the ballast water fee has been made permanent. The maximum administrative civil penalty is $27,500 per violation for a person who intentionally or negligently fails to comply with the law. (*Environmental Fees Newsletter*, California Department of Tax and Fee Administration, January 2007)

Relief from liability.—Persons may be relieved from liability for the payment of the fee, including any interest or penalties, when their liability resulted from a failure to timely file a return or make a payment and that failure is found by the CDTFA to be due to reasonable reliance on written advice given by the CDTFA in a manner prescribed by Reg. 4902, 18 CCR. (Reg. 3502, 18 CCR)

- *Volatile organic compounds emissions fee*

The State Air Resources Control Board must impose a fee for any consumer product or any architectural coating sold in the state if the manufacturer's total sales of consumer products or architectural coatings will result in the emission in the state of 250 tons per year or more of volatile organic compounds. (Sec. 39613, Hlth. & Sfty. Code)

• *Electronic waste recycling fee*

Consumers purchasing a covered electronic device from a retailer must pay a California electronic waste recycling (Ewaste) fee. The fee is collected by the California Department of Tax and Fee Administration (CDTFA). Effective January 1, 2020, the fee is:

— for a screen size less than four inches, but less than 15 inches, $4;

— for a screen size of at least 15 inches, but less than 35 inches, $5; and

— for a screen size of at 35 inches or more, $6.

(https://www.cdtfa.ca.gov/taxes-and-fees/tax-rates-stfd.htm)

The California Integrated Waste Management Board, in collaboration with the California Department of Toxic Substances Control (DTSC), must review the covered electronic waste recycling fee at least every two years and make any adjustments to the fee to ensure that there are sufficient revenues to fund the covered electronic waste recycling program. (Sec. 42464.2, Pub. Res. Code)

A "covered electronic device" is defined as a cathode ray tube, cathode ray tube device, flat panel screen, or any other video display device with a screen size that is greater than four inches in size measured diagonally and which, when discarded or disposed, would be a hazardous waste under regulations set by the DTSC. (Sec. 42463, Pub. Res. Code) Covered electronic devices include

(1) computer monitors,

(2) laptop computers,

(3) portable DVD players with liquid crystal (LCD) screens,

(4) bare cathode ray tubes and devices containing cathode ray tube, and

(5) televisions with

— LCD screens,

— plasma screens, or

— cathode ray tubes.

(*BOE Publication 95, Electronic Waste Recycling Fee*, California Department of Tax and Fee Administration)

A retailer may pay the fee to the retailer's vendor on behalf of consumers if the vendor is registered with the State Board of Equalization to collect and remit the fee, the vendor holds a valid seller's permit, the retailer pays the fee as separately stated on the vendor's invoice to the retailer, and the retailer states on the consumer's invoice that the fee has been paid on behalf of the consumer. If a retailer elects to pay the fee to the vendor, the fee becomes a debt owed by the vendor to the state and the vendor may retain 3% of the fee for collection costs. (Sec. 42464, Pub. Res. Code)

A "vendor" is an entity that makes a sale of a covered electronic device for resale to a retailer who is the lessor of the device to a consumer under a lease that is a continuing sale and purchase. (Sec. 42463, Pub. Res. Code)

• *Propane safety inspection and enforcement fee and surcharge*

A fee is imposed on every propane storage system in order to pay for the cost of inspecting and regulating such systems. (Sec. 13244.5, Hlth. & Sfty. Code) In addition, to support the Public Utilities Commission's Propane Safety Inspection and Enforcement Program, a surcharge on the sale of propane is imposed on operators of propane distribution systems. Operators may pass on the cost of the surcharge to the ultimate consumers. (Sec. 4458, Pub. Util. Code)

The surcharge does not apply to:

(1) propane used by agricultural systems;

(2) commercial systems serving less than 10 customers;

(3) industrial and refinery systems;

    (4) recreational vehicles and appliances;

    (5) vehicular fuel;

    (6) single customers served by single tanks;

    (7) multicustomer systems (other than mobile home parks) that serve less than 10 customers; or

    (8) cylinder exchange operations.

(Sec. 4452, Pub. Util. Code)

The propane storage system fee is set by the State Fire Marshal in an amount not to exceed $250 per system and not to exceed the cost of inspection and regulation. (Sec. 13244.5, Hlth. & Sfty. Code) The rate for the surcharge is set by the Public Utilities Commission in an amount not to exceed 25¢ per lot or space per month. (Sec. 4458, Pub. Util. Code)

• *Underground storage tank fee*

Underground storage tank owners who are required to procure owner/operator permits must pay the State Board of Equalization (CDTFA) a storage fee. From January 1, 2015, through December 31, 2025, the fee will be $0.02 per gallon. The increase will not be operative beginning January 1, 2026. (Sec. 25299.43(g)(1), Hlth. & Sfty. Code)

The underground storage tank maintenance fee applies to:

    — gasoline and additives;

    — aviation gasoline and additives;

    — jet fuel and additives;

    — diesel fuels and additives;

    — lubrication oils;

    — heating and lighting oils; and

    — solvents.

The fee does not apply to motor fuel or heating oil used for noncommercial purposes and placed in tanks that have a capacity of 1,100 gallons or less, located on a farm or residence. (CDTFA Publication 88, Underground Storage Tank Fee, California Department of Tax and Fee Administration)

Fees, along with storage fee returns, must be filed with the Board on or before the 25th day of the month following the quarter for which the fee is due. The Board may require returns and payments to be made for periods other than quarterly. (Sec. 50109, Rev. & Tax. Code; Sec. 50110, Rev. & Tax. Code) Persons whose estimated underground storage tank maintenance fee liability averages $20,000 or more per month, as determined by the CDTFA pursuant to methods of calculation prescribed by the CDTFA, must remit amounts due by electronic funds transfer. Persons whose estimated liability averages less than $20,000 per month may elect to remit amounts due by electronic funds transfer with the approval of the CDTFA. The election is operative for a minimum of one year. (Sec. 50112.7, Rev. & Tax. Code)

Returns filed under the underground storage tank law may be filed electronically. (Sec. 50109, Rev. & Tax. Code; Sec. 50112.10, Rev. & Tax. Code)

Owner liability.—Liability for underground storage tank fees lies with owners, whether or not the owner is also the operator of the tank, and even if an agreement between the owner and operator requires the operator to pay the fees due. Fees are due, whether or not fees were previously paid for petroleum that was removed and transferred to another tank or redeposited in the same tank in which it was previously stored. Moreover, owners are liable for fees on all fuel deposited in tanks they own, even if the operator deposits a brand of fuel in the tank different from the brand deposited by the owner, and even if such action by the operator violates the lease agreement between the owner and operator. Fee liability lies with tank owners, even if the owner claims lack of awareness that the fee was due or claims inability to procure information from an operator about the gallons of fuel deposited. In this regard, the CDTFA may furnish to the fee payer otherwise confidential information from the tank operator, provided such information is necessary to assess, administer, and verify the fee. (Reg. 1212, 18 CCR)

Presumption of ownership.—There is a rebuttable presumption that the owner of real property is liable for California underground storage fees as the owner of any underground storage tank located on the property, even if the property is leased to another person. (Reg. 1205, 18 CCR) To overcome this presumption, proof that ownership of the tank rests with another person includes, but is not limited to, evidence that:

— the lessee installed the tank and is authorized under the lease agreement to remove the tank when the lease terminates, whether or not the lessor's approval is required;

— the lessee installed the tank, and the lease agreement stipulates that any improvements installed by the lessee are the property of the lessee during the term of the lease;

— documentation, such as a bill of sale, shows the transfer of ownership of the tank to a person other than the real property owner;

— the tank is depreciated on the state or federal income tax returns of someone other than the real property owner; or

— the tank was located on the premises when the lease agreement was signed, and the lessee's ownership of, and vested title to, the tank during the term of the lease are specified in the lease agreement.

(Reg. 1205, 18 CCR)

Operator fee payment and filing.—In order to facilitate operator fee payments on behalf of owners, owners and operators may each execute and file notarized documents with the CDTFA, showing their intention and acknowledging their respective responsibilities and liabilities. If both forms are satisfactory, the CDTFA will send fee returns and notices for the owner's account to the operator. Each document is effective until the CDTFA receives written notice of any change from either the owner or operator.

If the required documents are not filed, the CDTFA does not recognize fees received from operators as payments on the owner's account. The owner remains liable for fees, penalties and interest without credit for fees paid by the operator, and the operator may request a refund. If the CDTFA discovers such a discrepancy, the owner and operator may request in writing that fee payments from the operator be transferred to the owner's account. (Reg. 1213, 18 CCR)

Exemptions.—Entities not subject to underground tank storage fees are:

— The State of California, its agencies and departments;

— The United States, its unincorporated agencies and instrumentalities;

— Incorporated agencies and instrumentalities of the United States, wholly-owned by the United States or by a corporation wholly-owned by the United States;

— Banks and other financial institutions;

— Insurance companies; and

— Persons of Native American descent who are entitled to services as Indians from the United States Department of the Interior, if an underground storage tank is located on an Indian reservation, rancheria, or land held by the United States in trust for an Indian tribe or individual Indian. (Reg. 1220, 18 CCR)

Relief pursuant to written advice.—Relief is available from liability for fees, interest and penalties that results from failure to file timely returns or payments, provided that such failure is due to reasonable reliance on CDTFA written advice under conditions prescribed by regulation. For liability relief purposes, qualified written advice must be furnished in response to a specific written inquiry that identifies the specific person for whom such advice is requested; the inquiry must also fully describe the facts and circumstances of the activity or transaction for which such advice is requested. Presentation of books and records for an auditor's examination constitutes a written request for an audit report for liability relief purposes. Prior audit reports that contain written evidence demonstrating that the issue in question was examined constitutes qualified CDTFA written advice. (Reg. 1248, 18 CCR)

Recordkeeping.—Fee payers are required to maintain and submit records as required and requested by the CDTFA, including books of account; bills, receipts, invoices, cash register tapes, and other original documents that support the books of account; and schedules of working papers. Machine-sensible records accompanied by identifiable supporting details meet the prescribed recordkeeping standards. Records maintained with electronic data interchange processes and technology are sufficient, provided they meet prescribed standards and replicate acceptable paper records. Fee payers must submit information at CDTFA request about business processes used to maintain records; provide the CDTFA access to machine-sensible records; conform to hardcopy and alternative storage media record requirements; and comply with prescribed parameters of recordkeeping discretion. Fee payers may engage the CDTFA in record retention limitation agreements that waive or modify regulatory requirements; the CDTFA may conduct tests to verify the accuracy of machine-sensible records retained under such agreements. Failure to maintain complete and accurate records is evidence of fee payer negligence or intent to evade fees that may result in penalties or administrative action. (Reg. 1271, 18 CCR)

Waiver of penalties.—Penalties for the late payment of an underground storage tank maintenance fee or the late filing of a return may be waived without a showing of reasonable cause for tardiness under criteria to be developed by the State Board of Equalization. The goal of the criteria must be to foster efficient resolution of requests for relief from penalties. The Board may not require taxpayers to file statements supporting their claims for relief under penalty of perjury, as is the case when a person seeks waiver under a claim of reasonable cause for tardiness. (Sec. 50112.2, Rev. & Tax. Code)

A taxpayer may be relieved of penalties for late payment of an underground storage tank maintenance fee if the taxpayer enters into an installment plan for paying the fee within 45 days after a notice of determination or redetermination is final. The taxpayer must comply with the agreement for the waiver to remain effective, and waiver may not be granted in cases of fraud. (Sec. 50138.6, Rev. & Tax. Code)

Statement itemizing installment payments.—Taxpayers who have entered into installment agreements to pay an underground storage tank maintenance fee must receive an annual statement from the State Board of Equalization itemizing the balance of the fee owed at the beginning and end of a year and the amount of the fee paid during the year. (Sec. 50138.7, Rev. & Tax. Code)

Refund claims by the disabled.—The limitations period for filing refund claims for underground storage tank maintenance fees is suspended during the period that a person is unable to manage financial affairs because of a physical or mental impairment that is life threatening or that is expected to last for at least 12 months. There is no waiver for individuals who are represented in their financial matters by their spouses or other persons. (Sec. 50140.1, Rev. & Tax. Code)

Cost reimbursements for unreasonable assessments.—Taxpayers who have been unreasonably assessed an underground storage tank maintenance fee by the State Board of Equalization are entitled to reimbursement of their fees and expenses for attending Board hearings. They may be reimbursed for costs incurred as of the filing of a notice of determination, jeopardy determination, or refund claim. (Sec. 50156.9, Rev. & Tax. Code)

Employer withholding order.—An employer that has been ordered by the California Department of Tax and Fee Administration to withhold wages from an employee to satisfy the employee's debt for an unpaid underground storage tank maintenance fee, but that has failed to remit the withheld amount to the Board, may be held liable by the Board for the unremitted amount, which may be treated as a fee deficiency of the employer. The Board has seven years from the first day on which the employer withheld wages from an employee to assess the deficiency, with interest. The employee's liability for the fee must be credited for the unremitted amount and no further action may be taken to collect that sum from the employee. (Sec. 50136.5, Rev. & Tax. Code)

Confidentiality of fee information.—Preparers of underground storage tank maintenance fee returns who, without a client's consent, knowingly or recklessly disclose the client's confidential fee information for any purpose other than return preparation may be convicted of a misdemeanor, fined up to $1,000, and imprisoned up to one year. A preparer also may be liable for prosecution costs. (Sec. 50155.5, Rev. & Tax. Code)

• *Motor oil fee*

A motor oil fee is to be paid by the first person who produces motor oil when it is sold to any retail establishment or motor oil dealer, including any sold to the federal government or its agencies. Retailers are subject to the fee when they transport motor oil into the state from outside the state. The fee does not apply to motor oil exported for sale outside the state. The fee is imposed at a maximum rate of $0.05 per gallon, depending on administration and enforcement costs. However, prior to adoption of regulations for the fee, the Secretary of Food and Agriculture may apply a fee of $0.03 per gallon. (Sec. 13430—Sec. 13434, Bus. & Prof. Code)

• *Lubricating oil fee*

A tax is imposed on lubricating oil sold or transferred in California or imported into California. Oil manufacturers must remit taxes due to the California Integrated Waste Management Board, on or before the last day of the month following each quarter. The general rate for lubricating oil is 6¢ per quart or 24¢ per gallon of lubricating oil (or 3¢ for each quart or 12¢ for each gallon of 70% re-refined base lubricant). For lubricating oil sold by weight, a weight to volume conversion factor of 7.5 pounds per gallon is used to determine the amount of the fee. Reports are due to the Board when payment is or would be due. (Sec. 48650, Pub. Res. Code; Sec. 48671, Pub. Res. Code)

Returns filed under the integrated waste management law (lubricating oil tax) may be filed electronically. (Sec. 45151, Rev. & Tax. Code)

Payment is not required with respect to:

(1) oil for which the Board has already received payment under this provision;

(2) oil exported or sold for export from the state;

(3) oil sold for use in vessels operated in interstate or foreign commerce by a person engaged in the business of a common or contract carrier;

(4) oil imported into the state in the engine crankcase, transmission, gear box, or differential of an automobile, bus, truck, vessel, plane, train, or heavy equipment or machinery;

(5) bulk oil imported into, transferred in, or sold in the state to a motor carrier and used in motortrucks of three or more axles that are more than 6,000 pounds unladen weight or truck tractors.

An exemption applies to oil in volume of five gallons or less per quarter. (Sec. 48650, Pub. Res. Code)

A taxpayer may request a refund of the California lubricating oil tax paid on oil that was subsequently sold or used for an exempt purpose pursuant to Public Resource Code Sec. 48650. An exempt purpose includes subsequent sales to an agency of the federal government on which tax was not paid. The request for a refund must include all information required by Regulation 18613. (Reg. 18627, California Integrated Waste Management Board)

- *Fire prevention fee*

> **COMPLIANCE ALERT: Suspension of collection; repeal of law.**—Effective July 1, 2017, imposition of the California fire prevention fee is suspended. The suspension becomes inoperative on January 1, 2031, on which date the fee law is repealed, unless a law is enacted that deletes or extends that date.
>
> Ch. 135 (A.B. 398), Laws 2017, effective and operative as noted

---

The California Department of Forest and Fire Protection is authorized to determine the annual amount of the state fire prevention fee to be imposed on structures that are intended to be used for human habitation if they are located in state responsibility areas (SRAs). (Sec. 4212, Pub. Res. Code; Sec. 4213, Pub. Res. Code) A person from whom the fire prevention fee is determined to be due may petition the California Department of Forestry and Fire Protection for a redetermination of whether or not he or she is subject to the fee within 30 days of receiving a notice of the determination. (Sec. 4220, Pub. Res. Code)

The fee is $152.33 ($150 for FY 2011-2012 and 2012-2013) per habitable structure within an SRA. (*Tax Rates—Special Taxes and Fees*, California Department of Tax and Fee Administration, January 7, 2014) However, owners of habitable structures within the boundaries of a local fire protection agency will receive a reduction of $35 per habitable structure. (Special Notice L-383, California Department of Tax and Fee Administration, August 2012)

The CDTFA provides guidance to property tax assessors regarding the fire prevention fee. The fee is assessed annually to the owners of habitable structures located within the SRA as recorded on the county rolls or as recorded by the Department of Housing and Community Development on July 1 of the fiscal year for which the fee is due. CAL FIRE must identify owners subject to the fee and determine the fee amount. The CDTFA must issue bills on behalf of CAL FIRE. For fiscal year 2012-13, the fee is $150 per habitable structure, but owners of habitable structures within the boundaries of a local fire protection agency will receive a reduction of $35 per habitable structure. In anticipation that feepayers may contact local county assessors regarding this issue, information is provided regarding the billing cycle and contact information to assist assessors in directing feepayers to the proper agency. (*Letter to County Assessors*, No. 2013/036, California Department of Tax and Fee Administration, July 19, 2013)

January 1, 2015.—Effective January 1, 2015, there are definition changes/additions, as well as amendments relating to appeals and penalty provisions.

The term "structure" is changed "habitable structure," which refers to a building that contains one or more dwelling units or than can be occupied for residential use and includes single family homes, multidwelling structures, mobile and manufactured homes, and condominiums. The term does not include commercial, industrial, or incidental buildings such as detached garages, barns, outdoor sanitation facilities, and sheds. A definition is added for the term "person," which includes an individual, a business entity, or a state or federal governmental unit. In addition, an "owner of a habitable structure" is newly defined as the person that is the owner of record of a habitable structure on July 1 of the state fiscal year for which the fee is due. (Sec. 4211, Pub. Res. Code)

The fee is imposed on the owner of a habitable structure within a state responsibility area. A habitable structure may be exempted from the fee if the owner:

— certifies that the structure is not habitable as a result of a natural disaster; and

— either documents that the structure passed a defensible space inspection within one year of the date the structure was damaged or destroyed or certifies that clearance was in place at the time that the structure was damaged or destroyed as a result of a natural disaster.

(Sec. 4213.1, Pub. Res. Code)

If an untimely petition for redetermination is filed, it may be treated as an administrative protest or claim for refund if it is determined that the, as originally determined, may have been excessive or that the fee may have been the result of an error by the state Department of Forest and Fire Protection, its agent, or the State Board of Equalization (CDTFA). Such petitions shall be reviewed in the same manner as a timely petition for redetermination. (Sec. 4220.1, Pub. Res. Code)

The 20% penalty for nonpayment or untimely payment of the fee will no longer apply. Instead, nonpayment or late payment of the fee will be subject to the terms of the Fee Collection Procedures Law. (Sec. 4225, Pub. Res. Code)

• *Managed audits*

Taxpayers may voluntarily participate in managed audits of qualifying hazardous substances tax (Sec. 43507, Rev. & Tax. Code, *et seq.*), integrated waste management fee (Sec. 45855.6, Rev. & Tax. Code, *et seq*), oil spill response fee (Sec. 46607, Rev. & Tax. Code, *et seq*), and underground storage tank maintenance fee (Sec. 50155.6, Rev. & Tax. Code, *et seq.*) accounts with the State Board of Equalization. An account will qualify for managed audits if:

— the taxpayer's business involves few or no statutory exemptions;

— the taxpayer's business involves a single or a small number of clearly defined taxability issues;

— the taxpayer is taxed pursuant to a qualifying tax or fee law at issue and agrees to participate in the program; and

— the taxpayer has the resources to comply with the managed audit instructions provided by the CDTFA.

(Sec. 43507.1, Rev. & Tax. Code; Sec. 45855.6.1, Rev. & Tax. Code; Sec. 46607.1, Rev. & Tax. Code; Sec. 50155.6.1, Rev. & Tax. Code)

A taxpayer wishing to participate in the program must examine its books and records to determine if it has any unreported tax liability for the audit period and make available to the CDTFA for verification all computations and books and records examined. (Sec. 43507.2(a)(2), Rev. & Tax. Code; Sec. 45855.6.2(a)(2), Rev. & Tax.

Code; Sec. 46607(a)(2), Rev. & Tax. Code; Sec. 50155.6.2(a)(2), Rev. & Tax. Code) After the audit is verified by the CDTFA, interest on any unpaid liability will be imposed at 1/2 the rate that would otherwise be imposed during the audit period. (Sec. 43507.4, Rev. & Tax. Code; Sec. 45855.6.4, Rev. & Tax. Code; Sec. 46607.4, Rev. & Tax. Code; Sec. 50155.6.4, Rev. & Tax. Code)

[¶37-300]
SEVERANCE TAXES

[¶37-301] Severance Taxes

California imposes a tax on severance of petroleum and natural gas and a timber yield tax.

> **COMMENT: Transfer of BOE powers.**—Beginning July 1, 2017, all California State Board of Equalization (BOE) administrative powers, duties, and responsibilities that are not constitutionally mandated to the BOE, with certain exceptions in the short term, were transferred to the California Department of Tax and Fee Administration (CDTFA). The Timber Yield Tax Program was transferred to the CDTFA.
>
> The following programs, however, returned to the BOE Property Tax Division effective February 1, 2018, because the duties of staff in these programs are intertwined with the constitutional duties that remain with the BOE:
>
> — Tax Area Services Section (TASS);
>
> — Legal Entity Ownership Program (LEOP); and
>
> — Welfare Exemption Program.
>
> (Ch. 6 (A.B. 102), Laws 2017; Ch. 37 (A.B. 1817), Laws 2018, effective June 27, 2018)

• *Oil and gas production tax*

Oil well operators are subject to an annual charge based on the number of barrels produced. (Sec. 3402, Pub. Res. Code) Operators of gas wells are subject to an annual charge per 10,000 cubic feet of gas produced, excepting gas used for recycling or in oil-producing operations. (Sec. 3403, Pub. Res. Code) An annual charge applies to operators of underground gas storage facilities to defray the regulatory costs incurred by the state in maintaining surveillance over facilities that are partially or fully depleted oil or gas reservoirs. (Sec. 3403.5, Pub. Res. Code) With respect to oil and gas produced from a well that qualifies as hazardous or idle-deserted, or that has been inactive for at least the preceding five consecutive years, the annual charge is reduced to zero for a period of ten years. (Sec. 3238, Pub. Res. Code)

Rates.—A uniform rate of charges is determined annually by the Department of Conservation. (Sec. 3412, Pub. Res. Code)

Current rate.—The assessment rate per barrel of oil and each 10,000 cubic feet of natural gas produced for fiscal year 2019-2020 is $0.565336900.

Previous rates.—Rates for previous fiscal years were:

2018-2019	$0.5547977
2017-2018	$0.5038349
2016-2017	$0.3626051
2015-2016	$0.3243123
2014-2015	$0.2863572
2013-2014	$0.1426683
2012-2013	$0.1406207

2011-2012	$0.1266251
2010-2011	$0.1062988
2009-2010	$0.0880312
2008-2009	$0.0790758
2007-2008	$0.0702257
2006-2007	$0.061889
2005-2006	$0.0538953
2004-2005	$0.0508980
2003-2004	$0.0443089
2002-2003	$0.0421689
2001-2002	$0.0373354

These charges apply in addition to all other taxes assessed. (Sec. 3404, Pub. Res. Code)

Reports.—Oil and gas producers are required to file a monthly report on or before the last day of each month, and an annual report on or before March 1 of each year. (Sec. 3227, Pub. Res. Code)

Owners must also file notices of intention to drill or otherwise permanently alter well casings or to deepen or redrill the well, of any operation involving the plugging of the well, and of any change of well number designations. (Sec. 3200, Pub. Res. Code through Sec. 3203, Pub. Res. Code)

All reports are filed with the Department of Conservation.

Payment.—The annual oil and gas production charge is due and payable on the first day of July in each year for assessments of more than $10 but less than $500, and is delinquent if not paid on or before August 15 of each year. With respect to assessments of $500 or more, the charges are due and payable on July 1; one-half of such charges are delinquent if not paid on or before August 15 and the remaining one-half of such charges are delinquent if not paid on or before February 1 of the following year. (Sec. 3420, Pub. Res. Code)

Forms.—The Department of Conservation prescribes the form and content of all reports relating to the oil and gas production tax. Forms are available on the department website at http://www.conservation.ca.gov/dog/pubs_stats/Pages/forms.aspx.

Acute orphan well operators.—The California Department of Conservation is required to impose a severance fee on persons operating oil or gas wells in the state, those owning royalty or other interests in the production of those wells, and persons operating idle wells in the state, beginning on March 1, 2006. Unless authorized by the Legislature, these fees will not be collected after 2007. (Sec. 3263, Pub. Res. Code)

The fee on production is at a uniform rate per barrel of oil and at a uniform rate per 10,000 cubic feet of natural gas produced from a well for the preceding year for an aggregate total of $500,000. The charge on idle wells in California is determined by dividing equally the maximum aggregate annual charge of $500,000 by the total number of idle wells as of December 31 of the preceding year. (Sec. 3263, Pub. Res. Code)

• *Timber yield tax*

Owners of harvested timber, and owners of felled or downed timber that acquire title thereto in California from a tax-exempt person or agency, are subject to a timber yield tax. The statutory tax rate is 6% of the total immediate harvest value of the timber, or "such other rate as may be fixed" by the California Department of Tax and Fee Administration (CDTFA). (Sec. 38115, Rev. & Tax. Code)

¶37-301

Tax rate.—The timber yield tax rate is currently 2.9%. This rate has been in effect since 2002. On or before December 31 of each year, the yield tax rate is adjusted to the nearest 0.1%, in the same proportion that the average rate of general property taxation in the rate adjustment counties in the current tax year differs from the average rate of general property tax in such counties in the preceding tax year. (Sec. 38202, Rev. & Tax. Code; *Form CDTFA-401-HVSI*, California Department of Tax and Fee Administration, January 2020)

Returns.—Tax returns are filed with the CDTFA on or before the last day of the month following each calendar quarter. (Sec. 38402, Rev. & Tax. Code) Tax payments are due on or before the last day of the month following each quarterly period in which the scaling date for the harvested timber occurs. (Sec. 38401, Rev. & Tax. Code)

PLANNING NOTE: Timber yield taxpayers receive two forms— CDTFA-401-APT, Timber Tax Harvest Report, which is used to report basic information about their harvest and to calculate total harvest value, and CDTFA-401-1PT, Timber Tax Return. Forms also can be downloaded from the BOE website at http://www.boe.ca.gov/proptaxes/timbertax.htm. (*BOE Publication 87, Guide to the California Timber Yield Tax*, California State Board of Equalization)

Timber is exempt from tax, provided that its immediate harvest value within a calendar quarter does not exceed $3,000. (Sec. 38116, Rev. & Tax. Code; Reg. 1024, 18 CCR) The exemption prevents harvest value tax collection and administration costs that would otherwise exceed tax revenues collected from low timber yields.

Waiver of penalties.—Penalties for the late payment of timber yield tax or the late filing of a return may be waived without a showing of reasonable cause for tardiness under criteria to be developed by the CDTFA. The goal of the criteria must be to foster efficient resolution of requests for relief from penalties. (Sec. 38452, Rev. & Tax. Code)

A taxpayer may be relieved of penalties for late payment of timber yield tax if the taxpayer enters into an installment plan for paying the tax within 45 days after a notice of determination or redetermination is final. The taxpayer must comply with the agreement for the waiver to remain effective, and the waiver may not be granted in cases of fraud. (Sec. 38504, Rev. & Tax. Code)

Statement itemizing installment payments.—Taxpayers that have entered into installment agreements to pay timber yield tax must receive an annual statement from the CDTFA itemizing the balance of tax owed at the beginning and end of a year and the amount of tax paid during the year. (Sec. 38504.5, Rev. & Tax. Code)

Refund claims by the disabled.—The limitations period for filing refund claims for timber yield tax is suspended during the period that an individual is unable to manage financial affairs because of a physical or mental impairment that is life threatening or that is expected to last for at least 12 months. There is no waiver for individuals who are represented in their financial matters by their spouses or other persons. (Sec. 38602.5, Rev. & Tax. Code)

Cost reimbursements for unreasonable assessments.—Taxpayers that have been unreasonably assessed timber yield tax by the CDTFA are entitled to reimbursement of their fees and expenses for attending CDTFA hearings. They may be reimbursed for costs incurred as a result of the filing of a notice of determination, jeopardy determination, or refund claim. (Sec. 38708, Rev. & Tax. Code)

Employer withholding order.—An employer that has been ordered by the CDTFA to withhold wages from an employee to satisfy the employee's debt for unpaid timber yield tax, but that has failed to remit the withheld amount to the CDTFA, may be held liable for the unremitted amount, which may be treated as a tax deficiency of the employer. The CDTFA has seven years from the first day on which the employer withheld wages from an employee to assess the deficiency, with interest. The employee's liability for tax must be credited for the unremitted amount and no further action may be taken to collect that sum from the employee. (Sec. 38503.5, Rev. & Tax. Code)

Confidentiality of tax information.—Preparers of timber yield tax returns who, without a client's consent, knowingly or recklessly disclose the client's confidential tax information for any purpose other than return preparation may be convicted of a misdemeanor, fined up to $1,000, and imprisoned up to one year. A preparer also may be liable for prosecution costs. (Sec. 38707, Rev. & Tax. Code)

UNCLAIMED PROPERTY

[¶37-350]

UNCLAIMED PROPERTY

[¶37-351] Unclaimed Property

Generally, property that is unclaimed by its rightful owner is presumed abandoned after a specified period of years following the date upon which the owner may demand the property or the date upon which the obligation to pay or distribute the property arises, whichever comes first.

What is unclaimed property?

"Unclaimed property" is all property that:

— is presently unclaimed, abandoned, escheated, permanently escheated, or distributed to the state;

— will become unclaimed, abandoned, escheated, permanently escheated, or distributed to the state; or

— will become the possession of the state, if not claimed within the time allowed by law, even if there is no judicial determination that the property is unclaimed, abandoned, escheated, permanently escheated, or distributed to the state. (Sec. 1300, Code of Civ. Proc.)

COMMENT: Escheat is an area of potential federal/state conflict. A federal statute may preempt state escheat provisions, as for instance Sec. 514(a) of the Employee Retirement Income Security Act of 1974 (ERISA). Pursuant to this provision, the Department of Labor and Workforce Development has been of the opinion that funds of missing participants in a qualified employee benefit plan must stay in the plan despite a state escheat provision because ERISA preempts application of the state escheat laws with respect to such funds (Advisory Opinion 94-41A, Department of Labor, Pension and Welfare Benefit Administration, Dec. 7, 1994). Some states have challenged the federal position on this and similar narrowly delineated situations. In the case of federal tax refunds, IRC Sec. 6408 disallows refunds if the refund would escheat to a state.

Practitioners are thus advised that a specific situation where federal and state policy cross on the issue of escheat may, at this time, be an area of unsettled law.

What are the dormancy periods for unclaimed property?

General rule. Generally, all tangible and intangible personal property that is held, issued, or owing in the ordinary course of a holder's business and that has remained unclaimed by the owner for more than three years, either from the date of the last activity of the owner or after the property became payable or distributable, depending on the type of property, is presumed abandoned.

Checks and drafts. Any sum payable on any other written instrument on which a banking or financial organization is directly liable, including any draft, cashier's check, teller's check, or certified check, that has been outstanding for more than three years from the date it was payable, or from the date of its issuance if payable on demand, is presumed abandoned when the owner has not corresponded electronically or in writing with the banking or financial organization, or otherwise indicated interest, concerning the item for more than three years.

Bank accounts. Any demand, savings, or matured time deposit, or account subject to a negotiable order of withdrawal, made with a banking organization, together with any interest or dividends thereon, are presumed abandoned when the owner has not indicated an interest in the deposit for more than three years.

Property distributable in the course of demutualization or related reorganization of an insurance company. Property distributable in the course of demutualization or related reorganization of an insurance company is presumed abandoned by:

(1) the date of demutualization if the owner address is known to be incorrect;

(2) two years after the date of demutualization if notices to the owner are returned undeliverable; or

(3) three years after the date of demutualization if the notices are not returned.

Gift certificates, gift cards and credit memos. Generally, gift certificates and gift cards are exempt from reporting requirements in California. However, gift certificates having an expiration date that are given in exchange for money or other things of value are presumed abandoned if left unclaimed by the owner for more than three years after the gift certificate became payable or distributable.

Stock and other intangibles. Any dividend, profit, distribution, interest, payment on principal, or other sum held or owing by a business association for or to its shareholder, certificate holder, member, bondholder, or other security holder, or a participating patron of a cooperative, who has not claimed it, or corresponded in writing with the business association concerning it, within three years after the date prescribed for payment or delivery, escheats to the state.

Other dormancy periods. Most states also have specified dormancy periods for:

Business association dissolutions/refunds,

Insurance policies,

IRAs/retirement funds,

Money orders,

Proceeds from class action suits,

Property held by fiduciaries,

Safe deposit boxes,

Shares in a financial institution,

Traveler's checks,

Utilities,

Wages/salaries, and

Property held by courts/public agencies.

Is there a business-to-business exemption for unclaimed property?

There is no business-to-business exemption in California.

What are the notice requirements for unclaimed property?

Not less than six months nor more than 12 months before property becomes reportable, holders generally must send notices to owners of the property with a value of $50 or more prior to reporting the accounts to the Controller. The notice must clearly state that the property will escheat to the state if a timely response to the notification is not received. Notices must be sent if the holder has in its records an address for the apparent owner, which the holder's records do not disclose to be inaccurate. The notice can be sent electronically with the owner's consent or mailed to the owner's last known address.

In addition, banks and financial organizations with records of an apparent owner for unclaimed property must make a reasonable effort to give notice to owners that their property will escheat to the state either:

(1) not less than two years nor more than two and one-half years after the date of last activity by, or communication with, the owner with respect to the account, deposit, shares, or other interest, as shown on the record of the banking or financial organization; or

(2) not less than six months nor more than 12 months before the time the item becomes reportable to the Controller.

What are the reporting requirements for unclaimed property?

General requirements. Persons holding property that has escheated to the state by reason of a presumption of abandonment are required to submit information reports. The report is made to the State Controller on Form UFS-1 and is due before November 1 for each year ending as of June 30 or earlier. The reports of life insurance companies and all insurance corporation demutualization proceeds must be filed by May 1 of each year ending as of December 31 or earlier. The report requires identification of the property and its former owner and dates when the property became payable and when the last transaction with the owner occurred.

Negative reporting. Organizations that neither hold nor owe unclaimed property are not required to submit a report, although it is recommended that they do so by completing and filing Form UFS-1 only. The Controller may require the filing of such a report by sending notification to the holder. (State of California Unclaimed Property Holder Handbook, Office of California State Controller)

Minimum reporting. California does not have a minimum report requirement.

Aggregate reporting. Items of value under $25 each may be reported in the aggregate. Banking and finance organizations' holder reports must include, among other items and except with respect to traveler's checks and money orders, the name, if known, and last known address of each person appearing from the records of the holder to be the owner of any property of value of at least $25. The State Controller's Officer "strongly discourage[s]" the use of aggregate reporting where account information is available. (State of California Unclaimed Property Holder Handbook, Office of California State Controller)

Electronic reporting. Reports that include 10 or more properties must be submitted electronically. (State of California Unclaimed Property Holder Handbook, Office of California State Controller)

Recordkeeping. Holders must retain all records pertaining to unclaimed property for a period of seven years after the property was, or should have been, reported.

[¶37-400]
UNEMPLOYMENT COMPENSATION

[¶37-401] Unemployment Insurance

California's Unemployment Insurance Tax is covered in Revenue and Taxation Code, Division 6 Withholding Tax on Wages. Comprehensive coverage of unemployment insurance is provided in Wolters Kluwer, CCH Unemployment/Social Security Reporter. For more information go to CCHGroup.com or contact an account representative at 888-CCH-REPS (888-224-7377).

[¶40-000]
MOTOR FUELS

[¶40-001] Gasoline Taxes

California has a motor vehicle fuel tax, a diesel fuel tax, a tax on aircraft jet fuel, and a use fuel tax. California also participates in the International Fuel Tax Agreement (IFTA), and imposes tax on other fuels.

> **COMPLIANCE ALERT: CDTFA assumes responsibility for motor fuel taxes administration.**—As a result of 2017 legislation that stripped the State Board of Equalization (BOE) of all but its constitutionally mandated duties, responsibilities, and powers, the California Department of Tax and Fee Administration (CDTFA) assumed responsibility for administration of all the taxes not contained in the BOE's constitutional duties, including motor fuel taxes. The change was effective July 1, 2017. (Ch. 16 (A.B. 102), Laws 2017, effective June 27, 2017) In subsequent legislation, a provision was added to specify that, in the Revenue and Taxation Code or any other code, references to the "board, itself" or "State Board of Equalization meeting as a public body" for purposes of the duties, powers, and responsibilities transferred to CDTFA means CDTFA. (Sec. 20.5, Rev. & Tax. Code, added by Sec. 16, Ch. 252 (A.B. 131), Laws 2017, effective September 16, 2017)

> **COMPLIANCE ALERT: Gas-tax swap discontinued.**—The annual rate adjustment required by the gas-tax swap instituted in 2010 (beginning with fiscal year 2011-2012) is discontinued. Instead, on July 1, 2020, the tax rates will be adjusted by a percentage amount equal to the increase in the California Consumer Price Index (CCPI) from November 1, 2017, through November 1, 2019. Every July 1 thereafter, the base rates and any subsequent rate increases will be increased by a percentage amount equal to the increase in CCPI in the subsequent 12-month period rounded to the nearest one-tenth of one cent.

Discussed here is the motor vehicle fuel tax. Specific topics covered include:

— products subject to tax,

— point of taxation,

— license requirements,

— basis of tax,

— rate of tax,

— exemptions,

— reports and payments,

— credits, refunds, and reimbursements, and

— local taxes.

• *Products subject to tax*

For purposes of the tax, motor vehicle fuel means gasoline and aviation gasoline. It does not include jet fuel, diesel fuel, kerosene, liquefied petroleum gas, natural gas in liquid or gaseous form, or racing fuel.

By regulation, "motor vehicle fuel" also means:

— gasohol;

— finished gasoline;

— gasoline blendstocks, which includes alkylate, butane, butene, catalytically cracked gasoline, coker gasoline, ethyl tertiary butyl ether (ETBE), hexane, hydrocrackate, isomerate, light naphtha, methyol tertiary butyl ether (MTBE), mixed xylene (not including any separated isomer of xylene), naphtha, natural gasoline, pentane, pentane mixture, polymer gasoline, raffinate, reformate, straight-run gasoline, straight-run naphtha, tertiary amyl methyl ether (TAME), tertiary butyl alcohol (gasoline grade) (TBA), thermally cracked gasoline, toluene, and transmix containing gasoline; and

— blended motor vehicle fuel.

By the same regulation, the "motor vehicle fuel" also does not include:

— ethanol (ethyl alcohol),

— methanol (methyl alcohol), or

— blends of gasoline and alcohol (including any denaturant) containing 15 percent, or less, gasoline.

Storage tax.—Suppliers, wholesalers, and retailers owning 1,000 gallons or more of tax-paid gasoline or diesel fuel on November 1, 2017, must pay a storage tax on those fuels. Anyone owing storage tax must file a form and pay the tax owed by January 1, 2018.

• *Point of taxation*

In California, the motor vehicle fuel tax generally is imposed on the removal of motor vehicle fuel from a terminal if the fuel is removed at the rack. The tax also is imposed on:

— removal from a refinery by bulk transfer if the refiner or owner of the fuel immediately before the removal is not a licensed supplier or at the refinery rack;

— entry of motor vehicle fuel into California entry of motor vehicle fuel into the state for sale, consumption, use, or warehousing if the entry is either by bulk transfer and the refiner or the owner of the fuel immediately before the removal is not a licensed supplier, or at the refinery rack;

— removal or sale of motor vehicle fuel in this state to an unlicensed person unless there was a prior taxable removal, entry, or sale of the motor vehicle fuel;

— blended motor vehicle fuelby the blender thereof;

— delivery into the fuel tank of a qualifying motor vehicle of any motor vehicle fuel on which a claim for refund has been allowed, or any liquid on which the motor vehicle fuel tax, the use fuel tax, or the diesel fuel tax has not been imposed.

There also are incidence of tax provisions for:

— position holders;

— terminal operators;

— enterers;

— blenders;

— highway vehicle operator/fueler;

— suppliers; and

— two-party exchange contracts.

• *License requirements*

California requires licenses for several types of persons subject to the motor vehicle fuel tax. Included in that group are:

— suppliers;

— industrial users;

— pipeline operators;

— pipeline operators; and

— train operators.

The CDTFA also may require any person to deposit with it an appropriate security.

• *Basis of tax*

The motor vehicle fuel tax is imposed on each gallon of motor vehicle fuel in California from a terminal if the motor vehicle fuel is removed at the rack.

• *Rate of tax*

The gasoline (motor vehicle fuel) excise tax rate is:

— $0.505 per gallon effective July 1, 2020 through June 30, 2021;

— $0.473 per gallon effective July 1, 2019 through June 30, 2020;

— $0.417 per gallon effective November 1, 2017 through June 30, 2019;

— $0.297 per gallon effective July 1, 2017 through October 31, 2017;

— $0.278 per gallon effective July 1, 2016 through June 30, 2017;

— $0.30 per gallon effective July 1, 2015 through June 30, 2016;

— $0.36 per gallon effective July 1, 2014 through June 30, 2015;

— $0.395 per gallon effective July 1, 2013 through June 30, 2014;

— $0.36 per gallon effective July 1, 2012 through June 30, 2013; and

— $0.357 per gallon effective July 1, 2011 through June 30, 2012.

(*Special Notice L-739*, California Department of Tax and Fee Administration, May 2020; *Special Notice L-561*, California Department of Tax and Fee Administration, June 2018; Tax Rates—Special Taxes and Fees, California State Board of Equalization, March 28, 2017)

Annual increases.—In addition, the annual rate adjustment required by the gas-tax swap instituted in 2010 for gasoline (beginning with fiscal year 2011-2012) is discontinued. Instead, on July 1, 2020, the tax rates will be adjusted by a percentage amount equal to the increase in the California Consumer Price Index (CCPI) from November 1, 2017, through November 1, 2019. Every July 1 thereafter, the base rates and any subsequent rate increases will be increased by a percentage amount equal to the increase in CCPI in the subsequent 12-month period rounded to the nearest one-tenth of one cent.

• *Exemptions*

Motor vehicle fuel tax does not apply to:

— any entry or removal from a terminal or refinery of fuel transferred in bulk if the persons involved are licensed suppliers;

— the removal of motor vehicle fuel if:

(1) the motor vehicle fuel is removed by railroad car from an approved refinery and is received at an approved terminal,

(2) the refinery and the terminal are operated by the same licensed supplier, and

(3) The refinery is not served by a specified pipeline or vessel;

— motor vehicle fuel exported outside the state by a supplier by means of

(1) facilities operated by the supplier,

(2) delivery to a carrier, customs broker, or forwarding agency, whether hired by the purchaser or not, for shipment to the out-of-state point, or

(3) delivery by the supplier to any vessel clearing from a port of this state for a port outside of this state and actually exported from this state in the vessel;

— motor vehicle fuel sold by credit card certified by the U.S. Department of State to consulate officers or employees of a foreign government;

— motor vehicle fuel sold to the U.S. armed forces for use in ships or aircraft or for use outside the state;

— qualifying entries or removals of gasoline blendstocks; and

— motor vehicle fuel sold by a supplier to a train operator for use in a fuel-powered train or for other off-highway use.

- *Reports and payments*

COMPLIANCE ALERT: Storage tax report, payment due January 1, 2018.— On or before January 1, 2018, each person subject to the storage tax enacted in 2017 (see discussion above) must prepare and file a return showing the total number of gallons of tax-paid motor vehicle fuel owned by the person on November 1, 2017 and the amount of the storage tax. The return must be accompanied by a remittance payable to the CDTFA.

Before the last day of each calendar month, those who must prepare and file with the CDTFA a motor fuel tax return for the previous month include the following:

— suppliers (BOE-501-PS);

— terminal operators (BOE-506-PO);

— pipeline operators (BOE-506-PT); and

— train operators (BOE-506-PT).

Payments.—Motor vehicle fuel tax is paid to the State Controller with reports. Persons whose estimated tax liability averages $20,000 or more per month, as determined by the California Department of Tax and Fee Administration (CDTFA) pursuant to methods of calculation prescribed by the CDTFA, must remit amounts due by electronic funds transfer (EFT). Persons whose estimated liability averages less than $20,000 per month may elect to remit amounts due by EFT with the approval of the CDTFA. The election is operative for a minimum of one year.

Persons whose estimated tax liability averages $900,000 or more per month must make a prepayment of tax on or before the 15th day of each month. The prepayment amount must be at least 95% of the tax liability for the month to which the prepayment applies or at least 95% of the tax liability reported for the previous month.

- *Credits, refunds, and reimbursements*

Motor vehicle fuel tax refunds are available to:

— persons buying and using motor fuel for purposes other than operating motor vehicles upon public highways; however, no refund is allowed for fuel used in recreational vehicles or in off-highway recreational vehicles;

— fuel exporters;

— construction equipment operators;

— persons selling fuel to armed forces, if such sales by distributors would be exempt;

— certain foreign government consulate employees and officers;

— any supplier that removes motor vehicle fuel at a rack and pays tax on that removal or that purchases tax-paid motor vehicle fuel outside the bulk transfer/terminal system and then delivers the tax-paid fuel to another approved terminal from which that supplier subsequently removes the fuel at the terminal rack, but only to the extent that the supplier can show that tax on the same amount of fuel has been paid more than once by the same supplier;

— any supplier that purchases tax-paid motor vehicle fuel in the bulk transfer/terminal system and subsequently removes the fuel at the terminal rack, but only to the extent that the supplier can show that tax on the same amount of fuel tax has been paid more than once by the same supplier; or

— qualifying persons who buy and use motor vehicle fuel that has been taxed under the California motor vehicle fuel tax law to produce a blended fuel that will be subject to the California use fuel tax.

Refunds are allowed for tax paid on fuel used in the operation of a vehicle on a highway under the jurisdiction of the U.S. Department of Agriculture.

Refunds of $0.06 per gallon are allowed on motor fuel used in propelling certain public transportation vehicles that carry persons for hire, compensation, or profit.

Refunds are allowed on motor fuel used to propel a vessel in California, only if the vessel is operated by its owner on waters located on private property owned or controlled by the vessel owner.

Refund claims must be filed within the later of three years from the date the fuel was purchased or six months from the date the taxpayer received the invoice for the tax.

Cost reimbursements for unreasonable assessments.—Taxpayers who have been unreasonably assessed motor vehicle fuel tax are entitled to reimbursement of fees and expenses for attending CDTFA hearings. They may be reimbursed for costs incurred as of the filing of a notice of determination, jeopardy determination, or refund claim.

Tax paid twice.—When a supplier needs to remove motor vehicle fuel from one terminal rack and transport it to another terminal to be stored above the rack, the supplier may obtain a credit or refund of the tax paid when the fuel is removed from the rack for a second time. The credit for the twice-paid tax must be taken on a tax return filed within 3 months after the close of the calendar month in which the second tax was reported to the state.

Returned fuel.—When motor vehicle fuel is returned by the supplier to a refinery or an approved terminal, the supplier can avoid paying tax a second time on the same fuel by either filing a claim for refund with the State Controller or taking a credit on the supplier's tax return filed with the CDTFA.

• *Local taxes*

A county (other than a county with a transit development board or a county under the jurisdiction of a county transportation commission), a city and county, a county transportation commission, a transit development board, a transit district, or a city with a population in excess of 500,000 located within a transit district may impose a $0.01 per gallon (or in the case of compressed natural gas, $0.01 per 100 cubic feet) tax on the sale, storage, or use of motor vehicle fuel, if approved by two-thirds of the voters voting at a qualifying special election. The California Department of Tax and Fee Administration (CDTFA) will administer the tax.

¶40-001

Subject to voter approval, counties are authorized to impose an additional tax on motor vehicle fuel in increments of $0.01 per gallon or, in the case of compressed natural gas, $0.01 per 100 cubic feet. No local tax may be imposed on fuel used in propelling an aircraft or a vessel. Any tax so imposed will be administered by the CDTFA.

[¶40-003] Diesel Fuel Taxes

> *COMPLIANCE ALERT: CDTFA assumes responsibility for diesel fuel taxes administration.*—As a result of 2017 legislation that stripped the State Board of Equalization (BOE) of all but its constitutionally mandated duties, responsibilities, and powers, the California Department of Tax and Fee Administration (CDTFA) assumed responsibility for administration of all the taxes not contained in the BOE's constitutional duties, including diesel fuel taxes. The change was applicable July 1, 2017. (Ch. 16 (A.B. 102), Laws 2017, effective June 27, 2017) In subsequent legislation, a provision was added to specify that, in the Revenue and Taxation Code or any other code, references to the "board, itself" or "State Board of Equalization meeting as a public body" for purposes of the duties, powers, and responsibilities transferred to CDTFA means CDTFA. (Sec. 20.5, Rev. & Tax. Code, added by Sec. 16, Ch. 252 (A.B. 131), Laws 2017, effective September 16, 2017)

> *COMPLIANCE ALERT: Gas-tax swap discontinued.*—The annual rate adjustment required by the gas-tax swap instituted in 2010 for diesel (beginning with fiscal year 2012-2013) is discontinued. Instead, on July 1, 2020, the tax rates will be adjusted by a percentage amount equal to the increase in the California Consumer Price Index (CCPI) from November 1, 2017, through November 1, 2019. Every July 1 thereafter, the base rates and any subsequent rate increases will be increased by a percentage amount equal to the increase in CCPI in the subsequent 12-month period rounded to the nearest one-tenth of one cent.

California imposes a diesel fuel tax. See ¶40-009 for information on the interstate user tax and the use fuel tax. Discussed here are:

— products subject to tax,

— point of taxation,

— license requirements,

— basis of tax,

— rate of tax,

— exemptions,

— reports and payments, and

— credits, refunds, and reimbursements.

• *Products subject to tax*

Diesel fuel means any liquid that is commonly or commercially known or sold as a fuel that is suitable for use in a diesel-powered highway vehicle. A liquid meets this requirement if, without further processing or blending, the liquid has practical and commercial fitness for use in the engine of a diesel-powered highway vehicle. However, a liquid does not possess this practical and commercial fitness solely by reason of its possible or rare use as a fuel in the engine of a diesel-powered highway vehicle. The term does not include kerosene, gasoline, liquefied petroleum gas, natural gas in liquid or gaseous form, or alcohol.

¶40-003

According to the California State Board of Equalization, "biodiesel" and "bi-ofuel" are fuels used as alternatives to petroleum based diesel fuel. The most common such fuels are biodiesel, straight vegetable oil, and waste vegetable oil. The diesel tax applies to biodiesel fuels, "whether they are called biodiesel, B100, methyl esters or by any other name, and whether the fuel meets the specification of ASTM D6751." Publication 96, California State Board of Equalization.

Storage tax.—Suppliers, wholesalers, and retailers owning 1,000 gallons or more of tax-paid diesel fuel on November 1, 2017, must pay a storage tax on those fuels. Anyone owing storage tax must file a form and pay the tax owed by January 1, 2018.

• *Point of taxation*

The diesel fuel tax generally is imposed on the removal of diesel fuel from a terminal if the diesel fuel is removed at the rack. It also is imposed on fuel:

— removed from refineries under some circumstances;

— entered into the state for sale, consumption, use, or warehousing under some circumstances;

— removed or sold to an unregistered person unless there was a prior removal, entry, or sale of the fuel; and

— removed or sold, if blended diesel fuel, by the blender.

Refiners, position holders, and diesel fuel blenders are subject to a diesel fuel tax in specified circumstances involving the removal or entry of the fuel within the state. The removal, import, or sale of fuel, and the status of a supplier as a blender, enterer, position holder, refiner, terminal operator, or throughputter, determine when the supplier is subject to tax.

Diesel fuel tax liability also arises from successor business or stock of goods purchases, provided that such transactions are governed by contract. Upon written request, the California Department of Tax and Fee Administration (CDTFA) issues certificates to suppliers in appropriate circumstances to provide assurance of release from tax liability. Otherwise, a CDTFA notice of successor liability enforces tax liability, and is timely, if served no later than three years after the CDTFA receives written notice of a stock or business goods purchase.

Highway vehicle operators, end sellers, and terminal operators may be jointly and severally liable for diesel fuel tax imposed as a backup tax on dyed diesel fuel used on highways or the sale of any diesel fuel on which a refund has been allowed.

Government entities that use exempt diesel fuel on California highways are required to pay an amount equal to the diesel fuel tax.

Suppliers are required to collect tax from purchasers of diesel fuel. The purchaser may elect to remit tax to the supplier on mutually agreeable terms. Alternatively, the purchaser may remit tax on or before five working days before the last day of the calendar month following the monthly period to which the tax relates. The election is available to purchasers remitting tax by electronic funds transfer.

• *License requirements*

Certain persons subject to the diesel fuel tax are required to apply for a license before engaging in business affected by the tax. These persons include

— suppliers;

— exempt bus operators;

— ultimate vendors; and

— highway vehicle operators and end sellers.

In addition, each government entity operating a diesel-powered highway vehicle upon the state's highways must apply for a diesel fuel tax license. The California

Department of Tax and Fee Administration (CDTFA) has issued a publication dealing with vehicle operators who need to have, among other things, an IFTA license, a California fuel trip permit, or an interstate user diesel fuel tax license.

Manufacturers, producers, and importers of biodiesel fuel and those who sell or use biodiesel that has not been taxed as diesel fuel are required to register with the CDTFA.

• *Basis of tax*

The diesel fuel tax generally is imposed on each gallon of diesel fuel removed from a terminal.

• *Rate of tax*

The diesel fuel excise tax rate is 36¢ per gallon effective July 1, 2018, through June 30, 2020, and 38.5¢ per gallon effective July 1, 2020, through June 30, 2021. (Sec. 60050, Rev. & Tax. Code; *Special Notice L-739*, California Department of Tax and Fee Administration, May 2020; *Special Notice L-633*, California Department of Tax and Fee Administration, May 2019; *Special Notice L-561*, California Department of Tax and Fee Administration, June 2018; *Special Notice L-540*, California Department of Tax and Fee Administration, May 2018)

Suppliers, wholesalers, and retailers owning 1,000 gallons or more of tax-paid gasoline or diesel fuel on November 1, 2017, must pay a storage tax on those fuels. Anyone owing a storage tax must file a form and pay the tax owed by January 1, 2018. (California State Board of Equalization, Fuel Tax Division—Tax Rates)

• *Exemptions*

Exemptions from diesel fuel tax are allowed for the following:

— the removal from a terminal or refinery of, or the entry or sale of, any diesel fuel if:

(1) the person otherwise liable for tax is a diesel fuel registrant,

(2) in the case of a removal from a terminal the terminal is an approved terminal, and

(3) the diesel fuel satisfies dyeing and marking requirements;

— any entry or removal from a terminal or refinery of taxable diesel fuel transferred in bulk to a refinery or terminal if the persons involved (including the terminal operator) are registered;

— the removal of diesel fuel, if:

(1) removed by railroad car from an approved refinery and received at an approved terminal,

(2) the refinery and terminal are operated by the same diesel fuel registrant, and

(3) the refinery is not served by pipeline (other than a pipeline for the receipt of crude oil) or vessel;

— diesel fuel shipped pursuant to terms in a sales contract, to a destination outside California by a supplier, via

(1) facilities operated by the supplier,

(2) delivery by the supplier to a carrier, customers broker, or forwarding agent, whether hired by the purchaser or not, for shipment to the out-of-state destination, or

(3) delivery by the supplier to a vessel clearing from a California port for a port outside the state, provided that the fuel is actually exported from California in the vessel;

¶40-003

— diesel fuel sold by credit card certified by the U.S. Department of State to any consulate officer or consulate employee of a foreign government:

(1) who is not engaged in any private occupation for gain within the state,

(2) who uses the fuel in a motor vehicle that is registered with the U.S. Department of State, and

(3) whose government has entered into a treaty with the United States providing for the exemption of its representatives or has granted a similar exemption to representatives of the United States;

— diesel fuel sold by a supplier to a train operator for use in a diesel-powered train or for other off-highway use when the supplier has on hand an exemption certificate from the train operator; and

— diesel fuel sold by a supplier to the United States and its agencies and instrumentalities.

In addition, backup tax does not apply to delivery of diesel fuel into the fuel tank of a diesel-powered highway vehicle for:

— farming purposes;

— exempt bus operation;

— off-highway operation;

— use in a diesel-powered highway vehicle that is owned and operated by the state or its political subdivisions; or

— use by the United States and its agencies or instrumentalities.

• *Reports and payments*

COMPLIANCE ALERT: Storage tax report, payment due January 1, 2018.— On or before January 1, 2018, each person subject to the storage tax enacted in 2017 (see discussion above) must prepare and file a return showing the total number of gallons of tax-paid diesel fuel owned by the person on November 1, 2017 and the amount of the storage tax. The return must be accompanied by a remittance payable to the CDTFA.

Diesel fuel supplier tax reports and accompanying payments are due at the California Department of Tax and Fee Administration (CDTFA) on or before the last day of the month following the calendar month in which a supplier's tax liability accrues. State and local government entities must file monthly reports with, and make monthly payments to, the CDTFA on or before the last day of each month for the preceding month. Diesel fuel tax returns may be filed electronically.

Payments.—Persons whose estimated diesel fuel tax liability averages $20,000 or more per month must remit amounts due by electronic funds transfer (EFT). Persons whose estimated liability averages less than $20,000 per month may elect to remit amounts due by EFT with the approval of the CDTFA. The election is operative for a minimum of one year.

Taxpayers who have entered into installment agreements to pay diesel fuel tax must receive an annual statement from the CDTFA itemizing the balance of tax owed at the beginning and end of a year and the amount of tax paid during the year.

• *Refunds, credits, and reimbursements*

The claim for a refund must be filed within three years from the date of purchase of the diesel fuel. A taxpayer requesting deferral of a refund claim action may be required to waive refund interest credit for the period of time action on the refund claim is deferred. The diesel fuel refund claim limitations period is suspended during the period that a person is unable to manage financial affairs because of a physical or mental impairment that is life threatening or that is expected to last for at least 12 months. There is no waiver for individuals who are represented in their financial matters by their spouses or other persons.

Persons who have paid tax for diesel fuel used for a nontaxable purpose (other than farming or exempt bus operations) may file a tax refund claim. Refund claims are allowed for diesel fuel:

— used for purposes other than motor vehicle operation on public highways;

— exported for use outside the state;

— used in construction equipment exempt from vehicle registration while operated within the confines and limits of a construction project;

— used to operate motor vehicles on highways under the jurisdiction of the U.S. Department of Agriculture;

— used in government vehicles on a military reservation;

— sold by suppliers to consulate officers or consulate employees under circumstances that would have entitled the supplier to an exemption;

— lost in the ordinary course of handling, transportation, or storage;

— sold to the United States or any of its agencies in exempt transactions;

— sold to train operators for use in diesel-powered trains or for other off-highway use under circumstances that would have entitled the person to an exemption had the person been a supplier of the diesel fuel; or

— removed from an approved terminal at the terminal rack, but only to the extent that the supplier can show that the tax on the same amount of diesel fuel has been paid more than once by the same supplier.

In lieu of the refund allowed to government entities, a credit may be taken on the government entity's tax return.

Each diesel fuel tax refund claim generally must be filed for a calendar year. However, if more than $750 is refundable at the close of any of the first three quarters of the calendar year with respect to diesel fuel used or exported during that quarter or any prior quarter during that calendar year, the taxpayer may file a refund claim for the quarterly period. Also, the California Department of Tax and Fee Administration (CDTFA) may require the filing of refund claims for other than yearly periods.

When remitting the tax, a credit is allowed for any diesel fuel tax paid to a retail vendor.

A credit is allowed for tax paid on worthless accounts.

Cost reimbursements for unreasonable assessments.—Taxpayers who have been unreasonably assessed diesel fuel tax are entitled to reimbursement of fees and expenses for attending CDTFA hearings. They may be reimbursed for costs incurred as of the filing of a notice of determination, jeopardy determination, or refund claim.

Claim filings 2017.—Effective January 1, 2017, taxpayers making installment payments on a final notice of determination and disputing their liability may file one timely claim for refund to cover all future payments applied to that billing. The filing also will apply to any prior payments that remain within the applicable statutes of limitations. A taxpayer disputing more than one billing must file a timely claim for refund for each separate billing. Payments made to release liens are subject to the six month statute, as they are considered voluntary. Payments submitted prior to January 1, 2017, will not cover any future payments. (*Special Notice L-479*, California California Department of Tax and Fee Administration, November 2016)

Tax paid twice.—When a supplier needs to remove diesel fuel from one terminal rack and transport it to another terminal to be stored above the rack, the supplier may obtain a credit or refund of the tax paid when the fuel is removed from the rack for a second time. For ease of both administration and compliance purposes, the process for credits and refunds is similar to federal law, and the reporting requirements are patterned after forms adopted by the IRS.

Blended fuel.—If California fuel tax is not imposed on dyed blended diesel fuel upon removal from an approved terminal at a terminal rack, a claim for refund may be allowed if tax previously was imposed on the biodiesel fuel portion of the blended fuel. However, the claim will be allowed only to the extent a supplier can show that the tax on the biodiesel fuel was paid by the same supplier.

Returned fuel.—When motor vehicle fuel is returned by the supplier to a refinery or an approved terminal, or when diesel fuel is returned to the supplier by a customer and delivered into a refinery or an approved terminal, the supplier can avoid paying tax a second time on the same fuel by either filing a claim for refund with the State Controller or taking a credit on the supplier's tax return filed with the CDTFA.

[¶40-005] Aviation Fuel Taxes

COMPLIANCE ALERT: CDTFA assumes responsibility for motor fuel taxes administration.—As a result of 2017 legislation that stripped the State Board of Equalization (BOE) of all but its constitutionally mandated duties, responsibilities, and powers, the California Department of Tax and Fee Administration (CDTFA) assumed responsibility for administration of all the taxes not contained in the BOE's constitutional duties, including motor fuel taxes. The change was effective July 1, 2017. (Ch. 16 (A.B. 102), Laws 2017, effective June 27, 2017) In subsequent legislation, a provision was added to specify that, in the Revenue and Taxation Code or any other code, references to the "board, itself" or "State Board of Equalization meeting as a public body" for purposes of the duties, powers, and responsibilities transferred to CDTFA means CDTFA. (Sec. 20.5, Rev. & Tax. Code, added by Sec. 16, Ch. 252 (A.B. 131), Laws 2017, effective September 16, 2017)

California motor vehicle fuel tax applies to aviation fuel and the state imposes a tax on aircraft jet fuel. (Sec. 7301, Rev. & Tax. Code; Sec. 7392, Rev. & Tax. Code) Discussed here are:

— products subject to tax,

— point of taxation,

— license requirements,

— basis of tax,

— rate of tax,

— exemptions,

— reports and payments, and

— credits, refunds, and reimbursements.

• *Products subject to tax*

For purposes of the aircraft jet fuel tax, aircraft jet fuel means any inflammable liquid which is used or sold for use in propelling aircraft operated by the jet or turbine type of engine. Aviation gasoline means all special grades of gasoline that are suitable for use in aviation reciprocating engines.

• *Point of taxation*

The point of collection of aviation fuel is the same as it is for gasoline in general. Administrative provisions relating the aircraft jet fuel tax generally are governed by administrative provisions of the motor vehicle fuel tax law. See the discussion at ¶ 40-001.

• *License requirements*

License requirements for aviation gasoline are the same as they are for gasoline in general. See the discussion at ¶ 40-001. For aircraft jet fuel tax purposes, a permit must be secured from the California Department of Tax and Fee Administration (CDTFA) by dealers.

• *Basis of tax*

The aircraft jet fuel tax is imposed on each gallon of aircraft jet fuel that is sold by a dealer or used by the dealer as an aircraft jet fuel user.

• *Rate of tax*

Excise tax rates applicable to California aviation gasoline and aircraft jet fuel effective July 1, 2018, through June 30, 2021, are:

aviation gasoline	$0.18 per gallon
aircraft jet fuel	$0.02 per gallon

(*Special Notice L-739*, California Department of Tax and Fee Administration, May 2020; *Special Notice L-633*, California Department of Tax and Fee Administration, May 2019; *Special Notice L-561*, California Department of Tax and Fee Administration, June 2018)

• *Exemptions*

Exemptions for the motor vehicle fuel tax also apply to the tax on aviation gasoline. See ¶ 40-001.

The aircraft jet fuel tax does not apply to:

— common carriers operating under a certificate of public convenience and necessity issued by California, the federal government, or a foreign government;

— persons constructing, reconstructing, modifying, overhauling, repairing, maintaining or servicing aircraft; or

— the U.S. armed forces.

• *Reports and payments*

Aircraft jet fuel tax returns and payments are due as provided for suppliers under the motor vehicle fuel tax. Reporting and payment provisions for the motor vehicle fuel tax also apply to the tax on aviation gasoline. See ¶ 40-001 for details.

Retailers of aviation fuel or jet fuel.—Beginning January 1, 2020, retailers of aviation fuel or jet fuel must report their sales of fuel by airport location. The Federal Aviation Administration (FAA) adopted a rule clarification that limits the proceeds from taxes imposed on jet fuel by state and local governments to airport-related expenses. With this new rule in effect, aviation and jet fuel retailers are required to report their sales of jet fuel by airport location. (*Special Notice L-712*, California Department of Tax and Fee Administration, November 2019)

Retailers of jet fuel at an airport need to track and report sales of jet fuel by airport location on a new supplementary form called CDTFA-531-JF, Aircraft Jet Fuel Retailers—Sales by Airport Location, for return periods beginning January 1, 2020. The amounts of jet fuel sold by airport location must be reported, including total taxable jet fuel sales and the amount of tax collected. The return will also include a separate line for taxable sales of jet fuel at non-airport locations. Reporting an amount

¶ 40-005

on the new form will not change any other part of the return. (*Special Notice L-712, California Department of Tax and Fee Administration, November 2019*)

•*Credits, refunds, and reimbursements*

No refund of any tax is allowed on motor vehicle fuel used to propel aircraft in California.

[¶40-007] Other Fuel Taxes

As a result of 2017 legislation that stripped the State Board of Equalization (BOE) of all but its constitutionally mandated duties, responsibilities, and powers, the California Department of Tax and Fee Administration (CDTFA) assumed responsibility for administration of all the taxes not contained in the BOE's constitutional duties, including motor fuel taxes. The change was effective July 1, 2017. (Ch. 16 (A.B. 102), Laws 2017) In subsequent legislation, a provision was added to specify that, in the Revenue and Taxation Code or any other code, references to the "board, itself" or "State Board of Equalization meeting as a public body" for purposes of the duties, powers, and responsibilities transferred to CDTFA means CDTFA. (Sec. 20.5, Rev. & Tax. Code)

Use fuel tax rate.—The use fuel tax rate is $0.18 per gallon. Alternative fuel is subject to an excise tax imposed for the use of fuel. (Sec. 8651, Rev. & Tax. Code; *Tax Rates—Special Taxes and Fees*, California Department of Tax and Fee Administration, October 2020)

California imposes a use fuel tax on a variety of alternative fuels. Specific motor fuel types discussed below are:

— A55 / A-21,

— biodiesel,

— compressed natural gas (CNG),

— dimethyl ether (DME);

— E-85,

— ethanol,

— gasohol,

— liquefied natural gas (LNG),

— liquefied petroleum gas (LPG),

— M-85,

— methanol, and

— propane.

• *A55 / A-21*

A55 is taxed at the rate of $0.385 per gallon effective July 1, 2020 through June 30, 2021.

• *Biodiesel*

Biodiesel is taxed at the rate of $0.385 per gallon effective July 1, 2020 through June 30, 2021. (Sec. 60050, Rev. & Tax. Code; *Tax Rates—Special Taxes and Fees*, California Department of Tax and Fee Administration, October 2020)

• *Compressed natural gas (CNG)*

CNG is taxed at the rate of $0.0887 per 126.67 cubic feet or 5.66 pounds. (Sec. 8651.6, Rev. & Tax. Code; *Tax Rates—Special Taxes and Fees*, California Department of Tax and Fee Administration, October 2020)

- *Dimethyl ether*

Applicable July 1, 2021, dimethyl ether (DME) and DME-liquefied petroleum gas fuel blend is taxed at the rate of $0.06 per gallon. (Sec. 8651.4, Rev. & Tax. Code; Sec. 8651.9, Rev. & Tax. Code)

- *E-85*

E-85 is taxed at the rate of $0.18 per gallon.

- *Ethanol*

Ethanol is taxed at the rate of $0.09 per gallon. (Sec. 8651.8, Rev. & Tax. Code; *Tax Rates—Special Taxes and Fees*, California Department of Tax and Fee Administration, October 2020)

- *Gasohol*

Gasohol is taxed at the rate of $0.505 per gallon effective July 1, 2020 through June 30, 2021. (*Special Notice L-739*, California Department of Tax and Fee Administration, May 2020)

- *Liquefied natural gas (LNG)*

LNG is taxed at the rate of $0.1017 per 6.06 pounds. (Sec. 8651.6, Rev. & Tax. Code; *Tax Rates—Special Taxes and Fees*, California Department of Tax and Fee Administration, October 2020)

- *Liquefied petroleum gas (LPG)*

LPG is taxed at the rate of $0.06 per gallon. (Sec. 8651.5, Rev. & Tax. Code; *Tax Rates—Special Taxes and Fees*, California Department of Tax and Fee Administration, October 2020)

- *M-85*

M-85 is taxed at the rate of $0.18 per gallon.

- *Methanol*

Methanol is taxed at the rate of $0.09 per gallon. (Sec. 8651.8, Rev. & Tax. Code; *Tax Rates—Special Taxes and Fees*, California Department of Tax and Fee Administration, October 2020)

- *Propane*

Propane is taxed at the rate of $0.18 per gallon.

[¶40-009] Motor Carriers, International Fuel Tax Agreement

> *COMPLIANCE ALERT: CDTFA assumes responsibility for motor fuel taxes administration.*—As a result of 2017 legislation that stripped the State Board of Equalization (BOE) of all but its constitutionally mandated duties, responsibilities, and powers, the California Department of Tax and Fee Administration (CDTFA) assumed responsibility for administration of all taxes not contained in the BOE's constitutional duties, including motor fuel taxes. The change became effective July 1, 2017. (Ch. 16 (A.B. 102), Laws 2017, effective June 27, 2017) In subsequent legislation, a provision was added to specify that, in the Revenue and Taxation Code or any other code, references to the "board, itself" or "State Board of Equalization meeting as a public body" for purposes of the duties, powers, and responsibilities transferred to CDTFA means the CDTFA. (Sec. 20.5, Rev. & Tax. Code, added by Sec. 16, Ch. 252 (A.B. 131), Laws 2017, effective September 16, 2017)

For most U.S. states and Canadian provinces, fuel taxes applicable to qualifying vehicles are governed to an extent under the terms of the International Fuel Tax Agreement (IFTA). In California, the law on IFTA is administered in conjunction with the state's Use Fuel Tax Law and Diesel Fuel Tax Law, which encompasses the state Interstate User Diesel Fuel Tax Law. To the extent there is any inconsistency between the state fuel laws and the IFTA, the IFTA prevails to the extent permitted under the California Constitution and the U.S. Constitution.

In California, IFTA is administered by the California Department of Tax and Fee Administration. Contact information for IFTA or Interstate User Diesel Fuel Tax issues is as follows:

Motor Carrier Section, Fuel Taxes Division

MIC: 65

State Board of Equalization

P.O. Box 942879

Sacramento, CA 94279-0065

800-400-7115

916-322-9669

Fax: 916-373-3070

The CDTFA has issued the following pertinent publications:

— Publication 12, California Use Fuel Tax, a Guide for Vendors and Users

— Publication 50, Guide to the International Fuel Tax Agreement

— Publication 84, Do You Need a California Fuel Permit or License?

The California Department of Tax and Fee Administration, with the approval of the Department of Finance and on behalf of the state, may become a party to a reciprocal fuel tax agreement between California and another jurisdiction providing for the administration, collection, and enforcement by a party to the agreement of taxes imposed upon motor fuels by the other jurisdiction and for the forwarding of collections to the jurisdiction on behalf of which the tax was collected.

•*IFTA, Interstate User Diesel Fuel Tax rates*

Effective July 1, 2020, the per gallon rate for the International Fuel Tax Agreement (IFTA) and the Interstate User Diesel Fuel Tax (DI) is increased from $0.76 to $0.795 per gallon.

This rate:

• is in effect until June 30, 2021;

• should be used starting with the third quarter 2020 return (July 1, 2020 through September 30, 2020); and

• is reported and paid with quarterly IFTA or DI tax returns for diesel fuel purchased outside California and used in California.

(*CDTFA-863-IFT*, California Department of Tax and Fee Administration, June 2020)

The $0.795 per gallon rate includes:

• $0.385 per gallon of diesel fuel tax, adjusted July 1, 2020, and then annually, effective July 1 of each year; and

• an additional excise tax of $0.410 per gallon.

(*CDTFA-863-IFT*, California Department of Tax and Fee Administration, June 2020)

Beginning July 1, 2020, IFTA and DI licensees may claim a credit of $0.795 per gallon for tax-paid diesel fuel purchased in California and used both inside and outside California. (*CDTFA-863-IFT*, California Department of Tax and Fee Administration, June 2020)

• *Use fuel tax*

For purposes of the use fuel tax, fuel includes any combustible gas or liquid, by whatever name the gas or liquid may be known or sold, of a kind used in an internal combustion engine for the generation of power to propel a motor vehicle on the highways, except fuel that is subject to the motor vehicle fuel tax or the diesel fuel tax or that is not used on highways. It does not include any combustible gas or liquid specifically manufactured and used for racing motor vehicles at a racetrack. In addition, alcohol produced for use in or as a fuel to propel vehicles will be taxed as a use fuel and not as an alcoholic beverage.

By regulation, "fuel" also includes, but is not limited to, liquefied petroleum gases (LPG, propane, and butane—see Publication 12, *California Use Fuel Tax*, California State Board of Equalization), kerosene, distillate, stove oil, natural gas in liquid or gaseous form, and alcohol fuels.

For purposes of the tax, use includes the placing of fuel into any receptacle on a motor vehicle from which fuel is supplied for the propulsion of the vehicle unless the operator of the vehicle establishes that the fuel was consumed for a purpose other than the operation of a motor vehicle within California and, with respect to fuel brought into California in any such receptacle, the consumption of the fuel in California. A person placing fuel in a receptacle on a motor vehicle of another who holds a valid use fuel tax permit is not deemed to have used the fuel.

Persons subject to tax.—A tax is imposed on vendors or users of fuel used to propel vehicles on the highway. Users are allowed a credit for tax paid to vendors.

Basis of tax.—The use fuel tax is imposed on fuel that either:

— is used in an internal combustion engine to propel a motor vehicle on a California highway, or

— is placed in a container on the vehicle, such as a fuel tank, from which fuel is supplied to run the vehicle on a highway.

Rate of tax.—The use fuel tax generally is imposed at the rate of $0.18 per gallon. However, certain fuels are assessed at a different rate. See generally ¶ 40-007.

Owners or operators, other than interstate users, of a vehicle propelled by a system using liquefied petroleum gas (LPG), liquid natural gas (LNG), or compressed natural gas (CNG) may pay the fuel tax for those fuels by paying an annual flat rate fuel tax, as follows:

— passenger cars and other vehicles 4,000 lbs. or less, $36;

— more than 4,000 lbs. but less than 8,001 lbs., $72;

— more than 8,000 lbs. but less than 12,001 lbs., $120; or

— 12,001 lbs. or more, $168;

Exemptions.—Use fuel tax does not apply to:

(1) fuel subject to the motor fuels tax or diesel fuel tax;

(2) fuel used generally off the highway in agricultural and construction operations in vehicles exempt from registration;

(3) fuel used for a purpose other than generating power to propel a motor vehicle;

(4) fuel used in operating a motor vehicle off the highway;

(5) fuel used in motor vehicles owned by a county, city, district, or other political subdivision or public agency when operated within a military reservation in California;

¶40-009

(6) fuel used by transit districts, private entities providing transportation services for people under contracts or agreements with public agencies authorized to provide public transportation services, municipal passenger carriers, and public school buses (however, a $0.01 tax is imposed on exempt gallons for use on state highways); and

(7) combustible gas or liquid specifically manufactured and used for racing motor vehicles at a racetrack.

Reports and payments.—Vendors and users, except users whose sole use of the fuel is to propel privately operated passenger vehicles, must report to the CDTFA on or before the last day of the calendar month following each quarterly period. However, in certain cases, returns and payments may be required for designated periods other than quarterly periods.

Subject to prescribed conditions, use fuel tax permit and return filing requirements do not apply to the interstate operation of recreational vehicles, or of certain motor vehicles whose gross vehicle weight does not exceed 26,000 pounds. Such requirements are waived, provided that all fuel used in California, excepting fuel brought into the state in the vehicle's fuel tank, is purchased from a California vendor who collects the tax from the user; or if the flat rate fuel tax has been paid.

The use fuel tax payment is due and payable quarterly on or before the last day of the calendar month next succeeding each quarterly period in which a taxable use of fuel occurs. Tax payment accompanies the report. Persons whose estimated tax liability averages $20,000 or more per month, as determined by the California Department of Tax and Fee Administration (CDTFA) pursuant to methods of calculation prescribed by the CDTFA, must remit amounts due by electronic funds transfer (EFT). Persons whose estimated liability averages less than $20,000 per month may elect to remit amounts due by EFT with CDTFA approval. The election is operative for a minimum of one year.

Taxpayers who have entered into installment agreements to pay use fuel tax must receive an annual statement from the CDTFA itemizing the balance of tax owed at the beginning and end of a year and the amount of tax paid during the year.

Refunds, credits, and reimbursements.—The claim for a use fuel tax refund must be filed must be filed by the latest of three years from the last day of the month following the reporting period for which the overpayment was made, six months from the date a deficiency determination or jeopardy determination becomes final, or six months from the date of overpayment. A taxpayer requesting deferral of a refund claim action may be required to waive refund interest credit for the period of time action on the refund claim is deferred.

Taxpayers who have been unreasonably assessed use fuel tax are entitled to reimbursement of their fees and expenses for attending CDTFA hearings. They may be reimbursed for costs incurred as of the filing of a notice of determination, jeopardy determination, or refund claim.

The tax paid to a vendor may be applied by the purchaser as a credit against the tax due from the purchaser on all fuel used in this state in the reporting period in which the fuel, with respect to which the tax was paid to the vendor, was used. The amount of credit allowable is the amount of tax separately stated or included in the selling price on the receipts (invoices) issued by the vendor to the purchaser for purchases of fuel delivered into vehicle fuel tanks. Vendors also are allowed credit for bad debt losses.

The limitations period for filing refund claims for use fuel tax is suspended during the period that a person is unable to manage financial affairs because of a physical or mental impairment that is life threatening or that is expected to last for at least 12 months. (Sec. 9152.1, Rev. & Tax. Code) There is no waiver for individuals who are represented in their financial matters by their spouses or other persons.

• *Interstate users fuel tax*

Interstate user diesel fuel tax.—California imposes a tax on interstate users for the privilege of using diesel fuel in a qualified motor vehicle in the state. The tax consists of two components: the state diesel fuel tax rate and an amount determined by a formula that derives from combined state and local sales taxes. An international user diesel fuel tax license or a California fuel trip permit is required if an interstate user:

— travels only in California and Mexico, or

— travels in California and the user's business is based outside California in a U.S. or Canadian jurisdiction that is not an IFTA member.

The resulting rate is the same rate as charged under IFTA. The definition for "qualified motor vehicle" is the same for this tax as it is for IFTA purposes. (BOE-400-DC, *California Interstate User Diesel Fuel Tax License*, California State Board of Equalization)

Exemptions.—IFTA provisions generally do not apply to qualifying motor vehicles that operate:

— on gasoline or gasohol that is taxed under the motor vehicle fuel tax;

— only in California; or

— only between California and Mexico.

However, if the qualifying motor vehicle travels to jurisdictions that tax interstate carriers for gasoline use, an IFTA license or fuel trip permit will be required. Also, qualifying motor vehicles that use diesel fuel travelling only between California and Mexico must have an interstate user diesel fuel tax license or fuel trip permit. Similarly, qualifying motor vehicles that use use fuel travelling only within California or between California and Mexico must have a user use fuel tax license. (CDTFA Publication 50, Guide to the International Fuel Tax Agreement, California Department of Tax and Fee Administration)

Rates.—For the period July 1, 2017 through June 30, 2018, the California rate of tax for IFTA and the interstate user diesel fuel tax is $0.37/gallon (formerly, $0.40/gallon). That rate is comprised of $0.16 per gallon of diesel fuel tax and $0.210 per gallon of excise tax. (Tax Rates—Special Taxes and Fees, California State Board of Equalization, March 28, 2017)

Credits and refunds.—Refunds and credits are available for IFTA taxes paid. Taxpayers can apply for refunds in the form of adjustments for tax-exempt miles. California considers only those miles traveled under a valid California Fuel Trip Permit to be tax-exempt miles for purposes of the quarterly IFTA return.

In addition, refunds are available for tax paid on fuel used in a nontaxable manner. The most common nontaxable uses include use of fuel:

— to power a vehicle on roads other than the state's public highways (off-highway use);

— to operate devices mounted on the vehicle and powered by a power take-off attached to the vehicle's transmission;

— to power a refrigeration unit, generator, or any similar equipment where fuel is not used to power the tractor;

— on a highway under qualified U.S. Department of Agriculture jurisdiction; or

— (diesel fuel only) in a motor vehicle owned and operated by a political subdivision on qualifying highways within a military reservation.

Refund claims must be filed within three years of the date the fuel in a nontaxable manner was purchased. Generally, refunds can be claimed once a year, although quarterly claims may be filed if the claim will total at least $750 for the quarter. (CDTFA Publication 50, Guide to the International Fuel Tax Agreement, California Department of Tax and Fee Administration)

• *International Fuel Tax Agreement*

Citations (e.g., R212) in this discussion of IFTA are to the IFTA Articles of Agreement (e.g., R212), Audit Manual (e.g., A310), or Procedures Manual (e.g., P410), each of which can be reviewed on the International Fuel Tax Association Web site. IFTA does not apply in the states of Alaska or Hawaii; the District of Columbia; or the Canadian provinces of Yukon Territory, Northwest Territories, or Nunavut.

The IFTA is a tax collection agreement among the 48 contiguous states and member Canadian provinces. The agreement is intended to provide uniform administration of motor fuels use taxation laws with respect to qualified motor vehicles operated in more than one member jurisdiction. Concepts at the core of the agreement include:

— base jurisdiction;

— retention of sovereign authority to exercise substantive tax authority over matters such as tax rates and exemptions; and

— uniform definition of vehicles to which the agreement applies.

(R130.100)

Definitions.—For purposes of IFTA, "base jurisdiction" means the member jurisdiction where

— qualified motor vehicles are based for vehicle registration purposes,

— operational control and operational records of a licensee's qualified motor vehicles are maintained or can be made available, and

— some travel is accrued by qualified motor vehicles within the licensee's fleet.

The commissioners of two or more affected jurisdictions may allow a person to consolidate several fleets that otherwise would be based in two or more jurisdictions. (R212)

A "qualified motor vehicle" is a motor vehicle used, designed, or maintained for transportation of persons or property, and either:

— having two axles with a gross vehicle or registered gross vehicle weight over 26,000 pounds or 11,797 kilograms;

— having three or more axles, regardless of weight; or

— used in combination and the gross vehicle or the registered vehicle weight of the combined vehicle weight exceeds 26,000 pounds or 11,797 kilograms.

"Qualified motor vehicle" does not include recreational vehicles. (R245)

"Motor fuel" means all fuels placed in the supply tank of qualified motor vehicles. (R239)

Licensing requirements, alternative.—Generally, persons based in a member jurisdiction operating a qualified motor vehicle in two or more member jurisdictions are required to be licensed under this Agreement. (R305) In lieu of such motor fuel tax licensing, persons may elect to satisfy motor fuels use tax obligations on a trip-by-trip basis. (R310) Persons required to register must file an application for licensing with their base jurisdiction and annually must renew their licenses, which expire December 31. (R610)

Recordkeeping requirements.—Generally, licensees must preserve records related to quarterly tax returns for four years from the later of the tax return due date or filing date. (IFTA Procedure Manual, P510.100) The records must be made available to any member jurisdiction upon request. (IFTA Procedure Manual, P520.100)

Reporting periods, due dates, requirements.—Generally, licensees must file a quarterly report on or before the last day of the month immediately following the close of each calendar quarter, even if no operations were conducted or no taxable fuel was used during the reporting period. (R930.100, R960.100) However, a licensee whose operations total less than 5,000 miles or 8,000 kilometers in all member jurisdictions other than the base jurisdiction during 12 consecutive months may ask to report on an annual basis. The request must be approved by the base jurisdiction. (R930.200) If the request is approved, the licensee's annual return will be due on January 31 following the close of the annual tax reporting period. (R960.100)

Payment.—Licensees must pay all taxes due to all member jurisdictions with the remittances payable to the base jurisdictions on the same dates that reports are due. (R910) Payments may be made by hand delivery, postal service delivery, or by electronic means approved by the base jurisdiction. (R960)

Licensee responsibility.—The timely filing of the tax return and the payment of taxes due to the base jurisdiction for all member jurisdiction discharges the responsibility of the licensee for filing of tax returns and payment of individual taxes to all member jurisdictions. (R920)

Refunds.—Licensees can claim a tax-paid credit on the IFTA tax return for fuel purchased at retail only when the fuel is placed into the fuel tank of a qualified motor vehicle and the purchase price includes fuel tax paid to a member jurisdiction. (R1010) For storage fuel purchased in bulk, a credit can be claimed on the IFTA return only when

— the fuel is placed into the fuel tank of a qualified motor vehicle;

— the bulk storage tank is owned, leased, or controlled by the licensee; and either

— the purchase price of the fuel includes fuel tax paid to the member jurisdiction where the bulk fuel storage tan is located or

— the licensee has paid fuel tax to the member jurisdiction where the bulk fuel storage tank is located.

(R1020.200)

Licensees can receive full credit or refund for tax-paid fuel used outside the jurisdiction where the fuel was purchased. The base jurisdiction must allow credits and issue refunds for all of its licensees on behalf of all member jurisdictions, as long as the licensee has satisfied all tax liability, including audit assessments, to all member jurisdictions. (R1100) If a credit is not refunded, it shall be carried over to offset the licensee's liabilities for the earlier of

(1) the time at which the credit is fully offset or

(2) eight calendar quarters.

(R1120.100) A licensee may apply an overpayment generated in one jurisdiction to taxes owed to another jurisdiction. (R1120.200)

If a refund is paid more than 90 days after an application was made, the refund is subject to interest at the rate of 1% per month or part of a month calculated from the date the refund was due. (R1150)

¶40-009

Assessment and collection.—A base jurisdiction may, among other things, assess tax against any licensee that

— fails, neglects, or refuses to file a tax return when due;

— fails to make records available upon written request; or

— fails to maintain records from which the licensee's true liability can be determined.

The assessment made by the base jurisdiction will be presumed correct. (R1200)

Penalties, interest.—For failing to file a tax return, filing a late tax return, or underpaying taxes due, a licensee may be assessed a penalty equaling the greater of $50.00 or 10% of delinquent taxes. Nothing in the IFTA limits the authority of a base jurisdiction to impose any other penalties provided by the laws of the base jurisdiction. (R1220)

The base jurisdiction shall assess interest on qualifying delinquent taxes at the rate of 1% per month. (R1230.100) Interest will be calculated separately for each jurisdiction from the date tax was due for each month or fraction of a month. (1230.300) All interest collected shall be remitted to the appropriate jurisdiction. (R1230.400)

A base jurisdiction may waive penalties for reasonable cause. If the base jurisdiction's laws permit waiver of interest and a licensee demonstrates that a tax return was filed late due to misinformation given by the base jurisdiction, the base jurisdiction may waive interest, also. However, to waive interest for another jurisdiction, the base jurisdiction must receive written approval from that jurisdiction. (R1260)

Audits.—While each base jurisdiction must audit its licensees on behalf of all member jurisdictions, other jurisdictions are not precluded from also auditing those licensees. (R1310) Audits conducted by member jurisdictions must be in compliance with IFTA Articles of Agreement, Procedures Manual, and Audit Manual. (R1330)

Appeal Procedures.—While IFTA has appeal procedures for licensees, those procedures only apply if the base jurisdiction does not have provisions for appeals of actions or audit findings. (R1400)

In order to appeal an action or audit finding, a licensee must make a written request for a hearing within 30 days after service of notice of the original action or finding. (R1410) The hearing must be held "expeditiously," and the base jurisdiction must give at least 20 days' notice of the time and place of the hearing. (R1420)

The licensee may appear in person and/or be represented by counsel and may produce witnesses, documents, or other pertinent material. (R1430.100) If the licensee appeals an assessment for one or more jurisdictions, the base jurisdiction will be responsible for participating in the appeal on behalf of the other jurisdictions. (R1430.200) The base jurisdiction will notify the licensee of the findings of fact and the ruling on the appeal. (R1440)

An appeal of any jurisdiction's findings will proceed in accordance with that jurisdiction's laws. (1450.100) In the case of an audit, the licensee may request any or every jurisdiction to audit the licensee's records. Each jurisdiction can accept or deny the request, and those electing to audit the record will audit only for its own portion of the licensee's operations. (R1450.200)

[¶40-011] Fuel Taxes Practice and Procedure

COMPLIANCE ALERT: CDTFA assumes responsibility for motor fuel taxes administration.—As a result of 2017 legislation that stripped the State Board of Equalization (BOE) of all but its constitutionally mandated duties, responsibilities, and powers, the California Department of Tax and Fee Administration

(CDTFA) assumed responsibility for administration of all the taxes not contained in the BOE's constitutional duties, including motor fuel taxes. The change was effective July 1, 2017. (Ch. 16 (A.B. 102), Laws 2017, effective June 27, 2017) In subsequent legislation, a provision was added to specify that, in the Revenue and Taxation Code or any other code, references to the "board, itself" or "State Board of Equalization meeting as a public body" for purposes of the duties, powers, and responsibilities transferred to CDTFA means CDTFA. (Sec. 20.5, Rev. & Tax. Code, added by Sec. 16, Ch. 252 (A.B. 131), Laws 2017, effective September 16, 2017)

California has a motor vehicle fuel tax (including an aviation tax), a tax on aircraft jet fuel, a diesel fuel tax, an interstate users tax, and a use fuel tax. California also participates in the International Fuel Tax Agreement (IFTA), and imposes tax on other fuels.

Discussed here are general topics and administrative matters relating to all the tax types. Specific topics covered include:

— administration,

— penalties,

— recordkeeping,

— assessment and collection,

— audits,

— appeal procedures,

— forms, and

— federal constitutional issues.

• *Administration*

California motor fuel taxes are administered by the California Department of Tax and Fee Administration.

Fuel Industry Section, Fuel Taxes Division

MIC: 30

State Board of Equalization

P.O. Box 942879

Sacramento, CA 94279-0030

800-400-7115

916-322-9669

Fax: 916-323-9352

The Fuel Taxes Division also maintains a motor fuel tax Web site.

• *Penalties*

There are a variety of actions or failures to act that can be subject to fines or penalties.

Motor vehicle fuel tax.—For purposes of the motor vehicle fuel tax, it is illegal to:

— obtain fuel for export and fail to export it;

— divert fuel from interstate or foreign transit begun in California;

— return fuel to California and sell or use it without complying with the law provisions or notification requirements;

— fail to pay tax;

¶40-011

— fail, neglect, or refuse to make any required statement;

— make any false statement or conceal any material fact in any required record, report, affidavit, or claim;

— conduct any activities requiring a license under this part without a license or after a license has been surrendered, canceled, or revoked;

— make, render, sign, or verify any return or report who makes any false or fraudulent return or report with intent to defeat or evade the determination of an amount due;

— willfully aid or assist in the preparation or presentation of a fraudulent or false document as to any material matter, whether or not the falsity or fraud is with knowledge or consent of the person authorized or required to present the document;

Any person violating any of the previous provisions will be subject to a fine of not less than one thousand dollars ($1,000) nor more than five thousand dollars ($5,000), or by imprisonment in the county jail not exceeding six months, or by both fine and imprisonment.

It is a misdemeanor for any person to willfully evade or attempt to evade or defeat the payment of the tax, and it is punishable by a fine of not less than five thousand dollars ($5,000) and not more than twenty thousand dollars ($20,000), imprisonment, or both the fine and imprisonment in the discretion of the court. In addition to those penalties, each person convicted under this section shall pay up to $2 for each gallon of motor vehicle involved in the misdemeanor.

Any prosecution for violation of the penal provisions of the motor vehicle fuel tax law must be instituted within three years after the commission of the offense or within two years after the violation is discovered, whichever is later. Civil penalties and interest are imposed for failure to timely pay the tax (10% of tax due plus interest) or file a return (10% of tax due).

Use fuel tax.—Under the terms of the use fuel tax law, it is illegal for any person to:

— place into a receptacle on a motor vehicle or to acquire fuel outside the state and use it for propulsion of a motor vehicle, unless the person is a vendor who collects the tax, a user who holds a valid use fuel, or a person excluded from the collection requirement (fine between $100 and $1,000, six months in prison, or both);

— failure to file a return (misdemeanor subject to $1,000 fine);

— any violation of use fuel tax provisions (punishable as a misdemeanor);

— violation of use fuel provision with intent to evade tax (felony if liability aggregates $25,000 in an 12-month consecutive period; fine of $5,000-$25,000; imprisonment of 16 months, two years or three years; or both fine and imprisonment).

Any prosecution for violation of the penal provisions of the use fuel tax law must be instituted within three years after the commission of the offense or within two years after the violation is discovered, whichever is later. Civil penalties and interest are imposed for failure to timely pay the tax (10% of tax due plus interest) or file a return (10% of tax due).

Diesel fuel tax, interstate user tax.—For purposes of the diesel fuel tax and the interstate user tax it is illegal to:

— obtain fuel for export and fail to export it;

— divert fuel from interstate or foreign transit begun in California;

— return fuel to California and sell or use it without complying with the law provisions or notification requirements;

— conspire to withhold diesel fuel from export or to divert it from interstate or foreign transit begun in the state or return it for sale in the state so as to avoid taxes;

— make a false claim for a refund;

— conduct any activities requiring a license under this part without a license or a valid diesel fuel trip permit;

— make, render, sign, or verify any return or report who makes any false or fraudulent return or report with intent to defeat or evade the determination of an amount due;

— willfully aid or assist in the preparation or presentation of a fraudulent or false document as to any material matter, whether or not the falsity or fraud is with knowledge or consent of the person authorized or required to present the document;

Any person violating any of the previous provisions will be subject to a fine of not less than one thousand dollars ($1,000) nor more than five thousand dollars ($5,000); imprisonment up to six months; or both fine and imprisonment.

It is a misdemeanor for any person to willfully evade or attempt to evade the payment of the tax, and it is punishable by a fine of not less than five thousand dollars ($5,000) and not more than twenty thousand dollars ($20,000), imprisonment, or both the fine and imprisonment in the discretion of the court. In addition to those penalties, each person convicted under this section shall pay up to $2 for each gallon of motor vehicle involved in the misdemeanor.

Any prosecution for violation of the penal provisions of the motor vehicle fuel tax law must be instituted within three years after the commission of the offense or within two years after the violation is discovered, whichever is later. Civil penalties and interest are imposed for failure to timely pay the tax (10% of tax due plus interest) or file a return (10% of tax due).

Waiver of penalties.—For purposes of the motor vehicle fuel tax, use fuel tax, and the diesel fuel tax, penalties for the late payment or the late filing of a return may be waived without a showing of reasonable cause for tardiness under criteria to be developed by the CDTFA. The goal of the criteria must be to foster efficient resolution of requests for relief from penalties. The CDTFA may not require taxpayers to file statements supporting their claims for relief under penalty of perjury, as is the case when a person seeks waiver under a claim of reasonable cause for tardiness.

Disaster relief.—If a person's failure to make a motor vehicle tax, use fuel tax, or diesel fuel tax return or payment is due to a disaster, and occurred notwithstanding the exercise of ordinary care and in the absence of willful neglect, the person may be relieved of paying interest.

Advice from CDTFA.—If a person's failure to make a timely motor vehicle tax, use fuel tax, or diesel fuel tax return or payment is due to the person's reasonable reliance on written advice from the CDTFA, the person may be relieved of taxes, penalties, and interest. Also, if a person's failure to pay motor vehicle tax, use fuel tax, or diesel fuel tax is due to an unreasonable error or delay by an employee of the CDTFA acting in his or her official capacity, the person may be relieved of paying interest.

EFTs.—If a person's failure to make a motor vehicle tax, use fuel tax, or diesel fuel tax payment by an appropriate EFT is due to reasonable cause and circumstances beyond the person's control, and occurred notwithstanding the exercise of ordinary care and in the absence of willful neglect, the person may be relieved of the penalty for failure to remit payment by an appropriate means.

Installment agreements.—Except in cases of fraud, if a person enters an installment payment agreement within 45 days from the date on which a notice of determination or redetermination becomes final, and the person complies with the terms of the installment payment agreement, the person may be relieved of the penalty for failure to pay a use fuel tax or diesel fuel tax determination when due.

Innocent spouse relief.—Innocent spouse relief is available for qualifying individuals under the motor vehicle fuel, use fuel tax, and diesel fuel taxes. Generally, if the failure to file a return, a filing of an erroneous return, or a failure to timely pay a tax is attributable to one spouse and the other spouse had no knowledge of the issue, the unknowing spouse can be relieved of liability for the understatement or nonpayment.

• *Recordkeeping*

Generally, fuel tax record keeping requirements are set out under Reg. 4901, 18 CCR. Records required to be maintained must be maintained for at least four years, unless the CDTFA authorizes in writing their destruction within a lesser period.

Persons subject to those record keeping requirements are dictated in each taxes law provisions, as follows:

— for motor vehicle fuel tax purposes, every highway vehicle operator/ fueler, industrial user, pipeline operator, supplier, train operator, vessel operator and every person dealing in, removing, transporting, or storing motor vehicle fuel;

— for use fuel tax purposes, every user and every person dealing in, transporting, or storing fuel in the state; and

— for diesel fuel tax and interstate user tax purposes, every interstate user, supplier, exempt bus operator, government entity, ultimate vendor, highway vehicle operator, highway vehicle operator/fuelers, train operator, pipeline operator, vessel operator, and person dealing in, removing, transporting, or storing diesel fuel in the state.

Each tax also is subject to specific recordkeeping requirements.

Motor vehicle fuel tax.—Generally, for purposes of the motor vehicle fuel tax, suppliers must maintain complete records of all rack removals, sales, imports, and certain exempt dispositions. Those records include, but are not limited to:

(1) refinery reports;

(2) inventory reconciliation by location;

(3) storage inventory reports;

(4) list of storage locations;

(5) tax returns from other states;

(6) cardlock statements;

(7) calculations or formulas to support off-highway exempt usage; and

(8) first taxpayer reports.

Aircraft jet fuel.—An aircraft jet fuel dealer must maintain:

— a complete record of all sales or other dispositions of jet fuel;

— a record of inventories, purchases, and tank gaugings or meter readings of jet fuels; and

— qualifying sales invoices.

¶40-011

Use fuel tax.—Vendors must maintaincomplete records of all sales or other dispositions, including self-consumed fuel and any other use of fuel subject to the use fuel tax, and prepare a serially numbered invoice for each sale of fuel, whether the fuel is sold for use in a motor vehicle or for other uses. A sales invoice must contain the:

— name and address of the vendor;

— the date of the sale;

— number of gallons or units of fuel sold, price per gallon or unit, and the total amount of the sale;

— amount of use fuel collected, if delivery is into a fuel tank of a motor vehicle, along with the separately stated tax, if the invoice does not bear the notation that the price includes tax; and

— the type of receptacle, other than a fuel tank of a motor vehicle, into which the vendor delivered less than 250 gallons or units of fuel without collecting the use fuel tax.

Users of fuel subject to the tax must obtain an invoice from the vendor and retain the invoice in their files. In addition, users should keep a detail of figures upon which the totals reflected on their returns are based.

Diesel fuel tax.—Taxpayers must maintain and submit diesel fuel tax records as required and requested by the CDTFA, including books of account; bills, receipts, invoices, cash register tapes, and other original documents that support the books of account; and schedules of working papers. In addition, suppliers, ultimate vendors, retail vendors, and users of diesel fuel must maintain complete records of all:

— rack removals;

— sales;

— imports; and

— exempt dispositions, including exemption certificates, self-consumed diesel fuel, inventories, purchases, receipts, and tank gaugings or meter readings.

• *Assessment and collection*

Motor vehicle fuel taxes and diesel fuel taxes are delinquent if not paid by the last day of the month following the monthly period to which the report relates. Use fuel taxes are delinquent if not paid by the last day of the calendar month following each quarterly period.

If a supplier fails, neglects, or refuses to timely file a motor vehicle fuel tax return, the CDTFA may estimate fuel removals, entries, or sales and, based on that estimate, shall determine the tax due from and add a 10% penalty to the total. Until paid, those determination amounts are subject to a monthly interest rate set by the CDTFA. (See ¶89-204, Interest Rates.) If the supplier's neglect or refusal is due to fraud or an intent to evade taxes, an additional penalty of 25% will be added to the determination amount.

If a delinquency determination remains unpaid, the state controller may, within 10 years after the date the payments become delinquent, file a state tax lien against the supplier. In addition, the controller may seize and sell any property of the supplier and sell it at public auction to pay the tax due.

There are similar law provisions for the CDTFA to:

(1) make use fuel tax and diesel fuel tax deficiency determinations subject to a 10% penalty;

(2) monthly assess interest on the use fuel tax and diesel fuel tax deficiency; and

(3) add a 25% fraud penalty for use fuel tax and diesel fuel tax.

Within three years after the use fuel tax or diesel fuel tax becomes delinquent, the CDTFA may bring a court action to collect the delinquent amount of taxes, plus interest and penalties. In addition, the CDTFA may seize and sell any property of the supplier and sell it at public auction to pay the use fuel tax or diesel fuel tax due.

Personal liability may be imposed on a business purchaser for unpaid use fuel tax and diesel fuel tax incurred by a former owner. Also, unless notice of the discontinuation of a business is provided to the CDTFA by the date of discontinuance, the purchaser or transferee of a business is liable for all motor vehicle fuel taxes and penalties accrued against the vendor or transferor, up to the value of the property and business transferred.

• *Audits*

Taxpayers subject to the motor vehicle fuel, use fuel, and diesel fuel taxes are subject to the CDTFA's general audit power. See generally ¶89-134, Audits by Tax Type.

Specifically, the CDTFA may examine the books of:

— for motor vehicle fuel tax purposes, highway vehicle operators/fuelers, industrial users, pipeline operators, suppliers, train operators, and vessel operators;

— for use fuel tax purposes, any user or person dealing in, transporting, or storing fuel; and

— for diesel fuel tax purposes, any interstate user, supplier, exempt bus operator, government entity, ultimate vendor, highway vehicle operator, train operator, or person dealing in, removing, transporting, or storing diesel fuel.

The general limitations period for audits for each of those taxes is three years, or eight years if no return is filed or there is fraud involved (motor vehicle fuel tax; use fuel tax; diesel fuel tax).

Managed audits—2015.—Effective January 1, 2015, taxpayers may voluntarily participate in managed audits of qualifying motor vehicle fuel tax, use fuel tax, and diesel fuel tax accounts with the California Department of Tax and Fee Administration. An account will qualify for managed audits if:

— the taxpayer's business involves few or no statutory exemptions;

— the taxpayer's business involves a single or a small number of clearly defined taxability issues;

— the taxpayer is taxed pursuant to a qualifying tax or fee law at issue and agrees to participate in the program; and

— the taxpayer has the resources to comply with the managed audit instructions provided by the CDTFA.

(Motor vehicle fuel tax; use fuel tax; diesel fuel tax)

A motor vehicle fuel, use fuel, or diesel fuel taxpayer wishing to participate in the program must examine its books and records to determine if it has any unreported tax liability for the audit period and make available to the CDTFA for verification all computations and books and records examined. After the audit is verified by the CDTFA, interest on any unpaid liability will be imposed at 1/2 the rate that otherwise would be imposed during the audit period. (Motor vehicle fuel tax, use fuel tax, and diesel fuel tax.)

• *Appeal procedures*

Taxpayers subject to the motor vehicle fuel, use fuel, and diesel fuel taxes may appeal assessments under subject to the CDTFA's appeal provisions.

• *Forms*

The California State Board of Equalization makes current forms for fuel taxes available on its Web site.

• *Federal constitutional issues*

The constitutionality of state motor fuels tax laws is governed, to an extent, by an assortment of U.S. Supreme Court decisions. While an individual state may generally impose a tax on the use, sale, or delivery of gasoline and other motor fuels within its borders, the state is subject to certain federal constitutional limitations. Primary among these restrictions are the U.S. Constitution's provisions that prohibit a state from:

     — taxing the federal government;

     — violating either the Due Process Clause or the Equal Protection Clause of the federal Constitution's Fourteenth Amendment:

     — imposing an undue burden on interstate commercial transactions:

     — interfering with an Indian Nation's sovereignty; and

     — bypassing the limitations generally placed on the taxation of property.

A select number of U.S. Supreme Court decisions addressing these federal constitutional limitations are briefly summarized below.

General parameters of federal and state authority.—The regulation of all inter-state commerce is within the exclusive power of the federal government under the Commerce Clause of the U.S. Constitution. A state may, however, tax a motor fuel as long as the free flow of interstate commerce is not impeded and the federal Due Process Clause or Equal Protection Clause is not violated. (*National Private Truck Council, Inc. v. Oklahoma Tax Commission* (1995), 515 U.S. 582, 115 S.Ct. 2351)

Taxation of the federal government.—Tennessee could impose a storage tax on gasoline owned by the federal government that was stored by a private company. The applicable tax was not based on the worth of the government's property but was imposed on the privilege of storing such property. The federal Constitution did not extend sovereign immunity from state taxation to a corporation or an individual contracting with the United States merely because the activities of such parties were useful to the federal government. Therefore, federal sovereign immunity did not prohibit this tax. Although the final tax burden was borne by the federal government, federal ownership alone did not immunize a private person. (*Esso Standard Oil Co. v. Evans* (1953), 345 U.S. 495, 73 S. Ct. 800) See, also, *Panhandle Oil Co. v. Mississippi* (1928), 277 U.S. 218, 48 S. Ct. 45, and *Graves v. Texas Co.* (1936), 298 U.S. 393, 56 S. Ct. 818.

Due Process Clause.—A state statute requiring a seller of gasoline to file a motor fuels tax report and to remit to the state any tax collected from the purchaser of such gasoline, and that also assessed a penalty for a seller's failure to do so, did not involve a deprivation of property and did not violate the federal Constitution's Due Process Clause. It was proper for a state to pass these reporting and collection responsibilities to a seller, even though such efforts entailed both an inconvenience and an expense to the seller. (*Pierce Oil Corp. v. Hopkins* (1924), 264 U.S. 137, 44 S. Ct. 251)

A foreign corporation that was a licensed Idaho dealer in motor fuels that sold and transferred gasoline in Utah for importation into Idaho by a federal agency could not be constitutionally taxed by Idaho on the theory that the dealer constructively "received" the gasoline in Idaho upon its importation. The fact that a foreign corporation had an Idaho gasoline dealer's license and engaged in business in Idaho did not permit Idaho to tax the corporation's out-of-state sale of gasoline to a federal agency for use in Idaho. The Utah sale was not related to the corporation's business activity in Idaho. In the absence of any indication that the taxpayer's activity in Idaho contributed to the procurement or performance of its out-of-state contract with the federal government, the federal Due Process Clause did not permit the imposition of a tax on the out-of-state sale. (*American Oil Co. v. Neill* (1965), 380 U.S. 451)

Equal Protection Clause.—A Montana motor fuels tax did not violate the federal Equal Protection Clause where the basis of the tax was the sale of gasoline within the state by a distributor or dealer refining or importing gasoline, and the tax was only applied to an in-state refiner. The tax was not extended to include gasoline shipped in from other states. (*Hart Refineries v. Harmon* (1929), 278 U.S. 499, 49 S. Ct. 188)

Burden on interstate commerce.—A Kentucky tax on gasoline sold within the state at wholesale ("wholesale" being defined to include gasoline obtained from outside the state and used within the state) was unconstitutional as a direct burden on interstate commerce when applied to gasoline purchased in Illinois and consumed in a ferry boat operating mostly in Kentucky. (*Helson v. Kentucky* (1929), 279 U.S. 245, 49 S. Ct. 279)

A South Carolina tax on the privilege of selling gasoline within the state was upheld when applied to an air transport company doing business mainly interstate but purchasing its gasoline within South Carolina. The mere purchase of supplies or equipment for use in conducting an interstate business was not so identified with that commerce as to make the purchase immune from a nondiscriminatory state tax. A nondiscriminatory tax upon a local sale was not regarded as imposing a direct burden upon interstate commerce. (*Eastern Air Transport, Inc. v. South Carolina Tax Commission* (1932), 285 U.S. 147, 52 S. Ct. 340; See, also, *Gregg Dyeing Co. v. Query* (1932), 286 U.S. 472, 52 S. Ct. 631)

A tax imposed on the storage or withdrawal from storage of gasoline for sale or use within the state was constitutionally applied to gasoline shipped into the state by a railroad for storage and subsequent consumption in the operation of its equipment in interstate commerce. This tax was not a direct burden on interstate commerce. (*Nashville, C & St. L. Ry. v. Wallace* (1933), 288 U.S. 249, 53 S. Ct. 345)

A Pennsylvania tax imposed upon a distributor of liquid motor fuels used or sold within the state was constitutional as applied to a Pittsburgh corporation that sold fuel at wholesale as a distributor throughout Pennsylvania. Since the applicable sales contracts were made in Pennsylvania, and interstate transportation was not required or contemplated, any resulting interstate transport was deemed to be merely incidental. Accordingly, interstate commerce was not burdened by this tax. (*Wiloil Corp. v. Pennsylvania* (1935), 294 U.S. 169, 55 S. Ct. 358)

An Arkansas tax imposed on the gasoline in the fuel and storage tanks of a bus entering the state was a federally unconstitutional burden on interstate commerce. While a state may charge reasonable compensation for the use of its highways, this gasoline tax, without regard to the amount actually used within the state, had no reasonable relationship to compensation for highway use. (*McCarroll v. Dixie Greyhound Lines, Inc.* (1940), 309 U.S. 176, 60 S. Ct. 504) See also, *Bingaman v. Golden Eagle Western Lines, Inc.* (1936), 297 U.S. 626, 56 S. Ct. 624.

A Pennsylvania motor fuels identification marker fee was an unconstitutional burden on interstate commerce. (*American Trucking Association, Inc. v. Scheiner* (1987), 483 U.S. 266)

An Ohio motor vehicle fuels sales tax credit that was available to an in-state producer of ethanol and also to an out-of-state producer whose home state granted a reciprocal credit for ethanol produced in Ohio clearly discriminated against interstate commerce and was not justified by a valid purpose unrelated to economic protectionism. The purpose of the credit was not to promote health or commerce, but rather to provide favorable tax treatment for ethanol produced in Ohio. Furthermore, even if there was neither a widespread advantage to in-state interests nor a widespread disadvantage to out-of-state competitors, when such discrimination was patent, the Court was required to invalidate such a law. (*New Energy Co. of Indiana v. Limbach, Tax Commissioner of Ohio* (1988), 486 U.S. 269, 108 S. Ct. 1803)

Indian Nation's sovereignty.—An Oklahoma motor fuels excise tax imposed on fuel sold by an Indian retail store on an Indian tribe's trust land was prohibited under the doctrine of Indian sovereignty because the legal incidence of the tax ultimately rested on the tribe as the retailer. Although the state's excise tax law did not expressly provide that the tax was imposed on the retailer, the legal incidence of the tax rested upon the retailer, rather than on the distributor or consumer, because:

(1) the tax had to be remitted on behalf of a licensed retailer;

(2) a retailer was liable for any tax not paid by the consumer;

(3) a retailer was not compensated for collecting the tax; and

(4) the tax was imposed when the fuel was sold by a distributor to a retailer without regard to whether the fuel was later purchased by a consumer.

(*Oklahoma Tax Commission v. Chickasaw Nation* (1995), 515 U.S. 450, 115 S. Ct. 2214)

A Kansas tax on motor fuels received by a non-Indian distributor, but subsequently delivered to an Indian reservation's gas station, was constitutionally valid and did not affront a tribe's sovereignty. The distributor paid the tax on its initial receipt of the fuel and then merely passed the tax cost onto its customers, including a retailer located on an Indian reservation. The implementation of this tax did not adversely impact Indian sovereignty because this nondiscriminatory tax was imposed on an off-reservation transaction between non-Indians. The legal incidence of the tax was on the non-Indian distributor and it was the distributor's off-reservation receipt of the fuel that established the tax liability. (*Wagnon v. Prairie Band Potawatomi Nation* (2005), 546 U.S. 95, 126 S. Ct. 676)

Property tax limitations.—A New Mexico motor fuels tax that was measured by the number of gallons of gasoline bought, sold, or used in the state was not unconstitutional. The tax, applicable to a distributor, was an excise tax that was not subject to the federal constitutional limitations generally placed on the taxation of property. While an excise tax could not be imposed upon interstate commerce, it was valid as applied to intrastate commerce. However, gasoline brought from outside the state and sold in its original containers could not be subject to such a tax since any enforcement would be a direct burden on interstate commerce. But gasoline brought from outside the state and sold from broken packages in quantities to suit customers or used by a distributor in the operation of its stations was validly subject to the excise tax, since it had gone beyond interstate commerce. (*Bowman v. Continental Oil Co.* (1921), 256 U.S. 642, 41 S. Ct. 606)

CIGARETTES, TOBACCO PRODUCTS

[¶55-000]
CIGARETTES, TOBACCO PRODUCTS

[¶55-001] Cigarettes

California imposes a tax on the distribution, use, or consumption of cigarettes. Cigarettes also are subject to sales tax in the state.

CDTFA responsible for cigarette, tobacco products taxes administration.—As a result of 2017 legislation that stripped the State Board of Equalization (BOE) of all but its constitutionally mandated duties, responsibilities, and powers, the California Department of Tax and Fee Administration (CDTFA) assumed responsibility for administration of all the taxes not contained in the BOE's constitutional duties, including cigarette and tobacco products taxes. The change was effective July 1, 2017. (Ch. 16 (A.B. 102), Laws 2017) In subsequent legislation, a provision was added to specify that, in the Revenue and Taxation Code or any other code, references to the "board, itself" or "State Board of Equalization meeting as a public body" for purposes of the duties, powers, and responsibilities transferred to CDTFA means CDTFA. (Sec. 20.5, Rev. & Tax. Code)

For a discussion of California's tax on tobacco products, see Tobacco Products. Administrative and procedural provisions are discussed at Cigarette, Tobacco Products Tax Practice and Procedure.

COMPLIANCE ALERT: Proposition 56.—On November 8, 2016, California voters approved initiative Proposition 56. Effective April 1, 2017, Proposition 56 increases the cigarette tax rate and redefines "tobacco products" to include any type of tobacco, nicotine, little cigars, and electronic cigarettes sold in combination with nicotine. It also imposes a floor tax and a stamp adjustment tax on cigarettes. See generally Special Notice L-488, California State Board of Equalization, January 1, 2017.

Discussed here in relation to the cigarette tax are:

— Persons and products subject to tax,

— Exemptions,

— Basis of tax,

— Rate of tax,

— Reports,

— Payment,

— Credits, refunds, discounts,

— Licenses and permits, and

— Local taxes.

Little cigars are taxed as a tobacco product and do not require cigarette tax stamps. (Special Notice L-488, California State Board of Equalization, January 1, 2017; see ¶55-005)

The California Department of Tax and Fee Administration (CDTFA) provides guidance on cigarette distributor licensing and tax stamps. (Publication 63, Cigarette Distributor Licensing and Tax Stamp Guide, California State Board of Equalization)

• *Persons and products subject to tax*

The cigarette tax is imposed on the distribution of cigarettes in the state. (Sec. 30101, Rev. & Tax. Code; Sec. 30123, Rev. & Tax. Code; Sec. 30131.2, Rev. & Tax. Code) As defined for purposes of the tax, "distribution" in the state includes:

— the sale of cigarettes;

— the use or consumption of cigarettes; or

— the placing of untaxed cigarettes in a vending machine or in retail stock.

(Sec. 30008, Rev. & Tax. Code)

Sample distribution of a cigarette or tobacco product clearly identified as a "sample" is permitted for advertising purposes, as specified by state law and the November 23, 1998 Master Settlement Agreement with the state. However, such distributions are subject to tax. (Reg. 4081, 18 CCR)

The tax does not apply to electronic cigarettes (eCigarettes). Although the U.S. Food and Drug Administration (FDA) has issued a notice that eCigarettes shall be regulated as a tobacco product, eCigarettes do not fall under the California cigarette law definition of "cigarette" or "tobacco" because they do not contain tobacco. (*BOE Publication 204, Cigarette and Tobacco Products Newsletter*, BOE, October 2011)

Under federal law, flavored cigarettes cannot be manufactured, imported, or sold in the U.S., and those cigarettes have been and may continue to be removed from the California Tobacco Directory. It is illegal for distributors to affix a California cigarette tax stamp on packages of cigarettes or pay the tax on roll-your-own product unless the manufacturer and the brand family are listed in the directory. (*Special Notice, BOE-400-LSC*, California State Board of Equalization, December 2012)

Master Settlement Agreement.—California has entered into the Master Settlement Agreement, which in part requires participating cigarette manufacturers to pay substantial sums of money to the state. Nonparticipating manufacturers must make payments into a separate escrow fund for each non-exempt cigarette sold in the state and are subject to separate reporting requirements. (Sec. 30165.1, Rev. & Tax. Code; Sec. 104556, Hlth. & Saf. Code)

Internet, mail-order, and other types of delivery sales.—Generally, no person may engage in a retail sale of cigarettes in California unless the sale is a vendor-assisted, face-to-face sale. However, the state permits qualifying delivery sales. A person may engage in delivery sales if the delivery seller:

— fully complies with the federal Jenkins Act,

— obtains and maintains applicable licenses,

— maintains any required escrow accounts, and

— complies with any reporting requirements.

(Sec. 30101.7(d), Rev. & Tax. Code)

Sales on Indian nation or tribal reservations.—For purposes of collection of all cigarette-related taxes, the term "Indian country" has the same meaning as provided in Section 1151 of Title 18 of the United States Code, and includes any other land held by the United States in trust or restricted status for one or more Indian tribes. In addition, the term "interstate commerce" means, among other things, "... commerce between a state and Indian country in the state, or commerce between points in the same state but through a place outside of the state or through any Indian country." (Sec. 30101.7, Rev. & Tax. Code) The cigarette tax law makes no further reference to either "Indian" or "Indian country."

However, the U.S. Supreme Court ruled that the legal incidence of California's cigarette tax falls on non-Indian purchasers of cigarettes sold by the Chemehuevi Indian Tribe on its reservation. The incidence of the tax falls on the consuming purchaser if the vendor is exempt. Therefore, the State Board of Equalization (now the California Department of Tax and Fee Administration) can rightfully require the tribe to collect and remit the tax to the state. (*California State Board of Equalization v. Chemehuevi Indian Tribe*, 474 U.S. 9 (1985))

• *Exemptions*

The cigarette tax does not apply to the following:

— sales to Army, Air Force, Navy, Marine, or Coast Guard exchanges and commissaries and ship's stores or to the Veterans Administration, but only until the first day of the first month beginning more than 60 days after federal law is amended to permit state taxation of cigarette sales by or through federal military installations; (Sec. 30102, Rev. & Tax. Code)

— distribution of cigarettes that are non-tax-paid under Chapter 52 of the Internal Revenue Act and the cigarettes are under Internal Revenue Bond or customs control; (Sec. 30102.5, Rev. & Tax. Code)

— sales by the manufacturer to a licensed distributor; (Sec. 30103, Rev. & Tax. Code)

— sales or transfers of untaxed cigarettes to law enforcement agencies for use in criminal investigations when authorized by the California Department of Tax and Fee Administration; (Sec. 30103.5, Rev. & Tax. Code)

— sales by a distributor to a common carrier engaged in interstate or foreign passenger service or to a person authorized to sell cigarettes on the facilities of such carrier (sales by the carrier or authorized persons on the carrier's facilities are subject to tax); (Sec. 30104, Rev. & Tax. Code)

— sales of cigarettes by the original importer to a licensed distributor if the cigarettes are manufactured outside the U.S.; (Sec. 30105, Rev. & Tax. Code)

— sales or gifts of cigarettes to veterans' homes or to a veterans' hospital, provided cigarettes are delivered directly by manufacturer under Internal Revenue bond, and (Sec. 30105.5, Rev. & Tax. Code)

— cigarettes brought into the state in a single shipment of less than 400 cigarettes for use or consumption by either an individual for his own use or consumption or by Army, Air Force, Navy, Marine, or Coast Guard exchanges and commissaries and ship's stores or the Veterans Administration. (Sec. 30106, Rev. & Tax. Code)

• *Basis of tax*

The cigarette tax is imposed on the distribution of cigarettes by distributors. (Sec. 30101, Rev. & Tax. Code; Sec. 30123, Rev. & Tax. Code; Sec. 30131.2, Rev. & Tax. Code)

• *Rate of tax*

Effective July 1, 2020 through June 30, 2021, cigarettes are taxed at the rate of $2.87 per 20-pack ($0.1435 per cigarette). On a per-cigarette basis, that rate is comprised of:

— a tax of six mills; (Sec. 30101, Rev. & Tax. Code)

— a tax of 12.5 mills; (Sec. 30123, Rev. & Tax. Code)

— a surtax of 25 mills; and (Sec. 30131.2, Rev. & Tax. Code)

— a tax of 100 mills. (Sec. 30130.51, Rev. & Tax. Code)

Master Settlement Agreement.—Pursuant to the terms of the Master Settlement Agreement laws in California, after 2006 nonparticipating manufacturers are required by the model statute to make a yearly deposit into a qualified escrow account. The base escrow amount is $0.0188482 for each cigarette (unit) sold in a year, prior to the inflation adjustment. The deposit is to be made by each April 15 for units sold during the previous calendar year. (Sec. 104557, Hlth. & Saf. Code) "Units sold" means the number of cigarettes sold to consumers regardless of whether the state excise tax was due or collected, but the term does not include cigarettes sold on federal military installations, sold by a Native American tribe to a member of that tribe on that tribe's land, or that are otherwise exempt from state tax under federal law. (Sec. 104556, Hlth. & Saf. Code)

• *Reports*

Except as discussed below, distributors, carriers, wholesalers, and consumers must file reports or returns with the California Department of Tax and Fee Administration (CDTFA) by the 25th of each month. (Sec. 30182, Rev. & Tax Code; Sec. 30183, Rev. & Tax. Code; Sec. 30186, Rev. & Tax Code; Sec. 30188, Rev. & Tax Code)

All cigarette distributors must file a report by the 25th day of the month with respect to those distributions of cigarettes and purchases of stamps and meter register settings that were made during the preceding month. (Sec. 30182, Rev. & Tax Code) On the last day of the month following the end of a quarter, consumers and users of cigarettes from whom the cigarette tax has not been collected must file a report with the CDTFA of the amount of cigarettes received during the preceding quarter. (Sec. 30187, Rev. & Tax Code)

Cigarette tax returns may be filed electronically. (Sec. 30181, Rev. & Tax. Code through Sec. 30183, Rev. & Tax. Code; Sec. 30193, Rev. & Tax. Code)

Manufacturer's monthly report.—Each manufacturer of cigarettes must file a certified report of all releases and deliveries and all shipments of cigarettes from outside the state to locations within the state. This report must be filed with the CDTFA by the 20th day of each month. In addition, the report must show the following:

— the date of release, delivery, or shipment,

— the location from which the release, delivery, or shipment was made,

— the name and address of the purchaser,

— the address to which the release, delivery, or shipment was made,

— the number of cigarettes or type, quantity,

— the invoice or document number and date,

— the license number, if released to a licensed distributor, and

— the information indicating the cancellation of any release, delivery, or shipment.

(Reg. 4027, 18 CCR)

Jenkins Act registration and reporting.—The federal Jenkins Act (15 U.S.C. §§375-378), as amended in 2010 by the Prevent All Cigarette Trafficking Act of 2009 (PACT Act), Pub. L. No. 111-154, imposes certain registration and reporting requirements on those who sell, transfer, or ship (or who advertise or offer to do so) cigarettes, roll-your-own tobacco, and smokeless tobacco for profit in interstate commerce to a state, locality, or Indian country of an Indian tribe that taxes the sale or use of such products.

Registration requirement: A statement must be filed with the U.S. Attorney General and with the tobacco tax administrators of the state and place into which the products are shipped (or where advertisements or offers are directed). The statement must provide the name and trade name (if any) of the seller, transferor, or shipper, and the address of its principal place of business and of any other place of business. (15 U.S.C. §376(a)) Additionally, the statement must include telephone numbers for each place of business, a principal e-mail address, any website addresses, and the name, address, and telephone number of an agent in the state authorized to accept service on behalf of the seller, transferor, or shipper. (15 U.S.C. § 376(a))

As an alternative to filing a statement with the U.S. Attorney General, Form 5070.1 can be filed with the Bureau of Alcohol, Tobacco, Firearms and Explosives (ATF). This federal form is available on the ATF's website at http://www.atf.gov/.

Reporting requirement: The Jenkins Act also imposes a duty to file on the 10th of each month with the relevant state tobacco tax administrator a report of the names and addresses of all of the seller's in-state cigarette and smokeless tobacco purchasers, the brand and quantity of cigarettes or smokeless tobacco, and the name, address, and phone number of the person delivering the shipment. (15 U.S.C. § 376(a)) A copy of the report must be filed with the chief law enforcement officer of the local government and any Indian tribe that applies its own local or tribal taxes on the cigarettes or smokeless tobacco purchased. (15 U.S.C. § 376(a)) These reports can be used by the state tobacco tax administrators and the local chief law enforcement officers that receive them to enforce the collection of any taxes owed on the sales. (15 U.S.C. § 376(c))

Master Settlement Agreement.—Every tobacco product manufacturer selling cigarettes in the state must file a report with the California Attorney General certifying that it is either a participating manufacturer under the terms of the Master Settlement Agreement, or that it is a nonparticipating manufacturer in full compliance with California requirements for nonparticipating manufacturers. (Sec. 30165.1, Rev. & Tax. Code)

• *Payment*

Generally, the cigarette tax is paid by distributors through the use of stamps or meter impressions. (Sec. 30161, Rev. & Tax. Code) When the tax is not paid through use of stamps or meter impressions, it is due and payable on the 25th of the month following the month in which:

— a distribution of cigarettes occurs; or

— in the case of common carrier of passengers, a sale of cigarettes on the facilities of the carrier occurs.

(Sec. 30181, Rev. & Tax. Code)

However, the cigarette tax may be prepaid by the use of stamps and metering machines. (Sec. 30161, Rev. & Tax. Code) Cigarette distributors that defer payment for stamps and meter register settings and that elect to remit tax on a twice-monthly basis must remit their first monthly payment by the 5th day of the month; their first monthly payment must equal the greater of one half the tax due on purchases made during the preceding month or the total tax due on purchases made between the 1st and the 15th of the preceding month; and they must remit their second monthly payment by the 25th day of the month for the remainder of the prior month's purchases. Cigarette distributors that defer payment for stamps and meter register settings and that elect to remit tax on a monthly basis must remit their monthly payment by the 25th day of each month. Cigarette distributors that defer payment for stamps and meter register settings must remit payment by the 25th day of the month following the month in which the payments were deferred. Beginning in 2007, if a distributor elects to make the payment on a weekly basis, the distributor shall remit the payment on or before Wednesday following the week in which the stamps and meter register settings were approved and released. Every distributor electing to make payment on a weekly basis shall provide an electronic mail address for the purpose of receiving payment information. (Sec. 30168, Rev. & Tax. Code)

Consumers or users of untaxed cigarettes within the state are required to pay any amount of tax due by the last day of the month following the calendar quarter in which the untaxed cigarettes were received. (Sec. 30187, Rev. & Tax. Code)

Persons with an estimated monthly tax or fee liability of at least $20,000 are required to remit amounts due by electronic funds transfer. Persons with a liability of less than $20,000 per month may elect to pay electronically. (Sec. 30190, Rev. & Tax. Code; Reg. 4031.1, 18 CCR; Reg. 4905, 18 CCR)

• *Credits, refunds, discounts*

Distributors that affix stamps or meter impressions are allowed a discount of 0.85% of the face value of the stamps. (Sec. 30166, Rev. & Tax. Code)

Refunds or credits are allowed for tax paid on cigarettes that have become unfit for use, are unmarketable, or have been destroyed. (Sec. 30177, Rev. & Tax. Code)

A claim for a refund must be filed by the later of three years from the 25th day after the close of the monthly period for which the overpayment was made, six months from the date a deficiency determination becomes final, or six months from the date of overpayment. (Sec. 30362, Rev. & Tax. Code) Taxpayers making install-ment payments on a final notice of determination and disputing their liability may file one timely claim for refund to cover all future payments applied to that billing. The filing also will apply to any prior payments that remain within the applicable statutes of limitations. A taxpayer disputing more than one billing must file a timely claim for refund for each separate billing. Payments made to release liens are subject to the six month statute as they are considered voluntary. Payments submitted prior to January 1, 2017, will not cover any future payments. (Sec. 30362.2, Rev. & Tax. Code; *Special Notice L-479*, California State Board of Equalization, November 2016)

An unused stamp is a tax stamp on a roll or undistributed package of cigarettes with at least four characters of the five-character serial number affixed. If fewer than four characters are identifiable, the distributor must show that the remainder of the stamp is not affixed to a distributed package of cigarettes. (Reg. 4061, 18 CCR)

The claim form must be filed with the CDTFA and contain information regarding the number and types of cigarette stamps being claimed for refund, the amount of the claim for each type of stamp, and the reason for the claim. In addition, the CDTFA must acknowledge receipt of the cigarette tax stamps relating to the claim and certify receipt and destruction of these stamps. Moreover, an authorized CDTFA employee must verify the refund or credit and obliterate the stamp using a permanent marker. However, if the stamps are on a roll, the roll must be returned to the CDTFA after verification of the refund or credit. (Reg. 4061, 18 CCR)

• *Licenses and permits*

Distributors, including common carriers, must obtain a license for each place of business at which they distribute cigarettes. Persons selling or accepting orders for cigarettes that are to be transported from out of state to a consumer within the state need not be registered. (Sec. 30140, Rev. & Tax. Code)

Wholesalers must also apply for and obtain a license for each place of business. (Sec. 30155, Rev. & Tax. Code)

Retailers can apply for a license to sell cigarettes directly to the public from a qualifying "retail location." A retail location is either any building from which cigarettes are sold at retail or a vending machine. (Sec. 22971, Bus. and Prof. Code; Sec. 22972, Bus. and Prof. Code) Under a CDTFA policy, special purpose commercial coaches, such as catering trucks or lunch wagons, cannot be licensed as a retail location because they were not buildings. For mobile sellers, licenses will no longer be issued. (Special Notice: Mobile Sellers of Cigarettes and Tobacco Products, Califor-nia State Board of Equalization, March 2013)

Distributors of cigarettes who are not doing business in California may apply for a California distributor's license for California cigarette tax purposes. These licensed distributors must file a monthly report or return. In addition, these licensed distributors must collect tax, give a receipt for the tax collected, and remit the tax to the CDTFA in the same manner as licensed distributors doing business in the state. (Reg. 4011, 18 CCR)

Licensed distributors must stamp and meter cigarette packages in conformity with federal labeling requirements before distributing products for sale, and must refrain from doing so as prescribed by statute. Licenses of noncompliant distributors are subject to revocation by the CDTFA. Products stamped or metered in violation of statutory requirements are subject to both seizure by the CDTFA and forfeiture to the state. (Sec. 30163, Rev. & Tax. Code; Sec. 30436, Rev. & Tax. Code)

The CDTFA sells and allows the application of only those tax stamps that utilize technology capable of being read by a scanning or similar device, as required by California law. (Sec. 30162, Rev. & Tax. Code)

• *Local taxes*

The cigarette tax is in lieu of all other state, county, municipal, or district taxes on the privilege of distributing cigarettes. (Sec. 30111, Rev. & Tax. Code)

[¶55-005] Tobacco Products

California imposes a tax on tobacco products at an annually adjusted rate. The CDTFA issues a publication on cigarette and tobacco products taxes. (Publication 93, Cigarette and Tobacco Products Tax, California Department of Tax and Fee Administration)

Tobacco products also are subject to sales tax in the state.

CDTFA responsible for cigarette and tobacco products taxes administration.— As a result of 2017 legislation that stripped the State Board of Equalization (BOE) of all but its constitutionally mandated duties, responsibilities, and powers, the California Department of Tax and Fee Administration (CDTFA) assumed responsibility for administration of all the taxes not contained in the BOE's constitutional duties, including cigarette and tobacco products taxes. The change was effective July 1, 2017. (Ch. 16 (A.B. 102), Laws 2017) In subsequent legislation, a provision was added to specify that, in the Revenue and Taxation Code or any other code, references to the "board, itself" or "State Board of Equalization meeting as a public body" for purposes of the duties, powers, and responsibilities transferred to CDTFA means CDTFA. (Sec. 20.5, Rev. & Tax. Code)

For a discussion of the cigarette tax, see Cigarettes (¶55-001). Administrative and procedural provisions are discussed at Cigarette, Tobacco Products Tax Practice and Procedure (¶55-010).

COMPLIANCE ALERT: Proposition 56.—On November 8, 2016, California voters approved initiative Proposition 56. Effective April 1, 2017, Proposition 56 increases the cigarette tax rate and redefines "tobacco products" to include any type of tobacco, nicotine, little cigars, and electronic cigarettes sold in combination with nicotine. It also imposes a floor tax and a stamp adjustment tax on cigarettes. See generally Special Notice L-488, California State Board of Equalization, January 1, 2017.

Discussed here in relation to the tobacco products tax are:

— Persons and products subject to tax,

— Exemptions,

— Basis of tax,

— Rate of tax,

— Reports,

— Payment,

— Credits, refunds, discounts,

— Licenses and permits, and

— Local taxes.

• *Persons and products subject to tax*

On April 1, 2017, as a result of Proposition 56, distribution of the following products became subject to the tobacco products tax:

— little cigars (cigarette tax stamps will no longer be required);

— any product made, derived, or containing any amount of tobacco that is intended for human consumption (previously products had to contain at least 50% tobacco and be a smoking or chewing tobacco or snuff);

— nicotine intended for human consumption (sold with or without a nicotine delivery device); and

— nicotine delivery devices (including electronic cigarettes, e-cigars, e-pipes, vape pens and e-hookahs) sold in combination with substances containing nicotine.

(Sec. 30121, Rev. & Tax. Code)

As defined in relevant part for purposes of the tax, "distribution" in the state includes:

— the sale of tobacco products;

— the use or consumption of tobacco products; or

— the placing of untaxed tobacco products in a vending machine or in retail stock.

(Sec. 30008, Rev. & Tax. Code)

• *Exemptions*

The tobacco products tax does not apply to the following:

— sales to Army, Air Force, Navy, Marine, or Coast Guard exchanges and commissaries and ship's stores or to the Veterans Administration, but only until the first day of the first month beginning more than 60 days after federal law is amended to permit state taxation of cigarette sales by or through federal military installations; (Sec. 30102, Rev. & Tax. Code)

— sales by the manufacturer to a licensed distributor; (Sec. 30103, Rev. & Tax. Code)

— sales or transfers of untaxed tobacco products to law enforcement agencies for use in criminal investigations when authorized by the CDTFA; (Sec. 30103.5, Rev. & Tax. Code)

— sales by a distributor to a common carrier engaged in interstate or foreign passenger service or to a person authorized to sell tobacco products on the facilities of such carrier (sales by the carrier or authorized persons on the carrier's facilities are subject to tax); (Sec. 30104, Rev. & Tax. Code)

— sales of tobacco products by the original importer to a licensed distributor if the tobacco products are manufactured outside the U.S.; and (Sec. 30105, Rev. & Tax. Code)

— sales or gifts of tobacco products to veterans' homes or to a veterans' hospital, provided tobacco products are delivered directly by manufacturer under Internal Revenue bond. (Sec. 30105.5, Rev. & Tax. Code)

• *Basis of tax*

The tobacco products tax is imposed based on the wholesale cost of tobacco products distributed in the state. (Sec. 30123(b), Rev. & Tax. Code; Sec. 30131.2(b), Rev. & Tax. Code)

• *Rate of tax*

The tobacco products tax rate, adjusted each state fiscal year by the CDTFA, is equivalent to the combined rate of tax imposed on cigarettes. (Sec. 30123(b), Rev. & Tax. Code; Sec. 30131.2(b), Rev. & Tax. Code)

Effective July 1, 2020 through June 30, 2021, the tax rate on other tobacco products is 56.93% of wholesale cost. (*Special Notice L-747*, California Department of Tax and Fee Administration, April 2020)

Effective July 1, 2019 through June 30, 2020, the tax rate on other tobacco products is 59.27% of wholesale cost. (*Special Notice L-657*, California Department of Tax and Fee Administration, May 2019)

Previous rates were:

— 62.78% from July 1, 2018 through June 30, 2019;

— 65.08% from July 1, 2017 through June 30, 2018;

— 27.30% from July 1, 2016 through June 30, 2017;

— 28.13% from July 1, 2015 through June 30, 2016;

— 29.95% from July 1, 2014 through June 30, 2015;

— 29.82% from July 1, 2013 through June 30, 2014;

— 30.68% from July 1, 2012 through June 30, 2013;

— 31.73% from July 1, 2011 through June 30, 2012;

— 33.02% from July 1, 2010 through June 30, 2011;

— 41.11% from July 1, 2009 through June 30, 2010;

— 45.13% from July 1, 2007 through June 30, 2009;

— 46.76% from July 1, 2003 through June 30, 2007;

— 48.89% from July 1, 2002 through June 30, 2003; and

— 52.65% from September 10, 2001 through June 30, 2002.

• *Reports*

Except as discussed below, distributors, carriers, wholesalers, and consumers must file reports or returns with the CDTFA by the 25th of each month. (Sec. 30183(b), Rev. & Tax. Code; Sec. 30186, Rev. & Tax Code; Sec. 30188, Rev. & Tax Code)

COMPLIANCE NOTE: Beginning January 1, 2020, tobacco products distributors are required to report the wholesale cost of electronic cigarettes and vaping products that contain nicotine separately from the wholesale cost of all other tobacco products they distribute. Distributors are also required to report their total sales of electronic cigarettes and vaping products that contain nicotine by customer (buyer) as of the same date. Form CDTFA-501-CT, Tobacco Products Distributor Tax Return, is revised and schedule CDTFA-810-CTN, Electronic Cigarettes and Vaping Products That Contain Nicotine—Tax Disbursement Schedule, is added to meet these requirements. (*Executive Order N-18-19*, Office of California Gov. Gavin Newsom, September 16, 2019)

On the last day of the month following the end of a quarter, consumers and users of tobacco products from whom the cigarette tax has not been collected must file a report with the CDTFA of the amount of tobacco products received during the preceding quarter. (Sec. 30187, Rev. & Tax Code)

Tobacco tax returns may be filed electronically. (Sec. 30181, Rev. & Tax. Code; Sec. 30183, Rev. & Tax. Code)

• *Payment*

Each distributor of tobacco products must include with each report or return due a remittance payable to the CDTFA for the amount of tax due. (Sec. 30181, Rev. & Tax. Code; Sec. 30184, Rev. & Tax. Code)

Consumers or users of untaxed tobacco products within the state are required to pay any amount of tax due by the last day of the month following the calendar quarter in which the untaxed tobacco products were received. (Sec. 30187, Rev. & Tax. Code)

Persons with an estimated monthly tax liability of at least $20,000 are required to remit amounts due by electronic funds transfer. Those with an estimated monthly liability of less than $20,000 may elect to remit their payments electronically with CDTFA approval. (Sec. 30190, Rev. & Tax. Code; Reg. 4031.1, 18 CCR; Reg. 4905, 18 CCR)

• *Credits, refunds, discounts*

The CDTFA must refund or credit to a distributor the tax that is paid on tobacco products that are shipped to a point outside the state for subsequent use or sale out of state. (Sec. 30176.1, Rev. & Tax. Code)

Refunds or credits are allowed for tax paid on tobacco products that have been returned by a customer, provided that the distributor refunds the entire amount the customer paid for the tobacco products, either in cash or as a credit. The entire amount will be deemed to be refunded to the customer when the purchase price less rehandling and restocking costs, determined by reference to average costs during the previous accounting cycle, is refunded or credited. (Sec. 30176.2, Rev. & Tax. Code)

A claim for a refund must be filed by the later of three years from the 25th day after the close of the monthly period for which the overpayment was made, six months from the date a deficiency determination becomes final, or six months from the date of overpayment. (Sec. 30362, Rev. & Tax. Code) Taxpayers making install-ment payments on a final notice of determination and disputing their liability may file one timely claim for refund to cover all future payments applied to that billing. The filing also will apply to any prior payments that remain within the applicable statutes of limitations. A taxpayer disputing more than one billing must file a timely claim for refund for each separate billing. Payments made to release liens are subject to the six month statute as they are considered voluntary. Payments submitted prior to January 1, 2017, will not cover any future payments. (Sec. 30362.2, Rev. & Tax. Code; *Special Notice L-479*, California State Board of Equalization, November 2016)

• *Licenses and permits*

Distributors, including common carriers, must obtain a license for each place of business at which they distribute tobacco products. Persons selling or accepting orders for tobacco products that are to be transported from out of state to a consumer within the state need not be registered. (Sec. 30140, Rev. & Tax. Code)

Wholesalers must also apply for and obtain a license for each place of business. (Sec. 30155, Rev. & Tax. Code)

Retailers can apply for a license to sell tobacco products directly to the public from a qualifying "retail location." A retail location is either any building from which tobacco products are sold at retail or a vending machine. (Sec. 22971, Bus. and Prof. Code; Sec. 22972, Bus. and Prof. Code) In March 2013, the BOE implemented a policy that special purpose commercial coaches, such as catering trucks or lunch wagons, cannot be licensed as a retail location because they were not buildings. Licenses will no longer be issued for mobile sellers. (*Special Notice: Mobile Sellers of Cigarettes and Tobacco Products*, California State Board of Equalization, March 2013)

Distributors of tobacco products who are not doing business in California may apply for a California distributor's license for tobacco products excise tax purposes. These licensed distributors must file a monthly report or return using form CDTFA-501-CT. In addition, these licensed distributors must collect tax, give a receipt for the tax collected, and remit the tax to the CDTFA in the same manner as licensed distributors doing business in the state. (Reg. 4011, 18 CCR)

• *Local taxes*

The tobacco products tax is in lieu of all other state, county, municipal, or district taxes on the privilege of distributing tobacco products. (Sec. 30111, Rev. & Tax. Code)

[¶55-010] Cigarette, Tobacco Products Tax Practice and Procedure

---

COMPLIANCE ALERT: CDTFA assumes responsibility for cigarette, tobacco products taxes administration.—As a result of 2017 legislation that stripped the State Board of Equalization (BOE) of all but its constitutionally mandated duties, responsibilities, and powers, the California Department of Tax and Fee Administration (CDTFA) assumed responsibility for administration of all the taxes not contained in the BOE's constitutional duties, including cigarette and tobacco products taxes. The change was effective July 1, 2017. (Ch. 16 (A.B. 102), Laws 2017, effective June 27, 2017) In subsequent legislation, a provision was added to specify that, in the Revenue and Taxation Code or any other code, references to the "board, itself" or "State Board of Equalization meeting as a public body" for purposes of the duties, powers, and responsibilities transferred to CDTFA means CDTFA. (Sec. 20.5, Rev. & Tax. Code, added by Sec. 16, Ch. 252 (A.B. 131), Laws 2017, effective September 16, 2017)

Discussed here are administrative and procedural issues involved in compliance and enforcement of the cigarette and tobacco products taxes.

Specific topics covered include:

— Administration,

— Penalties,

— Record keeping,

— Assessment and collection,

— Audits,

— Appeal procedures, and

— Forms.

• *Administration*

The California Department of Tax and Fee Administration (CDTFA) is authorized to enforce the provisions of the cigarette and tobacco products tax laws. It may prescribe, adopt, and enforce rules and regulations relating to the administration and enforcement of the tax and prescribe the extent to which any ruling or regulation shall be applied without retroactive effect. (Sec. 30451, Rev. & Tax. Code)

The BOE has issued a publication to discuss generally the cigarette tax and the cigarette and tobacco products surtax. Topics discussed include registration requirements, out-of-state purchases by consumers, and exempt transactions. (Publication 93, Cigarette and Tobacco Products Tax, California Department of Tax and Fee Administration)

• *Penalties*

There are a variety of civil and criminal penalties prescribed for violations of different parts of the laws governing the California taxes on cigarettes and tobacco products.

Violations of restrictions on delivery sales is a misdemeanor. Each violation is punishable by a $5,000 fine and up to one year in jail. (Sec. 30101.7(e), Rev. & Tax. Code) The attorney general or a city attorney, county counsel, or district attorney may bring a civil action to enforce the delivery sales provisions that may subject a person in violation of the provisions to civil penalties ranging from $1,000-$2,000 for a first violation up to $10,000 for a fifth or subsequent violation within a five-year period. (Sec. 30101.7(g), Rev. & Tax. Code)

The CDTFA may revoke the license of any distributor who does not comply with license and bonding requirements. (Sec. 30148, Rev. & Tax. Code) Any person who engages in the distribution or wholesale sales of cigarettes or tobacco products in California without a license or after the person's license has been canceled, suspended, or revoked is guilty of a misdemeanor. The misdemeanor penalty is extended to each officer of any corporation that engages in business in that manner. (Sec. 30149, Rev. & Tax. Code; Sec. 30159, Rev. & Tax. Code)

Failure to timely pay any amount owing for the purchase of cigarette stamps or meter register setting will subject a distributor to a penalty of 10% of the amount due. (Sec. 30171, Rev. & Tax. Code)

If any part of a deficiency determination by the CDTFA is due to negligence or intentional disregard of rules and regulations related to the taxes, a penalty of 10% of the determination amount is added to the determination. (Sec. 30204, Rev. & Tax. Code) If any part of a deficiency determination by the CDTFA is due to fraud, a 25% penalty is added to the determination. (Sec. 30205, Rev. & Tax. Code)

For persons who become distributors without first obtaining a license, any tax, interest, and interest become immediately due and payable. (Sec. 30210, Rev. & Tax. Code) After ascertaining, as best as it may, the amount of tax due, the CDTFA shall add to the tax due the greater of 25% of the determination amount or $500. In this situation, any person who signs a statement asserting a truth that the signer knows to be false is guilty of a misdemeanor and subject to penalties of up to one year in county jail, a fine of up to $1,000, or both. (Sec. 30211, Rev. & Tax. Code)

If the failure of any person to file a report is due to fraud, a penalty of 25% of the amount due will be added to the amount required to be paid by the person, exclusive of penalties. (Sec. 30224, Rev. & Tax. Code)

Except for taxes determined by the CDTFA either in deficiency determination proceedings or in proceedings where no report was made, any person who fails to timely pay any tax must pay a penalty of 10% of the tax due plus the current underpayment interest rate charged by the CDTFA (see ¶ 89-204). Any distributor who fails to timely file a report is subject to a penalty of 10% of the amount of tax due. The penalties here are limited to 10% of the tax for which the return is required for anyone return. (Sec. 30281, Rev. & Tax. Code)

Misdemeanor violations.—In addition, there are criminal penalties for other specific violations. The violations listed below are misdemeanors and, except for the first item in the list, violators are subject to imprisonment of up to one year either as an alternative to the fine listed or in addition to it. The violations are

— refusal to file any required report; refusal to furnish a supplemental report or other data; refusal to allow an inspection; or rendering of a false or fraudulent report (up to $1,000 fine for each offense); (Sec. 30471, Rev. & Tax. Code)

— any false or fraudulent report ($300-$5,000 fine); (Sec. 30472, Rev. & Tax. Code)

— any counterfeiting of stamps or meter impressions (felony, imprisonment of 2-4 years, fines ranging from $1,000 -$25,000, or both fine and imprisonment); (Sec. 30473, Rev. & Tax. Code)

— buying or selling fewer than 2,000 false, fraudulent, or unaffixed stamps (fine not to exceed $5,000); (Sec. 30473.5, Rev. & Tax. Code)

— buying or selling at least 2,000 false, fraudulent, or unaffixed stamps (fine not to exceed $50,000); (Sec. 30473.5, Rev. & Tax. Code)

— selling of untaxed cigarettes (fine up to $25,000); (Sec. 30474, Rev. & Tax. Code)

— sale of counterfeit cigarettes or tobacco products by a manufacturer, distributor, wholesaler, or retailer (seizure and destruction of product, maximum fines of $5,000 (less than two cartons of cigarettes) or $25,000 (at least two cartons of cigarettes)); (Sec. 30474.1, Rev. & Tax. Code)

— violation of transporter provisions (fine up to $1,000 or, if the violation involves more than 40,000 cigarettes or $5,000 worth of tobacco products, $25,000); (Sec. 30475, Rev. & Tax. Code)

— placement of untaxed cigarettes in a vending machine (fine of up to $1,000); (Sec. 30476, Rev. & Tax. Code)

Felony violations.—Under certain circumstances, any of the misdemeanor violations noted immediately above would become a felony. Specifically, if the violation would be classified as a felony if it was intended to defeat or evade the determination of an amount due and the amount of the violator's tax liability over any 12-month consecutive period aggregated $25,000 or more. In that event, the penalties would be a maximum fine of $20,000, 16 months' imprisonment, or both a fine and imprisonment. (Sec. 30480, Rev. & Tax. Code)

In addition, it is a felony to counterfeit stamps or meter impressions. A violation is punishable by a fine ranging from $1,000-$25,000, imprisonment of 2-4 years, or both fine and imprisonment. (Sec. 30473, Rev. & Tax. Code)

Statute of limitations, costs.—Any prosecution for any of the crimes noted above must be instituted within six years after commission of the offense. (Sec. 30481, Rev. & Tax. Code) A person convicted of a crime may also be charged the costs of the prosecution. (Sec. 30482, Rev. & Tax. Code)

• *Record keeping*

Distributors or wholesalers must maintain and produce for examination, if requested, all records necessary to determine their correct tax liability. Use of electronic data interchange processes and technology and electronic data processing systems is permitted if record detail is equivalent to that contained in acceptable paper records, or the processing system meets the same requirements for a manual accounting system. However, the distributor or wholesaler must retain hardcopy records that are created or received in the ordinary conduct of their business. Penalties or other appropriate administrative action may apply when the distributor or wholesaler fails to maintain and keep complete and accurate records. (Reg. 4026, 18 CCR; Reg. 4901, 18 CCR)

In addition, every distributor, wholesaler, and manufacturer of cigarettes and tobacco products must maintain and make available for examination, on CDTFA request, records maintained in the manner prescribed by Reg. 4901, 18 CCR. If a distributor, wholesaler, or manufacturer is engaged in transporting, storing, or warehousing cigarettes or tobacco products in California, then they must maintain a record of all releases or deliveries from each storage place in the state and a record of the manufacturer's shipments from outside the state to locations within the state. (Reg. 4026, 18 CCR)

• *Assessment and collection*

Except in the case of fraud, intent to evade tax, or failure to make a report or return, every notice of a deficiency determination by the CDTFA must be given within three years after:

— the 25th day of the month following the month for which the amount should have been paid or the report or return was due;

— the report or return was due; or

— or the report or return was filed.

(Sec. 30207, Rev. & Tax. Code)

In the case of failure to file a report or return, the notice of determination must be mailed within eight years after the report or return was due. If a fiduciary of an estate requests a deficiency determination for a deficiency arising during the lifetime of a decedent, a notice of determination must be mailed within four months after the written request is received. (Sec. 30207.1, Rev. & Tax. Code)

If the CDTFA is dissatisfied with the report or return filed by any person, it may compute and determine the amount to be paid upon the basis of any information available to it. One or more deficiency determinations may be made on the amount of tax due for one or for more than one month. (Sec. 30201, Rev. & Tax. Code) Interest will be due from the date on which the tax should have been reported until the date it is paid. (Sec. 30202, Rev. & Tax. Code) In making a determination, the CDTFA may offset overpayments from one or more months against underpayments for other months.

If any person becomes a cigarette or tobacco products distributor without first securing a license, the tax, and applicable penalties and interest, if any, become immediately due and payable on account of all cigarettes or tobacco products distributed. Moreover, all cigarettes or tobacco products manufactured in or transported to California no longer in the possession of the unlicensed distributor are considered to have been distributed. (Sec. 30210, Rev. & Tax. Code) The CDTFA shall determine the amount of the cigarettes or tobacco products distributed and shall further immediately determine the tax due on that amount, adding a penalty of either 25% of the amount of tax or $500, whichever is greater. (Sec. 30211, Rev. & Tax. Code)

Where a person fails to make a report or return for a month or months, the CDTFA must make an estimate of the number of cigarettes or the wholesale cost of the tobacco products. The estimate shall be made based upon any information available to the CDTFA, which shall compute and determine the amount required to be paid. (Sec. 30221, Rev. & Tax. Code)

Jeopardy assessments.—If the CDTFA believes that any amount of tax required to be paid by any person will be jeopardized by delay, it should make a determination of the amount due, which will become immediately due and payable. (Sec. 30241, Rev. & Tax. Code) If that amount, along with any interest and penalties due, is not paid within 10 days after service of the notice of determination and no petition for redetermination is filed, the determination becomes final and delinquency interest and penalties attach. (Sec. 30242, Rev. & Tax. Code) The person may file a petition for redetermination or ask for an administrative hearing. (Sec. 30243, Rev. & Tax. Code; Sec. 30243.5, Rev. & Tax. Code)

• *Audits*

Distributors and wholesalers must maintain and produce for examination upon request all records necessary to determine their tax liability. (Reg. 4026, 18 CCR; Reg. 4901, 18 CCR) In making determinations, the CDTFA may use any information available to it. (Sec. 30201, Rev. & Tax. Code) The CDTFA provides Publication 152 Cigarette and Tobacco Product Inspections, which details what licensees can expect if the CDTFA conducts a routine inspection of their business.

Managed audits.—Taxpayers may voluntarily participate in managed audits of qualifying cigarette and tobacco products tax accounts with the California Department of Tax and Fee Administration. (Sec. 30457, Rev. & Tax. Code, *et seq.*) An account will qualify for managed audits if:

— the taxpayer's business involves few or no statutory exemptions;

— the taxpayer's business involves a single or a small number of clearly defined taxability issues;

— the taxpayer is taxed pursuant to a qualifying tax or fee law at issue and agrees to participate in the program; and

— the taxpayer has the resources to comply with the managed audit instructions provided by the CDTFA.

(Sec. 30457.1, Rev. & Tax. Code)

A taxpayer wishing to participate in the program must examine its books and records to determine if it has any unreported tax liability for the audit period and make available to the CDTFA for verification all computations and books and records examined. (Sec. 30457(a)(2), Rev. & Tax. Code) After the audit is verified by the CDTFA, interest on any unpaid liability will be imposed at 1/2 the rate that would otherwise be imposed during the audit period. (Sec. 30457.4, Rev. & Tax. Code)

• *Appeal procedures*

Any person against whom a determination, other than a jeopardy determination, has been made may petition for a redetermination within 30 days after service of the notice of determination. (Sec. 30261, Rev. & Tax. Code) The written petition must specify the grounds of the petition, and the petitioner may request an oral hearing. (Sec. 30261.5, Rev. & Tax. Code) The order or decision of the CDTFA upon a petition for redetermination becomes final 30 days after notice of it is mailed. (Sec. 30262, Rev. & Tax. Code) All determinations are due and payable when they become final. (Sec. 30264, Rev. & Tax. Code)

[¶60-000]

INTRODUCTION

[¶60-020] Application of Sales and Use Taxes

California sales tax is imposed on every retailer for the privilege of making retail sales of tangible personal property in the state. (Sec. 6051, Rev. & Tax. Code)

California use tax is imposed on the purchase of tangible personal property from any retailer for storage, use, or consumption in California when California sales tax was not paid. (Sec. 6202, Rev. & Tax. Code)

Which transactions are generally subject to sales tax in California?

California sales tax is applied to the gross receipts from the sale at retail of tangible personal property in the state. Sales tax generally does not apply to services. With specific exceptions, leases of tangible personal property in California are treated as "sales."

California sales tax must be collected by every retailer for the privilege of making retail sales of tangible personal property in the state.

COMMENT: The CDTFA provides guidance regarding the applicability of California sales tax to transactions in which products are sold and shipped directly to the purchaser at an out-of-state location for use outside California. Among the topics discussed are special delivery conditions (such as products bound for a foreign country in an airplane, ship, or other conveyance furnished by the purchaser), the documentation of the sale and delivery, and proper completion of sales and use tax returns. (*CDTFA Publication 101, Sales Delivered Outside California*, California Department of Tax and Fee Administration)

COMMENT: The CDTFA provides guidance to consumers regarding sales and use tax. (CDTFA Publication 452, California Buyer's Guide to Tax, California Department of Tax and Fee Administration)

COMMENT: The CDTFA provides guidance regarding sales and use tax laws and regulations as they apply to sales to purchasers from Mexico. Since there is no general exemption for sales to residents of other states or countries, sales in California to purchasers from Mexico are normally subject to tax. However, some sales to Mexican residents may qualify as exempt sales for export or nontaxable sales for resale. The CDTFA publication discusses these sales and explains what taxpayers must do to document their claim that a sale to a Mexican purchaser is an exempt sale for export or a nontaxable sale for resale. (*CDTFA Publication 32, Sales to Purchasers from Mexico*, California Department of Tax and Fee Administration)

Presumption of taxability. It is presumed that all gross receipts are subject to tax until the contrary is established. The burden of proving that a sale of tangible personal property is not a retail sale is upon the person making the sale, unless he or she obtains a certificate from the purchaser indicating that the property is purchased for resale.

Sales at wholesale. While California statutes generally do not refer to "sales at wholesale", these transactions generally are exempt from sales or use tax. A resale certificate taken in good faith from a person that is engaged in the business of selling tangible personal property relieves the seller from the liability for sales tax and the duty to collect use tax.

Counterfeit marks. A "retail sale" or "sale at retail," for California sales and use tax purposes, includes a sale by a convicted seller of tangible personal property with a counterfeit mark, a counterfeit label, or an illicit label on that property, or in connection with that sale, regardless of whether the sale is for resale in the regular course of business. Moreover, "storage" and "use" each include a purchase by a convicted purchaser of tangible personal property with a counterfeit mark, a counterfeit label, or an illicit label on that property, or in connection with that purchase, regardless of whether the purchase is for resale in the regular course of business. (Sec. 6007, Rev. & Tax. Code; Sec. 6009.2, Rev. & Tax. Code)

The definitions of "convicted seller" and "convicted purchaser" include a person convicted of a counterfeiting offense, including, but not limited to, specified counterfeiting-related violations. Also, there is no sale for resale exclusion for tangible personal property sold or purchased with counterfeit or illicit labeling. (Sec. 6007, Rev. & Tax. Code; Sec. 6009.2, Rev. & Tax. Code)

The CDTFA must mail a determination for any unreported tax to a convicted seller or purchaser within one year from the date of the last month of conviction. Any fine imposed or restitution amount awarded as a result of such a conviction must be satisfied before the CDTFA can collect the tax. (Sec. 6007, Rev. & Tax. Code; Sec. 6009.2, Rev. & Tax. Code)

Sales tax definitions.

Place of sale. The "place of sale" or purchase is the location where the property is situated at the time that the sale or purchase occurs.

Purchase. A "purchase" is defined in substantially the same manner as a sale. A purchase is:

— any transfer of title or possession, exchange, or barter of tangible personal property for a consideration;

— a transaction that transfers possession of property, but retains title in the seller for security purposes;

— customer special orders produced, fabricated, or printed for a consideration, and in which title or possession passes; and

— leases of tangible personal property, with certain exceptions (see Leases and Rentals).

Retail sale. "Retail sale" is a sale for any purpose other than resale in the regular course of business in the form of tangible personal property. Anyone that delivers merchandise in California that was sold by an out-of-state merchant is a "retailer", and the delivery is a taxable retail sale.

Retailers. A "retailer" is any seller that makes any retail sale or sales of tangible personal property and any person engaged in the business of making sales for storage, use, or other consumption.

Persons are considered retailers if they make more than two retail sales during any 12-month period.

The term "person" includes individuals or any group or combination acting as a unit.

The following are not considered to be retailers, but are consumers with respect to the materials used or furnished in the performance of their professional services:

— optometrists, physicians and surgeons, pharmacists (with respect to replacement contact lenses), or registered dispensing opticians;

— licensed veterinarians;

— licensed chiropractors; and

— licensed podiatrists.

The CDTFA may treat as retailers the dealers, distributors, supervisors, or employers under whom salespersons, representatives, peddlers, and canvassers operate or from whom they obtain the tangible personal property that they sell, even if the salespersons, etc., are making sales on their own behalf.

Retailers of tangible personal property must:

— obtain a seller's permit for each place of business in the state;

— file returns and pay tax;

— collect use tax, when applicable, and remit the tax with returns; and

— keep records and give resale certificates.

PLANNING NOTE: The CDTFA provides guidance regarding seller's permits, which are generally required of sellers or lessors of merchandise, vehicles, and other tangible personal property in California. (*CDTFA Publication 73, Your California Seller's Permit; CDTFA Publication 74, Closing Out Your Seller's Permit;* and *CDTFA Publication 107, Do You Need a California Seller's Permit?,* California Department of Tax and Fee Administration)

Sale. A "sale" means any transfer of title or possession, exchange, or barter, conditional or otherwise, in any manner or by any means whatsoever, of tangible personal property for a consideration.

A "sale" also includes the following:

— the production, fabrication, processing, printing, or imprinting of tangible personal property for consumers that furnish the materials;

— the furnishing for consideration of tangible personal property by social clubs and fraternal organizations to their members or others;

— the furnishing, preparing, or serving for consideration of food, meals, or drinks (although sales of bona fide food products are exempt);

— a transaction whereby possession is transferred, but the seller retains title for security purposes;

— transfer of title or possession of property that has been produced, fabricated, or printed to the special order of the customer; or

— leases of tangible personal property, with certain exceptions.

Sales price. "Sales price" means the total amount in money for which tangible personal property is sold, leased, or rented, without deduction for the cost of property sold, material used, labor or service, interest, losses, other expenses, or transportation costs. However, transportation costs are excludable if certain conditions are satisfied.

The sales price total includes all receipts, cash, credit, and property of any kind, as well as any amount for which credit is allowed by the seller to the purchaser.

Tangible personal property. "Tangible personal property" is personal property that may be seen, weighed, measured, felt, touched, or that is in any other manner perceptible to the senses. The term excludes telephone and telegraph lines, electrical transmission and distribution lines, and the poles, towers, or conduit by which they are supported or in which they are contained.

Transfer of possession. "Transfer of possession" means only those transactions that the CDTFA finds to be in lieu of transfer of title, exchange, or barter.

Wholesaler. The term "wholesaler" does not include anyone dealing in motor vehicle fuel or diesel fuel in the capacity of an operator of a service station.

Which transactions are generally subject to use tax in California?

California use tax is imposed on the purchase of tangible personal property from any retailer for storage, use, or consumption in California when California sales tax was not paid.

Transactions that are exempt from sales tax or on which sales tax has been paid (except for leases, to which special provisions may apply) are exempt from use tax.

COMMENT: The CDTFA provides information on purchases from out-of-state vendors in *CDTFA Publication 112*. (*CDTFA Publication 112, Purchases from Out-of-State Vendors*, California Department of Tax and Fee Administration)

The CDTFA discusses California use tax, which applies to the use, storage, or other consumption of physical merchandise, including vehicles, in California. Guidance regarding applicability, liability, rates, and payment is provided. (*CDTFA Publication 79-B, California Use Tax* and *CDTFA Publication 110, California Use Tax Basics*, California Department of Tax and Fee Administration)

The CDTFA also provides guidance to California businesses on how to identify use tax due. The CDTFA explains how to examine records to establish the use tax due on purchases of physical merchandise (e.g., supplies, furniture, fixtures, and equipment) from out-of-state sellers. (*CDTFA Publication 123, California Businesses: How to Identify and Report California Use Tax Due*, California Department of Tax and Fee Administration)

Whether use tax applies to transactions involving out-of-state parties implicates federal constitutional and state statutory provisions. For a discussion of these issues, see Nexus–Doing Business in California.

Alternative use tax reporting method. Retailers may request the CDTFA's approval of an alternative use tax reporting method for qualified purchases subject to use tax. The CDTFA has issued guidelines to assist retailers in determining:

— eligibility for the program;

— criteria for CDTFA approval;

— notification requirements;

— termination/cancellation for noncompliance with program requirements; and

— renewal of the CDTFA-approved reporting method.

See Resales, for a discussion on withdrawals from inventory.

¶60-020

Exemption for military personnel. Through January 1, 2019, the storage, use, or other consumption in California of qualified tangible personal property purchased by a qualified service member or a qualified service member's spouse or registered domestic partner while outside California and prior to the report date on official orders transferring the service member to California is exempt from use tax. A "qualified service member" is defined as a member of the Armed Forces of the United States on active duty, a member of reserve components of the Armed Forces of the United States on active duty, or a member of the National Guard on active duty.

"Qualified tangible personal property" is defined as tangible personal property other than a vehicle, vessel, or aircraft.

"Registered domestic partner" is defined as a person that meets certain Family Code requirements and includes a person in a union recognized as a valid domestic partnership, as provided.

Payment of use tax. Purchasers or lessees of property that is subject to use tax must pay the tax to the seller or lessor if the seller or lessor holds a seller's permit or a "Certificate of Registration—Use Tax." If a seller or lessor lacks a qualifying permit or certificate, then the purchaser or lessee is liable for and should make payment to the CDTFA. Purchasers and lessees, as a general rule, are liable for payment of tax to the CDTFA unless a receipt is obtained from the sellers or lessors holding a seller's permit or a Certificate of Registration—Use Tax. (Sec. 6202, Rev. & Tax. Code; Reg. 1685, 18 CCR)

Property delivered to California resident. Property delivered out-of-state to a purchaser that is known by the retailer to be a California resident is presumed to be purchased for storage, use, or other consumption in California. This presumption may be rebutted by a written statement, signed by the purchaser or purchaser's representative, that the property was purchased for out-of-state use.

Property shipped or brought to California. There is a presumption that tangible personal property shipped or brought to California by a purchaser was purchased from a retailer for storage, use, or consumption in California.

Use, storage, or consumption. "Use" is defined as the exercise of any right or power over tangible personal property incident to the ownership of the property, as well as possession of or exercise of any right or power over such property by a lessee under a lease. The term "use" does not include a sale of property in the regular course of business.

"Storage" includes the keeping or retention in California, for any purposes except sale in the regular course of business or subsequent use solely outside California, of property purchased from a retailer.

There is no statutory definition of "consumption" for purposes of California use tax.

Does California follow destination or origin based sourcing for general retail sales?

California generally sources interstate and intrastate retail sales using origin-based sourcing. (Sec. 6010.5, Rev. & Tax. Code; Sec. 6396, Rev. & Tax. Code; Sec. 7205, Rev. & Tax. Code; Sec. 7262, Rev. & Tax. Code; Sec. 7263, Rev. & Tax. Code; Reg. 1620, 18 CCR; Reg. 1802, 18 CCR)

Does California provide any other information concerning the general applicability of sales and use taxes?

Yes. California provides information on various aspects of sales and use tax. In addition, the California Department of Tax and Fee Administration (CDTFA) provides general information for consumers and business people (CDTFA Publication 53-A, Consumer Sales and Use Tax Questions and CDTFA Publication 53-B, Sales and Use Tax Questions for the Business Person) as well as a Taxpayer Educational Consultation Program, under which a CDTFA representative goes to a taxpayer's place of business to: (1) provide a review of business operations, record-keeping, and tax preparation systems; (2) demonstrate methods to correctly file sales and use tax returns; and (3) answer questions about sales and use tax and the CDTFA.

Rates. California imposes a total statewide base sales and use tax rate as well as various local sales and use tax rates.

Due dates. For a discussion of due dates, see Returns, Payments, and Due Dates.

Filing and payment requirements. For a discussion of filing and payment requirements, see Returns, Payments, and Due Dates.

Services. Services are generally not subject to tax.

Tax holidays. California does not provide a tax holiday.

Credits. California provides a credit for taxes paid to another state.

[¶60-025] Nexus--Doing Business in State

Whether an obligation to collect California sales or use tax attaches to a sale by an out-of-seller is determined by a combination of federal and state restrictions. At the federal level, the determination revolves around whether a nexus (or connection) between the sale and California can be established. If there is sufficient nexus, it then must be determined whether the seller qualifies as a "retailer engaged in business" in the state.

What is sales and use tax nexus?

In the state tax area, nexus is an important concern for companies that have a multistate presence because it is a threshold issue that must be evaluated to determine whether a business has tax registration, filing, collection, and remittance obligations in a particular jurisdiction. "Sales and use tax nexus" refers to the amount and type of business activity that must be present before the business is subject to the state's taxing authority.

State tax nexus considerations differ by tax type and jurisdiction, and there has been limited guidance from tax authorities as to when nexus conclusively exists. State nexus statutes are subject to federal constitutional restrictions.

In a series of cases, the U.S. Supreme Court established a general rule of "substantial nexus" which required an out-of-state seller to have a physical presence in a state before that state could require the seller to register and collect and remit sales or use taxes. Physical presence can be created by employees or other agents, property owned or leased in the state, or other factors. There are many gray areas when it comes to determining whether nexus conclusively exists, particularly for ecommerce.

Timeline of Important U.S. Supreme Court Nexus Cases

However, in *South Dakota v. Wayfair, Inc.*, 585 U.S. ___ (2018), the U.S. Supreme Court held that physical presence is no longer required to establish substantial nexus. Rather, economic and virtual contacts in a state and minimum in-state sales thresholds can establish sales and use tax nexus.

PLANNING NOTE: Nexus determinations are based on a taxpayer's specific set of facts. Taxpayers must carefully evaluate whether specific activities or types of contact create/establish nexus in each state in which they do business, as well as how frequently such contacts must occur in order to create tax nexus. A certain combination of business activities or a specific aspect of an activity may result in a different conclusion. To have a complete picture of all tax reporting requirements, multistate businesses should conduct a nexus review. A nexus review helps businesses understand their exposure and avoid audit situations.

South Dakota v. Wayfair. In a 5 to 4 decision, the U.S. Supreme Court held that *Quill Corp. v. North Dakota*, 504 U.S. 298 (1992), and *National Bellas Hess, Inc. v. Department of Revenue of Ill.*, 386 U.S. 753 (1967), are overruled because *Quill's* physical presence rule is unsound and incorrect. As a result, physical presence is no longer required to establish sales and use tax nexus.

The Court held that the *Complete Auto* (*Complete Auto Transit v. Brady*, 430 U.S. 274 (1977)) substantial nexus requirement with the taxing state is satisfied based on both the economic and virtual contacts the respondents have with the state. As a result of this decision, states are now free to levy taxes on sales of goods and services regardless of whether the seller has a physical presence in the state. Due process requirements, unrelated to those required by the "Commerce Clause" of the Constitution still apply, as do other nexus tests of the Commerce Clause. Since the *Wayfair* decision was issued, many states have enacted economic nexus and/or marketplace nexus thresholds. (*South Dakota v. Wayfair, Inc.*, 585 U.S. ___ (2018))

How is nexus established in California?

Every retailer engaged in business in California and making sales of tangible personal property for storage, use, or other consumption in California that are not otherwise exempted, must collect sales or use tax from the purchaser. "Retailer engaged in business in this state" specifically includes but is not limited to any retailer who:

— maintains, occupies, or uses, permanently or temporarily, directly or indirectly, or through a subsidiary, or agent, by whatever name called, an office, place of distribution, sales or sample room or place, warehouse or storage place, or other place of business;

— has any representative, agent, salesperson, canvasser, independent contractor, or solicitor operating in this state under the authority of the retailer or its subsidiary for the purpose of selling, delivering, installing, assembling, or the taking of orders for any tangible personal property; and

— regarding a lease, any retailer who derives rentals from a lease of tangible personal property situated in California;

— in the preceding or current calendar year, has total combined sales of tangible personal property for delivery in California by the retailer, and all persons related to the retailer, that exceed $500,000 (economic nexus).

(Sec. 6203, Rev. & Tax. Code; Reg. 1684, 18 CCR; *Special Notice L-632*, California Department of Tax and Fee Administration, April 2019)

Related persons. For these purposes, and applicable April 1, 2019, a person is related to another person if both persons are related as indicated under the Marketplace Facilitator Act under the sub-heading "Related Persons". (Sec. 6203, Rev. & Tax. Code)

Annual certification. A person may complete *Form CDTFA-232, Annual Certification of No Solicitation*, or any document that satisfies the regulatory requirements, to annually certify under penalty of perjury that the person has not engaged in any prohibited solicitation activities in California at any time during the previous year. An organization may complete the "Additional Statement from Organization" section of *Form CDTFA-232*, or any document that satisfies the regulatory requirements, to annually certify under penalty of perjury that its website includes information directed at its members alerting them to the prohibition against the solicitation activities described above. The BOE recommends taxpayers retain this form or any other document that satisfies the annual certification requirements for a minimum of eight years.

Independent contractors. A retailer is not "engaged in business" in California based solely on its use of a representative or independent contractor in California to perform warranty or repair services on tangible personal property sold by the retailer, provided the ultimate ownership (i.e., stock holder, bond holder, partner, or other person who holds an ownership interest) of the representative or independent contractor and the retailer is not substantially similar.

Out-of-state businesses selling certain items into California. Out-of-state sellers required to register with the CDTFA and collect the use tax may have additional registration and collection requirements if they sell any of the following items into California:

— new tires or motor vehicles and equipment that include new tires;

— covered electronic devices;

— lead-acid batteries; and

— lumber products or engineered wood products.

Retailers located outside California (remote sellers) are required to register with the CDTFA and collect California use tax if, in the preceding or current calendar year, the total combined sales of tangible personal property for delivery in California by the retailer and all persons related to the retailer exceed $500,000. (*Special Notice L-632*, California Department of Tax and Fee Administration, April 2019)

Trade shows. An out-of-state retailer is not engaged in business in California based solely on the physical presence of the retailer or its agents at convention or trade show activities (as described in IRC § 513(d)(3)(A)) for 15 or fewer days in any 12-month period if the retailer did not derive more than $100,000 of net income from those activities in California during the prior calendar year. However, a retailer must collect use tax on any sales of tangible personal property made at those activities and with respect to any sale made pursuant to an order taken at those activities.

Does California have economic nexus?

Yes. California applies economic nexus provisions. (Sec. 6203, Rev. & Tax. Code; *Special Notice L-632*, California Department of Tax and Fee Administration, April 2019)

A "retailer engaged in business in this state" is defined as any retailer:

— that has substantial nexus with California for purposes of the commerce clause of the U.S. Constitution; and

— upon whom federal law permits California to impose a use tax collection duty.

The term specifically includes, but is not limited to, any of the following:

— any retailer maintaining, occupying, or using, permanently or temporarily, directly or indirectly, or through a subsidiary, or agent, by whatever name called, an office, place of distribution, sales or sample room or place, warehouse or storage place, or other place of business;

— any retailer with any representative, agent, salesperson, canvasser, independent contractor, or solicitor operating in California under the authority of the retailer or its subsidiary for the purpose of selling, delivering, installing, assembling, or the taking of orders for any property;

— as respects a lease, any retailer deriving rentals from a lease of property situated in California;

— any retailer that, in the preceding calendar year or the current calendar year, has total combined sales of property for delivery in California by the retailer and all persons related to the retailer that exceed $500,000 (economic nexus).

(Sec. 6203, Rev. & Tax. Code)

For purposes of this section, a person is related to another person if both persons are related as indicated under the Marketplace Facilitator Act under the sub-heading "Related Persons". (Sec. 6203, Rev. & Tax. Code)

Marketplace Facilitator Act. The "Marketplace Facilitator Act" is part of the California Revenue and Taxation Code. A marketplace facilitator is considered the seller and retailer for each sale facilitated through its marketplace. Such a facilitator that meets both of the following requirements is the retailer selling or making the sale of tangible personal property sold through its marketplace:

— the marketplace facilitator is registered or is required to register with the California Department of Tax and Fee Administration (CDTFA); and

— the marketplace facilitator facilitates a retail sale of property by a marketplace seller.

(Sec. 6043, Rev. & Tax. Code; Reg. 1684.5, 18 CCR)

A California sales and use tax regulation implements the Marketplace Facilitator Act. Moreover, the regulation, for marketplace facilitators and marketplace sellers:

• clarifies registration requirements with the California Department of Tax and Fee Administration for a seller's permit or Certificate of Registration—Use Tax; and

• as between marketplace facilitators and marketplace sellers, identifies the retailer responsible for paying sales tax or collecting and remitting use tax on marketplace sales.

(Reg. 1684.5, 18 CCR)

To determine the total combined sales of property for delivery into California:

— a marketplace facilitator must include all sales of property for delivery into California, including sales made on its own behalf and by all related persons and sales facilitated on behalf of marketplace sellers;

— a marketplace seller must include all sales of property for delivery into California, including sales made on its own behalf and sales facilitated through any marketplace facilitator's marketplace.

(Sec. 6044, Rev. & Tax. Code)

A marketplace seller must register with the CDTFA for retail sales made on its own behalf and not facilitated through a registered marketplace facilitator. (Sec. 6045, Rev. & Tax. Code)

California provides guidance regarding the Marketplace Facilitator Act. (*CDTFA Tax Guide for Marketplace Facilitator Act*, California Department of Tax and Fee Administration, August 2019)

Applicable definitions. The following definitions apply to the Marketplace Facilitator Act. (Sec. 6041, Rev. & Tax. Code; Sec. 6041.5, Rev. & Tax. Code; Reg. 1684.5, 18 CCR)

A "marketplace facilitator" is a person who contracts with marketplace sellers to facilitate for consideration, regardless of whether deducted as fees from the transaction, the sale of the marketplace seller's products through a marketplace operated by the person or a related person and who does both of the following:

— directly or indirectly, through one or more related persons, engages in any of the following: (1) transmitting or otherwise communicating the offer or acceptance between the buyer and seller; (2) owning or operating the infrastructure, electronic or physical, or technology that brings buyers and sellers together; (3) providing a virtual currency that buyers are allowed or required to use to purchase products from the seller; or (4) software development or research and development activities related to any of the activities described below, if such activities are directly related to a marketplace operated by the person or a related person; and

— directly or indirectly, through one or more related persons, engages in any of the following activities with respect to the marketplace seller's products: (1) payment processing services; (2) fulfillment or storage services; (3) listing products for sale; (4) setting prices; (5) branding sales as those of the marketplace facilitator; (6) order taking; or (7) providing customer service or accepting or assisting with returns or exchanges.

(Sec. 6041, Rev. & Tax. Code; Reg. 1684.5, 18 CCR)

A "marketplace seller" is a person:

— who has an agreement with a marketplace facilitator; and

— makes retail sales of property through a marketplace owned, operated, or controlled by a marketplace facilitator, even if that person would not have been required to hold a seller's permit or permits, or required to collect the tax, had the sale not been made through that marketplace.

(Sec. 6041, Rev. & Tax. Code; Reg. 1684.5, 18 CCR)

A "marketplace" is a physical or electronic place, including but not limited to a:

— store;

— booth;

— Internet website;

— catalog;

— television or radio broadcast; or

— dedicated sales software application.

(Sec. 6041, Rev. & Tax. Code; Reg. 1684.5, 18 CCR)

On such a marketplace, a seller sells or offers for sale property for delivery in California regardless of whether the property, marketplace seller, or marketplace has a physical presence in California.

A "delivery network company" is a business entity that maintains an Internet website or mobile application used to facilitate delivery services for the sale of local products. (Sec. 6041.5, Rev. & Tax. Code; Reg. 1684.5, 18 CCR)

"Delivery services" are defined as the pickup of one or more local products from a local merchant and delivery of the local products to a customer. The term does not include any delivery requiring over 75 miles of travel from the local merchant to the customer. (Sec. 6041.5, Rev. & Tax. Code; Reg. 1684.5, 18 CCR)

A "local merchant" is a third-party merchant, that is not under common ownership or control with the delivery network company, including but not limited to a:

— kitchen;

— restaurant;

— grocery store;

— retail store;

— convenience store; or

— business of another type.

(Sec. 6041.5, Rev. & Tax. Code; Reg. 1684.5, 18 CCR)

"Local product" means any item, including food, other than freight, mail, or a package to which postage has been affixed. (Sec. 6041.5, Rev. & Tax. Code; Reg. 1684.5, 18 CCR)

Marketplace facilitator relief. Applicable October 1, 2019, a marketplace facilitator who meets both of the following requirements will be relieved of liability for the tax for that retail sale:

— the facilitator demonstrates, to the satisfaction of the CDTFA, that the facilitator made a reasonable effort to get accurate and complete information from an unrelated marketplace seller about a retail sale; and

— the failure to remit the correct amount of tax was due to incorrect or incomplete information provided to the facilitator by the unrelated marketplace seller.

(Sec. 6046, Rev. & Tax. Code)

Where a marketplace facilitator is relieved of liability for the tax on a retail sale, the marketplace seller is the retailer for that retail sale. (Sec. 6046, Rev. & Tax. Code)

A facilitator will be relieved of the tax on retail sales facilitated through its marketplace provided the facilitator demonstrates all of the following to the satisfaction of the CDTFA:

— the retail sales were facilitated for a marketplace seller prior to January 1, 2023, through a marketplace of the marketplace facilitator;

— the marketplace facilitator is not the marketplace seller;

— the marketplace facilitator and the marketplace seller are not related; and

— the failure to collect sales and use tax was due to a good faith error other than an error in sourcing the sale.

(Sec. 6047, Rev. & Tax. Code)

To the extent a marketplace facilitator is relieved of liability in this way, the marketplace seller for whom the facilitator has facilitated the retail sale is also relieved of liability. This is so unless the marketplace seller is the retailer for those retail sales. (Sec. 6047, Rev. & Tax. Code)

Such marketplace facilitator relief will not exceed the following percentage of the total sales and use tax due on sales facilitated by a facilitator for marketplace sellers, which sales do not include sales by the facilitator or persons related to the facilitator:

— for sales facilitated during the fourth quarter of 2019, or during the 2020 calendar year, 7%;

— for sales facilitated during the 2021 calendar year, 5%;

— for sales facilitated during the 2022 calendar year, 3%.

(Sec. 6047, Rev. & Tax. Code)

Newspapers, Internet websites, and other entities. Newspapers, Internet websites, and other entities that advertise property for sale, refer purchasers to the seller by telephone, Internet link, or other similar means to complete the sale, and do not participate further in the sale, are not facilitating a sale, provided such entities:

— do not transmit or otherwise communicate the offer and acceptance for the sale of property between the seller and purchaser; and

— do not process payments directly or indirectly through third parties for the property sold.

(Sec. 6041.1, Rev. & Tax. Code)

Related persons. For purposes of the Marketplace Facilitator Act, a person is related to another person if the persons are:

— members of a family;

— an individual and a corporation more than 50% in value of the outstanding stock of which is owned, directly or indirectly by or for such individual;

— two corporations that are members of the same controlled group;

— a grantor and a fiduciary of any trust;

— a fiduciary of a trust and a fiduciary of another trust, if the same person is a grantor of both trusts;

— a fiduciary of a trust and a beneficiary of such trust;

— a fiduciary of a trust and a beneficiary of another trust, if the same person is a grantor of both trusts;

— a fiduciary of a trust and a corporation more than 50% in value of the outstanding stock of which is owned, directly or indirectly, by or for the trust or by or for a person who is a grantor of the trust;

— a person and an organization to which IRC Sec. 501, relating to certain educational and charitable organizations that are exempt from tax, applies and which is controlled, directly or indirectly, by such person or, if such person is an individual, by members of the family of such individual;

— a corporation and a partnership if the same persons own: (1) more than 50% in value of the outstanding stock of the corporation; and (2) more than 50% of the capital interest or the profits interest in the partnership;

— an S corporation and another S corporation if the same persons own more than 50% in value of the outstanding stock of each corporation;

— an S corporation and a C corporation if the same persons own more than 50% in value of the outstanding stock of each corporation; or

— except in the case of a sale or exchange in satisfaction of a pecuniary bequest, an executor of an estate and a beneficiary of such estate.

(Sec. 6041.2, Rev. & Tax. Code)

A person that is a delivery network company is not a marketplace facilitator.

These provisions are applicable October 1, 2019.

Relief from interest and penalties. The CDTFA may, in its discretion, relieve a retailer engaged in business in this state from certain penalties and interest. In order to do so, the following requirements must all be met:

— the retailer must be registered as a retailer engaged in business;

— the total combined sales from the retailer and all persons related to the retailer, within the preceding 12 months, of property in California or for delivery into California, does not exceed $1 million;

— the retailer was not previously registered or required to be registered;

— the retailer's failure to collect and remit use tax was due to a good faith error and occurred notwithstanding the exercise of ordinary care and the absence of willful neglect;

— the retailer is not a marketplace facilitator; and

— any other factors as deemed necessary by the CDTFA.

(Sec. 6203.1, Rev. & Tax. Code)

The CDTFA may grant relief only for interest or penalties imposed on use tax liabilities due and payable for tax reporting periods beginning April 1, 2019, and ending December 31, 2022. (Sec. 6203.1, Rev. & Tax. Code)

Relief from penalties. A qualifying retailer will be relieved of penalties with respect to sales made from April 1, 2016, to March 31, 2019, inclusive. A "qualifying retailer" is:

— the retailer is not registered or has not registered with the CDTFA prior to December 1, 2018;

— the retailer had not filed sales or use tax returns or made sales or use tax payments prior to being contacted by the CDTFA;

— the retailer voluntarily registers, files completed tax returns for all tax reporting periods for which a determination may be issued, and pays in full the taxes due or applies for an installment agreement, but only if final payment under the terms of that installment payment agreement is paid no later than December 31, 2021; and

— the retailer is or was engaged in business in California solely because the retailer used a marketplace facilitator to facilitate sales for delivery in California and the marketplace facilitator stored the retailer's inventory in California.

(Sec. 6487.07, Rev. & Tax. Code)

Local transactions and use taxes (district taxes). District taxes are the voter-approved sales and use taxes imposed by cities, counties, and other local jurisdictions (districts). These district taxes are added to California's base sales and use tax rate to fund local services. For purposes of local transactions and use taxes imposed, a "retailer engaged in business in the district" also includes any retailer that, in the preceding calendar year or the current calendar year, has total combined sales of property in California or for delivery in California by the retailer and all persons related to the retailer that exceeds $500,000. (Sec. 7262, Rev. & Tax. Code)

For these purposes, a person is related to another person if both persons are related as indicated above under the Marketplace Facilitator Act. (Sec. 7262, Rev. & Tax. Code)

Retailers are required to report and pay any district tax to the CDTFA on their sales and use tax return. (Sec. 6203, Rev. & Tax. Code)

All retailers are required to collect and remit the district use tax on all sales made for delivery in any district that imposes a district tax if, during the preceding or current calendar year the total combined sales of tangible personal property in California or for delivery in California by the retailer and all persons related to the retailer exceed $500,000. (*Special Notice L-684*, California Department of Tax and Fee Administration, July 2019)

If a retailer exceeded the $500,000 district use tax collection sales threshold in calendar year 2018 or during the period from January 1, 2019, through April 24, 2019, then starting on April 25, 2019, that retailer:

• is considered engaged in business in every district imposing a district tax; and

• is required to collect, report, and pay the district use tax to the CDTFA on all sales made for delivery in those districts.

A retailer is not responsible for collecting, reporting, and paying the district use tax to the CDTFA on sales made for delivery in a taxing district prior to April 25, 2019, unless the retailer was otherwise engaged in business in that district. However, if a retailer had already collected district use tax from its customers on sales made prior to April 25, 2019, either at the time of the sale or at a later date, the retailer must report and pay the collected tax amounts to the CDTFA on their sales and use tax return. (*Special Notice L-684*, California Department of Tax and Fee Administration, July 2019)

If a retailer is otherwise engaged in business in a district, the retailer's responsibility to collect and pay the district use tax is not affected by the collection requirement or the change in operative date, and such a retailer should continue to collect, report, and pay the district tax on all sales made for delivery into that district(s). (*Special Notice L-684*, California Department of Tax and Fee Administration, July 2019)

Does California have click-through nexus?

California does not have click-through nexus provisions per se. Although California eliminated its click-through nexus provision (former Sec. 6203(c)(5)) applicable April 1, 2019, it enacted economic nexus provisions. Those provisions state that a retailer engaged in business in this state includes any retailer who, in the preceding or current calendar year, has total combined sales of tangible personal property for delivery in California by the retailer, and all persons related to the retailer, that exceed $500,000 (economic nexus). (Sec. 6203, Rev. & Tax. Code)

Does California have affiliate nexus?

Yes. Applicable April 1, 2019, the term "retailer" includes any retailer that, in the preceding or current calendar year, has total combined sales of tangible personal property for delivery in California, by the retailer and all persons related to the retailer, that exceed $500,000. For purposes of this section, a person is related to another person if the persons are two corporations that are members of the same controlled group. (Sec. 6203, Rev. & Tax. Code)

[¶60-100]

RATES

[¶60-110] Rate of Tax

The total statewide base sales and use tax rate is 7.25%. Tax rates in certain areas are higher than the total statewide base rate depending on applicable district taxes. (Sec. 36(f)(1)(A), Art. XIII, Cal. Const.)

The statewide base sales and use tax rate is comprised of the following components:

— a 3.6875% state (General Fund) tax. (Sec. 6051, Rev. & Tax. Code; Sec. 6201, Rev. & Tax. Code);

— a 0.25% state (General Fund) tax (Sec. 6051.3, Rev. & Tax. Code; Sec. 6201.3, Rev. & Tax. Code);

— a 0.50% state (Local Public Safety Fund) tax imposed under the California Constitution beginning January 1, 1994, to support local criminal justice activities (Sec. 35, Art. XIII, Cal. Const.);

— a 0.50% state (Local Revenue Fund) tax to support local health and social services programs (Sec. 6051.2, Rev. & Tax. Code; Sec. 6201.2, Rev. & Tax. Code);

— a 1.0625% state (Local Revenue Fund) tax (Sec. 6051.15, Rev. & Tax. Code; Sec. 6201.15, Rev. & Tax. Code); and

— a 1.25% local (county/city) tax comprised of 0.25% for county transportation funds and 0.75% for city and county operations. (Sec. 7203.1, Rev. & Tax. Code)

Local (county/city) sales and use taxes are authorized under the Bradley-Burns Uniform Sales and Use Tax Law. Additional transactions (sales) and use taxes are authorized in local taxing jurisdictions.

• *Fuel sales tax rates*

Effective July 1, 2018, through June 30, 2021, the sales and use tax rates for fuels are:

— 2.25% for motor vehicle fuel (gasoline);

— 7.25% for aircraft jet fuel; and

— 13% for diesel fuel.

District taxes are added where applicable. (*Special Notice L-739*, California Department of Tax and Fee Administration, May 2020; *Special Notice L-633*, California Department of Tax and Fee Administration, May 2019; *Special Notice L-541*, California Department of Tax and Fee Administration, June 2018; *Special Notice L-540*, California Department of Tax and Fee Administration, May 2018)

(Sec. 6051.8, Rev. & Tax. Code; Sec. 6201.8, Rev. & Tax. Code; *Special Notice L-500*, California State Board of Equalization, May 2017; *Special Notice L-469*, California State Board of Equalization, December 2016)

The existing additional sales and use tax rate on diesel fuel is 5.75%. (Sec. 6051.8, Rev. & Tax. Code; Sec. 6201.8, Rev. & Tax. Code; *Special Notice L-504*, California Department of Tax and Fee Administration, August 2017)

Aircraft jet fuel.—The sales and use tax rate applicable to aircraft jet fuel is 7.25%. (Sec. 6357, Rev. & Tax. Code; Sec. 6480, Rev. & Tax. Code; Reg. 1598, 18 CCR; *Special Notice L-541*, California Department of Tax and Fee Administration, June 2018; *Special Notice L-540*, California Department of Tax and Fee Administration, May 2018)

Diesel fuel.—The sales and use tax rate applicable to sales of diesel fuel is 5.75% (13% combined with the state rate). (*Special Notice L-541*, California Department of Tax and Fee Administration, June 2018; *Special Notice L-540*, California Department of Tax and Fee Administration, May 2018)

(Sec. 6051.8, Rev. & Tax. Code; Sec. 6201.8, Rev. & Tax. Code; *Special Notice L-500*, California State Board of Equalization, May 2017)

Motor vehicle fuel (gasoline).—The applicable sales and use tax rate imposed on sales of motor vehicle fuel (excluding aviation gasoline) is 2.25%, plus any applicable district taxes. (Sec. 6051.2, Rev. & Tax. Code; Sec. 6051.5, Rev. & Tax. Code; Sec. 6201.2, Rev. & Tax. Code; Sec. 6201.5, Rev. & Tax. Code; *Special Notice L-541*, California Department of Tax and Fee Administration, June 2018; *Special Notice L-540*, California Department of Tax and Fee Administration, May 2018)

See Motor Fuels.

• *Partial state tax exemptions*

The partial state tax exemption rate is 5% for qualified sales and purchases of the following:

— teleproduction or other postproduction service equipment (Reg. 1532, 18 CCR);

— farm equipment and machinery (Reg. 1533.1, 18 CCR);

— timber harvesting equipment and machinery (Reg. 1534, 18 CCR); and

— racehorse breeding stock (Reg. 1535, 18 CCR).

(Sec. 6378, Rev. & Tax. Code; Sec. 6356.5, Rev. & Tax. Code; Sec. 6358.5, Rev. & Tax. Code; *BOE Publication 388, Tax Information Bulletin*, California State Board of Equalization, September 2015)

The partial exemption for diesel fuel used in farming activities or food processing is 6.75%. (Sec. 6357.1, Rev. & Tax. Code; Reg. 1533.2, 18 CCR)

• *Support services*

California sales tax imposed by Article 1 plus the rate imposed by Section 35 of Article XIII of the California Constitution is applicable to support service providers for the privilege of selling support services at retail. The tax is measured by the gross receipts from the sale of those services. See Services. (Sec. 6151, Rev. & Tax. Code)

¶60-110

[¶60-200]

TAXABILITY OF PERSONS AND TRANSACTIONS

[¶60-230] Admissions, Entertainment, and Dues

In general, charges for admission to recreational events are not taxable as sales of tangible personal property, unless such charges are imposed in connection with sale of otherwise taxable property. (Sec. 6006, Rev. & Tax. Code; Sec. 6016, Rev. & Tax. Code)

• *Membership fees*

Sales and use tax generally does not apply to organization membership fees. However, membership fees that exceed the nominal amount (which is adjusted every five years to reflect changes in the California Consumer Price Index) that are related to the anticipated retail sale of tangible personal property are includible in taxable gross receipts when the retailer sells its products only to members. Also, without regard to membership fee amounts, membership fees are taxable when lower prices are charged to individuals who have paid the membership fee as opposed to prices charged to individuals who have not paid the fee. (Sec. 6006, Rev. & Tax. Code; Sec. 6016, Rev. & Tax. Code; Reg. 1584, 18 CCR)

When membership fees related to an anticipated retail sale of tangible personal property are taxable and the memberships are sold by an entity other than the retailer of the tangible personal property, the gross receipts from the sale of the memberships are part of the consideration for the retailer's sale of tangible personal property, and must be included in the taxable measure of the retailer rather than that of the entity that actually sold the membership. (Reg. 1584, 18 CCR)

[¶60-240] Advertising

The following addresses the application of sales and use tax to advertising agencies, sales of advertising space, paid commercial advertising by out-of-state retailers, and advertising materials sold as marketing aids. In view of recent electronic and digital technological innovations affecting the business environment, the relevant Department of Tax and Fee Administration (CDTFA) regulation, as amended, addresses the taxability of the transfer of electronic or digital art to clients or to third parties on a client's behalf, and clarifies whether transactions are taxable transfers of tangible personal property or nontaxable service transactions. (Reg. 1540, 18 CCR)

The CDTFA provides guidance regarding graphic design. (*Publication 37, Graphic Design, Printing, and Publishing*)

• *Agent status*

For tax purposes, advertising agencies acting as agents for clients to acquire tangible personal property are neither purchasers nor sellers of property that they buy and sell. On the other hand, advertising agencies acting on their own behalf when acquiring tangible personal property are purchasers and sellers of property so acquired when delivered to clients or third parties for the benefit of clients. An advertising agency's status as agent and a client's status as principal are rebuttably presumed when an agency acquires tangible personal property on the client's behalf. Sales or use tax is due on an agency's purchase price from the supplier, and an agency may not issue a resale certificate on its purchases as an agent. Agencies are liable for use tax if a resale certificate is issued in error, unless the agency has already paid tax or the client has self-reported the tax. (Reg. 1540, 18 CCR)

Agency charges to clients for reimbursement charged by suppliers, including tax reimbursement, are not subject to tax. Nor does tax apply to agency service charges or to fees directly related to property acquisitions. After agreeing to act as a client's agent, an advertising agency that issues resale certificates to vendors and marks up its cost in billing the client is acting on its own behalf for tax purposes, rather than as the client's agent (see SUTA Series 100, Advertising Agencies, Commercial Artists, and Designers). (Reg. 1540, 18 CCR)

• *Non-agent retailer status*

Agencies may elect non-agent status as retailers and may issue resale certificates to suppliers regarding tangible personal property they sell to clients. A written statement by the agency in the client contract, agreement, or invoice must support the election. (Reg. 1540, 18 CCR)

There is no principal-agent relationship, and agencies are retailers, with respect to property fabricated in-house for sale to clients. Excepting intermediate production aids, printing aids, or artwork and items that become an ingredient or component part of artwork, tax is due on the taxable selling price of property. A resale certificate should be issued for qualified property. (Reg. 1540, 18 CCR)

Agencies engaged in contracts to sell tangible personal property for lump-sum amounts are retailers. Except for artwork, tax applies to the lump-sum selling price of the property. (Reg. 1540, 18 CCR)

• *Taxable transactions*

When charges for nontaxable services are combined with taxable retail charges, selling price tax reporting and recordkeeping must include the cost of:

— direct labor;

— purchased items that become an ingredient or component part of tangible personal property;

— intermediate production or printing aids; and

— a reasonable markup.

(Reg. 1540, 18 CCR)

Specific separately stated charges aside, fees, commissions, and services exclusively related to tangible personal property production or fabrication, such as retouching that improves the quality of photographs or artwork, are taxable as direct labor costs. (Reg. 1540, 18 CCR)

When charges for finished art are combined with nontaxable services, tax may be reported on the prescribed calculated selling price, provided the selling price also includes the value of certain reproduction rights. Under an alternative election, nontaxable services sold along with artwork for a lump-sum are otherwise presumed to constitute 75% of the lump-sum amount. (Reg. 1540, 18 CCR)

Advertising agencies, commercial artists, and designers are regarded as consumers of tangible personal property used in their business operations, and their purchases of such property are subject to tax. (Reg. 1540, 18 CCR)

However, a digital pre-press instruction is a custom computer program, the sale of which is not subject to California sales tax if the pre-press instruction is prepared based on the purchaser's special order. In addition, the sale of a canned or pre-written digital pre-press instruction in tangible form is subject to sales tax. (Reg. 1540, 18 CCR)

¶60-240

Artwork transferred by modem is not a taxable sale of tangible personal property. Likewise, artwork transferred by floppy disk inserted into a customer's computer is not taxable, provided the artist removes and retains the disk without transferring title to, or possession of, the disk to the customer, and without allowing any intervening use of the disk by the customer (see SUTA Series 100, Advertising Agencies, Commercial Artists, and Designers).

• *Nontaxable transactions*

Certain fees, commission, and services imposed by advertising agencies are nontaxable, provided they are separately stated:

— agent fees added to tangible personal property purchases, provided there is a principal-agent relationship between the client and agent;

— media commissions for placement of advertising;

— commissions paid to agencies by suppliers;

— consultation and concept development fees;

— research or account planning;

— quality control supervision;

— assignment or licensing of a copyright interest as part of a technology transfer agreement; and

— separately stated charges for the formulation and writing of copy.

(Reg. 1540, 18 CCR)

For tax purposes, title to intermediate production or printing aids used by commercial artists or designers for in-house property fabrication purposes or to create finished art is presumed to pass to customers before they are actually used. Services rendered to create single copies of blueprints, diagrams, and instructions for signage provided due to environmental graphic design are not taxable. Nor does tax apply to the design, editing, or hosting of electronic websites, provided that tangible personal property is not transferred to the customer. (Reg. 1540, 18 CCR)

A written agreement that assigns or licenses a copyright interest in finished art for the purpose of reproducing and selling other property subject to the copyright interest is a technology transfer agreement, and California sales tax applies to amounts received for any tangible personal property transferred as part of the agreement. However, sales tax does not apply to amounts received for the assignment or licensing of a copyright interest as part of a technology transfer agreement. (Reg. 1540, 18 CCR)

"Finished art" means the final art used for actual reproduction by photomechanical or other processes, or used for display. Separate preliminary art and finished art contracts are not needed to establish "preliminary art" status. However, visualizations and layouts provided without subsequently provided finished art does not qualify as "preliminary art". Also, the title transfer to a client of layouts otherwise qualified as preliminary art renders separately stated charges for such art taxable, even if the layout is not incorporated into finished art. (Reg. 1540, 18 CCR) (SUTA Series 100, Advertising Agencies, Commercial Artists, and Designers)

Unless the client of a commercial artist or designer contractually acquires title to, or permanent possession of, hard copy or electronic media, charges for services that convey ideas, concepts, looks, or messages to the client are nontaxable, provided the charges are separately stated, clearly indicating they are imposed for such services rather than for finished art. However, creative or development services provided by an advertising agency in order to furnish finished art to clients is taxable. Charges for all rights related to finished art that is used for reproduction or display are taxable, including charges for copyrights, distribution and production rights. (Reg. 1540, 18 CCR)

The measure of sales tax on the sale of finished art transferred by an advertising agency or commercial artist as part of a technology transfer agreement is the separately stated sale price if the finished art is a permanent transfer, or the separately stated lease price if the finished art is a temporary transfer. However, if the sale or lease price is not separately stated, the measure of tax is the separate sale price at which the holder of the copyright interest in the finished art has sold or leased the finished art to an unrelated party, and there was no transfer of the copyright interest with the sale or lease, or the finished art was permanently transferred or temporarily leased at a separately stated price in another transaction. (Reg. 1540, 18 CCR)

The measure of tax is 200% of the combined cost of materials and labor used to produce or acquire the finished art if there is no separately stated price satisfying any of the above requirements. The cost of materials is the cost of materials used or incorporated into the finished art, or any tangible personal property transferred as part of the technology transfer agreement. The cost of labor is any charge for labor used to create the tangible personal property that the advertising agency or commercial artist purchased from a third party, or for labor performed by an employee of the agency or artist. (Reg. 1540, 18 CCR)

Charges for licenses, copyrights, or subparts of copyrights to exploit a photograph or finished art are taxable if sold with the photograph or finished art transferred by tangible media, or if sold pursuant to a subsequent contract executed within one year of the original transfer. (Reg. 1540, 18 CCR)

Charges for photo retouching, which ordinarily constitutes a step in the process of preparing photographs or other artwork for reproduction, are taxable unless it can be clearly demonstrated that the retouching is done solely for the purpose of repairing or restoring a photograph to its original condition. (Reg. 1540, 18 CCR)

• *Purchases by advertising agencies, artists, or designers*

Advertising agencies, commercial artists, and designers are consumers of tangible personal property they use for business purposes, and tax applies to their purchases of such property. (Reg. 1540, 18 CCR)

• *Impressed mats purchased by advertisers or advertising agencies*

Advertisers are the consumers of "impressed mats" furnished to newspapers for advertising purposes and must pay tax on their own purchase of such items. If the advertiser acquires the mats through an advertising agency that requires the mats for the advertiser's account, the agency pays tax on its purchase of the mats. If the agency acts as principal in obtaining and furnishing the mats to the advertiser, the agency may present a resale certificate when purchasing them and must collect and report tax on its sale to the advertiser. Impressed mats are paper matrices used in the stereotype production of duplicate printing plates bearing an impression of type or type and cuts (linecuts and halftones). (Reg. 1541(g), 18 CCR) The above definition also applies to parties other than advertisers or agencies.

• *Advertising space*

The definitions of "sale" and of "tangible personal property" do not include the sale of advertising space. In this regard, the sale of advertising space on maps, for example, does not constitute a sale of tangible personal property and is thus not taxable. However, sales of "spec ads" produced advertising space is sold are taxable, even if they are only in sketch form. (See SUTA Series 100, Advertising Agencies, Commercial Artists, and Designers) (Sec. 6006, Rev. & Tax. Code; Sec. 6016, Rev. & Tax. Code)

¶60-240

• *Advertising materials sold as marketing aids*

Tax applies to advertising materials sold as marketing aids to persons who buy such property for use in selling other property to customers. Such a marketing aid is deemed "sold" if at least 50% of the purchase price of the item is obtained from the customer, either through a separate charge or by an increase in the sales price of other merchandise sold with the marketing aid. (Reg. 1670(b), 18 CCR)

Manufacturers or others that provide marketing aids are the consumers of the items when there is a less-than-50% reimbursement; the tax applies to their purchase of the items for distribution, regardless of whether delivered directly to the person that sells their products or to a distributor or wholesaler for redelivery to the ultimate retailer. (Reg. 1670(b), 18 CCR)

• *Printed materials used in direct mail advertising*

California does not impose tax on sales of catalogs, letters, circulars, brochures, and pamphlets that consist of printed sales messages if the advertising material is:

— printed to the purchaser's special order;

— delivered by the seller, the seller's agent, or a mailing house acting as the purchaser's agent, via mail or common carrier; and

— received by any other person who becomes the owner of the material at no cost to the recipient.

(Sec. 6379.5, Rev. & Tax. Code)

However, if an agency is engaged in contract to sell camera-ready are that is incorporated into a printed sales message, tax applies to the agency's total gross receipts from the sale of camera-ready art, including charges for consultation, research, and supervision exclusively related to camera-ready art production. (Sec. 6379.5, Rev. & Tax. Code)

[¶60-250] Agriculture

Various factors determine the sales and use tax treatment of agricultural products. The California Department of Tax and Fee Administration (CDTFA) provides guidance to those in the agricultural industry. (*Publication 66, Agricultural Industry*)

• *Animal life and feed*

Guidance is provided regarding the application of California sales and use taxes to transactions that involve the buying and selling of dogs, cats and other non-food animals. (*Publication 122, Buying and Selling Dogs, Cats, and Other Non-Food Animals*)

California exempts the sale, storage, or use of animals of a kind ordinarily used for human consumption, and the feed for such animals or for animals sold in the purchaser's regular course of business. Cattle, sheep, swine, baby chicks, hatching eggs, fish, bees, ostriches, and emus are normally exempt; however, dogs, cats, horses, minks, and canaries are subject to tax. (Sec. 6358, Rev. & Tax. Code; Reg. 1587(a), 18 CCR)

Food animals that are exempt from California sales and use tax include any form of animal life intended for human consumption and classified in California Department of Food and Agriculture regulations as a dressed carcass of livestock or poultry, or as prepared meat or meat food products or poultry products, under the California Food and Agricultural Code. (Reg. 1587(a), 18 CCR)

Drugs.—Sales of medicines or drugs, including oxygen, administered directly to food animals, and medicines or drugs added to feed or drinking water for food animals or for nonfood animals held for sale in the regular course of business, are exempt from sales and use taxes if the primary purpose is the prevention and control of disease in the animals. (Sec. 6358, Rev. & Tax. Code; Sec. 6358.4, Rev. & Tax. Code; Reg. 1587(c), 18 CCR)

However, oxygen administered to nonfood animals to prevent or control disease is not exempt from sales and use taxes, whether or not such animals are held for sale in the regular course of business. Exempt status applies only to oxygen administered to food animals for qualified purposes, including oxygen injected into ponds or tanks that house or contain aquatic species raised, kept, or used as food for human consumption. (Sec. 6358, Rev. & Tax. Code; Sec. 6358.4, Rev. & Tax. Code; Reg. 1587(c), 18 CCR)

Exemption certificates from feed purchasers.—Sellers of feed must obtain exemption certificates from purchasers if the feed involved may be used for either exempt or nonexempt animals. No certificate is required if feed of any type is sold in small quantities (two standard sacks of grain or less and/or four bales of hay or less). Persons that buy drugs or medicines that are exempt from tax when administered directly to food animals or when mixed with feed or drinking water must supply the seller with an exemption certificate. (Reg. 1587(d), 18 CCR)

Feed.—"Feed," for exemption purposes, includes cod liver oil, salt, bone meal, calcium carbonate, double purpose limestone granulars, and oyster shells, but does not include medicines, sand, charcoal, granite grit, or sulphur. (Reg. 1587(b), 18 CCR)

EXAMPLE: Exempt sales.—Sales of llama are not exempt from tax. Horse feed purchased for breeding stock is exempt, provided that it is consumed by foals that are sold in the regular course of business; such feed is subject to tax if it is consumed by foals used as race horses instead of being sold. Subject to regulatory provisions, rabbit food is exempt from sales and use taxes, whether or not the rabbits are actually used as food for human consumption, because rabbits are animals of a kind ordinarily used for human consumption (see SUTA Series 110, Animal life and feed).

Inspection stamp.—Exempt status applies only to such products that bear the inspected and passed stamp of federal inspection or state inspection applied at the establishment where the animal was slaughtered and at the establishment where the meat or meat food product, or poultry or poultry product was prepared or manufactured. For tax exemption purposes, "poultry" is defined as domesticated fowl and domesticated rabbit intended for use as human food. Tax does not apply to qualified livestock or poultry sales on or after the date that the related food and agricultural regulation becomes effective. (Reg. 1587(a), 18 CCR)

Medicated feed.—California exempts the sale of medicated feed if its primary purpose is the prevention and control of disease in food animals or in nonfood animals that are to be sold in the regular course of business. California also exempts the sale of particular ingredients purchased from different sellers by a purchaser that combines them into a mixture to be fed to such exempt animals if the proportions of ingredients in the mixture make it an exempt medicated feed rather than a drug. (Reg. 1587(b)(2), 18 CCR)

• *Cannabis*

The following taxes are imposed on harvested cannabis:

— a cannabis excise tax on purchasers of cannabis or cannabis products sold in California at the rate of 15% of the average market price of any retail sale by a cannabis retailer; and

— a tax on cultivators of cannabis as follows: (1) $9.65 per dry-weight ounce of cannabis flowers; (2) $2.87 per dry-weight ounce of cannabis leaves; and (3) $1.35 per ounce of fresh cannabis plant.

(Sec. 34011, Rev. & Tax. Code; Sec. 34012, Rev. & Tax. Code; Reg. 3700, 18 CCR; *Special Notice L-720*, California Department of Tax and Fee Administration, November 21, 2019)

Cannabis tax return.—Effective November 9, 2020, the cannabis tax return will move to the CDTFA's online services system. The cannabis tax return revisions begin with the November 2020 reporting period for those who file on a monthly basis, and the fourth quarter 2020 reporting period (October through December) for those who file on a quarterly basis. Medicinal and adult-use cannabis entries are combined into one entry under both the Cannabis Excise Tax and the Cultivation Tax sections of the return. Taxpayers are prompted to provide their Bureau of Cannabis Control (BCC) license number if the CDTFA does not already have it on file. (*Cannabis Special Notice L-765*, California Department of Tax and Fee Administration, July 2020)

Application of sales and use tax.—Sales and use tax applies to retail sales of cannabis and cannabis products, but does not apply to sales of medicinal cannabis and cannabis products where a purchaser provides his/her Medical Marijuana Identification Card issued by the California Department of Public Health and a valid government identification card. (*Special Notice L-519*, California Department of Tax and Fee Administration, November 2017)

See Medical, Dental, and Optical Supplies and Drugs for a discussion of the sales and use tax exemption for medical cannabis.

Gross receipts from the sale of cannabis and cannabis products for purposes of sales and use tax include the excise tax. (*Special Notice L-519*, California Department of Tax and Fee Administration, November 2017)

Cannabis retailers, cultivators, manufacturers, and distributors making sales must register with the CDTFA for a seller's permit to report and pay any sales and use tax due to the CDTFA. If a cannabis business already has a seller's permit that was issued by the California Board of Equalization (BOE), it is not necessary to re-register for a seller's permit with the CDTFA. It is important that a cannabis business timely obtain a valid resale certificate that is accepted in good faith from the purchaser if the business makes sales for resale. (*Special Notice L-519*, California Department of Tax and Fee Administration, November 2017)

Average market price.—When the sale to the retailer is an "arm's length transaction," meaning the consideration received reflects the fair market value between two parties under no requirement to participate in the transaction, the "average market price" is:

• the wholesale cost of the cannabis or cannabis products sold or transferred to the retailer; plus

• a mark-up predetermined by the CDTFA.

(*Special Notice L-519*, California Department of Tax and Fee Administration, November 2017)

In order to collect the excise tax from customers, a retailer should apply the 15% excise tax to the average market price. The average market price can be calculated as either:

- the retailer's gross receipts, which is the retail selling price to the retailer's customer; or

- the retailer's wholesale cost plus a markup predetermined by the California Department of Tax and Fee Administration (CDTFA).

(*Special Notice L-537*, California Department of Tax and Fee Administration, March 2018)

Sales tax is due on the retailer's total gross receipts, which includes the excise tax. When invoicing a customer, a retailer is required to add the following statement on the invoice or receipt: "The excise taxes are included in the total amount of this invoice." (*Special Notice L-537*, California Department of Tax and Fee Administration, March 2018)

Regardless of the method chosen, a retailer must pay the tax collected to a distributor. The payment must be made by the 15th of the month following the date the tax was collected from the customer. Retailers should get a receipt from the licensed distributor that shows the amount of excise tax that was collected and paid. (*Special Notice L-537*, California Department of Tax and Fee Administration, March 2018)

California Cannabis Track-and-Trace.—New sales and use tax Regulation 3702 requires distributors and retailers to enter the following information into the California Cannabis Track-and-Trace (CCTT) system:

- the wholesale cost; and

- the retail selling price of cannabis or cannabis products.

(*Special Notice L-594*, California Department of Tax and Fee Administration, January 2019)

CalCannabis Cultivation Licensing (CalCannabis), a division of the California Department of Food and Agriculture, administers the CCTT system. (*Special Notice L-594*, California Department of Tax and Fee Administration, January 2019)

All commercial cannabis activity must be recorded in the CCTT system. Distributors and retailers that obtain an annual license with the Bureau of Cannabis Control must begin recording commercial cannabis activity in the CCTT system. (*Special Notice L-594*, California Department of Tax and Fee Administration, January 2019)

A distributor is required to enter into the CCTT system the retailer's wholesale cost of the cannabis or cannabis products that is sold or transferred to a retailer in an arm's length transaction. In an arm's length transaction, the distributor is required to calculate the average market price of the cannabis or cannabis products, which is:

- the retailer's wholesale cost; plus

- a mark-up established by the CDTFA.

The wholesale cost used to calculate the average market price is the amount entered into the CCTT system. (*Special Notice L-594*, California Department of Tax and Fee Administration, January 2019)

A cannabis retailer is required to enter into the CCTT system:

- the wholesale cost of the cannabis or cannabis products; and

- the retail selling price of the cannabis or cannabis products when the product is sold at retail.

Effective January 1, 2020, the "wholesale cost" is the amount paid by the cannabis retailer for cannabis or cannabis products, including transportation charges and after any discounts are provided. (*Cannabis Tax Fact*, California Department of Tax and Fee Administration, February 14, 2020)

¶60-250

Cannabidiol products that contain cannabis.—Cannabidiol (CBD) products that contain cannabis are subject to the cannabis excise tax. CBD products that do not contain cannabis are not subject to the cannabis excise tax, even if the CBD product contains trace amounts of tetrahydrocannabinol (THC). (*Cannabis Tax Fact*, California Department of Tax and Fee Administration, April 12, 2018; *Cannabis Tax Fact*, California Department of Tax and Fee Administration, April 16, 2018)

"Cannabis" is defined as all parts of the cannabis sativa L. plant and the term excludes industrial hemp. A "cannabis product" is defined as cannabis that has undergone a process that transforms the cannabis plant material into a concentrate, edible, topical, or other thing that contains cannabis.

In general, CBD products made from industrial hemp are not subject to the cannabis excise tax. The California Department of Food and Agriculture (CDFA) regulates the industrial hemp industry. (*Cannabis Tax Fact*, California Department of Tax and Fee Administration, April 12, 2018; *Cannabis Tax Fact*, California Department of Tax and Fee Administration, April 16, 2018)

Cannabis accessories that do not contain cannabis.—Cannabis accessories are not subject to the California 15% cannabis excise tax. Cannabis accessories include:

- pipes;
- pipe screens;
- vape pens;
- vape pen batteries (without cannabis);
- rolling papers; and
- grinders.

However, retail sales of cannabis accessories are subject to sales tax and must be reported on a retailer's sales and use tax return. (*Cannabis Tax Fact*, California Department of Tax and Fee Administration, April 30, 2018)

Cannabis retailers may purchase cannabis accessories that they plan to sell in their business from their vendor/supplier for resale. A retailer may issue a resale certificate to his or her vendor to buy cannabis accessories or other property the retailer will sell in regular business operations prior to making any use of the product. (*Cannabis Tax Fact*, California Department of Tax and Fee Administration, April 30, 2018)

Cannabis accessories such as vape pen batteries sold in preassembled units may include cannabis. Cannabis distributors who sell these preassembled units with cannabis should separately list the retailer's cost of the cannabis on the distributor's invoice to the retailer in order to properly apply the excise tax to the cannabis only. (*Cannabis Tax Fact*, California Department of Tax and Fee Administration, April 30, 2018)

The Bureau of Cannabis Control (BCC) regulates the activities of distributors and retailers. Taxpayers should contact the BCC to determine if the sale of a specific accessory or item is an allowable activity. (*Cannabis Tax Fact*, California Department of Tax and Fee Administration, April 30, 2018)

The retail sale of cannabis and products containing cannabis are subject to the 15% cannabis excise tax. Unless an exclusion or exemption applies, such transactions are also subject to sales tax. Cannabis products include:

- pre-rolls;
- oils;
- edibles (i.e., cookies, butters, candies, sodas, etc.);
- topicals;

- waxes; and

- balms.

(*Cannabis Tax Fact*, California Department of Tax and Fee Administration, April 30, 2018)

Cannabis cultivation tax.—The cultivation tax applies to all harvested cannabis that enters the commercial market. Cultivators must pay the cultivation tax to:

- the distributor; or

- to the manufacturer if the first transfer or sale of unprocessed cannabis is to a manufacturer.

(*Special Notice L-519*, California Department of Tax and Fee Administration, November 2017)

On or after January 1, 2020, the cultivation tax rates apply to cannabis that a cultivator sells or transfers to a manufacturer or distributor. (*Special Notice L-720*, California Department of Tax and Fee Administration, November 21, 2019)

The CDTFA is prohibited from adjusting for inflation the cannabis cultivation tax rates that are imposed in the 2021 calendar year unless the adjustment is for an inflation rate that is less than zero. Moreover, beginning January 1, 2023, the rates imposed for the previous calendar year must be annually adjusted for inflation by the CDTFA. (Sec. 34010, Rev. & Tax. Code; Sec. 34012, Rev. & Tax. Code)

Manufacturers who collect the cultivation tax are required to pay the tax to the distributor, and the distributor reports and pays the cultivation tax to the CDTFA. (*Special Notice L-519*, California Department of Tax and Fee Administration, November 2017; *News Release 2-18*, California Department of Tax and Fee Administration, January 10, 2018)

Cannabis cultivator guidance.—The CDTFA provides guidance for cultivators regarding the way to determine the tax on whole dry cannabis plants sold to manufacturers. Cannabis cultivators are responsible for the California cultivation tax on all harvested cannabis that enters the commercial market. Cannabis distributors or manufacturers are required to collect the cultivation tax from cannabis cultivators based on the category and weight of the cannabis. (*Cannabis Tax Fact*, California Department of Tax and Fee Administration, April 23, 2018)

Cannabis distributor invoicing and recordkeeping requirements.—Cannabis distributors must properly document the amount of cannabis excise tax collected. (*Special Notice L-530*, California Department of Tax and Fee Administration, January 2018)

Distributors should keep accurate records of their commercial cannabis activity. This includes retaining records to support when the cannabis was transferred or sold to the distributor from a cultivator or manufacturer, or when a distributor sells or transfers to a retailer, and the amount of cultivation tax and excise taxes collected. (*Special Notice L-530*, California Department of Tax and Fee Administration, January 2018)

Cannabis excise tax.—The cannabis excise tax is imposed on purchasers of all cannabis and cannabis products at a rate of 15% of the average market price when purchased at retail. Retailers must collect the cannabis excise tax from purchasers at the time of the retail sale and pay the tax to the distributor. The distributor reports and pays the cannabis excise tax to the CDTFA. (Sec. 34011, Rev. & Tax. Code; Sec. 34012, Rev. & Tax. Code; Sec. 34012.5, Rev. & Tax. Code; *Special Notice L-510*, California Department of Tax and Fee Administration, September 2017; *Special Notice L-519*, California Department of Tax and Fee Administration, November 2017)

The CDTFA is prohibited from increasing the mark-up amount during the period beginning on and after September 18, 2020, and before July 1, 2021. (Sec. 34010, Rev. & Tax. Code; Sec. 34012, Rev. & Tax. Code)

Distributors who sell or transfer cannabis or cannabis products to a cannabis retailer are required to collect the cannabis excise tax from the retailer. Cannabis retailers who acquired cannabis or cannabis products before that date and did not pay the excise tax to a distributor must collect the 15% tax from their customers. Retailers must pay the excise tax on those sales by the 15th of the following month in which they collected the tax to a licensed cannabis distributor with whom they have a business relationship. (*Special Notice L-530*, California Department of Tax and Fee Administration, January 2018)

Cannabis excise tax requirements for microbusinesses and multiple license businesses.—The following are subject to the same California cannabis excise tax collection and reporting requirements as independent or third party distributors:

- a cannabis business licensed as a microbusiness that is authorized to act as a distributor; and

- a cannabis business that holds multiple cannabis licenses to operate as both a distributor and retailer.

This notice provides details for businesses that are both a distributor and retailer of cannabis or cannabis products (i.e., a business) regarding how and when to report the cannabis excise tax. (*Cannabis Tax Fact*, California Department of Tax and Fee Administration, April 12, 2018; *Cannabis Tax Fact*, California Department of Tax and Fee Administration, April 16, 2018)

California explains how microbusinesses and businesses with multiple licenses should calculate the cannabis excise tax on nonarm's length transactions. (*Cannabis Tax Fact*, California Department of Tax and Fee Administration, February 6, 2019)

Distributors or microbusinesses authorized to operate as distributors are required to calculate and collect the 15% cannabis excise tax. The excise tax is collected from cannabis retailers on the sale or transfer of cannabis or cannabis products. The excise tax is based on the average market price of the cannabis. (*Cannabis Tax Fact*, California Department of Tax and Fee Administration, February 6, 2019)

In a nonarm's length transaction, generally when a cannabis retailer is also the distributor:

- the average market price of the cannabis is equal to the gross receipts; and

- the 15% cannabis excise tax is applied to the gross receipts of the retail sale of the cannabis.

(*Cannabis Tax Fact*, California Department of Tax and Fee Administration, February 6, 2019)

Gross receipts include all charges related to the sale of cannabis, such as:

- labor;

- services; and

- certain transportation charges.

(*Cannabis Tax Fact*, California Department of Tax and Fee Administration, February 6, 2019)

For example:

- when a retailer delivers cannabis to customers using the retailer's vehicles; and

- there is no explicit written agreement prior to the delivery that passes title to the purchaser before delivery;

- the charge for that delivery is included in the gross receipts subject to the cannabis excise tax.

A retailer may add a separate amount to customers' invoices or receipts to cover a city cannabis business tax. That amount is then included in the gross receipts subject to the cannabis excise tax. (*Cannabis Tax Fact*, California Department of Tax and Fee Administration, February 6, 2019)

Cannabis pre-rolls.—Cannabis cultivators, including processors, are responsible for paying the cultivation tax when selling or transferring cannabis to distributors or manufacturers based on the weight and category (flowers, leaves, or fresh cannabis plant) of the cannabis. With respect to pre-rolled cannabis, a processor owes the cultivation tax when the processor transfers or sells the pre-rolled cannabis to a distributor. (*Cannabis Tax Fact*, California Department of Tax and Fee Administration, July 2, 2018)

When a cultivator sells or transfers cannabis to a processor for further processing, including making cannabis pre-rolls, the cultivator is not responsible for the cultivation tax at this time. However, documentation such as an invoice or manifest should, in addition to other requirements, indicate the transaction was between a cultivator and a processor and that there was no cultivation tax collected on the transaction. When the processor sells or transfers the cannabis pre-rolls to a distributor, the processor must pay the cultivation tax to the distributor based on the weight and category of the cannabis that was used to make the cannabis pre-rolls. The invoice or manifest between the processor and distributor should indicate the weight and category of the cannabis used to make the cannabis pre-rolls. (*Cannabis Tax Fact*, California Department of Tax and Fee Administration, July 2, 2018)

The distributor that arranges for the required testing and conducts the quality assurance review is responsible for collecting and reporting the cultivation tax based on the weight and category of the cannabis used to make the cannabis pre-rolls. The distributor is required to report and pay the cultivation tax on their cannabis tax return during the reporting period that the cannabis enters the commercial market (that is, passed required testing and quality assurance review). (*Cannabis Tax Fact*, California Department of Tax and Fee Administration, July 2, 2018)

Cannabis retailer collection and invoicing requirements.—Cannabis retailers are not required to separately state the cannabis excise tax on receipts or invoices to customers. They should instead include the following statement: "The cannabis excise taxes are included in the total amount of the invoice." Retailer's sales of cannabis and cannabis products are generally subject to sales tax. The sales tax is due on the retail selling price of cannabis or cannabis products, including the cannabis excise tax. (*Special Notice L-530*, California Department of Tax and Fee Administration, January 2018)

Cultivation tax requirements for microbusinesses and multiple license businesses.—The following are subject to the same requirements as independent/third party distributors for California cannabis cultivation tax purposes:

- a cannabis business licensed as a microbusiness that is authorized to engage in distribution; and

- a cannabis business that holds multiple cannabis license types to operate as a distributor as well as a cultivator and/or manufacturer.

(*Cannabis Tax Fact*, California Department of Tax and Fee Administration, April 9, 2018)

This notice provides guidance on reporting the cultivation tax for those who are distributors that obtain cannabis or cannabis products from a related or affiliated cultivator and/or manufacturer. (*Cannabis Tax Fact*, California Department of Tax and Fee Administration, April 9, 2018)

Determining the retailer's wholesale cost when calculating the average market price.—Cannabis distributors are required to collect the cannabis excise tax from retailers that they supply based on the average market price of the cannabis or cannabis products. In an arm's length transaction, such a cannabis distributor must calculate the average market price by using the retailer's wholesale cost of the cannabis or cannabis products plus a mark-up predetermined by CDTFA. (*Cannabis Tax Fact*, California Department of Tax and Fee Administration, June 27, 2018)

The wholesale cost includes:

- the amount the retailer paid for the cannabis or cannabis products, and

- the transportation charges to the retailer.

(*Cannabis Tax Fact*, California Department of Tax and Fee Administration, June 27, 2018)

Discount or trade allowance.—In addition, a cannabis distributor must add back any discounts or trade allowances given to the retailer. A discount or trade allowance is when there are price reductions, or allowances of any kind, whether stated or unstated. Examples include:

- short-term promotional incentives, such as receiving a discount or allowance for early payment;

- placing a large order; or

- having preferred-customer status.

However, if the selling price is given to all retailers, the amount of the reduction is not considered a discount or trade allowance and may be excluded from the retailer's wholesale cost. (*Cannabis Tax Fact*, California Department of Tax and Fee Administration, June 27, 2018)

A discount or trade allowance is when there are price reductions, or allowances of any kind, whether stated or unstated. Examples include but are not limited to, short-term promotional incentives, such as receiving a discount or allowance for early payment, placing a large order, or having preferred-customer status. Discounts or allowances of this nature must be included in the wholesale cost. If distributors reduce their selling price to all retailers and the price reduction is not a short-term promotional incentive, but a drop in the market price of the cannabis or cannabis product, the amount of the reduction would not be considered a discount or trade allowance required to be added back in when calculating your wholesale cost. (*Tax Guide for Cannabis Businesses*, California Department of Tax and Fee Administration, June 2019)

Donated medicinal cannabis.—Beginning March 1, 2020, cannabis retailers may donate free medicinal cannabis or medicinal cannabis products (medicinal cannabis) to medicinal cannabis patients, or cannabis licensees may donate free medicinal cannabis to cannabis retailers for subsequent donation to medicinal cannabis patients, without payment of certain taxes. The following taxes are not applicable to donated medicinal cannabis:

> — the cultivation tax will not apply to medicinal cannabis when the cultivator designates for donation in the California Cannabis Track-and-Trace system;

> — the cannabis excise tax does not apply when a cannabis retailer donates free medicinal cannabis to a medicinal cannabis patient; and

> — the use tax will not apply when a cannabis retailer donates free medicinal cannabis to a medicinal cannabis patient, or when another licensee, such as a distributor or manufacturer, donates free medicinal cannabis to a retailer for subsequent donation to a medicinal cannabis patient.

(*Special Notice L-729*, California Department of Tax and Fee Administration, January 2020)

See Medical, Dental, and Optical Supplies and Drugs for further information.

Electronic payment requirements temporarily waived.—California temporarily waives the electronic payment requirements for licensed cannabis sellers' payments of:

- the cannabis excise tax;
- the cannabis cultivation tax; and
- sales and use taxes.

(Sec. 6479.3, Rev. & Tax. Code; Sec. 34013, Rev. & Tax. Code)

California will allow payments by other means if the CDTFA finds it necessary to facilitate tax collection. This means sellers will not be subject to penalties for making cash payments of these taxes. The waiver of the electronic payment requirement extends until January 1, 2022.

Generally, any person whose estimated sales and use tax liability averages $10,000 or more per month must remit taxes electronically. A penalty applies if the person remits taxes by other means. California temporarily exempted licensed medical cannabis dispensaries from the requirement. To create equity within the industry, California extends the exemption to licensed adult-use cannabis sellers. (Sec. 6479.3, Rev. & Tax. Code; Sec. 34013, Rev. & Tax. Code)

Also, any person whose estimated liability for certain other taxes averages $20,000 or more per month must remit taxes electronically. A penalty applies if the person remits taxes by other means. Previously, California provided no exception to the requirement. California now provides an exception for persons who must pay or collect cannabis excise and cultivation taxes. (Sec. 6479.3, Rev. & Tax. Code; Sec. 34013, Rev. & Tax. Code)

According to the bill analysis of the legislation that enacted this temporary waiver of electronic payment requirements for licensed cannabis seller payments, since Federal law classifies cannabis as a Schedule 1 drug, most banks do not allow cannabis businesses to open bank accounts. Therefore, most cannabis businesses must operate and pay taxes in cash. The electronic payment exemptions provide incentives for these businesses to pay their California taxes. (*Assembly Floor Analysis*, A.B. 1741, August 10, 2018)

Free medicinal cannabis.—Cannabis retailers are prohibited from giving away any amount of cannabis or cannabis products unless authorized to do so by the Bureau of Cannabis Control (BCC), for California cannabis excise and sales and use tax purposes. The BCC administers cannabis licensing activities for retailers and distributors. If a retailer is authorized to give cannabis or cannabis products away free of charge, the cannabis excise tax does not apply. However, the retailer does owe use tax on the retailer's purchase price of the cannabis or cannabis products. (*Cannabis Tax Fact*, California Department of Tax and Fee Administration, April 26, 2018)

See Medical, Dental, and Optical Supplies and Drugs for further information.

Guidance from CDTFA.—The California Department of Tax and Fee Administration (CDTFA) provides guidance regarding cannabis. (*Publication 557, Tax Help for the Cannabis Industry*, California Department of Tax and Fee Administration, January 2020)

Immature plants, clones, and seeds.—In general, the cultivation tax does not apply to immature plants, clones, and seeds. However, the cannabis excise tax and the sales and use tax do apply to the retail sale of immature plants, clones and seeds. (*Cannabis Tax Fact*, California Department of Tax and Fee Administration, June 25, 2018)

The cultivation tax does not apply to the sale or transfer of immature plants, including clones, or seeds. The cultivation tax is imposed on cultivators for harvested cannabis that enters the commercial market; however, the definition of "enters the commercial market" specifically excludes immature plants and seeds. (*Cannabis Tax Fact*, California Department of Tax and Fee Administration, June 25, 2018)

Immature plants, clones, and seeds are subject to the 15% cannabis excise tax when sold at retail. Nurseries may sell immature plants, clones, or seeds to another cannabis licensee. However, a distributor is required to transport the cannabis from the nursery to the licensee and when the immature plants, clones, or seeds are sold or transported to a retailer, the distributor is also required to collect the 15% cannabis excise tax from the retailer based on the average market price of the immature plants, clones, or seeds. The retailer is responsible for collecting the cannabis excise tax from their retail customers when the immature plants, clones, or seeds are sold at retail. (*Cannabis Tax Fact*, California Department of Tax and Fee Administration, June 25, 2018)

Sales tax applies to the retail sale of immature plants, clones, and seeds, unless otherwise exempt. Sales and use tax does not apply to a cultivator's purchase of immature plants, clones, and seeds when the products grown from them will be resold as part of the cultivator's regular business activities. The seller should obtain and keep a valid and timely resale certificate from the purchaser as support that the sale was for resale. (*Cannabis Tax Fact*, California Department of Tax and Fee Administration, June 25, 2018)

Local government cannabis business taxes.—Some cities have enacted measures requiring that cannabis businesses located in their jurisdictions pay a cannabis business tax. If a separate amount is added to customer invoices or receipts to cover the cannabis business tax, sales tax applies to the business tax amount. Generally, whenever an expense of the retailer is separately added to any taxable sale, the expense is also subject to sales tax. (*Tax Guide for Cannabis Businesses*, California Department of Tax and Fee Administration, June 2019)

Losses due to theft for cannabis taxes and sales and use tax.—Cannabis retailers are required to pay the cannabis excise tax to their distributor based on the average market price of the cannabis or the cannabis products sold or transferred to the retailer. However, if the retailer already paid the cannabis excise tax to the distributor and the associated cannabis or cannabis products were subsequently stolen from the retailer, the retailer can request a refund of the tax from the distributor. The retailer must provide their distributor with documentation substantiating the theft. Examples of documentation include police reports, insurance claims, etc. When a refund is issued to the retailer, the distributor is required to provide the retailer with a receipt that indicates the amount of cannabis excise tax refunded. There is no exemption or deduction of the cannabis excise tax for the loss of proceeds due to theft of cash. (*Cannabis Tax Fact*, California Department of Tax and Fee Administration, July 17, 2020)

Distributors are required to collect the cannabis excise tax from cannabis retailers that the distributor supplies with cannabis or cannabis products. The cannabis excise tax does not apply to cannabis or cannabis products that the distributor sells or transfers to a cannabis retailer that is subsequently stolen from the retailer. When a theft of cannabis or cannabis products from a retailer occurs, and the cannabis excise tax was already paid to the distributor, the retailer can request a refund from the distributor for the cannabis excise tax paid to the distributor. For the distributor's records, and for any claim for refund you the distributor file, the distributor should get documentation from the cannabis retailer that supports the theft. The distributor is required to provide the cannabis retailer with a receipt or similar documentation that indicates the amount of the cannabis excise tax returned to the retailer. (*Cannabis Tax Fact*, California Department of Tax and Fee Administration, July 17, 2020)

The cultivation tax is due on cannabis that enters the commercial market (i.e., it passes the required testing and quality assurance review) even if the cannabis is subsequently lost due to theft. However, the cultivation tax is not due on cannabis stolen before the cannabis entered the commercial market. If a distributor collected the cultivation tax on cannabis that never entered the commercial market, the distributor is required to return the cultivation tax to the originating cultivator. If the cultivation tax cannot be returned to the cultivator, the distributor must report and pay the cultivation tax to the CDTFA. (*Cannabis Tax Fact*, California Department of Tax and Fee Administration, July 17, 2020)

Sales tax must be paid on all taxable sales despite the theft of cash. Losses of merchandise due to theft are not deductible for sales and use tax purposes since no sale occurred. However, since the loss of merchandise from theft may affect the cost of goods sold, documentation should be maintained in case of an audit. (*Cannabis Tax Fact*, California Department of Tax and Fee Administration, July 17, 2020)

Mark-up rate on wholesale cost.—Effective January 1 2020, the wholesale cost is the amount paid by the cannabis retailer (retailer) for cannabis or cannabis products, including transportation charges and after any discounts are provided. In an arm's length transaction, the excise tax is not based on the retailer's gross receipts. When the sale or transaction is not at arm's length, the average market price is the cannabis retailer's gross receipts from the retail sale of the cannabis or cannabis products. (*Cannabis Tax Fact*, California Department of Tax and Fee Administration, February 14, 2020)

The mark-up rate is 80% for the 2020 calendar year. (*Special Notice L-749*, California Department of Tax and Fee Administration, May 2020; *Special Notice L-720*, California Department of Tax and Fee Administration, November 21, 2019)

Registration.—Sellers of cannabis or cannabis products must register with the CDTFA for a seller's permit. Cannabis cultivators, processors, manufacturers, retailers, microbusinesses, and distributors making sales are required to obtain and maintain a seller's permit as a prerequisite for applying for a license with the California Department of Food and Agriculture, the California Department of Consumer Affairs, or the California Department of Public Health. Distributors of cannabis and cannabis products must also register with the CDTFA for a cannabis tax permit to report and pay the two new cannabis taxes to the CDTFA. The cannabis tax permit is in addition to seller's permits. (*Special Notice L-510*, California Department of Tax and Fee Administration, September 2017)

All cannabis businesses making sales are required to register online with the CDTFA for a seller's permit and file sales and use tax returns electronically and pay any sales and use tax to the CDTFA. Even if none of a seller's sales are subject to sales tax, cannabis sellers are still required to file a return and report their activities on their returns to the CDTFA. (*Special Notice L-510*, California Department of Tax and Fee Administration, September 2017)

A cannabis business can register for all the proper tax permits on the CDTFA website at: https://www.cdtfa.ca.gov. From the CDTFA homepage, taxpayers should click on the "Register" link and follow the prompt. When registering business activity, a cannabis business should select box number 3, cannabis business activities. (*Special Notice L-519*, California Department of Tax and Fee Administration, November 2017)

In addition, cannabis distributors must:

— collect the excise tax from retailers they supply;

— collect the cultivation tax from cultivators or manufacturers that send or transfer cannabis and cannabis products to them; and

— file both cannabis tax and sales and use tax returns electronically and pay any tax amounts due to the CDTFA.

(*Special Notice L-510*, California Department of Tax and Fee Administration, September 2017)

Regulations.—Three regulations have been adopted by the CDTFA in regard to cannabis excise and cultivation taxes. (Reg. 3700; Reg. 3701; Reg. 3702)

Regulation 3700:

— creates a new category of "fresh cannabis plant;"

— provides definitions for various terrms;

— reiterates the statutorily set penalties for failing to timely pay the cannabis excise and cultivation taxes;

— sets cultivation tax rates for cannabis flowers, cannabis leaves, and fresh cannabis plants;

— defines when the cultivation tax is collected;

— provides when cannabis is presumed sold; and

— specifies when a distributor is required to report and remit the cannabis excise tax due.

(Reg. 3700, 18 CCR)

Regulation 3701 establishes procedures relating to the collection and remittance of the cannabis excise tax. (Reg. 3701, 18 CCR)

Regulation 3702 specifies the information that must be entered in the California Cannabis Track-and-Trace (CCTT) system by a distributor or cannabis retailer that is required to record commercial cannabis activity in the system. (Reg. 3702)

Reporting and remitting.—Distributors must register with the CDTFA for a cannabis tax permit to report and pay the cultivation tax and cannabis excise tax to the CDTFA. A microbusiness licensee is licensed to act as a distributor, among other things, and must comply with all the same requirements as a distributor. (*Special Notice L-519*, California Department of Tax and Fee Administration, November 2017)

Electronic cannabis returns are now available online. Cannabis distributors must report and pay both the:

- cannabis excise tax collected from retailers to whom they sold or transferred cannabis or cannabis products; and

- cultivation tax which they collected from cultivators and manufacturers.

Cannabis distributors must report both cannabis taxes on the same electronic return. (*Cannabis Tax Fact*, California Department of Tax and Fee Administration, April 5, 2018)

Reporting the cannabis excise tax.—To report the excise tax, the cannabis distributor must enter the average market price of the distributor's sales or transfers of cannabis or cannabis products to a retailer during the reporting period in which the sale or transfer occurred. The total average market price on sales of medicinal cannabis and on sales of adult-use cannabis must be separately entered. The cannabis return will automatically calculate the excise tax due based on the amounts entered. (*Cannabis Tax Fact*, California Department of Tax and Fee Administration, April 5, 2018)

The box on the return that is labeled "Add Excess Excise Tax Collected, if any" is used to report:

- any amount of tax that was collected in excess of the amount of tax that is due and was not returned to the retailer and/or retail purchaser; and

- the cannabis excise tax retailers paid to a cannabis distributor on cannabis or cannabis products that were not purchased from the distributor prior to January 1, 2018, and sold at retail on or after January 1, 2018.

(*Cannabis Tax Fact*, California Department of Tax and Fee Administration, April 5, 2018)

Businesses that are both the distributor and retailer of cannabis or cannabis products must report and pay the cannabis excise tax on all cannabis or cannabis products transferred to the business' retail sales area or activity of the business. The tax is reported on the electronic cannabis tax return during the reporting period that the transfer of the cannabis or cannabis products occurred. The electronic cannabis tax return and payment of the excise tax are due on the last day of the month following the reporting period. (*Cannabis Tax Fact*, California Department of Tax and Fee Administration, April 12, 2018; *Cannabis Tax Fact*, California Department of Tax and Fee Administration, April 16, 2018)

Reporting the cultivation tax.—To report the cultivation tax, a cannabis distributor must enter the category (e.g., flowers, leaves, or fresh cannabis plant) and ounces of cannabis acquired from a cultivator or a manufacturer during the reporting period that the cannabis enters the commercial market (i.e., passes the required testing and quality assurance review). The weight and category for medicinal cannabis and for adult-use cannabis must be entered separately. The cannabis return will automatically calculate the cultivation tax due based on the amounts entered. (*Cannabis Tax Fact*, California Department of Tax and Fee Administration, April 5, 2018)

Distributors are required to report and pay the cultivation tax to the CDTFA during the reporting period that the cannabis or cannabis products passes the required testing and quality assurance review and is considered to have entered the commercial market. The electronic return and payment of the cultivation tax is due the last day of the month following the reporting period. (*Cannabis Tax Fact*, California Department of Tax and Fee Administration, April 9, 2018)

Samples.—Distributors, manufacturers, or cultivators may sell samples or promotional items to cannabis retailers. Whether the cannabis excise tax and the sales and use tax apply depends on whether the samples are sold to the retailer for marketing purposes for the retailer's use, or whether the samples are sold to the retailer for resale to the retailer's customers. (*Cannabis Tax Fact*, California Department of Tax and Fee Administration, June 13, 2018)

If samples are sold to a retailer for marketing purposes (i.e., the retailer does not resell the samples to their customers), the retailer is the consumer of those items. Samples or promotional items not sold for resale should be labeled as "not for resale." Cannabis excise tax applies when cannabis or cannabis products are sold by a cannabis retailer to their retail customer. As a result, a distributor is not required to collect the cannabis excise tax on sales of samples to a cannabis retailer when the retailer is the consumer of the samples and does not resell them. (*Cannabis Tax Fact*, California Department of Tax and Fee Administration, June 13, 2018)

Generally, a seller owes sales tax on sales of samples to cannabis retailers when the retailer is not purchasing them for resale. The sales tax is based on the seller's selling price. However, if the sample or promotional items are sold for less than 50% of cost when the value of the merchandise is not obsolete or about to expire, the seller does not owe sales tax, but instead owes use tax based on the cost of the product sold. (*Cannabis Tax Fact*, California Department of Tax and Fee Administration, June 13, 2018)

Regarding the application of the cannabis excise tax to samples sold for resale to a retailer, the sale to the cannabis retailer is not subject to sales tax. The seller should get and keep a valid and timely resale certificate from the purchaser as support that the sale was for resale. (*Cannabis Tax Fact*, California Department of Tax and Fee Administration, June 13, 2018)

Regarding the application of the cannabis sales and use tax to samples sold for resale to a retailer, the sale to the cannabis retailer is not subject to sales tax. The seller should obtain and keep a valid and timely resale certificate from the purchaser as support that the sale was for resale. (*Cannabis Tax Fact*, California Department of Tax and Fee Administration, June 13, 2018)

Tax collected in excess of amount owed.—A distributor or manufacturer that has collected any amount of tax in excess of the amount of tax imposed by these provisions and actually due from a cultivator or cannabis retailer, can refund that amount to the cultivator or cannabis retailer, even though that tax amount has already been paid over to the CDTFA and no corresponding credit or refund has yet been secured. The distributor or manufacturer may claim credit for that overpayment against the amount of tax imposed that is due upon any other quarterly return, providing that credit is claimed in a return dated no later than three years from the date of overpayment. (Sec. 34012.5, Rev. & Tax. Code)

Any tax collected from a cultivator or cannabis retailer that has not been remitted to the CDTFA is a debt owed to the state of California by the person required to collect and remit the tax. (Sec. 34012.5, Rev. & Tax. Code)

When cultivator supplies cannabis to a related/affiliated manufacturer.—A microbusiness that cultivates and manufactures cannabis, or a related/affiliated cultivator and manufacturer, must calculate the cultivation tax due based on the weight and category of the cannabis that is transferred from the cultivation part of the business to the manufacturing part of the business. (*Cannabis Tax Fact*, California Department of Tax and Fee Administration, April 9, 2018)

When distributing cannabis or cannabis products for a related/affiliated cultivator or manufacturer.—A distributor who distributes cannabis or cannabis products for a related/affiliated cultivator or manufacturer must keep track of the weight and category of the cannabis or cannabis products. If such a distributor is also the distributor who arranges for the required testing and conducts the quality assurance review, then that distributor must:

- report the weight and category of the cannabis or cannabis products entering the commercial market; and

- pay the cultivation tax due to the California Department of Tax and Fee Administration (CDTFA) on the cannabis tax return.

(*Cannabis Tax Fact*, California Department of Tax and Fee Administration, April 9, 2018)

When a distributor supplies cannabis or cannabis products to a related or affiliated retailer.—It is considered a "nonarm's length" transaction when a cannabis business that is both a distributor and a retailer transfers cannabis or cannabis products to the retail portion of that business. In a nonarm's length transaction, the average market price is the gross receipts from the retail sale of the cannabis or cannabis products. Such businesses must calculate the excise tax based on the gross receipts (i.e., all charges related to the sale of the cannabis or cannabis products). (*Cannabis Tax Fact*, California Department of Tax and Fee Administration, April 12, 2018; *Cannabis Tax Fact*, California Department of Tax and Fee Administration, April 16, 2018)

When a manufacturer supplies cannabis products to a related/affiliated distributor.—A manufacturer must keep track of the weight and category of the cannabis used to make a cannabis product. Such manufacturers should provide the weight and category of the cannabis to their related/affiliated distributors. (*Cannabis Tax Fact*, California Department of Tax and Fee Administration, April 9, 2018)

- *Diesel fuel*

California exempts from sales and use tax the gross receipts from the sale, use, or other consumption of diesel fuel used in farming activities and food processing. Farming activities include the transportation and delivery of farm products to the marketplace. The partial sales and use tax exemption applies to all portions of the state sales and use tax rate (see Rate of Tax). The partial exemption does not apply to the sales and use tax component authorized by the Bradley-Burns Uniform Local Sales and Use Tax Law or the Transaction and Use Tax Law. (Sec. 6357.1, Rev. & Tax. Code; Reg. 1533.2, 18 CCR)

Partial exemption certificate.—A qualified person that purchases diesel fuel for use in a qualified activity must provide the retailer with a partial exemption certificate in order for a retailer to claim the partial exemption. The partial exemption certificate may be in the form of a letter or purchase order, or any other document if it contains, along with information identifying the purchaser and the property:

— the signature of the purchaser, purchaser's employee, or purchaser's authorized representative;

— the purchaser's name, address, and telephone number;

— the seller's permit number held by the purchaser; or a sufficient explanation as to why the purchaser is not required to hold a California seller's permit;

— a statement of how much or what percentage of the diesel fuel is purchased for use in a qualified farming or food processing activity;

— a statement that the purchaser is engaged in an agricultural business or is a person that performs an agricultural service for a person engaged in an agricultural business; and

— the date of execution of the document.

(Reg. 1533.2, 18 CCR)

A purchaser is liable for the sales and use tax and related interest if, after timely submitting a copy of a partial exemption certificate to a retailer or to the CDTFA, the purchaser improperly uses the diesel fuel or does not qualify for the partial exemption. (Reg. 1533.2, 18 CCR)

A retailer may issue a resale certificate with respect to the amount of tax otherwise required to be prepaid when purchasing diesel fuel to be used by a consumer in farming activities or food processing. (Sec. 6480.9, Rev. & Tax. Code)

• *Farm equipment and machinery*

California partially exempts from sales and use taxes: farm equipment and machinery, and the parts purchased for use primarily in producing and harvesting agricultural products; and timber harvesting equipment and machinery, and the parts purchased by a qualified person primarily for use in timber harvesting. (Sec. 6356.5, Rev. & Tax. Code; Reg. 1534, 18 CCR)

The partial exemption applies to all portions of the state sales and use tax rate (see Rate of Tax). The partial exemption does not apply to the sales and use tax component authorized by the Bradley-Burns Uniform Local Sales and Use Tax Law or the Transaction and Use Tax Law. (Sec. 6356.5, Rev. & Tax. Code; Reg. 1534, 18 CCR; Reg. 1533.1, 18 CCR)

Partial exemption certificate.—A qualified person that purchases or leases qualified property from a retailer obligated to collect use tax must provide the retailer with a partial exemption certificate in order for a retailer to claim the partial exemption. The partial exemption certificate may be in the form of a letter or purchase order, or any other document if it contains:

— the signature of the purchaser, or the purchaser's employee, or authorized representative;

— the purchaser's name, address, and telephone number;

— the seller's permit number held by the purchaser;

— a statement that the property is purchased to be used primarily, or exclusively as to qualifying vehicles, in producing and harvesting agricultural products;

— a statement that the purchaser is engaged in an agricultural business or is a person that performs an agricultural service for a person engaged in an agricultural business;

— a description of the property purchased; and

— the date that the document was executed.

(Sec. 6356.5, Rev. & Tax. Code; Reg. 1534, 18 CCR; Reg. 1533.1, 18 CCR)

Qualifying for the partial exemption.—Eligible persons who purchase qualifying farm equipment and machinery that is used at least 50% in the production and harvesting of agricultural products may claim the partial exemption. If a taxpayer otherwise qualifies for the farm equipment and machinery partial exemption, the taxpayer's solar power facilities that are tied to the local power grid but are not directly attached to qualifying farm equipment may qualify provided they are designed to generate power for such equipment and machinery. (Reg. 1533.1, 18 CCR; *Special Notice L-330*, California State Board of Equalization, November 2012)

To determine whether a solar power facility is used at least 50% in the production and harvesting of agricultural products, taxpayers are instructed to divide the total annual amount of power consumed by qualifying farm equipment and machinery by the total annual amount of power generated by the solar power facility. For example, a solar facility producing 1000 kilowatts of electricity annually to power qualified agricultural equipment that consumes 600 kilowatts of electricity annually would qualify for the partial exemption (600/1000 = .60, or 60%). (Reg. 1533.1, 18 CCR; *Special Notice L-330*, California State Board of Equalization, November 2012)

Required documentation.—To support a claim that a solar power facility is eligible for the partial tax exemption, taxpayers must document the annual amount of electricity consumed by qualifying farm equipment and machinery for the first 12 months after the solar power facility is operating. Documentation should include data obtained from the meters on qualifying farm equipment. If meter information is not available, an analysis of the electricity demands for qualifying property versus nonqualifying property should be performed. For recordkeeping purposes, taxpayers must retain any supporting documentation for at least four years after the purchase date of the solar power facility. (Reg. 1533.1, 18 CCR; *Special Notice L-330*, California State Board of Equalization, November 2012)

Solar power facilities.—Under certain circumstances, solar power facilities may qualify for the farm equipment and machinery partial exemption from sales and use tax. Sales and leases of farm equipment and machinery, including solar power facilities, that meet certain criteria are partially exempt. The farm equipment and machinery partial exemption applies to the state general fund portion of the sales and use tax rate (see Rate of Tax). According to the BOE, this partial exemption would apply even if the electricity generated first goes to the electrical grid before being used in qualified agricultural activities. (Reg. 1533.1, 18 CCR; *Special Notice L-330*, California State Board of Equalization, November 2012)

A seller of solar power facilities is not liable for the state portion of sales or use tax if they take a partial exemption certificate from a qualified purchaser that states that the property will be used in a qualifying manner. The certificate should be retained by the seller for at least four years. (Reg. 1533.1, 18 CCR)

Timber harvesting equipment and machinery.—If the partial exemption relates to a sale of timber harvesting equipment and machinery, the document must contain:

— the seller's permit number held by the purchaser;

— a statement that the purchaser is engaged in commercial timber harvesting operations, and the property purchased is designed for off-road commercial timber harvesting and will be used primarily in timber harvesting; and

— the date of execution of the document.

(Reg. 1534, 18 CCR)

A purchaser is liable for sales and use taxes and the related interest if, after timely submitting a copy of a partial exemption certificate to a retailer or a partial exemption certificate for use tax to the CDTFA, the purchaser improperly uses or takes delivery of the property or does not qualify for the exemption. (Reg. 1534, 18 CCR)

This exemption also applies to equipment and machinery designed primarily for off-road use in commercial timber harvesting operations, including parts purchased for use primarily in harvesting timber. (Sec. 6356.6, Rev. & Tax. Code)

Vehicles that qualify for partial exemption.—In order for a vehicle to be considered "farm equipment and machinery," it must meet both of the following conditions:

— the vehicle must be designated as an implement of husbandry (i.e., a vehicle used exclusively in the conduct of agricultural operations) by the Department of Motor Vehicles; and

— the vehicle must be used exclusively in agricultural operations by a "qualified person," which generally includes farmers, ranchers, or other persons who produce and harvest agricultural products.

(*Special Notice L-436*, California State Board of Equalization, January 2016)

Examples of implements of husbandry include but are not limited to:

— lift carriers;

— nurse rigs;

— bale wagons;

— farm trailers;

— trap wagons;

— farm tractors;

— row dusters; and

— fertilizer rigs.

(*Special Notice L-436*, California State Board of Equalization, January 2016)

Implements of husbandry also include any vehicle: (1) operated on a highway for the sole purpose of transporting agricultural products; and (2) that is never operated on the highway for a total distance greater than one mile from the point of origin of the trip. (*Special Notice L-436*, California State Board of Equalization, January 2016)

• *Organic and waste products used as fuel*

California exempts organic products grown for fuel, and waste by-products from agricultural or forest production (or from municipal refuse or manufacturing operations; see Manufacturing, Processing, Assembling, or Refining). The products must be delivered in bulk and used as industrial fuel in lieu of oil, natural gas, or coal. (Sec. 6358.1, Rev. & Tax. Code)

See Utilities, for Sales Tax Counsel rulings relating to this provision.

• *Poultry litter*

California exempts the sale or use of wood shavings, sawdust, rice hulls, or other products that are used as litter in poultry and egg production and resold or incorporated into fertilizer products. (Sec. 6358.2, Rev. & Tax. Code)

• *Racehorse breeding stock*

California exempts from sales and use taxes the gross receipts from the sale, use, or other consumption in this state of any racehorse breeding stock. (Sec. 6358.5, Rev. & Tax. Code)

A partial exemption from California sales and use tax applies to sales of, and the storage, use, or other consumption in this state of, racehorse breeding stock purchased by a person solely with the intent and purpose of breeding. The partial exemption applies to all portions of the state sales and use tax rate (see Rate of Tax). The partial exemption, however, does not apply to local taxes authorized under the Bradley-Burns Uniform Local Sales and Use Tax Law or the Transactions and Use Tax Law (Reg. 1535, 18 CCR)

A "racehorse breeding stock" is a live horse that:

— is or will be eligible to participate in a California horseracing contest wherein pari-mutuel wagering is permitted under rules and regulations prescribed by the California Horse Racing Board;

— is capable of producing foals which will be eligible to participate in a California horseracing contest wherein pari-mutuel wagering is permitted under rules and regulations prescribed by the Board; and

— is or was registered with an agency recognized by the Board, unless the agency does not consider the horse eligible for breeding stock.

(Reg. 1535, 18 CCR)

A retailer that paid sales tax on a qualified sale or a person that paid use tax on a qualified purchase and that failed to claim the partial exemption may file a claim for refund equal to the amount of the partial exemption that could have been claimed. (Reg. 1535, 18 CCR)

Partial exemption certificate.—A qualified person who purchases or leases qualified property from a retailer obligated to collect use tax must provide the retailer with a partial exemption certificate in order for a retailer to claim the partial exemption. The partial exemption is allowed only if the retailer claims the exemption on its sales and use tax return for the reporting period during which the transaction giving rise to the partial exemption occurred. The partial exemption certificate may be in the form of a letter or purchase order, or any other document, if, in addition to providing information that identifies the purchaser and the property, it contains:

— the seller's permit number held by the purchaser;

— a statement that the purchaser will use the property solely for the purpose of breeding;

— a statement that the property is capable of reproduction; and

— the date of execution of the document.

(Reg. 1535, 18 CCR)

A purchaser is liable for the sales and use taxes and related interest if, after timely submitting a copy of a partial exemption certificate to a retailer or a partial exemption certificate for use tax to the California Department of Tax and Fee Administration (CDTFA), the purchaser improperly uses or takes delivery of the property or does not qualify for the exemption.

• *Seeds, plants, and fertilizer*

California exempts the sale of seeds and annual plants whose products are ordinarily used for human consumption, and the sale of fertilizer used in producing such products. Sales of all plants whose products are ordinarily used for human consumption are exempt from tax as well. Also exempt are sales of seeds and fertilizers used to grow feed for any form of animal life whose products are normally used for human consumption. The exemption includes sales of both seeds and plants that will produce either (1) a product that ordinarily would constitute food for human consumption, or (2) a product the purchaser will resell, such as flowers. "Fertilizer" for purposes of the exemption, includes commercial fertilizers, agricultural minerals, and manure, and carbon dioxide. "Fertilizer," for purposes of the exemption, does not include soil amendments or auxiliary soil and plant substances. (Sec. 6358, Rev. & Tax. Code; Reg. 1588, 18 CCR)

• *Veterinary medicine*

Licensed veterinarians are consumers of the drugs and medicines that they administer in performing their services; therefore, tax does not apply to a veterinarian's charges to clients for such items. Tax applies to the sale of drugs and medicines to veterinarians and to drugs and medicines that veterinarians sell without performing specific related professional services. However, drugs or medicines purchased by a veterinarian and used primarily for the prevention or control of disease are exempt from tax. (Sec. 6018.1, Rev. & Tax. Code; Reg. 1506(h), 18 CCR)

Veterinarians are consumers of (and must pay tax on) items, other than drugs and medicines, that they either use or furnish to clients without separately stated charges; if such charges to clients are separately stated, then the charges are taxable to the clients. Also taxable are separately stated charges for X-rays if the X-rays are delivered to clients. (Sec. 6018.1, Rev. & Tax. Code; Reg. 1506(h), 18 CCR)

[¶60-260] Alcoholic Beverages

California does not provide a statutory exemption for sales for consumption of wine, beer, and spirituous liquors. The tax on such sales is based on the full amount charged, including any other federal and state taxes. (Reg. 1568, 18 CCR)

The California Department of Tax and Fee Administration (CDTFA) provides guidance regarding sales and use tax laws and regulations as they apply to the dining and beverage industry. (*Publication 22, Dining and Beverage Industry*, California Department of Tax and Fee Administration)

The CDTFA provides information regarding California sales and use tax law as it applies to liquor stores. (*Publication 24, Liquor Stores*, California Department of Tax and Fee Administration)

Federal areas and military installations.—Sellers of alcoholic beverages to persons on federal reservations (e.g., national parks, Native American reservations, etc.) are liable for the sales tax on the selling price except when the sales are made to federal instrumentalities or to persons who purchase for resale. Sales of alcoholic beverages to officers' and noncommissioned officers' clubs and messes on military installations are exempt if the purchasing organizations have been authorized under federal regulations to sell alcoholic beverages to authorized purchasers. (Reg. 1616, 18 CCR)

[¶60-290] Clothing

Generally, there are no special provisions in California law or regulations regarding clothing. There is, however, an exemption for new children's clothing that is sold to a nonprofit organization for its distribution without charge to elementary school children. See ¶60-580 Nonprofit Organizations, Private Schools and Churches.

Diapers.—A sales and use tax exemption is available for diapers designed, manufactured, processed, fabricated, or packaged for use by infants, toddlers, and children. This exemption sunsets on July 1, 2023. (Sec. 6363.9, Rev. & Tax. Code)

[¶60-310] Computers, Software, and Services

In general, computer hardware and canned software are taxable, but custom software and computer services are exempt. (Sec. 6010.9, Rev. & Tax. Code; Sec. 6051, Rev. & Tax. Code; Reg. 1502(g), 18 CCR)

Is computer hardware subject to sales tax in California?

Computer hardware is tangible personal property and, as such, is subject to sales and use tax. (Sec. 6051, Rev. & Tax. Code)

Is computer software subject to sales tax in California?

Canned software is taxable but custom software is exempt. (Sec. 6010.9, Rev. & Tax. Code)

Canned software. California taxes the sale of "canned" computer software, which is software designed and manufactured for general retail sale and not under the specifications or demands of any individual client. (Sec. 6010.9, Rev. & Tax. Code)

Tax applies whether title to the storage media on which the program is recorded, coded, or punched passes to the customer, or the program is recorded, coded, or punched on storage media furnished by the customer. Tax applies to the entire charge made to the customer, including any license or royalty fees. However, tax does not apply to license fees or royalties paid for the right to reproduce or copy a federally copyrighted program, even if a tangible copy of the program is transferred concurrently with the granting of the right. (Reg. 1502, 18 CCR)

In addition, tax does not apply to sales of canned software that are transmitted electronically from the seller's place of business to or through the purchaser's computer as long as the purchaser does not obtain possession of any tangible personal property in the transaction. Sales of canned software also are not taxable if the software is installed by the seller on the customer's computer unless the seller transfers title to or possession of storage media in the transaction or the installation of the program is a part of the sale of the computer. (Reg. 1502, 18 CCR)

Custom software. California exempts sales and leases of computer programs, other than basic operational programs, that are prepared to the customer's special order. (Sec. 6010.9, Rev. & Tax. Code)

A "basic operational program" is a computer program that is fundamental and necessary to the functioning of a computer. (Sec. 995.2, Rev. & Tax. Code)

Transfers of custom software. Transfers of custom programs, or custom programming services performed in connection with the sale or lease of computer equipment, are exempt regardless of whether the charges for the custom program or programming are separately stated. (Sec. 6010.9, Rev. & Tax. Code)

Custom-ordered modifications. Charges for custom-ordered modifications to existing, prewritten programs are exempt, provided that such charges are separately stated. (Sec. 6010.9(d), Rev. & Tax. Code; Reg. 1502(f)(2)(B), 18 CCR)

If the charges are not separately stated, then tax applies to the entire charge made for the modified program unless the modification is so significant that the new program qualifies as a custom program. If the prewritten program was previously marketed, then the new program will qualify as a custom program if the price of the prewritten program was 50% or less of the price of the new program. In the case of a prewritten program that has not previously been marketed, the new program will qualify as a custom program if the charge made to the customer for custom programming services is more than 50% of the contract price to the customer. (Reg. 1502(f)(2)(B), 18 CCR)

Digital pre-press instruction. Tax does not apply to a seller's transfer of original information created by digital pre-press instruction if the original information is a custom computer program. (Reg. 1502, 18 CCR)

The term "digital pre-press instruction" means the creation of original information in electronic form by combining more than one computer program into specific instructions or information necessary to prepare and link files for electronic transmission for output, within the printing industry, to film, plate, or direct to press, which is then transferred on electronic media such as tape or compact disc. (Reg. 1502, 18 CCR)

The process of transferring information known as "digital pre-press instruction" creates a new program that is considered a custom computer program and is not subject to tax if the digital pre-press instruction is prepared to the special order of the customer. However, the digital pre-press instruction is not regarded as a custom computer program if it is a canned or prewritten computer program that is held or exists for general or repeated sale or lease, even if the digital pre-press instruction was initially developed on a custom basis or for in-house use. (Reg. 1502, 18 CCR)

Are computer services taxable?

The taxability of services in California depends on the nature of the transaction involved.

Exempt services. Charges for the performance of the following services are not subject to tax unless the services are performed as a part of the sale of tangible personal property:

— designing and implementing computer systems (e.g. determining equipment and personnel required and the ways in which they will be used);

— designing storage and data retrieval systems (e.g., determining what data communications and high-speed input-output terminals are required);

— consulting services (e.g., the study of all or part of a data processing system);

— feasibility studies (e.g., studies to determine what benefits would be derived if procedures were automated);

— evaluation of bids (e.g., studies to determine which manufacturer's proposal for computer equipment would be most beneficial);

— providing technical help, analysts, and programmers usually on an hourly basis;

— training services;

— equipment maintenance; and

— consultation regarding the use of equipment.

(Reg. 1502, 18 CCR)

The following services are also exempt from tax in California.

Researching and developing original information for a customer is generally not taxable.

Charges for processing customer-furnished information (e.g., sales, data, payroll data, etc.) are generally not taxable.

Time-sharing charges for use of computers in remote facilities are generally not taxable.

Charges for addressing material for mailing when the customer furnishes information are generally not taxable.

Charges for training services are nontaxable except where the services are provided as part of the sale of tangible personal property.

Charges for testing a prewritten program on the purchaser's computer to insure that such a program operates as required are installation charges and are not taxable.

(Reg. 1502, 18 CCR)

Taxable services. Charges for producing, fabricating, processing, printing, imprinting or otherwise physically altering, modifying, or treating consumer-furnished tangible personal property (e.g., cards, tapes, disks, etc.) are generally taxable. (Reg. 1502, 18 CCR)

Transfer of computer-generated output (e.g., artwork, graphics, and designs) is taxable where the true object of the contract is the output and not the services rendered in producing the output.

Tax is applicable to pickup and delivery charges that are made in conjunction with the sale of tangible personal property or the processing of customer-furnished tangible personal property. (Reg. 1502, 18 CCR)

Maintenance contracts. If the purchase of a maintenance contract is optional with the purchaser, and there is a single lump-sum charge for the contract, then 50% of the lump-sum charge for the contract is subject to California sales and use taxes as a taxable sale of tangible personal property. The remaining 50% of the charge constitutes a nontaxable charge for repairs. However, sales and use taxes do not apply to any portion of the charge if there was no transfer of tangible personal property to the purchaser during the period of the maintenance contract. Furthermore, sales and use taxes do not apply to a separately stated charge for consultation services when the purchase of these services is not required as part of the purchase or lease of any tangible personal property, such as a prewritten computer program or a maintenance contract. If the purchase of the maintenance contract is not optional, then the charges for the maintenance contract are taxable, including the charges for any consultation services. (Reg. 1502, 18 CCR)

When a consumer purchases a prewritten program in an electronic download or load-and-leave transaction that does not include the transfer of tangible storage media, and also purchases a separate optional maintenance contract that includes the transfer of a backup copy of the same or similar prewritten program recorded on tangible storage media (which the customer can use to restore lost or corrupted data), then:

— tax does not apply to the charge for the prewritten program itself; and

— tax applies to 50% of the lump-sum charge for the optional maintenance contract.

(Reg. 1502, 18 CCR)

Technology transfer agreements. California sales and use tax applies to amounts received for any tangible personal property transferred in a technology transfer agreement (TTA). In addition, tax applies to all amounts received from the sale or storage, use, or other consumption of property transferred with a patent or copyright interest. Moreover, sales and use tax specifically applies to the sale or storage, use, or other consumption of artwork and commercial photography. (Reg. 1507, CCR)

However, California excludes from the tax base the amount charged for intangible personal property that is transferred with tangible personal property in connection with a technology transfer agreement, provided the agreement separately states a reasonable price for the tangible property. (Sec. 6011(c)(10), Rev. & Tax. Code; Sec. 6012(c)(10), Rev. & Tax. Code)

Definition. A "technology transfer agreement" is defined as a written agreement under which a person holding a patent or copyright interest agreement assigns or licenses to another the right to make and sell a product or to use a process that is subject to the patent or copyright interest. A technology transfer agreement is neither an agreement for the transfer of tangible personal property manufactured pursuant to a technology transfer agreement nor an agreement for the transfer of any property derived, created, manufactured, or otherwise processed by property manufactured pursuant to a transfer technology agreement. (Reg. 1507, CCR)

¶60-310

Non-custom software. Generally, if patent or copyright interests in non-custom software are held, and retail sales of the software are made on tangible media, then a portion of the proceeds from those retail sales may be excluded from the taxpayer's gross receipts subject to sales tax. If non-custom software is purchased on tangible media in a transaction that is subject to use tax from a retailer who holds patent or copyright interests in the software, then a portion of the price paid for the software may be excluded from the sales price of the software that is subject to use tax. (*Software Technology Transfer Agreements*, California State Board of Equalization, October 2012, updated August 2016)

COMMENT: *Tender of software on discs under TTA did not convert it into taxable tangible property.* The assessment of California sales tax on the intangible portions of transactions engaged in by a manufacturer who sells telecommunications equipment to telephone companies, who then use that equipment to provide telephone and Internet services to their customers, was erroneous. The transmission of software using a tape or disc in conjunction with the grant of a license to copy or use that software is not a taxable transaction because the tape or disc is merely a convenient storage medium used to transfer the copyrighted content and is not in itself essential or physically useful to the later use of the intangible personal property. (*Lucent Technologies, Inc. v. State Board of Equalization*, Court of Appeal of California, Second District, No. B257808, October 8, 2015; petition for review denied, California Supreme Court, No. S230657, January 20, 2016)

COMMENT: *Licensed software was exempt under TTA statutes.* Software licensed by the taxpayers was, as a matter of law, exempt from California sales and use tax under statutory technology transfer agreement (TTA) provisions. The taxpayers manufactured and sold switching equipment to their telephone customers that allowed the customers to provide telephone calling and other services to end customers. The switches required software, provided on storage media, in order to operate. The software was provided to the telephone customers pursuant to written agreements. The transfer involved both tangible and intangible personal property. California law provides that intangible personal property transferred with tangible personal property in any TTA is exempt from sales and use taxes provided the agreement separately states a reasonable price for the tangible personal property. A "technology transfer agreement" is statutorily defined as any agreement under which a person who holds a patent or copyright interest assigns or licenses to another person the right to make and sell a product or to use a process that is subject to the patent or copyright interest. (*Lucent Technologies, Inc. v. State Board of Equalization of the State of California*, Superior Court, Los Angeles County (California), No. BC402036, September 27, 2013; affirmed, Court of Appeal of California, Second District, No. B257808, October 8, 2015; petition for review denied, California Supreme Court, No. S230657, January 20, 2016)

Establishing agreement qualifies as TTA. In order to establish that an agreement qualifies as a TTA, the taxpayer must be able to document that the retailer of the non-custom software sold in tangible form held patent or copyright interests in the software, and transferred the patent or copyright interests to the purchaser of the software under the terms of the agreement. The retailer must be able to provide documentation from the United States Patent and Trademark Office documenting that the retailer obtained the patent, or, in the case of a copyright, the retailer must be able to provide a certificate from the U.S Copyright office or other reasonable and satisfactory documentation to establish original ownership or authorship of the copyrighted work. If the retailer obtained the patent or copyright interests from another party, then the retailer must be able to provide written documentation to show that it held the patent or copyright interests at the time of sale. If you are the purchaser of the software seeking a refund, then you will still be required to provide written documentation establishing that the retailer held the patent or copyright interests at the time of the sale. (*Software Technology Transfer Agreements*, California State Board of Equalization, October 2012, updated August 2016)

Amount subject to tax. When tangible personal property is transferred with patent or copyright interests under a TTA, the gross receipts from the sale of the tangible personal property or the sales price of the tangible personal property is:

— the separately stated reasonable price for the tangible personal property stated in the TTA; or

— if there is no separately stated reasonable price in the TTA, then the separately stated reasonable price at which the tangible property or like tangible personal property was previously sold by this retailer or by a third party; or

— if there is no separately stated reasonable price available, then 200% of the cost of the materials and labor used to produce the tangible personal property. (Sec. 6011(c)(10), Rev. & Tax. Code; Sec. 6012(c)(10), Rev. & Tax. Code); *Software Technology Transfer Agreements*, California State Board of Equalization, October 2012, updated August 2016)

The cost of the materials and labor used to produce tangible personal property includes the software development costs of non-custom software imprinted on tangible media. We recognize that establishing the software development costs for each sale of software may be difficult. (*Software Technology Transfer Agreements*, California State Board of Equalization, October 2012, updated August 2016)

Retailers will be required to establish that sales tax has been added to the total amount of the sale price and has not been absorbed by them. (Sec. 6012, Rev. & Tax. Code)

Claim for refund. For those who purchased non-custom software from a California retailer under a TTA and paid sales tax reimbursement to the retailer, they must contact the retailer to apply for a refund of any excess sales tax reimbursement that the retailer may have collected from the purchaser on the purchase of the software. However, if the purchaser paid use tax, as opposed to sales tax, on the purchase and the non-custom software was transferred under a TTA, then the purchaser may file a claim for refund with the CDTFA for any use tax that was overpaid. Such a purchaser will be required to provide documentation that the transaction qualified as a TTA, including that the retailer held the patent and copyright interests at the time the software was purchased, and to support the amount claimed as a refund. If tangible personal property was not sold or received (for example, the software was downloaded electronically from the retailer's website), then the sale or purchase is not subject to sales or use tax and there is no TTA at issue. (*Software Technology Transfer Agreements*, California State Board of Equalization, October 2012, updated August 2016)

Claims for refund based upon software transactions that were similar to the software TTAs in Lucent are ready to be processed provided staff can verify that the claims relate to a software TTA, specifically:

— between an exclusive holder-retailer, such as Lucent, and a licensee, such as the telephone companies involved in Lucent's software TTAs; and

— pursuant to which software was transmitted to the licensee on tangible storage media that was wholly collateral to the licensee's use of the licenses regarding that software, such as the tapes and discs used to transfer Lucent's software.

Also, an exclusive holder-retailer's agreement is similar to the software TTAs in Lucent if the agreement assigns or licenses the right to reproduce or copy non-custom software, subject to the exclusive holder-retailer's copyright or patent interest, that is transmitted on wholly collateral storage media. BOE staff will send a questionnaire to taxpayers that previously filed claims for refunds that may relate to one or more software transactions that are similar to the software TTAs in Lucent to help BOE staff identify claims that are ready to be processed. (*Special Notice L-468*, California State Board of Equalization, August 24, 2016)

Considerations for those who sell non-custom software in tangible form that is transferred under a TTA. Those who sell non-custom software in tangible form that is then transferred under a TTA should:

— Document that the sale of software qualifies as a TTA. There must be a written agreement and the retailer of the software must also be the holder of the patent or copyright interests transferred. Otherwise, the transaction does not qualify as a TTA and the entire sales price of the software is subject to tax.

— Set a selling price for the tangible personal property portion of the transaction that is reasonable pursuant to the statutory provisions. By doing so, the seller will not be required to use the 200% cost mark-up method provided in the statute. (*Software Technology Transfer Agreements*, California State Board of Equalization, October 2012, updated August 2016)

Word-processing. Generally, tax applies to charges for producing multiple copies of documents through the use of word-processing equipment. However, tax does not apply to charges for furnishing original documents or carbon copies made simultaneously with the originals prepared with a typewriter or word- processing equipment, because the true object of such a transaction is the performance of a service and not the furnishing of tangible personal property. In such a situation, the word-processing company is considered the consumer of the property used in providing the service. (Reg. 1502.1, 18 CCR)

In the case of multiple copies, tax applies to the entire charge without deduction for any charges for setting up the machine, keyboarding, or assembling the material. Multiple copies include form letters produced with a slight variation that personalizes essentially the same letter. Charges for providing the additional copies are subject to tax regardless of whether the original was prepared using a typewriter or word-processing equipment and regardless of whether the copies were produced by computers, word processors, copying machines, or other methods. (Reg. 1502.1, 18 CCR)

Tax does not apply to charges made by a word-processing company for keyboarding original names and addresses, setting up and sorting, or for printing the names and addresses onto mailing labels. (Reg. 1502.1, 18 CCR; Reg. 1504(b), 18 CCR)

Tax also does not apply to charges made when a word processor is used to produce copy that was acquired and used exclusively for reproduction purposes. (Sec. 6010.3, Rev. & Tax. Code)

Is cloud computing taxable?

The taxability of cloud computing depends on the category under which the activity is classified. "Cloud computing" is a term used to describe the delivery of computing resources, including software applications, development tools, storage, and servers over the Internet. Rather than purchasing hardware or software, a consumer may purchase access to a cloud computing provider's hardware or software. Cloud computing offerings are generally divided into three categories: software as a service (SaaS), infrastructure as a service (IaaS), and platform as a service (PaaS).

Software as a service. Under the SaaS model, a consumer purchases access to a software application that is owned, operated, and maintained by a SaaS provider. The consumer accesses the application over the Internet. The software is located on a server that is owned or leased by the SaaS provider. The software is not transferred to the customer, and the customer does not have the right to download, copy, or modify the software.

Sales tax authority on SaaS transactions is still evolving. Some states have taken the position that SaaS transactions are a sale of software, reasoning that using software by electronically accessing it is no different than downloading it. Other states have deemed it a service based on the fact that no software is transferred. In some states, the taxability may depend on the specific facts and whether the object of the transaction is the use of software or some other purpose.

Some software providers may use the "Software as a Service" or a similar model in which: (1) customers can access the software on a remote network or location; (2) customers do not receive a copy of the software, electronic or otherwise; and (3) the seller retains possession and control of the software at all times. Under these conditions, tax does not apply to charges for SaaS and similar transactions. In order for there to be a taxable event under California Sales and Use Tax Law, there must be a transfer of tangible personal property. There is normally no transfer of possession or control of tangible personal property when consumers use SaaS. (Sec. 6006, Rev. & Tax. Code; Sec. 6016, Rev. & Tax. Code; Reg. 1502, 18 CCR)

Infrastructure as a service. IaaS providers sell access to storage, networks, equipment, and other computing resources that the provider operates and maintains. A consumer purchases the ability to store data or deploy and run software using the provider's equipment. The consumer does not manage or control the cloud infrastructure but has control over its applications and data.

California does not currently have any provisions regarding IaaS.

Platform as a service. Under the PaaS model, the provider sells access to a platform and software development tools that a consumer uses to create its own applications. A consumer deploys the applications it creates onto the provider's infrastructure. The consumer has control over its deployed applications but does not control the underlying infrastructure.

California does not currently have any provisions regarding PaaS.

Does a sales tax holiday apply to computer items in California?

No, California does not provide a sales tax holiday that applies to computer items.

[¶60-330] Construction

In general, construction materials and supplies are taxable, but the treatment of construction related services varies depending on the nature of the transaction. (Sec. 6006, Rev. & Tax. Code; Reg. 1521, 18 CCR)

Are construction materials and supplies taxable in California?

Yes, in general, construction contractors are consumers of materials they use in performing their contracts, and tax applies to sales to contractors of such items, unless the sales are specifically exempted. Construction contractors are the retailers of fixtures that they provide and install provided that the contract explicitly transfers title to the materials before installation, and separately states the sales price of the materials, exclusive of installation charges. Consequently, they may purchase those items exempt as resales and must collect tax from the ultimate consumer on the selling price. Construction contractors are also the retailers of machinery and equipment they provide in the performance of a construction contract.

Materials, fixtures, machinery, and equipment. Taxable construction contract supplies are classified as:

— materials—i.e., lumber, bricks, etc., which lose their identity on becoming incorporated into the property; or

— fixtures—i.e., furnaces, elevators, etc., which retain their identity after installation; or

— machinery and equipment—i.e., machine tools, drill presses, etc., which are not essential to the fixed works of a structure and are readily removable.

Miscellaneous personal property. In addition to fixtures, machinery, and equipment, miscellaneous personal property sold at retail by contractors is also subject to sales tax. The sale of buildings severed, or to be severed, by the contractor; furniture sold with a building; and of other items, such as parts, supplies, tools, and equipment, are subject to tax.

Supplies and tools for self-use. Contractors must pay sales tax on all purchases of supplies, such as oxygen, acetylene, gasoline, acid, oil, and tools and parts for tools that they use in performing contracts.

Solar cells, panels and modules. Photovoltaic (PV) cells, solar panels, and solar modules, including both solar thermal panels and solar electric PV panels, are considered materials when they function in the same manner as other materials such as roofing, windows, or walls and are incorporated into, attached to, or affixed to real property, and as such, lose their identity by becoming an integral and inseparable part of the real property. Construction contractors are generally the consumers of the materials they use. As consumers, they owe tax on the cost of materials they use in the performance of a construction contract.

> *EXAMPLE:* Examples of these types of solar panels include but are not limited to PV integrated skylights, PV panels used to function as a roof on a parking lot shade structure, and PV integrated roofing tiles. Other materials include wiring, wiring harnesses, strapping, piping, and mounting systems.

Other types of photovoltaic (PV) cells, solar panels, and solar modules, including both solar thermal panels and solar electric PV panels, are considered fixtures when they are accessory to a building or other structure and do not lose their identity as accessories when installed. Construction contractors are the retailers of fixtures that they provide and install. As retailers, they owe tax on the selling price of fixtures they provide and install in the performance of a construction contract.

> *EXAMPLE:* Examples of these types of solar panels include but are not limited to rack mounted solar panels installed on roofs and solar panels used in free-standing solar arrays. Other items included in a solar energy system that are considered fixtures include terminal boxes, DC and AC disconnect boxes, inverters, transformers, batteries and pumps.

Solar power facilities. Construction contractors who furnish and install solar power facilities under a construction contract to improve realty are generally regarded as retailers of fixtures and consumers of materials. Sales and leases of farm equipment and machinery, including solar power facilities, that meet certain criteria are partially exempt from California's sales and use tax. The farm equipment and machinery partial exemption applies to the state general fund portion of the sales and use tax rate. The partial exemption may apply to the sale of the solar power facility if the contractor is regarded as a retailer. If the contractor is regarded as a consumer of materials, the partial exemption does not apply to the contractor's purchases of materials used in the construction of the solar power facility. (*Special Notice L-330,* California State Board of Equalization, November 2012)

How does California tax construction related services?

The treatment of construction related services varies depending on the nature of the transaction.

Buildings and other property affixed to realty. If an agreement for the sale of buildings or other property attached to land includes a provision that the seller will remove the property, the transaction is taxable as a retail sale of personal property. However, if it is understood that the purchaser will sever or remove the property, no tax is due. The transfer of timber to be severed from land is subject to tax without regard to which party severs the timber.

> **Fixtures, draperies, and machinery, and equipment.** If a contract for the sale "in place" of fixtures, draperies, or machinery and equipment affixed to real property includes the removal of the items by either the seller or purchaser, the transaction is taxable. The measure of the tax does not include any value attributed to the physical attachment of the items to real property, even if this value is included in the agreed price. If the agreed price does include this value, the tax should be determined by multiplying the agreed price by the ratio of: (a) the original cost of the affixed items; to (b) the total of that cost plus the cost of attachment.

Construction contracts. Whether sales and use tax applies to construction contracts depends on the type of contract, how contractors purchase materials, fixtures, machinery, and equipment, and how they install such items under contracts to improve real property. Construction contractors are considered to be consumers of materials they use and retailers of fixtures they install. A "construction contract" is any agreement, including one by a subcontractor or specialty contractor, to:

> — erect, construct, alter, or repair real property or such fixed works as waterways or hydroelectric plants;

> — pave surfaces; or

> — furnish and install various accessories on land or in a structure.

¶60-330

However, the sale and installation of machinery, equipment, or other tangible personal property, does not qualify as a construction contract. Moreover, a contract to furnish tangible personal property in connection with a construction project does not constitute a construction contract if the person providing the property is not responsible for its final installation or affixation.

Construction contractor. "Construction contractors" are defined as persons engaged to perform work in various building trades, in conjunction with, by, or through others. Persons organized within or outside California, who are required to hold a license under the California Contractors' State License Law, or who are engaged in contract with the United States to perform construction contracts, qualify as construction contractors.

Local taxes. Construction contractors are subject to local sales and use taxes under the Bradley-Burns Uniform Sales and Use Tax Law. All state sales and use tax laws and regulations affecting construction contractors, except laws and regulations related to tax rates, apply to local taxes. For local tax purposes, the sale of fixtures and use of materials occur at the jobsite, rather than the contractor's place of business.

State-administered local sales tax applies in the county or district in which the fixtures are sold. A local use tax applies to the use of materials unless purchased in a county having a state-administered local tax and not purchased under a resale certificate. If a jobsite is in a county or district that does not have a state-administered local sales tax, local tax is not imposed on the sale of fixtures even though the contractor's principal place of business in a county or district with a local tax.

U.S. government contractors, consumers of both materials and fixtures, are also regarded as doing business at the jobsite; hence, the use of materials and fixtures is a liability of the contractor in the county or district in which the jobsite is located, unless the property was purchased tax-paid in another jurisdiction. If a contractor purchases and pays tax on fixtures in a county or district having a local tax, the contractor, upon installing the fixtures in a county or district without local taxes, may take a credit for the tax paid.

All of the provisions of the state Sales and Use Tax Law and regulations relating to construction contractors, including subcontractors, (other than those relating to the rate of tax) are applicable to state-administered transactions (sales) and use taxes.

Exemption for building materials and supplies used by a nonprofit to construct veterans facility. Applicable on and after January 1, 2019, and before January 1, 2025, building materials and supplies purchased by a qualified person and used in the construction of a qualified facility are exempt from state and local sales and use taxes. (Sec. 6369.7, Rev. & Tax. Code)

Building materials and supplies. "Building materials and supplies" include any machinery, equipment, materials, accessories, appliances, contrivances, furniture, fixtures, and all technical equipment or other tangible personal property that:

- are necessary to construct and equip a qualified facility;
- become part of the completed facility; and
- are transferred to the U.S. Department of Defense or the U.S. Department of Veterans Affairs as a gift.

(Sec. 6369.7, Rev. & Tax. Code)

Qualified person. A "qualified person" is either or both of the following:

- a qualified nonprofit organization; and/or

- a contractor, subcontractor, or builder working under contract with a qualified nonprofit organization to construct a qualified facility.

(Sec. 6369.7, Rev. & Tax. Code)

Qualified facility. A "qualified facility" is either:

- a medical facility, or a temporary residential facility for families of patients receiving care, including either or both inpatient and outpatient care, at a medical facility, located on a U.S. military base located in California; or

- a U.S. Department of Veterans Affairs medical center, or a temporary residential facility for families of patients receiving care at or as part of a U.S. Department of Veterans Affairs medical center, located in California.

(Sec. 6369.7, Rev. & Tax. Code)

Qualified nonprofit organization. A "qualified nonprofit organization" is an organization exempt from taxation under IRC Sec. 501(c)(3) that constructs a qualified facility as a gift to:

- the U.S. Department of Defense; or

- the U.S. Department of Veterans Affairs.

(Sec. 6369.7, Rev. & Tax. Code)

Factory-built housing. Tax applies to only 40% of the price to the consumer of factory-built housing, provided that the property is to be used for residential dwelling purposes or as an institution for resident or patient care. If any other use is made of the factory-built housing, tax applies to the full sales price (or to the remaining 60% if the 40% tax has already been paid). Taxable use of such property bought under a resale certificate occurs when the property is allocated for use in construction; tax should be reported and paid with the return for that period. (Sec. 6012.7, Rev. & Tax. Code; Reg. 1521.4(c), 18 CCR)

Exclusion certificate. To claim the 60% exemption, the retailer must obtain from the purchaser a signed certificate stating that the factory-built housing will be used for residential purposes or as an institution or part thereof for resident or patient care; the regulation contains a model of such a certificate. If the purchaser then uses the property in any other manner, the purchaser becomes liable for tax on the remaining 60% amount. (Sec. 6012.7(d), Rev. & Tax. Code; Reg. 1521.4(d), 18 CCR)

What constitutes factory-built housing. Only particular models or units approved by the California Department of Housing and Community Development or by the local building authority under contract with the Department are considered factory-built housing; the models or units must bear an insignia of approval, issued by the Department, which must be attached at the factory before shipment.

"Factory-built housing" includes:

— a home, or combination of rooms, designed as a dwelling or for patient care, manufactured so that concealed processes of manufacture cannot be inspected at the building site without disassembly of or damage to the component, and designed to be assembled at the site in accordance with applicable building requirements;

— modular housing, designed as a cube or cubes comprising one or more rooms of a residence or of an institution for resident or patient care;

— sectionalized housing, generally consisting of two modules forming a living unit or an institution for resident or patient care; and

— modular, utility, or wet cores, that are rooms or modules comprising a kitchen or a bathroom or bathrooms of a residential building, or of an institution for resident or patient care.

(Sec. 6012.7, Rev. & Tax. Code; Reg. 1521.4(b), 18 CCR)

Factory-built housing does not include mobile homes, pre-cut housing packages when more than 50% of the package is only pre-cut lumber, panelized construction components (such as walls) that do not form a manufacturer's complete housing structure, or porches or awnings that are not purchased as part of a total housing unit. Finally, freestanding appliances (such as stoves, washers, dryers), rugs (excluding wall- to-wall carpets), draperies, furniture, and other furnishings are not factory-built housing. (Sec. 6012.7, Rev. & Tax. Code; Reg. 1521.4(b), 18 CCR)

Factory-built school buildings. Tax applies to only 40% of the sales price to the consumer of factory-built school buildings. "Factory-built school building" means any building designed in compliance with state laws for school construction and approved by the structural safety section of the office of the state architect. In addition, the building must be wholly, or in substantial part, manufactured at an off-site location to be assembled, erected, or installed on a site owned or leased by a school district or a community college district. The place of sale or purchase of a factory-built school building is the retailer's place of business, regardless of whether the sale includes installation of the building or placement upon a permanent foundation. (Sec. 6012.6, Rev. & Tax. Code; Reg. 1521(c), 18 CCR)

For Bradley-Burns uniform local sales and use tax and for transaction (sales) and use tax purposes, the sale or purchase of a factory-built school building occurs at the building retailer's place of business, regardless of whether the sale includes installation or whether the building is placed on a permanent foundation. (Reg. 1802, 18 CCR; Reg. 1822, 18 CCR; Reg. 1806, 18 CCR; Reg. 1826, 18 CCR)

Modular systems furniture. Persons who contract to sell and install modular systems furniture are retailers of the items they sell and install, and tax applies to the entire contract price less those charges excludable from gross receipts or sales price. A contract to sell and install modular systems furniture is a contract for the retail sale of the tangible personal property and not a construction contract, regardless of whether the systems are affixed to realty. Those selling and installing the modular systems may claim 10% of the total contract price, excluding charges attributable to free-standing furniture, as the charge for nontaxable installation labor. A subcontractor who has contracted with the seller to assemble and install a modular system (the system components being provided by a prime contractor or others) or reconfigure an existing system, the allowable 10% deduction is inapplicable to such contracts. Taxpayers should report and separately account for their taxable and nontaxable labor charges. (CDTFA Publication 9, Construction and Building Contractors)

Are labor charges taxable in California?

No. In general, sales and use tax does not apply to itemized charges for repair labor (i.e., work performed on a product to repair or restore it to its intended use), and it also does not apply to charges for installation labor. (Sec. 6006, Rev. & Tax. Code; Sec. 6010, Rev. & Tax. Code; Sec. 6011, Rev. & Tax. Code; Sec. 6012, Rev. & Tax. Code; Reg. 1546, 18 CCR)

What incentives or credits are available for contractors in California?

California offers construction contractors a partial sales and use tax rate for certain jobs when contracted by qualified companies engaged in manufacturing or research and development (R&D). (Sec. 6377.1, Rev. & Tax. Code; Reg. 1525.4, 18 CCR; *Special Notice L-430*, California State Board of Equalization, January 2016)

Manufacturing and R&D partial exemption. The California Department of Tax and Fee Administration (CDTFA) advises construction contractors that they may be able to purchase and/or sell materials and fixtures at a partial sales and use tax rate (3.5625%, plus applicable district taxes, from January 1, 2017 to June 30, 2022) for certain jobs when contracted by qualified companies engaged in manufacturing or research and development (R&D). Certain companies engaged in manufacturing or R&D are allowed to make annual purchases of up to $200 million of qualifying property at a reduced sales and use tax rate. The partial exemption also applies to qualifying property purchased for use in constructing or reconstructing a special purpose building. The CDTFA advises that the law is unusual because qualified companies can authorize the construction contractor to make purchases of materials and fixtures for the special purpose building at a reduced tax rate and pass the tax savings back to the qualified manufacturing or R&D company. (Sec. 6377.1, Rev. & Tax. Code; Reg. 1525.4, 18 CCR; *Special Notice L-430*, California State Board of Equalization, January 2016) For a detailed discussion of this partial exemption, see Manufacturing, Processing, Assembling, or Refining.

Exemption certificates. Contractors are required to get a partial exemption certificate from qualified persons. Construction contractors need to retain records that support their purchases of materials and fixtures at the reduced sales and use tax rate. There are two separate exemption certificates that construction contractors may need:

— CDTFA-230-M, Partial Exemption Certificate for Manufacturing, Research & Development Equipment; and

— CDTFA-230-MC, Construction Contracts—Partial Exemption Certificate for Manufacturing, Research & Development Equipment.

(*Special Notice L-430*, California State Board of Equalization, January 2016)

To make qualifying purchases using the partial exemption, construction contractors must first get a signed exemption certificate CDTFA-230-M from the manufacturing or R&D company that certifies they are a qualified person, and that the special purpose building qualifies for the partial exemption. General contractors who hire subcontractors to furnish materials, fixtures, machinery, or equipment for a qualifying job, must provide the subcontractors with a copy of the CDTFA-230-M partial exemption certificate received from the qualified person, and issue the subcontractor a CDTFA-230-MC. (*Special Notice L-430*, California State Board of Equalization, January 2016)

Once a construction contractor has obtained the CDTFA-230-M from the qualified person, or once a subcontractor has obtained a CDTFA-230-M and CDTFA-230-MC from the general contractor, the contractor may then issue a separate CDTFA-230-MC partial exemption certificate to the contractor's supplier to make qualifying purchases at the reduced sales and use tax rate. (*Special Notice L-430*, California State Board of Equalization, January 2016)

Special purpose buildings and foundations. The special purpose building must be used exclusively for manufacturing, processing, refining, fabricating, or recycling, or as a research or storage facility for these activities in order to qualify for the partial exemption. Buildings such as warehouses used solely to store a product after it has completed the manufacturing process are ineligible for the partial exemption. (*Special Notice L-430*, California State Board of Equalization, January 2016)

What certificate or form must a contractor use to claim an exemption in California?

A seller's permit is required of any construction contractor who makes a retail sale of personal property; a permit is not necessary for any contractor who fulfills an agreement without making a retail transaction.

With a valid seller's permit, a contractor may purchase fixtures and machinery and equipment for resale by giving a resale certificate to the supplier; materials may not be purchased for resale unless the contractor is also in the business of retailing materials. Purchases of tangible personal property to be used on an out-of-state contract are exempt from tax, provided that the contractor holds a seller's permit. The contractor must certify in writing at the time of purchase that the property will be used outside California. A deduction is available with respect to property that is resold, rather than used, by the contractor, provided that the contractor paid tax at the time of purchase.

Exemption certificates. Contractors are required to get a partial exemption certificate from qualified persons in order to claim the partial sales and use tax rate for certain jobs when contracted by qualified companies engaged in manufacturing or research and development (R&D). Construction contractors need to retain records that support their purchases of materials and fixtures at the reduced sales and use tax rate. There are two separate exemption certificates that construction contractors may need:

— CDTFA-230-M, Partial Exemption Certificate for Manufacturing, Research & Development Equipment; and

— CDTFA-230-MC, Construction Contracts—Partial Exemption Certificate for Manufacturing, Research & Development Equipment.

(*Special Notice L-430*, California State Board of Equalization, January 2016)

Does California have special rules concerning subcontractors?

Yes. Generally, subcontractors owe tax on the cost of materials they use and owe tax on either the cost price or selling price of fixtures, machinery, and equipment they furnish and install. Prime contractor's charges to clients for subcontracted improvements to real property are not taxable. The subcontractor is responsible for reporting and paying the tax. If a client pays a subcontractor directly, the subcontractor may bill the prime contractor's client for tax. General contractors may not give their subcontractors a resale certificate for materials or fixtures installed in a construction contract.

Does California have other provisions related to construction?

Yes, the California Department of Tax and Fee Administration (CDTFA) provides guidance, CDTFA Publication 9, Construction and Building Contractors, regarding California sales and use tax law as it applies to construction and building contractors.

Building on Native American land. The application of tax to a particular purchase by a Native American depends on whether ownership of the item being sold or purchased transfers to the Native American purchaser on Native American land. When a non-Native American retailer makes a sale on or off Native American land to a non-Native American customer or a sale to an Native American customer off a reservation, sales or use tax applies unless the sale is otherwise nontaxable. However, a non-Native American retailer's sale of tangible personal property to a Native American is not taxable if the delivery is made to the Native American purchaser on a reservation and title (ownership) transfers to the purchaser on the reservation. For a complete discussion, see Construction Contracts on Indian Land, Guidance and Requirements.

Lumber products assessment. In addition to any other California sales and use taxes, an assessment is imposed on a person who purchases a lumber product or an engineered wood product for storage, use, or other consumption in California, at the rate of 1% of the sales price. The assessment is administered by the California Department of Tax and Fee Administration (CDTFA). For a complete discussion, see *CDTFA Publication 256, Lumber Products and Engineered Wood Products.*

Consumers. Consumers who purchase lumber products and engineered wood products for use in California and do not pay the 1% assessment to a California retailer or purchase these products from outside California for use in California are required to report and pay the assessment directly to the CDTFA.

Construction contractors. Construction contractors may be either consumers or retailers of lumber products or engineered wood products. (*Special Notices L-339 and L-343*, California State Board of Equalization, November 2012; *Special Notice L-340*, California State Board of Equalization, December 2012)

As consumers of lumber products or engineered wood products, construction contractors are required to pay the assessment to their California vendors. In addition, as consumers of lumber products or engineered wood products, construction contractors are required to pay the assessment directly to the CDTFA on purchases made from outside California for use in the state. (*Special Notices L-339 and L-343*, California State Board of Equalization, November 2012; *Special Notice L-340*, California State Board of Equalization, December 2012)

As retailers of lumber products, construction contractors are required to charge and collect the assessment from their customers and report and pay the assessment to the CDTFA on their sales and use tax returns. Moreover, as a retailer of items that a construction contractor manufactures, assembles, processes, or produces from lumber products or engineered wood products (e.g., prefabricated cabinets), no assessment is due on either the contractor's purchase or on the contractor's subsequent sale of these items. (*Special Notices L-339 and L-343*, California State Board of Equalization, November 2012; *Special Notice L-340*, California State Board of Equalization, December 2012)

Definitions. "Engineered wood product" is defined as a building product, including but not limited to veneer-based sheeting material, plywood, laminated veneer lumber (LVL), parallel-laminated veneer (PLV), laminated beams, I-joists, edge-glued material, or composite material such as cellulosic fiberboard, hardboard, decking, particleboard, waferboard, flakeboard, oriented strand board (OSB), or any other panel or composite product where wood is a component part, that is identified in regulations adopted by the board. The definition only includes products that consist of at least 10% wood.

A "lumber product" is defined as a product in which wood or wood fiber is a principal component part, including but not limited to a solid wood product, or an engineered wood product, that is identified in regulations adopted by the board. The definition does not include furniture, paper products, indoor flooring products such as hardwood or laminated flooring, bark or cork products, firewood, or other products not typically regarded as lumber products.

Products subject to the assessment. In general, lumber products and engineered wood products subject to the assessment are primary wood products produced directly from forest trees in which wood is a principal component (at least 10% of total content). However, wood products that have been manufactured, assembled, processed, or produced from primary wood products are not subject to the assessment. These include secondary wood products, where additional labor has added significant value to the product. Products that are subject to the 1% assessment include:

— lumber;

— plywood particle board;

— fiberboard;

— poles;

— posts;

— structural panels;

— decking;

— railings;

— fencing (poles, solid board);

— roofing (shakes and wooden shingles);

— siding;

— sub-flooring;

— oriented strandboard;

— glue-laminated timber;

— laminated veneer lumber; and

— lath (e.g., a thin narrow strip of wood used for support).

Products that are not subject to the assessment include:

— furniture;

— firewood;

— paper products;

— indoor finished flooring;

— wainscoting (facing or paneling applied to walls);

— paneling;

— shutters;

— blinds;

— frames;

— windows;

— doors;

— cabinets;

— molding;

— millwork (e.g., baseboards);

— trusses;

— pre-constructed railing sections; and

— carvings and craft products.

(*Special Notices L-339 and L-343*, California State Board of Equalization, November 2012; *Special Notice L-340*, California State Board of Equalization, December 2012)

Purchasers. Every person who purchases a lumber product or an engineered wood product for storage, use, or other consumption in California is liable for the assessment until it has been paid to the state, except that payment to a retailer relieves the person from further liability for the assessment. Any assessment collected from a person that has not been remitted to the CDTFA shall be a debt owed to the state by the retailer required to collect and remit the assessment.

Purchasers, including construction contractors, who purchase lumber products or engineered wood products for use in California without paying the assessment to a registered California retailer at the time of their purchase must register with the CDTFA to report and pay the assessment directly to the CDTFA. (*Special Notices L-339 and L-343*, California State Board of Equalization, November 2012; *Special Notice L-340*, California State Board of Equalization, December 2012)

Registration. Every person required to pay the lumber products assessment is required to register with the CDTFA. Every application for registration must be made in a form prescribed by the CDTFA and must provide the name under which the applicant transacts or intends to transact business, the location of his or her place or places of business, and such other information as the CDTFA may require.

Reimbursement. A retailer required to collect this assessment may retain $250 per location, plus an additional reimbursement of $485 per location, as reimbursement for startup costs associated with the collection of the assessment. This reimbursement is to be taken on the retailer's first return on which the lumber products assessment is reported, or if the amount of the assessment is less than the reimbursement, on the retailer's next consecutive returns until the allowed reimbursement amount is retained. (Sec. 4629.4, Pub. Res. Code; Reg. 2000, 18 CCR; Reg. 2001, 18 CCR)

"Location," for these purposes, is defined as a business location registered under the retailer's seller's permit as of January 1, 2013, where sales of products subject to the assessment are made. (Reg. 2000, 18 CCR; Reg. 2001, 18 CCR)

Reporting requirements. The lumber products assessment is due to the CDTFA quarterly on or before the last day of the month following each quarterly period. In addition, on or before the last day of the month following each quarterly period, a return for the preceding quarterly period is required to be filed with the CDTFA using electronic media, in the form prescribed by the CDTFA.

Retailer's requirements. The retailer is required to collect the assessment from the purchaser and remit the amounts collected pursuant to the procedures in the Fee Collection Procedures Law. A retailer is required to charge the purchaser the amount of the assessment as a charge that is separate from, and not included in, any other fee, charge, or other amount paid by the purchaser. The retailer is also required to separately state the amount of the assessment on the sales receipt given by the retailer to the person at the time of sale.

Retailers who sell lumber products and engineered wood products are required to:

— charge and collect the 1% assessment on sales of lumber products or engineered wood products;

— separately state the amount of the assessment on the sales receipt given to the customer (the separately stated amount may be designated as "lumber products assessment" or "LPA" or "lumber assessment" or "lumber fee" or "lumber");

— report and pay the assessment to the California Department of Tax and Fee Administration (CDTFA) as part of their electronically filed sales and use tax return (eFile); and

— notify the CDTFA if their sales and use tax return does not include the lumber assessment schedule.

(*Special Notices L-339 and L-343*, California State Board of Equalization, November 2012; *Special Notice L-340*, California State Board of Equalization, December 2012)

Retailers with de minimis sales. A retailer with de minimis sales of qualified lumber products and engineered wood products of less than $25,000 during the previous calendar year is not a retailer for purposes of the provisions regarding the assessment. An excluded retailer is required to provide a notice to a purchaser of qualified lumber products or engineered wood products regarding the purchaser's obligation to remit the assessment to the CDTFA.

[¶60-340] Drop Shipments

The term "drop shipment" does not appear in the California Revenue and Taxation Code. However, the transaction is described in the definition of "retail sale." Anyone who delivers tangible personal property, either to a California consumer or to a person for redelivery to a California consumer pursuant to a retail sale made to the consumer by a retailer that does not do business in California, is the retailer of the property for California sales and use tax purposes. The deliverer must include the retail selling price of the property in the gross receipts or sales price of the property. (Sec. 6007, Rev. & Tax. Code)

The Department of Tax and Fee Administration has issued a publication that discusses application of sales tax to drop shipment transactions, including who owes the tax and why. (*CDTFA Publication 121, Drop Shipments*, California Department of Tax and Fee Administration)

Application of tax.—As a general rule, a drop shipper calculates the taxable retail selling price of its drop shipments based on the selling price from the true retailer to the consumer plus a mark-up of 10%. However, if the drop shipper can show that a lower mark-up percentage accurately reflects the retail selling price charged by the true retailer, that lower percentage can be used. (Reg. 1706, 18 CCR)

If a mark-up percentage lower than 10% is developed in an audit of a drop shipper, that percentage will be used for subsequent reporting periods provided the drop shipper has no significant change in business operations. Otherwise, a higher percentage mark-up will apply up to a maximum of 10%. (Reg. 1706, 18 CCR)

Drop shipment examples.—Taxable sales that lead to drop shipments begin with a sale of tangible personal property from a retailer that does not do business in California (true retailer) to a California consumer. Generally, the true retailer then purchases the property from a supplier with instructions to deliver the property directly to the consumer. The delivery of the property to the consumer is a drop shipment, and the supplier making the delivery is a drop shipper. For all drop shipments involving nonexempt sales, the drop shipper is reclassified as the retailer and must report and pay applicable California sales and use tax. (Reg. 1706, 18 CCR)

CCH EXAMPLE: *Simple drop shipment scenario.*—A true retailer, Goodsales, Inc., sells a vase to a California consumer. Goodsales then contracts with a supplier, Vasesales Corp., to purchase the vase and instructs Vasesales to deliver it to the consumer. When Vasesales Corp. delivers the vase, it becomes the drop shipper, is reclassified as a retailer, and must report and pay the applicable sales tax.

A drop shipment can involve more than two sales. When it does, the drop shipper is the first person who is a retailer engaged in business in California in the series of transactions beginning with the purchase by the true retailer. (Reg. 1706, 18 CCR)

> **CCH EXAMPLE:** *Two-sale drop shipment.*—A true retailer, Goodsales, Inc., sells a vase to a California consumer and then contracts to purchase the vase from Vasesales Corp., a retailer engaged in business in California. Goodsales instructs Vasesales to deliver the vase to the consumer. Vasesales, in turn, contracts with Speedy Co. to deliver the vase. Because Vasesales is a retailer engaged in business in California, it is the drop shipper. It does not matter whether Speedy is a retailer engaged in business in California.

> Use the same example except that Vasesales is not engaged in business in California. In that event, Speedy becomes the first retailer engaged in business in California in the series of transactions beginning with the purchase by Goodsales. Once Speedy makes the delivery, it becomes the drop shipper, is reclassified as a retailer, and must report and pay any applicable sales tax.

A person otherwise qualifying as, and presumed to be, a drop shipper can overcome the presumption by accepting a timely resale certificate from the purchaser. Similarly, the presumption that a delivery is to a consumer can be overcome if the person making the delivery accepts a qualifying resale certificate from the person to whom the property is delivered. (Reg. 1706, 18 CCR)

Generally, drop shipment transactions involve one consumer, two sales, and two businesses:

— the consumer in California who buys and receives a product;

— the "true retailer," that is, a business located outside the state and not registered to collect California tax, that sells the product to the California consumer; and

— the "drop shipper" who sells the product to the true retailer but ships the product directly to the California consumer on behalf of the retailer.

Drop shippers generally owe tax on the retail selling price the consumer paid the true retailer. However, if that amount is unknown to the drop shipper, tax may be calculated based on the drop shipper's selling price to the true retailer plus a 10% markup. (*Tax Information Bulletin*, California State Board of Equalization, March 2007)

> *Drop shipment that involves more than one California retailer.*—Generally, the first retailer engaged in business in California (the in-state retailer that receives the order from the out-of-state retailer) in the series of drop shipment transactions is liable for the sales tax. The first retailer knows the selling price to the true retailer and must report and pay tax accordingly. (*CDTFA Publication 121, Drop Shipments*, California Department of Tax and Fee Administration)

> *Liability for tax.*—When an out-of-state retailer holds a valid California seller's permit or a California Certificate of Registration-Use Tax, the out-of-state retailer is liable for tax due on any sale made in California, even if the product is delivered by another California retailer. However, if the out-of-state retailer does not hold a seller's permit or certificate of registration–use tax and the retail sale of the property

is subject to California sales or use tax, the California retailer (drop shipper) is liable for the tax. (*CDTFA Publication 121, Drop Shipments*, California Department of Tax and Fee Administration)

Who does the drop shipper charge for sales tax.—If the out-of-state retailer holds a permit, it should issue the drop shipper a resale certificate for the sale and the drop shipper is relieved of the responsibility to report and pay the tax. However, if the true retailer does not hold a permit:

— the drop shipper is responsible for reporting and paying the tax;

— the drop shipper should charge the true retailer tax based on the retail amount and report and pay it to the CDTFA;

— the true retailer may choose to seek reimbursement from the in-state consumer for the cost of sales tax charged to them by the drop shipper either by increasing the selling price of the product or adding an additional line on the invoice for reimbursement; and

— the true retailer cannot issue an invoice with a line called "California tax" or "California sales tax" (However, the true retailer can use a phrase such as "California tax paid to California drop shipper" or similar terminology on their sales invoice, indicating that California tax has been paid to a drop-shipper, which will also alert the in-state consumer that California tax has been paid on their purchase).

(*CDTFA Publication 121, Drop Shipments*, California Department of Tax and Fee Administration)

[¶60-360] Enterprise Zones and Similar Tax Incentives

While California has enterprise zones, it does not offer any zone-related sales and use tax exemptions.

[¶60-390] Food and Grocery Items

Gross receipts from sales of food and beverages for human consumption are exempt. The exemption extends to most of the common food products sold at retail to consumers, but excludes alcoholic beverages (see ¶60-260 Alcoholic Beverages), dietary supplements and food adjuncts, meals served for consumption in or on the seller's premises, hot prepared foods, food served at places charging admissions, and certain cold take-out foods; these exceptions are discussed separately in the subparagraphs that follow. (Sec. 6359, Rev. & Tax. Code)

Although meals served in a restaurant are subject to tax, exemptions apply to meals that are served to, or furnished by, specified persons and organizations:

— student meals at schools;

— meals served by certain associated organizations and blind vendors;

— hot prepared food products furnished by caterers or vendors to airline passengers;

— meals served by religious organizations to raise operating revenue;

— meals served to residents or patients of institutions, boarding houses, and residential care facilities for the elderly;

— meals delivered to homebound elderly or disabled persons;

— meals served to the low-income elderly at, or below, cost; and

— meals served regularly to persons 62 years of age or older who are residents of a condominium, or to residents of any housing financed by state or federal programs that primarily serves older persons.

(Sec. 6359, Rev. & Tax. Code)

The California Department of Tax and Fee Administration (CDTFA) provides guidance for taxpayers in the dining and beverage industry. (*CDTFA Publication 22, Dining and Beverage Industry*, California Department of Tax and Fee Administration)

The CDTFA also provides guidance regarding tips, gratuities, and service charges. (*CDTFA Publication 115, Tips, Gratuities, and Service Charges*, California Department of Tax and Fee Administration)

The CDTFA also provides guidance for mobile food vendors. (*CDTFA Publication 287*, California Department of Tax and Fee Administration, June 2014)

The California Constitution prohibits the state and any of its political subdivisions from imposing sales or use taxes on food products, except as already provided by statute as of January 1, 1993. Accordingly, additional sales or use taxes can be imposed and existing exemptions can be removed only if approved by the voters. (Art. XIII, Sec. 34, Cal. Const.)

See ¶61-220 Returns, Payments, and Due dates, for a discussion of registration, reporting, and recordkeeping requirements for mobile food vendors.

• *General exemption*

California exempts sales of the basic food groups (meats and fish, cereals, milk and dairy products, and fruits and vegetables) as well as most spices and condiments, coffee, tea, and cocoa. Beverages such as fruit and vegetable juices are exempt, but alcoholic and carbonated drinks are subject to tax. Preparations sold as dietary supplements and food adjuncts are generally taxable, with certain exceptions (see below under "Dietary supplements"). (Sec. 6359, Rev. & Tax. Code)

• *Airlines*

Hot prepared food products sold by caterers or other vendors to interstate or international air carriers for consumption by passengers are exempt, as are hot prepared food products sold or served by such carriers to passengers for in-flight consumption. Crew members are not defined as "passengers" in this context. Any caterer or vendor claiming this exemption must have an exemption certificate from the air carrier. (Sec. 6359.1, Rev. & Tax. Code; Reg. 1603(e)(2), 18 CCR)

• *Beverages sold by carriers*

Tax applies to the sale or use of taxable beverages in California by carriers, except when the sale occurs during a "trans-state trip," *i.e.*, a trip across California territory or airspace during a continuous journey between points outside the state without any stops or landings in the state. Tax applies to taxable beverages, whether they are sold or served on a complimentary basis to passengers or crew. (Reg. 1620.2, 18 CCR)

Carriers may compute tax on beverages using the "California passenger miles method." This computation requires carriers to attribute a portion of total gross receipts, and of the total cost of taxable beverages served on a complimentary basis, to California according to a prescribed ratio: passenger miles in California, divided by total system-wide passenger miles. Carriers may also use any other reporting that accurately reports the tax due, and must be prepared to demonstrate the accuracy of the method applied with records that can be verified by audit. Amtrak is not considered a "carrier" for purposes of this provision. (Reg. 1620.2, 18 CCR)

• *Carbon dioxide packing*

The sale, storage, use, or other consumption of carbon dioxide is exempt from tax, provided that it is used or employed in packing and shipping or transporting fruits or vegetables for human consumption and the package that is purchased by the ultimate consumer does not contain the carbon dioxide. The exemption also applies to any nonreturnable materials containing the carbon dioxide atmosphere used in the packing and shipping or transportation of fruits and vegetables for human consumption. (Sec. 6359.8, Rev. & Tax. Code)

• *Caterers*

Tax applies to the entire charge caterers impose to serve meals, food, and drinks, including charges for labor and for the use of dishes, silverware, glasses, chairs, and tables. Charges for preparing and serving food and drinks are subject to tax, even if the food is not provided by the caterer. The rental of dishes and other utensils, purchased tax-paid, is not subject to tax, provided that no food is provided or served by the caterer. (Reg. 1603(h), 18 CCR)

Sales of meals by caterers to social clubs, fraternal organizations, or other persons are sales for resale (and thus not taxed) if those entities or persons are retailers of the meals and provide valid resale certificates to the caterers. (Reg. 1603(h), 18 CCR)

Caterers are generally considered the consumers of tangible personal property used to serve meals, food, or drinks, except for separately stated charges for the lease of such property by the caterer from a third party. Property used to serve food includes disposable plates, napkins, utensils, glasses, cups, stemware, placemats, trays, covers, and toothpicks. (Reg. 1603(h)(2), 18 CCR)

A caterer is the lessor of property unrelated to the serving or furnishing of meals, food, or drinks when the caterer also rents or leases such property from a third party, and tax applies to the lease. Property unrelated to the serving of meals, food, or drinks includes decorative props related solely to optional entertainment, special lighting for guest speakers, sound or video systems, dance floors, and stages. (Reg. 1603(h)(3)(B)(1), 18 CCR)

Tax applies to charges by a caterer for event planning, design, coordination, and/ or supervision when such charges are made in connection with the furnishing of meals, food, or drinks for the event. However, tax does not apply to separately stated charges for:

— services such as optional entertainment, which are unrelated to the furnishing and serving of meals, food, or drinks; or

— any staff such as coat check clerks, parking attendants, and security guards, who do not directly participate in the preparation, furnishing, or serving of meals, food, or drinks.

(Reg. 1603(h)(3)(C)(1), 18 CCR)

Sales of meals or hot prepared food products by restaurants, concessionaires, hotels, boarding houses, soda fountains, and similar establishments to persons such as event planners, party coordinators, or fundraisers, who buy and sell on their own account, are sales for resale for which resale certificates may be accepted. (Reg. 1603(a)(2)(A), 18 CCR)

Separately stated charges for the lease of premises on which meals, food, or drinks are served are nontaxable. However, in instances where a charge for leased premises is a guarantee against a minimum purchase of meals, food, or drinks, the charge for the guarantee is subject to tax. Moreover, when a person contracts to provide both premises and meals, food, or drinks, the charge for the meals, food, or drinks must be reasonable in order for the charge for the premises to be nontaxable. (Reg. 1603(h), 18 CCR)

Sales by caterers of meals or food products to students of a school are exempt from tax if:

— the premises used by the caterer to serve the lunches to the students are used by the school during the remainder of the day for other purposes such as sporting events and school activities;

— the fixtures and equipment used by the caterer are owned and maintained by the school; and

— the students purchasing the meals cannot distinguish the caterer from school employees.

(Reg. 1603(j)(2)(D), 18 CCR)

Snacks sold through an honor system snack sale are taxable when the snacks are sold at or near a lunchroom, break room, or other facility that provides tables and chairs, where it is contemplated the snacks will normally be consumed. An "honor system snack sale" is a sale where customers take snacks from a box or tray and pay by depositing money in a container provided by the seller. Such sales do not include hotel room mini-bars or snack baskets. (Reg. 1603(t), 18 CCR)

Event planners.—Generally, fees or markups charged by event planners for design, coordination and supervision of events and special venues are subject to tax when they involve sales of tangible personal property. Contracts that are presented as a lump sum charge, a portion of which applies to serving meals, food, drinks or other transfers of tangible personal property, are taxable. Such charges are regarded as retail sales of tangible personal property. The event planner must hold a California seller's permit and report and pay sales tax on their retail sales. (*Tax Information Bulletin*, California State Board of Equalization, December 2007)

Tax does not apply to separately stated charges for services unrelated to taxable sales such as optional entertainment or any staff such as coast-check clerks, parking attendants or security guards who do not directly participate in preparing, furnishing or serving food. If, however, charges are not itemized on the event planners' records, the entire charge may be taxable. (*Tax Information Bulletin*, California State Board of Equalization, December 2007)

• *Cold take-out food*

California sales and use tax applies to consumer purchases of cold food products that are suitable for consumption on the seller's premises, including separately priced hot bakery goods and hot beverages, provided that food products yield more than 80% of the seller's gross receipts, and provided that more than 80% of the seller's qualified retail food sales are subject to tax. The computation excludes revenues from the sale of alcoholic beverages, carbonated beverages, and cold food that is not suitable for consumption on the seller's premises. Also, the operations of each physically separate seller location are considered separately for computation purposes. Qualifying food purchases from sellers that meet the criteria outlined are taxable. However, sales of cold food products that are suitable for consumption on the seller's premises, but are actually consumed off premises, are exempt from tax, provided that the seller properly documents and separately accounts for such sales. (Sec. 6359(f), Rev. & Tax. Code; Reg. 1603(c), 18 CCR)

Cold food products are in a form suitable for consumption on the seller's premises if furnished (1) in a form that requires no further processing by the purchaser and (2) in a size that may be immediately consumed by one person. Cold food products furnished in containers larger than a pint are not considered to be in a form suitable for immediate consumption. (Reg. 1603(c), 18 CCR)

If cold food products are suitable for consumption on the seller's premises, the quantity purchased is irrelevant. For example, a sale of 40 one-half-pint containers of milk would be taxable if the seller qualifies under the 80-80 rule. However, pieces of candy sold in bulk quantities of one pound or greater are deemed to be sold in a form not suitable for consumption on the seller's premises. Also, purchases of cold food products that are not suitable for consumption on the seller's premises, such as party trays or whole cold chickens, are not subject to tax. (Reg. 1603(c), 18 CCR)

• *Combination packages*

A clear standard is provided by regulation regarding the applicability of California sales and use tax to combination packages that include food and non-food products (e.g., gift baskets) that are sold for a single price. When a package contains both food products (e.g., dried fruit) and non-food products (e.g., wine or toys), the application of tax depends on the essential character of the complete package. If more than 10% of the retail value of the complete package, exclusive of the container, represents the value of the non-food products, a segregation has to be made. When that segregation is made and the retailer has documentation that establishes the cost of the individual component parts of the package, the tax is measured by the retail selling price of the non-food products. When the retailer does not have documentation that evidences the cost of the individual component parts of the package, and the package exclusive of the container consists of non-food products whose retail selling price would exceed 10% of the retail selling price for the entire package, the tax is measured by the retail selling price of the entire package. If the retail value of the non-food products is 10% or less, exclusive of the container, and the retail value of the container is 50% or less of the retail value of the entire package, the selling price of the entire package is not subject to tax. (Reg. 1602, 18 CCR)

• *Dietary supplements*

Dietary supplements or adjunct products, sold in liquid, powdered, granular, tablet, capsule, lozenge, or pill form, are excluded from the definition of nontaxable "food products". Such products are taxable unless they qualify for a separate exemption (e.g., as a prescription medicine). These products are (1) described on their labels as food or dietary supplements or adjuncts, or (2) prescribed to remedy specific dietary deficiencies or to increase or decrease areas of human nutrition, such as vitamins, proteins, and minerals, or caloric intake. Products manufactured from specially mixed or compounded ingredients that yield a high nutritional source, such as protein supplements and vitamin pills, are taxable as food supplements. Cod liver oil, halibut liver oil, and wheat germ oil, even though not specially compounded, are also treated as taxable dietary supplements. However, unusual foods, (e.g., brewer's yeast, wheat germ, and seaweed), that are not manufactured from specially mixed or compounded ingredients, are exempt from tax unless the package label identifies the product as a food supplement or the equivalent. Vitamin-enriched milk and high protein flour are also exempt. (Sec. 6359(c), Rev. & Tax. Code; Reg. 1602(a)(5), 18 CCR)

Complete dietary foods that provide, in the recommended daily dosage, substantial amounts of vitamins, proteins, minerals, and adequate caloric intake, are exempt from tax. For example, a food that provides a daily consumer 70 grams of high quality protein, 900 calories, and minimum FDA daily requirements of vitamins A, B_1, C, D, riboflavin, niacin, calcium, phosphorous, iron, and iodine, qualifies for exemption. (Reg. 1602(a)(5), 18 CCR)

Food products and nutritional supplements.—Changes made to the product labels of various food products and nutritional supplements can affect the application of California sales and use tax to sales of such products. The label may claim the product helps remedy specific dietary deficiencies or improves health, but the California Department of Tax and Fee Administration (CDTFA) considers the details contained on the label, including the form of the product, when it determines whether an item qualifies as a food product or a food supplement. The CDTFA also takes into consideration the calories, proteins, minerals, and caloric intake when they make that determination. (*Tax Information Bulletin, Publication 388*, California State Board of Equalization, September 2013)

Tax applies to sales of products that are:

— in liquid, powdered, granular, tablet capsule, lozenge, or pill form; and

— described on its label or package as a food supplement, food adjunct, dietary supplement, or dietary adjunct; or

— prescribed or designed to remedy specific dietary deficiencies or to increase or decrease generally those areas of human nutrition dealing with vitamins, proteins, minerals, or calories.

(*Tax Information Bulletin, Publication 388*, California State Board of Equalization, September 2013)

According to the CDTFA, the following products are not taxable because their labels meet the definition of a nontaxable "food product:" Ensure™, Ensure Plus™, and Glucerna™. However, Ensure Bone Health™, Ensure Immune Health™, Ensure Muscle Health™, and Ensure High Protein™ are subject to tax because the products are food supplements. (*Tax Information Bulletin, Publication 388*, California State Board of Equalization, September 2013)

Supplements used to treat obesity.—When dietary supplements and adjunct products do not qualify as food products, as specified, and are furnished by a physician to his or her own patients as part of a medically supervised weight loss program to treat obesity, such products are regarded as medicine and are exempt from California sales and use taxes. Very low calorie meal replacement products meet the definition of "medicine" because they are intended for use by internal application to the human body in the treatment of obesity which is commonly recognized as a disease. (Reg. 1591(e)(7), 18 CCR; Reg. 1602(a)(4), 18 CCR)

• *Discount coupons for taxable food and beverages*

When a business that sells meals, alcoholic beverages, or both, such as a bar, delicatessen, restaurant, or catering operation, accepts two-for-one coupons or other discount coupons or cards that allow customers to purchase food or beverages at a reduced price, the sales and use tax liability is based on the total amount the business receives from the sale. This total amount includes any reimbursement the business receives from any other sponsor or promoter. Any tip that is added as an additional amount by the customer is not included in the taxable measure. When a discount is offered by a sponsor or promoter, the amount received must be included as part of the total sales subject to tax. (*Tax Information Bulletin*, California State Board of Equalization, September 2009)

• *Drive-ins*

Food and beverages sold for immediate consumption at or near parking facilities are taxable, even though they are sold on a take-out or to-go basis and are actually packaged and wrapped and taken off the premises. Products sold in bulk or in a form not suitable for consumption on the premises are exempt. The validity of deductions for such receipts requires complete and detailed recordkeeping by the retailer. (Sec. 6359(d), Rev. & Tax. Code; Reg. 1603(b), 18 CCR)

• *Food service companies*

California does not currently provide any specific guidance regarding food service companies, food service management companies, food management entities, or other such companies. California sales tax is imposed on every retailer for the privilege of making retail sales of tangible personal property in the state. California use tax is imposed on the purchase of tangible personal property from any retailer for storage, use, or consumption in California. See ¶ 60-020 Application of Sales and Use Taxes.

There are specific California provisions regarding caterers. See below.

• *Food stamps (aka CalFresh benefits)*

Purchases made with CalFresh benefits (formerly known as federal food stamp coupons) are tax exempt, as mandated by P.L. 95-113. With respect to purchases made partly with cash and partly with CalFresh benefits, CalFresh benefits are first attributed to receipts that would have been taxed had the coupons not been redeemed. (Sec. 6373, Rev. & Tax. Code; Reg. 1603(s), 18 CCR)

Retailers who receive CalFresh benefits for purchases that are entirely or partly taxable may, in lieu of separately accounting for such sales, deduct on their sales tax returns 2% of the total amount of CalFresh benefits redeemed during the applicable tax period. Grocers may claim a deduction in excess of 2% if a percentage greater than 2% results from dividing the total taxable purchases eligible to be purchased with CalFresh benefits by the total exempt food product purchases plus the taxable purchases eligible to be purchased with CalFresh benefits. In the alternative, the Department of Tax and Fee Administration is authorized to supply a method of computing a sales tax deduction for retailers who elect not to account separately for the proceeds from the CalFresh benefits, provided the method supplied results in a deduction that equals at least 2% of the total amount of food stamps redeemed by the retailer during the return period. (Sec. 6373, Rev. & Tax. Code; Reg. 1602.5(c), 18 CCR)

• *Grocers*

In reporting sales of exempt food products, grocers may use the purchase-ratio method, the modified purchase-ratio method, the retail inventory method, the markup or other similar method, or an electronic scanning system. (Reg. 1602.5, 18 CCR)

The California Department of Tax and Fee Administration (CDTFA) provides guidance regarding sales and use tax laws and regulations as they apply to grocery stores. (*CDTFA Publication 31, Grocery Stores*, California Department of Tax and Fee Administration)

Purchase-ratio method.—Under the purchase-ratio method, otherwise known as a "grocer's formula," grocers may claim as exempt the proportion of their total gross receipts from grocery items that equals the ratio of total purchases of exempt food to total purchases of grocery items. This method may be used only by grocers and only for grocery item sales; drug stores selling food products cannot use this method. (Reg. 1602.5(b)(1), 18 CCR)

Modified purchase-ratio method.—Modified purchase-ratio methods are also available. For example, grocers can include self-performed processing, manufacturing, warehousing, or transportation costs. Grocers must show that the modified method applied does not overstate food product exemptions. (Reg. 1602.5(b)(2), 18 CCR)

Retail inventory or markup methods.—Grocers engaged in manufacturing, processing, warehousing, or transporting their own products may prefer to use a retail inventory or markup method.

The retail inventory method procedure follows:

— opening inventory is extended to retail and segregated as to exempt food products and taxable merchandise;

— as invoices for merchandise are received, they are extended to retail and segregated as to exempt food products and taxable merchandise;

— the ending inventory at retail is segregated as to exempt food products and taxable merchandise;

— the total of the segregated amounts determined in (1) and (2) less (3) represent anticipated exempt and taxable sales;

— the segregated amounts determined in (4) are adjusted for net markons, markdowns, and shrinkage to determine realized exempt and taxable sales; and

— physical inventories are taken periodically to adjust book inventories.

(Reg. 1602.5(b)(3)(A), 18 CCR)

Under the cost-plus markup method, all taxable merchandise is marked up from cost to anticipated selling prices. Records are kept of net markups, net markdowns, and shrinkage, and the records are used to adjust the anticipated selling price to the realized price. The grocer should determine the markup factor percentages applicable to taxable merchandise by a shelf-test sample of representative purchases. The sample should cover a minimum one-month purchasing cycle within a three-year period and be segregated by commodity groupings such as for beer, wine, carbonated beverages, tobacco and related products, paper products, pet food, and soap and detergents. (Reg. 1602.5(b)(3)(B), 18 CCR)

As an alternative to the markup factor percentage procedure, an overall markup factor percentage for all taxable commodity groupings may be used. The overall average markup factor percentage is determined by obtaining markup factor percentages by commodity groupings on the basis of shelf test covering a minimum one-month purchasing cycle within a three-year period. (Reg. 1602.5, 18 CCR)

Electronic scanning system.—Using an electronic scanning system, grocers may automatically compile and record taxable and nontaxable sales, sales tax, and related data from scanned products. Grocers must ensure that proper controls are maintained for monitoring and verifying the accuracy of their scanning results and tax returns. Records that clearly segregate taxable and nontaxable purchases may aid in monitoring and verifying scanning accuracy. In addition, grocers must retain documentation relating to product identity, price, sales tax code, scanning program changes, and corrections to programs. (Reg. 1602.5(b)(4), 18 CCR)

• *Herbal products*

Sales of herbal products, including teas and tea capsules are subject to tax provided: (1) medicinal claims are made on the label or packaging or in catalogs, brochures, or other informational material distributed with the products; or (2) the products are labeled, packaged, or otherwise marketed as food supplements or adjuncts (i.e., food additives). Medicinal claims do not have to be made in English for tax to apply. A medicinal claim on a product's label does not convert a food product into a medicine. Products sold as medicines are not excluded from the definition of "food products;" actual medicines are excluded from food products. If a product is a medicine, then it is not a food product. In order to determine if the sale of an herbal product, including teas and tea capsules, falls within the food products exemption, it is irrelevant if specific medicinal claims are made regarding the product. Instead, the product must actually be a medicine. In determining if a product is a medicine, it must first be determined if the product is approved for use by the U.S. Food and Drug Administration to diagnose, cure, mitigate, treat, or prevent any disease, illness, or medical condition. If a product is so approved, it is a medicine and is not a food product. (*Tax Information Bulletin*, California State Board of Education, December 2009)

• *Hot prepared food*

Purchases of "hot prepared foods", defined as products, items, or components prepared for sale in a heated condition, and sold at a temperature higher than room temperature, even if served cold because of delay, are subject to tax in California. (Sec. 6359(d) and (e), Rev. & Tax. Code; Reg. 1603(e), 18 CCR)

The mere heating of a food product constitutes preparation of a hot prepared food, provided that the food is intended to be served heated. Products sold at cold temperatures are exempt from tax, even if preparation requires heating, such as a cold tuna sandwich on toast. Tax applies to the total gross receipts from a combination of hot and cold food items if a single price has been established for the combination. For example, hot coffee included in the price for a meal of cold foods subjects the entire charge to tax. (Sec. 6359(e), Rev. & Tax. Code; Reg. 1603(e), 18 CCR)

Hot bakery goods and beverages, including coffee, although considered "hot prepared foods," are exempt if sold for a separate price, unless they are sold for consumption on the retailer's premises, at a drive-in, or at a place that charges admission. Sales of hot take-out bakery goods and beverages also may be taxable under the 80-80 rule. See discussion of "Cold take-out food" above. (Reg. 1603(e), 18 CCR)

• *Local taxes on groceries*

The Keep Groceries Affordable Act of 2018 prohibits any new local California sales or use tax, fee, or other assessment on groceries. (Sec. 7284.8, Rev. & Tax. Code; Sec. 7284.12, Rev. & Tax. Code; *Special Notice L-597*, California Department of Tax and Fee Administration, January 2019)

Application of prohibition.—The prohibition applies to the imposition, increase, levy, collection, or enforcement of such a local:

- tax;
- fee; or
- assessment.

(Sec. 7284.8, Rev. & Tax. Code; Sec. 7284.12, Rev. & Tax. Code; *Special Notice L-597*, California Department of Tax and Fee Administration, January 2019)

Local taxes, fees, or assessments imposed on groceries before January 1, 2018.— Cities, counties, and local agencies may continue to levy and collect, enforce, or reauthorize any tax, fee, or other assessment on groceries imposed, extended, or increased on or before January 1, 2018. (Sec. 7284.8, Rev. & Tax. Code; Sec. 7284.12, Rev. & Tax. Code; *Special Notice L-597*, California Department of Tax and Fee Administration, January 2019)

Moreover, the act does not prohibit the imposition, extension, increase, levy and collection, or enforcement of any generally applicable tax, fee, or other assessment, including:

- taxes levied under the Bradley-Burns Uniform Local Sales and Use Tax Law; or

- the Transactions and Use (District) Tax Law.

(Sec. 7284.8, Rev. & Tax. Code; Sec. 7284.12, Rev. & Tax. Code; *Special Notice L-597*, California Department of Tax and Fee Administration, January 2019)

Consequences of local action taken in conflict with act.—If a local agency acts in conflict with the act, the California Department of Tax and Fee Administration (CDTFA) will terminate its contract to administer any local sales or use tax ordinance. This action will be taken under the Bradley-Burns Uniform Local Sales and Use Tax Law. (Sec. 7284.15, Rev. & Tax. Code; *Special Notice L-597*, California Department of Tax and Fee Administration, January 2019)

Any civil court action that arises from this law:

- will be given priority over other actions; and
- the venue will be Sacramento County.

(Sec. 7284.15, Rev. & Tax. Code; *Special Notice L-597*, California Department of Tax and Fee Administration, January 2019)

Local taxes, fees, or assessments imposed on groceries after January 1, 2018.—Any new taxes, fees, or assessments on groceries imposed by a local agency after January 1, 2018:

- are inoperative as of June 28, 2018, and
- cease to be imposed, levied, collected, and enforced as of that date.

(Sec. 7284.12, Rev. & Tax. Code; *Special Notice L-597*, California Department of Tax and Fee Administration, January 2019)

Definitions.—"Groceries" are defined as any raw or processed food or beverage intended for human consumption, including the:

- packaging;
- wrapper;
- container; or
- any ingredient of such food or beverage.

(Sec. 7284.10, Rev. & Tax. Code; *Special Notice L-597*, California Department of Tax and Fee Administration, January 2019)

Examples include:

- meat;
- poultry;
- fish;
- fruits;
- vegetables;
- grains;
- bread;
- milk;
- cheese and other dairy products; or
- any carbonated or noncarbonated nonalcoholic beverages.

(Sec. 7284.10, Rev. & Tax. Code; *Special Notice L-597*, California Department of Tax and Fee Administration, January 2019)

Groceries do not include:

- alcoholic beverages;
- cannabis;
- cannabis products;
- cigarettes;
- tobacco products; and
- electronic cigarettes.

(Sec. 7284.10, Rev. & Tax. Code; *Special Notice L-597*, California Department of Tax and Fee Administration, January 2019)

"Tax, fee, or other assessment on groceries" includes:

- taxes;
- fees;
- surcharges;
- any similar levy, charge, or exaction of any kind on groceries; or
- the manufacture, supply, distribution, sale, acquisition, possession, ownership, transfer, transportation, delivery, use, or consumption of groceries.

(Sec. 7284.10, Rev. & Tax. Code; *Special Notice L-597*, California Department of Tax and Fee Administration, January 2019)

Sunset.—These provisions are repealed as of January 1, 2031. (Sec. 7284.16, Rev. & Tax. Code; *Special Notice L-597*, California Department of Tax and Fee Administration, January 2019)

• *Meals provided at summer conference programs*

Some colleges lease their facilities for various summer conference programs such as high school enrichment programs, music or sports camps, or training seminars organized by professional or educational groups. Generally, each conference participant is charged a lump sum fee that includes meals provided by the college. The college charges the group a daily rate per participant, which includes such items as the use of dorm rooms and classrooms, catered meals and services for breakfast, lunch, refreshment breaks, and dinner, or banquet services. Although the participants are attending the conference on college facilities, they are not considered students of the college. As such, any sales of meals made to those participants are taxable sales when the group sponsoring the summer conference program is not a school or educational institution. When, however, summer conference programs are directly run by a college, the participants are considered students of the college and meals that are provided to such participants under a college program are considered exempt sales of meals to students. (Reg. 1603, 18 CCR; Reg. 1506(g), 18 CCR; *Tax Information Bulletin*, California State Board of Equalization, June 2009)

• *Meals served to the elderly or disabled*

California exempts the sale, storage, use, or other consumption of meals and food products furnished or served to low-income elderly persons at or below cost by a nonprofit organization or government agency under a program funded for that purpose by the state or the federal government. (Sec. 6374, Rev. & Tax. Code)

California also exempts the sale, use, or other consumption of meals and food products to condominium residents aged 62 or older, provided that the meals are prepared and served to such residents at the common kitchen facility of the condominium on a regular basis and the elderly to whom the meals are served own equal shares in the kitchen facility. (Sec. 6376.5, Rev. & Tax. Code)

The sale, storage, use, or other consumption of meals delivered to homebound elderly or disabled persons by nonprofit volunteer home delivery meal providers is also exempt from sales and use tax. (Sec. 6363.7, Rev. & Tax. Code)

• *Meals served to employees*

The sale of meals to employees by an employer is subject to tax if an average of five or more employees purchase such meals during the calendar quarter and a specific charge is imposed for the meals. Any employer or employee organization in the business of selling meals, such as a restaurant, hotel, club, or association, must include receipts from employee meals in its taxable receipts if a specific charge is made for such meals. Tax does not apply to cash paid to an employee in lieu of meals. (Reg. 1603(k), 18 CCR)

A "specific charge" is imposed if:

— the employee pays cash for consumed meals;

— a value for the meals is deducted from the employee's wages;

— meals are received instead of cash to reach the legal minimum wage (in such a case, tax applies to the amount by which the minimum wage exceeds the amount otherwise paid to the employee, up to the value of the meals so credited); or

— the employee has the option of receiving cash for meals not consumed.

(Reg. 1603(k), 18 CCR)

If no specific charge is imposed, the employer is the consumer of food products purchased. Although purchases of exempt food products are not taxable, employer purchases of nonfood items, such as cigarettes or soft drinks, furnished with employee meals, are subject to tax. (Reg. 1603(k), 18 CCR)

• *Meals served in health care facilities or boarding houses*

California exempts meals and food products served to and consumed by residents or patients of:

— qualified "health facilities" and "community care facilities", as defined in the Health and Safety Code;

— a "residential care facility for the elderly", as defined in the Health and Safety Code;

— any institution supplying board and room for a flat monthly rate and serving as a principal residence exclusively for persons aged 62 or older;

— any housing financed by state or federal programs that primarily serves older persons; or

— qualified alcoholism or drug abuse recovery facilities.

(Sec. 6363.6, Rev. & Tax. Code; Reg. 1503, 18 CCR)

Also exempt are sales of meals and food products to such institutions that serve such meals to residents or patients. (Reg. 1503(b)(1), 18 CCR) Meals served by hospitals to outpatients are also exempt (Sales Tax Counsel Ruling 300.0080), as are meals served by food service contractors to the residents or patients of the qualified facilities described above (Sales Tax Counsel Ruling 300.0040).

See ¶ 60-580 Nonprofit Organizations, Private Schools and Churches, for treatment of sales and purchases of tangible personal property in general by the institutions described above.

•*Meals served by religious organizations*

Meals and food products sold by a religious organization at its gatherings are exempt, provided that the sales revenues are collected to help the organization to function and the receipts are actually used for that purpose. (Sec. 6363.5, Rev. & Tax. Code)

•*Meals served to students*

California exempts meals served to public or private school students by schools, student or parent-teacher organizations, or any qualified blind person operating a restaurant or vending stand. The exemption does not apply when food products are sold for consumption within a place to which admission is charged, except state and national parks and monuments. Soft drinks not sold as part of an exempt meal, meals sold to school employees, and caterer's meals sold directly to students, are all subject to tax. (Sec. 6363, Rev. & Tax. Code; Reg. 1603(j), 18 CCR)

•*Meals served at summer camps*

Unless a summer camp qualifies as a school or educational institution, meals sold at a summer camp are taxable, whether the camp is operated by municipal or private corporations or other parties. A summer camp that conducts regularly scheduled classes led by competent instructors qualifies as an educational institution, provided that class attendance is required. With respect to qualified summer camps, meals are treated as if sold by a school. (Reg. 1506(f), 18 CCR)

•*Meals served by veterans' organizations*

California allows a sales and use tax exemption for meals and food products that are furnished or served by any nonprofit veterans' organizations for fundraising purposes. (Sec. 6363.8, Rev. & Tax. Code; Reg. 1603, 18 CCR)

•*Nonprofit youth organizations*

Certain nonprofit youth organizations are regarded as consumers, rather than retailers, of food products, nonalcoholic beverages, or other tangible personal property made or produced by members of the organization, which the organization sells on an "irregular or intermittent" basis. "Irregular or intermittent" refers to direct association with a particular event, including refreshment stands or booths. The profits of the sale must be used exclusively to advance the organization's mission. (Sec. 6361, Rev. & Tax. Code; Reg. 1597(d), 18 CCR)

The organization must qualify under one of three categories:

— it must qualify for tax-exempt status under IRC Sec. 501(c), its primary purpose must be to provide a supervised program of competitive sports for youth or to promote good citizenship in youth, and it must not discriminate on the basis of race, sex, nationality, or religion;

— it must be a youth group sponsored by, or affiliated with, a qualified educational institution as defined in the law; or

— it must be a Little League; Bobby Sox; Boy Scouts; Cub Scouts; Girl Scouts; Campfire, Inc.; YMCA; YWCA; FFA; FHA; 4-H Clubs; Distributive Education Clubs of America; Future Business Leaders of America; Vocational Industrial Clubs of America; Collegiate Young Farmers; Boys' Clubs; Girls' Clubs; Special Olympics, Inc; American Youth Soccer Association; California Youth Soccer Association, North; California Youth Soccer Association, South; or Pop Warner Football.

(Sec. 6361, Rev. & Tax. Code; Reg. 1597(d), 18 CCR)

• *Nutritional drinks*

California sales and use tax does not generally apply to the sale of food products for human consumption, including most nutritional drinks. However, tax generally does apply to the sale of nutritional drinks described on their label or package as food supplements or food adjuncts or that meets other criteria. Nutritional drink products are generally milk or juice based products that often promote themselves as having additional nutrients. Such drinks are mixed or enriched for the purpose of providing general nutrition, are not carbonated, and do not contain alcohol. (*Special Notice L-456*, California State Board of Equalization, June 2016)

Sales of nutritional drinks are generally not subject to tax when they have "Nutrition Facts" on their label or package unless:

— the label or package describes the product as a food supplement or adjunct; or

— the product is prescribed or designed to remedy specific dietary deficiencies or to increase or decrease: vitamins, proteins, minerals, or caloric intake.

(*Special Notice L-456*, California State Board of Equalization, June 2016)

Sales of powder mixes with substantially the same ingredients and labeling as their ready-to-drink counterparts are also not subject to tax when the sale of the nutritional drink is not subject to tax. (*Special Notice L-456*, California State Board of Equalization, June 2016)

Sales of nutritional drinks are generally subject to tax when they have "Supplement Facts" on their label or package and/or are described as a food supplement, food adjunct, dietary supplement, or dietary adjunct on the label or package. However, sales of nutritional drinks that are a complete dietary food, regardless of labeling or packaging, are not subject to tax. Complete dietary foods provide 70 grams of protein, 900 calories, and the minimum daily requirements of vitamins and minerals A, B1, C, D, riboflavin, niacin, calcium, phosphorus, iron, and iodine set by the Food and Drug Administration (FDA) within three servings. (*Special Notice L-456*, California State Board of Equalization, June 2016)

• *Packing ice*

Ice or dry ice used in packing or shipping food products for human consumption is exempt, provided that the food products are shipped or transported in intrastate, interstate, or foreign commerce by common carriers, contract carriers, or proprietary carriers. (Sec. 6359.7, Rev. & Tax. Code)

• *Paper bag surcharges*

Sales and use tax is inapplicable to local paper bag surcharges. Some cities and counties have enacted ordinances that prohibit certain retailers from providing plastic bags to customers. Under certain ordinances, the customer is generally required to pay the retailer a specific amount for each paper bag the customer is provided. Some of these ordinances specifically require that the retailer indicate on the customer's receipt the number of paper bags provided and the total amount charged for the paper bags. Under these circumstances, the charge is imposed by the local jurisdiction upon the customer, not the retailer. As such, this charge is not included in the retailer's gross receipts and is not subject to sales or use tax. (*Special Notice L-282*, California State Board of Equalization, June 2011)

• *Places that charge admissions*

Tax applies to sales of food products sold for consumption within a place that charges admission. There is a presumption that food products are sold at such establishments for consumption on the premises. If an exemption is claimed, the retailer must retain evidence for it, such as proof that sales were of items in forms unlikely to be consumed in the place sold. (Sec. 6359(d), Rev. & Tax. Code; Reg. 1603(d), 18 CCR)

"Admission charge" does not include guest charges or dues in an organization that grants members entrance to a fenced area containing a club house, tennis court, or swimming pool. Also, fees for identification cards that entitle a student to attend school events, golf course green fees, swimming pool use charges, and charges for bowling in a public place, do not constitute "admission charges." (Sec. 6359(d), Rev. & Tax. Code; Reg. 1603(d), 18 CCR)

The exemption granting student meals does not apply to food sold to students in places that charge admission, unless the food is sold by a nonprofit parent teacher association. Sales of food products by a student organization to students and non-students at an athletic event where admission is charged are taxable. (Sec. 6359(d), Rev. & Tax. Code; Reg. 1603(d), 18 CCR)

National and state parks and monuments, and marinas, campgrounds, and recreational vehicle parks are not considered places that charge admission for sales and use tax purposes. (Sec. 6359(d), Rev. & Tax. Code; Reg. 1603(d), 18 CCR)

• *Places that sell food*

The general exemption for food products does not apply to food:

— sold as meals on or off the retailer's premises;

— furnished in a form suitable for consumption on the seller's premises, if 80% of the seller's gross receipts are from the sale of food products and over 80% of the seller's retail sales of food products are taxable sales of the kind discussed in (1) above, or (3), (4) or (7) below (this is known as the 80-80 rule);

— furnished for consumption at the retailer's tables, counters, trays, etc.;

— sold for consumption on or near parking facilities;

— sold from vending machines;

— sold for consumption at a place that charges admission, except for state or national parks and monuments, or marinas, campgrounds, and recreational vehicle parks; or

— sold as hot prepared food products.

(Sec. 6359(d), Rev. & Tax. Code)

Sales of otherwise nontaxable food products that are taxed as a result of application of the 80-80 rule may still qualify for exemption if the retailer elects to separately account for the nontaxable sales and provides full documentation substantiating such sales. (Sec. 6359(f), Rev. & Tax. Code)

• *Restaurants, hotels, and similar establishments*

Tax applies to sales of meals or hot prepared food products furnished by restaurants, concessionaires, hotels, boarding houses, soda fountains, and similar establishments, whether served on or off premises. American Plan hotels and boarding houses are required to reasonably segregate room charges from meal charges. Charges for delivering meals or hot prepared food products to rooms of guests are taxable, whether or not separately stated. Charges for parking attendants, security guards, and wrap attendants are excludable from taxable receipts if the charges for their services can be identified on the retailers' records and if the personnel performing these services did not also participate in the service of food and drinks. (Reg. 1603, 18 CCR)

A "boarding house" is any establishment regularly serving meals to an average of five or more paying guests and includes a guest home, residential care home, halfway house, or any other establishment providing room and board or board only that is not a health-care or related kind of institution. (Reg. 1603(a), 18 CCR)

"American Plan hotels" are lodging establishments that charge a fixed sum for room and meals combined. (Reg. 1603(a), 18 CCR)

"Average retail value" of complimentary food and beverages is equivalent to their total cost for the preceding calendar year, marked up 100% and divided by the number of rooms rented. Delivery charges are included in a lodging establishment's total costs, but discounts taken and sales tax reimbursements paid to vendors are excluded. The 100% markup factor includes costs of food preparation by hotel employees, the fair rental value of hotel facilities used for food and beverage preparation and service, and profit. (Reg. 1603(a), 18 CCR)

"Average daily rate" is calculated by dividing a hotel's gross room revenue for the preceding calendar year by the number of rooms rented for that year. (Reg. 1603(a), 18 CCR)

"Gross room revenue" includes hotel guest charges, but excludes separately stated occupancy taxes and revenue from contract and group rentals that do not qualify for complimentary food and beverages. Revenue from special packages that combine food and beverages with room accommodations is also excluded, unless the documented retail value of the food and beverages does not exceed 10% of the total charge for the package. (Reg. 1603(a), 18 CCR)

"Number of rooms rented for that year" is the total number of nightly room rentals that are reflected in gross room revenue. (Reg. 1603(a), 18 CCR)

Complimentary hotel meals.—Food and beverages of *de minimis* retail value, provided to hotel guests on a complimentary basis, are not subject to tax. In this regard, a lodging establishment is a consumer, rather than a retailer, of complimentary food and beverages for sales and use tax purposes, provided that the average retail value of complimentary food and beverages it has furnished during the preceding year is incidental. Average retail value that does not exceed 10% of a hotel's average daily rate for room accommodations for that year qualifies as incidental. Food and beverages provided to transient guests are complimentary, provided that guest bills do not reflect separate charges for accommodations and food, and provided that guests may not choose to decline food and beverages in exchange for discounted room rentals. The formula is calculated separately with respect to the operations of a hotel's concierge floor, club level, or similar program, to determine if the average retail value of complimentary food and beverages furnished to program participants is incidental. Likewise, the operations of a lodging establishment's multiple locations are considered separately in determining if each location's complimentary food and beverages are incidental. Food and beverages provided as part of an American Plan hotel's special packages do not qualify as complimentary. (Reg. 1603(a), 18 CCR)

A lodging establishment is also a consumer, rather than a retailer, with respect to complimentary food and beverages furnished in exchange for certain non-transferable coupons and similar documents that are redeemed by guests in an area of the hotel where food and beverages are also sold on a regular basis to the general public. (Reg. 1603(a), 18 CCR)

Prohibition against double taxation of food products.—Food products that are subject to California sales and use tax are not subject to a city, county, city and county, or charter city's transient occupancy tax. With respect to this prohibition, "food products" means food and beverages of every kind, regardless of how or where served. "Food products" specifically includes, but is not limited to, alcoholic beverages and carbonated beverages of every kind. (Sec. 7282.3, Rev. & Tax. Code)

Restaurant surcharge.—California sales tax applies to a separate surcharge added by a restaurant owner or operator to a customer's bill to cover required employer costs, such as increases to minimum wage, healthcare contributions, and paid sick leave. Whenever a surcharge is separately added to any taxable sale, the surcharge is also subject to sales tax. Restaurant owners or operators may not claim the cost of the surcharge as a deduction on their sales and use tax returns because California law does not allow a specific exemption for added surcharges. (*Special Notice L-491,* California State Board of Equalization, February 2017)

Two-for-one meal promotions.—When a restaurant agrees to furnish a "free" meal to a customer who purchases another meal and presents a coupon or card that the customer purchased either from the restaurant or through a sales promotional agency, the restaurant must include in its taxable receipts the price of the paid meal, plus either the additional receipts for the coupon (if purchased by the customer from the restaurant) or for any additional compensation that the restaurant received from the agency. (Reg. 1603(r), 18 CCR)

• *Social clubs and fraternal organizations*

Meals, food, and drink furnished by social clubs or fraternal organizations exclusively to members are not subject to tax in California, provided that such sales occur less frequently than once a week. If the club or organization furnishes such items to nonmembers as well as members, receipts from both members and nonmembers are subject to tax. Meals, food, and drinks paid for by members are "furnished" to the members, even if consumed by nonmember guests. (Reg. 1603(i), 18 CCR)

• *Tips and service charges*

A distinction is made between optional tips, gratuities and service charges that are paid at the customer's discretion and mandatory tips, gratuities and service charges that are added to the bill by the retailer and are part of the selling price of meals for purposes of the application of tax to such charges. An optional payment designated as a tip, gratuity or service charge is not subject to tax but a mandatory payment so designated is included in taxable gross receipts even if the amount is subsequently paid by the retailer to employees. (Reg. 1603(g), 18 CCR)

The CDTFA also provides guidance regarding tips, gratuities, and service charges. (*CDTFA Publication 115, Tips, Gratuities, and Service Charges,* California State Board of Equalization)

• *Vitamin enhanced water*

Sales of non-carbonated vitamin enhanced water beverages are not subject to California sales and use tax because they are considered to be food products. Medicinal claims made on the labels of such beverages do not change their classification as food products. A medicinal claim made on the label of a food product by a manufacturer does not necessarily render the food product taxable. The product must actually be a medicine to not qualify for the food products exemption. Compounding nutritional elements, such as vitamins, in an item traditionally accepted as food does not make the sale of the product taxable nor does inclusion of the word "vitamin" in a food product name, description, or product advertising. Sales of products in liquid, powdered, granular, tablet, capsule, lozenge, or pill form and described on their package as food supplements, food adjuncts, dietary supplements, or dietary adjuncts are subject to tax. Such products include but are not limited to over-the-counter vitamins, liquid vitamins, and concentrated vitamin boosts and shots that are designed to give a quick concentrated boost or shot of vitamins and/or energy. (Reg. 1602, 18 CCR; *Tax Information Bulletin*, California State Board of Equalization, September 2009)

[¶60-420] Government Transactions

Generally, sales to the government of the United States are exempt from the sales and use taxes both by California statute (Sec. 6381, Rev. & Tax. Code) and due to constitutional constraints discussed below.

The California Department of Tax and Fee Administration (CDTFA) provides guidance regarding sales and leases of merchandise to the U.S. government. (*CDTFA Publication 102, Sales to the United States Government*, California Department of Tax and Fee Administration, November 2018)

Sales to state or local governmental units are subject to the tax. The discussion below is separated into U.S. government transactions, state and local transactions, and public school transactions.

• *U.S. government transactions*

Sales to the following entities are exempt:

— the U.S. government and its unincorporated agencies and instrumentalities;

— any incorporated agency or instrumentality of the U.S. that is wholly owned by the U.S. or by a corporation wholly owned by the U.S.;

— the American National Red Cross, and;

— incorporated federal instrumentalities not wholly owned by the U.S. (unless federal law permits taxation of the instrumentality).

(Sec. 6381, Rev. & Tax. Code)

The use tax may not be imposed on the storage, use, or other consumption of property by the government unless specifically allowed under federal law. (Reg. 1614(a)(4), 18 CCR)

In addition, the Supremacy Clause of the U.S. Constitution declares that the U.S. Constitution and laws are the supreme law of the land, and the U.S. Supreme Court held early that this clause invalidated a state tax imposed directly on a federal instrumentality. (*McCulloch v. Maryland*, 17 US 316 (US SCt 1819))

To qualify for exemption, payment for the sale must be made directly to the vendor by the federal government or exempt agency (Reg. 1614(a), 18 CCR) and the sale itself must be supported by a government purchase order or documents that demonstrate direct payment by the United States. (Reg. 1614(g), 18 CCR) If a nonexempt person or entity makes full payment for a sale, the entire amount is taxable even if the federal government or an exempt agency fully or partially reimburses the payor. If payment is made partly by the federal government or exempt agency and partly by nonexempt parties, only the portion paid directly to the vendor by the federal government is exempt.

As an example of the above rule, a sale to a federally financed city housing authority was taxable. Purchases under the Soil Conservation Act that were made jointly by individual farmers and by the federal government were exempt only on the amount paid by the U.S.

Federal areas.—Under the Buck Act (4 U.S.C. Secs. 105—110), states may collect sales and use taxes within federal areas to the same extent as in nonfederal areas.

With respect to California, tax applies to the sale or use of tangible personal property in federal areas to the same extent it applies in nonfederal areas. Motor fuel sold on military or other federal reservations also is subject to state tax. (4 U.S.C. Sec. 104) (Reg. 1616(a), 18 CCR)

Sellers of alcoholic beverages to persons on federal reservations (e.g., national parks, Indian reservations, etc.) are liable for the sales tax on the selling price, except when the sales are made to federal instrumentalities or to persons who purchase for resale. (Reg. 1616(b), 18 CCR)

Foreign consuls and diplomatic personnel.—Tax does not apply to purchases or use of tangible personal property by foreign consular officers, employees, or members of their families exempt from taxation under treaty or diplomatic agreement with the United States. Persons identified as exempt from taxation pursuant to treaty or diplomatic agreement with the United States are issued an exemption card by the U.S. Department of State, Office of Foreign Missions (OFM), that identifies the bearer as exempt and specifies the extent of the exemption. The exemption does not extend to U.S. nationals performing consular duties for foreign governments. (Reg. 1619, 18 CCR)

In order for the exemption to apply to the sale or lease of vehicles to foreign consular officers, employees, or members of their families, the following requirements must be met:

— the purchaser must provide a valid tax exemption card (personal or mission) or a protocol identification card to the retailer; and

— the retailer must contact and obtain directly from the OFM a letter that states the vehicle sale or lease to the purchaser is eligible for exemption (otherwise known as an "OFM Eligibility Letter").

Moreover, in addition to other recordkeeping requirements, retailers must retain a copy of the tax exemption card, whether personal or mission, or protocol identification card, as well as the OFM Eligibility Letter to support each transaction claimed as an exempt sale or lease. (Reg. 1619(a)(2), (b), 18 CCR)

To support any deduction claimed for sales to foreign counsels, retailers must prepare invoices or written records of sales, including the name and exemption number of the purchaser, the name of the mission, the expiration date of the exemption card, and the minimum level of exemption specified on the exemption card. Generally, purchases of tangible personal property are exempt only if a valid exemption card is presented at the time of purchase. (Reg. 1619, 18 CCR)

The Office of Foreign Missions of the U.S. Department of State administers California sales tax exemption privileges to eligible foreign government offices and diplomatic or consular personnel on assignment in the United States. The Office issues Mission Tax Exemption Cards and Personal Tax Exemption Cards, both of which are valid nationwide and in the Commonwealth of Puerto Rico, Guam, and the U.S. Virgin Islands. The exemption cards may be used to claim exemption from state sales tax, lodging/occupancy tax, and other similar taxes charged to customers. The card does not authorize an exemption for utilities, gasoline, or vehicle purchases. Personal Tax Exemption Cards can only be used by foreign consular officers, employees, or members of their families who have been identified by the State Department as exempt. Mission Tax Exemption Cards are used only for official purchases by a foreign consulate. The person whose name and photo appears on such a card does not need to be present for the mission's official purchases. The back of the card should be checked for specific restrictions. Vendors must retain a copy of the front and back of the card for each transaction and must attach that copy to the receipt or invoice for their files. (*Tax Information Bulletin*, California State Board of Equalization, March 2009)

Government contractors.—Goods purchased for use under a construction contract fall into three categories:

— materials that become component parts of real property, such as bricks, doors, and cement;

— fixtures, that are accessories attached to real property, such as air conditioners, signs, and lighting fixtures; and

— machinery and equipment furnished in connection with a construction contract, such as lathes and machine tools. Purchases by federal contractors of the above items are treated as follows below.

(Reg. 1521(a)(1)(B), 18 CCR)

Machinery and equipment.—Federal contractors are retailers of machinery and equipment furnished in connection with construction contracts with the U.S. Sales of such property to federal contractors are exempt, provided that title passes to the U.S. before the contractor uses the property; such sales are considered sales for resale, and the purchasing contractor may issue a resale certificate. A contractor who uses such property before title passes to the U.S. is the consumer, and either sales or use tax applies to the sale to or use by the contractor. (Reg. 1521(b)(1)(B), 18 CCR)

Machinery and equipment v. improvements to realty.—The definition of "machinery and equipment" is limited to property that is used in producing, manufacturing, or processing tangible personal property, in performing services, or for other purposes (such as research and testing) not essential to the fixed works of a structure and that, if attached, is readily removable. For example, reinforcing steel, transformers, switch gear, and other miscellaneous items installed on military airfields were not machinery and equipment, which would have made their sales to federal contractors exempt as sales for resale, but improvements to property, and, as such, taxable to the contractor as consumer. Similarly, electric transmission cable that was purchased by a contractor for resale to the federal government and that was installed to replace worn-out lines constituted a fixture, and thus the contractor was liable for use tax on the purchase. (Reg. 1521(a), 18 CCR)

There are special provisions regarding contracts with the U.S. government to furnish or fabricate and furnish tangible personal property when title to items purchased by the contractor for use in performing the contract passes to the U.S. pursuant to title provisions contained in the contract before the contractor uses the items. Typical of such contracts are contracts to fabricate and furnish to the U.S. government ships, aircraft, ordnance, or equipment. The main issues in such contracts are taxability of the contractor's purchase of "direct consumable supplies" and "overhead materials," which are discussed below. (Reg. 1618, 18 CCR)

A federal government contractor's purchase of "direct consumable supplies" or "overhead materials" qualifies as a sale for resale to the federal government, provided that the federal government takes title pursuant to a U.S. government supply contract before the contractor uses the property for the purpose it was manufactured. Supplies, tools, or equipment consumed in performance of contractual obligations qualify as "direct consumable supplies," provided that they are identified to the contract and provided that the actual cost of such materials is charged as a direct cost to the specific contract. (Reg. 1618(a), 18 CCR)

The term "tools" includes "special tooling" that was previously covered by Federal Acquisition Regulation 52.245-17. (Reg. 1618(a), 18 CCR)

"Overhead materials" are defined as supplies consumed in the performance of a contract, the cost of which is charged to an overhead expense account and then allocated to various contracts based on generally accepted accounting principles and consistent with government cost accounting standards. (Reg. 1618(a), 18 CCR)

Whether title to direct consumable supplies or indirect consumable supplies (i.e., overhead materials) passes to the U.S. under a U.S. government supply contract, and the time at which title passes, is determined according to contractual title provisions, if any exist. For direct consumable supplies, which are charged direct to the U.S. government contract, title passes to the U.S. government pursuant to the title passage clause(s) associated with that specific contract. For indirect consumable supplies (i.e., overhead materials), which are charged to an expense account which is then allocated to various locations, cost centers or contracts, it will be considered that title passed to the U.S. government prior to use of the property, and tax will not apply with respect to the purchase or use of the property charged to the expense account, if the item is allocated to a specific U.S. government supply contract, pursuant to the terms of which title passes to the United States prior to the use of the item. (Reg. 1618(b), 18 CCR)

Materials and fixtures.—Federal contractors are consumers of materials and fixtures that they furnish and install in performing their contracts. Thus, either the sales tax or the use tax applies to sales of tangible personal property—including materials, fixtures, supplies, and equipment—to contractors for use in performing their contracts with the U.S. for constructing improvements on or to real property or for repairing fixtures. Sales tax, but not use tax, applies when the contractor purchases property as the agent of the federal government. (Sec. 6384, Rev. & Tax. Code; Reg. 1521(b)(1)(A), 18 CCR; Reg. 1521(c)(6), 18 CCR)

Military reservations.—Sellers of alcoholic beverages to officers' and non-commissioned officers' clubs and messes are exempt if the purchasing organizations have been authorized to sell alcoholic beverages to authorized purchasers. (Reg. 1616(b), 18 CCR)

Sales tax applies to gross receipts of operators of vending machines on Army, Navy, or Air Force installations. Tax does not apply to operators who lease machines to military exchanges or other U.S. instrumentalities (such as Post Restaurants and Navy Civilian Cafeteria Associations) if the instrumentality contractually acquires title to the merchandise and sells it through the leased machines. (Sec. 6021, Rev. & Tax. Code; Reg. 1616(c), 18 CCR)

California exempts sales to military exchanges and exchange services, open messes, and officers' messes, established under armed services regulations. Tax applies, however, to sales to military personnel, even if the merchandise is billed through such organizations. Tax does not apply to sales to civilian welfare funds operated at military installations in the state; exemption of such sales requires filing a special certificate obtained from the buyer. (Reg. 1614, 18 CCR)

Person insured under federal Medicare program.—California exempts sales to a person insured under the federal Medicare program, provided that the government makes direct payment to the seller; such sales are treated as exempt sales to the U.S. Sales of items under "Part B" of the Medicare Act, in which the patient's claim for reimbursement is assigned to the supplier and the supplier files the claim with the carrier, are taxable. Payments by patients, even if reimbursed by the U.S., are taxable. (Reg. 1614(f), 18 CCR)

Property purchased from any unincorporated agency or instrumentality of the U.S.—California exempts from the use tax property purchased from any unincorporated agency or instrumentality of the United States. The exemption does not apply to property reported as surplus property by an owning agency to the General Services Administration and to property included in contractor inventory. ("Surplus property," "owning agency," and "contractor inventory" have the meanings given them in the Surplus Property Act of 1944.) As examples of how the above provision applies, the use tax was imposed on property purchased from the Public Housing Administration, which is an incorporated federal instrumentality, and on a vessel declared surplus property and purchased from the Maritime Commission. However, use tax did not apply to a yacht sold by U.S. Marshal under a federal court order in an admiralty matter. (Sec. 6402, Rev. & Tax. Code)

Sales of property to a national bank.—California's right to collect tax on sales of property to a national bank was previously denied by the U.S. Supreme Court in a 1976 decision, *Diamond National Corp. v. BOE*, No. 75-1038, 425 US 268, 96 SCt 1530 (US SCt 1976), in which the Court held that the incidence of the state's sales tax is on the purchaser and is invalid when that purchaser is an exempt U.S. instrumentality. In *U.S. v. BOE*, 536 F2d 294 (US CA-9 1976), a federal appellate court ruled that former Revenue and Taxation Code Sec. 6381.5, which imposed a tax on leases to the federal government, was invalid. Although the taxes were levied on the lessors, the incidence of the tax fell on the government in violation of its constitutional immunity from state taxation. In response to this decision, the California legislature enacted Ch. 1211, Laws 1978, which amended sales and use tax law to clarify that the tax is imposed on the retailer, not on the purchaser. (Sec. 6051, Rev. & Tax. Code)

• *State and local transactions*

Under California sales and use tax law, the state of California and any county, city, or other political subdivision are considered "persons". (Sec. 6005, Rev. & Tax. Code) Generally, there is no specific exemption for sales to or purchases from such entities. However, animals transferred as pets to individuals by localities, local government animal shelters, and nonprofit animal welfare organizations are exempt from tax. (Sec. 6010.40, Rev. & Tax. Code)

A state department or agency may not enter into a contract for the purchase of tangible personal property from any vendor, contractor, or affiliate of a vendor or contractor unless the vendor, contractor, and all affiliates that make sales for delivery into California have a valid seller's permit or are registered with the California Department of Tax and Fee Administration (CDTFA) for sales and use tax purposes. Every vendor, contractor, or affiliate of a vendor or contractor offered such a contract is required to submit a copy of its, and any affiliate's, seller's permit or certificate of registration. An exception to this requirement is provided if the executive director of the state department or agency determines that the contract is necessary to meet a compelling state interest. The term "compelling state interest" includes, but is not limited to, situations ensuring the provision of essential services or the public health, safety, or welfare, or responding to an emergency as defined by law. (Sec. 10295.1, Pub. Contracts Code)

Tire retailers.—The California Department of Tax and Fee Administration provides information for tire retailers who signed a dealer agreement with any tire manufacturer agreeing to make sales to eligible state government entities honoring the pricing set through Western States Contracting Alliance (WSCA) contracts. The WSCA offers cooperative purchasing benefits for states as well as cities, counties, public schools, institutions of higher education, and other eligible entities. (*Special Notice L-371*, California State Board of Equalization, January 2014)

If the contracted WSCA price is lower than the tire retailer's dealer cost, a credit is generally applied to the retailer's vendor account to reimburse the retailer for the difference between that cost and the contracted price. This is a nontaxable reduction in the cost of the tires to retailer. (*Special Notice L-371*, California State Board of Equalization, January 2014)

If the retailer's vendor pays the retailer an additional credit, the additional credit amount the retailer will receive in the transaction is generally taxable. Sometimes these credits are called a "service allowance" and the credit is paid as a set percentage of the total sales amount. These additional credit amounts must be included in the taxable sales reported on the retailer's sales tax return in the same period that the sale occurred. (*Special Notice L-371*, California State Board of Equalization, January 2014)

The tire retailer may collect sales tax reimbursement on the additional taxable credit amount by listing the taxable amount on invoices. The tire retailer is required to disclose to its customers the amount of any taxable discounts, rebates, or incentives offered or paid to the retailer by third parties upon which sales or use tax is collected. (*Special Notice L-371*, California State Board of Equalization, January 2014)

All authorized governmental entities in any state are welcome to use WSCA cooperative contracts with the approval of that state's Chief Procurement Official by signing a participating addendum. (*Special Notice L-371*, California State Board of Equalization, January 2014)

• *Public school transactions*

Charitable donations by retailers to government or schools.—A use tax exemption applies to property (including motor vehicles) donated by retailers to certain federally exempt organizations described in IRC Sec. 170(b)(1)(A) and located in California:

— educational organizations maintaining a faculty and curriculum and having a regular student body;

— public colleges and universities that receive substantial financial support from federal, state, or local governments, or from the general public; and

— federal, state, or local governments, U.S. possessions, and the District of Columbia, provided that the donated property is used exclusively for public purposes.

(Sec. 6403, Rev. & Tax. Code; Reg. 1669.5(a)(5), 18 CCR; Reg. 1669(e), 18 CCR)

Property loans to schools.—California exempts from the use tax loans by retailers of (1) tangible personal property (including motor vehicles) to a school district for any of its educational programs and (2) motor vehicles to the University of California or to the California State University for exclusive use in driver education teacher certification programs. (Sec. 6404, Rev. & Tax. Code; Reg. 1669.5(a)(4), 18 CCR) For an exemption for motor vehicles loaned to private high schools for driver education programs, see ¶ 60-580 Nonprofit Organizations, Private Schools, and Churches.

A partial use tax exemption applies to motor vehicle loans by retailers to University of California or California State University employees. If the loan meets specified criteria, the retailer is liable for tax that would apply if the vehicle were leased at fair rental value during the loan term, rather than for an amount based on the vehicle's sales price. The partial exemption is available, provided that:

— the vehicle is furnished for the employee's exclusive use;

— the loan is approved by the chancellor of the university or the president of the state university, and

— the vehicle loan is independent of other automotive related business transactions between the retailer and the university or state university.

(Sec. 6202.7, Rev. & Tax. Code)

School yearbooks and catalogs.—Schools, school districts, county offices of education, and student organizations are consumers of yearbooks and catalogs prepared for or by them and distributed to students; tax does not apply therefore to sales of such items to students. (Sec. 6361.5, Rev. & Tax. Code; Reg. 1590(b)(9), 18 CCR) Tax does apply to charges made by printers, engravers, photographers, and the like to the above entities for preparing such publications. (Reg. 1590(b)(9), 18 CCR)

See ¶ 60-390 Food and Grocery Items, for school meals.

• *Space travel*

Gross receipts from the sale, storage, use, or other consumption in California of tangible personal property for use in connection with a space flight are exempt. Fuel produced, sold, and used exclusively for space flight is also exempt, provided that the fuel is not adaptable for use in ordinary motor vehicles; however, material not intended to be launched into space does not qualify for the exemption. (Sec. 6380, Rev. & Tax. Code)

[¶60-445] Internet/Electronic Commerce

Sales or use tax may apply to a variety of transactions in an electronic commerce environment. Such transactions include (1) purchases over the Internet of taxable services and property that are delivered in a nonelectronic form and (2) purchases of services or property that are delivered electronically and that may or may not be the equivalent of services or property that also can be delivered by nonelectronic means. General principles concerning the taxability of such transactions are discussed below.

CCH COMMENT: Click-through and affiliate nexus.—California has enacted click-through and affiliate nexus. See Nexus—Doing Business in California.

The California Department of Tax and Fee Administration (CDTFA) provides information regarding Internet sales. (*CDTFA Publication 109, Internet Sales*, California Department of Tax and Fee Administration)

The CDTFA also provides guidance on Internet auction sales and purchases. (*CDTFA Publication 177, Internet Auction Sales and Purchases*, California Department of Tax and Fee Administration)

Taxes on sales of computer software and services are discussed at Computers, Software, and Services.

If a transaction in an electronic commerce environment is taxable, the seller may or may not have a sufficient taxable connection, or nexus, with the taxing jurisdiction to be required to collect and remit tax on that transaction. Nexus issues in an electronic commerce environment are discussed below.

Under the federal Internet Tax Freedom Act (ITFA) and its amendments (P.L. 105-277, 112 Stat. 2681, 47 U.S.C. Sec. 151 note, amended by P.L. 107-75, P.L. 108-435, P.L. 110-108, P.L. 113-164, P.L. 113-235, P.L. 114-53, P.L. 114-113, and P.L. 114-125), state and local governments are barred from imposing multiple or discriminatory taxes on electronic commerce and taxes on Internet access, except for Internet access taxes allowed under grandfather clauses. The Internet Tax Freedom Act and its amendments are discussed below.

• *Taxability of transactions in electronic commerce*

The federal Internet Tax Freedom Act (ITFA), defines "electronic commerce" as any transaction conducted over the Internet or through Internet access, comprising the sale, lease, license, offer, or delivery of property, goods, services, or information, whether or not for consideration, and includes the provision of Internet access.

Transactions involving nonelectronic delivery.—Sales over the Internet may include the purchase of services that are delivered in a nonelectronic form, tangible personal property that is commonly delivered by mail or common carrier, or property in an electronic form capable of being processed by a computer ("digital property") that is stored on tangible storage media that is commonly delivered by mail or common carrier.

The taxability of such sales over the Internet generally is governed by the same rules as the purchase of such services or property in a traditional Main Street environment. However, the obligation of the seller to collect tax on such remote sales depends on whether the seller has nexus with the taxing jurisdiction, which is discussed below. If a sale is taxable and the seller does not collect tax, then the buyer generally is responsible for remitting use tax on the transaction.

A state may consider digital property stored on tangible storage media to be included in the definition of "tangible personal property" and, therefore, subject to the same taxability standard. Many states have special rules concerning the taxability of software and these are discussed at Computers, Software, and Services.

While most states impose sales and use tax generally on all sales of tangible personal property, the taxability of sales of digital property delivered electronically varies among the states. In some states, a sale of certain types of digital property delivered electronically is considered a taxable sale of tangible personal property. In other states, such a sale is treated as not involving the transfer of tangible personal property and, therefore, is nontaxable. In yet other states, sales of some software delivered electronically are taxable while sales of other items delivered electronically are nontaxable.

Some states may also draw a distinction based on whether the digital property delivered electronically would be considered tangible personal property if the same content were transferred on tangible storage media. That is, some states may only tax sales involving the electronic delivery of property if the property is the digital equivalent of tangible personal property.

Most states apply a true object of the transaction test in making taxability determinations. For example, if a state does not tax legal services, the delivery of a will electronically would not be taxable even if the state taxes the digital equivalent of tangible personal property, just as delivery of a will prepared on paper would not be taxable as the sale of tangible personal property.

The taxability of services varies among the states. The California sales and use taxes apply to services that are defined as sales of tangible personal property. The following are examples of services that are sales of tangible personal property:

— 50% of the lump-sum charge for the purchase of an optional software maintenance contract and the purchase or lease of a pre-written software program for such purchases made after 2002;

— charges for consultation services before 2003, where the purchase of an optional maintenence contract did not include an option to purchase consultation services in addition to the sale of the storage media containing program improvements or error corrections;

— any charge for consultation services provided in connection with a maintenance contract;

— fabrication services on garments or furniture furnished by a customer;

— charges for manipulating customer furnished data; and

— charges for producing multiple copies of documents through the use of word processing equipment.

See also Services and Computers, Software, and Services.

The taxability of information services and information databases also varies among the states.

• *Nexus and collection responsibility*

Once it is determined that a taxable transaction is involved, it must be determined whether nexus is sufficient to trigger tax liability and on whom tax collection responsibility rests.

CCH COMMENT: *Click-through nexus.*—California has enacted click-through nexus. See ¶ 60-025 Nexus—Doing Business in California.

In the absence of specific statutes or other defined policy governing taxation of sales of personal property that are made over the Internet, the law and issues applicable to mail order sales may provide a basis for determining sales and use tax treatment of sales made by electronic commerce.

As with mail order sales, a transaction involving an electronic sale to a purchaser by a vendor that has no physical presence in the purchaser's state raises nexus issues. Under *Quill Corp. v. North Dakota*, 504 US 298 (1992), unless a vendor has substantial nexus with the purchaser's state, the state has no constitutional basis for the imposition of sales and use tax collection responsibility on that vendor. Sales and use tax nexus and other constitutional issues are discussed at Nexus—Doing Business in California.

Among the factors specific to an electronic commerce environment that may be taken into account in determining whether nexus exists is the maintenance of a web page on a computer server located in the taxing state and the nature and extent of in-state services performed for a vendor by a company maintaining the vendor's website.

• *Federal Internet Tax Freedom Act*

The federal Internet Tax Freedom Act (ITFA) (P.L. 105-277, 112 Stat. 2681, 47 U.S.C. Sec. 151 note, amended by P.L. 107-75, P.L. 108-435, P.L. 110-108,. P.L. 113-164, P.L. 113-235, P.L. 114-53, P.L. 114-113, and P.L. 114-125) bars state and local governments from imposing multiple or discriminatory taxes on electronic commerce and taxes on Internet access.

Tax on Internet access.—The term "tax on Internet access" applies regardless of whether such a tax is imposed on a provider of Internet access or a buyer of Internet access and regardless of the terminology used to describe the tax. However, the term "tax on Internet access" does not include taxes on or measured by net income, capital stock, net worth, or property value, or other state general business taxes, such as gross receipts taxes, that are structured in such a way as to be a substitute for or supplement the state corporate income tax.

Grandfather provision.—A state or local government may continue to tax Internet access through June 30, 2020, if the tax was generally imposed and actually enforced prior to October 1, 1998. However, this grandfather clause does not apply to any state that, prior to November 1, 2005, repealed its tax on Internet access or issued a rule that it no longer applies such a tax.

Internet access definition.—"Internet access" means a service that enables users to connect to the Internet to access content, information, or other services. The definition includes the purchase, use, or sale of telecommunications by an Internet service provider to provide the service or otherwise enable users to access content, information, or other services offered over the Internet. It also includes incidental services such as home pages, electronic mail, instant messaging, video clips, and personal electronic storage capacity, whether or not packaged with service to access the Internet. However, "Internet access" does not include voice, audio or video programming, or other products and services using Internet protocol for which there is a charge, regardless of whether the charge is bundled with charges for "Internet access."

Telecommunications services.—Under the Internet Tax Freedom Act Amendments Act of 2007, state and local governments that continued to impose tax on telecommunications service purchased, used, or sold by a provider of Internet access had until June 30, 2008, to end these disputed taxes. However, this provision only operated if a public ruling applying such a tax was issued prior to July 1, 2007, or such a tax was the subject of litigation that was begun prior to July 1, 2007.

Bundled services.—The Act allows the taxation of otherwise exempt Internet access service charges that are aggregated (i.e. bundled) with and not separately stated from charges for telecommunications services or other taxable services, unless the Internet access provider can reasonably identify the charges for Internet access from its books and records kept in the regular course of business.

Discriminatory taxes.—Under the Act, prohibited discriminatory taxes are defined as:

— taxes imposed on electronic commerce transactions that are not generally imposed and legally collectible on other transactions that involve similar property, goods, services or information;

— taxes imposed on electronic commerce transactions at a different rate from that imposed on other transactions involving similar property, goods, services or information, unless the rate is lower as part of a phase-out of the tax over a five-year or lesser period;

— collection or payment obligations imposed upon a different person or entity than would apply if the transaction were not transacted via electronic commerce;

— classification of Internet access service providers or online service providers for purposes of imposing on such providers a higher rate of tax than is imposed on providers of similar information delivered through other means;

— collection obligations imposed on a remote seller on the basis of the in-state accessibility of the seller's out-of-state computer server; and

— collection obligations imposed on a remote seller solely because the Internet access service or online service provider is deemed to be the remote seller's agent on the basis of the remote seller's display of information or content on the out-of-state server or because orders are processed through the out-of-state server.

Multiple taxes.—Prohibited multiple taxes are taxes imposed by a state or local government on the same, or essentially the same, transactions in electronic commerce that are also subject to a tax imposed by another state or local government without a corresponding credit or resale exemption certificate for taxes paid in other jurisdictions.

The moratorium against multiple taxes does not include taxes imposed within a state by the state or by one or more local governments within the state on the same electronic commerce.

The moratorium against multiple taxes does not prohibit other taxes from being imposed on persons who are engaged in electronic commerce even though that commerce has been subject to a sales or use tax.

State Internet access taxes.—California had a state Internet Tax Freedom Act that expired on January 1, 2004.

[¶60-460] Leases and Rentals

Leases and rentals of tangible personal property are subject to sales and use tax in California.

Are leases and rentals taxable in California?

Yes. The lease of tangible personal property for consideration is subject to sales and use tax as a sale or purchase, subject to certain exceptions. Generally, the tax applicable to leases is the use tax, which is measured by the rental receipts; the lessor is responsible for collecting the tax and giving the lessee a receipt. The lessee remains liable for the tax until this receipt is obtained. However, the lessor has the option of paying tax upon its acquisition of the property to be leased and not collecting tax on the lease payments.

A "lease" is defined as a "continuing sale," and possession of the leased property is a "continuing purchase" However, the definition of "lease" excludes any use of tangible personal property for less than one day and for a charge of less than $20, if the privilege of using the property is restricted to the premises or a business location of the grantor. The grantors of these services are consumers of the property, and the rental receipts are not taxable.

The California Department of Tax and Fee Administration (CDTFA) provides guidance regarding the leasing of tangible personal property.

Assignment of leases. When a lessor assigns to another party the right to receive rental payments, liability for collection of tax shifts to the assignee only if there is a transfer of title; the title holder is responsible for collecting use tax on the rental receipts of any taxable lease. This is the case even if title is assigned temporarily for security reasons and is to revert to the lessor/assignor at the end of the lease. When title to the property is assigned, the assignee assumes the position of lessor and is required to hold a seller's permit and to collect and pay tax to the state; in such a situation, the assignor, when assigning the property, should obtain a resale certificate from the assignee covering the assigned property. An assignee/purchaser who uses the property after termination of the lease is subject to use tax measured by the purchase price.

Basis of tax. In computing a lessee's liability for use tax, the terms "sales price" and "gross receipts" include the total amount for which the property is leased, any services provided as part of the transaction, and any credits given. In the case of a lease that is a "sale" and "purchase" the tax is measured by the rentals payable. Included in the amount subject to tax are personal property taxes on the leased property, whether assessed against the lessee or lessor. The amount subject to tax does not include amounts paid to the lessor for:

— collection costs, including attorney's fees and repossession charges (however, tax does apply to delinquent rental payments, including those collected by court action);

— costs of insuring or repairing the property following a default;

— costs incurred in defending a court action or in paying a judgment arising out of the lessee's operation of the leased property, or any insurance premiums paid on policies covering such court actions or judgments;

— costs of disposing of the property at expiration or earlier termination of the lease;

— late charges and interest for delinquent rental payments; and

— separately stated insurance charges or maintenance or warranty contracts, provided that these charges are optional.

Chemical and portable toilets. Leases of chemical and portable toilets are taxable regardless of whether tax was paid on the purchase price when they were acquired or whether they are leased in the same form as acquired.

Leases to exempt entities and the federal government. When the lessee (other than the federal government and its instrumentalities) is not subject to the use tax, e.g., insurance companies, sales tax applies and is measured by the rental receipts imposed on the lessor. Leases to the federal government or its instrumentalities are exempt from both sales and use taxes, unless federal law permits taxation of the instrumentality. For a complete discussion of transactions with the federal government, see Government Transactions.

Lessor's use of property. If a lessor uses property after leasing it and reporting tax on the rental receipts, the lessor is liable for use tax measured by the property's full purchase price. Tax paid on the rental receipts is credited against the use tax paid on the purchase price, and any excess remaining tax due may be applied at a later date against any tax liability on subsequent leases of the same property.

Options to purchase and sales under security agreements. A lease that affords the lessee an option to purchase is a taxable sale if that option is exercised; the tax is measured by the amount that must be paid by the lessee/purchaser upon exercising the option. In addition, California taxes a "sale under a security agreement," not as a lease, but as a transaction in which the lessee is contractually bound for a fixed term and either is to obtain title to the property at the end of the term upon completing lease payments or has the option at that time of purchasing the property for a nominal amount. The option price is considered "nominal" if it does not exceed the lesser of $100 or 1% of the purchase price.

Are there any special exemptions for leases or rentals in California?

Yes. California has various exemptions for leases or rentals.

Airport customer facility charges. Customer facility charges or any other facility financing fees required by an airport to be collected from customers of rental car companies operating in or near an airport are not subject to California sales or use tax.

Credit for tax paid in another state. California allows a lessor that leases property in California that was purchased out of state to take a credit for tax paid to another state. This credit is allowed only for out-of-state taxes measured by the purchase price of the property, not by rental receipts from out-of-state leases. If the out-of-state tax equals or exceeds the tax due in California, the lessor qualifies automatically for the credit, and the California rental receipts are not taxable. However, if the out-of-state tax is less than the tax due in California, the lessor, in the reporting period in which the property is first leased, must elect to pay use tax measured by the purchase price. If this timely election is not made, the rental receipts are taxed. If the lessee is not subject to use tax, a lessor that has not made the timely election may still not take this credit, since in such a situation the tax due is a sales tax rather than a use tax.

Exceptions for certain tangible personal property. California does not consider leases of certain kinds of tangible personal property to be either a "sale" or a "purchase," and as a result, such leases are not subject to tax. Leases that are not subject to tax include:

Household furnishings. A lease of household furnishings that are part of a lease of living quarters in which they are to be used is not a taxable sale provided that the lessor of the household furnishings is also the lessor of the living quarters. (Sec. 6006(g), Rev. & Tax. Code; Reg. 1660(b)(1), 18 CCR)

Linens. If the recurrent service of laundering or cleaning is an essential part of a lease agreement, the furnishing of linens and similar articles is not a sale and thus not taxable. This also applies to items such as towels, uniforms, coveralls, shop coats, dust cloths, caps and gowns. (Sec. 6006(g), Rev. & Tax. Code; Reg. 1660(b)(1), 18 CCR)

Manufacturing property. A post-1996 lease of qualified manufacturing property by a manufacturer to a qualified person in a form not substantially the same as when acquired is not considered a "sale" or "purchase" if the lessor makes a timely election to report and pay tax measured by the cost price of the property. See ¶60-510 Manufacturing, Processing, Assembling, or Refining, for a discussion of the requirements for making such an election. (Reg. 1660(b)(1), 18 CCR)

Mobile homes. The lease of a new mobile home purchased by a retailer without payment of sales tax reimbursement or use tax and first leased on or after July 1, 1980, is excluded from classification as a continuing sale and the lessor's use of such property by leasing is subject to the use tax.

Mobile transportation equipment. Leasing mobile transportation equipment for use in transporting persons or property does not constitute a taxable sale or purchase. For a complete discussion, see Transportation.

Motion pictures. Leases of motion pictures, including television, films, or tapes, are not "sales" and are, as a result, not taxable. However, the rental or lease of a videocassette, videotape, or videodisk for private use is taxable. "Private use" means that the lessee does not acquire the right to license, broadcast, exhibit, or reproduce the property. Tax applies to the rental receipts regardless of whether the property is leased in substantially the same form as acquired and regardless of whether the lessor has paid sales or use tax on the purchase price of the property. (Sec. 6006(g), Rev. & Tax. Code; Reg. 1660(b)(1) and (d)(2), 18 CCR)

Tax paid property. Tangible personal property leased in substantially the same form as acquired by the lessor or a transferor, as to which the lessor or transferor has paid sales tax reimbursement or has paid use tax measured by the purchase price of the property, is not considered a sale or a purchase, and is not subject to tax.

Option to pay tax on purchase price. California does not tax any lease of property that is in substantially the same form as when acquired by the lessor and on which the lessor has paid sales or use tax measured by the purchase price. Payment of use tax or sales tax reimbursement on these properties at the time of acquisition is an irrevocable election to measure tax by the purchase price and may not be changed by reporting tax on rental receipts and claiming a deduction for tax-paid property resold. If the tax on the purchase price was not paid by the lessor at the time of acquisition, the lessor may elect to pay this tax; the election must be made on the lessor's return for the reporting period in which the property is first leased.

Property acquired in a business transfer. A lessor who acquired property as the transferee in a transfer of substantially all of the personal property of a transferor in a retail business (or other activity requiring a seller's permit) with no real change in ownership does not have to report tax on the rental receipts if the transferor paid sales or use tax on the purchase price to the transferor of the property. If the transferor did not pay tax when it acquired the property, the transferee may elect to pay use tax measured by the purchase price; the election must be made on the transferee's return for the reporting period in which the property is initially leased.

Property acquired from deceased. The exemption for rental receipts from the lease of property as to which tax was paid on the purchase price also applies to property acquired by a transferee/lessor from a decedent by will or law of succession, where the decedent/transferor had already paid sales or use tax measured by the property's purchase price.

Property acquired in an occasional sale. A lessor of property that was purchased by the lessor in an occasional sale may elect to pay use tax on the purchase price instead of tax measured by rental receipts; the election must be made on the lessor's return for the reporting period in which the property is initially leased.

Out of state property. California exempts leases of tangible personal property that is situated outside California.

Property affixed to realty. Fixtures essential to a structure (such as air-conditioning units) being rented out by the lessor of the structure are considered real property and are, consequently, not subject to sales or use tax, while components of a structure leased by someone other than the lessor of the real property are treated as leases of tangible personal property. Fixtures that are attached to realty are treated as personal property when leased with property that the lessor does not own and when the lessor has the right to remove the fixtures upon termination or breach of the lease. Structures that are firmly attached to realty, together with the component parts of such structures (e.g., plumbing fixtures, air conditioners, etc.), are regarded as real property when leased; this provision does not apply to prefabricated mobile homes or portable buildings attached to real property only through plumbing and electrical hookups.

Factory-built school buildings. Leases of factory-built school buildings (i.e., relocatable classrooms) are leases of real property, and the lessor is treated as the consumer. If the lessor is the manufacturer of the building, tax applies to the costs of all tangible personal property used to construct the building. If the lessor is not the manufacturer of the building, tax applies to 40% of the sales price of the building to the lessor.

Repair parts used in maintaining leased property. A lessor may purchase, under a resale certificate, any repair parts that the lessor uses in maintaining leased equipment under a mandatory maintenance contract, provided the rental receipts are subject to tax. Charges paid by the lessee under the mandatory maintenance contract are part of the taxable rental payments.

Sale and leaseback transactions. Generally, California does not tax sale and leaseback transactions.

Acquisition sale and leaseback. An acquisition sale and leaseback arrangement executed after 1990 is exempt from sales and use tax. A "sale" and "purchase" do not include any transfer of title to, or lease of, tangible personal property under an acquisition sale and leaseback.

An "acquisition sale and leaseback" is a sale by a person and a leaseback to that person of tangible personal property when: (1) that person has paid sales tax reimbursement or use tax with respect to that person's purchase of the property; and (2) the acquisition sale and leaseback is consummated within 90 days of the person's first functional use of the property.

Other sale and leaseback transactions. California treats as a nontaxable financing arrangement a sale and leaseback transaction if:

— the lease would qualify as a "sale under a security agreement," i.e., the lease binds the lessee for a fixed term and gives the lessee, upon completion of the payments at the end of the term, either: (a) title to the property; or (b) an option to buy the property for a nominal amount (1% of the total contract price or $100, whichever is least);

— the purchaser/lessor claims no federal or state income tax deduction, credit, or exemption with respect to the property; and

— the amount attributable to interest, had the transaction been originally structured as a financing agreement, is not usurious under California law.

A sale and leaseback transaction used to finance the initial purchase of tangible personal property is also treated as a nontaxable financing arrangement, provided that all of the following conditions are met:

— the seller/lessee of the property has not paid the entire initial purchase price to the original vendor;

— in the purchase order and invoice for the property, the interest of the seller/lessee is assigned to the purchaser/ lessor;

— the purchaser/lessor, on behalf of the seller/lessee, pays the balance due on the purchase price;

— the purchaser/lessor claims no federal or state income tax deduction, credit, or exemption with respect to the property;

— the amount attributable to interest, if the arrangement had been structured as a financing agreement, would not be usurious under California law; and

— the seller/lessee has the option to purchase the property at the end of the lease term at a price no higher than fair market value.

Safe-harbor leases. Sales and use tax does not apply to "safe-harbor" sale and leaseback transactions that were set up under former IRC § 168(f)(8). This exemption also applies to: (1) arrangements that the California Department of Transportation entered into with private corporations for passenger transportation vehicles; and (2) the transfer of a qualified mass commuting vehicle in a safe-harbor transaction.

Subleases. California does not tax subleases of property leased in substantially the same form as acquired by the prime lessor and for which tax has been paid either: (1) by the prime lessor on the purchase price; or (2) on rental receipts derived under the prime lease or any prior sublease.

[¶60-480] Lodging

The sales and use tax is not imposed on lodging or room rentals, campsite rentals, etc. However, certain redevelopment agencies and the legislative bodies of cities and counties may impose transient occupancy taxes for short-term hotel, motel, tourist home, and mobile home lodgings.

The California State Board of Equalization (CDTFA) provides guidance regarding the application of sales and use tax to transactions engaged in by organized camps, such as sales of meals and other tangible personal property sold to campers, staff, and guests. (*Publication 127, Organized Camps*, California Department of Tax and Fee Administration)

• *Banquet and meeting rooms*

California Department of Tax and Fee Administration (CDTFA) Publication 22 provides that charges by restaurants, hotels, and similar establishments for the use of premises where meals, food, or drinks are served are taxable, regardless of whether the charge is separately stated on the invoice. (Reg. 1603(i)(4), 18 CCR; Publication 22, Dining and Beverage Industry, California Department of Tax and Fee Administration)

> **EXAMPLE:** *Banquet charges*—If a $100 fee is charged for the use of a banquet room for a holiday party, the fee is taxable. (Publication 22, Dining and Beverage Industry, California Department of Tax and Fee Administration)

According to the BOE, a charge for the use of a conference room not generally used for food service is generally non-taxable. The BOE considers the value of the food in the total charge (the portion of the total charge attributable to food) to determine taxability. If a room rental charge would ordinarily be $500 but the invoice for the use of the room for a conference states the charge was $2,000, then because the value of the food, as compared to the fee for the use of the room, is in excess of the room rental fee, the charge would be taxable. (*Telephone conversation*, California State Board of Equalization, June 25, 2015)

[¶60-510] Manufacturing, Processing, Assembling, or Refining

The taxability of a manufacturer's purchases of certain materials and equipment varies depending on the nature of the transaction, and its sales of tangible personal property are taxable.

Are purchases by manufacturers, processors, assemblers, or refiners taxable in California?

Purchases by manufacturers, processors, assemblers, or refiners may be:

— exempt;

— taxable;

— partially exempt; or

— possibly excluded from tax.

Exempt purchases. Tax does not apply to purchases of certain property by manufacturers. (Reg. 1525, 18 CCR)

Property incorporated into a manufactured article. Tax does not apply to purchases of property to be incorporated into a manufactured article, such as raw materials becoming ingredients or components of the manufactured article. For the exemption to apply, the primary purpose of the purchase of the property must be its actual incorporation into a manufactured article to be sold. (Reg. 1525, 18 CCR)

Oak wine and brandy barrels. Tax does not apply to oak wine or brandy barrels purchased to incorporate oak into the wine or brandy to be sold. The use of oak barrels as containers during the manufacturing process is incidental to the primary purpose of incorporating the oak into the wine or brandy. (Reg. 1525, 18 CCR)

Taxable purchases. Tax applies to certain purchases made by manufacturers.

Property not physically incorporated into manufactured article. Tax applies to purchases of tangible personal property for use in manufacturing, producing, or processing tangible personal property and not physically incorporated into the manufactured article. Examples include machinery, tools, furniture, office equipment, and chemicals used as catalysts. (Reg. 1525, 18 CCR)

Items used and consumed in production. Manufacturers and refiners must pay tax on their purchase of tangible personal property to be used and consumed in the manufacturing or refining process, including the portion of purchased raw materials that comprise by-products that are produced and consumed during the manufacturing process. (Reg. 1525.5, 18 CCR)

When a manufacturer or refiner, prior to or during manufacturing or refining, physically commingles property purchased for resale with property not so purchased, but that is so similar that the separate identity of the materials in the commingled mass cannot be determined, any by-products produced from the commingled mass and consumed are treated as if first consumed from the property not purchased for resale until a quantity of commingled goods equal to the quantity of property not purchased for resale has been consumed. (Reg. 1525.5(c), 18 CCR)

Manufacturing aids. Tax applies to sales of manufacturing aids, such as dies, patterns, jigs, and tooling, that are used in manufacturing, even if the aid is subsequently delivered to, or held as property of, the purchaser of the manufactured article. If title to the manufacturing aid contractually passes to the customer before it is used in the manufacturing process, then the manufacturer may purchase the aid (or raw materials used by the manufacturer in its fabrication) under a resale certificate; in this instance, tax applies to the sale of the aid to the customer. Also, although items used as manufacturing aids may not be transferred to the customer, the transaction includes a taxable sale of such items to the customer if the sales contract indicates that title to the item passes to the customer. See SUTA Series 440, Property used in manufacturing. (Reg. 1525.1, 18 CCR)

Purchases of coke by foundries. Tax applies to 55% of the receipts from the sale of coke to foundries for manufacturing castings by the cupola process. This percentage represents that portion of the coke consumed in the process. The remaining 45% is not taxable because it represents that portion of the coke that the foundry purchases for resale. (Reg. 1530, 18 CCR)

Partially exempt purchases. From July 1, 2014 through June 30, 2030, a partial sales and use tax exemption is applicable to the gross receipts from the sale, storage, use, or other consumption in California of any qualified tangible personal property purchased for use by:

— a qualified person to be used primarily (i.e., 50% or more of the time) in any stage of the manufacturing, processing, refining, fabricating, or recycling of tangible personal property, beginning at the point any raw materials are received by the qualified person and introduced into the process and ending at the point at which the manufacturing, processing, refining, fabricating, or recycling has altered tangible personal property to its completed form, including packaging, if required;

— a qualified person to be used primarily in R&D;

— a qualified person to be used primarily to maintain, repair, measure, or test any qualified tangible personal property described above;

— a contractor purchasing that property for use in the performance of a construction contract for the qualified person that will use that property as an integral part of the manufacturing, processing, refining, fabricating, or recycling process, the generation or production, or storage and distribution, of electric power, or as a research or storage facility for use in connection with those processes; and

— a qualified person to be used primarily in the generation or production, or storage and distribution, of electric power.

(Sec. 6377.1, Rev. & Tax. Code)

See Construction, for a discussion of the ways in which this manufacturing and R&D partial exemption may be used by construction contractors.

The exemption is inapplicable to either of the following:

— purchases of qualified tangible personal property for which this exemption is claimed by a qualified person that exceed $200 million; or

— the sale or storage, use, or other consumption of property that, within one year from the date of purchase, is removed from California, converted from an exempt use to some other use not qualifying for exemption, or used in a manner not qualifying for exemption. (Sec. 6377.1, Rev. & Tax. Code)

Application of partial exemption. The partial exemption from sales and use taxes applies to 4.1875% of the current total statewide base sales and use tax rate from July 1, 2014 to December 31, 2016, and to 3.9375% of the total statewide base sales and use tax rate from January 1, 2017 to June 30, 2030. Consequently, the reduced tax rate applicable to qualifying purchases and leases is:

— 3.3125% from July 1, 2014 to December 31, 2016; and

— 3.5625% from January 1, 2017 to June 30, 2030. (Reg. 1525.4, 18 CCR)

July 1, 2014, through December 31, 2016. For the period beginning July 1, 2014, and ending on December 31, 2016, the partial exemption applies to the taxes imposed by Revenue and Taxation Code Sections 6051 (except the taxes deposited pursuant to section 6051.15), 6051.3, 6201 (except the taxes deposited pursuant to section 6201.15), and 6201.3, and Section 36 of Article XIII of the California Constitution (an exemption of 4.1875%). The partial exemption does not apply to the taxes imposed or deposited pursuant to Revenue and Taxation Code Sections 6051.2, 6051.5, 6051.15, 6201.2, 6201.5, or 6201.1, the Bradley-Burns Uniform Local Sales and Use Tax Law, the Transactions and Use Tax Law, or Section 35 of Article XIII of the California Constitution. (Reg. 1525.4, 18 CCR)

January 1, 2017, through June 30, 2022. For the period beginning January 1, 2017, and ending on June 30, 2030, the partial exemption applies to the taxes imposed by Revenue and Taxation Code Sections 6051 (except the taxes deposited pursuant to section 6051.15), 6051.3, 6201 (except the taxes deposited pursuant to section 6201.15), and 6201.3 (an exemption of 3.9375%). The partial exemption does not apply to the taxes imposed or deposited pursuant to Revenue and Taxation Code Sections 6051.2, 6051.5, 6051.15, 6201.2, 6201.5, or

6201.15, the Bradley-Burns Uniform Local Sales and Use Tax Law, the Transactions and Use Tax Law, or Section 35 of Article XIII of the California Constitution. (Reg. 1525.4, 18 CCR)

Qualified person. Prior to January 1, 2018, a "qualified person" is defined as a person that is primarily engaged in those lines of business described in Codes 3111 to 3399, inclusive, 541711, or 541712 of the North American Industry Classification System (NAICS) published by the United States Office of Management and Budget (OMB), 2012 edition. Examples of types of manufacturing companies represented by the applicable NAICS codes include R&D in biotechnology, physical engineering, and life sciences. On and after January 1, 2018, and before July 1, 2030, Codes 22111 to 221118, inclusive, 221122 are added. (Sec. 6377.1, Rev. & Tax. Code; Reg. 1525.4, 18 CCR)

Qualified tangible personal property. "Qualified tangible personal property" includes:

— machinery and equipment, including component parts and contrivances such as belts, shafts, moving parts, and operating structures;

— equipment or devices used or required to operate, control, regulate, or maintain the machinery, including but not limited to computers, data-processing equipment, and computer software, together with all repair and replacement parts with a useful life of one or more years, whether purchased separately or in conjunction with a complete machine and regardless of whether the machine or component parts are assembled by the qualified person or another party;

— tangible personal property used in pollution control that meets standards established by the state or any local or regional governmental agency within the state;

— prior to January 1, 2018, special purpose buildings and foundations used as an integral part of the manufacturing, processing, refining, fabricating, or recycling process, or that constitute a research or storage facility used during those processes (buildings used solely for warehousing purposes after completion of those processes are not included); and

— on and after January 1, 2018, and before July 1, 2030, special purpose buildings and foundations used as an integral part of the manufacturing, processing, refining, fabricating, or recycling process, or that constitute a research or storage facility used during those processes, or the generation or production or storage and distribution of electric power (buildings used solely for warehousing purposes after completion of those processes are not included). (Sec. 6377.1, Rev. & Tax. Code; Reg. 1525.4, 18 CCR)

The following are not included within the definition of "qualified tangible personal property" for purposes of the exemption:

— consumables with a useful life of less than one year;

— furniture, inventory, and equipment used in the extraction process, or equipment used to store finished products that have completed the manufacturing, processing, refining, fabricating, or recycling process; and

— tangible personal property used primarily in administration, general management, or marketing. (Sec. 6377.1, Rev. & Tax. Code)

The California Department of Tax and Fee Administration (CDTFA) is required to cancel any outstanding and unpaid deficiency determination and any related penalties and interest and will not issue any deficiency determination or notice of determination, with respect to unpaid sales and use tax on qualified property with a useful life that was purchased or leased on or after July 1, 2014, and before January 1, 2018. Any amounts paid by a qualified person pursuant to such a determination will be refunded by the department to the qualified person. Any such cancellation or refund is contingent upon a qualified person making a request to the department, in a manner prescribed by the department, by June 30, 2018. (Sec. 6377.1, Rev. & Tax. Code)

Exemption certificate. The exemption is not allowed unless the purchaser furnishes the retailer with an exemption certificate and the retailer retains the exemption certificate in its records and furnishes it to the California Department of Tax and Fee Administration upon request. (Sec. 6377.1, Rev. & Tax. Code)

In order to document the partially exempt sale, taxpayers must get a timely exemption certificate from their customers. The certificate should include:

— the date;

— the signature of the purchaser, the purchaser's agent, or the purchaser's employee;

— the name and address of the purchaser;

— the purchaser's seller's permit number, or if the purchaser is not required to hold a seller's permit, a notation to that effect and the reason;

— a description of the property purchased under the certificate; and

— a statement of the manner in which, or the purpose for which, the property will be used that demonstrates why the exemption is applicable. (Invoices on sales claimed by a seller as exempt should specify the names of the purchasers in order to relate them to exemption certificates.) (*Manufacturing Exemption*, California Department of Tax and Fee Administration)

If a purchaser certifies in writing to the seller that the tangible personal property purchased without payment of the tax will be used in a manner entitling the seller to the exemption, and the purchase exceeds the $200 million limitation, or, within one year from the date of purchase, the purchaser removes that property from California, converts that property for use in a manner not qualifying for the exemption, or uses that property in a manner not qualifying for the exemption, then the purchaser will be liable for payment of sales tax with applicable interest as if the purchaser were a retailer making a retail sale of the property at the time the property is so purchased, removed, converted, or used. Tax will be calculated on the cost of the property to the purchaser. (Sec. 6377.1, Rev. & Tax. Code)

The exemption is inapplicable to local sales and use taxes imposed under the Bradley-Burns Uniform Local Sales and Use Tax Law, transactions and use taxes imposed under the Transactions and Use Tax Law, and certain state taxes, as specified, from which revenues are deposited into certain funds including the Local Public Safety Fund, the Local Revenue Fund, and the Local Revenue Fund 2011. (Sec. 6377.1, Rev. & Tax. Code)

Sunset. The exemption is repealed effective January 1, 2031. (Sec. 6377.1, Rev. & Tax. Code)

Possibly excluded purchases. Some purchases made by manufacturers may be excluded from tax.

Green manufacturing exclusion. The California Alternative Energy and Advanced Transportation Financing Authority is authorized to approve a sales and use tax exclusion on tangible personal property used for the design, manufacture, production, or assembly of advanced transportation technologies or alternative source products, components, or systems, otherwise known as a "green manufacturing exclusion."

Are sales by manufacturers, processors, assemblers, or refiners taxable in California?

Yes, tax applies to retail sales by manufacturers to consumers of tangible personal property that is not exempt. (Reg. 1524, 18 CCR)

Are self-produced goods used in manufacturing, processing, assembling, or refining taxable in California?

California does not currently have sales and use tax provisions specifically concerning self-produced and self-consumed goods used in manufacturing, processing, assembling, or refining.

Are labor and services related to manufacturing, processing, assembling, or refining taxable in California?

Yes, charges for producing, fabricating, processing, printing, or imprinting tangible personal property for consumers who furnish the materials used in those procedures are taxable. (Sec. 6006(b), Rev. & Tax. Code; Reg. 1526, 18 CCR) Guidance is provided regarding the application of sales and use tax to particular labor charges, including fabrication. (*CDTFA Publication 108, Labor Charges*, California Department of Tax and Fee Administration)

Fabrication. In determining whether tax applies, the phrase "producing, fabricating, and processing" is defined as any operation that results in, or any step in a process or series of operations that result in, the creation or production of tangible personal property. For example, tax generally applies to charges for alterations to new clothing, whether or not the alterations are performed by the seller of the garment or by another person. However, charges for alterations to new or used clothing by a dry cleaner or clothes dyeing establishment are not subject to tax as long as 75% or more of the establishment's total gross receipts are from cleaning or dyeing services and no more than 20% of the gross receipts from the preceding calendar year were from charges for alterations of new and used clothing. Charges for painting, polishing, and otherwise finishing tangible personal property in connection with the production of a finished product are also subject to tax, whether the article to be finished is supplied by the customer or by the finisher. (Reg. 1526, 18 CCR)

Not included in the operations subject to tax is the mere repair or reconditioning of property to refit it for the use for which it was originally produced; charges for mere repair or reconditioning, if separately stated, are exempt, and tax applies only to the retail value of the parts used. Labor charges for repair are taxable, however, when they do result in the creation of a new or enhanced piece of property rather than in one that is merely returned to its original condition. For example, although servicing a neon light by replacing an electrode and refilling a tube with gas would be exempt as repair, cutting, bending, filling, and sealing a new tube would be a taxable fabrication. However, the conversion of a piston-engine airplane to a jet airplane was not so extensive as to constitute a taxable fabrication; since it was a nontaxable reconditioning or modification, tax applied to the parts and materials used in the conversion. See SUTA Series 435, Producing, fabricating, and processing property furnished by consumers—General rules. (Reg. 1526(b), 18 CCR; *CDTFA Publication 108, Labor Charges*, California Department of Tax and Fee Administration)

Stretch limousines. When a dealer, at a customer's request, has a conversion company "stretch" a vehicle into a limousine, the conversion company's charge to the dealer is not taxable, but the dealer's charge to the customer for the conversion is taxable. If the customer provides the conversion company with a vehicle, then the conversion company's entire charge to the customer is taxable. (Reg. 1526(c), 18 CCR)

Are there refunds and/or credit provisions for manufacturers, processors, assemblers, or refiners in California?

California does not currently have sales and use tax provisions specifically concerning refunds and/or credits for manufacturing, processing, assembling, or refining.

For a general discussion of refunds and credits, see ¶ 61-270 Credits and ¶ 61-610 Application for Refund.

[¶60-520] Medical, Dental, and Optical Supplies and Drugs

Exemption from California sales and use tax applies to prescription drugs, and to medicines, that are furnished by licensed physicians, dentists, and podiatrists in treating their patients, or that are furnished by health facilities (including health facilities maintained by any division of state government) in treating patients pursuant to the order of licensed physicians, dentists, or podiatrists. Exemption eligibility instead requires products to satisfy requirements set forth in the controlling statute and regulation. (Sec. 6369, Rev. & Tax. Code; Reg. 1591, 18 CCR)

See Food and Grocery Items, under the subheading "Vitamin enhanced water," for a discussion of medicinal claims made on food products.

• *Blood and human body parts*

Exempt from taxation for any purpose are human whole blood, plasma, blood products, and blood derivatives, or any human body parts held in a bank for medical purposes. (Sec. 33, Rev. & Tax. Code) Containers used to collect or store tax-exempt human whole blood, plasma, blood products, or blood derivatives are also exempt. (Sec. 6364.5, Rev. & Tax. Code; Reg. 1589(b)(1), 18 CCR) The exemption extends to blood collection units and blood pack units, as defined.

• *Catheters*

Intra-aortic balloon pump catheters and coronary angioplasty balloon catheters are exempt from tax. Other catheters are also exempt if they are:

— permanently implanted in the human body, and help a natural organ, artery, vein, or limb to function, and remain or dissolve in the body;

— used for drainage through an artificial opening in the human body, qualifying as ostomy materials and related supplies; or

— used for drainage through a natural opening in the human body to help a natural body part to function or to replace such a part, qualifying as a prosthetic device.

(Reg. 1591.1, 18 CCR)

Supplies related to catheters are subject to tax. "Related supplies" includes, but is not limited to, coronary guiding catheters, coronary guide wires, guide wire introducers, sheath introducer systems, torquing devices, hemostatic valves, inflation devices, and syringes. (Reg. 1591.1, 18 CCR)

The CDTFA legal division regards other catheters are taxable except for catheters that are:

— permanently implanted;

— used for drainage; or

— an integral and necessary part of another exempt item.

See SUTA Series 425, Prescription Medicines.

• *Dental items*

Not qualifying as exempt medicines are most dental works, including dentures, plates, fixed permanent bridges, and permanently implanted teeth, crowns, caps, inlays, other dental prosthetic materials and devices, and orthodontic devices, and appliances. (Sec. 6369(c), Rev. & Tax. Code; Reg. 1591.2, 18 CCR)

See Services, for a discussion of dentists and dental laboratories.

• *Drug stores*

Guidance is provided regarding the application of sales and use taxes to common drug store transactions such as sales of prescription drugs, magazines, beauty supplies, and food products. The publication is designed for individuals who are responsible for drug store sales and purchases. (CDTFA Publication 27, Drug Stores, California Department of Tax and Fee Administration)

• *Hearing aids*

Hearing aids furnished by licensed hearing aid dispensers are exempt from sales and use tax, but are taxable to the dispensers when they purchase such items. (Sec. 6018.7, Rev. & Tax. Code; Reg. 1506(e), 18 CCR) Tax applies to the retail sale of such items by persons who are not licensed hearing aid dispensers. (Reg. 1506(e), 18 CCR)

• *Hemodialysis products*

California exempts the sale or use of hemodialysis products supplied under the order of a medical doctor to a patient by a registered pharmacist or by a supplier authorized under California law to distribute such products directly. (Sec. 6369.1, Rev. & Tax. Code; Reg. 1591, 18 CCR)

• *Herbal products*

Sales of herbal products, including teas and tea capsules, are subject to tax provided: (1) medicinal claims are made on the label or packaging, or in catalogs, brochures or other informational material distributed with the products; or (2) the products are labeled, packaged or otherwise marketed as food supplements or adjuncts (i.e., a food additive). Medicinal claims do not have to be in English for tax to apply. Tax applies to sales of herbal products that have a medicinal claim in a foreign language on the label or packaging as specified above. (Reg. 1602, 18 CCR; *Tax Information Bulletin*, California State Board of Equalization, June 2008)

A medicinal claim on a product's label does not convert a food product into a medicine. Products sold as medicines are not excluded from the definition of "food products;" actual medicines are excluded from food products. If a product is a medicine, then it is not a food product. In order to determine if the sale of an herbal product, including teas and tea capsules, falls within the food products exemption, it is irrelevant if specific medicinal claims are made regarding the product. Instead, the product must actually be a medicine. In determining if a product is a medicine, it must first be determined if the product is approved for use by the U.S. Food and Drug Administration to diagnose, cure, mitigate, treat, or prevent any disease, illness, or medical condition. If a product is so approved, it is a medicine and is not a food product. (*Tax Information Bulletin*, California State Board of Equalization, December 2009)

• *Hospitals and other medical service facilities*

Guidance is provided regarding the application of California sales and use taxes to transactions that involve hospitals and other medical service facilities, as defined. Although institutions operated by the federal government are not covered by this publication, the following institutions are: health facilities, community care facilities, residential care facilities for the elderly, alcoholism or drug abuse recovery or treatment facilities, housing for older persons, and surgery centers or other medical or psychological outpatient health facilities. (*CDTFA Publication 45, Hospitals and Other Medical Facilities*, California State Board of Equalization, February 2009)

• *Insurance coverage*

The prescription medicine exemption applies, even if prescription medicine charges are covered in whole or in part by insurance or by an employer-furnished health contract, whether or not the retailer issues a joint billing in the name of both the consumer and the insurer. (Reg. 1591, 18 CCR)

Sales to persons insured under Part A of the Medicare Act are exempt from California sales and use tax as sales to the United States, whether or not items sold qualify as exempt "medicines," because health care providers are engaged in contract with the federal government to provide certain services. Unless sales to persons insured under Medicare Act Part B are otherwise not subject to tax, however, such sales are taxable since patients, not sellers, are under contract with the federal government with respect to Part B claims. See SUTA Series 425, Prescription Medicines. (Reg. 1591, 18 CCR)

See for the CDTFA legal division's position concerning the tax treatment of items provided to patients by health maintenance organizations (HMOs). See SUTA Series 425, Prescription Medicines.

• *Medical identification tags*

See Nonprofit Organizations, Private Schools, and Churches.

• *Medical oxygen delivery systems*

Medical oxygen delivery systems, defined as systems used to administer oxygen directly into a patient's lungs to relieve an abnormal deficiency or inadequate supply of oxygen, are exempt from tax. Liquid oxygen containers, high pressure cylinders, regulators, oxygen concentrators, tubes, masks, and related items necessary for delivery of oxygen to a person qualify for exemption from tax. However, devices that only assist breathing, but do not deliver air or oxygen directly into the lungs, do not qualify as exempt medical oxygen delivery systems. Qualifying systems are exempt, provided they are sold, leased, or rented to an individual for that person's use under the direction of a medical doctor. Systems used by patients while on the premises of hospitals, immediate care facilities, physicians, or other health care providers, however, are subject to tax. Insurance coverage does not affect the exempt status of qualifying sales of oxygen delivery systems and replacement parts, even if the retailer issues a joint billing in the name of the individual and the insurer. (Sec. 6369.5, Rev. & Tax. Code; Reg. 1591.4, 18 CCR)

For qualifying system delivery purposes, "physicians" are persons authorized by a currently valid and unrevoked license to practice their respective professions in California. Persons holding a valid and unrevoked physician's and surgeon's certificate or certificate to practice medicine and surgery, issued by the Medical Board of California or the Osteopathic Medical Board of California, qualify as physicians. Unlicensed persons lawfully practicing medicine as a graduate of an approved medical school, registered with the Division of Licensing, and enrolled in an approved postgraduate training program, also qualify as physicians, provided they satisfy all other conditions requisite to the practice of medicine as postgraduates. (Reg. 1591.4, 18 CCR)

Qualifying system rentals or leases to health facilities are exempt from tax, provided the facility intends to lease or rent the system to an individual for personal use and such transaction is actually consummated, with direction and control of the equipment transferred to the patient. Separate billing to the patient for using the system does not constitute an exempt lease or rental if the patient's use of the system is limited to the health facility's premises. (Reg. 1591.4, 18 CCR)

• *Medicinal cannabis*

On November 8, 2016, California voters approved Proposition 64, The Control, Regulate, and Tax Adult Use of Marijuana Act. (*Special Notice L-481*, California State Board of Equalization, October 2016; *Tax Guide for Medical Marijuana Businesses*, California State Board of Equalization, November 2016)

Retail sales of medicinal cannabis to persons who have a valid Medical Marijuana Identification Card (MMIC) issued by the California Department of Public Health (CDPH) and a valid government-issued identification card (ID) are exempt from sales and use tax.

The California Department of Tax and Fee Administration (CDTFA) provides guidance regarding marijuana. (*Publication 557, Tax Help for the Cannabis Industry*, CDTFA, January 2020)

Donated medicinal cannabis.—Beginning March 1, 2020, cannabis retailers may donate free medicinal cannabis or medicinal cannabis products (medicinal cannabis) to medicinal cannabis patients, or cannabis licensees may donate free medicinal cannabis to cannabis retailers for subsequent donation to medicinal cannabis patients, without payment of certain taxes. The following taxes are not applicable to donated medicinal cannabis:

— the cultivation tax will not apply to medicinal cannabis when the cultivator designates for donation in the California Cannabis Track-and-Trace system;

— the cannabis excise tax does not apply when a cannabis retailer donates free medicinal cannabis to a medicinal cannabis patient; and

— the use tax will not apply when a cannabis retailer donates free medicinal cannabis to a medicinal cannabis patient, or when another licensee, such as a distributor or manufacturer, donates free medicinal cannabis to a retailer for subsequent donation to a medicinal cannabis patient.

(*Special Notice L-729*, California Department of Tax and Fee Administration, January 2020)

A "medicinal cannabis patient" is a qualified patient who possesses a qualifying physician's recommendation, or a qualified patient or the patient's primary caregiver with a valid Medical Marijuana Identification Card issued by the California Department of Public Health. (*Special Notice L-729*, California Department of Tax and Fee Administration, January 2020)

The cannabis licensee that receives medicinal cannabis for donation must certify in writing to the licensee donating it that the medicinal cannabis will ultimately be donated to a medicinal cannabis patient. Cannabis licensees can use a written document, such as a letter, note, purchase order, or preprinted form, as a cannabis donation certificate. In the alternative, a cannabis licensee may use form CDTFA-230-CD, Cannabis Donation Certificate, as a written certification that the medicinal cannabis will be donated to a medicinal cannabis patient. (*Special Notice L-729*, California Department of Tax and Fee Administration, January 2020)

When taken in good faith by the licensee donating the medicinal cannabis, the written certification relieves:

— the cultivator from the liability of the cultivation tax;

— the manufacturer from its responsibility to collect the cultivation tax from the cultivator;

— the distributor from its responsibility to collect the cultivation tax from the cultivator and the cannabis excise tax from the retailer; and

— each licensee from liability of the use tax when donating the medicinal cannabis.

If a cannabis licensee certifies in writing that medicinal cannabis will be donated to a medicinal cannabis patient and later sells or uses the medicinal cannabis in some other manner than for donation, the certifying licensee will be liable for any taxes that would be due, including the cultivation tax, cannabis excise tax, and use tax. (*Special Notice L-729*, California Department of Tax and Fee Administration, January 2020)

Guidance issued to retailers on free medicinal cannabis.—Cannabis retailers are prohibited from giving away any amount of cannabis or cannabis products unless authorized to do so by the Bureau of Cannabis Control (BCC), for California cannabis excise and sales and use tax purposes. The BCC administers cannabis licensing activities for retailers and distributors. If a retailer is authorized to give cannabis or cannabis products away free of charge, the cannabis excise tax does not apply. However, the retailer does owe use tax on the retailer's purchase price of the cannabis or cannabis products. (*Cannabis Tax Fact*, California Department of Tax and Fee Administration, April 26, 2018)

The BCC provides that free cannabis or cannabis products can be provided to medicinal cannabis patients or primary caregivers in possession of valid Medical Marijuana Identification Cards issued by the California Department of Public Health. The cannabis excise tax does not apply to medicinal cannabis provided for free to qualified patients. If a retailer already paid the excise tax to a cannabis distributor, the retailer may request a return of the tax from the distributor who supplied the retailer with the cannabis or cannabis product. (*Cannabis Tax Fact*, California Department of Tax and Fee Administration, April 26, 2018)

A cannabis retailer owes use tax based on the retailer's purchase price of the cannabis or cannabis products the retailer provides to medicinal cannabis patients or primary caregivers free of charge. Or, if a retailer is also a licensed manufacturer, such a retailer owes tax on the cost of the taxable items used to manufacture the cannabis products. To pay use tax, the purchase price of the cannabis is reported as "Purchases Subject to Use Tax" on the sales and use tax return. Those purchases become part of the total amount that is subject to tax. (*Cannabis Tax Fact*, California Department of Tax and Fee Administration, April 26, 2018)

To qualify for the exemption.—Retail sales of the following types of medical cannabis are exempt from sales and use tax:

— medical cannabis;

— medical cannabis concentrate;

— edible medical cannabis products; and

— topical cannabis (as defined in Sec. 19300.5 of the Business and Professions Code).

(*Special Notice L-486*, California State Board of Equalization, November 2016; *Special Notice L-481*, California State Board of Equalization, October 2016; *Tax Guide for Medical Marijuana Businesses*, California State Board of Equalization, November 2016)

To obtain the exemption, qualified patients or their primary caregiver must provide their valid Medical Marijuana Identification Card issued by the California Department of Public Health (pursuant to Sec. 11362.71 of the Health and Safety Code) and a valid government issued identification card at the time of purchase. In order to properly claim the sales and use tax exemption, a medical marijuana business should not collect sales tax reimbursement on the qualifying exempt sales of medical marijuana, and should claim a deduction on its sales and use tax return for the qualifying exempt medical marijuana sales. (*Special Notice L-486*, California State Board of Equalization, November 2016; *Tax Guide for Medical Marijuana Businesses*, California State Board of Equalization, November 2016)

What retailers need to do to properly claim the exemption.—Medical marijuana retailers can claim the exemption on their sales and use tax return. Retailers should retain supporting documentation (either physical or electronic) to substantiate exempt transactions, including:

— the purchaser's nine-digit ID number and expiration date, as shown on the qualified patient's or primary caregiver's unexpired Medical Marijuana Identification Card; and

— the related sales invoice or other original record of sale.

(*Special Notice L-486*, California State Board of Equalization, November 2016; *Special Notice L-481*, California State Board of Equalization, October 2016; *Tax Guide for Medical Marijuana Businesses*, California State Board of Equalization, November 2016)

A valid MMIC is issued by the CDPH and indicates:

— that the card is issued by the State of California and includes the state seal;

— whether the purchaser is a "Patient" or "Caregiver;"

— the patient's or primary caregiver's photo;

— a nine-digit ID number;

— the CDPH website to verify the ID number;

— the expiration date; and

— the county that issued the card, with the county phone number.

Retailers can verify the validity of the nine-digit ID number on the website of the California Department of Public Health at http://www.calmmp.ca.gov/MMIC_Search.aspx. (*Special Notice L-486*, California State Board of Equalization, November 2016; *Tax Guide for Medical Marijuana Businesses*, California State Board of Equalization, November 2016)

See Agriculture, for a discussion of an excise tax imposed upon purchasers of all marijuana and marijuana products effective January 1, 2018, and a tax on marijuana cultivators also effective January 1, 2018.

• *Medicine*

Medicines sold to licensed physicians, dentists, or podiatrists, health facilities, or to any division of state government for use in treating patients are also exempt. However, medicines furnished by surgical centers to patients pursuant to a doctor's order are not exempt because surgical centers are regarded as the consumers of medicines they dispense. (See SUTA Series 425, Prescription Medicines)

A sales and use tax exemption also applies to prescription medicines furnished without charge by pharmaceutical manufacturers or distributors to medical doctors or health care facilities for treatment purposes, and furnished to institutions of higher education for instruction or research purposes. The exemption also specifically applies to the cost of medicine packaging materials, and to constituent elements and ingredients used to produce medicines. Dual purpose devices used to administer and to package medicine, such as pre-filled syringes, are exempt. However, delivery devices furnished separately or included in distributed packages are subject to tax. (Sec. 6369, Rev. & Tax. Code; Reg. 1591, 18 CCR)

For exemption purposes, "medicine" means any product fully implanted or injected in the human body, or any drug or any biologic approved by the U.S. Food and Drug Administration to diagnose, cure, mitigate, treat, or prevent any disease, illness, or medical condition regardless of ultimate use, or any substance or preparation intended for use by external or internal application to the human body in the diagnosis, cure, mitigation, treatment or prevention of disease and which is commonly recognized as a substance or preparation intended for that use. "Health facilities" is defined to include facilities, places, and buildings organized, maintained, and operated to diagnose, prevent, and treat human illness for at least a 24-hour period. (Sec. 1250, Hlth. & Sfty. Code; Reg. 1591, 18 CCR)

California sales and use tax is inapplicable to the sale of all permanently implanted articles. This includes an implant's interdependent internal and external components that operate together as one device in and on a person in whom the device is implanted (including ear implants), unless the device is excluded from the definition of "medicines." (Reg. 1591(b)(2), 18 CCR)

Botox.—Botox and Botox Cosmetic are injected biologics and are considered to be medicines under Regulation 1591. The FDA states that Botox and Botox Cosmetic are approved to treat moderate to severe frown lines between the eyebrows, a medical condition that is not serious. As such, CDTFA staff accepts that doctors only give patients injections of Botox and Botox Cosmetic when, in their judgment, they are treating a medical condition. (*Tax Information Bulletin*, California State Board of Equalization, December 2006)

Breast implants.—Breast implants are approved by the FDA for use in both reconstructive and cosmetic surgeries and are considered to be medicines regardless of the type of surgery performed. (*Tax Information Bulletin*, California State Board of Equalization, December 2006)

Exempt medicine.—In general, the exemption applies to qualified items in these categories:

— artificial eyes or limbs and their replacement parts;

— catheters;

— permanently implanted articles;

— insulin, and insulin syringes, as well as glucose test strips and skin puncture lancets used to determine a diabetic patient's blood sugar level, insulin amounts needed, and other diabetic control medication, furnished by a pharmacist as required under a physician's instructions for treatment of diabetes as directed by a physician;

— mammary prostheses and ostomy appliances and supplies;

— medical oxygen delivery systems (see "Medical oxygen delivery systems" below);

— orthotic devices and their replacement parts (however, orthopedic shoes and supportive devices for the foot are not exempt unless they are an integral part of a leg brace or artificial leg);

— programmable drug infusion devices to be worn on or implanted in the body;

— prosthetic devices or their replacement parts (other than dentures and auditory, ophthalmic, or ocular devices). Included in this exempt category are stump socks, stockings worn with artificial legs, intraocular lenses, ear implants, and breast and tissue expanders;

— sutures, whether or not permanently implanted;

— wheelchairs, crutches, canes, quad canes, and walkers; and

— vehicles and vehicle modifications for the physically handicapped.

(Sec. 6369, Rev. & Tax. Code; Reg. 1591, 18 CCR; Reg. 1591.1, 18 CCR; Reg. 1591.2, 18 CCR; Reg. 1591.4, 18 CCR)

Devices used to insert medication into patients may qualify as exempt "nonreturnable containers" if they are prefilled with medication, are disposable, and may be used to administer medication only to one patient. See SUTA Series 425, Prescription Medicines.

Injected collagen and other dermal implants.—Injected collagen and similar products require FDA approval because they are injected under the patient's skin. Generally, such implants are approved by the FDA for correction of skin contour deficiencies such as wrinkles and acne scars and are considered to be medicines regardless of their ultimate use (whether used to correct scarring or the appearance of lines and wrinkles from aging). (*Tax Information Bulletin*, California State Board of Equalization, December 2006)

Supplements used to treat obesity.—When dietary supplements and adjunct products do not qualify as food products, as specified, and are furnished by a physician to his or her own patients as part of a medically supervised weight loss program to treat obesity, such products are regarded as medicine and are exempt from California sales and use taxes. Very low calorie meal replacement products meet the definition of "medicine" because they are intended for use by internal application to the human body in the treatment of obesity which is commonly recognized as a disease. (Reg. 1591(e)(7), 18 CCR; Reg. 1602(a)(4), 18 CCR)

Taxable medical devices and items.—The exemption for medicines and drugs is inapplicable to:

— alcoholic beverages;

— dentures, including removable plates, fixed permanent bridges, and permanently implanted artificial teeth, crowns, caps, and other dental prosthetic materials and devices;

— hospital beds (including specialized or therapeutic beds);

— orthodontic, auditory, ophthalmic, or ocular devices or appliances; and

— splints, bandages, pads, dressings, instruments, appliances, devices, or other mechanical, electronic, optical, or physical equipment or articles (or their components or accessories).

(Sec. 6369, Rev. & Tax. Code; Reg. 1591, 18 CCR; Reg. 1591.1, 18 CCR; Reg. 1591.2, 18 CCR; Reg. 1591.4, 18 CCR)

• *Menstrual hygiene products*

A sales and use tax exemption is available for menstrual hygiene products. "Menstrual hygiene products" are defined as: tampons; sanitary napkins primarily designed and labeled for menstrual hygiene use; menstrual sponges; and menstrual cups. This exemption sunsets on July 1, 2023. (Sec. 6363.10, Rev. & Tax. Code)

• *Optical goods*

Physicians, surgeons, or optometrists are the consumers, and are therefore taxable on their purchases, of materials such as eyeglasses, frames, and lenses used or furnished in performing their professional services. Sunglasses without correction, including clip-on sunglasses, are covered by this provision if furnished to correct a condition pursuant to a diagnosis. In all other instances, the physician, optometrist, or dispensing optician is the retailer of the sunglasses. (Sec. 6018, Rev. & Tax. Code; Reg. 1592, 18 CCR)

A dispensing optician who fills a prescription prepared by a physician, surgeon, or optometrist for glasses, frames, sunglasses, including clip-on sunglasses, or other materials, or a licensed pharmacist who fills a prescription prepared by a physician or optometrist for replacement contact lenses, is also deemed to be the consumer of those items and must pay tax on his or her own purchase of such items. (Sec. 6018, Rev. & Tax. Code; Reg. 1592(b), 18 CCR)

For a related discussion of sales, purchases, and services of ophthalmologists and optometrists, see ¶ 60-665 Services.

• *Prosthetic devices and equipment*

California's exemption for prescription medicines and drugs generally covers prosthetic devices and equipment (other than dental prostheses or auditory, ophthalmic, or ocular devices) furnished under a physician's written order. (Sec. 6369, Rev. & Tax. Code; Sec. 6369.2, Rev. & Tax. Code; Reg. 1591, 18 CCR)

Mammary prostheses and ostomy appliances and supplies.—Medicine distribution exemption criteria do not apply to mammary prostheses and ostomy appliances and related supplies, provided such items are dispensed pursuant to a written order by a person authorized to issue a prescription. Ostomy appliances and related supplies used to accommodate patients after surgery are exempt from tax; however, such items are subject to tax when used as an adjunct to surgical procedure unless they remain in the patient for postoperative purposes. Exempt ostomy appliances include endotracheal and tracheostomy tubes used post-operatively or for home care to evacuate metabolic waste. Kidney dialysis machines and accessories are also exempt as ostomy appliances and related supplies. An accessory qualifies as a related supply item, provided it is either a necessary and integral part of the machine itself or it is a substance or preparation for external or internal application to the dialysis patient's body. (Reg. 1591, 18 CCR)

Wheelchairs, crutches, and canes.—Wheelchairs, crutches, canes (including white canes used by the blind), quad canes, and walkers, and replacement parts for such items are exempt, provided they are sold to an individual for that person's personal use as directed by a licensed physician. (Sec. 6369.2, Rev. & Tax. Code; Reg. 1591.2, 18 CCR) Three-wheel scooters that are similar in design and function to conventional wheelchairs qualify as wheelchairs for exemption purposes. (Reg. 1591.2, 18 CCR)

Replacement parts eligible for exemption from tax include, but are not limited to, batteries for electric wheelchairs; belts and cushions sold to replace or supplement the basic items originally sold with wheelchairs, lap boards and trays attached to wheelchairs and considered a part of the wheelchair; and rubber tips, wheels, and other such items prescribed to replace an original component of the device. Mechanical devices that help a patient to eat or write do not qualify as exempt replacement parts unless they are part of the device itself. Restraints and similar items that do not become a part of a wheelchair or other such prescribed service are also not exempt replacement parts. (Reg. 1591.2, 18 CCR)

• *Recordkeeping requirements*

Pharmacies must keep records supporting all deductions claimed under the prescription medicine exemption. Physicians, surgeons, and podiatrists must keep accurate records of drugs furnished by them. Any deduction for sales of medicines must be supported by appropriate records. This requirement is satisfied when records show the name of the purchaser, the name of the doctor, the date of sale, the item sold, and the sale price. All prescriptions filled must be kept on file and open for inspection by duly constituted authorities. (Reg. 1591, 18 CCR)

• *Vehicles and vehicle modifications for the physically handicapped*

Items and materials used to modify a vehicle for use by a handicapped person also are exempt, provided they are necessary to enable the vehicle to transport a handicapped person. Also, when a handicapped person purchases a vehicle, gross receipts attributable to the portion of the vehicle modified to enable it to transport physically handicapped persons are not subject to tax. For exemption purposes, such materials must be incorporated into the vehicle; tax does not apply to such materials, whether or not they are installed by the retailer. (Sec. 6369.4, Rev. & Tax. Code; Reg. 1591.3, 18 CCR)

Items eligible for exemption include, but are not limited to:

— interlock systems;

— upper torso restraints;

— air bags of a unique type to raise or lower the vehicle for loading or unloading;

— running boards on lower side of vehicle;

— bolt cams used to restrain a wheelchair inside a van;

— seat belts;

— tire carriers to hold a spare, installed within a handicapped person's reach;

— AC lights to illuminate the ramp or elevator area;

— hardware for privacy curtains;

— air compressors for use with medical equipment;

— 12-volt receptacles to supply power to medical equipment;

— 4-point tie-down systems to restrain a wheelchair; and

— allocable portions of various interior packages, interior materials, and conversions necessary to modify a vehicle to transport physically handicapped persons.

(Reg. 1591.3, 18 CCR)

Certain items do not qualify for exemption from tax, whether or not they are installed on a vehicle to transport physically handicapped persons. Such items include, but are not limited to:

— upper torso durable pads (unless part of the restraint);

— portable ramps (telescopic);

— air conditioners (unless necessary to transport certain types of disabled persons);

— fire extinguishers;

— CB radios (unless shown to be necessary to transport certain types of disabled individuals);

— leather seat covers;

— extra windows and their accessories;

— upgrades to the interior (upgrade to leather seats); and

— engine covers.

(Reg. 1591.3, 18 CCR)

• *Vitamins, minerals, herbs, and dietary supplements*

Vitamins, minerals, herbs, and other supplements sold or furnished under qualifying criteria, are exempt, provided they are used to cure, mitigate, treat or prevent disease, and provided they are commonly recognized as intended for such use. (Reg. 1591, 18 CCR) However, food products in liquid, powdered, granular, tablet, capsule, lozenge, or pill form that are sold as dietary supplements or adjuncts are subject to tax (Sec. 6359(c), Rev. & Tax. Code; Reg. 1602(a)(5), 18 CCR) unless they qualify as exempt prescription medicines.

See ¶ 60-390 Food and Grocery Items, for a more complete discussion of food products, food supplements, and dietary supplements.

[¶60-560] Motor Fuels

California taxes the sale or use of motor vehicle and aircraft fuels, with the exception of "aviation gasoline."

An exemption for fuel used in space flights is discussed at ¶ 60-420 Government Transactions.

• *Aircraft jet fuel*

Sales and use tax applies to aircraft jet fuel. Aircraft fuel sold to an air common carrier is exempt if sold for immediate consumption or shipment in the air common carrier business on a flight whose final destination is a foreign destination. (Sec. 6357, Rev. & Tax. Code; Sec. 6480(b), Rev. & Tax. Code; Reg. 1598, 18 CCR)

Quarterly information returns required by aircraft jet fuel retailers.—Beginning January 1, 2020, on or before the last day of the month next following each quarterly period, a retailer of aircraft jet fuel must provide a quarterly information return to the California Department of Tax and Fee Administration (CDTFA) for sales and use tax purposes. (Sec. 6452.05, Rev. & Tax. Code)

The CDTFA will collect the information from the returns and post the following each quarter on its website:

• the amount of reported tax revenue derived from the sale, storage, use, or consumption of aircraft jet fuel in California;

• the amount of reported tax revenue derived from the sale, storage, use, or consumption of aircraft jet fuel with respect to taxes imposed by a city, county, city and county, or other governmental entity pursuant to the Transactions and Use Tax Law.

(Sec. 6452.05, Rev. & Tax. Code)

Such an aircraft jet fuel retailer who fails or refuses to timely furnish an information return or other data required by the CDTFA will pay a penalty of $5,000. Moreover, an accuracy-related penalty of $5,000 will be imposed if a person fails to accurately disclose required information in the information return for each return not accurately filed. The accuracy-related penalty will not be assessed if the penalty for failure or refusal to timely furnish an information return is imposed. (Sec. 6452.05, Rev. & Tax. Code; Sec. 6591.3, Rev. & Tax. Code)

Aviation gasoline.—California sales and use tax does not apply to the sale or use of "aviation gasoline," which is any flammable liquid used in propelling aircraft in an explosion-type engine, provided that the motor vehicle fuel (gasoline) tax is paid on the gasoline and that the purchaser does not claim a refund of this latter tax. (Sec. 6357, Rev. & Tax. Code; Sec. 6480(b), Rev. & Tax. Code; Reg. 1598, 18 CCR)

Counties may impose local sales and use and transactions and use taxes on sales of fuel or petroleum products to aircraft operators. (Reg. 1825, 18 CCR)

See ¶ 60-110 Rate of Tax, for the current rate.

Documentation requirements.—Sellers of "aviation gasoline" must secure and retain documentation to support exempt sales. For gasoline sold and delivered directly into an aircraft's fuel tank, the exemption may be supported by either a properly completed sales invoice or an aircraft fuel exemption certificate. For retail sales delivered into the purchaser's storage facilities or receptacles (other than fuel tanks), the exemption must be supported by an invoice and an aircraft fuel exemption certificate. (Reg. 1598(h), 18 CCR)

See "Fuel and petroleum products sold to common carriers" below for an exemption for sales to air carriers flying directly to a foreign destination.

• *Basis of tax on fuels*

When motor fuels are subject to the sales or use tax, the taxable amount includes the following:

— the federal tax on gasoline, diesel, and jet fuel producers or importers, except as noted below;

— the California tax on gasoline and other fuel distributors (i.e., the state motor vehicle fuel tax) that has not been refunded, and, if applicable;

— the California tax on aircraft jet fuel.

(Reg. 1598(c), 18 CCR; Sec. 6011(b)(3), Rev. & Tax. Code; Sec. 6012(a)(4), Rev. & Tax. Code).

Not included in the taxable amount are the following:

— the California use fuel tax (including the annual flat rate fuel tax);

— the California diesel fuel tax;

— any federal retailer's excise taxes on gasoline or jet fuel used in noncommercial aircraft and on diesel fuel and special motor fuels; or

— any federal excise tax on gasoline, diesel, or jet fuel for which the purchaser is entitled to a direct refund or credit against income tax.

(Reg. 1598(c), 18 CCR)

• *Diesel fuel*

The retail sale of diesel fuel is subject to the statewide base sales and use tax rate plus an additional sales and use (excise) tax. (Sec. 6051.8, Rev. & Tax. Code; Sec. 6201.8, Rev. & Tax. Code)

See ¶ 60-110 Rate of Tax, for the current rate.

• *Fuel and petroleum products sold to common carriers*

Fuel and petroleum products sold to common carriers are discussed.

¶60-560

Fuel sold to air carriers flying to foreign destinations.—California exempts fuel and petroleum products sold to an air common carrier for immediate consumption or shipment in the conduct of its business, provided that the consumption or shipment is on an international flight whose final destination is to a point outside the United States. The seller must deliver the fuel or petroleum products directly into the aircraft for consumption or transportation outside the U.S. and not for storage by the purchaser or any third party. The air carrier must furnish to the seller a written exemption certificate stating the quantity of fuel or petroleum products claimed as exempt and the carrier's valid seller's permit or fuel exemption registration number. A seller who accepts such an exemption certificate in good faith is not liable for sales and use tax on the products covered by the certificate. (Sec. 6357.5, Rev. & Tax. Code)

Fuel and petroleum products sold to water common carriers.—Sales of fuel or petroleum products to water common carriers for immediate shipment and consumption outside the state are exempt from sales tax. This provision sunsets effective January 1, 2024. (Sec. 6385, Rev. & Tax. Code)

• *Fuel surcharge*

Some businesses add a fuel surcharge, also known as a "trip or service charge," to their charges. Depending on the transaction, a fuel surcharge may be nontaxable, partially taxable, or fully taxable:

— when none of the charges for a job are taxable, tax does not apply to the trip or service charges (tax does not apply when the job involves only nontaxable labor or services and materials or merchandise are not transferred to the customer);

— if all or part of the charges for a job are taxable, tax applies to all or part of the trip charges (if services are provided and materials or merchandise are also transferred to a customer, some or all of the trip charges are taxable);

— if all of the other charges for a job are taxable, the full amount of a trip charge is also taxable; and

— when a job includes both taxable and nontaxable charges, part of the trip charge is taxable.

(*Tax Information Bulletin*, California State Board of Equalization, March 2007)

• *Fuel tax swap*

In March 2010, two bills were enacted to effect a "fuel tax swap" (also referred to as the "gas tax swap"). Although a sales and use tax exemption for motor vehicle fuel is enacted applicable July 1, 2010, there is a corresponding increase in the motor vehicle fuels tax rate. In addition, although there is an increase in the sales and use tax rate imposed on diesel fuel applicable July 1, 2011, there is a corresponding decrease in the motor vehicle fuel tax rate. According to the bill analysis, the legislature intended the effect of this legislation to be revenue neutral. (A.B. 6 (8th Ext. Sess.) and S.B. 70, Laws 2010, *Bill Analysis*, Senate Committee on Budget and Fiscal Review, March 22, 2010)

In 2011, legislation was enacted that repeals and reenacts the California motor "fuel tax swap" in order to comply with Proposition 26. Enacted in 2010, the tax swap also raised the sales tax rate applicable to sales of diesel fuel and simultaneously lowered the state excise diesel fuel tax, effective July 1, 2011. Proposition 26, approved by the voters on November 2, 2010, amended the California Constitution to, among other things, require a two-thirds vote of both houses of the legislature for any change in statute that results in any taxpayer paying a higher tax. Proposition 26 also provides that any tax adopted after January 1, 2010, but prior to November 3, 2010, that was not adopted in compliance with the two-thirds vote requirement is void on

November 3, 2011, unless the tax is reenacted by the legislature with a two-thirds vote. Since the legislation that enacted the fuel tax swap in 2010 was enacted after January 1, 2010, with a simple majority vote, legislation was required to reenact these provisions with a two-thirds vote to ensure the fuel tax swap meets the new constitutional requirements.

According to the bill analysis, the reenacted swap is similar to the swap enacted in 2010, but some of the diesel rates have changed slightly to address the requirements of Proposition 22, which was also approved by voters on the November 2010 ballot, as well as to address changes in the forecast of quantity and price of diesel fuel. This swap, like the one before, is revenue-neutral and an adjustment is made each July 1 to maintain that neutrality. In addition, the reenacted swap excludes off-road users, such as railroads, farm equipment, and aviation gasoline from certain provisions of the swap to maintain the tax neutrality for those users that already enjoy certain exemptions. (*Bill Analysis*, Office of Senate Floor Analyses, March 17, 2011; *Fuel Tax Swap FAQs*, California State Board of Equalization, May 2011)

• *Local taxes*

Under the Bradley-Burns Uniform Local Sales and Use Tax Law, local tax is allocated to the place of sale. For sales of jet fuel, the "place of sale" of jet fuel is the point of delivery of the fuel into the aircraft, regardless of how many places of business the retailer has in California or where the retailer negotiates his or her sales. Taxpayers are instructed to report the local tax collected under the Bradley-Burns Uniform Local Sales and Use Tax Law to the local jurisdiction (or multi-jurisdictional airport) where the jet fuel is delivered into the aircraft. (Sec. 7205, Rev. & Tax. Code; Reg. 1802, 18 CCR)

• *Motor vehicle fuel (gasoline)*

A partial sales and use tax exemption from the statewide base sales and use tax rate is applicable to motor vehicle fuel (i.e., gasoline). (Sec. 6051.2, Rev. & Tax. Code; Sec. 6051.5, Rev. & Tax. Code; Sec. 6201.2, Rev. & Tax. Code; Sec. 6201.5, Rev. & Tax. Code; *Fuel Tax Swap FAQs*, California State Board of Equalization, May 2011; *Special Notice L-352*, California State Board of Equalization, May 2013)

See ¶ 60-110 Rate of Tax, for the current rate.

The partial exemption is inapplicable to the following portions of the state sales and use tax rate:

— the 0.50% state tax allocated to the Local Revenue Fund (Revenue and Taxation Code section 6051.2 and 6201.2);

— the 0.25% state tax allocated to the Fiscal Recovery Fund (Revenue and Taxation Code section 6051.5 and 6201.5);

— the 0.50% state tax allocated to the Local Public Safety Fund (Section 35 of Article XIII of the California Constitution);

— the 1% tax allocated to local cities and/or counties (Part 1.5 of Division 2 of the Revenue and Taxation Code); and

— any applicable district taxes imposed by a special taxing jurisdiction (Part 1.6 of Division 2 of the Revenue and Taxation Code).

(Sec. 6051.2, Rev. & Tax. Code; Sec. 6051.5, Rev. & Tax. Code; Sec. 6201.2, Rev. & Tax. Code; Sec. 6201.5, Rev. & Tax. Code; *Fuel Tax Swap FAQs*, California State Board of Equalization, May 2011)

As specified above, the partial exemption is inapplicable to local sales and use taxes imposed under either the Bradley-Burns Uniform Local Sales and Use Tax Law or the Transactions and Use Tax Law. (Sec. 6357.7, Rev. & Tax. Code)

The exemption is disallowed unless the purchaser furnishes the seller with a properly completed exemption certificate. (Sec. 6051.2, Rev. & Tax. Code; Sec. 6051.5, Rev. & Tax. Code; Sec. 6201.2, Rev. & Tax. Code; Sec. 6201.5, Rev. & Tax. Code)

The California Department of Tax and Fee Administration (CDTFA) provides guidance regarding the fuel tax swap, including rate information. (*Fuel Tax Swap Frequently Asked Questions (FAQ)*, California State Board of Equalization, May 2011)

• *Prepayment of tax on motor vehicle fuel distributions*

Distributors and brokers of motor vehicle fuel must collect prepayment of retail sales tax from persons to whom they distribute or transfer any fuel that is subject to the motor vehicle fuel tax, except aviation gasoline and any fuel distributed to bonded distributors.

[¶60-570] Motor Vehicles

This paragraph discusses sales and use tax treatment of various transactions involving motor vehicles.

See ¶60-740 Transportation, for treatment of vehicles used in transportation as well as of vessels and aircraft in general.

See ¶60-420 Government Transactions, for treatment of motor vehicle loans to public schools.

• *Automobile dealers and salespeople*

Scenarios involving both automobile dealers and salespeople are discussed.

Dealer aid to salespeople.—An automobile dealer is the retailer of property sold by its salespeople, and is thus liable for collecting and reporting tax, if the dealer aids the salespeople by either (1) reporting the sales on the dealer's report to the Department of Motor Vehicles (DMV) or (2) executing conditional sales agreements in which the dealer appears as the seller. If, however, the dealer's aid is limited to acting as guarantor on conditional sales made by the salespeople or to allowing or requiring them to use its showrooms or other facilities, the dealer incurs no tax liability; in this latter case, use tax must be paid to the DMV by the purchaser. (Reg. 1566(a), 18 CCR)

The California Department of Tax and Fee Administration (CDTFA) provides guidance regarding sales and use tax laws and regulations as they apply to motor vehicle dealers. (*CDTFA Publication 34, Motor Vehicle Dealers*, California Department of Tax and Fee Administration)

Exclusion for returned used vehicle or price of contract cancellation option agreement.—Dealers must offer customers a contract cancellation option on certain used vehicles sales (those with a purchase price of less than $40,000), and if a buyer chooses to purchase such an option, the buyer will have the right to cancel the purchase and receive a full refund, including amounts charged for sales tax, under certain conditions. That portion of the sales price returned to the buyer of a used vehicle or the purchase price of the contract cancellation option agreement are excluded from the terms "gross receipts" and "sales price" for California sales and use tax purposes. (Sec. 6012.3, Rev. & Tax. Code; Sec. 11713.21, Veh. Code; *Special Notice L-152*, California State Board of Equalization, June 2006)

The cancellation option agreement must state:

— the time period within which the buyer may cancel the purchase and return the vehicle (the deadline may not be before close of business on the second day after the day the dealer delivers the vehicle to the customer);

— the maximum number of miles the vehicle may be driven before it is returned under the agreement (may not be less than 250 miles);

— the buyer must pay a restocking fee if the buyer cancels the purchase; and

— the specific requirements for return of the vehicle for a refund.

(*Special Notice L-152*, California State Board of Equalization, June 2006)

Dealers may charge a restocking fee, that is not subject to sales and use tax, for used vehicles returned in this manner:

— $175 for a vehicle with a cash price of $5,000 or less;

— $350 for a vehicle with a cash price of between $5,000 and $10,000; and

— $500 for a vehicle with a cash price of $10,000 or more.

(*Special Notice L-152*, California State Board of Equalization, June 2006)

Exclusion for vehicle fees and taxes.—California excludes from the measure of the tax the amount of any motor vehicle fee or tax that is paid to the state and that has been included in the vehicle's sales price. (Sec. 6011(c)(9), Rev. & Tax. Code; Sec. 6012(c)(9), Rev. & Tax. Code)

Farm equipment and machinery partial exemption.—The California Department of Tax and Fee Administration (CDTFA) advises that, generally, car dealers' sales or leases of vehicles designed primarily for transportation of persons or property on a highway, including sales or leases of pickup trucks, heavy duty trucks, and tractor trucks, do not qualify for the partial sales and use tax exemption provided for farm equipment and machinery. (Sec. 6356.5, Rev. & Tax. Code; Reg. 1534, 18 CCR; *Special Notice L-436*, California State Board of Equalization, January 2016)

In order for a vehicle to be considered "farm equipment and machinery," it must meet both of the following conditions:

— the vehicle must be designated as an implement of husbandry (i.e., a vehicle used exclusively in the conduct of agricultural operations) by the Department of Motor Vehicles; and

— the vehicle must be used exclusively in agricultural operations by a "qualified person," which generally includes farmers, ranchers, or other persons who produce and harvest agricultural products.

(*Special Notice L-436*, California State Board of Equalization, January 2016)

Examples of implements of husbandry include but are not limited to:

— lift carriers;

— nurse rigs;

— bale wagons;

— farm trailers;

— trap wagons;

— farm tractors;

— row dusters; and

— fertilizer rigs.

(*Special Notice L-436*, California State Board of Equalization, January 2016)

¶60-570

Implements of husbandry also include any vehicle: (1) operated on a highway for the sole purpose of transporting agricultural products; and (2) that is never operated on the highway for a total distance greater than one mile from the point of origin of the trip. (*Special Notice L-436*, California State Board of Equalization, January 2016)

For sales to qualified persons, a car dealer may only accept a partial exemption certificate from the purchaser and claim the partial exemption on the dealer's sales and use tax return in the limited circumstances in which the car dealer sells or leases a vehicle that meets both of the requirements to be considered "farm equipment and machinery." If the qualified person is buying the property of a kind not normally used in producing and harvesting agricultural products, such as a passenger vehicle or pickup, the car dealer should require a statement as to how the specific property purchased will be used. An exemption certificate cannot be accepted in good faith, however, in situations in which the car dealer has knowledge that the property will not be used in an exempt manner. (*Special Notice L-436*, California State Board of Equalization, January 2016)

The California Department of Tax and Fee Administration provides a list of items that generally do not qualify for the partial sales and use tax exemption for sales of farm equipment and machinery to persons engaged in qualifying farming or ranching activities (qualified persons). The full tax rate applies to sales of these items (although this is not an exhaustive list): abrasives, tape; air compressors and accessories; audio equipment; automobile accessories; battery chargers; cables; carbonated beverages; cargo supplies; cleaning agents; collectables, toys, games; consumables; containers; decals; electrical equipment for an automobile or pickup truck; fasteners, hardware; floor mats, seat covers; hand cleaner, soap; janitorial supplies; lighting equipment; locks and lock kits; logo items; lubricants; marine parts and accessories; office computers, paper, printers; phone systems; promotional products (items typically given away to customers); ramps; repair manuals; repair/replacement parts for automobiles; repair/replacement parts for pickup trucks; shipping supplies; shop heating and cooling equipment; shop supplies, shop towels; tire chains for automobiles; tire chains for pickup trucks; tire changing and service equipment; tool storage equipment; travel accessories; truck bed and tailgate accessories; warehouse supplies; welding equipment; wheel balancers; winter accessories; and video equipment. (*Special Notice L-461*, California State Board of Equalization, June 2016)

See ¶60-250 Agriculture, for a detailed discussion of the farm equipment and machinery partial exemption.

Leases.—If a certificated dealer leases a vehicle and registers it in the name of the lessee only, use tax is applicable and is measured by the sales price to the dealer/ lessor. (Reg. 1610(d)(1), 18 CCR)

If a certificated dealer sells a vehicle to a lessor that is not a certificated dealer, dismantler, manufacturer, or lessor/retailer, the dealer reports the sale to the DMV and the vehicle is registered in the name of the lessee only; sales tax, measured by the sales price to the lessor, applies. (Reg. 1610(d)(1), 18 CCR)

Resale certificates from nondealer retailers.—A licensed or certified dealer that makes a sale to a retailer that is not an automobile dealer may accept a resale certificate from the nondealer only if the certificate states that the vehicle is being purchased for resale and if the designated purchaser on the certificate is named on the dealer's report of sale and on the application for registration. If all these conditions are not met, the transaction is a retail sale for which the dealer must collect and report tax. (Reg. 1566(b), 18 CCR)

Used motor vehicle dealers.—Applicable January 1, 2021, any licensed car dealers, other than new vehicle dealers, are required to collect and remit to the Department of Motor Vehicles (DMV) applicable California sales tax, measured by the sales price of the vehicle with the registration fee. In addition, used motor vehicle dealers are required to remit applicable sales tax along with the Report of Sale (ROS) and registration fees to DMV within 30 days from the date of sale. (Sec. 6295, Rev. & Tax. Code; Sec. 4750.6, Veh. Code)

The DMV must withhold registration of vehicles purchased from used motor vehicle dealers until the dealer pays to the DMV the sales tax measured by the sales price together with any penalty. A penalty is imposed on a used motor vehicle dealer for failure to timely remit sales tax if that dealer is subject to the DMV penalty for failure to make a timely application for registration. Used motor vehicle dealers are also required to continue to file sales tax returns with the California Department of Tax and Fee Administration and impose interest and penalties for sales tax not timely paid. (Sec. 6295, Rev. & Tax. Code; Sec. 4750.6, Veh. Code)

• *Demonstration, display, or other use of vehicles held for resale*

California permits vehicles held for resale to be used for demonstration and display without the retailer incurring tax liability, but taxes other uses of vehicles prior to their retail sale. (Sec. 6094, Rev. & Tax. Code; Sec. 6244, Rev. & Tax. Code; Reg. 1669.5, 18 CCR)

• *DMV registration*

The California Department of Tax and Fee Administration (CDTFA) provides guidance regarding use tax clearance for Department of Motor Vehicle (DMV) registration for vehicles and vessels. This publication also provides examples of vehicle and vessel transfers that are not subject to California use tax. (CDTFA Publication 52, California Department of Tax and Fee Administration)

• *Lessee's sale of vehicle to third party*

A special provision addresses document processing delays when a vehicle lessee wishes to transfer title to a third party, instead of buying the vehicle, when the lease expires or terminates. There is a rebuttable presumption that a lessor's transfer to a lessee is a nontaxable sale for resale, provided the lessee transfers title and registration to a third party within ten days after the lessee acquires title upon termination or expiration of the lease. This presumption may be rebutted by evidence that the sale was not for resale prior to use. Transfer of title and registration to the third party occurs when the lessee endorses the certificate of ownership. (Sec. 6277, Rev. & Tax. Code; Reg. 1610(d)(2), 18 CCR)

• *Nondealer sales and leases*

California exempts from the sales tax (but not necessarily from the use tax) motor vehicle sales by a seller who is (1) not licensed or certificated as a dealer, manufacturer, remanufacturer, dismantler, or lessor/retailer, or (2) not required to hold a seller's permit by reason of the number, scope, and character of its sales of such vehicles. (Sec. 6282, Rev. & Tax. Code; Sec. 6283, Rev. & Tax. Code)

In these circumstances, the seller is not required to collect and remit tax; the purchaser, however, must pay use tax to the Department of Motor Vehicles (DMV). Application to the DMV relieves the purchaser from use tax return filing requirements. Use tax does not apply if the transaction qualifies as an inter-family transaction, or if the purchaser is a serviceman qualifying for the exemption for certain out-of-state purchases. The above sales tax exemption does not apply to rental fees payable under a lease. (Sec. 6291, Rev. & Tax. Code; Sec. 6292, Rev. & Tax. Code; Reg. 1610(c)(1), 18 CCR)

Exemption or clearance certificates.—The CDTFA provides for exemption or other tax clearance certificates to be obtained by qualified applicants either from the CDTFA or from qualified vehicle retailers. The certificates allow completion of registration by the DMV, and may indicate that the CDTFA finds no use tax is due, or that tax has or will be paid so that registration will not be withheld. The certificate form is prescribed by the CDTFA, and any issuing, altering, forgery, or contrary use of a certificate is a misdemeanor. (Sec. 6422.1, Rev. & Tax. Code)

Leases by nondealers.—The measure of use tax applied when a lessor who is not a certificated dealer or dismantler leases a vehicle and registers it in the name of the lessee only depends upon the circumstances:

— if the vehicle was purchased from a bona fide dealer outside California, the use tax is measured by the sales price to the lessor, and is payable by the lessor to the DMV;

— if the vehicle was purchased neither from a certificated California dealer nor from a bona fide out-of-state dealer, and if no evidence is presented of the actual sales price to the lessor, the measure of tax is the vehicle's fair market value (as determined under the Vehicle Code), multiplied by 1.2 for a noncommercial vehicle, or by 1.8 for a commercial vehicle.

(Reg. 1610(d)(1), 18 CCR)

See ¶60-740 Transportation, for similar provisions on nondealer sales of vessels or aircraft.

• *Reorganizations, consolidations, mergers*

California has special provisions exempting vehicles (as well as vessels and aircraft; see ¶60-740 Transportation) transferred with substantially all of the seller's business property, provided that the real or ultimate ownership is substantially similar to that existing before the transfer. (Sec. 6281, Rev. & Tax. Code)

• *Sales to family members or revocable trusts*

California exempts the sale or use of vehicles (as well as vessels and aircraft; see ¶60-740 Transportation) if the seller is the parent, grandparent, child, grandchild, or spouse of the purchaser or if the seller and purchaser are minor brothers or sisters. The seller must not be in the business of selling the type of property for which the exemption is claimed. Those claiming this exemption must submit proof of the relationship. Sales by a stepchild to a stepparent, or vice versa, are not exempt. (Sec. 6285, Rev. & Tax. Code; Reg. 1610(b)(2), 18 CCR)

The sale of a motor vehicle to a revocable trust is exempt, provided that the sale does not change beneficial ownership of the property. Also, the trust must provide for reversion of the property to the seller upon revocation of the trust, and consideration for the sale must be limited to assumption by the trust of an existing loan for which the property being transferred is the sole collateral. (Sec. 6285, Rev. & Tax. Code)

• *Stretch limousines*

When a dealer, at a customer's request, has a conversion company "stretch" a vehicle into a limousine, the conversion company's charge to the dealer is not taxable; however, the dealer's charge to the customer for the conversion is subject to tax. If the customer provides the vehicle for conversion, the conversion company's entire charge to the customer is taxable. (Reg. 1526(c), 18 CCR)

- *Vehicles purchased by foreigners*

The sale of a new motor vehicle to a foreign country resident who, before arriving in the U.S., arranges the purchase through an authorized dealer in the foreign country, is exempt from tax, provided that:

— an in-transit permit is issued to the purchaser under Veh. Code Sec. 6700.1, and

— the retailer ships or drives the vehicle to a point outside the U.S. before the in-transit permit expires, by way of the retailer's own facilities or by delivery to a carrier, customs broker, or forwarding agent for shipment to that point.

(Sec. 6366.2, Rev. & Tax. Code)

- *Vehicles, vessels, and aircraft purchased out of state*

Any vehicle brought into California after being purchased outside the state is deemed to have been purchased for use in California, provided that the vehicle's first functional use is in the state. (Reg. 1620(b)(5), 18 CCR)

A rebuttable presumption exists that a vehicle, vessel, or aircraft shipped or brought into California within 12 months from the date of its purchase was purchased from a retailer for storage, use, or other consumption in California, under specific circumstances, and is therefore subject to use tax, provided such vehicle, vessel, or aircraft is:

— purchased by a California resident;

— subject to California's registration or property tax laws during the first 12 months of ownership; or

— used or stored in California more than half the time during the first 12 months of ownership.

(Sec. 6248, Rev. & Tax. Code; Reg. 1620(b)(5), 18 CCR)

Application of the presumption to residents includes a closely held corporation or limited liability company (LLC) if 50% or more of the shares or membership interests are held by shareholders or members who are California residents. (Sec. 6248, Rev. & Tax. Code)

The presumption may be controverted by documentary evidence, as provided. Moreover, the presumption is inapplicable to: (1) any vehicle, vessel, or aircraft used in interstate or foreign commerce, as provided; and (2) any aircraft or vessel brought into California for the purpose of repair, retrofit, or modification. Moreover, repair, retrofit, or modification work must be performed by a qualifying licensed repair facility for vessels and by a certified repair station or manufacturer's maintenance facility for aircraft. (Sec. 6248, Rev. & Tax. Code)

In the case of a vessel purchased outside California and brought into California within the first 12 months of ownership for the exclusive purpose of repair, retrofit, or modification, the vessel is not considered purchased for use in California if that repair, retrofit, or modification is performed by a repair facility that holds an appropriate permit issued by the CDTFA and is licensed to do business by the county, city, or city and county in which it is located if the city, county, or city and county so requires. (Sec. 6248, Rev. & Tax. Code)

Auto dealers and repair shops should indicate specific dates on their invoices or work orders when warranty or repair service work is performed on vehicles brought into California. In this manner, customers can more readily indicate, if necessary, that the vehicle qualifies for the use tax exclusion applicable to vehicles brought into the state only for warranty or repair service. In order to qualify for the exclusion, the vehicle must be used or stored in California for 30 days or less, including all travel time in the state. (*Tax Information Bulletin*, California State Board of Equalization, March 2007)

Out-of-state purchases by servicemen.—Use in California of a vehicle purchased and delivered outside the state to an active duty member of the U.S. Armed Forces is not subject to tax, provided the serviceman's intention to use the vehicle in California resulted from official transfer orders, rather than from the serviceman's own independent determination. A serviceman's independent determination to use the vehicle in California is indicated if the purchase contract is made after the serviceman receives transfer orders, or if the serviceman arranges to receive the vehicle in California when the purchase contract is made. (Reg. 1610(b)(2), 18 CCR; Reg. 1566(c), 18 CCR)

A licensed California dealer must collect and remit use tax on an out-of-state vehicle sale to a serviceman for use in California if a contract is made after the purchaser's transfer orders to California. (Sec. 6249, Rev. & Tax. Code; Reg. 1566(c), 18 CCR; Reg. 1610(b)(2), 18 CCR)

Sales to servicemen in California.—Licensed California dealers, manufacturers, or dismantlers must collect and remit tax on sales of vehicles in California to servicemen, regardless of the purchaser's place of residence. (Reg. 1566(c), 18 CCR)

• *Local taxes*

Based on the Bradley-Burns Uniform Local Sales and Use Tax Law, leased vehicles are subject to a 1% local use tax. The place of use of leased vehicles with lease terms that exceed four months must be defined for the purpose of reporting and transmitting the local use tax. If the lessor is a new motor vehicle dealer, the place of use of the leased vehicle is the city, city and county, or county in which the lessor's business is located. If the lessor is not a new motor vehicle dealer but purchases the vehicle from a new motor vehicle dealer, the place of use is the city, city and county, or county in which the dealer's place of business is located. The place of use in the above instances will remain the same for the duration of the lease contract, even if the lessor sells the vehicle and assigns the lease contract to a third party. Finally, if the lessor is not a new motor vehicle dealer and purchases the vehicle from someone other than a new motor vehicle dealer, the use tax must be reported to and distributed through the countywide pool of the county in which the lessee resides. (Sec. 7205.1, Rev. & Tax. Code)

The place of use of a vehicle leased by a leasing company or purchased by a lessor from a leasing company will be determined in the same manner as for a vehicle leased by a new motor vehicle dealer or purchased by a lessor from a new motor vehicle dealer. A "leasing company" is a company that:

— originates lease contracts that constitute continuing sales and purchases of motor vehicles;

— does not sell or assign those lease contracts; and

— has annual motor vehicle lease receipts of $15 million or more per location.

(Sec. 7205.1, Rev. & Tax. Code)

The definition of "motor vehicle" in the Bradley-Burns Uniform Local Sales and Use Tax Law is limited to self-propelled passenger vehicles and pickup trucks rated less than one ton for the purpose of allocating local use tax imposed with respect to a lease of a new or used motor vehicle. (Sec. 7205.1, Rev. & Tax. Code)

[¶60-580] Nonprofit Organizations, Private Schools, and Churches

California law does not provide a general exemption for sales or purchases of nonprofit organizations. However, there are various provisions, discussed below, treating specific nonprofit entities (such as charitable organizations) and specific types of property.

The California Department of Tax and Fee Administration (CDTFA) provides guidance regarding the sales and use tax law and regulations as they apply to nonprofit organizations. (*CDTFA Publication 18, Nonprofit Organizations*, California Department of Tax and Fee Administration)

•*Animals and plants of zoological societies*

The gross receipts from the sale, storage, use, or other in-state consumption of endangered or threatened animal or plant species are exempt from sales and use taxes if both the seller and the purchaser are nonprofit zoological societies. (Sec. 6366.5, Rev. & Tax. Code)

"Endangered or threatened animal or plant species" means animals or plants that are listed in Appendix I, II, or III to the Convention for International Trade of Endangered Species or listed by the U.S. Department of the Interior, Fish and Wildlife Service, as endangered or threatened. For purposes of the exemption, a "nonprofit zoological society" is either a zoological society operated for charitable, educational, or scientific purposes and qualified for exemption under IRC Sec. 501(c)(3) or a zoological park owned or operated by a city, county, or other instrumentality of any state or foreign government. (Sec. 6010.50, Rev. & Tax. Code)

•*Art purchased for a museum*

The existing California sales and use tax exemption for sales of original works of art purchased by certain governmental entities or nonprofit organizations includes the lease of original works of art, as specified, if both the lessor and lessee are nonprofit organizations qualified for exemption from state income tax. The term of the lease must be at least 35 years in order for the art collection to be considered part of the permanent collection of the lessee. (Sec. 6365, Rev. & Tax. Code)

The exemption is also applicable to works of art that are purchased and become part of the permanent collection of a governmental entity that leases art for public display from another governmental entity. In addition, the exemption is clarified to specify that purchases of clothing, costumes, dresses, and personal adornment that are works of art as defined by regulation are also exempt. (Sec. 6365, Rev. & Tax. Code)

The only exemption for sales of art provided under California law is for purchases of original works of art by or on behalf of state or local governments or by nonprofit organizations for public display. (Sec. 6365, Rev. & Tax. Code; Reg. 1586, 18 CCR)

•*Charitable donations by retailers*

California provides a use tax exemption for property (including motor vehicles) donated by a seller to any federally exempt organization described in IRC 170(b)(1)(A) that is located in the state. In addition to public or government entities, the following private organizations are described in the federal statute:

— churches and conventions or associations of churches;

— educational organizations maintaining a faculty and curriculum and having a regular student body;

— medical organizations that provide medical or hospital care, medical education, or medical research;

— corporations, trusts, community chests, funds, and foundations that normally receive substantial support from federal, state, or local governments; and

— certain private foundations.

(Sec. 6403, Rev. & Tax. Code; Reg. 1669(e), 18 CCR; Reg. 1669(e), 18 CCR; Reg. 1669.5(a)(5), 18 CCR)

Museums qualify as donee organizations only if they use the property solely for display purposes and are nonprofit museums, as provided. "Museum" refers to any museum that has a significant portion of its space open to the public without charge, that is open to the public without charge for at least six hours during any month the museum is open to the public, or that is open to a segment of the student or adult population without charge. (Sec. 6366.4(c), Rev. & Tax. Code)

• *Charitable organizations*

Sales and donations by charitable organizations.—California exempts sales and donations by charitable organizations that assist the needy, provided all of the following conditions are met:

— the organization must be exempt from California property taxation under the "welfare exemption" in Sec. 214, Rev. & Tax. Code. (This exemption is available only for property owned by the charitable organization and actually used for charitable purposes. Property used merely to raise funds is not used in a charitable activity, even if the funds are devoted to charitable purposes. The organization must have a welfare exemption for the same retail outlet for which a seller's permit is held or, if it does not own the outlet, the exemption must cover its tangible personal property such as inventory or fixtures. However, since an organization can operate on leased premises, a California court of appeal ruled that lack of a property tax "welfare exemption" is not a bar to claiming sales and use tax exemption);

— the organization must be engaged in relieving poverty and distress;

— the organization's sales and donations must be made principally as an assistance to purchasers in distressed financial conditions; and

— the property sold or donated must have been made, prepared, assembled, or manufactured by the organization. (This condition is satisfied when the property is picked up at various locations and brought together at one or more locations for purposes of sale, even though nothing further needs to be done to make the property saleable. Property is "prepared" if it is made ready for sale by such processes as cleaning, repairing, or reconditioning.)

(Sec. 6375, Rev. & Tax. Code; Reg. 1570(a) and (b), 18 CCR)

Nonprofit organizations that do not meet the property tax "welfare exemption" may still be exempt from sales and use tax; see "Thrift stores operated by certain nonprofit organizations," below.

Sales to charitable organizations.—Neither the sales tax nor the use tax is applicable to tangible personal property purchased by qualifying organizations for the purpose of donation. However, tax is imposed on sales to these organizations of supplies and other articles not otherwise exempt. (Reg. 1570(c), 18 CCR)

Seller's permits and exemption certificates.—Even though their sales are exempt, qualified charitable organizations must hold seller's permits and must fill out an exemption certificate. (Reg. 1570, 18 CCR)

• *Flags provided by veterans' organizations*

A nonprofit veteran's organization is the consumer of U.S. flags that it sells if the profits are used for purposes of the organization. Thus, it may not present a resale certificate when purchasing such items; however, its own sales are exempt. (Sec. 6359.3, Rev. & Tax. Code; Reg. 1597, 18 CCR)

For exemption provisions concerning fund-raising meals that are furnished or served by nonprofit veterans' organizations, see ¶ 60-390 Food and Grocery Items.

• *Hospitals, institutions, and homes for the care of persons*

"Institution," as it pertains to the following discussion, is defined as:

— qualified "health facilities" and "community care facilities" as defined in the Health and Safety Code;

— any institution supplying board and room for a flat monthly rate and serving as a principal residence exclusively for persons aged 62 or older; or

— qualified alcoholism or drug abuse recovery facilities.

(Sec. 6363.6, Rev. & Tax. Code; Reg. 1503(a), 18 CCR)

Health facility includes any "clinic" as defined by the Health and Safety Code. (Sec. 6369, Rev. & Tax. Code)

Sales to institutions.—Tax applies to sales of tangible personal property to institutions for which a separate charge is not made upon transfer of the property to patients, residents, nurses, doctors, or others. Sales to institutions for which the institution does make a separate charge are tax-exempt sales for resale. This provision does not apply to sales of exempted medicines, meals, or food products furnished to and consumed by residents or patients. (Reg. 1503(b), 18 CCR)

Sales by institutions.—Tax is inapplicable to charges made by institutions to residents or patients for meals or food products (see ¶ 60-390, "Food and Grocery Items") or rooms or services. Tax does apply to charges made to residents or patients for appliances, dressings, and other supplies except for those items that qualify as exempt medicines (see ¶ 60-520 Medical, Dental, and Optical Supplies and Drugs). (Reg. 1503(b), 18 CCR)

If a charge is made for property administered to a resident or patient and no separate charge is made that identifies the actual administration charges, the total charge is nontaxable and the institution is treated as the consumer of the administered property. This provision covers property requiring technical or professional administration, such as injections or other internal applications or applying casts, splints, dressings, or bandages; oral applications or external applications such as rubbing on the skin are not considered "administrations" for purposes of this provision. If a separate charge is made for administering the property, the institution is the retailer and tax applies to charges for the property but not to the administration charge. (Reg. 1503(b), 18 CCR)

If the institution adds sales tax reimbursement to any charge including the furnishing of tangible property, there is a rebuttable presumption that the institution has made a retail sale. (Reg. 1503(b), 18 CCR)

Laboratory charges for blood or blood counts.—Laboratory charges, such as for blood counts, are not taxable. Purchases, sales, or donations of whole blood or blood plasma for transfusion also are exempt. (Reg. 1503(b)(3), 18 CCR)

¶60-580

• *Meals served to the elderly or disabled*

California exempts the sale, storage, use, or other consumption of meals and food products furnished or served to low-income elderly persons at or below cost by a nonprofit organization or government agency under a program funded for that purpose by the state or the federal government. (Sec. 6374, Rev. & Tax. Code) The sale, storage, use, or other consumption of meals delivered to homebound elderly or disabled persons by a nonprofit volunteer home delivery meal provider is also exempt from sales and use tax. (Sec. 6363.7, Rev. & Tax. Code)

• *Meals served by religious organizations*

California exempts meals and food products sold by a religious organization at its gatherings, provided that the sales are for obtaining revenue for the organization's functioning and the receipts are so used. (Sec. 6363.5, Rev. & Tax. Code)

• *Meals served to students*

California exempts meals served to private or public school students by schools, student or parent-teacher organizations, or any qualified blind person operating a restaurant or vending stand. The exemption does not apply when food products are sold for consumption within a place to which admission is charged, except state and national parks and monuments. (Sec. 6363, Rev. & Tax. Code; Reg. 1603(j), 18 CCR)

• *Medical health information and health and safety materials*

Use tax does not apply to medical health literature or health and safety educational materials or insignias purchased by a qualifying charity from its national or branch office if it is engaged in the dissemination of such information. A qualifying charity is one that qualifies for the "welfare exemption" from California property taxation under Sec. 214, Rev. & Tax. Code (see "Charitable organizations" above for a discussion of the welfare exemption). (Sec. 6408, Rev. & Tax. Code; Sec. 6409, Rev. & Tax. Code)

• *Medical identification tags*

California exempts the sale or use of medical identification (worn to alert others of a medical disability or allergic reaction to certain treatments) furnished by nonprofit organizations that are exempt from the corporate (franchise) income tax. (Sec. 6371, Rev. & Tax. Code)

• *New children's clothing*

Operative January 1, 2014, California exempts the gross receipts from the sale, storage, use or other consumption of new children's clothing that is sold to a nonprofit organization for its distribution without charge to elementary school children. A "nonprofit organization" is defined as an organization that: (1) is organized and operated for charitable purposes; (2) has exempt status under Section 23701d of the Revenue and Taxation Code; (3) is engaged in the relief of poverty and distress; and (4) distributes new children's clothing principally as a matter of assistance to recipients in distressed financial conditions. (Sec. 6375.5, Rev. & Tax. Code; Reg. 1570(c), 18 CCR)

• *Nonprofit organizations characterized as consumers*

An IRC § 501(c) nonprofit membership organization will be characterized as a consumer rather than as a retailer in regards to specified tangible personal property that the organization provides or sells to its members. Accordingly, the retail sale that will be subject to tax is the sale of the applicable property to the organization itself.

The organization will not have to act as a tax collector in such specified sales to its members. To qualify, however, the specified sales must meet the following requirements:

— the tangible personal property must bear a logo or other identifying mark of the organization and must be a promotional item or other item commonly associated with use by a member to demonstrate that member's association with, or membership in, the organization;

— the cost to the member for the acquisition of this property may not be more than the cost to the organization itself to obtain and transfer the property to the member, including any applicable sales or use tax paid by the organization;

— reasonable steps must be taken by the organization to ensure that no member acquires more than 30 identical items of such property or resells the items to another person; and

— the property may not be distributed for purposes of organized political campaigning or issue advocacy.

(Sec. 6018.9, Rev. & Tax. Code; Reg. 1597, 18 CCR)

These provisions sunset effective January 1, 2015. (Sec. 6018.9, Rev. & Tax. Code; Reg. 1597, 18 CCR)

• *Nonprofit youth group sales*

See ¶ 60-390 Food and Grocery Items.

• *Prisoner-of-war bracelets distributed by charitable organizations*

A charitable organization that qualifies for the "welfare exemption" from California property taxation under Sec. 214, Rev. & Tax. Code, is the consumer of bracelets that commemorate American POWs and that it distributes, regardless of whether a contribution is made, if any profits are used for purposes of the organization. (Sec. 6360, Rev. & Tax. Code; Reg. 1597(c), 18 CCR) Thus, it may not present a resale certificate when purchasing such items. (Reg. 1597(g), 18 CCR)

• *Property sold at auction to fund homeless shelters*

Sales and use tax does not apply to property sold at auctions conducted to provide funding for homeless shelters if:

— the auction is conducted by or for a nonprofit organization that is exempt from tax under Sec. 23701d, Rev. & Tax. Code;

— no more than one such auction is conducted by or for the organization annually; and

— the proceeds of the auction are actually used to fund a homeless shelter.

(Sec. 6363.2, Rev. & Tax. Code)

• *PTAs, cooperative nursery schools, and Friends of the Library*

Nonprofit parent-teacher associations, nonprofit parent cooperative nursery schools, and authorized nonprofit Friends of the Library associations are consumers of personal property that they sell, provided that the profits are used exclusively for the purposes of the organizations. These organizations may not present resale certificates when they purchase such property. (Sec. 6370, Rev. & Tax. Code; Reg. 1597(g), 18 CCR)

• *Rummage sales by auxiliaries of public museums*

A nonprofit association or equivalent organization that performs auxiliary services for a city or county museum and that sells tangible personal property at an annual rummage sale is the consumer of property sold at the rummage sale and thus does not have to collect and report tax on such sales. To benefit from this provision, the organization must be authorized by the governing authority of the museum to operate within the museum, must have held an annual rummage sale for at least five consecutive years prior to the current sale, and must use the profits exclusively for furthering the purposes of the organization. (Sec. 6370.5, Rev. & Tax. Code)

• *Sales benefiting certain disabled or disturbed persons*

Qualified organizations that provide services to developmentally disabled persons or to severely emotionally disturbed children are considered consumers, rather than retailers, of tangible personal property, provided that the property is hand-crafted or artistic in nature and is designed, created, or made by individuals with developmental disabilities or by children with severe emotional disturbances who are members of, or are receiving services from, the qualified organization. (Sec. 6361.1(a), Rev. & Tax. Code; Reg. 1597(d), 18 CCR)

To be eligible for this sales and use tax exemption, the price of an item sold by the organization may not exceed $20, sales must be made on an irregular basis, and the profits from such sales must be used to further the purposes of the organization. "Qualified organizations" are those that are exempt under IRC Sec. 501(c)(3), that are devoted primarily to providing services to persons with developmental disabilities or to children with severe emotional disturbances, and that do not discriminate on the basis of race, sex, nationality, or religion. (Sec. 6361.1, Rev. & Tax. Code; Reg. 1597(d), 18 CCR)

• *School yearbooks and catalogs*

Private schools and their student organizations are consumers of yearbooks and catalogs prepared for or by them and distributed to students; tax does not apply therefore to sales of such items to students. (This exemption also applies to public schools; see ¶ 60-420 Government Transactions.) Tax does apply to charges made by printers, engravers, photographers, and the like to schools and student organizations for preparing such publications. (Sec. 6361.5, Rev. & Tax. Code; Reg. 1590(b)(9), 18 CCR)

• *Social clubs and fraternal organizations*

With a limited exception for sales of food and drink to members, California taxes sales of tangible personal property by social clubs and fraternal organizations to their members or other persons. (Sec. 6006(c), Rev. & Tax. Code)

California does not tax meals, food, and drinks furnished by social clubs or fraternal organizations exclusively to members, provided that such sales occur less frequently than once a week. If the club or organization furnishes such items to nonmembers as well as members, all member and nonmember receipts are subject to tax. Meals, food, and drink paid for by members are "furnished" to the members even if consumed by nonmember guests. (Reg. 1603(i), 18 CCR)

Sales of meals by caterers to social clubs and fraternal organizations are sales for resale (and thus not taxed) if those entities or persons are retailers of the meals and provide valid resale certificates to the caterers. (Reg. 1603(h), 18 CCR)

• *Thrift stores*

Provisions apply to items sold by thrift stores operated by certain nonprofit organizations and to tangible personal property sold by thrift stores located on military installations.

Thrift stores operated by nonprofit organizations.—Sales and use tax does not apply to used pieces of clothing, household items, or other retail items sold by thrift stores operated by nonprofit organizations that provide medical, hospice, or social services to individuals with human immunodeficiency virus (HIV) disease or acquired immune deficiency syndrome (AIDS). To qualify for the exemption, at least 75% of the thrift store's net revenue must be used to fund these services. The exemption expires January 1, 2019. (Sec. 6363.3, Rev. & Tax. Code)

In order to be eligible for the exemption, the purpose of the thrift store must be to obtain revenue for the funding of medical, hospice, or social services to chronically ill individuals, and at least 75% of the net income derived from the operations of the thrift store must be actually expended for those purposes. (Sec. 6363.3, Rev. & Tax. Code)

Thrift stores located on military installations.—Tangible personal property sold by a thrift store located on a military installation and operated by a designated entity that, in partnership with the U.S. Department of Defense, provides financial, educational, and other assistance to members of the U.S. Armed Forces, eligible family members, and survivors that are in need, is exempt from sales and use tax. "Designated entity," for purposes of this exemption, is defined as a military welfare society, as provided. This exemption sunsets on January 1, 2024. (Sec. 6363.4, Rev. & Tax. Code)

The exemption applies to thrift stores operated by the Navy-Marine Corps Relief Society on bases in San Diego, Twentynine Palms, Miramar, Camp Pendleton, Port Imperial Beach, Port Hueneme, and Lemoore. These thrift stores sell nominally-priced used clothing, uniforms, and household goods to military families and Department of Defense employees, including retirees, and civilian contractors, and are closed to the general public. Income from sales at these stores supports relief services to Navy and Marine Corps communities on and near their respective bases. (*News Release 78-13-G*, California State Board of Equalization, August 21, 2014)

• *Vehicles loaned to schools or veterans' hospitals for training programs*

California exempts from the use tax the loan by any retailer of a motor vehicle to an accredited private or parochial high school for state-approved driver education and training programs or to a veterans' hospital or such other nonprofit facility or institution to provide disabled veterans with instruction in operating specially equipped vehicles. (Sec. 6404, Rev. & Tax. Code)

[¶60-650] Resales

Sales for resale are generally exempt from sales or use tax. The sales tax applies only to retail sales, defined as a sale for any purpose other than resale in the regular course of business, while the use tax is imposed on the storage, use, or other consumption in the state of tangible personal property purchased from a retailer. (Sec. 6051, Rev. & Tax. Code; Sec. 6201, Rev. & Tax. Code)

PLANNING NOTE: The CDTFA explains California sales and use tax law for businesses that make sales for resale to Mexican merchants and sales for export to Mexican purchasers. (*CDTFA Publication 32, Sales to Purchasers from Mexico*, California Department of Tax and Fee Administration)

The California Department of Tax and Fee Administration (CDTFA) provides guidance regarding resale certificates. (*CDTFA Publication 42, Resale Certificate Tips*, California Department of Tax and Fee Administration)

The CDTFA also addresses seller's permits. (*CDTFA Publication 73, Your California Seller's Permit*, California Department of Tax and Fee Administration)

The CDTFA provides guidance regarding sales for resale and resale certificates. Among the issues discussed are the legitimacy of purchases for resale, the content of a resale certificate, timely acceptance of a resale certificate, verifying a seller's permit number, and proper completion of sales and use tax returns. (*CDTFA Publication 103, Sales for Resale*, California Department of Tax and Fee Administration)

There is a rebuttable presumption that all gross receipts are subject to sales tax (Sec. 6091, Rev. & Tax. Code) and that tangible personal property sold for delivery in the state is sold for storage, use, or consumption in the state. (Sec. 6241, Rev. & Tax. Code)

The burden of proving that a sale of tangible personal property is not at retail is upon the seller unless the seller timely takes in good faith a certificate from the purchaser that the property is purchased for resale. If a seller takes such a certificate in good faith from a person who is engaged in the business of selling tangible personal property and who holds a California seller's permit, the certificate relieves the seller from liability for the sales tax and the duty of collecting the use tax. A certificate will be considered timely if it is taken at any time before the seller bills the purchaser for the property, or any time within the seller's normal billing and payment cycle, or any time at or prior to delivery of the property to the purchaser. A resale certificate remains in effect until revoked in writing. (Sec. 6092, Rev. & Tax. Code; Sec. 6242, Rev. & Tax. Code; Reg. 1668, 18 CCR)

If the purchaser insists that property not normally resold is bought for resale, a specific resale certificate so stating is required. A certificate is timely taken if taken before the seller bills the purchaser, within the seller's normal billing and payment cycle, or at any time at or prior to delivery of the property. (Reg. 1668(a), 18 CCR) See ¶ 61-020 Exemption Certificates.

A seller who does not timely obtain a resale certificate is not relieved from tax liability or from the burden of proving that the sale was for resale merely by the fact that the purchaser deletes the tax or tax reimbursement from the seller's billing, provides the seller with a permit number, or informs the seller that the transaction is not taxable. (Reg. 1668(b)(5), 18 CCR)

Moreover, a resale certificate that is not timely taken is not retroactive. Consequently, a seller will be relieved of tax liability only upon satisfactory evidence that the property:

— was actually resold by the purchaser and was not used for any purpose other than retention, demonstration, and display while being held for resale;

— is being held for resale and has not been used by the purchaser for any purpose other than retention, demonstration, or display; or

— has been used or consumed by the purchaser and the purchaser has paid use tax directly to the state.

(Reg. 1668(c), 18 CCR)

• *Auto dismantlers and auctioneers*

Licensed auto dismantlers and auto auctioneers are prohibited from accepting resale certificates from purchasers of vehicles, mobile homes, and commercial coaches, unless the purchasers are licensed dealers, dismantlers, auto repair dealers, or scrap metal processors, as specified and defined, for California sales and use tax purposes. Every qualified person making any sale of a mobilehome or commercial coach required to be registered annually under the Health and Safety Code, or of a vehicle required to be registered under the Vehicle Code or subject to identification under the Vehicle Code, or a vehicle that qualifies under the permanent trailer identification plate program pursuant to the Vehicle Code, or of any salvage certificate vehicle as defined in the Vehicle Code, as provided, is presumed to be making a sale at retail and not a sale for resale. (Sec. 6092.5, Rev. & Tax. Code; Reg. 1566.1, 18 CCR)

Rebuttal of presumption.—The presumption may be rebutted by taking a resale certificate from any of the following: (1) a person that certifies it is licensed, registered, regulated, or certificated under the Health and Safety Code or the Vehicle Code as a dealer or dismantler; (2) a person that certifies it is licensed, registered, regulated, or certificated under the Business and Professions Code as an automotive repair dealer, or is qualified as a scrap metal processor as described in the Vehicle Code; (3) a person that certifies it is licensed, registered, regulated, certificated, or otherwise authorized by another state, country, or jurisdiction to do business as a dealer, dismantler, automotive repairer, or scrap metal processor. For these purposes, a "qualified person" means a person making a sale at auction or a dismantler licensed under the Vehicle Code. (Sec. 6092.5, Rev. & Tax. Code; Reg. 1566.1, 18 CCR)

Resale certificates.—Sales of vehicles, motorhomes, commercial coaches, and salvage vehicles by dismantlers and auctioneers are taxable unless the dismantler or auctioneer accepts a resale certificate from someone who is licensed to sell vehicles, vehicle parts, or scrap metal. Under previous law (applicable prior to September 29, 2012), dismantlers and auction houses could accept a resale certificate from any person with a seller's permit, not just a licensed dealer. For example, a person with a seller's permit for the operation of a restaurant could have issued a resale certificate for the purchase of a salvage vehicle from an auto auction. (*Special Notice L-333*, California State Board of Equalization, October 2012)

A dismantler or auctioneer may only accept a resale certificate from the following persons:

— auto dealers;

— automotive repair dealers;

— dismantlers; and

— scrap metal processors.

(*Special Notice L-333*, California State Board of Equalization, October 2012)

Any document (e.g., a letter or purchase order) will be considered a resale certificate provided it is timely provided by the purchaser to the seller and contains all of the following information:

— the signature of the purchaser, purchaser's employee, or authorized representative of the purchaser;

— the purchaser's name and address;

— the number of the seller's permit held by the purchaser;

— a statement that the property described in the document is purchased for resale in the regular course of business;

— a statement that the purchaser is licensed, registered, regulated, or certificated under the Health and Safety Code or the Vehicle Code as a dealer or dismantler, or is licensed, registered, regulated, or certificated under the Business and Professions Code as an automotive repair dealer, or is qualified as a scrap metal processor as described in the Vehicle Code, or is licensed, registered, regulated, certificated, or otherwise authorized by another state, country, or jurisdiction to do business as a dealer, dismantler, automotive repairer, or scrap metal processor; and

— the date the document is executed.

(Reg. 1566.1, 18 CCR)

Reg. 1566.1 provides the form of the resale certificate. (Reg. 1566.1, 18 CCR)

The resale certificate must include all of the required elements as provided in Regulation 1668, Sales for Resale, in addition to the applicable license or registration number of the dealer, dismantler, automotive repair dealer, or scrap metal processor providing the resale certificate. If the purchaser is not required to hold a seller's permit, the purchaser must provide on line 1 of the resale certificate, where the permit number is requested, a sufficient explanation regarding the reasons the purchaser is not required to hold a California seller's permit. (Reg. 1668, 18 CCR; *Special Notice L-333*, California State Board of Equalization, October 2012)

A dismantler or auctioneer who fails to obtain a timely valid resale certificate may use alternative methods as prescribed by the CDTFA to rebut the presumption that the sale was not a sale at retail. The purchaser must include their applicable license or registration number on the form. (Reg. 1668, 18 CCR; *Special Notice L-333*, California State Board of Equalization, October 2012)

• *Commingled fungible goods*

If fungible goods purchased under a resale certificate are commingled with similar goods that were not so purchased and the identities of the two groups cannot be determined, sales from the commingled mass are treated as sales for resale until the amount sold is equal to the amount purchased under a resale certificate. Conversely, if goods are removed from the commingled mass for the purpose of consumption, the amounts removed are treated as if purchased for consumption until an amount has been removed that equals the amount of the commingled mass that was *not* purchased under a resale certificate. (Sec. 6095, Rev. & Tax. Code; Sec. 6245, Rev. & Tax. Code)

• *Form of resale certificate*

A resale certificate may be in any form, such as a note, letter, or memorandum. It must, however, contain the following information:

— the name and address of the purchaser;

— the number of the seller's permit held by the purchaser if the purchaser is required to have a seller's permit. If the purchaser does not have a seller's permit, the statement must include a statement to that effect and an explanation as to why the purchaser does not have a seller's permit;

— a description of the property to be purchased;

— a statement that the described property is being purchased for resale (the word "resale" must be specifically stated, the use of words such as "nontaxable," "exempt," or similar terms is not acceptable);

— the date of the document; and

— the signature of the purchaser or someone approved to act on the purchaser's behalf.

(Sec. 6093, Rev. & Tax. Code; Sec. 6243, Rev. & Tax. Code; Reg. 1668, 18 CCR)

• *Tax-paid purchases resold*

Retailers may deduct the amount of sales or use tax that they have paid on property that they purchased for purposes other than resale, but that they do in fact resell prior to making any taxable use. If a retailer takes this deduction, no refund or credit will be allowed to the retailer's vendor with respect to the sale of the property. The deduction should be taken on the retailer's return in which the sale of the property is reported. If the deduction is not taken at this time, a refund claim must be filed. (Sec. 6012(a)(1), Rev. & Tax. Code; Reg. 1701, 18 CCR)

This deduction could arise in the following situations:

— the retailer intends to use the property but resells it before making use of it;

— the property is not of a type normally sold by the retailer but is the subject of an unusual sale;

— a portion of the property generally used by the retailer is incidentally sold; or

— the retailer, through error, pays tax on purchases of property that is intended for resale.

(Reg. 1701(b), 18 CCR)

California does not permit this deduction with respect to property purchased tax-paid and placed in "standby service" at the location where it is intended to be used, even if the property is ultimately removed and sold. (Reg. 1701(c), 18 CCR)

• *Withdrawals from inventory*

California generally taxes the use, other than demonstration or display, of property held for resale, including items withdrawn from inventory. Property that is used for any purpose other than or in addition to demonstration or display, such as making deliveries, personal use of employees, etc., is subject to use tax. In addition, tax applies to the subsequent retail sale of the property. (Sec. 6094(a), Rev. & Tax. Code; Reg. 1669, 18 CCR)

The measure of the use tax is the purchase price of the property, unless the use of the property is limited to the loan of the property to customers as an accommodation while awaiting delivery of property purchased or leased from the lender or while property is being repaired for customers by the lender. In such case, the measure of the tax is the fair rental value of the property for the duration of each loan so made. The measure of the tax for property that is used frequently for purposes of demonstration or display while holding it for sale in the regular course of business, and that is also is used partly for other purposes, is the fair rental value of the property for the period of such other use or uses. (Sec. 6094(a), Rev. & Tax. Code)

For information concerning the use of mobile transportation equipment, see ¶ 60-740 Transportation.

• *XYZ letters*

A taxpayer has the option of using XYZ letters to indicate the character of property and application of sales and use tax to help the CDTFA determine if the use tax has already been reported or if the seller's sale was a sale for resale. In the absence of any valid resale documentation or evidence of tax payment to the CDTFA, an auditor may determine that it is appropriate for a seller to use the CDTFA 504 series of forms, referred to as "XYZ letters." Those letters are used to help satisfy the seller's burden of proving that a sale was not at retail even though a valid resale certificate was not obtained or to confirm a claim that the purchaser paid the tax directly to the state. When the CDTFA accepts the purchaser's response to an XYZ letter as valid, the CDTFA relieves the seller of liability for sale or use tax collection. An XYZ letter, however, is not treated as a resale certificate in that it does not relieve a seller from liability for sales tax. (*Tax Information Bulletin*, California State Board of Education, December 2009)

[¶60-665] Services

Services are generally exempt from sales and use tax in California.

What services are taxable in California?

Certain fabrication services are subject to tax.

California sales tax is also imposed on providers of support services at retail measured by the gross receipts from the sale of those services.

What about transactions that also involve tangible personal property?

Amounts received for services that are a part of the sale or lease of tangible personal property are taxable if the true object of the sale is the transfer of the tangible personal property. However, if the true object is a service, tax does not apply even though some property may be transferred.

> **EXAMPLE:** A business advisory firm that performs record keeping, payroll, and tax services and furnishes forms, binders, and other property to its clients as an incident to the rendition of its services is the consumer, and not the retailer, of that tangible personal property. The true object of the contract between the firm and its client is the performance of a service and not the furnishing of tangible personal property. If it is determined that a transaction is a sale of tangible personal property, tax applies to the gross receipts without any deduction for work, labor, skill, thought, time, or other expenses of production.

How is tangible personal property purchased by the service provider treated?

Tangible personal property purchased and consumed by a service provider is subject to tax. If property is purchased by a service provider for sale to customers, however, the purchase would be exempt and sales tax would be collected on the sale of that property. (See Resales.)

Does California provide any detailed guidance on specific services?

Yes, the California Department of Tax and Fee Administration (CDTFA) provides detailed guidance on several services.

Architects. Fees paid to licensed architects for their designs, concepts, ideas, and specifications are not subject to tax. Any instruments of service integral to the licensed architect's services such as plans, specifications, renderings, or models, are likewise not subject to tax. A licensed architect is the consumer of any tangible personal property used or transferred in the performance of professional services, regardless of whether the charge for such property is added to and separately stated on a customer's bill. Architectural perspectivists and modelers however are the retailers of renderings, prints, drawings and models they provide to architects or other consumers, and tax applies to the entire charge for such items.

Barbers and beauty shops. Barbers and beauty shop operators are consumers of, and must pay tax on their purchase of, the supplies and other property used in performing their services. They are retailers of any supplies, used articles, or other property that they sell to consumers in the regular course of business; tax applies to the gross receipts from such sales.

Chiropractors. Licensed chiropractors are the consumers of, and must pay tax on their purchase of, vitamins, minerals, dietary supplements, and orthotic devices used or furnished in performing their professional services.

Circulating libraries. Tax does not apply to charges made by a circulating library for renting books, provided that the library has already paid either sales or use tax on the books. However, a circulating library is the retailer of books that it sells to consumers in the regular course of business.

Dentists and dental laboratories. Dentists are consumers of, and must pay tax on their purchase of, the materials, supplies, dental laboratory products, and other property that they use in their profession. Dental laboratories are the retailers of the plates, inlays, and other products that they manufacture for dentists and other consumers. Tax applies to the entire price that is charged for such products, regardless of whether they segregate charges for materials and manufacturing services.

Employment services. California has no specific provisions relating to the tax treatment of temporary employment agencies, employment agencies, professional employers, executive search services, job search or placement services, employment counseling, or resume writing services. California currently taxes only selected services, and employment services are not listed as taxable services.

Fabrication. Tax applies to producing, fabricating, processing, printing, or the imprinting of tangible personal property for a consideration for customers who furnish, either directly or indirectly, the materials used in those processes.

Fur repairers, alterers, and remodelers. Sales tax generally applies to fabrication services on garments or furniture furnished by a customer. When services performed on a fur garment by repairers, alterers, or remodelers result in producing, processing, or fabricating tangible personal property, or are a step in producing, processing, or fabricating tangible personal property, the entire charge, including fabrication labor and materials, is subject to tax.

Reupholsterers. Charges for fabrication labor are taxable. Cutting and sewing materials for coverings for furniture being reupholstered, including back and seat cushions, are steps in the process of completing a new article and are fabrication labor. Labor for making new furniture from material furnished directly or indirectly by the customer is fabrication labor.

Gift wrapping. Tax applies to the entire charge for gift wrapping, (i.e., furnishing the materials and labor required to wrap an item for a customer), regardless of whether the person who wraps the gift is also the seller of the contents. If the person who wraps the gift is the seller, the gift wrapping is considered sold together with the contents, regardless of whether the gift wrapping charge is separately stated. Also, a person who engages in gift wrapping may purchase the materials free of tax for resale.

The CDTFA provides information regarding gift wrapping. (CDTFA Publication 106, Combination Packages and Gift-Wrapping, California Department of Tax and Fee Administration)

Gun clubs. Gun clubs are consumers of, and must pay tax on their purchase of, clay pigeons or blue rocks furnished to members or patrons for trapshooting or similar sports, even though the charge for the service is measured by the number of clay pigeons or blue rocks used.

Hearing aid dispensers. Licensed hearing aid dispensers are consumers of, and must pay tax on their purchase of, hearing aids that they sell or furnish. Tax applies to the retail sale of such items by persons who are not licensed hearing aid dispensers.

Interior designers. Fees for the professional services of an interior designer or decorator are not subject to tax when the fees have no relation to the sale of merchandise. Such fees are taxable, however, when the fees are directly related to the taxable sale of merchandise. Typical services include consulting, design, layout, selection of color schemes, coordination of furniture and fabrics, supervision of installations, and so on. The fee may be a negotiated fixed amount or a percentage of the selling price of furnishings, labor, and installation charges. Tax does not apply to charges for professional services that are not directly related to the sale of merchandise. Charges for the professional services should be separately stated.

Fees related to the sale of merchandise. Tax does apply to charges for fees that are directly related to acquiring and providing furnishings and other merchandise an interior decorator or designer sells to a client. For example, fees charged to accompany a client to a showroom to select furniture the client is buying from the decorator are taxable. (CDTFA Publication 35, Interior Designers and Decorators, California Department of Tax and Fee Administration)

Guidance. The California Department of Tax and Fee Administration (CDTFA) provides guidance regarding the application of sales and use taxes to transactions that involve interior designers and decorators. Topics discussed include designer fees and charges related to the sale of merchandise, improvements to real property, purchases, resale certificates, use tax, and record-keeping requirements. (CDTFA Publication 35, Interior Designers and Decorators, California Department of Tax and Fee Administration)

Landscaping. Landscape contractors who enter into contracts for landscaping in which they furnish and install plants, trees, and lawns are construction contractors. The installation of a lawn is an improvement to realty. In a lump sum contract, the contractor is generally a consumer of the materials installed. Plants and trees installed in landscaping contracts are considered fixtures. Landscape contractors are considered to be the retailer liable for the tax on their sales of plants and trees furnished and installed in connection with their services. In the case of lump sum contracts, the selling price of the plants and trees is generally regarded as the cost price to the landscape contractor. If nurseries install plants or trees under a lump sum contract, which have been grown or produced by them, the cost price is considered to be the price at which similar plants or trees in similar quantities ready for installation are sold by the nursery to other contractors.

Deduction. The landscaper may be entitled to a deduction for "tax-paid purchases resold prior to use" on their sales and use tax return if they make the taxable sale of materials and fixtures and: (1) purchase plants and trees (fixtures) from nurseries to install in a construction contract; (2) pay an amount as sales tax reimbursement on those purchases; and (3) make no use of them prior to installation (other than retention, demonstration, or display while holding them for resale).

Guidance. The CDTFA provides guidance on such contracts. (**CDTFA Publication 9, Construction and Building Contractors**, California Department of Tax and Fee Administration)

Locksmiths. When a locksmith sells merchandise, such as locks, locksets, lubricating spray, and lock parts, without providing any labor or services, the sale is usually subject to sales tax. For jobs that involve labor or services only, generally, if the locksmith does not furnish any materials in the course of the job and the locksmith's charge does not include amounts for materials, the work is not taxable. For jobs that involve labor or services and charges for materials, sales tax may apply to the entire charge or only to the locksmith's charges for materials. The application of tax depends on the circumstances of the transaction. In general, tax applies to charges for fabrication labor, but not to charges for work considered installation or repair.

Guidance. The CDTFA provides guidance regarding the taxability of locksmith charges, sales, and purchases. (CDTFA Publication 62, Locksmiths, California Department of Tax and Fee Administration)

Optometrists and opticians. Tax applies to the sale of ophthalmic materials including eyeglasses, frames, and lenses used or furnished in the performance of the optometrist's or optician's professional services in the diagnosis, treatment, or correction of conditions of the human eye. An optometrist or optician is the consumer of such ophthalmic materials and tax applies to the sale of such materials to optometrists and opticians.

Sunglasses. When sunglasses, including clip-on sunglasses, are dispensed pursuant to a prescription prepared by a physician and surgeon or optometrist for a particular class of plano, the dispensing optician is the consumer of the lenses and frames or sunglasses, and tax applies to the sale of those glasses to the optician. In all other instances, the optician is the retailer of such lenses and frames or sunglasses and tax applies to such a retail sale.

Opthalmic materials. See Medical, Dental, and Optical Supplies and Drugs, for a discussion of ophthalmic materials.

Painting, polishing, and finishing. Tax applies to charges for painting, polishing, and otherwise finishing tangible personal property if these services are part of the production of a finished product for consumers, regardless of whether the article to be finished is supplied by the customer or by the finisher. Tax does not apply to charges for painting or finishing real property.

Podiatrists. Podiatrists are the consumers of, and must pay tax on their purchases of, prosthetic materials and inlays, including arch supports or special footgear, that are used or furnished by them in performing their professional services.

Repainting and refinishing. A single or lump-sum charge to a customer for repainting or refinishing the customer's used article is not taxable; the repainter or refinisher is the consumer of, and must pay tax on the purchase of, materials used in the operation. If the repainter buys materials under a resale certificate or purchases materials out of state without paying use tax, the repainter must report and pay tax on the cost of the materials. However, if a separate charge for materials is billed to the customer at a fair retail selling price, this charge is a retail sale and the materials may be purchased by the repainter under a resale certificate.

Work done for sellers. California treats, as a sale for resale, any charges for materials (such as paint) that become a component of repainted or refinished articles if the customers are themselves retailers of and will resell the articles; in such situations, the repainter or refinisher should take a resale certificate from the customer/retailer.

Storage services. California does not specifically provide guidance regarding storage services. However, the application of sales and use tax to storage charges depends on whether there is a related sale of tangible personal property. If a transaction involves the sale or rental of tangible personal property in addition to the sale of a service, such as storage services, then the transaction is taxable. If there is no sale or rental of such property, then the transaction is not subject to tax. For example, charges imposed to rent or lease storage space is not subject to California sales and use tax because there is no sale of tangible personal property, only the rental of storage space. The true object of the transaction is the purchase of the storage service, there is no purchase of a product. (Sec. 6012, Rev. & Tax. Code; Reg. 1501, 18 CCR)

True object test. The basic distinction in determining whether a particular transaction involves a sale of tangible personal property or the transfer of tangible personal property incidental to the performance of a service is one of the true objects of the contract. Is the real object sought by the buyer the service per se or the property produced by the service? If the true object of the contract is the service per se, the transaction is not subject to tax even though some tangible personal property is transferred. (Sec. 6012, Rev. & Tax. Code; Reg. 1501, 18 CCR)

Support services. California sales tax is imposed on providers of support services at retail measured by the gross receipts from the sale of those services.

See Rate of Tax, for the current rate.

The tax is operative provided specified federal approval requests for matching funds are granted.

"Support services," for purposes of the tax, are defined as:

domestic services and services related to domestic services;

heavy cleaning;

personal care services, as defined;

accompaniment when needed during necessary travel to health-related appointments or to alternative resource sites;

yard hazard abatement;

protective supervision;

teaching and demonstration directed at reducing the need for other supportive services; and

paramedical services that make it possible for the recipient to establish and maintain an independent living arrangement, including necessary paramedical services ordered by a licensed health care professional, as provided.

"Seller" is defined to include:

the California Department of Social Services in its capacity as the state agency that oversees the In-Home Supportive Services (IHSS) program;

a county in which county staff serve as homemakers, as provided;

a county that contracts with a nongovernmental contractor to arrange for the retail sale of support services; or

any other nongovernmental person that arranges for the retail sale of support services.

Compliance. Sellers that are actively engaged in arranging for the retail sale of support services are required to register with the California Department of Tax and Fee Administration (CDTFA), collect tax from the provider, and report and pay the tax to the CDTFA. Sales tax prepayments are inapplicable to sellers until no later than three months after the date that federal approval is obtained.

Implementation date. The implementation date of the California sales tax on providers of support services at retail measured by the gross receipts from the sale of those services is January 1, 2012.

In addition, the Director of the Department of Health Care Services is required to seek federal approval from the federal Centers for Medicare and Medicaid Services to implement these provisions, and to notify the CDTFA within 10 days of receipt of that approval.

Provider. "Provider" is defined as a natural person who is authorized by law to provide all such support services and who makes a retail sale. Moreover, the term includes nongovernmental persons that arrange for the retail sale of all support services.

Taxidermists. Taxidermists are consumers of, and must pay tax on their purchase of, materials used in the operations that they perform on the animals, birds, etc., furnished by their customers; if, however, a separate charge at the fair retail selling price is made for such property on the customer's invoice, the taxidermist is the retailer of the property, and tax applies to the separate charge. Tax applies to a taxidermist's retail sales of skins, heads, mountings, or other tangible personal property.

Veterinarians. Veterinary services are exempt. Licensed veterinarians are consumers of the drugs and medicines that they administer in performing their services. Tax does not apply to a veterinarian's charges to clients for such items, even if separately stated. Tax applies to the sale of medicines and drugs to veterinarians and to drugs and medicines that veterinarians sell without performing specific related professional services are taxable. However, medicines and drugs purchased by a veterinarian and used primarily for the prevention and control of disease are exempt from tax (see Agriculture, for a discussion of this exemption).

Veterinarians as consumers. Veterinarians are consumers of and must pay tax on items, other than drugs and medicines, that they either use or furnish to clients without separately stated charges; if such charges are separately stated, the charges are taxable to the clients. Also taxable are separately stated charges for X-rays if the X-ray films are delivered to clients.

Guidance. The California Department of Tax and Fee Administration (CDTFA) provides guidance regarding sales and use tax laws and regulations as they apply to veterinarians. (CDTFA Publication 36, Veterinarians, California Department of Tax and Fee Administration)

[¶60-740] Transportation

In general, transportation equipment and supplies and transportation services are exempt from sales and use tax in California.

¶60-740

How does California tax transportation equipment and supplies?

In general, transportation equipment and supplies are exempt from sales and use tax.

Aircraft sold or leased to common carriers. California exempts the sale or lease of aircraft to persons using the aircraft as common carriers and to persons who will lease the aircraft to others for such use. To qualify for the exemption, the aircraft must be used as a common carrier for more than one-half of its operational use during the first 12 consecutive months after its first operational use.

The California Department of Tax and Fee Administration (CDTFA) provides guidance regarding aircraft.

Component parts of qualified aircraft. Tangible personal property that becomes a component part of a qualified aircraft as the result of maintenance, repair, overhaul, or improvements required by the Federal Aviation Administration is also exempt, as is the cost of labor and services rendered in connection with required maintenance, repair, overhaul, or improvements. It is rebuttably presumed that aircraft is not used in the business of a common carrier if annual gross receipts from using the aircraft do not exceed 20% of its cost or $50,000, whichever is less.

Exclusions. Common carrier use does not include:

— student training flights;

— ferry flights;

— flights for crop dusting, bird chasing, banner towing, fire fighting, aerial photography or surveying, powerline or pipeline patrol, search and rescue, and sightseeing;

— helicopter flights to perform construction or repair work, in the lumber industry to reposition fallen lumber, or to move large equipment; and

— flights to transport injured persons to medical facilities.

Exemption certificates. Exemption certificates are available for the purchase of common carrier aircraft and aircraft parts. An exemption certificate relieves the seller from liability for sales or use tax collection if it is taken timely and in good faith.

Leased aircraft. Aircraft that is leased, or that is sold for the purpose of leasing is also rebuttably presumed not to be used regularly in the business of transporting property or persons for hire, absent contrary evidence satisfactory to the CDTFA, provided that the lessor's annual gross receipts from leasing the aircraft to others for use as a common carrier of property or persons do not exceed 20% of the aircraft's cost to the lessor, or $50,000, whichever is less. Gross receipts do not include compensation paid by the owner or lessor or by related parties for use of the aircraft as a common carrier. Members of the owner's or lessor's immediate family, employees of the owner or lessor while on company business, and entities in which the owner, lessor, or immediate family member holds at least 50% interest, qualify as "related parties."

Activities that do not affect the exemption. The exemption is not affected by:

— test flights made to determine if the aircraft flies according to specifications or is in proper operating condition, even if the flights are made after the aircraft is sold and delivered to the purchaser;

— modifications, repairs, or replacements made after delivery of the aircraft and prior to its being placed in service;

— operation of the aircraft, either prior to or after delivery, to train the customer's pilots or other personnel in proper operation or maintenance, provided that the training period is not longer than what is reasonably required; and

— operation of the aircraft, after its delivery but prior to its being placed in regular service, for a short period in transporting nonrevenue passengers or property.

Aircraft sold or leased to nonresidents or to foreign governments. California exempts the sale or lease of aircraft to foreign governments or to nonresidents for use outside California. Also exempt is tangible personal property that becomes a component part of a qualified aircraft as the result of maintenance, repair, overhaul, or improvements required by the Federal Aviation Administration, and the cost of labor and services rendered in connection with required maintenance, repair, overhaul, or improvements. The "use outside California" requirement is satisfied if the foreign government or nonresident, as owner or lessee, removes the aircraft from California and does not bring it back in (except for warranty or repair work) within 12 months after its removal.

Activities that do not affect the exemption. The exemption is not affected if:

— the aircraft is returned to California within the 12-month period solely for repair or warranty service covered by warranty;

— test flights are conducted to determine if an aircraft will fly according to specifications, or that it is in proper operating condition, regardless of whether such flights occur before or after the sale and delivery of the aircraft;

— modification, repair, or replacement work is performed on an aircraft, after its delivery but before the aircraft is placed in regular operation by a common carrier, or in the case of a foreign government or nonresident, before the aircraft's removal from California; and

— the aircraft is operated, either before or after delivery, to train the customer's pilots or other personnel in proper operation or maintenance, provided the training period is not longer than what is reasonably required.

Common carriers and foreign air carriers. California exempts sales of tangible personal property or fuel to a common carrier or foreign air carrier for use in its operations outside California, subject to certain conditions.

See Motor Fuels.

Hot prepared food products sold to interstate air carriers. California exempts hot prepared food productswhen sold to air carriers engaged in interstate or foreign commerce as well as when sold or served by the carriers to their passengers, but taxes the sale or use of taxable beverages in California by carriers, except for sales occurring during trips across California territory or airspace without any stops or landings in the state.

See Food and Grocery Items.

Ground control stations sold to nonresidents or foreign governments. California exempts the sale of any ground control station to any foreign government or nonresident for use outside the state. The term "ground control station" means a portable facility used to operate aircraft in the air without a pilot on board, including controls, video equipment, computers, generators, and communications equipment, sold as an integral part of the station, and antennas used to control the aircraft. The term does not include trucks, tractor-trailers, or other devices solely used to transport the station.

Intermodal cargo containers used in interstate or foreign commerce. California exempts from use tax intermodal cargo containers that are:

— first used in interstate or foreign commerce;

— under a sales or lease contract prior to their entry into the state;

— brought into the state for the specific purpose of being loaded with freight and transported outside the state; and

— used continuously in interstate or foreign commerce both within and outside of the state and not exclusively in the state.

Leases of mobile transportation equipment. Leasing mobile transportation equipment for use in transporting persons or property does not constitute a taxable sale or purchase. "Mobile transportation equipment" is defined as railroad cars and locomotives, buses, trucks (excluding one-way rental trucks), truck tractors or trailers, dollies, bogies, chassis, reusable cargo shipping containers, aircraft, ships, and any tangible personal property that is or becomes a component part of such equipment. To qualify for the exemption, equipment is required to be intended for transporting passengers and property for substantial distances. Not included are passenger vehicles, trailers, and baggage containers designed for hauling by passenger vehicles or one-way rental trucks. Bogies, chassis, dollies, and other special terms are defined.

A lessor is considered to be the consumer of qualifying mobile equipment, and leases of such equipment are not continuing sales and purchases. The lessor's purchase or the use of mobile transportation equipment in California is therefore generally subject to tax, which may be paid when the equipment is purchased.

Alternatively, the lessor of mobile transportation equipment purchased without payment of tax or tax reimbursement may irrevocably elect to pay use tax measured by fair rental value, provided that the lessor does not use the equipment for purposes other than leasing.

The election must be made by the due date of the return for the later of the period in which the property is first leased or the period in which the equipment first enters California after being leased outside the state. Under this election, the lessor thereafter reports use tax on the rental value in all periods in which the equipment is leased, whether or not the equipment is within or outside the state. Lessors may purchase equipment under a resale certificate for the limited purpose of reporting use tax based on fair rental value.

If the CDTFA determines that the rentals paid under the lease are nominal, the tax is redetermined to reflect fair rental value. Fair rental value, in turn, does not include any use tax reimbursement paid by the lessee, which must either be returned to the lessee or remitted to the state.

If the lessor's tax liability is measured by fair rental value, the tax rate in effect when the equipment is first leased applies for all periods during the first, and any subsequent, lease. To report rental receipts subject to a tax rate before the rate reduction, Schedule T is required.

Pursuant to a lessor's election to pay tax measured by the fair rental value of leased mobile transportation equipment, tax applies for all periods during which the equipment is leased, even if the lessee does not make the required rental payments.

The rate of tax in effect at the time the equipment is first leased will continue to be the rate for all periods during which the equipment is leased, except if the equipment is sold while subject to an existing lease and the new purchaser elects to pay tax measured by fair rental value. In such a situation, the applicable rate will be the rate in effect at the time of the sale of the equipment.

Equipment purchased outside California. Mobile transportation equipment purchased outside California is subject to use tax when leased in California; use tax is measured by the lessor's purchase price, absent a timely election to pay tax on fair rental value, as discussed above. Equipment purchased outside California that enters California in interstate commerce and thereafter remains only in interstate commerce is exempt.

One-way rental trucks. One-way rental trucks are excluded from the definition of "mobile transportation equipment," with the result that rental receipts from leasing are taxable, as is the initial purchase of the vehicle. They are defined as motor trucks that are required to be registered, do not exceed the manufacturer's gross vehicle weight rating of 24,000 pounds, and are principally employed by a rental business in being leased out for periods of not more than 31 days to individual customers for one-way or local hauling of personal property.

Local taxes. Under the Bradley-Burns Uniform Local Sales and Use Tax Law, retailers of vehicles, aircraft, and vessels must collect local use tax based on where the vehicle, aircraft, or vessel is registered or licensed. Even though the sale of the vehicle, aircraft, or vessel may be exempt from state and local sales tax, if the property is used or stored principally in a district with a transactions tax, local use tax must be collected. The dealer is required to collect the use tax from any purchaser who registers or licenses a vehicle, aircraft, or vessel at an address in a district imposing the tax. The buyer is required to sign a written declaration that the address of registry is the buyer's principal residence.

Aircraft common carrier local tax partial exemption. The local California sales and use tax exemption for qualifying sales to, and purchases by, aircraft common carriers is 1%. (*Special Notice L-434*, California State Board of Equalization, November 2015)

If a retailer claims the exemption from the local tax, the retailer must complete and attach CDTFA-531-X, Schedule X Detailed Allocation by County of Sales Exempt from Local Tax, to the retailer's return. Retailers do not need to obtain a new blanket exemption certificate from their customers. Properly completed certificates already on file may be used to support partially exempt sales made under the new rate. (*Special Notice L-434*, California State Board of Equalization, November 2015)

Aircraft exemption. Local use tax ordinances must contain provisions exempting tangible personal property (other than fuel or petroleum products) that is sold or leased to operators of aircraft if is to be used outside the taxing city or county in transporting persons or property. The exemption applies to 75% of the gross receipts from qualified transaction in the case of a Bradley-Burns sales and use tax, or 100% in the case of a transactions (sales) and use tax. The 75% exemption continues until the first day of the first calendar quarter commencing more than 90 days after the California Director of Finance notifies the California Department of Tax and Fee Administration that all state deficit financing bonds have been repaid or that sufficient funds have been set aside to fully repay the bonds.

Aircraft used outside the county. Sales of tangible personal property to operators of aircraft to be used or consumed outside the county in which the sale is made is exempt from local use tax only if the property is used or consumed "directly and exclusively" in the use of the aircraft as a common carrier. The exemption does not include office or shop equipment or supplies not directly used or consumed in the carriage of persons or property.

Certificate of Exclusion from district use tax. A sample certificate of exclusion (declaration) from California local district use tax is available for purchasers to submit to retailers substantiating their claim that district use tax is inapplicable to a particular purchase of tangible personal property delivered and for use outside the district. According to the California Department of Tax and Fee Administration (CDTFA), when retailers collect district use tax, they often use software programs that locate jurisdictions based on ZIP codes. District boundaries, however, like city and county boundaries, do not coincide with ZIP code boundaries. The regulation is necessary, according to the CDTFA, to provide guidance to retailers who may be reluctant to accept purchasers' unsubstantiated statements that they do not live in a district when the purchasers' ZIP codes are within a district. The sample declaration, signed by the purchaser under penalty of perjury, includes statements that the tangible personal property was both delivered and purchased for use at a location outside the subject district.

Retailers of registered vehicles, undocumented vessels, and licensed aircraft. Retailers of any vehicle subject to registration and any licensed aircraft and registered undocumented vessels are subject to the local use tax.

The CDTFA must make information concerning the cities and counties located within districts imposing the transactions and use tax and the rates at which the tax is imposed available to dealers.

Supplies and equipment used directly in the carriage of persons or property. Local tax does not apply to certain sales to, or purchases by, aircraft common carriers if the property is used or consumed in a qualifying manner. This exemption is limited to supplies and equipment (excluding fuel and petroleum products) used or consumed directly in the carriage of persons or property. It does not include office supplies, shop equipment, or any other property not directly used or consumed in the carriage of persons or property. (*Special Notice L-434*, California State Board of Equalization, November 2015)

Nondealer sales of vessels and aircraft. California exempts from the sales tax, though not necessarily the use tax, sales in California of vessels and aircraft if the retailer is not a person required to hold a seller's permit by reason of the number, scope, and character of the sales.

The CDTFA provides guidance regarding documented vessels.

Broker-arranged sales. The exemption does not apply to any sale of a vessel or aircraft when a broker arranges the sale between two private parties and the broker collects sales tax reimbursement on the transaction.

Credit for tax paid. When a person purchases a vessel or aircraft from another person through a broker, the purchaser will be relieved of liability for the use tax if the purchaser has paid an amount as sales or use tax to the broker and has obtained and retained a receipt from the broker showing the payment of tax. The amount collected by the broker constitutes a debt owed by the broker to the state, as if the broker were a retailer engaged in business in California.

See Motor Vehicles.

Undocumented vessels. In the case of an undocumented vessel required to be registered with the Department of Motor Vehicles (DMV), the purchaser must pay use tax to the DMV.

Use tax. Unless specifically exempted under another provision, the purchaser must pay use tax measured by the sales price to the purchaser.

Rail cars used in interstate or foreign commerce. California exempts from the sales and use tax rail freight cars that are for use in interstate or foreign commerce.

Railroad equipment component parts. California exempts from use tax gross receipts from the storage, use, or other consumption in the state of tangible personal property that becomes a component part of any railroad equipment in the course of repairing, cleaning, altering, or improving the equipment outside the state.

Labor and services for railroad equipment component parts. Also exempt are charges made for labor and services rendered with respect to such repair, cleaning, alteration, or improvement. "Railroad equipment" is defined for purposes of the exemption as locomotives, freight and passenger cars, maintenance of way equipment, and any other equipment riding on flanged wheels and owned or used by a common carrier engaged in interstate or foreign commerce, or by any person for the purpose of leasing that equipment to a common carrier engaged in interstate or foreign commerce.

Sales to family members or revocable trusts. California exempts the sale or use of vessels and aircraft (as well as motor vehicles; see Motor Vehicles) if the seller is the parent, grandparent, child, grandchild, or spouse of the purchaser or if the seller and purchaser are minor brothers or sisters. The seller must not be in the business of selling the type of property for which the exemption is claimed. Those claiming this exemption must submit proof of the relationship. Sales by a stepchild to a stepparent or vice-versa are not exempt.

Revocable trusts. The sale of a vessel or aircraft to a revocable trust is exempt if the sale does not result in any change in the beneficial ownership of the property, the trust provides that upon revocation the property will revert wholly to the seller, and the only consideration for the sale is the assumption by the trust of an existing loan for which the property being transferred is the sole collateral. (Sec. 6285, Rev. & Tax. Code)

Trailers or semi-trailers moved under "one-trip" permit. California exempts from the use tax the storage, use, or other consumption of new or used trailers or semitrailers in connection with the moving or "operation laden" of such vehicles in accordance with a one-trip permit issued by the DMV. Such permits are issued to a manufacturer or dealer of (1) new trailers or semitrailers not previously registered in any state, and (2) used trailers or semitrailers not currently registered in California so they may be moved or operated laden within, entering, or leaving California for not more than five days as part of a continuous trip from the place of manufacture or dispatch to the place where they will be offered for sale.

Trucks and trailers purchased for out-of-state use. California exempts sales and purchases of new or remanufactured trucks, truck tractors, semitrailers, or trailers with a minimum unladen weight of 6,000 pounds or more when purchased outside California for use outside the state, but delivered by the manufacturer or remanufacturer to a nonresident purchaser in California, provided that the vehicle is moved outside the state within 30 days. The exemption also applies to trailer coaches or auxiliary dollies.

Exemption requirements. In order to qualify for the exemption, the purchaser must provide the manufacturer or remanufacturer with:

— written evidence of the vehicle's out-of-state registration;

— an affidavit that the purchaser is not a California resident, and

— an affidavit that the vehicle has been moved or driven to a point outside California within 30 days of the delivery date.

Trucks and trailers purchased in California. A sales and use tax exemption applies to trailers or semitrailers with a minimum unladen weight of 6,000 pounds or more that are manufactured or remanufactured out of state, purchased for use outside California, and delivered to the purchaser in California, provided that the trailer or semitrailer is moved from the state within 30 days. (Sec. 6388.5, Rev. & Tax. Code)

The sales and use tax exemption applies to the gross receipts from the sale, storage, use, or other consumption of the vehicle in California whenever a:

— new, used, or remanufactured truck, trailer, or semitrailer, that has an unladen weight of 6,000 pounds or more, that has been manufactured or remanufactured outside California, is purchased for use outside California, and is delivered by the manufacturer, remanufacturer, or dealer to the purchaser in California, and the purchaser drives or moves the vehicle to any point outside California within 30 days from and after the date of delivery;: or

— new, used, or remanufactured truck, trailer, or semitrailer that has an unladen weight of 6,000 pounds or more, that has been manufactured or remanufactured in California, is purchased for use outside California, and is delivered by the manufacturer, remanufacturer, or dealer to the purchaser in California, and the purchaser drives or moves the vehicle to any point outside California within 75 days from and after the date of delivery.

The exemption applies provided the purchaser or the purchaser's agent furnishes all the following to the manufacturer, remanufacturer, or dealer:

— written evidence of an out-of-state license and registration for the vehicle;

— with regard to a vehicle subject to the permanent trailer identification plate program that is used exclusively in interstate or foreign commerce or both, written evidence of the purchaser's or lessee's U.S. Department of Transportation number or Single State Registration System (effective January 1, 2021, "Unified Carrier Registration System") filing may be substituted for the written evidence of an out-of-state license and registration for the vehicle;

— effective January 1, 2021, and until January 1, 2024, with regard to a vehicle registered under the International Registration Plan (an international highway program that facilitates commercial vehicle registration and operation among states and Canada) that is used exclusively in interstate or foreign commerce, or both, written evidence of the purchaser's or lessee's U.S. Department of Transportation number or Unified Carrier Registration System filing may be substituted for the written evidence of an out-of-state license and registration for the vehicle (this provision is repealed effective January 1, 2024);

— the purchaser's affidavit that the purchaser purchased the vehicle from a dealer at a specified location for use exclusively outside California, or exclusively in interstate or foreign commerce or both; and

— the purchaser's affidavit that the vehicle has been moved or driven to a point outside California within the appropriate period of either 30 days or 75 days of the date of the delivery of the vehicle to the purchaser.

(Sec. 6388.5, Rev. & Tax. Code; Reg. 1620.1, 18 CCR)

To meet these documentation requirements, a purchaser may use CDTFA-837, Affidavit for Section 6388 or 6388.5 Exemption from California Sales and Use Tax, or an alternative acceptable affdavit that includes all the essential elements outlined above. The purchaser must provide a CDTFA-837, or an acceptable alternative, to the manufacturer, remanufacturer, or dealer of the truck or trailer no later than 30 days from the date the truck or trailer is taken outside California. Both the seller and the purchaser must retain these documents in their records for four years from the date of sale. (*Special Notice L-721*, California Department of Tax and Fee Administration, November 2019)

Vehicles purchased out of state. Any vehicle brought into California after being purchased outside the state is deemed to have been purchased for use in California, and is subject to use tax, provided that the vehicle's first functional use is in the state.

Rebuttable presumption. A rebuttable presumption exists that a vehicle, vessel, or aircraft shipped or brought into California within 12 months from the date of its purchase was purchased from a retailer for storage, use, or other consumption in California, under specific circumstances, and is therefore subject to use tax, provided such vehicle, vessel, or aircraft is:

— purchased by a California resident;

— subject to California's registration or property tax laws during the first 12 months of ownership; or

— used or stored in California more than half the time during the first 12 months of ownership.

Application of the presumption to residents includes a closely held corporation or limited liability company (LLC) if 50% or more of the shares or membership interests are held by shareholders or members who are California residents.

The presumption may be controverted by documentary evidence. Moreover, the presumption is inapplicable to: (1) any vehicle, vessel, or aircraft used in interstate or foreign commerce, as provided; and (2) any aircraft or vessel brought into California for the purpose of repair, retrofit, or modification. Moreover, repair, retrofit, or modification work must be performed by a qualifying licensed repair facility for vessels and by a certified repair station or manufacturer's maintenance facility for aircraft.

Repair, retrofit, or modification. In the case of a vessel purchased outside California and brought into California within the first 12 months of ownership for the exclusive purpose of repair, retrofit, or modification, the vessel is not considered purchased for use in California if that repair, retrofit, or modification is performed by a repair facility that holds an appropriate permit issued by the CDTFA and is licensed to do business by the county, city, or city and county in which it is located if the city, county, or city and county so requires.

Vessels or aircraft transferred in reorganizations or mergers. In accord with its provisions on "occasional sales," California has special provisions exempting vessels and aircraft (as well as motor vehicles) transferred with substantially all of the seller's business property, provided that the real or ultimate ownership is substantially similar to that existing before the transfer.

Vessels of more than 1,000 tons burden. California provides a sales tax exemption for sales by builders of vessels of more than 1,000 tons burden.

Watercraft used outside California's territorial waters. Sales and uses of watercraft are exempt, if the watercraft is used in:

— interstate or foreign commerce, for more than one-half of the vessel's operational use, by persons whose gross annual receipts from such commerce exceed the lesser of 10% of the watercraft's cost or $25,000;

— commercial deep sea fishing, during more than one-half of the vessel's operational use, outside of California's territorial waters by one regularly engaged in such fishing; and

— transporting for hire, during at least 80% of the vessel's functional use, persons or property to vessels or offshore drilling platforms located outside California's territorial waters.

Commercial deep sea fishing. There is a rebuttable presumption that a person is engaged in commercial deep sea fishing only if such operations produce $20,000 or more per year in receipts; such receipts are measured either by the first consecutive 12-month period beginning with the first functional use of the vessel after purchase of the boat (by a person not engaged in commercial deep sea fishing at the time of purchase) or, if the purchaser is already a commercial fisherman at the time of purchase, by any consecutive 12-month period in which the first functional use of the watercraft occurs. Receipts from both territorial and extraterritorial fishing are considered in making this determination, but the watercraft is not exempt if its principal use will be in territorial waters.

Component parts. This exemption also applies to sales of tangible personal property that becomes a component part of such watercraft during construction, repair, cleaning, altering, or improvement, along with related charges for labor and services; such materials include radio equipment, anchors, lifeboats, chains, cables, and items affixed to the hull for passenger or crew comfort, but exclude portable equipment and nonattached furniture such as chairs. The exemption also applies to sales of such watercraft to, and their use by, persons who lease such watercraft.

The CDTFA provides guidance regarding sales and use tax laws and regulations as they apply to the watercraft industry.

Watercraft operating between points within the state. Watercraft, such as ferry boats, barges, or tugs, that operate between points within the state may qualify for exemption if they are principally used either to transport interstate passengers or cargo or to convoy or aid the departure or arrival of vessels to or from points outside California. However, the exemption does not apply to watercraft used principally in intrastate commerce even if voyages are sometimes made in interstate or foreign commerce.

Special exemption certificate. A seller of watercraft is relieved of sales tax liability by taking a special exemption certificate that states that the watercraft qualifies for the exemption for watercraft that operates between points within the state.

Zero-emission transit buses. A partial California sales and use tax exemption is available on eligible purchases and leases of zero-emission technology transit buses by the following qualifying purchasers:

- city, county, or city and county;
- transportation or transit district; or
- public agencies that provide transit services to the public.

This exemption is effective October 9, 2019, and it sunsets on January 1, 2024. (Sec. 6377(d), Rev. & Tax. Code)

Hybrid and Zero-Emission Truck and Bus Voucher Incentive Project (HVIP). The California Air Resources Board (CARB) administers the HVIP to encourage the use of hybrid and zero-emission trucks and buses in California. HVIP provides discounts to vehicle purchasers by issuing voucher incentives for the purchase of qualifying trucks or buses. (*Special Notice L-716*, California Department of Tax and Fee Administration, November 2019)

Eligible zero-emission technology transit buses. The legislation enacted a partial exemption on purchases and leases, by eligible purchasers, of zero-emission buses on the HVIP eligible vehicles list and the following bus types:

- articulated bus;

- bus;

- cutaway bus;

- double decker bus;

- over-the-road bus;

- shuttle bus;

- transit bus; and

- trolley bus.

(*Special Notice L-716*, California Department of Tax and Fee Administration, November 2019)

Dealers. Sales to qualifying purchasers by dealers of eligible buses are subject to tax at a reduced rate of 3.3125% (7.25% current statewide tax rate less the 3.9375% partial exemption) plus any applicable district taxes. The reduced sales or use tax rate is applied to the total selling price of the vehicle before any incentives, such as a voucher from HVIP, are applied. (Sec. 6377(d), Rev. & Tax. Code; *Special Notice L-716*, California Department of Tax and Fee Administration, November 2019)

To report sales of eligible zero-emission technology buses on the sales and use tax return, taxpayers must report the total selling price in their total sales. The partial exemption for eligible sales of eligible buses to qualifying purchasers may be claimed as a "Zero-Emission Transit Bus" deduction the return. Taxpayers should obtain a timely partial exemption certificate from their customers to document the partially exempt sale. (*Special Notice L-716*, California Department of Tax and Fee Administration, November 2019)

Buyers. A qualifying purchaser making a purchase or lease of an eligible zero-emission technology transit bus must provide the retailer with a timely partial exemption certificate to obtain the reduced tax rate. (*Special Notice L-716*, California Department of Tax and Fee Administration, November 2019)

Exemption certificate. A partial exemption certificate must be issued to the retailer to document the partially exempt sale. We have a form exemption certificate, CDTFA-230-HB, Partial Exemption - Zero-Emission Transit Bus, on our website for your use in documenting the partial exemption. (*Special Notice L-716*, California Department of Tax and Fee Administration, November 2019)

What is the tax treatment of transportation services in California?

In general, transportation services are exempt from sales and use tax in California.

Passenger tickets. Federal law prohibits a state and its political subdivisions from collecting or levying a tax, fee, head charge, or other charge on:

— a passenger traveling in interstate commerce by motor carrier;

— the transportation of a passenger traveling in interstate commerce by motor carrier;

— the sale of passenger transportation in interstate commerce by motor carrier; or

— the gross receipts derived from such transportation.

(Sec. 14505, Title 49 U.S.C.)

[¶60-750] Utilities

California exempts the sale, use, or other consumption of gas or electricity delivered to consumers through mains, lines, or pipes. California also exempts the sale, furnishing, use, or other consumption of liquefied petroleum gas for household use or for use in producing and harvesting agricultural products. The liquefied petroleum must be delivered into a tank with a storage capacity equal to or greater than 30 gallons. The exemption also applies to steam and geothermal steam, brines, and heat when delivered to the consumer through mains, lines, or pipes, as well as to exhaust steam, waste steam, heat, and resultant energy produced through "cogeneration" (Sec. 6353, Rev. & Tax. Code; Reg. 1533, 18 CCR; SUTA Series 275, Gas, Electricity, and Water, California Department of Tax and Fee Administration)

A purchaser of qualified liquefied petroleum gas must provide a retailer with an exemption certificate in order for the retailer to claim the exemption. The exemption certificate may be in the form of a letter or purchase order, or any other document if it contains, along with information identifying the purchaser:

— the seller's permit number held by the purchaser; and

— a statement that incorporates certain specified information regarding the ultimate use of the gas.

(Sec. 6353, Rev. & Tax. Code; Reg. 1533, 18 CCR)

A purchaser of qualified liquefied petroleum gas may present a blanket exemption certificate in lieu of an exemption certificate for each transaction. (Sec. 6353, Rev. & Tax. Code; Reg. 1533, 18 CCR)

A purchaser is liable for the sales and use tax and related interest if, after timely submitting a copy of an exemption certificate to a retailer or to the CDTFA, the purchaser improperly uses or takes delivery of the liquefied petroleum gas or does not qualify for the exemption. (Sec. 6353, Rev. & Tax. Code; Reg. 1533, 18 CCR)

The exemption does not apply to fuel oil even if the oil is delivered through pipes and serves the same function as gas (SUTA Series 275, Gas, Electricity, and Water, California Department of Tax and Fee Administration). Sales of butane and propane gas from vendors' tanks through customers' pipes are exempt, unless the gas is sold in liquid form when it passes through the meter to the consumer. (Sec. 6353, Rev. & Tax. Code)

California also exempts organic products grown for fuel and waste by-products from agricultural or forest production, municipal refuse, or manufacturing operations. The products must be delivered in bulk and used as industrial fuel in lieu of oil, natural gas, or coal. (Sec. 6358.1, Rev. & Tax. Code)

See ¶ 60-560 Motor Fuels, for treatment of motor fuels.

California exempts a utility's sale of water to consumers through mains, lines, or pipes, and bulk sales of water to individuals for home use in quantities of 50 gallons or more, provided that the home is not in an area serviced by mains, lines, or pipes. Delivery of water by barge to ships at anchor is taxable because the delivery is not through mains, lines, or pipes. (SUTA Series 275, Gas, Electricity, and Water, California Department of Tax and Fee Administration) However, sales of water delivered by canals are exempt because the canals are considered the equivalent of mains, lines, or pipes. Sales of water delivered through a meter on a hydrant to the customer's tank trucks are exempt. (Sec. 6353, Rev. & Tax. Code)

See ¶ 60-390 Food and Grocery Items, for sales and use tax treatment of bottled water.

• *Property used by utilities in rendering services*

There are no special provisions on tangible personal property used by utilities in rendering their services, with the exception of the following: California excludes from the definition of "tangible personal property" (and thus excludes from the tax) telephone and telegraph lines, electrical transmission and distribution lines, and the poles, towers, or conduit by which they are supported or in which they are contained. (Sec. 6016.5, Rev. & Tax. Code)

[¶60-770] Sales Tax Holidays

California does not currently have any sales tax holidays.

[¶61-000]

EXEMPTIONS

[¶61-020] Exemption Certificates

There is a rebuttable presumption that all gross receipts are subject to tax. (Sec. 6091, Rev. & Tax. Code; Reg. 1667(a), 18 CCR) The seller is relieved of liability for sales tax if the seller takes in good faith from the purchaser a timely exemption certificate or resale certificate. (Sec. 6421, Rev. & Tax. Code; Reg. 1667(a), 18 CCR)

Resale certificates are discussed at ¶ 60-650 Resales.

• *Exemption certificates*

For transactions for which no specific exemption certificate is prescribed under California regulations (see below), a valid exemption certificate must include the following:

— the date;

— the signature of the purchaser or of an agent or employee of the purchaser;

— the purchaser's name and address;

— the purchaser's seller's permit number or a note stating why the purchaser is not required to hold such a permit;

— a description of the property purchased; and

— a statement of the manner in which or purpose for which the property will be used so as to qualify for exemption.

(Reg. 1667(c), 18 CCR)

A certificate is timely taken if taken before the seller bills the purchaser, within the seller's normal billing and payment cycle, or at any time at or prior to delivery of the property. (Reg. 1667(b), 18 CCR)

Good faith acceptance.—A purchaser is liable for tax if the purchaser uses the property in any way or for any purpose other than those specified in the certificate; the tax is measured by the cost of the property to the purchaser. (Sec. 6421, Rev. & Tax. Code)

Expiration date.—A California exemption certificate is valid until revoked in writing by the issuer, unless the certificate is issued for a specific transaction, in which case it is generally valid for one year. (Sec. 6421, Rev. & Tax. Code; Reg. 1667, 18 CCR)

• *Specialized certificates*

California has specially prescribed exemption certificates for the following kinds of property or transactions:

— animal or livestock feed (see ¶60-250 Agriculture);

— aviation gasoline (see ¶60-560 Motor Fuels);

— construction contractor exemption from tax rate increase (see ¶60-330 Construction);

— factory-built housing (see ¶60-330 Construction);

— hot prepared food sold to air carriers in interstate or foreign commerce (see ¶60-390 Food and Grocery Items);

— newspapers and periodicals: property becoming ingredient of;

— qualified sales and purchases of farm equipment and machinery (see ¶60-250 Agriculture);

— qualified sales and purchases of liquefied petroleum gas (see ¶60-750 Utilities);

— sales of printed sales messages delivered by the U.S. Postal Service or by common carrier;

— sales to an auto body repair and/or paint business (see ¶60-650 Resales);

— sales to civilian welfare funds at military bases (see ¶60-420 Government Transactions);

— sales to common carriers for use outside California; and

— watercraft used outside state territorial waters (see ¶60-740 Transportation).

• *Electronic exemption certificates*

California does not have any provisions regarding the acceptance of electronic exemption certificates.

• *Multiple point of use certificates (MPUs)*

California does not have any provisions for MPUs.

• *MTC and SST certificates*

Under the Multistate Tax Compact, a vendor is relieved of liability for sales or use tax with respect to a transaction for which the vendor accepts in good faith a resale or other exemption certificate, or other authorized written evidence of exemption. The Commission has adopted a Uniform Multijurisdiction Exemption Certificate that is to be filled out by buyers claiming sales tax exemptions and is maintained on file by sellers. In order for the certificate to be accepted in good faith by a seller, the seller must exercise caution that the transaction, or property being sold, is of a type that normally qualifies for exemption in the state. This certificate is not valid as an exemption certificate in California.

California is not a member of the Agreement because, although it has enacted legislation authorizing it to enter into the Agreement, it has not yet enacted the changes to its laws necessary to comply with the Agreement's requirements. The SST Governing Board has approved a uniform exemption certificate. Although full member states may continue to use their pre-existing exemption certificates, they must also accept the uniform certificate. Associate member and nonmember states may, but are not required to, accept the certificate.

[¶61-100]

BASIS OF TAX

[¶61-110] Tax Base

"Gross receipts," upon which the sales tax is imposed, and "sales price," upon which the use tax is imposed, are similarly defined as the total amount for which tangible personal property is sold, leased, or rented, valued in money (whether paid in money or otherwise), without any deduction for (a) the cost of the property sold; (b) the cost of materials used, labor or service costs, interest paid ("interest charged" for use tax purposes), losses, or any other expenses; or (c) the cost of transporting the property, except as otherwise provided. (Sec. 6011, Rev. & Tax. Code; Sec. 6012, Rev. & Tax. Code)

The "total amount for which property is sold, leased, or rented" includes:

— any services that are a part of the sale;

— any amount for which credit is given to the purchaser by the seller; and, in the definition of "gross receipts;"

— all receipts, cash, credits, and property of any kind.

(Sec. 6011, Rev. & Tax. Code; Sec. 6012, Rev. & Tax. Code)

Sales tax does not apply to automated teller machine (ATM) charges when an access device (e.g., a debit card or credit card) is issued to make a cash withdrawal from, or to engage in any other transaction that is not subject to tax, at an ATM. In addition, gross receipts from a retail sale of tangible personal property do not include debit card charges collected by the retailer if:

— the debit card charges are separately stated;

— the consumer would not otherwise incur the charge if he or she did not use the debit card;

— the fee is not calculated as a percentage of the amount of the purchase; and

— the charge is reasonably related to the cost of the transaction to the retailer.

(Reg. 1643, 18 CCR)

Taxable receipts of rentals or leases.—See ¶ 60-460 Leases and Rentals, for a discussion of special factors, if any, that can affect the basis of the tax in the case of rentals or leases.

• *Goods withdrawn from inventory*

The measure of the use tax for goods withdrawn from inventory (see ¶ 60-650 Resales) is the purchase price of the property, unless the use of the property is limited to the loan of the property to customers as an accommodation while awaiting delivery of property purchased or leased from the lender or while property is being repaired for customers by the lender. In such case, the measure of the tax is the fair rental value of the property for the duration of each loan so made. The measure of the tax for property that is used frequently for purposes of demonstration or display while holding it for sale in the regular course of business, and that is also is used partly for other purposes, is the fair rental value of the property for the period of such other use or uses. (Sec. 6094, Rev. & Tax. Code)

For information concerning the use of mobile transportation equipment, see ¶ 60-740 Transportation.

• *Goods damaged in transit*

If merchandise is damaged while en route to the consumer and after the sale has occurred, tax applies to the full purchase price. If the damage occurs prior to when the sale occurs, the following provisions apply: (1) if the goods are destroyed, tax does not apply to damages paid to the retailer; and (2) if the goods are not destroyed and are subsequently sold at retail in their damaged condition, tax applies to the portion of the total amount paid to the retailer representing the fair retail value of the goods in their damaged condition. (Reg. 1629, 18 CCR)

No use tax liability accrues on merchandise destroyed prior to the purchaser's use; however, if the property is used or stored in its damaged condition, use tax applies to the portion of the total price paid to the retailer that represents the fair market value of the damaged merchandise. (Reg. 1629, 18 CCR)

[¶61-200]

RETURNS, PAYMENT, AND RECORDS

[¶61-220] Returns, Payments, and Due Dates

Returns must be filed by sellers and by every person liable for sales tax. Out-of-state retailers engaged in business in the state and consumers subject to use tax who have not paid it to a retailer must also file returns. Sales and use tax returns must also be authenticated in a form or pursuant to methods prescribed by the California Department of Tax and Fee Administration (CDTFA). Likewise, applications to the CDTFA for permits to conduct business as a seller in the state must also be authenticated in a form or pursuant to methods prescribed by the CDTFA. Returns and permit applications may be filed by computer modem, magnetic media, optical disk, facsimile machine, telephone, or other electronic media. (Sec. 6452, Rev. & Tax. Code)

Except as noted below, sales and use taxes are due and payable to the CDTFA quarterly, on or before the last day of the month following each quarterly period. (Sec. 6451, Rev. & Tax. Code)

The quarterly return due for sales tax and some use tax filings must be signed by the filer or agent. If the return is prepared by a paid preparer, the preparer is required to include his or her name, social security number, federal employee identification number, and business name and address on the return. Failure to comply with this requirement will result in a $50 fine. The preparation of a substantial portion of a return is considered equivalent to preparing the entire return. A person is not deemed a paid preparer if his or her involvement is limited to typing, reproduction, or other mechanical assistance or if the return is prepared for another person in a fiduciary capacity. (Sec. 6452, Rev. & Tax. Code)

Collection cost recovery fee.—The California Department of Tax and Fee Administration (CDTFA) can impose a collection cost recovery fee on any person that fails to pay an amount of sales and use tax, interest, penalty, or other amount due and payable. The fee will be in an amount equal to the CDTFA's costs for collection as reasonably determined by the CDTFA, and will be imposed only if the CDTFA has mailed its demand notice that advises that continued failure to pay the amount due may result in collection action, including the imposition of a collection cost recovery fee. (Sec. 6833, Rev. & Tax. Code)

Extensions.—For good cause, the CDTFA may grant a one-month extension of time for filing a return or paying the tax. However, interest is imposed at the adjusted prime rate plus three percentage points until the payment date. In addition, the CDTFA is authorized, in the case of a disaster, to extend the time for making a return or paying the tax for a period not to exceed three months. Any person granted a disaster extension is required to pay, in addition to the tax or fee amount, interest at the modified adjusted rate per month, or fraction of that, from the date on which the payment would have been due without the extension to the date of actual payment. (Sec. 6459, Rev. & Tax. Code; Sec. 6591.5, Rev. & Tax. Code)

Return periods.—The CDTFA may grant an extension of more than one month if the taxpayer requesting the extension is a creditor of the state who has not been paid because the legislature failed to adopt a budget by July 1. (Sec. 6459, Rev. & Tax. Code) An extension granted under this provision expires on the last day of the month following the month in which the budget is passed. Interest at the modified adjusted rate applies from the date on which the tax would have been due until the date of payment; however, the portion of the payment that is equivalent to the amount due the taxpayer from the state accrues no interest. (Sec. 6591.5, Rev. & Tax. Code)

The CDTFA may require returns and tax payments for periods other than calendar quarters in order to ensure payment and facilitate collection. Reports for these "designated" periods must be filed on or by the last day of the month following each such period. (Sec. 6455, Rev. & Tax. Code)

For sales tax, the return must show the seller's gross receipts during the preceding reporting period, and for a nonseller, the return must show gross receipts for the period in which liability was incurred. With respect to use tax, the retailer return must show the total sales price of the property that became subject to tax during the preceding reporting period. A purchaser filing a use tax return (except purchasers that make an irrevocable election to report and remit use tax on their California personal income tax, corporation franchise or income tax, partnership, limited liability company, or estate or trust tax or information returns), on the other hand, must show the total sales price of the property that was purchased and used by the purchaser during the preceding reporting period. The return must also show tax amounts for the period covered by the return. (Sec. 6453, Rev. & Tax. Code)

Retailers may request the CDTFA's approval of an alternative use tax reporting method for qualified purchases subject to use tax. The CDTFA has issued guidelines to assist retailers in determining eligibility for the program, criteria for CDTFA approval, notification requirements, termination/cancellation for noncompliance with program requirements, and renewal of the CDTFA-approved reporting method. (See *Alternative Method of Reporting Use Tax (AMRUT) Program Guidelines*, BOE, Public Information and Administration Section, November 5, 2002).

A lessor's return must report the rental fees paid by a lessee during the preceding reporting period; a lessee's return should show the rents paid during the preceding period upon which tax has not been paid to the lessor. (Sec. 6457, Rev. & Tax. Code)

If a retailer filing yearly tax returns transfers or discontinues the business before the end of the yearly period, a closing return must be filed by the last day of the month following the close of the calendar quarter in which the business was transferred or discontinued. (Reg. 1699(f), 18 CCR)

The methods for notifying the CDTFA when a seller's permit becomes inactive are clarified by regulation. In addition, the fraud penalty can be imposed on a predecessor when the ownership of the successor who committed fraud is substantially the same as the predecessor ownership. (Reg. 1699(f), 18 CCR)

• *Calculation of estimated use tax and Use Tax Lookup Table*

Regulation 1685.5 prescribes:

— the specific use tax table that taxpayers can use to estimate their calendar year use taxes based upon their adjusted gross income (AGI);

— the manner in which the CDTFA must annually calculate the estimated amount of use tax due according to a person's AGI; and

— the format of the use tax table the CDTFA is required to make available to the FTB each year.

(Reg. 1685.5, 18 CCR)

Safe harbor.—If eligible consumers use the use tax tables included in the instructions to their FTB returns to estimate their use tax liabilities for qualified nonbusiness purchases and correctly report those liabilities in accordance with their AGI ranges, then the CDTFA may not assess the difference, if any, between the estimated use tax liabilities reported in accordance with the use tax tables and the consumers' actual use tax liabilities for qualified nonbusiness purchases. (Reg. 1685.5, 18 CCR)

Those eligible to use CDTFA use tax tables.—Consumers may elect, and are not required, to use the use tax table included in the instructions to their state income tax returns to report their estimated use tax liabilities for one or more single nonbusiness purchases of individual items of tangible personal property each with a sales price of less than $1,000 on their state income tax returns. However, eligible consumers may still calculate their actual use tax liabilities using the worksheets in the instructions to their FTB returns and report their actual use tax liabilities on their returns. (Reg. 1685.5, 18 CCR)

The Use Tax Lookup Table may not be used to estimate use tax liabilities for business purchases, including purchases made by businesses required to hold a seller's permit or to register with the CDTFA under the Sales and Use Tax Law and report their use tax liabilities directly to the CDTFA. (Reg. 1685.5, 18 CCR)

This table can only be used to report use tax on the 2019 California Income Tax Return:

— AGI of less than $10,000 = $1 use tax liability;

— AGI of $10,000 to $19,999 = $3 use tax liability;

— AGI of $20,000 to $29,999 = $5 use tax liability;

— AGI of $30,000 to $39,999 = $7 use tax liability;

— AGI of $40,000 to $49,999 = $9 use tax liability;

— AGI of $50,000 to $59,999 = $12 use tax liability;

— AGI of $60,000 to $69,999 = $14 use tax liability;

— AGI of $70,000 to $79,999 = $16 use tax liability;

— AGI of $80,000 to $89,999 = $18 use tax liability;

— AGI of $90,000 to $99,999 = $20 use tax liability;

— AGI of $100,000 to $124,999 = $24 use tax liability;

— AGI of $125,000 to $149,999 = $29 use tax liability;

— AGI of $150,000 to $174,999 = $34 use tax liability;

— AGI of $175,000 to $199,999 = $39 use tax liability;

— AGI of more than $199,999 = multiply AGI by 0.021% (0.00021).

(*California Use Tax Table*, California Department of Tax and Fee Administration)

This table can only be used to report use tax on the California Income Tax Return. This table may not be used to report use tax on business purchases. The table and instructions are provided in the state income tax return instructions for forms 540 and 540 2EZ. (*California Use Tax Table*, California Department of Tax and Fee Administration)

Total spending on taxable purchases.—On June 1 each year, the use tax liability factor or use tax table percentage for the current calendar year is calculated by multiplying the percentage of income spent on taxable purchases for the preceding calendar year by 0.036, multiplying the product by the average state, local, and district sales and use tax rate, and then rounding the result to the nearest thousandth of a percent. (Reg. 1685.5, 18 CCR)

• *Confidentiality*

Information in returns is confidential, excepting certain cases when the Governor authorizes inspection by federal or state officials and when a city or county resolution authorizes an employee or other person to make such an inspection. The CDTFA may give successors, predecessors, receivers, trustees, executors, administrators, assignees, and grantors, if directly interested, information about the items included in the measure and amounts of any unpaid tax or amounts of tax required to be collected, including interest and penalties. (Sec. 7056, Rev. & Tax. Code)

Information contained in certificates of use tax registration and the terms of certain settlements approved by the State Board of Control may also be disclosed without violating the confidentiality statute. The statute grants officers of a city, county, or transit district access to information relevant to collection of the local sales and use or transactions tax. The willful unauthorized inspection, or unauthorized disclosure or use, of confidential taxpayer information furnished pursuant to California tax laws or other laws constitutes a misdemeanor. (Sec. 7056.5, Rev. & Tax. Code)

Preparers of sales and use tax returns who, without a client's consent, knowingly or recklessly disclose the client's confidential tax information for any purpose other than return preparation may be convicted of a misdemeanor, fined up to $1,000, and imprisoned up to one year. A preparer also may be liable for prosecution costs. (Sec. 7056.6, Rev. & Tax. Code)

• *Credit card payment*

For California sales and use tax purposes, the California Department of Tax and Fee Administration (CDTFA) indicates that in addition to being able to use the Discover/Novus, MasterCard and American Express credit cards, taxpayers may now make sales and use tax payments using their Visa credit card. In addition, the CDTFA has updated the credit card payment program for sales and use taxes and the following information is provided:

— conditions that apply when charging sales and use tax payments using a credit card;

— frequently asked questions (FAQs) regarding the program; and

— necessary information to have available when calling to make a credit card payment.

(*Credit Card Payment Program for Sales and Use Tax*, California State Board of Equalization, July 11, 2005)

A convenience fee of 2.5% of the transaction amount is charged by the card processing vendor. (*Credit Card Payment Program for Sales and Use Tax*, California State Board of Equalization, July 11, 2005)

To charge payments, taxpayers must:

— complete the return or prepayment form to determine how much tax is due;

— call 1-800-272-9829 and follow the recorded instructions;

— check the box on the return or prepayment form indicating payment by credit card; and

— sign and mail the completed return or form.

(*Credit Card Payment Program for Sales and Use Tax*, California State Board of Equalization, July 11, 2005)

The BOE provides guidance regarding credit card payment. (Publication 159CCG, Credit Card Payment Guide, California State Board of Equalization)

• *Electronic funds transfer (EFT)*

Except as discussed below, persons, other than those who collect use tax voluntarily, whose estimated tax liability averages $10,000 or more per month (formerly, $20,000 or more per month) must remit the tax due by an electronic funds transfer. Persons whose estimated tax liability is less than the threshold amount, and those who voluntarily collect use tax, may remit tax due by electronic funds transfer for a minimum of one year with the approval of the CDTFA. (Sec. 6479.3, Rev. & Tax. Code; Reg. 1707(b), 18 CCR)

Electronic funds transfers must comply with the usual due dates. Payment is deemed complete on the date the taxpayer initiates the transfer, if settlement to the state's demand account occurs on or before the banking day following the date the transfer is initiated; otherwise payment is deemed to occur on the date settlement occurs. Payment is deemed timely for electronically filed returns if the transmission is completed on or before the due date of the return. Before January 1, 2022, a person issued a seller's permit for a place of business that is a "dispensary," as defined in the Medical Cannabis Regulation and Safety Act, may remit amounts due for retail sales at the dispensary by a means other than electronic funds transfer. (Sec. 6479.3, Rev. & Tax. Code; Reg. 1707(b), 18 CCR)

The California State Board of Equalization provides guidance regarding e-filing for sales and use tax purposes. (*BOE Publication 159EFT, E-file Guide for EFT Accounts*, California State Board of Equalization)

Annual review.—The CDTFA will conduct an annual review of all taxpayers with sales and use tax permits to identify mandatory participants. Taxpayers registering to report and pay sales and use tax for the first time will not be required to participate in the electronic funds transfer program. Successors will be required to participate in the electronic funds transfer program if their predecessor was a mandatory participant. Once a taxpayer drops below the threshold for mandatory participation in the electronic funds transfer program, the taxpayer may submit a written request to the CDTFA to discontinue the payments. However, the taxpayer must continue to make payments by electronic funds transfer until notified by the CDTFA of the effective date of their withdrawal from the program. (Reg. 1707(b), 18 CCR)

A person required to remit taxes by electronic funds transfer must, on or before the due date of the remittance, file a return for the preceding reporting period. (Sec. 6479.3, Rev. & Tax. Code; Reg. 1703, 18 CCR) When no tax is due from a mandatory participant, a zero-dollar transaction must be made by electronic funds transfer or the CDTFA must receive written notification from the taxpayer stating that no tax was due. (Reg. 1707(g), 18 CCR)

Penalties.—Failure to timely file a return results in a penalty of 10% of the amount of taxes, excluding prepayments, with respect to the quarter for which the return is required. Taxes remitted by means other than electronic funds transfer are subject to a penalty of 10% of amounts incorrectly remitted for any one return. No penalty applies, absent the taxpayer's willful neglect, provided the improper mode of payment is due to reasonable cause and circumstances beyond the taxpayer's control, and occurred notwithstanding the taxpayer's exercise of ordinary care. (Sec. 6479.4, Rev. & Tax. Code)

A taxpayer who is required to make payments by electronic funds transfer and who receives a deficiency determination after failing to timely remit tax, is subject to a 10% penalty, assessed on the amount of tax due for any one return, in addition to any other penalties that may be imposed. Penalties prescribed for the delinquent payment of sales and use tax remitted by electronic funds transfer are exclusive of penalties imposed for sales and use tax delinquencies applicable to other payment methods. (Sec. 6479.3, Rev. & Tax. Code)

An "electronic funds transfer" is any transfer of funds (excepting transactions originated by check, draft, or similar paper instrument) that is initiated through an electronic terminal, telephone, or computer or magnetic tape, and that is executed by automated clearinghouse debit or credit, or by Federal Reserve Wire Transfer. (Sec. 6479.5, Rev. & Tax. Code) Payments by Federal Reserve Wire Transfer are accepted only with the CDTFA's prior authorization and are generally not approved for recurring transactions. (Reg. 1707(h), 18 CCR)

• *Free e-file service*

The CDTFA offers free electronic filing or "BOE-File" service for California sales and use tax returns of eligible taxpayers. The BOE provides guidance regarding e-filing. (*BOE Publication 159 eFile Guide*, California State Board of Equalization)

• *Information returns*

Information returns must be filed by any person who solicits orders for sales of tangible personal property that are subject to use tax if the seller is not engaged in business in the state (and does not hold a seller's permit) and does not hold a Certificate of Registration—Use Tax. Returns are required for each calendar quarter, and must be filed on or before the last day of the month following the quarterly period. Returns must show the name and address of each purchaser from whom an order was taken, a description and the sales price of the property, the date when the order was taken, and the date on which the property is to be delivered to the purchaser. (Sec. 7055, Rev. & Tax. Code; Reg. 1687, 18 CCR)

• *Innocent spouse relief from liability*

Taxpayer liabilities resulting from underreporting tax, failure to file tax reports, or underpayment or nonpayment of taxes as reported on a return, are not imputed to an innocent spouse. An innocent spouse may be relieved of tax liability (including interest, penalties, and other amounts), provided that:

— any underreporting, omission, underpayment, or nonpayment is attributable to the other spouse;

— the innocent spouse can establish a lack of knowledge that was reasonable; and

— relief from liability is deemed to be equitable under the circumstances.

(Reg. 1699(f), 18 CCR)

Facts and circumstances impact any determination that holding liable a spouse who claims to be innocent is, or is not, equitable. This determination is also affected by any significant benefits beyond normal support, measured relative to the family's standard of living, that are derived by the claiming spouse because of the liability, whether such benefits are direct or indirect. (Reg. 1699(f), 18 CCR)

A claim may be filed if, at the time relief is requested, the claiming spouse is no longer married to, is legally separated from, or is no longer a member of the same household as the nonclaiming spouse. (Reg. 1705.1, 18 CCR)

If an individual fails to qualify for innocent spouse status under these criteria, that status still may be conferred if facts and circumstances indicate that holding the individual liable for tax is inequitable. (Sec. 6456, Rev. & Tax. Code)

Factors that the CDTFA may consider for purposes of granting equitable relief include, but are not limited to, whether:

— the claiming spouse is separated or divorced from the nonclaiming spouse;

— the claiming spouse would suffer economic hardship if relief is not granted;

— the claiming spouse, under duress from the nonclaiming spouse, failed to pay the liability;

— the claiming spouse did not know, and had no reason to know, about the items causing the understatement of tax or that the tax would not be paid;

— the nonclaiming spouse has a legal obligation under a divorce decree or agreement to pay the tax and the claiming spouse did not know, or have reason to know, at the time the divorce decree or agreement was entered into, that the nonclaiming spouse would not pay the tax; and

— the tax for which relief is sought is attributable to the nonclaiming spouse.

(Reg. 1705.1, 18 CCR)

Relief is not available in any calendar quarter that is the latest of the following:

— more than five years from the final date on an CDTFA determination;

— more than five years from the return due date for nonpayment on a return;

— more than one year from the first contact with the innocent spouse claiming relief; or

— closed by *res judicata*.

(Sec. 6456, Rev. & Tax. Code; Reg. 1705.1, 18 CCR)

Determining the spouse to whom items of understatement or nonpayment are attributable is made without regard to community property laws. Attributing failure to file or omission of an item from a return to one spouse, rather than both, depends upon a conclusion that a spouse rendered substantial service as a retailer of the taxable items to which the understatement relates. If neither spouse rendered substantial services as a retailer, the items of understatement are treated as community property. An erroneous deduction or credit is attributed to the spouse who caused that deduction or credit to be entered on the return. (Sec. 6456, Rev. & Tax. Code)

The CDTFA must send notice of a claim for innocent spouse relief and the basis for that claim to the non-claiming spouse. (Reg. 1705.1, 18 CCR)

The BOE provides guidance regarding innocent spouse relief from sales and use tax. (*BOE Publication 57, Innocent Spouse Relief from Sales and Use Tax*, California State Board of Equalization)

• *Irrevocable election to report use tax on income tax returns*

Taxpayers who are not required to hold a seller's permit or to be registered with the CDTFA may make an irrevocable election to report their qualified use tax obligations from purchases of tangible personal property on their California personal income tax, corporation franchise or income tax, partnership, limited liability company, or estate or trust tax or information returns. These provisions are inapplicable to purchases of mobile homes, vehicles, aircraft, and vessels, leases of tangible personal property, and certain purchases of cigarettes, tobacco, and tobacco products. Qualified use tax will be considered timely reported and remitted if it is included with a timely filed original return. (Sec. 6452.1, Rev. & Tax Code)

Effective January 1, 2018, the phrase "timely filed" is eliminated from the definition of an "acceptable return" for purposes of remitting qualified California use tax on an income tax return. Until January 1, 2018, income tax filers may fill-in the amount of use tax due on their income tax returns. In cases where a taxpayer underpaid income taxes owed, the Franchise Tax Board can apply the use taxes paid to the income tax obligation, and the taxpayer does not face late payment penalties from the California Department of Tax and Fee Administration (CDTFA) for underpaying their use tax if the income tax return is timely filed. Effective January 1, 2018, the requirement that an income tax return be timely filed for a taxpayer to avoid late payment penalties from the CDTFA in cases where the use tax reported on the income tax return is used to satisfy underpaid income taxes is eliminated. (Sec. 6452.1, Rev. & Tax Code)

Payments and credits on a return of a taxpayer that reports use tax on the return will be applied first to satisfy the use tax liability, with any excess amount then being applied to the outstanding taxes, penalties, and interest owed to the Franchise Tax Board. (Sec. 6452.1, Rev. & Tax Code)

The qualified use tax of an eligible purchaser is due and payable on or before April 15 following the close of the calendar year in which the liability for use tax was incurred. (Sec. 6452.2, Rev. & Tax Code)

An eligible person is authorized for one or more single non-business purchases of individual items of tangible personal property, each with a sales price of less than $1,000, to either report the estimated amount of use tax due based on the person's California adjusted gross income as reflected in the use tax table shown in the instructions of the acceptable tax return or the actual amount of use tax that was not paid to a registered retailer. (Sec. 6452.1, Rev. & Tax Code)

"Qualified use tax" is defined as a taxpayer's actual unpaid use tax liability after applying the state use taxes imposed under the California Sales and Use Tax Law, section 35 of article XIII of the California Constitution, and the local and district use taxes imposed in conformity with the Bradley-Burns Uniform Local Sales and Use

Tax Law or in accordance with the Transactions and Use Tax Law, to the taxpayer's purchases of tangible personal property subject to use tax. (Sec. 6452.1, Rev. & Tax Code)

• *Mobile food vendors*

The CDTFA provides guidance to mobile food vendors who may be unaware of their registration, reporting, and recordkeeping requirements under the state and local sales and use tax laws. "Mobile food vendors" include those who operate food trucks, stands, or carts that do not have a fixed physical location. Such vendors are required to register with the CDTFA, file sales and use tax returns, and maintain books and records that are adequate for sales and use tax purposes. (*Special Notices L-348 and L-348A,* California State Board of Equalization, June 2013)

The BOE provides guidance for mobile food vendors. (*BOE Publication 287,* California State Board of Equalization, June 2014)

Those required to hold a seller's permit must keep books and records that are necessary to accurately determine tax liability. Such books and records include sales receipts or register tapes, books of account, and bills, invoices, and other documents that support business transactions. In addition, such taxpayers should keep the schedules and working papers used to prepare tax returns. Mobile food vendors whose menu item prices include sales tax are required to post a notice for customers that states: "All prices of taxable items include sales tax." Such vendors should report sales tax at the rate in effect at the location the sales are made. (*Special Notices L-348 and L-348A,* California State Board of Equalization, June 2013)

Unless a separate amount for tax reimbursement is added to the price, mobile food vendors' sales of taxable items are presumed to be made on a tax included basis. However, the presumption is inapplicable when a mobile food vendor is making sales as a caterer, as defined. (Reg. 1603(u), 18 CCR)

• *Sales at state-designated fairs*

Applicable July 1, 2018, a return filed with the California Department of Tax and Fee Administration (CDTFA) to report gross receipts for sales and use tax purposes must segregate the gross receipts of the seller and the sales price of the property on a line or a separate form when the place of sale in California or for use in California is on or within the real property of a state-designated fair or any real property of a state-designated fair that is leased to another party. (Sec. 19620.15, Bus. & Prof. Code)

Retailers who make sales of tangible personal property on the real property of a California state-designated fair must separately state the amount of those sales on their sales and use tax returns. There is no additional tax or fee due on these sales. (*Special Notice L-549,* California Department of Tax and Fee Administration, May 2018)

"State-designated fair" means the California Exposition and State Fair in Sacramento and:

- district agricultural fairs;
- county fairs; and
- citrus fruit fairs.

(*Special Notice L-549,* California Department of Tax and Fee Administration, May 2018)

Reporting requirement.—The separately-stated amount must include sales that take place at any time and at any event on the state-designated fairground, not just during an actual fair. Sales that take place on state-designated fairgrounds include:

- over-the-counter sales on the fairgrounds; and

- sales in which the property sold is shipped or delivered to or from the fairgrounds.

(*Special Notice L-549*, California Department of Tax and Fee Administration, May 2018)

How to separately report state-designated fairground sales.—For return periods starting July 1, 2018, the online and paper returns will include an additional line for sales that take place on a California state-designated fairground. Reporting an amount on this line will not change any other part of the return. Sellers are instructed to continue to report such transactions as they currently do, and in addition, report them on the new line for fairground sales. (*Special Notice L-549*, California Department of Tax and Fee Administration, May 2018)

• *Voluntary use tax reporting program*

California offers a voluntary use tax reporting program. A deficiency determination mailed to a qualifying purchaser is limited to the three-year period beginning after the last day of the calendar month following the quarterly period for which the amount is proposed to be determined. This reduces the period of time for which the CDTFA may issue a determination from eight years to three years when unregistered in-state purchasers, as defined, voluntarily report to the CDTFA purchases subject to use tax. (Sec. 6487.06, Rev. & Tax. Code)

A "qualifying purchaser" is a person that: (1) voluntarily files an individual use tax return for tangible personal property that is purchased from a retailer outside California for storage, use, or other consumption within California; and (2) meets all of the following conditions:

— the purchaser resides or is located within California and has not previously registered with the CDTFA, filed an individual use tax return with the CDTFA, or reported an amount on his or her individual California income tax return;

— the purchaser is not engaged in business in California as a retailer, as defined;

— the purchaser has not been contacted by the CDTFA regarding failure to report the use tax imposed as specified; and

— the CDTFA has made a determination that the purchaser's failure to file an individual use tax return or to otherwise report or pay the use tax imposed, as specified, was due to reasonable cause and was not caused by reason of negligence, intentional disregard of the law, or by an intent to evade taxes.

(Sec. 6487.06, Rev. & Tax. Code)

If the CDTFA makes a determination that the purchaser's failure to timely report or remit the taxes imposed, as specified, is due to reasonable cause or circumstances beyond the purchaser's control, the purchaser may be relieved of any penalties imposed. Moreover, this provision is inapplicable to purchases of vehicles, vessels, or aircraft, as specified. (Sec. 6487.06, Rev. & Tax. Code)

Taxpayers who wish to apply for the program must complete *Form BOE-38-1, Application for In-State Voluntary Disclosure*. By signing the form, a taxpayer indicates they are a qualified purchaser who meets all of the qualifying criteria. (*Form BOE-38-1, Application for In-State Voluntary Disclosure*, California State Board of Equalization)

• *Whole-dollar reporting*

On any return, statement, supporting schedule, or other document, taxpayers may elect to round the dollar amounts to the nearest whole dollar amount. This election is made at the time of filing the return (or other document) and is irrevocable for that return, although a new election may be made on any subsequent return. Under the whole-dollar reporting method, a fractional part of a dollar is disregarded unless it amounts to one-half dollar or more, in which case the amount is increased to the next whole dollar. This method applies only to cumulative amounts required to be reported, and the total amount to be reported at the nearest whole dollar must be computed from the aggregate sum of the individual items including cents. (Reg. 1704, 18 CCR)

[¶61-240] Vendor Registration

Any person that wants to conduct business as a seller in California must apply for a permit from the California Department of Tax and Fee Administration (CDTFA) for each place of business. (Sec. 6066, Rev. & Tax. Code) The application must be on a prescribed form and be signed by the owner, partner, or corporate officer, with the signatory certifying that the applicant will actively conduct business as a seller of tangible personal property. Conducting such operations in California without a seller's permit or with a suspended or revoked permit is a misdemeanor punishable by a fine of not less than $1,000 or more than $5,000, or imprisonment not exceeding one year in county jail, or both. (Sec. 6071, Rev. & Tax. Code)

The CDTFA provides information regarding what is required of operators of swap meets, flea markets, and special events. (*CDTFA Publication 111, Operators of Swap Meets, Flea Markets, and Special Events*, California Department of Tax and Fee Administration)

The CDTFA also provides guidance regarding seller's permits. (*CDTFA Publication 73, Your California Seller's Permit*, California Department of Tax and Fee Administration)

In addition, the CDTFA provides guidance regarding its statewide compliance and outreach program. (*Publication 164, Statewide Compliance and Outreach Program*, California Department of Tax and Fee Administration; *Publication 165, Statewide Compliance and Outreach Program*, California Department of Tax and Fee Administration)

Changes made to permit requirements for selling at temporary locations.—The CDTFA requires business owners (taxpayers) who hold a seller's permit for a permanent place of business and who also make sales at temporary locations (such as swap meets, flea markets, trade or specialty shows, fairs, festivals, and similar limited-term events), to register and hold a sub-permit for each selling location for sales and use tax purposes. Registration of these selling locations ensures cities and counties receive the appropriate local and district taxes. Taxpayers will report the sales made at these locations when they file their sales and use tax returns. (*Special Notice L-306*, California State Board of Equalization, April 2012)

Those who make or will make sales at temporary locations need to register for a permit for the temporary location, even if they already hold a seller's permit for a permanent place of business. To register and obtain a sub-permit, taxpayers should call the CDTFA Taxpayer Information Section at 800-400-7115 or their local CDTFA office and state that they would like to register and obtain a sub-permit for the temporary selling location(s). The CDTFA will offer an Internet-based registration called "eReg" that will allow businesses to register for permits and/or licenses online for most of the tax and fee programs administered by BOE. This service will also allow taxpayers who have existing seller's permits to register any future temporary selling locations online. (*Special Notice L-306*, California State Board of Equalization, April 2012)

Swap meet, flea market, or special event operators are required by state law to document, in writing, the seller's permit status of all people who sell at their event. They may not rent space to sellers unless they have a seller's permit or sub-permit that indicates the address of the temporary selling location. (*Special Notice L-306*, California State Board of Equalization, April 2012)

Taxpayers must notify the CDTFA when any of their business locations (including these types of selling locations registered under your account) become inactive and no longer make sales. If a taxpayer's seller's permit is revoked, a fee of $100 per active business location plus any outstanding balance of tax, penalty, and interest due, will be required to be paid to reinstate the revoked account. (*Special Notice L-306*, California State Board of Equalization, April 2012)

• *Collection and transmission of information by local jurisdictions*

A city, county, or city and county may collect seller's permit application information from persons desiring to engage in the business of selling tangible personal property in the jurisdiction and may submit that information to the CDTFA. (Sec. 6066.3, Rev. & Tax. Code)

The information submitted to the CDTFA serves as all of the following:

— the preliminary application for a seller's permit;

— notice to the CDTFA by the local jurisdiction of a person desiring to engage in the business of selling tangible personal property in the jurisdiction; and

— notice to the CDTFA for purposes of the redistribution of tax between counties. (The local jurisdiction may not charge a fee for collecting and transmitting the information.)

(Sec. 6066.3, Rev. & Tax. Code)

The CDTFA must issue determinations regarding the issuance of seller's permits as follows:

— within 30 days of receipt of the information if a determination can be made on the basis of the information submitted or

— within 120 days of receipt of the information if additional information is required before a determination can be made.

(Sec. 6066.3, Rev. & Tax. Code)

A local jurisdiction may require persons desiring to engage in the business of selling tangible personal property in the jurisdiction to provide their seller's permit account numbers, if any. (Sec. 6066.4, Rev. & Tax. Code)

• *Non-issuance or revocation of seller's permit*

The CDTFA may refuse to issue a seller's permit to any person who has an outstanding liability with the CDTFA and has not entered into an installment payment agreement. In addition, the CDTFA can refuse to issue a seller's permit if:

— the person who desires to engage in or conduct business as a seller within California is not a natural person or individual; and

— any person controlling the person who desires to engage in or conduct business as a seller within California has an outstanding final liability with the CDTFA.

(Sec. 6070.5, Rev. & Tax. Code; Reg. 1699(g), 18 CCR)

¶61-240

The CDTFA must provide notice to the person who applied for a seller's permit who was refused the permit under this provision, and such a person may request reconsideration of that decision by submitting a written request within 30 days of the notice of denial. Timely submission of a written request for reconsideration will afford the person a hearing. (Sec. 6070.5, Rev. & Tax. Code; Reg. 1699(g), 18 CCR)

A final liability will not be considered outstanding if the person with the outstanding liability has entered into a payment plan, as provided, and remains in full compliance with that plan. If the person submitting an application for a seller's permit has entered into a payment plan and fails to comply with the terms of the plan, the CDTFA may seek to revoke the seller's permit obtained by the person. (Sec. 6070.5, Rev. & Tax. Code; Reg. 1699(g), 18 CCR)

The CDTFA is required to consider offers in compromise when determining whether to issue a seller's permit. If a seller's permit is conditioned on an offer in compromise being entered into, then a final liability will not be deemed outstanding if the offer in compromise has been accepted by the CDTFA and the person has paid the amount in full or remains in full compliance with the compromise plan. If the person submitting a seller's permit application has entered into an offer in compromise and fails to comply with those terms, the CDTFA may revoke the seller's permit obtained by the person. (Sec. 6070.5, Rev. & Tax. Code; Reg. 1699(g), 18 CCR)

• *Permit application*

An individual applying for a seller's permit must furnish:

— his or her social security number;

— the name and location of banks where he or she does business;

— the applicant's driver's license number;

— addresses of property owned, its value, the amount owed, and to whom payments are made;

— names of suppliers;

— the name of the applicant's bookkeeper or accountant;

— names and addresses of three personal references;

— estimated monthly operating expenses for the applicant's business; and

— anticipated average monthly sales and the amount of those sales that will not be taxable.

In the case of a partnership or corporation, the partners or corporate officers, respectively, must provide the required information. (*Application for Seller's Permit, Individual/Partnership*, Form CDTFA-400-MIP)

• *Permit requirements*

A separate, nonassignable permit must be held for each place of business and conspicuously displayed at each such place. (Sec. 6067, Rev. & Tax. Code) A permit holder who changes a business address will be issued a new permit after notifying the CDTFA of the new address; a new application need not be filed. (Sec. 6068, Rev. & Tax. Code)

A permit is required for any branch office that receives orders, even if no merchandise is stocked on the premises. However, a facility used merely for storage and maintained as part of a business that has a permit need not have a separate permit. Only one permit is needed if more than one business is carried on at the same location by the same person (e.g., a gas station operator having a restaurant in addition to the station on the same premises). (Reg. 1699(a), 18 CCR)

Sellers of animal feed exempt from sales and use taxes are exempt from the requirement to obtain a seller's permit (discussed below).

Buying companies.—A buying company is regarded as the seller of tangible personal property it sells or leases and will be issued a seller's permit for purposes of California sales and use tax. (Reg. 1699(a), 18 CCR)

A presumption applies that the buying company is formed specifically for the operational reasons of the entity that owns or controls it or to which it is otherwise related (other entity). A buying company formed for the sole purpose of purchasing tangible personal property tax-free for resale to the other entity in order to redirect local sales tax from the location of the vendor to the location of the buying company will not be recognized as a separate legal entity and will not be issued a seller's permit. Sales of tangible personal property to third parties will be regarded as having been made by the entity that owns, controls, or is related to the buying company. (Reg. 1699(a), 18 CCR)

A buying company formed to redirect local sales tax is evidenced by one or more of the following elements: (1) the addition of markup to its cost of goods sold in an amount sufficient to cover its operating and overhead expenses; and (2) the issuance of an invoice or an accounting for the transaction in any way. (Reg. 1699(a), 18 CCR)

Defined as a legal entity that is separate from another legal entity that owns or controls it or to which it is otherwise related, a "buying company" is created for the purpose of performing administrative functions, including acquiring goods and services, for the other entity. (Reg. 1699(a), 18 CCR)

The location of a computer server on which a website resides may not be issued a seller's permit except when the retailer has a proprietary interest in the server and the activities at that location otherwise qualify for a seller's permit. (Reg. 1699(a), 18 CCR)

Concessionaires and agents.—Persons operate as concessionaires if they are independent retailers authorized by contract with, or permission of, a primary retailer, to operate on the premises of the primary retailer, under the guise that their operations are controlled by the primary retailer and their sales are reasonably believed by the general public to be the sales of the primary retailer. (Reg. 1699(d), 18 CCR)

Persons do not operate as concessionaires under the following conditions:

— operations appear to the public to be separate and autonomous from the primary retailer;

— business records are maintained separately from those of the primary retailer, particularly with respect to sales;

— selling prices are established independently;

— business decisions are made independently;

— registration with other regulatory agents is as a separate business; and

— funds are deposited into separate accounts.

(Reg. 1699(d), 18 CCR)

The primary retailer is jointly and severally liable for any sales and use tax imposed or unreported during the period that a retailer operates on his/her premises as a concessionaire. The primary retailer is relieved of this liability, however, during the period that the concessionaire holds a seller's permit to operate at the primary retailer's location or the primary retailer takes in good faith the concessionaire's written affirmation that he or she holds a seller's permit for the primary retailer's location. (Reg. 1699(d), 18 CCR)

Moreover, the written statement must include the following:

— the permit number;

— the location for which the permit is issued, including the concessionaire's location upon the primary retailer's premises;

— the signature of the concessionaire; and

— the date.

(Reg. 1699(d), 18 CCR)

The statement should contain language identifying the responsible party for reporting and remitting the sales and use tax due on the concessionaire's sales.

Persons leasing or granting permission to another to occupy retail space are not liable for the sales and use tax if:

— they are primary retailers and the lessee is not operating on their premises as a concessionaire;

— they are not retailers themselves; or

— they are retailers but the lessee is an independent retailer who is not operating within the perimeters of their business.

(Reg. 1699(d), 18 CCR)

Itinerant agents of a principal who has a permit for each of his or her business locations do not have to have permits, but if the principal does not carry a permit for each of his or her businesses in the state, each agent must obtain a permit. (Reg. 1699(e), 18 CCR)

• *Qualified itinerant vendors*

Certain itinerant veteran vendors are regarded as consumers rather than retailers of tangible personal property owned and sold by the qualified itinerant vendors, except for alcoholic beverages or items sold for more than $100. A "qualified itinerant vendor" is a person who:

— was a member of the armed forces of the United States who received an honorable discharge or a release from active duty under honorable conditions from service;

— is unable to obtain a livelihood by manual labor due to service-connected disability;

— is a sole proprietor with no employees for the purposes of selling tangible personal property; and

— has no permanent place of business in California.

(Sec. 6018.3, Rev. & Tax. Code)

Advice.—Those persons who are uncertain whether they qualify as a consumer may submit a written request for advice to: Audit and Information Section, MIC:44; Department of Tax and Fee Administration; P.O. Box 942879; Sacramento, CA 94279-0044. If the CDTFA finds that a person's failure to make a timely return or payment is due to the person's reasonable reliance on written advice from the CDTFA, the person may be relieved from future tax liabilities. (*Special Notice L-251*, California State Board of Equalization, March 2010)

Consumers who hold seller's permits.—Consumers are not required to hold a seller's permit and should complete *CDTFA-65, Notice of Close Out for Seller's Permit*. If a person who qualifies as a consumer issued resale certificates to suppliers, that person should provide the suppliers with written notification of the person's consumer status so that tax is charged on that person's purchases of taxable products. Such persons should reapply for a seller's permit if they make sales after the statutory sunset date of January 1, 2022. (*Special Notice L-251*, California State Board of Equalization, March 2010)

Difference between retailers and consumers.—There are differences between retailers and consumers, according to the CDTFA. In general, a retailer is required to hold a seller's permit and report tax based on the taxable sales of products to the retailer's customers. When certain persons are considered the consumers of tangible personal property sold by retailers, sales to those consumers are retail sales for which either the sales or use tax applies. Resale certificates may not be issued by such consumers when making purchases. Since businesses generally owe tax on sales made to consumers, a qualified itinerant vendor should expect to pay an amount as "tax" when purchasing merchandise from their suppliers. As a consumer, a qualified itinerant vendor is not required to hold a seller's permit. (*Special Notice L-251*, California State Board of Equalization, March 2010)

Exceptions.—These provisions are inapplicable to the sale of alcoholic beverages and single items sold for more than $100. Therefore, qualifying veterans continue to be regarded as retailers, rather than consumers, with respect to their sales of alcoholic beverages and single items for more than $100. Furthermore, the new provisions do not apply to a person who operates a vending machine or to a person engaged in the business of serving meals, food, or drinks to a customer at a location owned, rented, or supplied by the customer. (*Special Notice L-251*, California State Board of Equalization, March 2010)

Permanent place of business.—For these purposes, a "permanent place of business" is any building or other permanently affixed structure, including a residence, used for the purpose of making sales, or taking orders and arranging property for shipment. The term does not include any building or permanently affixed structure, including a residence, used for the storage of tangible personal property or the cleaning of equipment or other property used in connection with the manufacture or sale of tangible personal property. Persons who are generally considered to not have a permanent place of business may include: vendors who only sell from mobile food carts or beverage stands, lunch wagons, and vendors who only sell at swap meets or other special events. (Sec. 6018.3, Rev. & Tax. Code)

The treatment of the itinerant veteran vendors as consumers sunsets effective January 1, 2022. (Sec. 6018.3, Rev. & Tax. Code)

• *Registration of qualified purchaser*

Service industry businesses with gross receipts of over $100,000 are required to register with the CDTFA as a qualified purchaser for purposes of paying use tax. (Sec. 6225, Rev. & Tax. Code)

A qualified purchaser is required to register with the CDTFA and provide the name under which the qualified purchaser transacts or intends to transact business, the location of the qualified purchaser's place or places of business, and other information as the CDTFA may require. Moreover, qualified purchasers are required to file a return, along with their remittance of the amount of tax due, on or before April 15. (Sec. 6225, Rev. & Tax. Code)

A "qualified purchaser" is defined as a person that meets all of the following conditions:

— the person is not required to hold a seller's permit;

— the person is not required to be registered, as specified;

— the person is not a holder of a use tax direct payment permit, as described;

— the person receives at least $100,000 in gross receipts from business operations per calendar year; and

— the person is not otherwise registered with the CDTFA to report use tax.

(Sec. 6225, Rev. & Tax. Code; Reg. 1699(j), 18 CCR; *Special Notice L-232*, California State Board of Equalization, September 2009)

FAQs available.—The California State Board of Equalization (CDTFA) provides a list of frequently asked questions regarding the use tax registration requirements. (*Frequently Asked Questions (FAQ) for ABx4-18 (Registration for Use Tax)*, California State Board of Equalization, November 2009)

Gross receipts less than $100,000 for the last two consecutive years.—If a QP's gross receipts from business operations fell below $100,000 for the last two consecutive years, the QP is allowed to close out their QP use tax account. This closeout process is not automatic. As a result, QPs who meet this criteria must contact their local CDTFA field office. The QP will be required to provide sufficient documentation that indicates their gross receipts from business operations fell below $100,000 for the last two consecutive years. (*Special Notice L-299*, California State Board of Equalization, February 2012)

Guidance provided.—The CDTFA has also issued a publication regarding the use tax registration requirement. (*CDTFA Publication 126, Mandatory Use Tax Registration for Service Enterprises*, California Department of Tax and Fee Administration)

Purchases subject to use tax after QP use tax account is closed.—After a QP's use tax account is closed, the QP must re-register for a QP use tax account and file a return annually if the QP's gross receipts increase to meet the $100,000 threshold and the QP makes purchases subject to use tax. If a QP does not meet the $100,000 gross receipts threshold after the QP's use tax account is closed, the QP may use CDTFA Form CDTFA-401-DS, Use Tax Return, or their Franchise Tax Board income tax return to report any use tax due. Use tax is due when items are purchased from a retailer such as a mail order catalog, an Internet seller, an online auction, or a television shopping network located outside California and tax was not paid to the retailer. (*Special Notice L-299*, California State Board of Equalization, February 2012)

Registration requirements.—Qualified purchasers may download Form CDTFA-404-A, Qualified Purchaser Use Tax Registration, or Form CDTFA-400-CSU, California Consumer Use Tax Account Application, and furnish either one to their local CDTFA field office. A due date of April 15 is imposed for use tax reported by qualified purchasers. Penalty and interest applies to payments received after the due date of each return period. (*Special Notice L-232*, California State Board of Equalization, September 2009)

Once registered, the taxpayer will be assigned an account number. (*Frequently Asked Questions (FAQ) for ABx4-18 (Registration for Use Tax)*, California State Board of Equalization, November 2009)

The registration requirement applies to taxpayers who operate service businesses that are either an individual, partnership, corporation, or other business entity that meets the following criteria: (1) the business receives at least $100,000 in gross receipts from business operations, both in-state and out-of-state, per calendar year; (2) the business is not required to hold a seller's permit or certificate of registration for use tax; (3) the business is not a holder of a use tax direct payment permit; and (4) the business is not otherwise registered with the CDTFA to report use tax. (*News Release 41-10-Y*, California State Board of Equalization, April 1, 2010)

Although a 10% penalty applies for all late returns, qualified purchasers may request relief of late payment penalties imposed pursuant to the use tax registration requirement. Taxpayers are instructed to use *Form CDTFA-735 Request for Relief of Penalty*, for this purpose. Qualified purchasers who have not received a letter from the CDTFA are still obligated to comply with the registration requirement. Upon registration, a taxpayer will be furnished with an account number and express login code. Taxpayers who register in CDTFA field offices can immediately file their returns at e-filing kiosks in each office. Payment options available while e-filing are: (1) electronic payment through ACH Debit (eCheck); (2) credit card; or (3) paper check. (*News Release 41-10-Y*, California State Board of Equalization, April 1, 2010)

Three consecutive returns reporting $0.00 purchases subject to use tax.—The CDTFA will close QP use tax accounts where three consecutive annual use tax returns were filed with no purchases subject to use tax were reported. The CDTFA will notify QPs prior to the closeout of their account. If a QP incurs a use tax liability in a future year, the QP must re-register for a QP use tax account and file a return annually. (*Special Notice L-299*, California State Board of Equalization, February 2012)

Vehicles, vessels, or aircraft.—These provisions are inapplicable to the purchase of a vehicle, vessel, or aircraft. A "qualified purchaser" includes businesses with at least $100,000 in annual gross receipts from business operations, and "gross receipts" are considered to be the total of all receipts from both in-state and out-of-state business operations. (Sec. 6225, Rev. & Tax. Code; Reg. 1699(j), 18 CCR; *Special Notice L-232*, California State Board of Equalization, September 2009)

• *Revocation or suspension of permits and inactive permits*

A seller's permit is valid only so long as the holder is actively engaged in business. (*CDTFA Publication 73, Your California Seller's Permit*, California Department of Tax and Fee Administration)

Any noncomplying retailer will be given ten days' written notice by the CDTFA of a hearing requiring the retailer to show cause why any one or more of his or her seller's permits should not be suspended or revoked. (Sec. 6070, Rev. & Tax. Code)

The notice of hearing or written notice of an actual suspension or revocation will be served personally or by mail. The CDTFA can not issue a new permit until it is satisfied that the former holder will comply with the sales and use tax law. A fee of $100 is charged for renewal of a suspended or revoked permit. (Sec. 6069, Rev. & Tax. Code)

Inactive permits.—When a business is discontinued or transferred, the retailer's permits must be surrendered to the CDTFA for cancellation. (Sec. 6072, Rev. & Tax. Code; Reg. 1699(f), 18 CCR)

The CDTFA is authorized to revoke the permit of any person found not to be actively engaged in business as a seller. A person who knowingly issues a resale certificate while not actively engaged in business is liable not only for the tax due on the transaction but also for a penalty of 10% or $500, whichever is greater. (Sec. 6072, Rev. & Tax. Code)

Transfer or discontinuance of business.—If ownership of a business is transferred, whether by outright sale or by the withdrawal of a principal, the transferor should notify the CDTFA and deliver its permit(s) to the CDTFA for cancellation. (Reg. 1699, 18 CCR)

Although the successor's application for a permit also puts the CDTFA on notice of the transfer, a transferor who does not initially notify the CDTFA or surrender its permit(s) may be held liable for all taxes, interest, and penalties (except those for fraud or intent to evade tax) incurred by the successor for the quarter in which the business is transferred and the three subsequent quarters. (Sec. 6071.1, Rev. & Tax. Code)

This limitation of liability is unavailable if, after the transfer, 80% or more of the real or ultimate ownership of the business transferred is held by the predecessor. Stockholders, bondholders, partners, or other persons holding an ownership interest in the entity are regarded as having real or ultimate ownership of the entity. (Sec. 6071.1, Rev. & Tax. Code)

If a retailer filing yearly tax returns transfers the business to another person or discontinues it before the end of the yearly period, a closing return must be filed by the last day of the month following the close of the calendar quarter in which the business was transferred or discontinued. (Reg. 1699, 18 CCR)

• *Security deposit*

The CDTFA may require a taxpayer to deposit security to ensure compliance with the tax law. The security may not exceed the lesser of (1) $50,000 or (2) twice the average liability for a quarterly taxpayer or three times that of one paying on a monthly basis. In the case of a taxpayer whose permit has been revoked or suspended or who has been notified of a revocation hearing, the amount of security may not exceed the lesser of (1) $50,000 or (2) three times the quarterly or five times the monthly average liability. Within these limitations, the CDTFA may increase or decrease the security required. (Sec. 6701, Rev. & Tax. Code)

• *Sellers of exempt animal feed*

Any person who sells animal feed in California that is exempt from sales and use taxes as feed for animals ordinarily used for human consumption or for animals sold in the purchaser's regular course of business (see Agriculture) and who does not sell other taxable personal property at retail is exempt from the requirement to obtain a seller's permit. However, a seller of hay who is also a grower of hay is exempt only if the grower (1) produces hay for sale only to beef cattle feedlots or dairies, or (2) sells exclusively through a farmer-owned cooperative. A person who grows hay that is not exempt animal feed is required to obtain a seller's permit. (Sec. 6075, Rev. & Tax. Code; Reg. 1595(c), 18 CCR)

• *Swap meets, flea markets, special events, catering trucks, and retail florists*

Various provisions regarding these topics are discussed:

Persons who sell to catering truck operators.—By written demand not more than three times a year, the CDTFA may require any person who makes sales to catering truck operators to obtain evidence that the operators hold valid seller's permits and to provide the CDTFA with a list of such operators within 30 days of the CDTFA's notice. The list must show the operators' valid seller's permits and, for those operators not providing such information, the operators' names, addresses, and telephone numbers. (Sec. 6074, Rev. & Tax. Code)

The CDTFA, by written notice, may also require those selling to catering truck operators to promptly notify the CDTFA if a newly purchasing operator fails to provide, within 30 days of the first purchase, evidence of a valid seller's permit. A penalty of up to $500 per violation may be imposed on any person who submits such evidence after receiving a written demand from the CDTFA. Persons who make sales to catering truck operators who do not hold valid seller's permits must report and pay tax on the merchandise as if the merchandise were sold at retail at the time of sale. (Sec. 6074, Rev. & Tax. Code)

Retail florists.—In addition to any other penalty, a penalty of $500 may be imposed on retail florists who fail to obtain permits before engaging in or conducting business as a seller. "Retail florist" does not include any flower or ornamental plant grower who sells his or her own products. (Sec. 6077, Rev. & Tax. Code; Reg. 1703(c)(6), 18 CCR)

Mobile retail florists must have a copy of the permit at each sales location. "Mobile retail florist" is defined as any retail florist who does not sell from a structure or retail shop, including, but not limited to, florists who sell from vehicles, pushcarts, wagons, or other portable methods, or who sell at swap meets, flea markets, or similar transient locations. (Sec. 6077, Rev. & Tax. Code)

Swap meets, flea markets, or special events.—The CDTFA may require the operator of a swap meet, flea market, or special event to obtain written evidence, before space is rented, that sellers on the operator's premises hold permits or are making exempt sales, except as specified below. "Swap meets, flea markets, or special events" are defined as activities involving a series of sales sufficient in number, scope, and character to constitute a regular course of business or as any event at which two or more persons offer tangible personal property for sale or exchange and at which a fee is charged for the privilege of displaying the property. (Sec. 6073, Rev. & Tax. Code)

An operator of such an event satisfies the evidence requirement by verifying that a seller has a valid seller's permit or by obtaining from the seller a certificate stating that the seller is not offering for sale any item that is subject to sales tax and by completing the reporting form required of vendors under Sec. 21663 of the Business and Professions Code. (Sec. 6073.1, Rev. & Tax. Code) Swap meet, flea market, and special event operators may also be required to provide the CDTFA with a list of vendors conducting business on the operator's premises. (Sec. 6073, Rev. & Tax. Code)

The list must include the names, addresses, and social security numbers of vendors who do not have seller's permits, as well as the names and seller's permit numbers of vendors who are permit holders. An operator may not be required to furnish such a list more than three times within a calendar year.

The CDTFA cannot require operators to obtain evidence that sellers on their premises hold valid sellers' permits or are making exempt sales at any of the following:

— an event or show for which all exhibitors' contracts prohibit any sale of tangible personal property at the event or show and at which no tangible personal property is actually sold;

— an event or show that is conducted for informational or educational purposes only and at which no tangible personal property is sold; or

— a trade show.

(Sec. 6073.2, Rev. & Tax. Code)

A "trade show" is defined as an event or show that is not open to the general public, that is operated by an organization that qualifies for federal tax-exempt status, and at which only orders for tangible personal property are solicited or taken from sellers for subsequent resale. The CDTFA may require the operator of a trade show to provide, within 10 days of the close of the show, a list of the names and addresses of the agents or representatives soliciting orders at the show and their principals, including, but not limited to, manufacturers, wholesalers, distributors, and suppliers. An operator who willfully fails to comply with this requirement is subject to a penalty of up to $1,000 for each offense. (Sec. 6073.2, Rev. & Tax. Code)

• *Use tax registration requirements*

Every retailer selling tangible personal property for storage, use, or other consumption in California must register with the CDTFA and give the name and address of all agents operating in the state and the location of all distribution or sales houses, offices, or other business places in the state. (Sec. 6226, Rev. & Tax. Code; Reg. 1684, 18 CCR) Such retailers must hold seller's permits since they are considered to be engaging in business in the state. Retailers not "engaged in business in the state" (see Application of Sales and Use Taxes for criteria) may apply for a Certificate of Registration—Use Tax. Holders of such a certificate are required to collect use tax from, and give use tax receipts to, purchasers and to remit the tax to the CDTFA. (Reg. 1684(b), 18 CCR)

[¶61-270] Credits

A credit is allowed against California use tax for sales or use taxes paid to another state prior to the use, storage, or consumption of the property in California. California does not provide a credit in the form of a prompt payment discount for collection of the tax. A credit or refund is also allowed for erroneous or overpaid taxes. (Sec. 6901, Rev. & Tax. Code; Sec. 6901.5, Rev. & Tax. Code)

See ¶ 60-020 Application of Sales and Use Taxes.

See ¶ 61-610 Application for Refund.

Hiring credit for qualified small business employers

Effective September 9, 2020, and applicable as noted, a hiring credit against California sales and use taxes is enacted for qualified small business employers. A qualified small business employer must submit an application to the California Department of Tax and Fee Administration (CDTFA) for a tentative credit reservation amount for the small business hiring tax credit allowed to such an employer. Qualified small business employers may claim the credit against corporate and personal income taxes or they may irrevocably elect to apply the credit against qualified sales and use taxes. (Sec. 6902.7, Rev. & Tax. Code; Sec. 6902.8, Rev. & Tax. Code)

Application required.—The application must include:

— the net increase in qualified employees;

— whether the credit will be applied against corporate or personal income taxes or both;

— whether the qualified small business employer makes an irrevocable election to apply the credit against qualified sales and use taxes in lieu of claiming the credit against their corporate or personal income taxes; and

— any other information the CDTFA determines to be necessary.

(Sec. 6902.8, Rev. & Tax. Code)

Applications will be accepted by the CDTFA beginning December 1, 2020, and ending January 15, 2021, or any earlier date when the maximum cumulative total allocation limit is reached. Applications will not be accepted after January 15, 2021. (Sec. 6902.8, Rev. & Tax. Code)

The CDTFA will:

— notify the applicant of the tentative credit reservation amount no more than 30 days after the application is received; and

— allocate the credit reservations on a first-come, first-served basis, not to cumulatively exceed $100 million.

(Sec. 6902.8, Rev. & Tax. Code)

Tentative credit reservation amount.—The tentative credit reservation amount will be equal to the net increase in qualified employees as reported on the application multiplied by $1,000, and will not exceed $100,000 per qualified small business employer. (Sec. 6902.7, Rev. & Tax. Code)

The CDTFA will allow a qualified small business employer that received a tentative credit reservation and made an irrevocable election to apply the hiring credit against qualified sales and use taxes imposed on the employer, as follows:

— for monthly filers, the credit will apply to amounts due and payable for the month of March 1, 2021, and due April 30, 2021;

— for quarterly filers, the credit will apply to amounts due and payable for the January through March 2021 quarter and due April 30, 2021; and

— for annual filers, fiscal year filers, or a qualified small business owner on any other reporting basis, the credit will apply to amounts due and payable on the first return due on or after April 30, 2021.

(Sec. 6902.7, Rev. & Tax. Code)

Any excess credit will be carried over and will not be refunded. When the credit amount exceeds the sales and use taxes due and payable, the CDTFA will apply the excess credit against amounts due and payable for periods following those above (i.e., monthly, quarterly, and annual filers) on returns due and filed on or before April 30, 2026. Any remaining excess credit amount after April 30, 2026:

— will not be refunded; and

— will be forfeited.

(Sec. 6902.7, Rev. & Tax. Code)

Applicable definitions.—"Qualified sales or use taxes" are defined as any state and local sales and use taxes. (Sec. 6902.7, Rev. & Tax. Code)

A "qualified small business employer" is a taxpayer that:

— as of December 31, 2019, employed a total of 100 or fewer employees; and

— had a 50% decrease in gross receipts determined by comparing gross receipts from April 1 to June 30, 2020, with the gross receipts from April 1 to June 30, 2019.

(Sec. 6902.7, Rev. & Tax. Code)

The term does not include any taxpayer required or authorized to be included in a combined report. (Sec. 6902.7, Rev. & Tax. Code)

Legislative purpose.—According to the legislative analysis, the credit was enacted in response to the effects of COVID-19 on the economy which left thousands unemployed. (Ch. 41 (S.B. 1447), Laws 2020, effective September 9, 2020, and applicable as noted; *Senate Floor Analysis*, California State Senate, August 31, 2020; *News Release*, Office of California Gov. Gavin Newsom, September 9, 2020)

Motion picture production credit

In lieu of claiming a credit against corporation franchise and income taxes or credit against personal income taxes, a taxpayer may make an election to claim a credit against the state sales and use tax. The taxpayer has the option of claiming a refundable sales and use tax credit or offsetting any excess credit against sales and use taxes due for the subsequent five reporting periods. (Sec. 6902.5, Rev. & Tax. Code)

Qualified motion picture production credit

For taxable years beginning on or after January 1, 2016, a California corporation franchise and income and personal income tax credit is available to qualified taxpayers for qualified motion picture production expenditures paid or incurred. The credit is provided in addition to the already existing (original) motion picture production credit. However, the new credit will not be allowed for any qualified expenditures for which the original motion picture production credit has been claimed. A qualified taxpayer may, in lieu of claiming the new credit or the original motion picture production credit, make an irrevocable election to apply the credit amount against the qualified sales and use taxes imposed on the taxpayer. (Sec. 6902.5, Rev. & Tax. Code)

[¶61-600]
TAXPAYER REMEDIES

[¶61-610] Application for refund

Refund claims for erroneous or overpaid taxes, penalties, or interest must be in writing and state the specific grounds on which the claims are founded. (Sec. 6904, Rev. & Tax. Code)

The factual and legal bases of the claim should be stated as completely as possible because any subsequent court action against the Department of Tax and Fee Administration (CDTFA) will be limited to the grounds specified. (Sec. 6933, Rev. & Tax. Code; Sec. 6591.5, Rev. & Tax. Code)

The CDTFA must serve notice on the claimant within 30 days after disallowing a refund claim in whole or in part. (Sec. 6906, Rev. & Tax. Code) The claimant has 90 days from service of the notice in which to bring court action. If the claimant does not receive notice of the CDTFA's action within six months after the claim is filed, the taxpayer may consider the claim disallowed and may bring court action. (Sec. 6934, Rev. & Tax. Code)

PLANNING NOTE: The CDTFA provides guidance regarding the filing of a claim for refund when a taxpayer has paid more California sales or use tax than that owed. Among the topics discussed are filing deadlines, how a claim is filed, how much detail should be provided, supporting documents, and where to send a claim for refund. (*CDTFA Publication 117, Filing a Claim for Refund*, California Department of Tax and Fee Administration)

Use tax on sales-tax paid transactions.—No credit or refund of use tax paid will be allowed on the ground that the sales price was included in the measure of the sales tax unless the person satisfies the CDTFA that the vendor has remitted the sales tax to the state. (Sec. 6903, Rev. & Tax. Code)

Class action claims.—A claim filed on behalf of a class of taxpayers must:

— be accompanied by written authorization from each taxpayer sought to be included in the class;

— be signed by each taxpayer or taxpayer's representative; and

— state the specific grounds on which the claim is founded.

(Sec. 6904, Rev. & Tax. Code)

Time limits on filing.—A refund claim must be filed within three years from the due date of the return for which the overpayment is alleged. (Sec. 6902, Rev. & Tax. Code)

However, a taxpayer has three years from the date of overpayment to file a claim for refund of an overpayment of any tax, penalty, or interest collected by the CDTFA through the use of a levy, lien, or other enforcement procedure. (Sec. 6902.3, Rev. & Tax. Code)

After deficiency determinations, determinations when no return is filed, or jeopardy determinations, a refund claim must be filed within six months from the time the determination becomes final or from the date of overpayment, whichever is later. Failure to file a claim within the prescribed time is a waiver of any demand against the state. (Sec. 6905, Rev. & Tax. Code)

The limitations period for filing a refund claim is suspended during the period that a person is unable to manage financial affairs because of a physical or mental impairment that is life-threatening or that is expected to last for at least 12 months. There is no waiver for individuals who are represented in their financial matters by their spouses or other persons. (Sec. 6902.4, Rev. & Tax. Code)

Interest.—Interest is payable by the state on refunds at the modified adjusted rate per month, which is the modified adjusted rate per annum divided by 12. But see CCH Comment, below, concerning the legislature's intent to equalize the interest rate paid on underpayments and overpayments. For refund purposes, the modified adjusted rate per annum is determined by applying the bond equivalent rate of 13-week treasury bills established at auctions in January and July, as follows:

— The bond equivalent rate of 13-week treasury bills established at the first auction held each January applies for the second half of that calendar year.

— The bond equivalent rate of 13-week treasury bills established at the first auction held each July applies for the first half of the following calendar year.

(Sec. 6591.5, Rev. & Tax. Code)

Interest is payable from the first day of the calendar month following the month during which the overpayment was made to (1) the last day of the calendar month in which the taxpayer is notified that the claim may be filed or (2) the date the claim is approved by the CDTFA, whichever is earlier.

Interest rates on refunds applicable to designated periods are discussed at ¶ 89-204 Interest Rates.

Credit interest is not allowed when statutorily prohibited, or if the CDTFA determines that any overpayment is intentional or is the result of taxpayer fraud, negligence, or carelessness. (Sec. 6908, Rev. & Tax. Code; Reg. 1703, 18 CCR)

For credit interest purposes, taxpayer carelessness occurs when overpayments result from clerical errors or from computational errors on a return or supporting schedules, provided that the CDTFA has given the taxpayer written notice of the same or similar errors on one or more previous returns. If the taxpayer requests the CDTFA to defer action on a refund claim, the CDTFA may require a waiver of interest for the deferred period. (Sec. 6908, Rev. & Tax. Code)

CDTFA claim approval.—If the overpayment amount exceeds $50,000, the CDTFA must make the record available to the public at least 10 days prior to the effective date of the refund determination. (Sec. 6901, Rev. & Tax. Code)

¶61-610

CDTFA claim denial.—If the CDTFA denies a refund (Sec. 6933, Rev. & Tax. Code) or fails to act on the request within six months, (Sec. 6934, Rev. & Tax. Code) the taxpayer may commence a suit for refund in superior court.

Return of excess tax to customer.—Tax reimbursements collected from customers on nontaxable amounts or on amounts in excess of the taxable amount must be returned by the retailer to the customer upon notification by the CDTFA or by the customer. (Sec. 6901.5, Rev. & Tax. Code)

A purchaser generally cannot bring a sales tax refund suit against the CDTFA since the retailer, not the purchaser, is the taxpayer for sales tax purposes. (Sec. 6933, Rev. & Tax. Code)

Petitions for redetermination of a tax assessment are discussed at ¶ 61-620 Administrative Remedies.

• *Offset for Labor Commission judgments*

When a judgment is entered against a taxpayer in an action for the enforcement of state-mandated labor standards, the Controller is authorized, upon request from the Labor Commissioner, to offset the amount of such judgment that remains unpaid for 90 days against any claim by the taxpayer for a refund of sales and use tax from the CDTFA. When amounts available for refund are insufficient to satisfy an offset request, the Controller may allocate the funds among the requests for offset, after first applying the available funds to any amount due a state agency. (Sec. 12419.11, Gov. Code)

• *Unconstitutional local taxes*

Retailers or purchasers required to report and/or pay sales or use tax in a taxing district imposing an unconstitutional tax may obtain refunds of illegally collected taxes. (Sec. 7275, Rev. & Tax. Code)

Taxpayers who are required to report and pay sales or use tax to the state and who reside or conduct business in a district in which an invalid tax was imposed must continue to report sales and use tax at the current combined state and local rate, but may take a 0.75% credit against the total amount of taxes reported. The amount of sales or use taxes collected from purchasers by such taxpayers must also be reduced by the 0.75% credit amount. (Sec. 7276, Rev. & Tax. Code)

Persons other than retailers who pay a local sales and use tax that is subsequently held invalid must file written claims for refund. (Sec. 7277, Rev. & Tax. Code)

Only single purchases or aggregate purchases of $5,000 or more are eligible for refund claims by purchasers. The written claim must set forth the specific ground on which the claim is based, accompanied by proof of payment of the tax to a retailer or wholesaler that indicates the date of purchase, a description of the property purchased, the purchase price, and the amount of transactions and use tax collected or, if such amount was not separately stated, the rate of the transactions and use tax imposed. (Sec. 7277, Rev. & Tax. Code) Interest is payable on refunds at the modified adjusted rate, (Sec. 6907, Rev. & Tax. Code) discussed above.

Written claims by purchasers must be filed within one year of the effective date of the refund statute or the first day of the calendar quarter commencing after the date on which the final court decision was rendered declaring the tax invalid, whichever is later. (Sec. 7277, Rev. & Tax. Code)

The six-month period within which to file a court action for recovery of an overpayment does not commence until the one-year period claim period has expired. (Sec. 7275, Rev. & Tax. Code)

[¶61-620] Administrative Remedies

Other than a petition for redetermination (for those taxpayers against whom a deficiency or jeopardy determination has been made), a claim for refund is the only action available to taxpayers prior to bringing suit against the California Department of Tax and Fee Administration (CDTFA). The refund claim is a prerequisite to any court action on the taxpayer's part, and any suit against the state must be on the ground set forth in the refund claim. (Sec. 6932, Rev. & Tax. Code; Sec. 6933, Rev. & Tax. Code)

See ¶61-610 Application for Refund, for a discussion of refund claims.

COMMENT: *California Department of Tax and Fee Administration.*—Legislation enacted in 2017, the Taxpayer Transparency and Fairness Act of 2017, restructured the California State Board of Equalization (BOE) into three separate entities: the BOE, the California Department of Tax and Fee Administration (CDTFA), and the Office of Tax Appeals (OTA). As of July 1, 2017, all BOE administrative powers, duties, and responsibilities that are not constitutionally mandated to the BOE are transferred to the CDTFA. The BOE is left with responsibility for:

— property tax assessment and equalization functions and assessment of taxes on insurers authorized by Article XIII of the state constitution; and

— assessment and collection of excise taxes on alcohol pursuant to Article XX of the state constitution.

Although the BOE formerly heard corporation franchise and income tax and personal income tax appeals from the Franchise Tax Board (FTB), the Office of Tax Appeals (OTA) currently hears franchise and personal income tax appeals, sales and use tax appeals, and other special taxes and fee appeals. (Ch. 6 (A.B. 102), Laws 2017, effective June 27, 2017, and operative as noted; *Special Notice L-507*, California Department of Tax and Fee Administration, July 2017)

The CDTFA provides guidance regarding free sales and use tax products and services. (*BOE Publication 51, Resource Guide to Free Tax Products and Services*, California State Board of Equalization)

The CDTFA also provides guidance regarding the rights of California taxpayers. (*BOE Publication 70, Understanding Your Rights as a California Taxpayer*, California State Board of Equalization)

•*CDTFA settlement program*

The CDTFA provides a settlement program to taxpayers or feepayers who have a petition for redetermination, administrative protest, or claim for refund pending in connection with a tax or fee liability administered by the CDTFA. Settlement proposals may be considered for civil tax or fee matters in dispute under the sales and use tax program or certain special tax and fee programs. The settlement program does not include audits in progress or collection matters. Litigation cases are handled outside the settlement program. The settlement program is intended to expedite the resolution of tax and fee disputes consistent with a reasonable evaluation of litigation risks and costs. Therefore, a taxpayer's inability to pay the disputed liability is not considered under the settlement program. (*Settlement Program—Sales and Use Tax—Special Tax and Fee Cases*, California State Board of Equalization, March 2012)

To initiate settlement, a taxpayer must first submit a proposal on *Form BOE-393, Settlement Proposal for Sales and Use Tax and Special Tax and Fee Cases*, or on a signed and dated written request for settlement that includes: the taxpayer's or feepayer's name, phone number, and current address; if applicable, the name, address, fax, and phone number of the taxpayer's or feepayer's representative, as well as a copy of the representative's power of attorney; the taxpayer's or feepayer's account number; the tax or fee period involved; the tax or fee involved; and a good faith settlement offer, including factual and legal grounds in support of the offer. If the taxpayer has requested a CDTFA hearing for their appeals case or is already scheduled for a Board hearing, the case will not be considered for settlement unless the proposal is submitted at least 15 days before the date scheduled for a hearing of your case before the five-member Board. (*Settlement Program—Sales and Use Tax—Special Tax and Fee Cases*, California State Board of Equalization, March 2012)

• *Hearing*

If the petition cannot be resolved by staff members, it will proceed to an informal, nonadversarial CDTFA appeals conference, in which an appeals attorney or appeals auditor who is not associated with the assessing departments will discuss with the taxpayer the factual basis of the petition, along with the taxpayer's position regarding applicable laws and regulations. After the conference, the appeals attorney or appeals auditor will prepare a written decision and recommendation concerning the taxpayer's case. The taxpayer may request reconsideration of the case and/or an oral hearing before the board members of the CDTFA. If a hearing is requested prior to, or within 30 days of, the date that the decision and recommendation was mailed to the taxpayer, the CDTFA will hold an oral hearing. If a hearing is not requested, the CDTFA will mail notice of its action on the decision and recommendation to the taxpayer. (Sec. 6562, Rev. & Tax. Code)

After the CDTFA board members issue an order or decision on a petition for redetermination indicating that tax is due, the tax must be paid within 30 days, or a 10% penalty applies. (Sec. 6564, Rev. & Tax. Code; Sec. 6565, Rev. & Tax. Code)

The CDTFA has issued guidance regarding oral appeal hearings for purposes of California sales and use taxes and certain other taxes and fees administered by the CDTFA. Information is provided regarding filing a response to a Notice of Hearing, postponement requests, representation at the hearing, contribution disclosure statements, settlement requests, advance payment and interest charges, and hearing exhibits. (*BOE Publication 143, Your Appeal Hearing Before the Board Members*, California State Board of Equalization)

• *Hearing procedures*

Protest hearings before the CDTFA must be held at the time and places that are reasonable and convenient to the taxpayer. A hearing may be recorded only if prior notice is given to the taxpayer, who is entitled to receive a copy of the recording. Prior to the hearing, the taxpayer must be informed of the right to have an attorney, accountant, or other agent present. (Sec. 7090, Rev. & Tax. Code)

Reimbursement for hearing-related expenses.—The taxpayer is entitled to reimbursement for reasonable hearing-related fees and expenses incurred after the filing of a notice of determination, jeopardy determination, or refund claim and only if the taxpayer seeks review of an unfavorable Decision and Recommendation issued by the CDTFA's Appeals Section. (Sec. 7091, Rev. & Tax. Code; Reg. 5601, 18 CCR)

The taxpayer must file a claim for reimbursement with the CDTFA within one year of the date the CDTFA's decision becomes final, although extensions may be granted for good cause. Finally, payment is contingent on an CDTFA finding that its staff acted unreasonably. As a prerequisite to this finding, CDTFA staff must establish that its position was substantially justified. (Sec. 7091, Rev. & Tax. Code; Reg. 5603, 18 CCR)

The CDTFA must hold an oral hearing on a reimbursement claim. (Reg. 5604, 18 CCR)

The CDTFA's decision on such a claim is final 30 days from the date it is mailed. (Reg. 5605, 18 CCR)

• *Installment payment agreements*

The CDTFA may enter into installment payment agreements for the payment of any tax due, together with penalties and interest. The CDTFA may terminate an agreement upon failure of a taxpayer to comply with the terms. (Sec. 6832, Rev. & Tax. Code)

Taxpayers who have entered into installment agreements to pay California sales and use tax must receive an annual statement from the CDTFA itemizing the balance of tax owed at the beginning and end of a year and the amount of tax paid during the year. (Sec. 6832.5, Rev. & Tax. Code)

A taxpayer may be relieved of penalties for late payment of sales and use tax if the taxpayer enters into an installment plan for paying tax within 45 days after a tax due date. The taxpayer must comply with the agreement for the waiver to remain effective, and waiver may not be granted in cases of fraud. (Sec. 6832, Rev. & Tax. Code)

Buyers of used vehicles, used aircraft from private parties, used boats or other vessels, and goods from foreign countries must be notified by the State Board of Equalization that they may pay California use tax for their purchases under an installment plan. Notice must be mailed to taxpayers with any return, notice of determination, or notice of redetermination that is mailed by the Board to a taxpayer. (Sec. 6832.6, Rev. & Tax. Code)

• *Petition for redetermination*

A taxpayer seeking a redetermination of a deficiency assessment must file a written petition within 30 days after the taxpayer has been served notice of the deficiency; otherwise, the assessment becomes final. (Sec. 6561, Rev. & Tax. Code)

The petition must state the grounds for redetermination and the amount, if any, that the taxpayer concedes is owing. Additional grounds may be added to the petition any time before the CDTFA issues its decision. (Sec. 6561.5, Rev. & Tax. Code)

The taxpayer will be granted an oral hearing, provided that a request for such a hearing is made in a timely filed petition. (Sec. 6562, Rev. & Tax. Code)

The CDTFA will give the taxpayer 10 days notice of the hearing's time and place. The CDTFA may increase or decrease the deficiency assessment before it becomes final, but the amount may be increased only if the CDTFA asserts a claim for such an increase at or before the hearing. The CDTFA must specify the information on which it bases its claim for increase. (Sec. 6563, Rev. & Tax. Code)

Unless a penalty for fraud or evasion of tax applies to the original or the increased assessment, the CDTFA must assert the claim for increase within one of the two following time periods, as applicable:

— for taxpayers whose reported gross receipts and total sales price of property sold or purchased for each calendar quarter of the period(s) to which the assessment applies was less than $10 million, the claim must be asserted within three years after the first deficiency determination or the time tax records requested by the CDTFA are made available, whichever is later; or

— for all other taxpayers, the claim must be asserted within eight years after the first deficiency determination or the time tax records requested by the CDTFA are made available, whichever is later.

(Sec. 6563, Rev. & Tax. Code)

These time limits may be waived by mutual agreement of the taxpayer and the CDTFA. (Sec. 6563, Rev. & Tax. Code)

The order or decision on a petition for redetermination becomes final 30 days after the order is served to the petitioner. (Sec. 6564, Rev. & Tax. Code) All determinations are due and payable when they become final, and if not paid by that time are subject to a 10% penalty. (Sec. 6565, Rev. & Tax. Code)

Further appeal may be obtained only by paying the tax under protest and by filing a claim for refund pursuant to statutory provisions. See ¶ 61-610 Application for Refund.

• *Preliminary notice prior to tax lien*

A taxpayer is entitled to preliminary notice of the proposed filing or recording of a tax lien, mailed at least 30 days beforehand, and the opportunity in the interim to demonstrate by substantial evidence that the lien would be in error. If the CDTFA finds that its action was in error, it must mail a release to the taxpayer and the lien recorder within seven days. The CDTFA may release or subordinate a lien if it determines that release or subordination will facilitate the collection of the tax liability or will be in the best interest of the state and the taxpayer. (Sec. 7097, Rev. & Tax. Code)

Except where the CDTFA finds collection of the tax to be in jeopardy, if property has been levied upon, the property or proceeds from the sale must be returned to the taxpayer if the board determines that:

— the levy on the property was not in accordance with the law;

— the taxpayer has entered into and is in compliance with an installment payment agreement, as provided; or

— the return of the property will facilitate the collection of the tax liability or will be in the best interest of the state and taxpayer.

(Sec. 7094.1, Rev. & Tax. Code)

• *Protections against tax levies*

Except for seizures of property resulting from a jeopardy assessment, a previously issued levy or notice to withhold must be released whenever: (1) the expense of selling the levied property would exceed the taxpayer's liability; or (2) the "Taxpayers' Rights Advocate" determines that the levy or notice to withhold threatens the health or welfare of the taxpayer or the taxpayer's family. (Sec. 7094, Rev. & Tax. Code)

The Taxpayers' Rights Advocate may also order the return of up to $1,500 of the funds received pursuant to a levy or notice to withhold if he or she determines that the levy or notice to withhold threatens the health or welfare of the taxpayer or the taxpayer's family. Certain household and other goods are exempted from levy under the California Code of Civil Procedure. The taxpayer must be notified in writing of these exemptions prior to the sale of any seized property. The taxpayer may be reimbursed for bank charges and any other reasonable third-party charge fees incurred as a result of an erroneous levy or notice to withhold, erroneous processing action, or erroneous collection action by the CDTFA. (Sec. 7096, Rev. & Tax. Code)

• *Reliance on CDTFA's written advice*

Failure to timely file or pay tax based upon reasonable reliance on written advice from the CDTFA, entitles a taxpayer to relief from taxes, penalties, and interest that would otherwise be imposed. In order to qualify for relief, four conditions must be satisfied:

— the taxpayer has requested in writing that the CDTFA give advice as to whether a particular activity or transaction is subject to tax, and the request fully described the specific facts and circumstances of the activity or transaction and identified the specific person for whom the advice was requested;

— the CDTFA has provided written response stating whether or not the activity or transaction is subject to tax, or the conditions under which the activity or transaction would be subject to tax;

— in reasonable reliance upon the CDTFA's written advice, the taxpayer has not charged or collected use tax or sales tax reimbursement from customers, or has not paid use tax on the storage, use, or other consumption in California of tangible personal property; and

— the particular activity or transaction took place (a) before the CDTFA rescinded or modified its advice by sending written notice of the rescinded or modified advice, or (b) before the CDTFA's written advice was rendered invalid by a change in statutory or constitutional law, a change in CDTFA's regulations, or a final decision of a court.

(Sec. 6596, Rev. & Tax. Code; Reg. 1705, 18 CCR)

Approval of use tax reporting methodology.—An agreement approving a use tax reporting methodology can be struck between a taxpayer and the Board that constitutes written communication from the Board. (Sec. 6596, Rev. & Tax. Code; Reg. 1705, 18 CCR)

Subsequent to a taxpayer's written submission of a proposal for a use tax reporting methodology for qualified purchases, the Board may write to the taxpayer approving the method, if the Board determines that the methodology accurately reflects the taxpayer's use tax liability for the defined population. The Board's approval is subject to certain conditions including:

— the defined population of the purchases that will be included in the reporting method;

— the percentage of purchases of the defined population that is subject to tax;

— the length of time the writing will remain in effect;

— the definition of a significant or material change that will require rescinding the method; and

— other conditions as required.

(Reg. 1705, 18 CCR)

Written approval of the method is void and cannot be relied upon if the taxpayer files a claim for refund of tax that was reported based upon the agreed-upon method. (Reg. 1705, 18 CCR)

Books and records presented for examination by auditor.—Presentation of books and records for examination by an auditor is deemed to be a written request for the audit report. Accordingly, if an audit report contains written evidence that demonstrates that an issue in question was examined, the evidence is regarded as "written advice from the CDTFA." Such audit reports may relieve the taxpayer from liability if the conditions relating to the activity or transaction have not changed, and if the taxpayer is unaware that the written advice is erroneous. (Reg. 1705, 18 CCR)

Filing requirements.—Taxpayers must file the following with the CDTFA: (1) a copy of the written request and the CDTFA's written advice; (2) a statement under penalty of perjury setting forth the facts on which the claim for relief is based; and (3) any other information the CDTFA may require. Only the person who requested the advice may rely on it to seek relief under the above provisions. (Sec. 6596, Rev. & Tax. Code; Reg. 1705, 18 CCR)

Informing businesses of their right to request and rely on CDTFA written advice.—The CDTFA is required to explore and use every available means of regularly informing California businesses of their right to request and rely on written advice from the CDTFA. For example, the CDTFA must seek the addition to city business license applications of notices that inform businesses about such requests. Such notices must state that sales and use taxes may apply to the applicant's business activities and that the applicant may seek written advice from the CDTFA about the application of the tax. (Sec. 6596, Rev. & Tax. Code; Reg. 1705, 18 CCR)

Person with shared accounting and common ownership with audited person.—Effective July 1, 2014, Reg. 1705 provides that relief of liability for the payment of sales and use taxes, including penalties and interest, is extended when the liability resulted from the failure to make a timely return in reliance upon written advice given by the CDTFA to a person with shared accounting and common ownership with the audited person. (Reg. 1705, 18 CCR)

Relief, under Sec. 6596, Rev. & Tax. Code, can apply to a person who the CDTFA would reasonably expect to rely on written advice provided by CDTFA staff in a prior audit of another related person because the two persons are:

— in the same industry;

— under common ownership; and

— share accounting functions and accounting staff.

(Reg. 1705, 18 CCR)

• *Reliance on legal rulings and annotations as written advice*

Taxpayers seeking relief from liability for tax, penalties and interest imposed for failure to timely file returns or payments, may rely upon CDTFA legal rulings and annotations of counsel as written advice, provided:

— the underlying legal ruling of counsel involving the facts at issue is addressed to the person, or to the person's representative, who submitted a specific written inquiry seeking relief from liability; or

— the annotation or legal ruling of counsel is provided to the person, or to the person's representative, by the CDTFA within the body of a written communication, and involves the same facts as presented in the subject annotation or legal ruling of counsel.

(Reg. 1705, 18 CCR)

Trade or industry associations that request advice on behalf of their members and franchisors that request advice on behalf of their franchisees, must identify and include in the request specific member or franchisee name(s) for whom the advice is requested for relief from liability. In order for a member or franchisee to receive relief based on the advice, the activity or transactions in question must involve the same facts and circumstances as those presented in the written inquiry by the association or franchisor. (Reg. 1705(e), 18 CCR)

• *Special procedures for settling certain tax disputes*

The executive officer of the CDTFA (or the officer's designee) may settle any disputed civil tax matter involving a tax liability of $5,000 or less. (Sec. 7093.5, Rev. & Tax. Code) The terms of any such settlement must be made available to the public.

In addition, the CDTFA's Executive Director and the Chief Counsel may recommend to the CDTFA board members a settlement of any civil tax matter. Prior to any submittal to the CDTFA board members, however, the Executive Director and the Chief Counsel must present their recommendations to the Attorney General for review. However, such settlements may be made by the Executive Director and the Chief Counsel without review by the Attorney General. (Sec. 7093.5, Rev. & Tax. Code)

The board members are required to act on the Executive Director's or Chief Counsel's recommendation within 45 days. Any recommendation for settlement that is not acted upon within 45 days will be treated as approved. If disapproved by a majority vote of the board members, a proposed settlement may be renegotiated and resubmitted for further consideration. Settlements achieved by means of this special procedure are final and may not be appealed, unless there is proof of fraud or misrepresentation. (Sec. 7093.5(e) and (f), Rev. & Tax. Code)

• *Taxpayers' Bill of Rights*

Although the CDTFA is specifically exempted from Administrative Procedure Act provisions governing adjudicatory hearings, (Sec. 15609.5, Govt. Code) the "California Taxpayers' Bill of Rights" (Sec. 7080, Rev. & Tax. Code—Sec. 7099, Rev. & Tax. Code) affords a wide range of protections to taxpayers dealing with the CDTFA.

See ¶ 89-222 Taxpayers' Bill of Rights.

• *Taxpayer rights advocates*

The CDTFA is obligated to create "Taxpayer Rights Advocate" positions. (Sec. 7083, Rev. & Tax. Code)

Such advocates are responsible for investigating taxpayer complaints and for staying actions when the taxpayer has suffered or will suffer irreparable loss as a result of those actions. The CDTFA is also required to undertake extensive taxpayer education and information programs. (Sec. 7084, Rev. & Tax. Code)

CDTFA officers and employees are prohibited from authorizing, requiring, or conducting the investigation or surveillance of taxpayers for reasons unrelated to tax administration. (Sec. 7092, Rev. & Tax. Code)

[¶61-700]

LOCAL TAXES

[¶61-710] Local Taxes and Administration

This explanation paragraph discusses the local sales and use taxes that local jurisdictions may be authorized to impose in California. For local sales and use tax rates, see Local Tax Rates.

• *Application of local taxes*

California cities and counties are authorized by the Bradley-Burns Uniform Local Sales and Use Tax Law to impose a total tax of 1% on the sale or use of tangible personal property. (Sec. 7202, Rev. & Tax. Code)

¶61-700

The tax is paid with the state tax, and one reporting form is used for both state and local taxes. To levy the tax, counties must adopt by reference all the provisions of, and amendments to, the state sales and use tax law. County legislation must include a provision making the ordinance inoperative upon noncompliance with Sec. 29530, Govt. Code, which provides for the establishment of, and deposit of revenue into, a transportation fund, or upon an increase by a city of its tax rate above the rate in effect when the county law was enacted. (Sec. 7203.2, Rev. & Tax. Code)

The California Department of Tax and Fee Administration (CDTFA) provides guidance regarding voter-approved special transactions (sales) and use tax districts. In such districts, the total tax rate includes the standard statewide tax rate plus the district tax rate (which varies from district to district). (*CDTFA Publication 105, District Taxes and Delivered Sales*, California Department of Tax and Fee Administration)

In counties that have levied the tax, cities may levy a conforming tax (80% of the total local tax), and the counties must allow cities a credit against the county rate in their ordinances. Adoption of the Bradley-Burns Law is not subject to referendum; it may be enacted by the board of supervisors of any county by adopting legislation to conform to all the provisions set out in the enabling legislation. (Sec. 7202, Rev. & Tax. Code)

The city/county tax is in addition to the state rate. Every California county has adopted the sales and use tax provided under the Bradley-Burns Law. See Rate of Tax, for the current rate.

The CDTFA provides guidance for city and county officials. (*CDTFA Publication 28, Tax Information for City and County Officials*, California Department of Tax and Fee Administration)

Although Bradley-Burns preempts local sales and use taxation, a city or county may levy and collect "any other substantially different tax authorized by the California Constitution or by statute or by the charter of any charter city." (Sec. 7203.5, Rev. & Tax. Code)

One of the most common local taxes other than Bradley-Burns is the transactions and use tax, a local tax imposed within the boundaries of various transit, traffic, or other districts, as allowed by state law to finance district operations. The maximum transactions and use tax rate in any county is 2%. Transactions and use tax applies in addition to the state sales and use tax. (Sec. 7251.1, Rev. & Tax. Code)

The CDTFA provides guidance regarding district taxes. (*CDTFA Publication 44, District Taxes (Sales and Use Taxes)*, California Department of Tax and Fee Administration)

A list of local tax rates by city can be found at Local Tax Rates.

Auctioneers.—Retail sales made by auctioneers are subject to local tax. (Reg. 1802, 18 CCR)

Construction contractors.—Sales of fixtures and use of materials by construction contractors are subject to local sales and use taxes. (Reg. 1806, 18 CCR; Reg. 1826, 18 CCR)

See Construction.

Jet fuel.—Jet fuel is subject to local sales and use tax. (Sec. 7205, Rev. & Tax. Code; Reg. 1802, 18 CCR)

See Motor Fuels.

Leased vehicles.—Leased vehicles with terms of at least four months are subject to a 1% local use tax. (Sec. 7205.1, Rev. & Tax. Code)

For details of the leased vehicle local use tax, see Motor Vehicles.

Local use tax.—Local use tax is due when the property is used in a county or district that has enacted a local tax if any of the following conditions exists:

— title to the property passes out of state,

— the sale is in a jurisdiction in the state that has no local tax (there are no such jurisdictions at present),

— the sale of the property is exempt but its use is not, or

— the property was purchased under a valid resale certificate and then used in a taxable manner.

(Reg. 1803, 18 CCR; Reg. 1823, 18 CCR)

Local use tax does not apply to property stored or processed for use outside the state or in a nontaxing jurisdiction. The obligation of out-of-state retailers collecting use tax is not affected by the fact that the taxable use occurs in a county or city other than the one in which the retailer is engaged in business.

Place of sale.—The Bradley-Burns Uniform Local Sales and Use Tax Law requires that all sales and use taxes collected by the CDTFA under contract with a city or county are to be returned to that jurisdiction. (Sec. 7204, Rev. & Tax. Code)

The CDTFA requires retailers to make a county-by-county allocation of local tax liabilities on the return. All retail sales are consummated at the place of business of the retailer unless the property is delivered by the seller, the seller's agent, or a common carrier to an out-of-state point. (Sec. 7205, Rev. & Tax. Code)

The regulations govern the place of sale in cases not covered in the law. If a retailer has more than one place of business in the state, but only one location participates in the sale, the sale is deemed to occur at that location. If a retailer has more than one place of business involved in a sale, the transaction is regarded as having taken place where the principal negotiations are carried on or where the order is taken. As long as title passes within the state, it is immaterial that it passes outside the taxing jurisdiction in which the retailer's business is located. (Reg. 1802, 18 CCR; Reg. 1822, 18 CCR)

For transactions of $500,000 or more, if a seller is required to collect local use tax on a transaction, except with respect to persons who register with the California Department of Tax and Fee Administration (CDTFA) to collect use tax under Regulation 1684(c), then the seller is obligated to report the local use tax revenues derived therefrom directly to the participating jurisdiction where the first functional use is made. Persons who voluntarily collect use tax under Regulation 1684(c) may, solely at their own discretion, report the local use tax revenues on transactions of $500,000 or more directly to the participating jurisdiction where first functional use is made. (Reg. 1802, 18 CCR)

If an out-of-state retailer does not have a permanent place of business in California other than for the maintenance of a stock of tangible personal property, the place of sale is the city, county, or city and county from which delivery or shipment is made. (Reg. 1802, 18 CCR)

If a property order is sent by a purchaser directly to an out-of-state retailer and the property is shipped directly to the in-state purchaser, the transaction is subject to local use tax in the jurisdiction where the first functional use of the property is made. Unless the seller possesses a Use Tax Certificate of Registration (see Vendor Registration), the seller is required to report local use tax revenues from non-lease transactions of $500,000 or more directly to the local taxing jurisdiction. In addition, any person that is required to report and pay local use tax directly to the CDTFA that makes a purchase in the amount of $500,000 or more is also required to report the local use tax revenues directly to the local taxing jurisdiction in which the first functional use of the property is made. (Reg. 1802, 18 CCR)

Scope of local taxes.—Under both the Bradley-Burns uniform local sales and use tax and the transactions (sales) and use taxes, with the exception of the local tax exemption provided for common carrier aircraft, stocks, bonds, and securities, and direct-to-home satellite services, the state-administered local sales and use taxes are applicable to every transaction, including leases, that are subject to the state sales and use tax, and the local sales and use taxes do not apply to transactions that are exempt under the state sales and use tax. The measure of tax includes any state taxable delivery charges. (Reg. 1803, 18 CCR; Reg. 1823, 18 CCR)

The local tax must include, in addition to the state exemptions, a provision that the amount subject to tax does not include any state imposed sales and use tax. (Sec. 7203, Rev. & Tax. Code)

The transactions (sales) and use taxes must also exclude from tax any amount of sales and use tax imposed by a city, county, or district of California. (Sec. 7261, Rev. & Tax. Code)

Unless otherwise exempt, a lease that is a continuing sale is subject to use tax to be collected by the lessor on receipts from leases of property in districts with a transaction (sales) and use tax. (Reg. 1823, 18 CCR)

Stocks, bonds, and other securities.—Local taxing agencies are specifically prohibited from imposing any tax, fee, or charge on or measured by the sale of stocks, bonds, or any other securities. (Sec. 50026.5, Govt. Code)

Vehicles, aircraft, and vessels.—A dealer is required to collect local use tax from any purchaser who registers or licenses a vehicle, vessel, or aircraft at an address in a district imposing the tax. (Sec. 7262, Rev. & Tax. Code)

For details of the vehicle, aircraft, and vessel local use tax, see ¶60-740 Transportation.

Vending machines.—Vending machine sales are subject to local tax at the place where the machine is located. (Reg. 1802, 18 CCR; Reg. 1822, 18 CCR)

• *Prohibition on local governments imposing taxes on groceries*

A local agency cannot impose, increase, levy and collect, or enforce any California sales and use tax, fee, or other assessment on groceries. (Sec. 7284.12, Rev. & Tax. Code)

A local agency may continue to levy and collect, enforce, or reauthorize any tax, fee, or other assessment on groceries imposed, extended, or increased on or before January 1, 2018. Any such tax or fee on groceries imposed by a local agency after January 1, 2018, and before June 28, 2018, is inoperative as of June 28, 2018, and ceases to be imposed, levied and collected, and enforced as of that date. (Sec. 7284.12, Rev. & Tax. Code)

"Tax, fee, or other assessment on groceries" includes but is not limited to a sales tax, gross receipts tax, business and occupation tax, business license tax, excise tax, privilege tax, surcharge, or any other similar levy, charge, or exaction of any kind on:

- groceries; or
- the manufacture, supply, distribution, sale, acquisition, possession, ownership, transfer, transportation, delivery, use, or consumption of groceries.

(Sec. 7284.10, Rev. & Tax. Code)

"Groceries" are defined as any raw or processed food or beverage, including its packaging, wrapper, or container, or any ingredient of such food or beverage, intended for human consumption, including but not limited to:

- meat;
- poultry;
- fish;
- fruits;
- vegetables;
- grains;
- bread;
- milk;
- cheese and other dairy products;
- carbonated and noncarbonated nonalcoholic beverages;
- kombucha with less than 0.5% alcohol by volume;
- condiments;
- spices;
- cereals;
- seasonings;
- leavening agents;
- eggs;
- cocoa; and
- raw or processed teas and coffees.

(Sec. 7284.10, Rev. & Tax. Code)

The term does not include:

- alcoholic beverages;
- cannabis products;
- cigarettes;
- tobacco products; and
- electronic cigarettes.

"Local agency" includes a: county; city (whether general law or chartered); city and county; school district; municipal corporation; district; political subdivision; or any board, commission, or agency of such an jurisdiction; other local public agency; or entities that are legislative bodies of a local agency. (Sec. 7284.10, Rev. & Tax. Code)

(Sec. 7284.10, Rev. & Tax. Code)

The imposition, extension, increase, levy and collection, or enforcement of a tax, fee, or other assessment on groceries is not prohibited by a local agency if both of the following apply:

- the tax, fee, or other assessment is generally applicable to a broad range of businesses, business activity, or products; and

- the tax, fee, or other assessment does not establish or rely on a classification related to or involving groceries or a subset of groceries for purposes of establishing or otherwise resulting in a higher tax rate due to that classification.

(Sec. 7284.12, Rev. & Tax. Code)

These provisions sunset on January 1, 2031, and are repealed as of that date. (Sec. 7284.16, Rev. & Tax. Code)

¶61-710

• Transactions and use taxes

Although the Bradley-Burns Law preempts the area of sales and use taxation by a city or county, nothing in that law prohibits the levy and collection by a city or county "of any other substantially different tax authorized by the Constitution of California or by statute or by the charter of any charter city." (Sec. 7203.5, Rev. & Tax. Code)

In 1970, a California court of appeal overturned a 5% "tipplers' tax" imposed by the city of Los Angeles on the purchase and consumption of alcoholic beverages, holding that it was not "substantially different" from state laws enacted to regulate the sale of alcoholic beverages. (*Century Plaza Hotel Co. v. City of Los Angeles*, 7 CalApp3d 616 87 CalRptr 166 (1970))

On the other hand, the California Supreme Court in 1971 held that a 5% utility users' tax imposed by the city of Fresno on intrastate telephone services was valid because it was "substantially different" from any other tax in the statewide system. (*Rivera v. City of Fresno*, 6 Cal3d 132, 490 P2d 793 (1971))

Other than Bradley-Burns, the most common local sales and use taxes are transactions and use taxes imposed within the boundaries of various transit, traffic, or other districts, as allowed by state law to finance operations of the district. The maximum rate at which such taxes may be imposed in any county is 2%. Like Bradley-Burns, the transactions and use tax is in addition to the state sales and use tax. (Sec. 7251.1, Rev. & Tax. Code)

The board of supervisors of any county may levy a transactions and use tax at a rate of 0.125% or any multiple thereof. Alternatively, the board of supervisors of any county may establish an authority for specific purposes. The authority may then impose a transactions and use tax at a rate of 0.125% for the purpose for which it is established if the tax is approved by a two-thirds vote of the authority, is subsequently approved by a vote of the qualified voters in an amount that is otherwise required by law, and conforms to other requirements. (Sec. 7285, Rev. & Tax. Code; Sec. 7285.5, Rev. & Tax. Code)

A county's board of supervisors may levy, increase, or extend a general purpose California local transactions and use tax throughout the entire county or within the unincorporated area of the county if the ordinance proposing that tax is approved by a two-thirds vote of all members of the board of supervisors and the tax is approved by a majority vote of the qualified voters of the entire county if levied on the entire county, or the unincorporated area of the county if levied on the unincorporated area of the county, voting in an election on the issue. (Sec. 7285, Rev. & Tax. Code)

In addition, a county's board of supervisors may levy, increase, or extend a special purpose transactions and use tax throughout the entire county or within the unincorporated area of the county, as applicable, provided:

— the ordinance proposing that tax is approved by a two-thirds vote of all members of the board of supervisors and is subsequently approved by a two-thirds vote of the qualified voters of the entire county if levied on the entire county, or the unincorporated area of the county if levied on the unincorporated area of the county, voting in an election on the issue;

— the tax conforms to the Transactions and Use Tax Law, as provided; and

— the ordinance includes an expenditure plan describing the specific projects for which the revenues from the tax may be expended.

(Sec. 7285.5, Rev. & Tax. Code)

County boards of supervisors are also authorized to impose special taxes, (Sec. 50075, et seq., Govt. Code) provided the ordinance or resolution proposing the imposition of any special tax is approved by a two-thirds majority of the voters voting on the issue. The special tax must be applied uniformly to all taxpayers within the county. (Sec. 23027, Govt. Code)

Transactions (sales) and use taxes imposed by districts incorporate most of the provisions of the state sales and use taxes and generally have the same tax base as the Bradley-Burns uniform local sales and use taxes imposed by cities and counties. (Reg. 1821, 18 CCR)

The primary differences between the transactions (sales) and use tax of a district and the state and Bradley-Burns uniform local sales and use taxes are as follows:

— the transactions tax of a district is not applicable to the gross receipts from the sale or lease of tangible personal property that the seller or lessor is obligated to furnish for a fixed price pursuant to a contract entered into prior to the operative date of the tax (see ¶60-110 Rate of Tax, for a general discussion of the application of tax rate changes to fixed-price contracts and leases);

— the transactions tax does not apply to gross receipts from the sale of property to be used outside the district when the property is shipped to a point outside the district by the retailer or common carrier;

— the use tax of a district is not applicable to the storage, use, or other consumption in the district of tangible personal property that the purchaser or lessee is obligated to purchase or lease for a fixed price pursuant to a contract entered into prior to the operative date of the tax (see Rate of Tax, for a general discussion of the application of tax rate changes to fixed-price contracts and leases);

— the district use tax must be collected by retailers engaged in business in the district and paid to the Department of Tax and Fee Administration (CDTFA) when the retailer ships or delivers the property sold into the district or partici-pates within the district in making the sale; the state and Bradley-Burns uniform local use tax must be collected by retailers engaged in business in the state; and

— retailers of vehicles, aircraft, or undocumented vessels in a district impos-ing a transactions and use tax are required to collect the use tax from the purchaser and pay it to the CDTFA when the vehicle, aircraft, or vessel is registered or licensed in that district.

(Reg. 1821, 18 CCR)

Credit.—The use tax portion of any transactions and use tax ordinance must include a provision that any person subject to use tax under the ordinance may credit against that tax any transactions tax or reimbursement for transactions tax paid another district or a retailer in another district. (Reg. 1823.5, 18 CCR)

When the transactions tax has been paid in one transit district where the property was purchased and the district use tax is owed to a second district where the property is actually used and where the rate (or combined rate) is higher, a credit is allowed against the second district's use tax in an amount equal to but not exceeding the transactions tax reimbursement paid to the first district or to a retailer in the first district. (Reg. 1823.5, 18 CCR)

If the taxable use occurs in two or more districts whose boundaries are over-lapped or coextensive, the credit must be applied first against any use tax liability imposed by the district that first adopted its transactions and use tax ordinance; any remaining credit amount is then applied against the use tax imposed by the district having the next-earliest transactions and use tax ordinance, and so forth until the amount of the credit is exhausted. (Reg. 1823.5, 18 CCR)

Exemptions.—In addition to the exemptions provided for in state law, the district transactions and use tax ordinance (Sec. 7251, Rev. & Tax. Code through Sec. 7274, Rev. & Tax. Code) must contain the following exemptions:

— the amount of any state or uniform local sales or use tax is to be excluded from the measure of tax;

— property that is required to be and is shipped out of the district by a retailer or his agent is not subject to that district's tax;

— property obligated to be sold or leased for a price fixed pursuant to a contract or lease entered into before the operative date of the local transactions and use tax ordinance is exempt (see Rate of Tax, for a general discussion of the application of tax rate changes to fixed-price contracts and leases); and

— the transactions and use tax does not apply to property (other than fuel or petroleum products) sold to or purchased by operators of commercial aircraft if the property is used directly and exclusively in the use of the aircraft as common carriers of people or property and, in the case of a transactions tax, is used principally outside the county of sale.

(Sec. 7261, Rev. & Tax. Code; Reg. 1823, 18 CCR)

Legal challenges attacking validity of tax.—In order to prevent the expenditure of revenues received from a local tax when the validity of that tax is being legally challenged, local taxing districts are required to deposit any revenues received pursuant to such a tax into an interest-bearing escrow account until the issue of the tax's legality is resolved by a final and nonappealable decision rendered by a court of competent jurisdiction. (Sec. 7270, Rev. & Tax. Code)

However, any actions challenging the constitutionality or validity of a local transactions (sales) and use tax in its entirety (as opposed to its application to a particular taxpayer or type of transaction) must be brought within 60 days of its adoption and approval by the voters. (Sec. 7270.5, Rev. & Tax. Code)

The State may not be named as a party to any action or proceeding challenging the validity of a local tax and may not be held liable for any refunds, fees, or costs associated with the challenge. (Sec. 7270.5, Rev. & Tax. Code)

Nevertheless, if the tax is found to be invalid, the local taxing district must transmit any funds to the state for the purpose of refunding the revenues to the affected taxpayers. (Sec. 7267, Rev. & Tax. Code)

• *City transactions and use tax*

The governing body of any city may levy, increase, or extend a transactions and use tax at a rate of 0.125% or a multiple thereof, subject to voter approval. The governing body may levy, increase, or extend more than one transaction and use tax as long as each is adopted in the required manner. (Sec. 7285.9, Rev. & Tax Code; Sec. 7261, Rev. & Tax. Code; Sec. 7262, Rev. & Tax. Code)

Alternatively, the governing body of any city may levy, increase, or extend a transactions and use tax at a rate of 0.125%, or a multiple thereof, for specific purposes. To levy the tax, all of the following requirements must be met:

— The ordinance proposing the tax is approved by a two-thirds vote of all members of the governing body and is subsequently approved by a two-thirds vote of the qualified voters of the city voting in an election on the issue.

— The transactions and use tax conforms to the Transactions and Use Tax Law.

— The ordinance includes an expenditure plan describing the specific projects for which the revenues from the tax may be expended.

(Sec. 7285.91, Rev. & Tax Code)

The authority of a city to impose the transactions and use tax is in addition to any authority to impose the tax discussed below. However, no city may impose the tax at a rate of more than 2%. (Sec. 7285.92, Rev. & Code)

Alameda.—The city of Alameda is authorized to impose a general purpose district tax that, in combination with all district taxes imposed, would not exceed the existing 2% limitation by more than 0.5% provided all of the following requirements are met:

— the city adopts an ordinance proposing a district tax by any applicable voting approval requirement;

— the city ordinance proposing the district tax is submitted to the electorate of the adopting city, and is approved by the voters voting on the ordinance in accordance with Article XIII C of the California Constitution (the election on the ordinance proposing the district tax may occur after January 1, 2017); and

— the district tax conforms to the Transactions and Use Tax Law (the bill also specifies that the tax rate authorized by this bill will not be included in the calculation of the 2% rate limitation).

(Sec. 7292.5, Rev. & Tax. Code)

If the proposed district tax ordinance is not approved by the electorate by January 1, 2025, these provisions are repealed as of that date. (Sec. 7292.6, Rev. & Tax. Code)

Berkeley.—The City of Berkeley may impose a California transactions and use tax for general or specific purposes. (Sec. 7299, Rev. & Tax. Code)

The tax may be imposed at a rate of no more than 0.5%. The rate could, in combination with all taxes imposed under the Transactions and Use Tax Law, exceed the 2% statutory cap. To impose such a tax, the city must:

• adopt an ordinance proposing the transactions and use tax by any applicable voting approval requirement;

• submit the ordinance proposing the transactions and use tax to the electorate and obtain the approval of voters voting on the ordinance pursuant to Article XIIIC of the California Constitution; and

• conform the tax to the Transactions and Use Tax Law.

(Sec. 7299, Rev. & Tax. Code)

Clearlake.—The city of Clearlake is authorized to impose a transactions and use tax of 0.25% or 0.5% to be used solely for the provision of public safety services, as defined in Govt. Code Sec. 30052, provided that any ordinance or resolution proposing the taxes is approved by a majority vote from the city council and two-thirds of qualified city voters voting on the issue. (Sec. 7286.45, Rev. & Tax. Code)

Clearlake is authorized to levy a California local transactions (sales) and use tax of at a rate of 0.25%, or a multiple thereof not to exceed 1% for the maintenance, repair, replacement, construction, or reconstruction of its road systems. However, the city's authority to levy this tax is subject to approval by a majority vote of all members of its city council and approval by a two-thirds vote of the qualified voters voting in an election on the issue. (Sec. 7286.24, Rev. & Tax. Code)

Clovis.—The city of Clovis is authorized to impose a transactions and use tax at the rate of 0.3% to provide revenue solely for police and fire facilities, furnishings, and equipment. The levy must be approved by a majority of the city council and two-thirds of the qualified electors voting in an election on the issue. (Sec. 7286.48, Rev. & Tax. Code)

Davis.—The city of Davis is authorized to levy a 0.25% or 0.5% California local transactions (sales) and use tax. However, the city's authority to levy this tax is subject to approval by a two-thirds vote of all members of its city council and approval by a two-thirds or majority vote of the qualified voters voting in an election on the issue. (Sec. 7290, Rev. & Tax. Code)

El Cerrito.—The city of El Cerrito is authorized to impose a California transactions and use tax for general purposes at a rate of no more than 0.5% that would, in combination with other taxes, exceed the 2% statutory limit provided the following conditions are met:

— the city adopts an ordinance proposing the tax subject to any applicable voter approval requirement;

— the city ordinance proposing the tax is submitted to the electorate of the adopting city and is approved by voters voting on the ordinance, as required by Article XIII C of the California Constitution (the election on the ordinance proposing the tax may occur on or after November 4, 2014);

— the tax conforms to the Transactions and Use Tax Law, as provided; and

— the tax is imposed on or after January 1, 2015.

(Sec. 7293, Rev. & Tax. Code)

If an ordinance proposing a transactions and use tax has not been approved by January 1, 2022, these provisions are repealed as of that date. (Sec. 7294, Rev. & Tax. Code)

Fort Bragg.—Fort Bragg is authorized to levy a California local transactions (sales) and use tax of at a rate of 0.25%, or a multiple thereof not to exceed 1% for the maintenance, repair, replacement, construction, or reconstruction of its road systems. However, the city's authority to levy this tax is subject to approval by a majority vote of all members of its city council and approval by a two-thirds vote of the qualified voters voting in an election on the issue. (Sec. 7286.24, Rev. & Tax. Code)

Lakeport.—The city of Lakeport is authorized to impose a transactions and use tax of 0.25% or a multiple thereof, not to exceed 1%, to be used solely for the repair, replacement, construction, or reconstruction of the city's streets and roads. Any ordinance or resolution proposing the tax must be approved by a majority vote from the city council and two-thirds of qualified city voters voting on the issue. (Sec. 7286.40, Rev. & Tax. Code)

Madera.—The city of Madera is authorized to levy a transactions (sales) and use tax of 0.25% if the tax is approved by a majority of the city council and two-thirds of the qualified voters voting on the issue. (Sec. 7286.65, Rev. & Tax. Code)

Placerville.—The city of Placerville is authorized to levy a transactions (sales) and use tax at a rate of either 0.125% or 0.25% in order to fund police services, as defined by the resolution or ordinance that proposes the tax, provided that the tax is approved by a majority vote of all city council members and is also approved by two-thirds of the city's qualified voters who vote at an election on the issue. (Sec. 7286.70, Rev. & Tax. Code)

Point Arena.—The city of Point Arena is authorized to levy a California local transactions (sales) and use tax of at a rate of 0.25%, or a multiple thereof not to exceed 1% for the maintenance, repair, replacement, construction, or reconstruction of its road systems. However, the city's authority to levy this tax is subject to approval by a majority vote of all members of the city council and approval by a two-thirds vote of the qualified voters voting in an election on the issue. (Sec. 7286.24, Rev. & Tax. Code)

San Diego.—The San Diego Metropolitan Transit System (MTS) may impose, subject to the approval of two-thirds of the voters and in accordance with the Transactions and Use Tax Law and Article XIII C of the California Constitution, a retail transactions and use tax within the portions of San Diego County and use the revenues for public transit purposes. The MTS Board of Directors may impose a maximum tax rate of 0.5%. (Sec. 120480, Pub. Util. Code; Sec. 125480, Pub. Util. Code)

Santa Fe Springs.—The city of Santa Fe Springs may impose, subject to voter approval pursuant to Article XIII C of the California Constitution, a retail transactions and use tax that would, in combination with all other such taxes, exceed the 2% limit, subject to certain restrictions. The tax rate authorized is no more than 1% for Santa Fe Springs. (Sec. 7286.27, Rev. & Tax. Code) If this authorized tax has not been approved by voters by December 31, 2022, it will be repealed on that date. (Sec. 7286.28, Rev. & Tax. Code)

Sebastopol.—The city of Sebastopol is authorized to levy a 0.125% transactions and use tax, provided that an ordinance or resolution proposing the tax is approved by a majority of city council members, and by two-thirds of qualified voters of the city voting in an election on the issue. (Sec. 7286.80, Rev. & Tax. Code)

Ukiah.—The city of Ukiah is authorized to levy a California local transactions (sales) and use tax of at a rate of 0.25%, or a multiple thereof not to exceed 1% for the maintenance, repair, replacement, construction, or reconstruction of its road systems. However, the city's authority to levy this tax is subject to approval by a majority vote of all members of the city council and approval by a two-thirds vote of the qualified voters voting in an election on the issue. (Sec. 7286.24, Rev. & Tax. Code)

Visalia.—The city of Visalia is authorized to levy a 0.25% California local transactions (sales) and use tax for the purpose of improving its public safety, fire, and law enforcement services. However, the city's authority to levy this tax is subject to approval by a majority vote of all members of its city council and approval by a two-thirds vote of the qualified voters voting in an election on the issue. (Sec. 7286.44, Rev. & Tax. Code)

West Sacramento.—The city of West Sacramento is authorized to levy a transactions and use tax at a rate of 0.25% or 0.5%, if approved by a two-thirds vote of the city council and a majority vote of the electorate. (Sec. 7286.75, Rev. & Tax. Code)

Willits.—The city of Willits is authorized to levy a California local transactions (sales) and use tax of at a rate of 0.25%, or a multiple thereof not to exceed 1% for the maintenance, repair, replacement, construction, or reconstruction of its road systems. However, the city's authority to levy this tax is subject to approval by a majority vote of all members of the city council and approval by a two-thirds vote of the qualified voters voting in an election on the issue. (Sec. 7286.24, Rev. & Tax. Code)

Woodland.—The city of Woodland is authorized to levy an additional transactions and use tax at a rate of 0.25% or 0.5%, if approved by a two-thirds vote of the city council and a majority vote of the electorate. (Sec. 7286.52, Rev. & Tax. Code)

• *County transactions and use taxes*

The board of supervisors of any county may levy a transactions and use tax at a rate of 0.125% or any multiple thereof. Alternatively, the board of supervisors of any county may establish an authority for specific purposes. The authority may then impose a transactions and use tax at a rate of 0.125% for the purpose for which it is established, provided that the tax is approved by a two-thirds vote of the authority, and if the tax is subsequently approved by a vote of the qualified voters in an amount otherwise required by law, and the tax conforms to other requirements. (Sec. 7285, Rev. & Tax. Code; Sec. 7285.5, Rev. & Tax. Code; Sec. 7261, Rev. & Tax. Code; Sec. 7262, Rev. & Tax. Code)

The CDTFA provides guidance regarding voter-approved special California transactions (sales) and use tax districts. (*CDTFA Publication 105, District Taxes and Delivered Sales*, California Department of Tax and Fee Administration)

Alameda County.—Alameda County is authorized to impose, subject to voter approval pursuant to Article XIII C of the California Constitution, a retail transactions and use tax that would, in combination with all other such taxes, exceed the 2% limit, subject to certain restrictions. The tax rate authorized is no more than 0.5% for Alameda County. (Sec. 7292.2, Rev. & Tax. Code) If this tax has not been approved by voters by December 31, 2022, it will be repealed on that date. (Sec. 7292.3, Rev. & Tax. Code)

Contra Costa Transportation Authority.—The Contra Costa Transportation Authority is authorized to impose a transactions and use tax for the support of county-wide transportation programs at a rate of no more than 0.5% that would, in combination with all other transactions and use taxes, exceed the 2% limit established in existing law if all the following conditions are met:

— the Contra Costa Transportation Authority adopts an ordinance proposing the transactions and use tax by any applicable voting approval requirement;

— the ordinance proposing the transactions and use tax is submitted to the electorate and is approved by the voters voting on the ordinance pursuant to Article XIII C of the California Constitution; and

— the transactions and use tax conforms to the Transactions and Use Tax Law, as provided.

(Sec. 7291, Rev. & Tax. Code; Sec. 7292, Rev. & Tax. Code)

Effective January 1, 2021, Contra Costa County and cities within the county have flexibility to impose local transactions and use taxes. A transactions and use tax rate imposed by the Contra Costa Transportation Authority is not considered for purposes of the combined rate limit. (Sec. 7291, Rev. & Tax. Code)

County library programs tax.—The board of supervisors of any county may impose a transactions and use tax at a rate of 0.125% or 0.25% to fund public library construction, acquisition, programs, and operations within the county. The tax may be imposed in lieu of, but not in addition to, any transactions and use tax imposed under Rev. & Tax. Code Sec. 7285.5 by an authority established by a county board of supervisors specifically for public library purposes. (Sec. 7286.59, Rev. & Tax. Code)

The ordinance imposing the tax must be submitted to, and approved by, two-thirds of county voters voting on the ordinance. Revenues from the tax must be used only to supplement existing expenditures for public libraries and must not be used to supplant existing funding for public libraries. The tax may be imposed for an initial period of up to 16 years, and may be imposed for additional 16-year periods only if all of the requisite conditions are satisfied, including submission of the tax ordinance to voters for approval. (Sec. 7286.59, Rev. & Tax. Code)

The county of San Joaquin may impose a 1.25% transactions and use tax to be used solely to fund countywide library programs and operations, provided that the ordinance imposing the tax is submitted to and approved by two-thirds of the voters of the county voting on the issue. If approved, the tax may be imposed initially for up to 10 years and reimposed for succeeding 10-year periods if it continues to receive the support of the County Board of Supervisors and two-thirds of the voters of the county voting on the issue. (Sec. 7286.55, Rev. & Tax. Code)

Fresno County zoological tax.—The Fresno County board of supervisors may establish an authority that may impose an 0.1% transactions and use tax in accordance with the Transaction and Use Tax Law for the support of zoos, zoological facilities, and related zoological purposes in the county, if the ordinance imposing the tax:

— is approved by a two-thirds vote of the governing board of the authority;

— is approved by a two-thirds vote of the voters of the county voting on the ordinance; and

— requires the revenues, net of refunds, to be used exclusively for zoos, zoological facilities, and related zoological purposes in the county.

(Sec. 7286.43, Rev. & Tax. Code)

Los Angeles County Metropolitan Transportation Authority (MTA).—The Los Angeles County Metropolitan Transportation Authority (MTA) is authorized to impose, in addition to any other tax that it is authorized to impose, a California local transactions and use tax at the rate of 0.5%. The tax may be imposed only if the proposing ordinance is approved by two-thirds of the voters in an election. The proposing ordinance must specify, in addition to the rate of tax and other matters, that the tax is to be imposed for a period not to exceed 30 years. The Legislature intends that the net revenues derived from the tax be used to fund a transportation investment program. (Sec. 130350.4, Pub. Util. Code; Sec. 130350.5, Pub. Util. Code)

The MTA is authorized, in addition to any other tax it is authorized to impose or has imposed, to impose an additional 0.5% California transactions and use tax (district tax), for a period to be determined by the MTA, and applicable in the incorporated and unincorporated areas of the county, to fund transportation-related projects. Such a tax, when combined with the existing 0.5% district tax for transportation, cannot exceed 1%. (Sec. 130350.7, Pub. Util. Code)

Monterey County.—Monterey County is authorized to impose a countywide transactions and use tax at a rate of no more than 0.375% for transportation purposes that would, in combination with all other locally-imposed sales tax, exceed the 2% tax rate cap if all of the following requirements are met:

— the Transportation Agency for Monterey County adopts an ordinance proposing the transactions and use tax by an applicable voting approval requirement;

— the ordinance proposing the transactions and use tax is submitted to the electorate and is approved by the voters voting on the ordinance in accordance with Article XIII C of the California Constitution; and

— the transactions and use tax conforms to the Transactions and Use Tax Law, as specified.

(Sec. 7297, Rev. & Tax. Code)

This provision is repealed if county voters do not approve a proposed tax increase before January 1, 2026. (Sec. 7298, Rev. & Tax. Code)

¶61-710

North County Transit District.—Effective January 1, 2018, the North County Transit District (NCTD) may impose, subject to the approval of two-thirds of the voters and in accordance with the Transactions and Use Tax Law and Article XIII C of the California Constitution, a retail transactions and use tax within the portions of San Diego County and use the revenues for public transit purposes. The NCTD Board of Directors may impose a maximum tax rate of 0.5%. (Sec. 120480, Pub. Util. Code; Sec. 125480, Pub. Util. Code)

Peninsula Corridor Joint Powers Board.—Effective January 1, 2018, the Peninsula Corridor Joint Powers Board may, subject to certain restrictions, impose a regional retail transaction and use tax in excess of the 2% limit in accordance with the transactions and use tax law and Article XIII C of the California Constitution. Imposition of the tax is subject to approval by the boards of supervisors of the counties of San Francisco, San Mateo, and Santa Clara, and each of those counties' transportation entity's governing board. Then the measure must be approved by two-thirds of the voters from the three counties voting on the measure. The tax may not exceed 0.125%. (Sec. 7286.65, Rev. & Tax. Code)

San Diego County.—The San Diego County Regional Transportation Commission is authorized to increase the California local transactions (sales) and use tax rate in the county to the maximum rate authorized under existing law subject to voter approval. Such an ordinance adopted under these provisions would become operative on the first day of the calendar quarter commencing more than 110 days after adoption of the ordinance. (Sec. 132320, Pub. Util. Code)

Sonoma County.—Effective January 1, 2019, Sonoma County or any city within the county may impose a transactions and use tax for general purposes, and the county, any city within the county, or the Sonoma County Transportation Authority may impose a transactions and use tax for specific purposes, at a rate of no more than 1% that would, in combination with all taxes imposed in accordance with the Transactions and Use Tax Law, exceed the 2% limit. The tax may be imposed if: (1) the County of Sonoma, a city within the county, or the Sonoma County Transportation Authority adopts an ordinance proposing the transactions and use tax by any applicable voting approval requirement; and (2) the ordinance is approved by the voters in accordance with Article XIII C of the California Constitution. The election on the ordinance proposing the transactions and use tax may occur on or after November 6, 2018. If, as of January 1, 2026, an ordinance has not been approved, this provision is repealed as of that same date. (Sec. 7292.8, Rev. & Tax. Code; Sec. 7292.9, Rev. & Tax. Code)

Riverside County.—Effective January 1, 2018, the Riverside County Transportation Commission is authorized to impose a maximum transactions and use tax rate for transportation purposes of 1% (previously 0.5%), subject to voter approval. The commission is prohibited from imposing a tax rate other than 1%, 0.75%, 0.5%, or 0.25% unless specifically authorized by statute. In addition, the tax rate imposed by the commission will not be considered for purposes of the 2% combined transactions and use tax rate limit. (Sec. 240306, Pub. Util. Code)

San Mateo County tax for education purposes.—The San Mateo County board of supervisors may establish an authority that may impose an 0.5% transactions and use tax for the support of public elementary and secondary education in the county if:

— the ordinance imposing the tax is approved by a two-thirds vote of the governing board of the authority and is subject to any voter approval requirement;

— the ordinance requires the revenues to be allocated only for educational purposes in the county; and

— the tax complies with the Transactions and Use Tax Law.

(Sec. 7285.8, Rev. & Tax. Code)

San Mateo County is authorized to impose a California transactions (sales) and use tax at a rate of 0.125% or 0.25% for a specified period of time provided the ordinance that imposes the tax is approved by two-thirds of all members of the Board of Supervisors and is subsequently approved by two-thirds of the county voters. An expenditure plan that describes the purposes for which the tax revenue may be used must be included with the ordinance that imposes the tax. (Sec. 7286.90, Rev. & Tax. Code)

If the tax is imposed, (1) tax revenue may be used only for park and recreation acquisition, improvements, maintenance, programs, and operations within the incorporated and unincorporated areas of the county; and (2) it would be in lieu of and not in addition to a tax imposed for park and recreation purposes as specified. Under current statutory provisions, the combined rate of all transactions and use taxes imposed in any county cannot exceed 2%. (Sec. 7286.90, Rev. & Tax. Code)

San Mateo County tax for transportation purposes.—Effective January 1, 2016, San Mateo County is authorized to impose a countywide California transactions and use tax at a rate of no more than 0.5% for transportation purposes that would, in combination with all other locally imposed sales tax, exceed the 2% tax rate cap provided it otherwise conforms to the Bay Area County Traffic and Transportation Funding Act. (Sec. 7295, Rev. & Tax. Code)

If the ordinance proposing the transactions and use tax is not approved as indicated above, this provision is repealed as of January 1, 2026. (Sec. 7296, Rev. & Tax. Code)

Effective January 1, 2018, the San Mateo County Transit District is authorized, subject to voter approval pursuant to Article XIII C of the California Constitution, to impose a California retail transactions and use tax that would, in combination with all other such taxes in San Mateo County, exceed the 2% limit provided: (1) the tax is set at a rate of no more than 0.5%; (2) the San Mateo County Transit District Board of Directors adopts the ordinance approving the tax before January 1, 2026; and, (3) the tax conforms to the Transactions and Use Tax law. (Sec. 7295, Rev. & Tax. Code; Sec. 103350, Pub. Util. Code; Sec. 131057, Pub. Util. Code)

Santa Clara County.—Effective January 1, 2018, Santa Clara County may impose, subject to voter approval pursuant to Article XIII C of the California Constitution, a retail transactions and use tax that would, in combination with all other such taxes, exceed the 2% limit, subject to certain restrictions. The tax rate authorized is no more than 0.625% for Santa Clara County. (Sec. 7292.4, Rev. & Tax. Code) If this authorized tax has not been approved by voters by December 31, 2022, it will be repealed on that date. (Sec. 7292.41, Rev. & Tax. Code)

Santa Clara Valley Transportation Authority.—The Santa Clara Valley Transportation Authority, with two-thirds approval of the voters of the County of Santa Clara, is authorized to adopt an ordinance imposing a California transactions and use tax at a rate of 0.125% for transit facilities and services, provided that certain provisions of the Revenue and Taxation Code and the Public Utilities Code are complied with by the Authority. (Sec. 7262.3, Rev. & Tax. Code)

• *Local Transportation Authority and Improvement Act*

The Local Transportation Authority and Improvement Act authorizes a local transportation authority to impose a voter-approved retail transactions and use tax in the incorporated and unincorporated territory of a county for purposes of raising revenue for highway improvement and other transportation-related projects. (Sec. 180201, Pub. Util. Code)

A county board of supervisors may create a local transportation authority to carry out the provisions of the Act or may designate an existing transportation planning agency or county transportation commission to serve as a local transportation authority. (Sec. 180050, Pub. Util. Code)

The ordinance must be adopted by a two-thirds majority vote of the authority, and subsequently approved by a majority of the electors voting on the measure at a special election called for that purpose by the board of supervisors. (Sec. 180201, Pub. Util. Code) The ordinance must state the nature of the tax to be imposed, the tax rate or maximum tax rate to be imposed, the period during which the tax will be imposed, and the purposes for which the revenue derived from the tax will be used. (Sec. 180202, Pub. Util. Code)

The tax rate or maximum tax rate to be imposed may be 0.25%, 0.5%, 0.75%, or 1%. (Sec. 180202, Pub. Util. Code) Such a tax will remain in effect for the period of time specified in the ordinance, even if the time period is more than 20 years. (Sec. 180201, Pub. Util. Code)

A transactions and use tax imposed by a local transportation authority becomes operative on the first day of the first calendar quarter starting more than 110 days after adoption of the taxing ordinance. Prior to the operative date, the authority must contract with the Department of Tax and Fee Administration to administer the tax. (Sec. 180204, Pub. Util. Code)

•*Districts authorized to impose a transactions and use tax*

Cities, counties, and special districts are authorized to impose transactions and use tax in increments of 0.125% upon voter approval. (Sec. 7261, Rev. & Tax. Code; Sec. 7262, Rev. & Tax. Code)

A local public finance authority may adopt an ordinance imposing a transactions and use tax at a rate of 0.25% or 0.5% to finance drug abuse prevention, crime prevention, health care services, and public education. (Sec. 7288.3, Rev. & Tax. Code)

The ordinance must be approved by two-thirds of the authority's board of directors and by a majority of the voters. The finance authority may be established if the county board of supervisors adopts a resolution declaring an intent to propose an increase in the transactions and use tax in the county, or if the county superintendent of schools receives resolutions from a majority of the school districts in the county declaring their intent to propose an increase in the transactions and use tax in the county. (Sec. 7288.1, Rev. & Tax. Code)

The tax cannot be imposed before the first day of the first calendar quarter commencing more than 90 days after the election results are certified by the county registrar. (Sec. 7288.4, Rev. & Tax. Code)

Bay Area County Traffic and Transportation Funding Act.—The Bay Area County Traffic and Transportation Funding Act authorizes a transactions and use tax of 0.5% or 1%, if approved by the voters, for any of nine counties in the San Francisco Bay Area: Alameda, Contra Costa, Marin, Napa, San Mateo, San Francisco (city and county), Solano, Sonoma, and Santa Clara. (Sec. 131102, Pub. Util. Code)

Since no county can assess more than a total of 1% transactions and use tax, counties already imposing a 0.5% tax are limited to an additional 0.5%. Effective January 1, 2014, the 1% limitation on the combined local rate under the Act is eliminated. (Sec. 131001, Pub. Util. Code)

County Regional Justice Facilities Financing Act and Orange County Regional Justice Facilities Act.—The County Regional Justice Facilities Financing Act authorizes the creation of county regional justice facility agencies in Humboldt, Los Angeles, Riverside, San Bernardino, and Ventura counties, and the Orange County Regional Justice Facilities Act establishes the Orange County Regional Justice Commission. These bodies are empowered to adopt transactions and use taxes of 0.5% with the approval of two-thirds of the agency or commission members and a majority of voters in the specified counties. However, these bodies may also, if they wish, adopt local tax ordinances that require the approval of two-thirds of the electors, rather than a simple majority. Receipts from these taxes, if adopted, generally must be used for the financing, construction, acquisition, furnishing, maintenance, and operation of adult and juvenile detention facilities, courthouse facilities, and related structures. (Sec. 26299.041, Govt. Code; Sec. 26298.2, Govt. Code)

North Lake Tahoe Transportation Authority Act.—The North Lake Tahoe Transportation Authority Act authorizes the creation of the North Lake Tahoe Transportation Authority, which is empowered to impose a transactions and use tax not to exceed a maximum tax rate of 1% if approved by two-thirds of the qualified voters voting in an election on the measure. (Sec. 67970, Govt. Code; Sec. 67972, Govt. Code)

Other local districts.—The following special purpose districts are authorized to impose special taxes with the approval of a two-thirds majority of the local electorate: school districts, public library districts, community college districts, community services districts, harbor districts, port districts, public cemetery districts, memorial districts, resource conservation districts, resort improvement districts, municipal utility districts, public utility districts, airport districts, the Alameda-Contra Costa Transit District, irrigation districts, and county and municipal water districts. Generally, the special taxes must be applied uniformly to all taxpayers. (Sec. 50079, Govt. Code; Sec. 53717, Govt. Code; Sec. 50079.1, Govt. Code; Sec. 61615.1, Govt. Code; Sec. 6092.5, Harb. & Nav. Code; Sec. 6364, Harb. & Nav. Code; Sec. 8981.5, Hlth. & Sfty. Code; Sec. 1192.5, Mil. & Vets. Code; Sec. 9513, Pub. Res. Code; Sec. 13161.5, Pub. Res. Code; Sec. 12891.5, Pub. Util. Code; Sec. 16641.5, Pub. Util. Code; Sec. 22909, Pub. Util. Code; Sec. 25892.1, Pub. Util. Code; Sec. 22078.5, Water Code; Sec. 31653, Water Code; Sec. 72090.5, Water Code)

San Diego County Justice Facilities Financing Act.—The San Diego County Justice Facilities Financing Act authorizes the board of supervisors of San Diego County to impose a 0.5% transactions and use tax with the approval of two-thirds of the qualified voters voting in an election on the measure. Revenues generated by the tax are to be used solely for the provision, construction, and operation of justice facilities, the funding of law enforcement and crime prevention projects, the costs incurred to conduct a special election on the measure, and the costs of any legal action incurred by the county in connection with the tax. (Sec. 7286.30, Rev. & Tax. Code—Sec. 7286.38, Rev. & Tax. Code)

• *Graffiti tax*

Any city, county, or city and county may levy a tax, with the approval of two-thirds of the voters, on sales of aerosol paint containers, containers of any other marking substance, felt-tip markers, and any other marking instrument. The tax may not exceed ten cents per container of aerosol paint or other marking substance, and five cents per felt-tip marker or other marking instrument. (Sec. 7287, Rev. & Tax. Code—Sec. 7287.10, Rev. & Tax. Code)

• *Calexico hospital district tax*

The city of Calexico is authorized to impose a 0.5% transactions and use tax for the Heffernan Memorial Hospital District. (Sec. 7286.20, Rev. & Tax. Code)

• *Avalon hospital tax*

The city of Avalon may impose a 0.5% transactions and use tax to be used exclusively for the Avalon Municipal Hospital and Clinic if an ordinance or resolution proposing the tax is approved by a majority vote of the city council and by two-thirds of the voters of the city voting on the issue. (Sec. 7286.25, Rev. & Tax. Code; Sec. 7286.26, Rev. & Tax. Code)

However, the tax may not be submitted for voter approval until every tax imposed by the City of Avalon that was not previously approved by the voters in a manner consistent with the California Supreme Court's opinion in *Santa Clara County Local Transportation Authority v. Guardino* is placed before the voters for continued approval or rescission. In *Guardino*, the Supreme Court upheld Proposition 62 provisions that require a majority of voters to pass a new or increased general tax and a two-thirds vote of the voters to approve a special tax. (*Santa Clara County Local Transportation Authority v. Guardino*, 11 CalApp4th 220 (1995))

• *Special tax measures must include accountability requirements*

Any local California special tax measure that is subject to voter approval and would provide for imposition of a special tax by a local agency must include accountability measures that include, but are not limited to the following measures:

— a statement indicating the specific purposes of the special tax;

— a statement indicating the specific purposes of the special tax;

— the creation of an account into which the proceeds must be deposited; and

— a requirement that the chief fiscal officer of the local agency provide a report at least annually that states the amount of funds collected and expended and the status of any project required or authorized to be funded with the tax proceeds.

(Sec. 50075.1, Govt. Code; Sec. 50075.3, Govt. Code)

For purposes of these requirements, "local agency" means any city, county, or city and county, including a charter city or county, or any special district. A "special district" is an agency of the state formed pursuant to general law or a special act for the performance of governmental or proprietary functions, with limited geographic boundaries, including but not limited to a school district and a community college district. (Sec. 50075.1, Govt. Code; Sec. 50075.3, Govt. Code)

• *Petition for redistribution of local or district tax*

There is a process for the review by the CDTFA of requests by local jurisdictions to investigate suspected misallocation of local sales and use taxes imposed under the Bradley-Burns Uniform Local Sales and Use Tax Law as well as suspected improper distribution or nondistribution of district transactions and use taxes. (Reg. 35056, 18 CCR)

• *Transient occupancy tax*

Certain redevelopment agencies and the legislative bodies of cities and counties may impose transient occupancy taxes for short-term hotel, motel, tourist home, and mobile home lodgings. (Sec. 7280, Rev. & Tax. Code; Sec. 7280.5, Rev. & Tax. Code; Sec. 7281, Rev. & Tax. Code) The authority to impose transient occupancy taxes does not, however, extend to campsites located in state parks. (Sec. 7282, Rev. & Tax. Code)

Furthermore, a city, county, city or county, or charter city may not levy the transient occupancy tax on any food products already subject to sales and use tax. In this context, "food products" means food and beverages of every kind, regardless of how or where served. In addition, the term "food products" specifically includes but is not limited to alcoholic beverages and carbonated beverages of every kind. (Sec. 7282.3, Rev. & Tax. Code)

• *Proposition 11*

In the general election of November 3, 1998, California voters approved Proposition 11, which amends the California Constitution, authorizing local jurisdictions to engage in contract with each other to apportion local sales and use taxes derived from the Bradley-Burns Local Sales and Use Tax Law (Sec. 7202, Rev. & Tax. Code) or any successor provision. Contractual apportionment of such revenue is subject to a two-thirds majority vote approval of the ordinance or resolution that proposes the apportionment, by the governing body of each jurisdiction that is a party to the contract. (Sec. 29, Art. XIII, Cal. Const.)

The state legislature may also authorize contractual sales and use tax apportionment between counties, cities and counties, and cities, subject to majority approval by the voting electorate in each jurisdiction at a general or primary election. Local jurisdictional authority to engage in such contracts was limited to these prerequisites prior to the November 3, 1998 general election. (Sec. 29, Art. XIII, Cal. Const.)

• *Proposition 13*

Cities, counties, and special districts may impose special taxes, subject to a two-thirds vote of the electorate; (Sec. 4, Art. XIIIA, Cal. Const.; Sec. 50075, Govt. Code; Sec. 23027, Govt. Code) however, no transactions (sales) or use taxes on the sale of real property may be imposed within such cities, counties, or special districts. (Sec. 4, Art. XIIIA, Cal. Const.)

The California Supreme Court held in 1982 that the special districts referred to in Sec. 4, Art. XIIIA, of the California Constitution (Proposition 13), were only those districts with power to levy a tax on real property. (*Los Angeles County Transportation Commission v. Richmond*, 31 Cal3d 197, 643 P2d 941 (1982)) However, in 1991, the California Supreme Court construed the term "special district" to include any local taxing agency, whether or not it has property-taxing power, if it was created after the passage of Proposition 13 to raise funds for city or county purposes to replace revenues foregone because of Proposition 13's restrictions on property taxation. (*Rider v. County of San Diego*, 1 Cal4th 1, 1 CalRptr2d 490 (1991)) The law defines the term "district" as a state agency formed for the local performance of governmental or proprietary functions within limited boundaries. (Sec. 50075, Govt. Code)

The court also has held that special taxes requiring a two-thirds vote of the electorate are those taxes that are levied for a specific purpose rather than those placed in the general fund to be utilized for general governmental purposes. Consequently, a payroll and gross receipts tax imposed by a city on businesses within its boundaries was not a special tax and did not need two-thirds voter approval, because it was not levied for a special purpose. The proceeds of the payroll and gross receipts tax were to be placed in the city's general fund and used for general city governmental purposes. The law states that the term "special tax" does not include any fee that does not exceed the reasonable cost of providing the service or regulatory activity for which the fee is charged and that is not levied for general revenue purposes. (Sec. 50076, Govt. Code)

The supermajority voter approval requirement also does not apply to any retail transactions (sales) and use tax imposed by an ordinance that was adopted by a transportation agency organized under the Public Utilities Code and approved prior to December 19, 1991, by a majority of the voters. (Sec. 99550, Pub. Util. Code)

¶61-710

Accountability requirements.—Any local California special tax measure that is subject to voter approval and would provide for imposition of a special tax by a local agency must include accountability measures that include, but are not limited to the following measures:

— a statement indicating the specific purposes of the special tax;

— a requirement that the proceeds be applied only to the stated specific purposes;

— the creation of an account into which the proceeds must be deposited; and

— a requirement that the chief fiscal officer of the local agency provide a report at least annually that states the amount of funds collected and expended and the status of any project required or authorized to be funded with the tax proceeds.

(Sec. 50075.1, Govt. Code; Sec. 50075.3, Govt. Code)

For purposes of these requirements, "local agency" means any city, county, or city and county, including a charter city or county, or any special district. A "special district" is an agency of the state formed pursuant to general law or a special act for the performance of governmental or proprietary functions, with limited geographic boundaries, including but not limited to a school district and a community college district. (Sec. 50075.1, Govt. Code; Sec. 50075.3, Govt. Code)

• *Proposition 62*

In the general election on November 4, 1986, California voters approved Proposition 62, which amended the Government Code to provide that any new or higher general tax must be approved by two-thirds of a local government's or district's legislative body and by a majority of the voters. Also, any new or higher special tax had to be approved by at least two-thirds of the voters. Finally, local governments and districts were required to stop collecting any new or higher taxes that were adopted during the so-called "window period" from August 1, 1985, to November 5, 1986, the date of adoption of Proposition 62, unless such taxes were approved by a majority of the electorate within two years of the adoption of the proposition. (Sec. 53720, Govt. Code)

The California Supreme Court has held that Proposition 62 is constitutional to the extent that it requires a majority of the voting electorate to pass a new or increased general tax, and a two-thirds majority vote of the voting electorate to approve a special tax. However, the California Supreme Court has not ruled on the constitutionality of the provision that requires voters to approve those taxes in existance prior to Proposition 62's passage during the "window period" discussed above. A California appellate court concluded that the "window period" provision was invalid because it required voters to approve an already existing tax and, thus, amounted to an unconstitutional referendum on a tax. (*City of Westminster v. County of Orange*, 204 CalApp3d 623 (1988))

• *Proposition 218*

In the general election on November 5, 1996, California voters approved Proposition 218, which added provisions to the California Constitution to: (1) prohibit all local governments, including charter cities, from imposing, extending, or increasing any general tax after November 5, 1996, without the approval of a majority of the local electorate; and (2) require that any general tax imposed, extended, or increased from January 1, 1995, through November 5, 1996, by any local government without voter approval be submitted to voters for approval by November 6, 1998, and be approved by a majority of the voters in order for the tax to continue to be imposed.

Proposition 218 also reiterated that a local government may not impose, extend, or increase any special tax until the tax is submitted to the voters and approved by a two-thirds vote. (Sec. 2, Art. XIIIC, Cal. Const.)

"Tax" is defined to mean any levy, charge, or exaction of any kind imposed by a local government, except:

— a charge imposed for a specific benefit conferred or privilege granted directly to the payor that is not provided to those not charged, and which does not exceed the reasonable costs to the local government of conferring the benefit or granting the privilege;

— a charge imposed for a specific government service or product provided directly to the payor that is not provided to those not charged, and which does not exceed the reasonable costs to the local government of providing the service or product;

— a charge imposed for the reasonable regulatory costs to a local government for issuing licenses and permits, performing investigations, inspections, and audits, enforcing agricultural marketing orders, and the administrative enforcement and adjudication thereof;

— a charge imposed for entrance to or use of local government property, or the purchase, rental, or lease of local government property;

— a fine, penalty, or other monetary charge imposed by the judicial branch of government or a local government, as a result of a violation of law;

— a charge imposed as a condition of property development; and

— assessments and property-related fees imposed in accordance with the provisions of Art. XIII D.

(Sec. 3, Art. XIII C, Cal. Const.)

An ordinance or resolution presented for voter approval pursuant to the requirements of Proposition 218 may propose a range of tax rates or amounts and may provide for inflation adjustments to those rates or amounts, provided that if a rate or amount is determined by using a percentage calculation, the ordinance or resolution may not provide for inflation adjustments to the percentage. A general or special tax will not be deemed to have been increased if it is imposed at a rate or amount not higher than the maximum rate approved by the electorate. (Sec. 2, Art. XIIIC, Cal. Const.; Sec. 53739, Govt. Code)

Under Proposition 218, all taxes imposed by local governments are deemed to be either general taxes or special taxes, and special purpose districts or agencies, including school districts, are without power to levy general taxes. (Sec. 2, Art. XIIIC, Cal. Const.)

Finally, notwithstanding any other provision of the California Constitution, there must not be any limitation on the use of the initiative power to reduce or repeal any local tax, assessment, fee, or charge. Also, neither the legislature nor any local government charter may impose a signature requirement for local initiatives that is higher than that applicable to statewide statutory initiatives. (Sec. 3, Art. XIIIC, Cal. Const.)

• *Administration of local taxes*

Prior to the adoption of conforming legislation, the local taxing jurisdiction must contract with the Department of Tax and Fee Administration (CDTFA) to administer the ordinance. An amount equal to 0.82% of the taxes collected is retained by the CDTFA for administrative expenses. (Sec. 7202, Rev. & Tax. Code; Reg. 1803, 18 CCR) Similar provisions require jurisdictions imposing a transactions and use tax to contract with the CDTFA for administration and collection of the tax. (Sec. 7270, Rev. & Tax. Code; Reg. 1823, 18 CCR)

The California Department of Tax and Fee Administration (CDTFA) provides a guide to CDTFA services. (*CDTFA Publication 51, Board of Equalization Resource Guide to Free Tax Products and Services*, California Department of Tax and Fee Administration)

The CDTFA must terminate its contract with a city, county, or city and county if that taxing entity imposes a similar sales or use tax in addition to that authorized by and conforming to state law. (Sec. 7203.5, Rev. & Tax. Code)

Furthermore, if the prohibition against a city, county, city and county, or charter city levying the transient occupancy tax on any food products already subject to sales and use tax is held to be inapplicable to charter cities, the CDTFA must terminate its contract for administration with a city, county, or city and county that imposes a tax on the privilege of occupying a room or rooms in a hotel, motel, bed and breakfast inn or similar transient lodging establishment if:

— the lodging establishment provides food products to its guests;

— the cost of the food products is included in the price of the transient occupancy accommodation;

— that portion of the price for the transient occupancy accommodation that is allocable to the food products is subject to sales or use tax and local tax upon occupancy; and

— the operator of the establishment provides a specified allocation of the value of the food products.

(Sec. 7203.5, Rev. & Tax. Code)

"Food products" means food and beverages of every kind, regardless of how or where served, and specifically includes, but is not limited to, alcoholic beverages and carbonated beverages of every kind. A "hotel," "motel," "bed and breakfast inn," or "similar transient lodging establishment" is an establishment containing guest room accommodations with respect to which the predominant relationship existing between the occupants thereof and the owner or operator of the establishment is that of innkeeper and guest. (Sec. 7282.3, Rev. & Tax. Code)

Obligation of the retailer to collect.—A seller doing business in a transactions tax district is not required to collect use tax unless the seller ships or delivers the property into the district or participates in the sale there. However, according to the regulation, a retailer must collect use tax if the retailer delivers property outside the district to a purchaser known by the retailer to be a resident of a district imposing the tax, if the retailer is in business in that district and takes part in the sale. The presumption that the property is to be used in a taxing jurisdiction may be refuted by a written statement from the buyer, or other evidence satisfactory to the CDTFA, that the property will be used in a nontaxing district. (Reg. 1827, 18 CCR)

"Retailers engaged in business in the district," for transactions and use tax purposes, are defined as any of the following:

— any retailer maintaining, occupying, or using, permanently or temporarily, directly or indirectly, or through a subsidiary or agent, by whatever name called, an office, place of distribution, sales or sample room or place, warehouse or storage place, or other place of business in the district;

— any retailer having any representative, agent, salesman, canvasser, or solicitor operating in the district under the authority of the retailer or its subsidiary for the purpose of selling, delivering, or the taking of orders for any tangible personal property;

— as respects a lease, any retailer deriving rentals from a lease of tangible personal property situated in the district;

— any retailer of vehicles subject to registration pursuant to Chapter 1 (commencing with Section 4000) of Division 3 of the Vehicle Code, aircraft licensed in compliance with Section 21411 of the Public Utilities Code, or undocumented vessels registered under Article 2 (commencing with Section 680) of Chapter 5 of Division 3 of the Harbors and Navigation Code.

(Reg. 1827, 18 CCR)

Retailers not doing business in the district may obtain a Certificate of Registration—Use Tax, requiring the holder to collect use tax and pay it to the board. (Sec. 7262, Rev. & Tax. Code)

Retailers holding permits under the state law are not required to obtain additional local permits. (Sec. 7202, Rev. & Tax. Code)

[¶61-735] Local Tax Rates

California has many special taxing jurisdictions that are funded by a transactions (sales) and use tax rate that is added to the standard statewide rate. The tax rates for these districts range from 0.10% to 2% per district. In some areas, there is more than one district tax in effect, and in others, there is no district tax in effect. Local sales and use taxes are authorized by the Bradley-Burns Uniform Local Sales and Use Tax Law.

Taxpayers may find current local sales and use tax rates at http://cdtfa.ca.gov/taxes-and-fees/sales-use-tax-rates.htm.

The term "local tax" is the general term for sales and use taxes imposed under the Bradley-Burns Uniform Sales and Use Tax Law. See Rate of Tax, for the current state tax rate. (Sec. 7200, Rev. & Tax. Code—Sec. 7212, Rev. & Tax. Code)

In addition, "district taxes" are imposed locally under the Transactions and Use Tax Law within the boundaries of various transit, traffic, or other districts where allowed by state law. As a consequence of these special taxing jurisdictions (districts) that are funded by a transactions (sales) and use tax rate that is added to the standard statewide rate, the tax rate in a particular area in California may be higher than the standard statewide rate depending on whether a district tax applies. Moreover, there is more than one district tax in some areas while there is no district tax in effect in other areas. (*California City and County Sales and Use Tax Rates*, California Department of Tax and Fee Administration)

Local and district taxes collected within each county are reported on *Form CDTFA-401-A, State, Local, and District Sales and Use Tax Return* and *Form CDTFA-531-A2, Schedule A2, Computation Schedule for District Tax—Long Form*. (*CDTFA Publication 44, District Taxes (Sales and Use Taxes)*, California Department of Tax and Fee Administration)

• *Recent rate changes*

Recent rate changes are discussed.

Rate changes effective October 1, 2020.—California announced new local (district) sales and use tax rates effective October 1, 2020. The rate changes apply only within the indicated city limits. The following are new citywide local (district) sales and use tax rates:

• Blythe, located in Riverside County, increases its tax rate from 7.75% to 8.75%;

• Hawaiian Gardens, located in Los Angeles County, increases its tax rate from 9.5% to 10.25%; and

• Vernon, located in Los Angeles County, increases its tax rate from 9.5% to 10.25%.

(*Special Notice L-761*, California Department of Tax and Fee Administration, August 2020)

Rate changes effective July 1, 2020.—California announced new local (district) sales and use tax rates effective July 1, 2020. The rate changes apply only within the indicated city limits. (*Special Notice L-743 REV.1*, California Department of Tax and Fee Administration, May 2020)

The following are new citywide local (district) sales and use tax rates:

• Alhambra, located in Los Angeles County, increases its tax rate from 9.5% to 10.25%;

• Azusa, located in Los Angeles County, increases its tax rate from 9.5% 10.25%;

• Carmel-by-the-Sea, located in Monterey County, increases its tax rate from 8.75% to 9.25%;

• Duarte, located in Los Angeles County, increases its tax rate from 9.5% to 10.25%;

• Emeryville, located in Alameda County, increases its tax rate from 9.25% to 10%;

• Gardena, located in Los Angeles County, increases its tax rate from 9.5% to 10.25%;

• Lakewood, located in Los Angeles County, increases its tax rate from 9.5% to 10.25%;

• La Verne, located in Los Angeles County, increases its tax rate from 9.5% to 10.25%;

• Lompoc, located in Santa Barbara County, increases its tax rate from 7.75% to 8.75%;

• Montebello, located in Los Angeles County, increases its tax rate from 9.5% to 10.25%;

• Monterey, located in Monterey County, increases its tax rate from 8.75% to 9.25%;

• Norwalk, located in Los Angeles County, increases its tax rate from 9.5% to 10.25%;

• Paramount, located in Los Angeles County, increases its tax rate from 9.5% to 10.25%;

• Reedley, located in Fresno County, increases its tax rate from 8.475% to 9.225%;

• San Gabriel, located in Los Angeles County, increases its tax rate from 9.5% to 10.25%;

• Scotts Valley, located in Santa Cruz County, increases its tax rate from 9% to 9.75%; and

• Whittier, located in Los Angeles County, increases its tax rate from 9.5% to 10.25%.

(*Special Notice L-743 REV.1*, California Department of Tax and Fee Administration, May 2020)

The following citywide local (district) sales and use tax rates are extended:

- the 10.25% tax rate imposed in Culver City, located in Los Angeles County, is extended until March 31, 2033;

- the 8.25% tax rate imposed in Davis, located in Yolo County, is extended indefinitely;

- the 9.25% tax rate imposed in Del Rey Oaks, located in Monterey County, is extended indefinitely; and

- the 9.25% tax rate imposed in Watsonville, located in Santa Cruz County, is likewise extended indefinitely.

(*Special Notice L-743 REV.1*, California Department of Tax and Fee Administration, May 2020)

The CDTFA advises that the 0.50% Alameda County tax proposed by Measure C on the March 3, 2020, ballot is subject to pending litigation and is not included on the special notice. Information regarding this tax will be updated if it becomes operative. (*Special Notice L-743 REV.1*, California Department of Tax and Fee Administration, May 2020)

• *Ballot Measure M (Los Angeles County Traffic Improvement Plan)*

Voters approved Ballot Measure M on November 8, 2016. The measure authorizes the Los Angeles County Traffic Improvement Plan, which imposes a 0.5% sales tax and continues the existing 0.5% traffic relief tax until voters decide to end it (originally set to expire in 2039). According to the Los Angeles County Counsel, the approval of Measure M adopted the ordinance known as the "Los Angeles County Traffic Improvement Plan" ("ordinance") proposed by the Los Angeles County Metropolitan Transportation Authority ("Metro"), which placed the measure on the ballot by resolution dated June 23, 2016. (Los Angeles County Counsel, January 24, 2017)

The ordinance imposes a retail transactions and use tax at the rate of 0.5% within Los Angeles County beginning on the first day of the first calendar quarter commencing not less than 180 days after adoption of the ordinance. The sales tax will increase to 1% on July 1, 2039, when the Measure R tax of 0.5% tax imposed by Metro by Ordinance number 08-01 expires. The sales tax is in addition to any other taxes authorized by law, and has no expiration date. (Los Angeles County Counsel, January 24, 2017)

The Measure M Ordinance states: "Prior to the operative date, Metro shall contract with the Board of Equalization to perform all functions incident to the administration and operation of this Ordinance; provided, that if Metro shall not have contracted with the Board of Equalization prior to the operative date, it shall nevertheless so contract and in such a case the operative date shall be the first day of the first calendar quarter following the execution of such a contract." The ordinance was adopted by voters in November of 2016. (Los Angeles County Counsel, January 24, 2017)

Measure M sales tax will increase to 1% on July 1, 2039, when the Measure R tax of 0.5% tax imposed by Metro by Ordinance Number 08-01 expires. (Los Angeles County Counsel, January 24, 2017)

The 0.50% California sales and use tax rate increase, as provided by Ballot Measure M and operative July 1, 2017, applies to the county of Los Angeles, including all cities and unincorporated areas. (*Special Notice L-499*, California State Board of Equalization, May 2017)

Operative July 1, 2017, the sales and use tax rate changes in Los Angeles County and areas and cities within the county are as follows:

— an increase from 8.75% to 9.25% in Los Angeles County (the 9.25% tax rate applies to all unincorporated areas and cities, and the incorporated cities that do not have city district taxes);

— an increase from 9.25% to 9.75% in the cities of Avalon, Commerce, Culver City, Downey, El Monte, Inglewood, San Fernando, and South El Monte;

— an increase from 9.75% to 10.25% in the cities of Compton, La Mirada, Long Beach, Lynwood, Pico Rivera, Santa Monica, and South Gate.

(*Special Notice L-499*, California State Board of Equalization, May 2017)

Incorporated cities in Los Angeles County that do not have city district taxes are: Agoura Hills, Alhambra, Arcadia, Artesia, Azusa, Baldwin Park, Bell, Bell Gardens, Bellflower, Beverly Hills, Bradbury, Burbank, Calabasas, Carson, Cerritos, City of Industry, Claremont, Covina, Cudahy, Diamond Bar, Duarte, El Segundo, Gardena, Glendale, Glendora, Hawaiian Gardens, Hawthorne, Hermosa Beach, Hidden Hills, Huntington Park, Irwindale, La Canada-Flintridge, La Habra Heights, La Puente, La Verne, Lakewood, Lancaster, Lawndale, Lomita, Los Angeles, Malibu, Manhattan Beach, Maywood, Monrovia, Montebello, Monterey Park, Norwalk, Palmdale, Palos Verdes Estates, Paramount, Pasadena, Pomona, Rancho Palos Verdes, Redondo Beach, Rolling Hills, Rolling Hills Estates, Rosemead, San Dimas, San Gabriel, San Marino, Santa Clarita, Santa Fe Springs, Sierra Madre, Signal Hill, South Pasadena, Temple City, Torrance, Vernon, View Park, Walnut, West Covina, West Hollywood, Westlake Village, and Whittier. (*Special Notice L-499*, California State Board of Equalization, May 2017)

The tax rates listed above do not include the rate increases approved by Measure H. (*Special Notice L-499*, California State Board of Equalization, May 2017)

• *Measure H*

On March 7, 2017, Los Angeles County voters approved Measure H, Sales Tax for Homeless Services and Prevention, which imposes a transactions and use tax at a rate of 0.25% for the support of countywide programs and services to prevent and combat homelessness within the incorporated and unincorporated areas of the county. The Legislature has found that the transactions and use tax (i.e., district tax) imposed by Measure H is valid and authorized and conforms to the California Transactions and Use Tax Law. (Sec. 7286.40, Rev. & Tax. Code)

The 0.25% tax is not imposed in the cities of Compton, La Mirada, Long Beach, Lynwood, Pico Rivera, Santa Monica, and South Gate because doing so would cause the rate in those cities to exceed the 10.25% maximum tax rate allowed under the law in Los Angeles County. If and when an existing tax in one of these cities expires, the Measure H tax will be imposed in that city immediately. (*News Release 17-14*, California Department of Tax and Fee Administration, September 20, 2017)

UTILITIES

[¶80-100]
PUBLIC UTILITIES TAXES AND FEES

[¶80-110] Utilities Subject to Tax

In general, the gross receipts of public utilities from the sale and service of gas, electricity, water, and derivative products are exempt from California sales and use taxes. (Sec. 6353, Rev. & Tax. Code)

California now imposes no special excise tax on public utilities. However, the state constitution authorizes the California State Board of Equalization (BOE) to centrally assess certain types of utility property. Centrally assessed (unit-valued) utility property is not subject to the 2% annual assessment increase limitation imposed under Proposition 13. However, the limitation does apply to independent generator property and to other locally assessed property.

Although the constitution prohibits other taxes on public utilities different from those imposed on other business corporations, it also provides that this restriction does not release utility companies from payments for special privileges or franchises granted by a government body. Therefore, payments by utilities to local governments as compensation for franchises to operate toll bridges, erect utility poles, etc., are not taxes. (*Tulare County v. City of Dinuba*, 188 Cal 664, 206 P 983 (1922)) These franchises are covered under the Public Utilities Code, Streets and Highways Code, and Harbors and Navigation Code.

•*Public utilities defined*

The state constitution defines "public utilities" as common carriers, and private corporations and persons that own, operate, control, or manage a line, plant or system for the transportation of people or property; the transmission of telephone or telegraph messages; or the production, generation, transmission, or furnishing of heat, light, water, power, storage, or wharfage, directly or indirectly to or for the public. (Sec. 3, Art. XII, Cal. Const.) As authorized by the constitution, the legislature has added toll bridge and sewer system corporations to the definition of "public utilities" for property tax purposes. (Sec. 216, Pub. Util. Code) Motor carriers of property are specifically excluded from the definition of "public utilities." (Sec. 216.2, Pub. Util. Code) Motor carrier taxes are discussed at ¶37-101.

•*Corporate franchise tax*

Utility companies are subject to the corporate franchise tax.

•*San Francisco tax on rides provided by transportation network companies (TNCs)*

Effective January 1, 2019, San Francisco is authorized to impose a California tax on each transportation network company (TNC) ride originating in the city and county. This authorization is pursuant to the Transportation Assistance Funding Act, and is subject to voter approval. (Sec. 5446, Pub. Util. Code)

The city and county of San Francisco may impose a tax on each ride originating in the city and county. The ride must be provided by a participating driver in an amount not to exceed:

- 1.5% of net rider fares for a shared ride in which, before the start of the ride, a passenger requests through the TNC's online-enabled application or platform to share the ride with one or more passengers, and each passenger is charged a fare that is calculated, in whole or in part, based on the passenger's request to share all or part of the ride with one or more passengers, regardless of whether the passenger actually shares all or part of the ride; and

- 3.25% of the net rider fare for any other types of rides provided by a TNC.

(Sec. 5446, Pub. Util. Code)

The city and county of San Francisco may impose a tax on each ride originating in the city and county. The ride must be provided by an autonomous vehicle, whether facilitated by a TNC or any other person, in an amount not to exceed:

- 1.5% of net rider fares for a shared ride in which, before the start of the ride, a passenger requests to share the ride with one or more passengers and each passenger is charged a fare that is calculated, in whole or in part, based on the passenger's request to share all or part of the ride with one or more passengers, regardless of whether the passenger actually shares all or part of the ride; and

- 3.25% of the net rider fare for any other types of rides provided by an autonomous vehicle.

(Sec. 5446, Pub. Util. Code)

The city and county of San Francisco may set a lower tax rate for net rider fares for a ride originating in the city and county. The ride must be provided by a zero-emission vehicle. The purpose of this provision is to further incentivize deployment of zero-emission vehicles. (Sec. 5446, Pub. Util. Code)

"Net rider fare" means all charges for a ride, including but not limited to charges based on:

- time;
- distance; or
- both.

(Sec. 5446, Pub. Util. Code)

The term excludes any additional charges such as:

- taxes;
- airport or venue fees; or
- fees imposed by the Public Utilities Commission.

(Sec. 5446, Pub. Util. Code)

A tax imposed under these provisions is subject to applicable voter approval requirements. Moreover, such a tax, if imposed, will expire no later than November 5, 2045. (Sec. 5446, Pub. Util. Code)

• *Property taxes*

The California Constitution authorizes the BOE to assess property taxes on pipelines, flumes, canals, ditches, and aqueducts lying within two or more counties, and on property, except franchises, owned or used by regulated railway, telegraph, or telephone companies, car companies operating on railways in the state, and companies transmitting or selling gas or electricity. Utility property, other than centrally assessed (unit valued) property, is subject to taxation to the same extent and in the same manner as all other property. The legislature may authorize the BOE to assess the property of other public utilities. (Sec. 19, Art. XIII, Cal. Const.)

• *Regulatory fees and utility service surcharges*

Fees charged by the Public Utilities Commission for regulating freight transportation rates and the electric utility and telephone user surcharges are discussed below. Permit or registration fees for specific carriers are covered at ¶ 37-101.

¶80-110

• *Deaf and Disabled Telecommunications Program*

The surcharge on intrastate telephone services to cover the costs for providing telecommunications devices capable of serving the needs of the deaf and hearing impaired is imposed until January 1, 2020. The surcharge, which is not to exceed 0.5%, is uniformly applied to a subscriber's intrastate telephone service, other than one-way radio paging and universal telephone services. (Sec. 2881, Pub. Util. Code)

[¶80-130] Energy Resources Surcharge

A surcharge applies to the consumption of energy resources purchased from an electric utility. This surcharge is commonly referred to as the "electrical energy surcharge." (Sec. 40016, Rev. & Tax. Code) The tax is collected by electric utilities from consumers. The surcharge rate is set yearly by the California Energy Commission (CEC) and is collected by the California Department of Tax and Fee Administration (CDTFA) and may not exceed $0.0003 per kilowatt hour. (Special Notice L-528, California Department of Tax and Fee Administration, December 2017)

• *Rate*

Effective January 1 through December 31, 2019, the electrical energy resources surcharge rate is $0.0003 (three-tenths mill) per kilowatt hour, according to the California Energy Commission (CEC). The rate was formerly set at $0.00029 (twenty-nine hundredths mill). (*Special Notice L-590*, California Department of Tax and Fee Administration, December 2018)

• *Exemptions*

The surcharge does not apply to consumption that is not subject to tax due to federal and state constitutional restrictions. (Sec. 40041, Rev. & Tax. Code) Consumption by an electric utility of purchased electrical energy that is used directly, lost by dissipation, or unaccounted for by the utility in the generation, transmission, and distribution of electrical energy, is also exempt. (Sec. 40043, Rev. & Tax. Code)

• *Reports and payments*

Returns and payments from electric utilities are due by the last day of the month following each calendar quarter. (Sec. 40051, Rev. & Tax. Code; Sec. 40061, Rev. & Tax. Code) If a return is not filed, the CDTFA may estimate the amount due and add a 10% penalty. (Sec. 40081, Rev. & Tax. Code) An additional 25% penalty applies if the failure to file is due to fraud or intent to evade the surcharge. (Sec. 40084, Rev. & Tax. Code)

Energy resources surcharge returns may be filed electronically. (Sec. 40061, Rev. & Tax. Code; Sec. 40063, Rev. & Tax. Code; Sec. 40069, Rev. & Tax. Code)

Persons whose estimated energy resources surcharge liability averages $20,000 or more per month, as determined by the CDTFA pursuant to methods of calculation prescribed by the CDTFA, must remit amounts due by electronic funds transfer (EFT). Persons whose estimated liability averages less than $20,000 per month may elect to remit amounts due by EFT with the approval of the CDTFA. The election is operative for a minimum of one year. (Sec. 40067, Rev. & Tax. Code)

• *Recordkeeping requirements*

A taxpayer must maintain and make available for examination, upon CDTFA request, records in the manner required by Reg. 4901, 18 CCR. In addition to these recordkeeping requirements, every electric utility must maintain records that show:

— the electrical energy generated, purchased, transmitted, distributed, consumed, and sold in the state;

— meter readings and other records to determine the kilowatt-hours of electrical energy generated, purchased, transmitted, distributed, consumed, and sold in the state;

— all deductions claimed in filing returns, except for the electrical energy used or lost in generation, transmission, and/or distribution; and

— the methods and amounts used in computing its reports of estimates of future availability, generation, sales, and consumption of electrical energy. (Reg. 2343, 18 CCR)

• *Refunds*

Any amount erroneously or illegally collected is credited against amounts due and any balance is refunded to the person from whom it was collected. Any overpayment by a consumer to the state is credited or refunded by the state to the consumer. Any overpayment by a consumer to an electric utility required to collect the surcharge is also refunded by the state to the consumer. However, if an electric utility has paid the CDTFA the amount due, and has not collected the amount due from the consumer or has refunded the amount to the consumer, the overpayment may be credited or refunded by the state to the electric utility. A refund will not be approved after three years from the last day of the month following the close of the quarterly period for which the overpayment was made, unless a claim is filed within that time. If the CDTFA determines the amount due when a return has not been filed, or if there is a deficiency determination, no refund will be made after six months from the date the determination becomes final or after six months from the date of overpayment, whichever is later, unless a claim is filed within that time. (Sec. 40111, Rev. & Tax. Code; Sec. 40112, Rev. & Tax. Code)

A suit for refund cannot be maintained in court unless a claim for refund has been filed. (Sec. 40126, Rev. & Tax. Code) A suit can be brought within 90 days after the mailing of the notice of the CDTFA's action on the refund claim, or six months after the refund claim is filed if no notice is mailed within that time. (Sec. 40127, Rev. & Tax. Code; Sec. 40128, Rev. & Tax. Code)

Taxpayers requesting deferral of a refund claim action may be required to waive refund interest credit for the period of time action on the refund claim is deferred. (Sec. 40117, Rev. & Tax. Code)

• *Managed audits*

Taxpayers may voluntarily participate in managed audits of qualifying energy resources surcharge accounts with the CDTFA. (Sec. 40177, Rev. & Tax. Code, *et seq.*) An account will qualify for managed audits if:

— the taxpayer's business involves few or no statutory exemptions;

— the taxpayer's business involves a single or a small number of clearly defined taxability issues;

— the taxpayer is taxed pursuant to a qualifying tax or fee law at issue and agrees to participate in the program; and

— the taxpayer has the resources to comply with the managed audit instructions provided by the CDTFA.

(Sec. 40177.1, Rev. & Tax. Code)

A taxpayer wishing to participate in the program must examine its books and records to determine if it has any unreported tax liability for the audit period and make available to the CDTFA for verification all computations and books and records examined. (Sec. 40177(a)(2), Rev. & Tax. Code) After the audit is verified by the CDTFA, interest on any unpaid liability will be imposed at 1/2 the rate that would otherwise be imposed during the audit period. (Sec. 40177.4, Rev. & Tax. Code)

¶80-130

• *Taxpayer remedies*

Waiver of penalties.—Persons may be relieved from the liability of payment of the energy resources surcharge, including any interest or penalties, when their liability resulted from a failure to timely file a return or make a payment and that failure is found by the CDTFA to be due to reasonable reliance on written advice given by the CDTFA in a manner prescribed by Reg. 4902, 18 CCR. (Reg. 2343, 18 CCR) Penalties for the late payment of an energy resources surcharge or the late filing of a return may be waived without a showing of reasonable cause for tardiness under criteria to be developed by the CDTFA. (Sec. 40102, Rev. & Tax. Code) The goal of the criteria must be to foster efficient resolution of requests for relief from penalties. The CDTFA may not require taxpayers to file statements supporting their claims for relief under penalty of perjury, as is the case when a person seeks waiver under a claim of reasonable cause for tardiness.

Relief from California special tax and fee liabilities is extended to provide relief due to reasonable reliance on written advice from the CDTFA to a person who relies on advice provided in a prior audit of a related person, under specific circumstances. Written advice from the CDTFA that was received during a prior audit of the person, as provided, may be relied upon by the person audited or a person with shared accounting and common ownership with the audited person or by a legal or statutory successor to those persons. A person is considered to have shared accounting and common ownership if the person:

— is engaged in the same line of business as the audited person;

— has common verifiable controlling ownership of 50% or greater ownership or has a common majority shareholder with the audited person; and

— shares centralized accounting functions with the audited person (i.e., the audited person routinely follows the same business practices that are followed by each entity involved).

(Reg. 4902, 18 CCR)

Evidence that may indicate sharing of centralized accounting functions includes, but is not limited to:

— quantifiable control of the accounting practices of each business by the common ownership or management that dictates office policies for accounting and tax return preparation;

— shared accounting staff or an outside firm that maintains books and records and prepares returns for special tax and fee programs, as provided; and

— shared accounting policies and procedures.

(Reg. 4902, 18 CCR)

In addition, the taxpayer is required to establish that these requirements existed during the periods for which relief is sought. A subsequent written notification from the CDTFA that provides that the advice was not valid at the time it was issued, or was subsequently rendered invalid to any party with shared accounting and common ownership, including the audited party, serves as notification to all parties with shared accounting and common ownership, including the audited party, that the prior written advice may not be relied upon as of the notification date. (Reg. 4902, 18 CCR)

A taxpayer may be relieved of penalties for late payment of an energy resources surcharge if the taxpayer enters into an installment plan for paying the surcharge within 45 days after a notice of determination or redetermination is final. (Sec. 40167, Rev. & Tax. Code) The taxpayer must comply with the agreement for the waiver to remain effective, and waiver may not be granted in cases of fraud.

Statement itemizing installment payments.—Taxpayers that have entered into installment agreements to pay an energy resources surcharge must receive an annual statement from the CDTFA itemizing the balance of the surcharge owed at the beginning and end of a year and the amount of the surcharge paid during the year. (Sec. 40167.5, Rev. & Tax. Code)

Refund claims by the disabled.—The limitations period for filing refund claims for energy resources surcharges is suspended during the period that a person is unable to manage financial affairs because of a physical or mental impairment that is life threatening or that is expected to last for at least 12 months. (Sec. 40112.1, Rev. & Tax. Code) There is no waiver for individuals who are represented in their financial matters by their spouses or other persons.

Cost reimbursements for unreasonable assessments.—Taxpayers that have been unreasonably assessed an energy resources surcharge by the CDTFA are entitled to reimbursement of their fees and expenses for attending CDTFA hearings. (Sec. 40209, Rev. & Tax. Code) They may be reimbursed for costs incurred as of the filing of a notice of determination, jeopardy determination, or refund claim.

Employer withholding order.—An employer that has been ordered by the CDTFA to withhold wages from an employee to satisfy the employee's debt for an unpaid energy resources surcharge, but that has failed to remit the withheld amount to the CDTFA, may be held liable by the CDTFA for the unremitted amount, which may be treated as a surcharge deficiency of the employer. (Sec. 40156, Rev. & Tax. Code) The CDTFA has seven years from the first day on which the employer withheld wages from an employee to assess the deficiency, with interest. The employee's liability for the surcharge must be credited for the unremitted amount and no further action may be taken to collect that sum from the employee.

Confidentiality of surcharge information.—Preparers of energy resources surcharge returns that, without a client's consent, knowingly or recklessly disclose the client's confidential surcharge information for any purpose other than return preparation may be convicted of a misdemeanor, fined up to $1,000, and imprisoned for up to one year. (Sec. 40176, Rev. & Tax. Code) A preparer also may be liable for prosecution costs.

[¶80-140] Emergency Telephone Users Surcharge

Applicable January 1, 2020, an Emergency Telephone Users (911) Surcharge is imposed on purchasers (consumers) of prepaid mobile telephony services (MTS) at a flat rate. Sellers of prepaid MTS are required to collect, report, and pay the 911 Surcharge on each purchase made by a prepaid MTS consumer. The 911 Surcharge is due on each retail transaction that involves a sale of prepaid MTS. The amount of the 911 Surcharge and local charges (if applicable) must be separately stated on an invoice, receipt, or other similar document provided to the prepaid consumer of MTS by the seller, or otherwise disclosed electronically to the prepaid consumer, at the time of the retail transaction. (Sec. 41020, Rev. & Tax. Code; Sec. 41028, Rev. & Tax. Code)

The Local Prepaid MTS Collection Act, which requires sellers of prepaid MTS to collect applicable local charges on their sales of prepaid MTS, is extended through December 31, 2020. Sellers of prepaid MTS at retail location(s) in areas with an applicable local charge or sellers that make sales made online or remotely to California customers in areas with local charges that have retail sales of prepaid MTS of more than $15,000 in the prior calendar year must continue to collect the local charges on sales of prepaid MTS through December 31, 2020. (*Special Notice L-713*, California Department of Tax and Fee Administration, October 2019)

Applicable January 1, 2020, service suppliers will collect the Emergency Telephone Users (911) Surcharge based on:

- Each access line a service user subscribes for use in California each month or partial month.

- Each purchase of prepaid mobile telephony services (MTS) by a prepaid MTS consumer for each retail transaction in California.

(*Special Notice L-703*, California Department of Tax and Fee Administration, September 2019)

Formerly (prior to January 1, 2020) the surcharge was percentage-based. Effective January 1, 2020, the surcharge is imposed at a flat rate. (*Special Notice L-703*, California Department of Tax and Fee Administration, September 2019)

The California Governor's Office of Emergency Services (Cal OES) determines the surcharge rate amount annually by October 1 each year and the rate is effective on January 1 of the following year. The surcharge rate will not exceed $0.80 per access line or retail transaction and is subject to a minimum of 0.5%. (Sec. 41030, Rev. & Tax. Code; *Special Notice L-703*, California Department of Tax and Fee Administration, September 2019)

Current rate.—Effective for calendar year 2020, the emergency telephone users surcharge amount for each access line a service user subscribes for use in California, and for each retail transaction of prepaid mobile telephony services purchased in California is $0.30. (*Emergency Telephone Users Surcharge and Prepaid 911 Surcharge for Telecommunication Service Suppliers*, California Department of Tax and Fee Administration, October 2019)

Sourcing.—Sourcing rules for mobile telecommunication services conform to the Mobile Telecommunication Sourcing Act (P.L. 106-252). In accordance with these rules, relevant terminology for the imposition of surcharges and fees is uniformly defined and the surcharges or fees do not apply for mobile telecommunication services provided to a customer whose primary place of use is outside the state. (Sec. 247.1, Public Utilities Code)

• *Applicable definitions*

The following definitions apply.

Access line.—Applicable January 1, 2020, an "access line" means any of the following:

- a wireline communication service line;

- a wireless communications service line, excluding prepaid wireless; or

- a VoIP service line.

(Sec. 41007.1, Rev. & Tax. Code; *2019 Emergency Telephone Users Surcharge Rate Meeting Minutes*, California Department of Tax and Fee Administration, October 25, 2018)

Prepaid mobile telephony services.—Effective July 1, 2019, "prepaid mobile telephony services" means the right to use a mobile device for mobile telecommunications services or information service, or both telecommunications services and information services, that must be purchased in advance of usage in predetermined units or dollars. (Sec. 41007.5, Rev. & Tax. Code)

Service supplier.—Applicable January 1, 2020, a "service supplier" is any person supplying an access line to a service user in California. Service suppliers that sell prepaid MTS are required to collect the 911 surcharge from their prepaid consumers on each retail transaction. (Sec. 41007, Rev. & Tax. Code; *2019 Emergency Telephone Users Surcharge Rate Meeting Minutes*, California Department of Tax and Fee Administration, October 25, 2018)

Service user.—Applicable January 1, 2020, a "service user" is any person that subscribes for the right to utilize an access line in California. (*2019 Emergency Telephone Users Surcharge Rate Meeting Minutes*, California Department of Tax and Fee Administration, October 25, 2018)

VoIP service.—Applicable January 1, 2020, "VoIP service" means any service that does all of the following:

> — enables real-time, two-way voice communication that originates from and terminates to the user's location using Internet Protocol (IP) or any successor protocol;

> — requires a broadband connection from the user's location; and

> — permits users, generally, to receive calls that originate on the public switched telephone network and to terminate calls to the public switched telephone network.

(Sec. 41016.5, Rev. & Tax. Code; *2019 Emergency Telephone Users Surcharge Rate Meeting Minutes*, California Department of Tax and Fee Administration, October 25, 2018)

Moreover, such service does at least one of the following:

> • requires Internet Protocol-compatible customer premises equipment (CPE);

> • when necessary, is converted to or from transmission control protocol (TCP)/IP by the service user's service supplier before or after being switched by the public switched telephone network; or

> • is a service that the Federal Communications Commission (FCC) has affirmatively required to provide 911 service.

(Sec. 41016.5, Rev. & Tax. Code; *2019 Emergency Telephone Users Surcharge Rate Meeting Minutes*, California Department of Tax and Fee Administration, October 25, 2018)

• *Exemptions*

Applicable January 1, 2020, there are exempt from the Emergency Telephone Users (911) Surcharge the following access lines and nonaccess line services:

> — those lines supplying lifeline service;

> — those lines connected to public telephones; and

> — those lines for which no charges are billed by a service supplier to a service user.

(Sec. 41046, Rev. & Tax. Code)

The surcharge is not applied in violation of the federal Constitution, federal law, or state law. (Sec. 41027, Rev. & Tax. Code; Sec. 41003, Rev. & Tax. Code)

No surcharge applies to charges imposed for service or equipment furnished by a service supplier while the same or similar service or equipment is also available for sale or lease from persons other than a service supplier that is subject to public utility regulation. (Sec. 41019, Rev. & Tax. Code)

• *Managed audits*

Taxpayers may voluntarily participate in managed audits of qualifying emergency telephone users surcharge accounts with the State Board of Equalization. (Sec. 41133, Rev. & Tax. Code, *et seq.*) An account will qualify for managed audits if:

> — the taxpayer's business involves few or no statutory exemptions;

> — the taxpayer's business involves a single or a small number of clearly defined taxability issues;

> — the taxpayer is taxed pursuant to a qualifying tax or fee law at issue and agrees to participate in the program; and

> — the taxpayer has the resources to comply with the managed audit instructions provided by the CDTFA.

(Sec. 41133.1, Rev. & Tax. Code)

A taxpayer wishing to participate in the program must examine its books and records to determine if it has any unreported tax liability for the audit period and make available to the CDTFA for verification all computations and books and records examined. (Sec. 41133(a)(2), Rev. & Tax. Code) After the audit is verified by the CDTFA, interest on any unpaid liability will be imposed at 1/2 the rate that would otherwise be imposed during the audit period. (Sec. 41133.4, Rev. & Tax. Code)

• *Prepaid mobile telephony surcharge*

Effective January 1, 2019, the prepaid mobile telephony services (MTS) surcharge no longer applies, and intrastate prepaid telephone services are subject to the emergency telephone users surcharge (ETUS). (*L-592*, California Department of Tax and Fee Administration, December 2018)

The surcharge was imposed and collected by a seller from a prepaid consumer at the time of a retail transaction in California. The prepaid MTS surcharge was imposed as a percentage of the sales price of each retail transaction that occurs in California and was imposed in lieu of any charges imposed pursuant to the emergency telephone users surcharge act and the Public Utilities Commission (PUC) surcharges for prepaid mobile telephony services. The surcharge rate was calculated annually by the CDTFA no later than November 1, by adding the emergency telephone users surcharge rate and the PUC reimbursement fee and surcharges. (Sec. 42010, Rev. & Tax. Code)

Effective January 1, 2019, sellers of prepaid MTS must not charge or collect the state surcharge from customers. They must collect only the local MTS surcharge. They must also continue to file a MTS report and pay all surcharge amounts collected from customers. Sellers should not refund any state MTS surcharges they collected from customers. California will send a separate refund notice and provide new information when it is available. (*L-592*, California Department of Tax and Fee Administration, December 2018)

COMPLIANCE NOTE: **Effective January 1, 2019, prepaid mobile telephony service surcharge no longer applies.** Effective January 1, 2019, the prepaid mobile telephony services surcharge no longer applies. The CDTFA issued instructions on the reformatted emergency telephone users surcharge return to reflect a federal court decision that held the Prepaid Mobile Telephony Services (MTS) Surcharge Collection Act:

- unconstitutional;

- preempted by federal law; and

- as a result, unenforceable.

(*MetroPCS California, LLC v. Picker et al*, U.S. District Court, Northern District of California, Case No. 17-cv-05959-SI; *Special Notice L-599*, California Department of Tax and Fee Administration, January 2019)

Although a notice of appeal of the district court's decision was filed on December 14, 2018, a judicial stay of the injunction was not requested, thereby ending CDTFA's enforcement of the prepaid MTS program.

Injunction issued against enforcement of the state MTS surcharge. The federal district court issued an injunction against enforcement of the state MTS surcharge. Effective January 1, 2019:

- the prepaid mobile telephony services surcharge no longer applies;

• intrastate prepaid telephone services are subject to the emergency telephone users surcharge (ETUS); and

• prepaid MTS service suppliers must revert back to collecting the ETUS on all charges for intrastate telecommunication service, including VoIP and prepaid and postpaid wireless services.

(*Special Notice L-599*, California Department of Tax and Fee Administration, January 2019)

The ETUS Return has been reformatted to a single-column return beginning with the January 2019 reporting period. Total charges due from service users for all postpaid intrastate telecommunication services subject to the surcharge other than charges for VoIP services must be reported on Line 1. Total charges due from service users for all prepaid intrastate telecommunication services subject to the surcharge other than charges for VoIP services should be reported on Line 2. (*Special Notice L-599*, California Department of Tax and Fee Administration, January 2019)

• *Recordkeeping requirements*

A service supplier must maintain and make available for examination, on CDTFA request, records maintained in the manner prescribed by Reg. 4901, 18 CCR. In addition, every service supplier that is liable for payment of the emergency telephone users surcharge which it collects from service users must maintain records that show:

— totals for intrastate telephone communication billed to service users;

— all exemptions allowed by law; and

— amounts of emergency telephone users surcharge collected.

(Reg. 2431, 18 CCR)

• *Refunds*

Any amount erroneously or illegally collected is credited against amounts due and any balance is refunded to the person from whom it was collected. (Sec. 41100, Rev. & Tax. Code) Refunds are not paid after three years from the last day of the second month following the close of the quarterly period for which the overpayment was made, unless a refund claim is filed during that time period. A claim for refund must be filed within three years from the last day of the second month following the close of the *month* the overpayment was made. If the CDTFA makes a determination of the amount due when a return is not filed, or if there is a deficiency determination, no refund is paid after six months from the date the determination becomes final, or after six months from the date of overpayment, whichever is later, unless a claim is filed during that time period. (Sec. 41101, Rev. & Tax. Code)

A suit for a refund cannot be maintained in court unless a claim for refund has been filed. (Sec. 41109, Rev. & Tax. Code) A suit can be brought within 90 days after the mailing of the notice of the CDTFA's action on the refund claim, or six months after the refund claim is filed if no notice is mailed within that time. (Sec. 41110, Rev. & Tax. Code; Sec. 41111, Rev. & Tax. Code)

Taxpayers requesting deferral of a refund claim action may be required to waive refund interest credit for the period of time action on the refund claim is deferred. (Sec. 41106, Rev. & Tax. Code)

• *Reports and payments*

Applicable January 1, 2020, service suppliers that formerly filed surcharge returns on a quarterly or annual basis will be changed to a monthly basis beginning with the January 2020 reporting period. (*Special Notice L-703*, California Department of Tax and Fee Administration, September 2019)

Until January 1, 2020, returns must be filed with the California Department of Tax and Fee Administration (CDTFA) on or before the last day of the second month of each calendar quarter covering the preceding quarter. Payments are due with the returns. Monthly returns and payments are required. (Sec. 41051, Rev. & Tax. Code; Sec. 41052, Rev. & Tax. Code)

The Emergency Telephone Users Surcharge Return and emergency telephone users surcharge accounts are included in the CDTFA's online services system effective November 9, 2020. (*Special Notice L-768*, California Department of Tax and Fee Admnistration, August 2020)

Emergency telephone users surcharge returns may be filed electronically. (Sec. 41052, Rev. & Tax. Code; Sec. 41063, Rev. & Tax. Code)

Persons whose estimated emergency telephone users surcharge liability averages $20,000 or more per month, as determined by the CDTFA pursuant to methods of calculation prescribed by the CDTFA, must remit amounts due by electronic funds transfer (EFT). Persons whose estimated liability averages less than $20,000 per month may elect to remit amounts due by EFT with the approval of the CDTFA. The election is operative for a minimum of one year. (Sec. 41060, Rev. & Tax. Code)

The surcharge amount collected in one calendar month by the service supplier must be paid to, and an accompanying return filed with, the CDTFA on or before the last day of the second month following the month in which the surcharges were collected. The CDTFA may also require different filing and payment schedules in order to ensure payment or facilitate surcharge collection. (Sec. 41052.1, Rev. & Tax. Code)

The CDTFA may make deficiency determinations if it is not satisfied with returns, and may make determinations of the amount due if no return is filed. (Sec. 41070, Rev. & Tax. Code; Sec. 41080, Rev. & Tax. Code) Penalties equal to 10% of the determination amount or $10, whichever is greater, also apply. The penalty amount applied pursuant to fraud is 25% of the determination amount or $25, whichever is greater. (Sec. 41073, Rev. & Tax. Code; Sec. 41074, Rev. & Tax. Code; Sec. 41083, Rev. & Tax. Code; Sec. 41095, Rev. & Tax. Code) Taxpayers may file a petition for redetermination. (Sec. 41085, Rev. & Tax. Code)

Subject to regulatory requirements, intrastate telecommunication service billing aggregators may file returns and pay surcharges due on behalf of telephone service suppliers registered with the CDTFA. (Reg. 2401, 18 CCR; Reg. 2406, 18 CCR)

• *Taxpayer remedies*

Taxpayers are afforded a number of remedies.

Waiver of penalties.—Persons may be relieved from the liability of payment of the emergency telephone users surcharge, including any interest or penalties, when their liability resulted from a failure to timely file a return or make a payment and that failure is found by the CDTFA to be due to reasonable reliance on written advice given by the CDTFA in a manner prescribed by Reg. 4902, 18 CCR. (Reg. 2432, 18 CCR)

Penalties for the late payment of an emergency telephone users surcharge or the late filing of a return may be waived without a showing of reasonable cause for tardiness under criteria to be developed by the CDTFA. The goal of the criteria must be to foster efficient resolution of requests for relief from penalties. The CDTFA may not require taxpayers to file statements supporting their claims for relief under penalty of perjury, as is the case when a person seeks waiver under a claim of reasonable cause for tardiness. (Sec. 41096, Rev. & Tax. Code)

Relief from California special tax and fee liabilities is extended to provide relief due to reasonable reliance on written advice from the California Department of Tax and Fee Administration (CDTFA) to a person who relies on advice provided in a prior audit of a related person, under specific circumstances. Written advice from the CDTFA that was received during a prior audit of the person, as provided, may be relied upon by the person audited or a person with shared accounting and common ownership with the audited person or by a legal or statutory successor to those persons. A person is considered to have shared accounting and common ownership if the person:

— is engaged in the same line of business as the audited person;

— has common verifiable controlling ownership of 50% or greater owner-ship or has a common majority shareholder with the audited person; and

— shares centralized accounting functions with the audited person (i.e., the audited person routinely follows the same business practices that are followed by each entity involved).

(Reg. 4902, 18 CCR)

Evidence that may indicate sharing of centralized accounting functions includes, but is not limited to:

— quantifiable control of the accounting practices of each business by the common ownership or management that dictates office policies for accounting and tax return preparation;

— shared accounting staff or an outside firm that maintains books and records and prepares returns for special tax and fee programs, as provided; and

— shared accounting policies and procedures.

(Reg. 4902, 18 CCR)

In addition, the taxpayer is required to establish that these requirements existed during the periods for which relief is sought. A subsequent written notification from the CDTFA that provides that the advice was not valid at the time it was issued, or was subsequently rendered invalid to any party with shared accounting and common ownership, including the audited party, serves as notification to all parties with shared accounting and common ownership, including the audited party, that the prior written advice may not be relied upon as of the notification date. (Reg. 4902, 18 CCR)

A taxpayer may be relieved of penalties for late payment of an emergency telephone users surcharge if the taxpayer enters into an installment plan for paying the surcharge within 45 days after a notice of determination or redetermination is final. (Sec. 41127.6, Rev. & Tax. Code) The taxpayer must comply with the agreement for the waiver to remain effective, and waiver may not be granted in cases of fraud.

Statement itemizing installment payments.—Taxpayers that have entered into installment agreements to pay an emergency telephone users surcharge must receive an annual statement from the CDTFA itemizing the balance of the surcharge owed at the beginning and end of a year and the amount of the surcharge paid during the year. (Sec. 41127.7, Rev. & Tax. Code)

Refund claims by the disabled.—The limitations period for filing refund claims for emergency telephone users surcharges is suspended during the period that a person is unable to manage financial affairs because of a physical or mental impair-ment that is life threatening or that is expected to last for at least 12 months. (Sec. 41101.1, Rev. & Tax. Code) There is no waiver for individuals who are represented in their financial matters by their spouses or other persons.

Cost reimbursements for unreasonable assessments.—Taxpayers that have been unreasonably assessed an emergency telephone users surcharge by the CDTFA are entitled to reimbursement of their fees and expenses for attending CDTFA hearings. (Sec. 41169, Rev. & Tax. Code) They may be reimbursed for costs incurred as of the filing of a notice of determination, jeopardy determination, or refund claim.

Employer withholding order.—An employer that has been ordered by the CDTFA to withhold wages from an employee to satisfy the employee's debt for an unpaid emergency telephone users surcharge, but that has failed to remit the withheld amount to the CDTFA, may be held liable by the CDTFA for the unremitted amount, which may be treated as a surcharge deficiency of the employer. (Sec. 41123.6, Rev. & Tax. Code) The CDTFA has seven years from the first day on which the employer withheld wages from an employee to assess the deficiency, with interest. The employee's liability for the surcharge must be credited for the unremitted amount and no further action may be taken to collect that sum from the employee.

Confidentiality of surcharge information.—Preparers of emergency telephone users surcharge returns that, without a client's consent, knowingly or recklessly disclose the client's confidential surcharge information for any purpose other than return preparation may be convicted of a misdemeanor, fined up to $1,000, and imprisoned for up to one year. (Sec. 41132, Rev. & Tax. Code) A preparer also may be liable for prosecution costs.

INSURANCE

[¶88-000]
INSURANCE

[¶88-001] Overview

Insurance companies that have received authority from the Department of Insurance (DOI) to transact insurance business in California are called admitted insurers and may be subject to a gross premiums insurance tax, a retaliatory tax, and/or an ocean marine tax. Surplus line brokers, who are licensed brokers that sell policies for nonadmitted (non-licensed) insurance companies are also subject to tax on premiums for California insureds. If a California insured purchases the insurance directly from a nonadmitted insurer, the premiums are subjected to a nonadmitted insurance tax.

The insurance tax program is jointly administered by the Board of Equalization (BOE), Department of Insurance (DOI) and the State Controller's Office (SCO).

[¶88-030] Rates

The tax applied to insurers is equal to 2.35%, except as noted below (Sec. 12202, Rev. & Tax. Code):

— Premiums from certain federally exempt pension and profit sharing plans (Sec. 12202, Rev. & Tax. Code) 0.5%

— Ocean marine insurers (Sec. 12101, Rev. & Tax. Code) 5%

— Surplus line brokers and nonadmitted insurance (Sec. 1775.5, Ins. Code) 3%

(Sec. 685, Ins. Code)

The retaliatory tax is equal to the aggregate taxing burden imposed upon California insurers by another state and the aggregate taxing burden imposed on insurers located within that state. The taxing burden is determined by aggregating all taxes, licenses and other fees, fines, penalties, deposit requirements or other material obligations, prohibitions or restrictions that is applied to the California insurer.

[¶88-035] Credits

The credits discussed below may be claimed against the insurance premiums tax. (Sec. 12207, Rev. & Tax. Code) The credits are claimed on the insurance tax form filed with the California Department of Insurance.

CCH PRACTICE TIP: 2020, 2021, and 2022 limitation on credit amounts.— For the 2020, 2021, and 2022 tax years, the amount of credits and credit carryovers (other than low-income housing credits and carryovers) that may reduce a taxpayer's tax is limited to $5 million per year. Any unused credit may be carried over. The carryover period is extended by the number of taxable years the credit, or any portion thereof, was not allowed as a result of the limitation. (Sec. 12209, Rev. & Tax. Code)

• *Low-income housing credit*

California law allows taxpayers that build, rehabilitate, or acquire low-income housing to claim a credit, generally based on IRC Sec. 42, the federal low-income housing credit, for a percentage of the portion of a housing project's qualified basis that is attributable to the project's low-income units. Insurers that invest in qualified low-income housing projects in California are eligible for the credit. A maximum aggregate low-income housing credit amount is allocable by the California Tax Credit Allocation Committee (CTCAC) for each calendar year against the insurance premium tax, the corporation franchise and income taxes, and the personal income tax. (Sec. 12206, Rev. & Tax. Code).

• *College access tax credit*

For tax years beginning on or after January 1, 2017, and before January 1, 2023, insurers may claim a credit in an amount equal to 50% of the amount contributed to the College Access Tax Credit Fund, as allocated and certified by the California Educational Facilities Authority. Total credits that may be authorized for all taxpayers may not exceed $500 million. (Sec. 12207, Rev. & Tax. Code) For tax years beginning on or after January 1, 2020, and before January 1, 2023, the total amount of a taxpayer's credits for college access tax fund contributions and for premiums tax due on pilot project insurance for previously uninsured motorists, including carryovers, cannot reduce the taxpayer's tax by more than $5 million per year. The amount of any credit not allowed because of the limit will remain a credit carryover. The credit carryover period for any credit not allowed because of the limit will be increased by the number of years the credit or any part of it was not allowed. (Sec. 12209, Rev. & Tax. Code)

• *Low cost driver's insurance*

Insurers may claim a credit equal to the amount of gross premiums tax due on account of pilot project insurance issued for certain previously uninsured motorists. The pilot project requires certain insurers to provide low-cost insurance to qualified low-income residents of the City and County of San Francisco, California, and Los Angeles County, California. (Sec. 12208, Rev. & Tax. Code) For tax years beginning on or after January 1, 2020, and before January 1, 2023, the total amount of a taxpayer's credits for college access tax fund contributions and for premiums tax due on pilot project insurance for previously uninsured motorists, including carryovers, cannot reduce the taxpayer's tax by more than $5 million per year. The amount of any credit not allowed because of the limit will remain a credit carryover until the credit is exhausted. (Sec. 12209, Rev. & Tax. Code)

[¶88-040] Practice and Procedure

California has extensive administrative and procedural provisions concerning its insurance taxes. For details, refer to the following paragraphs.

For filing deadlines and other significant dates for California taxes, see ¶89-012 (annual calendar), ¶89-014 (quarterly calendar), and ¶89-016 (monthly calendar). For other topics, refer to the following:

— Assessment of delinquent tax;

— Civil action;

— Protest and appeal of assessments;

— Interest rates;

— Civil penalties; and

— Abatement of interest, penalties, or additions to Tax.

• *Return filing and payment of tax*

Every insurer must file an annual return with the Insurance Commissioner. (Sec. 1774, Ins. Code; Sec. 12281, Rev. & Tax. Code; Sec. 12302, Rev. & Tax. Code)

Taxes are due at the same time as the return. (Sec. 1775.5, Ins. Code; Sec. 12287, Rev. & Tax. Code; Sec. 12301, Rev. & Tax. Code)

Every insurer must file a return with the Commissioner on or before April 1 (June 15, with respect to taxes on ocean marine insurance) annually. (Sec. 12302, Rev. & Tax. Code) The Commissioner, for good cause shown, may extend for up to 30 days the time for filing a tax return or paying any amount required to be paid with the return. (Sec. 12306, Rev. & Tax. Code) Each insurer subject to the retaliatory tax must file a retaliatory tax return with the Insurance Commissioner on or before April 1 annually (an ocean marine insurer must amend its return by filing an amended ocean marine retaliatory tax return on or before June 15). (Sec. 12281, Rev. & Tax. Code)

Surplus line brokers placing business for a home state insured must file an annual return on or before March 1. The return must contain an account of the business done by the broker for the prior year. When two or more licensed surplus lines brokers are involved in placing an insurance policy, only the licensed surplus lines broker who is responsible for filing the confidential written report on the transaction, or who is delegated the responsibility for filing the report pursuant to a written agreement between the surplus lines brokers, must include the policy in the broker's sworn statement of business transacted. (Sec. 1774, Ins. Code)

Every person subject to the tax on nonadmitted insurance must file a return with the Franchise Tax Board on or before the first day of the third month following the close of the calendar quarter during which a taxable insurance contract took effect or was renewed. (Sec. 13220, Rev. & Tax. Code)

Taxes, other than taxes on ocean marine insurance and surplus line brokers, are payable to the Insurance Commissioner on or before April 1. Taxes on ocean marine insurance are due June 15. (Sec. 12301, Rev. & Tax. Code) Surplus line brokers' taxes are paid on or before March 1 to the Insurance Commissioner. (Sec. 1775.5, Ins. Code) Retaliatory taxes are paid to the Controller on or before April 1, except that any additional retaliatory tax due on account of ocean marine insurance must be paid on or before June 15. (Sec. 12287, Rev. & Tax. Code)

Below are the forms that need to be filed:

— CDI FS-001, All Classes of Insurance Except Ocean Marine, Life, Title, And Home Protection Tax Return Form

— CDI FS-002, Life Companies Including Accident and Health Insurance Tax Return Form

— CDI FS-003, Title Insurance Tax Return Form

— CDI FS-004, Home Protection Tax Return Form

— CDI FS-005, Ocean Marine Insurance Tax Return Form

— CDI FS-006, Surplus Line Broker and Special Lines Surplus Line Broker Tax Return Form

— CDI FS-006-0, Zero Tax Return Surplus Line Broker and Special Lines Surplus Line Broker Form

— CDI FS-007, Surplus Line Broker's Monthly Tax Payment Voucher Form

— FTB Form 570, Nonadmitted Insurance Tax Return

• *Prepayment requirements*

Insurers transacting business in California whose annual tax for the preceding calendar year was $20,000 or more must prepay their tax for the current calendar year, except that no prepayments are required of ocean marine insurers tax or any retaliatory tax. (Sec. 12251, Rev. & Tax. Code) The Commissioner may relieve an insurer of its obligation to make prepayments if the insurer establishes that either the insurer has ceased to transact insurance in California, or the insurer's annual tax for the current year will be less than $20,000. (Sec. 12260, Rev. & Tax. Code)

Prepayments are due on or before April 1, June 1, September 1, and December 1 of the current year. The prepayments must be made payable to the State Controller and be remitted to the Insurance Commissioner. (Sec. 12253, Rev. & Tax. Code) Each prepayment must be 25% of the insurer's annual tax for the preceding calendar year. (Sec. 12254, Rev. & Tax. Code) Prepayments are made with CIA-T-4, Premium Tax Voucher for the 1st Quarter Prepayment Form.

The Commissioner may extend the time for making a prepayment for up to 10 days for good cause, provided that an extension request is filed before the prepayment is due. Interest is applied from the date the original prepayment was due. (Sec. 12255, Rev. & Tax. Code)

Surplus line brokers.—Surplus line brokers whose annual tax for the preceding calendar year was $20,000 or more must make monthly installment payments by the first day of the third calendar month following the end of the accounting month in which the business was done. The monthly payments must be made payable to the State Controller and be remitted to the Insurance Commissioner. (Sec. 1775.1, Ins. Code) The monthly payments are made with CDI FS-007, Surplus Line Broker's Monthly Tax Payment Voucher Form.

The annual payment is in lieu of an installment payment for the accounting month of December. (Sec. 1775.3, Ins. Code)

PRACTICE AND PROCEDURE

[¶89-010]

TAX CALENDARS

[¶89-012] Annual Tax Calendar

Some California taxes are reported or paid once a year or on a periodic basis other than quarterly or monthly. The following calendar, arranged, by month, lists the principal dates for tax assessments, declarations, notices, returns, statements, reports, and payments. The following calendar indicates that taxpayers operate on a calendar year basis. Dates will need to be adjusted for taxpayers operating on a fiscal year basis.

January

31st—Employers' withholding statements to employees due .... ¶89-102

Deadline for furnishing statements to persons named in certain information returns .... ¶89-104

February

1st—One-half of oil and gas production charges becomes delinquent for assessments of $500 or more .... ¶37-301

March

1st—Annual oil and gas production report due .... ¶37-301

Surplus line brokers' returns and payment due .... ¶88-040

Insurance tax liens attach .... ¶88-040

15th—S corporation returns and payment due .... ¶89-102

15th—Partnership returns due .... ¶89-102

April

1st—Insurers' (other than ocean marine insurers' and surplus line brokers') returns and tax due .... ¶88-040

15th—Personal income tax returns and payment due .... ¶89-102

15th—Corporation franchise (income) tax returns and payment due ... ¶89-102

May

15th—Exempt organizations' information returns due .... ¶89-102

June

15th—Ocean marine insurers' returns and tax due .... ¶88-040

July

1st—Oil and gas production charges due .... ¶37-301

August

15th—Oil and gas production charges become delinquent for assessments of more than $10 but less than $500 (or one-half of the charges becomes delinquent for assessments of $500 or more) .... ¶37-301

September

15th—Agricultural cooperatives' income tax returns due . . . . ¶ 89-102

[¶ 89-014] Quarterly Tax Calendar

Some California taxes are reported or paid on a quarterly basis. The following list highlights the principal dates for quarterly tax returns, statements, reports, and payments.

Jan., Apr., Jul., and Oct.

25th—Underground storage tank fee returns and payment due . . . . ¶ 37-151

Last day—Quarterly reports and payment of withheld personal income tax due . . . . ¶ 89-102

Use fuel vendors' and users' reports and tax due . . . . ¶ 40-007

Lubricating oil tax reports and payment due . . . . ¶ 37-151

Interstate users' diesel fuel tax reports and payment due . . . . ¶ 40-009

Quarterly returns and payment of sales and use taxes due . . . . ¶ 61-220

Quarterly returns and payment of timber yield tax due . . . . ¶ 37-301

Mar., May/Jun., Sep., and Dec.

24th—Sales and use tax prepayment reports and prepayments due

Apr., Jun., Sep., and Dec.

15th—Insurance tax prepayments due, except April prepayment due April 1st . . . . ¶ 89-104

Estimated tax installments for calendar year corporation franchise (income) taxpayers due . . . . ¶ 89-104

Apr., Jun., Sep., and Jan.

15th—Estimated tax installments for calendar year personal income taxpayers due . . . . ¶ 89-104

[¶ 89-016] Monthly Tax Calendar

Some California taxes are reported or paid on a monthly basis. The following list highlights the principal monthly dates.

1st—Common carriers' alcoholic beverage tax reports and payment due . . . . ¶ 37-001

Surplus line brokers' installment payments due . . . . ¶ 89-104

15th—Alcoholic beverage tax reports and payment due . . . . ¶ 37-001

25th—Motor fuel distributors', producers', and brokers' reports and tax due . . . . ¶ 40-001

Aircraft jet fuel reports and tax due . . . . ¶ 40-005

Cigarette, tobacco products tax reports or returns and tax payment due . ¶ 55-001; ¶ 55-005

Last day—Diesel fuel suppliers' reports and payment due . . . . ¶ 40-003

Oil and gas producers' monthly reports due . . . . ¶ 37-301

[¶89-050]
ADMINISTRATION OF TAXES

[¶89-060] State Taxing Authority

The Franchise Tax Board (FTB) administers the corporation franchise (income) and personal income taxes. (Sec. 19501, Rev. & Tax. Code)

The California State Board of Equalization (BOE) administers the property tax. The BOE and the California Department of Tax and Fee Administration (CDTFA) jointly administer the insurance tax. As part of an interagency agreement, the CDTFA collects the alcoholic beverage tax and administers the program in cooperation with the BOE. The BOE hears all appeals for claims for refund or petition for redetermination denials regarding the alcoholic beverage tax. (*Business Taxes and Fee in California*, California Department of Tax and Fee Administration; *Alcoholic Beverage Tax Program*, California State Board of Equalization)

The CDTFA administers the:

— alcoholic beverage tax;

— cannabis tax;

— childhood lead poisoning prevention fee;

— cigarette and tobacco products licensing program;

— cigarette and tobacco products tax;

— cigarette tax stamp program;

— covered electronic waste recycling fee;

— diesel fuel tax;

— emergency telephone users surcharge;

— emergency telephone users (911) surcharge and local charges;

— energy resources (electrical) surcharge;

— fire prevention fee;

— hazardous waste disposal fee;

— hazardous waste environmental fee;

— hazardous waste facility fee;

— hazardous waste generator fee;

— insurance tax;

— integrated waste management fee (solid waste and wood waste);

— International Fuel Tax Agreement (IFTA) and Interstate User Diesel Fuel Tax;

— Interstate User Diesel Fuel Tax;

— jet fuel tax;

— lead-acid battery fee;

— lumber products assessment;

— marine invasive special (ballast water) fee;

— motor vehicle fuel tax;

— natural gas surcharge;

— occupational lead poisoning prevention fee;

— oil spill prevention, response, and administration fee;

— sales and use tax;

— timber yield tax program;

— tire fee;

— underground storage tank maintenance fee;

— use fuel tax; and

— water rights fee.

(*Business Taxes and Fee in California*, California Department of Tax and Fee Administration)

CAUTION: Transfer of BOE powers.—As of July 1, 2017, all California State Board of Equalization (BOE) administrative powers, duties, and responsibilities that are not constitutionally mandated to the BOE are transferred to the California Department of Tax and Fee Administration (CDTFA). The BOE is responsible for property tax assessment, equalization functions, and assessment of taxes on insurers authorized by Article XIII of the state constitution. Moreover, the BOE is prohibited from hearing corporation franchise and income tax and personal income tax appeals from the Franchise Tax Board (FTB). The Office of Tax Appeals (OTA) now hears those appeals. (Ch. 6 (A.B. 102), Laws 2017, effective June 27, 2017, and operative as noted)

• *FTB*

The FTB is made up of the State Controller, the Director of the Department of Finance, and the Chairman of the BOE. (Sec. 15700, Govt. Code) An executive officer administers the day-to-day activities of the FTB and exercises the power and authority conferred on the FTB under the direction of the FTB members. (Sec. 15701, Govt. Code; Sec. 15702, Govt. Code; Reg. 17000.11, 18 CCR) There are powers and duties specifically reserved to the FTB that cannot be delegated to the executive officer. This restriction applies to:

— the adoption of rules and regulations;

— determination of the retroactive effect of a rule or regulation;

— appointment and removal of an executive officer; and

— any other power or duty that must be exclusively performed by the FTB.

(Reg. 17000.11, 18 CCR)

All of the powers and duties not specifically reserved to the FTB may be exercised and performed by the executive officer, subject to the general supervision and direction of the FTB. (Reg. 17000.10, 18 CCR)

As authorized by law, the FTB has divided the state into districts with branch offices maintained as necessary. (Sec. 19501, Rev. & Tax. Code) The FTB may appoint deputies and assistants to conduct hearings, prescribe regulations, or perform other duties imposed upon the FTB. (Sec. 19506, Rev. & Tax. Code)

• *BOE*

The BOE is composed of four elected members plus the State Controller, who is also an elected official. (Sec. 17, Art. XIII, Cal. Const.)

•*California Department of Tax and Fee Administration (CDTFA)*

The CDTFA possesses all administrative powers, duties, and responsibilities of the BOE that are not constitutionally mandated to the BOE.

•*Additional administrative personnel*

Employment Development Department.—The Employment Development Department administers the wage withholding system, the unemployment insurance program, and the state disability insurance program.

Secretary of State.—The Secretary of State administers and collects corporate organization and qualification fees.

State Controller.—The State Controller administers estate and generation-skipping transfer taxes and the unclaimed property law.

Also, the State Controller supervises tax sales, tax deeds, and property redemptions through regulations governing the conduct of county officials. (Sec. 158, Rev. & Tax. Code) The State Controller must direct tax collectors regarding their collection duties and must prescribe tax levying and collecting procedures. (Sec. 30300, Govt. Code; Sec. 30301, Govt. Code)

Department of Motor Vehicles.—The Department of Motor Vehicles administers and collects motor vehicle license and registration fees and motor carrier permit fees.

[¶89-100]
RETURN FILING AND PAYMENT OF TAX

[¶89-102] Returns and Payments in General

The return filing and payment requirements for income and sales and use taxes imposed by California are summarized in the paragraphs below.

What returns must be filed in California?

Forms required to report California corporation franchise and income tax, personal income tax, and sales and use taxes are discussed below.

Corporation franchise and income tax returns. Form 100, California Corporation Franchise or Income Tax Return, must be filed by corporations subject to California's corporation franchise or income tax. (Sec. 18601, Rev. & Tax. Code) Corporations electing to file on a water's-edge basis use Form 100-W, California Corporation Franchise or Income Tax Return—Water's-Edge Filers.

COMPLIANCE ALERT: **Required information.** Every return, statement, or other document required to be filed under the corporation franchise or income tax law must contain the corporation's identifying number, any tax return preparer's identifying number, and a written declaration that the document is made under penalty of perjury. (Sec. 18621, Rev. & Tax. Code)

Federal form attachment. Corporations using the federal reconciliation method to figure net income must attach a copy of their federal return, along with all supporting schedules. In addition, taxpayers filing federal Schedule M-3 must attach either:

— a copy of the federal Schedule M-3 (Form 1120) and related attachments;

— a complete copy of the taxpayer's federal return; or

— the federal Schedule M-3 (Form 1120) in a spreadsheet format.

If applicable, corporations must also attach the following federal forms:

— Form 926 (return by a U.S. transferor of property to a foreign corporation);

— Form 1066 (U.S. real estate mortgage investment conduit (REMIC) income tax return);

— Form 3115 (application for change in accounting method);

— Form 5471 (information return of U.S. persons with respect to certain foreign corporations);

— Form 5472 (information return of a 25% foreign owned U.S. corporation or a foreign corporation engaged in a U.S. trade or business);

— Form 8886 (reportable transaction disclosure statement);

— Form 8938 (statement of specified foreign financial assets);

— Form 8975 (country-by-country report) and accompanying Schedule A (tax jurisdiction and constituent entity information); and

— Schedule UTP (uncertain tax position statement).

(Instructions, Form 100, California Corporation Franchise or Income Tax Return)

Amended returns. Taxpayers must use Form 100X, Amended Corporation Franchise or Income Tax Return, when making amendments to a Form 100 or Form 100W that was already filed. (Instructions, Form 100X, Amended Corporation Franchise or Income Tax Return)

Short period returns. A corporate taxpayer must file a California short-period return under any of the following circumstances:

— the taxpayer, with California Franchise Tax Board (FTB) approval, changes its annual accounting period;

— the taxpayer exists for only part of a taxable year;

— the FTB terminates the taxpayer's taxable year for jeopardy; or

— federal law requires the taxpayer to file a short-period return.

A short period return is not required if a corporation terminates because of a reorganization under IRC Section 368(a)(1)(F) (*i.e.*, because of a mere change in identity, form, or place of organization). (Sec. 24634, Rev. & Tax. Code)

Composite returns. Corporations may file a California group nonresident income tax return on behalf of at least one electing nonresident director who receive wages, salaries, fees, or other compensation for director services, such as attendance at board of directors' meetings that take place in California. The group return is filed on a Form 540NR, California Nonresident or Part-Year Resident Income Tax Return. A Schedule 1067A, Nonresident Group Return Schedule, and a Form 3864, Group Nonresident Return Election, must be attached. Corporations that file the group return are liable for the nonresident director's payments of tax, additions to tax, interest, and penalties associated with the director's compensation. Nonresidents that elect to participate in the group return are not required to file a nonresident personal income tax return to report director compensation attributable to California. To qualify, a nonresident director must be a nonresident for the full taxable year and must not have any other California-source income, unless the other California-source income is being reported on another group nonresident return. In making the election, the nonresident agrees to be taxed at the highest marginal personal income tax rate. (Sec. 18536, Rev. & Tax. Code; *FTB Pub. 1067, Guidelines for Filing a Group Form 540NR Return*)

CAUTION: **Deductions and credits.** Directors are not allowed to claim any deductions or credits on the group nonresident return. This includes, but is not limited to, deductions for expenses related to their director compensation, itemized deductions, standard deduction, net operating losses, and adjustments to income such as individual retirement account deductions. It also included the personal, blind, senior, or dependent exemption credit and all special credits such as the other state tax credit. (*FTB Pub. 1067, Guidelines for Filing a Group Form 540NR Return; Tax News,* California Franchise Tax Board, July 2015)

S corporation returns. A business electing to be treated as an S corporation for California purposes must file a return on Form 100S, California S Corporation Franchise or Income Tax Return. An S corporation required to file a California return also must furnish each person who is a shareholder at any time during the taxable year a copy of the information shown on the return. (Sec. 18601, Rev. & Tax. Code)

Federal form attachment. S corporations using the federal reconciliation method to figure net income must attach a copy of their federal return, along with all supporting schedules. In addition, taxpayers filing federal Schedule M-3 must attach either:

— a copy of the federal Schedule M-3 (Form 1120S) and related attachments;

— a complete copy of the taxpayer's federal return; or

— the federal Schedule M-3 (Form 1120S) in a spreadsheet format.

If applicable, S corporations must also attach the following federal forms:

— Form 926 (return by a U.S. transferor of property to a foreign corporation);

— Form 3115 (application for change in accounting method);

— Form 5471 (information return of U.S. persons with respect to certain foreign corporations);

— Form 5472 (information return of a 25% foreign owned U.S. corporation or a foreign corporation engaged in a U.S. trade or business);

— Form 8825 (rental real estate income and expenses of a partnership or an S corporation);

— Form 8869 (qualified subchapter S subsidiary election);

— Form 8886 (reportable transaction disclosure statement);

— Form 8938 (statement of specified foreign financial assets); and

— Form 8975 (country-by-country report) and accompanying Schedule A (tax jurisdiction and constituent entity information).

(Instructions, Form 100S, California S Corporation Franchise or Income Tax Return)

Amended returns. To correct or change a previously filed Form 100S, an S corporation should use the most current version of Form 100X, Amended Corporation Franchise or Income Tax Return. (Instructions, Form 100S, California S Corporation Franchise or Income Tax Return)

Composite returns. Nonresident individual shareholders of an S corporation doing business in California may elect to file a group nonresident return on Form 540NR, California Nonresident or Part-Year Resident Income Tax Return. The S corporation, as agent for the electing shareholders, must make payments of tax, interest, and penalties. (Sec. 18535, Rev. & Tax. Code; Instructions, Form 100S, California S Corporation Franchise or Income Tax Return)

The S corporation is responsible for allowing each nonresident individual shareholder the annual option of being included in a group nonresident return, and for informing the individuals of the terms and conditions for being included in a group nonresident return. To qualify, a nonresident shareholder must be a nonresident for the full taxable year. The irrevocable election to file a group nonresident return is made on Form 3864, Group Nonresident Return Election, which must be attached to the Form 540NR filed for the group. A new election must be signed and attached to the group return each year. The group nonresident return must be filed for a calendar year reporting all of the individual's distributive share of California-source income from the S corporation's taxable year ending in the calendar year for which the group return is filed. This is true, even if the S corporation files on a fiscal-year basis. (*FTB Pub. 1067, Guidelines for Filing a Group Form 540NR Return*)

The income reported on the group return is taxed at the highest marginal rate. Individual deductions are not allowed on the group nonresident return, and only credits directly attributable to the S corporation's business activities can be claimed. Capital losses claimed on the group return are applied at the individual level. Consequently, each nonresident is treated as a single individual and is limited to a $3,000 capital loss. Conversely, the S corporation completes a single Form 3801, Passive Activity Loss Limitations, for the group return. Net operating loss carryovers cannot be claimed on a group return, nor can a deduction for a contribution to a deferred compensation plan. (*FTB Pub. 1067, Guidelines for Filing a Group Form 540NR Return*)

Tiered S corporations are not allowed to file a group return to combine all of their business entities and individual nonresident members on one group return. Each of the tiered entities must file a separate group nonresident return for their electing individual nonresident shareholders and cannot include any business entities in the group nonresident return. (*FTB Pub. 1067, Guidelines for Filing a Group Form 540NR Return*)

Partnership returns. A partnership, including a real estate mortgage investment conduit (REMIC) classified as a partnership, that engages in a trade or business in California or has income from a California source must file Form 565, Partnership Return of Income. Limited liability companies (LLCs) classified as partnerships generally must file Form 568, Limited Liability Company Return of Income. However, nonregistered foreign LLCs and limited partnerships (excluding disregarded entities/single member LLCs) that are not doing business in California, but are deriving income from California or filing to report an election on behalf of a California resident, must file Form 565. Nonregistered foreign LLCs that are members of an LLC doing business in California or general partners in a limited partnership doing business in California are considered to be doing business in California and should file Form 568, while nonregistered foreign partnerships that are a member of an LLC doing business in California or a general partner of a partnership doing business in California are considered doing business in California and should file Form 565. Certain publicly traded partnerships treated as corporations under IRC § 7704 must file Form 100, California Corporation Franchise or Income Tax Return. (Sec. 18633, Rev. & Tax. Code; Instructions, Form 565, Partnership Return of Income; Instructions, Form 568, Limited Liability Company Return of Income)

¶89-102

COMPLIANCE ALERT: **LLCs with nonresident members.** A multi-member LLC with nonresident members must file Form 3832, Limited Liability Company Nonresident Members' Consent, with Form 568 when one of its members is a nonresident of California. Form 3832 must be filed for the first taxable period for which the LLC became subject to tax and for any taxable year in which the LLC had a nonresident member not previously listed on form FTB 3832. Both the nonresident and the nonresident's spouse are required to sign the form. The LLC is responsible for paying tax on a member's share of distributive income at the highest individual tax rate for any nonresident member that fails to sign FTB 3832. (Instructions, Form 3832, Limited Liability Company Nonresident Members' Consent) Single member LLCs (SMLLCs) do not complete form FTB 3832. Instead, a SMLLC consents to be taxed under California jurisdiction by signing the "Single Member LLC Information and Consent" on Form 568. (Instructions, Form 568, Limited Liability Company Return of Income)

CAUTION: **Penalties may be imposed for failure to file proper return.** Many LLCs classified as a partnership, especially foreign LLCs, mistakenly file a Form 565, rather than a Form 568. When this happens, the FTB processes the return as a partnership, creates a new account, and applies any payments made to that new account number. Because a Form 568 is not filed, the FTB also issues a delinquent notice and assesses penalties for not filing. In some instances, though the incorrect tax return was filed, the correct LLC tax voucher (Form 3522) is submitted with the payment. The payment is then applied to the LLC account, but the return is on the new account number. (*Tax News*, California Franchise Tax Board, March 1, 2011)

Federal form attachment. Partnerships and LLCs filing federal Schedule M-1 must attach either:

— a copy of the federal Schedule M-3 (Form 1065) and related attachments;

— a complete copy of the taxpayer's federal return; or

— the federal Schedule M-3 (Form 1065) in a spreadsheet format.

If applicable, partnerships and LLCs must also attach the following federal forms:

— Form 8825 (rental real estate income and expenses of a partnership or an S corporation);

— Form 8832 (entity classification election);

— Form 8886 (reportable transaction disclosure statement); and

— Schedule F (profit or loss from farming).

(Instructions, Form 565, Partnership Return of Income; Instructions, Form 568, Limited Liability Company Return of Income)

Amended returns. If, after the partnership or LLC files its return, it becomes aware of changes it must make, the partnership or LLC should file an amended Form 565 or an amended Form 568, and an amended paper Schedule K-1 (565 or 568) for each affected partner/member, if applicable. The "amended return" box on the form must be checked. In addition, a corrected Schedule K-1 (565 or 568) labeled "amended" must be given to each affected partner/member. If the partnership or LLC originally filed a group nonresident partner Form 540NR,

California Nonresident or Part-Year Resident Income Tax Return, the partnership or LLC must also file an amended Form 540NR. (Instructions, Form 565, Partnership Return of Income; Instructions, Form 568, Limited Liability Company Return of Income)

If a partnership elects to pass a federal partnership-level audit adjustment through to its partners, it must file an amended California nonresident group return for all nonresident direct partners and pay the additional amount of tax that would have been due had the federal adjustments been reported properly. Partners not included in the amended California nonresident group return must individually report their share of the adjustment. (Sec. 18622.5, Rev. & Tax. Code)

The FTB will assume that a publicly traded partnership has elected to pass federal partnership-level audit adjustments through to its partners unless it files a request to make a different election. However, it does not have to file an amended California nonresident group return for nonresident direct partners or pay the additional amount of tax that would have been due had the federal adjustments been properly reported. It only needs to report direct partners' shares of any federal adjustments to the FTB. (Sec. 18622.5, Rev. & Tax. Code)

Composite returns. Nonresident individual partners/members of a partnership or LLC doing business in California or deriving income from California sources may elect to file a group nonresident return on Form 540NR, California Nonresident or Part-Year Resident Income Tax Return. The partnership or LLC, as agent for the electing shareholders, must make payments of tax, interest, and penalties. (Sec. 18535, Rev. & Tax. Code; Instructions, Form 565, Partnership Return of Income; Instructions, Form 568, Limited Liability Company Return of Income)

The partnership or LLC is responsible for allowing each nonresident individual partner/member the annual option of being included in a group nonresident return, and for informing the individuals of the terms and conditions for being included in a group nonresident return. To qualify, a nonresident partner/member must be a nonresident for the full taxable year. The irrevocable election to file a group nonresident return is made on Form 3864, Group Nonresident Return Election, which must be attached to the Form 540NR filed for the group. A new election must be signed and attached to the group return each year. The group nonresident return must be filed for a calendar year reporting all of the individual's distributive share of California-source income from the partnership or LLC's taxable year ending in the calendar year for which the group return is filed. This is true, even if the partnership or LLC files on a fiscal-year basis. (*FTB Pub. 1067, Guidelines for Filing a Group Form 540NR Return*)

The income reported on the group return is taxed at the highest marginal rate. Individual deductions are not allowed on the group nonresident return (exception for the deduction for contributions to a deferred compensation plan), and only credits directly attributable to the partnership or LLC's business activities can be claimed. Capital losses claimed on the group return are applied at the individual level. Consequently, each nonresident is treated as a single individual and is limited to a $3,000 capital loss. Conversely, the partnership or LLC completes a single Form 3801, Passive Activity Loss Limitations, for the group return. Furthermore, net operating loss carryovers cannot be claimed on a group return. (*FTB Pub. 1067, Guidelines for Filing a Group Form 540NR Return*)

Tiered partnerships and LLCs are not allowed to file a group return to combine all of their business entities and individual nonresident partners on one group return. Each of the tiered entities must file a separate group nonresident return for their electing individual nonresident partners/members and cannot include any business entities in the group nonresident return. (*FTB Pub. 1067, Guidelines for Filing a Group Form 540NR Return*)

Exempt organization returns. Exempt organizations subject to tax on unrelated business taxable income must file a return on Form 109, California Exempt Organization Business Income Tax Return, if the gross income from an unrelated trade or business is more than $1,000. An exempt organization is not required to file Form 109 if (1) t is formed to carry out a function of the state, (2) it is carrying out that function, and (3) it is controlled by the state. (Sec. 23771, Rev. & Tax. Code; Reg. 23771, 18 CCR; Instructions, Form 109, California Exempt Organization Business Income Tax Return)

In addition, exempt organizations generally must file an annual information return on Form 199, California Exempt Organization Annual Information Return, if gross receipts are normally more than $50,000. However, they are not required to file in their first year unless their gross receipts exceed $75,000. In an organization's second year a return is only required if the average of the gross receipts exceeded $60,000 its first two years. Private foundations must file Form 199 regardless of the amount of their gross receipts. Churches, pension trusts, IRAs, political organizations, and government entities are not required to file Form 199. (Sec. 23772, Rev. & Tax. Code; Instructions, Form 199, California Exempt Organization Annual Information Return; *FTB Pub. 1068, Exempt Organizations—Filing Requirements and Fees*)

Small tax-exempt organizations with gross receipts normally equal to or less than $50,000 are required to electronically file Form 199N, Annual Electronic Filing Requirement for Small Tax-Exempt Organizations (California e-Postcard). (Sec. 23772(b)(13), Rev. & Tax. Code; Instructions, Form 199, California Exempt Organization Annual Information Return)

PRACTICE TIP: **Substantiation requirement.** If an organization does not have financial records to support its claim that it did not exceed the $50,000 threshold, the FTB may accept a signed statement of a duly elected officer or board member attesting to the fact that the entity did not have gross receipts normally exceeding $50,000 for certain years. The FTB has the authority to exercise judgment to determine what supporting documentation is sufficient. (*FTB Technical Advice Memorandum 2011-4*, May 31, 2011)

Until January 1, 2021, organizations required to file Form 199 (including private foundations) must pay a $10 filing fee, increased to $25 if the fee is paid after the original or extended due date. (Sec. 23772, Rev. & Tax. Code) Effective January 1, 2021, California eliminated the fee.

PRACTICE TIP: **Filing requirements for organizations granted exemptions retroactively.** An organization that has filed corporation franchise and income tax returns for prior tax years and subsequently is granted exemption status retroactively to cover those tax years is not required to file Form 199s for those prior tax years as the information reported on the Form 100s should provide sufficient information. However, the FTB may request that a Form 199 be filed if there is a business need. Any taxes paid with the Form 100s would be credited against the taxpayer's account, so unless the Form 199 fee is more than the amount previously paid each year, there would be no remaining amount due. (*FTB Technical Advice Memorandum 2011-4*, May 31, 2011)

A tax-exempt homeowners' association must file a regular corporate return (Form 100) for any taxable year that its taxable income exceeds $100, and it must also file an annual exempt organization information return (Form 199). (Sec. 23701t, Rev. & Tax. Code)

A tax-exempt political organization must file a regular corporate return (Form 100) for any taxable year in which its taxable income exceeds $100, but it is not required to file an exempt organization annual information return (Form 199). (Sec. 23701r, Rev. & Tax. Code)

Federal form attachment. Exempt organizations filing Form 109 must attach federal Form 8886, Reportable Transaction Disclosure Statement, if it was involved in a reportable transaction. (Instructions, Form 109, California Exempt Organization Business Income Tax Return)

With regard to the filing of Form 199, exempt organizations must either (1) complete Part II of Form 199; or (2) attach a completed copy of federal Form 990, Return of Organization Exempt From Income Tax, including all appropriate schedules. Private foundations must either (1) complete Part II of Form 199; (2) attach a completed copy of federal Form 990-PF for private foundations, including all appropriate schedules; or (3) attach a complete copy of the current report filed with the Registry of Charitable Trusts. Tax-exempt labor organizations must attach a copy of the federal Department of Labor Form LM-2 or LM-3, Labor Organization Annual Report, as appropriate, in lieu of completing Part II of Form 199. An IRC § 4947(a)(1) charitable trust must attach federal Schedule A (Form 990 or 990-EZ), Public Charity Status and Public Support, or federal Form 990-PF, Return of Private Foundation or Section 4947(a)(1) Trust Treated as a Private Foundation. (Instructions, Form 199, California Exempt Organization Annual Information Return)

Amended returns. To correct or change a previously filed Form 109, a new Form 109 should be filed with the "amended return" box checked. A statement that identifies the line number of each amended item, corrected amount, and explanation of the reason(s) for each change must be attached to the new Form 109. (Instructions, Form 109, California Exempt Organization Business Income Tax Return) Form 199 also has an "amended return" box that should be checked when using the form to file an amended return.

Composite returns. A group information return (Form 199) may be filed by a central organization for its subordinate organizations if the subordinate organizations:

— are affiliated with the central organization at the close of the central organization's annual accounting period;

— are subject to the general supervision and control of the central organization; and

— do not have unrelated trade or business income in excess of $1,000.

All subordinates/affiliates must have tax-exempt status before being included in a group return. In addition, each local organization must annually authorize the central organization in writing to include it in the group return and must declare, under penalty of perjury, that the authorization and the information it submits to be included in the group return are true and complete. A private foundation may not be included in a group return. (Reg. 23772(d), 18 CCR; Instructions, Form 199, California Exempt Organization Annual Information Return)

Withholding of income tax. Employers withholding personal income tax from employee wages must file Form DE 9, Quarterly Contribution Return and Report of Wages, and Form DE 9C, Quarterly Contribution Return and Report of Wages

(Continuation). These fore must be filed even if the employer paid no wages during the quarter. (Sec. 13021, Unempl. Ins. Code; Form DE-44, California Employer's Guide, California Employment Development Department)

Form 592, Resident and Nonresident Withholding Statement, must be filed by the payor of various types of California-source income subject to withholding (similar to federal "backup withholding"), such as payments to independent contractors, prizes and winnings, trust and estate distributions, rents and royalties, elective withholding (included by Indian tribes), compensation for personal services, or distributions to domestic nonresident owners of pass-through entities. (Sec. 18662, Rev. & Tax. Code; Instructions, Form 592, Resident and Nonresident Withholding Statement)

With regard to the withholding requirements for sales of California real property, Form 593, Real Estate Withholding Tax Statement, is used to report real estate withholding on sales closing, installment payments made, or exchanges that were completed or failed during the tax year. (Instructions, Form 593, Real Estate Withholding Tax Statement)

Amended returns. Employers use Form DE 9ADJ, Quarterly Contribution and Wage Adjustment Form, to make corrections to previously filed quarterly reports. Corrections may also be made electronically at www.edd.ca.gov/e-Services_for_Business. (Form DE-44, California Employer's Guide, California Employment Development Department)

If an error is discovered after a Form 592 has been filed, an amended Form 592 must be filed to correct the error (check the "Amended" box at the top of the form). Only withholding agents can file amended forms. (Instructions, Form 592, Resident and Nonresident Withholding Statement)

For real estate withholding, a previously filed Form 593 can be corrected by filing a new Form 592 and checking the "Amended" box at the top of the form. However, only a real estate escrow person can file an amended form. (Instructions, Form 593, Real Estate Withholding Tax Statement)

Information returns (1099 series). The FTB recommends filing federal 1099-series forms through the IRS Combined Federal/State Filing program, because taxpayers that use the program only have to file once (the IRS will forward California information returns to the FTB). The following 1099 forms may be filed under this program:

— 1099-DIV;

— 1099-G;

— 1099-INT;

— 1099-MISC;

— 1099-OID;

— 1099-PATR; and

— 1099-R.

Taxpayers not participating in the Combined Federal/State Filing program and filing 250 or more information returns of one type must file directly with the FTB electronically. Taxpayers that file less than 250 information returns electronically with the IRS should use the same method to file the federal forms with the FTB. Taxpayers that file paper information returns with the IRS should not send a paper copy to the FTB. Instead, the IRS will forward the information to the FTB. Generally, the FTB's reporting requirements are the same as the IRS reporting requirements. (Form DE-44,

California Employer's Guide, California Employment Development Department; FTB Publication 4227A, Guide to Information Returns Filed With California)

Filing thresholds. The filing threshold amounts for California 1099-series information returns are the same as the federal threshold amounts. (Form DE-44, California Employer's Guide, California Employment Development Department; FTB Publication 4227A, Guide to Information Returns Filed With California)

Health insurance coverage information returns. Beginning January 1, 2020, entities that provide minimum essential coverage to individuals, as required under the California Individual Healthcare Mandate, during the calendar year must file information returns with the FTB. The returns are due by March 31 following that calendar year. The entities also must provide written statements to the covered individuals. The statements are due by January 31 following the calendar year for which a return is required. (Sec. 61005, Rev. & Tax. Code)

Personal income tax returns. California resident taxpayers may file Form 540, California Resident Income Tax Return, or Form 540 2EZ, California Resident Income Tax Return. Nonresident and part-year resident taxpayers file Form 540NR (Long), California Nonresident or Part-Year Resident Income Tax Return, or Form 540NR (Short), California Nonresident or Part-Year Resident Income Tax Return.

COMPLIANCE NOTE: A single or head of household taxpayer whose total income is $100,000 or less, or a married taxpayer filing a joint return or qualified widow(er) whose total income is $200,000 or less, may use Form 540 2EZ. "Total income" means taxable wages, dividends, interest, and pension income for this purpose. (Sec. 19582.5, Rev. & Tax. Code)

COMPLIANCE NOTE: **Identifying numbers.** For tax years beginning on or after January 1, 2021, and until January 1, 2026, the FTB will not require a nonresident alien who is not eligible for or has not been issued a Social Security Number (SSN) or individual tax identification number (ITIN) to provide a SSN or ITIN in order to file a state return, statement, or other income tax document. If the nonresident alien subsequently becomes eligible for and receives a SSN or ITIN, the FTB may require a letter or other form documenting the SSN or ITIN. (Sec. 18624, Rev. & Tax. Code)

Federal form attachment. Residents filing Form 540 who attached federal forms or schedules, other than federal Schedules A or B, to their federal Form 1040 must attach federal Form 1040 and all supporting schedules and forms to their California return. Residents who do not itemize deductions on their federal return, but do itemize deductions on their California return, must attach a pro forma copy of federal Schedule A to Form 540. In addition, residents filing Form 540 must attach all federal Forms W-2 and W-2G, and any federal 1099 forms showing California income tax withheld. If applicable, federal Form 8886, Reportable Transaction Disclosure Statement, must also be attached to California Form 540. (Instructions, Form 540, California Resident Income Tax Return) Residents filing Form 540 2EZ must attach all federal W-2 forms to their California return. (Instructions, Form 540 2EZ, California Resident Income Tax Return)

Nonresidents and part-year residents filing Form 540NR (Long) must attach a copy of their federal income tax return, along with all supporting federal forms and schedules. If they do not itemize deductions on their federal return, but do itemize deductions on their California return, they must also attach a pro forma copy of federal Schedule A. In addition, nonresidents and part-year residents filing Form 540NR (Long) must attach all federal Forms W-2 and W-2G, and any federal 1099 forms showing California income tax withheld. If applicable, federal Form 8886, Reportable Transaction Disclosure Statement, must also be attached to California Form 540NR (Long). (Instructions, Form 540NR (Long), California Nonresident or Part-Year Resident Income Tax Return) Nonresidents and part-year residents filing Form 540NR (Short) must attach all federal W-2 and 1099 forms to their California return. (Instructions, Form 540NR (Short), California Nonresident or Part-Year Resident Income Tax Return)

Amended returns. Taxpayers must use Form 540X, Amended Individual Income Tax Return, to amend previously filed Forms 540, 540 2EZ, 540NR (Long), or 540NR (Short). A claim for refund of an overpayment of tax should also be made by filing Form 540X. Form 540X should not be used to correct the taxpayer's Social Security number, name, or address, or to correct a use tax error reported on an original tax return. (Instructions, Form 540X, Amended Individual Income Tax Return)

Nonresident group return for nonresident aliens. For tax years beginning on or after January 1, 2021, and until January 1, 2026, California allows the filing of a nonresident group return on behalf of electing nonresident aliens receiving California source income. The nonresident group return will be in lieu of nonresident aliens filing individual returns. The entity filing the group return, as agent for the electing nonresident aliens, must make payments of tax, additions to tax, interest, and penalties otherwise required to be paid by the electing nonresident aliens. (Sec. 18537, Rev. & Tax. Code)

COMPLIANCE NOTE: **Identifying numbers.** The FTB will not require a nonresident alien who is not eligible for or has not been issued a SSN or ITIN to provide a SSN or ITIN in order to be included in a nonresident group return. If the nonresident alien subsequently becomes eligible for and receives a SSN or ITIN, the FTB may require a letter or other form documenting the SSN or ITIN. (Sec. 18537, Rev. & Tax. Code)

For a nonresident alien electing to file in a group return, taxable income for services performed in California is subject to tax at the highest marginal personal income tax rate(s), plus, if applicable, the additional mental health tax. No deductions or credits are allowed on the return, except credits for tax withheld. (Sec. 18537, Rev. & Tax. Code)

Fiduciary income tax returns. California fiduciary income tax returns are filed on Form 541, California Fiduciary Income Tax Return, to report income received by an estate or trust, income that is accumulated or currently distributed to beneficiaries, or an applicable tax liability of an estate or trust. A fiduciary includes a trustee of a trust (including a qualified settlement fund), or an executor, administrator, or person in possession of property of a decedent's estate. (Instructions, Form 541, California Fiduciary Income Tax Return)

Federal form attachment. If applicable, fiduciaries must also attach the following federal forms:

— Form 1066 (U.S. real estate mortgage investment conduit (REMIC) income tax return);

— Form 8886 (reportable transaction disclosure statement);

— Schedule C or C-EZ (1040) using California amounts (profit or loss from business);

— Schedule E (1040) using California amounts (supplemental income and loss);

— Schedule F (1040) using California amounts (profit and loss from farmning);

— Form W-2 (wage and tax statement);

— Form W-2G (certain gambling winnings); and

— Form 1099-R (distributions from pensions, annuities, retirement or profit-sharing plans, IRAs, insurance contracts, etc.).

(Instructions, Form 541, California Fiduciary Income Tax Return)

Amended returns. To correct or change a previously filed Form 541, a new Form 541 should be filed with the "Amended tax return" box checked. The fiduciary must complete the entire tax return, correct the lines needing new information, and recompute the tax liability. On an attached sheet, the fiduciary must explain the reason for the amendments and identify the lines and amounts being changed on the amended tax return. The fiduciary's name and federal taxpayer identification number must be on each attachment. (Instructions, Form 541, California Fiduciary Income Tax Return)

If the amended tax return results in a change to income, or a change in distribution of any income or other information provided to a beneficiary, an amended Schedule K-1 (541) must also be filed with the amended Form 541 and given to each beneficiary. The "Amended" box must be checked on the Schedule K-1 (541). (Instructions, Form 541, California Fiduciary Income Tax Return)

Sales and use tax and other taxes administered by the CDTFA. Sellers and anyone liable for sales or use tax are required to file BOE-401-A2, State, Local and District Sales and Use Tax Return.

Effective November 9, 2020, the online services system of the California Department of Tax and Fee Administration (CDTFA) will expand to include all the tax and fee programs the agency administers. As of that date, returns, schedules, and reports will be filed using the CDTFA's Centralized Revenue Opportunity System (CROS) and paper returns will no longer be mailed. The following special tax and fee programs will move to the online system on November 9, 2020:

— Cannabis Taxes;

— Childhood Lead Poisoning Prevention Fee;

— Emergency Telephone Users Surcharge;

— Energy Resources Surcharge;

— Hazardous Substances Taxes (Disposal, Environmental, Facility, Generator);

— Integrated Waste Management Fee;

— Lead-Acid Battery Fees;

— Marine Invasive Species Fee (formerly Ballast Water Management Fee);

— Natural Gas Surcharge;

— Occupational Lead Poisoning Prevention Fee;

— Public Warehouse – Alcoholic Beverage Tax;

— Tax on Insurers; and

— Water Rights Fee.

(*Special Notice L-744*, California Department of Tax and Fee Administration, April 2020)

This is in addition to the taxes that are already on the online system:

- — Sales and Use Tax;

- — Cigarette Retailer License Fee;

- — Covered Electronic Waste Recycling Fee;

- — Lumber Products Assessment;

- — California Tire Fee;

- — Prepaid MTS Surcharge;

- — Cigarette & Tobacco Internet Purchases;

- — Alcoholic Beverage Tax;

- — Cigarette and Tobacco Products Tax;

- — Cigarette and Tobacco Products Licensing (Distributors, Importers, Manufacturers, Wholesalers);

- — Fuel Taxes (Aircraft Jet Fuel, Diesel Fuel, including Interstate User Diesel Fuel Tax, International Fuel Tax Agreement (IFTA), Motor Vehicle Fuel, and Alternative Use Fuel);

- — Oil Spill Response, Prevention & Administration Fees;

- — Timber Yield Tax; and

- — Underground Storage Tank Maintenance Fee.

(*Special Notice L-744*, California Department of Tax and Fee Administration, April 2020)

When are returns due?

Corporation franchise and income tax returns. Generally, corporations reporting income on a calendar year basis must file returns and pay taxes by April 15 (March 15 for taxable years beginning before 2016). Corporations reporting on a fiscal year basis must file returns by the 15th day of the fourth month following the close of the fiscal year (15th day of third month for taxable years beginning before 2016). (Sec. 18601, Rev. & Tax. Code; Sec. 19001, Rev. & Tax. Code)

Agricultural cooperatives must file returns and pay taxes by September 15 (15th day of the ninth month after the close of fiscal year). (Sec. 18601, Rev. & Tax. Code; Sec. 19001, Rev. & Tax. Code)

Extensions. Corporations in good standing filing Form 100 or 100W are allowed an automatic six-month extension of time to file a return without making any written request for an extension (six months for the 2016-2018 taxable years). However, an extension of time to file is not an extension of time to pay the tax. To avoid underpayment penalties, taxpayers must submit a payment voucher (Form 3539) with full payment of any tax due by the original due date for filing the return. (Sec. 18604, Rev. & Tax. Code; Reg. 25402, 18 CCR; *FTB Notice 2019-07*, California Franchise Tax Board, December 2, 2019; Instructions, Form 3539, Payment Voucher for Automatic Extension for Corporations and Exempt Organizations) The FTB may also extend return filing deadlines, tax payment periods, and refund claim filing deadlines for up to one year for taxpayers affected by disasters, terrorist attacks, or military actions. (Sec. 18572, Rev. & Tax. Code)

CAUTION: **Payment of tax by electronic funds transfer (EFT).** If a corporation is required to pay its tax liability by EFT, all payments must be remitted by EFT to avoid noncompliance penalties, in which case the corporation should not use a Form 3539 payment voucher. (Instructions, Form 100, California Corporation Franchise or Income Tax Return)

For taxable years beginning on or after January 1, 2015, California generally conforms to the federal provision (IRC §6164) that allows a corporation expecting a net operating loss (NOL) carryback to extend the time for payment of taxes for the immediately preceding taxable year. However, IRC §6164(d)(2), relating to the period of extension if an application for tentative carryback adjustment is filed, does not apply for California purposes. (Sec. 19131.5, Rev. & Tax. Code)

Reporting federal changes. If any amount required to be reported on a corporation's federal income tax return is changed or corrected by the IRS or any other competent federal authority, or a renegotiated contract with the United States results in a change in gross income or deductions, the taxpayer must report the federal change or correction to the FTB within six months of the final federal determination, or as otherwise required by the FTB. The change must be reported even if it does not result in an increase in the amount of tax due. The taxpayer must concede the accuracy of the determination or state where it is erroneous. In addition, if for any reason a taxpayer files an amended federal income tax return, the taxpayer must file an amended state return or notification with the FTB within six months. (Sec. 18622, Rev. & Tax. Code) The corporation must also include a copy of the final federal determination and all underlying data and schedules that explain or support the federal adjustments. (Instructions, Form 100X, Amended Corporation Franchise or Income Tax Return)

Short period returns. A California short-period corporation franchise or income tax return is due on the same due date as the federal short-period return that includes the taxpayer's net income for that short period. If a federal short-period return is not required for a short period, a California short-period return is due by April 15 for calendar-year filers, or the 15th day of the fourth month following the close of fiscal year (March 15, or 15th day of third month for taxable years beginning before 2016). (Sec. 18601, Rev. & Tax. Code)

S corporation returns. S corporations must file their returns by the 15th day of the third month after the close of the taxable year (March 15 for calendar-year filers), unless the return is for a short-period. A California short-period corporation franchise or income tax return is due on the same due date as the federal short-period return that includes the taxpayer's net income for that short period. If a federal short-period return is not required for a short period, a California short-period return is due by March 15 for calendar-year filers, or the 15th day of the third month following the close of fiscal year. (Sec. 18601, Rev. & Tax. Code; Instructions, Form 100S, California S Corporation Franchise or Income Tax Return)

COMPLIANCE NOTE: **Short-year returns.** An S corporation that converts to another type of entity, such as an LLC or limited partnership, must file two California returns. It must file a short-period return for the taxable year ending on the day before the effective date of the conversion, and it is subject to all other filing requirements and tax obligations from the date of conversion. (Instructions, Form 100S, California S Corporation Franchise or Income Tax Return) Or, if an S corporation has a change in ownership that causes the corporation to cease to be a small business, such as having more than 100 shareholders, the S corporation will terminate (also commonly referred to as a technical termination). If there is a technical termination mid-year, the S corporation will have to file two short-year tax returns. Both tax returns will be due on the same day. (*Tax News*, California Franchise Tax Board, August 2013)

Extensions. An S corporation is allowed an automatic six-month filing extension without making any written request for extension (seven months prior to the 2016 taxable year). Suspended S corporations do not qualify for the automatic extension. An extension of time to file is not an extension of time to pay the tax. To avoid underpayment penalties, taxpayers must submit Form 3539, Payment Voucher for Automatic Extension for Corporations and Exempt Organizations, with full payment of any tax due, or they must remit payment by EFT, if required to pay by EFT, by the original due date for filing the return. (Sec. 18604, Rev. & Tax. Code; *FTB Notice 2019-07*, California Franchise Tax Board, December 2, 2019; Instructions, Form 100S, California S Corporation Franchise or Income Tax Return)

Reporting federal changes. If any amount required to be reported on a S corporation's federal income tax return is changed or corrected by the IRS or any other competent federal authority, or a renegotiated contract with the United States results in a change in gross income or deductions, the taxpayer must report the federal change or correction to the FTB within six months of the final federal determination, or as otherwise required by the FTB. The change must be reported even if it does not result in an increase in the amount of tax due. The taxpayer must concede the accuracy of the determination or state where it is erroneous. In addition, if for any reason a taxpayer files an amended federal income tax return, the taxpayer must file an amended state return or notification with the FTB within six months. (Sec. 18622, Rev. & Tax. Code) The corporation must also include a copy of the final federal determination and all underlying data and schedules that explain or support the federal adjustments. (Instructions, Form 100X, Amended Corporation Franchise or Income Tax Return)

Composite returns. A group nonresident return must be filed by the 15th day of the fourth month after the close of the taxable year (April 15 for calendar-year filers). (Sec. 18601, Rev. & Tax. Code; *FTB Pub. 1067, Guidelines for Filing a Group Form 540NR Return*; Instructions, Form 540NR (Long), California Nonresident or Part-Year Resident Income Tax Return) An automatic six-month filing extension without making any written request for extension is allowed for group returns. However, an extension of time to file is not an extension of time to pay the tax. To avoid underpayment penalties, taxpayers must submit Form 3519, Payment for Automatic Extension for Individuals, with full payment of any tax due by the original due date. (Sec. 18604, Rev. & Tax. Code; *FTB Pub. 1067, Guidelines for Filing a Group Form 540NR Return*; Instructions, Form 540NR (Long), California Nonresident or Part-Year Resident Income Tax Return)

Partnership returns. Returns (Form 565) and payments for calendar-year partnerships are due on March 15 (April 15 prior to the 2016 taxable year), while returns and payments for fiscal-year partnerships are due on the 15th day of the third month following the end of the taxable year (15th day of fourth month prior to the 2016 taxable year). (Sec. 18633, Rev. & Tax. Code) For LLCs classified as partnerships and SMLLCs owned by pass-through entities, the due dates for returns (Form 568) and payments are the same as for partnerships. For SMLLCs that are not owned by pass-through entities, the due date is the 15th day of the fourth month following the close of the owner's taxable year. (Sec. 18633.5, Rev. & Tax. Code; Instructions, Form 568, Limited Liability Company Return of Income)

COMPLIANCE NOTE: **Short-year returns.** An LLC classified as a partnership will be treated as terminated when there is a change of 50% or more of the total interests in the LLC within a 12-month period (commonly referred to as a technical termination). If there is a technical termination mid-year, the LLC will have to file two short-year tax returns and pay the annual tax and fee for two entities because the FTB treats each short-period return as covering a separate taxable year. The due date for filing and payment will be based on the beginning and ending of each separate taxable year. (*Tax News*, California Franchise Tax Board, August 2013)

Extensions. Partnerships and LLCs classified as partnerships are allowed an automatic six-month filing extension without making any written request for extension (seven months after the 2016 taxable year). An extension of time to file is not an extension of time to pay any tax due. To avoid underpayment penalties, partnerships must submit Form 3538, Payment Voucher for Automatic Extension for LPs, LLPs, and REMICs, and LLCs must submit Form 3537, Payment for Automatic Extension for LLCs, with full payment of any tax due by the original due date for filing a return. (Sec. 18567, Rev. & Tax. Code; Instructions, Form 3537, Payment for Automatic Extension for LLCs; Instructions, Form 3538, Automatic Extension for LPs, LLPs, and REMICs)

Reporting federal changes. If a partnership or LLC federal return is changed for any reason, including changes made because of an examination, the federal change may affect the entity's California return. In such a case, the partnership or LLC must file an amended California return within six months of the final federal adjustments, and must attach a copy of the federal Revenue Agent's Report or other notice of the adjustments to the amended return. The partnership or LLC must also inform its owners that they may also be required to file amended returns based on any changes made by the IRS within six months of the date of the final federal adjustments. (Sec. 18622, Rev. & Tax. Code; Instructions, Form 565, Partnership Return of Income; Instructions, Form 568, Limited Liability Company Return of Income)

If a partnership's federal return is changed or corrected by federal authorities and the partnership is issued an adjustment under the federal partnership audit rules or makes a federal election for alternative payment as part of the partnership-level audit, the partnership must report the change or correction to the FTB within six months after the final federal determination. The partnership must provide enough detail to calculate the California tax change resulting from the federal adjustment. This applies to final federal determinations assessed under the rules as in effect January 1, 2018. (Sec. 18622.5, Rev. & Tax. Code)

PRACTICE NOTE: **Effect of federal election.** A federal election to pay the imputed underpayment resulting from a partnership-level audit adjustment or to pass the underpayment through to partners generally will apply for California purposes, with no separate state election allowed. However, a unitary partner whose share of a partnership's income and apportionment factors is includible as business income on the partner's original California return is not bound by the federal election. The partner will be treated as having filed an amended federal return and must file an amended state return to separately report its California share of the adjustments. Also, any partnership can file a request to make a state election different from its federal election. The FTB must grant the request if the partnership establishes that the election would not impede the FTB's tax collection. (Sec. 18622.5, Rev. & Tax. Code)

Composite returns. A group nonresident return must be filed by the 15th day of the fourth month after the close of the taxable year (April 15 for calendar-year filers). (Sec. 18601, Rev. & Tax. Code; *FTB Pub. 1067, Guidelines for Filing a Group Form 540NR Return*; Instructions, Form 540NR (Long), California Nonresident or Part-Year Resident Income Tax Return) An automatic six-month filing extension without making any written request for extension is allowed for group returns. However, an extension of time to file is not an extension of time to pay the tax. To avoid underpayment penalties, taxpayers must submit Form 3519, Payment for Automatic Extension for Individuals, with full payment of any tax due by the original due date. (Sec. 18604, Rev. & Tax. Code; *FTB Pub. 1067, Guidelines for Filing a Group Form 540NR Return*; Instructions, Form 540NR (Long), California Nonresident or Part-Year Resident Income Tax Return)

Exempt organization returns. Exempt organizations subject to tax on their unrelated business income must file returns (Form 109 and Form 199) and pay taxes by the 15th day of the fifth month following the close of their taxable year. However, an employees' trust (IRC § 401(a)), an IRA, or a Coverdell Education Savings Account must file Form 109 by the 15th day of the fourth month after the end of the taxable year. (Sec. 23771, Rev. & Tax. Code; Sec. 23772, Rev. & Tax. Code; Instructions, Form 109, California Exempt Organization Business Income Tax Return; Instructions, Form 199, California Exempt Organization Annual Information Return)

Extensions. Exempt organizations in good standing are allowed an automatic six-month extension of time to file a return without making any written request for an extension (seven months prior to the 2016 taxable year). However, an extension of time to file is not an extension of time to pay the tax. To avoid underpayment penalties, taxpayers must submit a payment voucher (Form 3539) with full payment of any tax due by the original due date for filing the return. (Sec. 18604, Rev. & Tax. Code; Reg. 25402, 18 CCR; Instructions, Form 3539, Payment Voucher for Automatic Extension for Corporations and Exempt Organizations)

Withholding of income tax. Form DE 9 and Form DE 9C are due on April 1, July 1, October 1, and January 1, and become delinquent if not filed by April 30, July 31, October 31, and January 31, respectively. (Sec. 13021, Unempl. Ins. Code; Form DE-44, California Employer's Guide, California Employment Development Department)

For withholding on other California-source income (similar to federal "backup withholding"), Form 592 is due January 15, April 15, June 15, and September 15. (Sec. 18662, Rev. & Tax. Code; Reg. 18662-8, CCR; Instructions, Form 592, Resident and Nonresident Withholding Statement) Form 592-V, which is used to remit withholding payments reported on Form 592 to the FTB, is due on the same dates as Form 592. (Reg. 18662-8, CCR; Instructions, Form 592-V, Payment Voucher for Resident and Nonresident Withholding)

With regard to the withholding requirements for sales of California real property, Form 593 is due by the 20th day of the calendar month following the month escrow closes. (Reg. 18662-8, CCR; Instructions, Form 593, Real Estate Withholding Tax Statement) Form 593-V, which is used to remit withholding payments reported on Form 592 to the FTB, is due on the same dates as Form 592. (Reg. 18662-8, CCR; Instructions, Form 593-V, Payment Voucher for Real Estate Withholding)

NEW DEVELOPMENTS: Beginning January 1, 2020, a new Form 593, *Real Estate Withholding Statement*, must be submitted to the FTB whenever a sale of real property occurs. The form, which replaces Forms 593, 593-C, 593-E, and 593-I, is due to the FTB and the seller by the 20th day of the month following the close of the transaction. Form 593-V, *Payment Voucher for Real Estate Withholding*, must still be included with any payment sent to the FTB. (Reg. 18662-3, 18 CCR; Real Estate Withholding Statement Instructions)

Information returns (1099 series). Taxpayers filing federal 1099-series forms through the IRS Combined Federal/State Filing program must follow established federal due dates (February 28 if filing paper returns; March 31 if filing electronically). Otherwise, taxpayers must file 1099-series forms with the FTB by February 28. (Form DE-44, California Employer's Guide, California Employment Development Department; FTB Publication 4227A, Guide to Information Returns Filed With California)

Personal income tax returns. Generally, taxpayers must file their personal income tax returns and pay the tax by April 15 following the close of the calendar year. Taxpayers with a fiscal year different from the calendar year must file their returns and pay the tax by the 15th day of the fourth month following the close of the fiscal year. (Sec. 18566, Rev. & Tax. Code; Sec. 19001, Rev. & Tax. Code)

Taxpayers residing or traveling abroad must file their returns and pay the tax by the June 15, or by the 15th day of the sixth month following the close of the taxable year. However, interest will accrue from the regular due date for returns (the 15th day of the fourth month following the close of the taxable year) to the date of payment. (Sec. 18566, Rev. & Tax. Code; Sec. 18567, Rev. & Tax. Code; Instructions, Form 3519, Payment for Automatic Extension for Individuals)

A return for a decedent's last taxable year must be filed by April 15 of the calendar year following death, or by the 15th day of the fourth month following the close of the decedent's fiscal year. Returns for any prior years for which required returns were not filed by the decedent should be filed as soon as possible, and must be filed before the estate is distributed. (Reg. 18505-4, 18 CCR)

Extensions. Taxpayers are allowed an automatic six-month extension to file a personal income tax return without making any written request for extension. However, an extension of time to file is not an extension of time to pay any tax due. To avoid underpayment penalties, taxpayers must submit a payment voucher (Form 3519) with full payment of any tax due by the original due date for filing the return. (Sec. 18567, Rev. & Tax. Code; Reg. 18567, 18 CCR)

Taxpayers residing or traveling abroad are also allowed an automatic six-month extension, which is in addition to the additional two months allowed for filing an original return (i.e., to June 15). Thus, the overall extension is to December 15. (Instructions, Form 3519, Payment for Automatic Extension for Individuals)

Military personnel and members of the merchant marine serving outside the United States are granted an automatic extension to file returns and pay tax until 180 days after their return to the United States. Similar extensions are available to military personnel or individuals serving in support of military personnel serving in a combat zone and persons deployed outside the United States away from their permanent duty station while participating in a contingency operation. (Sec. 18570, Rev. & Tax. Code; Sec. 18571, Rev. & Tax. Code; *FTB Pub. 1032*, Tax Information for Military Personnel)

¶89-102

In addition, the FTB may extend return filing deadlines and tax payment periods for up to one year for taxpayers affected by disasters, terrorist attacks, or military actions. (Sec. 18572, Rev. & Tax. Code)

Reporting federal changes. If any amount required to be reported on a taxpayer's federal income tax return is changed or corrected by the IRS or any other competent federal authority, or a renegotiated contract with the United States results in a change in gross income or deductions, the taxpayer must report the federal change or correction to the FTB within six months of the final federal determination, or as otherwise required by the FTB. The change must be reported even if it does not result in an increase in the amount of tax due. The taxpayer must concede the accuracy of the determination or state where it is erroneous. In addition, if for any reason a taxpayer files an amended federal income tax return, the taxpayer must file an amended state return or notification with the FTB within six months. (Sec. 18622, Rev. & Tax. Code) The taxpayer must also include a copy of the final federal determination and all underlying data and schedules that explain or support the federal adjustments. (Instructions, Form 540X, Amended Individual Income Tax Return)

Fiduciary income tax returns. Generally, fiduciary returns (Form 541) must be filed and the tax paid by April 15 following the close of the calendar year. Taxpayers with a fiscal year different from the calendar year must file their returns and pay the tax by the 15th day of the fourth month following the close of the fiscal year. (Sec. 18566, Rev. & Tax. Code; Sec. 19001, Rev. & Tax. Code; Instructions, Form 541, California Fiduciary Income Tax Return)

Extensions. Fiduciaries are allowed an automatic six-month extension to file a personal income tax return without making any written request for extension. However, an extension of time to file is not an extension of time to pay any tax due. To avoid underpayment penalties, taxpayers must submit a payment voucher (Form 3563) with full payment of any tax due by the original due date for filing the return. (Sec. 18567, Rev. & Tax. Code; Reg. 18567, 18 CCR)

Reporting federal changes. If any amount required to be reported on a fiduciary's federal income tax return is changed or corrected by the IRS or any other competent federal authority, or a renegotiated contract with the United States results in a change in gross income or deductions, the fiduciary must report the federal change or correction to the FTB within six months of the final federal determination, or as otherwise required by the FTB. The change must be reported even if it does not result in an increase in the amount of tax due. The fiduciary must concede the accuracy of the determination or state where it is erroneous. In addition, if for any reason a fiduciary files an amended federal income tax return, the fiduciary must file an amended state return or notification with the FTB within six months. (Sec. 18622, Rev. & Tax. Code)

Sales and use tax. Quarterly returns must be filed with the State Board of Equalization (BOE) by the last day of the month following each quarterly period.

For good cause, the BOE may grant a one-month extension of time for filing a return. In the case of a disaster, the BOE is authorized grant an extension for a period not to exceed three months. "Disaster" is defined as fire, flood, storm, tidal wave, earthquake, or similar public calamity, regardless of whether the disaster results from natural causes. (Sec. 6459, Rev. & Tax. Code)

Taxpayers who are not required to hold a seller's permit or to be registered with the BOE may report their qualified use tax obligations from purchases of tangible personal property on their California personal income tax, corporation franchise or income tax, partnership, limited liability company, or estate or trust tax or information returns. Qualified use tax will be considered timely reported if it is included with a timely filed return.

How and when are tax payments made?

The due date for tax payments is the same as the due date for filing for the following California tax returns:

— corporation franchise and income tax returns;

— S corporation returns;

— partnership returns;

— exempt organization returns;

— withholding of income tax;

— information returns (1099 series);

— personal income tax returns; and

— fiduciary returns.

California allows a variety of tax payment methods.

Withholding of income tax. If an employer is required to remit, for federal income tax purposes, the total amount of withheld federal income tax in accordance with IRC Sec. 6302 and regulations thereunder, and the accumulated amount of state income tax withheld is more than $500, the employer must remit the total amount of income tax withheld for state income tax purposes within the number of business days as specified for withheld federal income taxes. However, an employer required to withhold any tax that is not required to make payment in accordance with IRC Sec. 6302 must remit the total amount of income tax withheld during each month of each calendar quarter, on or before the 15th day of the subsequent month if the income tax withheld for any of the three months or, cumulatively for two or more months, exceeds $350. (Sec. 13021, Unempl. Ins. Code) Beginning January 1, 2017, a requirement is phased in to remit all payments of withheld income taxes by electronic funds transfer. (See ¶ 89-108) Tax payments are submitted with Form DE 88ALL, Payroll Tax Deposit.

Any state income tax that is withheld, but that is not subject to the requirements outlined above or that is required to be submitted by electronic funds transfer, must be remitted to the state by the last day of the month following the end of the quarter. Payment that is not required to be made by electronic funds transfer is generally deemed complete when it is placed in a properly addressed envelope bearing the correct postage and deposited in the United States mail. (Sec. 13021, Unempl. Ins. Code)

COMMENT: **California deposit schedule.** California's deposit schedule is dependent upon the employer's federal deposit schedule as follows:

— If the employer's federal deposit schedule is next business day, the employer must pay quarterly if accumulated state personal income tax withholding is $350 or less, monthly if accumulated state personal income tax withholding is $350 to $500, and the next business day if accumulated state personal income tax withholding is $500 or more.

— If the employer's federal deposit schedule is semiweekly, the employer must pay quarterly if accumulated state personal income tax withholding is less than $350, monthly if state personal income tax withholding accumulated is $350 to $500, or the following Wednesday if accumulated personal income tax withholding is $500 or more and the payday is Wednesday, Thursday, or Friday (the following Friday for other paydays).

— If the employer's federal deposit schedule is monthly, the employer must pay quarterly if accumulated state personal income tax withholding is less than $350, or monthly if accumulated state personal income tax withholding is $350 or more.

— If the employer's federal schedule is quarterly or annually, the employer must pay quarterly if accumulated state personal income tax withholding is less than $350, or monthly if accumulated state personal income tax withholding is $350 or more.

(Form DE-44, California Employer's Guide, California Employment Development Department)

For good cause, the Employment Development Department (EDD) may extend the time for filing a return, report, or payment up to 60 days. (Sec. 1111, Unempl. Ins. Code; Sec. 13059, Unempl. Ins. Code) In addition, if the EDD finds that collection of taxes is jeopardized because an employer is insolvent or going out of business, or because the employer's business is temporary or seasonal, the director may provide the employer ten days' notice, requiring payment of withheld taxes from the beginning of the calendar quarter in which notice is given to the date designated in the notice. Such payments are due and payable on the date specified in the notice, and are delinquent if not paid within ten days of that date. The EDD may also require payment of withheld taxes for reporting periods shorter than calendar quarters. These payments are due on the day following the close of each reporting period, and are delinquent if not paid within ten days. (Sec. 1115, Unempl. Ins. Code)

Sales and use tax. Sales tax is due and payable to the BOE quarterly by the last day of the month following each quarterly period. Use tax imposed on gross receipts from the storage, use, or other consumption in the state of tangible personal property is due on or before the 15th day of the fourth month following the tax year in which the property first becomes taxable.

For good cause, the BOE may grant a one-month extension of time for paying the tax, but interest will be imposed until the payment date.

Where else can I find information on returns and payments in California?

Additional information relating to California returns and payments is provided in the discussions of:

— estimated tax returns and payments;

— electronic filing;

— electronic funds transfer (EFT) and other payment methods;

— civil penalties;

— audit and assessment limitation periods; and

— refunds.

California insurance premiums tax returns and payments are discussed in the Insurance Division.

The California Franchise Tax Board provides a comprehensive listing of tax forms, instructions, schedules, and publications on its website at https://www.ftb.ca.gov/forms/. California sales and use forms are available at http://www.boe.ca.gov/sutax/staxforms.htm on the Board of Equalization website.

[¶89-104] Estimated Payments and Returns

California has provisions for making estimated payments of various taxes and for filing various information returns.

Are payments of estimated tax required?

Corporations. Corporations must make estimated tax payments regardless of estimated liability. Entities constituting "corporations" that must pay estimated tax include:

corporations incorporated or qualified under the laws of California or doing business in California;

banks;

financial corporations;

certain associations;

regulated investment companies (RICs);

real estate investment trusts (REITs);

exempt organizations with unrelated business taxable income;

exempt homeowners' associations with non-exempt function income;

limited liability companies (LLCs) and limited partnerships (LPs) that have elected to be taxed as corporations for federal tax purposes; and

S corporations.

(Instructions, Form 100-ES, Corporation Estimated Tax)

Safe harbor calculation. The required estimated payment to avoid an underpayment of estimated tax penalty is the lesser of:

— 100% of the tax shown on the current year's tax return;

— 100% of the tax shown on the preceding year's tax return.

— 100% of the amount the corporation would owe if its estimated tax was computed on annualized current year income; or

— 100% of the amount the corporation would owe if its estimated tax was computed on annualized seasonal income.

For a corporation's first taxable year, the prior year tax exception does not apply. For the second taxable year, the prior year tax exception does not apply if no tax liability existed in the first taxable year or the business operated for less than 12 full months. (Instructions, Form 100-ES, Corporation Estimated Tax)

If a corporation had California net income (computed without regard to the net operating loss deduction) of $1 million or more for any of the three immediately preceding tax years, then it may use the prior year's tax exception for only the first installment and must add any reduction in the first installment to the second installment. (Instructions, Form 100-ES, Corporation Estimated Tax)

Unitary group. Estimated tax for a unitary group of corporations filing a group return must generally be paid by the designated "key corporation" on behalf of the group members. The required estimated tax is the total estimated group liability for the current year. (Instructions, Sch. R, Apportionment and Allocation of Income)

Nonresident directors. A corporation must make estimated tax payments on behalf of its nonresident directors if the corporation files a group nonresident return and the net tax on the return is $500 or more. (FTB Pub. 1067, Guidelines for Filing a Group Form 540NR)

Pass-through entities.

S corporations. S corporations are subject to the same estimated payment requirements as C corporations. (Instructions, Form 100-ES, Corporation Estimated Tax) An S corporation must make estimated tax payments on behalf of nonresident shareholders if the entity files a group return for the shareholders and the net tax on the return after allowable credits is $500 or more. (FTB Pub. 1067, Guidelines for Filing a Group Form 540NR)

Partnerships. A partnership must make estimated tax payments on behalf of nonresident partners if the entity files a group return for the partners and the net tax on the return after allowable credits is $500 or more. (FTB Pub. 1067, Guidelines for Filing a Group Form 540NR)

LLCs. An LLC must make estimated tax payments on behalf of nonresident members if the entity files a group return for the members and the net tax on the return after allowable credits is $500 or more. (FTB Pub. 1067, Guidelines for Filing a Group Form 540NR)

LLCs are also required to make an estimated LLC fee payment.

Withholding requirements. S corporations must withhold tax at a rate of 7% on California source income distributed to a nonresident shareholder if the income distributed exceeds $1,500 in the calendar year. Withholding is not required if the shareholder has received authorization from the FTB to waive the withholding requirement.

Partnerships and LLCs must withhold tax if California source income is allocable to a foreign nonresident partner/member or the California source income distributed to a nonresident partner/member exceeds $1,500 in the calendar year. The withholding rates are 8.84% for foreign corporate partners/members, the highest personal income tax rate (currently, 12.3% through 2030, 9% thereafter) for foreign nonresident individual partners/members, and 7% for all domestic nonresident partners/members. Withholding is not required if the partner or member has received authorization from the FTB to waive the withholding requirement.

Personal income tax An individual must make estimated tax payments if the individual expects to owe at least $500 ($250 if married or a registered domestic partner (RDP) filing separately) in tax for the tax year (after subtracting withholding and credits). Estimated payments are not required if the individual is a nonresident or new resident of California in the current tax year and did not have a California tax liability in the previous tax year. (Instructions, Form 540-ES, Estimated Tax for Individuals)

Safe harbor calculation. Generally, the required estimated payment to avoid an underpayment of estimated tax penalty is the lesser of:

— 90% of the tax shown on the individual's current year tax return; or

— 100% of the tax shown on the individual's preceding year tax return, including alternative minimum tax (AMT).

Individuals who are required to make estimated tax payments and whose California adjusted gross income for the preceding year exceeds $150,000 ($75,000 if married filing separately) must figure estimated tax based on the smaller of 90% of the tax shown on the individual's current year tax return or 110% of the tax shown on the individual's preceding year tax return, including AMT. This rule does not apply to farmers or fishermen.

Individuals with California adjusted gross income for the current year that is equal to or greater than $1 million ($500,000 if married/RDP filing separately) must figure estimated tax based only on their current year's tax.

Sales and use tax. Persons whose estimated taxable sales and use tax receipts average $17,000 or more per month (although the average threshold may increase to $50,000 under some circumstances) must file a quarterly prepayment report and prepay the tax.

How are payments of estimated tax made?

C corporations. C corporations must make estimated tax payments in four installments. Corporations remitting an estimated tax payment or extension payment in excess of $20,000 or having a total tax liability in excess of $80,000 must remit all payments through electronic fund transfer (EFT). Corporations required to file electronically may use Web Pay or a credit card. Those not required to file electronically may do so voluntarily or may mail a check as payment. (Instructions, Form 100-ES, Corporation Estimated Tax) The installments of the estimated tax are equal to 30% for the first quarter, 40% for the second quarter, 0% for the third quarter, and 30% for the fourth quarter.

Pass-through entities. S corporations must make estimated tax payments in four installments. S corporations remitting an estimated tax payment or extension payment in excess of $20,000 or having a total tax liability in excess of $80,000 must remit all payments through EFT. S corporations required to file electronically may use Web Pay or a credit card. Those not required to file electronically may do so voluntarily or may mail a check as payment. (Instructions, Form 100-ES, Corporation Estimated Tax) The installments of the estimated tax are equal to 30% for the first quarter, 40% for the second quarter, 0% for the third quarter, and 30% for the fourth quarter.

Estimated tax on behalf of nonresident shareholders, partners, or members must be paid in four installments in the amounts discussed below for personal income tax. (FTB Pub. 1067, Guidelines for Filing a Group Form 540NR)

Personal income tax. Individuals must make estimated tax payments in four installments. Individuals remitting an estimated tax payment or extension payment in excess of $20,000 or having a total tax liability in excess of $80,000 must remit all payments electronically. Once that threshold is met, all subsequent payments regardless of amount, tax type, or taxable year must be remitted electronically. Instructions, Form 540-ES, Estimated Tax for Individuals. The installments of the estimated tax are equal to 30% for the first quarter, 40% for the second quarter, 0% for the third quarter, and 30% for the fourth quarter.

Annualized income installment method. Individuals who do not receive their income evenly throughout the year may calculate their required installments by annualizing their income This method allows individuals to match their estimated tax payments to the actual period when they earned the income. (Instructions, Form 540-ES, Estimated Tax for Individuals)

Sales and use tax. Prepayments of sales and use tax must be made electronically.

What are the due dates for estimated tax?

C corporations. Generally, four income tax installments are due and payable by the 15th day of the fourth, sixth, ninth, and 12th months of the taxable year. If the amount of estimated tax does not exceed $800 ($25 in the case of an inactive gold mining or quicksilver mining corporation), the entire amount of the minimum tax is payable as an estimate by the 15th day of the fourth month of the corporation's current year.

If a corporation first meets the requirements for paying estimated tax after the first day of the fourth month of the taxable year, the payments are spread over the appropriate remaining quarters, depending on the quarter in which the requirements are met.

Pass-through entities. Estimated tax for S corporations generally is due and payable in four installments on the 15th day of the fourth, sixth, ninth, and 12th months of the taxable year. (Instructions, Form 100-ES, Corporation Estimated Tax) Estimated tax on behalf of nonresident shareholders and partners generally is due and payable in four installments on the 15th day of the fourth, sixth, and ninth months of the taxable year, and the first month of the following taxable year. (Instructions, Form 540-ES, Estimated Tax for Individuals)

Personal income tax. Estimated personal income tax payments generally are due and payable on April 15, June 15, and September 15 of the taxable year, and January 15 of the following year (the fourth, sixth, and ninth months of the taxable year, and the first month of the following taxable year, for fiscal year filers). The fourth installment is not required if the taxpayer files a return by January 31 of that year and pays the balance of tax due at that time. (Instructions, Form 540-ES, Estimated Tax for Individuals)

Farmers and anglers. Estimated tax for farmers and anglers is due and payable by January 15 of the succeeding year.

Sales and use tax. The first, third, and fourth quarter prepayments and reports are due by March 24, September 24, and December 24, respectively. In the second quarter, the first prepayment and report is due by May 24 and the second prepayment is due by June 24.

What forms are required for filing estimated tax?

C corporations. Corporations must use Form 100-ES, Corporation Estimated Tax.

Pass-through entities. S corporations must use Form 100-ES, Corporation Estimated Tax, to pay estimated tax or Form 540-ES to make estimated payments on behalf of nonresident shareholders. Partnerships, LLPs, and LLCs making estimated tax payments on behalf of nonresident partners must use Form 540-ES, Estimated Tax for Individuals.

Personal income tax. Individuals must use Form 540-ES, Estimated Tax for Individuals.

Sales and use tax. Prepayments are made electronically. (EFT Filing Instructions for Sales and Use Tax Prepayment Accounts, BOE-367-EFT)

Where can I find other information on estimated payments and returns?

The California Franchise Tax Board has a Forms and Publications page on its website at https://www.ftb.ca.gov/forms/. In addition, the California State Board of Equalization has websites for sales and use tax forms and publications.

Additional information may be found under:

— returns and payments in general;

— electronic filing;

— electronic funds transfer and other payment methods; and

— civil penalties;

[¶89-106] Electronic Filing

California has provisions for electronic filing in various situations. California laws conform to federal laws that allow electronic postmarks as proof of the file date of electronically filed tax returns. See Sec. 21027, Rev. & Tax Code. Electronic payment of taxes is discussed at ¶89-108.

CCH PRACTICE TIP: Protecting clients' privacy on the Internet.—Businesses are required to use safeguards to ensure the security of Californians' personal information, including their customers' Social Security numbers, driver's license/state identification number, and financial account numbers. Businesses must also contractually require third parties, such as payroll, tax return preparation, or record disposal services, to do the same. Customers must be notified if there are any security breaches. (Sec. 1798.80, Civ. Code, *et seq.*)

Businesses and state and local agencies are prohibited from publicly posting or displaying Social Security numbers, nor embedding SSNs on a card or document using a bar code, chip, magnetic strip or other technology, in place of removing the number as required by law. (Sec. 1798.85, Civ. Code, *et seq.*)

Penalties that may be imposed against tax preparers for violating a client's personal information are discussed in the paragraphs covering Tax Preparers and Taxpayers' Bill of Rights.

• *Corporation tax returns*

California participates in the Modernized e-File (MeF) program for corporation tax returns. (*FTB Pub. 1345, Handbook for Authorized e-file Providers*)

Mandates and options.—If an original or amended corporation franchise or income tax return of a C corporation, S corporation, or exempt organization, other than a return for unrelated business taxable income, is prepared using tax preparation software, then the return must be filed electronically in the form and manner prescribed by the Franchise Tax Board (FTB). (Sec. 18621.10, Rev. & Tax. Code; *FTB Pub. 1345, Handbook for Authorized e-file Providers*)

Waiver.—A business entity required to file a return electronically may annually request a waiver of the requirement from the FTB. The FTB may grant a waiver if it determines that the business entity is unable to comply with the requirement due to, but not limited to, technology constraints, where compliance would result in undue financial burden, or due to circumstances that constitute reasonable cause and not willful neglect. (Sec. 18621.10, Rev. & Tax. Code)

Penalties.—For taxable years beginning on or after January 1, 2017, if a business entity required to file a return electronically fails to comply with the requirement, a penalty will be imposed in the amount of $100 for an initial failure and in the amount of $500 for each subsequent failure, unless the failure is due to reasonable cause and not willful neglect. If a group return is filed on behalf of eligible electing taxpayer members of a combined reporting group, the penalty will apply to the combined reporting group and not to a taxpayer member of the combined reporting group. (Sec. 19171, Rev. & Tax. Code)

Forms and schedules.—Form 100 and Form 100S as well as related schedules are accepted for e-filing.

Extensions.—No paper or electronic state extension applications are required.

• *Partnership, LLP, and LLC returns*

California participates in the Modernized e-File (MeF) program for partnership, limited liability partnership (LLP), and limited liability company tax returns. (*FTB Pub. 1345, Handbook for Authorized e-file Providers*)

Mandates and options.—If an original or amended corporation franchise or income tax return of a partnership, LLP, or LLC is prepared using tax preparation software, then the return must be filed electronically in the form and manner prescribed by the FTB. (Sec. 18621.10, Rev. & Tax. Code; *FTB Pub. 1345, Handbook for Authorized e-file Providers*)

Waiver.—A business entity required to file a return electronically may annually request a waiver of the requirement from the FTB. The FTB may grant a waiver if it determines that the business entity is unable to comply with the requirement due to, but not limited to, technology constraints, where compliance would result in undue financial burden, or due to circumstances that constitute reasonable cause and not willful neglect. (Sec. 18621.10, Rev. & Tax. Code)

Penalties.—For taxable years beginning on or after January 1, 2017, if a business entity required to file a return electronically fails to comply with the requirement, a penalty will be imposed in the amount of $100 for an initial failure and in the amount of $500 for each subsequent failure, unless the failure is due to reasonable cause and not willful neglect. (Sec. 19171, Rev. & Tax. Code)

Forms and schedules.—Form 565, Partnership Return of Income, and Form 568, Limited Liability Company Return of Income, as well as related schedules are accepted for e-filing.

Extensions.—No paper or electronic state extension applications are required.

• *Individual income tax returns*

California participates in the Modernized e-File (MeF) program for individual income tax returns.

Mandates and options.—Individual income taxpayers and tax preparers are allowed to electronically file. (*FTB Pub. 1345, E-File Handbook for Authorized e-file Providers*) Tax return preparers who have prepared and filed more than 100 timely original California personal income tax returns and who prepare at least one personal income tax return using tax preparation software in the current calendar year must file all personal income returns for the current calendar year and subsequent calendar years using electronic technology. The requirement will cease to apply to a tax return preparer if, during the previous calendar year, the tax return preparer prepared no more than 25 original personal income tax returns. (Sec. 18621.9, Rev. & Tax. Code)

Waiver and taxpayer opt-out.—If a taxpayer elects not to have a return filed electronically or if a tax preparer is unable to electronically file due to reasonable cause, the taxpayer can opt out of electronic filing by filing FTB 8454, e-file Opt-Out Record.

Penalties.—A penalty of $50 per return is imposed for failure to e-file, if due to willful neglect and not reasonable cause. (Sec. 19170, Rev. & Tax. Code)

Forms and schedules.—Form 540 as well as related schedules are accepted for e-filing.

Extensions.—No paper or electronic state extension applications are required.

• *Fiduciary return*

Mandates and options.—Fiduciaries are allowed, but not required, to electronically file Form 541. (*Tax News,* Franchise Tax Board, October 2013)

Extensions.—No paper or electronic state extension applications are required.

• *Special taxes programs*

All special taxes accounts (including most environmental fees, excise, and fuel tax accounts) whose average monthly tax or fee payments equal or exceed $20,000 are required to participate in the electronic fund transfer (EFT) program. Each qualifying account will be notified in writing by the SBE of their mandatory EFT status. Once notified, a taxpayer must continue to make tax or fee payments electronically for a mandatory EFT account until notified in writing of the taxpayer's eligibility to withdraw from the program. (Reg. 4905, 18 CCR)

Taxpayers not required to participate in the EFT nevertheless may choose to do so voluntarily. To make the election, a taxpayer must notify the SBE and complete an Authorization Agreement for Electronic Funds Transfer form (BOE-555-EFT).

(1) motor fuel tax; (Sec. 7403.2, Rev. & Tax. Code; Sec. 7651, Rev. & Tax. Code; Sec. 7652.5 Rev. & Tax. Code)

(2) use fuel tax; (Sec. 8752, Rev. & Tax. Code; Sec. 8763, Rev. & Tax. Code; Reg. 1331.2, 18 CCR)

(3) cigarette and tobacco products tax; (Sec. 30181, Rev. & Tax. Code —Sec. 30188, Rev. & Tax. Code; Sec. 30193, Rev. & Tax. Code; Reg. 4031.1, 18 CCR)

(4) alcoholic beverage tax; (Sec. 32251, Rev. & Tax. Code)

(5) energy resources surcharge; (Sec. 40061, Rev. & Tax. Code; Sec. 40063, Rev. & Tax. Code; Sec. 40069, Rev. & Tax. Code; Reg. 2333, 18 CCR)

(6) emergency telephone users surcharge; (Sec. 41052, Rev. & Tax. Code; Sec. 41063, Rev. & Tax. Code; Reg. 2425, 18 CCR)

(7) hazardous substances tax; (Sec. 43152.9, Rev. & Tax. Code; Sec. 43173, Rev. & Tax. Code; Reg. 3005, 18 CCR)

(8) integrated waste management fee (lubricating oil tax); (Sec. 45151, Rev. & Tax. Code; Reg. 3303, 18 CCR)

(9) oil spill response, prevention, and administration fee; (Sec. 45163, Rev. & Tax. Code)

(10) underground storage tank maintenance fee; (Sec. 50109, Rev. & Tax. Code; Sec. 50112.10, Rev. & Tax. Code; Reg. 1214, 18 CCR)

(11) fee collection procedures; (Reg. 3503, 18 CCR) and

(12) diesel fuel tax. (Sec. 60201, Rev. & Tax. Code—Sec. 60205.5, Rev. & Tax. Code; Sec. 60107, Rev. & Tax. Code; Reg. 1425, 18 CCR)

• *Withholding of tax*

Employers required under IRC Sec. 6011 to file magnetic media returns for federal withholding tax purposes must:

(1) file any subsequent reports of wages electronically; or

(2) establish a lack of automation, severe economic hardship, current exemption from submitting magnetic media or electronic information returns for federal purposes, or other good cause for not filing reports of wages electronically.

Effective January 1, 2017, all employers with 10 or more employees must file their report of contributions, quarterly return, and report of wages electronically. Effective January 1, 2018, the requirement is extended to all employers to file the report of contributions, quarterly return, and report of wages electronically. However, an employer may request a waiver from the electronic filing requirements. The Employment Development Department may grant a waiver if the employer establishes to the satisfaction of the director that there is a lack of automation, a severe economic hardship, a current exemption from filing electronically for federal purposes, or other good cause. An approved waiver shall wibe valid for one year or longer, at the discretion of the director. (Sec. 1088, Unempl. Ins. Code)

• *Sales and use taxes*

Sales and use tax returns and permit applications may be filed by computer modem, magnetic media, optical disk, facsimile machine, telephone, or other electronic media. (Sec. 6479.31, Rev. & Tax. Code)

Taxpayers, who currently file Form BOE-401-A, with Schedule A only; or form BOE-401-EZ and who conduct their business from a single location can file their sales and use tax returns electronically. Taxpayers can obtain additional information about the E-file program by accessing the taxpayer website at (www.boe.ca.gov/) or by calling the BOE Information Center at (800) 400-7115. See *News Release, No. 26-P*, California State Board of Equalization, June 8, 2001.

The SBE launched its first free sales and use tax E-file system in 2005. Effective May 7, 2007, the option of the free Sales Tax E-file service is expanded to be offered to businesses with only one location that pre-ay on a quarterly basis. (*News Release 26-Y*, California State Board of Equalization, May 7, 2007)

[¶89-108] Payment Methods

Depending on the type of tax owed, payments may be made online, by cash, check, credit card, or electronic funds transfer (EFT).

• *Online payments*

Income taxes.—Personal income taxpayers and businesses may make payments on the Franchise Tax Board's (FTB) website through the FTB's Web-Pay program found on the FTB's website at: https://www.ftb.ca.gov/pay/bank-account/index.asp.

Special taxes.—The State Board of Equalization (BOE) EFT program allows taxpayers to electronically pay amounts due for special taxes and fees accounts. Electronic payment is required if a taxpayer's monthly tax or fee payments are at least $20,000. (Publication 89ST, EFT Quick Reference Guide, California State Board of Equalization)

• *Check or credit card*

State and local agencies must accept in-state checks in payment of any license, permit, fee, or other obligation if the person issuing the check furnishes satisfactory proof of residence in the state. (Sec. 5157, Govt. Code)

In addition, all state agencies, with limited exceptions, must accept payments made by credit cards or other payment devices for all forms of government-to-consumer transactions. (Sec. 6163, Govt. Code)

Income taxes.—Corporation franchise (income) taxes and personal income taxes are payable directly to the Franchise Tax Board (FTB) by credit cards issued by Discover, MasterCard, Visa, or American Express or by check payable in U.S. funds. Credit card payments are accepted for current-year tax return payment, extension payment (FTB 3519), estimated tax payment (Form 540-ES), any amount owed for prior years, or any bill that includes an insert about credit card payments. To pay by credit card (1) call 1-800-272-9829 and enter the jurisdiction code 1555 and payment information, or (2) access the FTB website at https://www.ftb.ca.gov/pay/credit-card.html, then go to Official Payments Corp. and provide payment information. Credit card payments are subject to a convenience fee (minimum fee of $1.00) which is retained by the credit card vendor.

Amounts not paid by the bank on which a credit card or check is drawn, including amounts not paid because the taxpayer later reverses the credit card transaction, remain the liability of the taxpayer, with interest, penalties, and other fees imposed for nonpayment or late payment of taxes. (Sec. 19005, Rev. & Tax. Code)

Taxes, fees collected by the SBE.—The SBE has broadened the option to make credit card payments to all taxes and fees it collects. Taxpayers may use credit cards issued by Discover, MasterCard, Visa, and American Express. (*News Release 26-Y*, California State Board of Equalization, May 7, 2007) Credit card payments are subject to a convenience fee of 2.5% of the transaction amount. This fee is retained by the credit card vendor and is not revenue to the SBE. Credit card payment is not acceptable for tax liabilities billed by the SBE or tax liabilities required to be paid by EFT (see discussion below). However, taxpayers who are currently a voluntary electronic funds transfer account may pay their tax by credit card. (California SBE Website at www.boe.ca.gov/elecsrv/faqcc.htm)

To remit sales and use tax payments by credit card, taxpayers must:

(1) complete the return or prepayment form to determine how much tax is due;

(2) call 1-800-272-9829, enter jurisdiction code 1599, and follow the recorded instructions;

(3) check the box on the return or prepayment form indicating payment by credit card; and

(4) sign and timely mail the completed return or form.

General questions about remittance by credit card should be directed to the SBE Information Center at 1-800-400-7115. (*News Release 41-G*, California SBE, August 16, 1999; *News Release 8-G*, California SBE, February 9, 1998)

Alternatively, payments may be remitted over the Internet at http://www.boe.ca.gov. (*Tax Information Bulletin*, California SBE, June 2000)

• *Electronic funds transfer*

Depending on the type and amount of tax owed, a taxpayer may be required to make payments by EFT.

Income taxes.—Banks and corporations must make payments of corporation franchise or income tax by EFT if:

(1) any estimated tax installment payment exceeds $20,000 or

(2) total tax liability exceeds $80,000 in any taxable year.

In determining whether an installment payment or total tax liability exceeds the threshold amount, corporations whose California income is required to be determined by a combined report must be aggregated, and the aggregate payment or total tax liability must be treated as the income of a single taxpayer. Taxpayers may elect to discontinue making payments by EFT if the threshold amounts are not met for the preceding taxable year. (Sec. 19011, Rev. & Tax. Code; *FTB Pub. 3817, Electronic Funds Transfer Information Guide (1998)*)

Personal income taxpayers must make their tax payments electronically, including utilizing a pay by phone option, if their estimated personal income tax installment payment or extension request payment exceeds $20,000 or if their tax liability exceeds $80,000. The total tax liability is that amount as shown on the taxpayer's original return with any adjustments made to correct clerical or mathematical errors. (Sec. 19011.5, Rev. & Tax. Code)

PRACTICE TIP: *Notice of mandatory e-pay requirement.*—Within a few days of receiving a payment or a posting to the FTB system that triggers the mandatory e-pay requirement, the FTB will send taxpayers an FTB Form 4106 MEO, Mandatory e-pay Program Participation Notice, that advises the taxpayers they must remit future payments electronically, and provides them with their options, including how to request a waiver from the requirement. (*Tax News*, California Franchise Tax Board, August 2011)

Taxpayers may make a written election to not make their payments electronically if they did not meet the $20,000 or $80,000 threshold requirements for the preceding taxable year. In addition, the FTB may waive the electronic payment requirement if it determines that the particular amounts paid in excess of the threshold amounts were not representative of the taxpayer's tax liability. (Sec. 19011, Rev. & Tax. Code; Sec. 19011.5, Rev. & Tax. Code)

PRACTICE TIP: *General waiver from requirement.*—Taxpayers whose tax thresholds fall below the mandatory electronic payment amounts may request to discontinue making electronic payments by filing FTB 4107, Mandatory e-pay Election to Discontinue or Waiver Request. The FTB will notify the taxpayer in writing if the request is approved or denied. If the individual is granted a waiver and later meets e-pay requirements, the individual must resume making payments electronically. (*Tax News*, California Franchise Tax Board, March 2011)

Permanent waiver from requirement.—Taxpayers may request a permanent waiver from the mandatory e-pay requirements by completing FTB 4107PC, Mandatory e-pay Election to Discontinue or Waiver Request, and have a physician complete and sign page 3 of the form. This signed affidavit must be attached to FTB 4107PC when it is submitted. Taxpayers may also check a box on the form to have the FTB review the taxpayer's account for possible waiver of a previously imposed mandatory e-pay penalty if all the following conditions exist:

— the taxpayer received a mandatory e-pay penalty for payments made before receiving approval of his/her permanent physical or mental impairment request;

— the date on the physician's affidavit of permanent physical or mental impairment pre-dates the assessment of the penalty; and

— the statute of limitations for filing a claim for refund is still open.

The FTB will notify taxpayers as to whether the request for a permanent waiver has been accepted or denied. (*Mandatory E-Pay for Individuals*, California Franchise Tax Board, updated March 2012)

Taxpayers receiving a permanent disability waiver that file a joint return with a spouse or registered domestic partner who has not received a general or mandatory waiver from the requirements must continue to make all future payments electronically regardless of the taxable year, type of payment, or amount if they have met the mandatory e-pay requirement. (*Public Service Bulletin 12-09*, California Franchise Tax Board, March 29, 2012)

Corporation franchise and income tax and personal income tax taxpayers not required to remit payments by EFT may voluntarily remit payments by EFT if they obtain the FTB's approval by completing and submitting form FTB 3815 to the FTB.

Payments of corporation franchise or income tax and personal income tax by EFT may be made by automated clearinghouse debit, automated clearinghouse credit, Federal Reserve Wire Transfer (Fedwire), or international funds transfer. (Sec. 19011, Rev. & Tax. Code)

Penalties are imposed for failure to comply with the EFT requirements. (see ¶89-206) The FTB has released a legal ruling providing guidance as to when these penalties will be imposed and when the FTB may waive the penalties. (*Legal Ruling 96-4*, California Franchise Tax Board, July 3, 1996)

Withholding of tax.—Prior to January 1, 2017, any employer whose cumulative average payment for deposit periods in the 12-month period ending June 30 of the prior year was $20,000 or more must, for one calendar year beginning January 1, remit the total amount of withheld state income taxes by EFT. Effective January 1, 2017, all employers subject to the electronic filing requirements of Sec. 1088, Unemp. Ins. Code, must remit the total amount of income tax withheld by EFT. Any employer required to remit payments by EFT may request a waiver of the requirement from the Employment Development Department (EDD). The EDD may grant a waiver only if it determines that the taxpayer's payments in excess of the threshold amount were not representative of the taxpayer's actual tax liability and were the result of an unprecedented occurrence. Employers not required to pay by EFT may elect to do so with the approval of the EDD. (Sec. 13021, Unempl. Ins. Code)

Sales and use taxes.—Except as discussed below, persons whose estimated sales and use tax liability averages $10,000 or more per month ($20,000 or more per month under the law in effect prior to January 1, 2006), other than those who collect use tax voluntarily, must remit the taxes due by EFT. Persons whose estimated tax liability is less than the threshold amount, and those who voluntarily collect use tax, may elect to remit the tax due by EFT with State Board of Equalization approval, using form BOE-555-EFT, of the SBE. Payment is deemed complete on the date the taxpayer initiates the transfer, provided settlement to the state's demand account occurs by the following banking day; otherwise, payment is deemed complete on the date settlement occurs. Before January 1, 2022, a person issued a seller's permit for a place of business that is a "dispensary," as defined in the Medical Cannabis Regulation and Safety Act, may remit amounts due for retail sales at the dispensary by a means other than electronic funds transfer. (Sec. 6479.3, Rev. & Tax. Code)

Payment is deemed timely for electronically filed returns if the transmission is completed by the due date of the return. (Sec. 6479.31, Rev. & Tax. Code)

Payments of sales and use taxes by EFT may be made by automated clearinghouse debit, automated clearinghouse credit, or Federal Reserve Wire Transfer (Fedwire). (Sec. 6479.5, Rev. & Tax. Code)

The California State Board of Equalization (SBE) provides guidance regarding EFT. (*SBE Publication 80-D, EFT Quick Reference Guide*, August 2008)

Insurance taxes.—Insurers whose annual insurance taxes exceed $20,000 must make EFT payments. (Sec. 1531, Ins. Code; Sec. 1775.8, Ins. Code; Sec. 12602, Rev. & Tax. Code; Reg. 2330.1, 10 CCR) In the case of Medi-Cal managed care plans, all payments must be made by EFT. (Sec. 12602, Rev. & Tax. Code)

Other taxes.—Persons whose estimated tax liability for any of the following taxes averages $20,000 or more per month, as determined by the SBE, must remit amounts due by EFT:

— alcoholic beverage tax; (Sec. 32260, Rev. & Tax. Code)

— motor vehicle fuel tax; (Sec. 7659.9, Rev. & Tax. Code)

— use fuel tax; (Sec. 8760, Rev. & Tax. Code)

— cigarette tax; (Sec. 30190, Rev. & Tax. Code)

— energy resources surcharge; (Sec. 40067, Rev. & Tax. Code)

— emergency telephone users surcharge; (Sec. 41060, Rev. & Tax. Code)

— hazardous substances tax; (Sec. 43170, Rev. & Tax. Code)

— integrated waste management fee; (Sec. 45160, Rev. & Tax. Code)

— oil spill prevention and administration fee; (Sec. 46160, Rev. & Tax. Code)

— oil spill response fee; (Sec. 46160, Rev. & Tax. Code)

— underground storage tank maintenance fee; (Sec. 50112.7, Rev. & Tax. Code) or

— diesel fuel tax. (Sec. 60250, Rev. & Tax. Code)

Persons whose estimated tax liability for any of these taxes averages less than $20,000 per month may elect to remit amounts due by EFT with the approval of the SBE. The election is operative for a minimum of one year until January 1, 2006, when this minimum is no longer required. (Reg. 4905, 18 CCR)

• *Payment by warrant*

Income taxes.—A taxpayer who is a payee named in a registered warrant received in payment of an obligation of the state may pay any income tax liability, including any liability for periodic estimated tax payments, by submitting a check in an amount not exceeding the amount of the warrant, excluding interest, along with a copy of the warrant. The check must not be presented for payment by the state or be paid by the bank on which it is drawn until the warrant becomes payable. The taxpayer may not collect any interest on the warrant from the date the check for the payment of taxes is submitted. (Sec. 17280.1, Govt. Code; Sec. 17280.2, Govt. Code; Sec. 17280.3, Govt. Code)

[¶89-110] Mailing Rules and Legal Holidays

A return sent through the U.S. mail or a bona fide commercial delivery service is generally deemed filed on the date shown by the cancellation mark (e.g., the postmark) on the envelope containing the return, provided the return is properly addressed and the postage is prepaid. It may be possible to establish that the return was actually mailed on an earlier date if satisfactory proof is presented to the state agency. (Sec. 11003, Govt. Code)

If the last day for filing a return falls on a Saturday, Sunday, or legal holiday, the return is deemed timely if filed on the next business day. (Sec. 6707, Govt. Code)

Any federal legal holiday recognized by the Internal Revenue Service under IRC §7503 will automatically be considered a legal holiday for California corporation franchise and income and personal income tax purposes. (Sec. 18410, Rev. & Tax. Code)

[¶89-112] Whole Dollar Reporting

If filing a corporation franchise (income) or personal income tax return, the Franchise Tax Board allows the rounding up of fractional parts of a dollar to the nearest whole dollar if that is 50¢; and rounded down to the nearest whole dollar if the fractional part is less than 50¢. The rounding-off provision does not apply to computations necessary to determine each amount shown on the return, but applies only to the final amount. (Sec. 18623, Rev. & Tax. Code; FTB Instructions to Form 540 and telephone conversation with the FTB, Taxpayer Assistance, August 15, 2001)

Any amount reported on a sales and use tax return filed with the State Board of Equalization should be rounded to the nearest whole dollar amount (i.e., a fractional part of a dollar is disregarded unless it amounts to 50¢ or more, in which case the amount is increased to the next whole dollar). This rounding-off method applies only to cumulative amounts reported on the return. (Reg. 1704, 18 CCR)

[¶89-130]

AUDITS

[¶89-132] Audits in General

In general, audits of taxes administered by the State Board of Equalization (BOE) and by the Franchise Tax Board (FTB) cover returns filed over the past three years or four years, respectively. Audits may cover a longer period if no returns have been filed. (see ¶89-144)

Auditors are not evaluated based on revenue quotas or goals; see ¶89-222 for a list of statutory sections barring such quotas or goals.

California is a member of the Multistate Tax Commission, which maintains a Joint Audit Program that audits businesses for several states concurrently for sales and use and corporate income taxes. (see ¶89-184) The article of the Multistate Tax Compact relating to interstate audits is made applicable in California. (Sec. 38021, Rev. & Tax. Code)

For California sales and use tax purposes, the BOE provides guidance regarding computer-assisted audits in a publication designed to help taxpayers understand what to expect when the agency, as part of an audit, examines the taxpayers' electronic records. Taxpayers are reminded that, under BOE regulations, the BOE is permitted to access all records, including electronic (machine-sensible) records and data. Computer data is considered part of the taxpayers' books and records. In a computer-assisted audit, the taxpayer downloads data that the BOE analyzes using specialized software and a computer audit specialist to assist the auditor. By requiring the retrieval of fewer source documents, such as invoices, the computer assisted audit saves the taxpayer time and money, according to the BOE. Other topics discussed are what the auditor will need to know about a taxpayer's electronic records, confidentiality of records, the steps in a computer assisted audit, and statistical sampling standards. (*BOE Publication 147, What To Expect in a Computer-Assisted Audit*, California State Board of Equalization)

[¶89-134] Audits by Tax Type

California has specific audit provisions applicable to various tax types, as discussed below.

• *Corporation franchise (income) and personal income*

The Franchise Tax Board (FTB) has the power to require that any person or entity provide information or make available for examination or copying any relevant books, papers, records, and other data to determine the correctness of a return, to reconstruct a return when none is filed, and to determine and collect all liabilities. It may require the attendance of any person and proof of any matter, and may administer oaths and issue subpoenas for those purposes. (Sec. 19504, Rev. & Tax. Code) Generally, subpoenas must be signed by a member of the FTB. However, for taxpayers that have been contacted by the FTB regarding the use of an abusive tax avoidance transaction, subpoenas may be signed by a member of the FTB, the Executive Officer of the FTB, or any designee.

The FTB is not required to disclose the standards used for audit selection when such disclosure would seriously impair tax assessment, collection, or enforcement. (Sec. 19544, Rev. & Tax. Code)

PRACTICE POINTER: The FTB has alerted taxpayers to the fact that sales and use tax audits can lead to franchise and income tax audits. The State Board of Equalization provides the FTB with copies of sales and use tax audit reports for the audits that result in adjustments of additional gross receipts (total sales). The FTB reviews these sales and use tax reports to determine if an income tax adjustment is warranted, then advises the taxpayer in writing before making the appropriate adjustments. The FTB has found that the most common income tax items affected by a sales and use tax audit are total sales (gross receipts) and cost of goods sold. At the conclusion of a sales and use tax examination, the audit report should be reviewed to determine if any changes were made to reported sales (total sales and/or taxable sales). In situations where total sales were adjusted, the corresponding income tax return should be reviewed to determine if an adjustment is needed. If the changes made by the SBE result in a change in California income tax liability for the corresponding tax years, the taxpayer should file an amended income tax return. (*Tax News*, California Franchise Tax Board, November 2008)

Water's-edge taxpayers.—The FTB must examine the returns filed by any taxpayer that has made a water's-edge election. If an examination reveals that there may be potential noncompliance with arm's-length standards involving the transfer of goods, services or intangibles, or the lending of money between entities, the FTB *may* conduct a detailed examination/audit, unless the taxpayer has been, or is currently, under examination by the Internal Revenue Service (IRS) with respect to the same year on the same issue. (Sec. 25114, Rev. & Tax. Code; Reg. 25114, 18 CCR)

• *Sales and use*

The State Board of Equalization (SBE) or its authorized representative may examine the books, papers, records, and equipment of any seller of tangible personal property or of any person liable for use tax and may investigate the character of the business to verify the accuracy of the tax returns or, if no returns are filed, to determine the proper tax amount due. (Sec. 7054, Rev. & Tax. Code)

• *Other taxes and fees*

The SBE or its authorized representative may examine the books and records of the following persons and may make other investigations it deems necessary in carrying out the provisions of the applicable tax laws:

— for cigarette tax purposes, every distributor and every person dealing in, transporting, or storing cigarettes or other tobacco products in the state; (Sec. 30454, Rev. & Tax. Code)

— for diesel fuel tax purposes, see ¶ 40-011;

— for emergency telephone users' surcharge purposes, any service supplier; (Sec. 41130, Rev. & Tax. Code)

— for energy resources surcharge purposes, any person generating, transmitting, distributing, consuming, purchasing, or selling electrical energy; (Sec. 40174, Rev. & Tax. Code)

— for hazardous substances tax purposes, any taxpayer; (Sec. 43502, Rev. & Tax. Code)

— for motor vehicle fuel tax purposes, see ¶ 40-011;

— for oil spill fee purposes, any fee payer; (Sec. 46603, Rev. & Tax. Code)

— for solid waste management fee purposes, any fee payer; (Sec. 45852, Rev. & Tax. Code)

— for underground storage tank maintenance fee purposes, any fee payer; (Sec. 46603, Rev. & Tax. Code); and

— for use fuel tax purposes, see ¶ 40-011.

[¶89-142] Record Maintenance and Production

Provisions relating to record maintenance and production are discussed below.

• *Income taxes*

Tax practitioners involved in an ongoing California corporation franchise and income or personal income tax audit or legal case may securely exchange confidential, case-related documents electronically with the Franchise Tax Board (FTB) using the FTB's Secure Electronic Communications System without compromising their clients' privacy. To get started, tax practitioners should simply tell their current FTB contact that they want to use the system. The FTB will initiate the registration process and upon completion of the registration process will send an e-mail confirmation along with information on how to use the system. The system is available 24 hours a day, seven days a week. No special hardware or software is required to use the system; all that is needed are a browser that supports 128-bit encryption and the latest virus protection software. (*Tax News*, California Franchise Tax Board, July/August 2005)

Water's-edge taxpayers.—Any taxpayer apportioning its income or making a water's-edge election is required to maintain and make available upon request by the FTB all of the following:

(1) records to determine the correct treatment of the components that are a part of one or more unitary businesses;

(2) records to determine the correct treatment of amounts that are classified as business or nonbusiness income;

(3) records to determine the proper apportionment factors; and

(4) documents and information necessary to resolve audit issues involving the attribution of income to the United States or to foreign jurisdictions.

(Sec. 19141.6, Rev. & Tax. Code)

A regulation provides that a taxpayer will be deemed to have met the record-keeping requirements if it maintains or causes another person to maintain those records listed in the "safe harbor" provision of the regulation that are relevant to the issues outlined above. The records to be maintained for the safe harbor are organized into the following categories:

(1) financial and tax data;

(2) profit and loss statements;

(3) apportionment factor records;

(4) foreign country and third party filings;

(5) ownership and capital structure records;

(6) management structure;

(7) records of sales transactions; and

(8) records of loans, services, and other non-sales transactions.

Upon a taxpayer's written request, the FTB may also enter into agreements with taxpayers specifying which particular records must actually be maintained (which may be even less than the number required for the safe harbor). (Reg. 19141.6, 18 CCR)

Record maintenance generally does not require the creation of records that are not ordinarily created by the taxpayer or any related parties in the ordinary course of business. However, a taxpayer must create basic accounting records that are sufficient to document the California effects of transactions between related parties if such records do not exist. Also, a taxpayer must create records sufficient to produce material profit and loss statements that are relevant for determining the California tax treatment of transactions between the taxpayer's unitary group and any excluded entity if such records are not maintained in the ordinary course of business. (Reg. 19141.6, 18 CCR)

Records generally must be retained for the longer of the following:

(1) the period of time in which the taxpayer's California franchise or income tax liability is subject to adjustment, including all periods in which additional taxes may be assessed, but not to exceed eight years from the due date (including extensions) of the return;

(2) the period of time during which a protest is pending before the FTB;

(3) the period of time during which an appeal is pending before the State Board of Equalization; or

(4) the period of time during which a refund lawsuit is pending in a state or federal court.

However, a taxpayer need not maintain records beyond the period specified in (1) above if the particular records are irrelevant to the subject matter of any dispute existing at the end of that period. (Reg. 19141.6, 18 CCR)

If a taxpayer fails to maintain or cause another to maintain the records, documents, or information described above, the taxpayer will be subject to a penalty of $10,000 for each income year with respect to which the failure occurs upon approval by a majority of the members of the FTB. Moreover, if any such failure continues for more than 90 days after the FTB mails notice of the failure to the taxpayer, the taxpayer will be subject to an additional penalty of $10,000 with respect to each related party for which the failure occurs for each 30-day period (or fraction thereof) during which the failure continues after the 90-day period expires.

Although failure to maintain records (and any associated penalty) may be excused for reasonable cause, it is the taxpayer's burden to affirmatively show that there is reasonable cause. Reasonable cause includes, but is not limited to, destruction resulting from theft, riot, war, or natural disaster. The reasonable cause standard is applied liberally to banks and corporations whose gross receipts or net assets for a taxable year total $50 million or less, provided that the bank or corporation had no knowledge of the recordkeeping requirements, has a limited presence in and contact with California, and fully complies with all FTB requests for books, records, or other relevant materials. If the FTB finds no reasonable cause, the taxpayer may file a petition for review with the FTB, within 60 days of receiving notification of the FTB's determination. (Reg. 19141.6, 18 CCR)

The FTB may issue a subpoena or subpoena duces tecum requesting a taxpayer to produce any of the above records, documents, or information or related testimony. A taxpayer may file suit to quash a subpoena or subpoena duces tecum no later than 90 days after it is issued; all statutes of limitation regarding tax assessment and collection or criminal prosecution are suspended while the action is pending. (Sec. 19141.6, Rev. & Tax. Code)

If the taxpayer is unable to comply with the subpoena or subpoena duces tecum, the FTB, in its sole discretion and based on its own knowledge and information from other sources, may determine the components of any unitary business of which the taxpayer is a part, the apportionment factors of such business, the classification of items as business or nonbusiness income, and the attribution of income to the United States or foreign jurisdictions. A taxpayer may appeal the FTB's determination to the State Board of Equalization (BOE) or to the appropriate court. However, review by the BOE or a court is limited to whether the determination was arbitrary, capricious, or not supported by substantial evidence. (Sec. 19141.6, Rev. & Tax. Code)

The FTB may not exercise its power to determine the component parts of a unitary business for the purpose of circumventing a water's-edge election. (Sec. 19141.6, Rev. & Tax. Code)

The FTB may also make its own determinations if a taxpayer is not authorized to act as the limited agent of all of the taxpayer's related parties with respect to requests by the FTB to examine or furnish records or testimony. Any such authorization must be submitted in a form preapproved by the FTB. (Reg. 19141.6, 18 CCR)

Recordkeeping requirements for corporate taxpayers electing to file on a water's-edge basis are discussed in detail at ¶ 11-550 Combined Reports.

Recordkeeping requirements.—The FTB is required to preserve tax returns for a minimum of three years from the due date until it orders them to be destroyed. The FTB may charge fees for providing taxpayers copies of tax returns, including the costs of handling requests, copying documents, and postage. (Sec. 19530, Rev. & Tax. Code; Sec. 19561, Rev. & Tax. Code)

• *Other taxes and fees*

CDTFA Publication 76, *Audits*, by the California Department of Tax and Fee Administration, lists the types of records an BOE auditor may need when performing an audit. Persons are required to keep records and other data as the CDTFA may prescribe for the applicable tax laws defined in Reg. 4901, 18 CCR, including the following tax laws:

— for cigarette tax purposes, every distributor and every person dealing in, transporting, or storing cigarettes or other tobacco products in the state; (Sec. 30453, Rev. & Tax. Code)

— for diesel fuel tax purposes, see ¶ 40-011

— for emergency telephone users' surcharge purposes, every service supplier in the state; (Sec. 41129, Rev. & Tax. Code)

— for energy resources surcharge purposes, every electric utility engaged in generating, purchasing, transmitting, distributing, consuming, or selling electrical energy in the state; (Sec. 40172, Rev. & Tax. Code; Sec. 40173, Rev. & Tax. Code)

— for motor vehicle fuel tax purposes, see ¶ 40-011;

— for sales and use tax purposes, every seller, retailer, and person storing, using, or otherwise consuming tangible personal property in the state that has been purchased from a retailer; (Sec. 7053, Rev. & Tax. Code) and

— for use fuel tax purposes, see ¶ 40-011.

PLANNING NOTE: The CDTFA provides guidance regarding audits in *CDTFA Publication 76, Audits.* Issues discussed include initial contact, scheduling an appointment, records that will be reviewed, discussion with the auditor, examination and testing, audit findings, the exit conference, notice of audit results, what to do if you disagree with the audit results, prepaying a liability, Notices of Determination (billing), Notices of Refund, and other appeal procedures. (*CDTFA Publication 76, Audits,* California Department of Tax and Fee Administration)

A person required to pay taxes under any of the applicable tax laws listed above must make available for CDTFA examination, on request, the following records:

— books of account or other similar summary information;

— bills, receipts, invoices, cash register tapes, or other documents of original entry supporting entries in the books of account; and

— schedules of working papers used in connection with the preparation of tax returns and reports.

(Reg. 4901, 18 CCR)

Sales or use tax transactions.—Taxpayers should keep all records in regard to transactions that involve sales or use tax liability for four years unless the CDTFA has provided written authorization to destroy such records sooner. Moreover, if the CDTFA conducts an audit of a taxpayer's records, the taxpayer should retain all records for the period being audited until the audit is completed, or until the case is resolved if a taxpayer appeals audit findings or files a claim for refund. (*Tax Information Bulletin,* California State Board of Equalization, March 2006)

Machine-sensible records.—Machine-sensible records are "records" used to establish tax compliance. These records must contain sufficient source document (transaction-level) information to identify the details underlying the machine-sensible records and be capable of being retrieved and converted to a standard magnetic record format. A taxpayer that uses electronic data interchange (EDI) processes and technology or electronic data processing (EDP) systems must satisfy the requirements specified in Reg. 4901, 18 CCR.

A taxpayer must provide, upon CDTFA request, a description of the business process that created the retained records, including the relationship between the records and the tax documents prepared by the taxpayer, and the measures employed to ensure the integrity of the records. The taxpayer must demonstrate the:

— function being performed;

— internal controls used to ensure accurate and reliable processing; and

— internal controls used to prevent unauthorized addition, alteration, or deletion of retained records.

(Reg. 4901, 18 CCR)

The specific documentation required for the retention of machine-sensible records include:

— record formats or layouts;

— field definitions, including the meaning of all codes used to represent information;

— file descriptions; and

— detailed charts of accounts and account descriptions.

(Reg. 4901, 18 CCR)

Hardcopy records.—Taxpayers must retain hardcopy records that are created or received in the ordinary course of business, including those generated at the time of a transaction using a credit or debit card. Taxpayer do not have to retain hardcopies of computer printouts created for validation, control, or other temporary purposes. (Reg. 4901, 18 CCR)

Alternative storage media.—Taxpayers may convert hardcopy documents received or produced in the normal course of business and required to be retained to storage-only imaging media (*i.e.*, microfilm, microfiche, or other media used in electronic imaging). Taxpayers that convert to storage-only imaging media must:

— retain and make available on request the documentation establishing the procedures for converting hardcopy documents to storage-only imaging system;

— establish procedures for the identification, processing, storage, and preservation of the stored documents;

— provide, upon CDTFA request, facilities and equipment for reading, locating, and reproducing the documents; and

— maintain and arrange documents in a manner that permits the location of any particular record.

In addition, the documents, when displayed on storage-only imaging media or reproduced on paper, must exhibit a high degree of legibility and readability. For these purposes, "legibility" means the quality of a letter or numeral that enables the observer to identify it positively and quickly. "Readability" means the quality of a group of letters or numerals being recognizable as words or complete numbers. There must be no substantial evidence that the storage-only imaging medium lacks authenticity or integrity. (Reg. 4901, 18 CCR)

Record retention.—Taxpayers must retain all records required for retention for a period of at least four years, unless the CDTFA gives written authorization for an earlier destruction. (Reg. 4901, 18 CCR)

Record retention limitation agreement.—The CDTFA may enter into or revoke a record retention agreement. A taxpayer's request for this agreement must specify those records that will not be retained and the reasons. Only the records included in a CDTFA-approved agreement are subject to the agreement. However, the agreement does not relieve the taxpayer of the responsibility to maintain adequate and complete records supporting any tax or information return. (Reg. 4901, 18 CCR)

A request for an agreement to limit the taxpayer's retention of machine-sensible records must:

— document the understandings reached with the CDTFA, including the conversion of files created on an obsolete computer system, restoration of lost or damaged files and the action to be taken, and the use of taxpayer computer resources;

— specifically identify which of the records that the CDTFA determines are not necessary for retention and which records may be discarded; and

— authorize any variance from the normal regulation provisions.

(Reg. 4901, 18 CCR)

When a record retention limitation agreement exists, the taxpayer's record retention practices are subject to the CDTFA's evaluation. The evaluation may include a review of the taxpayer's relevant data processing and accounting systems, including systems using electronic data interchange (EDI) technology. The evaluation does not determine tax reporting accuracy and, therefore, is not an "examination of records." (Reg. 4901, 18 CCR)

In addition to the record retention evaluation, the CDTFA may conduct tests to establish the authenticity, readability, completeness, and integrity of the machine-sensible records retained under a record retention limitation agreement. This testing may include the testing of EDI and a review of the internal controls and security procedures associated with the storage of these records. (Reg. 4901, 18 CCR)

Unless otherwise specified, the agreement does not apply to accounting and tax systems added subsequent to the completion of the evaluation, or to any person, company, corporation, or organization that acquires the taxpayer or is acquired by the taxpayer subsequent to the taxpayer's signing of the agreement. (Reg. 4901, 18 CCR)

Failure to maintain records.—A taxpayer's failure to maintain complete and accurate records is considered evidence of negligence or intent to evade tax, and may be subject to penalties or other administrative action. (Reg. 4901, 18 CCR)

Reliance on CDTFA advice.—A person may be relieved from liability for the payment of any tax or fees defined in Reg. 4901, 18 CCR, including any interest or penalties, when the liability resulted from a failure to timely file a return or make a payment and that failure is found by the CDTFA to be due to reasonable reliance on:

— written advice given by the CDTFA to the person in response to a specific written inquiry seeking relief from liability that fully describes the circumstances of the activity or transactions for which the advice was requested;

— written advice from the CDTFA in the form of an annotation or legal ruling of counsel, but only if the underlying legal ruling involving the fact pattern at issue is addressed to the person in response to a specific written inquiry seeking relief from liability, or the annotation or legal ruling is provided to the person by the CDTFA within the body of a written communication and involves the same fact pattern as that presented in the subject annotation or legal ruling; and

— written advice given by the CDTFA in a prior audit.

(Reg. 1124, 18 CCR; Reg. 1422, 18 CCR; Reg. 4902, 18 CCR)

Moreover, a trade or industry association requesting advice for its members must identify the member for whom the advice is requested in order for the relief from liability to apply. (Reg. 4902, 18 CCR)

Relief from California special tax and fee liabilities is extended to provide relief due to reasonable reliance on written advice from the CDTFA to a person who relies on advice provided in a prior audit of a related person, under specific circumstances. Written advice from the CDTFA that was received during a prior audit of the person, as provided, may be relied upon by the person audited or a person with shared accounting and common ownership with the audited person or by a legal or statutory successor to those persons. A person is considered to have shared accounting and common ownership if the person:

— is engaged in the same line of business as the audited person;

— has common verifiable controlling ownership of 50% or greater ownership or has a common majority shareholder with the audited person; and

— shares centralized accounting functions with the audited person (i.e., the audited person routinely follows the same business practices that are followed by each entity involved).

(Reg. 4902, 18 CCR)

Evidence that may indicate sharing of centralized accounting functions includes, but is not limited to:

— quantifiable control of the accounting practices of each business by the common ownership or management that dictates office policies for accounting and tax return preparation;

— shared accounting staff or an outside firm that maintains books and records and prepares returns for special tax and fee programs, as provided; and

— shared accounting policies and procedures.

(Reg. 4902, 18 CCR)

In addition, the taxpayer is required to establish that these requirements existed during the periods for which relief is sought. A subsequent written notification from the CDTFA that provides that the advice was not valid at the time it was issued, or was subsequently rendered invalid to any party with shared accounting and common ownership, including the audited party, serves as notification to all parties with shared accounting and common ownership, including the audited party, that the prior written advice may not be relied upon as of the notification date. (Reg. 4902, 18 CCR)

[¶89-144] Limitations Period for Audits

The following summarizes limitations periods applicable to taxes administered by the State Board of Equalization (BOE) and by the Franchise Tax Board (FTB).

•*BOE*

Sales and use.—In general, a sales and use tax audit covers returns filed over the past three years. Audits may cover the past eight years if no returns have been filed or if the taxpayer's gross receipts and total quarterly sales price of property sold or purchased equals or exceeds $10 million. Although a taxpayer's signature on a Waiver of Limitation document extends limitations periods that would otherwise expire, it also extends the time period available to file refund claims and allows credit arising from that period to offset tax liability. (Sec. 6487, Rev. & Tax. Code; Sec. 6563, Rev. & Tax. Code)

Other taxes and fees.—General limitations periods for the following taxes and fees are also three years, or eight years if no return is filed:

— alcoholic beverage tax; (Sec. 32272, Rev. & Tax. Code)

— cigarette tax; (Sec. 30207, Rev. & Tax. Code)

— diesel fuel tax, see ¶ 40-011;

— emergency telephone users' surcharge; (Sec. 41076, Rev. & Tax. Code)

— energy resources surcharge; (Sec. 40077, Rev. & Tax. Code)

— hazardous substances tax; (Sec. 43202, Rev. & Tax. Code)

— motor vehicle fuel tax, see ¶ 40-011;

— oil spill fees; (Sec. 46203, Rev. & Tax. Code)

— solid waste management fees; (Sec. 45202, Rev. & Tax. Code)

— timber yield tax; (Sec. 38417, Rev. & Tax. Code)

— underground storage tank maintenance fees; (Sec. 50113.1, Rev. & Tax. Code); and

— use fuel tax, see ¶ 40-011.

The general limitations period for insurance taxes is four years, or eight years if no return is filed. (Sec. 12432, Rev. & Tax. Code)

• *FTB*

For corporation franchise or income tax and personal income tax purposes, notices of proposed assessment must be issued within prescribed limitations periods. Circumstances, beginning with "Normal" in the following table, determine the limitations period applicable:

Circumstances	Limitations Period
Normal	4 years after original due date or 4 years after date filed, whichever is later (Sec. 19057, Rev. & Tax. Code; Sec. 19066, Rev. & Tax. Code)
State waiver	Period agreed upon (Sec. 19067, Rev. & Tax. Code)
Joint return after filing separate returns	1 year, in addition to time period under (Sec. 19057, Rev. & Tax. Code) through (Sec. 19067, Rev. & Tax. Code), after joint return filed (Sec. 18529, Rev. & Tax. Code)
Gain on sale of principal residence	4 years after notification by taxpayer of cost of new residence, intention not to purchase, or failure to purchase within period specified (Sec. 17024.5, Rev. & Tax. Code)
Request fiduciary	18 months after written request to invoke provisions of (Sec. 19517, Rev. & Tax. Code) made subsequent to or concurrently with
Substantially disproportionate redemptions	1 year after notice by taxpayer of reacquisition of stock (Sec. 17322, Rev. & Tax. Code)
Fraud; or no return filed	No limitation; assessment may be made at any time (Sec. 19057, Rev. & Tax. Code)
Unreported installment income (Corporation franchise (income))	4 years after taxpayer ceases to be subject to tax (Sec. 24672, Rev. & Tax. Code)
Original transferee (Corporation franchise (income))	1 year beyond the normal statute of limitations (Sec. 19074, Rev. & Tax. Code)
Transferee of a transferee (Corporation franchise (income))	1 year after the expiration of the period of limitation of the preceding transfer, except as provided under Sec. 19074(b), Rev. & Tax. Code)
Omission of 25% of gross income	6 years after date return filed or original due date, whichever is later. (Sec. 19058, Rev. & Tax. Code; Sec. 19066, Rev. & Tax. Code)

Circumstances	Limitations Period
Federal waiver signed	Normal statute or 6 months after expiration of federal waiver, whichever is later (Sec. 19065, Rev. & Tax. Code)
Federal change reported by taxpayer (or state return amended for federal change) 6 months after the final determination	4 years after the date the tapayer notifies the FTB or files return (applicable for federal adjustments only) (Sec. 18622, Rev. & Tax. Code; Sec. 18622.5, Rev. & Tax. Code; Sec. 19060, Rev. & Tax. Code)
Federal change reported by taxpayer (or state return amended for federal change) within 6 months of federal determination	Normal statute or 2 years from the date the notice or amended return is filed with the FTB, whichever is later (applicable for federal adjustments only) (Sec. 18622.5, Rev. & Tax. Code; Sec. 19059, Rev. & Tax. Code)
Federal change not reported, or amended state return for federal change not filed	At any time; statute of limitations suspended (Sec. 18622.5, Rev. & Tax. Code; Sec. 19060, Rev. & Tax. Code)
Bankruptcy	Running of statute suspended up to two years (Sec. 19089, Rev. & Tax. Code)
Abusive tax avoidance transaction	8 years (increased to 12 years for taxable years that have not been closed by a statute of limitations, res judicata, or otherwise, as of August 1, 2011) after the return was filed or within the period otherwise provided in Article 3 (commencing with Sec. 19031, Rev. & Tax. Code) of Chapter 4 of Part 10.2 of Division 2 of the Rev. & Tax. Code, whichever expires later (Sec. 19755, Rev. & Tax. Code)

An "abusive tax avoidance transaction" is:

— a California tax shelter;

— a reportable transaction that is not adequately disclosed;

— a listed transaction;

— a gross misstatement; or

— transaction subject to the noneconomic substance transaction (NEST) penalty.

(Sec. 19777(b), Rev. & Tax. Code)

CCH POINTER: *Penalty for omission of 25% of gross income.*—The six-year statute of limitations applicable to assessments related to omitted income in instances in which the taxpayer omitted an income item greater than 25% of the gross income stated on the return does not apply if the return, including all schedules and statements, contains sufficient information so that the FTB can tell the nature and amount of the income that is not included on the return. (*Tax News*, California Franchise Tax Board, May 31, 2010)

Mailing of notice.—A timely mailed notice is valid even though the taxpayer alleges that the notice was not received, because the statute requires only that the notice be mailed by the FTB. (*Appeal of Anderson*, SBE, 81-SBE-117, September 29, 1981) A notice of action that clarifies a timely notice of proposed assessment is also timely. (*Appeal of Sierra Pacific Industries*, SBE, 94-SBE-002, January 5, 1994)

Reporting federal changes.—The California Supreme Court has ruled that the four-year statute of limitations period for issuing a deficiency assessment does not apply in cases in which a federal change is made. (*Ordlock v. FTB*, California Supreme Court, No. S127649, June 8, 2006)

Annual minimum LLC tax.—In a nonprecedential summary decision, the BOE held that a taxpayer's failure to report and pay the annual minimum LLC tax was akin to a mathematical error, and therefore the provision governing the statute of limitations on issuing a deficiency assessment was inapplicable. Similarly, the corresponding late filing and late payment penalties were not governed by the deficiency assessment limitations period statute and thus could be issued after the four year period for issuing a deficiency assessment had lapsed. (*Appeal of Auto Theft R.F. Systems, LLC*, California Board of Equalization, No. 336033, March 22, 2011)

Gain on involuntary conversion.—A taxpayer may elect not to recognize gain on the involuntary conversion of property owned by the taxpayer into similar property. Generally, the tax on any gain is deferred, provided the proceeds from the original property are invested in replacement property or in a corporation owning replacement property within a specified period, see ¶10-640 and ¶15-710. An election to defer recognition of any gain from an involuntary conversion results in two special periods of assessment that override, in respect only to the conversion gain, any other limitation period that would otherwise bar an assessment. (Sec. 19061, Rev. & Tax. Code)

The first special period of assessment begins when the taxpayer notifies the FTB that (1) the replacement property was purchased within the specified period, or (2) the taxpayer does not intend to purchase replacement property. The FTB has four years from the date of notification to assess any deficiency attributable to any part of the deferred gain on involuntary conversion for any tax year in which any part of the gain is realized.

The second period of assessment is applicable if the replacement property is purchased in a tax year preceding the tax year or years in which the proceeds from the disposition of the original property are realized. In this situation, the amount of any gain cannot be determined until the final year of realization. Under the second assessment period, a deficiency may be assessed at any time before the expiration of the period within which a deficiency for the final year of realization may be assessed. (Sec. 19061, Rev. & Tax. Code; Sec. 24946, Rev. & Tax. Code)

Installment sales between related parties.—A special period of assessment applies to a taxpayer that makes an installment sale to a related party that is followed by a resale by the related party. To the extent that a deficiency was attributable to the early recognition of gain by the first seller, the deficiency may be assessed against the first seller at any time within two years after the date the first seller notifies the FTB that there was a resale by the related party to which the early recognition rules may apply. This special assessment period overrides all other limitation periods that would otherwise bar an assessment. (Sec. 24667(a), Rev. & Tax. Code; IRC Sec. 453(e)(8))

Partners of federally registered partnerships.—A special assessment period applies to deficiencies attributable to a partnership item of a federally registered partnership. The period for assessing a deficiency attributable to any such partnership item is the later of (1) five years after the date of filing (or, if later, the date prescribed for filing) the partnership return for the partnership tax year in which the item arose, or, (2) if the name and address of the partner to be assessed does not appear on the partnership return, one year after the FTB is furnished with this information. (Sec. 19063, Rev. & Tax. Code)

Noncash patronage allocations.—On receipt of noncash patronage allocations from farmers' cooperative associations, a taxpayer may elect either to include the allocations in gross income in the year received or to exclude them from gross income until redeemed or realized. (Sec. 17086(a), Rev. & Tax Code; Sec. 24273.5(a), Rev. & Tax. Code) Any deficiency attributable to the receipt of noncash patronage allocations may be assessed at any time up to four years after the date the FTB is first notified that the deferred allocations have been redeemed or realized. (Sec. 17086(f), Rev. & Tax Code; Sec. 24273.5(f), Rev. & Tax. Code)

[¶89-160]
COLLECTION OF TAX

[¶89-164] Assessment of Delinquent Tax

Tax delinquency dates and notice requirements vary according to the type of tax collected and the action taken.

• *Date of delinquency*

Income taxes.—Generally, personal income taxes are delinquent if not paid by the 15th day of the fourth month following the close of the taxable year. Corporation franchise (income) taxes are delinquent if not paid by the 15th day of the third month following the close of the taxable year. (Sec. 18566, Rev. & Tax. Code; Sec. 18601, Rev. & Tax. Code; Sec. 19001, Rev. & Tax. Code)

Exempt organization taxes on unrelated business income are delinquent if not paid by the 15th day of the fifth month following the close of the taxable year. (Sec. 23771, Rev. & Tax. Code)

Estimated income taxes.—Payments of estimated income tax by calendar year taxpayers are delinquent if not made by April 15, June 15, and September 15 of the taxable year and January 15 of the following year. These dates are adjusted accordingly for fiscal year taxpayers. (Sec. 19025, Rev. & Tax. Code; Sec. 19136, Rev. & Tax. Code)

Sales and use taxes.—Sales and use taxes are delinquent if not paid by the last day of the month following each quarterly period. (Sec. 6451, Rev. & Tax. Code)

Severance taxes.—The annual oil and gas production charge for assessments of more than $10 but less than $500 becomes delinquent if not paid by August 15. For assessments of $500 or more, one-half of the charge is delinquent if not paid by August 15 and the remaining one-half of the charge is delinquent if not paid by February 1 of the following year. (Sec. 3420, Pub. Res. Code)

Timber yield taxes are delinquent if not paid by the last day of the month following each quarterly period in which the scaling date for the harvested timber occurs. (Sec. 38401, Rev. & Tax. Code)

Lubricating oil tax.—Lubricating oil taxes are delinquent if not paid by the last day of the month following each quarter. (Sec. 48650, Pub. Res. Code)

Underground storage tank fee.—Underground storage tank fees are delinquent if not paid by the 25th day of the month following the quarter for which the fees are due. (Sec. 50109, Rev. & Tax. Code)

Alcoholic beverage taxes.—Alcoholic beverage taxes are delinquent if not paid by the 15th day of the month following each monthly period. (Sec. 32251, Rev. & Tax. Code)

Cigarette and other tobacco products taxes.—Payments by cigarette distributors that defer payment for stamps and meter register settings are delinquent if not paid by the 25th day of the month (if electing to pay on a monthly basis) or by the 5th and 25th days of the month (if electing to pay on a twice-monthly basis). Payments are due on Wednesday of every week from distributors who elect to pay on a weekly basis. (Sec. 30168, Rev. & Tax. Code) Other cigarette and tobacco products taxes are delinquent if not paid by the 25th of the month following the calendar month in which a distribution of cigarettes occurs (if electing to pay on a monthly basis) or by the 5th and 25th days of the month (if electing to pay on a twice-monthly basis). (Sec. 30181, Rev. & Tax. Code)

¶89-160

Payments by cigarette distributors that defer payment for stamps and meter register settings are delinquent if not paid by the 25th day of the month following the month in which the payments were deferred, and payments by other distributors are delinquent if not paid by the 25th day of the month following the month during which the tobacco products were distributed. (Sec. 30168, Rev. & Tax. Code; Sec. 30181, Rev. & Tax. Code)

Insurance taxes.—Insurance taxes, other than taxes on ocean marine insurance and surplus line brokers, are delinquent if not paid by April 1. Taxes on ocean marine insurance are delinquent if not paid by June 15. (Sec. 12301, Rev. & Tax. Code) Surplus line brokers' taxes are delinquent if not paid by March 1. (Sec. 1775.5, Ins. Code)

Energy resources surcharge; emergency telephone users surcharge.—Energy resources surcharges are delinquent if not paid by the last day of the month following each calendar quarter. (Sec. 40051, Rev. & Tax. Code) Emergency telephone users surcharges are delinquent if not paid by the last day of the second month following each calendar quarter. (Sec. 41051, Rev. & Tax. Code)

• *Deficiency assessments*

Discussed below are general procedurs for issuing deficiency assessments. See ¶ 89-144 for a discussion of the limitation periods for deficiency assessments.

Income taxes.—If the Franchise Tax Board (FTB) determines that the tax disclosed by a taxpayer on an original or amended return is less than the tax disclosed by its examination, or if no return is filed, the FTB may mail the taxpayer a notice of proposed deficiency assessment, which must be postmarked by the U.S. Postal Service. (Sec. 19033, Rev. & Tax. Code; Sec. 19087, Rev. & Tax. Code) Until January 1, 2025, the FTB is also authorized to communicate with taxpayers via electronic means. (Sec. 18416.5, Rev. & Tax. Code) The FTB has adopted a regulation that establishes alternative communication method procedures. The regulation allows the FTB, at the request of a taxpayer or the taxpayer's authorized representative, to provide notification to the taxpayer in a preferred electronic communication method designated by the taxpayer that a bill, notice, or other required communication is available for viewing on the FTB's limited access secure website (MyFTB). The regulation also allows a taxpayer or the taxpayer's representative to electronically file a protest, notification, or other communication with the FTB via MyFTB. The regulation specifies the procedures for electing an alternative communication method; the consequences of an election; how an election may be revoked; the consequences of a delivery failure; and the procedures for filing a protest, notification, or other communication via MyFTB. (Reg. 18416.5, 18 CCR)

COMMENT: Last known address requirement.—The FTB is required to mail the notice to the address that appears on the taxpayer's last return filed with the FTB, unless the taxpayer has provided to the FTB clear and concise written or electronic notification of a different address, or the FTB has an address it has reason to believe is the most current address for the taxpayer. (Sec. 18416, Rev. & Tax. Code)

The FTB must examine an original or amended return or related electronically stored return data prior to issuing a proposed deficiency assessment unless the return or data is unavailable and the taxpayer fails to provide a copy of the return within 30 days of a request by the FTB. A taxpayer may be granted an additional 30 days to provide the FTB a copy of the return if reasonable cause exists. (Sec. 19033, Rev. & Tax. Code; Sec. 19087, Rev. & Tax. Code)

The FTB may require employers, persons, or financial institutions to provide information or make available for examination or copying, any relevant books, papers, records, or other data to determine the correctness of a return, to reconstruct a return, and to determine and collect all liabilities. The FTB may also require the attendance of any person and proof of the matter; however the FTB is prohibited from issuing a subpoena in a civil action to produce or analyze any tax-related computer software source code unless certain requirements are satisfied. (Sec. 19504, Rev. & Tax. Code; Sec. 19504.5, Rev. & Tax. Code)

A deficiency notice must set forth reasons for the proposed assessment, details of the computation, and the last date, as determined by the FTB, the taxpayer may file a written protest. The FTB may not contact any person other than the taxpayer with respect to the determination and collection of the taxpayer's tax liability without notifying the taxpayer in advance unless: the taxpayer has authorizes notice; the FTB determines that the notice would jeopardize the collection of tax; a criminal investigation is pending; or the unpaid tax is consolidated for collection purposes with a preexisting unpaid tax for which notice has been given. (Sec. 19034, Rev. & Tax. Code; Sec. 19504.7, Rev. & Tax. Code)

The FTB may serve a taxpayer with notice of a proposed carryover adjustment and a proposed adjusted carryover amount if the FTB determines that the amount disclosed by the taxpayer is greater than that disclosed by the FTB's own examination. For purposes of this provision, "carryover" means the amount of credit, loss, deduction, or other item shown on an original or amended return, including an amended return reporting federal adjustments. The proposed adjustment becomes final 30 days after its determination, unless either the FTB or the taxpayer files a petition for rehearing within that 30-day period. Once final, the FTB's carryover adjustment is binding and conclusive except in certain circumstances. In addition, a provision that included in the definition of "deficiency" the amount by which a credit carryover is reduced by the FTB was deleted. (Sec. 19043, Rev. & Tax. Code; Sec. 19043.5, Rev. & Tax. Code)

Personal income tax withholding.—The Unemployment Insurance Code provides for assessment of taxes when an employer fails to make a report or return of taxes withheld from wages or fails to timely file a report or return. (Sec. 1126, Unempl. Ins. Code —Sec. 1141, Unempl. Ins. Code) If an employer fails to make a report or return, or if the Director of the Employment Development Department is not satisfied that a correct report or return has been filed, the Director is required to recompute or estimate the amount due and assess that amount. (Sec. 1126, Unempl. Ins. Code; Sec. 1127, Unempl. Ins. Code)

In cases of failure to file a return with good cause, assessment notices must be served within three years; in cases without good cause, the Director has eight years in which to serve an assessment notice. (Sec. 1132, Unempl. Ins. Code) The Director may cancel an erroneous assessment where no appeal has been filed or before a referee decision has been mailed. After a decision has been issued, an assessment may be canceled if the decision was on grounds other than the merits and the Appeals Board approves. (Sec. 1136, Unempl. Ins. Code)

When an employer or other person fails to collect or pay over tax required by the FTB to be withheld at the source, the employer or other person must be be notified by registered mail or hand delivered notice of the failure. The tax becomes collectible after delivery of the notice, and the employer or other person is required to deposit the tax in a bank in trust for the FTB no later than the end of the second banking day after the tax is collected. The FTB may cancel the notification when it is satisfied that all requirements with respect to the tax have been met. (Sec. 19009, Rev. & Tax. Code)

The FTB is authorized to require information necessary for identification of persons subject to withholding at the source. (Sec. 18408, Rev. & Tax. Code)

Insurance taxes.—If the Commissioner determines that the amount of tax disclosed by an insurer's or surplus line broker's tax return and assessed by the SBE is less than the amount of tax disclosed by the Commissioner's examination, or if no return is filed, the Commissioner may propose in writing that the SBE issue a deficiency assessment for the amount of tax due. (Sec. 12422, Rev. & Tax. Code; Sec. 12423, Rev. & Tax. Code) The SBE must give written notice of the deficiency assessment to the insurer or surplus line broker by mail or by personal service. (Sec. 12427, Rev. & Tax. Code; Sec. 12434, Rev. & Tax. Code)

Sales and use taxes.—If the State Board of Equalization (SBE) is not satisfied with a return or the amount of tax paid, or if no return is made, the SBE may compute and determine the amount required to be paid upon the basis of the facts contained in the return or other information within its possession. (Sec. 6481, Rev. & Tax. Code; Sec. 6511, Rev. & Tax. Code) The SBE must give written notice of its determination by mail or by personal service. (Sec. 6486, Rev. & Tax. Code; Sec. 6515, Rev. & Tax. Code)

Other SBE-administered taxes and fees.—Provisions similar to those applicable under the sales and use tax law apply to the following SBE-administered taxes and fees:

— alcoholic beverage tax; (Sec. 32271, Rev. & Tax. Code; Sec. 32291, Rev. & Tax. Code)

— cigarette tax; (Sec. 30201, Rev. & Tax. Code; Sec. 30206, Rev. & Tax. Code; Sec. 30221, Rev. & Tax. Code; Sec. 30225, Rev. & Tax. Code)

— diesel fuel tax, see ¶40-001;

— emergency telephone users' surcharge; (Sec. 41070, Rev. & Tax. Code; Sec. 41075, Rev. & Tax. Code; Sec. 41080, Rev. & Tax. Code; Sec. 41084, Rev. & Tax. Code)

— energy resources surcharge; (Sec. 40071, Rev. & Tax. Code; Sec. 40076, Rev. & Tax. Code; Sec. 40081, Rev. & Tax. Code; Sec. 40085, Rev. & Tax. Code)

— hazardous substances tax; (Sec. 43201, Rev. & Tax. Code)

— motor vehicle fuel tax, see ¶40-001;

— oil spill fees; (Sec. 46201, Rev. & Tax. Code; Sec. 46202, Rev. & Tax. Code; Sec. 46251, Rev. & Tax. Code; Sec. 46255, Rev. & Tax. Code)

— solid waste management fee; (Sec. 45201, Rev. & Tax. Code)

— timber yield tax; (Sec. 38411, Rev. & Tax. Code; Sec. 38416, Rev. & Tax. Code; Sec. 38421, Rev. & Tax. Code; Sec. 38425, Rev. & Tax. Code);

— underground storage tank maintenance fee; (Sec. 50113, Rev. & Tax. Code)

— use fuel tax, see ¶40-001.

• *Annual notices of delinquency*

Income taxes.—The FTB must mail an annual notice to each taxpayer who has a delinquent corporation franchise (income) tax or personal income tax account, indicating the amount of the tax delinquency as of the date of the notice. (Sec. 21026, Rev. & Tax. Code)

[¶89-166] Other Liable Parties

Responsible persons, successors in interest, and fiduciaries may be held liable for the unpaid tax liabilities of another person or business.

• *Income taxes*

Corporation franchise (income) tax and personal income tax deficiencies may be assessed against persons secondarily liable at any time within which they are assessable against the principal, except that the running of the period of limitations for assessments against persons secondarily liable is suspended for the period during which the principal is pursuing the administrative remedies of protest and appeal. Such deficiencies may be assessed and collected in the same manner provided for persons principally liable. (Sec. 19071, Rev. & Tax. Code; Sec. 19072, Rev. & Tax. Code)

Assessments may be made against transferees for the unpaid taxes of their transferors. (Sec. 19073, Rev. & Tax. Code) Such assessments generally must be made within one year of the expiration of the period for assessments against the transferor. In a case involving a transferee of a transferee, the period for assessments is extended for an additional year after the expiration of the period for assessments against the preceding transferee, but for not more than three years altogether after the expiration of the period for assessments against the original transferor. However, if, before the expiration of the period for assessments against a transferee of a transferee, a court proceeding for the collection of the tax has begun against the original transferor or the last preceding transferee, then the period for assessments against the transferee of the transferee will expire one year after the return of execution in the court proceeding. Transferees may also extend the period for assessment by written agreement with the Franchise Tax Board (FTB). (Sec. 19074, Rev. & Tax. Code)

Income tax deficiency assessments may also be made against persons acting in a fiduciary capacity. (Sec. 19073, Rev. & Tax. Code) Such assessments must be made not later than one year after the tax liability arises or one year after the period for collection of the tax expires. Fiduciaries may also extend the period for assessment by written agreement with the FTB. (Sec. 19074, Rev. & Tax. Code)

• *Withholding of tax*

An employing unit that acquires the business or assets of another employer must withhold in trust money or property to cover any amount of unpaid withholding tax until the employer produces a certificate from the Employment Development Department stating that no payments, penalties, or interest are due. If the employer does not produce a certificate, the acquiring employer must pay the amount due at the time of acquisition, up to the amount of the purchase price. (Sec. 1731, Unempl. Ins. Code; Sec. 1732, Unempl. Ins. Code)

An acquiring employer who fails to withhold money or property or fails to pay the amount withheld is personally liable for the amounts due, including penalties and interest, up to the purchase price. (Sec. 1733, Unempl. Ins. Code)

An officer, major stockholder, or other person having charge of the affairs of a corporation, association, limited liability partnership, or limited liability company who willfully fails to pay the amounts due on the date on which they become delinquent will be personally liable for the amounts. (Sec. 1735, Unempl. Ins. Code)

A lender, surety, or other third party who pays wages directly to employees of an employer or group of employers is personally responsible for any required tax withholding on those wages. The third party is also liable for any interest or penalties accruing on these accounts. A third party who supplies funds to an employer so that the employer can pay employees' wages is also personally liable for withheld taxes on the wages if the third party has actual notice or knowledge that wages are to be paid out of the advanced funds and that the employer does not intend or will not be able to pay over any withheld taxes. However, the liability of the lender in such case is limited to 25% of the total amount advanced. (Sec. 13077, Unempl. Ins. Code; Sec. 18677, Rev. & Tax. Code)

• *Sales and use taxes; other taxes*

Upon termination, dissolution, or abandonment of a business, any person who has control of, or responsibility for, filing returns or paying taxes on behalf of the business may be held personally liable for sales and use tax that the person intentionally, consciously, and voluntarily failed to remit, plus interest and penalties. (Sec. 6829, Rev. & Tax. Code; Reg. 1702.5, 18 CCR)

Similarly, when a closely held corporation's powers, rights, and privileges are suspended, certain designated responsible persons may be held personally liable for the corporation's unpaid sales and use taxes incurred during the suspension period, plus interest and penalties. (Reg. 1702.6, 18 CCR)

Unless the State Board of Equalization (SBE) has issued a sales and use tax clearance certificate, the purchaser of a business must withhold a sufficient portion of the purchase price to cover any unpaid sales and use taxes until the former owner produces a receipt from the SBE showing that the tax has been paid or a certificate from the SBE stating no amount is due. (Sec. 6811, Rev. & Tax. Code; *Your California Seller's Permit: Your Rights and Responsibilities under the Sales and Use Tax Law,* State Board of Equalization, January 1996) Noncompliance with this requirement renders the purchaser personally liable for any unpaid taxes incurred by the former owner, up to the amount of the purchase price. (Sec. 6812, Rev. & Tax. Code; Reg. 1702(b), 18 CCR)

As under the sales and use tax law, personal liability may also be imposed on a purchaser for the following unpaid taxes and fees incurred by a former owner:

— diesel fuel tax, see ¶ 40-003;

— motor vehicle fuel tax, see ¶ 40-001;

— oil spill fees (Sec. 46451, Rev. & Tax. Code; Sec. 46452, Rev. & Tax. Code); and

— use fuel tax, see ¶ 40-007.

[¶ 89-168] Jeopardy Assessments

State taxing authorities may issue jeopardy assessments when the collection of tax will be jeopardized by delay.

Income taxes.—If the Franchise Tax Board (FTB) believes that the collection of any corporation franchise (income) tax or personal income tax for a current or past year will be jeopardized by delay, it will demand immediate payment of the tax with interest and penalties. (Sec. 19081, Rev. & Tax. Code)

If the tax is for a current period, the FTB may declare the current period immediately terminated. (Sec. 19082, Rev. & Tax. Code) Once a jeopardy assessment is made, a court proceeding to collect the amounts due may be commenced at once. (Sec. 19083, Rev. & Tax. Code)

The taxpayer may petition the FTB for review within 30 days after the taxpayer is furnished with a written statement of the information upon which the FTB relies or within 30 days after the last day of the period within which the written statement is required to be provided. The filing of a petition for review does not stay collection. Collection may be stayed only by posting a bond, as discussed at ¶ 89-178. (Sec. 19084(a)(2), Rev. & Tax. Code)

Withholding of tax.—If the Director of the Employment Development Department finds that the collection of any withheld tax will be jeopardized by delay, the Director may levy a jeopardy assessment and demand a deposit of security to ensure compliance. The amount of the assessment is immediately delinquent, but the penalty for failing to pay an assessment before it becomes delinquent does not attach to the jeopardy assessment unless the assessment is not paid or secured within 30 days after service of the jeopardy assessment. (Sec. 1137, Unempl. Ins. Code) A jeopardy assessment may be made only upon a finding by the Director, based on probable cause, that:

— the employing unit is insolvent;

— the employing unit has transferred, or is about to transfer, assets for less than fair market value and by so doing has rendered itself insolvent;

— the employing unit has been dissolved;

— any person liable for the employing unit's contribution has departed from the State of California and the departure is likely to deprive the Director of a source of payment of the employing unit's contribution;

— the person in charge of the employing unit, or liable for its contribution, is secreting assets, or moving and depositing assets, outside the state for the purpose of interfering with the orderly collection of the unit's liability; or

— the assessment to be issued against the employing unit or an individual includes a penalty for fraud, intent to evade taxation, or concealment of wages.

(Sec. 1137.1, Unempl. Ins. Code)

The employer may file a petition for reassessment of the jeopardy assessment within ten working days of notice of a jeopardy assessment (Sec. 1221, Unempl. Ins. Code) The deposit of security is not a condition for the exercise of review and appeal rights by the employer against whom the jeopardy assessment is made. However, the deposit of security will stay collection activities while the jeopardy assessment is under review. The filing of a petition for reassessment will stay the sale of all property, other than perishable goods, seized by the Director pursuant to the collection action until a final decision from the preliminary hearing is issued. (Sec. 1137, Unempl. Ins. Code)

Sales and use taxes.—If the State Board of Equalization (SBE) believes that the collection of any sales and use tax will be jeopardized by delay, it may make an assessment that is immediately due and payable. (Sec. 6536, Rev. & Tax. Code) If not paid within 10 days, the assessment becomes final and incurs interest and a deficiency penalty, unless a petition for redetermination is filed and a security deposit is posted within the 10-day period. (Sec. 6537, Rev. & Tax. Code; Sec. 6538, Rev. & Tax. Code)

The taxpayer may apply for an administrative hearing within 30 days after service of notice of the jeopardy assessment. No security deposit is required to file an application and obtain a hearing. However, absent a deposit within 10 days of service of notice, the filing of an application for hearing does not stay collection activities, except the sale of property seized after the jeopardy assessment. (Sec. 6538.5, Rev. & Tax. Code)

Other taxes and fees.—Taxing authorities may also issue jeopardy assessments if they believe that a delay will jeopardize collection of any of the following taxes and fees:

— cigarette tax; (Sec. 30241, Rev. & Tax. Code)

— diesel fuel tax; (Sec. 60330, Rev. & Tax. Code)

— hazardous substances tax; (Sec. 43350, Rev. & Tax. Code)

— motor vehicle fuel tax; (Sec. 7698, Rev. & Tax. Code)

— oil spill fees; (Sec. 46301, Rev. & Tax. Code)

— solid waste management fee; (Sec. 45351, Rev. & Tax. Code)

— underground storage tank fee; (Sec. 50120.1, Rev. & Tax. Code) and

— use fuel tax. (Sec. 8826, Rev. & Tax. Code)

[¶89-172] Tax Liens

If a person fails to pay any of the following taxes and fees when they become due and payable, the amount due, including interest, penalties, and costs will be a perfected and enforceable state tax lien:

— alcoholic beverage tax; (Sec. 32363, Rev. & Tax. Code)

— cigarette tax; (Sec. 30322, Rev. & Tax. Code)

— corporation franchise (income) taxes; (Sec. 19221, Rev. & Tax. Code; Sec. 19222, Rev. & Tax. Code)

— diesel fuel tax; (Sec. 60445, Rev. & Tax. Code)

— emergency telephone users surcharge; (Sec. 41124.1, Rev. & Tax. Code)

— energy resources surcharge; (Sec. 40158, Rev. & Tax. Code)

— hazardous substances tax; (Sec. 43413, Rev. & Tax. Code);

— motor vehicle fuel tax; (Sec. 7872, Rev. & Tax. Code)

— oil and gas production charge (Sec. 3423, Pub. Res. Code)

— oil spill fees; (Sec. 46421, Rev. & Tax. Code)

— personal income taxes; (Sec. 19221, Rev. & Tax. Code; Sec. 19222, Rev. & Tax. Code; Sec. 19223, Rev. & Tax. Code)

— sales and use taxes; (Sec. 6757, Rev. & Tax. Code)

— timber yield tax; (Sec. 38532, Rev. & Tax. Code)

— underground storage tank maintenance fee; (Sec. 50123, Rev. & Tax. Code)

— use fuel tax; (Sec. 8996, Rev. & Tax. Code) and

— withheld personal income tax. (Sec. 1703, Unempl. Ins. Code)

Under the state constitution, every tax is conclusively presumed to have been paid after 30 years from the time it became a lien unless the property subject to the lien is sold in the manner provided by the legislature for the payment of tax. (Sec. 30, Art. XIII, Cal. Const.) Under state statutory law, a state tax lien continues in effect for 10 years from the date of its creation unless it is released sooner or otherwise discharged, and it is extinguished 10 years from the date of its creation unless a notice of state tax lien is recorded or filed.

When a notice of a state tax lien is recorded or filed before the lien is extinguished, the lien continues in effect for 10 years from the date of recording or filing the notice of state tax lien unless it is released sooner or otherwise discharged, and it is extinguished 10 years from the date of recording or filing the notice of state tax lien unless it is extended. Within 10 years of the date of recording or filing of a notice of state tax lien or within 10 years of the date of the last extension of the lien, a state tax lien may be extended by recording in the office of the county recorder or by filing with the Secretary of State a new notice of state tax lien. From the time of such recording or filing, the lien is extended for 10 years unless released sooner or otherwise discharged. (Sec. 7172, Govt. Code)

Between competing state tax liens or between a state tax lien and a federal tax lien, the lien that first comes into existence has priority over any lien that later comes into existence. (Sec. 7170.5, Govt. Code)

Except for prior recorded liens and certain claims for personal services, the state's claim for unpaid income tax liabilities has priority when:

— the taxpayer is insolvent;

— the taxpayer makes a voluntary assignment of assets;

— an estate is insufficient to pay all the debts of a decedent; or

— the estate and effects of an absent, concealed, or absconding person are levied on by process of law.

(Sec. 19253, Rev. & Tax. Code; Sec. 1701, Unempl. Ins. Code; Sec. 1702, Unempl. Ins. Code)

The agency may file a notice of tax lien in the office of the county recorder of the county in which the real property is located. The notice and related documents may be filed electronically. (Sec. 7171, Govt. Code)

• *Income taxes*

A tax lien for delinquent income taxes will not attach during any period that an automatic stay has been issued in a federal bankruptcy proceeding pursuant to Title 11 U.S.C. Sec. 362, unless the taxes are a debt that will not be discharged in the bankruptcy proceeding and the property or its proceeds are transferred out of the bankruptcy estate to, or otherwise revested in, the debtor. (Sec. 19221, Rev. & Tax. Code)

According to the Franchise Tax Board's (FTB) *Collections Procedures Manual*, liens against real property will be recorded without regard to a minimum balance of unpaid income tax if the taxpayer has refused to comply and is

(1) known to own real property,

(2) self-employed,

(3) contemplating bankruptcy,

(4) terminally ill,

(5) engaged in any judicial proceeding in which failure to file a lien would jeopardize collection.

(Sec. 4320, *Collections Procedures Manual*, Franchise Tax Board)

The FTB's *Collections Procedures Manual* also outlines the FTB's policies regarding the release of income tax liens. (Sec. 4340, *Collections Procedures Manual*, Franchise Tax Board) At the request of a property owner whose property is subject to a lien for income taxes, the FTB must release the lien from the property if the owner is not the person whose unsatisfied tax liability gave rise to the lien and the owner posts a cash deposit or bond equal to the value of the state's interest in the property. (Sec. 19226, Rev. & Tax. Code)

CCH PRACTICE TIP: Partial lien releases.—Partial lien releases may be requested during short sales transactions if a taxpayer does not have enough funds in their escrow account to pay off the recorded state tax lien in full. In such instances, a taxpayer should request a partial lien release from the FTB by calling the Lien Resolution Unit at (916) 845-4350. A partial lien release releases a specific piece of property from a recorded state tax lien. However, it does not release the lien in its entirety. The lien remains in effect against the taxpayer and continues to encumber other property owned or acquired by the taxpayer. (*Tax News*, California Franchise Tax Board, October 31, 2010)

• *Sales and use taxes*

Also, a sales and use tax lien may not arise during any period in which a federal bankruptcy proceeding pursuant to Title 11 U.S.C. Sec. 362 applies to the taxpayer. (Sec. 6757, Rev. & Tax. Code)

[¶89-174] Warrants for Collection of Tax

State taxing authorities may issue warrants for the collection of tax, as discussed below.

Income taxes.—The Franchise Tax Board (FTB) may issue a warrant for the sale of property to recover delinquent corporation franchise (income) and personal income taxes, penalties, and interest and to enforce a tax lien. (Sec. 19231, Rev. & Tax. Code)

Warrants may be levied for the seizure and sale of the following types of property:

— vehicles;

— personal property of value that requires a sale or other action to convert the property to cash;

— cash and negotiable instruments from the debtor's business during business hours;

— real property;

— boats, motorcycles, and airplanes; and

— stocks, bonds, and mutual funds.

(Sec. 4605, *Collections Procedures Manual*, Franchise Tax Board)

The FTB must notify taxpayers in writing 30 days before first levy is made on a taxpayers' property or property rights. Taxpayers can contact the taxpayer advocate to request an independent departmental administrative review during the 30 day period before the first levy. Taxpayers can raise any relevant issue relating to the unpaid tax or the lien. (Sec. 21015.5, Rev. & Tax. Code)

The FTB, in a one-time action called a "till tap," may instruct a levying officer to seize all money or other negotiable instruments on the premises of a business. If the proceeds of the "till tap" do not satisfy the delinquency, the state may install a "keeper" at the taxpayer's business to take into custody the proceeds of all sales during a continuous period of up to 10 days. (Sec. 4615, *Collections Procedures Manual*, Franchise Tax Board)

The seizure and sale of a principal residence requires a court order. Also, no warrant may be levied on any real property used as a residence by the taxpayer or any nonrental real property used as a residence by any other individual if the amount of liability to be satisfied is $5,000 or less. Furthermore, the FTB may not levy a warrant on tangible personal property or nonrental real property used in a trade or business unless

(1) the levy is approved in writing by the FTB's assistant officer for collections or a delegate or

(2) the FTB finds that the collection of tax is in jeopardy.

(Sec. 19236, Rev. & Tax. Code)

A warrant must not be issued if

(1) it constitutes a means of harassment,

(2) the proceeds from the sale will not result in a reasonable reduction of the tax liability, or

(3) the sale will result in undue hardship.

(Sec. 4605, *Collections Procedures Manual*, Franchise Tax Board)

A taxpayer's bona fide residence is exempt from levy, up to the amount of the applicable homestead exemption. (Sec. 704.710, Code of Civ. Proc.—Sec. 704.730, Code of Civ. Proc.) A natural person may exempt up to $1900 of any combination of the following:

(1) the person's aggregate equity in motor vehicles;

(2) the proceeds of an execution sale of a motor vehicle; and

(3) the proceeds of insurance or other indemnification for the loss, damage, or destruction of a motor vehicle.

(Sec. 704.010, Code of Civ. Proc.)

Withholding of tax.—The Director of the Employment Development Department may issue a warrant for the enforcement of any lien for withheld taxes and for the collection of any withheld tax required to be paid. The warrant must be issued within three years after the payment becomes delinquent, within 10 years after the last entry of a judgment, or within 10 years after the filing of a lien. (Sec. 1785, Unempl. Ins. Code)

Oil spill fees; underground storage tank fee.—At any time within three years after any person is delinquent in the payment of any oil spill fee or underground storage tank fee or after the last recording or filing of a notice of state tax lien, the SBE may issue a warrant for the enforcement of any lien and for the collection of any amount required to be paid. (Sec. 46431, Rev. & Tax. Code; Sec. 50125, Rev. & Tax. Code)

Energy resources surcharge; emergency telephone users surcharge.—At any time within five years after any person is delinquent in the payment of any energy resources surcharge or emergency telephone users surcharge, the SBE may issue a warrant for the collection of the delinquent amount. (Sec. 40161, Rev. & Tax. Code; Sec. 41125, Rev. & Tax. Code)

Other taxes.—For the following taxes and fees, the SBE may issue a warrant to enforce any lien and to collect any delinquent amount at any time within three years after the amount becomes delinquent or 10 years after the last recording of an abstract or notice of lien:

— alcoholic beverage tax; (Sec. 32365, Rev. & Tax. Code)

— cigarette tax; (Sec. 30341, Rev. & Tax. Code)

— diesel fuel tax; (Sec. 60451, Rev. & Tax. Code)

— hazardous substances tax; (Sec. 43421, Rev. & Tax. Code)

— motor vehicle fuel tax; (Sec. 7881, Rev. & Tax. Code)

— sales and use taxes; (Sec. 6776, Rev. & Tax. Code)

— timber yield tax; (Sec. 38541, Rev. & Tax. Code) and

— use fuel tax. (Sec. 9001, Rev. & Tax. Code)

Also, the State Controller may issue a warrant for the collection of oil and gas production charges, interest, and penalties and for the enforcement of any lien for such charges. (Sec. 3423.3, Pub. Res. Code)

[¶89-176] Other Collection Methods

The following additional collection methods are available to the state. Also discussed below are the tax shelter registration and reporting requirements administered by the California Franchise Tax Board (FTB).

• *Summary judgment*

Personal income tax withholding.—The Director of the Employment Development Department (EDD) may file with the Office of the County Clerk of Sacramento County, or with the clerk of the superior court of the county in which the employer has its principal place of business, a certificate specifying the amount of delinquent payments and requesting that a judgment be entered against the employer in that amount. The certificate must be filed no later than 10 years after:

— the payment became delinquent;

— the last entry of judgment; or

— the last filing of a tax lien.

The county clerk with whom the certificate is filed must immediately enter such a judgment. (Sec. 1815, Unempl. Ins. Code) The Director may use the summary judgment procedure in addition to any other authorized collection procedure. (Sec. 1818, Unempl. Ins. Code)

The amount of the judgment constitutes a lien on the real property of the employer in the county in which it is entered and continues for 10 years, unless released or discharged sooner. The lien may be extended. (Sec. 1816, Unempl. Ins. Code) The Director may release the lien at any time the Director determines that payments have been sufficiently secured or that the release will not jeopardize collection. The Director may also subordinate the lien imposed by Unempl. Ins. Code Sec. 1816 to other liens and encumbrances. (Sec. 1817, Unempl. Ins. Code)

• *Injunction*

At the FTB's request, a civil action may be brought in the name of the state to enjoin any person or corporation from promoting abusive tax shelters or aiding and abetting an understatement of corporation franchise (income) tax or personal income tax liability. At the FTB's request, civil actions may also be brought in the name of the state to enjoin any failure by a tax shelter organizer to register a tax shelter or failure by a tax shelter organizer, seller, or material organizer to maintain and provide a list of investors. (Sec. 19715, Rev. & Tax. Code)

No action may be taken against the state to prevent or enjoin the collection of tax. (Sec. 32, Art. XIII, Cal. Const.)

• *Financial institutions record match system*

The FTB is mandated to establish a financial institutions record match (FIRM) system with specified financial institutions doing business in California for purposes of improving collections from taxpayers with outstanding California income tax liabilities or other debts that the FTB is required to collect. Effective June 27, 2012, the FIRM program is expanded to also apply to the collection of various delinquent amounts payable to the BOE and the EDD. (Sec. 19266, Rev. & Tax. Code)

Under the FIRM system, financial institutions must provide the FTB quarterly reports including the account holder's name, record address, and other addresses, Social Security number or other taxpayer identification number, and other identifying information for each delinquent tax debtor, as identified by the FTB. Financial institutions that fail to comply, without reasonable cause, will be subject to a penalty equal to $50 for each record not provided, up to a total of $100,000 annually. Financial institutions may be reimbursed for specified program implementation costs. (Sec. 19266, Rev. & Tax. Code)

No action may be taken against the state to prevent or enjoin the collection of tax. (Sec. 32, Art. XIII, Cal. Const.)

Taxpayer and financial institution inquiries concerning the FIRM program can be directed as follows:

— For information regarding bank garnishments, including why they are issued and how to release them, taxpayers can go to https://www.ftb.ca.gov and search for "bank garnishment".

— Personal income taxpayers can call the phone number on their notice or call (800) 689-4776 or (916) 845-4470 (if outside the United States)

— Business tax taxpayers can call (888) 635-0494 or (916) 845-7033 (if outside the United States)

— Vehicle Registration Collection inquiries can be directed to (888) 355-6872 or (916) 845-6872 (if outside the United States)

— For Court Ordered Debt questions, call (916) 845-7064

— Financial institutions can contact the FIRM Administrator for additional information at zCATAX@informatixinc.com or (866) 576-5986

(*Public Service Bulletin 2012-11*, California Franchise Tax Board, April 5, 2012)

• *Order to withhold*

Income taxes.—The FTB may issue an order to withhold (OTW) requiring any employer, corporation, person, officer or department of the state, political subdivision or agency of the state, charter city, or other political body controlling or possessing credits, personal property, or other things of value belonging to a taxpayer to withhold from the credits, personal property, or other things of value in the amount of any unpaid income tax, interest, or penalties due from the taxpayer. (Sec. 18670, Rev. & Tax. Code) The FTB may issue a continuous order to withhold (COTW), for a period of up to one year, requiring a person to withhold from payments that are due to a taxpayer or that will become due after the COTW is received. The FTB may serve the notice to withhold personally, by first-class mail, or beginning January 1, 2021, by electronic transmission or other electronic technology. (Sec. 18671, Rev. & Tax. Code) The FTB generally issues an OTW or a COTW only if a taxpayer does any of the following:

— has not responded to a demand for payment;

— has previously promised to pay but failed to do so;

— has a history of delinquency;

— does not make full financial disclosure; or

— defaults on a payment agreement.

(Secs. 2410.02, 2420.02, 3510.02, and 3515.02, *Collection Procedures Manual*, Franchise Tax Board)

When the FTB issues an order to a financial institution, securities intermediary, or other person to withhold all, or a portion, of a financial asset for the purpose of collecting a delinquent tax liability from a taxpayer, the financial institution, securities intermediary, or other person must liquidate the financial asset in a commercially reasonable manner within 90 days of the issuance of the order and must remit the proceeds of the liquidation, less any reasonable commissions and fees, to the FTB within five days of the liquidation. If the value of the financial assets to be liquidated exceeds the taxpayer's tax liability, the taxpayer may, within 60 days after the service of the order to withhold, give instructions as to which financial assets to liquidate first. If the taxpayer does not provide such instructions, the holder of the financial assets must liquidate the financial assets beginning with those purchased most recently. (Sec. 18670, Rev. & Tax. Code)

CCH COMMENT: Employee orders to withhold taxes.—The FTB will issue an earnings withholding order for taxes (EWOT) in instances in which a taxpayer fails to respond to a demand for payment; fails to make promised payments, including installment payments; has a history of delinquency; or does not make a full disclosure of the taxpayer's financial condition when required to do so. An EWOT is a continuing wage garnishment on earnings due to a taxpayer from an employer. The FTB does not have to obtain a court order to issue an EWOT unless the FTB wants to reach more than the established 25% of disposable income or to levy on the earnings of a nonliable spouse. An EWOT creates a levy upon the earnings of the taxpayer, including bonuses and commissions, in the amount of the taxpayer's outstanding personal income tax liabilities. Periodic payments pursuant to a pension or retirement program may not be subjected to an EWOT. (*Tax News*, California Franchise Tax Board, May 31, 2010)

While the FTB may adjust an EWOT payment amount if the taxpayer has a financial hardship, the FTB will not release a valid EWOT to set up an installment agreement unless there are exceptional circumstances. Therefore, taxpayers who receive collection notices and cannot pay are encouraged to pay what they can and then contact the FTB. Taxpayers may be able to prevent collection actions if they: pay their tax liability in full; enter into an installment agreement; file all required tax returns or provide proof that they have no filing requirement; make an offer in compromise that the FTB accepts; or establish that a financial hardship prevents them from paying their liability. (*Tax News*, California Franchise Tax Board, February 2012)

In the priority ranking of various levies that may be issued against earnings, an EWOT falls below an earnings assignment order for support or a withholding order for child support or alimony, but is above an earnings withholding order for other nontax debt and civil judgments.

The FTB answers frequently asked questions concerning employer's withholding orders in an FTB pamphlet. (*FTB Pub. 1014, Earnings Withholding Orders for Taxes—Commonly Asked Questions for Employers*)

Personal income tax withholding.—The EDD may direct any employer, person, officer or department of the state, state agency, city organized under a freehold charter, or any other political body controlling or possessing assets belonging to a taxpayer or an employer to withhold amounts due from credits or other personal property of the taxpayer or employer liable for unpaid personal income tax withholding. (Sec. 13072, Unempl. Ins. Code) There is no comparable federal provision. Any person or employer failing to withhold and transmit the unpaid taxes after service of a notice to withhold is liable for the amounts. (Sec. 13073, Unempl. Ins. Code)

To be effective service on the state of California, a notice to withhold must be made on the appropriate state agency before the agency submits a claim for payment to the State Controller. (Sec. 13075, Unempl. Ins. Code)

Employers and other persons are required to deduct and transmit the amounts due without resort to legal or equitable action. (Sec. 13074, Unempl. Ins. Code) An employer or other individual paying to the Department amounts required to be deducted is not liable to the person from whom they are withheld unless the taxes are refunded to the withholding agent.

Sales and use taxes.—The BOE may send a notice to withhold to holders of credits or other property belonging to any delinquent sales and use taxpayer. Upon receipt of the notice, holders must advise the BOE of any credits, personal property, or debts belonging to the delinquent taxpayer that are in their possession or control. No transfer or other disposition of such assets may be made until the BOE gives consent or until 60 days have passed, whichever is earlier. (Sec. 6702, Rev. & Tax. Code)

Other taxes and fees.—Notices to withhold may also be issued for the following taxes and fees:

— diesel fuel tax; (Sec. 60402, Rev. & Tax. Code)

— motor vehicle fuel tax; (Sec. 7851, Rev. & Tax. Code)

— oil spill fees; (Sec. 46402, Rev. & Tax. Code)

— timber yield tax; (Sec. 38502, Rev. & Tax. Code) and

— use fuel tax. (Sec. 8952, Rev. & Tax. Code)

• *Notice of levy*

Personal income tax withholding.—The Director of the EDD may collect delinquent payments of personal income tax withholding or enforce any liens by serving notices of levy on all persons controlling any credits or other property belonging to a delinquent employer. (Sec. 1755, Unempl. Ins. Code—Sec. 1758, Unempl. Ins. Code) The person on whom a levy is served is required to surrender the credits or property or pay to the department the amount of any debt owed to the delinquent employer within five days of service. Credits, property, or debts owed that come into the possession, or under the control, of the person on whom the levy is served within one year after the receipt of the notice of levy, must be surrendered within five days of the date on which the person served came into possession or control. (Sec. 1755, Unempl. Ins. Code—Sec. 1758, Unempl. Ins. Code) Anyone who refuses to comply with this requirement is personally liable for an amount equal to the value of the garnished credits or other personal property if, solely by reason of his failure or refusal, the department is unable to recover the delinquent amounts. (Sec. 1757, Unempl. Ins. Code) If the garnished credits are paid to the department, the payor is not liable to the delinquent employer. (Sec. 1755, Unempl. Ins. Code) Notice of levy to the state must be given to the appropriate department before the department has presented the delinquent employer's claim to the state controller for payment. (Sec. 1756, Unempl. Ins. Code)

Sales and use taxes.—The BOE may issue a notice of levy to holders of credits or other property belonging to a delinquent sales and use taxpayer. This notice requires the holders to withhold any payments or deliveries to the taxpayer and to turn over the withheld amounts at times designated by the BOE. (Sec. 6703, Rev. & Tax. Code)

Other taxes and fees.—Notices of levy may also be issued for the following taxes and fees:

— diesel fuel tax; (Sec. 60407, Rev. & Tax. Code)

— motor vehicle fuel tax; (Sec. 7855, Rev. & Tax. Code)

— oil spill fees; (Sec. 46406, Rev. & Tax. Code) and

— use fuel tax. (Sec. 8957, Rev. & Tax. Code)

• *Wage garnishment*

The state may serve an earnings withholding order for taxes (EWOT) to collect a state tax liability if the existence of the liability either appears on the face of the taxpayer's return or has been assessed or determined in a proceeding in which the taxpayer had notice and opportunity for administrative review. (Sec. 706.072, Code of Civ. Proc.) For purposes of an earnings withholding order for taxes issued by the Franchise Tax Board, "state tax liability" also includes any liability under Part 10 (commencing with Section 17001), Part 10.2 (commencing with Section 18401), or Part 11 (commencing with Section 23001) of Division 2 of the Revenue and Taxation Code that is due and payable and unpaid. (Sec. 706.070, Code of Civ. Proc.) The amount that may be withheld pursuant to an EWOT is determined by reference to a federal provision that limits garnishment of an individual's aggregate disposable earnings for any work week to the lesser of

(1) 25% of the individual's disposable earnings for the week or

(2) the amount by which the individual's disposable earnings for the work exceeds 30 times the federal minimum hourly wage.

(Sec. 706.074, Code of Civ. Proc.)

The FTB's policy for issuing an EWOT is the same as its policy for issuing an OTW or a COTW (see above). (Sec. 2420.02, *Collection Procedures Manual*, Franchise Tax Board)

• *Collection of other obligations*

Included among the obligations that the FTB may also collect in the same manner authorized for the collection of personal income tax delinquencies are the following:

— court-imposed fines;

— effective January 1, 2021, monetary sanctions;

— any amounts imposed by a California court upon a person or any other entity;

— effective January 1, 2021, any payment from the State Bar of California's Client Security Fund that is part of a final determination from the Client Security Fund;

— state or local penalties;

— bail;

— forfeitures;

— restitution fines;

— restitution orders;

— debts;

— labor code violation payments;

— student loan amounts;

— criminal restitution;

— certain court-imposed amounts for debts due to the State Bar; and

— penalties imposed on employers under the CalSavers Retirement Savings Program.

(Sec. 19280, Rev. & Tax. Code; Sec. 19286, Rev. & Tax. Code; Sec. 19722, Rev. & Tax. Code; Sec. 3000.5, Penal Code)

• *Tax shelter registration and reporting requirements*

Taxpayer requirements.—California generally conforms to IRC Sec. 6011(a) and the regulations issued thereunder, which require the disclosure of certain "reportable transactions." California modifies the federal law to additionally provide that the term "reportable transaction" includes any transaction of a type that the Secretary of Treasury for federal income tax purposes or the Franchise Tax Board (FTB) for California franchise or income tax purposes determines as having a potential for tax avoidance or evasion including deductions, basis, credits, entity classification, dividend elimination, or omission of income. (Sec. 18407(a), Rev. & Tax. Code)

Also, California modifies the federal law to additionally provide that the term "listed transaction" includes any transaction that is the same as, or substantially similar to, a transaction specifically identified by the Secretary of Treasury for federal income tax purposes or the FTB for California franchise or income tax purposes as a tax avoidance transaction. All reportable transactions must be disclosed on California returns or statements. (Sec. 18407(a), Rev. & Tax. Code)

COMMENT: Listed transactions.—The FTB must identify listed transactions through the use of FTB Notices and other published positions, and this information must be published on the FTB's website at http://www.ftb.ca.gov. (Sec. 18407(a), Rev. & Tax. Code)

The FTB has become aware of transactions involving apportioning corporate taxpayers that use one or more partnerships to improperly inflate the denominator of their California sales factor, thereby reducing the amount of business income apportioned to California. The FTB warns taxpayers and their representatives that it considers these transactions to be tax avoidance transactions, and it intends to disallow any tax benefits claimed as a result of the sales factor manipulation. Furthermore, the FTB identifies these transactions, and substantially similar transactions, as listed transactions. The identified transactions involve the use of special sales factor rules in Reg. 25137-1(f)(3) to include intercompany sales in the denominator of the sales factor even though the gain or loss generated by those sales is eliminated from the calculation of apportionable business income. The FTB provides examples of two common variations of the business structures used to facilitate these tax avoidance transactions and provides a nonexclusive list of the types of factors it will consider in determining whether to assess tax and/or penalties. (*FTB Notice 2011-01*, California Franchise Tax Board, January 6, 2011)

Another type of transaction that has been identified as a listed transaction involves circular cash flow transactions in which parent corporations artificially increase their basis in the stock of their subsidiaries, without any outlay of cash or property, prior to the parent selling the subsidiary's stock to an unrelated third party, thereby minimizing the taxable gain from the stock sale. One way in which this is accomplished is by the parent contributing a promissory note or other instrument to the subsidiary in a transaction intended to qualify as a contribution to capital under IRC § 351. The parent's contribution to the subsidiary's capital is temporary and transitory in nature, and is intended to remain with the subsidiary for a short period of time. The subsidiary then takes steps to generate what the subsidiary alleges are earnings and profits through the sale or transfer of intangible property to a related entity in a manner that avoids the application of California's intercompany transaction rules. Around the same time, the parent pays off the promissory note or other instrument issued to the subsidiary and the subsidiary distributes the cash back or a substantially equivalent amount of property back to the parent. The parent claims that this repayment is essentially a dividend, which is either deductible or excludable on the parent's California return. In addition, because it is a dividend, the parent does not have to reduce its basis in the subsidiary. Consequently, the parent gets an increased basis in the subsidiary for the promissory note, which never actually remained with the subsidiary, and upon the subsidiary's sale the parent recognizes minimal gain as a result of the increased basis in the subsidiary. (*FTB Notice 2011-04*, California Franchise Tax Board, August 4, 2011)

Generally, taxpayers that are involved in a reportable transaction and/or a listed transaction must attach a copy of the federal Form 8666 to their original or amended California return. A copy must also be sent to the FTB the first time a reportable transaction is disclosed on the taxpayer's return. (*FTB Notice 2007-3*, California Franchise Tax Board, July 31, 2007; Instructions, Form 100, Corporation Franchise or Income Tax Return)

A penalty is imposed for failure to disclose reportable or listed transactions.

Material advisor requirements.—California incorporates, with modifications, federal law (IRC Sec. 6111) requiring specified material advisors to file information returns disclosing reportable transactions. Material advisors are required to send a duplicate of the federal return or the same information required to be provided on the federal reportable transactions return for California reportable transactions to the FTB no later than the date specified by the FTB or the U.S. Secretary of the Treasury. Additional information may be required if specified in an FTB Notice. (Sec. 18628, Rev. & Tax. Code)

Material advisors must file with the FTB a copy of IRS Form 8918, or a Form 8918 completed on a California-only basis if there is a filing requirement under California law but not under federal law, on the same date Form 8918 is required to be filed with the IRS for a reportable transaction that is not a listed transaction. Under the final regulations, a material advisor must file Form 8918 by the last day of the month that follows the end of the calendar quarter in which the advisor becomes a material advisor with respect to a reportable transaction or in which the circumstances necessitating an amended disclosure statement occur. For listed transactions, California law requires material advisor disclosure by the later of 60 days after entering into the transaction or 60 days after the transaction becomes listed. (*FTB Notice 2008-1*, California Franchise Tax Board, January 11, 2008)

COMMENT: *Multiple material advisors.*—A material advisor may enter into a designation agreement that allows multiple material advisors to the same reportable transaction to designate a single material advisor to disclose the transaction. However, if the designated material advisor does not disclose the transaction, the other material advisors are not relieved of their obligations to disclose the transaction in a timely manner. (*FTB Notice 2008-1*, California Franchise Tax Board, January 11, 2008)

Material advisors are subject to the California reporting requirements if they are:

— organized in California;

— doing business in California;

— deriving income from California sources; or

— providing any material aid, assistance, or advice with respect to organizing, managing, promoting, selling, implementing, insuring, or carrying out any reportable transaction with respect to a taxpayer that is organized in California, does business in California, or derives income from California sources.

California also conforms to federal law (IRC Sec. 6112) requiring material advisors of reportable transactions to keep lists of advisees. The lists must be maintained for California purposes in the form and manner prescribed by the FTB. For transactions that become listed transactions (as defined in IRC Sec. 6707A(c)(12)) at any time and that are specifically identified by the FTB as listed transactions at any time, the lists must be provided to the FTB by the later of 60 days after entering into the transactions, or 60 days after the transaction becomes a listed transaction. (Sec. 18648, Rev. & Tax. Code)

[¶89-178] Requirement to Post Bond or Security

Various bond and security requirements are discussed below.

Income taxes.—A taxpayer may stay the collection of a jeopardy assessment for corporation franchise (income) or personal income taxes by posting

(1) a bond equal to the amount, plus interest, with respect to which the stay is sought or

(2) other security in an amount that the Franchise Tax Board deems necessary, not to exceed double the amount, plus interest, with respect to which the stay is sought.

The taxpayer can waive the stay of collection by payment (in whole or in part) of the assessment, and, to the extent the assessment is abated, the bond or other security may be proportionately reduced at the taxpayer's request. (Sec. 19083, Rev. & Tax. Code)

Withholding of tax.—In levying a jeopardy assessment for withheld personal income tax, the Director of the Employment Development Department may demand a deposit of security as the Director deems necessary to ensure compliance with the tax laws. (Sec. 1137, Unempl. Ins. Code)

Other taxes.—Before granting a person a motor vehicle fuel tax or diesel fuel tax license, the California Department of Tax and Fee Administration (CDTFA) may require the person to file a bond. (Sec. 7486, Rev. & Tax. Code; Sec. 60121, Rev. & Tax. Code; Sec. 60133, Rev. & Tax. Code; Sec. 60143, Rev. & Tax. Code; Sec. 60163, Rev. & Tax. Code; Reg. 35031, 18 CCR)

Also, whenever necessary to ensure compliance with the use fuel tax law or the diesel fuel tax law, the SBE may require a person to deposit security with the SBE. (Sec. 8951, Rev. & Tax. Code; Sec. 60401, Rev. & Tax. Code)

Every applicant for a cigarette tax license must file security in an amount and form prescribed by the CDTFA. (Sec. 30141, Rev. & Tax. Code)

For oil and gas production charge purposes, an operator may be required to file an indemnity bond. (Sec. 3204, Rev. & Tax. Code; Sec. 3205, Rev. & Tax. Code)

Whenever necessary to ensure compliance with the timber yield tax law, a person may be required to deposit security with the CDTFA. (Sec. 38501, Rev. & Tax. Code)

A person petitioning for redetermination or reassessment of a jeopardy determination or jeopardy assessment for any of the following taxes must deposit security with the CDTFA as the CDTFA deems necessary to secure compliance with the tax laws or to insure payment of the amount due:

— alcoholic beverage tax;

— cigarette and tobacco products taxes;

— diesel fuel tax;

— hazardous substances tax;

— solid waste management fee;

— motor vehicle fuel tax;

— occupational lead poisoning prevention fees;

— oil spill fees;

— sales and use taxes;

— tire recycling fee;

— underground storage tank maintenance fee; and

— use fuel tax.

Tax return preparers.—Tax return preparers must maintain a $5,000 bond per individual preparing tax returns, up to a $125,000 maximum. (Sec. 22250, Bus. & Prof. Code; renumbered to Sec. 22250.1, Bus. & Prof. Code, effective January 1, 2019)

[¶89-180] Civil Action

California law authorizes various civil actions to collect tax.

Income taxes.—The Franchise Tax Board may bring a court action to collect corporation franchise (income) or personal income taxes, penalties, and interest at any time within 10 years after the determination of liability for the amount due or within the period during which a lien is in force. (Sec. 19371, Rev. & Tax. Code)

Withholding of tax.—The Employment Development Department may bring an action to collect the amount of any delinquent withholding not paid over by the employer, together with penalties and interest. The action must be brought not later than

(1) three years after the amount due on a return, report, or assessment becomes delinquent or

(2) 10 years after the entry of summary judgment or the recording of a tax lien.

(Sec. 1852, Rev. & Tax. Code)

Sales and use taxes.—The State Board of Equalization (SBE) may bring suit to collect sales and use taxes, penalties, and interest at any time within three years after an amount becomes due and payable or delinquent or during any time a lien is in force. (Sec. 6711, Rev. & Tax. Code)

Severance taxes.—The State Controller has until May 30 following any oil and gas production charge delinquency to bring an action to collect the delinquent charge or assessment, plus penalties and costs. (Sec. 3426, Pub. Res. Code)

The SBE may bring an action to collect delinquent timber yield tax and penalties at any time within three years after the tax becomes due and payable or delinquent or during any time a lien is in force. (Sec. 38511, Rev. & Tax. Code)

Insurance taxes.—The State Controller may bring suit to collect delinquent insurance taxes, penalties, and interest at any time within four years after an amount becomes due and payable and at any time within two years after a deficiency assessment becomes due and payable. (Sec. 12676, Rev. & Tax. Code)

Cigarette tax.—At any time within three years after a cigarette tax amount becomes due and payable, and at any time within 10 years after the last recording or filing of a notice of state tax lien, the SBE may transmit notice of the delinquency to the Attorney General, who may bring an action to collect the amount due. (Sec. 30301, Rev. & Tax. Code)

Motor fuel taxes.—The State Controller may request that the Attorney General bring suit for the recovery of any unpaid motor vehicle fuel tax, interest, penalties, and costs. (Sec. 7861, Rev. & Tax. Code)

The SBE may bring an action to collect delinquent use fuel tax or diesel fuel tax, penalties, and interest at any time within three years after the tax becomes due and payable or delinquent or during any time a lien is in force. (Sec. 8971, Rev. & Tax. Code; Sec. 60421, Rev. & Tax. Code)

Energy resources surcharge; emergency telephone users surcharge.—The SBE may bring an action to collect any delinquent surcharge and penalties at any time within 10 years after the surcharge becomes due and payable and at any time after any determined deficiency becomes due and payable. (Sec. 40141, Rev. & Tax. Code; Sec. 41115, Rev. & Tax. Code)

Other taxes and fees.—The SBE may bring any action necessary to collect an alcoholic beverage tax, hazardous substances tax, oil spill fee, or underground storage tank fee deficiency and, upon the SBE's request, the Attorney General must bring the action. (Sec. 32351, Rev. & Tax. Code; Sec. 43401, Rev. & Tax. Code; Sec. 46411, Rev. & Tax. Code; Sec. 50121, Rev. & Tax. Code)

See ¶89-224 for information on civil actions to recover erroneous refunds or credits.

[¶89-182] Civil Action in Another Jurisdiction

The Attorney General or an appropriate official of any political subdivision of California may bring suit in the courts of another state to collect taxes legally due the state or the political subdivision. Officials of other states that extend a like comity to California officials may sue for the collection of taxes in California courts. (Sec. 30, Rev. & Tax. Code; Sec. 31, Rev. & Tax. Code)

[¶89-184] Intergovernmental Tax Collection Agreements

There are a number of agreements among governmental agencies to provide for assistance in tax collection, both between the Internal Revenue Service and the states, and among the states themselves.

• *Reciprocal collection agreements with IRS, other states*

Both the BOE and the FTB are authorized to enter into agreements to collect any delinquent tax debt due to the IRS or any other state imposing an income tax, a tax measured by income, sales and use tax, or a similar tax, provided that the IRS and the other states agree to collect delinquent tax debts due to the BOE and the FTB. Under any such agreement, the California Controller would offset any delinquent tax debt due to that other state from a person or entity against any refund to that person or entity under the California sales and use tax law, personal income tax law, or corporation tax law. (Sec. 6835, Rev. & Tax. Code; Sec. 6850, Rev. & Tax. Code; Sec. 19291, Rev. & Tax. Code; Sec. 19377.5, Rev. & Tax. Code)

Participation in any such agreement is subject to a condition that the agreement not cause the net displacement of civil servants. At the discretion of the BOE and the FTB, the IRS may, as part of the collection process, refer the tax debt for litigation by its legal representatives in the name of the BOE. (Sec. 6835, Rev. & Tax. Code; Sec. 6850, Rev. & Tax. Code; Sec. 19291, Rev. & Tax. Code; Sec. 19377.5, Rev. & Tax. Code)

CCH PRACTICE TIP: *Federal Treasury Offset Program (FSOP).*—When more than one debt is submitted for the same taxpayer, the federal debt collection agency applies money in the following order:

— federal tax

— child support

— federal non-tax

— state income tax

FTB staff will select cases for the FSOP and generate Form FTB 1102BC, Intent to Offset Federal Payments, by certified mail with a return receipt. In order for taxpayers to avoid the offset, they must: pay the balance in full or provide proof that the debt is not past due or legally enforceable. If the taxpayer does not respond within 60 days, the debt will be referred to the Department of Treasury's Financial Management Service (FMS) for offset of federal payments. A $22.00 fee is assessed for each offset and is adjusted yearly.

Taxpayers can direct inquiries to the FTB's Offset Desk at (916) 845-2867 or send mail to Interagency Intercept Collections, MS-A460, FTB, P.O. Box 2966, Rancho Cordova, CA 95741-2966. (*Public Service Bulletin 2012-14*, California Franchise Tax Board, April 16, 2012)

PRACTICE TIP: *Reciprocal offset program with New York State.*—Beginning October 29, 2013, the FTB commenced a reciprocal refund offset program with New York State, whereby personal income tax refunds may be applied to pay a taxpayer's debts owed to the other state. Once a refund offset occurs, the offsetting state will issue a notice to the taxpayer with the offset date and amount. The notice will include contact information for the state to which the refund was offset. No fee is assessed for reciprocal state refund offsets. If the FTB receives more than one agency offset request, its priority is as follows:

— child support

— spousal support

— unemployment

— FTB – registration collection unit/other state agencies

— cities or counties

— private and post secondary education

— Internal Revenue Service

— multistate offset program

(*Public Service Bulletin 13-33*, California Franchise Tax Board, October 14, 2013)

• *Abusive Tax Avoidance Transactions (ATAT) Memorandum of Understanding*

The Small Business/Self-Employed Division of the Internal Revenue Service signed ATAT Memorandums of Understanding with 40 states and the District of Columbia on September 16, 2003, that provide for information sharing on abusive tax avoidance transactions. (*Memorandum of Understanding*, Internal Revenue Service, September 16, 2003) The Memorandum authorizes the IRS and a state to:

— exchange tax returns and return information,

— share audit results from ATAT participant cases,

— exchange information on identified types of ATAT schemes, and

— share audit technique guides.

The IRS will provide states with a list of participants in a particular ATAT scheme on a semi-annual basis on July 31 and January 31. The IRS generally refers to an abusive tax shelter arrangement as the promise of tax benefits with no meaningful change in the taxpayer's control over or benefit from the taxpayer's income or assets.

California has signed the ATAT Memorandum of Understanding with the IRS. (*Memorandum of Understanding*, Internal Revenue Service, September 16, 2003)

• *Multistate agreements*

Multistate Tax Compact.—California is a member of the Multistate Tax Commission, an agency of state governments created through a Multistate Tax Compact. The Commission maintains a Joint Audit Program that audits businesses for several states concurrently for sales and use and corporate income taxes. The Commission also maintains a National Nexus Program to help ensure compliance with state filing requirements.

Uniform Exchange of Information Agreement.—California is also a member of the Federation of Tax Administrators, which has developed a Uniform Exchange of Information Agreement that enables states to exchange tax information with each other.

International Fuel Tax Agreement.—California participates in the International Fuel Tax Agreement, which is intended to provide uniformity in the administration of motor fuel use tax laws for motor vehicles operated interstate and to enable states to act cooperatively in the administration and collection of motor fuel use taxes.

• *Agreement between state agencies*

Taxpayers who are delinquent in paying California corporate and personal income taxes and sales and use taxes may have their California state licenses revoked or suspended.

Generally, a state licensing agency that issues professional or occupational licenses, certificates, registrations, or permits must suspend, revoke, and refuse to issue a license if the licensee's name is included on a certified list published by the BOE or the FTB. A "certified list" means the list provided by either the BOE or the FTB of the persons whose names appear on the list of the 500 largest tax delinquencies. (Sec. 494.5, Bus. & Prof. Code)

The agencies would also be required to collect identifying information from each license applicant to match it against the lists. There are specific terms for some agencies, including the Department of Motor Vehicles, the State Bar of California, and the Alcoholic Beverage Control Board. (Sec. 494.5, Bus. & Prof. Code)

In addition, state agencies generally are prohibited from entering into any contract for the acquisition of goods or services with a contractor whose name appears on either of the lists. (Sec. 10295.4, Pub. Cont. Code)

From January 1, 2019, until January 1, 2023, the California Tax Education Council may enter into an agreement with the FTB to reimburse the FTB for its assistance carrying out enforcement activities consistent with The Tax Preparation Act. (Sec. 22253, Bus. & Prof. Code)

¶89-184

Joint Enforcement Strike Force.—The Employment Development Department, Department of Consumer Affairs, Department of Industrial Relations, and Department of Insurance are part of a Joint Enforcement Strike Force on the Underground Economy, which has duties to:

— encourage participating agencies to develop and share information necessary to combat the underground economy;

— develop methods to pool, focus, and target enforcement resources to deter tax evasion and maximize recoveries from tax evaders and those who violate the wage withholding reporting laws;

— coordinate the enforcement activities of participating agencies; and

— reduce enforcement costs by eliminating duplicative audits and investigations.

Other agencies, such as the Franchise Tax Board, State Board of Equalization, and Department of Justice, which are not part of the strike force, are encouraged to participate. (Sec. 329, Unempl. Ins. Code)

[¶89-186] Agreements in Compromise of Tax Due

Under specific circumstances, state taxing authorities have the authority to compromise tax liabilities.

COMMENT: Multi-agency form.—The FTB, California Department of Tax and Fee Administration (CDTFA), and Employment Development Department (EDD) have developed a single form, Form DE 999CA, Multi-Agency Form for Offer in Compromise, that individuals can use to apply for offers in compromise of nondisputed final tax liabilities owed to the FTB, CDTFA, and EDD. Businesses should not use Form DE 999CA to request offers in compromise, but should instead use Form FTB 4905BE, Offer in Compromise for Business Entities, for FTB offers, and Form CDTFA-490-C, Offer In Compromise Application For Corporations, Limited Liability Companies, Partnerships, Trusts, and Unidentified Business Organizations, for CDTFA offers. The state agencies will negotiate each offer in compromise separately for their respective taxes. (*News Release*, California Tax Service Center, August 23, 2006)

• *Income taxes*

Tax settlement agreements.—The Executive Officer and the Chief Counsel of the Franchise Tax Board (FTB) may jointly approve the settlement of any corporation franchise or income tax or personal income tax dispute involving a reduction in tax and penalties of $8,100 or less. On January 1 of each calendar year, this threshold amount is increased to reflect inflation. All such settlements are final and nonappealable, except upon a showing of fraud or misrepresentation with respect to a material fact. For tax and penalty reductions that exceed $8,100, the Executive Officer and the Chief Counsel must present their settlement recommendations to the FTB board members for approval. Any settlement approved by the FTB itself is final and conclusive to the same extent as a closing agreement approved by the FTB itself. (Sec. 19442, Rev. & Tax. Code; *FTB Notice 2006-2*, Franchise Tax Board, February 14, 2006)

PRACTICE POINTER: Settlement procedures

Taxpayers who want to initiate a settlement should call for additional information or submit a written request to the Director of the Settlement Bureau.

A written request for settlement should include:

— the taxpayer's name and current address;

— any representative's name, current address, fax, and telephone number;

— the taxpayer's Social Security or taxpayer identification number;

— the taxable year(s) involved;

— the tax amount involved;

— the present status of the dispute (i.e., protest, appeal, or claim for refund);

— a copy of the representative's power of attorney (FTB Form 3520), unless a valid form is already on file with the FTB;

— a good faith settlement offer, including the grounds in support of the offer;

— identification and discussion of all issues in contention, including legal and factual grounds for positions taken by the taxpayer; and

— a listing of, including the present status of and amount involved in, all notices of proposed assessment and claims for refund for the taxable years involved that are not part of the settlement request.

The FTB Settlement Bureau reviews the information and notifies the taxpayer or the taxpayer's representative as to whether the case is accepted into the settlement program. If accepted, a tentative settlement is generally reached within nine months, subject to FTB approval. Final approval generally follows deposit of the required tax payment. Except with the Chief Counsel's approval, cases are removed from settlement consideration and returned to pre-settlement status if a tentative settlement has not been reached within nine months. (*FTB Notice 2007-2*, Franchise Tax Board, June 27, 2007)

PRACTICE NOTE: Admissibility of settlement negotiations.—Evidence of any settlement offer made during settlement negotiations between a taxpayer and the FTB is not admissible in any subsequent adjudicative proceeding or civil action, including any appeal to the State Board of Equalization. Nor is any evidence of any conduct or statements related to the settlement negotiations admissible to prove liability for any tax, penalty, fee, or interest, except to the extent provided for in Sec. 1152 of the Evidence Code. (Sec. 19442(g)(3), Rev. & Tax. Code)

Voluntary disclosure program.—Under terms established in a voluntary disclosure agreement, the FTB may waive additions to tax or penalties for noncompliance with specified registration, reporting, and payment requirements for the six taxable years immediately preceding the FTB's signing of the agreement. For taxable years ending more than six years prior to the agreement, income taxes, additions to tax, fees, or penalties may be waived. (Sec. 19191(d)(1), Rev. & Tax. Code)

The FTB may enter into these agreements with qualified business entities, nonresident S corporation shareholders, partners (effective after 2017), limited liability company (LLC) members, or trust beneficiaries. However, the FTB may not waive additions to tax or penalties for any of the six years immediately preceding the signing of the agreement during which a partner, S corporation shareholder, or an LLC member was a California resident required to file a California tax return. In addition, the FTB may not waive additions to tax or penalties attributable to a partner's, S corporation shareholder's, or a LLC member's income other than the California source income from the partnership, S corporation, or LLC. (Sec. 19191(a), Rev. & Tax. Code; Sec. 19192(a)(4), (6), (11), Rev. & Tax. Code)

> *DEPARTMENT OF REVENUE COMMENT: Participation in program not prevented by "doing business" rulings.*—The FTB notes that a request for a Chief Counsel Ruling regarding whether a putative taxpayer's activities constitute "doing business" in California under the general rule of Rev. & Tax. Code Sec. 23101(a) will not prevent the putative taxpayer from applying for the FTB's Voluntary Disclosure Program (VDP). Persons who request such advice must disclose the identity of the putative taxpayer. However, an applicant that otherwise meets the requirements for eligibility may still request admission into the VDP even if the guidance requested results in a preliminary determination by the Legal Division that the activities in question constitute "doing business" and, thus, that a return filing obligation exists, whether or not a Chief Counsel Ruling is ultimately issued. (*FTB Notice 2011-06*, California Franchise Tax Board, October 12, 2011)

Taxpayers who wish to participate in the Voluntary Disclosure Program should use Form 4925, Application for Voluntary Disclosure, to apply. It is not necessary for taxpayers to identify themselves to receive information.

Filing compliance agreements.—The FTB provides business entities, partnerships, and trusts the opportunity to voluntarily enter into a filing compliance agreement (FCA) if they have a filing requirement for past years, and an unpaid California tax liability. A nonresident shareholder of an S corporation, partner, LLC member, or beneficiary may apply for an FCA if the entity also files an FCA request. For taxpayers entering into an FCA, the FTB may on a case-by-case basis waive penalties for which reasonable cause is a defense. The most commonly waived penalties under the program are the failure to file and the failure to pay tax penalties.

Taxpayers eligible to enter into an FCA are those taxpayers in the class of taxpayers described in the authorizing statute for California's voluntary disclosure program (VDP) discussed above, but who failed to satisfy an eligibility requirement.

The primary differences between the FCA and the voluntary disclosure program are the following:

— the VDP is a statutory program, whereas the FCA program is authorized under the FTB's general authority to abate specified penalties for reasonable cause;

— a taxpayer may enter into a FCA even if the taxpayer was first contacted by the FTB, whereas a taxpayer may not enter into the VDP if the taxpayer was contacted by the FTB for a return prior to applying for the program;

— relief from penalties and additions to tax is limited to a six year look-back period under the VDP, whereas there is no specified look-back period under the FCA program; and

— the underpayment of estimated tax penalty may be waived under the VDP, but not under the FCA program.

A taxpayer interested in participating in an FCA should send a completed form FTB 5841 Request for Filing Compliance Agreement to the FTB.

Taxpayers allowed to enter into an FCA must submit the required tax returns and payment by the date specified in the agreement. Full payment is usually due within 30 days from the date of the agreement, unless the taxpayer enters into an installment payment agreement.

The FCA may be voided if at any time the information supplied by the taxpayers is subsequently determined by the FTB to be inaccurate or false. (*Filing Compliance Agreement*, California Franchise Tax Board, October 2013)

Offers in compromise.—An FTB program provides for "offers in compromise" (OIC) when a taxpayer's tax liability is not in dispute and there is little, if any, possibility that the tax can ever be paid in full. (Pub. FTB 4905BE, Offer in Compromise for Business Entities, Franchise Tax Board, October 2013; Pub. FTB 4905PIT, Offer in Compromise for Individuals, Franchise Tax Board, April 2009)

PRACTICE TIP: Criteria for offers in compromise.—The FTB requires tax-payers to prove that the amount offered is the most the FTB could expect to receive based on their present assets and income. In addition, the FTB determines whether taxpayers have reasonable prospects of acquiring additional income or assets that would allow them to satisfy a greater amount of the liability than the offered amount within a reasonable period. Depending on other factors, five years is usually considered a reasonable period. (*Tax News*, Franchise Tax Board, August 2010)

The Executive Officer and the Chief Counsel of the FTB, or their delegates, jointly, may administratively compromise any final tax liability if the resulting tax reduction is $7,500 or less. The FTB, upon the joint recommendation of the Executive Officer and the Chief Counsel, may compromise a final tax liability resulting in a tax reduction in excess of $7,500. The FTB may, by resolution, delegate to the Executive Officer and the Chief Counsel joint authority to compromise a final tax liability resulting in a tax reduction in excess of $7,500 but less than $10,000. (Sec. 19443, Rev. & Tax. Code) The FTB will not automatically accept an OIC that was accepted by the Internal Revenue Service. (Pub. FTB 4905BE, Offer in Compromise for Business Entities, Franchise Tax Board, October 2013; Pub. FTB 4905PIT, Offer in Compromise for Individuals, Franchise Tax Board, April 2009)

When a married couple files a joint return, the acceptance of an offer in compromise from one spouse does not relieve the other spouse from paying the joint liability. However, liability is reduced by the amount of the accepted offer. (Sec. 19443, Rev. & Tax. Code)

An offer in compromise may be rescinded if a taxpayer (1) conceals property or otherwise withholds information or makes false statements relating to the taxpayer's financial condition, (2) fails to comply with the terms of the program, or (3) fails to file reports or make payments within 20 days of the FTB's notice and demand. (Sec. 19443(h), Rev. & Tax. Code)

• *Withholding of tax*

Tax settlement agreements.—The Director of the EDD may approve settlements of civil employment tax disputes involving a tax reduction of $7,500 or less. However, the Director must submit a settlement of $7,500 or less to an administrative law judge for approval if an appeal has been filed with the Unemployment Insurance Appeals Board, the appeal has been assigned to an administrative law judge, and a notice of hearing has been issued. Furthermore, if an appeal from an administrative law judge's decision has been filed, the settlement must be approved by the Board. For tax reductions that exceed $7,500, the Director must present any settlement recommendations to the Board for approval. (Sec. 1236, Unempl. Ins. Code)

The Director must submit proposed settlement agreements of over $5,000 to the Attorney General for review prior to presenting their recommendations for approval to the Board. Within 30 days of receiving a settlement recommendation, the Attorney General must review the recommendation and make written findings concerning the reasonableness of the recommendation. The Board will review all recommendations made and hold any related proceedings concerning such recommendations in closed sessions. (Sec. 1236, Unempl. Ins. Code)

All settlements entered into are final and nonappealable except upon a showing of fraud or misrepresentation concerning a material fact. Approved settlements that result in a reduction in tax or penalties or total tax and penalties in excess of $500 become part of a public record kept on file in the office of the Director. (Sec. 1236, Unempl. Ins. Code)

Offers in compromise.—When an employer or other person formerly having charge of the affairs of an employing unit owes delinquent contributions, withholdings, penalties, or interest to the EDD, the Director may enter into an agreement to accept partial payment in satisfaction of the full liability if the Director believes that it would be in the best interest of the state and certain other requirements are met. Offers in compromise will be considered only for liabilities of employers with inactive out-of-business accounts and individuals or partners who no longer have a controlling interest in, or association with, the business that incurred the liabilities. An employer, individual, or partner submitting an offer in compromise must not have:

— access to current income sufficient to pay more than the accumulating interest and 6.7% of the liability on an annual basis;

— reasonable prospects of acquiring increased income or assets that would allow the liability to be liquidated in a reasonable period; or

— assets that, if sold, would satisfy the liability.

Only nondisputed, final tax liabilities will be considered for compromise. (Sec. 1870, Unempl. Ins. Code)

The amount offered in compromise must be more than the EDD could reasonably expect to collect through involuntary means during the four-year period beginning on the date the offer is made. The offer must be submitted in writing and must generally be accompanied by cash, a cashier's check, or a money order equal to the amount offered in compromise. However, the Director may permit payment of the agreed upon amount in installments over a period of up to five years if the Director believes that it would be in the best interest of the state. (Sec. 1870, Unempl. Ins. Code)

Any liability due to fraud or actions resulting in a violation of the Unemployment Insurance Code will not be compromised. An agreement that reduces liability by $10,000 or more will not be effective until it is approved by the Board. (Sec. 1871, Unempl. Ins. Code)

Once the terms of a compromise agreement are fulfilled, the liability will be considered satisfied in full, all withholding tax liens filed or recorded will be released, and a statement containing information relating to the compromise will be placed on file with the Department. (Sec. 1873, Unempl. Ins. Code)

Acceptance of a compromise offer may be rescinded, and all compromised liabilities may be reestablished without regard to any applicable statute of limitations if the Department determines that any person willfully did any of the following:

— concealed from the state any property belonging to the estate of the employer or other person liable for the tax;

— received, withheld, destroyed, mutilated, or falsified any book, document, or record;

— made any false statement relating to the estate or financial conditions of the employer or other person liable for the tax; or

— failed to pay any tax liability owed the Department for any subsequent active business in which the employer or person who previously submitted the offer in compromise has a controlling interest or association.

(Sec. 1875, Unempl. Ins. Code)

Voluntary non-wage withholding program.—The FTB has a withholding voluntary compliance program (WVCP) that allows eligible withholding agents to remit past-due, nonwage and real estate withholding for the previous two calendar years, including interest, in exchange for having specified withholding tax liabilities and penalties waived. The limited amnesty program is available to both business and individual withholding agents who have a requirement to withhold resident, nonresident, and real-estate withholding and have not previously withheld.

Withholding agents who participate in the program are eligible for the following benefits:

— Waiver of information return penalties for the two-year look-back period.

— Elimination of withholding audits prior to the two-year look-back period.

— Limitation of the tax withholding liability to the look-back period, plus interest.

Withholding agents are ineligible to participate in the program if they:

— Participated in the 2008 nonresident withholding incentive program.

— Have been audited by the FTB for nonwage withholding.

— Have had a withholding liability or information return penalty for nonwage withholding assessed against them by the FTB.

Eligible agents who would like to participate in the program should submit a completed FTB 4827, Withholding Voluntary Compliance Program Application, along with an estimate of the amount of withholding for each calendar year covered, and pay the required withholding amount, plus interest. (*FTB Tax NewsFlash—Withholding Voluntary Compliance Initiative,* July 15, 2013)

• *Sales and use taxes*

The Offer in Compromise (OIC) program is for taxpayers and feepayers that do not have, and will not have in the foreseeable future, the income, assets, or means to pay their tax liabilities. This program allows a taxpayer to offer a lesser amount for payment of a nondisputed final tax liability. A taxpayer wishing to compromise a liability through the OIC process must no longer own the personal property that incurred the tax that could result in an additional tax or fee assessment. Generally, the California Department of Tax and Fee Administration (CDTFA) approves an Offer in Compromise when the amount offered represents the most the agency can expect to receive from the taxpayer's current income or assets. (CDTFA-490 Offer in Compromise Application)

A CDTFA Offer in Compromise is evaluated separately from an offer reached with the IRS or FTB. However, in general, if the amount of the offer represents the most that the CDTFA can expect to collect within a reasonable period of time, such an Offer in Compromise will be accepted. (CDTFA-490 Offer in Compromise Application)

The Executive Officer and the Chief Counsel of the CDTFA may jointly approve the settlement of any disputed civil sales and use tax matter involving a reduction in tax and penalties of $5,000 or less. The Executive Director or the Chief Counsel may make recommendations to the CDTFA board members for settlement of any other disputed civil sales and use tax matter. The CDTFA is required to maintain records of settlement agreements with sales and use taxpayers for amounts of over $500 for a period of at least one year. (Sec. 7093.5, Rev. & Tax. Code)

Final tax liability.—The Executive Director and Chief Counsel of the CDTFA may compromise any final tax liability in which the reduction of tax is $7,500 or less. The CDTFA, upon recommendation by its Executive Director and Chief Counsel, jointly, may compromise a final tax liability involving a reduction in tax greater than $7,500, and a recommendation for approval of an offer in compromise that is not either approved or disapproved within 45 days of the submission of the recommendation is deemed approved. The CDTFA may itself by resolution delegate to the Executive Director and the Chief Counsel, jointly, the authority to compromise a final tax liability in which the reduction of tax is greater than $7,500 but less than $10,000. (Sec. 7093.6, Rev. & Tax. Code)

A "final tax liability" is any final tax liability that arises under the laws regarding Sales and Use Taxes, Uniform Local Sales and Use Taxes, Transactions and Use Taxes, and Additional Local Taxes of the Revenue and Taxation Code (i.e., Parts 1, 1.5, 1.6, and 1.7) or related interest, additions to tax, penalties, or other amounts assessed. (Sec. 7093.6, Rev. & Tax. Code)

Offers in compromise can be considered only for liabilities that were generated from a business that has been discontinued or transferred, where the taxpayer who makes the offer no longer has a controlling interest or association with the transferred business or has a controlling interest or association with a similar type of business as the transferred or discontinued business. (Sec. 7093.6, Rev. & Tax. Code)

Qualified final tax liability.—Until January 1, 2023, a qualified final tax liability can be compromised regardless of whether the business was discontinued or transferred or whether the taxpayer has a controlling interest or association with a similar type of business as the transferred or discontinued business. All provisions that apply to a final tax liability also apply to a qualified final tax liability. A "qualified final tax liability" is any of the following:

— that part of a final tax liability, including related interest, additions to tax, penalties, or other amounts assessed, arising from transactions in which the CDTFA found no evidence that the taxpayer collected sales tax reimbursements or use tax from the purchaser;

— a final tax liability, including related interest, additions to tax, penalties, or other amounts assessed, arising from the taxpayer's sale of the business to successors or assigns who withhold sufficient of the purchase price to cover the liability until the former owner produces a receipt from the CDTFA showing that it has been paid; or

— that part of a final tax liability for use tax, including related interest, additions to tax, penalties, or other amounts assessed, against a taxpayer who is a consumer that is not required to hold a seller's permit.

(Sec. 7093.6, Rev. & Tax. Code)

A qualified final tax liability may not be compromised with:

— a taxpayer who previously received a compromise for a liability arising from transactions substantially similar to transactions attributable to the liability for which the taxpayer is making the offer;

— a business transferred by a taxpayer who previously received a compromise and who has a controlling interest or association with the transferred business when the liability arises from transactions substantially similar to transactions attributable to the liability for which the taxpayer is making the offer; or

— a business in which a taxpayer who previously received a compromise has a controlling interest or association with a similar type of business for which the taxpayer received the compromise when the liability of the business making the offer arose from transactions substantially similar to the transactions for which the taxpayer's liability was previously compromised.

(Sec. 7093.6, Rev. & Tax. Code)

The CDTFA may permit the taxpayer to pay the compromise in installments for a period of up to a year, and the taxpayer may be required to pay by electronic funds transfer or any other means to facilitate the payment of each installment. (Sec. 7093.6, Rev. & Tax. Code) Other than making recommendations to the executive director and the chief counsel, CDTFA members may not participate in this offer in compromise procedure. (Sec. 7093.6, Rev. & Tax. Code)

A taxpayer receiving a compromise under this process may be required to enter into any collateral agreement deemed necessary to protect the interests of the state. A collateral agreement may include a provision allowing the CDTFA to reestablish the liability, or any part of it, if the taxpayer has sufficient annual income during the succeeding five-year period. (Sec. 7093.6, Rev. & Tax. Code) In addition, a taxpayer receiving a compromise shall file and pay by the due date all subsequently required tax returns for a five-year period from the date the liability is compromised or until the taxpayer no longer is required to file tax returns. (Sec. 7093.6, Rev. & Tax. Code)

Effective January 1, 2023, provisions regarding a qualified final tax liability are repealed. (Sec. 7093.6, Rev. & Tax. Code)

• *Other taxes and fees*

The Executive Director or the Chief Counsel of the BOE may also make recommendations to the BOE board members for settlement of any disputed civil matter involving the following taxes and fees:

— use fuel tax; (Sec. 9271, Rev. & Tax. Code)

— cigarette tax; (Sec. 30459.1, Rev. & Tax. Code)

— alcoholic beverage tax; (Sec. 32471, Rev. & Tax. Code)

— timber yield tax; (Sec. 38800, Rev. & Tax. Code)

— energy resources surcharge; (Sec. 40211, Rev. & Tax. Code)

— emergency telephone users surcharge; (Sec. 41171, Rev. & Tax. Code)

— hazardous substances tax; (Sec. 43522, Rev. & Tax. Code)

— integrated waste management fee; (Sec. 45867, Rev. & Tax. Code)

— oil spill fees; (Sec. 46622, Rev. & Tax. Code)

— underground storage tank maintenance fee; (Sec. 50156.11, Rev. & Tax. Code); and

— fee collection procedures law; (Sec. 55332, Rev. & Tax. Code)

— diesel fuel tax. (Sec. 60636, Rev. & Tax. Code)

Offers in compromise.—Several taxes and fees administered by the BOE have offer in compromise programs that closely parallel the BOE program for offers in compromise for sales and use tax liabilities described above, including the provisions that relate to transferred or discontinued businesses. In addition, the January 1, 2023, expiration date for offers in compromise provision relating to final tax liabilities also apply to several other taxes and fees, including

— use fuel tax; (Sec. 9278, Rev. & Tax. Code)

— cigarette tax; (Sec. 30459.15, Rev. & Tax. Code)

— alcoholic beverage tax; (Sec. 32471.5, Rev. & Tax. Code)

— emergency telephone users surcharge; (Sec. 41171.5, Rev. & Tax. Code)

— oil spill fees; (Sec. 46628, Rev. & Tax. Code)

— underground storage tank maintenance fee; (Sec. 50156.18, Rev. & Tax. Code)

— fee collection procedures law; (Sec. 55332.5, Rev. & Tax. Code) and

— diesel fuel tax. (Sec. 60637, Rev. & Tax. Code)

[¶89-188] Installment Payments

Various taxes may be paid in installments. For information on property tax installment payments, see ¶20-756.

• *Personal income and corporation franchise and income taxes*

The Franchise Tax Board (FTB) may enter into an agreement with a taxpayer that allows the taxpayer to pay the full or partial amount of outstanding personal income or corporation franchise or income taxes, interest, and penalties due in installments if the FTB determines that the taxpayer's situation is one of financial hardship. (Sec. 19008, Rev. & Tax. Code)

COMMENT: *Business entity applications.*—Business entities may request an installment payment arrangement for the payment of unpaid California corporation franchise or income taxes by calling the FTB at 1-888-635-0494. (*FTB Notice 2005-5*, California Franchise Tax Board, October 7, 2005; *Tax News*, California Franchise Tax Board, May 2010)

COMPLIANCE POINTER: *Skipping payments.*—Taxpayers who pay their personal income tax obligation through an installment agreement may request skipping a payment from the FTB's website or through the FTB's interactive voice response system. Taxpayers may be eligible to skip a payment if they (1) are in an existing active installment agreement, (2) have less than two previous skipped payments, and (3) submit their request more than five days but less than 30 days from the next payment due date. (*Tax News*, California Franchise Tax Board, November 2016)

Individual taxpayer eligibility.—The FTB *must* enter into an agreement to accept full payment of an individual's personal income tax liability in installments if, as of the date the individual offers to enter into the agreement, all of the following apply:

(1) the aggregate amount of the liability, determined without regard to interest, penalties, additions to tax, and additional amounts, does not exceed $10,000;

(2) the individual and, if the individual has filed a joint return, the individual's spouse has not during the preceding five years failed to file a personal income tax return, failed to pay any tax required to be shown on the return, or entered into an installment agreement for payment of any personal income tax;

(3) the FTB determines that the individual is financially unable to pay the liability in full when due and the individual submits any information that the FTB may require to make this determination;

(4) the agreement requires full payment of the liability within three years; and

(5) the individual agrees to comply with the provisions of the California personal income tax law and related administrative provisions for the period that the agreement is in effect.

(Sec. 19008, Rev. & Tax. Code)

Notwithstanding the above provisions, an individual taxpayer may be eligible for an installment agreement if he or she:

— owes a balance of $25,000 or less;

— agrees to pay the full amount in 60 months or less;

— has filed all required personal income tax returns; and

— is not in an existing installment agreement.

However, if the tax liability owed exceeds $10,000 or the installment agreement period for payment exceeds 36 months, or both, then the individual must certify that she or he has a financial hardship. Approval will be based on ability to pay and compliance history. A lien may be filed, and/or a financial statement requested, as a condition for approval. (*FTB 3567*, Installment Agreement Request)

Partial payments.—Agreements entered into for partial payment of tax liabilities must be reviewed by the FTB at least once every two years. (Sec. 19008(f), Rev. & Tax. Code)

Informal arrangements.—In the case of any taxpayer that is making payments to the FTB under an informal payment arrangement existing as of September 6, 2005, that informal payment arrangement will be treated as an installment payment agreement that was entered into on the later of (1) January 1, 2005, or (2) the date on which the arrangement was established. Arrangements entered into prior to February 1, 2005, are treated as an installment payment agreement entered into as of the start of the amnesty program. Consequently, taxpayers participating in such an arrangement would not be subject to tax amnesty penalties. (Sec. 19008(g), Rev. & Tax. Code)

Frivolous submissions—Generally applicable to submissions made after 2010, an application to enter into an installment agreement will be treated as it if were never submitted if the FTB determines that the application was a frivolous tax submission. The FTB's determination is not subject to any further administrative or judicial review. (Sec. 19443(i), Rev. & Tax. Code)

Fees.—The fee for individuals to enter into an installment payment plan is $34. The fee for business entities to enter into an installment payment plan is $50. However, the fee does not need to be paid until the payment plan is approved. The fee will be added to the balance due if the installment payment application is approved. No separate payment of the fee is required. (Reg. 19591, 18 CCR; *FTB Notice 2004-09*, California Franchise Tax Board, December 17, 2004; *FTB 3567*, Installment Agreement Request (Rev. 12-2009))

Termination.—The FTB may terminate an agreement for noncompliance. (Sec. 19008, Rev. & Tax. Code)

•*Other taxes*

The State Board of Equalization (SBE) may enter into installment payment agreements for the payment of any of the following taxes, together with penalties and interest:

— alcoholic beverage tax; (Sec. 32389, Rev. & Tax. Code)

— cigarette tax; (Sec. 30354, Rev. & Tax. Code)

— diesel fuel tax; (Sec. 60493, Rev. & Tax. Code)

— emergency telephone users surcharge; (Sec. 41127.6, Rev. & Tax. Code)

— energy resources surcharge; (Sec. 40167, Rev. & Tax. Code)

— oil spill fees; (Sec. 46464, Rev. & Tax. Code)

— hazardous substances tax; (Sec. 43448, Rev. & Tax. Code)

— sales and use taxes; (Sec. 6832, Rev. & Tax. Code)

— underground storage tank maintenance fee; (Sec. 50138.6, Rev. & Tax. Code) and

— use fuel tax. (Sec. 8958, Rev. & Tax. Code)

Upon failure of a person to fully comply with the terms of an installment payment agreement, the SBE may terminate the agreement.

[¶89-190] Recovery of Erroneous Refunds

Specific provisions on recovery of erroneous refunds or credits are as follows.

•*Income taxes*

Corporation franchise (income) tax and personal income tax amounts erroneously refunded or credited to a taxpayer due to Franchise Tax Board (FTB) error may be assessed and collected by the FTB after notice and demand. (Sec. 19368(a), Rev. & Tax. Code)

A misdirected income tax refund deposited via direct deposit into the bank account of a person other than the taxpayer entitled to the refund may be recovered upon notice and demand from the FTB to the recipient of the misdirected refund. Effective on the date that the notice and demand for repayment is mailed to the recipient of the misdirected refund, the taxpayer's account will be credited with the amount of the misdirected refund. This procedure for recovering misdirected tax refunds will apply only if the FTB determines that all of the following conditions are satisfied:

— a taxpayer filed a tax return that designated one or more direct deposit refunds;

— the taxpayer, tax return preparer, or electronic return originator entered an incorrect financial institution account or routing number that resulted in all or a portion of the refund not being received, directly or indirectly, by the taxpayer due the refund;

— the taxpayer did not receive the refund; and

— the recipient of the misdirected refund was not entitled to the refund.

Before any credit for a misdirected refund will be allowed to a taxpayer, the taxpayer must provide certain information to the FTB upon written request. (Sec. 19368(b), Rev. & Tax. Code)

Also, the FTB may bring an action in court to recover an income tax refund or credit erroneously made or allowed to a taxpayer or to any third party, including where the taxpayer or a related party caused, in any way, the erroneous refund, together with interest at the adjusted annual rate (see ¶ 89-204 Interest Rates). (Sec. 19411, Rev. & Tax. Code)

Abatement of interest on amounts due under these provisions is discussed at ¶ 89-210 Abatement of Interest, Penalties, or Additions to Tax.

• *Other taxes*

For each of the following taxes, the State Board of Equalization may pursue the collection of an erroneous refund or credit by issuing a deficiency determination or the State Controller may bring suit to recover an erroneous refund or credit:

— alcoholic beverage tax; (Sec. 32431, Rev. & Tax. Code)

— cigarette tax; (Sec. 30381, Rev. & Tax. Code)

— diesel fuel tax; (Sec. 60561, Rev. & Tax. Code)

— emergency telephone users surcharge; (Sec. 41114.1, Rev. & Tax. Code)

— energy resources surcharge; (Sec. 40135, Rev. & Tax. Code)

— hazardous substances tax; (Sec. 43481, Rev. & Tax. Code)

— motor vehicle fuel tax; (Sec. 8171, Rev. & Tax. Code)

— oil spill fees; (Sec. 46541, Rev. & Tax. Code)

— sales and use taxes; (Sec. 6961, Rev. & Tax. Code)

— timber yield tax; (Sec. 38621, Rev. & Tax. Code)

— underground storage tank maintenance fee; (Sec. 50150, Rev. & Tax. Code) and

— use fuel tax. (Sec. 9181, Rev. & Tax. Code)

Also, the State Controller may bring suit to recover an erroneous insurance tax refund or credit. (Sec. 12691, Rev. & Tax. Code)

[¶ 89-200]

INTEREST AND PENALTIES

[¶ 89-202] Interest and Penalties in General

California has separate provisions on interest and penalties for various tax types, instead of general administrative provisions for all taxes. For a discussion of applicable interest rates, see ¶ 89-204. For civil penalties, see ¶ 89-206, and for criminal penalties, see ¶ 89-208. For provisions relating to abatement of interest, penalties, or additions to tax, see ¶ 89-210.

Interest and penalties for late filing or late payments are reported on Form 540, California Resident Income Tax Return, for an individual taxpayer and Form 100, California Corporation Franchise or Income Tax Return, for a corporate taxpayer.

• *Deposits made to suspend running of interest on potential underpayments*

California incorporates, with modifications, federal law (IRC Sec. 6603) as of California's current federal conformity date, relating to deposits made to suspend the running of interest on potential underpayments. For California purposes, the deposit is not considered a payment of tax for purposes of filing a refund claim, converting an administrative refund claim into a judicial refund action, or filing a judicial refund action, unless the taxpayer provides a written notification to the Franchise Tax Board stating that the deposit is a payment of tax or the deposit is actually used to pay a final tax liability. (Sec. 19041.5, Rev. & Tax. Code)

Additional modifications to IRC Sec. 6603 substitute a "notice of proposed deficiency" for a "30-day letter" for purposes of defining a "disputable tax".

The FTB has announced that it will follow *Revenue Procedure 2005-18*, 2005-13 I.R.B. 798, which outlines the policies and procedures followed by the Internal Revenue Service in implementing the federal tax deposit provision. *FTB Notice 2005-6*, outlines the procedures taxpayers should follow for making tax deposits and for requesting returns of deposits. The Notice specifies to whom the written statements designating a remittance as a tax deposit and requests for return or transfers of tax deposits should be mailed to and the addresses of the appropriate staff person.

PRACTICAL ANALYSIS: Tax deposit forms.—Forms 3576-3579, Tax Deposit Voucher, should be used to designate a remittance as a tax deposit for a specific tax year. Form 3581, Tax Deposit Refund or Transfer Request, should be used to request a tax deposit refund, designate the application of a tax deposit to a different tax year, or apply a tax deposit to convert an administrative protest or appeal to an administrative refund action. (*Tax News*, California Franchise Tax Board, September 2006)

[¶89-204] Interest Rates

Interest on underpayments and overpayments of other taxes is imposed as follows.

See ¶20-752 Interest, for property tax interest information.

• *Corporation franchise (income) and personal income taxes*

The adjusted annual rate of interest on corporation franchise and income tax and personal income tax underpayments and overpayments is determined semiannually on the basis of the federal underpayment rate. Interest is compounded daily. (Sec. 19521, Rev. & Tax. Code)

For any corporations, the adjusted annual interest rate on overpayments of California corporation franchise and income taxes is the lesser of 5% or the bond equivalent rate of a 13-week U.S. Treasury bill. The bond equivalent of 13-week U.S. treasury bills that is established at the first auction held during the month of January is used to determine the interest rate for the following July 1 through December 31. This rate is rounded to the nearest full percent or, if the rate is a multiple of one-half of 1%, increased to the next highest full percent. The bond equivalent rate of 13-week U.S. Treasury bills established at the first auction held during the month of July is used to determine the interest rate for the following January 1 through June 30. (Sec. 19521, Rev. & Tax. Code)

The rates in effect for personal income tax underpayments and overpayments and for corporation franchise and income tax underpayments for the designated periods are:

From	Applicable Period To	Adjusted Annual Rate
January 1, 2020	December 31, 2020	5%
July 1, 2019	December 31, 2019	6%
January 1, 2019	June 30, 2019	5%
January 1, 2017	December 31, 2018	4%
July 1, 2012	December 31, 2016	3%
January 1, 2012	June 30, 2012	4%
July 1, 2011	December 31, 2011	3%
January 1, 2010	June 30, 2011	4%
January 1, 2009	December 31, 2009	5%
July 1, 2008	December 31, 2008	7%
January 1, 2007	June 30, 2008	8%

The interest rates on corporate overpayments for the designated periods are:

From	Applicable Period To	Adjusted Annual Rate
January 1, 2019	December 31, 2020	2%
July 1, 2017	December 31, 2018	1%
July 1, 2009	June 30, 2017	0%
January 1, 2009	June 30, 2009	2%
July 1, 2008	December 31, 2008	3%
January 1, 2007	June 30, 2008	5%

Large corporate underpayments accrue interest at 2% higher than the ordinary underpayment rate. A "large corporate underpayment" is an underpayment of tax by a C corporation that is in excess of $100,000 for any taxable period. (Sec. 19521, Rev. & Tax. Code)

Interest equal to 150% will be imposed if all of the following applies:

— the taxpayer files an amended return before being contacted by the IRS or FTB regarding a potentially abusive tax shelter;

— the taxpayer files an amended return to report an understatement of tax related to a reportable transaction (see ¶89-176); and

— the amended return is for a tax year beginning after December 31, 1998.

(Sec. 19778, Rev. & Tax. Code)

California does not follow the federal provision in IRC Sec. 6621(d), relating to the elimination of interest on overlapping periods of tax overpayments and underpayments. (Sec. 19521, Rev. & Tax. Code)

• *Withholding of tax*

Interest on delinquent payments of withheld personal income tax is imposed at the same rate that applies to underpayments of corporation franchise (income) and personal income taxes (see above). (Sec. 1113, Unempl. Ins. Code)

• *Sales and use taxes*

Interest on sales and use tax underpayments and overpayments is applied at the modified adjusted rate per month, or fraction thereof. The "modified adjusted rate per month" is the modified adjusted rate per annum divided by 12. (Sec. 6591, Rev. & Tax. Code; Sec. 6907, Rev. & Tax. Code)

CCH COMMENT: Daily interest rates: The California Department of Tax and Fee Administration (CDTFA) may compute interest at a modified adjusted daily rate for electronic payments if, in light of all facts and circumstances, it would be inequitable to compute interest at the modified adjusted rate per month. A "modified adjusted daily rate" is equal to the modified adjusted rate per annum divided by 365. The daily rate can only be charged if

— the payment of the fee was made one business day after the date it was due;

— the person was granted relief from all penalties that applied; and

— the person files a request for an oral hearing before the CDTFA.

This rate does not apply to any payment made pursuant to a deficiency determination, a determination where no return has been filed, or a jeopardy determination issued by the CDTFA. (Sec. 6591.6, Rev. & Tax. Code)

For underpayments, the modified adjusted rate per annum is three percentage points above an adjusted annual rate determined semiannually on the basis of the federal income tax underpayment rate. (Sec. 6591.5, Rev. & Tax. Code)

Interest rates on deficiencies (unpaid or underpaid taxes) effective for designated time periods are:

	Applicable Period	Modified Adjusted
From	To	Annual Rate
January 1, 2021	June 30, 2021	6%
January 1, 2020	December 31, 2020	8%
July 1, 2019	December 31, 2019	9%
January 1, 2017	June 30, 2019	7%
July 1, 2012	December 31, 2016	6%
January 1, 2012	June 30, 2012	7%
July 1, 2011	December 31, 2011	6%
January 1, 2011	June 30, 2011	7%
January 1, 2010	December 31, 2010	7%
July 1, 2009	December 31, 2009	8%
January 1, 2009	June 30, 2009	8%
July 1, 2008	December 31, 2008	10%
January 1, 2007	June 30, 2008	11%

Interest rates on refunds applicable to designated periods are as follows:

	Applicable Period	Interest Rate
From	To	
January 1, 2021	June 30, 2021	0%
January 1, 2019	December 31, 2020	2%
July 1, 2017	December 31, 2018	1%
July 1, 2009	June 30, 2017	0%
January 1, 2009	June 30, 2009	2%
July 1, 2008	December 31, 2008	3%
January 1, 2007	June 30, 2008	5%

For overpayments, the modified adjusted rate per annum is determined semiannually on the basis of the bond equivalent rate of 13-week treasury bills auctioned. (Sec. 6591.5, Rev. & Tax. Code)

• *Other taxes*

Interest on underpayments and overpayments of the following taxes is applied at the same rates that apply to underpayments and overpayments of sales and use taxes (see above):

— motor vehicle fuel taxes; (Sec. 7655.5, Rev. & Tax. Code; Sec. 7674, Rev. & Tax. Code; Sec. 8130, Rev. & Tax. Code)

— use fuel taxes. (Sec. 8876, Rev. & Tax. Code; Sec. 8876.5, Rev. & Tax. Code; Sec. 9155, Rev. & Tax. Code)

— insurance taxes; (Sec. 12631, Rev. & Tax. Code; Sec. 12631.5, Rev. & Tax. Code; Sec. 12983, Rev. & Tax. Code)

— cigarette taxes; (Sec. 30281, Rev. & Tax. Code; Sec. 30281.5, Rev. & Tax. Code; Sec. 30366, Rev. & Tax. Code)

— energy resources surcharges; (Sec. 40101, Rev. & Tax. Code; Sec. 40101.5, Rev. & Tax. Code; Sec. 40116, Rev. & Tax. Code)

— emergency telephone users surcharges; (Sec. 41095, Rev. & Tax. Code; Sec. 41095.5, Rev. & Tax. Code; Sec. 41105, Rev. & Tax. Code)

— hazardous waste taxes; (Sec. 43155.5, Rev. & Tax. Code; Sec. 43201, Rev. & Tax. Code; Sec. 43455, Rev. & Tax. Code);

— solid waste management fees; (Sec. 45153, Rev. & Tax. Code; Sec. 45153.5, Rev. & Tax. Code; Sec. 45655, Rev. & Tax. Code)

— oil spill fees; (Sec. 46154, Rev. & Tax. Code; Sec. 46154.5, Rev. & Tax. Code; Sec. 46506, Rev. & Tax. Code)

— underground storage tank fees; (Sec. 50112, Rev. & Tax. Code; Sec. 50112.1, Rev. & Tax. Code; Sec. 50142.1, Rev. & Tax. Code) and

— fee collection procedures law; (Sec. 55042, Rev. & Tax. Code; Sec. 55042.5, Rev. & Tax. Code; Sec. 55221, Rev. & Tax. Code)

— diesel fuel taxes; (Sec. 60207.5, Rev. & Tax. Code; Sec. 60314, Rev. & Tax. Code; Sec. 60511, Rev. & Tax. Code)

[¶89-206] Civil Penalties

Civil penalties apply to various violations of the tax provisions. See ¶89-208 Criminal Penalties, for penalties applicable to other violations.

• *Public disclosure of tax delinquencies*

The California Franchise Tax Board (FTB) and California Department of Tax and Fee Administration (CDTFA) are each authorized to make available as a matter of public record a list of the 500 largest tax delinquencies in excess of $100,000 under the Personal Income Tax Law, the Corporation Tax Law, and the Sales and Use Tax Law, as specified. Before making a delinquency a matter of public record, however, the FTB and CDTFA are required to provide preliminary written notice to the person or persons liable by certified mail, return receipt requested. If the amount due is not remitted or payment arrangements are not made within 30 days after issuance of the notice, the delinquency is included on the list. (Sec. 7063, Rev. & Tax. Code; Sec. 19195, Rev. & Tax. Code)

Taxpayers on the delinquency lists may lose any state licenses that have been issued to them or that they are applying for. Also, they may be precluded from competing for state contracts. See the discussion at ¶89-184.

As promptly as feasible, but no later than five business days from the occurrence of any of the following, the respective board must remove a taxpayer's name from the list:

(1) the person liable has contacted the appropriate board and resolution of the delinquency has been arranged;

(2) the board has verified that an active bankruptcy proceeding has been initiated;

(3) the board has verified that a bankruptcy proceeding has been completed and there are no assets available with which to pay the delinquency; or

(4) the board has determined the delinquency is uncollectible.

(Sec. 7063, Rev. & Tax. Code; Sec. 19195, Rev. & Tax. Code)

COMPLIANCE NOTE: The FTB has adopted regulations providing (1) procedures under which a taxpayer will be allowed a hearing on the issue of whether the FTB must provide a release, and (2) standards in determining whether the taxpayer has a financial hardship that will enable that taxpayer to obtain the requested release. (Reg. 19195-1, 18 CCR; Reg. 19195-2, 18 CCR) The FTB also announced that all notifications, notices, and requests to the FTB under the emergency regulations that are mailed to the FTB must be sent by first-class mail to the following address: Franchise Tax Board, P.O. Box 3065, Rancho Cordova, CA 95741-3065. As an alternative, all notifications, notices, and requests to the FTB that are related to release hearings may also be sent by facsimile to the following number: 916-843-0172. Notifications, notices, and requests to the FTB may not be sent by e-mail unless and until specified at a future date by the FTB. (*FTB Notice 2016-05*, California Franchise Tax Board, November 22, 2016)

The FTB is required to make the list available to the public at least twice each calendar year. A tax delinquency is defined as the total amount owed by a taxpayer for which a notice of state tax lien has been recorded. The term does not include a delinquency for which

  (1) payment arrangements have been made;

  (2) the taxpayer has filed for bankruptcy; or

  (3) the person liable has contacted the FTB and resolution has not yet been rejected by the FTB.

The FTB also must include additional information on the list with respect to each delinquency, including the type, status, and number of any occupational or professional license held by the person or persons liable for payment of the tax. The names and titles of the principal officers of the person liable for payment of the tax also must be included if that person is a limited liability company (LLC) or a corporation. (Sec. 19195, Rev. & Tax. Code)

The CDTFA is required to make the list available to the public on a quarterly basis. A tax delinquency is defined as an amount that has been either determined by the SBE or self-assessed by the taxpayer and that is delinquent for more than 90 days for which a state tax lien has been filed. The term does not include a delinquency

  (1) that is under litigation in a court of law;

  (2) for which payment arrangements have been made; or

  (3) for which the taxpayer has filed bankruptcy.

(Sec. 7063, Rev. & Tax. Code)

• *Corporation franchise and income and personal income taxes*

Following is a list of income tax violations, penalties, and the code sections under which civil penalties are imposed:

VIOLATION	PENALTY	REV. & TAX. CODE SECTION
failure to report personal services remuneration *	disallowance of deduction; unreported amount multiplied by the highest personal income tax rate	17299.8, 19175
failure to report real estate transaction *	disallowance of related deductions	17299.9
failure to comply with requirement to remit corporate franchise and income tax payment by electronic funds transfer	10% of amount paid	19011
failure to comply with requirement to remit personal income tax payment by electronic funds transfer	1% of amount paid	19011.5

VIOLATION	PENALTY	REV. & TAX. CODE SECTION
failure to file return	5% per month, up to 25%; for individuals, after 60 days, at least the lesser of $135 or 100% of the tax; if fraudulent, 15% per month, up to 75% maximum	19131
failure to pay amount on return by due date or within 15 days of notice and demand	5% of unpaid amount plus 0.5% per month of remaining tax to maximum of 25% of unpaid tax	19132
failure to furnish requested information or file return on notice and demand by FTB	25% of deficiency or of tax amount for which information or return was requested	19133
failure to make small business stock report *	$50 per report; $100 if failure due to negligence or intentional disregard	19133.5
dishonored check, credit card, or electronic funds transfer	$25 or amount of check, whichever is less, or, if check is for $1,250 or more, 2% of the amount of the check	19134
failure to file return if nonqualified, suspended, or forfeited corporation or limited liability company (LLC) is doing business in the state **	additional $2,000 per taxable year	19135
underpayment of estimated personal income tax*	determined under IRC Sec. 6654, as modified	19136
corporate understatements of the greater of $1 million or 20% of tax shown on return filed by extended due date (see details below)**	20% of understatement	19138
failure to file corporate organization statement **	$250 ($50 for nonprofit corporation)	19141
failure to furnish information concerning certain foreign corporations**	$1,000 for each annual accounting period; additional $1,000 for each 30-day period up to a maximum of $24,000 when failure continues after 90-day of notification	19141.2
failure to furnish information or maintain records concerning foreign-controlled corporation **	$10,000 per year of failure; additional $10,000 for each 30-day period when failure continues after 90-day of notification	19141.5
failure to furnish information on transfers to foreign persons **	10% of fair market value at time of exchange, plus recognition of gain required as if property sold based on that value; penalty capped at $100,000 unless failure due to intentional disregard.	19141.5
failure to report transactions or maintain records about foreign corporations doing business in the U.S. and its foreign investors **	$10,000 per year of failure; additional $10,000 for each 30-day period when failure continues after 90-day of notification	19141.5
failure to furnish information with respect to foreign financial assets (taxable years beginning on or after January 1, 2016)	$10,000 per year of failure; additional $10,000 for each 30-day period when failure continues after 90-day of notification, not to exceed $50,000 total penalty	19141.5
failure to keep water's-edge records **	$10,000 per year; if 90 days after notice by the FTB, $10,000 per 30-day period, not to exceed $50,000	19141.6
accuracy-related penalty—negligence	20% of underpayment attributable to violation; 40% unless certain exceptions apply for amnesty eligible years (pre-2003 tax years)	19164
accuracy related penalty—substantial valuation misstatement (underpayment must exceed $5,000 ($10,000 if C corporation))	20% of the portion of the underpayment of tax attributable to the misstatement;	19164

VIOLATION	PENALTY	REV. & TAX. CODE SECTION
fraud	75% of underpayment attributable to fraud	19164
accuracy-related penalty on reportable or listed transaction understatements	20% of understatement; 30% if not disclosed	19164.5
understatement by tax return preparer	the greater of $250 or 50% of the income derived by the return preparer from the return or refund claim for tax understatement due to unreasonable position; the greater of $1,000 or 50% of the income derived from the return or refund claim if position concerns noncompliance with reportable transaction requirements, listed transaction, or gross misstatement; the greater of $5,000 or 50% of the income derived from the return or refund claim if any part of understatement due to willful conduct or reckless or intentional disregard of rules or regulations	19166
failure of tax preparer to give taxpayer copy of return, furnish identifying number, or retain copy or list	$50 each failure up to $25,000 in a return period	19167
failure of tax preparer to register with California Tax Education Council	$5,000 ($2,500 for first offense)	19167
failure of tax preparer to exercise due diligence in determining eligibility for earned income credit	$500 per failure	19167
tax preparer negotiating client's refund check	$250 per check	19169
failure of tax preparer to file electronically *	$50 per return	19170
failure of business entity to file electronically (for taxable years beginning after 2016)	$100 for initial failure, $500 for each subsequent failure	19171
failure to file partnership return *	$18 per month multiplied by number of partners up to a 12-month maximum	19172
failure to file S corporation return	$18 per month multiplied by number of shareholders up to a 12-month maximum	19172.5
material advisor's failure to maintain list of advisees for reportable transaction	$10,000 for each day of failure if not provided within 20 days of request	19173
material advisor's failure to maintain list for listed transaction	the greater of (1) $100,000 or (2) 50% of advisor's gross income from activity, if not provided by prescribed due date	19173
failure to maintain records to substantiate tax shelter promoter return *	$1,000 multiplied by number of investors	19174 [repealed January 1, 2018]
false statements in connection with withholding	$500	19176
promoting abusive tax shelters	$1,000 or 100% of gross income derived or to be derived from violation, whichever is less, if a tax shelter promoter causes another to make a gross valuation overstatement as to any matter material to the tax shelter; 50% of gross income derived or to be derived from violation if a tax shelter promoter causes another to make a false or fraudulent tax benefits statement concerning participation in the tax shelter	19177
aiding and abetting understatement of tax liability	$1,000; $10,000 per corporate return or document	19178
filing frivolous return	$5,000	19179
failure to meet original issue discount reporting requirements	1% of aggregate issue price, up to $50,000 per-issue	19181
failure to furnish information concerning a reportable transaction	$50,000	19182

VIOLATION	PENALTY	REV. & TAX. CODE SECTION
failure to furnish information concerning listed transaction	the greater of (1) $200,000 or (2) 50% (75% if intentional) of material advisor's gross income derived with respect to transaction	19182
failure to file information return or furnish a payee statement, except in instances of intentional disregard of requirements *	up $100 per violation not to exceed $1,500,000 per year	19183
intentional disregard of required filing of information return or payee statement *	the greater of $250 or 5% or 10% of the items required to be reported, depending on the return involved	19183
failure to provide a written explanation *	$10 per failure up to $5,000	19183
failure to file copy of federal information return regarding large cash transactions **	$50 per return, up to $100,000 maximum per year; if intentional disregard, $100 per return, or, if greater, 5% of the aggregate amount of items required to be reported	19183
failure to file information report regarding individual retirement account or annuity *	$50 per failure	19184
overstatement of nondeductible IRA contributions without reasonable cause *	$100 per overstatement	19184
failure to timely file return with respect to medical savings accounts, qualified tuition programs, or education savings accounts	$50	19184
substantial and gross valuation misstatements attributable to incorrect appraisals	the lesser of (1) the greater of $1,000 or 10% of the tax underpayment amount attributable to the misstatement or (2) 125% of the gross income received by the appraiser for preparing the appraisal	19185
fraudulent identification of exempt use property	$10,000	19186
failure to file return; filing false return; aiding and abetting tax evasion; willful failure to pay	$5,000 maximum	19701
instituting protest or refund procedures frivolously	$5,000 maximum	19714
obtaining, endorsing, or negotiating a tax refund warrant or an electronic refund, generated by the filing of a return knowing the recipient is not entitled to the refund	$5,000 maximum	19720
willfully and with intent to defraud, obtaining, endorsing, or negotiating a tax refund warrant or an electronic refund, generated by the filing of a return knowing the recipient is not entitled to the refund	$10,000 maximum	19721
failure by taxpayer with taxable income greater than $200,000 to disclose reportable or listed transaction	maximum $15,000 per failure ($5,000 in the case of a natural person, for penalties assessed after 2015) for reportable transaction; $30,000 per failure ($15,000 in the case of a natural person, for penalties assessed after 2015) for listed transaction; minimum $2,500 penalty ($1,250 in the case of a natural person) for penalties assessed after 2015	19772
noneconomic substance transaction	40% of the understatement; 20% for underpayments to which the facts were disclosed in the return	19774

VIOLATION	PENALTY	REV. & TAX. CODE SECTION
Interest-based penalty if contacted by FTB concerning reportable transaction noncompliance, listed transaction, gross misstatement, or abusive tax avoidance transaction (ABAT)	100% of interest payable on underpayment, computed from original due date of return to date of notice of proposed assessment; 50% of interest attributable to ABAT if an amended return reporting the ABAT is filed after the taxpayer is contacted by the FTB regarding the ABAT but before a notice of proposed assessment is issued	19777

*personal income tax only
**corporation franchise and income tax only

For purposes of the above provisions, California modifies the federal definition of the term "information return" to include any information return that a check cashing business must file when it cashes checks totaling more than $10,000 from the same person. (Sec. 19183, Rev. & Tax. Code)

In addition, a taxpayer may file a civil action to require performance of a tax preparer's statutory duties, to recover a civil penalty of $1,000, or for both performance and recovery. (Sec. 22257, Bus. & Prof. Code)

Large corporate understatements.—Business entities that understate their corporation franchise or income tax liability by more than the greater of $1 million for any taxable year or 20% of the tax due as shown on the return filed by the extended due date are subject to a 20% understatement penalty, in addition to any other penalty that may be imposed. For pre-2010 tax returns, the penalty was imposed against all taxpayers who understated their liability by $1 million, regardless of what percentage the liability represented. For taxpayers required or allowed to be included in a combined report, the understatements of all the group members are aggregated for purposes of determining whether the $1 million or 20% threshold has been reached.

For taxable years beginning on or after January 1, 2015, an increase in tax shown on the first amended return reflecting a proper IRC § 338 election (relating to certain stock purchases treated as asset line acquisitions) will be treated as an amount of tax shown on an original return for purposes of the large corporate understatement penalty. (Sec. 19138, Rev. & Tax. Code)

CCH POINTER: Large corporate underpayment penalty avoidance planning.—A taxpayer could not make a single sales factor (SSF) election during the 2011 and 2012 tax years and then pay California corporation franchise and income tax computed as though no election was made in order to avoid the large corporate understatement penalty (LCUP) in the event that the taxpayer was later determined to be ineligible to use the SSF formula. Both the SSF election and the tax for measuring the LCUP understatement had to be reported on the last return filed on or before the extended due date of the return. Therefore, a taxpayer could not, for the same taxable year, make the SSF election and report tax based on income apportioned using the three-factor formula. (*Legal Division Guidance 2012-03-02*, California Franchise Tax Board, March 2012)

The penalty does not apply to understatements attributable to a change in law that is enacted, promulgated, issued, or becomes final after the earlier of either (1) the date the taxpayer files the return for the taxable year for which the change is operative, or (2) the extended due date for the taxpayer's return or the taxable year for which the change is operative. Nor can the penalty be imposed if the understatement resulted from the taxpayer's reliance on written advice contained in an FTB Chief Counsel Ruling. For taxable years beginning on or after January 1, 2015, the penalty also does not apply to an understatement attributable to a change to the taxpayer's federal method of accounting, but only to the extent of understatements for taxable years where the due date of the return, without regard to any extension of time for filing the return, is before the date the Secretary of the Treasury consents to that change. Further, applicable to understatements for any taxable year for which the statute of limitations on assessments has not expired as of September 30, 2015, the penalty does not apply to an understatement attributable to the imposition of an alternative apportionment or allocation method by the FTB under the authority of Rev. and Tax. Code § 25137 because the standard allocation and apportionment provisions do not fairly represent the extent of the taxpayer's business activity in the state. (Sec. 19138, Rev. & Tax. Code)

CCH COMMENT: Sec. 19138 ruled constitutional.—A California court of appeal has ruled that Sec. 19138 is a valid penalty and not an unconstitutional tax. In so holding, the court rejected a taxpayer association's claim that the governing provision was enacted for the purpose of raising revenues in order to help bridge California's large budget deficit and, therefore, was a tax that required a two-thirds vote of the Legislature in order to pass constitutional muster pursuant to Art. XIIIA, Sec. 3 (Proposition 13). The court also rejected a claim that the penalty provision violated taxpayers' procedural due process rights because it affords no pre- or post-payment review process. Although the penalty provision precludes a taxpayer from utilizing the administrative hearing venue to protest the penalty, there is nothing specifically in the statute that prohibits taxpayers from bringing a refund action in the courts, which provides a constitutionally adequate post-deprivation remedy. (*California Taxpayers' Association v. California Franchise Tax Board, et al.*, California Court of Appeal of California, Third District, No. C062791, December 13, 2010; review denied, California Supreme Court, No. S189996, March 16, 2011)

Underpayment of estimated tax.—An underpayment of estimated corporation franchise and income tax or personal income tax incurs an annual "addition to tax," which is a percentage of the underpayment. Although the addition is considered a penalty, it does not accrue interest like other penalties. However, the addition is computed at the adjusted annual rate of interest that applies to underpayments and overpayments of such taxes (see above). (Sec. 19101(d), Rev. & Tax. Code; Sec. 19136, Rev. & Tax. Code; Sec. 19142, Rev. & Tax. Code)

Liability for the penalty is determined on an installment basis. If the amount paid on or before any installment date is less than the amount that should have been paid by that date if the estimated tax were 100% of the tax shown on the return for the current year (or the applicable percentage of the correct tax liability if no return was filed), the difference is an underpayment subject to penalty. (Sec. 19144, Rev. & Tax. Code)

Underpayment of estimated tax and the exceptions to the penalty for underpayment are based on "the tax shown on the return." This language refers to the final return for the income year and to the tax after correction of any mathematical errors. For banks and financial corporations, the phrase means the tax as adjusted after final determination of the bank tax rate for the year. (Sec. 19144, Rev. & Tax. Code)

For personal income taxes, the period of underpayment runs from the due date of the installment to the earlier of the 15th day of the fourth month following the close of the tax year or the date when the underpayment is paid. (Sec. 19136, Rev. & Tax. Code)

For corporation franchise and income taxes, the period of underpayment runs from the due date of the installment to the earlier of the 15th day of the third month following the close of the taxable year (the 15th day of the fifth month of the taxable year for exempt organizations) or the date when the underpayment is paid. (Sec. 19145, Rev. & Tax. Code)

If the amount of estimated tax due from a corporation, other than a large corporation, is only the minimum tax, then the penalty for underpayment of estimated tax will be computed on the basis of only the minimum tax. The fact that a corporation may end the year with an income tax liability above the required minimum tax will be disregarded for purposes of imposing the penalty for underpayment of estimated tax. The penalty for underpayment of estimated tax is waived if an exception applies. (Sec. 19149, Rev. & Tax. Code)

The FTB will not assess a penalty for underpayment of estimated corporation franchise and income tax if:

— total payments for the corporation, other than a large corporation, equal or exceed the tax shown on the prior year's return; (Sec. 19147, Rev. & Tax. Code)

— the estimated tax paid by the installment due date equals or exceeds 100% of the amount the corporation would owe if its estimated tax was computed on an annualized basis; (Sec. 19147, Rev. & Tax. Code)

— the corporation does not have a permanent place of business in California and (1) the required percentage of tax is paid by withholding or (2) the required percentage of net income consists of income from which an amount was withheld and the first estimated tax installment equals at least the minimum franchise tax; (Sec. 19147, Rev. & Tax. Code) or

— the estimated tax paid by the installment due date equals or exceeds 100% of the amount the corporation would owe if its estimated tax was computed on an annualized seasonal income basis. (Sec. 19148, Rev. & Tax. Code)

Also, the penalty for underpayment of corporation franchise and income tax is not imposed on any exempt organization whose exemption is retroactively revoked, unless the organization has received notice that the estimated tax should have been paid. (Sec. 19151, Rev. & Tax. Code)

No penalty may be imposed for underpayment of estimated tax under Sec. 19136, Rev. & Tax. Code, or Sec. 19142, Rev. & Tax. Code, to the extent the underpayment was created or increased as the direct result of an erroneous levy, erroneous processing action, or erroneous collection action by the FTB. (Sec. 19136.7, Rev. & Tax. Code)

During the period that a taxpayer is in bankruptcy proceedings, the taxpayer may qualify for relief from the penalty for underpayment of corporation franchise and income tax. (Sec. 19161, Rev. & Tax. Code)

For the exceptions/abatements applicable to underpayment of estimated tax for personal income tax purposes, see Abatement of Interest, Penalties, or Additions to Tax.

For federal and California franchise (income) tax purposes, a "large corporation" that fails to make estimated tax payments as required of the current year's tax is subject to underpayment penalties even if its payments equal or exceed the amount of tax shown on its return for the prior year. However, the amount of the large corporation's tax liability for the prior year is used in determining the amount of estimated tax that must be paid in the first installment payment of the year. A large corporation will not be subject to an underpayment penalty if, as of the first installment date, it makes an estimated tax payment equal to 30% of its tax liability for the preceding year. The first installment may not be less than the amount of the minimum tax. A reduction in the first required installment resulting from the application of this rule is recaptured by increasing the amount of the next required installment by the amount of the reduction. A "large corporation" is one that had taxable income (computed without regard to net operating loss deductions) of $1 million or more during any of its three preceding income years. (Sec. 19147, Rev. & Tax. Code)

Limited liability companies.—An LLC is subject to a 10% underpayment penalty if the LLC's estimated fee payment is less than the amount of the fee actually due and payable with the LLC's return. However, no penalty will be imposed if the estimated fee equals or exceeds the amount of the fee paid by the LLC in the preceding taxable year. (Sec. 17942(d), Rev. & Tax. Code)

CCH POINTER: LLC fee penalty.—Unlike the corporation estimated tax prior tax year exception, there is no requirement that the prior tax year be a full 12 months and no penalty will be imposed for the LLC's first year filing in California. However, the penalty may not be waived for reasonable cause. (*Tax News*, California Franchise Tax Board, May 31, 2010)

Exempt organizations.—Exemption status may be revoked upon an exempt organization's failure to:

— file required statements or returns and pay amounts due within one year following the close of its taxable year;

— furnish required records to the California Franchise Tax Board (FTB); or

— restrict activities to those permitted under their exemption.

(Sec. 23777, Rev. & Tax. Code)

The underpayment penalty on any installment is not imposed on an exempt corporation whose exemption is retroactively revoked, unless the corporation has been notified that the estimated tax should have been paid. The denial of the organization's exemption application or the revocation of its exemption by the IRS satisfies the notice requirement. (Sec. 19151, Rev. & Tax. Code)

Spouses.—If the tax due on a joint return made after the filing of separate returns exceeds the aggregate amount of tax paid by the spouses on their separate returns, and if any part of the excess is the result of negligence, 20% of the total amount of the excess must be paid in addition to the tax due. If any part of the excess is attributable to fraud, 75% of the amount of the excess is added to the tax due. (Sec. 18530, Rev. & Tax. Code)

Individual healthcare mandate.—Beginning January 1, 2020, California will impose a penalty if a resident individual, the individual's spouse, or the individual's dependent fails to enroll in and maintain minimum essential health care coverage as required under the California Individual Healthcare Mandate, unless an exemption applies. The penalty, referred to as the individual shared responsibility penalty, will be included on an individual's California income tax return. (Sec. 61010, Rev. & Tax. Code) The penalty for a tax year equals the lesser of:

— the total monthly penalty amounts for the year; or

— 1/12 of the state average premium for California Health Benefit Exchange bronze plans, multiplied by the number of months in which the failure occurred.

For purposes of the above computation, the monthly penalty equals 1/12 of the greater of:

— the lesser of the (a) the sum of the applicable dollar amounts (for 2020 and 2021, $750 per adult and $375 per child) for all applicable household members that failed to maintain required coverage during the month or (b) 300% of the applicable dollar amount for the year; or

— 2.5% of the excess of the individual's household income for the year over the amount of gross income that would trigger a state income tax return filing requirement.

However, the maximum monthly penalty for an individual with a household size of five or more is limited to the same amount as for an individual with a household size of five. The specified dollar amounts are subject to cost of living adjustments. For taxable years during which a federal shared responsibility penalty applies, California will reduce the state penalty, but not below zero, by the amount of the federal penalty imposed on the responsible individual for each month during which the state penalty applies. (Sec. 61015, Rev. & Tax. Code; *Memorandum*, California Franchise Tax Board, September 1, 2020)

Collection and filing enforcement cost recovery fees.—A taxpayer (other than an exempt organization) that fails to pay any amount of income tax, penalty, interest, or other liability upon written notice by the FTB must pay a collection cost recovery fee. For the state's 2020-2021 fiscal year, the fee is $316 for an individual, partnership, limited liability company classified as a partnership for California income tax purposes, or fiduciary, and $322 for a corporation or limited liability company classified as a corporation for California income tax purposes. For the state's 2019-2020 fiscal year, the fee is $317 for an individual, partnership, limited liability company classified as a partnership for California income tax purposes, or fiduciary, and $355 for a corporation or limited liability company classified as a corporation for California income tax purposes. (Sec. 19254, Rev. & Tax. Code; Sec. 2.00, Ch. 23 (A.B. 74), Laws 2019; Sec. 91, Ch. 7 (A.B. 89), Laws 2020)

A taxpayer (other than an exempt organization) that fails to file a required income tax return within 25 days after a formal legal demand is mailed by the FTB must pay a filing enforcement cost recovery fee. For the state's 2020-2021 fiscal year, the fee is $97 for an individual, partnership, limited liability company classified as a partnership for California income tax purposes, or fiduciary, and $83 for a corporation or limited liability company classified as a corporation for California income tax purposes. For the state's 2019-2020 fiscal year, the fee is $93 for an individual, partnership, limited liability company classified as a partnership for California income tax purposes, or fiduciary, and $85 for a corporation or limited liability company classified as a corporation for California income tax purposes. (Sec. 19254, Rev. & Tax. Code; Sec. 2.00, Ch. 23 (A.B. 74), Laws 2019; Sec. 91, Ch. 7 (A.B. 89), Laws 2020)

Notice and demand penalty, personal income tax.—Personal income tax taxpayers are subject to a 25% notice and demand penalty in certain cases. The penalty will be imposed only if (1) the taxpayer fails to timely respond to a current demand for tax return in the manner prescribed, and (2) the Franchise Tax Board has proposed an assessment of tax after the taxpayer failed to timely respond to a request for tax return or a demand for tax return, in the manner prescribed, at any time during the four-taxable-year period preceding the taxable year for which the current demand for tax return is issued. (Reg. 19133, 18 CCR)

Suspension or disbarment from practice before the FTB.—If the U.S. Secretary of the Treasury suspends or disbars a person from practice before the Department of the Treasury, the FTB must, after notice and opportunity for a proceeding, suspend or disbar that person from practice before the FTB during the period of the federal suspension or disbarment, unless the FTB determines that the action of the Secretary of the Treasury was clearly erroneous. A person who practices before the FTB must provide written notice to the FTB within 45 days of the issuance of a final federal order disbarring or suspending the person from practice before the Department of the Treasury, and in such notice the person must concede the accuracy of the federal action or state the reason(s) why the federal action is clearly erroneous. A person who fails to notify the FTB as required will be subject to a penalty of $5,000. A person who has been suspended or disbarred from practice before the FTB may seek review of that determination. These provisions are effective for final federal orders of disbarment or suspension issued after July 18, 2005. (Sec. 19523, Rev. & Tax. Code)

Involuntary dissolution.—Beginning January 1, 2019, domestic corporations and LLCs may be subject to administrative dissolution if the FTB has suspended the entity's powers, rights and privileges for a period of not less than 60 continuous months. (Sec. 2205.5, Corp. Code; Sec. 17713.10.1, Corp. Code) Under the involuntary dissolution procedures, the FTB must provide written notice of the pending action, and must also send the business's name and file number to the California Secretary of State. After receiving this information, the SOS must provide a 60-day notice of the pending dissolution on its website.

The business may then file a written objection with the FTB. In that case, the business has an additional 90 days to:

— pay or otherwise satisfy all accrued taxes, penalties, and interest;

— file a current Statement of Information with the SOS;

— fulfill any other requirements to be eligible; and

— apply for revival.

If there is no written objection, the business is administratively dissolved. After the administrative dissolution is completed, the FTB will abate any minimum franchise or annual tax, interest, and penalties. However, an administrative dissolution does not affect the state's lawful ability to enforce any liability owed by the business. (Sec. 2205.5, Corp. Code; Sec. 17713.10.1, Corp. Code)

No administrative appeal or other judicial action is allowed against the FTB's or the SOS's action. However, reimbursement of amounts incorrectly paid after the administrative dissolution may be available. The business's rights, powers, and privileges cease when the administrative dissolution is completed. (Sec. 2205.5, Corp. Code; Sec. 17713.10.1, Corp. Code)

Registration of tax preparers.—Under limited circumstances, a licensed accountant from another state is authorized to prepare California personal income or estate tax returns for persons who are or were California residents, without obtaining a California permit to practice public accountancy. In addition, the provisions governing registration of tax preparers are amended to require the California Tax Education Council, after receiving notification from the Franchise Tax Board regarding the violation of the registration requirements, to notify the attorney general, a district attorney, or a city attorney, who would be authorized to levy a fine or issue a cease and desist order. The penalty is $2,500 for the first failure to register and $5,000 for subsequent instances of a failure to register. (Sec. 19167, Rev. & Tax. Code)

Abusive tax avoidance transactions.—An "abusive tax avoidance transaction" is:

— a California tax shelter;

— a reportable transaction that is not adequately disclosed;

— a listed transaction;

— a gross misstatement; or

— a transaction subject to the noneconomic substance transaction (NEST) penalty.

(Sec. 19777(b), Rev. & Tax. Code)

For these purposes, a gross misstatement includes both the omission of income equal to more than 25% of the gross income reported on a return and the substantial undervaluation of property as described in IRC § 6662(e) and (h)(2). (*Tax News*, California Franchise Tax Board, October 2011) More information on reportable and listed transactions is provided in the discussion of Other Collection Methods.

¶89-206

COMPLIANCE TIP: Tax shelters and transactions subject to the NEST penalty.—A tax shelter includes a partnership or other entity, an investment plan or arrangement, or any other plan or arrangement, if a significant purpose of the partnership, entity plan, or arrangement is the avoidance or evasion of federal or California income or franchise tax. The tax shelter scheme often overlaps with transactions subject to the noneconomic substance transaction penalty because a tax strategy set up for the primary purpose of avoiding taxes may also lack economic substance. Taxpayers should also be aware that the step transaction, sham transaction, and substance over form doctrines may be applied to conclude that a transaction is abusive when a tax strategy includes unnecessary or extra steps that create a tax savings that otherwise would not exist. Some examples of abusive transactions include:

— transactions that unreasonably defer or eliminate gain on the sale of assets through the use of a private annuity or promissory note between related parties;

— oil and gas partnerships in which the promoters promise substantial tax deductions that are primarily intangible drilling costs in the initial year and a substantial amount of the tax benefit is derived from the use of promoter-financed notes or loans;

— transactions that make a bona fide charitable organization a majority, nonmanaging, nonvoting owner of a pass-through entity (PTE) before liquidating appreciated property, where the PTE's income or gain is allocated to the charity, but the sales proceeds remain in the PTE and actual or effective control of the proceeds remains with the original property owner; and

— schemes in which taxpayers claim to breed race horses as a farming or trade or business activity, but where the promoter of the schemes charges participants inflated fees or expenses that are largely financed by promoter-granted loans that will never be collected.

(*Tax News*, California Franchise Tax Board, October 2011)

• *Employer contributions and withholding*

An employer who, without good cause, fails to make required employment contributions on time and by the prescribed method of payment must pay a penalty of 15% of the amounts due. However, employers required to remit payments electronically for the first time beginning on or after January 1, 2017, will not be subject to the penalty prior to January 1, 2019. (Sec. 1112, Unemp. Ins. Code)

An employer who is required to file a quarterly return electronically on or after January 1, 2017, pursuant to Sec. 1088, Unemp. Ins. Code, and without good cause fails to file a quarterly return electronically must pay a penalty of $50, in addition to any other penalties imposed. However, prior to January 1, 2019, an employer required to file a quarterly return electronically who files a quarterly return within the time required by means that are not electronic will not be subject to this penalty. (Sec. 1112.1, Unemp. Ins. Code)

An employer who, without good cause, fails to file a report of wages within 15 days after service and demand to do so will be fined $20 for each unreported wage item. Also, absent good cause, an employer required to file reports of wages by magnetic media or other electronic means who, without good cause, instead files by other electronic means is subject to a $20 penalty for each wage item. However, employers required to file a report of wages electronically for the first time beginning on or after January 1, 2017, will not be subject to the penalty prior to January 1, 2019. (Sec. 1114, Unemp. Ins. Code)

A penalty of 15% is added to the amount of any deficiency assessment if an employer fails to make a report or return for withheld tax, or files an unsatisfactory report or return, and the failure is the result of negligence or disregard of the withholding requirements. (Sec. 1126, Unempl. Ins. Code; Sec. 1127, Unempl. Ins. Code) If the failure to file a report or return, or any part of the deficiency assessment, was due to fraud or intent to evade, a 50% penalty is added to the assessment. Also, an additional 50% penalty will be added to any assessment that includes the 50% penalty for failure to file due to fraud or intent to evade if the employer pays wages and fails to file an information return required under Unemp. Ins. Code Sec. 13050 (concerning W-2 forms) or IRC Sec. 6041A (concerning payments of remuneration for services and direct sales). The 50% penalties are in addition to the 15% penalty for failing to file a report or return or filing an unsatisfactory report or return. (Sec. 1128, Unempl. Ins. Code)

Also, a penalty is imposed for failure to report amounts paid as remuneration for personal services. Any unreported amount is multiplied by the highest personal income tax rate. (Sec. 13062.5, Unemp. Ins. Code)

An individual may be subject to a $500 penalty for filing false withholding information. (Sec. 19176, Rev. & Tax. Code)

An employer may also be subject to a $50 penalty for furnishing an employee with a false, fraudulent, or untimely withholding statement. (Sec. 13052, Unemp. Ins. Code)

• *Unauthorized disclosures*

Persons making an unauthorized disclosure of tax returns and related information in an action or proceeding affecting the personnel rights of employees or former employees are subject to criminal penalty and civil liability. (Sec. 19556, Rev. & Tax. Code)

Accountants who violate a client's confidentiality may be subject to penalties of up to $5,000 ($10,000 for subsequent violations). (Sec. 5063.3, Bus. & Prof. Code; Sec. 5116.1, Bus. & Prof. Code) Unauthorized disclosure penalties that may be imposed against tax preparers are discussed at ¶35-001.

• *Sales and use taxes*

Late filing, late payment, nonpayment.—Except for late prepayments (see below), a 10% penalty is imposed for late filing of sales and use tax returns or payments. (Sec. 6591, Rev. & Tax. Code; Reg. 1703(c)(2), 18 CCR)

If a return is filed and a deficiency determination is made, a 10% penalty is imposed on any part of the deficiency that is due to negligence or intentional disregard and a 25% penalty is imposed on any part of the deficiency that is due to fraud or intent to evade tax. (Sec. 6484, Rev. & Tax. Code; Sec. 6485, Rev. & Tax. Code)

If no return is filed and a deficiency determination is made, a 10% penalty is imposed on the amount of the deficiency and an additional 25% penalty is imposed if the failure to file is due to fraud or intent to evade tax. (Sec. 6511, Rev. & Tax. Code; Sec. 6514, Rev. & Tax. Code) However, effective January 9, 2003, fraud or the intent to evade California sales and use taxes must be established by clear and convincing evidence, the standard applied in *Renovizor's, Inc. v. California State Board of Equalization*, 282 F.3d 1233 (9th Cir., 2002). Because the opinion in *Renovizor's, Inc.* was a federal bankruptcy decision that was not binding on California, and since the California Supreme Court has not spoken on this issue, the regulatory amendment serves to avoid confusion on the proper standard to be applied in such cases. (Reg. 1703, 18 CCR)

When a deficiency assessment becomes final and is not paid, a 10% penalty is imposed. (Sec. 6565, Rev. & Tax. Code)

Direct payment permit holders.—Direct payment permit holders who issue an exemption certificate to a retailer and fail or refuse to timely pay the retailer's tax liability are subject to the same penalty that would be imposed if the permit holder were the retailer. Also, if a direct payment permit holder misallocates any local sales and use tax or transactions (sales) and use tax on a return, a 10% penalty is imposed on the misallocated amount. (Sec. 7051.2, Rev. & Tax. Code; Reg. 1703(c)(5), 18 CCR)

Failure to obtain seller's permit.—A 50% penalty applies when a person knowingly fails to obtain a valid seller's permit prior to the date on which the person's first tax return is due. The penalty does not apply to persons whose taxable receipts during the period when they engaged in business without the permit averaged $1,000 or less per month, nor does it apply to persons subject to the 50% penalty for registering vehicles, vessels, or aircraft outside California to evade tax. (Sec. 7155, Rev. & Tax. Code; Reg. 1703(c)(3), 18 CCR)

A $500 penalty is imposed when a retail florist fails to obtain a permit before engaging in or conducting business as a seller. (Sec. 6077, Rev. & Tax. Code; Reg. 1703(c)(7), 18 CCR)

Late prepayments.—Generally, a 6% penalty is imposed when a required prepayment of tax is not timely. A 10% penalty is imposed when a late prepayment is due to negligence or intentional disregard. (Sec. 6477, Rev. & Tax. Code; Sec. 6478, Rev. & Tax. Code; Reg. 1703(c)(5), 18 CCR; Reg. 1703(c)(1), 18 CCR)

A 10% (25% prior to 2002) penalty is imposed on late prepayments by motor vehicle fuel distributors or brokers. (Sec. 6480.4, Rev. & Tax. Code; Reg. 1703(c)(1), 18 CCR)

Electronic funds transfers (EFTs).—For persons required to remit sales and use taxes by EFT, the failure to file a return by the due date for the remittance results in a penalty of 10% of the amount of taxes, excluding prepayments, with respect to the quarter for which the return is required. A person required to remit taxes by EFT who remits taxes by other means must pay a penalty of 10% of the taxes incorrectly remitted, except that a person required to remit prepayments by EFT who remits prepayments by other means must pay a penalty of 6% of the prepayment amount incorrectly remitted. (Sec. 6479.3, Rev. & Tax. Code; Reg. 1703, 18 CCR)

Improper use of resale certificate.—A person who knowingly issues a resale certificate while not actively engaged in business is liable not only for the tax due on the transaction but also for a penalty of 10% or $500, whichever is greater. (Sec. 6072, Rev. & Tax. Code; Reg. 1703(c)(4), 18 CCR)

Vehicles, vessels, aircraft.—When a party to the sale of a motor vehicle understates the sales price in a document submitted to the Department of Motor Vehicles, a penalty equal to the greater of 100% of the tax or $500 is imposed. (Sec. 12122, Veh. Code)

A 10% penalty is imposed for nonpayment of use tax on a vehicle purchased from someone other than a licensed dealer, manufacturer, dismantler, or lessor/retailer. (Sec. 6292, Rev. & Tax. Code)

A 50% penalty is imposed on the amount of any unpaid use tax when a purchaser registers a vehicle, vessel, or aircraft outside California in order to evade tax. (Sec. 6485.1, Rev. & Tax. Code; Sec. 6514.1, Rev. & Tax. Code)

Other penalties.—When a person who makes sales to catering truck operators fails to notify the state concerning whether the operators hold valid sellers' permits, there is a $500 penalty per violation. (Sec. 6074, Rev. & Tax. Code)

A $50 fine is imposed when a paid tax return preparer fails to include his or her name, social security number, federal employee identification number, and business name and address on a return. (Sec. 6452, Rev. & Tax. Code)

- *Severance taxes*

Oil and gas production charge.—A 10% penalty is imposed for failure to timely pay an oil and gas production charge. (Sec. 3420, Pub. Res. Code)

Timber yield tax.—If a timber yield tax return is filed and any deficiency is due to negligence or intentional disregard, a 10% penalty is added. (Sec. 38414, Rev. & Tax. Code) If a return is filed and any deficiency is due to fraud or an intent to evade tax, a 25% penalty is added. (Sec. 38415, Rev. & Tax. Code)

If no return is filed, the SBE estimates the amount due and adds a 10% penalty. (Sec. 38421, Rev. & Tax. Code) If the failure to file is due to fraud or an intent to evade tax, a 25% penalty is added to the 10% penalty. (Sec. 38424, Rev. & Tax. Code)

Failure to pay any amount when due is subject to a penalty of 10% of the amount of the tax. (Sec. 38446, Rev. & Tax. Code; Sec. 38451, Rev. & Tax. Code)

- *Insurance taxes*

A 10% penalty is imposed for a failure to do any of the following with respect to insurance taxes:

— remit taxes by EFT when required;

— timely pay any gross premiums tax; or

— timely pay any retaliatory tax.

(Sec. 1531, Ins. Code; Sec. 1775.8, Ins. Code; Sec. 12602, Rev. & Tax. Code; Sec. 12258, Rev. & Tax. Code; Sec. 12631, Rev. & Tax. Code; Sec. 12632, Rev. & Tax. Code; Sec. 12287, Rev. & Tax. Code; Reg. 2330.1, 10 CCR)

Also, a 10% penalty is imposed when deficiency assessments are made on the basis of certain proposals submitted by the Insurance Commissioner. (Sec. 12633, Rev. & Tax. Code; Sec. 12634, Rev. & Tax. Code) A 25% penalty is added if any part of a deficiency for which a deficiency assessment is made is due to fraud. (Sec. 12635, Rev. & Tax. Code)

A 10% penalty is also imposed for failure to timely pay any nonadmitted insurance tax or gross premiums tax on surplus line brokers. If the failure to timely pay is due to fraud, a 25% penalty is added. (Sec. 1775.5, Ins. Code; Sec. 13220, Rev. & Tax. Code)

- *Cigarette taxes*

A 10% penalty is imposed for failure to timely pay any amount owed for the purchase of cigarette tax stamps or metering settings. (Sec. 30171, Rev. & Tax. Code)

Also, a 10% penalty is imposed for failure to timely file a return, failure to timely pay any tax other than a tax determined pursuant to a deficiency determination, and failure to remit taxes by EFT when required. (Sec. 30190, Rev. & Tax. Code; Sec. 30281, Rev. & Tax. Code)

If a return is filed and a deficiency is due to negligence or intentional disregard, a 10% penalty is added. (Sec. 30204, Rev. & Tax. Code) If the deficiency is due to fraud or an intent to evade tax, a 25% penalty is added. (Sec. 30205, Rev. & Tax. Code)

If a person fails to file a return, the SBE estimates the amount due and adds a 10% penalty. (Sec. 30221, Rev. & Tax. Code) If the failure to file is due to fraud or an intent to evade tax, a 25% penalty is added to the 10% penalty. (Sec. 30224, Rev. & Tax. Code) If a deficiency determination is not paid when due, a penalty equal to 10% of the amount of the determination is added. (Sec. 30264, Rev. & Tax. Code)

- *Motor fuel taxes*

See ¶ 40-001.

- *Energy resources surcharge*

If an electric utility fails to file a return reporting energy resources surcharges, the SBE estimates the amount due and adds a 10% penalty. (Sec. 40081, Rev. & Tax. Code)

If a return is filed and any deficiency is due to negligence or intentional disregard, a 10% penalty is added. (Sec. 40074, Rev. & Tax. Code) An additional 25% penalty applies if a failure to file or any deficiency is due to fraud or intent to evade the surcharge. (Sec. 40075, Rev. & Tax. Code; Sec. 40084, Rev. & Tax. Code)

A 10% penalty applies if payment is not timely. (Sec. 40101, Rev. & Tax. Code) Also, a 10% penalty applies if a person fails to remit payment by EFT when required. (Sec. 40067, Rev. & Tax. Code)

- *Emergency telephone users surcharge*

If a service supplier fails to file a return reporting emergency telephone users surcharges, the SBE estimates the amount due and adds a penalty equal to the greater of 10% of the determined amount or $10. (Sec. 41080, Rev. & Tax. Code) If a return is filed and any deficiency is due to negligence or intentional disregard, a penalty is imposed in an amount equal to the greater of 10% of the determined amount or $10. (Sec. 41073, Rev. & Tax. Code)

If a failure to file or any part of a deficiency is due to fraud or intent to evade the surcharge, a penalty is imposed in an amount equal to the greater of 25% of the determined amount or $25. (Sec. 41074, Rev. & Tax. Code; Sec. 41083, Rev. & Tax. Code)

A penalty equal to the greater of 10% or $10 applies if payment is not timely. (Sec. 41095, Rev. & Tax. Code) Also, a 10% penalty applies if a person fails to remit payment by EFT when required. (Sec. 41060, Rev. & Tax. Code)

- *Collection cost recovery fee*

For a variety of taxes, surcharges, and fees that it administers, the California Department of Tax and Fee Administration (CDTFA) can impose a collection cost recovery fee (collection fee) on any person that fails to pay an amount of fee, interest, penalty, or other amount due and payable. The collection fees are operative with respect to any demand notices for payment that are mailed after 2010. The collection fee shall be imposed only if the CDTFA has mailed its demand notice to that person for payment that advises that continued failure to pay the amount due may result in collection action, including the imposition of the collection fee.

The CDTFA may assess a fee on each liability greater than $250 that remains unpaid for more than 90 days. The fee amount, adjusted annually to reflect the cost of collecting unpaid liabilities, ranges from $185 to $925 for calendar year 2011, as follows:

— $185 for a small liability amount of $250.01 - $2,000;

— $550 for a medium liability amount of $2,000.01 - $50,000; and

— $925 for a large liability amount of $50,000.01 or greater.

(*News Release 145-10-G*, California State Board of Equalization, December 27, 2010)

Interest shall not accrue with respect to the collection fee, which shall be collected in the same manner as the collection of any other fee imposed by the CDTFA for the tax, surcharge, or fee at issue. A person shall be relieved of the collection fee if the failure to pay any otherwise qualified amount:

(1) was due to reasonable cause and circumstances beyond the person's control and

(2) occurred notwithstanding the exercise of ordinary care and the absence of willful neglect.

Any person seeking to be relieved of the collection fee must file with the CDTFA a statement under penalty of perjury setting forth the facts upon which the person bases the claim for relief.

The fee applies to:

— sales and use tax; (Sec. 6833, Rev. & Tax. Code)

— use fuel tax; (Sec. 9035, Rev. & Tax. Code)

— cigarette tax; (Sec. 30354.7, Rev. & Tax. Code)

— alcoholic beverage tax; (Sec. 32390, Rev. & Tax. Code)

— energy resources surcharge; (Sec. 40168, Rev. & Tax. Code)

— emergency telephone users surcharge; (Sec. 41127.8, Rev. & Tax. Code)

— hazardous substances tax; (Sec. 43449, Rev. & Tax. Code)

— integrated waste management fee; (Sec. 45610, Rev. & Tax. Code)

— oil spill response, prevention, and administrative fee; (Sec. 46466, Rev. & Tax. Code)

— underground storage tank maintenance fee; (Sec. 50138.8, Rev. & Tax. Code)

— fee collection procedures law; (Sec. 55211, Rev. & Tax. Code) and

— diesel fuel tax. (Sec. 60495, Rev. & Tax. Code)

[¶89-208] Criminal Penalties

Criminal penalties apply to various violations of the tax provisions. See Civil Penalties for penalties applicable to other violations.

•*Income taxes*

Following is a list of income tax violations, penalties, and the code sections under which criminal penalties are imposed:

VIOLATION	REV. & TAX. CODE SECTION	PENALTY
failing to file return or furnish information	19701	misdemeanor; fine of up to $5,000, and/or up to 1 year in county jail, and costs of prosecution
filing false or fraudulent return or information	19701	misdemeanor; fine of up to $5,000, and/or up to 1 year in county jail, and costs of prosecution
aiding another to evade tax, fail to file return, or supply false information	19701	misdemeanor; fine of up to $5,000, and/or up to 1 year in county jail, and costs of prosecution
willfully failing to pay tax or estimated tax	19701	misdemeanor; fine of up to $5,000, and/or up to 1 year in county jail, and costs of prosecution
forging spouse's signature *	19701.5	misdemeanor; fine of up to $5,000 and/or up to 1 year in county jail
willfully making or signing a return or document containing a declaration made under penalty of perjury that the maker or signer does not believe to be materially true or correct	19705	felony; fine of up to $50,000 ($200,000 for corporations), and/or up to 3 years in state prison, and costs of investigation and prosecution

VIOLATION	REV. & TAX. CODE SECTION	PENALTY
willfully aiding preparation or presentation of a false return or document	19705	felony; fine of up to $50,000 ($200,000 for corporations), and/or up to 3 years in state prison, and costs of investigation and prosecution
falsely executing or signing a bond, permit, entry, or required document	19705	felony; fine of up to $50,000 ($200,000 for corporations), and/or up to 3 years in state prison, and costs of investigation and prosecution
removing, depositing, or concealing taxable goods to evade tax	19705	felony; fine of up to $50,000 ($200,000 for corporations), and/or up to 3 years in state prison, and costs of investigation and prosecution
concealing estate property or destroying or falsifying estate records in regard to a settlement, closing agreement, or compromise	19705	felony; fine of up to $50,000 ($200,000 for corporations), and/or up to 3 years in state prison, and costs of investigation and prosecution
concealing property or records or making a false statement in connection with a closing agreement	19705	felony; fine of up to $50,000 ($200,000 for corporations), and/or up to 3 years in state prison, and costs of investigation and prosecution
willfully failing to file a return or supply information with intent to evade tax	19706	misdemeanor/felony; fine of up to $20,000, and/or up to 1 year in county jail or up to 3 years in state prison, and costs of investigation and prosecution
willfully making, signing, or verifying false return or statement with intent to evade tax	19706	misdemeanor/felony; fine of up to $20,000, and/or up to 1 year in county jail or up to 3 years in state prison, and costs of investigation and prosecution
failing to collect and pay withholding	19708	felony; fine of up to $2,000 and/or up to 3 years in state prison
failing to withhold or pay over nonresident withholding *	19709	misdemeanor; fine of up to $1,000 and/or up to 1 year in county jail
filing false information with employer *	19711	misdemeanor; fine of up to $1,000 and/or up to 1 year in county jail
negotiating or endorsing client's refund check by tax preparer	19712	misdemeanor; fine of up to $1,000, and/or up to 1 year in county jail, and prosecution costs
failing to set up withholding account *	19713	misdemeanor; fine of up to $5,000, and/or up to 1 year in county jail, and costs of prosecution
exercising the powers of a corporation suspended for nonpayment of taxes or transacting intrastate business of a forfeited foreign corporation **	19719	misdemeanor; fine of $250 to $1,000 and/or up to 1 year in county jail
obtaining, endorsing, or negotiating a tax refund warrant, or effective January 1, 2005, an electronic tax refund, generated by the filing of a return knowing the recipient is not entitled to the refund	19720	misdemeanor; fine of up to $10,000, and/or up to 1 year in county jail, and costs of investigation and prosecution
willfully and with intent to defraud obtaining, endorsing, or negotiating a tax refund warrant, or effective January 1, 2005, an electronic tax refund, generated by the filing of a return knowing the recipient is not entitled to the refund	19721	misdemeanor/felony; fine of up to $50,000, and/or up to 1 year in county jail or up to 3 years in state prison, and costs of investigation and prosecution

* personal income tax only
** corporation franchise (income) tax only

The penalty under Sec. 19701, Rev. & Tax. Code for failing to file a return or furnish information, filing a false or fraudulent return or statement, or supplying false or fraudulent information may be imposed only if the violations occur repeatedly over a period of two or more years and result in an estimated delinquent tax liability of $15,000 or more. Also, the misdemeanor, fine, and imprisonment provisions in Rev. & Tax. Code Sec. 19701 for failure to pay any tax, including any estimated tax, may not be applied to any person who is mentally incompetent or suffers from dementia, Alzheimer's disease, or a similar condition. (Sec. 19701, Rev. & Tax. Code)

An income tax return preparer is subject to an injunction or restraining order and is guilty of a misdemeanor punishable by a fine of up to $1,000, imprisonment in county jail for up to one year, or both the fine and imprisonment, if the preparer does any of the following:

— makes or authorizes false, fraudulent, or misleading statements;

— has a taxpayer sign a tax return or authorizing document containing blank spaces to be filled in after it has been signed;

— fails to give a taxpayer a copy of any document requiring the taxpayer's signature within a reasonable time after it has been signed;

— fails to maintain a copy of any tax return prepared for a taxpayer for four years from the later of the date of completion or the due date of the return;

— engages in false, fraudulent, or misleading advertising practices;

— violates federal or state laws prohibiting the disclosure of information obtained in the course of preparing a tax return;

— fails to sign a taxpayer's return when payment for services rendered has been made;

— fails to return records or other data provided by a taxpayer upon the demand by, or on behalf of, the taxpayer and after payment for services has been made; or

— knowingly gives false or misleading information to a consumer, a surety company, or the California Tax Education Council.

(Sec. 22253, Bus. & Prof. Code; Sec. 22256, Bus. & Prof. Code)

Applicable to all California tax types, a tax preparer commits a Business and Professions Code violation if he or she fails or refuses to provide a copy of any document that requires a customer's signature to the customer within a reasonable time from the date the document was signed, or fails to register as a tax preparer with the California Tax Education Council. Moreover, the FTB may notify the council of the identity of an individual who fails to register with the Council. (Sec. 22253, Bus. & Prof. Code)

The attorney general, a district attorney, or a city attorney may, upon receipt of notification from the council:

— cite the individual who fails to register with the council;

— levy a fine of $1,000 for each violation; or

— issue a cease and desist order that remains in effect until the individual complies with the registration requirement.

(Sec. 22253.2, Bus. & Prof. Code)

The authority for tax preparers penalty enforcement is transferred to the FTB. The California Franchise Tax Board (FTB) is required to notify the California Tax Education Council (CTEC) when it identifies an individual who has violated specific provisions regulating tax preparers. The FTB also is authorized to:

— cite individuals preparing tax returns in violation of provisions governing tax preparers;

— levy a fine on such individuals not to exceed $5,000 per violation; and

— issue a cease and desist order effective until the tax preparer is in compliance with the registration requirement.

However, the FTB may not incur any costs associated with enforcement actions until funding is provided through either (1) an appropriation in the FTB's annual budget; or (2) an agreement executed between the CTEC and the FTB to reimburse the FTB for the costs. (Sec. 22253.2, Bus. & Prof. Code)

• *Withholding of tax*

A person who fails to file a withholding report or return or to supply required information, or who supplies false information or files a fraudulent report or return, with or without intent to evade, is guilty of a misdemeanor and liable for a penalty of not more than $1,000 or up to one year in prison or both. (Sec. 2117, Unemp. Ins. Code)

A person or employer who fails to withhold or pay over withheld tax is guilty of a misdemeanor and may be fined up to $1,000 or be imprisoned for up to one year or both. (Sec. 2118, Unemp. Ins. Code)

A person who willfully fails to file a report or return or to supply information with the intent to evade tax, or who willfully files a false or fraudulent report or return, is punishable by a fine of up to $20,000 or imprisonment for up to one year or both. (Sec. 2117.5, Unemp. Ins. Code)

A person who willfully fails to collect or truthfully pay over withheld taxes is guilty of a felony and may be fined up to $20,000 or be imprisoned or both. (Sec. 2118.5, Unemp. Ins. Code)

A fine of up to $1,000 or imprisonment for up to one year or both is imposed on any person or employer who willfully furnishes a false or fraudulent withholding statement or who willfully fails to furnish a withholding statement. (Sec. 2119, Unemp. Ins. Code)

An employee who willfully supplies an employer with false or fraudulent information regarding exemption allowances is punishable by a fine of up to $1,000 or imprisonment of up to one year or both. (Sec. 19711, Rev. & Tax. Code)

• *Sales and use taxes*

The following violations of the sales and use tax law are misdemeanors punishable by a fine of not less than $1,000 nor more than $5,000, imprisonment for not more than one year, or both (Sec. 7153, Rev. & Tax. Code):

— failure or refusal to furnish any required return or to furnish a supplemental return or other data requested by the California Department of Tax and Fee Administration (CDTFA); (Sec. 6452, Rev. & Tax. Code)

— filing a false or fraudulent return with intent to defeat or evade tax; (Sec. 7152, Rev. & Tax. Code)

— failure to collect use tax, advertising that use tax will be absorbed, or failure to disclose use tax separately; (Sec. 6207, Rev. & Tax. Code)

— issuing a resale certificate when purchasing property that will not be resold; (Sec. 6094.5, Rev. & Tax. Code)

— engaging in business without a permit or with a suspended or revoked permit; (Sec. 6071, Rev. & Tax. Code)

— understating the sales price of a motor vehicle in a document submitted to the Department of Motor Vehicles; (Sec. 12122, Veh. Code);

— issuing or using a vehicle use tax exemption certificate improperly; (Sec. 6422.1, Rev. & Tax. Code)

— making an unjustified claim for an exclusion from gross receipts or sales price for federal manufacturers' or importers' excise tax paid under IRC Sec. 4091 for diesel and non-gas aircraft fuels; (Sec. 6423, Rev. & Tax. Code) and

— willfully aiding. assisting, procuring, counseling, or advising in the preparation or submission of any return, affidavit, claim, or other document that is fraudulent or false regarding any material matter. (Sec. 7152, Rev. & Tax. Code)

Any violation of the sales and use tax law with the intent to defeat or evade the reporting, assessment, or payment of tax is a felony if the aggregate unreported tax liability involved is at least $25,000 during any 12-month period. The felony is punishable by a fine of up to $20,000, imprisonment in state prison for 16 months, two years, or three years, or both the fine and imprisonment. (Sec. 7153.5, Rev. & Tax. Code)

• *Severance taxes*

Every person who fails or neglects or refuses to furnish any required oil and gas production report or record, or who willfully furnishes a false or fraudulent report, is guilty of a misdemeanor punishable by a fine of not less than $100 and not more than $1,000 or by imprisonment for up to six months, or both, for each offense. (Sec. 3236, Pub. Res. Code)

• *Insurance taxes*

Except when rendered by a surplus line broker, the following acts are misdemeanors when performed in the state:

— acting as an agent for a nonadmitted insurer in the transaction of insurance business in the state for a home state insured;

— advertising a nonadmitted insurer in the state; and

— otherwise aiding a nonadmitted insurer in the transaction of insurance business in the state for a home state insured.

In addition to any penalty provided for the commission of misdemeanors, a person committing any of these acts must pay the state the sum of $500, together with $100 for each month or fraction thereof during which the acts continue. (Sec. 703, Ins. Code)

• *Cigarette taxes*

A person who does any of the following is guilty of a misdemeanor and subject to a fine of up to $1,000 for each offense:

— fails or refuses to file any required cigarette tax report;

— fails or refuses to furnish a supplemental report or other data required by the CDTFA;

— fails or refuses to allow an inspection by the CDTFA; or

— renders a false or fraudulent report.

(Sec. 30471, Rev. & Tax. Code)

A person who makes a false or fraudulent report with the intent to defeat or evade tax is guilty of a misdemeanor punishable by a fine of not less than $300 and not more than $5,000 or imprisonment or both a fine and imprisonment. (Sec. 30472, Rev. & Tax. Code)

A person who falsely or fraudulently counterfeits any tax stamp or meter impression or who knowingly and willfully passes as genuine any counterfeited tax stamp or meter impression is guilty of a felony punishable by a fine of not less than $1,000 and not more than $25,000 or imprisonment for two, three, or four years or both a fine and imprisonment. (Sec. 30473, Rev. & Tax. Code)

A person who possesses, buys, sells, offers to buy or sell, any false or fraudulent tax stamps or meter impressions in a quantity of less than 2,000 is guilty of a misdemeanor and subject to a fine of up to $5,000, imprisonment not to exceed one year in a county jail, or both a fine and imprisonment. A person who possesses, buys, sells, offers to buy or sell, any false or fraudulent tax stamps or meter impressions in a quantity of 2,000 or more is guilty of a misdemeanor and subject to a fine of up to $50,000, imprisonment not to exceed one year in a county jail, or both a fine and imprisonment. (Sec. 30473.5, Rev. & Tax. Code)

Any person who knowingly possesses, keeps, stores, or retains for sale or sells or offers to sell any cigarette packages without tax stamps or meter impressions is guilty of a misdemeanor and punishable by a fine of up to $25,000 for each offense, imprisonment for up to one year, or both. In addition, a penalty is imposed in an amount equal to $100 for each carton of 200 cigarettes knowingly kept for sale or sold in such a manner. These penalties do not apply to licensed distributors. (Sec. 30474, Rev. & Tax. Code)

The sale or possession for sale of counterfeit tobacco products or cigarettes by a manufacturer, importer, distributor, wholesaler, or retailer shall result in the seizure of those items by the BOE or any law enforcement agency. Moreover, such action shall constitute a misdemeanor punishable as follows:

— a violation with a total quantity of less than two cartons of cigarettes is punishable by a fine of up to $5,000 or imprisonment for up to one year, or both, and such a violation shall result in the entity's license revocation;

— a violation of two cartons of cigarettes or more is punishable by a fine of up to $50,000, or imprisonment for up to one year, or both, and such a violation shall likewise result in the entity's license revocation.

(Sec. 30474.1, Rev. & Tax. Code)

If a person knowingly or willfully places for sale in a vending machine any cigarette packages without tax stamps or meter impressions, the person is guilty of a misdemeanor punishable by a fine of up to $1,000, imprisonment for up to one year, or both. (Sec. 30476, Rev. & Tax. Code)

The statute of limitations for prosecution of these penal provisions is six years after commission of the offense. (Sec. 30481, Rev. & Tax. Code) Moreover, any person convicted of a crime under these provisions may be charged the costs of investigation and prosecution at the court's discretion. (Sec. 30482, Rev. & Tax. Code)

[¶89-210] Abatement of Interest, Penalties, or Additions to Tax

Provisions relating to the abatement of interest, penalties, or additions to tax vary by the type of tax. For a discussion of voluntary disclosure agreements and filing compliance agreements, see ¶89-186.

• *Income taxes*

Reasonable reliance on FTB written opinion.—The Franchise Tax Board (FTB) may waive interest, penalties, and additions to tax if the taxpayer reasonably relied on a written opinion issued by the FTB. All of the following conditions must be met before the FTB will grant the waiver:

— the taxpayer must request a written opinion regarding the tax consequences of a particular activity that is fully described;

— the FTB must issue a written opinion;

— the taxpayer must reasonably rely on that opinion; and

— the tax consequences expressed in that opinion must not be affected by a change in statutory or case law, federal interpretation, or material facts or circumstances relating to the taxpayer.

(Sec. 21012, Rev. & Tax. Code)

In addition, if all of the above conditions are met and the FTB's written opinion consists of a Chief Counsel Ruling or Opinion Letter, then the taxpayer may be relieved of the duty to pay the tax itself as well as any interest, penalty, or addition to the tax. No waiver will be granted if the taxpayer's request for an opinion contains a misrepresentation or omission of a material fact. (Sec. 21012, Rev. & Tax. Code)

COMMENT: *Applying for relief.*—If a taxpayer has requested and received written advice from the FTB and the FTB subsequently takes action against the taxpayer that the taxpayer believes is inconsistent with that written advice, the taxpayer must follow certain procedures to receive a waiver. Actions against the taxpayer include a denial of a claim for refund or imposition of an audit assessment. Taxpayers who have received written advice from the chief counsel or his or her designee must request the waiver in a letter addressed to the chief counsel. The letter must be accompanied by the items enumerated in *FTB Notice No. 2009-09*. The FTB may request additional information or documentation from the taxpayer to make this determination. (*FTB Notice No. 2009-09*, October 12, 2009)

Relief granted by Taxpayers' Rights Advocate.—The FTB's Taxpayers' Rights Advocate may abate any corporation franchise and income tax or personal income tax penalties, fees, additions to tax, or interest assessed against a taxpayer if (1) relief is not otherwise available, (2) the error or delay was not attributable to the taxpayer, and (3) the advocate determines that the penalties, fees, additions to tax, or interest have been assessed as a result of any of the following:

— the FTB's erroneous action or erroneous inaction in processing the taxpayer's documents or payments;

— the FTB's unreasonable delay; or

— erroneous written advice that does not otherwise qualify for relief by the Chief Counsel.

Such relief may be granted only in consultation with the Chief Counsel. The determination regarding whether to grant relief is not subject to administrative or judicial review.

Any relief granted in which the total reduction exceeds $500 must be submitted to the Executive Officer of the FTB for concurrence, and the total relief that may be granted pursuant to this authority must not exceed $10,000, adjusted for inflation after 2016 ($11,405 for 2020).

Refunds resulting from the Advocate's granting of relief may be granted only if a written request for relief was filed with the Advocate's office within the statute of limitations period for filing a refund claim. (Sec. 21004, Rev. & Tax. Code; *Memorandum*, California Franchise Tax Board, September 1, 2020)

Reasonable cause.—The following civil penalties will not be asserted against a taxpayer who for reasonable cause, and not with willful neglect, failed to report or pay the tax due:

— the penalty for failure to file a timely return; (Sec. 19131, Rev. & Tax. Code)

— the penalty for refusal to furnish information or to file a return on notice and demand; (Sec. 19133, Rev. & Tax. Code)

— the penalty for underpayment of tax; (Sec. 19132, Rev. & Tax. Code)

— the penalty for failure to file an annual corporate statement; (Sec. 2204, Corp. Code)

— the "accuracy-related" penalty for negligence, substantial understatement of tax, etc.; (Sec. 19164, Rev. & Tax. Code)

— the penalty for failure to report original issue discounts; (Sec. 19181, Rev. & Tax. Code)

— the penalty for failure to remit payment by means of electronic funds transfer (EFT) when payment by that method is required; (Sec. 19011, Rev. & Tax. Code) and

— the penalty imposed against small business corporations for failure to file reports concerning the exclusion of gain on the sale of small business corporation stock. (Sec. 19133.5, Rev. & Tax. Code)

For a discussion of the FTB's filing compliance agreement program whereby the FTB will waive penalties for out-of-state businesses that failed to file a return due to reasonable cause, see ¶ 89-186.

COMMENT: Reasonable cause for late payment penalty: Reasonable cause will be found and the late payment penalty will not normally be assessed if 90% of the tax shown on the return is paid by the original due date of the return. However, taxpayers may still be subject to the underpayment of estimated tax penalty and interest will still be imposed if the full amount of the tax liability is not paid by the original due date. This treatment differs from that under federal law, which requires that the remaining outstanding 10% be remitted with the return in order to qualify for the reasonable cause waiver. (*Technical Advice Memorandum 2006-1,* FTB, February 14, 2006)

PRACTICE TIP: Reasonable cause abatement forms: Although the FTB continues to accept and process handwritten reasonable cause abatement requests, it now recommends that taxpayers use FTB 2917, Reasonable Cause – Individual and Fiduciary Claim for Refund, and FTB 2924, Reasonable Cause – Business Entity Claim for Refund, for a quicker response. The forms make it easier for taxpayers to provide the FTB with the information it needs to evaluate their requests, prevent unneeded correspondence, and speed the processing of claims. (*Tax News,* California Franchise Tax Board, September 2014)

Waiver of late filing penalty.—A rebuttable presumption is created that the penalty for failure to timely file a return does not apply when, with respect to the same taxable year, all of the following conditions are met:

— the taxpayer files a federal return after its due date;

— the FTB proposes a deficiency assessment based upon a final federal determination; and

— the IRS abates the federal late filing penalty based upon reasonable cause and absence of willful neglect.

(Sec. 19131(f)(1), Rev. & Tax. Code)

The FTB may rebut the presumption by establishing by a preponderance of the evidence that the taxpayer's failure to make and file a return was not due to reasonable cause or was due to willful neglect. (Sec. 19131(f)(1), Rev. & Tax. Code)

Other waivers.—The FTB may refrain from imposing or may waive penalties for failure to comply with (1) the EFT requirements imposed on certain taxpayers and (2) the recordkeeping and reporting requirements concerning certain foreign-owned corporations. Relief from these penalties is conditioned on a determination that the taxpayer's failure to comply neither jeopardizes the best interests of the state nor resulted from the taxpayer's willful neglect or intent not to comply. (Sec. 21015, Rev. & Tax. Code)

Nonprofit corporations.—The FTB must, upon written request by a qualified nonprofit corporation, abate unpaid qualified taxes, interest, and penalties, for taxable years for which the nonprofit corporation certifies, under penalty of perjury, that it was not doing business in the state. Abatement will be conditioned on the dissolution of the qualified corporation within 12 months from the date of filing the request for abatement. (Sec. 23156, Rev. & Tax. Code)

CAUTION: Dissolution of qualified inactive nonprofit corporations: Beginning January 2017, the FTB will administratively dissolve qualified inactive nonprofit corporations that are suspended or forfeited by the FTB for a period of at least 48 continuous months and are no longer in business. The FTB will mail a contact letter to selected nonprofit corporations informing them of the pending administrative dissolution to the last known valid mailing address. A list of the selected corporations pending administrative dissolution will be posted on the California Secretary of State (SOS) website. If a corporation does not have a known valid mailing address, notification will only occur by the posting on the SOS website. Corporations will have 60 days to object in writing to the pending dissolution. If the corporation submits an objection, then it will have 90 days from the date of the written notice to pay any owed taxes, penalties, and interest and file any missing returns and a current Statement of Information with the SOS, or it will be administratively dissolved at the end of the 90 day period. The FTB is authorized to grant one 90-day extension. (*Tax News*, California Franchise Tax Board, January 2017)

Abusive tax shelter penalties.—No penalty will be imposed for failure to comply with providing information concerning reportable transactions required by the FTB if it was not identified in a FTB notice issued prior to the date the transaction or shelter was entered into. furnish. (Sec. 19182(c), Rev. & Tax. Code)

The Chief Counsel of the FTB may rescind all or any portion of the accuracy-related reportable transaction penalty or any penalty imposed for failure to maintain a list of advisees or to provide information concerning reportable transactions, or the penalty applicable to taxpayers with taxable income greater than $200,000 that fail to include reportable transactions information with their return if all of the following apply:

    — the violation is with respect to a reportable transaction other than a listed transaction;

    — the person on whom the penalty is imposed has a history of complying with the requirements of the California franchise or income tax laws;

    — the violation is due to an unintentional mistake of fact;

    — imposing the penalty would be against equity and good conscience; and

    — rescinding the penalty would promote compliance with the requirements of the California franchise or income tax laws and effective tax administration.

(Sec. 19164.5(d), Rev. & Tax. Code; Sec. 19173, Rev. & Tax. Code; Sec. 19182(d), Rev. & Tax. Code; Sec. 19772, Rev. & Tax. Code)

Also, the Chief Counsel may rescind all or any portion of any penalty imposed for filing a frivolous return if both of the following apply:

— imposing the penalty would be against equity and good conscience; and

— rescinding the penalty would promote compliance with the requirements of the California franchise or income tax laws and effective tax administration.

(Sec. 19179, Rev. & Tax. Code)

If the notice of proposed assessment of additional tax has been sent with respect to a noneconomic substance transaction understatement, only the Chief Counsel may compromise the penalty or any portion thereof. (Sec. 19774, Rev. & Tax. Code)

The exercise of authority by the Chief Counsel under the provisions discussed above may not be delegated. Furthermore, any determination under these provisions may not be reviewed in an administrative or judicial proceeding. (Sec. 19164.5(d), Rev. & Tax. Code; Sec. 19173, Rev. & Tax. Code; Sec. 19179, Rev. & Tax. Code; Sec. 19182(d), Rev. & Tax. Code; Sec. 19772, Rev. & Tax. Code; Sec. 19773, Rev. & Tax. Code; Sec. 19774, Rev. & Tax. Code)

Interest abatement.—The FTB may also abate interest when:

— a tax deficiency is attributable in whole or in part to an unreasonable error or delay by an FTB officer or employee;

— a delay in payment results from dilatory conduct on the part of an FTB officer or employee; or

— a deficiency is based on a final federal determination of tax for the same period that interest was abated on the related federal deficiency amount, provided that the error or delay to which the deficiency is attributable occurred by the date of issuance of the final federal determination.

(Sec. 19104, Rev. & Tax. Code)

Interest on an erroneous refund for which an action is provided must be abated until 30 days after the notice and demand for repayment is made, unless the taxpayer or any related party has in any way caused the erroneous refund.

The FTB may waive interest also for any period for which the taxpayer demonstrates inability to pay solely because of extreme financial hardship caused by significant disability or other catastrophic circumstances. A waiver of interest will be withdrawn retroactively if it is granted because of fraud, malfeasance, or misrepresentation or omission of any material fact. (Sec. 19112, Rev. & Tax. Code)

Disaster relief.—If any taxpayer located in a presidentially declared disaster area or in any California county or city declared by the Governor to be in a state of disaster and the individual has incurred a loss, the FTB must abate interest imposed for any period that the FTB has (1) extended the taxpayer's period for filing an income tax return and paying income tax with respect to the return and (2) waived any corresponding penalties. (Sec. 19109, Rev. & Tax. Code)

Innocent spouse relief.—A spouse may be relieved of liability for taxes, penalties, and interest if he or she did not know of, or have reason to know of, an understatement of tax and if, under the circumstances, it would be inequitable to hold the spouse liable for the deficiency. (Sec. 18533, Rev. & Tax. Code; Reg. 35055, 18 CCR) For additional information, see ¶ 15-310 Joint Filers.

Suspension of interest and penalties.—If an individual files a personal income tax return for a taxable year by the due date for the return, including extensions, and the FTB does not provide a notice to the individual specifically stating the individual's liability and its basis within the time specified, the FTB generally must suspend the imposition of any interest, civil penalty, addition to tax, or additional amount with respect to any failure relating to the return that is computed by reference to the period of time the failure continues to exist. The FTB must provide this notice within the 36-month period beginning on the later of the date on which the return was filed or the due date of the return, without regard to extensions. In instances in which a taxpayer provides signed, written documents to the FTB after the taxpayer files a return for the taxable year, and the document shows that the taxpayer owes an additional amount of tax for the taxable year, the notice must be provided within the 36-month period beginning on the date on which the documents were filed.

The imposition of any interest, civil penalty, addition to tax, or additional amount would resume 15 days after the FTB sends the required notice. The suspension requirement does not apply to:

— any penalty for failure to file or failure to pay;

— interest, penalty, addition to tax, or additional amounts involving fraud;

— interest, penalty, addition to tax, or additional amounts shown on the return;

— any criminal penalty;

— interest, penalty, addition to tax, or additional amounts related to any gross misstatement;

— interest, penalty, addition to tax, or additional amounts related to reportable transactions for which specified requirements are not met and listed transactions.

— interest, penalty, addition to tax, or additional amount relating to any abusive tax avoidance transaction.

(Sec. 19116(d), Rev. & Tax. Code)

The suspension requirement also does not apply to any taxpayer with taxable income greater than $200,000 if the taxpayer has been contacted by the FTB regarding the use of a potentially abusive tax shelter. Special rules apply to taxpayers required to report a federal change or correction to the state. (Sec. 19116(f), Rev. & Tax. Code)

Voluntary disclosure agreement.—See the discussion of voluntary disclosure agreements at ¶ 89-186

Underpayment of estimated tax.—The FTB may grant a waiver of the penalty for underpayment of estimated personal income tax when imposition of the penalty would be against equity and good conscience as a result of casualty, disaster, or other unusual circumstances. In addition, the FTB may waive the penalty if it finds that (1) underpayment was due to reasonable cause and not willful neglect and (2) the taxpayer is a person who retired after age 62 or became disabled in either the tax year for which estimated payments were required or the preceding tax year. (Sec. 19136, Rev. & Tax. Code)

Also, the FTB will not assess a penalty for underpayment of estimated personal income tax if the preceding year's tax or the current year's tax, after withholding and credits, is less than $500 for single or joint filers or $250 for married individuals filing separate return. For purposes of this safe harbor provision, the "tax" includes any alternative minimum tax, in addition to any regular tax, less credits other than the credit for amounts withheld. (Sec. 19136, Rev. & Tax. Code)

Penalties for underpayments of estimated personal income or corporation franchise or income taxes will not be imposed to the extent that the underpayment was created or increased by (1) legislation chaptered and operative for the taxable year of the underpayment or (2) applicable to penalties imposed on or after January

1, 2016, the earned income tax credit adjustment factor for the taxable year being less than the adjustment factor for the preceding taxable year. (Sec. 19136, Rev. & Tax. Code; Sec. 19142, Rev. & Tax. Code) The relief does not apply to federal law changes that may create an underpayment of state tax, because federal law is enacted without being chaptered. (*Bill Analysis*, Ch. 242 (S.B. 14), Laws 2005, Senate Floor, August 23, 2005)

No penalty will be imposed for underpayment of estimated tax under Sec. 19136, Rev. & Tax. Code, or Sec. 19142, Rev. & Tax. Code, to the extent the underpayment was created or increased as the direct result of an erroneous levy, erroneous processing action, or erroneous collection action by the FTB. (Sec. 19136.7, Rev. & Tax. Code)

During the period that a taxpayer is in bankruptcy proceedings, the taxpayer may qualify for relief from the penalty for underpayment of corporation franchise (income) tax or personal income tax. (Sec. 19161, Rev. & Tax. Code)

For other exceptions applicable to the corporation (franchise) income tax estimated tax underpayment penalty, see Civil Penalties.

• *Withholding of tax*

An employer who makes an underpayment of the amount due on a periodic report will be relieved of interest and penalties if the error was caused by excusable neglect and the employer makes a proper adjustment. (Sec. 1113.1, Unemp. Ins. Code)

The penalty for filing false withholding information may be waived if the individual's income tax for the year does not exceed allowable tax credits and estimated tax payments for the year. (Sec. 19176, Rev. & Tax. Code)

• *Sales and use taxes*

If the California Department of Tax and Fee Admministration (CDTFA) finds that a taxpayer's failure to timely file or pay is due to reasonable cause and circumstances beyond the taxpayer's control, the taxpayer may be relieved of penalties for late prepayments, failure to file and pay, and failure to pay a deficiency assessment when it becomes final. (Sec. 6592, Rev. & Tax. Code) In addition, if a taxpayer proves that a failure to timely file or pay is due to reasonable reliance on the CDTFA's written advice, the taxpayer may be relieved of taxes, penalties, and interest. (Sec. 6596, Rev. & Tax. Code)

A taxpayer may be relieved of penalties for late payment of sales and use taxes if the taxpayer enters into an installment plan for paying the taxes within 45 days after a notice of determination or redetermination is final. The taxpayer must comply with the agreement for the waiver to remain effective. Waiver may not be granted in cases of fraud. (Sec. 6832, Rev. & Tax. Code)

If the CDTFA determines that the failure of a qualifying out-of-state retailer to make a timely return or payment is due to reasonable cause and circumstances beyond the retailer's control, the CDTFA may waive any applicable penalties. (Sec. 6487.05(b), Rev. & Tax. Code)

A taxpayer may be relieved of the 6% penalty for late prepayments (Sec. 6592, Rev. & Tax. Code), but interest generally will not be waived. (Sec. 6592.5, Rev. & Tax. Code)

Interest may be waived if the CDTFA finds that a taxpayer's failure to timely file or pay was (1) due to a disaster and occurred in spite of the exercise of ordinary care and in the absence of willful neglect or (2) due to an unreasonable error or delay by an CDTFA employee. (Sec. 6593, Rev. & Tax. Code; Sec. 6593.5, Rev. & Tax. Code)

If a person's failure to pay sales and use taxes by EFT when required is due to reasonable cause and circumstances beyond the person's control, and occurred notwithstanding the person's exercise of ordinary care and in the absence of willful neglect, the penalty for remitting taxes by inappropriate means will not apply. (Sec. 6479.4, Rev. & Tax. Code)

Innocent spouse relief.—An innocent spouse may be relieved of liability for sales and use tax, interest, penalties, and other amounts, provided:

— any underreporting, omission, underpayment, or nonpayment is attributable to the other spouse;

— the innocent spouse can establish a lack of knowledge that was reasonable; and

— relief from liability is deemed equitable under the circumstances.

(Sec. 6456, Rev. & Tax. Code; Reg. 35055, 18 CCR)

Innocent spouse relief is not available in any calendar quarter that is (1) more than five years from the final date of an CDTFA determination, (2) more than five years from the return due date for nonpayment on a return, (3) more than one year from the first contact with the innocent spouse claiming relief, or (4) closed by res judicata, whichever is later. (Sec. 6456, Rev. & Tax. Code)

• *Miscellaneous taxes—innocent spouse relief*

Innocent spouse relief is available for a wide variety of taxes, surcharges and fees administered by the California Department of Tax and Fee Administration.

• *Severance taxes*

If a person's failure to make a timely timber yield tax return or payment is due to reasonable cause and circumstances beyond the person's control, and occurred notwithstanding the exercise of ordinary care and in the absence of willful neglect, the person may be relieved of the penalties for failure to make a return or payment. (Sec. 38453, Rev. & Tax. Code)

Disaster relief.—If a person's failure to make a return or payment is due to a disaster, and occurred notwithstanding the exercise of ordinary care and in the absence of willful neglect, the person may be relieved of paying interest. (Sec. 38453, Rev. & Tax. Code)

Advice from CDTFA.—If a person's failure to make a timely return or payment is due to the person's reasonable reliance on written advice from the CDTFA, the person may be relieved of taxes, penalties, and interest. (Sec. 38454, Rev. & Tax. Code) Also, if a person's failure to pay is due to an unreasonable error or delay by an employee of the CDTFA acting in his or her official capacity, the person may be relieved of paying interest. (Sec. 38455, Rev. & Tax. Code)

Installment agreements.—Except in cases of fraud, if a person enters an installment payment agreement within 45 days from the date on which a notice of determination or redetermination becomes final, and the person complies with the terms of the installment payment agreement, the person may be relieved of the penalty for failure to pay a determination when due. (Sec. 38504, Rev. & Tax. Code)

• *Insurance taxes*

If an insurer's failure to make payment by an appropriate EFT is due to reasonable cause or circumstances beyond the insurer's control, and occurred notwithstanding the exercise of ordinary care and in the absence of willful neglect, the insurer may be relieved of penalties for:

— failure to make payment by an appropriate means; (Sec. 1531, Ins. Code; Sec. 1775.8, Ins. Code; Sec. 12602, Rev. & Tax. Code; Reg. 2330.3, 10 CCR)

— failure to timely pay; (Sec. 1775.5, Ins. Code; Sec. 12636, Rev. & Tax. Code; Reg. 2330.4, 10 CCR) and

— any deficiency determination made on the basis of a proposal submitted by the Insurance Commissioner when no return has been filed. (Sec. 12636, Rev. & Tax. Code)

Also, if an insurer's failure to make a timely return or payment is due to disaster, and occurred notwithstanding the exercise of ordinary care and in the absence of willful neglect, the insurer may be relieved of paying interest. (Sec. 12637, Rev. & Tax. Code)

• *Cigarette taxes*

If a person's failure to make a cigarette tax return or payment is due to reasonable cause and circumstances beyond the person's control, and occurred notwithstanding the exercise of ordinary care and in the absence of willful neglect, the person may be relieved of the penalties for failure to make a return or payment. (Sec. 30282, Rev. & Tax. Code)

Disaster relief.—If a person's failure to make a return or payment is due to a disaster, and occurred notwithstanding the exercise of ordinary care and in the absence of willful neglect, the person may be relieved of paying interest. (Sec. 30283, Rev. & Tax. Code)

Advice from CDTFA.—If a person's failure to make a timely return or payment is due to the person's reasonable reliance on written advice from the CDTFA, the person may be relieved of taxes, penalties, and interest. (Sec. 30284, Rev. & Tax. Code) Also, if a person's failure to pay is due to an unreasonable error or delay by an employee of the CDTFA acting in his or her official capacity, the person may be relieved of paying interest. (Sec. 30283.5, Rev. & Tax. Code)

EFTs.—If a person's failure to make a cigarette tax payment by an appropriate EFT is due to reasonable cause and circumstances beyond the person's control, and occurred notwithstanding the exercise of ordinary care and in the absence of willful neglect, the person may be relieved of the penalty for failure to remit payment by an appropriate means. (Sec. 30191, Rev. & Tax. Code)

Installment agreements.—Except in cases of fraud, if a person enters an installment payment agreement within 45 days from the date on which a notice of determination or redetermination becomes final, and the person complies with the terms of the installment payment agreement, the person may be relieved of the penalty for failure to pay a determination when due. (Sec. 30354, Rev. & Tax. Code)

• *Motor fuel taxes*

See ¶ 40-001 (motor vehicle fuel tax); ¶ 40-003 (diesel fuel tax); and ¶ 40-007 (use fuel tax).

• *Energy resources surcharge; emergency telephone users surcharge*

Relief from energy resources surcharges and emergency telephone users surcharges, penalties, and interest is similar to that available under the cigarette tax and motor fuel tax laws. Generally, a person may be eligible for some relief if a failure to file or pay is due to:

— reasonable cause; (Sec. 40102, Rev. & Tax. Code; Sec. 41096, Rev. & Tax. Code)

— disaster; (Sec. 40103, Rev. & Tax. Code; Sec. 41097, Rev. & Tax. Code)

— reasonable reliance on written advice from the CDTFA; (Sec. 40104, Rev. & Tax. Code; Sec. 41098, Rev. & Tax. Code) or

— an unreasonable error or delay by an employee of the CDTFA. (Sec. 40103.5, Rev. & Tax. Code; Sec. 41097.5, Rev. & Tax. Code)

Also, a person may be relieved of the penalty for failure to make a surcharge payment by an appropriate EFT if the failure is due to reasonable cause. (Sec. 40068, Rev. & Tax. Code; Sec. 41061, Rev. & Tax. Code)

Installment agreements.—Except in cases of fraud, if a person enters an installment payment agreement within 45 days from the date on which a notice of determination or redetermination becomes final, and the person complies with the terms of the installment payment agreement, the person may be relieved of the penalty for failure to pay a surcharge determination when due. (Sec. 40167, Rev. & Tax. Code; Sec. 41127.6, Rev. & Tax. Code)

• *Miscellaneous fees*

Relief from miscellaneous fees administered by the CDTFA and related penalties and interest is available if a failure to file or pay is due to:

— reasonable cause; (Sec. 55044, Rev. & Tax. Code)

— disaster; (Sec. 55046.5, Rev. & Tax. Code)

— reasonable reliance on written advice from the CDTFA; (Sec. 55045, Rev. & Tax. Code) or

— an unreasonable error or delay by an employee of the CDTFA. (Sec. 55046, Rev. & Tax. Code)

Also, a person may be relieved of the penalty for failure to make a surcharge payment by an appropriate EFT if the failure is due to reasonable cause. (Sec. 55051, Rev. & Tax. Code)

Installment agreements.—Except in cases of fraud, if a person enters an installment payment agreement within 45 days from the date on which a notice of determination or redetermination becomes final, and the person complies with the terms of the installment payment agreement, the person may be relieved of the penalty for failure to pay a fee determination when due. (Sec. 55209, Rev. & Tax. Code)

[¶89-220]

TAXPAYER RIGHTS AND REMEDIES

[¶89-222] Taxpayers' Bill of Rights

The California Department of Tax and Fee Administration (CDTFA) provides a comprehensive list of contact information for taxpayer advocates in the following agencies:

— California Department of Tax and Fee Administration (CDTFA);

— Employment Development Department (EDD);

— Franchise Tax Board (FTB);

— Board of Equalization (BOE);

— Internal Revenue Service (IRS); and

— Governor's Office of Business and Economic Development (GO-Biz).

(*Publication 145*, California Department of Tax and Fee Administration)

CAUTION: Transfer of BOE powers.—Beginning July 1, 2017, all California State Board of Equalization (BOE) administrative powers, duties, and responsibilities that are not constitutionally mandated to the BOE, with certain exceptions in the short term, were transferred to the California Department of Tax and Fee Administration (CDTFA). The BOE is left with responsibility for property tax assessment and equalization functions and assessment of taxes on insurers authorized by Article XIII of the state constitution; assessment and collection of excise taxes on alcohol pursuant to Article XX of the state constitution; and the statutory duty to adjust the rate of the motor vehicle fuel tax for the 2018-19 fiscal year. Until January 1, 2018, the BOE heard corporation franchise and income tax and personal income tax appeals from the Franchise Tax Board (FTB). However, on that date, those functions were transferred to the Office of Tax Appeals, and the BOE is prohibited from hearing further appeals.

These changes are the result of 2017 legislation, Ch. 6 (A.B. 102), Laws 2017, effective June 27, 2017, and operative as noted.

The Franchise Tax Board (FTB) has established the position of Taxpayers' Rights Advocate, whose responsibilities include coordinating the resolution of taxpayer complaints and problems, including taxpayer complaints concerning the unsatisfactory treatment of taxpayers by FTB employees. (Sec. 21004, Rev. & Tax. Code) Taxpayers may describe problems that they are having with the FTB at the Taxpayers' Rights Advocate website.

See FTB 4058B, *Your Rights as a Taxpayer*, for a basic overview of taxpayer rights.

Abatement of penalties, interest, fees, and additions to tax.—The Advocate is authorized to abate penalties, interest, fees, and additions to tax under certain circumstances involving error or delay by the FTB. (Sec. 21004, Rev. & Tax. Code) The Advocate may grant relief under Sec. 21004 only if the taxpayer did not contribute to the error or delay in any significant way and relief is not otherwise available under the law, including under any regulation or FTB announcement. See the discussion of Abatement of Interest, Penalties, or Additions to Tax for more information.

Information and education programs.—The FTB, in consultation with the Taxpayers' Rights Advocate, is responsible for implementing taxpayer information and education programs designed to (1) point out common errors to taxpayer or industry groups identified in the annual report and (2) structure continuing education programs for FTB audit and compliance staff. As part of this effort, the FTB must:

— identify forms, procedures, regulations, or laws that are confusing to taxpayers; and

— take action, including recommending remedial legislation, to change the items causing taxpayer confusion.

(Sec. 21005, Rev. & Tax. Code)

Action for damages.—If an FTB officer or employee recklessly disregards published procedures, an aggrieved taxpayer may bring an action for damages in a state superior court. If the state is found liable, the state will compensate the taxpayer for (1) actual and direct monetary damages sustained by the taxpayer and (2) reasonable litigation costs. In awarding damages, however, the court will take into account negligence or omissions of the taxpayer, and a penalty of up to $10,000 may be imposed if the taxpayer's position is deemed frivolous. (Sec. 21021, Rev. & Tax. Code)

Following is a statutory listing of taxpayer rights and privileges applicable to various California taxes and fees:

Taxpayers' Bill of Rights Statutes
(Revenue and Taxation Code Sections)

Description	Property Taxes	Sales & Use Tax	Motor Vehicle Fuel License Tax	Use Fuel Tax	Private Railroad Car Tax	Personal Income, Bank & Corporation Taxes	Cigarette Tax	Alcoholic Beverage Tax
Administration	5902	7082	8260	9260	NA	21003	30458	32460
Taxpayers' Rights Advocate	5903 5904(a)&(b) 5911	7083	8261	9261	NA	21004	30458.1	32461
Education & Information Program	5905 5908	7084	8262	9262	NA	21005	30458.2	32462
Get It in Writing	5909(b)	NA	NA	NA	NA	21006	NA	NA
Taxpayer Noncompliance*	5906(a)(1) 5908	7085	NA	NA	NA	21006	NA	NA
Annual Hearing†	5906(d)	7085	8263	9263	NA	21007	30458.3***	32463
Statements in Simple/Clear Language	5906(b)	7086	8264	9264	NA	21008	30458.4	32464
Quotas/Goals Barred	5907	7087	8265	9265	NA	21009	30458.5	32465
Evaluation of Employee Contact	5907	7088	8266	9266	NA	21010	30458.6	32466
Timely Resolution of Petitions & Refunds	5904(a)(2) 5911(a)	7089	8267	9267	NA	21011	30458.7	32467
Hearing Procedures/Locations	5906(b)(3)	7090	8268	9268	NA	21013	30458.8	32468
Reimbursement of Hearing Expenses	NA	7091	8269	9269	NA	21014	30458.9	32469
Nontax Investigations Barred	NA	7092	8270	9270	NA	19442	30459	32470
Settlement of Disputed Liabilities	NA	7093.5	NA	9271	NA	21015.5	30459.1	32471
Notice and Review of Levy	NA	7094	NA	9272	NA	21016	30459.2	32472
Release of Levy	NA	7094	8272	9272	NA	NA	30459.2	32472
Return of Levied Property	NA	7094.1	NA	9272.1	11254	21017	30459.2A	32472.1
Exemptions from Levy	NA	7095	8273	9273	NA	NA	30459.3	32473
Reimbursement of Third-Party Charges or Fees	NA	7096	NA	9274	NA	21018	30459.4	32474
Notice Prior to Filing Lien	NA	7097	NA	9275	NA	21019	30459.4	32475
Notice Prior to Suspension	NA	7098	8276	9276	NA	21020	30459.6	NA
Disregard by Employee	NA	7099	8277	9277	NA	21021	30459.7	32476
Privileged Communications	NA	7099.1	NA	NA	NA	21028	NA	NA

* Only Property, Sales and Use, Personal Income, and Bank & Corporation Tax Laws have requirement to identify areas of taxpayer noncompliance.

† All programs include an Annual Hearing requirement.

*** Beginning January 1, 2005, two hearings per year are required. (Ch. 634 (A.B. 2030), Laws 2004)

This listing includes law sections that may not appear under the Taxpayers' Bill of Rights, but pertain to taxpayer rights.

In addition, certain confidentiality privileges are provided for personal income tax-withholding advice-related communications between a taxpayer and a federally-authorized tax practitioner who appears before the Employment Development Department. (Sec. 13019, Unemp. Ins. Code)

• *Corporation franchise (income) and personal income taxes*

Disclosure by FTB.—It is a misdemeanor for any member of the FTB, any officer of the state, or any other individual to disclose information (including business affairs of a corporation) contained in a tax or information return or report. (Sec. 19542, Rev. & Tax. Code) "The prohibition of disclosure applies to federal tax returns as well, on the theory that disclosure of a taxpayer's federal tax return is equivalent to disclosure of the taxpayer's California tax return. (*Webb v Standard Oil Co.*, 49 Cal 2d 509 (1959)) Business affairs" are the details of the business activities of the taxpayer, excluding extraneous matters such as corporate title, number, taxable years adopted, date of commencing business in the state and the like. (Sec. 19543, Rev. & Tax. Code) Misdemeanor infractions include the willful unauthorized inspection, or unauthorized disclosure or use, of confidential taxpayer information furnished pursuant to California tax laws or other laws. (Sec. 19542.1, Rev. & Tax. Code)

The FTB is prohibited from providing the California Wildlife Conservation Board with information relating to any natural heritage preservation tax credit claimed if it would disclose the tax return information of a taxpayer, unless the taxpayer has consented to the disclosure. (Sec. 19560, Rev. & Tax. Code)

Also, safeguards are provided to prevent improper disclosure by the FTB of trade secrets or other confidential information with respect to any software that comes into the FTB's possession or control in connection with a tax return examination. (Sec. 19504.5, Rev. & Tax. Code) Computer software source code and executable code are considered return information for disclosure purposes. Any person who willfully divulges or makes known to another person any computer software source code or executable code obtained in connection with a tax return examination may be punished by a fine or imprisonment or both. (Sec. 19542.3, Rev. & Tax. Code)

The FTB may not approve for electronic filing any proprietary filing software or electronic tax preparation forms that require a taxpayer, as a condition of accessing the software or forms, to consent to the disclosure of information that the law requires a separate consent to disclose. (Sec. 18621.7, Rev. & Tax. Code)

The following disclosures are allowed:

(1) Disclosure in a judicial or administrative tax proceeding (Sec. 19545, Rev. & Tax. Code) or to the Attorney General or other state legal representative (Sec. 19547, Rev. & Tax. Code) under the following circumstances:

(a) the taxpayer is a party to the proceeding or the proceeding arose out of, or in connection with, the taxpayer's civil or criminal liability,

(b) the treatment of an item reflected on the return is related to the resolution of an issue in the proceeding, or

(c) the return or information directly relates to a transactional relationship between the taxpayer and a party to the proceeding that directly affects the resolution of an issue in the proceeding.

For purposes of disclosures in a judicial or administrative proceeding or to the Attorney General, the terms "return," "return information," "taxpayer return information," and "tax administration" are statutorily defined. (Sec. 19549, Rev. & Tax. Code) In addition, the Attorney General may inspect any return in the enforcement of any public or charitable trust or in compelling adherence by a nonprofit corporation to any charitable purposes for which it was formed. (Sec. 19547, Rev. & Tax. Code)

(2) Disclosure to city tax officials pursuant to a written agreement and only with respect to taxpayers with an address within the city's jurisdictional boundaries, who report business income to the FTB. Disclosure is limited to a taxpayer's name, address, Social Security or taxpayer identification number, and business activity code, which can only be furnished to or used by an employee of the taxing authority and must be used in a form and manner that safeguards the tax information. From January 1, 2009, until January 1, 2019, city tax officials may enter into reciprocal agreements to obtain this tax information from the FTB. From January 1, 2016, until January 1, 2019, officials of any county or city and county may enter similar agreements. The disclosure is permitted only if a written executed agreement between a city, county, or city and county and the FTB provides for

(a) the payment by the city, county, or city and county to the FTB of all the first year's costs (includes costs for the purchase of equipment and the development of processes and labor) for providing the information prior to any of these costs being incurred by the FTB,

(b) the reimbursement by the city, county, or city and county of the annual costs incurred by the FTB in disclosing the allowed information.

The FTB must receive an amount equal to the first year's costs before it provides any of the outlined information. For any other type of information not specified above, officials may request information from the FTB by affidavit only. (Sec. 19551.1, Rev. & Tax. Code)

(3) Disclosures to a legislative committee upon request (Sec. 19546, Rev. & Tax. Code) or disclosures to a legislative committee by any person with current or prior authorized access to a return or return information if the person believes the return or return information relates to possible FTB misconduct, maladministration, or abuse of taxpayers. (Sec. 19546.5, Rev. & Tax. Code) It is a misdemeanor for any committee member or employee to disclose any information contained in a return or report except to law enforcement officers. (Sec. 19546, Rev. & Tax. Code)

(4) Disclosure to the U.S. Commissioner of Internal Revenue or the Commissioner's representative, tax officials of California or other states, or members of the Multistate Tax Commission, for state or federal tax purposes only. (Sec. 19551, Rev. & Tax. Code) The FTB may also disclose to tax officials of Mexico the income tax return of a Mexican national for tax purposes so long as there is a reciprocal agreement. Unwarranted disclosure or use of the information by an agency or individual is a misdemeanor. (Sec. 19552, Rev. & Tax. Code)

(5) Disclosure of information in an exemption application, together with related documents. On request, supporting papers may be withheld from public inspection if they contain information on a trade secret, patent process, style of work, or apparatus of the organization. The FTB may also withhold information if the disclosure would adversely affect the national defense. (Sec. 19565, Rev. & Tax. Code)

(6) Publication of statistics that do not identify particular reports or returns. (Sec. 19563, Rev. & Tax. Code)

(7) Disclosure of address information to the Department of Justice, a court, or any law enforcement agency, upon request, for person for whom there is an outstanding arrest warrant. (Sec. 19550(a), Rev. & Tax. Code)

(8) Disclosure of address information to the Department of Justice for purposes of locating unregistered sex offenders. (Sec. 19550(b), Rev. & Tax. Code)

(9) Disclosure to the State Controller's Office of specified information that is obtained from business entity returns filed with the FTB for purposes of assisting the Controller's office in locating owners of unclaimed property. The information is limited to the taxpayer's name, identification number, address, and principal business activity code. (Sec. 19554, Rev. & Tax. Code)

(10) Submission of a list to the Attorney General annually by November 30, based on income tax returns filed for the previous taxable year, identifying retail sellers and manufacturers doing business in the state that have annual world-wide gross receipts in excess of $100 million, who are required to disclose their efforts to eradicate slavery and human trafficking from their direct supply chains for tangible goods offered for sale. (Sec. 19547.5, Rev. & Tax. Code)

(11) Disclosure of the name and social security number or taxpayer identification number to designated financial institutions or their authorized processing agent for purposes of matching debtor records to account-holder records at the financial institution. (Sec. 19560.5, Rev. & Tax. Code)

COMMENT: *Waiver of privilege.*—Taxpayers may be required to waive or relinquish the privilege against disclosure to obtain non-tax-related benefits. For example, the Contractors' State License Board may refuse to issue or renew a contractor's license for failure to pay final tax liabilities assessed by the FTB. Therefore, the application for a contractor's license will include an authorization by the applicant for the FTB's disclosure of this information. (Sec. 7145.5, Bus. & Prof. Code)

---

(12) Disclosure to the California Health Benefit Exchange, the State Department of Health Care Services, the Managed Risk Medical Insurance Board, and county departments and agencies, returns or return information to verify or determine eligibility of an individual for Medi-Cal benefits, the Healthy Families Program, the Access for Infants and Mothers Program, health benefits, tax credits, health insurance subsidies, or cost-sharing reductions through the Exchange. (Sec. 19548.5, Rev. & Tax. Code)

(13) Disclosure to the State Department of Public Health to verify the modified adjusted gross income, tax-exempt interest and social security benefits, and foreign earned income of an applicant for, or recipient of, human immunodeficiency virus treatment services pursuant to Chapter 6 (commencing with Sec. 120950), Part 4, Div. 105, of the Health and Safety Code. (Sec. 19548.2, Rev. & Tax. Code)

(14) Disclosure to the Scholarshare Investment Board of income reported to the FTB for the purpose of verifying the eligibility of participants in a qualified tuition program. (Sec. 19548.3, Rev. & Tax. Code)

(15) Disclosure of individual income tax return and related information to the California Health Benefit Exchange. (Sec. 19548.8, Rev. & Tax. Code)

(16) Disclosure of information to the CalSavers Retirement Savings Board to facilitate collection and appeals. (Sec. 19567, Rev. & Tax. Code)

(17) Annually furnish the jury commissioner of each county with a list of resident state tax filers, for the purpose of expanding jury pools. (Sec. 19548.4, Rev. & Tax. Code)

(18) Disclosure of return information to the Employment Development Department (EDD) to verify income, when necessary for EDD unemployment program administration. (Sec. 19551.2, Rev. & Tax. Code)

(19) For tax years beginning on or after January 1, 2018, and before January 1, 2020, disclosure of return information to the State Department of Social Services, for purposes of informing individuals of the availability of federal stimulus payments. (Uncodified Sec. 26, A.B. 107, Laws 2020)

Disclosure to FTB.—The FTB may require any state licensing board, the State Bar, the Department of Real Estate, and the Insurance Commissioner to provide certain specified information, including the following:

(1) the licensee's name, address, and Social Security number (or federal employer identification number if a partnership) or, effective January 1, 2015, individual taxpayer identification number,

(2) type of license and its effective and expiration dates, and

(3) whether the license is new or a renewal and active or inactive.

The FTB may send a notice to a licensee that fails to provide a Social Security number, federal employer identification number, or individual taxpayer identification number on a license application, and after 30 days following the issuance of the notice may assess a $100 for failure to provide the information. (Sec. 19528, Rev. & Tax. Code)

A "licensee" is defined as any entity, other than a corporation, authorized by a license, certificate, registration, or other means to engage in a business or profession regulated by the Business and Professions Code, the chiropractors' initiative, or the Osteopathic Act. The disclosure of information must be used exclusively for state tax enforcement purposes. (Sec. 30, Bus. & Prof. Code)

The FTB may demand information from a financial institution only if the demand complies with the California Right to Financial Privacy Act (Chapter 20, Division 7, Title 1, Govt. Code). Under the Act, a financial institution may provide the following information to the FTB:

(1) whether the taxpayer has an account at the financial institution,

(2) the amount of security interest in the taxpayer's assets that are held by the institution, and

(3) financial records in connection with a tax return or return information required to be filed by the financial institution.

(Sec. 19504, Rev. & Tax. Code)

Also, a financial institution must furnish to the FTB the name and address of any co-owner, cosigner, or any other person who had access to the funds in an account following the date of a direct deposited income tax refund if the FTB certifies in writing to the financial institution that:

— a taxpayer filed a tax return that authorized a direct deposit refund with an incorrect financial institution account or routing number that resulted in all or a portion of the refund not being received, directly or indirectly, by the taxpayer;

— the direct deposit refund was not returned to the FTB; and

— the refund was deposited directly on a specified date into the account of an account holder of the financial institution who was not entitled to receive the refund.

If the account has been closed, the financial institution must furnish the name and address of the person who closed the account. (Sec. 7480, Govt. Code) However, the Legislature has stated its intent that this procedure, which provides an exception to the California Right to Financial Privacy Act, should be exercised by the FTB only after all other avenues to recover the misdirected refund have been exhausted. (Sec. 5, Ch. 234 (A.B. 2249), Laws 2008)

Effective September 29, 2020, State Department of Social Services may exchange data with the FTB, upon request, including, but not limited to, names, addresses, and contact information of individuals that may qualify for the California earned income tax credit. (Uncodified Sec. 26, A.B. 107, Laws 2020)

Disclosure by tax return preparer.—A person who discloses any information obtained in the business of preparing a federal or state income tax return is guilty of a misdemeanor unless the disclosure is (1) with the written consent of the taxpayer, (2) authorized by law, (3) necessary to the preparation of the return, or (4) pursuant to court order. Prohibited disclosures include disclosures of information obtained through an electronic medium and disclosures made internally within the entity preparing or assisting in preparing the tax return for any purpose other than tax preparation or made by that entity to any of its subsidiaries or affiliates. (Sec. 17530.5, Bus. & Prof. Code)

Disclosure in connection with financial or business related transaction.—Disclosures of state or federal income tax return information or any information obtained from a tax schedule submitted with the return by a consumer in connection with a financial or other business related transaction, including disclosures of information obtained through an electronic medium and disclosures made internally within an entity or made by that entity to any of its subsidiaries or affiliates, are generally prohibited. Also, no unrelated use may be made of state or federal tax return information submitted by a consumer in connection with such a transaction. (Sec. 1799.1a, Civ. Code)

A disclosure in connection with a financial or other business related transaction is allowed if it is:

— made with the written consent of the taxpayer;

— authorized by law;

— necessary to complete or service the financial or business related transaction or to effect, administer, or enforce such a transaction requested by the consumer; or

— pursuant to a court order.

(Sec. 1799.1a, Civ. Code)

Also, a disclosure of tax return information in connection with a financial or other business related transaction is allowed if the disclosure is required to complete the following:

— a proposed or actual sale, merger, transfer, or exchange of a business or operating unit;

— a proposed or actual securitization or secondary market sale, including the sale of servicing rights;

— the provision of information to insurance rate advisory organizations, guaranty funds, or agencies, rating agencies, and other persons assessing compliance with industry standards;

— the protection against or prevention of actual or potential fraud and unauthorized transactions and claims for institutional risk control activities.

(Sec. 1799.1a, Civ. Code)

The FTB may disclose tax returns and related information to:

— FTB employees or former employees who are a party to an administrative proceeding affecting their personnel rights;

— an authorized representative upon request by the employee or former employee;

— FTB officers and employees for use in any action or proceedings affecting the personnel rights of employees or former employees; and

— an administrative law judge, administrative board member, judge, justice, or authorized officer or employee with respect to an administrative procedure affecting the personnel rights of employees or former employees.

An action or proceeding affecting the personnel rights of employees or former employees is one arising under certain provisions of the State Civil Service Act or the Ralph C. Dills Act.

Such disclosures can be made only to the extent that the information is relevant or material to the action or proceeding.

Persons making an unauthorized disclosure are subject to criminal penalty and civil liability. (Sec. 19556, Rev. & Tax. Code)

Disclosure to Registrar of Contractors.—The Franchise Tax Board is required to notify the Registrar of Contractors of the Contractors State License Board, the Director of Employment Development, the Economic and Employment Enforcement Coalition, and the Joint Enforcement Strike Force on the Underground Economy upon the arraignment of, or the filing of, criminal charges against any individual for a failure to file a return or for filing a false return (beginning with Sec. 19701, Rev. & Tax. Code) if that individual engages in the business or acts in the capacity of a contractor within California pursuant to a license issued by the Contractors State License Board or if that individual unlawfully engages in the business or acts in the capacity of a contractor within this state without having the required license. (Sec. 19529, Rev. & Tax. Code)

COMMENT: Social Security number safeguards.—Unless prohibited by federal law, the FTB is required to redact the first five digits of a taxpayer's Social Security number on personal income and corporation franchise and income tax lien abstracts and any other public records created by the FTB that are disclosable under the Public Records Act. (Sec. 15705, Govt. Code)

• *City business tax/license information*

Each California city that assesses a city business tax or that requires a city business license must annually submit to the FTB, upon request of the FTB, specified information collected in the course of administration of the city's business tax or license program. Beginning January 1, 2016, this requirement also applies to any county or city and county that assesses a business tax or that requires a business license. The information required to be submitted is limited to the following:

— the name of the business if the business is a corporation, partnership, or limited liability company, or the owner's name if it the business is a sole proprietorship;

— the business mailing address;

— the federal employer identification number, if applicable, or the business owner's Social Security number;

— the Standard Industry Classification Code (SIC) or North American Industry Classification Code;

— the business start date;

— the business cease date;

— the city number; and

— the business ownership type.

However, a city, county, or city and county will not be required to provide this information to the FTB if the FTB fails to provide tax information to the city, county, or city and county pursuant to a reciprocal agreement with the city, county, or city and county for reasons other than the confidentiality of the information. (Sec. 19551.5, Rev. & Tax. Code)

[¶89-224] Refunds

In general, taxpayers are entitled to refunds of overpayments of tax, penalties, or interest.

CAUTION: Transfer of BOE powers.—Beginning July 1, 2017, all California State Board of Equalization (BOE) administrative powers, duties, and responsibilities that are not constitutionally mandated to the BOE, with certain exceptions in the short term, were transferred to the California Department of Tax and Fee Administration (CDTFA). The BOE is left with responsibility for property tax assessment and equalization functions and assessment of taxes on insurers authorized by Article XIII of the state constitution; assessment and collection of excise taxes on alcohol pursuant to Article XX of the state constitution; and the statutory duty to adjust the rate of the motor vehicle fuel tax for the 2018-19 fiscal year. Until January 1, 2018, the BOE continued to hear corporation franchise and income tax and personal income tax appeals from the Franchise Tax Board (FTB). However, on that date, those functions were transferred to the Office of Tax Appeals (OTA), and the BOE is prohibited from hearing further appeals.

These changes are the result of 2017 legislation, Ch. 6 (A.B. 102), Laws 2017, effective June 27, 2017, and operative as noted.

• *Income taxes*

Refunds for overpayments of corporation franchise and income tax or personal income tax must be claimed in writing, be signed under penalty of perjury by the taxpayer or the taxpayer's authorized representative, and state specific grounds for the claim. (Sec. 19322, Rev. & Tax. Code; Reg. 19322, 18 CCR) The taxpayer must affirmatively establish the right to a refund of the taxes by a preponderance of the evidence by supplying a sufficient level of support for their refund when they file their refund claims. Sufficient support includes forms, calculations, or schedules used in determining the amount of refund, as well as detailed explanations for the change. (*Tax News*, California Franchise Tax Board, December 2007)

In addition, claims filed on behalf of a class of taxpayers must be accompanied by written authorization from each taxpayer in the class, must be signed by each taxpayer or taxpayer's authorized representative, and must state specific grounds for the claim. (Sec. 19322, Rev. & Tax. Code; Reg. 19322, 18 CCR)

In order to file a claim for refund of an overpayment of corporation franchise or income tax, taxpayers must use Form 100X, to amend a previously filed Form 100, *California Corporation Franchise or Income Tax Return*, Form 100W, *California Corporation Franchise or Income Tax Return—Water's-Edge Filers*, or Form 100S, *California S Corporation Franchise or Income Tax Return*. (Instructions, Form 100X, Amended Corporation

Franchise or Income Tax Return) Taxpayers must indicate on Form 100X whether they wish to receive a refund of the overpayment or a credit towards their income tax liability for the succeeding year. Personal income tax refunds are made on Form 540X, Amended Individual Income Tax Return. Amended return forms are available on the California Franchise Tax Board (FTB) website.

The FTB must notify the taxpayer if it disallows a claim for refund, and the FTB must provide the taxpayer with an explanation of the reasons for disallowing the claim. (Sec. 19323, Rev. & Tax. Code) The FTB's denial of a refund claim becomes final if the taxpayer does not file an appeal to the CDTFA within 90 days of the *Notice of Action on Cancellation, Credit or Refund* or a *Claim for Refund Denial Letter*. (Sec. 19324, Rev. & Tax. Code; *Tax News*, California Franchise Tax Board, January 2017)

COMPLIANCE POINTER: Proper notice by FTB.—The FTB issues formal claim denials either by issuing a *Notice of Action on Cancellation, Credit or Refund* or a *Claim for Refund Denial Letter*. When it denies all or part of the claim for refund, taxpayers can either file an appeal with the CDTFA or file a suit in superior court. The FTB's internal procedure is that a formal notification of a claim denial should contain information regarding appeal rights. Therefore, the FTB will attach Forms 1084 or 1087 with the formal notification, which gives detailed information about the different options, where to file, and how to file it. If an auditor issues an *Audit Information Presentation Sheet* indicating the claim for refund is either fully or partially denied, this does not constitute a formal notification of a claim denial. (*Tax News*, California Franchise Tax Board, January 2017)

Statute of limitations.—A credit or refund claim for corporation franchise (income) tax or personal income tax generally must be made prior to the expiration of the later of:

— four years from the date the return was filed, if filed within the time prescribed by law, including extensions;

— four years from the last day prescribed for filing the return, determined without regard to any extensions; or

— one year from the date of overpayment.

(Sec. 19306, Rev. & Tax. Code)

A return filed within four years of the due date for the return showing an overpayment of withheld or estimated taxes will be treated as a claim for refund. (Sec. 19307, Rev. & Tax. Code)

An otherwise valid claim for refund that is made in the absence of full payment of the assessed or asserted tax (i.e., an "informal claim") is deemed filed only for purposes of tolling the four-year statute of limitations. For all other purposes, the claim is deemed filed on the date the tax is paid in full. (Sec. 19322.1, Rev. & Tax. Code; *Tax News*, California Franchise Tax Board, January 2017)

Extensions of time may be available to military personnel serving in a combat zone, persons deployed outside the United States away from their permanent duty station while participating in a contingency operation, or to individuals living in a presidentially declared disaster area. (Sec. 18570, Rev. & Tax. Code; Sec. 18571, Rev. & Tax. Code)

If the taxpayer signs a waiver granting the FTB or federal authorities an extension of time in which to propose additional assessments, the time limit for claiming a refund is extended to the later of four years after the return was filed or six months after the date of the expiration of the agreed period for assessing additional income tax deficiencies, whichever period expires later. (Sec. 19308, Rev. & Tax. Code; Sec. 19065, Rev. & Tax. Code) In the period before an extension agreement is made, the general four-year time limit applies. (Sec. 19309, Rev. & Tax. Code)

CCH CAUTION: *Voluntary payments made after statute of limitations period.*— In a nonprecedential summary decision, the BOE held that California does not follow the federal law that requires the Internal Revenue Service to refund voluntary payments made after the statute of limitations has lapsed. Under California law, the FTB is required to refund payments made after the limitations period has lapsed only if there was an actual overpayment. Consequently, the BOE held that as the taxpayer failed to establish that the amounts self-assessed on the taxpayer's return for the tax years at issue were incorrect, the FTB was not required to refund the amounts paid that were associated with the amount reflected on the taxpayer's returns. (*Appeal of Auto Theft R.F. Systems, LLC*, California Board of Equalization, No. 336033, March 22, 2011)

If a change or correction is made or allowed by federal authorities and the taxpayer notifies the FTB as required, the time for claiming a refund or credit extends to the later of:

— two years from the date of the final federal determination; or

— the period provided in (Sec. 19306, Sec. 19307, Sec. 19308, or Sec. 19316).

For adjustments under the federal partnership audit rules resulting in a tax on the partnership, the extended period for claiming a refund or credit is also available. This applies to final federal determinations assessed under the rules as in effect January 1, 2018. (Sec. 19311, Rev. & Tax. Code)

Similarly, taxpayers may file claims for refund or credits for taxes paid to other states within one year from the date the tax is paid to the other state even if the standard statute of limitations period has lapsed. (Sec. 19311.5, Rev. & Tax. Code)

PRACTICE TIP: *Overcollections.*—The FTB is not barred from returning taxes that were "overcollected" as a result of the FTB's mathematical or clerical error even after the statute of limitations period has expired. However, no interest is due on such overcollected amounts. An "overcollection" occurs when the amount collected exceeds the amount actually due under the law as the result of clerical or mechanical error. (*Technical Advisory Memorandum 2007-1*, California Franchise Tax Board, April 23, 2007)

If the taxpayer has overpaid taxes because a bad debt or worthless security has subsequently become deductible or because the taxpayer has erroneously included an amount as a bad debt recovery, the time limit for claiming a refund or credit is seven years from the due date of the return. (Sec. 19312, Rev. & Tax. Code)

Federally registered partnerships have five years from the filing of a partnership return or six months after the expiration of an extension to file a claim for refund or credit arising from an overpayment attributable to a partnership item. (Sec. 19313, Rev. & Tax. Code)

The running of the statute of limitations specified in Sec. 19306, Rev. & Tax. Code, Sec. 19308, Rev. & Tax. Code, Sec. 19311, Rev. & Tax. Code, Sec. 19312, Rev. & Tax. Code, or Sec. 19313, Rev. & Tax. Code for filing a claim for refund will be suspended during any period for which an individual is financially disabled. For this purpose, an individual is "financially disabled" if the individual is unable to manage his or her own financial affairs by reason of a medically determinable physical or mental impairment that is deemed to be a terminal impairment or expected to last for a continuous period of not less than 12 months. However, persons for whom a spouse or other person is legally authorized to act on that individual's behalf in financial matters are not considered financially disabled. (Sec. 19316, Rev. & Tax. Code)

A tax deposit made to stop the running of interest, is not considered a payment of tax for purposes of filing a claim for refund, converting an administrative action to a judicial refund action, or filing a judicial refund action until either of the following occurs:

— the taxpayer provides a written statement to the FTB specifying that the deposit is a payment of tax for purposes of Sec. 19306, Rev. & Tax. Code, Sec. 19335, Rev. & Tax. Code, or Sec. 19384, Rev. & Tax. Code; or

— the deposit is used to pay a final tax liability.

(Sec. 19041.5, Rev. & Tax. Code; *Notice 2005-6*, California Franchise Tax Board, November 28, 2005)

PRACTICAL ANALYSIS: *Conversion of protest to refund claim.*—A taxpayer that has a tax deposit amount on account and would like to convert a protest or appeal to a claim for refund must provide a statement in writing (preferably on Form 3581, Tax Deposit Refund or Transfer Request) asking the FTB to convert the administrative deficiency dispute into an administrative claim dispute. When the FTB receives the written request, it will finalize the deficiency and apply the tax deposit amount to the final deficiency amount, including interest and any amnesty penalty (if applicable). If there is an overpayment after all amounts due for the year have been paid, the balance will be refunded, unless the taxpayer has designated that excess amounts should be retained or applied differently, and the protest will then convert to a perfected claim upon which the FTB will take action. If the tax deposit amount is not enough to pay the final deficiency amount, including penalties, fees, and interest, the claim will become an informal claim, and the taxpayer will receive a bill for the remaining amount due. The FTB cannot act on a claim until it is perfected by full payment. (*Tax News*, California Franchise Tax Board, September 2006)

Interest.—Interest at the current rate (see ¶89-204) is generally payable on overpayments of income tax. (Sec. 19340, Rev. & Tax. Code) However, no interest is allowed if:

— an overpayment is the result of federal law that reduces taxes for taxable years prior to the federal law's enactment date; (Sec. 19325, Rev. & Tax. Code)

— an overpayment of corporation franchise (income) tax is refunded or credited within the later of 90 days after the return is filed or 90 days after the last day prescribed for filing the return (determined without regard to extensions); (Sec. 19341, Rev. & Tax. Code)

— an overpayment of personal income tax is refunded or credited to an individual or fiduciary within the later of 45 days after the return is filed or 45 days after the last day prescribed for filing the return (determined without regard to extensions); (Sec. 19341, Rev. & Tax. Code)

— a return is filed after the prescribed date (determined with regard to extensions), in which case no interest is allowed for any day before the date on which the return is filed. (Sec. 19341, Rev. & Tax. Code)

Direct deposit of refunds.—Individual taxpayers have the option of designating more than one account at a financial institution for direct deposit of a tax refund. (Sec. 19303, Rev. & Tax. Code) In addition, personal income tax return form instructions must include information about the ability of a taxpayer to directly deposit a portion of a refund of any overpayment of taxes into the Golden State Scholarshare College Savings Trust. The Scholarshare Investment Board must provide the FTB with a description of the Golden State Scholarshare College Savings Trust on or before a specified date provided by the FTB. (Sec. 19304, Rev. & Tax. Code)

> *CCH PRACTICE TIP: Misdirected direct deposit refunds.*—The FTB receives over 60,000 misdirected direct deposit refunds (DDR) each year. A client that has not received the DDR should wait at least 25 working days from the authorized date of the refund (seven days for e-file returns and eight weeks for paper-filed returns) before calling the FTB. Taxpayers will need to fax the FTB a bank statement showing that the deposit was not made to their account and will be sent a FTB 3851, Taxpayer Affidavit of Misdirected Refund Deposit to complete and return to the FTB. In addition, the taxpayer must notify the taxpayer's bank or financial institution in writing of the error and file a police report. Copies of the letter and the report must be attached to FTB 3851. After the FTB receives the FTB 3851 from the taxpayer, the FTB will contact the bank or financial institution where the misdirected refund was deposited to request information on the account holder who received the misdirected refund. Although the information is required to be sent within seven days, it frequently takes longer. Once the FTB receives the information from the bank or financial institution, a paper check refund will be issued to the correct taxpayer. (*Tax News*, California Franchise Tax Board, April 2012)

Voluntary contributions.—California permits taxpayers to make certain contributions by designating the desired amounts (full dollar amounts) on their returns as additions to their tax liability. Thus, the designated amounts increase the balance payable on the return or reduce the refund, if any. (Sec. 18701 to Sec. 18910, Rev. & Tax. Code) All designated contributions are permitted as charitable contributions. (Instructions, Form 540, California Resident Income Tax Return)

• *Personal income tax withholding*

Taxes withheld from wages are considered an overpayment to the extent they exceed the personal income tax imposed. (Sec. 19354, Rev. & Tax. Code) However, FTB refunds of excess taxes withheld are not to be regarded as constituting a determination of the correctness of the return. (Sec. 19355, Rev. & Tax. Code) The Unemployment Insurance Code provides for refunds or credits in situations in which an employer erroneously remits amounts that exceed the amount of tax that the employer has actually withheld from an employee. (Sec. 1177, Unempl. Ins. Code— Sec. 1184, Unempl. Ins. Code)

Failure to file a claim within the prescribed period, failure after denial of a claim to file a timely petition for review, or failure to file an appeal from an adverse referee decision results in a waiver of any claim for refund or credit. (Sec. 1179, Unempl. Ins. Code) Also, no claim for refund of amounts paid pursuant to an offer in compromise may be filed. (Sec. 1180.1, Unempl. Ins. Code)

To the extent that funds are available, the Employment Development Department (EDD) will pay interest on overpayments from the date of overpayment, unless the overpayment was made intentionally or as a result of negligence. (Sec. 1181, Unempl. Ins. Code) Regulations apply to the interpretation of the provision. (Reg. 1181-1, 18 CCR)

The Director of the EDD will assess the employer for the amount of any erroneous refund. (Sec. 1184, Unempl. Ins. Code) The assessment bears interest at the annual rate set by the FTB. Written notice of the assessment must be given to the employer within three years from the date the refund was made or credit allowed.

A person from whom tax is collected by withholding is entitled to the remedies outlined in Rev. & Tax. Code Sec. 19301 through Rev. & Tax. Code Sec. 19368, pertaining to overpayments and refunds, and Rev. & Tax. Code Sec. 19381 through Rev. & Tax. Code Sec. 19393, relating to suits for refund. (Sec. 18675, Rev. & Tax. Code) In the case of overpaid taxes withheld from wages paid to nonresidents and from nonwage payments, the employer or other withholding agent may obtain a refund only to the extent that the amount of the overpayment was not withheld from the employee or payee. (Sec. 19361, Rev. & Tax. Code)

If a withholding agent discovers that an amount was withheld in error, the withholding agent may request a refund or credit of the erroneously withheld amount to be refunded or credited either to the withholding agent or to the payee. If the withholding agent requests that the erroneously withheld amount be retained as a credit against the withholding agent's future withholding obligations (in cases where the withholding agent has repaid the erroneously withheld funds to the payee), the FTB will retain the withholding amount in the name of the withholding agent who can then apply the excess withholding on a later period remittance as a prior payment. (Reg. 18662-8, 18 CCR)

COMPLIANCE NOTE: The one-year and four-year statute of limitations periods under Rev. & Tax. Code Sec. 19306 apply to withholding agents. Therefore, they limit the period in which the FTB may allow a refund or credit to a withholding agent of the failure to withhold liability. The four-year limitations period starts to run from the due date of the original information return filed on FTB Form 592 or FTB Form 593. If no information return is filed, the statute of limitations period for a withholding agent claiming a refund or credit of the failure to withhold liability begins to run on the due date of the original information return that was required to be filed with respect to that withholding amount. (*Technical Advice Memorandum 2016-02*, California Franchise Tax Board, February 24, 2016)

• *Sales and use taxes*

Refund claims for erroneous or overpaid sales and use taxes, penalties, or interest must be in writing and state the specific grounds on which the claims are founded. (Sec. 6904, Rev. & Tax. Code)

Statute of limitations.—A refund claim must be filed within three years from the due date of the return for which the overpayment is alleged. (Sec. 6902, Rev. & Tax. Code) However, a taxpayer has three years from the date of overpayment to file a claim for refund of an overpayment of any tax, penalty, or interest collected by the State Board of Equalization (CDTFA) through the use of a levy, lien, or other enforcement procedure. (Sec. 6902.3, Rev. & Tax. Code) After deficiency determinations, determinations when no return is filed, or jeopardy determinations, a refund claim must be filed within six months from the time the determination becomes final or from the date of overpayment, whichever is later. (Sec. 6905, Rev. & Tax. Code) The limitations period for filing a refund claim is suspended during any period that a person is financially disabled. (Sec. 6902.4, Rev. & Tax. Code)

Claim filings.—Taxpayers making installment payments on a final notice of determination and disputing their liability may file one timely claim for refund to cover all future payments applied to that billing. The filing also will apply to any prior payments that remain within the applicable statutes of limitations. A taxpayer disputing more than one billing must file a timely claim for refund for each separate billing. Payments made to release liens are subject to the six month statute as they are considered voluntary. Payments submitted prior to January 1, 2017, will not cover any future payments. (Sec. 6902.6, Rev. & Tax. Code; *Special Notice L-479*, California State Board of Equalization, November 2016)

Interest.—Interest at the current rate (see ¶ 89-204) is generally payable on overpayments of sales and use taxes. (Sec. 6907, Rev. & Tax. Code) Interest is not allowed if the CDTFA determines that an overpayment has been made intentionally or by reason of carelessness. (Sec. 6908, Rev. & Tax. Code)

CDTFA approval, public record requirements.—If any proposed determination by the CDTFA involves a use tax refund in excess of $50,000 made by the state to a purchaser who had overpaid use tax to a retailer, the CDTFA must make the proposed determination available as a public record for at least 10 days prior to the effective date of the determination. (Sec. 6901, Rev. & Tax. Code)

Generally, if staff determines that a refund in excess of $100,000 should be granted or denied, the recommendation must be submitted to the Deputy Director of the assigned section's Department (the CDTFA, prior to March 2016) for approval. If the assigned staff or the Deputy Director of the assigned section's Department (Executive Director, prior to March 2016) determines that refunds in excess of $50,000 should be granted, the proposed determination must be available as a public record for at least 10 days prior to its effective date. (Reg. 35042, 18 CCR; Reg. 5237, 18 CCR)

If a staff decision and recommendation or supplemental decision and recommendation recommends that a petition, claim, or request for relief be granted in an amount in excess of $100,000, the recommendation must be submitted to the CDTFA for approval. For determinations pursuant to the Integrated Waste Management Fee Law in an amount in excess of $15,000 that does not need CDTFA approval, the 10-day public record posting is required. (Reg. 35066, 18 CCR; Reg. 5266, 18 CCR)

Unconstitutional local taxes.—Retailers or purchasers of $5,000 or more who are required to report and/or pay sales or use tax in a taxing district imposing an unconstitutional tax may obtain refunds of any illegally collected tax. (Sec. 7275, Rev. & Tax. Code)

Retailers must continue to report sales and use tax at the current combined state and local rate, but may take a credit against the total amount of taxes reported. (Sec. 7276, Rev. & Tax. Code)

Persons other than retailers who pay a local sales and use tax that is subsequently held invalid must file written claims for refund. The written claim must set forth the specific grounds on which the claim is based, accompanied by proof of payment of the tax to a retailer or wholesaler that indicates the date of purchase, a description of the property purchased, the purchase price, and the amount of local sales and use tax collected or, if such amount was not separately stated, the rate of local sales and use tax imposed. Written claims by purchasers must be filed within one year of the first day of the calendar quarter commencing after the date on which the final court decision was rendered declaring the tax invalid. (Sec. 7277, Rev. & Tax. Code)

• *Other taxes and fees*

General limitations periods for other tax refunds are discussed below. For the rate of interest on these tax refunds, see ¶ 89-204.

Cigarette tax.—See ¶ 55-001 (cigarettes) and ¶ 55-005 (tobacco products).

Emergency telephone users surcharge.—The claim for a refund must be filed by the later of three years from the last day of the second month following the close of the month for which the overpayment was made, six months from the date a deficiency determination becomes final, or six months from the date of overpayment. (Sec. 41101, Rev. & Tax. Code) Taxpayers making installment payments on a final notice of determination and disputing their liability may file one timely claim for refund to cover all future payments applied to that billing. The filing also will apply to any prior payments that remain within the applicable statutes of limitations. A taxpayer disputing more than one billing must file a timely claim for refund for each separate billing. Payments made to release liens are subject to the six month statute as they are considered voluntary. Payments submitted prior to January 1, 2017, will not cover any future payments. (Sec. 41101.3, Rev. & Tax. Code; *Special Notice L-479*, California State Board of Equalization, November 2016)

Energy resources surcharge.—The claim for a refund must be filed by the later of three years from the last day of the month following the close of the quarterly period for which the overpayment was made, six months from the date a deficiency determination becomes final, or six months from the date of overpayment. (Sec. 40112, Rev. & Tax. Code) Taxpayers making installment payments on a final notice of determination and disputing their liability may file one timely claim for refund to cover all future payments applied to that billing. The filing also will apply to any prior payments that remain within the applicable statutes of limitations. A taxpayer disputing more than one billing must file a timely claim for refund for each separate billing. Payments made to release liens are subject to the six month statute as they are considered voluntary. Payments submitted prior to January 1, 2017, will not cover any future payments. (Sec. 40112.3, Rev. & Tax. Code; *Special Notice L-479*, California State Board of Equalization, November 2016)

Fuel taxes.—For information on refund claims for motor vehicle fuel, use fuel and diesel fuel taxes, see ¶40-001.

Hazardous substances tax.—The claim for a refund must be filed by the later of three years from the date the taxes were due for the period for which the overpayment was made, six months from the date a deficiency determination becomes final, or six months from the date of overpayment. (Sec. 43452, Rev. & Tax. Code) Taxpayers making installment payments on a final notice of determination and disputing their liability may file one timely claim for refund to cover all future payments applied to that billing. The filing also will apply to any prior payments that remain within the applicable statutes of limitations. A taxpayer disputing more than one billing must file a timely claim for refund for each separate billing. Payments made to release liens are subject to the six month statute as they are considered voluntary. Payments submitted prior to January 1, 2017, will not cover any future payments. (Sec. 43452.3, Rev. & Tax. Code; *Special Notice L-479*, California State Board of Equalization, November 2016)

Insurance tax.—The claim for a refund must be filed by the later of four years after April 1 of the year following the year for which the overpayment was made, six months from the date a deficiency assessment becomes final, or six months from the date of overpayment. (Sec. 12978, Rev. & Tax. Code)

Motor oil fees.—A request for refund of the payment motor oil fees must be submitted no later than three years from the date the fees were paid. The request must be signed by an employee having knowledge of the transaction and supported by (1) a ledger of the related purchases and exports, (2) documentation of payment of the fees, and (3) documentation of the export of the motor oil from California. Requests for refunds not timely made or supported by the required documentation are not processed but are returned to the sender. (Reg. 4307, 4 CCR)

Oil spill fee.—The claim for a refund must be filed by the later of three years from the due date of the payment for the period for which the overpayment was made, six months after a deficiency determination or jeopardy determination becomes final, or six months from the date of overpayment. (Sec. 46502, Rev. & Tax. Code) Taxpayers making installment payments on a final notice of determination and disputing their liability may file one timely claim for refund to cover all future payments applied to that billing. The filing also will apply to any prior payments that remain within the applicable statutes of limitations. A taxpayer disputing more than one billing must file a timely claim for refund for each separate billing. Payments made to release liens are subject to the six month statute as they are considered voluntary. Payments submitted prior to January 1, 2017, will not cover any future payments. (Sec. 46502.3, Rev. & Tax. Code; *Special Notice L-479*, California State Board of Equalization, November 2016)

Solid waste management fee.—The claim for a refund must be filed by the later of three years from the due date of the payment for the period for which the overpayment was made, six months after a deficiency determination becomes final, or six months from the date of overpayment. (Sec. 45652, Rev. & Tax. Code) Taxpayers making installment payments on a final notice of determination and disputing their liability may file one timely claim for refund to cover all future payments applied to that billing. The filing also will apply to any prior payments that remain within the applicable statutes of limitations. A taxpayer disputing more than one billing must file a timely claim for refund for each separate billing. Payments made to release liens are subject to the six month statute as they are considered voluntary. Payments submitted prior to January 1, 2017, will not cover any future payments. (Sec. 45652.3, Rev. & Tax. Code; *Special Notice L-479*, California State Board of Equalization, November 2016)

Timber yield tax.—The claim for a refund must be filed by the later of three years from the last day of the month following the close of the quarterly period for which the overpayment was made, six months after a deficiency determination or jeopardy determination becomes final, or six months from the date of overpayment. (Sec. 38602, Rev. & Tax. Code)

Underground storage tank maintenance fee.—The claim for a refund must be filed by the later of three years after the due date of the payment for the period for which the overpayment was made, six months after a deficiency determination becomes final, or six months from the date of overpayment. (Sec. 50140, Rev. & Tax. Code) Taxpayers making installment payments on a final notice of determination and disputing their liability may file one timely claim for refund to cover all future payments applied to that billing. The filing also will apply to any prior payments that remain within the applicable statutes of limitations. A taxpayer disputing more than one billing must file a timely claim for refund for each separate billing. Payments made to release liens are subject to the six month statute as they are considered voluntary. Payments submitted prior to January 1, 2017, will not cover any future payments. (Sec. 50140.3, Rev. & Tax. Code; *Special Notice L-479*, California State Board of Equalization, November 2016)

[¶89-230] Taxpayer Conferences

An appeals conference with the California Department of Tax and Fee Administration (CDTFA) officials is available as an alternative to a full hearing for taxpayer complaints. (Reg. 35060, 18 CCR; Reg. 35061, 18 CCR; Reg. 35062, 18 CCR; Reg. 35063, 18 CCR; Reg. 35064, 18 CCR; 35065; Reg. 35066, 18 CCR; Reg. 35067, 18 CCR)

For a discussion of property tax appeals conferences, see ¶20-906.

> *CAUTION: Transfer of BOE powers.*—Beginning July 1, 2017, all California State Board of Equalization (BOE) administrative powers, duties, and responsibilities that are not constitutionally mandated to the BOE, with certain exceptions in the short term, were transferred to the California Department of Tax and Fee Administration (CDTFA). The BOE is left with responsibility for property tax assessment and equalization functions and assessment of taxes on insurers authorized by Article XIII of the state constitution; assessment and collection of excise taxes on alcohol pursuant to Article XX of the state constitution; and the statutory duty to adjust the rate of the motor vehicle fuel tax for the 2018-19 fiscal year. Until January 1, 2018, the BOE continued to hear corporation franchise and income tax and personal income tax appeals from the Franchise Tax Board (FTB). However, on that date, those functions were transferred to the Office of Tax Appeals (OTA), and the BOE is prohibited from hearing further appeals.
>
> These changes are the result of 2017 legislation, Ch. 6 (A.B. 102), Laws 2017, effective June 27, 2017, and operative as noted.

It is the responsibility of the Appeals Division of the CDTFA to "take a fresh look" at the law and the facts and make an objective recommendation. The conference is not an adversarial proceeding or an evidentiary hearing. It is an informal discussion of the relevant facts and applicable laws relating to the taxpayer's complaint. (Reg. 5264(d), 18 CCR)

• *Transition to CDTFA and OTA*

The California Department of Tax and Fee Administration (CDTFA) will conduct appeals conferences for taxes and fees it administers in the same manner as they were conducted under the State Board of Equalization (BOE). (Sec. 15570.50, Govt. Code) CDTFA appeals regulations have been adopted (Division 5). (Sec. 15570.52, Govt. Code) Anyone requesting relief in an appeals conference may thereafter request a hearing before the OTA, if the CDTFA denies the relief requested. (Sec. 15570.54, Govt. Code)

[¶89-234] Administrative Appeals

The California Department of Tax and Fee Administration (CDTFA) has promulgated a division of regulations known as Division 5 made effective March 19, 2018, that govern the administrative and appellate review process for all the tax and fee programs the CDTFA administers. (Reg. 5000, 18 CCR) For a discussion of property tax administrative appeals, see ¶20-906.

> *CAUTION: Transfer of BOE powers.*—Beginning July 1, 2017, all California State Board of Equalization (BOE) administrative powers, duties, and responsibilities that are not constitutionally mandated to the BOE, with certain exceptions in the short term, were transferred to the California Department of Tax and Fee Administration (CDTFA). The BOE is left with responsibility for property tax assessment and equalization functions and assessment of taxes on insurers authorized by Article XIII of the state constitution; assessment and collection of excise taxes on alcohol pursuant to Article XX of the state constitution; and the statutory duty to adjust the rate of the motor vehicle fuel tax for the 2018-19 fiscal year. Until January 1, 2018, the BOE continued to hear corporation franchise and income tax and personal income tax appeals from the Franchise Tax Board (FTB). However, on that date, those functions were transferred to the Office of Tax Appeals, and the BOE is prohibited from hearing further appeals.

These changes are the result of 2017 legislation, Ch. 6 (A.B. 102), Laws 2017, effective June 27, 2017, and operative as noted.

• *Appeal before one Administrative Law Judge*

The Office of Tax Appeals must establish a process under which a person filing an appeal may opt to appear before one administrative law judge if either of the following is true:

— if the appeal arises from a tax, fee, or penalty imposed pursuant to the Personal Income Tax Law, and the total amount in dispute, including penalties and fees, is less than $5,000; or

— if the appeal arises from a tax, fee, or penalty administered by the California Department of Tax and Fee Administration (CDTFA), and both of the following are satisfied:

• the entity filing the appeal has gross receipts of less than $20 million; and

• the total amount in dispute, including penalties and fees, is less than $50,000.

(Sec. 15676.2, Gov. Code)

The decision of one administrative law judge made pursuant to this process does not have precedential effect. (Sec. 15676.2, Gov. Code)

Sunset.—This provision sunsets effective January 1, 2030. (Sec. 15676.2, Gov. Code)

• *Appeals from action taken by FTB and CDTFA*

California has adopted regulations, made effective January 3, 2019, governing appeals before the Office of Tax Appeals (OTA) from action taken by:

• the Franchise Tax Board (FTB); and

• the California Department of Tax and Fee Administration (CDTFA).

The new regulations are referred to as the "Rules for Tax Appeals." In addition, existing regulations regarding appeals from actions of the FTB are repealed. (Regs. 30000, 30101, 30102, 30103, 30104, 30105, 30106, 30201, 30202, 30203, 30204, 30205, 30206, 30207, 30208, 30209, 30210, 30211, 30200.5, 30212, 30213, 30213.5, 30214, 30214.5, 30215, 30216, 30217, 30218, 30219, 30220, 30221, 30222, 30223, 30224, 30301, 30302, 30303, 30304, 30310, 30311, 30312, 30313, 30314, 30315, 30316, 30401, 30402, 30403, 30404, 30405, 30410, 30411, 30412, 30420, 30421, 30430, 30431, 30432, 30433, 30501, 30502, 30503, 30504, 30505, 30601, 30602, 30603, 30604, 30605, 30606, 30607, 30701, 30702, 30703, 30704, 30705, 30706, 30707, 18 CCR, Office of Tax Appeals, effective January 3, 2019; *California Regulatory Notice Register*, Office of Administrative Law, January 11, 2019)

The new division of regulations applies to appeals and petitions for rehearing submitted to the OTA under the:

• Franchise and Income Tax Laws;

• Cannabis Tax;

• Cigarette and Tobacco Products Tax Law;

• Diesel Fuel Tax Law;

• Emergency Telephone Users Surcharge Law;

• Energy Resources Surcharge Law;

- Hazardous Substances Tax Law;
- Childhood Lead Poisoning Prevention Fee and Occupational Lead Poisoning Prevention Fee, Integrated Waste Management Fee Law;
  - Lead-Acid Battery Recycling Act;
  - Motor Vehicle Fuel Tax Law;
  - Oil Spill Response, Prevention, and Administration Fees Law;
  - Sales and Use Tax Law;
  - Transactions and Use Tax Law and Additional Local Taxes;
  - Underground Storage Tank Maintenance Fee Law;
  - Uniform Local Sales and Use Tax Law;
  - Use Fuel Tax Law; and
  - Fee Collection Procedures Law.

(Regs. 30000, 30101, 30102, 30103, 30104, 30105, 30106, 30201, 30202, 30203, 30204, 30205, 30206, 30207, 30208, 30209, 30210, 30211, 30200.5, 30212, 30213, 30213.5, 30214, 30214.5, 30215, 30216, 30217, 30218, 30219, 30220, 30221, 30222, 30223, 30224, 30301, 30302, 30303, 30304, 30310, 30311, 30312, 30313, 30314, 30315, 30316, 30401, 30402, 30403, 30404, 30405, 30410, 30411, 30412, 30420, 30421, 30430, 30431, 30432, 30433, 30501, 30502, 30503, 30504, 30505, 30601, 30602, 30603, 30604, 30605, 30606, 30607, 30701, 30702, 30703, 30704, 30705, 30706, 30707, 18 CCR, Office of Tax Appeals, effective January 3, 2019; *California Regulatory Notice Register*, Office of Administrative Law, January 11, 2019)

• *CDTFA review of FTB actions*

Before a Franchise Tax Board (FTB) action on reconsideration of a corporation franchise (income) tax or personal income tax assessment or action to dismiss a taxpayer's corporation franchise (income) tax or personal income tax refund claim becomes final, the taxpayer may appeal the action to the CDTFA. The taxpayer may also appeal an FTB notice of determination not to abate interest. (Sec. 19045, Rev. & Tax. Code; Sec. 19085, Rev. & Tax. Code; Sec. 19104, Rev. & Tax. Code; Sec. 19324, Rev. & Tax. Code; Sec. 19343, Rev. & Tax. Code)

A taxpayer may appeal to the CDTFA after FTB review of a jeopardy determination. (Sec. 19084, Rev. & Tax. Code)

If the FTB does not mail a notice of action on a refund claim within six months after the claim is filed, the action is considered to be disallowed, and the taxpayer may appeal to the CDTFA.

Filing of the appeal.—Two copies of the appeal and any supporting documents must be mailed to the CDTFA in Sacramento, which shall forward one copy of each to the FTB. (Sec. 19046, Rev. & Tax. Code; Sec. 19085, Rev. & Tax. Code; Sec. 19332, Rev. & Tax. Code; Sec. 19344, Rev. & Tax. Code)

The Chief of Board Proceedings may grant a deferral or postponement for a period of up to 90 days in his sole discretion or for a longer period with the consent of the Chief Counsel under specific circumstances. (Reg. 5522.8(b)(1), 18 CCR)

Prehearing procedures.—Subpoenas are served at the expense of the issuing party. An application for a subpoena must be accompanied by an affidavit specifying the nature and materiality of the items to be produced. (Reg. 5523.5(b), 18 CCR)

The CDTFA may request, or the parties may agree, to file a stipulation of the facts in agreement and those in dispute. (Reg. 5523.6(c), 18 CCR) The appeal may be dismissed or deferred on the basis of a stipulation between the parties, at the request of the FTB, or at any time the appellant requests dismissal in writing. (Reg. 5522.8(a), 18 CCR) When all the information has been filed, the appeal will be submitted for decision on the basis of the written record unless the taxpayer requests an oral hearing. (Reg. 5522, 18 CCR)

General hearing procedures.—At the hearing, a member of the CDTFA's legal staff will summarize the undisputed facts and the issues. The appellant and the FTB will then state their positions and present evidence under oath. Either party, as well as the chair of the CDTFA, may call witnesses for testimony and cross-examination. The CDTFA may deny admission of evidence it considers irrelevant, untrustworthy, or repetitious. The parties may refute any matters of which the CDTFA has taken official notice, including records maintained by the CDTFA, tax returns filed with the FTB by the appellant, related FTB records, and any fact judicially noticed by the state courts. (Sec. 5079, Rev. & Tax. Code)

The burden of proof as to issues of fact is generally on the taxpayer, except in cases of fraud, in which case the FTB has the burden of proof (Reg. 5541, 18 CCR)

CDTFA determination.—The CDTFA will notify the taxpayer and the FTB of its determination. (Sec. 19047, Rev. & Tax. Code; Sec. 19085, Rev. & Tax. Code; Sec. 19333, Rev. & Tax. Code; Sec. 19345, Rev. & Tax. Code)

Generally, an CDTFA determination becomes final after 30 days from the date of the determination, unless the taxpayer or the FTB files a petition for rehearing with the CDTFA within that time. (Sec. 19048, Rev. & Tax. Code; Sec. 19085, Rev. & Tax. Code; Sec. 19334, Rev. & Tax. Code; Sec. 19346, Rev. & Tax. Code)

An CDTFA determination with respect to an FTB review of a jeopardy determination becomes final after 60 days from the day after the day by which the CDTFA must make its determination or the day it notifies the taxpayer of its determination, unless either party files a civil action. (Sec. 19084, Rev. & Tax. Code)

Unemployment Insurance Appeals Board procedures are outlined in the Sec. 403, Unempl. Ins. Code—Sec. 413, Unempl. Ins. Code, and Sec. 1951, Unempl. Ins. Code—Sec. 1959, Unempl. Ins. Code.

• *Personal income tax withholding*

An employer receiving a notice of assessment or denial of a claim for refund or credit with respect to withheld personal income taxes may, within 30 days of service, file a petition for review or reassessment with a referee. For good cause, a referee may grant an additional 30 days for filing. If no petition is filed within the prescribed period, the assessment or notice is final. In the case of a claim for refund or credit, the employer may consider the claim denied and file a petition for review if the director fails to serve a notice of action within 60 days after the claim was filed. (Sec. 1222, Unempl. Ins. Code)

Following a notice of jeopardy assessment, the employer may file a petition for reassessment within 10 days of service. (Sec. 1221, Unempl. Ins. Code)

A referee will review timely petitions and grant hearings where requested by the employer, unless a prior hearing has been afforded the employer involving the same issues and no new evidence is set forth by affidavit. The referee must give at least 20 days' notice of the time and place of the hearing. (Sec. 1223, Unempl. Ins. Code)

The referee may decrease or increase the amount of any assessment under review and must notify the employer and the Director of the Employment Development Department of his or her decision and reasons. (Sec. 1223, Unempl. Ins. Code)

The Director or the employer may, within 30 days of notice of the referee decision, file an appeal with the Unemployment Insurance Appeals Board. The Board may for good cause extend the appeal period. If the referee fails to serve notice of the decision on a petition for review of denial of a claim for refund or credit within 60 days after a petition is filed, the petitioner may consider the petition denied and file an appeal with the Board. (Sec. 1224, Unempl. Ins. Code)

If an appeal is not filed within the 30-day period or within the additional period granted by the Board, the referee's decision is final at the end of that period, except that in cases where a decision of the referee requires an adjustment of an assessment by granting a portion of a petition or by increasing an assessment, the assessment is final 30 days after service by the Director of a statement of amounts due setting forth the adjusted liability. (Sec. 1224, Unempl. Ins. Code)

On appeal, the Board may decrease or increase the amount of any assessment. In cases where an order or decision of the Board requires an adjustment of an assessment by granting a portion of a petition or by increasing an assessment, the order or decision and the assessment become final 30 days after service by the Director of a statement of amounts due setting forth the adjusted liability. In all other cases, the order or decision of the Board and any assessment become final 30 days after service of notice of the order or decision. (Sec. 1224, Unempl. Ins. Code)

• *CDTFA general appeal rules*

The CDTFA has, among other appeals rules, a general chapter that applies to a wide variety of taxes. To the extent that any rule in this chapter of general application varies from any rule in chapters of more specific application (e.g., income tax, sales and use tax, property tax), the more specific chapter rule applies. (Reg. 5510, 18 CCR)

Every taxpayer may file a written request for an oral hearing before the CDTFA regarding any appropriate tax matter. A request generally will be granted unless it is made for the primary purpose of delay or it is frivolous or groundless. (Reg. 5522, 18 CCR)

During hearings, taxpayers may be represented by any authorized person or persons, at least 18 years of age, including an attorney, appraiser, accountant, bookkeeper, employee, or business associate. (Reg. 35002, 18 CCR; Reg. 5523(a), 18 CCR) Taxpayers also can present evidence and call witnesses. (Reg. 5523.6, 18 CCR; Reg. 5523.7, 18 CCR) Generally, the burden of proof is on the taxpayer. However, the burden of proof is on the appropriate department of the CDTFA where the issue involves fraud with intent to evade tax. (Reg. 35003, 18 CCR; Reg. 5541, 18 CCR)

For general business taxes, the CDTFA will mail notice of its decision to all parties within 45 days from the date of the decision, except that it will mail notice to all parties within 30 days if the decision is to deny a claim for refund. For appeals from actions by the FTB, a copy of the decision or opinion will be mailed to all parties within three business days from the date of the decision. Notice of a property tax decision is mailed within 30 days of the decision. (Reg. 5560, 18 CCR)

After the CDTFA decides an appeal (see discussion on written opinions below), taxpayers generally may file a petition for rehearing within 30 days of the date on which notice of the decision is mailed to the taxpayer. (Reg. 5561, 18 CCR)

• *CDTFA written opinions*

Generally, the CDTFA is not required to issue a written opinion to decide an appeal. (Reg. 5551, 18 CCR) However, for appeals in which the amount in controversy is at least $500,000, the CDTFA must adopt a written opinion within 120 days after the date on which the board's vote to decide the appeal became final. (Reg. 5552, 18 CCR) The CDTFA issues three types of written opinions:

— a "formal opinion" forms the basis for the CDTFA decision on an appeal from an action by the FTB and sets precedent;

— a "memorandum opinion" sets precedence for appeals other than appeals from an action by the FTB; and

— a "summary decision" is not intended to set precedent.

(Reg. 5511, 18 CCR)

Amount in controversy.—For purposes of the opinion requirement, "amount in controversy" is the total amount of taxes, fees, penalties, interest and/or other charges directly contested by the parties to an appeal as of the date the appeal becomes final. Consolidated appeals are treated as one appeal in calculating the amount in controversy. The term does not include taxes, fees, penalties, interest, or other charges that may be ancillary or related to, or calculated with reference to, directly contested amounts, unless items are also directly contested. (Reg. 5552, 18 CCR)

If an appeal concerns the reallocation of local or district tax, amount in controversy includes directly contested taxes that were reported and paid to the Board prior to the date the Board's decision on the appeal became final (e.g., taxes reported and paid for the last quarter for which a return was filed prior to the finality date), and shall not include taxes that are reported and paid to the Board after the date the Board's vote to decide the appeal becomes final. (Reg. 5552, 18 CCR)

[¶89-236] Judicial Appeals and Remedies

Judicial remedies consist of suits for refund and proceeding to determine specific issues.

CAUTION: Transfer of BOE powers.—Beginning July 1, 2017, all California State Board of Equalization (BOE) administrative powers, duties, and responsibilities that are not constitutionally mandated to the BOE, with certain exceptions in the short term, were transferred to the California Department of Tax and Fee Administration (CDTFA). The BOE is left with responsibility for:

— property tax assessment and equalization functions and assessment of taxes on insurers authorized by Article XIII of the state constitution;

— assessment and collection of excise taxes on alcohol pursuant to Article XX of the state constitution; and

— the statutory duty to adjust the rate of the motor vehicle fuel tax for the 2018-19 fiscal year.

Until January 1, 2018, the BOE continued to hear corporation franchise and income tax and personal income tax appeals from the Franchise Tax Board (FTB). However, on that date, those functions were transferred to the Office of Tax Appeals (OTA), and the BOE is prohibited from hearing further appeals.

These changes are the result of 2017 legislation, Ch. 6 (A.B. 102), Laws 2017, effective June 27, 2017, and operative as noted.

Standing to sue local agency for wasteful or illegal spending.—Effective January 1, 2019, criteria to establish standing to sue a local agency is clarified for California income, sales, use, property, and business license tax purposes. An action can be brought to get a judgment that restrains and prevents any illegal spending of, waste of, or injury to, the estate, funds, or other local agency property. (Sec. 526a, Code of Civ. Pro.)

Until that date, an action may be brought to get a judgment that restrains and prevents any illegal expenditure of, waste of, or injury to, the estate, funds, or other property of a county, town, city, or city and county of the state. Such a suit may be maintained against any officer of such a local agency, or any agent, or other person, acting in its behalf, either by a citizen resident or by a corporation, who is assessed for and is liable to pay, or, within one year before the commencement of the action, has paid, a tax in that local jurisdiction. However, the provision does not require a person to have paid a property tax in order to have sufficient standing to maintain a taxpayer action. Instead, an allegation that a person has paid an assessed tax to the defendant locality is sufficient. (Sec. 526a, Code of Civ. Pro.; *Weatherford v. City of San Rafael*, Court of Appeal of California, First District, A138949, May 22, 2014)

A "local agency" is any of the following in California:

- city;
- town;
- county;
- city and county;
- district;
- public authority; or
- any other political subdivision.

(Sec. 526a, Code of Civ. Pro.)

The action can be brought by either a resident or a corporation. The resident or corporation must be assessed and liable to pay, or, within one year before the commencement of the action, has paid, a tax that funds the defendant local agency. Such an action can be brought against any officer or agent of a local agency, or other person acting on the agency's behalf. (Sec. 526a, Code of Civ. Pro.)

A "resident" is a person who lives, works, owns property, or attends school in the jurisdiction of the defendant local agency. (Sec. 526a, Code of Civ. Pro.)

The provision applies to the following types of taxes that fund the defendant local agency, including but not limited to:

- an income tax;
- a sales and use or transaction and use tax initially paid by a consumer to a retailer;
- a property tax, including a property tax paid by a tenant or lessee to a landlord or lessor under the terms of a written lease; and
- a business license tax.

(Sec. 526a, Code of Civ. Pro.)

• *Suits for refund*

Income taxes.—A taxpayer who has paid the amounts due and whose claim for a corporation franchise (income) or personal income tax refund has been denied by the California Franchise Tax Board (FTB) or the California Office of Tax Appeals (OTA) (prior to January 1, 2018, the California State Board of Equalization (BOE)) (see ¶89-234 Administrative Appeals) may file a suit for refund in superior court. (Sec. 32, Art. XIII, Cal. Const.; Sec. 19382, Rev. & Tax. Code)

PRACTICE TIP: *Amounts due.*—A California court of appeal has held that the payment prerequisite requirement for bringing a suit for refund does not apply to proposed assessments. Only final assessments that are due and payable must be paid. (*City National Corp. v. Franchise Tax Board*, Cal CtApp, 146 Cal. App. 4th 1040, 53 Cal. Rptr. 3d 411, (2007); petition for review denied, California Supreme Court, No. S150563, April 11, 2007)

A taxpayer may file suit against the FTB without appealing to the OTA if the FTB fails within six months after a refund claim was filed to mail its notice of action on the claim. (Sec. 15677, Govt. Code; Sec. 19385, Rev. & Tax. Code)

> *PRACTICE TIP: Exhaustion of administrative remedies.*—Although a taxpayer is not required to pursue an administrative appeal before the OTA prior to bringing a judicial action challenging a refund denial or deemed denial, a taxpayer is precluded from recovering any litigation costs, including attorney fees, incurred in pursuing a judicial action unless the taxpayer has exhausted his or her administrative remedies, including filing an administrative appeal. (*Information Letter 2007-2*, California FTB, August 23, 2007)

> *CCH COMMENT: Jury trial.*—A taxpayer does not have a right to a jury trial in a tax refund action. (*Franchise Tax Board v. The Superior Court of the City and County of San Francisco*, California Supreme Court, No. S176943, June 6, 2011)

A superior court action for refund must be filed within the later of:

— four years from the last date prescribed for filing the return;

— one year from the date the tax was paid;

— 90 days after notice of action by the FTB upon any claim for refund; or

— 90 days after the determination (including the issuance of a decision, opinion, or dismissal) by the OTA on an appeal from the action of the FTB on a claim for refund becomes final.

(Sec. 19384, Rev. & Tax. Code)

Withholding of tax.—An employer may bring suit in a court of competent jurisdiction in Sacramento County for recovery of personal income tax withholding payments erroneously assessed, provided the employer has previously filed a claim for refund or credit. The action must be brought within 90 days after service of notice of the Appeals Board decision. If the Board fails to serve notice of its decision within 90 days after the appeal was filed, the employer may consider the claim denied and may file suit. The Director may extend up to two years the period within which an action may be initiated if the employer files a written request for an extension within the 90-day period. (Sec. 1241, Unempl. Ins. Code)

Judgment in favor of the employer will include interest at the rate of 12 to the extent that funds are available. The amount of the judgment will first be credited toward payments due from the employer; any balance will be refunded. (Sec. 1242, Unempl. Ins. Code)

Other taxes and fees.—If the California Department of Tax and Fee Administration (CDTFA) (prior to 2018, the BOE) disallows a claim for refund or credit of any of the following taxes and fees, the claimant may bring an action to recover the whole or any part of the disallowed amount:

— alcoholic beverage tax; (Sec. 32413, Rev. & Tax. Code)

— cigarette tax; (Sec. 30403, Rev. & Tax. Code)

— diesel fuel tax; (Sec. 60543, Rev. & Tax. Code)

— emergency telephone users surcharge; (Sec. 41110, Rev. & Tax. Code)

— energy resources surcharge; (Sec. 40127, Rev. & Tax. Code)

— hazardous substances tax; (Sec. 43473, Rev. & Tax. Code)

— insurance taxes; (Sec. 13103, Rev. & Tax. Code)

— motor vehicle fuel tax; (Sec. 8148, Rev. & Tax. Code)

— oil spill fee; (Sec. 46523, Rev. & Tax. Code)

— sales and use taxes; (Sec. 6933, Rev. & Tax. Code)

— solid waste management fee; (Sec. 45703, Rev. & Tax. Code)

— timber yield tax; (Sec. 38613, Rev. & Tax. Code)

— underground storage tank maintenance fee; (Sec. 50145, Rev. & Tax. Code) and

— use fuel tax. (Sec. 9173, Rev. & Tax. Code)

For taxes and fees that it administers, the CDTFA (prior to 2018, the BOE) has the burden of proving any factual issue relevant to ascertaining the liability of a taxpayer for intent to evade or fraud in any civil action in which the CDTFA is a party. The standard of proof required is clear and convincing evidence, and a "taxpayer" includes a person on whom fees administered by the CDTFA are imposed. However, imposition of this burden of proof cannot be construed to override any requirement for a taxpayer to substantiate any item on a return or claim filed with the CDTFA. (Sec. 524, Evidence Code)

• *Action to determine reasonableness of jeopardy determination*

After appealing to the OTA to determine the reasonableness of a jeopardy determination made by the FTB, a taxpayer may bring a civil action in the Sacramento, Los Angeles, San Francisco, or San Diego Superior Court. The action must be brought within 60 days of the earlier of:

(1) the day the OTA notifies the taxpayer of its determination or

(2) the day after the last day prescribed for the OTA to make its determination.

The determination made by the superior court will be final and will not be reviewable by any other court. (Sec. 19084, Rev. & Tax. Code)

• *Suit to determine residency*

After protesting a notice of deficiency assessment issued on the grounds of residency and after appealing the FTB's action to the OTA, an individual may file suit in the Sacramento, Los Angeles, or San Francisco Superior Court to determine the issue of residency. The suit must be filed within 60 days after the OTA's action becomes final and must be based on the grounds stated in the protest. (Sec. 19381, Rev. & Tax. Code)

• *Federal court actions*

An assessment may be appealed to a federal court if there is a question involving the U.S. Constitution or a federal statute. However, the right to bring a federal suit is limited by the Tax Injunction Act and the fundamental principle of comity. The Tax Injunction Act prohibits injunctions in federal district courts against the assessment, levy, or collection of any state tax when there is a "plain, speedy, and efficient remedy" in state courts. (28 U.S.C. 1341) Because this federal provision has been the subject of considerable litigation, the case law interpreting this provision should be researched if a federal action is contemplated.

In addition, any appeal of a state tax case to a federal court would be subject to established principles of federal jurisdiction and abstention.

[¶89-238] Representation of Taxpayer

In appearances before the Office of Tax Appeals (OTA), a person may be represented by any authorized person, at least 18 year old, including an attorney, appraiser, certified public accountant, bookkeeper, employee, business associate, or any other person. Any regulations adopted by the OTA may not limit or impair the ability of certified public accountants and others to represent their clients before a tax appeals panel. (Sec. 15676, Govt. Code)

Similar representation is authorized by regulation for hearings before the Board of Equalizaiton (BOE). A Power of Attorney form, either FTB 3520 or BOE-392, must be filed to designate a representative. (Reg. 35002, 18 CCR; Reg. 5523, 18 CCR)

CAUTION: Transfer of BOE powers.—Beginning July 1, 2017, all California State Board of Equalization (BOE) administrative powers, duties, and responsibilities that are not constitutionally mandated to the BOE, with certain exceptions in the short term, were transferred to the California Department of Tax and Fee Administration (CDTFA).

The BOE retains responsibility for property tax assessment and equalization functions and assessment of taxes on insurers authorized by Article XIII of the state constitution; assessment and collection of excise taxes on alcohol pursuant to Article XX of the state constitution; and the statutory duty to adjust the rate of the motor vehicle fuel tax for the 2018-19 fiscal year (residual responsibilities).

Until January 1, 2018, the BOE heard corporation franchise and income tax and personal income tax appeals from the Franchise Tax Board (FTB). However, on that date, those functions were transferred to the Office of Tax Appeals (OTA), and the BOE is prohibited from hearing further appeals not related to its residual responsibilities.

These changes are the result of 2017 legislation, Ch. 6 (A.B. 102), Laws 2017, effective June 27, 2017, and operative as noted.

COMPLIANCE ALERT: Beginning January 1, 2018, the FTB uses new Power of Attorney (POA) declaration forms. The new POA declaration forms are split into two forms (individual/fiduciary and business entity/group nonresident), expire six years from the date signed, do not revoke previously submitted POA declarations with overlapping privileges, and can be revoked by using POA revocation forms. The FTB no longer processes non-FTB POA declaration forms or prior versions of FTB Form 3520 after January 1, 2018. POA declarations filed before January 1, 2018, remain in effect until revoked or expired. (*Tax News*, California Franchise Tax Board, August 2017; *Tax News*, California Franchise Tax Board, December 2017)

The burden of proof is on the taxpayer to prove all issues of fact by a preponderance of evidence. (Reg. 35003, 18 CCR)

In addition, a joint agency power of attorney form (Form BOE-392) will be accepted by the California State Board of Equalization (BOE), the California Employment Development Department (EDD), and the FTB. (*Tax News*, California Franchise Tax Board, January/February 2003)

In adopting regulations, a state agency must afford interested persons or their authorized representatives the opportunity to present statements, arguments, or contentions in writing and to request a public hearing. (Sec. 11346.8, Govt. Code)

For corporation franchise (income) and personal income tax purposes, the FTB must grant a taxpayer or the taxpayer's authorized representative an oral hearing when the taxpayer protests a deficiency assessment or petitions for review of a jeopardy assessment and requests such a hearing. (Sec. 19044, Rev. & Tax. Code)

Also, a taxpayer must be informed of the right to have an attorney, accountant, or other designated agent present at any protest hearing relating to corporation franchise (income), personal income, or sales and use taxes (Sec. 7090, Rev. & Tax. Code; Sec. 21011, Rev. & Tax. Code) or at any informal appeals conference for the following taxes and fees:

— alcoholic beverage tax; (Sec. 32468, Rev. & Tax. Code)

— cigarette and tobacco products taxes; (Sec. 30458.8, Rev. & Tax. Code)

— diesel fuel tax; (Sec. 60629, Rev. & Tax. Code)

— emergency telephone users surcharge; (Sec. 41168, Rev. & Tax. Code)

— energy resources surcharge; (Sec. 40208, Rev. & Tax. Code)

— hazardous substances tax; (Sec. 43519, Rev. & Tax. Code)

— motor vehicle fuel tax; (Sec. 8268, Rev. & Tax. Code)

— oil spill fees; (Sec. 46619, Rev. & Tax. Code)

— sales and use taxes; (Sec. 7090, Rev. & Tax. Code)

— solid waste management fee; (Sec. 45864, Rev. & Tax. Code);

— underground storage tank maintenance fee; (Sec. 50156.8, Rev. & Tax. Code) and

— use fuel tax. (Sec. 9268, Rev. & Tax. Code)

A Power of Attorney form must be filed to designate a representative for any of the above tax matters.

[¶89-240] Limitations Period for Appeals

CAUTION: Transfer of BOE powers.—Beginning July 1, 2017, all California State Board of Equalization (BOE) administrative powers, duties, and responsibilities that are not constitutionally mandated to the BOE, with certain exceptions in the short term, will be transferred to a new Department of Tax and Fee Administration. The BOE will be left with responsibility for property tax assessment and equalization functions and assessment of taxes on insurers authorized by Article XIII of the state constitution; assessment and collection of excise taxes on alcohol pursuant to Article XX of the state constitution; and the statutory duty to adjust the rate of the motor vehicle fuel tax for the 2018-19 fiscal year. Until January 1, 2018, the BOE also will continue to hear corporation franchise and income tax and personal income tax appeals from the Franchise Tax Board (FTB). However, on that date, those functions will be transferred to a new Office of Tax Appeals, and the BOE will be prohibited from hearing further appeals.

These changes are the result of 2017 legislation, Ch. 6 (A.B. 102), Laws 2017, effective June 27, 2017, and operative as noted.

The following time limitations apply:

• *Administrative appeals*

A taxpayer has 30 days from the date of mailing of a Franchise Tax Board (FTB) action on a corporation franchise (income) or personal income tax assessment protest in which to appeal to the State Board of Equalization (SBE). (Sec. 19045, Rev. & Tax. Code; Sec. 19085, Rev. & Tax. Code)

A taxpayer has 90 days from the date of mailing of the FTB's action on a corporation franchise (income) or personal income tax refund claim in which to appeal to the SBE. (Sec. 19324, Rev. & Tax. Code; Sec. 19343, Rev. & Tax. Code)

• *Suits to recover refunds*

Income taxes.—Suits to recover corporation franchise (income) tax or personal income tax refunds must be filed within the later of:

— four years from the due date of the return;

— one year from the date of payment; or

— 90 days after the FTB sends its notice of action on a claim for refund or the SBE's determination on an appeal of a claim for refund becomes final.

(Sec. 19384, Rev. & Tax. Code)

Other taxes.—Suits for refund of the following taxes and fees must be brought within 90 days after the mailing of notice of action upon the refund claim:

— cigarette tax; (Sec. 30403, Rev. & Tax. Code)

— diesel fuel tax; (Sec. 60543, Rev. & Tax. Code)

— emergency telephone users surcharge; (Sec. 41110, Rev. & Tax. Code)

— energy resources surcharge; (Sec. 40127, Rev. & Tax. Code)

— hazardous substances tax; (Sec. 43473, Rev. & Tax. Code)

— insurance taxes; (Sec. 13103, Rev. & Tax. Code)

— motor vehicle fuel tax; (Sec. 8148, Rev. & Tax. Code)

— oil spill fee; (Sec. 46523, Rev. & Tax. Code)

— sales and use taxes; (Sec. 6933, Rev. & Tax. Code)

— solid waste management fee; (Sec. 45703, Rev. & Tax. Code)

— underground storage tank maintenance fee; (Sec. 50145, Rev. & Tax. Code) and

— use fuel tax. (Sec. 9173, Rev. & Tax. Code)

TOPICAL INDEX

⟫⟫→ References are to paragraph (¶) numbers.

FOR